ENCYCLOPEDIA OF
WHITE-COLLAR &
CORPORATE CRIME

ENCYCLOPEDIA OF
WHITE-COLLAR &
CORPORATE CRIME

Volume 2

GENERAL EDITOR

LAWRENCE M. SALINGER, Ph.D.
ARKANSAS STATE UNIVERSITY

A SAGE Reference Publication

SAGE Publications
Thousand Oaks ■ London ■ New Delhi

For information:

 Sage Publications, Inc.
2455 Teller Road
Thousand Oaks, California 91320
E-mail: order@sagepub.com

Sage Publications Ltd.
1 Oliver's Yard
55 City Road
London EC1Y 1SP
United Kingdom

Sage Publications India Pvt. Ltd.
B-42, Panchsheel Enclave
Post Box 4109
New Delhi 110 017 India

Printed in the United States of America

Library of Congress Cataloging-in-Publication Data

Encyclopedia of white-collar and corporate crime / general editor,
Lawrence M. Salinger.
       p. cm.
"A Sage reference publication."
Includes bibliographical references and index.
ISBN 0-7619-3004-3 (hardcover)

1. White collar crimes—Encyclopedias. 2. Corporations—Corrupt practices—Encyclopedias.
3. Commercial crimes—Encyclopedias. 4. Misconduct in office—Encyclopedias. 5. Political corruption—Encyclopedias. 6. Administrative agencies—Corrupt practices—Encyclopedias.
I. Salinger, Lawrence M.
HV6768.E63 2005
364.16'8'03—dc22

                                    2004010753

This book is printed on acid-free paper.

04   05   06   07   10 9 8 7 6 5 4 3 2 1

GOLSON BOOKS, LTD. STAFF:		SAGE PUBLICATIONS STAFF:	
President and Editor:	Geoff Golson	*Acquiring Editor:*	Rolf Janke
Design Director:	Kevin Hanek	*Editorial Assistant:*	Sara Tauber
Copyeditor and Proofreader:	Laura Lawrie	*Production Editor:*	Denise Santoyo
Indexer:	Gail Liss	*Production Artist:*	Janet Foulger

ENCYCLOPEDIA OF

WHITE-COLLAR & CORPORATE CRIME

CONTENTS

J

Japan

THE COUNTRY OF JAPAN has developed the second-largest economy in the world. Yet its industrialization and economic development happened very rapidly, and in a context of previously extended isolationism from the rest of the world. As a result, many of the systems and practices developed in Japan, which were suitable for earlier periods of its development, have been found to be out of step with modern, international business practices. The method of development adopted was one that stressed the cooperation between all members of society (business, people, and government) in ways which can appear to be collusive and corrupt. Together with these practices, are aspects of Japanese society such as the *yakuza* (organized crime) which appear to represent obvious cases of organized crime.

JAPANESE BUSINESS SYSTEM

Developed in response to the external shock of realizing the outside world was stronger and more advanced, Japan created a system in which all of its constituent parts would work together for the benefit of the whole country, rather than the benefit of individuals. Japan is, by comparison with the region, an ethnically and culturally homogeneous country. For cultural reasons, Japanese hold themselves to be different from other people and are quite prepared to accept that state policies should benefit Japanese society rather than anyone else. The system of development fell into four stages: import substitution through technological absorption; domestic rivalry and export expansion; outbound foreign direct investment (FDI); and import expansion from Japanese overseas units. In each case, steps were taken to boost local Japanese capabilities and to exclude overseas firms from the domestic market. This is important because it helps to explain the level of self-reliance which overseas competitors consider unfair, and which contravenes many international trade agreements that require nationality to be of no concern in business decisions.

The Japanese system is manifested in the ways in which central and local government contracts are allocated to potential contractors. Much vital information is withheld from outside competitors who feel themselves unfairly treated. The line between maintaining close and cooperative contacts between businesses and illegal collusion is often difficult to distinguish. Further, much of Japanese law remains in a vague and undefined manner such that it requires interpretation by officials or bureaucrats; again, there is opportunity for outsiders to feel unfairly excluded. This exclusion, it is widely believed in the business community, may be overcome through paying bribes, which is a widespread part of a gift-giving culture. One particularly well-known example of bribery was that of the U.S. aviation manufacturer Lockheed Corporation which, in the 1970s, paid bribes to a number of officials to secure sales; one result of this case was the conviction of former prime minister of Japan, Kakeui Tanaka.

An example of business and government working together is in the program of overseas development assistance (ODA) in Asia. In this case, assistance, which tends to focus on resource-rich recipient countries, is designed to benefit Japanese corporations more than the recipients of assistance. There is also evidence that the Japanese government has linked ODA with obtaining support in international forums, for example in buying votes to support its position at the International Whaling Commission.

Japanese companies have become well-known for the loyalty and diligence of their workers, with the Japanese culture among "salary men" involving long hours, often becoming obsessive, and being susceptible to death from overwork and suicide in the event of career failure or bankruptcy. It is also the case that the machismo of Japanese society not only prevents women from obtaining high levels of seniority, but also means they can be subject to sexual harassment and the international problem of differential wage levels. These issues have also traveled overseas when Japanese companies have opened international branches and factories. This has led to difficulties with trades (labor) unions and with local people gaining access to executive levels. However, these problems are lessening in impact.

The large international networks established by Japanese corporations and the unity that each manages to obtain from other units means that acts of collusion are quite possible. This includes such activities as transfer pricing and dumping. Transfer pricing involves selling goods between units of the same corporation at non-market prices to avoid taxation, while dumping involves selling goods in foreign markets at below cost or at least lower prices to get rid of them quickly or to undercut competitors.

A number of cases have been brought against Japanese corporations for possible dumping, and these are dealt with through international trade organizations, such as the World Trade Organization In some cases, allegations appear to have been made for political purposes as a form of retaliation against Japan's high informal and formal barriers-to-entry that make it difficult and expensive for most foreign corporations to become successful within Japan. There is also evidence of corporate decisions that have contributed to the significant degradation of the Japanese physical environment.

YAKUZA AND BUSINESS

It is not illegal in itself to be a member of a gang (a *yakuza*), since these have been accepted as parts of society for a long time. However, additional legislation has been provided to regulate *yakuza* activities, such as their re-designation as *boryoku-dan* (violence groups), which led to a great rush by gangs to redefine themselves as legitimate business associations or even religious orders. The *yakuza* have long been involved in a large number of sectors of the economy, notably construction and local politics, although they have subsequently diversified widely into international markets. Profitable activities include protection rackets, prostitution, illegal gambling and extortion.

Much of the proceeds of these crimes have been laundered by investing them in legitimate businesses, which has been an important factor in preventing prosecutions. Another problem in prosecution has been political protection, especially by the "racketeer-friendly right-wing" parties. The *yakuza* are said to work for members of the leading political parties against their own colleagues and to be linked with very senior political figures. They are also responsible for about one quarter of the current (2004) record level of unscrupulous money-lending deals that are, in an economy that has been in a decade-long recession, causing a great deal of distress.

The *yakuza* are organized into a large number of different gangs and make much use of tattoos and rituals to bind members together and lend prestige to their activities. There are estimated to be some 78,000 *yakuza* in Japan, and their samurai-like code of conduct, with its hacking-off of fingers for transgressions and as a sign of membership, is symbolic of 400 years of history. Many have assiduously cultivated links with politicians for mutual gain. The development of the Kansai airport, for example, is believed to have been marred by the extortion that followed the revelation of the routes to be taken by access roads. Gang members used inside knowledge and brought pressure to bear upon residents of

Miyajima Island in Japan symbolizes the hundreds of years of religious, cultural, and social traditions that continue to influence the conduct of business, government, and organized crime in the homogeneous country.

houses along the routes to sell their houses, which could then be resold to the government at a profit, after it had been publicly revealed where the roads would be built.

The tolerance for prostitution in Japanese society and the constant demand for (mostly) women to provide the necessary sexual services has provided the *yakuza* with an opportunity to make high profits through controlling the import and exploitation of women from Southeast Asian countries and elsewhere. A gang controlling 10 such women is reportedly able to make one billion yen (approximately $7 million) annually, with low costs because of the use of intimidation and drugs to control the women. This trade attracts gang organizers from overseas, and there have been instances of murders of gang bosses. It is apparent that collusion with immigration and other officials permits this large-scale trade to continue.

The Japanese economic success story turned somewhat sour at the end of the 1980s and has continued in decline into the 21st century. In 2003, the economy fell back into recession, which was marked by comparatively low levels of consumer demand, business failures and (for Japan) high levels of unemployment. Underlying this recession was the role of banks in making loans to companies which later were unwilling or unable to repay them (these are non-performing loans or NPLs). Repeated governmental attempts to stimulate the economy, according to Keynesian methods by spending money, have failed because much of the money was directed into needless construction projects, at least in part, according to some reports, because the construction industry was controlled by *yakuza* who were close to government figures.

THE POLITICAL COST

Forcing banks with many NPLs to resolve the issue by forcing repayments or bankruptcies would, it is believed, lead to a string of bankruptcies and bank failures that would have too high a political cost attached. Consequently, banks were allowed to continue, and the recession was prolonged perhaps more than necessary. There have been claims that the *yakuza* took a strong role in this situation, not just in causing banks to make loans that would never be repaid, but also in taking over some debts and ensuring their continued existence. Some estimates placed yakuza involvement in NPLs as high as 50 percent, while they may have laundered up to $15 billion of money into legitimate businesses overseas as part of a bid to obtain a global presence.

This has been partly a result of overseas corporations, especially U.S. corporations, buying assets from distressed Japanese corporations and, in some cases with inadequate due process and diligence, later finding they had bought into businesses connected with the *yakuza*.

Yakuza operate front businesses known as *kigyo shatei* to hide the real nature of their businesses. Part of the Japanese economic development success resulted from the government-controlled banking system ensuring that Japanese corporations were able to obtain as much funding as they required at low levels of interest. However, the processes of globalization meant that, from about the 1980s onward, many such Japanese corporations were able to obtain better loan rates from international capital markets than from the Japanese banks that, shielded from real competition, were still inefficient in many ways. To cover the sudden lack of demand for their services, banks cast around for new customers and found them, knowingly or not, in the *kigyo shatei*. Many of the *yakuza* companies that benefited from loans at low interest rates had very little intention of ever repaying the money, and anticipated they would never be required to do so.

One example was Susumu Ishii, openly known to be a leading underworld figure who, before his death in 1991, obtained loans from 12 different banking organizations. Further, on the occasions when individuals within banks have endeavored rather bravely to recover the money, more than a dozen have been murdered or otherwise died in mysterious circumstances. Inevitably, there are many concerns about the decision-making processes in the banking system that permits banks to continue lending or avoid calling in their NPLs. However, most *yakuza* operate at a much lower level than this, being more concerned with minor extortion and the control of games of chance such as pachinko machines.

POLITICAL SYSTEM

The Japanese political system is structured to allow all agencies and organizations to work together, with outsiders effectively prevented from gaining access to power or even to equitable decision-making. This is achieved through an effective formal and informal consensus system in which all relevant parties are consulted to the extent necessary to ensure that they agree with a decision before it is announced. Japanese organizational culture frowns upon open discord, and so this system has arisen to prevent the loss of face that disagreement could cause. However, it also serves to exclude outsiders and to maintain the opacity of decisions. The political decision-making process led to a period of almost unchallenged rule by the Liberal Democratic Party (LDP) from 1955 onward. The party became almost institutionalized in power and many LDP sympathizers were placed in important organizations at all levels.

SOCIAL SYSTEMS

Informal networks, consisting of individuals who graduated from the same class or who hail from the same region, also reinforce the system and bind those already inside closer, while outsiders are excluded even more forcibly. With all parts of the system bound together so they move in the same direction, the line between mutual cooperation and illegal collusion becomes increasingly difficult to define. Added to this is the gift-giving culture in Japan in which visits, on nearly all occasions, are accompanied by often expensive gifts. The difference between corporate gift-giving and outright bribery is one which Western corporations, in particular, find difficult to establish and, fearing that they are losing business as a result, have pushed for all such activities to be deemed bribery and hence outlawed in international trade organizations.

In the political context, the system is ripe for collusion and bribery and this seems to have continued for many years on a staggering scale. Those included within decision-making circles are able to obtain privileged information to enable them to make successful bids for government tenders, to obtain scarce resources at favorable rates, and opportunities to negotiate directly with government figures. Certain ministries offer more opportunities for graft than others and assignment to them may be contested fiercely. Even when bribery is not involved, government treatment of the corporate sector is likely to be lenient because of the practice of *amakudari* (or descent from heaven) that occurs with the forced resignation of ministry officials whenever anyone younger obtains a more senior position to them. This system means they must seek employment elsewhere, and it is natural that they will look to the private sector with which they may have been dealing for some time.

The same situation applies to police officers who, similarly poorly paid by national standards, require additional employment once their official service is complete. Many of these forms of behavior are well-known and documented in public life but go unreported in the media because most media organizations are controlled by large corporate interests. Also, Japanese journalists, for cultural reasons that continue to be important, are reluctant to openly criticize establishment figures.

This does not all mean that all government officials or business people are corrupt or that people are generally insensitive to the slurs on the Japanese character that these instances suggest. There are government agencies and regulations to protect the vulnerable and some reformers and activists do manage to make some differences. However, the unified system acts against individuals and against those not part of the government-business system (who can be the same people in their role as consumers).

Meanwhile, the government agency charged with ensuring fair play in business, the Fair Trade Commission (FTC) is considered something of a toothless tiger because of its continued inability to bring to justice many of those against whom allegations have been made. One problem with the operation of the FTC is that it cannot respond to individuals wishing to bring forward complaints but, instead, must wait to investigate them itself before charges can be brought forward. Consequently, various delaying and diversionary tactics have been employed to ensure that cases are not satisfactorily investigated.

The same situation exists with respect to the protection of consumers: A law introduced in 1994 concerning product liability is considered inadequate as a consumer defense. The onus to prove deliberate design or technology misuse is particularly difficult in the area of complex and technologically advanced goods. A comparatively limited number of qualified lawyers in the general population also tends to act against the possibility of successful legal actions being taken against the corporations, which can afford to hire most of them pre-emptively.

SEE ALSO

graft; public corruption; Greenpeace; bribery; extortion; organized crime; Lockheed; ethics; Foreign Corrupt Practices Act.

BIBLIOGRAPHY. "Japan: Tycoons of Crime," *The Economist* (February 29, 1992); Brian Bremner, "Big Spenders and the Great Seaweed Slaughter" *BusinessWeek* (February 6, 2001): Tanya Clark, "Sayonara, Reformer," *Forbes* (July 6, 1998); Benjamin Fulford, "Japan's Dirty Secrets," *Forbes* (October 30, 2000); Greenpeace, "Japan Admits Buying Whaling Votes in Exchange for Aid," www.greenpeace.org (July 18th, 2001); Velisarios Kattoulas, "The Yakuza Recession," *Far Eastern Economic Review* (January 17, 2002); Inder P. Khera, "Business Ethics East vs. West: Myths and Realities," *Journal of Business Ethics* (v.30/1, 2001); Yayori Matsui, *Women in the New Asia* (Zed Books Ltd., 1999); Justin McCurry, "Loan Sharks Fuel Japan's Suicide Rise," *The Observer* (August 17, 2003); Gregory L. Miles, "Crime, Corruption and Multinational Business," *International Business* (July, 1995); Terutomo Ozawa, "Japan," *Governments, Globalization, and International Business* (Oxford University Press, 1997).

JOHN WALSH, PH.D.
MAHIDOL UNIVERSITY, THAILAND

Jesilow, Paul (1950–)

PAUL D. JESILOW WAS ONE of the first criminologists to systematically and rigorously explore the nature, causes, and consequences of fraud in the auto repair industry. Along with his colleagues at the University of California, Irvine (UCI), Jesilow also generated a great deal of research on the kinds of crimes committed in the healthcare field.

Jesilow did his undergraduate work in sociology and political science in the school of social sciences at UCI. His graduate work was done in the social ecology program at UCI, where he received his Ph.D. in 1982. While engaged in coursework, he also worked in a juvenile correction facility and in an educational opportunity program at UCI. His dissertation involved an examination of fraud in the automobile repair industry.

Jesilow has co-authored five books, including *In the Same Voice: Women and Men in Law Enforcement, Doing Justice in the People's Court, Prescription for Profit: How Doctors Defraud Medicaid, White-Collar Crime,* and *Myths that Cause Crime.* The last of these books won the Academy of Criminal Justice Sciences' outstanding book award shortly after it was published.

In the area of white-collar crime, Jesilow worked with his UCI colleagues to expand understanding about a number of different types of workplace offenses. His work on crime in the medical field and police misconduct is especially noteworthy. In medical-crime research, Jesilow has conducted several different studies covering different aspects of the problem. One study considered how the offenses are detected and investigated. Another study examined how prosecutors adjudicated cases involving doctors, while another looked at how medical programs in different countries perpetuated or prevented fraud. He has published his medical-crime research in the *Journal of the American Medical Association*, among others. This research eventually culminated in the *Prescription for Profit* book.

Jesilow's latest interest in white-collar crime has expanded to include research on police misconduct. Combining his interests in policing research with his ability to do public attitude surveys, Jesilow examined the effect that police misconduct has on opinions about the police.

SEE ALSO

automobile; police corruption; healthcare fraud; Pontell, Henry N.; Geis, Gilbert.

BIBLIOGRAPHY. Paul Jesilow, Henry N. Pontell, and Gilbert Geis, *Prescription for Profit: How Doctors Defraud Medicaid* (University of California Press, 1993); J. Meyer and Paul Jesilow, *Doing Justice in People's Court: Sentencing by Municipal Court Judges* (State University of New York Press, 1997); D. Parsons and Paul Jesilow, *In the Same Voice: Women and Men in Law Enforcement* (Seven Locks Press, 2001).

BRIAN K. PAYNE
OLD DOMINION UNIVERSITY

Jett, Joseph (1958–)

JOSEPH JETT WAS dismissed by the prestigious Wall Street firm Kidder Peabody in April 1994, accused of fraudulently booking $339 million in phony profits on bond trades in his position at the Kidder bond desk. With so many cases of rogue traders bringing down financial institutions, both on Wall Street and internationally, it was not hard to believe that the case of Jett at Kidder Peabody fit into the familiar pattern.

But Jett and some former colleagues insist that his case was different. In fact, they say, Jett, one of the few African-American traders on Wall Street, was being used as a scapegoat for larger problems at Kidder. They point out that Jett's superiors were aware of his trades, strategies, and profits, and not only allowed it, but rewarded his behavior in an effort to breed star traders, and window dress Kidder's balance sheet for Kidder's new owners at General Electric (GE).

As Saul Hensel of the *New York Times* states it, the central question is: "Can Jett be guilty of fraud if he hid nothing, falsified no records and was subject to several levels of oversight?" Jett and his colleagues were tasked with trying to profit on arcane trades which exploited the price differences between regular government bonds and zero-coupon bonds. Both sides agreed that more than half of the profits booked by Jett were not legitimate profits, but appeared on Kidder's computer screens due to a glitch in a complicated proprietary program that processed the stripping and reconstituting of these trades. Because of this glitch, the further out Jett set the settlement dates for these trades, the greater the profit recorded.

"By the end of 1993, Jett was made managing director, named man of the year, and awarded $9 million in bonuses on $150 million of reported trading profits," writes Hensel. With profits rolling in, it was easy for Kidder managers to fail to question how it all worked. And it was even easier to avoid embarrassment later by blaming the fiasco on one rogue trader, rather than address real flaws in Kidder's systems and oversight policies. As at least one trader testified at the Securities and Exchange Commission (SEC) hearing, more than one accountant questioned at the time had reassured senior management that the trades were real, not just paper transactions. Kidder's own internal auditors spent 400 hours reviewing Jett's zero-coupon desk in August and September 1993, but were apparently unable to detect the problem.

Then in the late fall of 1993, GE ordered Kidder to cut back on its bond holdings, and to comply with the order, Jett actually did engage in a number of paper transactions for the sole purpose of meeting the letter of the new balance sheet restrictions. While the SEC and Kidder asserted that this trading was an attempt by Jett to hide his fraudulent scheme, Jett said his superiors at Kidder ordered him to engage in the trading to deceive GE. Still, in January 1994, Jett's reported profits doubled, triggering another internal investigation by Kidder accountants, who finally figured out how their own systems were booking profits on the forward reconstitutions.

After a former SEC enforcement chief brought in by Kidder as an outside investigator accused Jett of deliberate manipulation of the system, GE officially blamed Jett for a $350 million charge against earnings and Jett was dismissed. GE ultimately sold Kidder for $600 million. In securities litigation filed by GE shareholders against Kidder, Kidder officers, and Jett and his supervisor, the court denied the defendants motion to dismiss, finding that the pattern of conduct alleged, if proven at trial, met the legal elements of fraud. The case remained in the courts in 2003.

SEE ALSO
Kidder, Peabody; bond fraud; securities fraud; Securities and Exchange Commission.

BIBLIOGRAPHY. David Bowman, "Wall Street Lynching," www.salon.com/books (May 27, 1999); British Broadcasting Service, "Nightmare on Wall Street," www.bbc.co.uk (October 18, 2000); Leah Nathans Spiro, "Now it's Joseph Jett's Turn," *BusinessWeek* (May 10, 1999); Saul Hansel, "Joseph Jett, Scoundrel or Scapegoat?" *New York Times* (April 6, 1997).

JANE G. HAIGH
UNIVERSITY OF ARIZONA

Johns-Manville

GREEK GEOGRAPHER Strabo and the Roman naturalist Pliny the Elder both noted that slaves weaving asbestos into cloth often developed a fatal sickness in the lungs. They were among the first to identify asbestosis, a lung disease caused by inhaling the fine fibers and particles of asbestos.

Johns-Manville, one of the modern companies using asbestos, began in 1858 as the H. W. Johns Manufacturing Company, founded on the principal use of asbestos as a fire-resistant roofing material. In 1901, the company added new asbestos products, including asbestos cement.

By the early 1930s, asbestos workers stricken with asbestosis were bringing damage suits against Johns-Manville, now the largest asbestos manufacturer in the country, and against other leading asbestos manufacturers. These manufacturers created a cover-up of the asbestos hazard that continued for more than 40 years. In 1933, Lewis Herold Brown, president of Johns-Manville, informed the company's board of directors of 11 pending lawsuits brought by employees who had developed asbestosis while working at the company's plant in Manville, New Jersey. He said that the cases could be settled out of court, provided that the attorney for the plaintiffs could be persuaded not to bring any more cases against the company.

.Over the next two decades, the cover-up continued. Memos and other written evidence revealed that Johns-Manville did not inform its employees when their chest X-rays showed they had developed asbestosis. In a 1952 symposium, the seventh one held at Saranac Laboratory, doctors informed the participants, including asbestos manufacturers, that medical evidence implicated asbestos as a powerful producer of lung cancer. The proceedings of the six other meetings had been published, but the proceedings of the seventh were not. Very little information about asbestos causing cancer found its way into the press for another decade.

The asbestos cover-up might have continued indefinitely, but in the 1960s, two developments in law and medicine exposed the asbestos manufacturers. In 1962 and 1963, Dr. Irving J. Selikoff, director of the Mount Sinai School of Medicine's Environmental Sciences Laboratory in New York City and two of his colleagues definitively linked industrial exposure to asbestos to extreme health hazards like cancer. And in 1965, the American Law Foundation defined tort law to make sellers of dangerous products liable to users and consumers unless they put adequate warning labels on their products.

In 1971, Ward Stephenson, a Texas trial lawyer, brought the first asbestos product liability lawsuit, and this case opened the way for other asbestos lawsuits. During the next decade, people filed about 15,000 lawsuits against Johns-Manville, Raybestos-Manhattan, and a dozen other asbestos insulation manufacturers. During these suits, hundreds of documents furnished overwhelming proof that these companies had covered up their knowledge of the hazards of asbestos. Juries all over the country awarded large compensatory damages to diseased asbestos workers and the survivors of workers who had died of asbestos disease. During 1981 and the first half of 1982, juries in 10 different cases found Manville liable for punitive damages worth more than $6 million. The company and its insurance carriers had already settled some 2,000 asbestos-disease cases out of court for tens of millions of dollars.

In August 1982, Manville, a corporation with assets of more than $2 billion, filed for protection under Chapter 11 of the Federal Bankruptcy Code, claiming it had been unfairly drained of assets by thousands of unwarranted lawsuits. During the next six-and-a-half years, while the case languished in the courts, Manville did not have to pay anything to the victims. When the final bankruptcy plan was approved, it only compensated 100,000 asbestos disease victims.

SEE ALSO

asbestos; employee safety; workplace deaths; unsafe products; Owens Corning.

BIBLIOGRAPHY. Eric Stallare, Kenneth G. Manton, and Joel E. Cohen, *Forecasting Product Liability Claims: Epidemiology and Modeling in the Manville Asbestos Case* (Statistics for Biology and Health, 2003); Paul Brodeur, "The Asbestos Tragedy," http://www.bumc.bu.edu/ (2003); Stephen J. Carroll, "Asbestos Litigation Costs and Compensation: An Interim Report," (Rand, Institute for Civil Justice, 2002).

KATHY WARNES, PH.D.
UNIVERSITY OF TOLEDO

Johnson, Lyndon B. (1908–1973)

THE FIRST ALLEGATION of Lyndon Baines Johnson (LBJ) exploiting his position in the government to benefit his personal business fortune came about while he was vice president, and such allegations persisted until he won the 1964 presidential election. Johnson appeared unable to separate his business work from his political career, and this greatly influenced people's perceptions of him as being a Texas "wheeler-dealer."

His administration was tainted by a past littered with claims of corruption. Most notorious was his victory over Coke Stevenson for the Texas Democratic Senate nomination in 1948, when he won by a mere 87 votes, and was widely believed to have "stuffed" Texas ballot boxes. In addition to allegations of political corruption, he had accumulated a multi-million dollar fortune through his LBJ Corporation and other business ventures, that raised allegations that he used his political influences to gain unfair business contracts for himself and his friends.

Business dealings caused LBJ the most problems, beginning in 1962 with the Billie Sol Estes scandal. A later scandal involving Johnson's protégé, Bobby Baker, would lead to more public scrutiny. The Baker affair helped fuel the bitter rivalry that Johnson had with Robert Kennedy, who was the attorney general during the John F. Kennedy administration in which Johnson served as vice president.

BILLIE SOL ESTES

The Billie Sol Estes scandal emerged in the summer of 1962 when Johnson was still Kennedy's vice president. Estes was a businessman from Pecos, Texas, who had established a lucrative business in agricultural products by mortgaging non-existent farm gear. He also created an illegal cotton-allotment business that eventually resulted in the dismissal of several members of the government's Department of Agriculture (DOA). With the help of government connections, Estes established his cotton business, and it became evident that such a deal would not have been possible without having some major influence within the government. This influence was immediately linked to Johnson. Estes was a major financial contributor to the Democratic Party and had been a major contributor to Johnson's many campaigns for the Senate and as vice president. The link to Johnson appeared strong.

Estes was arrested in March 1962 by the Federal Bureau of Investigation (FBI), charged with fraud and theft. In addition to those charges, the death of Henry Marshall, an official from DOA, cast further suspicion over Estes's affairs. Marshall was sent to Texas to investigate Estes's business deals. On June 3, 1961, Marshall was found dead, his body covered in bruises and shot five times. A bolt-action shotgun was found next to him and his death was ruled a suicide. Some observers considered this a bizarre ruling since a bolt-action shotgun would have to be pumped once before each shot was fired (obviously, one would think Marshall could not have pumped the shotgun after shooting himself with the first shot.)

Estes went to jail from 1965 until 1971, and again in 1979 until 1984, but never discussed his affairs and never disclosed any ties to Johnson. An FBI inquiry into the Estes case also revealed nothing that would incriminate Johnson. However, in 1984, upon his release from prison, Estes revealed allegations to a Robertson County Grand Jury in Texas that tied Johnson to not only the Marshall murder, but also seven other murders, including Kennedy's assassination.

Estes claimed that he had given Johnson millions of dollars in order to guarantee his unethical cotton business. When Marshall was sent to Texas to investigate, Estes claimed that LBJ contracted a man named Malcolm Wallace to kill Marshall. With the assistance of attorney Douglas Caddy, Estes tried to gain the protection of immunity from the Justice Department before further discussing these allegations in greater detail. Before any agreements could be reached, Estes decided against disclosing and refused any further information.

BOBBY BAKER

While Johnson was still dealing with the Estes scandal, another was uncovered involving the man whom Johnson referred to as a son, his protégé, Robert "Bobby" Baker. Baker was one of his top aides when Johnson was a Senator, and he became the secretary to the Senate majority leader by 1963. Baker was known as another wheeler-dealer because he had amassed a million-dollar fortune, which drew suspicions because he had always worked for the government for a modest salary.

Baker had, indeed, become entangled in many illegal deals, and his scandal in 1963 could have caused serious damage to not only Johnson, but also to Kennedy. In autumn 1963, Delaware Senator John Williams began to investigate Baker's suspicious business deals. On October 7, 1963, Baker resigned his position, hoping that would put the matter to rest and relieve suspicions of Johnson. However, his resignation did not save Johnson from claims of corruption.

The first issue tying Johnson to Baker was the claim by Dan Reynolds, a businessman from Maryland, that Baker and Walter Jenkins, another of Johnson's aides, had demanded him to pay Johnson kickbacks after LBJ purchased two life insurance policies from Reynolds. Furthermore, Reynolds claimed that he was pressured to buy advertising space on LBJ's television station in Texas, which was of no use to him since he lived in Maryland. Baker also received a nice commission on the sale of the life insurance policies while Johnson received an expensive hi-fi system from Reynolds, presumably as a kickback, which Johnson later claimed he thought was a present from Baker.

Johnson found himself in the heart of the Baker scandal when it was revealed that the life insurance policies had been sold to the LBJ Corporation with the guarantee that Johnson was a major employee. This contradicted Johnson's claims that his wife, Lady Bird, was in charge of handling all of the business's affairs; otherwise, Johnson could be accused of having conflicts of interests between his business deals and his government role. Unfortunately for Johnson, Baker's involvement in disreputable dealings was not confined solely to the insurance policy claim.

Baker posed such a great risk because he had known ties to gangsters, including the prominent, alleged mobster Sam Giancana. Baker, along with Giancana and organized-crime leaders Ed and Louis Levensen, had acquired the rights to expand Intercontinental Hotel Corporations to the Caribbean. This meant that they would be running illegal casinos throughout the Caribbean.

When rumors of this ploy reached the ears of the White House, Robert Kennedy had the FBI investigate Baker's dealings. After putting immense FBI pressure on Giancana, the gangster backed-off on the casino venture, but not before drawing more agitation from both Kennedys, who were becoming irritated by the constant allegations surrounding the vice president.

EMBROILED IN CONTROVERSY

Baker's illegal ties continued, as he was also an influential member of the Serve-U-Corporation, a company accused of strong-arming rival businesses into giving kickbacks. These various affairs portrayed Baker as an influence peddler who made his fortune by pushing government officials to give business contracts to his friends. Along with these ventures, Baker also found himself embroiled in more controversy when it was revealed that he had introduced John Kennedy to an attractive East German prostitute, Ellen Rometsch. Biographers have since discovered Kennedy and Rometsch probably carried out an affair with the president unaware that she had communist ties. When Robert Kennedy found out about Rometsch, he immediately had her and her husband deported to Europe before the relationship was publicly exposed. Had it been revealed to the public, the president would have been unlikely to survive the scandal.

Baker proved to be a major blemish for Johnson's image, which caused great tension between Johnson and the Kennedy administration. To make the situation worse for Johnson, it was widely known that he and Robert Kennedy were at odds. There were rumors circulating that Johnson would be dropped from the 1964 ticket and replaced by Robert Kennedy. This was not hard for LBJ to imagine, as he knew that the 1968 Democratic ticket would fall to either him or Robert Kennedy, and he believed that this would serve as a way to the top Democratic slot. However, the notion that the president intended to drop Johnson as his vice president is unlikely. Kennedy was fully aware that he needed Johnson in order to appease southern voters and without him he would struggle to win those votes.

SECRET RUMORS

When Johnson became president on November 22, 1963, following the assassination of Kennedy, his ties to the Baker scandal followed him to the White House. Johnson believed that Robert Kennedy was secretly circulating rumors linking LBJ to Baker in order to destroy Johnson's image. However, biographers show Robert Kennedy did his utmost to protect Johnson from the scandal.

Since it was Kennedy who was in charge of the investigation into the Baker situation, he could have inflicted serious damage to Johnson's character image and career. Instead, Kennedy reported that while Johnson may have had some unsavory connections with Baker, Johnson did nothing that was illegal. The close connections to Baker thus failed to significantly stain the reputation of Johnson's administration. Baker eventually served 18 months in prison in 1971, as a result of his illegal business deals.

Considering the nation was reeling from Kennedy's assassination and needed Johnson in the best light, inquiries died down after Johnson became president. Connections involving LBJ's role in the Kennedy assassination have produced many conspiracy theories, but nothing more.

Johnson was never found guilty of any wrongdoing in any of the scandalous allegations brought against him, although his suspect dealings and business relationships have forever cast suspicions. Johnson won the presidential election in 1964, but refused to run for re-election in 1968 following mounting death tolls from the war in Vietnam and domestic, social revolt.

SEE ALSO
Kennedy, Robert F.; elite crime; corruption.

BIBLIOGRAPHY. Michael R. Beschloss, ed., *Taking Charge: The Johnson White House Tapes, 1963–64* (Simon & Schuster, 1997); Joseph A Califano, *The Triumph & Tragedy of Lyndon Johnson: The White House Years* (Simon & Schuster, 1991); Robert Dalleck, *Flawed Giant: Lyndon Johnson And His Times, 1961–73* (Oxford University Press, 1998); Seymour Hersh, *The Dark Side of Camelot* (HarperCollins Publishers, 1997); Jeff Shesol, *Mutual Contempt: Lyndon Johnson, Robert Kennedy, and the Feud that Defined a Decade* (W.W. Norton, 1997).

DAVID W. MCBRIDE
UNIVERSITY OF NOTTINGHAM, ENGLAND

juries and awards

MULTIMILLION DOLLAR awards for damages granted by juries have garnered sensationalist headlines in the past decades. Usually resulting from product liability, workplace injury, and medical malpractice suits launched by individuals against corporations, these cases have cast much negative light on harmful business practices in the United States.

Lobbyists for corporations and allied politicians claim that juries are systematically biased toward the plaintiffs and unfairly award huge monetary damages solely to penalize corporate America. They argue further that such legal restrictions have affected the competitiveness of American business.

The most exhaustive empirical research to date, however, has demonstrated that there is no evidence of systematic jury bias nor that monetary damages awarded to plaintiffs has decreased the profitability of American business. Indeed, there is a strong case to be made, as Stephen Daniels and Joanne Martin contend, that "Punitive damages provide the only practical means of sanctioning large and flourishing economic actors in the face of weak administrative controls and the limits of criminal justice." An historical overview of juries and awards illustrates, moreover, that changing conceptions of liability for legal wrongdoings and monetary damages awarded by juries reflect shifting social and political attitudes and practices in society at large.

Civil cases involving juries and monetary damages fall under the general rubric of tort law, the law of civil wrongs. Tort law encompasses the legal concepts of liability and negligence. Liability can generally be defined as accountability and responsibility to other persons. Negligence involves a notion of failing to take care where it was reasonable to assume that injury would be caused. Both legal infractions are enforceable by civil and, in some cases, criminal sanctions. Under liability rules, plaintiffs usually only have to show that they were harmed by the defendant's conduct. Negligence laws are stricter and usually require plaintiffs to prove "unreasonable conduct" on the defendant's part.

Civil juries may award compulsory damages, that is, compensation for money, wages, property or emotional suffering lost due to liability or negligence on the part of the accused; and punitive damages, an extra award that penalizes the accused party in an effort to deter future illegal actions. The concepts of liability, negligence, and tort law, in general, therefore are highly ambiguous and inexact. What exactly constitutes accountability and responsibility is a question that historically has been decided by the context of specific political, legislative, and judicial decisions.

HISTORY OF ACCOUNTABILITY

The concept of liability and negligence for which plaintiffs could sue businesses for damages was narrowly defined until the 20th century. An individualist ethic in line with the ideology of free-market capitalism held sway in legal thinking. This ethic ran counter to the idea that corporate entities should be held liable for negligence and other injuries, and be required to pay compensation for individuals harmed under their auspices.

Thus, in the case of workers injured on the job in the 19th century, it was far more likely that courts would look for culpability among individuals (the injured worker or another employee) rather than the company itself.

The doctrine of contributory negligence also dominated legal discourse during this epoch. It held that X could not sue Y if X was partially responsible for an act of negligence. The markedly pro-business ideology of individualism was dominant at the highest levels of the judiciary. In 1873, a member of the New Hampshire Supreme Court characterized the idea of punitive damages in tort cases as a "monstrous heresy." Punitive damages were all but eliminated from tort cases brought against corporations after the Civil War, and 20th century notions of damages based on emotional distress were scarcely considered.

As a result, employees injured at the workplace or consumers harmed by products were frequently unsuccessful in suits against corporations. Lawrence Friedman reports that less than half the already limited number of cases against corporations in New York in 1910 were won by the plaintiff. Sometimes, other individuals could be found liable in such cases, but rarely corporate entities.

One famous case aptly demonstrates the limited concept of employer liability. In 1911, a fire at the Triangle Shirtwaist Factory in New York City killed 146 workers, mostly young immigrant women. The company was found to have committed numerous safety violations, yet a jury acquitted all the company owners from severe charges. Wrongful deaths suits settled out of court by family members resulted in the employers paying a paltry $75 for each of the 23 plaintiffs.

The nature of the jury system also played a role in limiting notions of liability. The relatively broad powers of the jury in the 18th century was superseded in the 19th century by the growing power of judges who adhered rigorously to the individualist ethic. Moreover, until the 1960s, jury members in state and federal courts were chosen from among people suggested by prominent civic or political leaders. The result was that juries were highly unrepresentative of the population at large and were composed of largely middle- and upper-class, white men who, it can be argued, were much less likely to find corporations at fault.

Throughout the late 19th and early 20th centuries, as the population expanded and the economy became more complex and interconnected, larger social and judicial changes slowly began to alter the doctrine of individual responsibility in favor of increased liability on the part of businesses. Much of this reform thrust originated from the skyrocketing growth in accidents in the increasingly industrial workplace of the early 20th century. In 1900, for instance, there were 2 million injuries and 35,000 deaths which occurred in the workplace. In 1907, 3,000 coal miners died in accidents across the country; in the same year, over 4,500 railroad workers lost their lives.

While the vast majority of those injured and the families of those killed were never compensated by employers, there was an increasing recognition that a modern, progressive economy required an expanded concept of liability. *MacPherson v. Buick Motor Company* (1916) and *Escola v. Coca Cola Bottling Company of Fresno* (1944) were both precedent-setting cases that witnessed injured persons successfully suing corporations and receiving damages. Reflecting a related trend, state governments also began to establish the first rudimentary elements of workers' compensation to deal with workplace injuries and deaths.

1960s REVOLUTION

In the 1960s, a veritable tort revolution occurred. Once again, legislative and court decisions reflected shifting social and political attitudes. Stricter rules for companies, wider definitions of product liability, and increasing numbers of criminal charges against corporate officers marked this era. All states expanded their concepts of negligence and liability and a definite trend toward increased monetary amounts can be discerned in court and state-agency awarded damages. The first settlement over $1 million was awarded by a jury in 1962.

Medical malpractice suits became more and more common in these years as the public increasingly sought new treatments, as medical techniques became more complex, and as the medical profession itself grew enormously. The introduction of more stringent safety laws and regulations, the rise of consumer protection agencies at the government level, and consumer advocacy groups in society at large contributed to these shifts, as did the general political climate which witnessed large-scale social movements and increasingly liberal social attitudes.

Legislative changes to jury composition in the late 1960s meant a shift toward a more representative section of the population who were willing to find verdicts against corporate entities. Shifting

ideas of social, economic, and environmental justice had therefore altered the social and political context of law by the 1970s.

Highly publicized product liability and workplace injury cases against large corporations, some of which were mass-action suits composed of numerous plaintiffs, blossomed in the 1970s. The first lawsuit related to asbestos poisoning, for example, was filed in 1966 in Texas by Claude Tomplait against 11 manufacturers of insulation products containing asbestos, including Johns-Manville, Fibreboard, and Owens Corning Fiberglass. Asbestos was found to be a highly toxic substance with often deadly consequences for workers who handled it. Yet Tomplait, who suffered from asbestosis, lost the case. A jury verdict found in favor of the defendants. The same law firm who handled this case, however, proceeded with another suit on behalf of Tomplait's co-worker, Clarence Borel.

This time, a jury returned a guilty verdict and granted $79,436.24 to the plaintiff. By the mid-1980s, claims against asbestos manufacturers had been launched by 30,000 individuals. These long-running cases have led to actual damages in the millions and punitive damages in the billions, although the mass declaration of bankruptcy by many defendants has considerably decreased the amount of damages actually paid. Punitive damages have been awarded on the basis that companies were aware of the health risks, but refused to put in place precautions. One lawyer uncovered a document from a company executive in the asbestos industry that said in part, "if you enjoyed the good life while working with asbestos products why not die from it?"

CONSUMER ADVOCACY

The majority of cases involving claims for damage have originated in product liability suits. Pioneering consumer advocate, Ralph Nader, was instrumental in encouraging a series of precedent-setting actions against Ford Motor Company in the 1970s. A faulty gas tank in one of the company's most popular models, the Pinto, was found to explode in certain kinds of rear-end accidents. While the company was aware of the potential threat from the launch of the model in 1969, they found the $11 cost of replacing the gas tanks with safer parts too expensive.

Only in 1977, did they begin to make the necessary alterations to adequately protect the gas tanks from exploding. A number of successful lawsuits were launched and substantial jury awarded damages were granted as a result of the estimated 500 deaths attributable to the Pinto's design flaw. Ford was initially confident that juries would find the drivers liable for the accidents and opted to fight the cases in court. However, the first few cases resulted in multimillion-dollar awards against the company. "We'll never go to a jury again," Ford spokesperson Al Stechter said in 1977. "Not in a fire case. Juries are just too sentimental. They see those charred remains and forget the evidence. No sir, we'll settle." Consequently, Ford settled the remainder of cases out of court.

ROBIN HOOD JURIES

Nevertheless, the tort revolution would be relatively short lived. In the late 1970s and 1980s, tort reform lobby groups, bankrolled by major businesses, predominantly in the insurance industry, undertook a concerted legislative lobby campaign to scale back expanded notions of industry liability. They widely publicized, in the words of Daniels and Martin, that the "system [had] run amok with skyrocketing awards ... " Empirical studies have clearly demonstrated, however, that the "frequency of claims, lawsuits filed, trials held, jury verdicts, and jury behavior" has not supported the case for tort reform. There is little data to back up the claim that juries are systematically pro-plaintiff, anti-business, and modern-day Robin Hoods.

A study by the National Center for State Courts found the win rate in civil jury tort trials with business defendants to be 52 percent; other studies of particular states found win rates to be as high as 72 percent and as low as 50 percent. In an exhaustive study of 378,000 state tort cases in 1990-91, the Department of Justice found that three out of four tort cases were settled out of court; only 3 percent went to trial and the plaintiffs won about half the cases.

A few high-profile cases of multimillion dollar awards has also masked the average award which tends to be modest. As Kenneth Jost has shown, plaintiffs "do not regularly win large amounts across all types of cases." In a study of 28 tort cases and eight contract cases, Valerie Hans found the median award was $115,000 and the mean award close to $700,000 due to five awards of more than $1 million. Other empirical studies similarly demonstrate modest median awards with the large majority resulting from compensatory damages. Moreover, punitive damages are rarely awarded. Judicial review of jury-awarded damages tends to reduce rather than increase awards, especially for punitive damages. The success rate of plaintiffs and the monetary value of awards has varied depending on the type of case, the nature of the injuries sustained, the state in which the case was tried, local settlement practices, and the particular mix of cases going to trial. Indeed, a Harvard Medical School malpractice study highlighted the great disparity between injuries suffered and claims or lawsuits filed. No overall trend toward massive awards granted by juries can be discerned across the array of evidence.

While largely unsuccessful at the federal level, many states, according to Valerie Hans, "have changed their tort systems, imposing new restrictions on the civil jury, including modification of liability rules and limits on monetary awards." Judicial decisions in the 1970s and 1980s would gradually weaken the extent of liability law. The Supreme Court gave judges greater control over which expert witnesses could testify, reduced the role of juries in patent cases, and approved restrictions on jury discretion.

Once again, it is clear that concepts of liability by corporate bodies, and the power of juries to regulate business conduct by awarding damages have been shaped by the shifting balance of political forces and social attitudes in the particular context of the 1980s and 1990s.

SEE ALSO

corporate criminal liability; *caveat emptor*; product deficiencies; Nader, Ralph; consumer deaths; asbestos; medical malpractice.

BIBLIOGRAPHY. Stephen Daniels and Joanne Martin, *Civil Juries and the Politics of Reform* (Northwestern University Press, 1995); Mark Dowie, "Pinto Madness," *Mother Jones* (September–October 1977); Lawrence Friedman, *American Law in the Twentieth Century* (Yale University Press, 2002); Valerie P. Hans, *Business on Trial: The Civil Jury and Corporate Responsibility* (Yale University Press, 2000); Kenneth Jost, "Tampering with Evidence: The Liability and Competitiveness Myth," *American Bar Association Journal* (v.44, 1992); Morton Keller, "Law and the Corporation," *Looking Back at Law's Century* (Cornell University Press, 2002); Stephen Rostoff, Henry N. Pontell, and Robert Tillman, *Profit Without Honor: White-Collar Crime and the Looting of*

America (Prentice Hall, 1998); U.S. Department of Justice, Press Release "Three out of Four Cases Settled Out of Court," (April 13, 1995).

SEAN PURDY, PH.D.
QUEEN'S UNIVERSITY, CANADA

Justice, Department of

THE U.S. Department of Justice (DOJ) is a cabinet department in the United States government that enforces the law and defends the interests of the United States according to the law, ensuring fair and impartial administration of justice for all Americans. The Department of Justice is administered by the U.S. attorney general, one of the original members of the president's cabinet.

The office of attorney general is older than the Department of Justice which the attorneys general have headed since 1870. The Judiciary Act of 1789 created the office of attorney general, providing for the appointment of "a meet person, learned in the law, to act as Attorney-General for the United States." The act stipulated that the duties of the attorney general were to prosecute and conduct all suits in the Supreme Court concerning the United States, and to give his advice and opinion upon questions of law when the president of the United States required it or when the heads of any of the departments required it.

The 1789 act did not make the attorney general a member of the presidential cabinet, but President George Washington decided that he needed the first attorney general of the United States, Edmund Randolph, to attend all of the cabinet meetings because of the numerous legal matters that he and his cabinet discussed. Since the attorney general continued to attend the cabinet meetings in the administrations of John Adams and Thomas Jefferson and beyond, the office became recognized as a cabinet post. The attorney general is directly appointed by the president and is confirmed by the Senate. From 1789 to 2003, there have been 79 attorneys general.

ATTORNEYS GENERAL

Congress routinely asked the first nine attorneys general Edmund Randolph, William Bradford, Charles Lee, Levi Lincoln, John Breckenridge, Caesar A. Rodney, William Pinkney, Richard Rush, and William Wirt to act as its counselor and render opinions of Congressional actions. But by this time, the duties of the attorney general had increased to almost unmanageable size.

The attorney general was expected to give opinions to the president, to the heads to the executive departments, and to Congress. William Wirt, the ninth attorney general, decided to remedy the situation. In 1819, Wirt wrote to President James Monroe, announcing that effective immediately, the office of the attorney general would revert to the original Judiciary Act of 1789 and render opinions only to the president and heads of the executive departments. Wirt's action did not decrease the workload of the attorneys general.

Roger B. Taney, of Dred-Scot case fame, Benjamin F. Butler and Felix Grundy served as attorneys general under Andrew Jackson and Martin Van Buren. Henry Dilworth Gilpin, the 14th attorney general from 1840–41 was born in Lancaster, England and came to the United States to earn his law degree from the University of Pennsylvania and work for Van Buren and his adopted country. John J. Crittenden served as the 15th attorney general in 1841 and the 22nd attorney general, from 1850 to 1853.

President James Buchanan appointed Edwin McMasters Stanton the 25th attorney general and he served from 1860 to 1861. In 1862, President Abraham Lincoln appointed him Secretary of War and he continued in that office until President Andrew Johnson suspended him on August 12, 1867. The Senate reinstated him on January 14, 1868, and he continued in office. President Ulysses Grant offered Stanton a justiceship on the Supreme Court, and he was confirmed on December 20, 1869, although he died before he could occupy the post.

President Abraham Lincoln appointed Edward Bates and James Speed as the 26th and 27th attorneys general. Bates, a prominent Whig anti-slavery proponent, spent one term in the House of Representatives and several terms in the Missouri state legislature. James Speed was elected to the Kentucky Legislature in 1861. Lincoln appointed him attorney general on December 2, 1864, and he remained in office until July 1866 when he resigned and resumed his practice of law.

After the Civil War, the amount of legal work involving the United States increased dramatically, prompting the government to hire hundreds of private attorneys to help handle the workload. Eighty-one years after the 1789 Act to appoint a "meet person learned in the law" as attorney general, Congress passed the Act to Establish the Department of Justice. Grant signed the bill to establish a Department of Justice into law on June 22, 1870 and the department officially began operations on July 1, 1870. The act designated the attorney general the head of the Department of Justice and established the office of the solicitor general to assist the attorney general. The act also gave the attorney general and the department control over federal law enforcement.

President Andrew Johnson appointed Henry Stanbery attorney general in July 1866, and on March 12, 1868, Stanbery resigned to defend the president during his impeachment trial. In an ironic conclusion, when the trial ended, Johnson renominated him attorney general and also to the Supreme Court, but the Senate did not confirm him.

William Maxwell Evarts, 29th attorney general, also helped defend Johnson in his impeachment trial as principal counsel to the president. On July 15, 1868, Johnson appointed him attorney general, and he later was secretary of state under President Rutherford B. Hayes, the U.S. delegate to the International Monetary Conference at Paris, and a U.S. Senator.

Grant appointed five attorneys general: Ebenezer R. Hoar, Amos T. Akerman, George H. Williams, Edwards Pierrepont and Alphonso Taft. Hoar also was a member of the Joint High Commission that framed the Treaty of Washington with Great Britain in 1873-75 and was also elected to the House of Representatives. During the Civil War, Amos T. Akerman served in the quartermaster's department in the Confederacy and as district attorney for Georgia in 1869. Grant appointed him attorney general on June 23, 1870. As a member of the Oregon Constitutional Convention, Williams helped form the state government and completed a term as Senator from Oregon.

In 1871, he was a member of the commission to settle the Confederate ship *Alabama* claims from the Treaty of Washington. Edwards Pierrepont served as attorney general from 1875 to 1876, and then became minister plenipotentiary of the United States to Great Britain. Alphonso Taft filled the cabinet post of secretary of war for Grant before he became the 34th attorney general on May 22, 1876.

After his term of office expired on March 11, 1877, he resumed practicing law, and eventually became minister to Austria and minister to Russia.

Charles Devens, attorney general for President Rutherford B. Hayes, was also Civil War hero and served as justice of the Supreme Court of Massachusetts. President James A. Garfield appointed Isaac Wayne McVeagh as attorney general and after Garfield's assassination, McVeagh continued to serve President Chester A. Arthur until October 24, 1881, when Benjamin H. Brewster took his place.

Augustus H. Garland of Arkansas, attorney general under President Grover Cleveland, won a seat in the Confederate Provisional Congress that assembled in 1861 and was elected a member of the House of Representatives of the First Congress of the Confederate States. In 1866, Garland won a seat in the U.S. Senate, but was not allowed to take his place since Arkansas had not yet been readmitted to the Union. Later Garland served as governor of Arkansas and as Senator. Cleveland appointed him the 38th attorney general in 1885. Garland died while arguing a case before the Supreme Court. William Henry Harrison Miller, Richard Olney, Judson Harmon and Joseph McKenna, attorneys general from 1889 to 1898 rounded out the 19th century attorneys general appointed by Grover Cleveland and William McKinley.

20TH-CENTURY ATTORNEYS GENERAL

As the department's workload continued to grow into the 20th century, the Justice Department expanded to include deputy attorneys general and several divisions to manage the workload. John William Griggs, McKinley's appointee for 43rd attorney general, was also one of the first members appointed to the Permanent Court of Arbitration at The Hague, Holland. Philander Chase Knox was secretary of state under President William Howard Taft in 1909 and also served in the Senate. During his Senate career he drafted pioneering legislation that created the Department of Commerce, Department of Labor, and established the regulatory power of the Interstate Commerce Commission over railroad rates. McKinley appointed him 44th attorney general on April 5, 1901.

President Theodore Roosevelt appointed William Moody and Charles Joseph Bonaparte attorneys general. Before he became attorney general,

The Department of Justice in Washington, D.C., uses its Antitrust Division to enforce corporate laws.

Moody was a Congressman and secretary of the navy. He resigned the office of attorney general on December 17, 1906, to become associate justice of the Supreme Court. Charles Joseph Bonaparte spent three years as attorney general, from 1906 to 1909, after being appointed by Roosevelt. He also served as secretary of the navy, and a member of the Board of Overseers of Harvard College.

Appointed by Taft, George Woodward Wickersham served as 47th attorney general from 1909 to 1913. Two other presidents used Wickersham's talents. President Woodrow Wilson named him to serve on the War Trade Board to Cuba shortly after the United States entered World War I, and in 1929, President Herbert Hoover named him to the National Commission on Law Observance and Enforcement.

Wilson appointed three attorneys general. On March 5, 1913, Wilson chose James Clark McReynolds to be the 48th attorney general. McReynolds specialized in antitrust laws and after his tenure from 1913 to 1914, he became associate justice of the Supreme Court. Thomas Watt Gregory spent eight years as a regent of the University of Texas and worked as special assistant to the attorney general in the investigation and proceedings against the New York, New Haven and Hartford Railroad Company. He worked as attorney general from 1914 to 1919. Alexander Mitchell Palmer

served in Congress from 1909 to 1915, was a judge of the U.S. Court of Claims, and was alien property custodian under the Trading with the Enemy Act. During his tenure as 50th attorney general from 1919 to 1921, Palmer spearheaded "the Red Scare," rounding up, imprisoning, and deporting thousands of suspected communists and other "undesirables."

Harry M. Daugherty, Harlan Fiske Stone, and John G. Sargent were respectively the 51st, 52nd, and 53rd attorneys general. Daugherty served under Warren G. Harding and Calvin Coolidge from 1921 to 1924. He was acquitted of charges of defrauding the U.S. government in the Teapot Dome Scandal. Harlin Fiske Stone was dean of Columbia Law School from 1910 to1923, and was appointed attorney general of the United States by Coolidge on April 7, 1924. Later he served as chief justice of the Supreme Court from 1941 until 1946. Coolidge appointed John Garibaldi Sargent as attorney general on March 17, 1925, and he remained in that office until March 5, 1929. Sargeant had served as chairman of the Vermont Commission on Uniform State Law, secretary for civil and military affairs of Vermont, and attorney general of Vermont.

William DeWitt Mitchell, 54th attorney general, served as an infantry officer during the Spanish American War and World War I. Hoover appointed him attorney general on March 4, 1929, and he held that office until March 4, 1933. After that he practiced law in New York City and served as chief counsel of the joint congressional committee investigating Pearl Harbor.

President Franklin D. Roosevelt appointed four attorneys general. Homer S. Cummings had been a U.S. Senator, state's attorney, and chairman of the committee on State Prison Conditions. After serving as attorney general from 1933 to 1939, he worked to improve the American prison system, and established Alcatraz Island prison in San Francisco Bay in 1934. Frank Murphy, 56th attorney general, filled a term as governor-general of the Philippine Islands in 1933, and first U.S. high commissioner to the Philippines from 1935 to 1936. He was also governor of Michigan, and an associate justice of the Supreme Court. Fifty-Seventh Attorney General Robert H. Jackson 's term lasted from 1940 to 1941.

He went on to become associate justice of the Supreme Court as well, and at the end of World War II, President Harry Truman appointed him as the U.S. representative in meetings with the "Big

Three" powers (England, Russia, and France) to negotiate agreement for the international trials of German war criminals. Justice Jackson was chief counsel of those trials, the International Military Tribunal at Nuremberg, Germany.

Francis Biddle functioned as a transition attorney general between Roosevelt and Truman from 1941 to 1945. A prolific author on legal issues, one of his books was *Mr. Justice Holmes,* a memoir of his experiences as private secretary to Justice Oliver Wendell Holmes. Thomas Campbell Clark began his political career as civil district attorney for Dallas County, Texas, and moved on to the Department of Justice. Truman appointed him attorney general on July 1, 1945. After he left in 1949, Clark was appointed to the Supreme Court.

Truman also appointed James H. McGrath and James P. McGranery as 60th and 61st attorneys general. James H. McGrath was elected governor of Rhode Island in 1946, and on August 24, 1949, Truman appointed him attorney general. He resigned on April 7, 1952, and entered private law practice. James P. McGranery served in World War I as an observation pilot with the Army Air Force and was elected Congressman from Pennsylvania. In November 1943, he was appointed assistant to the attorney general and was responsible for supervising the Federal Bureau of Investigation, Immigration and Naturalization Service, Bureau of Prisons and various divisions. His term as attorney general lasted from 1952 to 1953.

President Dwight David Eisenhower selected Herbert Brownell and William Pierce Rogers as the 62nd and 63rd attorneys general. Appointed on January 21, 1953, Brownell remained in office until November 8, 1957. After that he served as the U.S. member to the Permanent Court of Arbitration at The Hague. William Pierce Rogers practiced law in New York City, served as a lieutenant commander in the U.S. Navy, and worked as chief counsel of the Senate War Investigating Committee. Eisenhower appointed him as attorney general on November 8, 1957, and he served until January 20, 1961. In 1969, President Richard M. Nixon named him secretary of state and he held that office until 1973.

NEUTRALS AND ADVOCATES

In her study of attorneys general called *Conflicting Loyalties, Law and Politics in the Attorney General's Office, 1789–1990,* Nancy Baker argues that there have been two kinds of attorneys general in American history: the Advocate and the Neutral. Advocates are mainly concerned with the political priorities in the administration. An advocate attorney general acts as the unofficial "president's lawyer." Robert F. Kennedy is probably the best example of an advocate attorney general. He spoke out passionately about the issues of poverty, discrimination, and corruption and maintained some level of involvement in political activities during his term of office.

John Mitchell, Nixon's first attorney general, advocated for Nixon enough to become involved in the Watergate affair and spent 19 months in prison for perjury and obstruction of justice. President Ronald Reagan's attorneys general also were involved in his administration affairs. William French Smith, Reagan's first attorney general writes in his memoirs about the crusading spirit that he and his colleagues felt in Washington, D.C.

Reagan's second attorney general, Edwin Meese III, sought to overturn liberal Supreme Court decisions like *Miranda* and *Roe v. Wade* by means of strong arguments before the Supreme Court and by appointing only federal judges opposing *Roe v. Wade* (the Supreme Court decision allowing legal abortion).

In her examples of Neutral attorneys general, Baker cites Edward Levi, President Gerald Ford's attorney general. Appointed in a political atmosphere of chaos and distrust, Levi was a non-partisan academic, appointed to restore some credibility to the administration after the Watergate scandal. Griffin Bell, President Jimmy Carter's attorney general, was appointed in the same uncertain political atmosphere as Levi. Fiercely independent, Bell reportedly clashed with Carter on several occasions for refusing to adjust his advice to the president's views.

Baker considered President William J. Clinton's Attorney General Janet Reno, the first female attorney general in American history, to be a Neutral as well. Both supporters and opponents of Clinton criticized her handling of the Whitewater, fund-raising, and the Monica Lewinsky scandals.

The U.S. Senate confirmed John Ashcroft's appointment as 79th attorney general of the United States on December 22, 2000. Ashcroft pledged to renew the war on drugs, reduce gun violence and combat discrimination. He vowed to lead a professional Justice Department free from politics, and dedicated to upholding the rule of law.

DOJ ORGANIZATION

Over the 214 years since its inception in 1789, the Department of Justice has gone through several organizations and reorganizations, dictated by presidents, precedents, and politics. At the beginning of the 21st century, the Department of Justice is divided into approximately 60 sections. Following is a summary of a few of the Justice Department divisions.

The Antitrust Division has been enforcing antitrust laws for 60 years, monitoring practices like price-fixing, conspiracies, and corporate mergers that reduce competition, and predatory acts that strengthen monopolies. Its goal is to protect economic freedom and opportunity by promoting competition in the marketplace.

The Bureau of Alcohol, Tobacco, Firearms, and Explosives dates to 1789 when the first Congress taxed imported spirits to help finance the Revolutionary War debt. The bureau has taxing powers but cannot enact or amend the law.

Established in 1957, the Bureau of Civil Rights Division is responsible for enforcing federal laws that prohibit discrimination of the basis of race, sex, handicap, religion, and national origin.

The Criminal Division of the Department of Justice under the guidance of the assistant attorney general, develops, enforces, and supervises the enforcement of all federal criminal laws except those assigned to other divisions. The Criminal Division employees 93 U.S. attorneys to oversee criminal matters under more than 900 statutes and in certain civil litigation.

The Drug Enforcement Administration's mission is to enforce the drug laws of the United States and bring lawbreakers to justice.

The Environment and Natural Resources Division enforces pollution control laws, acquires property by eminent domain for the federal government, and tries cases under wildlife protection laws. It handles Native American rights and claims.

THE FBI AND ATF

Attorney General Charles Bonaparte created the Federal Bureau of Investigation (FBI) during the administration of Theodore Roosevelt. It began with a force of 34 agents to investigate violations of laws involving national banking, bankruptcy, naturalization, antitrusts, and land fraud. The FBI grew with America's expanding law enforcement needs. On May 10, 1924, Attorney General Harlan Fiske Stone selected J. Edgar Hoover to head the FBI. An employee of the Department of Justice since 1917, Hoover had directed enemy alien operations during World War I and, under Attorney General A. Mitchell Palmer, had investigated suspected anarchists and communists. For the next 48 years, Hoover headed the FBI until his death on May 2, 1972. His leadership of the FBI was often controversial, but he shaped it along the Progressive lines that Roosevelt had envisioned.

In the years after Hoover, the FBI. modernized and expanded its law enforcement capabilities, but not without continuing controversy. In August 1992, Deputy U.S. Marshal William Degan was killed at Ruby Ridge, Idaho, while tailing federal fugitive Randall Weaver. In the standoff, an FBI sniper killed Weaver's wife. In April 1993, at a compound in Waco, Texas, FBI agents tried to end a 51-day-standoff with a heavily armed religious sect that had killed four officers of the Bureau of Alcohol, Tobacco and Firearms (ATF). Members of the sect set the compound on fire and 80 people died. These two tragedies inspired the public and Congress to examine FBI methods and power, and the bureau has modernized and broadened itself to include more women and minorities and closer cooperation with other law enforcement agencies.

OTHER DOJ DIVISIONS

The Federal Bureau of Prisons administers prisons and strives to make them safe, humane, and secure and to assist offenders to become future law-abiding citizens.

On March 1, 2003, the Immigration and Naturalization Service became part of the U.S. Department of Homeland Security and its functions were divided into various bureaus of that department.

Established in 1993, the National Drug Intelligence Center is part of the Justice Department and a member of the intelligence community. Its purpose is to support national policymakers and law enforcement with strategic domestic drug intelligence, support counter-drug efforts and to produce national, regional, and state drug assessments.

The Office for Domestic Preparedness was established in 1993 to assist state and local governments in acquiring sufficient equipment and training to respond to and manage terrorist incidents involving weapons of mass destruction. When the Homeland Security Act of 2002 passed, the Office of Domestic Preparedness was transferred to the Department of Homeland Security from the Department of Justice's Office of Justice Programs.

Established and activated in September 2001 by Congressional directive, the Office of the Federal Detention Trustee detains federal prisoners and aliens awaiting trial or removal from the United States. The mission of the Federal Detention Trustee is to provide humane confinement of persons in federal custody awaiting trail or immigration proceedings.

The Office of Information and Privacy coordinates implementation of the Freedom of Information Act and decides all appeals pertaining to denials of access to information under the act.

The Office of the Solicitor General supervises and conducts government litigation in the Supreme Court. The United States is involved in about two-thirds of all the cases the. Supreme Court decides on each year.

The Office for Victims of Crime provides small grants up to $5,000 to grassroots community-based victim organizations and coalitions to improve outreach and services to crime victims through its Helping Outreach Programs to Expand (HOPE) initiative.

Established in 1995, the Office on Violence Against Women provides national and international leadership in addressing violence against women. It provides grants to states and territories to train personnel, establish specialized domestic violence and sexual assault units, assist victims of violence, and hold perpetrators accountable.

The Tax Division handles or supervises civil and criminal matters that originate from the internal revenue laws. Tax Division attorneys work closely with the Internal Revenue Service and U.S. attorneys to develop tax administration polices, handle tax litigation in federal and state courts, and handle criminal prosecutions and appeals.

SEE ALSO

antitrust; investigation techniques; prosecution; reform and regulation; Securities and Exchange Commission; Environmental Protection Agency.

BIBLIOGRAPHY. Cornell W. Clayton, *The Politics of Justice: The Attorney General and the Making of Legal Policy* (M. E. Sharpe, 1992); Arthur J. Dodge, *Origin and Development of the Office of the Attorney General* (Government Printing Office, 1929); Luther A. Huston, *The Department of Justice* (Praeger Publishers, 1967); Ross L. Malone, Jr., "The Department of Justice: The World's Largest Law Office," *American Bar Association Journal* (May 1953); Daniel J. Meador, *The President, the Attorney General, and the Department of Justice* (University of Virginia Press, 1980); H. Jefferson Powell, *The Constitution and Attorneys General* (Carolina Academic Press, 1999).

KATHY WARNES, PH.D.
UNIVERSITY OF TOLEDO

K

Keating, Charles (1924–)

THE SAVINGS and loan (S&L) scandals of the 1980s are considered to be one of the worst financial fiascoes in American history. Charles Keating, the head of Lincoln Savings and Loan, became the major villain of the S&L scandals. Keating has often been referred to as the "Hannibal Lecter of Finance," a reference to a cannibalistic character in the novel and movie, *Silence of the Lambs*. Keating's background should have made him an American hero rather than a villain. He had been a fighter pilot during World War II and afterward appeared to be headed for a successful business career as the executive vice president of American Financial in Cincinnati, Ohio. However, in 1979, both Keating and his boss were charged with defrauding stockholders when they approved $14 million in loans to company insiders and to themselves. Keating proclaimed his innocence and was fined. He than attempted to redeem himself through his campaigns against drugs and pornography and with his generous donations to charity.

In 1980, Keating moved to Phoenix, Arizona, and established a holding company, which he called American Continental Corporation. In 1984, Keating acquired the Lincoln Savings and Loan in Irvine, California. Within four years, Keating ostensibly increased the assets of Lincoln Savings from $2 billion to more than $5 billion. In reality, the assets were due to deceptive accounting practices. Keating and his cohorts at Lincoln S&L engaged in the practice of trading empty lots with other companies and listing them as profit-producing sales.

Compounding the company's accounting frauds, Keating invested two-thirds of the company's federally insured deposits in junk bonds and other various high-risk investments. In April 1989, federal regulators took control of the Lincoln S&L. Ultimately, the collapse of Lincoln Savings and Loan cost the American taxpayers $2.6 billion, and the overall bailout of the S&L industry amounted to approximately $500 billion.

When Keating began receiving unwanted attention from the federal government, he decided to use his contacts in the U.S. Senate, Alan Cranston (D-CA), Dennis DeConcini (D-AZ), John Glenn (D-OH), John McCain (R-AZ), and Donald Riegle (D-MI), for protection from government investigators. Keating was apparently so sure that his influence would pay off that he boasted about his "bribes" to reporters. The Senators subsequently became known as the Keating Five, and the ensuing investigation and scandal derailed the Congressional careers of two of the five senators involved in the affair, and stained the reputation of the entire U.S. Senate.

Keating faced a series of trials in both state and federal courts. Altogether, he was convicted of 90 counts of fraud, racketeering, and conspiracy and was sentenced to 12 years in prison. Most of the charges stemmed from the sale of junk bonds that were illegally marketed to thousands of clients, many who were elderly and ill able to deal with substantial financial losses. Keating was also forced to pay $156 million in fines, and the government auctioned off his home. While Keating was serving his sentence, a federal jury in Tucson, Arizona, awarded $3 billion in damages against Keating and his associates for damages to the investors in the S&L swindle.

In April 1996, U.S. District Court Judge Mariana Pfaelzer set aside Keating's state convictions and ordered a new trial, deciding that the jury had been prejudiced by prior knowledge of the Keating affair, and by the behavior of Judge Lance Ito who gave the jury incorrect instructions (Ito later presided over the controversial O. J. Simpson murder trial).

In December 1996, a federal judge also threw out Keating's federal convictions, claiming that they were tainted. In a separate decision, a three-judge panel decided that the evidence used to convict Keating was far from overwhelming. Overall, Keating spent four-and-a-half years in jail and continued to publicly insist that he was innocent of all charges.

SEE ALSO
Keating Five; accounting fraud; savings and loan fraud; bank fraud; land flipping.

BIBLIOGRAPHY. Sam Allis, et al., "Update: The Corporate Crime Files," *Time* (December 16, 1996); William F. Buckley, Jr., "The Anatomy of Corruption," *National Review* (December 22, 1989); William Black, "The Keating Five, April 18, 1987," *Eyewitness to Wall Street: 400 Years of Dreamers, Schemers, Busts, and Booms* (Broadway Books, 2001); "Financier Jailed," *Maclean's* (July 19, 1993); "Fall of the Mighty," *Time* (July 20, 1992); Warren B. Rudman, *Combat: Twelve Years in the Senate* (Random House, 1996); Skip Thurman, "Judge Throws out Keating Fraud Conviction," *Christian Science Monitor* (December 4, 1996); Adam Zagorin, "Charlie's An Angel?" *Time* (February 3, 1997).

ELIZABETH PURDY, PH.D.
INDEPENDENT SCHOLAR

Keating Five

IN 1990, THE U.S. Senate Select Committee on Ethics investigated charges that Senators Alan Cranston (D-CA), Dennis DeConcini (D-AZ), John Glenn (D-OH), John McCain (R-AZ), and Donald Riegle (D-MI) had improperly interfered with government investigators on behalf of Charles Keating who had become embroiled in savings and loan (S&L) banking scandals. Contributions from Keating to the five Senators had ranged from a few thousand dollars to more than $1 million. The five Senators strenuously objected to being lumped together and asked that each case be judged on its own merits. Nevertheless, it was almost a given that the press would view the five Senators as the "Keating Five" rather than as individuals. Objections were also made when the Senate investigating committee under the chairmanship of Republican Warren B. Rudman dealt with the five cases as a whole. In September 1989, the U.S. government brought criminal charges against Keating for fraud, racketeering and conspiracy, and the government took control of Keating's Lincoln Savings and Loan.

Much of the attention during the Senate investigation centered around two meetings that the Keating Five had with four government regulators who were investigating Keating. The investigators claimed that they were intimidated by the five senators and insisted that the purpose of the meeting was to stymie the investigation. In their view, DeConcini had been the most "hostile" of the group. Questions inevitably followed about Keating's influence on various political decisions made by the five senators, and whether the senators had intentionally interfered with the government investigation.

The American public reacted to the Senate investigation of the Keating Five with a mixture of outrage and scorn. With only one Republican among the five Senators accused of misconduct, it was a foregone conclusion that the investigation would be acrimonious and highly partisan. Rudman, chair of the Ethics Committee, claimed somewhat hopefully that the Democratic party was on the verge of collapse after losing three presidential elections and insisted that this made Democratic committee members hostile to the entire investigation. Senate rules dictated that the Ethics Committee be made up of three members of each party to avoid partisan annihilation of Senators brought before the committee. The committee had the option of either voting as bipartisans or of reporting a partisan deadlock to the Senate, which would have damaged the reputation of the entire Senate.

A number of complaints arose over leaks about the committee investigation. Democrats on the committee insisted that the leaks were coming from the Republicans. They also objected to the fact that Republicans were inclined to treat McCain and Glenn with kid gloves at the same time they were bitterly attacking Cranston, Riegle, and DeConcini.

After nine months of investigation, the committee's special counsel recommended that charges be dropped against McCain, the only Republican in the group, and Glenn who was treated with special respect an a former astronaut and a war hero. As expected, the committee split along party lines, and rejected the recommendations.

ALAN CRANSTON

The only one of the five senators rebuked by the Senate, Cranston had received more than $1 million from Keating in donations to his political campaigns and to his pet political projects. The Keating Five scandal caused the 30-year career of this senator, who had spent most of his political life trying to improve the conditions for people around the world, to end on a sour note. Keating had raised $10,000 for Cranston's unsuccessful 1984 presidential campaign and $39,000 for his 1986 Senate re-election campaign, and also made substantial contributions to the California Democratic Party and to various Political Action Committees (PACS) with which Cranston was associated. An additional $850,000 had been donated to three nonpartisan voter-education projects that Cranston supported.

At the time of the investigation, Cranston was suffering from prostate cancer and had decided not to run for re-election. He argued that the fact that he was leaving the Senate made him a perfect fall guy for the Ethics Committee. The Ethic Committee made a deal whereby Cranston would accept a formal Senate rebuke to avoid more serious charges. After the rebuke was announced on the floor of the Senate, Cranston apologized to his colleagues for focusing negative attention on the Senate but insisted that he had acted no differently than had most of his accusers. He may have been telling the truth because each of the 100 members of the Senate would have been loathe to face close scrutiny of their campaign contributions.

DENNIS DeCONCINI

After DeConcini and Keating, a fellow Arizonian, met during the course of anti-pornography work, the two men developed a political relationship. DeConcini reportedly launched an unsuccessful attempt to convince the Ronald Reagan administration to appoint Keating as ambassador to the Bahamas. Keating raised $33,000 and $48,000 for DeConcini's 1982 and 1988 campaigns respectively. In March 1987, Keating allegedly asked for DeConcini's help with his banking problems, setting in place an aggressive effort on DeConcini's part to help his political contributor. However, once the government filed formal charges against Keating, DeConcini returned the $48,000 that Keating had raised for his 1988 campaign. Republican members of the Ethics Committee believed that he should have also been rebuked by the Senate, but he was cleared of all charges.

JOHN GLENN

As a well-known astronaut and a fighter pilot from World War II, Glenn was an authentic American hero; and the public, the press and the Ethics Committee always viewed him as such. Keating and Glenn had been casual friends and political allies since 1970. James Grogan, who was employed by Keating as a lobbyist had once worked in Glenn's law office. In 1985, Keating donated $200,000 to a Political Action Committee (PAC), the National Council of Public Policy, with which Glenn was closely associated, to be used for state campaigns.

Keating also contributed $18,200 and $24,000 to Glenn's 1984 and 1986 campaigns respectively. Glenn seemed to have an innate distrust of political contributions from Keating in the midst of the ongoing S&L investigations and turned down Grogan's offer to help raise $100,000 for his 1984 re-election campaign. Glenn was cleared of charges.

JOHN McCAIN

Like Glenn, McCain was a certified war hero. McCain had been imprisoned for over five years by the North Vietnamese during the Vietnam War. Of the five senators involved in the Keating Five scandal, only McCain was a close personal friend of Keating. The two families had become so close that they vacationed together nine times, including a trip to Keating's vacation home in the Bahamas.

Keating had raised $112,000 for McCain's House elections in 1982 and 1984 and for McCain's 1986 Senate campaign. The Senator insisted that he thought his wife had sent Keating a check for $13,433 for the plane trip to the Bahamas, and he repaid Keating the $13,433 when he was informed that Keating had claimed the amount as a tax deduction. During the investigations, McCain and Keating allegedly had a heated confrontation, and the friendship ended. McCain was cleared of all charges by the Ethics Committee.

DONALD RIEGLE

After beginning his political life as a Republican, Riegle had become known as a highly partisan Democrat. Riegle met Keating in 1986 at the opening of Keating's Ponchartrain Hotel. By 1987, Riegle was in line to become the chair of the Senate Banking Committee, and Keating realized that Riegle was a person worth cultivating. He offered to host a fundraiser for Riegle at the Ponchartrain and eventually raised $78,250 for the Riegle campaign. Before that event had taken place, Riegle was allegedly asked for help in taking some of the investigative pressure off of Keating. Riegle decided not to run for re-election in 1994 even though he had been cleared of all charges.

In the wake of the Keating Five scandal, bipartisan support pushed the Ethics Reform Act of 1989 through both houses of Congress in an effort to identify what constituted ethical intervention by members of Congress in federal activities in which their constituents were involved. Congress was criticized, however, for not going far enough in specifying what constituted unethical intervention.

SEE ALSO
Keating, Charles; savings and loan fraud; Ethics Reform Act; corruption; ethics; prosecution.

BIBLIOGRAPHY. Chuck Alston, "Credibility of Senate Committee at Risk in Keating Five Probe," *Congressional Quarterly Weekly* (October 27, 1990); William Black, "The Keating Five, April 18, 1987," *Eyewitness to Wall Street* (Broadway Books, 2001); John R. Cranford, "Dennis DeConcini: Ran The Meeting," "Donald Riegle: Natural Ally," "John Glenn: Gray's Foe," "John McCain: Friend No More," "Keating and the Five Senators," *Congressional Quarterly Weekly Report* (January 26, 1991); Warren B. Rudman, *Combat: Twelve Years in the Senate* (Random House, 1996).

ELIZABETH PURDY, PH.D.
INDEPENDENT SCHOLAR

Kennedy, Robert F. (1925–1968)

DURING PRESIDENT John F. Kennedy's (JFK) administration from 1961 to 1963 the fight against crime, especially organized crime and its associated white-collar crime, was waged by Attorney General Robert F. Kennedy (RFK), the president's brother. The Kennedy brothers waged a crusade against organized crime once they realized the extent of the power it wielded. The result was the Organized Crime Bill of 1962.

Although the president's father, Joseph P. Kennedy, reputedly had mob connections in his business dealings and the president shared a mistress with a well-known mobster, and enjoyed social relations with some mob-related people, RFK had long been a foe of the rampant corruption in unions, bribery of law officials, and the ever increasing hold of organized crime on the United States. He thought that crime was paralyzing the country and that government subsequently played a secondary role in the affairs on the nation.

RFK, trained as a lawyer, began his formative experiences as assistant chief counsel of the Permanent Subcommittee on Investigations headed by Joseph McCarthy. However, he eventually disagreed with the investigative methods of the committee and resigned. From 1955 to 1957, RFK served as chief counsel under Senator John McClellan's Rackets Committee and became its driving force. His tenacious and relentless pursuit of Teamster David Beck and Jimmy Hoffa earned him nationwide notice. Racketeering in the labor unions, especially the fiscal corruption of the AFL-CIO and the Teamsters was exposed.

White-collar crime, prostitution, loan sharking and gambling were rampant and dominated many aspects of U.S. society. In 1960, RFK publicized the problems of the expansive reach of organized crime in the United States with a book, *The Enemy*

Within. The president agreed with his decision to fight organized crime using all of the government's capabilities.

As an activist attorney general, RFK fought legislatively against the organized crime figures who had helped his brother win the election in 1960. His clandestine adventures with the Federal Bureau of Narcotics convinced him that organized crime existed despite the strong denials of Federal Bureau of Investigation (FBI) director J.Edgar Hoover. For decades, the influence of the mob intimidated or fixed juries, killed witnesses, and paid off judicial officials, including judges and police officers. Moreover, they extracted billions of dollars from the American economy without paying taxes.

RFK believed that the legal violations committed by the criminal elements would eventually disrupt the country, so he expanded the Criminal Division of the Justice Department by increasing the numbers of lawyers from 17 to 50. Grand juries meant that days in court for Justice lawyers jumped from 61 to 1,364. Secured indictments also rose, from 0 to 683 (it was 0 because the FBI had not recognized organized crime, thus no one had ever been charged). Convictions also rose from 0 to 619. This was all due to the Organized Crime Bill. To counter the anarchic crime and corruption, RFK made the unprecedented move requiring the various judicial federal government agencies to cooperate, thereby facilitating various criminal investigations. The Internal Revenue Service (IRS), for example, was brought into partnership with the FBI resulting in numerous convictions of criminals.

When JFK was assassinated, the attorney general effectively lost the power he had enjoyed as the president's brother. One effect on RFK from the assassination was to be diverted from the battle against organized crime. RFK resigned as attorney general on September 3, 1964. He ran a successful campaign as Senator from New York, and waged a liberal presidential campaign in 1968 when he was assassinated.

SEE ALSO

organized crime; Cuba; Racketeer Influenced Corrupt Organizations Act; Johnson, Lyndon B.

BIBLIOGRAPHY. Henry Fairlie, *The Kennedy Promise: the Politics of Expectation* (Doubleday, 1973); Robert Goldfarb, *Perfect Villains, Imperfect Heroes: Robert Kennedy's War Against Organized Crime* (Random House,1995); C. David Heyman, *RFK: A Candid Biography of Robert F. Kennedy* (Penguin Group, 1998); Robert F. Kennedy, *The Enemy Within* (Harper & Row, 1960); Victor S. Navasky, *Kennedy Justice* (Atheneum, 1971).

ANNETTE RICHARDSON, PH.D.
UNIVERSITY OF ALBERTA, CANADA

Kepone Scandal

WITH THE JAMES River contaminated by the toxic pesticide kepone, Virginia authorities followed a do-nothing policy dictated by lack of clean-up funds. Fines levied against Allied Chemical, the company responsible for the contamination, had first been reduced, then managed incompetently, while the commercial fishing industry urged early reopening of the river.

Kepone, a grayish white powder, was used in ant traps and to kill potato and banana plants. It was banned in the United States in 1975, the same year that the state of Virginia closed a small kepone plant near the James River, citing workers who showed signs of over-exposure to the chemical Over-exposure first would lead to headaches, nervousness, tremors, slurred speech, muscle-twitching, poor memory, and visual disturbances, then lead to cancer, reproductive, kidney, and liver damage.

The plant, operated by Life Sciences Product Company after 1973, made kepone for Allied Chemical, had been an Allied Chemical facility from 1966 to 1973, and was owned by two former Allied employees. A state investigation discovered that the plant had illegally released kepone into the environment, first to the James River and later to the local sewage plant.

While Governor Godwin Mills immediately banned fishing on a 100-mile stretch of the James River, he also petitioned the U.S. Environmental Protection Agency (EPA) to raise the permissible level of kepone in fish, a move that would have allowed the river to be reopened. In late January 1977, U.S. District Judge Robert R. Merhige levied a record $13.2 million fine against Allied Chemical, which pleaded no contest to 940 counts of illegal dumping.

He then agreed to reduce the fine to $5 million if Allied Chemical created an $8 million environmental fund for Virginia. Merhige declared that the company's managers were "good boys in my book." That October, the *Washington Post* reported the state of Virginia levied its own $5.25 million fine for environmental clean-up.

Only about $5 million of the fines was earmarked for cleaning up the river and related contaminated sites. Investigations in 1985 determined that the money had been exhausted, while the James River remained choked with contaminated sediment. State officials admitted to the *Washington Post* that a natural disaster could stir up the sediment but noted that the state could afford neither the $225,000 a year needed for monitoring nor the estimated $2 billion required to dredge the river bottom. Available dredging methods were, by this time, as likely to do as much harm as good.

The money had been distributed among at least 50 programs, all coordinated by Roy N. Puckett, who was legendary for keeping his records in his head. After he died in 1981, the state took nine months to figure out how the money had been spent. Betty J. Diener, Virginia Secretary of Commerce and Resources, told the *Washington Post* in 1985 that the second-largest project funded from the fine had been a $516,000 marketing campaign to help Virginia's beleaguered seafood industry. The largest project was the replacement of a sewage plant that had been damaged by kepone-laced wastes; other projects included studies of the health effects of kepone and a plan for burning kepone at sea.

The ban on fishing in the James had been partially lifted in 1980, only to be reinstated by Governor John Dalton when kepone levels in fish spiked. A circuit judge overturned that ban on the grounds that public hearings were necessary. Within hours of the judge's decision, commercial fishing fleets were working on the James, just as they had jumped the gun on the abortive January 1 lifting of the ban. When fish showed three times the permissible level of kepone, the governor invoked his emergency powers to reinstate the ban. His successor, backed by the fishing industry, petitioned the EPA to triple the permissible level of kepone in fish. EPA documents suggest that the agency had not agreed to restate permissible levels of kepone since 1977.

Although environmentalists predicted that the James River could need hundreds of years to clean itself, the Virginia Board of Health declared in 1988 that kepone levels in fish were negligible and reopened the river for commercial fishing.

SEE ALSO
water pollution; Environmental Protection Agency; Allied Chemical.

BIBLIOGRAPHY. Paul G. Edwards, "Firm Pays $5 Million for Kepone Damage," *Washington Post* (October 14, 1977); Glenn Frankel, "Dalton Restores Ban on Fishing in James," *Washington Post* (May 14, 1980); Michael Isikoff, "Va. Agencies Seek to Ease Kepone Rules," Washington Post (June 20, 1982); Bill McAllister, "Allied's Fine Cut To $5 Million for Kepone Pollution," *Washington Post* (February 2, 1977); Bill McAllister, "Dangers of Kepone are Argued," *Washington Post* (January 27, 1977); Bill McAllister, "Lament for a River Befouled," *Washington Post* (May 24, 1980); Sandra Sugawara, "10 Years After Kepone Dumping, Problems Persist," *Washington Post* (July 29, 1985); U.S. Environmental Protection Agency (www.epa.gov); "Va. Lifts Last Ban On Commercial Fishing in James," *Washington Post* (May 11, 1988).

WENDE VYBORNEY FELLER, PH.D.
ST. MARY'S COLLEGE OF CALIFORNIA

Kerr-McGee

THE GIANT OKLAHOMA-based energy company's safety record became absorbed in national questions about nuclear energy after the mysterious death of laboratory analyst Karen Silkwood. However, the Cimarron River plutonium plant where Silkwood worked was not the only Kerr-McGee property where health and safety issues have been raised.

Although Kerr-McGee began as an oil drilling operation in the Oklahoma plains, its problems centered on Kerr-McGee Nuclear, a subsidiary corporation that processed uranium and plutonium for the federal government. Plutonium, like uranium, is used in nuclear bombs and nuclear power plants. Like all of the elements used for nuclear devices, plutonium emits alpha rays: radiation that, if absorbed in sufficient quantity, can cause cells in a seemingly healthy body to reproduce in a mutated form, ultimately resulting in cancer.

The Los Alamos National Laboratories call plutonium "a very dangerous radiological hazard" due to its high emission of alpha rays. Once plutonium enters the body, it can accumulate in the bones, lungs, and liver, where it continues to emit alpha rays long after the initial exposure.

The November 13, 1974, death of whistleblower Silkwood in a single-car accident as she drove to meet a *New York Times* reporter has spawned conspiracy theories that make it difficult to separate Kerr-McGee's actual misdeeds from plausible but unprovable notions of what might have happened. The facts that a jury accepted in 1979, awarding $10.5 million to Silkwood's heirs, were that Kerr-McGee's negligence in its safety procedures had caused Silkwood to become contaminated with plutonium in early November 1974, putting her at serious risk for cancer later in life. At the 11-week trial, workers testified about lapses in safety, including painting over the remnants of plutonium spills, failure to disclose cancer risks to workers, advance warning of government inspections, policies of operating the plant under conditions when it should have been temporarily shut down for decontamination, and insufficient security to prevent plutonium from being removed from the plant. Radiation expert Karl Z. Morgan testified that Kerr-McGee showed a "callous, almost cruel, hardened disregard" for employee safety.

Kerr-McGee management averred that the plant was in compliance with all government regulations; however, the jury accepted the argument that, with so hazardous a substance as plutonium, compliance was not sufficient to guarantee worker safety.

The documents that Karen Silkwood had promised to the reporter—which were not found at the accident scene—were supposed to prove the existence of serious safety problems at Kerr-McGee. Silkwood's own contamination almost certainly had not occurred at work, but in the apartment she shared with fellow lab analyst Sherri Ellis. The jury rejected Kerr-McGee's defense that Silkwood had spiked her own urine samples with plutonium or had deliberately contaminated herself. Journalist Richard Rashke, in his carefully documented account of Silkwood's death and the subsequent official investigations, suggests that someone at Kerr-McGee may have contaminated Silkwood to frighten her into dropping her union activism.

The negligence suit had originally been intended as one prong of two-part assault on Kerr-McGee Nuclear. Silkwood's father and activist lawyer Dan Sheehan planned to sue the company for conspiring to violate Silkwood's civil rights by preventing her from reporting problems. This suit was abandoned for lack of definitive evidence, even as it led into a tangle of alleged Federal Bureau of Investigation (FBI) actions against anti-nuclear activists. Government interest in protecting Kerr-McGee Nuclear would not be entirely surprising, thanks to founder Bob Kerr's long career as a powerful Oklahoma Senator.

CHASED OFF THE ROAD

Rashke theorizes that Silkwood's fatal accident, officially attributed to sleepiness and drugs, occurred when a vehicle from Kerr-McGee or the FBI chased her off the road, presumably to prevent her from delivering proof of Kerr-McGee's negligence. He cites the report of private investigator Bill Taylor, who claims an FBI source told him of files that describe the crash. Journalist Howard Kohn argues, with less explicit evidence, that Silkwood became aware of—and may have temporarily been part of—a plutonium smuggling ring. Records cited by Rashke indicate that the plant probably was "missing" enough plutonium to make a nuclear bomb.

The $10.5 million award was overturned on appeal. The appeals court ruled first that Silkwood's injuries had happened in the course of her work, so worker's compensation was the proper route for obtaining repayment; and second, that nuclear corporations working for the government were shielded from punitive damages by the Price-Anderson Act. Rather than pursuing a second trial, Kerr-McGee settled with the Silkwood estate for $1.38 million in 1986. Silkwood's story was made into a successful movie, *Silkwood*, in 1983. As late as 1992, Silkwood's father was still trying to find out what really happened in the fatal car crash.

OTHER PLANTS

The Cimarron River plant was closed in 1975. However, Rashke argues that Kerr-McGee's lack of interest in worker safety dates much further back than the Silkwood scandal and encompassed more than a single plant. There is evidence that, at Kerr-McGee's uranium mining operation on Navajo land in Arizona, Navajo workers were neither informed of the hazards of working with uranium nor provided with respirators to protect them from uranium dust, even though uranium had been implicated in miners' deaths since the 16th century.

The Atomic Energy Commission (since replaced by the Nuclear Regulatory Commission) did not express concern. There were also accidents with injuries at the Gore, Oklahoma, uranium plant in 1972 and 1986, both attributable to lack of safety precautions and inadequate worker training. Potentially radioactive liquid wastes from the Gore plant were used as fertilizer into the late 1980s.

Kerr-McGee was also casual about the fate of radioactive thorium tailings stored at a West Chicago, Illinois, plant that the company bought from American Potash in 1967 and operated until 1973. Originally owned and operated by Lindsay Light and Chemical Plant, the facility had processed thorium for decades, resulting in a 27-acre mound of tailings. With city encouragement, local homeowners turned to the four-story high pile of dirt behind the factory as a source of garden fill, not knowing that it was radioactive. After 75 nearby houses were found to have radiation levels above federal limits, Kerr-McGee officials starting negotiating clean-up arrangements. Other hot spots included a local park created from tailings fill. "No one seems to know where it all is," Larry Jensen of the regional Environmental Protection Agency (EPA) office told the *New York Times*.

RESIDENTIAL CLEAN UP

By fall 1998, Kerr-McGee had arranged for removal of more than 430,000 tons of contaminated soil from West Chicago. The scope of the clean up continued to expand, with negotiations starting for soil removal at an additional 600 houses and areas along Kress Creek. Contaminated soil was being shipped to a lined vault in Utah, a plan made after the community rejected Kerr-McGee's proposal to store the contaminated soil in local vaults.

By publication of its 2002 annual report, Kerr-McGee had completed clean up of the original residential areas and Reed-Keppler Park; clean up of the thorium plant was expected to finish in 2003. Two additional contaminated areas, Kress Creek and a sewage treatment plant, were still in negotiation with the EPA. Kerr-McGee was also responsible for removing contamination by toxic chemicals at a number of other closed facilities nationwide.

Kerr-McGee left the nuclear industry in 1987. As of 2003, the company's operations were in oil, gas, and titanium dioxide. Kerr-McGee's public relations notes that 11 facilities have been named Star

Worksites by the Occupational Safety and Health Administration (OSHA) in recognition of their excellent safety records. The official history on their internet site makes no mention of nuclear energy or Silkwood.

SEE ALSO

Silkwood, Karen; Occupational Safety and Health Act; whistleblower; employee safety.

BIBLIOGRAPHY. "$1.3 Million Accord Reached in Lawsuit by Silkwood's Heirs," *The New York Times* (August 23, 1986); Lisa Black, "Forest Preserve Seeks Thorium Cleanup," *Chicago Tribune* (September 17, 1998); Bill Curry and Paul Wenske, "Silkwood Family Awarded $10.5 Million in Damages," *Washington Post* (May 19, 1979); Kerr-McGee Corporation, www.kerrmcgee.com (2003); Kerr-McGee Corporation, *2002 Annual Report*; Howard Kohn, *Who Killed Karen Silkwood?* (Simon & Schuster, 1981); Los Alamos National Laboratories, "Plutonium," www.pearl1.lanl.gov/periodic/elements (2003); Richard Rashke, *The Killing of Karen Silkwood* (Cornell University Press, 2000); "Silkwood Radiation Trial," *Washington Post* (March 15, 1979); "Silkwood's Father Posts Reward for Crash Details," *Orlando Sentinel* (May 28, 1992); Ron Suskind, "Illinois Town's Battle Over Radioactive Waste," *The New York Times* (March 11, 1985).

WENDE VYBORNEY FELLER, PH.D.
ST. MARY'S COLLEGE OF CALIFORNIA

kickbacks

THE TERMS *bribery* and *graft* are often used when referring to kickbacks. Kickbacks are monetary and non-monetary benefits that are paid to gain influence over and profit from an individual or firm. They are widespread and often accepted as a cost of doing business in many segments of the economy at home and abroad. Indeed, there are some segments of the economy that are more susceptible to the kickbacks, and the practice is more prevalent within some occupations. Those often cited among those most susceptible are elected officials and police officers.

James W. Coleman notes that, in cases of commercial bribery, it is often argued that the amount paid in bribes is relatively small relative to the profits, and consumers bear little of the actual costs. However, the widespread practice of kickbacks gives an unfair advantage to large companies with the resources to defray the costs relative to smaller competitors. According to Coleman, companies are able to avoid the accounting problems that arise from bribes extended in the form of cash, stocks, bonds or other forms of monetary or non-monetary forms of payment by establishing dummy firms to absorb the cost. Another means of disguising kickbacks as a legitimate business expense occurs when multinational firms, unable to establish local offices, distribute payoffs through local sales agents. Firms find this an especially efficient way of conducting business because local agents are more knowledgeable about which local entities need to receive "gifts" according to cultural and structural norms. Moreover, once the sales agent is paid, multinational firms are able to plead ignorance of how money is subsequently distributed and for what purposes.

GOVERNMENT KICKBACKS

Bureaucratic departments and agencies are particularly susceptible to kickbacks because the government does not manufacture the products that it needs. Instead, contracts for materials and services are issued to businesses in the private sector. Officeholders are able to ensure their own financial gain through tactics such as awarding inflated contracts which then "kick back" the amount by which the contract has been inflated to the officeholders responsible for extending the contract.

Charles H. McCaghy notes another means through which kickbacks have been distributed is through donations to party campaign coffers. Contracts are extended to firms with the unspoken agreement that a voluntary campaign contribution will be forthcoming. Other times, officials might leak the amount of bids for government contracts to their preferred firms who are then able to seemingly win a contract by issuing the lowest bid.

That elected officials are particularly susceptible to the lure of kickbacks, often seeking them out, raises important questions not only about the honesty and integrity of elected officials, but also about their commitment to representing the interests of constituents. Kickbacks to politicians highlight the susceptibility of a political system to the interests of those most able to pay. Dishonesty on

Vice-President Spiro T. Agnew resigned after pleading no contest to charges he accepted $29,500 in kickbacks.

the part of elected officials contributes to an atmosphere of corruption and undermines the strength of laws. What makes a kickback to public officials more insidious is the inherent difficulty in determining the extent to which individual decision-makers are swayed.

The U.S. Department of Defense has come under intense scrutiny for the kickbacks enjoyed by its employees. As detailed by Coleman, in 1982 the General Accounting Office (GAO) reported a 91 percent chance that the average military contract would feature inflated costs, and that waste attributable to graft was costing the department at least $15 billion annually. Four years later, the U.S. attorney general for a southern California region around a high concentration of defense contractors testified that kickbacks on defense subcontracts posed a significant problem.

In 1987, coordinated efforts between the Department of Defense, the Federal Bureau of Investigation, and the Internal Revenue Service helped to hold dozens of individuals accountable for their actions. The intense scrutiny leveled at the Department of Defense uncovered egregious over-billing evidence, such as a $1,118.26 expense for a plastic cap for a leg of a stool, as Coleman reports.

AUTHORITARIAN REGIMES

The impact of graft is most acutely felt and widespread in developing nations. According to international watchdog or monitoring organizations, including Transparency International which has developed its own ranking of perceived corruption in over 100 nations, kickbacks are more frequent under authoritarian regimes and newly emerging democracies. Within these contexts, kickbacks are a significant impediment to economic growth and development because a disproportionate amount of monies earmarked for new schools, hospitals, and other institutions find their way into the pockets of government officials. Graft also inhibits growth by discouraging would-be investors who frequently refer to the Transparency International index to assess the investment climate and determine risk. Due to the efforts of Transparency International, with branches in more than 60 mostly poor nations, rich countries are more aware of how their foreign aid monies are being used and have responded by suspending aid to countries where graft is most pervasive.

Governments are collaborating to decrease this practice internationally. The Organization for Economic Cooperation and Development (OECD) members agreed in 1997 to draft a treaty making it illegal for firms from member countries to bribe foreign officials. The long-term effect of such an effort is contingent upon member countries actually drafting the legislation at home, making it illegal for firms based within their countries to bribe officials elsewhere, and then to find a way to actively enforce the new laws. The United States, which already has laws in place under the 1977 Foreign Corrupt Practice Act, is urging other countries to follow suit because it stands to lose money in bids awarded to less ethical competitors abroad.

The World Bank has also joined this effort, launching surprise audits of countries to make sure loan monies are being properly applied. The bank has also blacklisted multinational firms found bribing officials abroad. Another strategy has been to illustrate the growth potential that results from serious crackdowns on corruption in developing countries. Evidence shows that nations that bring graft under control experience an overall improvement in quality of life, because money that had previously lined the pockets of government officials is able to find its way into public programs.

Campaigns mounted by international organizations in their effort to discourage the practice of kickbacks frequently support measures that promote bureaucratic transparency. However, change is slow due to the fact that kickbacks have evolved into a public norm comparable to a cultural tradition. In fact, cultural differences do result in different cross-national understandings of what actually constitutes a kickback. Forging a universal definition is just one step in the right direction.

SEE ALSO

corruption; graft; bribery; government procurement fraud; government contract fraud; Arab nations; Asia; Japan; South America; Mexico.

BIBLIOGRAPHY. "Kickbacks," *The Economist* (May 31, 1997); Jay S. Albanese, *White-Collar Crime in America* (Prentice-Hall, 1995); James William Coleman, *The Criminal Elite: Understanding White-Collar Crime* (St. Martin's Press, 1998); Charles H. McCaghy, *Crime in American Society* (Macmillan, 1980); Paul Sweeney, "The World Bank Battles the Cancer of Corruption," *Global Finance* (October 1999); "Kickbacks," www.transparency.org (2003).

S. MARTIN
CORNELL UNIVERSITY

Kidder, Peabody

ONCE CONSIDERED a conservative second-tier investment firm, Kidder, Peabody survived two insider trading scandals in the 1980s before collapsing after bond trader Joseph Jett's schemes went awry. The first insider trading scandal broke in 1984, when *Wall Street Journal* columnist R. Foster Winans confessed to the Securities and Exchange Commission (SEC) that he had passed tips to broker Peter Brant. In 1985, Brant pled guilty and became the key witness against Winans, Winans' roommate David Carpenter, and Brant's long-time friend and fellow broker Kenneth Felis. All eventually served brief prison sentences.

Two years later, former Kidder, Peabody investment banker Martin Siegel, who had since moved to rival Drexel Burnham Lambert, pled guilty to selling insider secrets to arbitrageur Ivan Boesky. Siegel's testimony implicated two bankers at Kidder, Peabody; both were arrested, but charges were later dropped. The straw that broke Kidder, Peabody's back was the $350 million in phantom trades posted from 1992 to early 1994 by Jett, the company's Man of the Year and only African-American trader. Hired in 1991 for the company's government bond desk, Jett turned around his mediocre performance late the next year, when a glitch in newly installed software provided an opening for apparent profits.

Jett dealt in U.S. Treasury securities under the Separate Trading of Registered Interest and Principal of Securities (STRIPS) initiative. STRIPS allows traders to separate a bond into its principal and its interest, then trade the two separately. A bond would be stripped for trading, then reconstituted for its maturity date. Since bonds predictably increase in value as they near maturity, the securities market ordinarily offers low profits for low risks.

A quirk in how the software handled "forward settlements"—reconstitutions that were promised now but would take place in the future—allowed Jett to create large apparent profits. The system recorded a reconstitution as the purchase of a bond immediately and the sale of its related strips on the settlement date. Since the strips are inherently worth more later, this recording method created the illusion of large profits: the further away the settlement date, the larger the profit. However, when the trade was settled, the value of the bond and its strips would be nearly equal; only a small profit from recognizing undervalued strips could actually be realized. A paper profit of $300,000 might dwindle to a real profit of $30,000 at settlement.

By late 1993, Jett was habitually flipping strips: that is, bonds were reconstituted, then stripped again before their settlement dates, resulting in new settlement dates further in the future. The software recorded profits from each transaction, pushing his 1993 profit to over $150 million on a trading position limited to under $15 million. Upon firing Jett in spring 1994, Kidder, Peabody claimed he was a lone wolf who committed fraud to boost his annual performance bonuses. Jett contends he was the cat's paw in a larger scheme to hide Kidder, Peabody's financial position from parent company

General Electric (GE), which had acquired an 80 percent share in the investment house shortly before the Boesky scandal. His strips-flipping activities allowed his immediate superior, Ed Cerullo, to keep Kidder, Peabody's over-leveraged position off the books seen by GE. Jett argues that his superiors knew, approved of, even insisted on his activities. They swore to the Securities and Exchange Commission (SEC) that they never looked at his records.

The National Association of Securities Dealers (NASD) cleared Jett of fraud. A trial before an SEC administrative judge also cleared Jett of fraud but found him guilty of a books-and-records violation and ordered him to repay $8.21 million in phantom profits. Lawyer Gary Lynch's investigation for GE absolved Kidder, Peabody executives of conspiring to commit fraud, but the *New York Times* notes that Lynch had consulting ties to Kidder, Peabody.

Late in 1994, GE liquidated Kidder, Peabody, selling most assets to rival Paine Webber, part of UBS. In 2003, Jett headed his own capital investment firm.

SEE ALSO

investment trust fraud; Jett, Joseph; securities fraud; National Association of Securities Dealers.

BIBLIOGRAPHY. Reed Abelson, "Gary Lynch, Defender of Companies, Has His Critics," *New York Times* (September 3, 1996); Jett Capital Management, LLC, www.josephjett.com (2003); Joseph Jett, *Black and White on Wall Street* (William Morrow, 1999); "Lynch Report Concludes Jett Acted Alone at Kidder; Criticizes Oversight," PR Newswire (August 4, 1994); John Riley, "Cleared Trader Takes Swipe at Giuliani," *Newsday* (August 23, 1989); "Stockbroker Gets 8-Month Term on Insider Trading," *Los Angeles Times* (February 26, 1988); Securities and Exchange Commission, "Initial Decision of an Administrative Law Judge in the Matter of Orlando Joseph Jett," (July 21, 1988); R. Foster Winans, *Trading Secrets* (St. Martin's Press, 1986).

WENDE VYBORNEY FELLER, PH.D.
ST. MARY'S COLLEGE OF CALIFORNIA

Knapp Commission

NEW YORK CITY'S Knapp Commission Report on Police Corruption became public in 1972, and it comprises the most comprehensive collection of cases involving bribery of police officers. The city had experienced several previous corruption scandals prior to the Knapp Commission, including those in 1892 (quelled by Theodore Roosevelt), 1911, 1932, and 1951. The Knapp investigation was the result of information about police corruption brought to light in 1967 by former New York City detective Frank Serpico. The Knapp Commission, chaired by Whitman Knapp (who became a federal judge shortly after the commission ended), was in operation from 1967 through the end of 1972. It found pervasive corruption throughout virtually all lower ranks (through lieutenant) of the New York City Police Department, as well as among some higher officials. Not all police officers in the lower ranks were involved in blatant corruption, but most at least accepted "free" meals and services, and did not take steps to prevent what they knew or suspected as corrupt police activities.

The commission differentiated between two major forms of bribe-takers: meat eaters and grass eaters. Grass eating, the more common, refers to passively accepting bribes when appropriate situations present themselves. Meat eaters, on the other hand, are the police officers who aggressively seek out situations they can exploit for financial gain. These include gambling, drugs, and other offenses which can yield bribes totaling thousands of dollars. One highly placed police official told the commission that $5,000 to $50,000 payoffs to meat eaters were common; one narcotics bribe amounted to a quarter of a million dollars.

There are two types of bribes taken by the police: pads and scores. The pad refers to regularly scheduled (for example, weekly or monthly) bribes in exchange for non-enforcement of the law. Illegal gambling operations are probably the largest source of pad payments. Some detectives had collected monthly or every-other-week pads amounting to as much as $3,500 from each gambling establishment in their jurisdiction. The monthly share (or nut) per officer ranged from $300 or $400 in midtown Manhattan to $800 in the Bronx, $1,200 in Brooklyn, and $1,500 in Harlem. Supervisors' nuts often were a share-and-a-half. Newly assigned plainclothes officers were not given a share until after a few months in order to ascertain whether the newcomer was an informant.

A score is a one-time bribe that an officer solicits from (or is offered by) a citizen for not enforcing the law. A police officer can score from a motorist for not writing a traffic citation or from a narcotics peddler for not making an arrest. Many officers were implicated in the solicitation of payoffs for nebulous court testimony that would result in the dropping of charges. Additionally, narcotics officers took bribes in exchange for information about an impending arrest, for the results of telephone wiretaps or other confidential police information, and for influencing the justice process for known dealers or addicts.

Gratuities, variants of the pad, refer to free meals, free goods and services, and cash tips received by officers. Gratuities were by far the most widespread form of misconduct the commission found. Several thousand free meals were consumed by the New York officers each day. The sheer numbers of gratis meals posed problems for some establishments. Tips were often given at Christmas and for the performance of normal duties.

In addition to bribery, widespread thefts by New York City police were also uncovered by the Knapp Commission. Officers admitted to taking money and house keys (for later burglaries) from corpses in their charge. They also admitted to stealing from burglary scenes. The Knapp Commission concluded that an intense sense of organizational loyalty and a disdain for outside scrutiny were the major reasons why corruption flourished. The Knapp materials clearly indicated that rationales for bribery, as well as the techniques associated with it, were learned from other officers.

Twenty years after the Knapp Commission, a new anti-corruption commission was appointed to investigate the New York City Police Department. The Mollen Commission—named for its head, Milton Mollen, a former deputy mayor and appellate judge—began its hearings in September 1993. Evidence uncovered by the Mollen Commission included many of the same things found by its predecessor—extortion, pads, and scores. Additionally, some officers were implicated as drug dealers themselves. Although the police corruption uncovered by the Mollen Commission was more isolated than that found by Knapp, organized corruption was discovered within various pockets of the city

Taking bribes, which include anything of value (money, property, sexual or other favors), in exchange for official favors is punished under state bribery and extortion laws. Bribe-taking by federal agents and employees (or anyone working on behalf of the United States) is punishable under 18 U.S.C. §201. Nonfederal bribe-takers acting under "color of official right" are punished under 18 U.S.C. § 1951, (Hobbs Act).

SEE ALSO

police corruption; Mollen Commission; Hobbs Act; bribery; extortion; public corruption.

BIBLIOGRAPHY. Whitman Knapp, *The Knapp Commission Report on Police Corruption* (George Brazziler, 1973); John Noonan, *Bribes* (Macmillan, 1984); Warren Sloat, *Battle for the Soul of New York: Tammany Hall, Police Corruption, Vice, and Reverend Charles Parkhur* (Cooper Square Press, 2002).

GARY S. GREEN
CHRISTOPHER NEWPORT UNIVERSITY

L

labor crimes

LABOR CRIMES are violations of laws, treaties, or international conventions (referred to hereafter simply as laws) that govern workers' rights, labor unions, collective bargaining, and other aspects of employment for specific types of workers. The concept is sometimes used more generally to cover any abusive practices related to employment. Labor crimes can be committed by employers, by labor unions, or by individual workers.

Labor laws are based on the idea that there is an inequality of bargaining power between individual workers and employers, with employers holding a stronger position than workers. As a result, wages might be "too low," while other working conditions, such as workload and working hours, might also be worse than they should be.

To remedy this inequality, labor laws define rights for workers to organize into unions and bargain collectively with employers. The theory is that by bargaining collectively, unions have a more powerful position to deal with employers than do individual workers. Because the individual worker's livelihood depends on securing employment, while a business can almost always be profitable without any individual worker, the worker is in an inherently weaker bargaining position compared with the employer's position.

However, if a business must bargain with a large number of workers organized into a union, its cost of failure to reach agreement on terms of employment rises significantly. Labor laws further "up the ante" by exposing companies to legal action—usually civil but in some cases criminal—if they violate the relevant statutes.

LEGAL FRAMEWORK

In the United States before the 1930s, the law generally discouraged labor unions and took the side of employers. In the early 1800s, union organizing per se was sometimes seen as a crime and was prosecuted under criminal conspiracy statutes. Later courts ruled that unions could have justifiable objectives and were therefore not illegal in themselves. Subsequent cases focused on union tactics, such as pressuring non-members to support strikes.

By the 1880s, employers commonly used civil actions to thwart unions, seeking court injunctions to forbid union activities. Although the courts had recognized that unions did have legitimate objectives in advancing the interests of workers, they often ruled against union actions intended to achieve those objectives. Union activities had to be consistent with the courts' view of the "public welfare"; they could not use coercion to force workers to join unions, and could not use coercion to prevent other workers (scabs) from taking jobs of workers who were out on strike. In 1890, Congress passed the Sherman Antitrust Act, aimed mainly at restricting anti-competitive activities of giant business conglomerates (trusts) such as Standard Oil. The Sherman Act outlawed "conspiracies in restraint of trade" and monopolization, though it was lax in defining what these terms meant. As a result, the law was often applied not to business trusts but to labor unions, on the theory that they were conspiracies in restraint of trade. The first major application of the Sherman Act to labor unions was in the violent Pullman railroad strike of 1893.

In response to the Pullman strike, Congress in 1898 passed the Erdman Act, which applied only to workers operating interstate trains. The law prohibited employers from firing employees, or threatening to fire them, solely because they were union members. It provided that the chairman of the U.S. Interstate Commerce Commission (a federal agency originally set up mainly to regulate railroads) could intervene to mediate labor disputes. It also encouraged arbitration as an alternative to strikes. How-

ever, employers found it easy to evade the law, often by flatly refusing to negotiate with labor unions, and the U.S. Supreme Court ultimately struck it down.

In 1914, Congress passed the Clayton Act, which favored labor unions in two ways. First, recognizing that the Sherman Act and other antitrust laws had been used for actions Congress did not intend, the Clayton Act exempted labor unions from antitrust laws. Second, it prohibited the use of federal injunctions in disputes over terms or conditions of employment. Thus, in one fell swoop, the Clayton Act removed two of the most important weapons that businesses had used to thwart the growth of labor unions.

GROWTH OF UNIONS

In the six years following passage of the Clayton Act, U.S. labor union membership doubled, growing from 2.5 million to 5 million. In two cases from the same general time period, however, the U.S. Supreme Court considerably weakened the Clayton Act's protections for labor unions. In addition,

A road crew's labor representation would work with state, municipal, or utility company management.

A welder's salary and job benefits would usually be negotiated by an industrial union such as the AFL-CIO.

businesses found new ways to fight union membership, such as "yellow dog contracts," which the Court ruled legal in 1917. Such contracts required workers, as a condition of employment, to promise that they would not join labor unions.

In 1926, Congress passed the Railway Labor Act (RLA). Though it applied only to labor unions in the interstate railroad industry, it was amended in 1936 to include the airline industry. The RLA both legalized and formalized some aspects of collective bargaining. It set up a National Railroad Adjustment Board to arbitrate minor labor disputes and required labor and management to submit to such arbitration. It also declared that both labor and management had a duty to negotiate and to make every reasonable effort to maintain labor agreements. Finally, it set up both a mediation board and an investigative board to help push through agreements in intractable disputes. In 1930, the U.S. Supreme Court ruled that the RLA was constitutional.

During the Great Depression of 1929–41, massive unemployment led the federal government and courts to take a more supportive view of labor laws, labor unions, and collective bargaining. In 1932, Congress passed the Norris-LaGuardia Act, which removed the power of federal courts to issue injunctions against union activities unless those activities involved fraud or violence. However, it did not require employers to negotiate with unions.

WAGNER ACT

In 1935, the U.S. Congress passed the National Labor Relations Act, sometimes called the Wagner Act after its main legislative sponsor. The Wagner act was frankly pro-union. It affirmed rights of workers to form and join labor unions, to engage in collective bargaining with employers, and to engage in other activities related to collective bargaining. Most importantly, the Wagner Act imposed a duty on employers to negotiate with labor unions that represented their workers, and to do so "in good faith." It set out conditions under which a particular union might be designated as the legal representative of all the workers in a particular "bargaining

Unions gained the most membership from blue-collar workers, such as electricians and other trades.

A steelworker is represented by United Steelworkers of America, part of the AFL-CIO.

unit," ranging from an individual factory to an entire corporation. In the years following passage of the Wagner Act, U.S. union membership quintupled, growing from 3 million to 15 million.

In 1947, Congress passed the Labor-Management Relations Act, usually referred to as the Taft-Hartley Act. This law tried to rein in what its authors considered abuses by unions, such as secondary boycotts and restrictions on union membership. It established the Federal Mediation and Conciliation Service (FMCS) to help resolve disputes that could affect interstate commerce. It imposed a duty on both labor and management to inform the FMCS when they wanted changes in a collective bargaining agreement. Taft-Hartley also gave the U.S. president the power to obtain an injunction against strikes that might threaten national health and safety, postponing any strike for 80 days. Finally, the law prohibited "closed shops," collective bargaining agreements that require the employer to hire only union members.

In 1959, Congress passed the Labor-Management Reporting and Disclosure Act, also known as the Landrum-Griffin Act. This law attempted to remedy labor union corruption and abuses that had come to light in the 1950s. The law regulated some aspects of the internal management of labor unions and stated a "bill of rights" for their members.

NOTABLE CASES

Notable labor-crime cases would fill several volumes. A few of the most influential cases are:

Philadelphia Cordwainer's Case, 1806, 3.Doc. Hist. Of Am. Ind. Soc. 59. Employees struck for higher wages. The court ruled that unions themselves were illegal criminal conspiracies, even apart from any specific activities they undertook.

Commonwealth v. Hunt, 45 Mass. (4 Met.) 111 (1842). A Massachusetts union sought to impose a "closed shop," in which the employer would only hire union members. The court found that the union's "justifiable objectives" were sufficient for its actions to be legal. The court held that for union activities to be illegal, "abuse" had to be found.

Vegelahn v. Guntner, 167 Mass. 92 (1896). In this case, a labor union went on strike against and picketed a furniture manufacturer. The Massachusetts Supreme Court ruled that picketing constituted intimidation and that, therefore, the manufacturer could get an injunction to prohibit picketing. Ac-

cording to one popular labor law text, "The court seemed to imply that no matter how peaceful the picketing, if it might cause discomfort to strike-breakers or customers who saw it, the picketing was unlawful."

United States v. Debs, 64 F. 724 N.D. Illinois (1894); 158 U.S. 564 (1895). The first high-profile application of the Sherman Act to labor unions was in the Pullman strike of 1893. Debs was a co-founder of the American Railway Union, whose members struck against the Pullman Palace Car Company in 1893; Pullman was a manufacturer of railroad passenger cars. ARU members and others engaged in violence during the strike. The U.S. attorney general sought and received an injunction to stop the strike on the grounds that it violated the Sherman Act's prohibition on combinations in restraint of trade. Debs and others violated the injunction and were jailed. Both the Appeals Court and the Supreme Court upheld the government's injunction and ruled against Debs and the ARU.

Adair v. United States, 208 U.S. 161 (1908). Under the Erdman Act, it was illegal for railroads engaged in interstate commerce to fire workers solely because of their union membership. William Adair, an official of the Louisville and Nashville Railroad Company, violated the law when he fired a locomotive fireman for joining a union. (A train's fireman shoveled coal into the furnace that powered the train's engine.) The Supreme Court ruled in favor of Adair, striking down the Erdman Act as an unconstitutional interference with the freedom of contract between employers and workers.

Duplex Printing Press v. Deering, 254 U.S. 443 (1921) and *Bedford Cut Stone Co. v. Journeymen Stone Cutters Association of North America*, 274 U.S. 37 (1927). In both of these cases, the Supreme Court overruled the Clayton Act and allowed injunctions against union secondary boycotts of employers who refused to recognize other unions.

Though the precedent-setting labor crime cases listed above are older cases, battles are still being fought in this area. In November 2003, a settlement was reached in the case of *Ronald Walker et al v. Michael Swartz et al.*, which had been under litigation in the U.S. District Court for the Northern District of Ohio. When non-members of a union work in a bargaining unit represented by a union, they too are required to pay union dues. In this case, 223 non-union employees of Cleveland State University sued the union representing them to recover portions of their regular dues that had been used for political activities instead of for collective bargaining.

SEE ALSO

wage crimes; unions; boycotts; employee safety; Sherman Antitrust Act; Clayton Antitrust Act.

BIBLIOGRAPHY. Susan M. Collins, ed., *Imports, Exports, and the American Worker* (Brookings Institution Press, 1998); Melvyn Dubofsky, *The State and Labor in Modern America* (University of North Carolina Press, 1994); Stanley D. Henderson, *Labor Law: Cases and Comment* (Foundation Press, 2001); David Montgomery, *The Fall of the House of Labor: The Workplace, the State, and American Labor Activism 1865-1925* (Cambridge University Press, 1989); Douglas E. Ray, et al., *Understanding Labor Law* (Matthew Bender, 1999).

SCOTT PALMER, PH.D.
RGMS ECONOMICS

Leeson, Nick (1967–)

NICK LEESON, the financial trader whose trading losses led to the collapse of Barings Bank, was born in Watford, Essex, England, the son of a plasterer. After leaving Parmiter's School, aged 18 in 1985, Leeson got a job working as an accounts clerk for the bank Coutts & Company settling checks. In June 1987, Leeson moved to the London branch of the American investment bank Morgan Stanley where he worked in the Settlements Division for Futures and Options. In June 1989, Leeson left Morgan Stanley, taking a job in the Settlements Division for Futures and Options of Barings Securities, the trading arm of Barings Bank, Great Britain's oldest merchant bank, founded more than 240 years ago in 1762.

Leeson created a reputation as a settlements expert after clearing a £100 million backlog of share certificates at the bank's Jakarta, Indonesia, office during 1990 and 1991. In the spring of 1992, Barings sent Leeson to work at the Singapore International Monetary Exchange (SIMEX). A year after arriving in Singapore, Leeson had made more than £10 million, approximately 10 percent of Baring's total profit for 1993, and earned a bonus of £130,000 in addition to his salary of £50,000. In

reality, Leeson had taken huge losses, which he hid in a dormant error account. Leeson attempted to trade his way out of the situation.

However, his gamble failed spectacularly due to a downturn in the Asian financial markets that was exacerbated by the Kobe, Japan, earthquake; Leeson was left with losses of £208 million. He went on the run, fleeing to Malaysia and Borneo before attempting to return to the United Kingdom. On March 2, 1995, German police arrested Leeson at Frankfurt airport; he spent the next nine months in a Frankfurt jail resisting extradition to Singapore. An audit of Barings Singaporean operations revealed that Leeson had run up losses of £827 million, a sum nearly equal to the value of Baring's entire assets. Barings Bank collapsed on February 26, 1995, and was bought for £1 by the Dutch banking and insurance group ING.

A Bank of England investigation of the Barings collapse attributed the debacle to a failure of control. The report implicated numerous bank executives who chose to resign or were fired. On December 1, 1995, Leeson pleaded guilty to fraud and was sentenced to six-and-a-half years in Torah Merah prison, Changi, Singapore. While serving his prison sentence, Leeson published his autobiography, *Rogue Trader*, in which he condemned Barings for its failure to supervise his illicit trading activities.

In 1999, Leeson was diagnosed with cancer of the colon and released from prison on July 3having served three-and-a-half years of his sentence. On his arrival at London's Heathrow airport, the liquidators of Barings Bank served Leeson with an injunction for £100 million. In 2004, Leeson was making a living as an after-dinner speaker after completing an undergraduate degree in psychology at Middlesex University.

SEE ALSO

bank fraud; securities fraud; Barings Bank: Asia; investment trust fraud; accounting fraud.

BIBLIOGRAPHY. Nick Leeson with Edward Whitley, *Rogue Trader* (Little Brown, 1996); "Barings Bank," www.riskglossary.com (2003); Dee O'Connell, "What Happened Next?" *The Observer Magazine* (April 21, 2002).

MARK ROODHOUSE, PH.D.
UNIVERSITY OF YORK, ENGLAND

legal malpractice

LEGAL malpractice, sometimes also known as lawyers' professional liability, refers to wrongdoings by attorneys in the course of performing legal services which result in civil liability. There are three major areas in which legal malpractice may occur: 1) negligent actions; 2) breach of contract between lawyer and client; and 3) breaches of fiduciary duty (negligent financial practices in handling clients' money). Specific types of legal malpractice include tampering with or concealing evidence, negligent advice to clients, giving legal opinions to third parties, assisting others in committing crimes, misrepresentations of professional credentials, accepting illegal money and plagiarism of legal documents.

MALPRACTICE HISTORY

While legal malpractice was the subject of cases as far back as the 18th century in the United States, it has only been since the 1960s that lawyers' professional liability has been significantly expanded. Unlike most other professions, lawyers pervade most aspects of economics, society, and politics, and their actions affect others in very concrete ways.

Indeed, the fact that they are necessary for the conduct of such a wide range of personal, economic, and political practices has made attorneys particularly vulnerable to public and legislative censure. As in other areas of civil law, changing social, economic, and political attitudes by legislators, judges, and the general population have shaped the extent of liability for those practicing the legal profession.

The English common law of negligence was actually first applied in the 18th century to professionals such as lawyers who professed competency in a specialized field. In *Russell v. Palmer* (1767) and *Pitt v. Yalden* (1787), the courts held lawyers liable for negligent practices in relation to their clients. In reaction to such cases, judges attempted to protect their lawyer colleagues by holding that only certain types of lawyers were liable for negligence. Nonetheless, it soon became common to hold lawyers to "an ordinary degree of skill and care" in performing their services.

The 1776 case *Stevens v. White* was the first case in the United States involving lawyers' liability. The defendant lawyer claimed that his client, who had suffered damages due to the lawyers' actions, had not paid for his services so that he had no duty to properly represent his client. Yet, the court found that since the attorney had originally agreed to provide services to his client, he was judged liable for negligence. In the 1880s, the landmark U.S. Supreme Court case of *National Savings Bank v. Ward* further clarified the laws governing legal work. The lawyer in this case was employed by a bank to investigate if the land put up as collateral by a prospective borrower was sufficient to cover the loan. The bank loaned $3,500 to the client and then accepted the property as security for the loan. However, it turned out the borrower did not actually own the land and was bankrupt. The attorney was found liable for negligence.

In defending the decision, Justice Nathan Clifford offered a definition of negligent actions by lawyers which would prevail for the next century, "When a person adopts the legal profession... he must be understood as promising to employ a reasonable degree of care and skill in the performance of such duties, and if injury results to the client from the want of such a degree of reasonable care and skill, the attorney may be held to respond to damages to the extent of the injury sustained." He went on to say that proof of the employment relationship and a failure to perform duty in a reasonable manner were the only two prerequisites to winning a suit for negligence against a lawyer. This case thus established two precedents which would hold until the 1960s. To prove negligence, there had to be: 1) a contractual relationship between lawyer and client and; 2) a breach of duty.

In the century following this decision, judges and juries also debated the question of whether lawyers' liability should be tried within actions arising from breach of contract (contract law) or through breach of the standard of care (negligence under tort law.) If the case brought against a lawyer was argued as negligence, the court was responsible for deciding if negligence occurred. Yet cases brought against attorneys on the basis of breach of contract were also decided on the basis of duty in performing legal duties. The differences between the two approaches revolved around the extent of damages and the Statute of Limitations (limitations on the duration of time in which a client may legally sue for damages.)

Damages awarded to plaintiffs in breach of contract cases have generally been much more limited than in cases brought on the basis of negligence.

Furthermore, punitive damages were generally disallowed in such cases. The Statute of Limitations, however, is considerably longer in contract law than in tort law.

Often the most crucial points in legal malpractice cases was the question of privity, that is, the relationship between the lawyer and the plaintiff suing for damages. In this area, lawyers enjoyed considerable limitations on liability. Lawyers were only responsible to clients with whom they had a contractual relationship. Third-party claimants who suffered damages were generally ineligible to sue a lawyer for malpractice if they were not in privity. Another benefit granted to lawyers under this regime was the ambiguous nature of the concept of duty and reasonable care and the leeway that the Statute of Limitations offered to lawyers. Even though legal services gradually became more specialized over the course of the 20th century, lawyers were only held to an "ordinary" standard of care. As Mark Robert Fried concisely states, "A lawyer was held to the standard of care of a general practitioner even though he had represented himself as specially qualified in a particular area of law." Lawyers also enjoyed the protection of the Statute of Limitations since realistically clients were frequently unable to discover negligent actions within the time frame allowed.

THE LEGAL PROFESSION

It is also important to trace developments in the legal profession itself to understand professional liability for legal professionals. Only in the late 19th and early 20th century were professional standards and ethics gradually developed among lawyers. Well into the 20th century, states required varying levels of professional education and training among lawyers, and licensing regimes varied considerably by jurisdiction. Until the second half of the 20th century, many lawyers, for instance, did not belong to professional associations such as the American Bar Association which first passed a code of ethics in 1908. The legal profession preferred to govern itself and thus laid itself open to abuses by members of the profession, although by the post-war period, there were a plethora of codes of ethics and statements of professional conduct established by state and federal professional associations.

By the mid- to late-20th century, the legal profession found itself facing increasingly higher risks

of malpractice suits. The reasons for this vary. For one, the public itself had changed. Clients became increasingly educated and were not so ignorant of legal processes and their rights. As Dennis Gillen suggests, "The public [had] also become more resentful toward individuals who attempt to claim immunity by virtue of their profession." The development of malpractice insurance, moreover, fostered a willingness on the part of clients to rigorously pursue suits against what they perceived as negligent actions by their legal counsel. These developments corresponded to similar expansions of liability for corporate entities within tort law.

In the 1958 California Supreme Court case, *Biakanja v. Irving*, the judges held that lack of privity no longer prohibited actions for negligence against lawyers. From this decision onward, courts in many states have therefore found lawyers liable for damages incurred by certain third-parties. Cases since the 1960s have also found that legal malpractice constitutes both a tort and a breach of contract allowing plaintiffs to sue on a wider basis. Laws governing the Statute of Limitations have also been relaxed in favor of clients suing their lawyers. A simpler definition of negligence has been adopted in many jurisdictions making it easier to prove malpractice. Some states have abolished "good faith" defenses which were used in cases where lawyers erred, but acted in good faith. Lawyers have recently had to face courts which have defined "duty" and standard of care in a much more objective and stricter manner than lawyers faced in the past.

Cases of legal malpractice have usually arisen in civil law. It is worth mentioning, however, that state-appointed attorneys have also been found negligent in handling criminal cases. Several high-profile cases have surfaced in recent years focusing on the alleged malpractice of state-appointed lawyers in death-penalty cases. It was found that clients in these cases, often poor African-Americans and Hispanics unable to afford legal representation, suffered extensively from negligent practices by poorly trained lawyers.

The last two decades have seen dramatic increases in legal malpractice suits. Lawyers have finally been subjected to the same standards of accountability as doctors, accountants, surveyors, and inspectors. One reflection of this is that there has been a trend toward law firms shifting from partnerships to professional corporations, limited liability companies, or limited liability partnerships to lower the risk of financial penalties in the event of malpractice.

If current trends continue, the following decades will likely see an increasingly uniform use of objective standards of care and other broader notions of professional liability, bringing legal professionals in line with their peers in other professions.

SEE ALSO

fiduciary fraud; negligence; United States; United Kingdom.

BIBLIOGRAPHY. T.G. Bastedo, "A Note on Lawyers' Malpractice: Legal Boundaries and Judicial Regulations," *Osgood Hall Law Review* (v.7/3, 1969–70); Steven H. Felderstein, "Legal Malpractice: Is the Discovery Rule the Final Solution?" *Hastings Law Journal* (v.24, 1972–73); Mark Robert Fried, "New Developments in Legal Practice," *American University Law Review* (v.26, 1976–77); Lawrence Friedman, *American Law in the Twentieth Century* (Yale University Press, 2002); Warren Friedman, *A Guide to Malpractice Liability for Legal and Law-Related Professions* (Quorom Books, 1995); Dennis I. Gillen, "Legal Malpractice," *Washburn Law Journal* (v.281, 1972–73); Stephen Grant and Linda Rothstein, *Lawyers' Professional Liability* (Butterworth's, 1998); Steven K. Ward, "Developments in Legal Malpractice Liability," *South Texas Law Review* (v.121, 1990).

SEAN PURDY, PH.D.
QUEEN'S UNIVERSITY, CANADA

Levi, Michael (1948–)

IN 2004, MICHAEL LEVI was a professor of criminology at Cardiff University in Wales, England. Levi has addressed the problem of financial havens and bank secrecy in his work, as well as the process and rewards of becoming a white-collar criminal. Levi earned a M.A. degree from the University of Oxford, a Diploma in Criminology from the Institute of Criminology at the University of Cambridge, and finally a Ph.D. from the University of Southampton.

Most of Levi's research and writings have been about the prevention and criminal processing of white-collar and organized crime, including money laundering and asset confiscation. In 1997, he was chosen by the Strasbourg (France)-based Council of Europe to serve as its scientific expert on a new major initiative on organized crime. The council, Europe's oldest union of nations, is dedicated to promoting human rights and democracy, both of which are threatened by organized crime. Levi has also acted as a consultant to the United Nations and to the United Kingdom's Home Office Police Research Group.

Levi insists that it is inaccurate to think of the typical white-collar criminal as a person who just happened to take advantage of a criminal opportunity. Some white-collar criminals, like other types of entrepreneurs, may be people of vision who can detect possibilities of exploitation in their environment that remain invisible to others. People also become fraudsters via the transmission of information from people in the underworld who have carried out long-term frauds themselves, or who have learned the techniques from someone else.

The poor prosecution of white-collar crime has allowed many criminals to keep the profits. Levi discovered that British confiscation orders constitute a very small percentage of the estimated proceeds of drug trafficking. The orders are essentially civil in nature, making them out of place in the criminal justice system and making enforcement erratic. There is no organizational incentive for anyone to deal vigorously with confiscation matters in part because no percentage of assets confiscated is turned over to agencies for further use in combating drug trafficking.

Money laundering has emerged as one of the major types of white-collar crime. In a 1998 report prepared for the United Nations' Global Program Against Money Laundering, Levi acknowledged that criminal organizations have taken increasing advantage of financial havens and off-shore banking centers to launder money. These havens enforce strict financial secrecy, which serves to shield the criminal from regulatory authorities. Levi argues that all citizens must be legally accountable for government to work and that bank secrecy laws protect against legal accountability instead of privacy violations. Levi has called for an international convention on the privacy issues surrounding the electronic exchange of information and banks.

SEE ALSO

United Kingdom; money laundering; drug trafficking; organized crime; corruption; offshore entities.

BIBLIOGRAPHY. Michael Levi, *Fraud: Organization, Moderation, and Control* (Ashgate Dartmouth, 1999); Michael Levi, "The Crime of Corruption," *Corruption: The Enemy Within* (Kluwer Law International, 1997); Michael Levi and A. Pithouse, *White-Collar Crime and Its Victims* (Oxford University Press, 1995).

CARYN E. NEUMANN, PH.D.
OHIO STATE UNIVERSITY

Levine, Dennis (1952–)

INVESTMENT BANKER Dennis Levine's rise from working-class Queens (New York City) boy to multimillionaire seemed to justify the 1980s ethos of greed—until he was arrested for insider trading. On May 12, 1986, Levine fled Department of Justice (DOJ) officials who were waiting outside his office at Drexel Burnham Lambert.

In his autobiography, Levine remembers himself as an innocent young banker tempted into insider trading by colleague Robert Wilkis in his first job at Citibank. Investigative reporter Douglas Frantz argues that it was Levine who introduced Wilkis to insider trading after Levine had moved to Smith Barney and Wilkis to Lazard Frères. Levine envisioned creating a ring of sources at major investment houses, all pooling confidential information to make profitable trades ahead of the market. Meanwhile, his first secret overseas trading account was prospering.

Late in 1984, Drexel Burnham Lambert, home of junk bond manipulator Michael Milken, hired Levine as a managing director, intending to make him a mergers-and-acquisitions star. Invited in his first week to participate in Coastal Corporation's $2 billion acquisition of American Natural Resources (ANR), Levine turned his inside information into a $1.4 million personal profit. Levine blamed arbitrageurs such as Ivan Boesky for the heavy trading in ANR stock that forced Coastal to pay more for ANR. It was Levine who fed Boesky the inside information about ANR. Soon the two had a formal arrangement in which Boesky paid Levine for tips.

When an anonymous letter from Venezuela told brokerage Merrill Lynch that two of its people in Caracas were trading on insider information, the trail led first to Lynch broker Brian Campbell, then to Levine's $10 million secret trading account at Bank Leu in the Bahamas. After Levine surrendered to the DOJ, he turned in Boesky and the remainder of his insider trading ring, starting a long-running insider trading scandal. At his February 1987 sentencing for perjury, securities fraud, and tax evasion, the judge lauded Levine's "extraordinary" cooperation in leading investigators to "a nest of vipers." Levine was sentenced to two years in prison and a $362,000 fine.

Levine emerged briefly from prison in June 1987 to testify before a closed Congressional hearing on insider trading. Commented Representative Gerry Sikorski (D-MN): "It was not a story that engendered compassion. It was more akin to the curiosity one feels when one turns over a rock in a brook and looks to see what's underneath." In December 1988, Drexel settled with the DOJ for six felony counts and $650 million in fines, all related to employees implicated in Levine's ring. (Unrelated charges against Milken were not included.) Drexel went bankrupt and closed. After his release from prison, Levine became president of ADASAR Group, a financial consulting firm.

SEE ALSO
insider trading; Drexel Burnham Lambert; offshore entities; Justice, Department of; tax evasion.

BIBLIOGRAPHY. "Briefly: Dennis Levine Left Prison to Testify on Capitol Hill," *Los Angeles Times* (June 3, 1987); Douglas Frantz, *Levine & Co.* (Henry Holt and Company, 1987); Dennis B. Levine with William Hoffer, *Inside Out* (G.P. Putnam's Sons, 1991); John Riley, "Drexel Settles With U.S.," *Newsday* (December 22, 1988); Saundra Torrey, "Unpaid Federal Fines Drift Into Oblivion, Disorganization," *Washington Post* (September 18, 1989); "Wall Street Insider Gets 2-Year Sentence," *Chicago Tribune* (February 21, 1987).

WENDE VYBORNEY FELLER, PH.D.
ST. MARY'S COLLEGE OF CALIFORNIA

Lloyd's of London

FOR MORE THAN three centuries, Lloyd's of London evoked sterling images of respectability, dependability, and exclusivity. As an insurer, over the years, Lloyd's developed a reputation for promptly paying all legitimate claims. While Lloyd's had been involved in minor scandals in the past, in the late 1980s, Lloyd's became involved in the worst scandal of its illustrious career. The scandal resulted in hundreds of lost fortunes, totaling approximately $13 billion (£8 billion) and involving almost 2,000 of Lloyd's 34,000 "Names" (what Lloyd's calls its individual investors). The scandal also changed Lloyd's focus from investment by Names to corporate investors, particularly insurance companies from all over the world. By 1996, it was evident that Lloyd's would survive, but some of the Names were not so fortunate. Some of them had committed suicide during the crisis.

NAMES AND MORE NAMES

In 1950, Lloyd's of London limited its exclusive list of Names to 2,743 investors, most of whom were located in England. Over the next five years, the number of Names increased to 3,917. The next two decades saw steady increases in the number of Names as the list grew from 5,828 in 1965 to 7,660 in 1975. The most astonishing rise in Names began in 1975 and continued until the late 1980s as Lloyd's struggled to recoup substantial losses from a number of claims filed in the wake of disasters, both natural and human-made.

By 1985, Lloyd's boasted over 26,000 Names, and the number of investors continued to rise, with approximately 15 percent of the total being American and Canadian Names. Many of the North American Names were recruited by "members' agents" who received hefty commissions on the number of Names they recruited. It was later claimed that the North Americans Names, as well as those from other countries outside England, had been specifically recruited to bear the brunt of Lloyd's losses.

Most of Lloyd's North American Names were upper middle-class professionals and business people and their spouses. The Names were attracted to Lloyd's because of its stability and the guarantee of a quick return on what seemed to be a no-risk investment. On the surface, the method of investing in Lloyd's seemed simple: Individual names placed at least $150,000 in stocks and bonds in a Lloyd's account and pledged at least $400,000 in additional assets and credit. Technically, the funds were available to Lloyd's to pay out claims. However, Lloyd's rarely needed to tap the accounts for large sums, so

the funds steadily grew as premium payments were paid into trusts that each syndicate opened for its Names.

These approximately 400 syndicates made up what was essentially a lot of small companies under the Lloyd's of London umbrella. The amount received from premium payments varied according to the amount deposited in each Name's Lloyd's account. Likewise, when Lloyd's needed to withdraw funds to cover its losses, the amounts taken from each client were based on each Name's share of the total premiums issued by the syndicate. Each Name retained ownership of his/her Lloyd's deposit and earned profits according to the amount of pledged assets. It was common practice among English families who had inherited family property without sufficient funds to keep up their estates to become Names by pledging their lands as assets, allowing them to maintain their property with profits from Lloyd's accounts.

The practice of getting something for nothing from Lloyd's accounts ended in 1987 when a series of disasters placed an enormous drain on the financial assets of Names in certain syndicates. While it would seem that most of these claims were irrelevant to Lloyd's, the company was drawn in because of the practice of underwriting and reinsuring other insurance companies around the world. Lloyd's was well known for underwriting high-risk insurance policies. A large number of American claims were asbestos-related as scores of former asbestos workers became ill after being exposed to asbestos on their jobs decades before. Since their claims were made against valid policies, Lloyd's was required to honor them. Lloyd's also paid on American claims related to exposure to toxic wastes that had also occurred years before.

On October 15, 1987, Great Britain experienced its first hurricane in 200 years, resulting in losses to property amounting to some $3 billion; claims poured in to Lloyd's. The following year, a large number of disaster-related claims were filed with the company arising from the Piper Alpha oil rig explosion in the North Sea on July 7, 1988, in which 167 lives were lost. The crash of Pam Am flight 103 over Lockerbie, Scotland, on December 22, 1988, which claimed an additional 270 lives, further drained Lloyd's resources.

Additional claims were made after Hurricane Hugo touched down in the U.S. Carolinas on September 21, 1989, leaving behind over $7 million in damages. The following month, San Francisco, California was hit by a major earthquake. Both disasters generated numerous claims on Lloyd's resources. By that point, Lloyd's needed over $4 billion to meet incoming claims. When Lloyd's demanded that Names in some syndicates deliver their assets to meet Lloyd's shortfall, whole fortunes were wiped out. Thirty percent (about 7,000) Names were asked to bear the greatest share of the burden. American Names responded by filing numerous lawsuits, claiming that Lloyd's should have been forced to seek approval from the Securities and Exchange Commission (SEC) before doing business with Americans, and charging that agents had recruited Americans in order to bear the burden of Lloyd's losses.

In response to the serious economic crises it had caused for the Names, Lloyd's established a Hardship Committee to help investors locate necessary funds without wiping out all assets. Over 300 people applied for help, but Lloyd's never backed down from its demands. By 1991, close to 4,000 Names had resigned from membership in Lloyd's of London, while others scaled down their investments. Lloyd's also found itself in trouble with Inland Revenue, Britain's tax service, for depositing large sums of Names' investment money in offshore banks without their knowledge. Lloyd's was forced to pay the British government the money it has lost through the tax evasion scheme.

In the spring of 1995, Lloyd's announced a $3.8 billion settlement to be distributed among the Names that had been faced with financial ruin during Lloyd's crisis. Continuing its policy of using the private fortunes of its investors to mitigate its losses, Lloyd's asked Names who had not suffered losses to put up approximately $30 million of the settlement funds. Additional funds were solicited from insurance company investors.

SEE ALSO
securities fraud; insurance fraud; investment trust scandals; offshore entities; tax evasion.

BIBLIOGRAPHY. "A Decaf-Coffee House?" *The Economist* (February 20, 1999); Cathy Gunn, *Nightmare on Lime Street: Whatever Happened to Lloyd's of London?* (Smith Cryphon, 1992); Elizabeth Luessenhop and Martin Mayer, *Risky Business: An Insider's Account of The Disaster at Lloyd's of London* (Scribner, 1995); Richard Macve, *A Survey of Lloyd's Syndicate Accounts: Financial Reporting at Lloyd's in 1985* (Prentice Hall, 1986); Alexander MacLeod, "Lloyd's Near Settlement with Aggrieved Names," *Christian Science Monitor* (June 21, 1995).

ELIZABETH PURDY, PH.D.
INDEPENDENT SCHOLAR

Lockheed

IN 1909, AVIATOR Glenn L. Martin expanded his small aircraft construction business into Lockheed Martin Corporation, which became one of the most prominent aircraft suppliers in the world. In the years immediately after World War II, Europe was rebuilding its economy, and American businesses traded with former enemies as well as with former allies. International trade with developing countries was also on the rise. Expanded world markets offered enormous profits, and Lockheed was eager to make the most of its opportunities.

Money poured in from Lockheed sales to Japan, Germany, Italy, the Netherlands, West Germany, Indonesia, Turkey, Brazil, the Philippines, Saudi Arabia, and a number of other countries. Lockheed's problems started when William Findley, an independent auditor simply doing his job, discovered Lockheed's "unusual" accounting practices and began to wonder why Lockheed was making such huge contributions to a fund for widows and orphans in Djakarta, Indonesia, and to the Indonesian Air Force. Findley was most surprised by a Lockheed receipt that read: "I received One Hundred Peanuts." He was even more astonished when he learned that "One Hundred Peanuts" literally meant the receipt was for one million Japanese yen.

In June 1973, the head of Northrop Corporation, a Lockheed rival, admitted to a subcommittee of the U.S. Senate that his company had also paid "consultants" to facilitate business deals with foreign governments, adding that Northrop's secret agreements were patterned after those used by Lockheed. The resulting scandal led Senator Frank Church, chair of the Church Committee that investigated the Lockheed scandal, to remark that Lockheed's activities encompassed "a sordid tale of bribery, and of shadowy figures operating behind the scenes with a cast of characters [straight] out of a novel of international intrigue." Investigators discovered that between 1972 and 1974, the president of Lockheed, A. Carl Kotchian, had paid millions of dollars to Japanese sales consultants, secret agents, businessmen, and the Japanese government to facilitate the sale of Lockheed planes to All Nippon Airlines. Upon learning of the Lockheed scandal, Japanese merchants seized on the wording of the receipt that auditor Findley had discovered. Souvenir handkerchiefs were sold, which read: "I received One Hundred Peanuts." Foreign governments did not treat the scandals so lightly. Many of Lockheed's cohorts stood trial and received various punishments.

INTERNATIONAL BRIBERY

The Senate learned that money had been paid into Swiss bank accounts, dummy corporations, and "charities." Most Americans were horrified to learn that a share of the Japanese payments had been given to General Minoru Genda, the architect of the attack on Pearl Harbor on December 7, 1941, which had propelled the United States into World War II. Further investigation revealed that, in 1959, Genda visited Lockheed's Burbank, California, headquarters to test Lockheed's Starfighter. Japan had subsequently purchased 230 Starfighters. Yoshio Kadama, a Japanese agent who was considered one of the most powerful men in Japan and who was secretly on Lockheed's payroll, received $1.7 million for his services on the Starfighter deal. Overall, Lockheed paid over $12 million to various individuals in Japan through Kadama.

Lockheed had also sought to influence purchasing decisions in a number of other countries. In West Germany, for example, Lockheed worked with Franz Joseph Strauss, the Minister of Defense, who purchased 96 Lockheed planes in 1959. In return, Lockheed paid a percentage of the sales on all Lockheed planes sold to the West German government to the West German Air Force, Strauss's Christian Socialist Union political party, and various other West German political and military officials.

In the Netherlands, Lockheed paid Prince Bernhard, the husband of Queen Julianna, $1 million, depositing the money into a Swiss bank account. The prince later resigned in disgrace from all public offices, and the Dutch government purchased planes from the French. From 1969 to 1971, Lockheed paid Italian government agents over $2 million to facilitate the sale of Lockheed planes. The individuals who received payments from Lockheed were later brought to trial in the Italian courts.

Lockheed's relations with the Indonesian government went back as far as the mid-1950s. In 1966, the newly elected Indonesian president specified that no payments could be remitted to individuals but should instead be made to government-sponsored agencies. Initially, the Widows and Orphans fund in Djakarta, Indonesia, received 5 percent on all Lockheed sales to the Indonesian government but the payment was later raised to 10 percent. Few people believed that the Lockheed payments had actually supported widows and orphans.

Ironically, Lockheed's payments to foreign agents were not a violation of American law, and the practice of paying consultants and foreign governments was not uncommon. Nonetheless, Kotchian later acknowledged that he did not act ethically in the matter. He also admitted that Lockheed's profits would have suffered if he had not cooperated with foreign governments. The money realized on such sales had helped Lockheed to recover from a billion-dollar cost overrun that resulted from the production of Lockheed's first jumbo jet. It also saved thousands of jobs for employees of this company that was known for its frequent layoffs.

The Congressional investigation into Lockheed's activities motivated Congress to pass the Foreign Corrupt Practices, which President Jimmy Carter signed into law in 1977. The act made it a criminal offense to offer or pay money to government officials of foreign countries or to any individuals who intended to pass on such payments to foreign government officials for the purposes of obtaining or retaining business in those countries. Exceptions were made for payments to officials whose duties were chiefly ministerial or clerical. While the law established limits on the actions of American businesses doing business in foreign countries, its failure to distinguish between bribery and extortion was considered a major weakness.

SEE ALSO
bribery; extortion; Foreign Corrupt Practices Act; Northrop Grumman; corruption.

BIBLIOGRAPHY. David Boulton, *The Grease Machine* (Harper and Row, 1978); "History," www.lockheed.com (2003); George C. Kohn, *Encyclopedia of American Scandal* (Oxford University Press, 1989); A. Carl Kotchian,

"The Payoff: Lockheed's Seventy-Day Mission to Tokyo," *Saturday Review* (July 9, 1977); Christine Pierce, *How to Solve The Lockheed Case* (Social Philosophy and Policy Center, 1986).

ELIZABETH PURDY, PH.D.
INDEPENDENT SCHOLAR

Love Canal

WHEN MOST PEOPLE think of Niagara Falls, New York, they picture the beautiful spectacle and one of the world's wonders, that of Niagara Falls. However, many may not think of this awesome sight but instead images of toxic waste and houses that were rumored to glow. Just east of the Falls is the site of the Love Canal and the tragedy that fell on a small community.

In the 1890s, a man named William T. Love bought a small tract of land and dug a short canal between the upper and lower Niagara Rivers. He felt that power could be generated cheaply to fuel the industry and homes that would be developed. Unfortunately, Love's project was never finished and the canal that was supposed to be used as a way for a town to prosper was instead used as a dumping ground for a variety of municipal and industrial wastes.

The City of Niagara Falls started the dumping. In 1920, the canal was sold in a public auction to the municipality for use as a landfill. The U.S. Army was also responsible for dumping chemical warfare material. Hooker Chemical Company started to use the canal for a chemical dump site in 1942 when they negotiated with the city of Niagara Falls to buy the property. During the period 1942-53, Hooker owned the land and was the primary company disposing of its wastes into the canal. At this time, there were no regulations or laws prohibiting such activity. Hooker dumped over 21,800 tons of toxic chemical wastes on the site. Included in these chemicals were benzene hexachloride, chlorobenzenes, and 400,000 pounds of dioxin-contaminated trichlorophenol. All of these chemicals are highly carcinogenic (cancer-causing).

In 1952, the Niagara Falls School Board wanted to buy a part of the Love Canal property in order to build a new grade school so they approached Hooker. The population in Niagara Falls was growing and the local school board was pressuring Hooker to sell the undeveloped land. Hooker felt that it was not wise to build on the land since it was used as a dump site for over 10 years. The school board threatened the use of eminent domain and continued to pressure Hooker to give up the land. Hooker was still against the use of the land and tried to convince the school board that they should avoid building underground facilities of any kind, given the type and amount of chemicals that were disposed of on the property.

After much pressure, Hooker was willing to donate the property for $1, only if several conditions were guaranteed. Hooker wanted the school board to take the entire property and indemnify Hooker from any future claims. The school board refused and Hooker relinquished ownership when there was no other choice, and before the school board invoked eminent domain. Hooker covered the wastes with a protective clay cap and sold the 16-acre parcel for $1. Hooker tried to advise all of the parties involved about the chemicals that were buried on the site and that any building that was to be done should be done without disturbing the site. Parking lots and other above ground facilities would be appropriate, but building a school and houses would not be. In spite of these warnings, the city of Niagara Falls developed the land.

From 1954 through the mid-1970s, there were a series of incidents which showed the danger of breaking the ground around the canal. The ground subsided and old drums of toxic wastes rose to the surface. Complaints of foul odors and chemical residues, first reported in the 1960s, increased during the 1970s, as heavy rainfall caused the groundwater to rise, flooding area basements. Hooker was called to the site various times, but the company tried to explain to the city that they were no longer responsible for the site, the school board was since the site was transferred to them. However, the school board was protected by sovereign immunit (government officials cannot be held responsible for mistakes otherwise they would avoid making them, making it impossible to do their job). Therefore, the responsibility fell back on the Hooker Chemical Company.

During the summer of 1978, Love Canal first came to international attention. Through the courageous battle fought by Lois Gibbs, a local resident, and others in the area, the Love Canal area was declared a national emergency. In 1978, 239 families were evacuated and relocated by the U.S. government, and their homes destroyed. More families were relocated at a later date. There were 564 homes that were designated in the Emergency Declaration area. Residents of all but 72 of the 564 homes chose to move. More than 900 families were forced to leave their homes so the site could be cleaned.

CREATION OF THE EPA

It was not until the 1970s that the Environmental Protection Agency (EPA) was created to study the effects and regulate the thousands of chemicals used in the United States. President Richard M. Nixon declared his intention to establish the Environmental Protection Agency with Reorganization Plan Number 3, dated July 9, 1970. The EPA's mission would include: "The establishment and enforcement of environmental protection standards consistent with national environmental goals. The conduct of research on the adverse effects of pollution and on methods and equipment for controlling it; the gathering of information on pollution; and the use of this information in strengthening environmental protection programs and recommending policy changes ... assisting others, through grants, technical assistance and other means, in arresting pollution of the environment... assisting the Council on Environmental Quality in developing and recommending to the president new policies for the protection of the environment." After being cleared through hearings in the Senate and House of Representatives, the EPA was inaugurated on December 2, 1970.

Love Canal was the first hazardous waste disposal case to draw national attention, and it remains to this day a landmark case. The disaster at Love Canal led to the creation of the EPA's Superfund law in 1980. Superfund makes responsible parties liable for the cleanup costs of such environmental disasters. The Love Canal court battle provided one of the first tests of the Comprehensive Emergency Response, Compensation and Liability Act (CERCLA, also known as Superfund). The site was officially placed on EPA's list of hazardous waste sites needing cleanup in 1983. EPA worked with the state to cap the land to prevent rainwater from reaching the waste, built a system to clean water draining from the site, cleaned out debris from the sewers and surrounding creeks, and removed polluted soil from nearby schools and residential properties.

Even though Hooker tried to claim that they were not responsible for the disaster; they did settle and ended up paying over $227 million for the clean up. Since the dumping occurred before the EPA was created, no punitive damages were warranted because the actions of Hooker were not illegal at the time of the actual dumping. Even though Hooker settled and paid much of the cost of cleanup, the largest price paid for the cleanup came from the taxpayers. It cost over $30 million to evacuate the area and $250 million to clean up the site. If the Hooker Chemical Company had refused to sell to the city of Niagara Falls or cleaned up the site before the sale, or if the city of Niagara Falls had heeded Hooker's warnings, this disaster could have been avoided.

Early investigations of the Love Canal area confirmed the existence of toxins in the soil and determined that they were responsible for the area's unusually high rates of cancer, miscarriages, and birth defects. But, these results have been highly criticized. There have been no conclusive studies done of Love Canal's actual effects on its residents' health. This is mainly due to the lack of tracking of the families that had relocated. Residents of the area have complained of health problems, but whether or not Love Canal is to blame has not been conclusively determined.

Today, the waterway that gave the neighborhood its name is buried under a plastic liner with clay and topsoil in a fenced area that has been declared permanently off-limits. However, the EPA has declared the rest of Love Canal safe. Even though some still wonder if the area is truly safe, much of the property has been renovated and resold.

According to the Love Canal Revitalization Agency, 232 of the 239 homes have been renovated and recently sold, creating an environmentally safe neighborhood on land once contaminated. Love Canal, which symbolized hidden toxic wastelands, is now known as Black Creek Village. As a result of grass roots interest and media attention, Love Canal became a national symbol for the environmental threats the United States and the world face from hazardous waste.

In March 2004, the EPA reiterated Love Canal was clean and should be taken off Superfund list.

SEE ALSO

water pollution; Environmental Protection Agency; hazardous waste.

BIBLIOGRAPHY. Michael H. Brown, "A Toxic Ghost Town: Ten Years Later, Scientists Are Still Assessing The Damage From Love Canal," *The Atlantic* (v.263/1, 1989); Craig E. Colten and Peter Skinner, *The Road to Love Canal: Managing Industrial Waste before EPA* (University of Texas Press, 1996); Lois Gibbs, *Love Canal: The Story Continues* (New Society Publisher, 1998); Andrew J. Hoffman, "An Uneasy Rebirth at Love Canal," *Environment* (v.37/2, 1995); Willard Miller and Ruby M. Miller, *Environmental Hazards: Toxic Wastes and Hazardous Material* (ABC-CLIO, 1991); Environmental Protection Agency, www.epa.gov (2003).

DEBRA E. ROSS, PH.D.
GRAND VALLEY STATE UNIVERSITY

Luxembourg

LUXEMBOURG HAS LONG been known as a tax haven. One of the major hallmarks of tax havens is a strict policy of banking secrecy. In the Grand Duchy of Luxembourg it is illegal to disclose details of banking customers unless there is strong evidence of fraud. The Grand Duchy maintains that there is no contradiction between bank secrecy, which is intended to protect the individual's privacy, and effective crime fighting.

In January 2003, European Union (EU) finance ministers in Brussels, Belgium, agreed after 14 years of negotiation to terms that were meant to level the playing field on taxes and end tax havens. The Tax Package was formally agreed to six months later. The core of the package is the Savings Tax Directive which is intended to ensure that individuals do not escape taxes by investing in other EU countries. Terms were to have gone into effect the beginning of 2004 but have been delayed for one year. Twelve of the 15 EU countries (2003) are to share non-residents' savings accounts information.

The other three, Luxembourg, Austria, and Belgium, refused to waive their banking secrecy regulations and exchange customer information. Instead, those three agreed to levy a withholding tax on savings interest. The withholdings from each of these countries is to be distributed with 25 percent going to the banking country which collected it, and 75 percent to the country of the customer, but with no identification as to who the customer is. The three also agreed to join the information exchange only if Switzerland, which is not an EU member, drops its tradition of banking secrecy. Switzerland has agreed to join in withholding taxes on savings of EU residents.

Many scholars perceive financial centers that surround themselves with secrecy to be breeding grounds for crimes such as money laundering, as well as money sources for terrorists and other criminals. Luxembourg was among the first countries to adopt measures against money laundering in 1989. The Grand Duchy advises that it cooperates fully at the international level. A Luxembourg governmental web site says the country is an active member of FATF (Financial Action Task Force) which specializes in the fight against money laundering, and that the task force testified in its last evaluation that Luxembourg had completely respected all its recommendations.

Additionally, legislation in Luxembourg requires very strict conditions regarding access to the financial sector. This is especially true regarding the identity and worthiness of shareholders and directors of financial institutions. The law specifically demands that professionals in the financial sector know their customers. Anonymous accounts do not exist.

Luxembourg declares itself to be among the European countries which have "most completely and swiftly implemented the measures advocated by the American authorities in the fight against the financing of terrorism."

SEE ALSO

tax evasion; Bank Secrecy Act; Switzerland; offshore entities; Securities and Exchange Commission.

BIBLIOGRAPHY. Ronen Palan, "Tax Haven," *Routledge Encyclopedia of International Political Economy* (Routledge, 2001); "The Taxman Cometh," *The Economist* (January 25, 2003); "Critics See Flaws in Brussels Compromise," *International Money Marketing* (February 7, 2003); "Taxing Europe's Savings," *International Money Marketing* (July 21, 2003); Luxembourg government, www.gouvernement.lu (2003).

LINDA M. CREIBAUM
ARKANSAS STATE UNIVERSITY

M

Madison Guaranty

A SAVINGS AND LOAN bank, Madison Guaranty was part of President Bill Clinton's Whitewater scandal. In June 1978, Clinton and his wife Hillary joined their longtime friends, Jim and Susan McDougal, in the purchase of 230 acres near Flippin along north Arkansas' White River. Their Whitewater Development Corporation was formed to build and sell homes on lots on this land. The couples borrowed about $200,000 of the money to purchase the land from Citizens' Bank; the $10,000 down payment was borrowed from another bank but the investors did not inform Citizens. The Clintons were equal partners in the endeavor even though they did not invest as much as the McDougals.

In January 1982, Jim McDougal, who had been Arkansas Attorney General Bill Clinton's economic aide from 1978 to 1980, bought the Woodruff Savings and Loan in Augusta, Arkansas. He changed the named to Madison Guaranty and moved it to Little Rock. In the mid-1980s, the bank was making unwise loans, and in 1984, the Federal Home Loan Bank Board issued a "highly critical exam of Madison Guaranty," The Public Broadcasting System reported.

Madison entered into a supervisory agreement to correct its lending errors. The same year the McDougals borrowed $100,000 from the Madison Guaranty savings and loan (S&L) in order to pay down the Whitewater mortgage.

In April 1985, Jim McDougal held a fundraiser for Clinton, now governor after his tenure as attorney general) at the Madison Guaranty offices. An estimated $35,000 was raised, but later there were questions whether some of the funds were provided by depositors, or were given by the bank in the names of depositors without their knowledge.

McDougal and his friend Seth Ward (who was also a Madison Guaranty subsidy executive and father-in-law of Hillary Clinton's law partner Webb Hubbell) purchased the 1,050-acre Castle Grande property for $1.75 million in October 1985. Madison Financial, Madison Guaranty's real estate subsidy, provided $600,000, its legal limit, and Ward borrowed $1.15 million for his share from Madison Guaranty in a non-recourse loan.

By the end of 1985, Madison was in trouble. Attorney Hillary Clinton represented the S&L bank and helped persuade state officials to let Madison raise funds by selling preferred stock. This unusual course was approved by Beverly Bassett, Arkansas commissioner of securities and a Clinton appointee, but was never carried out.

In February 1986, developer Dean Paul borrowed $825,000 from Madison Guaranty to buy three properties from lender David Hale, whom

Clinton had appointed municipal judge. Hale loaned $150,000 to Jim Guy Tucker (later governor of Arkansas) and R.D. Randolph, who borrowed another $1.05 million from Madison Guaranty. Senator William Fulbright borrowed $700,000 from the S&L, then with Tucker and Randolph bought the majority of the Castle Grande property. Hale's company also loaned $300,000 to Susan Mc-Dougal's Master Marketing company; Hale said he was pressured by the governor and McDougal into approving the loan.

Jim and Susan McDougal were forced to resign from Madison Guaranty in July 1986 by the Federal Home Loan Bank Board. In 1989, Madison was taken over by the Resolution Trust Corp. (RTC), the federal agency managing the savings and loan crisis. Jim McDougal was indicted on bank fraud charges in late 1989 but acquitted by jury in 1990. The Mc-Dougals separated. Susan McDougal moved to California where she was later convicted of embezzlement. Hale was indicted on charges of defrauding the federal government with his Small Business Administration-backed loans in 1993. The S&L failure cost American taxpayers more than $60 million.

Governor Tucker, and Jim and Susan McDougal were indicted on multiple counts of bank fraud in August 1995, tried in April 1996, and convicted a month later. Susan McDougal refused to answer questions before the grand jury and was sent to prison. After his conviction, Jim McDougal began to cooperate with the independent counsel, Robert Fiske, appointed independent counsel to investigate Whitewater in 1994; he was followed seven months later by Kenneth Starr who broadened the inquiry wide enough to encompass the impeachment of the president of the United States, Bill Clinton.

SEE ALSO

Whitewater; Clinton William J.; bank fraud; accounting fraud; savings and loan fraud.

BIBLIOGRAPHY. Public Broadcasting System, "Frontline: Whitewater," www.pbs.org (2003); Cable News Network, "1997 In Focus, Whitewater," www.cnn.com (2003); Mark Hosenball, with Bob Cohn, and Tom Morganthau, "How Bad Is It?" *Newsweek* (January 17, 1994).

LINDA M. CREIBAUM
ARKANSAS STATE UNIVERSITY

mail fraud

THE FEDERAL MAIL fraud statute is codified under 18 USC §1341, and has two essential elements: 1) use of the United States mail; 2) use that is in furtherance of defrauding someone. The law has been utilized in diverse cases by federal prosecutors in pursuing everything from simple confidence games to bribery of public officials. §1341 has been used against virtually every new method of fraud, and sometimes has been the only way to prosecute and adequately punish sophisticated fraudsters. Despite the broad application and peculiar elements that give §1341 great prosecutorial power, those characteristics also place it in jeopardy of inappropriate and abusive usages.

Its offspring statute, wire fraud (18 USC §1343), is in almost all cases interpreted similarly to §1341. Mail fraud encompasses the use of the mails, either inter- or intrastate, whereas wire fraud outlaws the interstate use of wires for fraudulent purposes. Federal jurisdiction of both mail and wire fraud originate in the Constitution under Article 1, Section 8. However, mail fraud is based on Congress's control of the postal authorities and wire fraud is based on Congress's right to make laws affecting interstate and foreign commerce.

Mail fraud may be seen as more specific to the federal jurisdiction than wire fraud because its overt act is any use of the mails, which are owned and operated by the government, as a necessary means to complete the fraud scheme. Wire fraud, on the other hand, involves wires owned by entities other than the federal government, so federal jurisdiction is, like many federal offenses, based only on the Commerce Clause.

INSTRUMENTS OF CRIME

The underlying legal crime of mail fraud is not that associated with the scam, but rather the crime in using the mails, or trying to use them, as an instrument of defrauding the mail recipients. This allows extremely distinctive enforcement interpretations. First, the statute is completely unconcerned with the harm inflicted by the fraud. Second, the culpability structure of §1341 is much more inclusive than almost all other criminal offenses because the statute allows merely a "scheme" to be prosecuted, regardless of whether the scheme actually took place or was successful.

The interpretation is, in this sense, similar to a conspiracy to commit a crime, but a conspiracy necessitates at least two participants; there need be only one participant in the scheme to be prosecuted under mail fraud. Further, whereas conspiracy can be charged only once regardless of the number of separate overt acts committed as a result of the conspiracy, mail fraud law punishes each act of mailing as a separate count. Third, the intent to violate §1341 only need involve a broadly interpreted "foreseeable" use of the mails; most offenses require that the perpetrator have knowledge of the commission of the act and also intended its commission.

In 1994, Congress added to §1341 the use of common carriers to execute a fraud, and added financial institution victims in 1989. The maximum penalty for mail fraud affecting a financial institution was raised from 20 years to 30 years in 1990. The current §1341 is titled "Frauds and Swindles" and spells out the statute (albeit long-winded):

Whoever, having devised or intending to devise any scheme or artifice to defraud, or for obtaining money or property by means of false or fraudulent pretenses, representations, or promises, or to sell, dispose of, loan, exchange, alter, give away, distribute, supply, or furnish or procure for unlawful use any counterfeit or spurious coin, obligation, security, or other article, or anything represented to be or intimated or held out to be such counterfeit or spurious article, for the purpose of executing such scheme or artifice or attempting so to do, places in any post office or authorized depository for mail matter, any matter or thing whatever to be sent or delivered by the Postal Service, or deposits or causes to be deposited any matter or thing whatever to be sent or delivered by any private or commercial interstate carrier, or takes or receives therefrom, any such matter or thing, or knowingly causes to be delivered by mail or such carrier according to the direction thereon, or at the place at which it is directed to be delivered by the person to whom it is addressed, any such matter or thing, shall be fined under this title or imprisoned not more than five years, or both.

If the violation affects a financial institution, such person shall be fined not more than $1,000,000 or imprisoned not more than 30 years, or both.

HISTORY OF MAIL FRAUD

The two central legal questions that have dominated the history of this statute center on what constitutes the use of the mails and what constitutes fraudulent use. Prior to the Civil War, the general legal position was that the federal government had no right to open mail matter. This changed with the forerunner to the modern mail fraud statute, the "lottery law" of 1868, which made it illegal to mail any materials that involved a lottery or other similar prizes. The legal theory behind the lottery law, which is also the foundation of all subsequent mail fraud statutes, is based on the authorities first obtaining information about an illegal use of the mail and then securing a search warrant to inspect mail contents for evidence.

Given the large numbers of mail swindles during Reconstruction, there was a perceived need for federal help in combating frauds at the local level. Congress did not want the national postal system to be used as an instrument of crime and moral turpitude, so it passed the first mail fraud statute in 1872 as part of much larger legislation affecting the mails. The first section of the statute proscribed obscene and other objectionable materials, and the second section forbade lotteries. The third section, mail fraud, outlawed "having devised or intending to devise any scheme or artifice to defraud" that principally depended on the mail for execution.

The first mail fraud statute, then, projected a fairly limited conception of what is meant by the intended misuse of the mails. People were punished under the statute according to the extent "the abuse of the post-office establishment enters as an instrument into such fraudulent scheme or device." Judicial validation of this first statute came quickly in 1877 through the Supreme Court case, *Ex Parte Jackson* (96 U.S. 727, 1878). Although Jackson came to the Court under questions about the "lottery law," its opinion rang a sound constitutional endorsement for the mail fraud statute, finding that Congress controls the mails and that controlling the mails includes determining what will not be carried in those mails.

The most significant revision to mail fraud law took place in 1909, during the Progressive Era, and involved the major change in defining what constitutes the use of the mails to defraud. It deleted all specific language of the "instrumentality" theory requiring that the perpetrator intended to directly misuse the mails as a necessity to the fraud. In its place, Congress worded the statute to include any use of the mails in furtherance of a fraud, regardless of whether the perpetrator sent or received mail, regardless of whether the mails were intended to be used, and regardless of whether the mails represented a central or peripheral instrument of crime in the scheme.

This statutory language exploded the number and variety of cases in which the federal government could intervene jurisdictionally, and more than anything else reflected the federal government's desire, as was characteristic of the time's Progressivism, to become involved in innumerable types of acts that had been local matters. Since 1909, incidental, or even accidental, use of the mails during a fraud scheme would be enough to fall under the law.

Going back to 1909, the wording of the mail fraud statute has caused courts to grapple with many undefined issues because it does not address the kinds of "schemes" or "artifices" to defraud that fall under its punishment; rather, it counts only the number of times the mails were used. Courts have tried to focus on whether an act of mailing was somehow necessary for the offense's fruition, and the precedents seem to focus on a matter of timing. For example, a confidence artist can be convicted of mail fraud because he waited for his check to clear before absconding, and the check cleared through the mails—waiting for the cash was seen to be a part, however small, of the fraud scheme. On the other hand, a person who embezzles monies previously received through mailed donations is not punishable for mail fraud because the use of the mails occurred before the scheme to defraud. Mailing to a credit cardholder a statement with a fraudulent charge by another person does not constitute mail fraud for the thief, because the mailing occurred after the crime. The 1909 statute considers mail fraud to be present in all cases where mails are used to carry out the scheme in any way and where such use would be foreseeable by a reasonable person.

SERVICES, PROPERTY RIGHTS, AND TORTS

One strongly debated legal question has been whether mail fraud can be applied to both public officials and those in private business who use the mails to further a bribery scheme. Since the 1930s, the meaning of fraudulent schemes within the mail

fraud statute was interpreted to include depriving someone of an intangible right to honest service. This interpretation eventually encompassed under mail fraud any use of the mails associated with a solicitation or acceptance of corrupt, quid pro quo bribes by private individuals and public officials.

The use of mail fraud in bribery cases was consistently upheld by various courts until 1987, when the Supreme Court decided *McNally v. U.S.* (107 S.Ct. 2875, 1987). Here, the Court broke long tradition by finding that the historical intent of §1341 did not include as fraud depriving someone of something intangible, such as a right to honest services. Instead, according to McNally, the deprivation must involve actual or intended loss of property or property rights. Eventually, the McNally reversal was applied retroactively to those previously convicted of mail-related bribery that did not involve property losses.

Congress immediately exercised its check-and-balance role by passing in 1988 a completely new statute, 18 USC §1346, which stated simply, "For the purposes of this chapter [covering mail and wire fraud], the term 'scheme or artifice to defraud' includes a scheme or artifice to deprive another of the intangible right of honest services." §1346 was meant by Congress especially to reinstate the pre-McNally ability of federal prosecutors to go after bribery under the mail fraud and wire fraud statutes. It also tried to allow coverage of any other situation that involved deprivation of honest service using the mails or wires, including bribe-taking by a fiduciary.

The conflict over the idea of "dishonest services" among the courts, prosecutors, defendants, and Congress recurred in the allegation that the single sentence in §1346 is unconstitutionally vague because a reasonable person would not know what is meant by the statute's wording of depriving another of the intangible right to honest services. Further, there is no implication in §1346 about the circumstances in which it should be applied. At least three court-imposed restrictions have been placed on the applicability of §1346.

First, simple breaches of contract should not be considered a deprivation of honest services. Second, the focus in McNally on property rights for §1341 has been applied to §1346 through the requirement that something more than minimal economic harm to the victim must have been foreseeable by a reasonable person, if the statute's clause of deprivation of dishonest services is to be applied. Much to the dismay of Congress, this continuation of a property emphasis into §1346 may effectively eliminate the punishment of people who use the mails or wires to further a corrupt bribery scheme, but which does not involve economic harm.

Third, §1346 has been limited to torts. This means that the only time "dishonest services" actually occur in a mail or wire fraud is through wrongful behavior causing damage and for which a person can be sued civilly. Restricting §1341 to foreseeable property loss and restricting §1346 to torts should make their enforcement considerably more clear, but numerous issues remain to be resolved about exactly what constitutes using the mails or common carriers to defraud.

SEE ALSO

wire fraud; direct-mail fraud; bribery; scams.

BIBLIOGRAPHY. Jed Rakoff, "The Federal Mail Fraud Statute (Part 1)," *Duquesne Law Review* (v.18, 1980); John C. Coffee, Jr, "The Metastasis of Mail Fraud: The Continuing Story of the 'Evolution' of a White Collar Crime," *American Criminal Law Review* (v.21, 1983); Richard Beckler and Maury Epner, "Principal White Collar Crimes," *Business Crimes: A Guide for Corporate and Defense Counsel* (Practicing Law Institute, 1982); Pamela H. Bucy, *White Collar Crime: Cases and Materials* (West, 1992).

GARY S. GREEN
CHRISTOPHER NEWPORT UNIVERSITY

Major Fraud Act of 1988

SPONSORED BY U.S. Representative William Hughes from New Jersey, the Major Fraud Act (Public Law 100-700) was signed into law by President Ronald Reagan on November 11, 1988. The Major Fraud Act significantly increased the maximum penalties which could be assessed for certain major frauds committed against the United States government.

Title XVIII of the U.S. Code, primarily known as the Federal Criminal Code, was amended considerably to allow for increased penalties against anyone who knowingly and willingly commits or attempts to commit a plan to fraudulently receive property or services from the U.S. government valued at $1 million or more. The act increases the maximum penalty for a single count to $1 million and for multiple counts to $10 million. Criteria for the specified amounts of fines are set forth by the act, and fraud violators may also face prison terms of up to 10 years. The act authorizes the U.S. Sentencing Commission to come up with guidelines or to modify existing ones to better deal with frauds, especially those which have a high risk of potentially serious injuries as a possible result of the unlawful actions.

Employees who assist prosecutors with a fraud case are protected by the act if their employment is terminated or modified in a negative way as a result of the proceedings. However, in order for employees to receive this protection, they must not have acted with complicity in the fraud that was committed. If a person qualifies for this protection, the act stipulates specific remedies for adverse actions taken against employees.

The Major Fraud Act states that fraudulent contractors may not seek reimbursements for costs incurred during any fraud proceedings initiated by the federal government, or a state government, which deal with a violation or failure to comply, if the defendant is found to be guilty of the violation. The recovery of costs is permitted when the proceedings are ended by a compromise that results in an agreement between the contractor and the U.S. government. Usually, the amount which is to be reimbursed to the contractor is provided within the terms of the agreement. Also, costs may be recovered if the director of the department or agency which committed to do business with the contractor consents, under certain conditions, that the costs were covered under specific provisions within the original agreement between the contractor and the U.S. government.

In order to guarantee enforcement, the act provided for the creation of additional positions within the Department of Justice, including the addition of an assistant U.S. attorney, solely in order to investigate and prosecute fraud against the U.S. government. The U.S. attorney general is required by the act to report to Congress annually concerning statistics which record the number of referrals of fraud cases by government departments and agencies, number of investigations of contractors, number of attorneys, support, and agents utilized in cases, and number of convictions, acquittals, sentences, reimbursements, and penalties. Since its enactment, the Major Fraud Act has been amended numerous times, including some minor and major changes. Most of the amendments deal with specific types of fraudulent activities such as credit card fraud, computer fraud, bank fraud, among other fraud crimes. The fraud crimes which are most often prosecuted are usually not violations in excess of $1 million, but smaller violations such as false statements, false claims, and conspiracy to defraud.

Although smaller fraudulent acts are committed more frequently, violators of the Major Fraud Act are prosecuted often. For example, on February 16, 2000, Olson Electric Company of Daytona Beach, Florida, was sentenced to pay back $885,819 to the National Aeronautics and Space Administration (NASA) and pay a special assessment fee of $200. Olson Electric knowingly lied in official records to qualify for a NASA contract worth $3.2 million, specified for a woman-owned small business, to refurbish a shuttle launch pad at the Kennedy Space Center in Florida. Consequently, on November 17, 1999, Olson pleaded guilty to violating the Major Fraud Act and was forced to repay the over-billed amount at the sentencing on February 16, 2000. The verdict was only one success in the Department of Justice and the U.S. attorney general's ongoing battle against major fraud.

SEE ALSO

government contract fraud; government procurement fraud; Justice, Department of; conspiracy.

BIBLIOGRAPHY. 18 U.S.C. Sec. 1001, Transactional Record Access Clearinghouse, www.trac.syr.edu (2003); U.S. Nuclear Regulatory Commission, *OIG Fraud Bulletin* (v.1/2, June 2000); Major Fraud Act of 1988, Public Law 100-700, www.thomas.loc.gov (2003); U.S. Department of Justice, www.usdoj.gov (2003).

ARTHUR HOLST, PH.D.
WIDENER UNIVERSITY

maritime fraud

COMPOSED OF of several illegal activities, maritime fraud includes smuggling, money laundering, documentation and insurance fraud, and the illegal transport of persons. All of these examples present unique challenges to law enforcement authorities. The last few years have seen an alarming increase in international economic fraud, and much of it takes place during maritime transport. Due to the magnitude of operations, these crimes most always involve a complex and organized criminal element.

As the demand for and profit from illicit transportation of people, consumer contraband, and illegal drugs expands, so does the criminal scope. Transportation links present an attractive opportunity for business, and large profit margins are a driving force in motivation. By utilizing violence and intimidation, an organized crime system is able to secure help at various levels of transport. Complex schemes are planned and set into motion, many of which appear similar to those used by legitimate corporations. By the same token, legitimate businesses sometimes carry on illegal activities under the guise of business as usual.

Crime syndicates, drug cartels, and ethnic groups also compete for regional controls, which are carefully chosen to exploit weaknesses in the system. Areas that suffer a decrease in governmental controls are also targeted, as are areas which have affiliations with immigrant communities. Civil disturbances and international market conditions are often exploited in an attempt to take advantage of a temporary market and to shift suspicion onto other suspects. Growth of both black market and white-collar crime has greatly expanded due to advancements made in communications and transportation technologies.

The International Maritime Bureau (IMB), established in 1981, was formed to combat all types of maritime and trade crime. Their focus is often centered on aspects of cargo theft, deviation of ships, fraudulent documentation and illegal charter. Working closely with regional law enforcement agencies, they work to reduce piracy and fraud by carefully tracking cargos and shipments, verifying scheduled arrivals at different junctures. In order to expand their effectiveness, the IMB held an international conference in Geneva, Switzerland, where it established the International Maritime Organization (IMO), which investigates suspected criminal activities.

Maritime fraud is one of the end results of piracy, or violent crimes at sea. These may result from hit-and-run raids as well as theft of vessels and

Soaring maritime crime has created a surge in forged travel documents, both for the ship and the crew.

cargos. The result of piracy can be commercial devastation and often includes human tragedy; the busiest shipping lanes are prime hunting grounds. Piracy has soared worldwide. Armed with advanced weaponry and high-tech equipment, such as rocket launchers and global positioning equipment, criminals have a greater chance of successfully committing their crimes. The spoils of piracy are then fraudulently documented and millions of dollars are lost as the goods are sold to unsuspecting customers or other conspirators. A focus on piracy lead to two international treaties: the 1982 Convention, which provides an international definition for piracy, and the Rome Convention, which responds to the escalation in the global threat of terrorism.

Regulations in the declaration of ship ownership promises to be a great help to law enforcement in the fight against maritime crime. Secrecy is desired for purposes of theft or tax-evasion. False information presents an additional hurdle to maritime law enforcement. The inability to detect fraudulent certificates presents tremendous opportunities for illicit activities and presents a particular haven for terrorist opportunities.

FORGED PAPERS

The IMB reports that forged ship and crew travel documents are easily obtained, and difficult to de-

fend against. Recent investigations required the recall of several years' worth of maritime licenses and documents issued from San Juan, Puerto Rico. Hundreds of licenses contained blanks and a machine used for document printing was reported missing. Nearly 1,000 questionable mariner documents were targeted by the inspection teams and over 250 of them were confiscated. In 2001, there were 13,000 false certificates reported and it is estimated that many more went undetected. Two men were arrested; one was a formerly with the U.S. Coast Guard. The breech in maritime security was considered major.

Forgery was also evident in the majority of countries inspected. This well-organized deception required assistance from administrators, employers, manning agents, and training programs. Crimes of this magnitude must rely on participants from several layers of the organization, indicating widespread corruption.

On March 25, 2002, a new requirement was implemented was put into place which required all new ships be tagged with permanent identification numbers that are assigned by Lloyd's Registry Fairplay during ship construction. The number reads "IMO" followed by the seven-digit assigned number, which remains unchanged upon transfer of ownership. This requirement will make ownership transparent, and raises security standards by increasing the chances of prosecuting perpetrators of maritime fraud.

The volume of container shipping across the globe makes inspecting individual containers nearly impossible.

Another main target of maritime fraud is marine insurance underwriters who have to weigh out fictitious and legitimate insurance claims. This may take form as the intentional total loss of a vessel by the owner, or the over-insured loss of cargo. Another method used to defraud the underwriters is false documents used to substantiate such losses.

As the volume of commercial seaborne trade triples, identification of possible arms shipments becomes more difficult to defect. The demand for weapons and drugs continues to drive the black market and tempts those with access to the area. Violence and conflict stemming from ethnic or religious differences are prime business opportunities for criminal activity. The best laid criminal plans intermingle illicit cargo among the legitimate. Because the high success rate for fraudulent transport, more legitimate business people are lured by the desire of easy money, taking advantage of the confusion caused by jurisdiction differences.

On September 5, 2003, six Pacific Rim countries agreed to conduct joint maritime exercises for the following year in a united front to discourage the escalation of criminal activities. The maritime police in these areas are working to eradicate the crimes of piracy, smuggling, terrorism, and money laundering.

Compulsory disclosure of ship ownership, increased scrutiny of shipping documents, and amendments to international conventions to clarify links between vessels and flag states, can improve the efficiency of maritime law enforcement and provide a tighter security for the world at large. But an ongoing need will be for cutting-edge technology to combat the new complexities of maritime fraud.

SEE ALSO
drug trafficking; human trafficking; organized crime; forgery; globalization; money laundering.

BIBLIOGRAPHY. BBC News, "Shipping Fraud Heightens Terror Threat," (February 6, 2002); William Joseph Hackerman, "Transnational Crime and Terrorism and Its Effect on Maritime Industry," www.mrcinvestagations-.com (2003); Peter Goodspeed, "Piracy at Sea Reaches Record High," *National Post* (July 24, 2003); Llewellyn D. Howell, "The Open Seas Are Becoming No-Man's Land," *USA Today Magazine* (May 1,1999).

CYNTHIA CRISEL
ARKANSAS STATE UNIVERSITY

market manipulation

IN THE FALL of 2002, two international firms made headlines in the United States for their involvement in market manipulation. Specifically, Enron Corporation and Tyco International were charged with artificially inflating the value of their firms' respective stock. For example, the Federal Energy Regulatory Commission found that Enron had manipulated the price of its stock and hid the related transactions. There were several other large firms also charged in this time period, culminating in several task forces, commissions, reports, media coverage and ultimately resulting in structural reforms.

Manipulation has been formally defined by *Blacks' Law Dictionary*: "A series of transactions involving the buying or selling of a security for the purpose of creating a false or misleading appearance of active trading or to raise or depress the price to induce the purchase or sale by others."

Brokers who have a stake in a particular stock might be inclined to make misleading or false assertions to prospective clients. Often, this is done in order to create the impression that the price of a stock is soon to rise, and thereby such actions create an artificial demand for it (artificial inflation). There are many ways broker-dealers manipulate markets (upward or downward). Most frequently, market manipulation involves a brokerage firm purchasing large volumes of stock in a small (or sham) company that is frequently owned by the brokerage firm itself. The brokerage firm, which owns the overwhelming majority of shares, drives up the worthless stock by "cold-calling" scores of unsuspecting investors (often senior citizens). At some predetermined point (that is, price), the brokerage firms' insiders dump their shares, leaving the public with worthless stocks and the brokers with millions in ill-gotten gains. Though market manipulation can take place in virtually any securities exchange, it takes place most commonly in the penny-stock industry.

In general, penny stocks are considered those securities not listed on a recognized exchange, hence they are traded over-the-counter (OTC), and information about them is only available on the "pink sheets." Pink sheets refer to a weekly list of firms trading in over-the-counter stocks along with their price quotes on securities. The National Quotation Bureau, a private firm publishes the list, which is printed on pink paper. With respect to market manipulation, there is a key reason offenders target the pink sheets and the OTC market— lack of serious regulations.

For example, to get onto the National Association of Securities Dealers Automated Quotation System (NASDAQ), a company is required to have a minimum of several millions of dollars in assets and just slightly less in shareholders' equity. Perhaps more importantly, for a stock to be listed on NASDAQ it must have at least two market makers (a market maker is a broker-dealer that regularly buys and sells a particular security).

The reason for this should be obvious: a single market maker can, with ease and virtual impunity, illegally manipulate a security's price. Pink-sheet firms and the stocks they trade are only required to be registered with the Securities and Exchange Commission (SEC). NASDAQ securities average nine market makers per security, thus promoting competitiveness, while the pink sheet stocks typically have only one.

Thus, pink sheet firms are thought by a proportion of analysts and examiners to represent the true bottom-feeders of the securities world. Penny-stock market manipulations such as those above are frequently referred to as "pump-and-dump" schemes, and they are often run out of "boiler rooms," fake or temporary offices.

The contemporary penny-stock boiler room depends upon a large work force of telephone solicitors who are often deliberately chosen for their lack of experience in, and knowledge of, the securities industry. Many, in fact, quickly leave once they realize they are part of a criminal enterprise. Boiler rooms are run by energetic managers whose sole responsibility is to keep their sales representatives relentlessly on task, snaring unsophisticated people, and talking them into giving them money for nothing but a "dream," as one former stock scammer and boiler-room employee stated.

It is the relentless pressure by the managers on the callers-solicitors, and theirs, in turn, on the unsophisticated credulous public that is at the heart of the penny-stock swindle. Some of these criminal penny-stock boiler rooms gained infamy for their flamboyance. Stratton Oakmont, for example, was headed by Jordan Ross Belfort and Daniel Mark Porush and located in Lake Success, New York. The firm gained notoriety for its motto: "Never hang up the phone until the customer buys or dies." An-

other firm became the premise for the 2000 film *Boiler Room*, while several other real-life scenarios were portrayed in the popular HBO series *The Sopranos*.

Market manipulation, particularly in unregulated markets such as the pink sheets, is fairly simplistic. Successful manipulation schemes, such as those that wind up as news headlines and subplots for the mass media, require the artful assistance of accountants (to shield the scammer from regulatory bodies, hide money from investors and regulators), lawyers (to fend off regulatory, civil and criminal attacks, public relations), clearing firms (to provide guise of credibility) and banks (to house illicit proceeds). Thus, these are commonly organized criminal conspiracies in the truest sense.

SEE ALSO

securities fraud; National Association of Securities Dealers; stock fraud; telemarketing fraud.

BIBLIOGRAPHY. Associated Press, "Report: Enron Manipulated Market," (August 14, 2002); *Black's Law Dictionary* (West Publishing, 1991); Sean Patrick Griffin and Alan A. Block, "PennyWise: Accounting for Fraud in the Penny Stock Industry," *Contemporary Issues in Crime and Criminal Justice: Essays in Honor of Gilbert Geis* (Prentice Hall, 2000); North American Securities Administrators Association, *The NASAA Report on Fraud and Abuse in the Penny Stock Industry*, submitted to the Subcommittee on Telecommunications and Finance, Committee on Energy and Commerce, U.S. House of Representatives (September 1989); David Ratner, *Securities Regulation in a Nutshell* (West Publishing, 1978); Robert J. Stevenson, *The Boiler Room and Other Telephone Sales Scams* (University of Illinois Press, 1998); U.S. Senate, Permanent Subcommittee on Investigations (PSI) of the Committee on Governmental Affairs, *Fraud in the Micro-Capital Markets Including Penny Stock Fraud* (U.S. Government Printing Office, 1997).

SEAN PATRICK GRIFFIN, PH.D.
PENN STATE UNIVERSITY, ABINGTON

marketing fraud

MARKETING RELATES to all those functions relating to the creation, promotion, distribution and sale of goods and services for which there is a demand and on which a profit can be made. As a result, a wide range of business functions have a marketing component, particularly in the current business environment in which the marketing component of the value of finished goods and services increasingly takes a higher proportion as production costs decrease, as techniques improve. As a result, a very wide range of fraudulent opportunities are provided by the marketing process. However, it is more commonly understood that marketing fraud relates specifically to the failure to keep promises with the consumer and the hiding of negative consequences of consuming a product.

This form of behavior has become proverbial with the selling of snake oil and has been practiced for thousands of years. More recently, new technology, including the internet, has been used to multiply the effectiveness of such marketing frauds. An example is the cross-border telephone frauds involving Canadian and U.S. firms and individuals. These involve approximately 500 to 1,000 telephone "boiler rooms" (fake or temporary offices) in Canada offering fraudulent deals on credit cards, loan offers, and lottery prizes.

This industry may be grossing around $1 billion daily. These types of fraud have become characterized by rapidly increasing sophistication of methods, high levels of security and advanced processes of money transfer and laundering. In response to the jurisdictional difficulties involved in cross-border crime, states are creating bilateral and multilateral agreements to find new ways to monitor and regulate these activities.

Some examples of fraud result from, in part at least, ideological or political differences. For example, the United Kingdom Vegan Society is strongly opposed to the use of animals in producing food, and has produced literature based on research in which they claim that such food is unnecessary for nourishment, and the process is cruel to the animals. Hence, those involved in the dairy foods market are committing frauds on the public to persuade them they need these products. These claims of course are denied by the dairy and beef industries. Similar issues bedevil sectors related to genetically modified organisms (GMOs), about a number of contested claims have been made without incontrovertible scientific proof either way.

Another area of growing fraud involves companies apparently specializing in complex business and legal operations, who obtain money from customers but do not provide the services specified either at all or else in a substandard manner. One particular example of this is in advice and consultancy relating to patents and the protection of intellectual property. As this is a complex and continually changing field, the hopeful inventors are often eager to receive what they believe to be impartial and professional advice to support what has often been many hours of unpaid work on their part.

INTERNET FRAUDS

The increasing penetration of the internet has given rise to a variety of marketing fraud opportunities. The internet provides contact to large numbers of people through e-mail at a low cost. The anonymity provided by an online persona may be quite distinct from that of real-life situation where acts of selfishness and greed would be unconscionable in face-to-face dealings. These factors have ensured the internet as fertile ground for fraud. Four areas in particular have proved to be particularly problematic:

Making false claims with a view to obtaining the money of the victim: very well-known examples of this phenomenon include the mass e-mailing of letters purporting to be from individuals who have obtained very large sums of money through semi-legal or dangerous means. Commonly, the mailer claims to be the beneficiary of a rich individual in a country such as Nigeria, which is known for its high levels of corruption and inequitable distribution of wealth. The mailer claims to be looking for honest individuals able to assist in the cross-border transfer of sums of money amounting to many millions of dollars. The intended victim is requested to supply bank details and a handling fee which is then stolen by the fraudster, and the bank details are used to extract additional funds from the victim. In some cases, the interaction between fraudster and victim can become long-term.

Selling fake or substandard goods through mass e-mailing: One noted example of this has been the exploitation of public concern over the high costs of many prescription drugs by offering low cost supplies, often of sexual stimulants such as viagra about which people often feel reluctance to purchase openly.

Credit card and identity theft: sophisticated software is now able to be used to sift through many millions of communications to obtain, albeit in fragmentary form, personal details such as credit card account numbers. As online credit card transactions do not need the customer's signature, it is quite easy for people who have obtained these details to use them fraudulently to obtain goods and services.

Click-through schemes (also known as affiliate fraud): the click-through programs that at one stage seemed likely to dominate successful business models on the internet may be considered dishonest rather than fraudulent. They occupy one of the many areas in which technological development has leapt ahead of the ability of legislators to regulate efficiently, especially when dealing with an international context. In these schemes, website operators pay search engine companies a certain amount of money each time their site is listed as the result of an internet search and whenever any person clicks the link to their site as a result of that prompt. In the case of search terms with high money-making potential and intensive competition, such as home loans, online gambling, or web hosting, a single click-through referral may be worth $10 or more. Stakeholders in companies providing this service therefore have a significant incentive to use the service themselves and click-through to their customers' websites. As a result, a large proportion of hits recorded by the website may simply be the result of stakeholders artificially boosting the amount they must pay.

Other forms of marketing fraud may use the internet tangentially or else variations of the techniques developed in its context. For example, a recent series of high-quality frauds in the United Kingdom has featured cold-calling people with schemes based on investing in art, which either does not exist or else is valued much lower than advertised. These schemes may feature a supporting website supposedly offering endorsements of the products offered and even newspaper and magazine advertisements.

SEE ALSO

advertising fraud; internet fraud; Justice, Department of. bait-and-switch; scams.

BIBLIOGRAPHY. "Internet Share Site a Fraud," BBC News (January 6, 2000); Binational Working Group on Cross-Border Mass-Marketing Fraud, *Mass-Marketing Fraud: A Report to the Attorney General of the United States and the Solicitor General of Canada*, www.sgc.gc.ca (May 2003); Internet Marketing Research, "Overture Click Fraud," www.internet-marketing-research.net (2003); UK Vegan Society, "The Milk Marketing Fraud" (2003).

JOHN WALSH, PH.D.
MAHIDOL UNIVERSITY, THAILAND

Maxwell, Robert (1923–1991)

ROBERT MAXWELL was born Jan Ludvik Hoch in a small town on the Czechoslovakian border, to peasant parents who became victims of Adolf Hitler's holocaust during World War II. The fact that Maxwell rose from having nothing to heading up an international financial empire that encompassed publishing interests, television and cable stations, recording companies, and language schools affected most decisions he made throughout his life. Maxwell established a reputation as a user and abuser of people who frequently manipulated his own truths.

PUBLISHER EXTRAORDINAIRE

Many of Maxwell's critics were afraid to criticize him because he was known for bringing libel suits against those whom he thought defamed him. By all accounts, Maxwell relished being called "publisher extraordinaire" and delighted in his international acclaim. On one occasion, Maxwell approved a magazine layout that showed him with a halo superimposed on an existing photo-portrait. While Maxwell may have been an extraordinary publisher and financier, he was far from being an angel.

In 1951, Maxwell purchased Pergamon Press, which published textbooks and scientific journals, for £13,000. In 1969, questions arose over a failed attempt to sell Pergamon to Leasco, an American finance group, leading to a major investigation of both Maxwell and Pergamon. Investigators, who included the well-known accounting firm Price-Waterhouse, discovered that as head of Pergamon, Maxwell had manipulated financial records to hide the fact that most of Pergamon's profits were dependent on transactions with private companies owned by the Maxwell family. Price-Waterhouse reported that Pergamon's 1968 profits of £2.1 million had been over-reported by £1.6 million. In 1973, a no-holds-barred report issued by Britain's Department of Trade and Industry (DTI) made it clear that "notwithstanding Mr. Maxwell's acknowledged abilities and energy, he is not in our opinion a person who can be relied on to exercise proper stewardship of a publicly quoted company." Maxwell subsequently lost control of Pergamon but repurchased it in 1974 and continued to head the company until 1991 when he sold both Pergamon and Maxwell Directories for £440 million to Elsevier, a transnational publisher.

PRIME MINISTER MAXWELL

As part of his campaign to become prime minister of Great Britain, Maxwell ran for a Buckinghamshire seat in the House of Commons on the Labor Party ticket in 1964. For the next six years, Maxwell stirred up a number of controversies that led to various charges of dishonesty and deceit. For instance, in 1966, Maxwell surprisingly agreed to serve as chair of the House of Commons Catering Committee to determine why the commons kitchen had an overdraft of £53,000. Maxwell immediately fired the staff, reduced the quality of food, and sold off the entire contents of the House of Commons wine cellar. Afterwards, Maxwell claimed that he had earned a profit of £20,000 for the commons kitchen. Other committee members disagreed, claiming that Maxwell had manipulated records to hide the fact that he had actually increased the deficit to £57,000 within his four years at the helm. After being censured by the English High Court for his part in the Pergamon scandal, Maxwell decided not to run for re-election and gave up his dream of becoming prime minister.

In 1980, Maxwell took over the ailing British Printing Corporation, which he renamed the Maxwell Communications Corporation. In 1984, Maxwell purchased Mirror Group Newspapers (MGN), owners of the British tabloid *The Daily Mirror*, from Reed International. Maxwell chaired MGN until November 1991. Earlier that year, he had floated MGN as a public company in an effort to raise cash to avoid filing for bankruptcy because other Maxwell enterprises had amassed debts of over £2 billion. In 1988, Maxwell bought Macmillan Publishing Co., an established American publishing company and continued as chairman and chief executive officer until 1991.

In November 1991, Maxwell died aboard his yacht under mysterious circumstances that have never been explained, although many people believe that he committed suicide. On November 5, his body was found floating off the Canary Islands. In 1997, Ghislaine Maxwell, the youngest of Maxwell's nine children, told *Hello* magazine that she believed her father had been murdered.

After Maxwell's death, investigators discovered that lenders and shareholders in his various enterprises had lost around $3 billion. Subsequently, a report issued by Britain's DTI, which had conducted a nine-year investigation at a cost of over £8 million, revealed that Maxwell had bilked more than 30,000 Maxwell pensioners of £400 million by using employee retirement funds to manipulate the stock market to rescue various Maxwell enterprises from bankruptcy.

In 1995, Britain's Serious Fraud Office brought Maxwell's sons Kevin and Ian, and Larry Trachtenberg, a Maxwell financial adviser, to trial after charging them with misusing the pension funds of Maxwell employees and assisting Maxwell in risking employee funds by channeling them into other Maxwell companies. All three were acquitted in February 1996. The report by the Department of Trade and Industry stated that Kevin Maxwell bore "heavy responsibility" for the diversion of funds. Kevin Maxwell subsequently filed for bankruptcy, claiming that he was $610,000 in debt, although he continued to live in luxury. In addition to Kevin and Ian Maxwell and Larry Trachtenberg, various investment bankers and accountants were also faulted for their parts in the pensioners' scandal. Goldman Sachs and Coopers and Lybrand investment brokers were among those who paid a share of the £267 million settlement negotiated in February 1995, along with a £100 million payout by the British government to help rescue the retirement funds of the victimized pensioners.

A month after Maxwell's death in November 1991, the New York *Daily News*, which Maxwell had purchased earlier in the year, filed for bankruptcy. Three years later, it was revealed in bankruptcy proceedings that Maxwell's purchase of the failing *Daily News* had been motivated by his need to launder money. so that he could show a legitimate source of income for the huge sums that were being invested or channeled into other Maxwell enterprises. The bankruptcy judge accused Maxwell of fraud, misappropriation of funds, deceit, and unchecked self-interest during the time that he owned and operated the *Daily News*. Records revealed that within nine months, Maxwell had channeled $238 million through the newspaper, even though the newspaper's finances were so fragile that suppliers sometimes refused to deliver essentials such as newsprint.

Approximately 1,800 claims were filed against the *Daily News* after Maxwell's death, and *Daily News* employees were still owed around $1 million. In 1993, Mortimer Zuckerman purchased the newspaper for $26 million through the bankruptcy court.

SEE ALSO
money laundering; board of directors.

BIBLIOGRAPHY. Tow Bower, *Maxwell: The Outsider* (Auram Press, 1988); George Garneau, "Maxwell Money Laundry," *Editor and Publisher* (March 19, 1994); Joe Haines, *Maxwell* (Houghton Mifflin, 1988); "Maxwell Brothers Cleared," *Editor and Publisher* (February 19, 1996); "Maxwell Kin Suspects Murder," *Editor and Publisher* (March 15, 1997); "Maxwell Son Blamed in DTI Probe," www.bbc.com (March 30, 2001); "Robert Maxwell: A Profile," www.bbc.com (March 29, 2001); Alison Rogers, "Bankruptcy, Maxwell Style," *Fortune* (June 13, 1994).

ELIZABETH PURDY, PH.D.
INDEPENDENT SCHOLAR

Meat Inspection Act of 1906

SIGNED INTO LAW by President Theodore Roosevelt on June 30, 1906, the Federal Meat Inspection Act enacted sweeping reform of the meat packing industry, mandating that the U.S. Department of Agriculture (USDA) inspect all cattle, swine, sheep, goats, and horses both before and after they are slaughtered and processed into products for human consumption. The act prohibits the sale of adulterated or misbranded livestock and products as food and ensures that livestock and products are slaughtered and processed under sanitary conditions. The act applies to livestock and products within the United States as well as imports, which must be inspected under equivalent foreign inspection standards.

The 1906 legislation amended prior Meat Inspection Acts of 1890 and 1891 and other laws passed in 1897 that had provided for USDA inspection of slaughtered animals and meat products, but had proven ineffective in regulating many unsafe and unsanitary practices by the meat packing industry, also known as the Beef Trust. Beginning in the 1880s, Harvey W. Wiley, chief of the Bureau of Chemistry of the Department of Agriculture, had issued reports noting the health hazards posed by the adulteration of processed foods such as canned meat and the chemicals used as preservatives and coloring agents. The Association of Official Agricultural Chemists (an organization founded by Wiley) began a lobbying effort in favor of federal legislation governing the packing and purity of food products.

The first widespread public attention to the unsafe practices of the meatpacking industry was in 1898, when the press reported that Armour & Co. had supplied tons of rotten canned beef to the U.S. Army in Cuba during the Spanish-American War. The meat had been packed in tins along with a visible layer of boric acid that acted as a preservative and masked the stench of the rotten meat. Troops who consumed the meat fell ill, leaving them unfit for combat, and some died. Roosevelt, who served in Cuba as a colonel, testified in 1899 that he would as soon have eaten his old hat. Other soldiers and officers testified as well.

The canned meat scandal prompted Thomas F. Dolan, a former superintendent for Armour & Co., to sign an affidavit noting the ineffectiveness of government inspectors and stating that the company's common practice was to pack and sell "carrion." The *New York Journal* published Dolan's statement on March 4, 1899. Several states subsequently passed laws regulating the purity of food products, and the Senate formed the Pure-Food Investigating Committee that held hearings in Chicago, Washington, D.C., and New York City from 1899 to 1900. The committee declared such common meat preservatives as borax, salicylic acid, and formaldehyde to be "unwholesome," but lacked convincing evidence that these preservatives or other additives and coloring agents were actually harmful to human health. The press also reported from the committee's hearings that as much as 15 to 20 percent of the nation's food supply was adulterated—made impure by the addition of foreign or inferior substances. These concerns were in addition to the health problems posed by the packaging of substandard or condemned meat products.

Progressive journalists and activists called public attention to the meatpacking industry in the early 1900s.

At the center of public outrage were the Beef Trust and its base of meatpacking houses in Chicago's Packingtown. Journalists published pieces in radical and muckraking magazines, detailing the monopolistic and exploitive practices of Beef Trust businesses as well as the unsanitary conditions of the packing houses, and their tactics to evade minimal government inspection of animals and meat products. Of these journalists, Charles Edward Russell is perhaps best known for his series of articles about the Beef Trust that was published as a collection entitled *The Greatest Trust in the World* (1905).

The broadest public attention to the Chicago meatpacking houses came with the work of Upton Sinclair. In 1904, Sinclair covered a labor strike at Chicago's Union Stockyards for the Socialist news-paper *Appeal to Reason* and proposed that he spend a year in Chicago to write an expose of the Beef Trust's exploitation of workers. The result was Sinclair's best-known novel, *The Jungle* (1906). The novel first appeared serially in the *Appeal* beginning February 25, 1905, and was first published as a novel by Doubleday, Page a year later, after an independent investigation confirmed Sinclair's depiction of the meat packing houses.

The Jungle depicts the struggle of the fictional Lithuanian immigrant Jurgis Rudkus working in a Chicago meatpacking house. Sinclair's primary purpose with the novel was to demonstrate how the corruption and greed of American industry was destroying the lives of workers, but in so doing he rendered vivid descriptions of not only the working conditions of meatpacking houses, but also the horrific meatpacking practices that produced the food itself. Sinclair described in detail the slaughtering of diseased and dead animals, the packing of rotten meat, rats, and rat feces inadvertently adulterating the meat products, the absence of government inspectors during night-time processing, bribery of government inspectors, the debilitating effects of chemicals and dangerous working conditions on workers, and even the bodies of dead workers included in the final meat products.

Roosevelt, an avowed "trustbuster," was sent an advance copy of *The Jungle* and upon reading it initiated a full investigation of the Beef Trust's meatpacking practices. The novel was an instant international bestseller and prompted massive public outrage. It is worth noting that Sinclair had intended to promote Socialism as a solution to industrial ills, but readers responded primarily to the issues of sanitation and food contamination. Also contributing significantly to the broad public response was the larger movement of muckraking Progressive journalists and activists calling for reform in government regulation of industry. There also was growing support within the industry for regulation in response to heightened public awareness.

By early 1906, the Meat Inspection Act and the Pure Food and Drug Act had both long been stalled in Congress, but when the report of Labor Commissioner Charles P. Neill and social worker James Bronson Reynolds had fully confirmed Sinclair's charges, Roosevelt used the threat of disclosing its contents to speed along the passage of both acts, which both went into law on the same day.

SEE ALSO
Sinclair, Upton; Food and Drug Administration; Pure Food and Drug Act; Roosevelt, Theodore.

BIBLIOGRAPHY. Lorine Swainston Goodwin, *The Pure Food, Drink, and Drug Crusaders, 1879–1914* (McFarland, 1999); Ronald Gottesman, *Introduction to The Jungle* (Viking Penguin,1985); Upton Sinclair, *The Jungle* (Doubleday, Page, 1906) and "The Condemned-Meat Industry," *Everybody's Magazine* (v.14, 1906); Donna J. Wood, "The Strategic Use of Public Policy: Business Support for the 1906 Food and Drug Act," *Growth of the Regulatory State, 1900–17: State and Federal Regulation of Railroads and Other Enterprises* (Garland Publishing, 1994); U.S. Department of Agriculture, www.usda.gov (2003).

KRISTEN L. ROUSE
TALLAHASSEE COMMUNITY COLLEGE

medical malpractice

THE ISSUE OF medical malpractice has been a hot-button issue for politicians at both the federal and state levels since the mid-1970s. Liberals insist that plaintiffs who suffer at the hands of incompetent or neglectful medical personnel should be allowed to recover full damages, that unrestricted damages serve to promote accountability among the medical profession, and that juries should be free to respond to cases on an individual basis.

Conservatives counter with the claim that too many medical lawsuits are frivolous, that juries are more likely to favor plaintiffs than defendants, and that large jury awards are detrimental to business interests. Neither side contests the reality of the problems that exorbitant medical malpractice insurance rates have caused for the medical community, and both sides take it as given that rates for medical malpractice insurance will rise in relation to the amount of damages awarded in medical malpractice lawsuits.

In medical malpractice cases, the assumption is that a doctor, nurse, hospital, mental health professional, or other medical personnel has committed a wrongful act. In some cases, the plaintiff is able to prove negligence on the part of medical personnel through documenting that an act, a refusal to act, or a breach of duty resulted in injury. Other malpractice suits are brought on the grounds that a procedure was performed without the informed consent of the patient or the patients authorized representative or that a patient was abandoned before the professional relationship was terminated. An incident in which a patient's right to privacy is breached by releasing medical records to unauthorized third parties may also constitute grounds for medical malpractice. Patients may also file a breach of conduct malpractice lawsuit if a medical practitioner promises a certain result but does not produce it. For example, a botched nose surgery by a plastic surgeon could provide grounds for a breech of conduct malpractice suit.

The burden of proof in a medical malpractice suit is always on the plaintiff, and the plaintiff must show a clear relationship between the action of the medical practitioner and the damage suffered. Two tests are frequently used to document cause and effect in medical malpractice suites: The "but for" test must establish that the injury to the patient would not have happened but for the actions of the medical practitioner.

The "substantial factor" test is used to show that the defendant's actions were substantially responsible for the injury to the patient. The plaintiff's lawyer may call on expert witness to explain the normal course of care for a particular patient and how that care was violated in some way. The expert witness is also used to document the extent of a patient's injury.

Damages may be awarded in three categories: compensatory damages, punitive damages, and nominal damages. Compensatory damages are based on actual harm suffered, medical expenses, lost earnings, and pain and suffering. Punitive damages are aimed at punishing reckless, grossly negligent, or intentional actions that cause damage. Nominal damages are awarded to show that a patient had a legitimate complaint but that no substantive damages were inflicted.

A number of people accept what is called the "deep pocket theory," arguing that physicians are overpaid. As a result, they see no problem with huge medical malpractice awards or with high medical malpractice insurance rates. Yet, few people deny that a crisis exists when doctors refuse to deliver babies or when they refrain from performing risky operations for fear of being sued. A crisis also exists when whole communities suffer because they have been left without doctors because of the enormous costs involved in providing medical services to a country where citizens believe they have a constitutional right to sue over any injustice either real or perceived.

Malpractice reform continues to be the top priority for the American Medical Association (AMA). The AMA cites the disparity of jury awards, which vary from a few thousand dollars to several million dollars, as evidence that a cap on non-economic awards would promote more equitable treatment of the medical profession in malpractice lawsuits. In addition to jury awards, the defendant in a medical malpractice lawsuit spends an average of $25,000 in legal fees.

MALPRACTICE CASES

The issue of how medical malpractice insurance rates can affect an entire community is illustrated by the situation in which 10 Washington state neurosurgeons found themselves. The 10 physicians, who had formed Neurological Consultants of Washington in an effort to meet the rising malpractice costs, saw their rates increase from $21,000 a year in 1998 to $54,000 a few years later. Subsequently, their insurance carrier informed Neurological Consultants that they were uninsurable because of the high risks involved in neurosurgery and the large number of malpractice lawsuits that had been filed. With no insurance, the group was forced to cancel all scheduled surgery and refused to see new patients, leaving one large Washington hospital with only one neurosurgeon on call. Under a new carrier, the cost of medical malpractice insurance for the group was $133,000 a year.

The story of 17-year-old Jesica Santillan, on the other hand, provides support for the claims that medical malpractice is essential, and that juries need the option of awarding damages based on the facts of a particular case. Jesica's parents braved an illegal crossing into the United States from Mexico to receive a heart-lung transplant at Duke University in North Carolina. Jesica died because her surgeon failed to check her blood type against that of the donor. The physician admitted his mistake, and Duke accepted responsibility for the lack of cross-checks that could have saved the teenager's life.

It has been estimated that each year from 44,000 to 88,000 patients die in hospitals from medical negligence of some kind. The Harvard Medical Practice Study placed the total number of deaths, which includes those that take place outside of hospitals, at 180,000 people a year. According to the Association for Responsible Medicine (ARM), approximately 1 million people a year suffer injuries in response to medical mistakes. Even though studies show that doctors who make one serious mistake are more likely to commit others, most doctors who are found culpable in medical malpractice suits retain their licenses and their hospital privileges. The majority of medical mistakes are never reported, and most state laws prohibit release of this information to patients and their families who are involved in medical malpractice litigation, or to the general public.

The AMA has a powerful lobby, making the group a significant force in medical malpractice legislation. The AMA has been successful in shortening the statute of limitations for medical malpractice suits, limiting damages awarded by juries, and placing caps on legal fees for lawyers involved in malpractice suits. In March 2003, the House of Representatives passed the Medical Malpractice Awards Cap, the Republican-supported bill that placed a limit of $250,000 on jury awards for pain and suffering. In July 2003, the bill failed by one vote in the Senate. Republicans threatened Democrats with making the failure to pass the tort reform supported by President George W. Bush a campaign issue in 2004.

The failure of such tort reform is partly due to the influence of the National Conference of States Legislatures (NCSL) which believes that the bill would amount to federal interference in matters traditionally allotted to states. The American Bar Association (ABA) also opposed the bill, arguing that it would unfairly limit the rights of individuals to be compensated for non-economic suffering. The ABA also feels that the cap would have little if any effect on the overall costs of health care.

SEE ALSO
healthcare fraud; Medicare and Medicaid; negligence.

BIBLIOGRAPHY. "By The Numbers," *Modern Healthcare* (July 14, 2003); Avery Comarow, "Jesica's Story," *U.S. News and World Report* (July 28, 2003); Patricia M. Danzon, *Medical Malpractice: Theory, Evidence, And Public Policy* (Cambridge University Press, 1985); Margaret C. Jasper, *The Law of Medical Practice* (Oceana Publications, 2001); "Insurance Loss Leaves Doctors Scrambling for Coverage," *The Lancet* (August 2, 2003); Louise Lander, *Defective Medicine: Risk, Anger, and the Malpractice*

Crisis (Farrar, Straus, and Giroux, 1978); Chris Richard, "Number of Malpractice Cases Spikes," *Christian Science Monitor* (July 28, 2003); "States Weight In," *Modern Healthcare* (August 11, 2003); Sherry Gay Stolberg, "Short of Votes, Senate GOP Still Pushes Malpractice," *The New York Times* (July 6, 2003); Neil Vidmer, *Medical Malpractice and the American Jury: Confronting The Myths about Jury Incompetence, Deep Pockets, And Outrageous Damage Awards* (University of Michigan Press, 1995).

ELIZABETH PURDY, PH.D.
INDEPENDENT SCHOLAR

Medicaid and Medicare fraud

IN 1965, the Medicaid and Medicare programs were created in order to provide structured government mechanisms that would provide healthcare to the poor and elderly. Medicaid exists at the state level to provide healthcare to those who are unable to afford it. In all, over 36 million individuals receive healthcare through Medicaid. Medicare exists at the federal level to provide healthcare primarily to those 65 years of age and above, but also to vulnerable adults. Medicare is divided into Part A (providing hospital insurance) and Part B (providing medical insurance). Over 39 million individuals receive healthcare through Medicare.

When first created, there were no provisions for guarding against abusive activities, primarily because no one thought providers would defraud the healthcare systems. About 10 years after the programs developed, policy makers and legislators realized that the systems were being defrauded on a routine basis. To combat Medicaid fraud, many states began to develop Medicaid Fraud Control Units, which were given jurisdiction over fraud cases occurring at the state level. At the federal level, the Office of Inspector General in the Department of Health and Human Services maintained jurisdiction over the fraudulent and abusive activities.

Estimates suggest that 10 to 40 percent of the healthcare budget may be lost to fraudulent activities each year. In dollar terms, this means that billions are lost annually to criminal actions by fraudulent providers. It is important to note that a distinction exists between Medicaid/Medicare fraud and Medicaid/Medicare abuse. Fraud generally refers to instances where a provider intentionally steals from the healthcare system, while abuse refers to instances where the providers accidentally or unintentionally misuse the insurance systems. These distinctions are recognized in various state laws. Here's how the state of Florida, for instance, distinguishes between the two activities:

> Fraud is an intentional deception or misrepresentation made by a person with the knowledge that the deception results in unauthorized benefit to himself or another person. The term includes any act that constitutes fraud under applicable federal or state law. Abuse involves provider practices that are inconsistent with generally accepted business or medical practices and that result in an unnecessary cost to the Medicaid program or in reimbursement for goods or services that are not medically necessary or that fail to meet professionally recognized standards for healthcare.

The types of fraud can be discussed according to the occupations in which they are committed. In general, the three types of Medicaid/Medicare fraud that have been seen as rampant at one time or another include physician fraud, prescription fraud, and home healthcare fraud.

PHYSICIAN FRAUD

When public concern first surfaced about Medicaid/Medicare fraud, attention was directed toward activities by physicians, including doctors, dentists, psychologists, and other providers with practices in medicine. In the field of criminology, a host of researchers at the University of California, Irvine, were the first to discuss fraudulent activities by these medical professionals Their research focused on the types of fraudulent acts committed, the system's response, and their causes. Researchers agree that several specific types of Medicaid/Medicare fraud have been committed by doctors. Fee-for-service reimbursement includes situations where providers bill Medicare or Medicaid for services that the client never received.

This is believed to be one of the more common types of fraud committed, or at least uncovered. It is easy to establish that a service was never provided. Some providers have been known to bill for medical tests or supplies that were never provided in a routine basis.

Pingponging entails instances where providers recommend that patients seek additional services from other providers when those additional services are not needed. This type of fraud generally involves several providers working in concert with one another. It is a little more difficult to establish than fee-for-service reimbursement because services are being provided, but it is not clear whether those services are needed.

Upgrading entails situations where providers submit bills to Medicare or Medicaid for services that were more expensive than the services that were actually provided. Consider cases where dentists bill Medicaid for expensive fillings when they actually put in the cheapest filling possible.

Double-billing fraud entails instances where the provider bills more than one insurance company for the same services. There have even been instances when providers have billed patients and Medicare and Medicaid.

Finally, unnecessary surgery entails circumstances where unneeded surgery is performed on the victim. J. Reiman (1998) cites figures suggesting that 15,000 people die each year as a result of unnecessary surgeries. These unnecessary operations, he suggests, cost up to $4.8 billion each year. Again, the problem that comes up is that medical professionals vary in their determinations about what is necessary and unnecessary. Just as two auto mechanics may disagree on the appropriate way to maintain an automobile, two surgeons may disagree about the appropriateness of surgery.

Studies show that psychologists and psychiatrists are somewhat over-represented in terms of fraud allegations. The explanation for this disparity lies in the ways healthcare is delivered and billed for by different medical professionals. When patients visit physicians, they are often unaware of the services they received. Consequently, it is difficult for investigators to determine if the medical bills were submitted improperly. When patients visit psychologists, the provider bills for time. It is easy for investigators to ask patients how long their professional spent with them. If the patient says the provider only spent five minutes with her, and the provider billed for an entire hour, then a crime has occurred.

PRESCRIPTION FRAUD

In the mid- to late 1980s, the healthcare field witnessed what was in effect a "war on physician fraud." Investigations and prosecutions of these cases occurred more regularly than at any other time. In the early 1990s, the healthcare field witnessed a "war on prescription fraud." In addition to focusing on physician fraud, investigators and prosecutors began to target pharmacists, who were up until then, regularly cited in public opinion polls as one of the most trusted professions.

Several different varieties of prescription fraud exist. Generic drug substitution involves circumstances where pharmacists provide a generic drug but bill for a more expensive drug. This is especially easy to get away with because patients usually could not tell the difference between the two drugs. It would be as if someone paid for an expensive brand of gasoline, but actually received the lowest grade possible. How could they tell?

While easy to commit, this act is actually easy to catch through undercover sting operations, which were common in states such as New York and Massachusetts in the early 1990s. An off-duty police officer would take a prescription to a pharmacist, have it filled, and then the fraud control investigators would receive the filled prescription and wait for the bill to be submitted to Medicaid or Medicare. Once submitted, the investigator would be able to compare the drug in the prescription bottle with the drug on the bill. If they were different, then generic drug substitution may have occurred.

Short-counting occurs when a pharmacist bills Medicare or Medicaid for the amount prescribed by the doctor but provides less medicine to the patient. This fraud can also be somewhat easy to commit. Most people do not take their prescriptions home and count them. Those who do, will usually only alert the pharmacist if they have not received enough of their medicine. The pharmacist, then, excuses the short billing as an accident. As with generic drug substitution, undercover operations have alerted authorities to these practices.

Double-billing involves situations where pharmacists bill more than one insurance company for the same prescription (in the same way that doctors do it). Billing for nonexistent prescriptions involves billing for prescriptions that were never provided to the patient. Some billing for nonexistent prescription schemes have been quite complex, and administered as part of organized crime rings. In these cases, a pharmacist will hire drug addicts to go to the doctor and get a prescription for some fake ailment. The addict takes the prescription to the pharmacist and the pharmacist, rather than filling the prescription, gives the addict a small amount of cash or a couple of pills of codeine. The pharmacist will then bill Medicaid or Medicare for that prescription as if it were filled. Some of these schemes uncovered by authorities netted offenders over $1 million.

Altering the prescription is an example of forgery. In these cases, pharmacists may be involved in self-prescribing drugs. Believing that they are aware of all of a certain drugs' effects, and their own medical needs, a handful of pharmacists have been known to fill out their own prescriptions.

Finally, over-billing occurs when a pharmacist charges Medicare or Medicaid more than regulations permit. This occurs when fraudulent pharmacists find ways to overcharge Medicare or Medicaid, or the patient. Tight restrictions on allowable charges minimize the ability of pharmacists to commit this act.

HOME HEALTHCARE FRAUD

In the mid-1990s, the federal government expanded its focus on fraudulent healthcare providers to include home healthcare fraud. As an industry, home healthcare grew significantly in the 1980s and 1990s. Technological advances coupled with a higher number of elderly persons in society contributed to home healthcare's expansion. The unbridled growth included a number of home healthcare providers who found ways to dupe Medicare and Medicaid out of billions of dollars.

Federal authorities increased their investigations, and uncovered numerous examples of fraud. In *Crime in the Home Healthcare Field* (2003), Brian Payne points out that between 1987 and 1993, just 23 cases of home health fraud were described in the official publication of Medicaid Fraud Control Units. Between 1993 and 2000, more than 273 cases were cited in this same report. The kinds of cases uncovered by the fraud control units included the following: the provision of unnecessary services, billing for services not provided, overcharging, forgery, negative charting, substitute providers, double-billing, and kickbacks.

The provision of unnecessary services entails instances where home healthcare providers provide services which were unwarranted, but billed Medicare or Medicaid for those services. According to Medicare regulations, for a service to be neces-

sary, four criteria must be present: 1) the patient must be homebound; 2) the patient must be under a physician's care with a signed care plan; 3) the patient must need intermittent or part-time skilled nursing or therapy; 4) the services must be provided by a Medicare-certified agency. If any of these conditions are not present and the provider bills Medicare for services they had indeed given, then fraud has occurred.

Billing for services to patients who are not homebound are among the most common examples of this type of fraud. Concern about these crimes surfaced when the U.S. Government Accounting Office published a report describing instances where supposed homebound patients traveled regularly, held jobs, and even attended social clubs.

Billing for services not provided is similar to instances where doctors bill for services that did not happen, but different in that these services were supposed to occur in the patient's home. Many of these cases came to light when bills were submitted to Medicaid or Medicare that detailed services that clearly could not have been provided. Some providers have billed for services when they were actually in another state; others have billed for services when they were incarcerated; and others have billed for services they supposedly provided to deceased patients.

Overcharging occurs in the home healthcare field when providers bill Medicaid or Medicare more than they should. Unlike the previous fraud type, in these cases, services are provided, the bill is just higher than it should be. One of the more common varieties of overcharging by home healthcare providers entails situations where providers bill for more time than they actually spent with the patient.

To commit many of these acts, fraudulent home healthcare providers must sometimes commit forgery. Some may forge a patient's name suggesting that services were provided, when they were not. Others may forge a doctor's name, suggesting that the patient was homebound when she was not. Still others may forge documentation suggesting that they are licensed providers when they are not.

Related to forgery is negative charting. Negative charting occurs when home healthcare providers alter medical records to make it appear that patients are sicker than they actually are. Providers do this in order to increase the likelihood that a patient will be seen as homebound by Medicaid or Medicare regulators.

Substitute providers, as a type of home healthcare fraud, describes instances in which an unlicensed aide provided care to patients, but bills Medicare or Medicaid as if a licensed professional provided the care. More often than not, this type of fraud is actually committed by an agency rather than an individual home healthcare provider. The agency, wanting to maintain a certain level of productivity, may allow unqualified home healthcare employees to work for them.

As with prescription fraud and physician fraud, double billing is also found in the home healthcare field. More often in home healthcare, however, are instances where fraudulent providers encourage their vulnerable patients to pay out of their own pockets more than regulations permit. Finally, kickbacks occur when providers work together, referring patients back and forth between one another in order to generate a profit. In home healthcare, kickbacks are especially problematic when doctors or hospital staff receive cash or other property from home healthcare agencies in exchange for referrals.

CAUSES OF FRAUD

Three reasons fraud is committed by healthcare professionals include structural explanations, training, and systemic issues. In terms of structural explanations, providers often point to the reimbursement rates of Medicaid and Medicare. Both insurance schemes tend to reimburse doctors far less than they would actually receive from other patients. In effect, they are losing time and money, they say, by taking on patients covered under these programs. To make up for this lost time and money, some over-bill or mis-bill so they are billed fairly in their minds.

Training issues have to do with the fact that medical students often learn negative attitudes about government insurance programs even before they become doctors. The belief is that medical students learn from medical professionals about the horrors of dealing with the Medicaid and Medicare system. Even before dealing with the systems first hand, many learn about the low reimbursement rates, the complex rules, the unfair penalties (in their minds), and the bureaucratic nightmare that often comes along with dealing with government insurance agencies.

Systemic issues have to do with the fact that the justice system is not always equipped well enough to deal with these sorts of cases. Fraud control units exist in 47 states, but directors note that they are understaffed and under-funded.

Doctors are often able to blame the billing problems on their billing clerks, and they are also able to hire the best attorneys to keep them out of trouble. They are seen as upstanding members of their communities. While it is common to hear of citizens complaining about dangerous neighborhoods, drugs, and other community problems, it is unheard of that one would complain about doctors. Prosecutors are in political positions, and generally respond to the will of the voting public. This lack of outrage further insulates doctors from prosecution.

It is important to note that most providers do not engage in these fraudulent or abusive activities. Indeed, most healthcare professionals abide by their strong ethical codes. The few providers who commit these criminal acts, however, create a great deal of problems for the entire medical profession.

SEE ALSO

healthcare fraud; insurance fraud; scams; elite crime; medical malpractice..

BIBLIOGRAPHY. E. Dudek, "Medicaid Fraud and Abuse in Florida: A New Approach to an Old Problem," *Florida Bar Journal* (v.72/4, 1998); Gilbert Geis, Paul Jesilow, Henry N. Pontell, and H. O'Brien, "Fraud and Abuse of Government Medical Benefit Programs by Psychiatrists," *American Journal of Psychiatry* (v.142, 1985); Paul Jesilow, Henry N. Pontell, and Gilbert Geis, "Medical Criminals," *Justice Quarterly* (v.2/2, 1985); Paul Jesilow, Henry N. Pontell, and Gilbert Geis, *Prescription for Profit: How Doctors Defraud Medicaid* (University of California Press, 1993); E. Constance Keenan, G.C. Brown, Henry N. Pontell, and Gilbert Geis, "Medical Student's Attitudes on Physician Fraud and Abuse in the Medicare and Medicaid Programs," *Journal of Medical Education* (v.60, 1985); Brian K. Payne, "Medicaid Fraud: Actions, Actors, and Policy," *Criminal Justice Policy Review* (v.9/3, 1995); Brian K. Payne, *Crime in the Home Healthcare Field* (Charles C. Thomas, 2003); Henry N. Pontell, Paul Jesilow, and Gilbert Geis, "Policing Physicians: Practitioner Fraud and Abuse in a Government Medical Program," *Social Problems* (v.30/1, 1982); J Reiman, *The Rich Get Richer and the Poor Get Prison* (Allyn & Bacon, 1998).

BRIAN K. PAYNE
OLD DOMINION UNIVERSITY

Merrill Lynch

HISTORICALLY, Merrill Lynch has been one of the most powerful securities firms on Wall Street since it was established in 1907 by Edmund C. Lynch. However, beginning in the 1990s, Merrill Lynch, like so many other securities firms, was caught up in a swirl of civil and criminal charges resulting from corporate greed.

In the 1990s, Merrill served as the financial adviser for the Orange County Fund of California, which announced a $1.5 billion loss on December 1, 1994, making it the largest municipal failure ever reported in America, and miring Merrill Lynch in the worst scandal of its history. Robert L. Citron, the treasurer of the Orange County Fund, had worked with Merrill employees to purchase high-risk securities with large returns rather than the safer, low-risk securities usually purchased by municipal entities. After Citron resigned, hundreds of lawsuits were filed, including a $2 billion lawsuit filed by Orange County against Merrill Lynch.

Other participants in the suits against Merrill included individual participants in the Orange County pool, private investors, Orange County taxpayers, bondholders, and five money markets. At issue in the suits was whether Merrill Lynch had acted ethically in selling the risky securities to the Orange County Fund without proper warnings. Merrill Lynch reportedly spent $3 million a month fighting the suits. The Securities and Exchange Commission (SEC) investigation came to an end in 1999 when Merrill Lynch paid a $2 million fine.

Merrill's problems were not limited to California. The Inspector General of Massachusetts also opened an investigation into Merrill's municipal bond underwriting activities and sent out subpoenas to the rest of the states and to cities and banks around the country. All told, Merrill's settlements with the SEC, the Commonwealth of Massachusetts, the Attorney General of Massachusetts, and the District of Columbia equaled $12 million. New York City's controller permanently banned Merrill Lynch from managing bond deals for the city.

A number or Merrill executives were targeted in the course of various investigations. Edward Scherer, who had served as a high-yield analyst for Merrill Lynch, was sentenced to six months in prison and two years on probation on charges of conspiracy, wire fraud, and bribery. Investigators maintained that Scherer had conspired with

Richard Kursman, a bond trader, to purchase bonds for their private accounts at rigged prices, resulting in millions of dollars of illegal profits. Kursman was allowed to plead guilty to the single charge of wire fraud in exchange for testifying against Scherer. In December 1996, Mark Ferber, a former partner in Lazard Freres, who had neglected to report over $2.6 million in secret payments from Merrill Lynch was sentenced to 33 months in jail and was required to pay a $1 million fine after being convicted on 31 counts of mail and wire fraud. Additionally, the SEC fined Ferber $650,000 and banned him from the securities industry for life.

SCANDALS

Various other Merrill Lynch employees also involved the company in scandals. Linda Bustin, who had been a broker in the Burlington, Massachusetts, office, was fined and sentenced to 18 months in prison and three years probation for embezzling over $300,000 in forged checks and fraudulent accounts from 12 Merrill Lynch clients. Naham Vaskevitch, the former managing director of Merrill Lynch London, pled guilty to insider trading. He had previously settled a civil suit brought by the SEC for $2.9 million. Merrill's office in Lugano, Switzerland, negotiated a $5 million settlement with a French candy merchant who had lost over $3 million dollars when Merrill employees had, without permission, used his funds in derivative trading. Merrill also settled a lawsuit brought by 3,500 investors who had lost substantial amounts by following Merrill employees' advice to invest in ancient art and rare coins.

George Yu, who had worked in Merrill's Fort Lee, New Jersey, office was charged with attempted murder and sentenced to 10 years in prison after he hired a hit man, who turned out to be an FBI agent, to kill a client. Merrill Lynch also suffered substantial embarrassment when Janie D. Thomas, the so-called "stockbroker to the stars," vanished after making false statements to at least 50 clients, including singer/songwriter Paul Anka. Thomas's actions cost Merrill $14 million.

In business circles, 2000 became known as the Year of Corporate Scandal. Merrill Lynch's part in the scandal resulted in a reduction of 22,000 to Merrill's payroll, including a number of senior executives. Former Merrill Lynch research analyst Henry Blodgett had a starring role in this scandal that led to a $100 million fine for Merrill. Charges arose from a tainted research deal that lost Merrill's clients millions of dollars. Blodgett's activities were well documented through various emails, which revealed that Blodgett and his accomplices had been involved in at least 52 separate transactions in which they had inflated stock ratings of various companies in conjunction with investment bank clients. Blodgett claimed that the deals had earned $115 million for Merrill Lynch between December 1999 and November 2000. Merrill records revealed that Blodgett's personal income had risen from $3 million to $12 million during the relevant period. Although he refused to admit any wrongdoing, Blodgett was required to pay a $4 million fine for his activities and was banned from the securities industry for life. In October 2001, a corporate e-mail was leaked to the press in which Merrill Lynch "requested" 50,000 employees to attend a seminar teaching them about the perils of using e-mail, which could be subpoenaed by prosecutors and used in court.

On March 17, 2003, civil fraud charges were leveled against Merrill Lynch and three former top executives for the part they played in Enron Corporation's scandalous attempts to inflate its earnings. Merrill Lynch agreed to pay $80 million in fines for two questionable transactions with Enron. One of the transactions involved a $7 million deal for a power-generating barge in Nigeria; the other transaction concerned various energy trading deals between the two companies.

While Merrill admitted no wrong in the Enron transactions, the company agreed to an injunction that ensures that the company will refrain from further violations of securities laws. Additionally, Merrill agreed to allow independent auditing of its activities over an 18-month period and was placed under the supervision of an attorney selected by the Department of Justice.

The executives charged in the Enron affair were Daniel Bayly, Merrill's former head of global investment; James A. Brown, Merrill's former head of strategic asset lease and finance group; and Robert S. Furst, the executive in charge of the Merrill/Enron relationship. Pleading not guilty to the charges of conspiracy, obstruction of justice, and perjury, the three Merrill executives were each released on a $100,000 bail, which included $50,000 in cash.

If convicted, the three could serve time in prison and would also be required to pay personal fines. Thomas W. Davis, the former vice chairman for private equity and research, and Schuyler M. Tiney, head of energy investment banking at Merrill's Houston office, were not formally charged, but both were fined for refusing to testify about Merrill's dealings with Enron. Merrill Lynch was also ordered to pay an additional $100 million to settle global securities disputes.

SEE ALSO
insider trading; securities fraud; Securities and Exchange Commission; Enron Corporation.

BIBLIOGRAPHY. David Colbert, *Eyewitness to Wall Street: 400 Years of Dreamers, Schemers, Busts, and Booms* (Broadway Books, 2001); Kurt Eichenwald, "Merrill Reaches Deal with United States in Enron Affair," *The New York Times* (September 17, 2003); "Merrill to Pay $80 Million to Settle Enron Inquiry," *The New York Times* (October 20, 2003): Edwin J. Perkins, *Wall Street and Main Street: Charles Merrill and Middle-Class Investors* (Cambridge University Press, 1999); Paul Stiles, *Riding the Bull: My Year in the Madness of Merrill Lynch* (Random House, 1998); Nicolas Varchaver and Katherine Bonamici, "The Perils of Email," *Fortune* (February 17, 2003); Gary Weiss, "The SEC: This Watchdog Must Sharpen Its Bite," *Business Week* (March 31, 2003).

ELIZABETH PURDY, PH.D.
INDEPENDENT SCHOLAR

Metallgesellschaft

A DERIVATIVES trading scheme launched by Metallgesellschaft's U.S. trading subsidiary, MG Corp., resulted in $1.9 billion in losses for the industrial conglomerate, bringing it to the edge of bankruptcy in early 1994. German banks, including Deutsche Bank, a major investor in Metallgesellschaft, provided a bailout worth more than $2 billion. MG Corp.'s adventures in futures trading started in 1991 when MG Refining and Marketing hired Arthur Benson, who later sued Metallgesellschaft for wrongful termination after he was held responsible for trading losses. He also claimed the company ignored his plan to recoup losses.

The original trading scheme was not illegal and might have succeeded on a smaller scale. MG Corp. sold long-term contracts to provide petroleum products to customers at a fixed rate. These contracts appealed to buyers by reducing risks associated with a volatile energy market.

If oil prices fell, MG Corp. would make a profit. If oil prices rose, however, MG Corp. would be committed to sell oil to its customers at a loss. The company therefore developed a hedging strategy that involved buying oil futures contracts on the New York Mercantile Exchange (NYMEX) and arranging private swaps. Derivatives theorist Anatoly Kuprianov explains that MG Corp. was practicing an accepted strategy known as a stack-and-roll hedge. MG Corp. repeatedly bought bundles (stacks) of oil futures, rolling them over at their maturity date to realize a small profit and obtain a new stack. Behind this strategy was the assumption that if oil prices dropped, the value of the derivatives would increase to cover the loss, and vice-versa. Because MG Corp. required so many futures contracts to hedge its long-term commitments—the company reached 55,000 open contracts on NYMEX, well over the ordinary 24,000-contract limit—other traders could predict its actions and bid against it.

MG Corp. had not anticipated plummeting oil prices in fall 1993, cash flow problems from a mismatch in timing between the long-term and short-term contracts, and NYMEX's demand that the company increase its margin to protect the exchange from a potential default. Nobel laureate Merton Miller argues that Metallgesellschaft's problems were the result of management and U.S. regulators failing to understand the strategy and thereby mishandling it.

Similarly, some experts aver that upper management's insistence that MG Corp. liquefy contracts to cover their margins was what turned paper losses into real losses. However, an investigation by the U.S. Commodity Futures Trading Commission (CFTC) determined that MG Corp. had gone on a sales drive in the last three months of 1993, after oil prices started to fall, thus improving year-end results while increasing the company's exposure by about one-third. The CFTC fined Metallgesellschaft $2.5 million in 1995 and declared many of its short-term contracts void.

Seventeen oil companies later sued MG Refining and Marketing, the U.S. subsidiary of Metallgesellschaft, for violating its long-term contracts to provide them with petroleum. The plaintiffs also claim that Metallgesellschaft lied to the CFTC in

order to have the contracts declared illegal. This suit was still in progress in early 2004.

In November 1993, before the scandal broke, Metallgesellschaft's directors had announced a loss of only $216 million on oil trading. After the true scope of the losses became apparent, the directors were fired. Both U.S. and German authorities considered criminal charges against the directors for breach of fiduciary duty, and questions were raised about MG Corp.'s contracts to buy petroleum from Castle Energy.

The Castle contracts allowed MG Corp. to pay itself for making a profitable investment. MG Corp. was one of the investors in Castle, a small U.S. oil company. MG Corp. signed off-take contracts to buy all of the output of Castle's two refineries at above-market prices, thus guaranteeing that Castle would remain profitable. When MG Corp. needed to escape from its loss-generating long-term oil contracts in late 1994, part of the deal was that it would cancel $375 million of Castle's debt. MG Corp. estimated that it lost more than $630 million on its relationship with Castle.

An independent auditor's report assigned the blame for Metallgesellschaft's near-bankruptcy on dismissed chairman Heinz Schimmelbusch and former finance director Meinhard Forster. Metallgesellschaft sued Schimmelbusch, who countersued for defamation. At last report, in 1996, settlement talks had fallen apart over Schimmelbusch's unwillingness to admit fault. No criminal charges against Schimmelbusch or other directors were pursued.

By 2000, a leaner, more focused Metallgesellschaft, divested of its trading activities, had returned to profitability and was on the verge of regaining its position among Germany's top 30 blue-chip stocks.

SEE ALSO

Germany; securities fraud; Securities and Exchange Commission; insider trading; fiduciary fraud.

BIBLIOGRAPHY. Energy Merchant Corp., www.energymerchant.com (2003); "Fired Head of German Firm's U.S. Division Sues," *Baltimore Sun* (March 4, 1994); Andrew Fisher, "Metallgesellschaft Fails to Settle Suits," *Financial Times* (July 22, 1996); Ed Krapels, "Re-examining the Metallgesellschaft Affair and Its Implications for Oil Traders," *Oil and Gas Journal* (March 26, 2001); Anatoly Kuprianov, "Derivatives Debacles," *Federal Reserve Bank of Richmond Economic Quarterly* (Fall 1995); Tony Major,

"Metallgesellschaft Seeks to Project a Snappier Image," *Financial Times* (January 11, 2000); Andrew Maykuth, "An Offer It Couldn't Refuse," *Philadelphia Inquirer* (September 16, 1994); "Metallgesellschaft: A Waste of Resources?" *The Economist* (September 24, 1994); Laurie Morse, "Derivative Instruments: U.S. Ruling on MG Puts Spotlight on Internal Controls," *Financial Times* (August 2, 1995); Richard Waters, "Survey of Derivatives," *Financial Times* (November 16, 1994).

WENDE VYBORNEY FELLER, PH.D.
ST. MARY'S COLLEGE OF CALIFORNIA

Mexico

THE COLLUSION between white-collar crime and organized crime in Mexico has been rampant. For much of the 20th century, the Mexican government controlled organized crime. After the Mexican Revolution of the 1910s, the Mexican elite formed an official political party that eventually became known as the PRI. The PRI had a monopoly over political power and used this power to manipulate and exploit organized crime. Authorities sought out successful organized criminal groups, such as drug traffickers, and forced them to do the government's bidding. The government provided immunity from prosecution in exchange for payments used for government programs, political campaigns, and personal enrichment. Authorities expected criminals to cooperate. Failure to do so could result in prosecution or even being killed.

Due the fact that many Mexican government institutions such as the police or the attorney general's office, traditionally had little or no budget, they had to seek out their own operating funds. In order to do so, authorities would arrest crime figures, confiscate their goods, and then submit the goods to the Ministry of the Treasury in exchange for a payment. Furthermore, local officials often forced criminals to turn over valuable possessions such as homes and automobiles.

At other times, criminals would give suitcases filled with money and other gifts to their own attorneys, who would then turn them over to low-ranking government officials, who in turn submitted the payments to senior officials. Some of this money made it as high as the presidential palace, where it went into a slush fund. A good example of the gov-ernment-organized crime connection is the 1997 arrest of General Jesús Gutiérrez Rebello, head of the National Institute to Combat Drugs (INCD). Gutiérrez was charged with protecting Amado Carrillo Fuentes, a major drug cartel leader, in exchange for gifts that included luxury apartments, vehicles, jewelry, and money. At the same time he provided protection for Carrillo Fuentes, Gutiérrez also cracked down on a rival drug cartel.

Exposing the connection between authorities and criminals could be dangerous. In 1984, journalist Manuel Buendía was killed after allegedly acquiring a video of a meeting between high-ranking government officials and drug dealers. In 1985, drug traffickers kidnapped, tortured and killed U.S. Drug Enforcement Agency agent Enrique Camarena Salazar. It was rumored that José Antonio Zorrilla, director of the security service Dirección Federal de Seguridad (DFS) protected the drug traffickers. Later, the brother-in-law of President Luís Echeverría was convicted by a federal court in Los Angeles, California, for his involvement. Eventually, the DFS was dissolved amid corruption charges, as Zorrilla was also convicted in the Buendía assassination.

AUTOCRACY TO DEMOCRACY

In the 1980s and 1990s, however, this system began to change. As the PRI lost its stranglehold on political power and Mexicans began to demand a more democratic government, authorities held less control over organized crime. A more pluralistic society has given criminals more autonomy from government domination. Such freedom has led to greater organized criminal activity that has become more aggressive and violent, an occurrence that often accompanies the transition from autocratic political systems to more democratic ones, as has been the case in Russia.

Perhaps the most significant example of the increased audacity and violence of organized criminals was the March 1994 assassination of presidential candidate Luis Donaldo Colosio. President Carlos Salinas had designated Colosio as his successor, as was the practice of Mexican leaders. Many believe that Salinas's political opponents along with Mexican drug lords ordered Colosio's murder in the belief that they would benefit from eliminating him. Many traditional politicians in the PRI were unhappy with the dramatic changes Sali-

The hotel zone in Cancun, Mexico, shares the country's legacy of major ties between the government, organized crime, and the financial community, even as Mexican authorities seek to limit the rise of corruption.

nas had implemented and worried that Colosio would continue the trend. Drug leaders, particularly the Gulf Cartel, worried that Colosio would crack down on their operations. The leaders of this cartel were especially upset when Colosio refused a meeting with them. He was assassinated two days after refusing this request.

DRUG TRAFFICKING

International syndicates and local organizations are involved in the production, transportation, and distribution of illegal drugs in Mexico. As a consequence, there has been an increase in violence and corruption in the country. The drug trade is not new to Mexico; since the early 1900s, Mexico supplied the United States with marijuana and heroin. A significant change took place in the 1980s when Colombian drug traffickers began sending cocaine to the United States through Mexico. By the 1990s, more than half of the cocaine entering the United States passed through Mexico and Mexican drug traffickers earned billions of dollars. By the late-1990s, Mexican traffickers even were bypassing the Colombian operators, setting up their own wholesale and retail operations in the United States, and making connections directly with producers in Peru and Bolivia. Thus, Mexican drug cartels had become sophisticated organized crime operations.

These developments had a significant influence on politics and corruption. Among the most notable examples of the link between drugs, politics, and crime was the 1994 murder of José Francisco Ruiz Massieu, secretary-general of the PRI, Mexico's leading political party. The victim's brother, Mario Ruiz Massieu, then the assistant attorney general was in charge of the investigation. He claimed that Mexican drug bosses had ordered the murder and that high-ranking politicians were also involved in the plot. He later argued that the PRI attempted to cover up the details of the assassination. Then in February 1995, Raúl Salinas, brother of President Salinas, was arrested in connection with the murder. Salinas was found guilty in 1999 and rumors circulated that former president must have known of the murder plot.

Money laundering has also become widespread in Mexico, largely a result of the narcotics trade. Drug money earned in the United States by both Mexican and Colombian cartels is often laundered through Mexico's foreign exchange market, especially on the black market. There are several forms of getting dollars from the United States to Mexico. Sometimes, cartel operatives simply physically carry the money across the border to be deposited in Mexican banks, which are often less vigilant than U.S. banks. Other times, they convert cash into checks or money orders in the United States, then ship them to Mexico.

Another option is to deposit the money in a U.S. bank and then wire transfer the funds to a Mexican bank. While some of the drug money stays in Mexico to meet expenses, much of it is subsequently sent out of the country for further laundering in places such as London, Panama, or the Cayman Islands. While it is impossible to know exactly how much drug money flows into Mexico to be laundered, it is estimated at over $2 billion.

BANK FRAUD

White-collar crime was rampant in the Mexican banking industry during the 1990s. Illustrative of this trend was a bank insurance fraud scandal that came to light in 1998 due to a campaign by the PRD political party to expose corrupt banking and political practices. In 1990, the Mexican government created the Banking Fund to Protect Savings (Fobaproa) in order to insure bank deposits. Salinas hoped to build confidence in a banking system that he had privatized. In this environment, banks made many large loans to wealthy Mexicans. When the Mexican peso collapsed in December 1994, many borrowers were unable to pay their debts. The government of Ernesto Zedillo poured money into Fobaproa in order to rescue the banking system.

The fund took over the debts of some of the country's richest citizens, many of whom happened to be prominent contributors to the PRI. This process essentially transformed the private debts of rich Mexicans into public debt, which had reached $55 billion by 1998. Many critics claim that corrupt bankers simply made loans to themselves that they never intended to pay back. They further complain that Zedillo bailed them out because they were important campaign contributors.

Among the most notorious bankers was Carlos Cabal Peniche, a wealthy businessman involved in both the food distribution industry and banking. He was also involved in drug dealing and money laundering. Cabal Peniche set up dummy corporations to which his banks lent money. He used the funds to acquire legitimate corporations and to make campaign contributions to the PRI. When the dummy corporations collapsed, Fobaproa absorbed the debts Cabal eventually fled the country with funds estimated at least $700 million and as much as $2 billion. He was eventually caught in Australia.

SEE ALSO
drug trafficking; bank fraud. United States; Central America; money laundering.

BIBLIOGRAPHY. Jorge Chabat, "Mexico's War on Drugs: No Margin For Maneuver," *The Annals of the*

American Academy of Political and Social Science (v.582, July 2002); Robert E. Grosse, Drugs and Money: Laundering Latin America's Cocaine Dollars (Praeger, 2001); David Jordan, *Drug Politics: Dirty Money and Democracies* (University of Oklahoma Press, 1999); Stanley A. Pimentel, "The Nexus of Organized Crime and Politics in Mexico," *Trends in Organized Crime* (v.4/3, Spring 1999); Fred Rosen, "The $55 Billion Bank-Bailout Scandal," NACLA *Report on the Americas* (v.32/3, 1998); Peter H. Smith, "Semiorganized International Crime: Drug Trafficking in Mexico," *Transnational Crime in the Americas* (Routledge, 1999).

RONALD YOUNG
GEORGIA SOUTHERN UNIVERSITY

Microsoft

SINCE THE 1990S, Microsoft (MS) has been targeted for investigation by the U.S. Department of Justice (DOJ), the European Commission, the Japanese government, and several software trade associations. Microsoft has also been sued by individuals, other companies, and a number of states. There are two schools of thought on Microsoft's legal problems. One school argues that the government and MS competitors are out to get Bill Gates and his company because Microsoft has been so successful. The other school of thought insists that Gates and Microsoft have consistently engaged in cutthroat competition designed to shut out all competition through any means available.

Specifically, Microsoft has been charged with violating the Sherman Antitrust Act by forcing computer vendors and manufacturers to load new computers with Microsoft Windows as an operating system. Secondly, the company has been charged with forcing out browser competition by requiring vendors and manufacturers to include Microsoft Internet Explorer (IE) as the browser of choice for Windows and by removing icons for other browsers, such as Netscape, from computer desktops. Consumer advocate Ralph Nader called Microsoft "the most dangerous company in America today."

There is little doubt that Microsoft has dominated the computer software industry since its introduction of Windows 95 operating system in August 1995. Microsoft had been working for years to provide an operating system for the PC that would be as user friendly as that of Apple Macintosh computers. In 1988, in a landmark case, MS convinced the courts to uphold its right to copy the Graphical User Interface (GUI) used in Apple computers. Microsoft then introduced Windows 3.0, a weak and bug-filled imitation of the Mac. While its operating system was being fine-tuned, MS worked on innovations for its basic Windows programs, which would extend the market for Microsoft products.

As far back as the mid-1970s, MS had begun developing a string of improvements in the way that computers operate. In 1975, MS introduced the first Basic programming language for the personal computer (PC). The next year, Microsoft Word 1.0 became the first PC-based word processor to support a mouse. Within the next two years, Word 3.0 became the first PC-based word processor to support a laser printer. In 1987, MS introduced Excel, the first spreadsheet for Windows and followed it up two years later by adding the capability of generating tables to MS Word. In 1989, MS Office introduced the first suite of business applications. In 1991, MS incorporated multimedia into MS Works and drag-and-drop was added to MS Word.

In 1994, MS and Timex united to provide the first wristwatch to accept data from a computer. The following year, MS combined Intel's hardware with its own software, and Windows 95 was introduced. The rest, as they say, is history. From that point on, Microsoft became the force to be reckoned with in the computer industry. Within the first few months, Windows 95 sold over 50 million copies. Further improvements were made in Windows 98, Windows NT, Windows 2000, and Windows XP.

As Microsoft expanded and cornered a greater share of software markets, MS marketing practices were challenged by Netscape, Sun Microsystems, Novell, Lotus, and Word Perfect. In 1998, Robert Bork, a nationally known antitrust scholar who was notorious for his part in Richard Nixon's "Saturday Night Massacre" and for unsuccessfully seeking a seat on the Supreme Court in 1987, joined Netscape, MS's closest competitor for the browser market, as a consultant.

Bork and Robert Dole, who unsuccessfully challenged Bill Clinton for the presidency in 1996, joined forces to lobby for charges against Microsoft. Senator Orrin Hatch later joined them in

their attack on MS. There was a certain amount of irony in seeing three staunch conservatives line up against big business with liberal Ralph Nader, arguing for restrictions on free trade.

WORLDWIDE DOMINATION

Microsoft's competitors argue that as far back as 1996, Gates and company developed their strategy for worldwide domination of personal computers. They argue that MS made plants to totally annihilate the Mac, IBM's OS/2 and UNIX operating systems, and the Netscape browser. Reportedly, by 1997, MS had a cash reserve of over $10 billion, allowing them to buy competitors who threatened them. Microsoft bought a dozen companies in 1997 alone by adopting an "absorb-and-extend" strategy in which MS copied the competitor's product, modified or extended it with MS-generated improvements, then re-offered it to consumers.

In 1980, Microsoft had licensed MS-DOS to IBM to be pre-installed on all new computers. Ten years later, Microsoft and IBM announced at an industry trade show that they would work together on developing future operating systems. Afterward, the Federal Trade Commission (FTC) decided to investigate IBM, the connection with Microsoft became evident. When FTC attention turned to MS, government investigators discovered that Microsoft's licensing agreements had required that computer manufacturers who sold computers loaded with MS-DOS 6.0 and Windows 3.1 pay MS royalties on all computers sold whether or not that particular computer contained MS software. MS licenses also mandated a minimum commitment and discouraged manufacturers from including non-Microsoft software on their computers.

The FTC decided not to pursue charges against MS. However, in 1993, the Department of Justice opened its own investigation into Microsoft. In 1994, Microsoft and DOJ negotiated a consent decree under which Microsoft agreed to change its licensing practices, but a district court judge overturned the decree the following year. The DOJ investigation of MS expanded at the same time that an appeals court restored the consent decree. Microsoft then accused DOJ of "harassment and abuse" in their investigation. In response, DOJ, egged on by Netscape, extended its investigation even further. In 1997, Attorney General Janet Reno fined MS $1 million per day until the company complied with the 1995 consent decree and charged MS with contempt.

In May 1998, in *U.S. v. Microsoft Corporation*, a federal district court was asked to determine whether or not Microsoft engaged in monopolistic practices with its Windows operating system and with Internet Explorer. The federal case combined 20 other suits against Microsoft with the case brought by the DOJ. In the initial decision, the judge found Microsoft guilty of antitrust violations and ordered Microsoft to divide its operating system and other software into two separate companies. Gates argued that Microsoft should be allowed to compete in a free market with no controls: "Unless we're allowed to enhance Windows, I don't know how to do my job."

Microsoft appealed the district court's decision, arguing that the company was innocent of all antitrust accusations, that there were problems with procedural and factual factors in the government's case, and that the judge acted unethically by making public remarks about the merits of the case while it was still pending. MS also asked that the judge's ruling be set aside due to partiality. The appeals court reversed the district court's finding that Microsoft had engaged in monopolistic practices, and remanded the case to a lower court.

In March 2004, a European Union (EU) court ruled in an EU antitrust case against Microsoft, stating that the company must offer two versions of its Windows program. The company promptly filed an appeal.

SEE ALSO

Sherman Antitrust Act; antitrust; Justice, Department of; illegal competition;

BIBLIOGRAPHY. Ted G. Lewis, *Microsoft Rising and Other Tales of Silicon Valley* (The Computer Society, 1999); Richard B. McKenzie, *Trust on Trial: How The Microsoft Case Is Reframing the Rules of Competition* (Perseus Publishing, 2000); Joshua Quittner and Michelle Slatalla, *Speeding The Net: The Inside Story of Netscape And How It Changed Microsoft* (Atlantic Monthly Press, 1998); Gary Rivlin, *The Plot to Get Bill Gates: An Irreverent Investigation into the World's Richest Man and the People Who Hate Him* (Random House, 1999); *U.S. v. Microsoft Corporation*, caselaw.lp.findlaw.com (2003).

ELIZABETH PURDY, PH.D.
INDEPENDENT SCHOLAR

Middle East

THE MIDDLE EAST CONTAINS a wide variety of nations and states that is as diverse in economic opportunities as it is in ethnicity, religion, and language. It ranges from Iran and Iraq bordering on the Afghanistan region in the east, the Persian Gulf states in the south, Israel, Palestine, Jordan and Syria on the coast of the Mediterranean Sea, Egypt and the north African Muslim states to the west. The cultural and economic patterns linking this region also link it in some contexts with Turkey and the island of Cyprus. It is, therefore, a complex region with a great deal of diversity.

It would be simplistic to classify it as the Muslim region of the world because that would be to ignore the many important ethnic and religious minority peoples contained within its scope, and also the other Muslim peoples in other parts of the world. Nevertheless, the majority of the region has been welded together historically through context, most notably the Ottoman Empire that was finally dismembered after centuries of rule at the end of World War I. The legacy of the bureaucracy of the Byzantine Empire and its inability to provide economic growth partly led to the institutionalized corruption that became endemic within its borders, symbolized by the Egyptian word and concept of *baksheesh*.

Political and religious divisions have led to widespread and longstanding violence in many areas and this has led to many business activities being kept secret. For reasons of cultural practice and habit, many agreements are made on the basis of mutual friendship or kinship and are not subject to wider scrutiny. This practice is seen both in government and private sectors. The results of this include a wide range of opportunities for corruption and bad practices to flourish.

OIL CORRUPTION

Corruption is believed to be particularly widespread in the oil and construction industries, both of which are of considerable importance in the Middle East as oil wealth from reserves discovered in the 20th century led both to a demand by external powers to control the oil through either military force or commercial domination, as well as a burst of infrastructure building and more general expenditure by the newly rich owners.

The discovery of oil in some Middle East nations has led to a widening of the gap in economic opportunities between rich and poor, and the importance of the industry has meant that political considerations have underscored some commercial decisions. The importance placed upon defense and security in many states has also inspired a thriving armaments import trade that has necessitated additional secrecy on many occasions. In these conditions, in which few decisions and the reasons for making them are made public, in which most countries are undemocratic and in which a free press has struggled to establish itself, it is not surprising that there have been many opportunities for corruption and other forms of white-collar crime.

These include gun running and smuggling, prostitution and human trafficking, money laundering, support for and sponsorship of terrorism, fraud and embezzlement, and other activities. The division of labor according to ethnicity in many countries has meant that some groups are discriminated against and this has taken the form of lower wages and less desirable working conditions. In recent years, for example, Palestinians wishing to work in Israel have been subject to various regulations and difficulties, which have arisen as a result of the violence of the Intifada (uprising).

ARMED CONFLICT AND CORRUPTION

Indeed, the whole of the Middle East must, in many ways, be seen against the backdrop of the Israeli-Arab struggle, for this has been instrumental in shaping many of the political regimes in the region and that, in turn, has a significant impact upon the business environment. The Jewish state of Israel was established in the years following World War II through, at length, the assistance of Western powers, and in the teeth of resistance by the Arab peoples, especially the Palestinians who were forcibly displaced as a result.

Intensive but largely inconclusive debate concerning historical ownership and precedent of the land and its resources has been punctuated by a series of violent wars, each won by Israeli forces armed with superior technology and organization. Arms and other support have been supplied to Israel by the United States and also other players in the arms trade. The British arms trade with Israel continues to rise to significant numbers and reached £22 million (approximately $35.2 million) in 2001. However, this continues to be dwarfed by American dealings with Israel. Weapons sales, like overseas development assistance, are only occasionally linked to human rights issues, which are frequently ignored or brought back to prominence for short-term political reasons.

Palestinians and their supporters, including many terrorist groups, have been secretly and not so secretly supported by states such as Syria, Iran, and Iraq, partly through proxy organizations such as Hamas and Hizbullah. Coming under attack by rockets and mortars from southern Lebanon, the Israeli army invaded and occupied the area for years, which contributed to the intensification of civil war in Lebanon.

The crisis in Lebanon led to the exodus of a large number of companies, many of which had been conducting business successfully in the multicultural, sophisticated environs of Beirut (Lebanese capital) for years. Those firms, notably banks and financial institutions, sought an alternative base in the Middle East and found it in oil-rich Gulf states seeking to diversify sources of income.

The conflict between Israel and the Arab nations has featured military force and terrorist attacks, together with the widespread expropriation of Palestinian property by Israeli authorities and the denial of some fundamental labor rights for Palestinian and Arab labor in Israel. It has also led to high levels of smuggling, particularly in weapons but also in other merchandise to pay for weapons and other expertise. In the breakdown of civil order inevitable in such situations, there have been numerous opportunities for petty corruption, bribery, and extortion.

The armed struggle has also seen the blurring of the line between state and individual action. The first Arab-Israeli cyberwar was staged in 2000, when a group of Israeli hackers crippled the Hizbullah website. The next such war may possibly erupt at any time and may take a number of forms more dangerous than defacing existing materials. These actions are a form of economic warfare by individuals and private groups and, therefore, properly classified as white-collar crime.

The internet offers additional opportunities for criminal organizations, as reports of attempts to arrange illegal gambling rings and also to fix international cricket matches in the United Arab Emirates state of Sharjah by individuals linked to the Indian underworld attest.

IRREDENTISM

The Arab-Israeli conflict is not the only example of armed struggle within the region. In the 1980s, a particularly bloody war erupted between Iraq and Iran and, subsequently, Iraq invaded its oil-rich southern neighbor of Kuwait. In addition to the desire to control resources and enforce religious and political supremacy, armed conflicts have also been motivated by irredentism, the wish to redraw political boundaries so that they match historical cultural patterns. The current political boundaries were mainly drawn by the Western powers upon the collapse of the Ottoman Empire and in the wake of world war. Consequently, there are numerous examples of a mismatch between nations as represented on the map and nations as many people believe they should be. This leads both to cross-border personal and commercial networks that are adept at eluding official inspections, and also the widespread desire to circumvent the authorities who are not fully considered to be acting with appropriate jurisdiction.

The Iraq invasion of Kuwait and the subsequent Persian Gulf War in 1991 led to Iraqi withdrawal but the continuance of the ruling regime under Saddam Hussein. This regime was known to have committed numerous atrocities against its own people and the international community decided the best way of preventing it from committing further acts of aggression was to impose sanctions on the import of any materials that might be used to manufacture further weapons, together with a program of inspections by United Nations officials searching for existing weapons or programs that might lead to biological, chemical, or nuclear weapons capabilities. Sanctions proved very difficult to police, as the borders of Iraq are very lengthy and difficult to patrol and, as mentioned above, many local networks exist quite capable of avoiding officials.

There was also considerable incentive for firms to break the sanctions, as the Iraqi government was willing to pay high fees for importing banned equipment. In the United Kingdom, as one example, the Churchill Matrix firm was accused of exporting to Iraq material that may have been used to create a "super gun" (basically, a huge cannon capable of shooting missiles capable of reaching Israel). The trial of the directors of the company collapsed when it was revealed they were acting with the connivance of the British government, and had even been involved in spying for them. Legend has it the inventor of the super gun, and the man who sold the concept to Iraq, Canadian inventor Gerald Bull was eliminated by Israel's intelligence service, Mossad.

Sanctions imposed against Iran and Libya for what was considered to be their roles in sponsoring terrorism also inspired many cases of smuggling and secret dealings. In these cases, there was much less international unanimity that sanctions would be an appropriate tool; some Western European states had considerable interests in those countries and were unwilling to abandon them.

ILLICIT DRUGS

The Middle East has long faced the problem of illegal drugs—mainly the opium and heroin created from the poppy. It is estimated that there are approximately 2 million drug addicts in Iran, for example. Much of the supply of such drugs derives from the wilder regions of Afghanistan, where it has historically proved difficult for central authorities to control activities. This is no better demonstrated than by the establishment of al-Qaeda terrorist training camps in the remote and desolate land.

In the 1980s, drug production was accelerated in Afghanistan to get cash to fund resistance to the Soviet Union invasion of the 1980s, although it had existed at some level for hundreds of years. Following the U.S.-led war against al-Qaeda and its sponsor, the Taliban, in Afghanistan in 2002, a hiatus in drug production was followed by greatly enhanced production levels that threaten stability in the region. Distribution networks through central Asia and through Iran and Iraq are frequently unpoliced as a result of lack of resources, and the effects of warfare, corruption, and bribery. This has led to rapid distribution of drugs and associated problems of HIV infection through shared needles, and organized crime gangs seeking control of trade routes.

MONEY LAUNDERING

The al-Qaeda terrorist network is only the most visible example of terrorist gangs in the region. Most groups receive money from supporters, often in other countries, which is then used to buy weapons and other materiel. The degree of legality or illegality in these transactions is contested, since terrorists

Cairo, Egypt, represents the modern, urban side of the Middle East. Yet, ancient criminal customs prevail.

The city of Sana'a in Yemen suggests the labyrinths of crime inherited from the Byzantine Empire.

appear to be freedom fighters or justified warriors to at least their supporters. Nevertheless, it is clear that a great deal of weapons smuggling does take place and the weapons are paid for using money for which proper accounting procedures have not been followed. International charities, or non-governmental organizations (NGOs) have been accused of being part of this system, especially Islamic charities that are supported by those professing a conservative social order and radical foreign policies. This is in addition to the regular defense trade in the region, much of which itself is subject to suspicion of corruption and other forms of illegality.

LABOR LAWS

Labor laws are little respected in many Middle Eastern countries and scrutiny of their observation is hampered by the banning of trades (labor) unions, and the absence of international monitoring organizations such as the International Labor Organization (ILO). Middle Eastern nations, among others, have generally been unwilling to make concessions to the ILO or to acknowledge workers' rights.

Refusal to entertain international labor standards is, in part, a political and religious issue as it is believed that such standards pay insufficient attention to Muslim practices that restrict the ability of women to participate in the labor force in many countries. However, more important is the traditional and tribal mentality of governance in many

states. This means that a small elite, generally connected by family ties to the ruler, controls all important posts either directly, through appointment or through the unwillingness of anyone to be disobedient for fear of punishment.

This ruling style is seen very clearly in the six Gulf states of the Gulf Co-operation Council (the Kingdom of Saudi Arabia, the United Arab Emirates, Bahrain, Qatar, Oman, and Kuwait), as well as in Yemen. States which have nominally undergone political revolution to replace tribal rule have, in some cases, instead substituted dynastic one-party politics (for example, Syria and Libya) or have political systems mired in the controversies of vote-buying or voter intimidation (for example, Algeria and to some extent Egypt). Generally, the ruling elite is supported by the teachings of clerics who generally preach in favor of a conservative social order that translates into support for the status quo. Consequently, change delivered by democratic means is generally slow to arrive and when, for example, several women were allowed to stand for office in some local elections in Bahrain, the conservative tendencies of voters ensured that not one was elected.

For the labor market, this tends to mean few safeguards against extortion or means of workplace protection. The large pools of migrant labor in most countries, especially those funded by oil wealth, find themselves particularly vulnerable to exploitation. There are reports of some laborers remaining unpaid for months at a time when there is a prospect of political upheaval leading to their rapid repatriation. Few avenues of appeal or protest are available and anyone considered to be a trouble-maker may be swiftly deported. In some cases, migrant workers are cheated by the job brokers who facilitate their journey overseas, and then are cheated by their employers when they arrive.

Inevitably, women are particularly vulnerable to this form of treatment. Many women are destined for domestic service or for service industries in which they have very little opportunity to make complaints about inappropriate or unfair treatment. Local women are in many cases prevented from entering the workforce at all or, if they are permitted entry, restricted to a limited number of positions and occupations that are deemed socially appropriate. In some countries, such as the UAE, local people's wages are subsidized, as are many

The Mosque of Abu El Abbas near Alexandria, Egypt, is one symbol of the moral force of Islam in the region.

other aspects of their lifestlye and, throughout the region, nepotism is the accepted and unavoidable norm. In many cases, the real administrative and managerial work is conducted by shadow managers who receive a fraction of the compensation provided to the ostensible executives, and who have very few opportunities to influence policies or important decisions, most of which are made behind closed doors.

An additional implication of this situation of autocratic rule is that few people genuinely believe that reform is either possible or really to be attempted. Throughout most parts of the region, the media have been hampered in any investigative activities because of widespread suppression of dissident voices, corporate ownership of many large media outlets, and a continued sense of deference toward the ruling elites.

Consequently, policy and commercial decisions are not routinely scrutinized in any detail and scandals and incidents that are well-known in the public sphere go unreported. One example of this censorship is the very large incidence of fraud at Dubai Islamic Bank; the story was effectively placed under embargo by the UAE government. Vulnerable workers at the lower levels of the labor market can expect no such protection.

However, there is evidence that this double standard is changing. A new form of investigative media is emerging, sparked by the communication and organization facilitated by the internet and symbolized by the intrusive and challenging presence of the Al Jazeera television network so prominent during the 2003 Iraq War.

The fertility of the region, in combination with historically low life expectancies, has meant that large proportions of people are in young age categories, and more likely to be in favor of change, democracy, and the welcome impacts of globalization. When these voices become more prominent in decision-making processes, it is likely that many of the current practices will necessarily be reformed. Already some landmark cases of corruption have been reported, for example the jailing of the former chief spy of Jordan.

However, the recent United Nations Universal Declaration on Human Rights outlawed discrimination of individuals on grounds of sexual preference, among other rights, and this has been found unacceptable by many of the Middle Eastern nations, which has further removed them from international negotiations and therefore lessened accountability for other actions.

SEE ALSO

gender discrimination; drug trafficking; oligopoly; Israel; labor crimes.

BIBLIOGRAPHY. "Ex-Spymaster of Jordan Gets Eight Years," www.gulfnews.com (July 11, 2003); Robin Allen, "Survey: Bahrain," *Financial Times* (November 20, 2000); Mohammad Almezel, "Bahrain: A Year to Celebrate," www.gulfnews.com (January 1, 2003); Noam Chomsky, *Powers and Prospects: Reflections on Human Nature and the Social Order* (Allen & Unwin, 1996): Craig Francis, "Drug Trade Threatens Afghanistan," www.cnn.com (February 27, 2002); William D. Hartung and Frida Berrigan, "U.S. Arms Transfers and Security Assistance to Israel," Arms Trade Resource Center Fact Sheet, www.worldpolicy.org (May 6, 2002); David Landes, *The Wealth and Poverty of Nations* (Abacus, 1999). Marco Michelotti and Chris Nyland, "The ILO, International Trade and the 1998 Declaration on Fundamental Principles and Rights at Work," *Readings in International Business: an Asia Pacific Perspective* (Prentice Hall-Sprint Print, 2000); Richard Norton-Taylor, "Compensation for Arms to Iraq Pair," *The Guardian* (November 9, 2001); Neil Sammonds, "UK-Israel Arms Trade Blossoms amid the Rubble," *Middle East* (v.329, December 2002): Giles Trendle, "Cyberwars: The Coming Arab E-Jihad," *Middle East* (v.329, April 2002); Brian Whitaker, "Government Disorientation," *The Guardian* (April 29, 2003).

JOHN WALSH, PH.D.
MAHIDOL UNIVERSITY, THAILAND

military-industrial complex

FIRST COINED by outgoing President Dwight D. Eisenhower in his farewell address to the nation, the military-industrial complex is a tight-knit group of interchangeable parts and people, for example, retired military officers moving into defense companies, defense company leaders moving into government. Eisenhower warned the country to be wary of the military-industrial complex. Indeed, the opportunity for fraud and white-collar crime, may not be matched by another segment of society. The collusion between the military and industry has grown significantly since Eisenhower's 1950s.

Before World War II, between 1922 and 1939, annual military budgets averaged 1 percent of the Gross National Product, only $744 million. Purchasing was by public advertisement for fixed quantities. Bids were sealed, and awards went to low bidders. Government business was not lucrative, and companies solicited it reluctantly.

World War II changed that. Between 1940 and late 1941, the War Department spent $36 billion, more than the army and navy combined in World War I. And the contracts were cost-plus (allowing for profit), granted to large firms. The top 10 contractors got 30 percent, with General Motors alone getting 8 percent. The top 10 research and development (R&D) contractors received almost 40 percent of the funds. Government invested $17 billion in industrial plants after the war. Government largesse and protection proved irresistible, and the military-industrial complex was born. Over the next half century, the military-industrial complex cost over $10 trillion in 2002 dollars.

COLLUSION

The relationship was intimate as industry leaders moved back and forth between government and corporations. They met young military officers who, on retiring, used their connections to move by the thousands into the industries they had worked with at the Pentagon.

Government valued the contractors, bailing out Lockheed, Litton, General Dynamics, Chrysler, Grumman, and others instead of holding them to their contractual obligations. Department of Defense (DOD) money subsidized loans, facilities, and R&D. Congress recognized the value of military spending in the home district.

The proposed $21-billion Boeing tanker lease deal of 2003 was typical. The air force initially did not want the planes. Boeing used insiders in the air force to develop specifications that excluded Boeing's rivals. Perhaps an insider provided proprietary information; possibly the air force used Boeing's documents and arguments to lobby for the tankers once it accepted their value.

The working together of Boeing and air force insiders typified the method by which the military-industrial complex bought planes and ships and most other DOD needs. The military-industrial complex also buys electronic voting devices. In this case, a maker of electronic voting machines reputedly containing defects, that make vote fraud easy and undetectable, has a management team replete with retired military and intelligence personnel. On the VoteHere board is ex-CIA director Robert Gates, for example. VoteHere also interlocks with the Carlyle Group and Halliburton. Conspiracists see the connection as rife with potential for fraud and stolen elections.

The aftermath of the Iraq War in 2003 epitomized the military-industrial complex at its worst. The Center for Public Integrity documented that 30 members of the Defense Policy Board (non-elected formulators of defense policy in the Pentagon) had ties to companies that received over $76 billion in defense contracts in 2001 and 2002 alone. Bechtel made hundreds of millions dealing with the Iraqi regime then got hundreds of millions in non-competitive and open-ended rebuilding contracts. Halliburton, another top contractor reaping millions from the Iraq War, once employed Vice-President Dick Cheney. The spoils of war could top $100 billion.

Some experts assume that the expansion of NATO (North Atlantic Treaty Organization) is but another opportunity to enrich the ever-shrinking number of defense contractors, because the new NATO forces will have to acquire equipment compatible with that of the United States, that is, the arms made in the United States by the handful of defense contractors.

THE CARLYLE GROUP

Conspiracists really get exercised over the Carlyle Group, which buys struggling companies (defense, telecommunications, and aerospace), turns them around, and sells them for large profits. Carlyle, the 11th-largest defense contractor with assets of $12 billion, is reportedly the gate-keeper between private business and defense spending. Carlyle members include former U.S. president, George H.W. Bush, former British prime minister John Major, and former Philippine president Fidel Ramos.

Carlyle also has ties to the Saudi Arabian royal family, including members of Osama bin Laden's family. Moreover, Carlyle tied itself to George W. Bush by placing him on the board of one of its companies, Caterair International, in 1991. Critics decry Carlyle as the exemplar of crony capitalism and a potential subverter of the democratic process because it is the strongest in the iron triangle, with

no significant competitors. And it's secretive. In the latest manifestation of the military-industrial complex, defense contractor DynCorp hired mercenaries, private military companies, stocked with military veterans, who provide contract services ranging from logistics to, sometimes, actual combat capabilities. DynCorp began in the 1950s as an air force contractor, and evolved as part of the military-industrial complex into a prime contractor for the Central Intelligence Agency (CIA) and DOD. By subcontracting, the DOD can disclaim responsibility.

CONSPIRACY

To conspiracists, the military-industrial complex engages in more than business collusion. Thierry Meyssan argues in *l'Effroyable Imposture* (*The Horrifying Fraud*) that the September 11, 2001 terrorist attacks were the work of the military-industrial complex. Or, they can track the post-9/11 anthrax scare to weapons-grade anthrax linked circuitously to the CIA and DOD. They can link the military-industrial complex to the assassination of John F. Kennedy, arguing that the complex feared Kennedy would spoil its profits by withdrawing from Vietnam. The ultimate conspiracists see the military-industrial complex as preparing a coup, a switch from behind-the-scenes control to outright takeover of the United States.

SEE ALSO

government procurement fraud; government contract fraud; Eisenhower, Dwight D.; conspiracy.

BIBLIOGRAPHY. Julian E. Barnes and Christopher H. Schmitt, "Under The Radar; The Inside Story of a Pentagon Deal that Will Cost Taxpayers Billions," *U.S. News* (September 8, 2003); Dan Briody, *The Iron Triangle: Inside the Secret World of the Carlyle Group* (Wiley, 2003); Bruce Crumley, "France's No. 1 Bestseller Claims the U.S. Orchestrated the Sept. 11 Attacks: Why Do People Read this Stuff?" *Time Europe* (May 20, 2002); Uri Dowbenko, "Dirty Tricks, Inc.: The DynCorp-Government Connection," www.conspiracydigest.com (2003); "The Carlyle Group; C for capitalism," *The Economist* (June 26, 2003); James Fallows, "The Military-Industrial Complex," *Foreign Policy* (November–December 2002); Lynn Landes, "Voting Machine Fiasco: SAIC, Behemoth Military Contractor, Wants to Be inside Every Voting Machine; Three Way Scam on Diebold Review?" www.opednews.com (2003); Renae Merle, "Documents

Detail Maneuvers For Boeing Lease," *Washington Post* (August 31, 2003); Jonathan Wells, Jack Meyers, and Maggie Mulvihill, "Bush Advisers Cashed in on Saudi Gravy Train," *Common Dreams News Center*, www.commondreams.org (October 1, 2003).

JOHN H. BARNHILL, PH.D.
INDEPENDENT SCHOLAR

Milken, Michael (1946–)

DURING THE 1970s, Michael Milken developed a financial scheme that made him one of the richest and most powerful men in the United States. He found that he could make enormous profits from rescuing "fallen angels" by engineering financial deals that offered high yields on low-priced debt notes. These so-called junk bonds were financed by Milken and his company, Drexel Burnham Lambert, for small, high-risk companies that had faced financial troubles or even bankruptcy but who still showed potential for recovery. Because of the risks involved, these companies had been generally ignored by investment bankers.

Milken was a master at convincing perspective investors that junk bonds were more lucrative than the more stable low-risk bonds. By the late 1980s, Milken who had become known as the "junk bond king" or simply "the king," seemed to be at the top of the world. However, Drexel appeared more profitable on paper than it actually was because of innovative accounting practices. Before the decade was over, however, both Milken and Drexel were brought down by an insider trading scandal.

In May 1986, Milkin received a subpoena from the office of Rudy Giuliani, U.S. attorney for the Southern District of New York. As Giuliani's investigation unfolded, along with an ongoing investigation by the Securities and Exchange Commission (SEC), numerous charges surfaced. In March 1989, both Milken and his brother Lowell were charged with 98 counts of racketeering and securities fraud. Milken hired one of the most impressive legal/public relations teams ever put together to help him fight the charges. Since he was afraid that he might be vulnerable before a jury composed of minorities, Milken's public relations experts worked hard to improve his image with minorities. Reportedly, Drexel, who footed the bill for the enormous fees

for the attorneys and the public relations team, put Milken on a monthly budget of only $1.2 million. When ordered to appear before Congress, Milken followed his lawyer's advice and claimed the Fifth Amendment, which protected him from having to say anything that might incriminate him. He was wise enough to know, however, that pleading the Fifth did not solve his problems.

In April 1990, Milken pleaded guilty to six felonies and was forced to pay a $600 million fine. Drexel Burnham Lambert declared bankruptcy, and the junk bond market collapsed, although it slowly recovered over the course of the next decade. Overall, Milken paid $1.1 billion to settle the hundreds of lawsuits filed against him and Drexel Burnham Lambert by government agencies, corporations, service providers, and investors.

When the judge read out the verdict that sentenced Milken to two years on each of five counts to be served consecutively, Milken was apparently so stunned that he failed to realize the significance of the term. He later collapsed when he understood that he was actually sentenced to 10 years in prison for violations of securities laws. While Milken could have been sentenced to 28 years in prison, few people thought he would receive a sentence of more than a couple of years. A two- or three-year sentence was typical for white-collar criminals convicted of securities violations.

On March 3, 1991, Milken entered a minimum-security work camp in Pleasanton, California, where he worked 37 hours a week in maintenance and construction. According to his sentence, Milken was not eligible for parole for two years, although the judge had recommended that Milken serve 36 to 40 months before being paroled. In fact, in 1993, Judge Kimba Wood reduced Milken's sentence to the time already served. Many people felt that Milken had been sandbagged by both state and federal prosecutors and wondered why Milken had not been pardoned along with others criminals in the final days of the Clinton administration.

Milken was banned from the securities industry for life. Despite the ban, he later engineered a securities deal that involved Rupert Murdoch's News Corporation (NCI) and Ron Perelman's New World Entertainment. Milken was forced to pay back the $42 million that he received for the deal, plus another $5 million dollars in interest. Even while he was imprisoned, Milken received profits from the book, *Portraits of the American Dream*, which Lorraine Spurge, a former Drexel Burnham secretary, published with Milken's support. The book chronicled the successes of the companies that Drexel Burnham Lambert had financed.

After being released from prison, Milken, who was reportedly worth $500 million at this point, accepted a job as a legal researcher for his lawyer at a salary of $1,300 a week. Milken was diagnosed with terminal prostate cancer and told that he had no more than 18 months to live. He responded by taking charge of his illness, becoming a vegetarian and taking up yoga. In September 1998, Milken published *The Taste for Living Cookbook: Michael Milken's Favorite Recipes for Fighting Cancer.* His cancer went into remission, and Milken reinvented himself.

He gave away $250 million to charities and raised $120 million for cancer research through his charity CaPCURE. With his brother Lowell and Larry Ellison, the head of Oracle software, Milken established Knowledge Universe, which was billed as a "cradle-to-the-grave" educational service. The company provides worldwide educational training.

SEE ALSO

Drexel, Burnham, Lambert; insider trading; securities fraud; Giuliani, Rudolph; accounting fraud; Boesky, Ivan.

BIBLIOGRAPHY. Connie Bruck, "The Predator's Ball," *Eyewitness to Wall Street: 400 Years of Dreamers, Schemers, Bust, and Booms* (Broadway Books, 2001); "Michael Milken, Comeback King," *The Economist* (March 27, 1999); Kathleen Morris and John Carrey, "The Reincarnation of Mike Milken," *BusinessWeek* (March 10, 1999); Roy C. Smith, "After the Ball," *Wilson Quarterly* (Autumn 1992); James B. Stewart, *Den of Thieves* (Simon & Schuster, 1991).

ELIZABETH PURDY, PH.D.
INDEPENDENT SCHOLAR

Misappropriation Theory

THE MISAPPROPRIATION Theory is associated with insider-trading law. It is not in the statutes, but has evolved through case law since 1981. Until federal securities laws were enacted in the 1930s, it was generally not a crime for officers, directors, or controlling shareholders to trade stock in their own corporations on the basis of inside information. This is still the situation in many other countries; it is considered to be a privilege of corporate status.

Before 1980, insider trading cases were prosecuted using Section 10(b) and Rule 10b-5, which prohibits a corporate insider from buying or selling shares in her own company based on non-public information. This is the basis for the traditional or classic theory of insider trading. The Misappropriation Theory extends insider trading cases to include people, beyond these employees, who trade on information which they are under a fiduciary duty to keep confidential. Any person, not just traditional corporate insiders, with material facts has a duty to either disclose this information or refrain from trading stocks.

NONPUBLIC INFORMATION

Interestingly, the Misappropriation Theory began with a failure. Vincent F. Chiarella, a low-level employee at a financial printing house, was able to discern information relevant to company mergers and sales. He made investments based on the information he discovered and was convicted of securities fraud for trading on inside information. He won an appeal to the Supreme Court in 1980, with the justices ruling that he was not guilty because, not being affiliated with the company, he had no duty to other investors.

In a dissenting opinion, Chief Justice Warren E. Burger said Chiarella violated an obligation to his employer to keep its clients' secrets and had "misappropriated," or stolen, valuable nonpublic information. Within a year, the New York federal appeals court had upheld the conviction using the new Misappropriation Theory in a case involving securities trader James M. Newman. Newman's appeal to the Supreme Court went unheard.

In 1983, Anthony Materia, another low-level printing company employee, was convicted of inside trading in a civil suit brought by the Securities and Exchange Commission (SEC), under circumstances similar to those of Chiarella's case. A fiduciary duty to refrain from trading or providing information to others was found, in that doing those things would damage his employer's reputation and business. The court found that this duty was sufficient, even though the employer was not in any way involved with the securities that were bought or sold.

R. Foster Winans wrote a financial column in the *Wall Street Journal* which often affected the stock price of companies mentioned. In 1983 and 1984, Winans (and other brokers he told about the column contents) traded stocks in companies mentioned prior to the columns being published. He was fired from this action and for breaking conflict-of-interest rules, and was convicted of securities fraud using the Misappropriation Theory. The mail and wire fraud convictions were upheld by the U.S. Supreme Court in November 1987. However, the court split evenly on the securities fraud conviction. Because of the even split, this case will not set legal precedent but did lead many to believe the SEC needed to produce a clearer definition of insider trading. There was no tie-break vote because the court had one vacancy at the time.

James O'Hagan was a partner in a law firm which was to be local counsel for an attempted corporate takeover of Pillsbury Company. O'Hagan, who did not work on the takeover himself, bought shares and options based on conversations with another partner who did, prior to the announcement of the takeover. O'Hagan's conviction of mail and securities fraud was reversed by the 8th Circuit Court in a rejection of the Misappropriation Theory. This reversal was appealed, and with its 1997 opinion endorsing the theory in *U.S. v. O'Hagan*, "the U.S. Supreme Court has succeeded in both significantly extending the parameters of 'insider trading' liability and blurring the boundary line between permissible and impermissible trading activity." As the first time the Supreme Court endorsed the Misappropriation Theory, the decision allows the SEC the authority to impose criminal liability for fraud where there is no proof of a breach of fiduciary duty.

SEE ALSO

securities fraud; stock fraud; insider trading; Insider Trading Sanctions Act; mail fraud.

BIBLIOGRAPHY. William B. Glaberson, "Insider Trading: A Widening Net Catches the Small Fry," *BusinessWeek* (February 11, 1985); Reuters, "High Court Gets Pleas on Winans," *New York Times* (October 8, 1987); "Not Rain, Nor Snow, Nor Insider Trading Must Stop the U.S. Mail," *The Economist* (November 21, 1987); John F.X. Peloso and Timothy P. Burke, "The 'Misappropriation Theory' of Outsider Trading Liability," *S&P's The Review of Securities & Commodities Regulation* (January 15, 1997); Kate Oberlies, "What It Prevents Must Be Fraud: Playing with Words in O'Hagan," *Business Crimes Bulletin: Compliance & Litigation* (September 1997).

LINDA M. CREIBAUM
ARKANSAS STATE UNIVERSITY

Mollen Commission

NAMED AFTER A FORMER deputy mayor of New York City, Milton Mollen, the Mollen Commission was created in 1994 to assess the extent of corruption in the New York City Police Department (NYPD). The 1980s saw a return to rampant misconduct by police officers after a purported decrease following the investigation by the Knapp Commission in the 1970s. The stakes had also escalated, moving from bribes and corruption related to vice, to huge sums of money generated by the crack cocaine trade.

Just as the NYPD was recovering from its battering at the hands of the Knapp Commission, Officer Michael Dowd and 15 to 20 fellow officers were found at the center of a criminal organization in Brooklyn. Dowd lived up to his billing as the most crooked cop in New York by continuing his illegal activities even after his arrest, reportedly corresponding with drug dealers from his jail cell. The Mollen Commission was formed one month after his arrest in an effort to determine why Dowd's superiors had not acted on 16 complaints that had been filed against him alleging that he had been taking bribes, robbing drug dealers, and selling cocaine over a period of six years.

The commission uncovered blatant corruption and cases of brutality, with officers in Brooklyn and Manhattan not only stealing and selling drugs, but sometimes shooting the dealers. The commission reported a "willful blindness" to corruption throughout the ranks of the NYPD. It further suggested that at least 40 corruption cases involving senior officers had been "buried" by the Internal Affairs Bureau, and that several previous police commissioners had been more interested in containing corruption scandals than containing corruption.

Heightened internal controls was one of two major recommendations of the Mollen Commission. The other was a proposal to increase external controls, through the creation of a small police commission independent of the NYPD. That body would be empowered to perform continuous assessments of the department's systems for preventing, detecting, and investigating corruption, and to conduct, whenever necessary, its own corruption investigations.

SEE ALSO
Knapp Commission; police corruption; bribery; extortion; organized crime; drug trafficking.

BIBLIOGRAPHY. "Mollen Commission: Excerpts," *The New York Times* (July 7, 1994); Stephen M. Rosoff, Henry N. Pontell, and Robert Tillman, *Profit Without Honor:: White-Collar Crime and the Looting of America* (Prentice Hall, 1998); Joseph B. Treaster, "Mollen Panel Says Buck Stops With Top Officers," *New York Times* (July 10, 1994); Craig Wolff, "Corruption in Uniform: Chronology; Tracking Police Corruption Over the Years," *New York Times* (July 7, 1994).

HENRY N. PONTELL
UNIVERSITY OF CALIFORNIA, IRVINE
STEPHEN M. ROSOFF
UNIVERSITY OF HOUSTON, CLEARLAKE

money laundering

MONEY LAUNDERING is an old business, as old as any other illicit business. Not until recently has money laundering been seen as the problem that it really is.

The effects of terrorism have brought money laundering to the public's attention as terrorists are funded usually through laundered money, one way or another. Money laundering is a pervasive problem in the United States, and throughout the world. Over the past couple of decades it has become clear that money laundering is a robust, corrosive, all-consuming and dynamic activity that has far reaching consequences and effects.

In order to understand the issue of money laundering one must first understand what it is: Money laundering is the process by which someone conceals the existence, illegal source, or illegal application of income, and disguises that income to make it appear legitimate. Money laundering is the process of converting quantities of cash to a form that can be used more conveniently in commerce and ideally conceals the origin of converted funds.

According to the Financial Crimes Enforcement Network (FinCEN) money laundering involves disguising financial assets so they can be used without detection of the illegal activity that produced them. Money laundering covers a vast array of illegal conduct. Anyone who gains money illegally must find a way to "clean" the money in order to use it in society. There are variations among the many different definitions; people view the crime of money laundering in several different ways.

Money laundering is basically the means used to convert funds that proceed from illegal activities, such as narcotics trafficking, prostitution, casino gambling, skimming, and many others, into financial uses that involve legal instruments. These instruments include bank deposits, investments in stocks and bonds, real estate, and others. Money gets into the banking system in a variety of ways: cash deposits over the counter, wire transfers from one bank to another, and letters of credit from legitimate businesses.

The laundering of money becomes effective when it penetrates the legitimate business world. Once money laundering infects the banking system, it opens the way for all kinds of illegal activities. The process of money laundering has devastating social consequences, as well as economic consequences. According to FinCEN, money laundering provides the fuel for drug dealers, terrorists, arms dealers, and other criminals to operate and expand their criminal enterprises. money laundering has the potential of eroding the integrity of financial institutions.

The term *money laundering* appears to have begun in the United States. It may have been Al Capone who began the using the term. During Capone's era, criminals were trying to hide the proceeds of their illicit businesses. In order to accomplish this task, launderettes and car washes were often purchased in order to mix dirty money with clean money. Capone used a string of coin-operated laundromats in Chicago to disguise his profits from gambling, prostitution, racketeering, and violation of the Prohibition laws. The cash businesses provided a perfect opportunity to combine the proceeds of legal and illegal activity.

There appear to be four factors common in money laundering. First, the ownership and source of the money must be concealed. Second, the form of the currency itself is changed. Third, the trail of the money laundering process must be hidden from beginning to end. Lastly, constant control must be maintained over the money laundering process itself. There are three distinct stages to the money laundering cycle. Initially there is immersion, which is consolidation and placement. The second step involves layering. Here, the money is separated from its original source. Money may be moved from account to account creating a diverse web of transactions, which are not easy to follow. Finally, the focus is on repatriation and integration. Here, the cleansed funds are brought back into circulation. Obviously the smaller the amount of money to be laundered, the quicker and easier the process.

WORLD'S THIRD-LARGEST BUSINESS

The profits of crime that make their way into the financial systems throughout the world are staggering and problematic. Officials suggest that between $200 billion and $500 billion are laundered throughout the world each year. After foreign exchange and the oil industry, the laundering of money is the world's third largest business. The Financial Action Task Force (FATF) calculates that between $400 and $500 billion in drug money is laundered each year. In 1995, the sum of $500 billion is equal to two percent of the total annual production of the world, and equal to the gross domestic product of Mexico. Clearly, money laundering is not only a criminal action, it also greatly affects the entire world economy.

Many people besides drug and arms dealers and terrorists launder money. Corporations launder money, in a sense, to avoid or evade taxes, to defraud shareholders, to get around currency control regulations, and to bribe prospective clients. Common citizens launder money in order to hide it from a divorcing spouse or to halt erosion of their assets. Governments may also launder money in order to subvert terrorists or to arm freedom fighters. Clearly a variety of individuals are involved in money laundering, at many different levels.

In the past few years, several factors may have led to the growth in money laundering. Globalization of markets and financial flows has increased dramatically due to the internet. The internet has basically established a single market, which allows money to be moved from country to country in mere seconds. Another factor is that there are no

real global anti-money laundering rules. Each country deals with the problem differently. In fact, some countries do not deal with the problem at all. Another factor leading to an increase in money laundering is poverty itself. Countries and people who are poverty stricken or have enormous debts may look for new economic opportunities. Offshore financial services offer a tremendous opportunity to struggling countries. The confluence of high technology, the global economy, and the secretive offshore banking centers has created a money launderer's dream. A simple click of the mouse on an individuals' computer can transfer huge sums of money within seconds. Some experts say the technology of international criminal activity is way ahead of any governmental response.

REGULATION IN THE UNITED STATES

Increased regulations have made the laundering of money in the United States much more difficult. In addition, the United States enforces and prosecutes those individuals it suspects to be involved in this illegal activity. The toughening of anti-money laundering laws in this country has caused many criminals to look for alternative areas to hide their funds. Even though the United States expends great effort and money to deal with this problem, top U.S. officials admit that the enforcement system is fragmented and rather weak.

Prior to October 1970, people were bringing bags full of illegally obtained cash into banks for deposit. Often, questions were not asked of cash-loaded customers. These clients answered to no authority and were not investigated. Only until there was a violation of tax laws did anyone pay much attention to customer transactions. Obviously, the lack of scrutiny and law enforcement opened the door to wonderful opportunities for money launderers. Several important changes have taken place over the years since 1970.

In response to the abuse, Congress enacted the statute commonly referred to as the Bank Secrecy Act (BSA) which consists of two sets of provisions. The first set authorizes the secretary of the Treasury to require banks and other financial institutions to retain records to assure that the details of financial transactions can be traced if investigators need to do so. The second set of provisions authorizes the secretary of the Treasury to require financial institutions and in some other cases, other businesses and private citizens to report financial transactions of certain kinds.

The most important aspect of the BSA are the reporting rules. A currency transaction report (CTR) must be filed for every deposit over $10,000. The BSA has been amended many times since 1970. New amendments have given the Treasury Department a wider variety of regulatory tools to combat money laundering, especially since the BSA has historically had widespread non-compliance. In 1986, the Money Laundering Control Act was passed. This statute made money laundering a crime in its own right, and strengthened the BSA. In April 1990, the Financial Crimes Enforcement Network (FinCEN) was created by the secretary of the Treasury. Since its creation, FinCEN has sought to maximize information sharing among law enforcement agencies and its other partners in the regulatory and financial communities. In 1994, the agency was enhanced and given the BSA regulatory responsibilities.

Further strengthening the government's hand is the 1990 Depository Institution Money Laundering Amendment Act. This Act re-emphasized that the burden to report is clearly on the banks. In 1993, the Annunzio-Wylie Money Laundering Act was enacted which authorizes the government to require any financial institution, and its officers, directors, employees and agents, to report any suspicious transaction relevant to a possible violation of law or regulation.

In addition, this amendment to the BSA, also authorized the secretary to require financial institutions to carry out anti-money laundering programs, authorized special record-keeping rules relating to funds transfer transactions, and created the BSA Advisory Committee. Finally, the Annunzio-Wylie Money Laundering Act made operation of an illegal money transmitting business a crime, and enacted provisions requiring a re-examination of the charters of federally insured depository institutions convicted of money laundering.

In 1994 the BSA was again amended. The amendment came by way of the money laundering Suppression Act of 1994 (MLSA). This act required liberalization of the rules for exemption of transactions from the currency transaction reporting requirement. The act also authorized the Treasury Department to designate a single agency to receive reports of suspicious transactions from financial institutions. In addition, the act required all money transmitting businesses to register with the Treasury.

In October 1994, the Treasury Department's Office of Financial Enforcement (OFE) was merged with FinCEN. This merger created a single anti-money laundering agency. In effect, it combined regulatory, intelligence, and enforcement missions. Since this merger, FinCen has sought to streamline and simplify the BSA obligations of financial institutions. In addition, the reporting system has been reformatted to make the available data more useful for law enforcement investigations.

PATRIOT ACT

President George W. Bush signed the Patriot Act into law on October 26, 2001. This act was created as a reaction to the terrorist attacks on September 11. Title III of this law is of particular concern to banks and other financial institutions as it deals with anti-money laundering and requires new areas of compliance, beyond the stipulations already in place. New requirements under the Patriot Act include the institutionalization of the "know your customer" procedures. In addition, heightened transparency requirements regarding correspondent relationships with foreign banks and private banking relationships with foreign individuals were added.

The most important aspect of the Patriot Act is that the regulations apply not only to banks and thrifts, but also to broker-dealers in securities and commodities, mutual funds, money services businesses (issuers, redeemers, or cashiers of travelers checks, money orders, or similar instruments, and money transmitters), operators of credit card systems, and casinos. A number of new businesses have been set up to aid financial institutions trying to comply with anti-money laundering rules, especially those established following the September 11 terrorist attacks.

With each new regulation, the need for such aid continues to grow. Banks, credit unions, investment houses, brokers and dealers outside of banks, and money-transmitting businesses have quickly looked to these new businesses for assistance. Even jewelers, car dealers, and travel agencies have new requirements meant to prevent money laundering.

The nature of fighting money laundering has obviously changed 2001. In the past, money laundering worried governments because it was used to evade taxation and to hide the proceeds of other crimes. Even though these issues are still real, the new focus on money laundering surrounds the used of these funds for terrorism. Recently, the international community has pressured the world's 35 offshore centers to tighten their banking regulations, scrutinize their customers, and relax some secrecy laws. Many nations have signed treaties that allow for limited cooperation with foreign governments when drug money is involved. These efforts are not nearly enough.

SEE ALSO

drug trafficking; bank fraud; organized crime; United States; globalization; offshore entities; Bank Secrecy Act.

BIBLIOGRAPHY. Herbert E. Alexander and Gerald E. Caiden, eds., *The Politics and Economics of Organized Crime* (D.C. Heath, 1985); Daniel H. April and Angelo M Grasso, "Money Laundering," *The American Criminal Law Review* (v.38/3, 2001); Rachel Ehrenfeld, *Evil Money: Encounters Along the Money Trail* (Harper Business, 1992); Financial Crimes Enforcement Network, www.Fincen.gov (2003); Robert E. Grosse, *Drugs and Money: Laundering Latin America's Cocaine Dollars* (Praeger, 2001); Peter Lilley, *Dirty Dealing: The Untold Truth About Global Money Laundering* (Kogan Page, 2003); Jeffrey Robinson, *The Laundrymen: Inside the World's Third Largest Business* (Simon & Schuster, 1994).

DEBRA E. ROSS, PH.D.
GRAND VALLEY STATE UNIVERSITY

Morgan Grenfell Asset Management

WHEN ACCUSED Morgan Grenfell rogue trader Peter Young appeared for his court hearing in a red sweater, matching red skirt, black high heels, and red lipstick, it certainly made a great stir in London financial circles. How did the esteemed firm, British successor firm to the original J.S. Morgan and Co. and a component of the House of Morgan find itself in this ignominious position?

For over 100 years, Morgan Grenfell concentrated on the merchant banking business as established by Junius Morgan. Then, in an effort to keep current, the firm established a subsidiary, Morgan Grenfell Asset Management. It was this successful subsidiary which was traumatized by a scandal involving the rogue employee.

Young established outsized positions in a number of speculative small companies, including in July 1995, Xavier, a small Canadian company with questionable investments in oil fields in southern Russia and western Siberia, and a $30 million stake in a company called Solv-Ex, in March 1996. Solv-ex assets included plans to exploit Canadian Athabasca tar sands for oil through innovative chemical processing. Young's purchases came just the day before a report that the Federal Bureau of Investigation and the Securities and Exchange Commission were investigating Solv-ex due to the possible involvement of convicted stock swindlers, which triggered massive selling of the company's stock.

In fact, Solv-ex had been a speculative company for over a decade, and the efficacy of the company's touted new technologies was highly questionable. The promoters consistently used the traditional con man's technique of obfuscation: creation of so many conflicting reviews and outside analyst's reports that the truth was impossible to really determine, especially for the uninitiated.

Further damaging was the disclosure that Young had set up paired holding companies in order to circumvent British securities and investment regulations, which prohibit a single fund from owning more than 10 percent of any company. Morgan Grenfell became suspicious of the large quantities of unlisted shares, and concurrent with investigations by London regulators, the company shut down trading in three funds, until parent company Deutsch Bank (which had only recently purchased Morgan Grenfell) replaced the questionable assets with $300 million in cash. However when trading resumed, investors removed $400 million of assets. The estimated cost of this fiasco was perhaps $800 million including fines and compensation paid to the government and investors.

Morgan Grenfell's own investigations began in September 1996. Most substantive issues took a back seat to the image of Young, the rogue trader in pantyhose. Many suspected him of putting on a show in order to get the charges against him dropped. However when he attempted self-inflicted castration, the court did find him mentally ill, and prosecutors eventually lost the case against indicted co-conspirators.

SEE ALSO

stock fraud; securities fraud; Securities and Exchange Commission; United Kingdom.

BIBLIOGRAPHY. Sara Calian and Greg Steinmetz, "Stock Pro Uses Unusual Strategy to Avoid Prison," *Wall Street Journal* (April 30, 1999); "The Solv-Ex Scam?" www.fool.com/features (1996); "UK Fund Manager Faces Fraud Trial," BBC News (April 30, 1999); Julia Finch, "City High Flyer Who Heard Voices Urging Him to Change Sex," *The Guardian* (January 25, 2002); "Case Study: Morgan Grenfell," www.erisk.com (June 14, 2003); Simon Bowers, "Final Blow for Fraud Team" *The Guardian* (January 25, 2002).

JANE G. HAIGH
UNIVERSITY OF ARIZONA

Morgan, J. Pierpont (1837–1913)

J. P. MORGAN became the quintessential gentleman banker of the last quarter of the 19th century through a combination of inherited wealth, British connections, and a very Protestant version of chutzpah. J. P. Morgan and Co. was the American successor company to his father's J. S. Morgan of London, England, itself a successor to George Peabody, the first American merchant banker in London.

By the time J. P. Morgan took over, merchant bankers in the United States had become financiers who controlled not only business, but also government borrowing and financing, and Morgan was at the pinnacle of the group. Morgan prevailed in the railroad combines and railroad bond debacles of the 1870s and 1880s. In 1901, Morgan engineered the conglomerate that became U.S. Steel, made up of John D. Rockefeller mines and shipping companies, and Andrew Carnegie steel enterprises. The new company was patterned on a vision spun by young Charles M. Schwab, at the time an aide to Carnegie.

Political, ethnic, and religious differences among bankers permeated Wall Street, just as it did the rest of American society. Morgan's competitors included Jacob Schiff, the firm of Kuhn Loeb, Goldman, and Joseph Seligman. Just as Morgan was a conduit for British investment capital, and represented British investors, the "Jewish bankers" had access to German and French money. Morgan biographer, Ron Chernow asserts that "Pierpont's anti-Semitism was well-known," although Morgan later signed a protest when Seligman was barred from a fashionable Saratoga, New York, hotel.

When a panic, sparked in part by speculation in mining and railroad stocks, threatened to deplete the U.S. gold supply in 1895, Morgan brought together the financiers of the age, forming a syndicate which purchased $62 million in gold from Europe and traded it to the government in exchange for U.S. bonds, thus, reinforcing the gold reserves of the United States and propping up the gold standard.

President Grover Cleveland's own Democratic party was heavily allied with the Populists at the time. His enemies immediately portrayed this as yet another deal with the controlling interests on Wall Street. It did not help that the bankers had, in turn, sold the bonds at a handsome profit. Ironically, while the Populist rhetoric hinted at a conspiracy of Jewish bankers, Morgan represented the solidly Anglo-Protestant elite.

While Morgan professed a high regard for the public interest, he was perfectly capable of participating in market "corners" as he did with E. H. Harriman in the great Northern Pacific corner of 1901. Morgan had financed James J. Hills's purchase of the Chicago Burlington and Quincy railroad, consolidating it with his Great Northern and Northern Pacific. Fearing the trans-continental competition, Harriman sought to buy a stake in the new combine, and when rebuffed, set about secretly buying up $78 million in Northern Pacific shares. To protect their assets, Morgan and Hill began buying the stock themselves. With three bankers buying, the Northern Pacific stock kept rising, even as short-interest grew with every speculator on Wall Street expecting an imminent collapse. Every other stock on the market sank, as speculators were forced to sell other stock to maintain their positions. From 73 on May 4, the stock shot up to 1,000 before the entire market crashed. "Giants of Wall Street in fierce battle may precipitate crash that brings ruin to hordes of pygmies!" screamed the *New York Herald*, echoing the fears of the man on the street. Yet, President William McKinley, elected as a supporter of business, ignored public concern.

Then on September 6, 1901, McKinley was assassinated, and Morgan had to deal with Teddy Roosevelt. Morgan's "finest hour" came as a financial panic loomed in 1907. Wall Street had been expecting it. Averted in the spring, it finally came in October.

Morgan again mobilized New York's banking and finance elite to avert total economic collapse. Morgan would have said that his actions in limiting the damage on Wall Street stemmed from his deep sense of obligation to be of public service. Yet, one end result was the convenient acquisition by Morgan's U.S. Steel of the assets of the Tennessee Coal, Iron and Railroad Co. (TC&I) headquartered in Birmingham, Alabama, one of the few remaining independent steel producers.

Morgan organized the U.S. Steel trust in 1901 as an efficient, national industry that would eliminate wasteful duplication. It had begun in 1898 with the organization of Federal Steel from a number of smaller steel companies, the Minnesota Iron Company, and two railroads. In 1901, Morgan purchased all of the assets of Carnegie Steel as the centerpiece of the new trust, paying $480 million, more than the annual budget of the U.S. government. The new concern was capitalized at $1.4 billion.

The proximate cause of the 1907 panic was a failed attempt by speculators F. Augustus Heinze and Charles W. Morse to corner the stock of United Copper. The failure of the corner itself bankrupted a mining company, two brokerage houses, and a bank. But the worst was yet to come. Heinze and Morse had financed their run on the stock with loans from several New York trust companies. Trust companies at the time were a kind of unregulated state-chartered institution that functioned like a commercial bank, but with no reserve requirements. When news of the involvement of the Knickerbocker Trust spread through New York, depositors tried to withdraw their money.

The city's bankers met the demands of Knickerbocker's depositors for a few days, hoping to avert a wider panic. Morgan returned from the Episcopal Convention on Saturday, October 19, to meet the crisis, putting together a committee of leading bankers and financiers.

But by Tuesday, the team agreed to let Knickerbocker fail, setting off the wider panic. As the week progressed, Morgan took charge of impromptu committees of bankers, which he charged with raising the millions necessary to stabilize the trusts, brokerage houses, and banks, all reeling from the pressure to cover margin loans as stock prices sank. In effect, Morgan played the role of central banker

at a time when there was no national banking or reserve system.

It was near the end of the panic, that Grant Schley of the brokerage firm Moore and Schley, one of the largest on Wall Street, announced his imminent personal and business failure to Morgan and his team of bankers. Schley had used the securities of the TC&I as collateral for more than $35 million in loans, valuing the stock at $130 a share. But as the panic progressed, there was no market for any of the shares at that price. Morgan and U.S. Steel always maintained that they had done a favor for Schley and the markets by buying out the TC&I stock at $100 a share, a total of $30 million. The company was poorly run, not very profitable and its assets overvalued, they said.

But it was this transfer that gained the most ire from a country that had little understanding of banking or financial systems. While the transaction, approved by Roosevelt in advance, had put an end to the panic, Senate and House committees held highly publicized investigations in 1909 and again in 1911.

The experience of the 1907 panic led to the call for the establishment of a rudimentary monetary system. However, the establishment of the Federal Reserve did not become a reality before Morgan's death in Rome, Italy, at the age of 75 in 1913.

SEE ALSO

U.S. Steel; antitrust; Roosevelt, Theodore; Rockefeller, John D.; robber barons; antitrust; Roosevelt, Theodore.

BIBLIOGRAPHY. Ron Chernow, *House of Morgan* (Simon & Schuster, 1990); Jean Strouse, *Morgan* (Random House, 1999).

JANE G. HAIGH
UNIVERSITY OF ARIZONA

Morton-Thiokol

MORTON-THIOKOL is best known for its role in the explosion of the space shuttle *Challenger* on January 28, 1986. In 1973, Thiokol Chemical Corporation (later the company became Morton Thiokol, Inc.) was awarded an $800 million contract to manufacture solid rocket boosters for the National Aeronautics and Space Administration (NASA)

Morton-Thiokol tests a redesign of the solid rocket booster after the explosion of the space shuttle Challenger.

space shuttle program. The faulty O-ring seals developed by Thiokol ultimately failed in the right side solid rocket booster and caused the explosion of the spacecraft.

A subsequent investigation by the President's Commission on the Space Shuttle *Challenger* Accident, 1986, (the Rogers Commission), concluded that the failure of the O-rings and field joint was the primary cause of the *Challenger* explosion.

Early tests conducted by Thiokol indicated severe problems with the field joints on solid rocket boosters. Instead of closing and preventing the seepage of gases, the field joints were open and allowed hot combustion gases to leak and erode the O-rings. The erosion of the O-rings would necessarily cause the joints to explode, destroying the entire booster in the process as well as the spacecraft.

The failure of the field joints even destroyed secondary or failsafe O-rings. NASA's Marshall Space Flight Center classified the O-ring seals as Criticality 1, meaning they did not meet space shuttle requirements for failsafe standards. As such, the O-rings were considered extremely hazardous because they were subject to metal erosion, burning, and explosion.

Several Thiokol engineers openly expressed their concerns about the potential catastrophic costs associated with the faulty O-rings. One engineer, Roger Boisjoly, wrote a memo expressing these concerns about the O-rings and strongly urged the company to develop a team dedicated to quickly solving the problems. A task force was formed to investigate problems with the O-rings and field joints. However, they never reached a conclusion or solution to the problem primarily because of a lack of resources and reluctance by management to fully investigate the problem.

At the time, the company was in the process of renegotiating its contract with NASA. Seriously researching and resolving the O-ring problem most likely would have resulted in a lengthy delay of the shuttle launch, jeopardized the potentially lucrative second contract with NASA, and ultimately adversely affected Thiokol's profits. Eventually, Thiokol requested that NASA consider the O-ring problem resolved and just five days before the *Challenger* launch, officials at Marshall considered the matter closed.

Beyond erosion problems, Thiokol engineers also had knowledge that cold weather conditions severely affected the ability of the O-rings to effectively compress and contract and therefore seal out hot gases. The day before the *Challenger* launch, Thiokol engineers were concerned about the unexpectedly low temperatures at the Kennedy Space Center in Florida and contacted NASA officials to discuss the potential hazards of launching under cold weather conditions. Thiokol engineers recommended that the launch be delayed and not take place until weather conditions were about 53 degrees Fahrenheit.

This recommendation was not well received by NASA officials who were adamantly opposed to any further delays and Thiokol's conclusions regarding temperature levels. In this respect, Thiokol was under tremendous pressure to change their launch recommendation. Despite strong objections from Thiokol engineers, officials at the company reversed their position and approved the launching of the *Challenger*.

At the time of the launch, the temperature had reached a low of 36 degrees Fahrenheit and there was ice build-up on the launch pad. The *Challenger* tragically exploded only 73 seconds after launch, killing seven crewmembers including a schoolteacher, Christa McAuliffe, who was to conduct a lesson for her students from space.

SEE ALSO

Challenger Disaster; unsafe products; corporate criminal liability; whistleblowers.

BIBLIOGRAPHY. President's Commission on the Space Shuttle *Challenger* Accident, *Accident Report* (U.S. Government Printing Office, 1986); Ronald C. Kramer, "The Space Shuttle Challenger Explosion," *White-Collar Crime Reconsidered* (Northeastern University Press, 1992); Diane Vaughn, *The Challenger Launch Decision: Risky Technology, Culture, and Deviance at NASA* (University of Chicago Press, 1996); R.S. Lewis, *Challenger: The Final Voyage* (Columbia University Press, 1988).

JASON DAVIS
UNIVERSITY OF SOUTH FLORIDA

multinational corporations

AN INTERNATIONAL corporation is one which pursues business activities in one or more countries other than its home country. A multinational company is one in which a significant proportion of activities occur away from the home country. A global company is one which does not recognize a home country, but which conducts its activities on the basis of whichever location happens to be the most appropriate and efficient. In each of these cases, the organization is motivated by profit and considers activities in countries where they can obtain either new resources or new markets.

Multinational corporations first emerged as early as ancient Assyria and Mesopotamia, when overseas trading ventures were organized by partnerships of private individuals and facilitated by state governments. With people moving away from their homelands for trade, the influence of foreign ideas and customs and the absence of moderating home influence led many to behave in ways which would not be considered appropriate or legal at home. This has included not just marital infidelity and immoderate behavior, but mistreatment of workers, dishonesty in dealings, and the deliberate sale of goods of unacceptable quality.

In subsequent centuries, multinational companies became identified with the idea of colonization and the expansion of mainly European empires into third world areas. As a result, multinational corporations such as the British and Dutch East India Company, among others, were granted privileges by their home governments that enabled them to use military means to obtain desired markets and resources. This license allowed corporations and their representatives ample opportunity to benefit from fees, fines, and compensations paid by defeated states to the victorious corporations, as was the case with Robert Clive and the East India Company in defeating the Moghul Empire in India.

The creation of multinational companies in support of colonial empires enabled truly international trading networks on a large and stable basis. One of the most well-known was the triangular trade in rum, molasses, and slaves connecting New England, the Caribbean, and Africa. Another network of international trade, which would now be considered illegal, involved the forced importation of opium into China by British companies in return for Chinese silks and precious goods.

The 19th and early 20th centuries saw an intensification of international trading and business activities, with the growth of industry improving transportation and communication links lending great assistance to cross-border activities. Investors, particularly in London, England, and other great financial centers, were able to establish sophisticated portfolios of investment. The railroad era for the first time necessitated the creation of private networks of capital for use domestically; previous networks had been supported or facilitated by states through the formation of empire.

This process was halted by World War I and greatly hampered by the subsequent retreat away from free trade and toward tariffs that followed. Subsequently, the Great Depression of the 1930s had a huge worldwide impact because of the reach of international companies. However, this period did witness a number of important international agreements which facilitated the growth in importance of multinational companies. World War II offered the opportunity for the Allied Powers to try to redefine the international economic system and avoid the chaos that had marked previous years. This was attempted through the creation of the Bretton Woods system, pegging currencies to the dollar, the establishment of the World Bank and the International Monetary Fund, together with the inauguration of the General Agreement on Tariffs and Trade.

At the same time, the desire to create an architecture of international order to prevent such terrible warfare from recurring contributed to the stability of international relations and hence the ability of corporations to undertake international business. The subsequent creation of trading blocs such as the European Economic Community in 1957 further contributed to this process. In addition to internationalization becoming more convenient, it also features the increasingly rapid dissemination of business knowledge and common business systems around the globe. This has included not just awareness of the skills and competencies necessary to be an effective manager but, also, common standards in such fields as accountancy and financial regulation. These have both resulted from and stimulated further internationalization, as well as more tortuous governmental negotiations.

These international arrangements have made it much harder for companies in certain industries to maintain the cartels they had previously operated, although it is still difficult to tell whether firms are acting similarly for sound business reasons or because of collusion. Legislation in a number of countries has outlawed cartel activity, which was seen as axiomatic of business people by economist Adam Smith. However, improvements in global communications and transportation have made transfer pricing (in which members of a single multinational firm sell inputs to each other at non-market prices to avoid tax) and dumping (deliberately undercutting competitors in some markets by selling at reduced prices, or even below production costs) more prevalent activities.

Since the late 1970s and 1980s, the Western world has undergone something of an ideological change with much greater credence being placed on the value of markets in regulating activities and in monitoring the behavior of actors within them. This has meant the progressive deregulation of business, the lowering of corporate rates of taxation, and the increasing willingness of government agencies to do as the business sector would wish them to do. Inevitably, this has led to occasions of corruption and crime, and challenges to definitions of what is considered to be acceptable and legal. The close collaboration between the U.S. government and U.S. corporations in the rebuilding of Iraq in 2004 is one example of this, as is the U.S. support in multilateral trade agreements of genetically modified food technology in which U.S. corporations have a significant interest.

At the same time, growing awareness among consumers and communities at large of the impact of business upon the environment and of the activities of corporations, together with the increased ability that people have to organize themselves through information technology, have provided an important counterweight to corporate power, with many forced revelations of practices concerning sustainable development and of executive compensation. Non-governmental organizations (NGOs) such as Greenpeace have been very active in revealing environmental mismanagement, such as happened with Union Carbide's chemical pollution in Bhopal, India, while Amnesty International and the International Labor Organization (ILO) have paid attention to abuses of human rights by some companies, as well as the use of child labor and other abuses of workers.

SEE ALSO

Greenpeace; Union Carbide; capitalism; globalization; global warming; labor crimes; Asia; South America.

BIBLIOGRAPHY. David Landes, *The Wealth and Poverty of Nations* (Abacus, 1999); Kenneth Pomeranz, *The Great Divergence: China, Europe, and the Making of the Modern World Economy* (Princeton University Press, 2000); Nigel Thrift, "The Globalization of the System of Business Knowledge," *Globalization and the Asia-Pacific: Contested Territories* (Routledge, 1999).

JOHN WALSH, PH.D.
MAHIDOL UNIVERSITY, THAILAND

N

19th-century regulation

THROUGHOUT THE 19th century, change characterized every aspect of life in the United States. The economy changed from a nation of farmers and shopkeepers living in small towns to a country where one out of three people lived in a city, and instead of working for themselves worked in a factory for a wage. Lawmakers responded to these economic changes in two very different ways.

From 1830 to 1890, the U.S. government promoted economic development enacting legislation that benefited the growth of business, particularly big business. Beginning in 1890, lawmakers responded to public outrage at big business by a changing its emphasis from promotion of economic activity, to one of regulation based on an increasingly bureaucratic model of public policy.

Many scholars characterize the governmental response to industrialization as *laissez-faire* capitalism. *Laissez-faire* refers to the government policy of letting the market regulate business without the interference of the government. The question was not whether there should be economic growth, but how that economic growth should be managed, and for whose benefit: business or the workers? During the last quarter of the 19th century, industrialization and urbanization generated enough social pressure that government policy, in particular the Congress, diverged from its policy of *laissez-faire* to a policy of limited regulation.

PROMOTING BUSINESS

Taking control of Congress in the 1860s, Republicans embraced policies and programs that promoted economic enterprise. Congress extended massive subsidies to transcontinental railroad developers through land grants. The Pacific Railroad Bill of 1862 granted enormous amounts of federal land to the Union Pacific-Central Pacific Railroad, the first of the transcontinentals.

Congress passed other measures that promoted economic enterprise, including the Morrill Land-Grant Act, a law that donated 30,000 acres of federal land to every state for each of its Senators and Representatives. These and other promotional activities were dramatic evidence of federal intervention in the economy.

State legislatures and local governments promoted business by adopting laws and policies favorable to business. For example, some states in the 1870s realized they could make themselves attractive to big business by offering a corporate charter that provided broad powers. The states of Delaware, West Virginia, and New Jersey offered such charters. During the 1870s, however, most direct and local aid came to a gradual end. Large-scale bankruptcies, swindlers, and defalcations on bonds following the depression of 1873, and helped put to an end many of the state programs designed to promote business.

Industrialization and urbanization released social changes that this traditional distributive scheme was incapable of accommodating. Third parties and social reform movements launched an attack on distributive politics by offering a new view of law and legal institutions designed to serve disaffected social constituencies. For example, the Populist Party traced the severe economic distresses caused by industrialization to the growing control of large corporations, especially railroads, over government. Opposition to distributive politics also came from the social elite of the cities (professionals, intellectuals, and old money), known as mugwumps, who pushed for reform of urban politics, the introduction of the secret ballot, and scientific corporate management rather than partisan management by government.

Through the last quarter of the 19th century, the states were the center of regulatory activity limiting corporate enterprise, protecting children and women laborers, and forming bureaus and independent regulatory commissions. As the economy became more national in scope, regulatory authority moved to the federal government.

STATE AND FEDERAL REGULATION

State regulation grew in response to the railroad. Massachusetts, in 1869, passed legislation giving its pre-Civil War railroad commission general supervision of all railroads, with authority to examine them and to make certain they complied with the law. The commission, as was typical of most early state regulatory bodies, had the power to set rates or to enforce what it deemed reasonable rates. Its role was strictly advisory. In most states with commissions, state legislatures retained the right to review and change any decisions of the railroad commission. As a result, state railroad commissions were subject to political influence of the railroad financiers.

The Industrial Revolution also prompted changes in the workplace and in the structure of the labor force. These enormous changes were translated into two separate developments. The first was an increasing incidence of violent confrontation between labor and capital. A cut in wages, for example, by the Baltimore and Ohio Railroad in 1877, precipitated nationwide rioting that culminated in the destruction of millions of dollars worth of railroad property. Unionization was the second response to industrialization. Just as capital sought to mobilize its resources, labor gradually accepted that it, too, would have to bring its collective power to bear.

State legislatures responded to developments in the labor market in often contradictory ways. On the one hand, the violence associated the labor movement was translated into harsh anti-union statutes. An 1885 Alabama law banned boycotts and picketing that blocked strikebreakers. The fear of social disorder that attended the labor movement was also a stimulus for reform.

Several states outlawed the blacklist, which employers used to keep union members, once fired, from being rehired. The "yellow dog" contract, which pledged a worker as a condition of employment not to join a union, was also outlawed in several states but persisted in others until the New Deal of the 1930s. Other statutes forbade paying workers in scrip (a certificate constituting a kind of money) and required regular paydays.

The regulatory efforts of Congress after the Civil War were tentative and often contradictory, pulled as they were, on the one hand, by the nationalizing forces of the economy and, on the other, by a traditional respect for the rights of the states and the democratic impulse of the era's mass two-party system. Congress was a political institution in an era in which party politics dominated legislation.

ADMINISTRATIVE AGENCIES

The late 19th century response to economic consolidation was the administrative agency, a hybrid governmental institution that combined executive, legislative, and judicial functions. These bodies were separate from both the legislature and courts. Yet they legislated, in that they adopted regulations that had the force of law; they also adjudicated in that they held hearings and rendered quasi-judicial opinions. This "fourth branch" of government, nowhere mentioned in the Constitution, exercised delegated powers from the legislature, fulfilling on a day-to-day basis the oversight functions of regulation that a legislative body was incapable of doing.

The two most important early federal regulatory measures were aimed at the new economy's most vital elements: railroads and manufacturing. The Interstate Commerce Commission (ICC) of 1887 and the Sherman Antitrust Act of 1890 reveal the mix of political and administrative solutions to the problems created by economic growth. Congress kept one foot in the old world of distributive politics, while stepping tentatively into a future of administrative regulation. The end result was an incoherent, unworkable policy from which no one benefited.

The ICC reflects the tentative policy of Congress toward regulating and reforming business practices. Only after the Supreme Court struck down an Illinois railroad regulation, in *Wabash, St. Louis & Pacific Railroad Company v. Illinois* (1886) did Congress enact legislation creating the ICC. This case struck the death knell for state regulation of railroads. The Interstate Commerce Act addressed the problem of railroads charging different customers different prices for the same service. The ICC Act provided that all customers had to be treated in a similar fashion and required that all charges be reasonable and just.

Congress created a commission of five members to hear complaints about railroad practices and to undertake investigations on its own initiative. The president appointed the members of the commission with the advice and consent of the Senate, and they served staggered terms at the pleasure of the president for a maximum of six years. No more than three commissioners could come from the same political party, diminishing fears of partisan control of commission policy, but falling short of the reformers' demands for apolitical experts.

Congress essentially paralyzed the ICC by demanding that the ICC balance the interests of too many parties, which resulted in deadlock and inactivity. Despite its shortcomings, the original ICC was an important event in the history of 19th century law in the United States. It provided the building block upon which the administrative state of the 20th century subsequently arose.

Congressional response, in the form of the Sherman Antitrust Act, to the problem of economic competition reflects the ambivalence with which Congress and the American people viewed direct governmental intervention in the market. However, both Congress and the American public recognized the genuine threat of monopoly power to the economic order of free enterprises created by new conglomerates, such as John D. Rockefeller's Standard Oil. Both Congress and the American people feared that if a single company was able to monopolize, or drive all other companies out of business that sold the product, consumers would be forced to pay a higher price for the product.

THE PROBLEMATIC SHERMAN ACT

The Sherman Antitrust Act declared that "every contract, combination in the form of trust or otherwise, or conspiracy, in restraint of trade or commerce among the several states or with foreign nations, is hereby declared illegal." The act created no administrative structure, as had the Interstate Commerce Act; instead, the task of enforcement fell to the Department of Justice and federal courts. Violators were susceptible to fine, imprisonment, and, in the case of corporations, dissolution. The lack of administrative structure reflects Congressional intent to both regulate and promote. This ambivalence is reflected in the fact that the Sherman Act does not ban all corporate combinations.

The Sherman Act was problematic in another way. While the act covered transportation of goods across state lines, there was at least reasonable debate about whether manufacturing (the production of goods, even by a corporation that operated in several states) was encompassed within the statute and the commerce clause of the Constitution. Manufacturing had traditionally been treated as a local enterprise, the control of which properly belonged to the states. But the rise of an industrial market economy of transcontinental proportions posed difficult regulatory problems for the states.

The overwhelming support for the measure, which passed the Senate by a vote of 52 to 1 and by voice vote in the House of Representatives, suggests that critics thought the Supreme Court would nullify it. In any case, in a pattern repeated throughout the legal history of the United States, members of Congress were willing, given the diverse political pressures that played on them, to permit the federal courts to give meaning to the nation's first and most important antitrust act.

SEE ALSO
Sherman Antitrust Act; antitrust; Interstate Commerce Commission Act.

BIBLIOGRAPHY. Kermit L. Hall, *The Magic Mirror: Law in American History* (Oxford University, 1989); Morton J. Horwitz, *The Transformation of American Law 1780–1860* (Harvard University Press, 1990); Lawrence Friedman, *A History of American Law* (Simon & Schuster, 1973); Harold Hyman, Harold and William M. Wiecek, *Equal Justice Under Law: Constitutional Developments 1835–75* (Harper and Row, 1982); Jonathon Lurie, *Law and the Nation 1865–1912* (Knopf, 1983); Charles W. McCurdy, "The Knight Sugar Decision of 1895 and the Modernization of American Corporation Law, 1869–1903," *Business History* (v.53, autumn 1979); Stephen Skowronek, *Building a New American State: The Expansion of National Administrative Capacities 1877–1920* (Cambridge University Press, 1982).

MICHAEL MCGREGOR
GEORGE MASON UNIVERSITY

Nader, Ralph (1924–)

CONSUMER ADVOCATE, lawyer, environmentalist, feminist, and presidential candidate, Ralph Nader has forged a unique place in American culture and politics. Nader was born in Winsted, Connecticut. He graduated from Princeton University in 1955 and earned a law degree from Harvard in 1958. After practicing law for a brief period in Hartford, Nader arrived in Washington, D.C., in 1963 to work for Daniel Moynihan, the assistant secretary of labor. Nader wrote numerous articles for such diverse publications as *The Nation* and the *Christian Science Monitor*.

Pursuing an interest developed at Harvard, Nader also served as a voluntary adviser to a Senate subcommittee investigating automobile safety. He soon developed a special interest in the Corvair produced by General Motors (GM). Consumers who had bought the Corvair between 1960 and 1963 had filed 106 lawsuits against General Motors for a total of over $40 million.

The chief problem with the Corvair was that ignition switches sometimes stuck causing drivers to lose steering control. In his book, *Unsafe at Any Speed: The Designed-In Dangers of the American Automobile*, Nader used his skills as a lawyer to prepare a scathing indictment of GM in such a way that he was safe from legal actions that GM could take against him.

Since GM had no legal grounds to go after Nader, they hoped to discover something that would discredit him. GM hired two private detectives to follow him. When Nader discovered the detectives, he sued GM for violation of privacy, and the huge corporation was forced to publicly admit its guilt. Nader received a $425,000 settlement, most of which he used to create the Public Interest Research Group (PIRG) to serve as a permanent watchdog for consumer interests. By May 1969, when GM stopped producing the Corvair, Nader had become a household name of consumer advocacy.

In June 1968, Nader gathered a group of seven young lawyers with similar watchdog interests who became known as Nader's Raiders. The following summer, Nader selected 200 applicants for Nader's Raiders from a pool of 30,000 applicants and targeted the Interstate Commerce Commission (ICC). Nader sent the young lawyers into various corporations and agencies to get information to protect workers, taxpayers, and the environment.

In 1969, Nader set out to make automobile tires safer. He had evidence that the polyester used in the production of tires was likely to cause dangerous failures on the open road. His research revealed that tire manufacturers were withholding information in advertisements for their products, including the results of road tests that indicated safety problems. Additionally, it was revealed that tire manufacturers were recouping their losses from recalled tires by using loopholes in existing laws to recycle the tires by selling them abroad.

Nader forced General Motors to agree to release results of tests when consumers requested them, engineered truth in advertising of tires, helped to close loopholes in laws, and lobbied for the rights of consumers to file class-action lawsuits against tire manufacturers. Even Congress was not sacred to Nader. In 1971, in his magazine article, "Making Congress Work," Nader accused Congress of being too heavily influenced by lobbyists and other special interest groups and contended that they were unable to check the abuses of campaign finance. More than 30 years later, campaign finance and its regulation remain top concerns for the U.S. public and Congress.

Beginning with his 1965 attack on General Motors, Nader has been instrumental in achieving improvements in automobile safety, including laminated windshields, collapsible steering assemblies, enhanced door locks, shoulder harnesses, head restraints, safer tires and fuel tanks, and automobile recalls. Additionally, Nader's consumer watchdog role has focused on nuclear power, tax reform, meatpacking, education, banking, communications, and rights for consumers, workers, nursing home patients, the elderly, the disabled, and airline passengers.

ENACTING LAWS

Nader, along with supporters and other independent organizations, successfully lobbied Congress to enact the National Traffic and Motor Vehicle Safety Act of 1966; the Wholesome Meat Act of 1967; the National Gas Pipeline Safety Act of 1968; the Radiation Control for Health and Safety Act of 1968; the Coal Mine and Safety Act of 1969; the Truth in Lending Act of 1968; the Fair Credit Report Act of 1970; the Occupational Safety Act of 1979; the Fair Credit Billing Act of 1974; the Equal Credit Opportunity Act; the Fair Credit Report Act; the Fair Credit Billing Act; the Clean Air Act; and the Freedom of Information Act.

The consumer protection agencies that Nader has founded include the Center for the Study of Responsive Law, the PIRG, the Center for Auto Safety, Public Citizen, the Clean Water Action Project, the Disability Rights Center, the Pension Rights Center, and the Project for Corporate Responsibility. He has also worked with others to form a number of other consumer protection groups.

In the 2000 election, one of the closest presidential elections in history, Nader garnered 2,858,843 popular votes (2.74 percent). Some analysts argued Nader took votes away from Democratic candidate Al Gore, allowing Republican George W. Bush to win the presidency amid bitter controversy. After the election, Nader returned to watchdog interests. In 2002, after reading an article in the *Washington Post* about the financial problems of the District of Columbia's public library, he set out on a rescue mission. In 2003, Nader chose the accounting profession as his target and formed the Association for Integrity to monitor the activities of the Securities and Exchange Commission (SEC) and various other regulatory agencies.

SEE ALSO

Unsafe at any Speed; Corvair; Truth in Lending Act; consumer deaths; automobiles; corporate liability; unsafe products; Securities and Exchange Commission; campaign finance.

BIBLIOGRAPHY. David Bollier, "Citizen Actions and Other Big Ideas: A History of Ralph Nader and the Modern Consumer Movement," www.nader.org (2003); Robert F. Buckhorn, *The People's Lawyer* (Prentice Hall, 1972); David Campbell, "Ralph Rides Again," CFO (May 2003); James Martin, *Nader: Crusader, Spoiler, Icon* (Perseus, 2000); Charles McCarry, *Citizen Nader* (Saturday Review Press, 1972); Ralph Nader, "Making Congress Work," *New Republic* (August 21, 1971; Ralph Nader, *Unsafe at Any Speed: The Designed-In Dangers of the American Automobile* (Grossman, 1972); Stuart M. Speiser, *Lawsuit* (Horizon, 1980).

ELIZABETH PURDY, PH.D.
INDEPENDENT SCHOLAR

National Association of Securities Dealers

THE NATIONAL Association of Securities Dealers (NASD), which operates subject to Securities and Exchange Commission (SEC) oversight, is the largest self-regulatory organization in the United States, with a membership that includes virtually every broker-dealer in the country that does a securities business with the public. The NASD develops rules and regulations, conducts regulatory reviews of members' business activities, and designs and operates marketplace services and facilities. Established under authority granted by the 1938 Maloney Act Amendments to the Securities Exchange Act of 1934, Congress established a system of self-regulation for securities brokers and dealers paralleling those earlier created for the securities exchanges.

Under federal law, virtually every securities firm doing business with the American public is a member of this organization. Roughly 5,300 brokerage firms, over 93,000 branch offices, and more than 664,000 registered securities representatives come under its jurisdiction. NASD carries out its regulatory responsibilities through a variety of activities.

First, NASD registers and tests securities professionals. Second, it conducts onsite examinations of securities firms to determine their compliance with federal securities laws. Third, NASD oversees the rules of the Municipal Securities Rulemaking

Board and NASD rules and regulations. Fourth, the NASD performs continuous automated surveillance of the markets operated by The NASDAQ stock market. Fifth, it reviews advertising, sales literature, and underwriting arrangements proposed by securities firms in connection with new securities offerings. Sixth, the NASD enters into cooperative programs with governmental agencies and industry organizations to solve problems affecting investors, public companies, and securities firms.

NASD also offers a variety of services, including arbitration and mediation to enable investors and broker-dealer firms to resolve disputes, and telephone inquiry service to provide investors with background information on securities firms and their sales personnel. Governance of NASD is provided by a board composed an equal mix of public representatives and industry professionals.

NASD EXAMINATIONS

All NASD members are subject to field examination by NASD. NASD members are examined either annually or periods of up to once every four years depending on the nature of the firm's business activities, method of operation, and type of products sold. NASD reviews both the financial and operational condition of the firm, as well as its sales practices. During a routine examination, a member's books and records are examined for currency and accuracy. Sales practices are reviewed to determine whether the firm has dealt fairly with customers when making recommendations, executing orders, and charging commissions or markups and markdowns. Routine examinations also seek to determine member compliance with anti-fraud provisions of the Securities Exchange Act of 1934, the Securities Act of 1933, the NASD advertising rules, and Regulation T of the Federal Reserve Board which governs the extension of credit (margin) by brokers and dealers.

In addition to routine field examinations, NASD conducts thousands of investigations each year involving matters such as customer complaints, terminations of registered persons for cause, financial problems, and questionable sales practices or fraud. NASD's market regulation employs a number of sophisticated computer systems to monitor trading on the Nasdaq stock market. Among these is the Nasdaq Equity Audit Trail, which provides a fully integrated database of second-by-second quotations, transactions, and clearing detail for all NASDAQ securities on a firm-by-firm basis. The historical record of trading in NASDAQ securities is used in a broad range of NASD surveillance systems, and provides an efficient and effective means of overseeing ongoing trading activity in the NASDAQ market.

NASD PENALTIES

NASD disciplinary procedures are not designed to recover damages or to obtain relief for any party. Instead, they are used to promote membership compliance with high standards of commercial honor, and just and equitable principles of trade by appropriately penalizing those who fail to comply. Depending on the nature of the violations, NASD may sanction a member or an associated person by imposing any one or more of the following penalties: censure, fine, suspension or expulsion of a firm from membership in the NASD, or the suspension or revocation of a person's license to sell securities. NASD's disciplinary procedures provide appropriate rights of appeal. The SEC also receives and may review NASD final decisions if disciplinary action has been taken against a member or an associated person.

Any securities professional associated with a member firm including partner, officers, directors, branch managers, department supervisors, and salespersons must register with the NASD. The registration application requires information about the individual's prior employment and disciplinary history. The NASD and five other self-regulatory organizations, along with 13 member firms, developed a continuing education program that is uniform across the securities industry. NASD evaluates members' communications with the public to assure that they are fair and not misleading. These communications might consist of advertisements, as well as brochures, form letters, or research reports. NASD regulations require members to submit for review certain communications with the public, such as mutual fund sales literature or advertising.

New members must file all advertising prior to use for a period of one year, and NASD investigates customer complaints involving member communications with the public, and conducts periodic spot checks of material that is not required to be filed on a routine basis.

SEE ALSO
securities fraud; Securities and Exchange Commission; stock fraud; accounting fraud; fiduciary fraud.

BIBLIOGRAPHY. National Association of Securities Dealers, Inc., *Manual* (2002); Richard W. Jennings, Harold Marsh, Jr., John C. Coffee, Jr., and Joel Seligman, *Securities Regulation: Cases and Materials* (Foundation Press, 1998).

MICHAEL MCGREGOR
GEORGE MASON UNIVERSITY

National Highway Traffic Administration

THE NATIONAL HIGHWAY Traffic Safety Administration (NHTSA) is responsible for "reducing deaths, injuries and economic losses resulting from motor vehicle crashes," through the means of "setting and enforcing safety performance standards" as well as "providing grants to local and state governments to enable them to conduct effective local highway safety programs," according to its public relations literature.

Following a decade-long period of rising traffic casualties, increased public outcry, and the publication of Ralph Nader's Unsafe at Any Speed, in 1966 Congress held a series of hearings to determine whether a regulatory agency for traffic safety should be created. In passing of Highway Safety Act, the National Highway Safety Bureau was established, which in 1970 became the National Highway Traffic Safety Administration under the newly established Department of Transportation. Joan Claybrook, who would later go on to run Nader's consumer advocacy group, Public Citizen, was chosen to be the automotive and traffic safety bureau's first administrator.

With an annual budget of $434 million and with more than 600 employees, the NHTSA has a multi-faceted approach to ensuring drivers' safety. In addition to routinely recommending recalls and creating programs to educate the public, the administration publishes valuable statistics through its subdivision, the National Center for Statistics and Analysis, which informs the public on the precise danger that lies on America's roads.

AUTOMOTIVE RATINGS

The administration also contains a subdivision called the New Car Assessment Program, which rates, on a five-star scale, the frontal, side, and rollover resistance protection of hundreds of motor vehicles by make, model, and year. About three car models per year receive a five-star rating in every category.

In conjunction with the Environmental Protection Agency (EPA), The NHTSA regulates the Corporate Average Fuel Economy (CAFE), a statistic that sets the standard for fuel economy, which is defined as the average mileage possible of an automobile per one gallon of gasoline. Fuel economy is separated to consider terrain: there is a city mileage average and a highway mileage average.

The NHTSA and its Resource Center publish annually the *Traffic Safety Materials Catalog*, a publication containing topics of information ranging from air bags to youth safety. As with most government publications, all of the information contained in the publication is available free to the public on request.

In 2004, the NHTSA reported that since its inception, the bureau has recalled over 300 million cars, trucks, buses, motorcycles, child seats, and other motor vehicle-related products due to safety defects, or simply not complying with a Federal Motor Vehicle Safety Standard.

SEE ALSO
Nader, Ralph; *Unsafe at Any Speed*; automobile; Corvair; Ford Pinto.

BIBLIOGRAPHY. National Highway Traffic Safety Administration, www.nhtsa.dot.gov (2004); John Peter Rothe, *Beyond Traffic Safety* (Transaction Publishers, 1994).

KEVIN G. GOLSON
GOLSON BOOKS, LTD.

National Medical Enterprises

ORIGINALLY A PRIVATE California-based healthcare chain, National Medical Enterprises (NME) expanded quickly during the early 1980s and operated psychiatric hospitals throughout many areas of the United States, but primarily in Texas. As a for-profit private company traded publicly on the stock market, NME was driven to succeed financially. During times when insurance companies and employers across the United States increasingly funded psychiatric, alcohol, and drug treatment services, the opportunities for NME to profit were many.

By the end of the 1980s, however, some alarming accusations and reports were circulating about NME. In 1985, NME was accused of bribing political officials. By 1991, rumors attributed NME's massive profits to unethical conduct, exploitation, and lies. During a televised special the same year, one of NME's senior executives, Dr. Robert Stuckey, acknowledged that if an insurance company would pay $10,000 for alcoholism treatments and $50,000 for depression treatments, company doctors were instructed to change diagnoses to depression.

In the aftermath of Stuckey's comments, many former NME patients came forward with stories of abuse, fraud, and misery. Senator Mike Moncrief of Texas initiated a Senate inquiry. A settlement was reached between the Texas attorney general's office and NME, resulting in a $10 million penalty, which was the maximum fineable amount.

Still, NME attempted to maintain and expand its hospital chain and continued to bring in around $4 billion in revenues for 1991. Commercials played on television, detailing the quality of NME care, were only one component of NME's advertising campaign. Allegations went further than television ads, and claimed that NME officials were bribing police and probation officers and joining care groups like Alcoholics Anonymous to play up the importance of NME treatment.

Beginning after the original revelations by the whistleblower, Stuckey, shareholders began to file lawsuits against NME for fraud. Oddly, Stuckey died alone on his boat only days before he was scheduled to provide evidence to an inquiry by the U.S. House of Representatives in 1992. Even without Stuckey's evidence, NME was still held accountable for its actions. In 1992, 19 insurance companies sued NME for fraud and the lawsuits were settled with NME agreeing to pay more than $214 million. In June 1994, NME reached an agreement with the U.S. government, resulting in one of the largest settlements ever. The agreement, settling charges that NME paid bribes to doctors, referral services, and

others, cost NME $379 million, of which $33 million was a fine for criminal activity. Later in 1998, NME was sued by the Canadian provincial government of Ontario for similar reasons and complaints.

Earlier, in an attempt to improve its image, NME changed its name to Tenet Healthcare Corporation in 1994. Following years of illegally detaining patients, bribing officials, overcharging, and acting unethically, Tenet worked to clean up its reputation. However, controversy arose once again in 2000 when a St. Louis, Missouri, woman received shock treatments for psychiatric purposes that neither she nor her son agreed to. As a result, this particular Tenet hospital was put under investigation, which lasted until a monitored program averted closure of the hospital.

In 2003, Tenet Healthcare Corporation was the second-largest healthcare corporation in the United States and, along with its subsidiaries, it operated 114 hospitals across the country and employed 116,500 people.

SEE ALSO

healthcare fraud; insurance fraud; unnecessary surgery; medical malpractice; whistleblowers; bribery.

BIBLIOGRAPHY. "Company Fact Sheet," Tenet Healthcare Corporation, www.tenethealth.com (2003); "Psychiatric Hospitals: Money Spinners," *The Economist* (February 22, 1992); Tenet Healthcare Corporation, "Timeline of Major Events in the History of the Second-Largest Healthcare Corporation in America," www.ect.org/tenet (2003).

ARTHUR HOLST, PH.D.
WIDENER UNIVERSITY

National White-Collar Crime Center

IN 1980, LAW enforcement agencies from several states banded together to shutdown criminal operations such as heavy equipment theft, money laundering, and related white-collar criminal activities. Members of the Leviticus Project Associations realized the advantages and benefits of sharing information and pooling investigative resources. They expanded their mission to include investigations of the oil and natural gas industries and the precious metals industry. Desiring to extend the benefits to local and state criminal justice agencies nationwide, the Leviticus Project gave birth to the National White Collar Crime Center (NW3C) in 1992.

According to their public relations, the center's mission is to "provide a nationwide support system for agencies involved in the prevention, investigation, and prosecution of economic and high-tech crimes and to support and partner with other appropriate entities in addressing homeland security initiatives, as they relate to economic and high-tech crimes." The purpose of the NW3C is to link criminal justice agencies across jurisdictional borders. The center fulfills their mission by providing support through a combination of research, training, and investigative services.

The center is developing and implementing strategies to combat a rapidly emerging and technically sophisticated body of crimes that threatens economic prosperity. It is a federally funded, non-profit corporation whose membership primarily comprises law enforcement agencies, state regulatory bodies with criminal investigative authority, and state and local prosecution offices. While NW3C has no investigative authority itself, its job is to help law enforcement agencies better understand and utilize tools to combat economic and high-tech crime.

NW3C helps law enforcement agencies with a wide variety of tools, including, training, research, programs, and conferences. The center sponsors an annual Economic Crime Summit, recognized as an important venue to spotlight global economic crime with a focus on public and private-sector investigation and prevention initiatives.

The Economic Crime Summit offers attendees an exploratory environment dedicated to education and networking. Attendees typically include fraud and high-tech crime investigators, prosecutors, certified fraud examiners, auditors, loss prevention specialists, victim services advocates, academicians interested in white collar crime, and crime prevention specialists. Starting in 2004, the annual conference will be broken down into three regional conferences.

The center offers law enforcement training courses that range from introductory to advanced levels, and are free to law enforcement agency members. Through a joint effort with the Federal Bureau of Investigation (FBI) the center created the Internet Fraud Complaint Center (IFCC). Launched in May 2000, the IFCC is a resource established for law enforcement by law enforcement, providing a mechanism for consumers and businesses nationwide to report incidents of internet crime and other forms of fraud. In immediate support of national security, NW3C transformed IFCC into a terrorist tip portal shortly after the terrorist attacks of September 11, 2001. Over 303,000 terrorist tips were reported through the IFCC portal.

The National White Collar Crime Center is headquartered in Richmond, Virginia, and operates offices in Morgantown and Fairmount areas of West Virginia. It is a source for a wealth of information on the understanding, prevention, investigation and prosecution of economic crime, cyber crime and other high-tech crimes.

SEE ALSO

Better Business Bureaus; Securities and Exchange Commission; Environmental Protection Agency; prosecution; Justice, Department of.

BIBLIOGRAPHY. The National White-Collar Crime Center, "Helping America Fight Economic Crime," (Bureau of Justice Assistance Program Brief, 2002); Internet Fraud Complaint Center, www.ifccfbi.gov (2003); National White-Collar Crime Center, www.nw3c.org (2003).

DEBRA E. ROSS, PH. D.
GRAND VALLEY STATE UNIVERSITY

NatWest Markets

NATWEST MARKETS, the largest clearing bank in the United Kingdom in the mid-1990s and a financial trading unit of National Westminster Bank of London, specialized in corporate, treasury, and investment banking. In 1997, it discovered mispricing errors in interest rate options trades that dated back to 1994. The errors were subsequently traced to a rogue trader who had elevated his paycheck through fraud and a manager who had neglected his duty to supervise.

Kyriacos Papouis was a relatively low-profile, and low-paid, London-based trader in the rate risk management division of NatWest Markets. He earned an annual salary of about £80,000. In 1996, he left NatWest Markets just before the end of the year for a similar position at Bear, Stearns, a worldwide investment banking and securities trading and brokerage firm. By leaving, Papouis lost a projected bonus of £100,000. This bonus, a sum that surpassed Papouis's salary, came from the profits that he had supposedly generated for NatWest Markets by making trades with the firm's capital in the highly volatile interest rate options market.

Shortly after Papouis left, NatWest Markets discovered that he had lost about £50 million of the bank's money. In time, a full investigation would reveal that Papouis and his manager, Neil Dodgson, had actually sustained losses of £90 million by trading options and swaptions. (A swaption is an option on a swap, usually an interest rate swap, which is an agreement to exchange net future cash flows.)

Papouis, who traded German Deutschemark interest rate options and swaptions, had mismarked option positions in the bank's books in a concerted attempt to cover up the losses. Dodgson, who traded Sterling (GBP) interest rate options and swaptions, also mismarked positions and failed to exercise the "due skill, care and diligence" required of him by his regulators at the Securities and Futures Authority (SFA). Poor trading and adverse market movements caused the damages, while weaknesses in operations and internal controls had permitted the crime to occur. The losses were confined to interest rate option trades at NatWest Markets. No third parties lost money.

News of the scandal became public in February 1997. The case pointed out the danger of paying traders large bonuses dependent on the profits they generate, and giving them wide discretion over the risk that they take with their employer's capital. NatWest Markets insisted that it knew nothing of the loss-making trades. Papouis was suspended from Bear, Stearns. He was subsequently expelled from the SFA and fined £50,000 plus costs of £2,500. The less culpable Dodgson received a formal reprimand, a fine of £5,000 and was ordered to

The chaos of a bank trading room might lead to understanding how a low-level broker could hide £90 million in trading losses from the scrutiny of supervisors, as was the case at NatWest Markets.

pay costs of £2,500. Dodgson and a number of senior managers at the bank left their positions under pressure. The SFA heavily criticized NatWest Markets for its control failings. It discovered that NatWest Markets risk management process had failed to identify a clear case of mispricing for almost a year and then failed to spot the concealment of losing positions because of "significant and widespread non-compliance with internal minimum control standards." It fined the bank £420,000 including costs.

This rogue trading scandal badly damaged the reputation of NatWest Markets and its parent, National Westminster Bank, although the losses in the capital markets were small in relation to the massive size of the bank. Investor and shareholder confidence in NatWest Markets' management was severely shaken. In June 1997, NatWest Markets lost its chief executive officer, Martin Owen, as a direct result of the episode. In July 1997, the Bank of England attempted to conclude the matter by instructing NatWest Markets to resist calls for the resignation of the rest of its senior executives.

Despite this effort, the scandal did not disappear and it ultimately forced National Westminster Bank to accept a takeover bid from the Royal Bank of Scotland in February 2000, thus eliminating one of the oldest and mightiest banks in the United Kingdom.

SEE ALSO
bank fraud; accounting fraud; investment trust fraud; securities fraud; United Kingdom.

BIBLIOGRAPHY. Jon Ashworth, "NatWest Counts the Cost of Damage to Its Reputation," *The Times* (March 14, 1997); Jon Ashworth, "NatWest Fined by SFA," *The Times* (May 19, 2000); Robert Miller, "Former NatWest Trader Sent on Leave," *The Times* (March 4, 1997); Martin Waller, "City Censured by Bank Over 'Bonus Culture,'" *The Times* (March 3, 1997).

CARYN E. NEUMANN, PH.D.
OHIO STATE UNIVERSITY

negligence

THERE ARE FEW CONCEPTS in law more hotly contested than negligence. In popular usage, negligence is defined as carelessness and is commonly contrasted with intentional or deliberate harm. In legislation and the courts, however, it has evolved over several centuries into a complex, multi-faceted concept which was subject to competing interpretations by legal theorists, politicians, and the courts.

Negligence is a key legal term in both criminal and civil law. While there have been some cases of criminal negligence in the area of white-collar and corporate crime, it is in civil law where negligence has been most utilized. Indeed, negligence is the most important component of modern tort law, the law of civil wrongs, and is frequently relied upon in cases involving personal injury or death related to product liabilities, malpractice, and employment-related activities. In the last two centuries, its development has been shaped by shifting social, political and economic beliefs among jurists, legal thinkers, and legislators.

HISTORY OF NEGLIGENCE LAW

Prior to the 19th century, unintentional accidents causing personal harm in the English and American common-law tradition were generally governed within tort law under the principle of strict liability. (In contrasting legal systems such as continental Europe, the Canadian province of Quebec, and Puerto Rico, negligence is regarded as a form of extra-contractual obligation within the Law of Obligations). Under liability rules, plaintiffs usually only had to show that they were harmed by the defendant's conduct and were not required to demonstrate "fault." In other words, citizens were responsible for the harm their actions caused. Negligence, on the other hand, was a more complex concept that required that plaintiffs also prove "unreasonable conduct" on the part of the defendant. In theory, it was thus much easier to win a liability case than a negligence case since the burden of proof required for success was considerably lesser.

From the 1840s onward, the negligence standard had begun to replace strict liability in American tort law. Legal theorists in the second half of the century successfully attempted to systematize civil law by deriving logical and foundational principles to guide torts. They criticized what they saw as the arbitrary character of juries and their supposed predilection to favor the ordinary person against the corporate defendant. The most dominant school of American legal historians, often called the subsidy theorists, have argued persuasively that judges and legal thinkers in the 19th century, largely sharing the interests of industrial capitalists, successfully sought to make the negligence principle central to tort law in order to encourage the free market and development of *laissez-faire* capitalism. Since negligence was usually more difficult to prove, such a legal development would be beneficial to corporations who would face a lesser risk in the event they were sued for their products or behavior as an employer. As Morton Horwitz argues, "it was the doctrine of an emerging entrepreneurial class that argued that there should be no liability for a socially desirable activity that caused injury without carelessness." Older notions of strict liability were seen by defenders of this viewpoint as anomalies to a scientific, ordered, and certain set of legal principles in line with the developing capitalist economy.

This consensus among historians has been modified recently under the impact of new studies which have shown that in local practice both liability and negligence principles were used by the courts in injury cases during the era. The harshest aspects of negligence were only implemented for a short period. Other scholars have emphasized that concepts of negligence and liability have been highly gendered processes. In the biased views of judges and legal thinkers towards women, concepts of fault and reasonableness often involved stereotypical notions of men and women, which would affect case outcomes and the development of the law. Nevertheless, a trend toward the restriction of liability and the compensatory function of tort law, in which negligence played a major part, can certainly be discerned in the dominant legal theories and court cases of the latter half of the 19th century.

It was after the tumultuous social and economic upheavals of the Civil War period that legal theorists and judges first instituted a rigorous notion of negligence. According to Horwitz, Oliver Wendell Holmes, Jr., the most influential legal theorist in late 19th century America and a long-time Supreme Court justice in the early 20th century, aimed to reorder civil law by ignoring the traditional appeal to morality and individual rights which characterized American law until the Civil War, and by constructing a more uniform, predictable, and scientific legal system. As Horwitz expresses, prevailing legal thought among Holmes and his contemporaries was rooted in the notion that "the existence of decen-

tralized political and economic institutions was the primary reason why America had managed to preserve its freedom. A self-regulating, competitive market economy presided over by a neutral, impartial and decentralized "night-watchman" state embodied the old conservative vision of why America had uniquely been able to avoid falling victim to tyranny."

NEW ECONOMIC RATIONALITY

In the context of the emergence of large-scale industry based on competition and the profit motive, the growing power of corporations and an increasingly complex economy, there emerged new ideas about economic rationality among judges and legal thinkers that favored the relatively unimpeded growth of industry. The law itself had thus become increasingly enmeshed in the process of promoting economic growth, as judges relaxed liability law to lower the risks to industry of potential damages. Negligence would form the centerpiece of this new legal system as notions of strict liability were gradually undermined.

An 1850 Supreme Court of Massachusetts case, *Brown v. Kendall*, saw one of the first precedent-setting cases in the development of negligence. The plaintiff in this case was a man who was accidentally injured by another while both were trying to break up a fight between their dogs. The case revolved around the issue of liability and the failure to exercise ordinary care in a case in which one unintentionally injured another while engaging in a lawful act. Justice Lemuel Shaw argued that the plaintiff had to show that the defendant had either an unlawful intention or that he had acted negligently and was therefore at fault. The justices found that the defendant only had a duty to exercise "ordinary" and not "extraordinary" care. A simple case, it nevertheless originated the concept of "ordinary care" that prevailed into the 20th century.

Strict liability was overturned in two significant cases in the United States in 1873, the New Hampshire case of *Brown v. Collins* and the New York case of *Losee v. Buchanan*. These cases decided that there was no absolute liability to strangers. The former case concerned a pair of horses that were scared by a passing train and ended up damaging a light post. The driver was deemed to have used ordinary care to try to restrain the horses. The presiding judge ruled that a defendant must be proven negligent before he is liable. As Amanda Owens observes, "tort liability was dependent on showing a lack of ordinary care and skill." In the *Losee* case, it was maintained that damages arising from accidents involving machinery, dams, and railroads are liable only when they were a nuisance. Accidental damage was not to be held liable. A similar 1918 case in Ohio involved an action against a city for negligence due to damages suffered when a dam burst and flooded farm land. The judge decided that the city was not liable since it was only responsible for "proper duty" to its neighbor and not "impossible" obligations.

Negligence would develop in the late 19th century based on several general tenets. The first was the idea that to be held liable a defendant had to be at fault. A second key trait was that people would only be found negligent if they failed to exercise the due care of a "reasonable" person. An 1856 judicial statement cogently illustrates this notion. In *Blyth v. Birmingham Water Works*, the judge said:

> The rule of negligence is the omission to do something which a reasonable man, guided upon those considerations which ordinarily regulate the conduct of human affairs, would do, or doing something which a prudent and reasonable man would not do. The defendants might have been liable for negligence, if, unintentionally, they omitted to do that which a reasonable person would have done, or did that which a person taking reasonable precautions would not have done.

A third trait was the notion of contributory negligence in which a defendant was not liable for damages if the plaintiffs' actions were also partially negligent and responsible for the action. The concept of "assumption of risk" in which it was held that certain persons, even workers, were responsible for assuming some risk for dangerous situations was also developed. A final component of negligence was causation. In order for a plaintiff to win damages, it had to be shown that the defendant was the actual or promixate cause of the injury.

The notoriously dangerous railway industry was where many of these doctrines of negligence were used most extensively to acquit corporate defendants. Before the enactment of federal regulations governing the railroad in 1906, railway employers successfully used a number of defenses

based on negligence law in cases of personal injury and death in which they were defendants. Powerful railroad conglomerates could defend themselves from suits on the basis of assumption of risk since it was held that railway employees knew that the industry was dangerous when they began their employment. If the injury was the result of a fellow employee, then the railway could also argue that it was not liable. If the employee bringing the case was partially negligent, then companies could successfully use the doctrine of contributory negligence. The employee also had to prove that the employer's negligence was the most probable cause of an injury. Using one or all of these defenses, the railway industry was incredibly successful in defending itself against law suits. Injured workers and the families of fatally injured workers were often forced to survive on family resources alone. Only in the late 19th century did a series of federal regulations begin to stipulate absolute liability in cases of railway equipment defects and safety appliances.

THE 20TH CENTURY

By 1900, negligence had become a universal rule in tort law. Yet, just as social and political changes in late 19th-century America shaped the development of the concept of negligence, so too did an increasingly complex economy and society of the 20th-century and resultant legal changes favoring consumers lead to challenges to negligence.

In the food industry, for example, courts revived notions of strict liability due to the well-documented and pervasive illegal practices of food producers, wholesalers, and retailers. In product liability cases, a series of crucial court decisions gradually expanded the concept of liability at mid-century. By the 1960s and 1970s, an increasingly widespread belief among the population that corporations should be held strictly responsible for their products and actions led to substantially broader notions of liability. Juries began to award substantial damages for cases involving injuries caused by corporate negligence. Recently tort reforms have worked to once again restrict companies' liabilities for its actions.

Yet negligence continues to form one of the key claims in civil law cases involving personal injuries. Modern negligence laws vary somewhat by jurisdiction, but there are common features, all of which have originally evolved from precedents set in the

19th century. All three of the following components must be shown in order for a plaintiff to win the case and receive damages:

1) The duty element refers to a person's responsibility in acting with a suitable standard of conduct to protect others from harm, that is, the concept of "reasonable person." What constitutes a "reasonable person," of course, is an ambiguous concept. Yet in *Carlson v. Chochonov* (1947), the deciding judges reckoned that while imperfect, it was justifiable: "the ideal of that person exists only in the minds of men, and exists in different forms in the minds of different men. The standard is therefore far from fixed as stable. But it is the best all-round guided that the law can devise."

2) Breaching that duty comprises the second element of a negligence case. Currently, there are objective standards of reasonable conduct which consider the behavior of a hypothetical person and a subjective standard that considers the actual defendant and if they think they acted in a reasonable way.

3) A third component of negligence claims is based on causation, that is, whether the defendant was the actual or proximate cause of the injuries sustained by the plaintiff.

Proving negligence is therefore a highly complicated and expensive task especially in an era in which corporations have proven that they will stop at no expense to defend themselves. Indeed, negligence laws may prove to be a disincentive to plaintiffs to launch cases because of the huge sums of money involved, and the elevated risk of losing the case given the difficulties in proving negligence. Corporation have experienced lawyers who specialize solely in negligence cases and are able to marshal substantial financial and legal resources to plead their cases.

The future of negligence law will depend on how future generations negotiate the degree of responsibility that corporate America should have towards consumers, employees, and the general public.

SEE ALSO

corporate criminal liability; medical malpractice; legal malpractice; unsafe products; defective products.

BIBLIOGRAPHY. Jay Albanese, *White-Collar Crime in America* (Prentice Hall, 1995); Lawrence Friedman, *American Law in the Twentieth Century* (Yale University Press, 2002); Lloyd Duhaime, "Standard of Care: The 'Reasonable Man,'" www.duhaime.org (2003); Nan Goodman, *Shifting the Blame: Literature, Law and the Theory of Accidents in Nineteenth-Century America* (Princeton University Press, 1998); Morton Horwitz, *The Transformation of American Law, 1870–1960* (Oxford University Press, 1992); Amanda Owens, "The Classical Law of Tort," *Coke's Institutes of the Law,* www.thelockeinstitute.org (2003); Stephen Rostoff, Henry N. Pontell and Robert Tillman, *Profit Without Honor: White-Collar Crime and the Looting of America* (Prentice-Hall, 1998); Denis W. Stearns, "An Introduction to Product Liability Law," (Marler Clark, LLP, 2001); "Product Liability Claims," (Ashcraft & Gerel, LLP, 2003); Barbara Welke, "Unreasonable Women: Gender and the Law of Accidental Injury, 1970–90," *Law and Social Inquiry* (v.19, 1994); "Negligence," The Crow Law Firm Library www.crowlaw.com (2003).

SEAN PURDY, PH.D.
QUEEN'S UNIVERSITY, CANADA

Nigerian 419

THE CLASSIC Nigerian fraud involves a letter, fax or e-mail to a prospective victim, promising a quick and generous return (often 20 percent or more) if he or she provides the scammer with his or her bank account numbers. The scammer says he or she needs American bank accounts to allow transfer by wire of several million dollars scammed from the Nigerian government. Once the scammer has the victim's account number, he or she cleans out the account by means of bank drafts, and the money is out of the country and gone forever. This is a $5 billion worldwide scam which has been operated since at least 1989 under successive governments of Nigeria. It is also referred to as advance fee fraud and 419 fraud after the relevant section of the 4-1-9 Nigerian penal code that addresses fraud schemes. It has been estimated that the 419 scam is the third largest industry in Nigeria. The scheme has history going back to the 1920s when it became known as the The Spanish prisoner con.

The scam is conducted in a variety of ways, but the most prevalent involves an individual or company receiving a letter from an official of a foreign government or agency offering to transfer millions of dollars into the person's or company's bank ac-

The advent of e-mail has created exponentially larger markets for the $5 billion Nigerian scam business.

count. The reason for the letter may vary from time to time, such as: My father left me $40 million in his will, but I have to bribe government officials to get it out; the Nigerian National Petroleum Company has discovered oil, and we as officials of that company want to acquire the land, but we need a U.S. front man to purchase it first for us; we just sold an illegal shipment of crude oil in Nigeria, but we have to bribe the banker to get it out; a foreigner had died and left behind money; or the Nigerian government overpaid on some contract, and they need a front man to get it out of the country before the government discovers its error.

The scam is typically that the government overpaid on some procurement contract and the official does not want to return the money to the government. Instead, the official wants to get it out of the country. In cases where the letter recipient refuses to join the scam, oftentimes an ancillary scam is run: a Nigerian "fraud task force" official contacts the recipient and asks for assistance in cooperating with the scam so that the police can identify and apprehend the suspects.

This scam works as it causes the recipient of the letter to believe that he or she is going to scam, in turn, the Nigerian government, the Central Bank of Nigeria, and other authorities, and obtain a high return of money on an investment, so high a return that it could only be generated from an illegal operation. Items that may indicate that the letter is a scam are as follows: there is always a sense of urgency, often a restriction is placed on the amount of time available to complete the transaction, for example 14 days; there are foreign-looking documents and often actual Nigerian officials involved, sometimes even actual Nigerian building addresses are used; the transaction must be kept confidential; a Nigerian residing in the United States or the United Kingdom acts an "intermediary" to close the transaction; often, someone claims to be of Nigerian royalty or fame. To make the scam look legitimate, the con artist sends the victim numerous documents that contain official-looking seals, stamps, and logos.

An adaptation of the Nigerian 419 fraud is called the advanced fee fraud. The underlying scam is once again an offer to achieve a large return on an investment through a fraud perpetrated upon the Nigerian government. However, in this format the victim is encouraged to pay large advance fees for various taxes, attorney fees, transaction fees, bribes, and sometimes to travel to Nigeria to facilitate the business deal.

If the victim pays the money up-front by wire-transfer or by mail, one of two things will happen: 1) the money will be simply lost and will never be seen again; or 2) and much more likely, within a couple of days contact will be made, either by phone, letter, or e-mail, telling the victim that something has gone wrong, and that to clear it up and release the funds more money will have to be sent. This latter scamming will go on literally for weeks and months, until the victim either runs out of money, or finally figures it out.

SEE ALSO
advance fee fraud; scams; Africa; globalization.

BIBLIOGRAPHY. T. Lesce, *Modern Frauds and Con Games* (Loompanics Unlimited, 2002); U.S. Department of State, "Tips for Business Travelers to Nigeria," www.state.gov (2001); U.S. Secret Service, "Public Awareness Advisory Regarding '4-1-9' or 'Advance Fee Fraud' Schemes," www.secretservice.gov (2002).

PATRICK D. WALSH
LOYOLA UNIVERSITY NEW ORLEANS

Nixon, Richard M. (1913–1994)

RICHARD MILHOUS Nixon was born in Yorba Linda, California, the son of Hannah Milhous and Francis Nixon. His mother was an Evangelical Quaker who hoped that her son would one day become a Quaker missionary. The effect of his mother's strict Quaker ideology was not strong enough to burn a lasting impression on the future president, who chose to enter politics once he returned from the Navy after World War II. Nixon would have one of the most tumultuous political careers of the 20th century, which subsequently saw him resign as president of the United States on August 9, 1974, following the Watergate Scandal. Nixon's troubles and allegations of scandals, however, were never solely confined to simply the Watergate issue.

In 1946, Nixon was elected to the House of Representatives from California. Four years later, he was elected to the Senate. During this time, Nixon was making head-waves as a major combatant against communism, especially regarding accusations of various government officials having communist ties. The anti-communist frenzy began following the war and intensified in 1950 due to the speeches of Senator Joseph McCarthy of Wisconsin, who made wild accusations that the State Department had over 200 communist supporters in its ranks. While McCarthy would become infamous for this red scare, Nixon also played a significant part.

In 1948, former State Department official Alger Hiss voluntarily appeared before the House Committee on Un-American Activities (HUAC), claiming his innocence against allegations that he had given secret documents to former American communist spy, Whittaker Chambers. Nixon was a member of HUAC, and passionately lobbied against Hiss, even accusing President Harry S Truman's administration of being sympathetic to communism for attempting to defend Hiss. In 1948, Nixon went before a federal grand jury and requested that Hiss be tried for espionage. Hiss had two trials, the latter in January 1950, in which he was found guilty on two charges of perjury. Nixon was instrumental in Hiss being called to trial, however, all of the information that Nixon was basing his claims on was illegally supplied to him from the Federal Bureau of Investigation (FBI). For Nixon, his anti-communist tactics did not solely result in

the Hiss trial. When he ran for Senator in 1950, his victory was aided by his accusations that his opponent, Helen Gahagan, was a communist.

In 1952, Dwight Eisenhower chose Nixon to be his vice-presidential candidate. During the election, Nixon became a source of controversy over allegations that he received illegal campaign funding from businessmen. However, Truman was able to use this controversy to gain public support by going on television and admitting that he had received a cocker spaniel, but refused to give it back because his daughters loved "Checkers." This speech not only helped Nixon to gain public support, but he was able to deflect the allegations and retain his position as Eisenhower's running mate.

After spending eight years as vice president, Nixon lost the 1960 presidential election to John F. Kennedy. In 1962, he lost the election for governor of California, stating afterward that his political career was over. Yet, in 1968, Nixon returned to the top of the Republican Party, becoming the Republican nominee and then defeating Hubert Humphrey, thus becoming the 37th president of the United States.

When Nixon ran for president in 1968, he lobbied hard for Republican supporters to help finance his election bid. Often, he mentioned how, in 1960, Kennedy had benefited from having more money behind his campaign. As a result, Nixon, like other presidents before and after, engaged in dubious affairs in order to secure campaign funding. One instance was in 1968: Nixon received over $250,000 from 15 donators, all of whom were subsequently appointed as U.S. ambassadors during Nixon's presidency. In 1972, Nixon was the beneficiary of a massive campaign budget, raising over $60 million. As a result, 21 business executives were convicted of illegally contributing corporation funds to Nixon's re-election bid.

The Vietnam War was the major event of Nixon's first term, and was in full force when he became president. Nixon escalated America's war effort by beginning a bombing campaign in Cambodia in 1969, where he believed Vietcong soldiers were located. Due to the mass protest that such an initiative would bring from the American public, Nixon kept this operation silent, all the while claiming he was in the process of pulling America out of the war, thus providing an early glimpse of Nixon's penchant for lying to the American public.

The Watergate Scandal, which accused Nixon of covering up a burglary of the Democratic Party offices at the Watergate office complex, effectively brought Nixon's presidency to a close. Rather than face an impeachment trial, Nixon resigned. Gerald Ford replaced him as president, and promptly decided to pardon Nixon of all charges.

One of the most fascinating aspects of Nixon's numerous, dubious, and at times, illegal actions during his political career, is that he was able to partake in such dishonest and immoral actions even though he was raised under conservative Quaker ideals. The transformation of Nixon is incredible, when it is considered that he was, as a Quaker, almost a conscientious objector to World War II. Perhaps the most fitting description of Nixon's mindset was provided by Nixon himself, when he stated that "when the president does it, that means it is not illegal," thus granting himself justification that the president was above the law.

While Nixon's presidency will forever be remembered for Watergate, and the former president remembered as "Tricky Dick," in the years prior to his death, he was able to reinvent himself to the public. He was often sought by various presidents for his advice in foreign affairs. Regardless of his dishonest dealings as president, he was always one of the brightest minds in foreign policy. On April 22, 1994, Nixon died at age 81.

SEE ALSO
Watergate Scandal; Ford, Gerald R.; Carter, James E.

BIBLIOGRAPHY. David Greenberg, *Nixon's Shadow: The History of an Image* (W. W. Norton, 2003); Iwan W. Morgan, *Nixon* (Arnold, 2002); Melvin Small, *The Presidency of Richard Milhous Nixon* (University Press of Kansas, 1999); Anthony Summers, *The Arrogance of Power: The Secret World of Richard Nixon* (Phoenix, 2001); Allen Weinstein, *Perjury: The Hiss-Chambers Case* (Knopf, 1978).

DAVID W. MCBRIDE
UNIVERSITY OF NOTTINGHAM, ENGLAND

The era of the imperial presidency, in which Richard Nixon (left) proclaimed "I am not a crook," came to an end on August 9, 1974, when Gerald Ford (right) assumed the presidency and promptly pardoned Nixon for his alleged crimes.

nonprofit organization fraud

A NONPROFIT ORGANIZATION is a business that has been granted exemption from federal corporate income tax because it engages in an activity that is in the public interest. A wide variety of businesses may apply for nonprofit status, including large national corporations such as arts organizations, schools, hospitals, and religious establishments, as well as smaller local businesses, such as daycare centers or small charities. Nonprofit organizations are affected by the same kinds of fraud that adversely affect the running of all businesses, such as embezzlement or fraudulent management practices. Fraud can cause substantial damage to nonprofits in two major ways: first in the loss of funding that was most likely limited to begin with, and second through the tainting of the nonprofit's reputation and credibility in the public eye. Nonprofits depend on public confidence and a sterling reputation because much of their funding is derived from governmental grants and private donations.

NONPROFIT SECTOR

Nonprofits generally are private companies that operate in the public sector and have a social mission. A recent book on nonprofit organizations management reports that nonprofit organizations number about 1.1 million, with about 10.2 million employees. Most of these organizations are quite small, with fewer than 100 employees. This very large number of nonprofit organizations and the great variety of industries in which they are concentrated, combined with the small size and local character of many of them, mean that broad oversight and fraud prevention are extremely difficult to institute and maintain.

Despite their key role in providing social services, nonprofit organizations are usually not as transparent in terms of financial records as are government organizations or publicly traded companies. For this reason, and due to various widely publicized scandals in the 1990s and early 2000s, the nonprofit sector has a reputation, deserved or not, for being more susceptible to fraud, waste, and bad management than the for-profit sector. The role of nonprofits in the business world has become more complex as the organizations evolve to meet market demand for services. For example, the nonprofit YMCA, founded to assist socially disadvantaged

youth, has expanded into the fitness services market for all adults because it is naturally poised to take advantage of this business opportunity with already existing fitness programs and facilities. For-profit companies argue that this constitutes unfair competition, because the YMCA has the advantage of having tax-exempt status. Beyond the tax and unfair competition issues, the expansion of the mission of nonprofits also raises the spectre of fraud, as nonprofits leave behind their original altruistic motivations and compete for customers. Concern about this issue has led to calls for financial and administrative oversight for nonprofits similar to those instituted for other kinds of businesses.

Nonprofit organizations also have special operating circumstances that may make them susceptible to fraud. One possible fraud is the disguising of a truly for-profit business as a nonprofit in order to avoid paying taxes. Nonprofits also may not be subject to the rigorous controls that owners and shareholders insist on in the case of for-profit businesses; lax oversight creates an environment in which fraud can flourish undetected.

The most prevalent kind of fraud affecting nonprofits is embezzlement and other mismanagement of funds by employees, and it results for the most part from lax financial controls. Embezzling continues to be an acute problem for nonprofits; news stories appear daily about churches, schools, and other local nonprofit organizations that have had funds stolen by employees who took advantage of less than rigorous oversight of their activities.

The problem of mismanagement of funds can be found on a national level as well, despite the stronger scrutiny paid to large organizations. In 1995, the chief executive of United Way was sentenced to seven years in prison for misusing the charity's funds for personal expenses. The financial loss to United Way was estimated at $1 million, and the lasting damage to the charity's reputation, resulting in donor hesitancy, is incalculable.

ABUSE OF TRUST

Nonprofit charities attract a great deal of media attention when fraud is discovered, because this kind of fraud abuses the trust of unsuspecting individuals. Charity fraud takes a number of forms, including the misuse of donated funds, the deception of consumers in order to elicit donations, or illegitimate companies posing as nonprofit charities in order to steal money intended for charitable causes. Members of the public may also not be precisely sure of the difference between a nonprofit and a for-profit business, and dishonest for-profit businesses often take advantage of this confusion and obtain contributions under false pretenses.

"CREDIT COUNSELING"

An industry traditionally dominated by nonprofit organizations that rocked by accusations of fraud in the early 2000s is that of consumer credit counseling. In this industry, nonprofit organizations counsel debt-ridden consumers, intervening on their behalf with credit card companies and other creditors, assisting them in lowering their payments, and advising them of the appropriateness of strategies such as bankruptcy in improving their financial situation. One such company, the nonprofit AmeriDebt, has been enmeshed for years in legal proceedings, accused of abusing the public trust by only posing as a nonprofit.

AmeriDebt is accused of charging excessive fees, selling customers debt consolidation packages with little or no accompanying counseling, and then turning customers' loan payments over to a for-profit affiliate. In 1999, the District of Columbia won a $2 million fraud suit against the company, which is also being sued by other states and investigated by the Federal Trade Commission. AmeriDebt is suspected of being more concerned with helping its sister businesses make money rather than assist consumers, an allegation that if proved would be a violation of the trust of consumers who approach nonprofits looking for assistance, as well the original intended social mission.

Nonprofit organizations often receive government funding, and it is the suspicion of the improper use of this funding that is often the engine that sets into motion the exposure of fraud. The nonprofit healthcare industry is notoriously plagued by fraud, including abuses ranging from improper billing of Medicare and Medicaid by hospitals, to the inability of local clinics to account for government payment for providing healthcare services. Other nonprofits accused of fraud have mismanaged government funds intended for the redevelopment of poor neighborhoods, or redirected public funding to an inappropriate purpose, such as support of a particular religious group or political candidate.

Finally, nonprofits may, perhaps, be more likely to have fraud engineered by employees disgruntled with their pay. Nonprofits are granted a special status because they are businesses that are not set up or meant to pursue economic wealth, meaning the employees of a nonprofit are not usually handsomely paid. Though the benefits of working at a nonprofit are perceived by the vast majority of nonprofit workers as more than financial, dishonest employees may be more susceptible to the temptation of padding a paltry nonprofit paycheck with fraud, especially when oversight is less than rigorous.

The Internal Revenue Service has a stake in overseeing nonprofit organizations, because of the benefits afforded to these organizations by their tax-exempt status. The Federal Trade Commission pursues nonprofits that defraud consumers because they are responsible for fair business practices. Newspapers such as the *Chronicle of Philanthropy* also monitor fraud in the nonprofit world. Finally, there are oversight organizations such as Guidestar, which publishes information about the operations and finances of nonprofit organizations and advises nonprofit companies on efficient and ethical business practices.

In general, it is recommended that nonprofit organizations have the same kind of internal controls that for-profit companies institute, including internal and external auditing, administrative controls, and mechanisms for ensuring that funds are used appropriately. Nonprofits are particularly vulnerable to the disastrous effect of fraud on public relations, because the discovery of fraud at nonprofits is especially badly received by the public.

Nonprofits may soon see the effects of the Corporate Fraud Accountability Act of 2002, commonly known as the Sarbanes-Oxley Act, which was passed in response to the corporate scandals of the first years of the new millennium; nonprofit organizations are, for the most part, outside the purview of this law in letter but certainly not in spirit, and may likely be expected to hew to the same new ethical standards as for-profit businesses.

SEE ALSO
charity fraud; embezzlement; employee crimes; Medicare and Medicaid fraud; healthcare fraud.

BIBLIOGRAPHY. Paul Light, *Making Nonprofits Work: A Report on the Tides of Nonprofit Management Reform*

(Aspen Institute, 2000); Lester Salamon, ed., *The State of Nonprofit America* (Brookings Institute Press, 2002); Lester Salamon and Helmut K. Anheier, *The Emerging Nonprofit Sector: An Overview* (Manchester University Press, 1996); Michael Sorkin, "Missouri Accuses AmeriDebt of Bilking Consumers," *St. Louis Post-Dispatch* (September 12, 2003) Alan Ware, *Between Profit and State: Intermediate Organizations in Britain and the United States* (Polity Press, 1989); Gerard Zack, *Fraud and Abuse in Nonprofit Organizations: A Guide to Prevention and Detection* (John Wiley, 2003).

MARGUERITE KEANE, PH.D.
INDEPENDENT SCHOLAR

North, Oliver (1943–)

ACQUITTED OF CRIMES because he was "just following orders," Oliver North first came to the attention of the American public in connection with the 1987 Iran-Contra Senate Hearings. The hearings were an effort to determine who had knowledge of and involvement in secret arms sales to Iran, and the subsequent funneling of the profits to Nicaraguan Contras (anti-communists). Congress had banned U.S. aid to the Contras. Along with other implications for careers and futures, the last 18 months of President Ronald Reagan's administration was at stake as well. If it were proved that Reagan knew of the Iran-Contra actions, the popular president would be implicated in criminal conspiracy, thus diminishing further his already flagging support in Congress and perhaps forcing his resignation or impeachment.

October 1986 found North trying to forge relations with Iranian moderates, hoping they would help win the release of American hostages in Lebanon. The White House aide reportedly authorized Middle Easterner Albert Hakim to tell the moderates that "the U.S. 'will cooperate to depose' Iraqi President Saddam Hussein and 'fight Russians in Iran.'" The decorated Marine Lieutenant Colonel North was fired in November 1986.

Although Justice Department attorney Charles Cooper and Representative Michael DeWine (R-OH) indicated they would not believe North's veracity, in early July 1987, when North's testimony was televised, polls showed he was rated favorably by 43 percent of respondents. The Vietnam War veteran did not offer proof that Reagan knew of the affair, but did testify that he, North, sent the president five memoranda which outlined the scheme, and that North's superiors who were in direct contact with Reagan had authorized the plan. North also testified that he had seen a presidential directive, signed by Reagan, which detailed the intent to trade arms with Iran for hostages.

In February 1989, North faced a federal jury on 12 charges, including obstructing Congressional presidential investigations, destroying government documents, and receipt of illegal gratuities. North paid for a home security system with proceeds from a Swiss bank account that had been controlled by retired Air Force Major General Richard Secord, an associate in the Iran-Contra dealings. On discovery of the transaction, North tried to falsify records to show he had paid for the system from his own funds.

The most serious charges, conspiracy to defraud the government and theft, were dropped because successful prosecution depended so closely on secret documents. He was convicted of shredding and altering documents, though he said he was ordered to do so by his superiors; preparing false testimony for CIA Director William Casey and Rear Admiral John Poindexter, former national security adviser and North's immediate supervisor; and accepting an illegal gratuity for $13,873 security fencing for his home.

Punishment could have included up to 10 years imprisonment and fines of $750,000, but was placed at $178,785, two years of probation, and 1,200 hours of community service. Jurors believed North's claim that he acted on orders and acquitted him of other charges. The trial did not prove what, if any, involvement there was by Reagan and Vice President George H. W. Bush. Both Reagan and Bush (who became president as the trial ended), declined to issue a pardon for the former National Security Council aide.

In July 1990 a federal appeals court suspended North's three convictions. By June 1994, North, who had regularly asked co-workers for gas and lunch money while working at the White House, was making $20,000 for a one-hour speech, living the good life on a 194-acre estate, and running a campaign for the U.S. Senate (which he lost). He was also accused of vote-buying and making questionable solicitations for one of the nonprofit organizations he founded.

SEE ALSO
Reagan, Ronald; Contra-Gate; Bush, George H. W.; Iran-Contra; Central America.

BIBLIOGRAPHY. Melissa Healy, "Week 5: The Strangest Tales Yet," *U.S. News & World Report* (June 15, 1987); Melissa Healy, "Who Will Believe Oliver North?" *U.S. News & World Report* (July 6, 1987); Brian Duffy with Melissa Healy, Kenneth T. Walsh, Dennis Mullin, Rene Riley and Jenny Walden, "Oliver's Twist," *U.S. News & World Report* (July 20, 1987); Stephen J. Hedges and Steven Emerson, "Ollie North's Troubles: The Sequel," *U.S. News & World Report* (February 6, 1989); William Lowther, "A Forgiving Sentence," *Maclean's* (July 17, 1989); Eloise Salholz, "A Second Chance for Ollie," *Newsweek* (July 30, 1990); Douglas Pasternak, "He Works Hard for the Money," *U.S. News & World Report* (June 6, 1994).

LINDA M. CREIBAUM
ARKANSAS STATE UNIVERSITY

Northrop Grumman

THIS DEFENSE contractor remains trusted by the U.S. government despite a number of actions for overbilling and providing false information. For example, Northrop pleaded guilty in 1990 to 34 counts of providing false statements to the government during its work on the Air Launched Cruise Missile and Navy Harrier Jet programs. The guilty plea was the culmination of pervasive management and production problems that also dominated Northrop's work on the MX missile program.

By the time the company delivered its first Internal Measurement Unit (IMU) for the MX missile in May 1986, 203 days late, the company had been rated "marginal" in an Air Force audit. The House Armed Services Committee reported that Northrop falsely certified that parts met specifications, billed the government for its own mistakes, allowed altered worker time cards, and set up illegal shell corporations to speed parts purchasing. The shell corporations also provided an end-run around quality certification procedures. While the U.S. Air Force withheld payments, the Department of Justice pursued a criminal investigation. Of Northrop's practice of ignoring the external audits that identified problems, Representative Ron Wyden (D-

OR) told the *New York Times*, "that just strikes me as incredible incompetence."

When whistleblowers claimed a year later that Northrop defrauded the government of more than $2 billion on Stealth bomber contracts, the federal government declined to join the suit. How much and how permanently Northrop cleaned up its operations are debatable. On the one hand, the company's public relations says the company earned a number of quality awards in 2003. On the other hand, Northrop's acquisitions the prior year generally brought with them lawsuits over defense contractor fraud, along with signs of production inefficiency.

By late 2003, the company was faced with absorbing 30 percent of a $22 million cost overrun on the new CVN 77, a nuclear aircraft carrier built at the company's recently purchased Newport News, Virginia, shipyard. The Newport News facility's additional problems included a civil lawsuit alleging that the facility had, before Northrop acquired it, billed the government for $72 million in tanker research and development that was actually performed for a commercial customer between 1994 and 1999. The government sought up to $216 million in damages; the case was settled for $60 million in early August 2003.

During the summer 2003, Northrop apparently made an aggressive effort to settle its own and its subsidiaries' problems with the government. In June, the company agreed to pay the federal government $111 million to settle charges that TRW, which Northrop had acquired in late 2002, overcharged for a number of space-related contracts. In late August, Northrop agreed to another $20 million in fines for selling defective aerial drones to the U.S. Navy.

The TRW prosecution, one of largest whistleblower cases ever, began when Richard Bagley, formerly chief financial officer at TRW's Redondo Beach, California, unit, sued the contractor on behalf of the federal government, an act allowed by the federal False Claims Act. The U.S. government credits whistleblower suits under this act for allowing it to recover more than $1 billion in 2002 alone.

Whistleblowers can hope to collect up to 25 percent of the ultimate settlement. Says Bagley, who gained $27.2 million in his action against TRW, "If I knew what I know now, I would not do it again." Bagley alleged that TRW had billed the government $56 million for research and development that never took place, notably a commercial satellite-based telephone system and a rocket system to launch satellites. The settlement was for a greater amount because the government can sue for treble damages.

When settling these cases, Northrop's stance has been to avoid admitting guilt and to frame its acquisition policy as a successful strategy of gaining resources and access to new government contracts. In October 2003, Northrop Grumman's new chief executive, Ron Sugar, assured the *Financial Times* that the company was poised for growth without further acquisitions. Optimism was fueled by increased military spending related to terrorism and the war in Iraq. In November 2003 alone, the company announced it had gained eight major military contracts.

SEE ALSO

government contract fraud; government procurement fraud; whistleblowers; military-industrial complex.

BIBLIOGRAPHY. Christopher Bowe, "Northrop Aims to Secure Its Strategy," *Financial Times* (October 1, 2003); John H. Cushman, Jr., "Northrop's Struggle with the MX," *New York Times* (November 22, 1987); Michael Kilian, "Northrop Settles 2 Federal Probes," *Chicago Times* (August 27, 2003); Ruth Marcus, "U.S. Urged to Join Contractor's Case," *Washington Post* (November 18, 1988); Renae Merle, "Northrop Settles Billing Case," *Washington Post* (August 9, 2003); "Northrop Struggles to Control Costs," *Los Angeles Times* (September 25, 2003); Northrop Grumman (www.northropgrumman.com); Peter Pae, "For Whistle-Blowers, Virtue May Be the Only Reward," *Los Angeles Times* (June 16, 2003); Peter Pae, "Northrop, U.S. Said to Reach Accord over Tanker Billing," *Los Angeles Times* (August 9, 2003).

WENDE VYBORNEY FELLER, PH.D.
ST. MARY'S COLLEGE OF CALIFORNIA

obstruction of justice

ACCOUNTING AND insider trading scandals of recent years have, to some extent, centered around the issue of obstruction of justice. Obstruction of justice may be defined as "the crime of offering interference of any sort to the work of police, investigators, regulatory agencies, prosecutors, or other officials." The offense is specifically defined by the United States Code as a violation of 18 U.S.C. 73, sections, 1501 through 1519.

The sections covering obstruction of justice include crimes such as: assault on a process server; obstructing examinations of financial institutions; resistance to extradition agent; influencing or injuring an officer or juror generally; influencing juror by writing; obstruction of proceedings before departments, agencies, and committees; theft or alteration of record or process; false bail; picketing or parading; obstruction of court orders; tampering with a witness, victim, or an informant; and obstruction of criminal investigations of health care offenses.

Historically, the sections of 18 U.S.C. 73 that have applied primarily to white-collar crimes have been sections 1503 and 1505. Section 1503 makes it a crime to illegally influence a grand juror, petit juror, or court officer by threats, force, or threatening letters, as well as protecting the "due administration of justice." Section 1505 criminalizes the same behaviors and makes them applicable to proceeding of federal regulatory agencies. In *United States v. Aguilar*, the Supreme Court ruled that to be convicted of obstruction of justices, the defendant had to form specific intent to obstruct a federal judicial or grand jury proceeding.

The Sarbanes-Oxley Act of 2002, was enacted by Congress to amend and extend 18 U.S.C. 73 as a response to numerous cases of accounting fraud in which records of suspect corporations were shredded, altered, or otherwise disposed of to hide illegal behaviors, including criminal facilitation by auditors. The Sarbanes-Oxley Act amended Section 1512 to include "alters, destroys, mutilates, or conceals a record, document, or other object, or attempts to," as an act of obstruction of justice. The Sarbanes-Oxley Act also created Section 1519 that bars similar destruction of documents "in relation to or contemplation of … any matter within the jurisdiction of any department or agency of the United States.

ARTHUR ANDERSEN

Of the numerous cases of obstruction of justice brought against corporations and their officers in recent years, perhaps the most prominent has been that against the Arthur Andersen accounting firm.

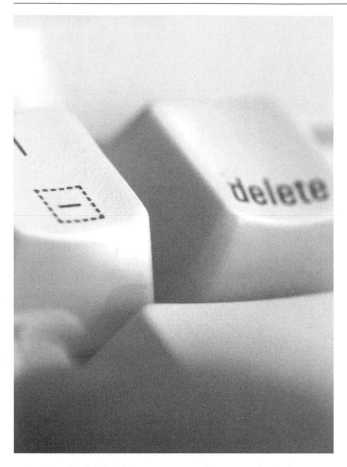

Pressing the "delete" key on accounting records during an investigation can constitute obstruction of justice.

Arthur Andersen was an international accounting and consulting firm that, until its demise in 2002, was responsible for auditing the accounting records of scores of large corporations and organizations, such as Featherlite, Landry's Restaurants, and Enron Corporation. It was in the context of its relationship with Enron that Andersen was caught obstructing justice.

Enron was a conglomerate that was based on a classic "house of cards," in which uncollected revenues were treated as profits in ledgers, even if the revenue never was received, and losses were hidden from regulators and stockholders through elaborate partnerships with ghost corporations created by the firm's officers. The collapse of Enron's shell-game brought questions of where the checks and balances had failed. Investigators repeatedly found corporate officers to have illegally profited on the company's malfeasance. The board of directors, which was meant to supervise the officers as a fiduciary responsibility to the stockholders, were found to be nothing more than figureheads who rubber-stamped officer's actions without question. The greatest blame, however, appeared to rest on Arthur Andersen as Enron's auditor, which did little, if anything to reign in the voodoo accounting practices at Enron, and may have indeed facilitated part of the fraudulent bookkeeping.

Once June 16, 2002, Arthur Andersen, LLP, was convicted of obstruction of justice under 18 U.S.C. 73 Section 1503. Separately, Andersen partner and lead Enron auditor David Duncan was also convicted of obstruction of justice. Duncan had directed the destruction of thousands of Enron accounting documents, electronic files, and e-mails over 17 days in 2001. These documents were destroyed in the face of an ongoing criminal investigation into Enron's accounting practices, and Arthur Andersen's participation in those fraudulent practices.

Andersen claimed it was only destroying "housekeeping" documents that were unrelated to the investigation. The destruction of documents only ended with the execution of a subpoena issued by the Securities and Exchange Commission (SEC), forcing Anderson to cooperate in the investigation by turning over all documents related to the case. Upon its conviction for obstruction on justice, Andersen was permanently barred from auditing the accounts of other corporations. In its response to the conviction, Andersen argued that the conviction was only technical in nature, and that it was wrongfully convicted for behaviors carried out by its competitors as well. In the course of a few months, over 80,000 Arthur Andersen employees worldwide lost their jobs. Andersen had fewer than 500 employees in 2004. Virtually unknown at the time was that Arthur Andersen had previously settled cases of suspected wrongdoing with regard to its audits of corporations such as Colonial Realty, Sunbeam Corporation, and Boston Market Trustee Corporation.

SEE ALSO

Enron Corporation; Securities and Exchange Commission; Arthur Andersen; accounting fraud.

BIBLIOGRAPHY. Luisa Beltran, Brett Gering, and Alice Martin. "Andersen Guilty," *Money* (June 16, 2002). Jonathan D. Polkes, "White-Collar Crime: Obstruction of Justice Nexus Requirement Unclear in New Statutes," *New York Law Journal* (July 7, 2003); Penelope Patsuris, "Andersen Clients Evacuate Post-Verdict,"

Forbes (August 14, 2002); "Response from Arthur Andersen LLP on Verdict," *Houston Chronicle* (June 15, 2002); United State Code Annotated, Title 18, Chapter 73. *United States v. Aguilar*, 515 U.S. 593 (1995).

LAWRENCE M. SALINGER, PH.D.
GENERAL EDITOR

occupational carcinogens

WHILE REPORTS OF occupational carcinogens were documented as early as the 17th century, it was only after World War II that a great deal of attention began to be paid to the reality of carcinogens in the workplace. By the beginning of the 21st century, it was known that industrial chemicals make up approximately one-half of all known carcinogens.

Even though most people are more likely to associate occupational carcinogens with workers who are employed in factories and mines, lethal substances may also be present in offices, laboratories, hospitals, work sites, and in many other places of business. Exposure to a cancer-causing agent does not mean that a worker will contract cancer, but it does increase risks of certain types of cancer.

In order to make the workplace as safe as possible, the Occupational Safety and Health Administration (OSHA) mandates the use of Material Safety Data Sheets (MSDS) in all areas where hazardous materials are used, and these sheets must include information about the presence of possible carcinogens. However, this information may be inaccurate, incomplete, or misinterpreted.

At best, the sheer volume of the information may be overwhelming to workers. Workers may also be unaware that occupational cancers can occur years after exposure to toxic substance occurred. For example, in asbestos-related cancers, the latency period has been identified as 30 years or more.

The study of occupational diseases can be traced as far back as the 17th century when Bernardino Ramazzini, an Italian physicist, developed a training method to help physicians diagnose work-related illnesses. Ramazzini believed that physicians should obtain information about all patients' occupations in order to identify possible causes for the symptoms the patient reported.

In the 18th century, information about occupational carcinogens became more specific. In 1775, Sir Percival Pott, a British surgeon, identified a connection between exposure to soot and cancer of the scrotum in chimney sweeps. Over the next several years, other physicians realized that workers who worked with coal tar and paraffin, or who were employed as shale oil workers or mule spinners in the textile industry, were also more likely than the general population to suffer from cancer of the scrotum.

As more physicians and researchers began to pay attention to occupational carcinogens, further evidence documented the link between pulmonary cancer and workers in metal mining. By 1895, a connection between exposure to coal tar and dyestuff and bladder cancer had been established.

In the early part of the 20th century, researchers first fully understood that cancer was not infectious but was a result of a number of variables that included heredity and environment. From this point on, the study of occupational carcinogens became common.

However, most medical schools continued to refuse to add the study of occupational carcinogens as a required course of study, leaving medical practitioners on their own as they dealt with increasing rates of work-related cancers. In 1976, Congress passed the Toxic Substances Control Act that mandated an inventory of all chemicals used in the workplace, giving physicians more data to use in diagnosing occupational cancers. This information also provided employers with details about possible carcinogens that could threaten their employees, however, many employers continued to ignore the problem.

Certain kinds of cancer have been linked to exposure to particular substances in the workplace. Lung cancer has been documented among workers who are exposed to alloys, aluminum, arsenic, asbestos, battery acids, chemicals, chloromethyl ethers, coal tars and pitches, coke, diesel emissions, nickel, radon, silica, soot, talc, textile fibers, wool fibers, and among those who are work in foundries.

Skin cancers have frequently occurred in workers who come in contact with arsenic, brick-making material, coal tars, coke, mineral oil, shale oils, soot, shoe-repair materials, and wood-preserving material. The chances of contracting leukemia are thought to be increased by coming into contact with boot and shoe repair work, ethylene oxide, paint, petroleum, radiation, rubber, and substances used in the chemical industry.

Studies on agricultural workers have also suggested possible links between exposure to various pesticides and leukemia, Hodgkin's disease, non-Hodgkin's lymphoma, multiple myeloma, and cerebral glioma. Electricians are more likely to contract leukemia and brain tumors than the general population.

A number of carcinogens have received particular attention because of the high incidences of cancer in workers who have been exposed to them. In addition to workers who have worked directly with asbestos, others who are at risk include construction workers, plumbers, shipyard workers, garage workers, and electricians. While all types of asbestos fibers are known to be associated with mesothelioma, it is thought that crucidolite is the most likely form of asbestos to produce cancer. For at least half a century, the link between exposure to beryllium and lung cancer was so well known that a condition called chronic beryllium disease has been identified. Beryllium is used in coal and oil combustors, nuclear reactors, X-ray windows, missile fuels, spacecraft, and space systems.

CHROMIUM EXPOSURE

The first case of cancer directly linked to exposure to chromium was reported in 1890. Studies throughout the following century supported the cancer-causing properties of this metal; however, it was estimated that by 1980 between 200,000 and 390,000 workers continued to be exposed to hexavalent chromium in the workplace. Those who are most likely to be exposed to chromium include any manufacturing plant where chrome ore or chromates are used, as well as places that engage in steel and cement production, paint and pigment manufacturing, and leather tanning.

The fact that heavy exposure to diesel emissions poses a lung cancer threat to workers in certain occupations has also been well documented. In November 2000, the Public Citizen Health Research Group estimated that controlling diesel emissions could prevent between 412 and 8,261 deaths among coal miners and from 636 to 11,444 deaths among metal and nonmetal miners over a span of 45 working years. Other occupations in which workers are exposed to diesel emissions include bridge and tunnel workers, railroad workers, loading dock workers, truck drivers, material handling machine operators, longshore workers, garage workers, and various transportation employees.

Lead has long been identified as a carcinogen and is known to be the leading cause of workplace-related illnesses. Workers who work with paints, battery manufacturing, construction, welding, cutting, fuels, solvents, radiator repair and firing ranges are constantly exposed to lead. Additionally, various metalworking fluids used in the manufacture of automobiles, farm equipment, aircraft, and heavy machinery have been linked to a variety of cancers. More than 1 million workers per year are exposed to silica crystalline in the workplace, and 250 of them die annually. The disease is preventable if exposure is reduced, but there is no known cure for silicosis.

According to the Surgeon General of the United States, radon is the second leading cause of lung cancer in the United States. Radon, which cannot be seen, smelled, or tasted, is present in many homes and work areas. Radon-testing kits can identify the presence of the substance so that it can be removed.

Experts who study occupational carcinogens have suggested a number of ways to reduce the risk of exposure to carcinogens in the workplace. The most effective remedy, of course, is to remove all carcinogens. When this is impossible, education, reductions in the extent of exposures, and protective clothing and equipment may reduce the risks.

SEE ALSO

asbestos; employee safety; employee deaths; Environmental Protection Agency; Occupational Safety and Health Act.

BIBLIOGRAPHY. American Cancer Society, "Known and Possible Carcinogens," www.cancer.org (2003); K.S. Cha and H.P. Lee, "Occupational Cancers," *Textbook of Occupational Medicine Practice* (World Scientific, 2001); John E. Craighead, Pathology of Environmental and Occupational Disease (Mosby, 1995); Raymond D. Harbison, Industrial Toxicology (Mosby, 1998); David Kohn, et al., eds., *Textbook of Occupational Medicine Practice* (World Scientific, 2001); *Occupational Safety and Health Administration*, "Carcinogens," www.osha.gov (2003); National Institute for Occupational Safety and Health, "NIOSH Carcinogen List" www.cdc.niosh/npotocca (2003); PCHRG, "Occupational Health Information Center" www.citizen.org (2003); "Radon Fact Sheet" www.radon.com (2003); Jack Siemiatycki, *Risk Factors for Cancer in the Workplace* (CRC Press, 1991).

ELIZABETH PURDY, PH.D.
INDEPENDENT SCHOLAR

occupational crime

SEE Introduction; employee crimes; embezzlement; differential association; Sutherland, Edwin H.; Geis, Gilbert.

Occupational Safety and Health Act

IN RESPONSE TO rising concerns about worker and workplace safety, the U.S. Congress passed the Occupational Safety and Health Act of 1970 (OSHA). Enacted under the federal government's Constitutional right to regulate interstate commerce, the legislation aims to guarantee that workers across the United States have a workplace which is free from hazards like machinery dangers, constant loud noises, temperature extremes, unsanitary conditions, and toxic chemicals. In order to achieve these goals, the act authorized the creation of the Occupational Safety and Health Administration (OSHA), which was established in 1971.

OSHA covers all employers and their employees in any U.S. state or territory. An employer is "any person engaged in a business affecting commerce who has employees, but does not include the United States or any state or political subdivision of a state." As a result, many industries and businesses are covered by the employer definition, granting OSHA control over safety regulations in manufacturing, agriculture, law, medicine, charity, and education, as well as other fields. However, the law doesn't encompass all U.S. workers; those who are self-employed, farms which rely only on family members, industries which interact with and run under the authority of other federal agencies and laws, and some government employees are not covered by OSHA.

The Occupational Safety and Health Act has two main requirements: setting safety and occupa-tional guidelines, and having regular inspections to guarantee compliance to safety and health standards. OSHA has the power to require employers to practice certain policies and methods in their workplaces and to become knowledgeable about OSHA standards. Although employers are mostly responsible for workplace safety, employees are also responsible for complying with OSHA standards.

Under the act, employers are bound under a "general duty" section of the legislation which affirms that employers must guarantee "a place of employment which is free from recognized hazards that are causing or are likely to cause death or serious physical harm to employees."

Federal OSHA regulations are standardized into four major categories: general industry, construction, maritime, and agriculture. Some standards apply to every category, but there are many that apply only to a specific category. Out of all these regulations, there are three main cross-category requirements. First, employers must give an employee access to any records that are kept about his health, as well as any additional records that document other specifics, such as toxic substance exposures. Second, the employers are required to provide the necessary equipment and protective gear to ensure a safe workplace. Third, employers that manufacture or use hazardous materials must regularly examine and test those hazardous materials for safety purposes.

OSHA regulations require that employers keep thorough records, report on OSHA compliance regularly, and post OSHA standards for employees. Any employer who has more than 10 employees, except for a few low-hazard exceptions, must keep three different types of records. These records are an OSHA Form 300 injury and illness log, an OSHA Form 301 individual incident report which provides more specific details of injuries, illnesses, or accidents from the OSHA form 300, and a national survey by the Department of Labor's Bureau of Labor Statistics on workplace safety which happens annually if a company is selected to participate by its state government.

Reports must be provided by all employers to the nearest OSHA office if there is an accident or occurrence which results in the death of any employee or the hospitalization of more than three employees. The report must be provided to the office within eight hours since an incident originally took place. As a result of the required report,

The Occupational Safety and Health Act aims to guarantee that workers in the United States have a workplace which is free from hazards like machinery dangers, loud noises, temperature extremes, unsanitary conditions, and toxic chemicals.

OSHA officials may examine the circumstances surrounding a death or hospitalization to determine if safety or health standards were violated.

In recent years, OSHA has pursued an initiative known as the Voluntary Protection Program (VPP), which aims to better meet the goals of the Occupational Safety and Health Act of 1970. The VPP is an attempt to extend work safety practices beyond the minimum requirements set forth in the legislation by recognizing employers and employees who have successfully incorporated health and safety into their workplace, motivating others to emulate those who are successful, and establishing a more cooperative relationship between employers and their local OSHA office.

EMPLOYEE RIGHTS

Most importantly, employees are given significant rights which are guaranteed to them by the act and which are inviolable by employers. Employees have the right to voice their relevant concerns to their local OSHA office without having their identities revealed to their employer, to participate in OSHA inspections of their workplace, and challenge OSHA's efforts to ameliorate hazards in their work-

place. Private sector workers are protected by the legislation and may not be fired in response to filing a complaint with OSHA. In order to achieve the standards set by OSHA and detailed in the Occupational Safety and Health Act, frequent standards updates are available in the federal government's publication, the *Federal Register*. Training assistance programs are available from the more than 70 field offices, which provide workers and management with educational materials on workplace hazards, as well as the opportunity to bring in OSHA officers as consultants for the creation of a compliance program at no cost to the employer.

Violations of OSHA and Occupational Safety and Health Act standards upon inspection may result in substantial fines and, in some severe cases, may result in criminal penalties. Penalties are determined by OSHA officials based upon a standard system of assessment. Fines for repeated and willful violation of standards may reach as high as $500,000 daily on each separate infringement for a corporation, and as high as $250,000 for an individual. OSHA also maintains a significant appeals process for both employers and employees in order to review penalties assessed by OSHA officials for workplace violations.

SEE ALSO
whistleblowers; employee safety; workplace deaths; unions; negligence; labor crimes.

BIBLIOGRAPHY. U.S. Code Collection: Title 29, Chapter 15: Occupational Safety and Health, Legal Information Institute, www4.law.cornell.edu (2003); U.S. Department of Labor, Occupational Safety & Health Administration, www.osha-slc.gov (2003); U.S. Department of Labor, Office of the Assistant Secretary for Policy, Employment Law Guide for Occupational Safety and Health, www.dol.gov (2003).

ARTHUR HOLST, PH.D.
WIDENER UNIVERSITY

Ocean Ranger

THE *OCEAN RANGER*, an oil-drilling sea rig, was built by Mitsubishi Heavy Industries of Japan and first operated in the Bering Sea off Alaska in 1976. From there it move to New Jersey, then Ireland, and in November 1980 arrived on the Grand Banks off eastern Canada. On the Grand Banks of Newfoundland, the rig was operated by ODECO Drilling of Canada, under contract to Mobil Oil of Canada. ODECO was to manage the operation of the rig and crew, whereas Mobil was responsible for the drilling program.

The *Ocean Ranger* was a massive oil rig touted as unsinkable and able to drill in areas too dangerous for other rigs. It was the pride of the offshore oil industry, the biggest rig of its day, more than 300 feet high and as long as two football fields. On February 15, 1982, the semi-submersible drilling rig capsized and sank in the Grand Banks, 170 miles east of St. John's. Poor training, inadequate safety equipment, design flaws, and 120-mile-an-hour winds sealed the fate of the 84 crew members. All of them died.

A Royal Commission was founded to determine the cause of the tragedy. The findings revealed a history of negligence regarding safety. ODECO failed to provide qualified marine personnel, had not replaced the lifeboats, and did not have a valid Certificate of Inspection at the time of the sinking. ODECO also neglected to provide any sort of survival suits for the crew. Mobil failed to ensure the crew had been through proper training as well as to instruct the captain of his duties.

The commission found neglect in safety, hiring, training of the crew and management, engineering design, and overall construction of the rig caused the *Ocean Ranger* to plunge to its destruction. A more strict inspection and regulation of the vessel should have been undertaken by the United States and Canadian governments in order to prevent the disaster. There should have been training provided on a regular basis for the operation of the rig, and evacuation in case of emergency. Many of the workers did not know the safety rules and escape procedure. Evacuations drills should have been mandatory. Families of the lost crewmembers sued the companies that owned and operated the *Ocean Ranger*. The companies were forced to pay out millions of dollars in lawsuits.

The oil company was held liable because its workers weren't trained for emergency procedures and didn't do any emergency drills. Experts found the *Ocean Ranger* could have survived the storm flooding if those in charge had understood how the ballast system worked. The two men working in the ballast room had never been tested for their competency. The senior operator had only reached the halfway point in his training but was promoted to the senior operator. The *Ocean Ranger* did not have enough safety equipment on board for the number of workers, just one example among other forms of gross negligence.

Although there were civil liabilities, no criminal charges were brought; this is often the case when death and injury is a product of violence from an employer's negligence, rather than that of a single individual outside the workplace.

SEE ALSO
employee safety; workplace deaths; Canada; negligence.

BIBLIOGRAPHY. Royal Commission on the Ocean Ranger Marine Disaster (Government of Canada, 1984–85); John Douglas House, *But Who Cares Now? The Tragedy of the* Ocean Ranger (Breakwater Books, 1987); John Douglas House, *Working Offshore: The Other Price of Newfoundland's Oil* (Institute of Social & Economic Research, Memorial University, 1985); Charles Reasons, Lois Ross, Craig Paterson, *Assault on the Worker: Occupational Health and Safety in Canada* (Butterworths Publishers, 1981).

CHARLES E. REASONS, LL.B. PH.D.
CENTRAL WASHINGTON UNIVERSITY

offshore bank accounts

OFFSHORE BANK ACCOUNTS are often associated with the darker side of major finance. Their high degree of confidentiality offers an ideal opportunity for tax evaders, arms and drug traffickers, terrorists, and corrupt politicians. Although most offshore banks offer a variety of legal services, many of these institutions have been tarnished as corrupt. These institutions are magnets for people wishing to profit from money laundering, fraud, corruption and tax evasion. The appeal is bank secrecy, which offers animosity to its clients. Offshore banking is a blue chip multi-billion dollar industry and involves international banks, major investment firms, and accounting firms. The special private banking services they provide allow big savings for big-money clients, who take advantage of the bank's discretion. Many of these clients fall in the $50 million to $100 million dollar range of assets, which allows for full advantage of overseas laws.

Offshore banking also offers an attraction for investors who want to diversify their portfolios and reduce their vulnerability in the face of domestic disturbances. They offer commercial services, such as loans, and foreign currency trades, investment and tax consulting; however, they often charge much higher interest on accounts than conventional banks. There are approximately 55 offshore zones, the largest being Switzerland. Five major clusters for offshore finance are the Caribbean, Europe, the Middle East, Southeast Asia, and the South Pacific.

The amount of money that moves about in offshore banking is staggering. According to information gathered by Lynch & Gemini Consulting, as of 2000, one-third of the money of the wealthiest individuals may now be held in offshore accounts. The amount of money being moved in and out of offshore accounts could be as high as $6 trillion. Experts think it is possible that one half of the world's money flows through these accounts. The International Monetary Fund (IMF) claims that up to $1.5 trillion in illicit money is laundered through offshore accounts each year, with an additional $5 billion in laundered drug money.

The United States and Europe both face the continuing and substantial loss of tax revenue due to hidden funds and many countries are now asking that reforms be made and enforced. A growing number of offshore banks specifically target professional people who can handle a minimum deposit of $80,000 or more. The IRS estimates that at least $100 billion in funds obtained through legal sources are placed in offshore accounts for the purpose of tax evasion.

Great secrecy is maintained concerning offshore accounts. Privacy is strictly upheld and account information cannot be divulged. Its non-regulated system of banking is allowed to interact with standard banks, which only serves to further their popularity. With the advent of electronic communications, monies can now be immediately transferred, making attempts to track the funds increasingly difficult. Funds can be transferred an infinite amount of times, and checkpoint areas can be rendered useless when transactions take place in person. By changing jurisdictions, it is easy to cause confusion over tax and fund amount issues.

99 PERCENT FAILURE

OXFAM International estimates a $50 billion loss to third world countries because of trade taking place through shell accounts. Attempts by Interpol, international police cooperation, to seize money from laundering rackets have yielded only about $3 billion over the last 20 years. Unfortunately, that amount is equivalent to the amount of money laundered in a typical three-day period. U.S. Treasury officials claim their efforts to combat money laundering has over a 99 percent failure rate.

More attention is being given to the subject of offshore banking due to the high profile discoveries, such as the account used by Osama bin Laden, who moved money to the Al Taqwa bank, which was registered in the Bahamas and operated from Switzerland. Enron Corporation set up 780 shell companies in the Grand Cayman islands, as well as an additional 80 companies in the Turk & Caicos Islands. This allowed them to manage insider trading, hide financial records, deceive investors and creditors, and avoid paying U.S. income taxes. The discoveries of these two cases have caused both politicians and the public to pay closer attention to the issue. Although the United States has been slow to call for radical reforms, the European public has called for an end to offshore banking.

In the Caribbean, Grenada's senate passed legislation to strengthen offshore regulations. It has closed more than 30 banks and has asked that two recently passed bills be signed by their governor and made into law. The Exchange of Information

Act is aimed at reducing opportunities for illegal acts such as tax evasion, money laundering, drug trafficking, and terrorism. The Offshore Banking Act would strengthen the power of the government to supervise, investigate, and administer licenses.

Nauru, the world's smallest republic and an island in the Pacific, was once considered the second largest provider of offshore banking, until it announced an end to its offshore operations. This action has taken place in an attempt to combat global criminal activities, money laundering, and terrorism. In the face of global threats, many changes can be expected in offshore banking practices and regulations, as their impact on world economy and prosperity becomes more evident.

SEE ALSO

offshore entities; Caribbean Islands; bank fraud; tax evasion; Switzerland; Luxembourg.

BIBLIOGRAPHY: Lucy Komisar, "Offshore Banking: The Secret Threat to America," *Dissent* (Spring 2003); Barney Warf, "Tailored for Panama: Offshore Banking at the Crossroads of the Americas," *Human Geography* (v.84/1, 2002); Melanie Warner, "Who Needs the Cayman Islands? The Sovereignty Loophole," *Fortune* (June 23, 1997).

CYNTHIA CRISEL
ARKANSAS STATE UNIVERSITY

offshore entities

OVER THE PAST 30 years, the number of offshore zones offering financial services proliferated. The growth of the offshore financial sector is routinely attributed to increased financial regulations, and higher taxes imposed on account holders in industrial countries. To avoid the scrutiny of regulators and lower tax burdens, Western firms and wealthy individuals relocated significant portions of their financial activities to offshore markets, which promise enhanced secrecy and client confidentiality with financial transactions conducted through offshore entities.

By some estimates, more than half of the global financial transactions pass through offshore centers, and nearly 20 percent of total private wealth is invested in offshore financial centers. Offshore financial centers also routinely offer an array of tax and regulatory incentives for non-resident investors. For individuals with significant assets, a number of jurisdictions, such as the Bahamas, Bermuda, the Cayman Islands, the Cook Islands, Gibraltar, and the Isle of Man, permit the establishment of offshore asset protection trusts. Individuals establish an asset protection trust by transferring ownership of financial assets to a trust that has only foreign trustees. The trustees, who have no formal office, manage the trust property through the offshore zones.

Asset protection trusts changes the character of the assets held by the debtor from one that can be easily seized and sold, to an asset that the creditor cannot legally seize and sell. When creditors attempt to seize assets, even if they discover the offshore trust, a foreign trustee, who is most often uncooperative during the investigation, holds the funds.

For example, courts in the United States have no jurisdiction over foreign trustees, and therefore are unable to provide any relief to creditors. The actual geographic distance between the creditor and the trustee also poses significant barriers to creditors, and law enforcement and regulatory agencies. Asset protection trust corporations routinely advertise their services (a means to avoid frivolous litigation, and seizures of funds by government agencies) for an initial cost of less than $1,000 for minimal trust protection, or more than $30,000 for complex trust protection schemes.

Individuals can also establish an offshore corporation, an entity recognized by law as a separate "person" with limited liability. Offshore corporations may issue shares, raise capital, make contracts, and maintain checking and saving accounts. Like the asset protection trusts, offshore corporations provide limited information to law enforcement and regulatory agencies. For example, under Panamanian law, the names of corporate officers, directors or shareholders are confidential, and not filed in the public registry.

Another financial instrument offered by offshore financial zones are bearer share certificates, which do not indicate the name of the owner of the certificate. Bearer shares facilitate the transfer of assets by permitting the transfer of ownership simply by the transferring of the certificate to another individual. Some offshore centers mandate that corporations issue only registered share certificates, that have the name of the owner on the document. But corporate records, which record the registered owner of the certificate, are an internal document available only to directors, officers, and shareholders. No public registry of shareholders is maintained. offshore zones also routinely offer customers the services of shelf companies, corporations that have been created to meet a client's immediate needs. The shelf companies only require a registered local agent who receives legal documents on behalf of the owner of the company.

Over the past two decades, the international community instituted a number of measures to reduce the comparative advantages of the offshore zones, and force tax havens to comply with international regulatory and accounting practices. For example, a number of global financial centers, such as London, England, and Frankfurt, Germany, have instituted massive deregulation, which reduced tax rates, and diminished the comparative advantages held by the offshore financial sector.

Additionally, new oversight bodies were created to monitor the offshore zones. For example, The Financial stability Form (FSF), which includes representatives of the International Monetary Fund (IMF), and regulatory bodies such as the Basel Committee on Banking Supervision, were created to examine offshore centers and to assess the quality of their respective regulatory environments offshore. The FSF submits a survey that requires banking, insurance, and securities supervisors to evaluate the level of resources devoted to supervision and international cooperation, and the degree of cooperation by individual offshore centers. Based on the survey results, the FSF identifies regulatory and enforcement weaknesses that facilitate the laundering of illicit capital in offshore zones.

REGULATORY RESPONSE

The responses of individual jurisdictions to these initiatives have varied widely. Some opponents of the international initiatives to mandate better oversight of offshore zones have urged resistance through formal legal action. However, most offshore zones responded positively, by strengthening their regulatory infrastructures for supervising offshore financial vehicles and service providers, and enacting anti-money laundering laws.

A number of these jurisdictions have explicitly committed to addressing FSF concerns and are to improve the transparency of their tax regimes and increase the effective exchange of criminal and civil tax information. Though numerous states have agreed to more closely monitor offshore zones, several countries in the Caribbean and South Pacific are boosting their limited economies with offshore sectors.

For example, in late 2000, domestic and international regulators expressed considerable concern after Vanuatu, a Southern Pacific island chain, passed a law that permits proprietors to establish web-based e-commerce sites, and conduct business from Vanuatu without the need to form an offshore corporation. The new legislation permits the establishment of a "cyber-suite," a Vanuatu-based website from which business can be conducted without revealing the identity of company directors and shareholders. Moreover, the owner of the cyber-suite does not have to maintain a physical presence in Vanuatu, such as a registered office.

Another unsettling trend is the concerted effort by countries throughout the Caribbean to become global centers for internet gaming, a $10 billion industry. Dominica, a country routinely criticized by international monitoring bodies for failing to institute anti-money laundering norms, established a regulatory framework that permits offshore operations of internet gaming through high-speed fiber-optic and satellite facilities. The gaming license permits the establishment of traditional forms of gaming over the internet, including slot machines, video poker, and gambling on a wide variety of sporting events, such as basketball, soccer, and auto racing. Criminal organizations are attracted to internet gaming because companies are exempt from income tax, withholding tax, sales tax, and foreign exchange controls.

While a number of regulatory controls have been instituted by offshore zones, domestic law enforcement and regulatory agencies that oversee offshore jurisdictions must also assure Western regulators that financial institutions are complying with international anti-money laundering standards. But more work must be done. This could be accomplished by removing secrecy provisions, increasing the number of unscheduled on-site inspections, and sanctioning financial institutions that fail to submit suspicious activities reports with fines and closures. This would allow offshore zones to adopt international anti-money laundering norms, and reduce the opprobrium routinely proffered by Western regulatory and law enforcement agencies.

SEE ALSO
offshore banking; bank fraud; money laundering; drug trafficking; reform and regulation; Caribbean Islands; Central America.

BIBLIOGRAPHY. Paolo Berbasconi, *Offshore Domiciliary Companies as Instruments of Corruption and Money Laundering* (Bertelsmann, 1999); Marcel Cassard, *IMF Working Paper No. 94/107: The Role of Offshore Centers in International Financial Intermediation* (International Monetary Fund, 1994); Alberto Musalem, and Luca Errico, *IMF Working Paper 99/5: Offshore Banking-An Analysis of Micro- and Macro-Prudential Issues* (International Monetary Fund, 1999).

TRIFIN ROULE
JOURNAL OF MONEY LAUNDERING CONTROL

oil crimes

OTHER THAN the food, water, shelter, and clothing necessary for survival, oil may be the single most valued substance in contemporary international society. Because the entire world has become so dependent on oil, this valuable resource has influenced population shifts in certain regions, elected or toppled the heads of nations, ignited and fueled wars, and affected foreign policy decisions. Oil crimes evolve from the fact that this coveted resource, in some form or another, is a negotiable resource that induces greed, ambition, and corruption. Oil crimes may be as simple as an individual at a gas pump driving away without paying, or they may be so complex that they involve millions of dollars and the citizens of several countries. Oil crimes may also be crimes against nature and the environment that range from a ship leaking oil to spills that discharge millions of barrels into the ocean and onto beaches.

AMERICAN OIL

After oil was discovered in 1859 in Titusville, Pennsylvania, it became a major element in the Industrial Revolution in the United States. In the early days of oil development, the American oil industry was controlled by only a few companies that created large trusts designed to cut out competition and retain as many profits as possible by controlling the entire process of petroleum or oil production and transportation.

These trusts were controlled by oil barons such as John D. Rockefeller of the Standard Oil Company, who ruthlessly squelched competition. The large oil companies manipulated prices in such as way that they received rebates from railroads while independent refineries were charged twice the going rate. When competitors or independents balked at the ruthless tactics of the oil barons, they were taken over or forced out of business. In the 1870s, the situation became so crucial that it led to the Oil War of 1872, which resulted in parades and mass meetings during which Rockefeller's effigy was burned. A Congressional investigating committee uncovered what it saw as "one of the most gigantic and dangerous conspiracies ever conceived." The oil barons claimed that the trusts benefited the consumers, but critics charged that rigged prices and wages threatened the American economy. The U.S. government agreed that monopolies restricted trade; and in 1911, the U.S. Supreme Court ordered Standard Oil to divest itself of its various subsidiaries.

During the 1930s and 1940s, the U.S. government began to work with privately owned oil corporations in the Middle East to produce sufficient oil to help swing the balance of power toward the Allies in World War II. By the end of the war, the economies of these oil-producing countries had changed forever. The three major players in the Middle East during this period were ARAMCO, an international oil cartel; the U.S. government, which promoted the Middle Eastern colonialism that sprang from the war years; and the government of Saudi Arabia, the largest oil producer in the Middle East and the motivating force in establishing oil prices and policies. In the more developed regions of the world, oil soon replaced coal as the major source of energy. Between 1945 and 1960, consumption of oil and gas doubled because oil was used to provide power for several essential industries such as steel, cement, metalworking, and glass. At the same time, an increase in the numbers of cars, trucks, and other motorized vehicles added to demands for more gasoline at cheaper prices.

In the 1970s, the United States was caught up in a major oil crisis that caused the prices of gas to soar and led to long lines at service stations in some parts of the country. With only a 30-day supply of oil left, the U.S. government restricted the amount of gasoline available to service stations and ordered oil refineries to turn their petroleum stacks into heating oil. Speed limits were lowered around the country to further conserve gasoline. The crisis was not an actual shortage in the production of oil, but an intentional oil embargo by the oil cartel (Organization of Petroleum Exporting Countries or OPEC) of the Middle East that had belatedly realized that it could become a major player on the global economic scene by controlling access to oil.

During the Arab-Israeli Yom Kippur War of 1973, the reigning oil powers in the Middle East had decided that they could use oil to force the West to honor Palestinian claims over those of Israel. By the time the embargo ended, oil prices had risen to more than five times the original consumer price. By the end of the 20th century, oil would become a major factor in funding international terrorist activities. Oil, fueled by politics and religion, would continue to heighten tensions in the area for generations to come.

OIL AND POLITICS

Just before World War II, Standard Oil of New Jersey was accused of being so obsessed with profits that it supplied Germany with oil products that helped to create the monstrous Nazi war machine, even though the company was well aware of Hitler's activities in Europe. Standard defended its action by claiming that it was just retribution for the theft of German secrets over the previous 15 years that had helped the Allies wage war against Germany.

During Richard Nixon's successful 1968 presidential campaign, several Texas oil companies were fined for illegally contributing thousands of dollars to Nixon's campaign with the hope that he would protect the domestic oil market. Four years later, contributions to Nixon's 1972 campaign created a scandal of major proportions.

In 1974, the Senate Watergate Investigating Committee began to probe illegal contributions made to Nixon's Committee to Re-Elect the President (CREEP) before the new Federal Election Campaign Act restricted large contributions to political campaigns. The trail led to the executives of several major American oil companies. Ashland Petroleum Corporation, the Gulf Oil Corporation, and Phillips Petroleum Corporation had each contributed $100,000 to the Nixon campaign at the request of CREEP representatives.

When the Watergate scandal became public, the money was returned. The three companies paid maximum fines of $5,000, and the executives who had initiated the contributions within each company were fined $1,000 each. The investigation also revealed that Gulf Oil had contributed to the unsuccessful presidential campaigns of Democratic candidates Wilbur D. Mills of Arkansas and Henry M. Jackson of Washington. W. W. Keller of Phillips Petroleum was believed to have coordinated the oil industry contributions, and he admitted that Phillips had also contributed to various House and Senate campaigns in 1970 and 1972, totaling some $60,000.

The oil industry's involvement in the Nixon campaign surfaced again when the Watergate Committee learned that Robert H. Allen, a Texas oilman who headed Gulf Resources and Chemical Corporation, had contributed the $100,000, routed through a Mexican bank, that had been deposited in the account of Bernard L. Barker. When Barker was arrested, he carried $89,000 of the Allen contribution with him. Barker pled guilty to conspiracy, burglary, and wiretapping on charges related to the Watergate break-in. It was estimated that at least 413 directors, senior officials, and stockholders of 170 oil and gas companies had contributed a total of $4.98 million to the Nixon re-election campaign, providing 10 percent of Nixon's total donations. As a result, Nixon was unable to put pressure on domestic oil companies during the energy crisis.

The oil industry also played a part in the scandal of George H. W. Bush's administration that became known as Iraq-Gate (since Watergate, most scandals somehow got the appendage "gate.") In 1989, representatives of several oil companies, along with representatives from General Motors, Westinghouse, and Xerox, accompanied members of Kissinger Associates, headed by former Secretary of State Henry Kissinger, to Baghdad, Iraq, to meet with Saddam Hussein. While the visit was geared toward finding ways that the United States could help Iraq defeat Iran, a secondary purpose was to increase the American oil supply. After the Bush administration made improved relations with Iraq a priority, the United States began to import more than 1 million barrels of Iraqi oil a day.

Christopher Dorgoul, an executive of BNL in Atlanta, pleaded guilty (but later recanted) to 60 felonies connected with his role in supplying Saddam Hussein with billions of dollars that were used to build ballistic and chemical weapons plants. This encouraged an environment in which mass killings and widespread political instability flourished, while Hussain tried to cover up his actions. Ultimately, Dorgoul pled guilty to three felonies and was sentenced to 37 months in jail.

INTERNATIONAL CRIME

A major scandal erupted in France in mid-2003 when it was discovered that the Elf-Aquitaine Oil Company operated an unofficial slush fund for the French government. French investigators learned that Elf routinely paid for everything from bribes to foreign governments to campaign contributions for the two major parties in France. Löik Floch-Prigent, Elf's chief executive, received a home that cost 9 million francs (about $2.25 million) and an Elf-funded 4.5-million-franc (about $1.15 million) divorce settlement. Floch-Prigent told investigators that President Francois Mitterand had ordered him to pay off his ex-wife so she would not blow the whistle on Elf's activities.

In October 2003, Mikhail Khorkovsky, the wealthiest man in Russia and the owner of Yukos Oil, was arrested by masked agents who boarded his plane at a Siberian airport. Khorkovsky was charged with tax evasion, fraud, forgery, embezzlement, and failing to abide by a court order. Khorkovsky is a strong supporter of the opposition party in Russia. His arrest was followed by the resignation of Russian President Vladimir V. Putin's chief of staff, Alexander S. Voloshin, who opposed the arrest. Voloshin was reportedly afraid that Khorkovsky's arrest could lead to capital flight and general economic instability.

In May 2003, a scandal erupted in Khazakhstan that involved American James H. Geffen, a counselor to President Nursultan Nazarbayev. Geffen was accused of channeling $60 million in oil commissions and bonuses into the president's account and another $17 million into the account of Nurlan Balgimbayev, the head of a state-owned oil company. After the scandal broke, Swiss banking officials opened an investigation into the scandal and froze a dozen accounts in the names of Geffen, Nazarbayev, and Balgimbayev.

Geffen was charged with 39 counts of money laundering and eight violations of the Foreign Corrupt Practices Act, which prevents Americans from paying bribes to obtain contracts in foreign countries. Geffen could face up to 20 years in jail and $84 million in penalties and fines. Investigators were also researching the activities of Mobil Oil, which paid bonuses to Geffen to ensure access to several oil fields in Khazakhstan. Two other Mobil executives were charged with failing to pay taxes on money received in kickbacks.

In March 2003, several churches in the Sudan charged Talisman Energy Company, a Canadian oil firm, with implicitly approving a campaign of genocide conducted by government officials against non-Muslim residents, that included kidnapping, rape, murder, and confiscation of land. The plaintiffs said that more than 2 million people had been killed since the genocide began.

The Nigerian Economic and Financial Crimes Commission announced in July 2003 that it was investigating two Americans who were suspected of being involved in the Halliburton scandal, in which American oil officials in Nigeria paid $2.4 million to a Nigerian firm to avoid paying taxes on its Nigerian subsidiary. The tax scheme was discovered by the Securities and Exchange Commission when Halliburton claimed a $5 million tax payment to Nigeria that never appeared in its books. The Bush administration denied that Vice President Dick Cheney, who had headed Halliburton at the time, was involved in the scandal.

OIL THEFT

A number of countries around the world are forced to devote a good deal of attention to problems that arise over oil theft. In Great Britain, for example, authorities estimate that robberies at service stations ranging from credit card fraud to major robberies resulted in approximately a $35 million loss to the oil industry in 1992. Thailand has such an enormous problem with smuggled oil that it began an intensive campaign in 2002 aimed at controlling the problem. The Thai government offered a bounty of 30 percent of the value of the property seized to encourage informers to notify the government about the activities of smugglers. The campaign quickly led to the arrest of three major smuggling rings.

In February 2002, Romanian authorities arrested five employees of the state-owned PETROM oil company in connection with the theft of more than 20 tons of petroleum fuel that was mixed with other fluids and sold in diesel fuel. The crackdown

An oil refinery is just one step in the oil production process that can include numerous varieties of white-collar crime.

on stolen oil led Thai legislators to pass a new law that mandates an 18-year sentence for the theft of oil from pipelines. Russian authorities estimate that more than 10 million tons of oil are stolen in that country every year. In 2002, the Interior Ministry reported that around 3,300 oil-related crimes had occurred in Russia, resulting in losses of more than 270 million rubles (about $10 million).

It is believed that organized crime is behind a large number of the oil-related crimes. In April 2003, Chinese authorities cracked down on a smuggling ring in Beijing, the capital, which involved 80 tons of oil products and eight boats. In one raid the month before, border police seized 25 yachts owned by the smugglers along with various oil products, tires, and computer equipment.

OIL SCAMS

In 1998, the U.S. Post Office investigated a mail scam that came to be known as The Nigerian Oil Letter, in which an individual who claimed to be a Nigerian prince and the head of a petroleum company offered recipients a 30 percent share of a $28.6 million pot if the recipient provided bank account information so the money could be deposited. Another scam in 1998 was identified as the first case of computer-aided gasoline fraud in the United States. Four employees of Mepco Oil in Los Angeles, California, aided by a pump technician, manipulated oil pumps at several service stations to pump a lower amount of gasoline than the pump registered. These scam artists managed to hoodwink station owners and inspectors before they were discovered. The oil company agreed to pay $640,000 in penalties, investigative costs, and inspector training. Between 1980 and 1981 Marc Rich and Pincus Green engaged in $105 million in fraudulent oil trades before they escaped to Switzerland. President Bill Clinton included Rich as one of his eleventh-hour pardons upon leaving office.

In Scotland, the McGovern crime family developed a scheme in which they sold gasoline at prices below any competitor. They used the money to generate cash to hide their illegal activities, including drug trafficking and money laundering at the local carwash. In South Korea, the chief executive of S-Oil, Kim Sun-dong, was sentenced to three years in jail in October 2002, after he was convicted of manipulating oil shares and accounting fraud. He and his partner, Yoo Ho-ki, who was quickly released after being sentenced to 10 months in jail, manipulated their accounts to show a $153 million profit for S-Oil, claiming that it was the way things were done in Korea.

OIL SPILLS

The damage inflicted on the environment by oil spills is extensive, and the effects can linger for years after a oil spill occurs. Because oil is transported thousands of miles through pipelines and in an ever-increasing number of tankers, the potential for accidents has accelerated in recent years. In March 1967, the 118,185-ton *Torrey Canyon* spilled 3.5 million gallons of Kuwaiti crude oil into the English Channel, polluting English and eventually, French beaches and presenting new pollution problems.

The ship's master was reportedly trying to beat the tide when the boat ran aground on the Seven Stones. When the ship hit the rocks, it broke open. Under British law, the owner or master of a ship that discharges oil into international waters may be prosecuted.

Because the *Torrey Canyon* spill was the world's first major spill, no one was sure what to do. The British attempted to mitigate the damage by flushing the oil spill with two million gallons of detergent, which was toxic to some marine life in the area. Ten days after the spill, the British government ordered aerial bombing of the tanker to burn off oil left on board. By the time the oil reached France, experts had devised a more eco-friendly method of using 3,000 tons of chalk to bind to the oil and force it downward into the water.

On March 24, 1989, the 211,469-ton Exxon *Valdez* entered Prince William Sound in the Gulf of Alaska. The captain of the ship was inebriated and asleep in his quarters while an unlicensed third mate steered the ship. When the vessel ran aground on Bligh Reef, it released 11 million gallons of crude oil into Prince William Sound. Immediately, a thick layer of black ooze covered the stones and rocks along the coast. It was estimated that seven killer whales died, along with 360 harbor seals, from 3,500 to 5,500 sea otters, 250,000 birds, from 1,500 to 2,000 pigeon guillemots, and 250 bald eagles. Traces of the oil spill will continue to be present for several generations to come. Exxon was required to pay $125 million to cover direct and unforeseen environmental damages. The jury also awarded plaintiffs $5 billion in punitive damages.

In March 2002, a Danish ship, the D/S *Progress* entered Baltimore Harbor while spewing oil from a leak in its hull. The captain had notified the shipping company, which told him not to report the leak to the U.S. Coast Guard. However, two crewmembers who believed that their lives were threatened by the leaking oil slipped Coast Guard inspectors a note explaining the situation. Under the Act to Prevent Pollution from Ships, the crewmen received $125,000 of the $250,000 fine levied against the shipping company.

While most oil spills are caused by accidents or human error, a new kind of environmental threat occurs when oil wells are set on fire, as they were during the Persian Gulf War in 1991. As Iraqi troops evacuated Kuwait before multinational forces moved in, they intentionally set fire to 650 of

Kuwait's 935 oil wells and spread oil slicks throughout the country. Approximately 525 million metric tons of crude oil were burned before the fires were extinguished. The Iraqis also opened pipelines at sea terminals to spread further havoc. The troops that had come to free Kuwait were attempting to manage the environmental chaos left by departing Iraqi troops. Environmentalists and meteorologists worried that the smoke could contribute to a change in the climate of Kuwait and Saudi Arabia, and some experts believed that the smoke affected Bangladesh and China by contributing to unusually heavy precipitation. Birds, fish, mammals, and invertebrates were killed by the oil. Fortunately, the extent of the damage was mitigated by heavier-than-normal monsoon rains.

OTHER ENVIRONMENTAL HAZARDS

Oil developers are required by law in many countries to protect the environment as much as possible. Before the rise of environmentalism in the 1970s, however, protecting the environment was not generally addressed by oil developers. For example, when the Blue Creek oil field was developed in West Virginia in 1968, residents were appalled at the amount of devastation that followed. One state legislator called it rape because oil developers destroyed fields, forests, and farmland and polluted much of the state's water supply.

In October 2003, a case involving ChevronTexaco's pollution of the Ecuadorian rain forest went to trial after eight years of wrangling over jurisdiction. The company was sued by 30,000 residents of the rain forest, who claimed that in the 1980s, the oil company refused to line its waste pits despite the potential hazards to residents and the environment.

The chief evidence in the case was a letter written in 1980 in which the company expressly rejected the possibility of relining or filling the waste pits because it would cost $4,197,958. In addition to the damage caused by the unlined waste pits, records revealed a long history of oil leaks in the pipelines that transport oil from Ecuador to the world market, with more than 297,000 barrels of oil leaking from 1972 to 1989.

SEE ALSO

Standard Oil; air pollution; water pollution; Arab nations; Middle East; Exxon *Valdez*; corruption; Rockefeller, John D.

BIBLIOGRAPHY. James Blair, "Keeping Tabs on Weights and Measures That Don't Add Up," *Christian Science Monitor* (November 4, 1998); James Blair, "Post Office's G-Men," *Christian Science Monitor* (September 10, 1998); Joanna Burger, *Oil Spills* (Rutgers University Press, 1997); Joel Carmichael, *Arabs Today* (Doubleday, 1972); David Colbert, *Eyewitness to Wall Street: 400 Years of Dreamers, Schemers, Busts, and Booms* (Broadway Books, 2001); "Comparative Corruption," *The Economist* (May 17, 2003); "Halliburton Scandal: Crime Commission Declares Two Wanted," *Africa News* (July 24, 2003); Mark Hamblett and Rich Kopstein Schwartz, "Suit Alleging Canadian Oil Firm Aided Sudan Genocide Proceeds," *Broward Daily Business Review* (March 25, 2003); William J. Kennedy, *Secret History of the Oil Companies in the Middle East* (Documentary Publications, 1979); John H. Lichtblau and Dillard P. Spriggs, *The Oil Depletion Issue* (Petroleum Industry Research Foundation, 1959); Peter Mantius, *Shell Game: A True Story of Banking, Spies, Lies, Politics, and the Arming of Saddam Hussein* (St. Martin's, 1995); Richard O'Connor, *The Oil Barons: Men of Greed and Grandeur* (Little, Brown, 1969); "Oil Scandal Hits Kazakhstan," *Washington Times* (May 17, 2003); Richard Petrow, *In the Wake of Torrey Canyon* (David McKay, 1968); Lester A. Sobel, ed., *Money and Politics: Contributions, Campaign Abuses of the Law* (Facts On File, 1974); Carl Solberg, *Oil Power* (Mason/Charter, 1976); George Ward Stocking, *The Oil Industry and the Competitive System* (Hyperion, 1975); "Tanker Company Sentenced for Conspiracy to Conceal Hazardous Conditions and Oil Pollution in Baltimore Harbor," *Department of Justice Report* (March 8, 2002); "Testimony Ends in ChevronTexaco's Pollution Trial in Ecuador," *Sacramento Bee* (October 30, 2003).

ELIZABETH PURDY, PH.D.
INDEPENDENT SCHOLAR

oligopoly

AN OLIGOPOLY IS A MARKET dominated by a small number of participants who are able to collectively exert control over supply and market prices. Usually if four or fewer firms control at least 50 percent of a given market in one product or service (for example, light bulbs, canned soup, razor blades, temporary workers) an oligopoly is said to exist.

Oligopolies are related to white-collar crime and deviance largely by attempts to limit competi-

tion or expand their markets. Oligopolies have developed a number of practices which serve to limit entry into the industry by new firms, to avoid price competition, and manipulate demand.

It is very costly to enter an industry dominated by a few well-known names. Large firms often purchase the successful smaller firms via mergers and acquisitions. Larger firms sometimes rely on their established relationships with customers or suppliers to limit the activities of smaller firms. Because market control by a few giant firms make it very difficult for smaller businesses to market new products or production processes, pricing and market share remain in the hands of larger corporations. This tends to keep the law of supply and demand from functioning and, consequently, prices remain artificially high. One study estimated that if oligopolies could be broken up, the cost of living for consumers would be reduced by 25 percent.

In many industries, one firm (usually the largest) becomes the established price leader. This firm is usually the first to raise prices in the face of rising costs. The others then also increase prices. This situation is informal and non-conspiratorial because any arrangement to raise prices among industry firms would constitute price-fixing, which is against the antitrust laws.

This practice serves to reward rich stockholders and corporate executives with rising stock prices, thereby funneling even more money to the richest segments of wealth holders and income earners. It also serves to make poorer those who do not own large blocks of stock—especially the middle class and the poor.

A large or diverse firm that can stand temporary losses by lowering its prices below its production costs until it either forces competitors out of business or becomes price leader, is said to conduct predatory pricing. Then it can re-raise prices. This is illegal, but very hard to prove in court. Collusion to fix prices is also used, even though it is illegal. Price-fixing is a major form of white-collar criminal activity that is very costly to the public. One study estimated that price-fixing may cost the American public as much as $78 billion per year.

Oligopolistic firms often create demand for their products via advertising. This sometimes results in the production of images instead of true product differences. What advertising leads to is brand recognition on the part of consumers. Advertising serves to limit competition because smaller firms can not afford commercials on large television networks. One advertising study estimated that 90 percent of all the commercials on prime time network television are sponsored by the largest 500 corporations in the United States. Advertising agencies make use of demographic research and psychological appeals. They use focus groups with sociological traits similar to their target markets and analyze these customers.

In discriminatory pricing, firms can increase profits by separating markets. Airlines do it all the time. They sell business customers high-priced seats since their demand is constant. Lower priced seats are sold to tourists, who tend to be bargain hunters and will fly only at lower price. Restrictions are developed to keep business customers from purchasing tickets at the tourist price.

In certain oligopolistic industries, some forms of criminal activity tend to become standard practice. One study of the criminal activity of the 582 largest publicly owned corporations between 1974 and 1976 found two-thirds of the criminal violations took place within just three industries: automobiles, petrochemicals (oil), and pharmaceuticals.

Study after study has demonstrated that oligopolistic corporations are the largest contributors to political campaigns in America. This has been accomplished by the formation of Political Action Committees (PACs) and so-called soft money contributions, which function to get around established campaign financing laws. Sometimes corporate lobbyists actually help politicians write legislation that they favor, or work in the political campaigns of the politicians they sponsor. Other times, members of large corporations actually run for office themselves, or accept posts as cabinet officers or undersecretaries in the executive branch of the federal government. Many corporations have also established foundations and associations that take positions on public issues.

All these practices function to keep political power in America entrenched within large corporations and inhibit reform of oligopoly practices.

SEE ALSO

campaign finance; price fixing; price discrimination; predatory practices; automobiles; pharmaceutical industry; oil crimes.

BIBLIOGRAPHY. Erik Barnouw, *The Sponsor* (Oxford University Press, 1978); Marshall Clinard and Peter Yeager (1978) "Corporate Crime: Issues in Research," *Criminology* (v.16, August 1978); Mark Green, Beverly Moore, Jr., and Bruce Wasserman, *The Closed Enterprise System* (Viking, 1972); David R. Simon, *Elite Deviance* (Allyn & Bacon, 2002).

DAVID R. SIMON
UNIVERSITY OF NORTH FLORIDA
UNIVERSITY OF CALIFORNIA, BERKELEY

Oraflex

ORAFLEX, A PAINKILLER for arthritis patients sold by Indianapolis, Indiana-based pharmaceutical giant Eli Lilly, is believed to have killed 49 people in the United States after the company illegally concealed evidence of several hundred deaths caused by the medication in overseas markets. Oraflex, known as Opren outside of the United States, went on the overseas market in 1980. From January 1981 to June 1982, Lilly received reports about problems with the medication in the United Kingdom and other countries where the drug was sold. The reports said that four people died from liver failure after taking Oraflex, three people suffered kidney or liver problems, and three developed jaundice. Lilly put Oraflex on the U.S. market in May 1982. On August 5, 1982, Britain banned the drug and Lilly voluntarily withdrew Oraflex from the U.S. and international markets.

Federal law requires companies to inform the Food and Drug Administration (FDA) of any adverse reactions from new drugs but Lilly did not do so. In 1985, Lilly pleaded guilty to 25 criminal counts for failing to inform federal officials of four deaths and six illnesses that occurred after patients took Oraflex. However, FDA officials declared that Oraflex had been linked to 49 deaths in the U.S. and several hundred abroad. The pharmaceutical company received the maximum penalty of $25,000, or $1,000 for each count. All of the counts were misdemeanors. Federal authorities did not charge the company with intentional deception. William Shedden, former vice president and chief medical officer of Lilly Research Laboratories, pleaded no contest to 15 criminal counts related to the drug and was fined $15,000.

In Britain, Lilly became the target of a lawsuit launched by 1,300 Britons who claimed that they had become ill, or that relatives died from taking Oraflex. In 1988, 1,000 of these plaintiffs settled with Lilly for an estimated £6 million ($10.9 million) to £7 million ($12.8 million). The company continued to deny that it intentionally withheld medically significant information.

SEE ALSO

Eli Lilly& Company; pharmaceutical industry; healthcare fraud; Food and Drug Administration.

BIBLIOGRAPHY. Joe Davidson and Carolyn Phillips, "Eli Lilly Admits It Failed to Inform U.S. of Deaths, Illnesses Tied to Oraflex," *Wall Street Journal* (August 22, 1985); "Lilly Says 1,000 Britons Settle in Oraflex Drug Case," *Wall Street Journal* (January 15, 1988).

CARYN E. NEUMANN, PH.D.
OHIO STATE UNIVERSITY

organized crime

THE ITALIAN MAFIA and its American counterpart has been the most high-profile organized crime genre for much of the 20th century. Increasingly, the term *Mafia* can be applied to any group of nefarious underground criminals, whether of Russian, Indian, Mexican, Jewish, or Italian heritage, who engage in organized crime. Organized crime, in turn, can be broadly defined as two or more persons conspiring together on a continuing and secretive basis to participate in profit-oriented illegal activities. Like other criminal organizations, the Mafia (also known in America as Cosa Nostra) is involved in a myriad of unsavory activities.

In addition to common organized criminal conspiracies, such as extortion, illegal gambling, smuggling, loan-sharking, and drug trafficking, the American mafia has been involved in what can be classified as white collar crimes, such as business and labor racketeering, insurance fraud, embezzlement, bankruptcy fraud, government (tax) fraud, and stock market manipulation.

ORIGINS

There has long been a debate about the origins of the Mafia, although there appears to be a consensus that it evolved from a patriarchic social network that has existed in Sicily, Italy, for centuries. Secret groups made up of ethnic Italians began to emerge in North America during the latter part of the 19th century with the massive Italian diaspora, or emigration. The debate circles around whether a secret criminal conspiracy, methods, and infrastructure was exported from Italy to North America around this time or conversely, if the origins of the North American Cosa Nostra can more accurately be traced to the cultural environment indigenous to the United States, and to a lesser extent, Canada.

As a reflection of its secretive nature, the Mafia, has been defined, conceptualized, and characterized in any number of different ways. Some have argued that the Mafia is a worldwide criminal organization headquartered in Sicily, with branch plant families located throughout the world, including North America.

Under this characterization, the Mafia is an inter-connected global criminal conspiracy, with the same historical origins, over-lapping memberships, and corresponding codes and membership rites of passage. Others have argued that the American Cosa Nostra is separate and distinct from the Sicilian Mafia in its origins, development, and operations.

OUR THING

Some scholars stress that the word *mafia* should not be used as a noun to describe a particular secret society or criminal conspiracy. Instead, it represents a philosophy that is based in historical Sicilian cultural traditions. Finally, there are those who reduce this debate to a simple question of semantics: whether one calls it the mafia, the Honored Society, the Yakuza, the Russian Mafia, La Cosa Nostra, the Syndicate, Our Thing, or any other name, it involves a group of men, mostly (but not exclusively) of a distinct ethnic heritage, that is involved in ongoing criminal conspiracies.

Historical evidence suggests that beginning in late 19th-century America, groups and networks made up of ethnic Italians, in particular Sicilians, increasingly were involved in organized criminal conspiracies. The growth of Italian organized crime in America was the result of a potent mix of sociological customs and traditions associated with the Sicilian Mafia. These combined with the foreign American urban environment (complete with a tradition of lawlessness, poverty, and discrimination) into which immigrants were acculturated. Italians as well as English, Irish, and Jewish immigrants were all major players in the formative years of organized crime in North America.

The earliest criminal activities undertaken by the Italian groups centered on the extortion of money from Italian immigrants and businesses. In addition, they increasingly offered goods and services, both legal and illegal, to satisfy the demands and vices of Italian communities in urban America. They ran lotteries and other games of chance and operated houses of prostitution. They were loan-sharks to gamblers and also served as bankers and moneylenders to those who could not borrow anywhere else, often charging usurious interest rates. They captured a monopoly on artichokes, olive oil, wine grapes, and other necessities of Italian life and extracted a price for permitting their distribution. They helped future Italian immigrants make their way to North America, often at a fee that placed the new arrival and their sponsors in a state of eternal debt to the Mafia benefactor.

PROHIBITION

It was the criminalization of liquor in 1920 that truly launched Italian-American criminal groups, and organized crime in general, into a more sophisticated and profitable epoch. The widespread demand for outlawed liquor in the United States led to the ongoing development of well-organized groups and networks of distillers and bootleggers. Prohibition expanded and organized the underworld, transforming the existing marauding gangs of smugglers and extortionists into sophisticated and extremely profitable criminal enterprises.

The organization of Italian-American criminals was also heightened in the early 1930s through the formal establishment of Cosa Nostra families in New York and other American cities, as well as the founding of the Commission, a ruling clique and arbitrator, made up of the heads of all the major Cosa Nostra families, that mapped out territories among the participating families and established rules and regulations, a code of honor, and dispute settlement mechanisms. While individuals and groups of any ethnic background could be part of or come before the Commission, binding decisions could only be made by Sicilian members.

The period between the repeal of Prohibition in 1934 and the outbreak of World War II (1939) was one of expansion and consolidation of the Cosa Nostra. According to organized-crime researcher Robert C. Stewart (1994) there are a number of reasons why Italian-American crime groups emerged and prospered in the underworld during Prohibition and the decades to come.

First, they had a scope, purpose, and membership that transcended that of any single conspiratorial episode. Second, members shared a deep sub-cultural bond that was reinforced by a Mafia code that emphasized loyalty and secrecy. Third, they emphasized a networking structure that enabled members to collaborate on joint business ventures with a wide variety of criminal groups and networks, including ties with criminal organizations in Italy. Fourth, Cosa Nostra members continuously exploited opportunities to make money in a systematic, expansive, protracted, and diversified manner. They were capitalist entrepreneurs in the true sense, and they fashioned their criminal operations to be highly synergistic in nature. For example, gambling operations fed their loan-sharking business, which in turn generated the indebted business person (who then forfeits a businesses) or the debtor warehouse worker (who pinpoints a valuable item in storage to be stolen).

Since they first appeared on the North American landscape, Mafia groups, members, and associates adroitly and successfully infiltrated a wide range of legitimate businesses to further their legal and illegal commercial activities, including companies involved in the production of alcoholic spirits, commercial transportation, entertainment, importing and exporting, hotels, restaurants, bars, automobile dealerships, construction, real estate, waste disposal, food distribution, garment manufacturing, and legalized gaming, to name just a few.

JUST BUSINESS

The Mafia also discovered that the techniques it used in the underworld, that is, extortion, violence, intimidation, and corruption could also be used in the legitimate commercial world with success. Mark H. Moore suggested in *Major Issues in Organized Crime* (1987) that the organized crime group should be viewed as a business firm pursuing profit with a portfolio that encompasses illicit as well as licit enterprises: "They coolly calculate how best to make money without worrying about whether a planned enterprise is illegal."

Annelise G. Anderson, in *The Business of Organized Crime* (1979), provides six reasons for organized criminal involvement in legitimate businesses.

Revenue and wages: For persons involved in organized crime, profit provides motivation; not all members of organized crime are able to make sufficient income from illicit activities. Anthony Russo, an underboss in Long Branch, New Jersey, once complained to Sam De Cavalcante that the *amici nostri* (friends of ours, meaning members of the Mafia) could not support themselves financially. In addition to legitimate revenue, cash-based companies provide a source of "skimming," which provide a source of tax-free income.

Diversification: Another reason that criminal entrepreneurs invest in legitimate businesses is for the diversification of capital; spreading investments into a number of different ventures. Diversification may entail moving into legitimate industries and introducing unfair and openly illegal tactics. A legitimate business provides the organized crime figure with income security that may not be available exclusively through illegal activities.

Transfer: Illegitimate enterprises are often difficult to legally transfer to dependents (particularly if they are female). Investing in legitimate enterprises such as a business or real estate ensures that an estate can be legally inherited.

Services: A criminal entrepreneur operating a legitimate business is in a position to act as a patron for a person in need of legitimate employment, such as associates on probation or parole.

Front: A legitimate business can provide a front or a base of operations for a host of illegal activities, including loan-sharking, gambling, and drug trafficking, to name a few.

Taxes: A legitimate business can provide a tax cover, thereby reducing the risk of being charged with income-tax evasion. Funds from an illegitimate enterprise can be mixed with those from the legitimate business, particularly if it is a cash-based business.

To this list, we can add a seventh reason: money laundering. While companies are established by criminal entrepreneurs for a number of reasons, arguably the greatest single reason for organized crime's present infiltration into the private sector is to launder the proceeds of their illicit activities. Especially attractive to money launderers are businesses that customarily handle a high volume of cash transactions, such as retail stores, restaurants, bars, currency exchange dealers, gas stations, etc. because the cash proceeds of illegal activities can be deposited into bank accounts as legitimate revenue (either alone or commingled with revenue actually produced from the business). Due to the immense profits generated by their illegal activities, in particular drug trafficking, which became a major source of revenue for the Mafia beginning in the 1950s, there was an increased reliance on money laundering through legitimate businesses.

CASINOS

It was during the late 1940s that the groups began to parlay their significant experience in illegal gambling, bookmaking, and underground casinos to legal gaming by financing and controlling some of the original casinos in Las Vegas, Nevada. Benjamin (Bugsy) Siegel, who had long been associated with some of the leading figures of the New York Mafia families (including Charles Luciano, Meyer Lansky, and Frank Costello) was sent to California to oversee the West Coast operations of the Cosa Nostra. This included overseeing the lucrative racing wire service, and increasing the mob's influence in Hollywood's labor unions. Siegel also scouted out Las Vegas as the possible site for a gambling casino and hotel that would be funded by the New York families. Soon after his beloved Flamingo Hotel opened, Siegel was killed by the very individuals who bankrolled his vision. After his death, Mafia families from New York and other parts of the country continued to invest in and ultimately controlled many of the casinos in Las Vegas, helping to situate the city as the gambling capital of North America.

UNIONS AND RACKETEERING

Mafia members also had a long-standing relationship with labor unions, influencing and even controlling certain union locals by relying on two tactical weapons: corruption (of union, business, and government officials) and the capacity to intimidate by threats of violence. The labor racketeering activities of the Mafia included extorting businesses by threatening union problems, raiding union pension funds, negotiating "sweetheart contracts" between unions and management, and providing union membership and fictitious jobs to Mafia members and associates. Labor racketeering provided a foray for the mafia to extort legitimate businesses and, in some cases, entire industries through intimidation, control over labor unions, or ties with corrupt government officials.

According to Howard Abadinsky in *Organized Crime* (2003) New York City's Fulton Fish Market, the source of much of New York's seafood, represents a classic saga in the ability of the mafia to control a legitimate industry through labor and business racketeering. Though the market was established in 1833, the organized crime connection began in the early 1920s, when Joseph (Socks) Lanza, a member of New York's Genovese crime family, organized workers into Local 359 of the United Seafood Worker's Union. As head of the local, Lanza extorted money from every dealer in the market and, along with his brother Nunzio, determined which businesses could operate in the market. Through his leadership of the union and influence over the supply of labor, Lanza asserted control over fishing boats.

He also controlled the Fulton Market's Watchmen's Protective Association, and any market vendor who failed to have a Lanza watchman look after his vehicles usually had slashed tires the next day. Lanza was convicted of racketeering in 1938, and in 1943, he was convicted of extorting local Teamster union officials. Convictions and imprisonment notwithstanding, Lanza continued to control the Fulton Market until his death in 1968, when the responsibility was passed to another Genovese family member.

Despite the fact that the market operated on city property, government controls remained absent for decades, creating a lawless atmosphere in which rules of operation evolved through violence and intimidation. In 1988, as a result of a civil action brought by the U.S. Department of Justice, U.S. Attorney Rudolph Giuliani convinced a federal judge that the market was dominated by organized crime and an outside administrator was appointed to monitor the market and rid it of illegal activities. Reforms established by the city have reduced, if not eliminated, the influence of organized crime. Ironically, this is seen as a mixed blessing by the market's wholesale dealers, who complain of rigid rules and increased overhead costs.

FRAUD

Beginning in the 1950s, the Mafia became increasingly involved in fraud, including government taxation fraud, insurance fraud, bankruptcy fraud, and stock market manipulation. Government taxation fraud primarily entailed the smuggling and distribution of high-taxed goods, such as liquor, cigarettes, and motor fuel. Contraband liquor and cigarettes were obtained from truck hijackings, and by illegally transporting cigarettes and liquor from low-tax states for sale in high-tax states.

Mafia groups in the United States and Canada are also known to cooperate with Russian crime groups in fuel-bootlegging scams designed to defraud the government of federal excise taxes (FET) levied on oil sales. In one type of FET fraud, numerous dummy companies are established to purchase home heating (diesel) oil, which is tax-free. The diesel oil is then sold through the fake companies as diesel fuel, which is subject to federal taxes. The taxes are collected by the criminals, but never submitted to the government, explains the Federal Bureau of Investigation (1995). Insurance fraud began with mafia members taking over businesses (often from recalcitrant debtors) and then committing arson to collect the insurance money. Government reports as far back as the early 1970s documented the involvement of mafia groups in bankruptcy fraud. Members would purchase or take over a business, and then buy merchandise on as large a scale as possible through the use of credit. The merchandise is turned into cash, much of which is skimmed. The business eventually is forced into bankruptcy by its creditors, which, of course, was the original intent of the scam.

For example, a principal in a major Italian-Canadian drug-trafficking organization in Canada regularly bankrupted his businesses. Once a business went bankrupt, he would arrange for a new company to be formed to buy out the assets of the failed business at a reduced cost. Bankruptcy was also used to void intentionally accrued debt. "Flipping" companies through fraudulent bankruptcies also facilitates money laundering; pumping illicit funds through a procession of businesses helps create an obfuscating layering process that is essential to legitimizing the proceeds of crime.

The initial foray of the mafia into the stock market began with the rudimentary theft of stock certificates and the use of intimidation to extort money and insider information from brokers. However, the securities market is also subject to more sophisticated manipulation and fraud by mafia groups. In a 1996 report, *BusinessWeek* alleged that some families had established a network of stock promoters, securities dealers, and "boiler rooms" that sold stocks nationwide through high-pressure sales tactics. The article estimated that four mafia families, as well as Russian criminal entrepreneurs, directly owned or controlled, through front men, two dozen brokerage firms. Citing court documents, the article stated that Philip Abramo, a ranking member in the New Jersey-based DeCavalcante family, controlled at least four brokerage firms through front men, and exerted influence upon still more firms. Other securities dealers and traders were believed to pay extortion money or "tribute" to the mafia as just another cost of doing business.

PUMP AND DUMP

In 2000, law enforcement officials in New York uncovered a coordinated effort between a mafia group and Russian criminals to steal millions from brokerage firms using threats, bribes, pension-fund raids, and "pump and dump" stock manipulations. The indictments allege the defendants profited by secretly controlling blocks of shares and pushing them onto ordinary investors through high-pressure "boiler room" sales calls. The price was kept artificially high by refusing to let anyone sell. Mafia enforcers would be stationed at the office's trading window to ensure none of the brokers could sell on behalf of their clients. After the stock value rose, mafia members cashed in by selling their secretly held shares, before the inflated value of the stocks plummeted.,

In court testimony, former members of the New Jersey DeCavalcante crime family provided a glimpse into organized crime activity on Wall Street, especially during the internet boom of the 1990s. Vincent (Vinnie Ocean) Palermo, a self-confessed murderer and former acting boss of the family, told the court that Philip Abramo was "always bragging about how much money he made on Wall Street, saying he was the best in the business." Victor DiChiara, another former associate of the DeCavalcante family, qualified as a broker in the early 1990s and worked for several Wall Street firms. DiChiara testified in court that he began his career as a broker at Hanover Sterling, which he stated was owned by two Genovese associates, Roy Ageloff and Bob Cataggio. Hanover was a "boiler-room operation" designed to "pump and dump" shares. DiChiara alleges that in 1994, Abramo asked him

for a list of house stocks, the shares Hanover controlled. DiChiara claims Abramo told him he had approached Hanover's bosses and warned them of the drop in price, which could be averted if they paid him $500,000. The offer was rebuffed. When the shares started falling, Abramo again offered to help, this time for $5 million. Hanover refused and true to his predictions, the value of these stocks crashed, causing Hanover clients to lose millions, and which eventually led Hanover to its bankruptcy.

Abramo's market manipulation activities were not confined to the United States. In Vancouver, Canada, stockbroker Jean Claude Hauchecorne, who worked at Pacific International Securities Inc. until mid-1999, was accosted by a client he knew as Louis Metzer (but was Abramo), whom he recognized from a photo in the 1996 *BusinessWeek* article. With Abramo was Philip Gurian, another mafia-connected figure who placed dozens of orders with Hauchecorne to buy and sell U.S. stocks, many of which had been identified by *BusinessWeek* as mob-manipulated stocks. They demanded that Hauchecorne return $1.75 million he had transferred to Switzerland on the instructions of another mafia operative, Eric Wynn, who had had a falling out with Abramo and Gurian. Otherwise, they would kill him.

The Ontario Securities Commission, the largest securities regulator in Canada, speculated that organized crime is active in the junior markets across Canada, through money laundering, manipulating share prices, and conducting insider trades. In the 1970s, William Obront, a loan shark and the financial brains behind Montreal's once-powerful Cotroni Mafia family, was charged with over 400 counts of fraudulently manipulating stock shares over a 15-year period.

INFILTRATION

In addition to the direct negative impact that extortion or fraud may have on businesses, the involvement of organized crime in the legitimate economy has enormous repercussions for individual companies and entire industries. Crime groups that have infiltrated businesses or labor unions often strive for monopolistic control over a particular industry, which they will pursue through fraud, corruption, labor racketeering, intimidation, and violence. Well-organized fraud and money laundering can distort the financial markets leading to market instability and deflate investor confidence. Illegal entrepreneurs may be able to use their criminal assets to assist their legal enterprises and disadvantage their non-criminal counterparts. Businesses run by organized crime groups have access to capital (produced by illegal activities) that is not available to legitimate business people, which can undercut competitors with below-cost prices.

SEE ALSO
gambling and lotteries; prostitution; drug trafficking; securities fraud; scams; Cuba; Capone, Alphonse.

BIBLIOGRAPHY. Howard Abadinsky, *Organized Crime* (Wadsworth Publishing, 2003); Joseph L. Albini, *American Mafia: Genesis of a Legend* (Appleton-Century-Crofts, 1971); Joseph L. Albini, "The Distribution of Drugs: Models of Criminal Organization and their Integration," *Drugs, Crime and Social Policy: Research Issues and Concerns* (Allyn and Bacon, 1992); Annelise Anderson, *The Business of Organized Crime: A Cosa Nostra Family* (Hoover Institution Press, 1979); Associated Press, "Mob Said to Infiltrate Wall Street," (March 2, 2000); "Troubled Waters: Pacific International Is Under the Microscope of the BC Securities Commission," *Canadian Business* (November 15, 2002); Donald R. Cressey, *Theft of a Nation: The Structure and Operations of Organized Crime in America* (Harper and Row, 1969); E.J. Defranco, *Anatomy of a Scam: A Case Study of a Planned Bankruptcy by Organized Crime* (U.S. Department of Justice, 1973); Ovid Demaris, *The Last Mafioso* (Times Books, 1981); Dow Jones News Service, "Federal Officials Charge 120 Individuals in Mob-Related Securities Fraud Case." June 15, 2000); Federal Bureau of Investigation, "Eurasian Criminal Enterprises," *Overview of International Organized Crime* (U.S. Department of Justice, 1995); Sean M. McSweeney, "The Sicilian Mafia and Its Impact on the United States," *FBI Law Enforcement Bulletin* (February, 1987); Mark H. Moore, "Organized Crime as a Business Enterprise," *Major Issues in Organized Crime* (National Institute of Justice, 1987); "Dirty Funds Haunt Small Exchanges," *National Post* (November 13, 2002); Quebec Police Commission Inquiry on Organized Crime, *Organized Crime and the World of Business* (Government of Quebec, 1977); Ed Reid, *Mafia* (Random House, 1952); Peter Reuter, "Racketeers as Cartel Organizers," *The Politics and Economics of Organized Crime* (Lexington Books, 1984); Robert C. Stewart, *An Introduction to the Elements of Traditional Organized Crime in America* (unpublished, 1994); "The Mafia on Wall Street," *Sunday Times* (May 18, 2003); Burton Turkus and Sid Feder, *Murder, Inc.: The Story of "the Syndicate"* (Farrar, Straus ,and Young, 1951); Gary Weiss, "The Mob on Wall Street," *BusinessWeek* (December 16, 1996).

STEPHEN SCHNEIDER, PH.D.
RYERSON UNIVERSITY, CANADA

outside directors

QUITE SIMPLY, outside directors are those members of a company's board of directors without executive responsibilities, and who often face information asymmetry about the company. They are usually appointed to the board of directors for their contribution to the expansion of the enterprise's strategy and to provide important knowledge not otherwise available to management. Outside directors, like inside directors, have two main roles: to ensure that the company delivers returns to shareholders (the performance function) and to ensure it acts in accordance with laws and regulations (the accountability function).

However, given the distance of their day-to-day operations, outside directors have more of a role to play in terms of the accountability function than in terms of the performance function. Outside directors are beneficial to an enterprise provided the company does not employ them in any other manner, including consulting contracts.

Outside directors provide access to valuable resources and information, but several corporate governance analysts insist on tighter rules of independence including a restriction on the number of directorships a single individual can hold, investor participation in the selection and appointment of outsiders, and mandated meetings with significant shareholders.

In the early 2000s, firms made significant changes to their programs, plans, and policies for members of their boards of directors. A struggle continues between the growing need for qualified persons and the reluctance by some candidates to join boards. This reluctance can be attributed to increased time requirements, and potential reputation and financial risk.

The result is increased competition for qualified board members, especially standing chief executive officers and candidates with substantial financial experience. This, in turn, impacts outside-director compensation. If outside directors are to provide meaningful protection for investors, they must be in a position to challenge the executive management and draw attention to dubious practices, even in apparently successful companies.

While independence is, above all, concerned with the integrity of the individual in question, it is not unreasonable to suggest that financial ties, whether personal, business, political or philanthropic, threaten the independence of outside directors and therefore their motivation to actively challenge management. But, rather than simply meeting some checklist of independence criteria, analysts say it is imperative that outsiders are able, in practice not just in theory, to express views to the board that are different from those of the chief executive officer. They must also be confident that, provided this is done in a considered way, they will not suffer reprisals.

Several proposals intend to set limits on how much money can be exchanged between the company for which an individual is a director, and another company for which she is an executive or employee. For example, the New York Stock Exchange (NYSE) proposed that if a director received fees in excess of $100,000 a year in direct payment from a company, then she should be presumed not to be independent until five years after such fees stop being received. Some proposals extend the scope of such fees to include nonemployment based compensation, such as executive consultancy work.

The collapse of Enron Corporation triggered corporate governance analysts to question whether outside directors should be accountable for, or simply be more aware of, a company's complex finances. In the United States, there are specific rules that aim to ensure that outside directors are independent, but in the light of financial high-profile events in the early 2000s, it is questionable whether these rules have had any real impact on the effectiveness of audit committees.

Of course, the level of diligence required in an increasingly demanding corporate environment may mean that outside directors need to devote more time to their role as ethical accountability partners, who also oversee efficiency of organizations' productivity.

SEE ALSO

board of directors; interlocking directorates.

BIBLIOGRAPHY. George Kassinis, "Corporate Boards and Outside Stakeholders as Determinants of Environmental Litigation," *Strategic Management Journal* (v.23/5, 2002); J.J. McConnel, "Outside Directors," *Financial Review* (v.38/1, 2003); Michael Weisbach, "Outside Directors and CEO Turnover," *Journal of Financial Economics* (v.20/1, 1988); W. Glenn Rowe and Debra Rankin, "Insiders or Outsiders: Who Should Have More Power on a Board?" *Ivey Business Journal* (v.67/2, 2002).

ALFREDO MANUEL COELHO
UNIVERSITY OF MONTPELLIER, FRANCE

Owens Corning

ALTHOUGH OWENS Corning, organized in 1938, sold less than 1 percent of all asbestos products, by 2000 it had been driven to bankruptcy by the settlement of 243,000 asbestos-related claims, with more claims pending. Owens-Illinois manufactured and sold Kaylo, a high-temperature calcium silicate pipe insulation which contained asbestos, from the late 1940s through the early 1950s. At that time Owens Corning agreed to sell the asbestos product. In the late 1950s, Owens Corning purchased Kaylo assets and began to manufacture and sell the product.

Following indications of potential health problems, Owens Corning, Johns-Manville, and other asbestos products manufacturers put warning labels on their products, and in 1972 Owens Corning removed asbestos from Kaylo, although it did continue to make that product with only calcium silicate. In 1980, the Occupational Safety and Health Administration (OSHA) began to require warnings on products that contained asbestos and to regulate their use.

In 1978, two shipyard workers who had developed asbestosis, an asbestos-related lung disease, filed a class-action lawsuit on behalf of 5,000 other workers against Toledo, Ohio -based Owens Corning and 14 other asbestos producers. The suit claimed these companies knew the hazardous nature of the mineral as early as 1938 but did not do enough to protect people working with it.

Huge settlements were awarded in asbestos-related suits, including an $18 million award for punitive damages to each of three New York victims. The amount was said to have been settled on because the number 18 symbolizes life in Hebrew. There was an additional $1.2 million in compensatory damages awarded in this case. Johns-Manville, who had an estimated 40-50 percent share of U.S. asbestos liability, filed for bankruptcy in 1982.

Over the next few years, companies with asbestos-related liabilities and their insurance carriers formed and disbanded organizations in attempts to control fallout from the issue. More of these manufacturers filed bankruptcy, and Owens Corning took its second major reserve ($1.1 billion) on its financial balance sheet with which to pay litigants in 1996.

Also in 1996, Owens Corning filed a Racketeer Influenced and Corrupt Organizations (RICO) suit against three testing laboratories, claiming the Mississippi, Louisiana, and Alabama companies manipulated medical tests so they would give false indications of asbestos injury. At the time the suit was filed, Owens Corning stated they had paid $2.6 billion for asbestos claims. This included some of the 40,000 claims which were from allegedly false lab reports.

In July 1997, Owens Corning acquired Fibreboard, another manufacturer of asbestos products. They filed suit against tobacco companies four months later, claiming that asbestos workers who smoked had a much higher rate of asbestos injury than those who did not, and asked that the tobacco companies be required to pay part of the settlements. This claim was dismissed by a Mississippi Circuit court in 2001. By the middle of 2000, Owens Corning had resolved over 243,000 asbestos claims and had another 27,000 pending. With these financial draws on the company and a weakening economy, Owens Corning's long-term debt grew to over $2 billion in 2000. The 62-year-old company filed for Chapter 11 bankruptcy on October 5, 2000.

SEE ALSO

asbestos; Occupational Safety and Health Act; Johns-Manville; employee safety.

BIBLIOGRAPHY. "Owens Corning, Asbestos," www.owenscorning.com; (2003); "Shipyard Workers Name 15 Asbestos Producers in $7 Billion Suit," *Chemical Week* (November 8, 1978); "Jurors Calculate Punitive Damages in Unusual Manner: Big Award in Asbestos Case Was Based on Number 18, Meaning Life in Hebrew," *Wall Street Journal* (April 14, 1994); Ann Shoket, "South," *The American Lawyer* (September, 1996); "Mississippi Judge Rejects Asbestos Company Claims Against R.J. Reynolds Tobacco Company and Other Tobacco Manufacturers," PR Newswire (May 24, 2001); Jim Brumm, "Asbestos Claims Push Owens Corning into Bankruptcy: $5.7B in Liabilities: Decline in Firm's Building Materials Sales Didn't Help," *National Post* (October 6, 2000).

LINDA M. CREIBAUM
ARKANSAS STATE UNIVERSITY

P

patent infringement

INNOVATION IS the motivating force in most businesses. Without new inventions and ideas, companies would be unable to keep up with competition and would stagnate. This has been true since America was made up of 13 separate colonies, and the United States of America was only a dream for visionaries. Benjamin Franklin, one of the Founding Fathers of the United States, who played a role in forming both the Declaration of Independence in 1776 and the United States Constitution in 1787, is often credited with discovering electricity.

In truth, Franklin invented the lightening rod that led to discoveries about how electricity works. He also invented bifocals, the odometer, and the Franklin stove. Inventors such as Franklin have an intellectual property right to own their inventions, and this right was considered so important that patent protection was included in the U.S. Constitution (Article 1, Section 8). Patent protection allows individuals and businesses to control who uses their inventions and provides them with recognition and monetary benefits. When others violate those rights, patent infringement occurs.

The U.S. Patent Office was created to administer all laws relating to federal patents and to advise the president and the Department of Commerce on all matters related to protecting patents and copyrights, and to offer advice on dealing with the ways that intellectual property is related to trade both domestically and internationally. In 1988, the name of the patenting agency was changed to the U.S. Patent and Trademark Office (PTO) to reflect the growing importance of protecting trademarks as intellectual property.

The PTO issues three types of patents: plant patents, design patents, and utility patents. Plant patents are given for new plants that have been asexually reproduced. Design patents are assigned for the design of a product, like a sofa or a beverage dispenser. Most patents approved by the Patent and Trademark Office are utility patents that protect inventions such as machines, processes, and improvements to existing machines and processes.

In addition to approving and renewing patents, the PTO maintains existing records of all federal and international patents to assist applicants who always bear the responsibility of searching for existing or similar patents before a patent application is filed. Once a patent application is approved, the owner of the patent has the right to exclude others from making, using, or selling the patented invention as long as the patent is valid.

The Patent and Trademark Office has no authority to hear cases of patent infringement because that authority is given to various courts of jurisdiction. Patent infringement occurs when another party makes use of a patented product or invention by making, using, or selling the invention without the patent owner's permission and without paying any licensing fees that may be required. Patent owners have a legal right to sue in order to protect their inventions. However, patent infringement is much harder to prove than infringement of trademarks or copyrights, which are more concrete. Patent infringement cases may be expensive, and they way take years to wind their way through the courts. In 2002, for example, less than 3,000 patent infringement cases were filed.

In order to win a patent infringement lawsuit, a plaintiff needs to show first of all that the alleged infringer willfully and intentionally violated the patent owner's rights. The burden of proof is always on the owner of the patent to show that patent infringement did indeed occur. The plaintiff must produce evidence to back up her claim to the patent, as well as documenting any damage that resulted from the infringement. Patent infringement evidence may be circumstantial, but it must be either substantially credible or persuasive.

NO USE REQUIREMENT

Federal courts have accepted infringement of patents in cases where the defendant has not actually used the patented invention, but has been prepared to use it in a way that violates the owner's patent. Plaintiffs have not always been required to show that the defendant profited monetarily from the infringement. For instance, in 1984 in *Trans-World Manufacturing Corporation v. Al Nyman and Sons*, a federal district court held that infringement occurred when Nyman and Sons provided a display rack free of charge to its customers even though Trans-World owned the patent on the display rack and Nyman and Sons had no right to use it.

Recoveries for patent infringement are limited to the six years preceding the filing of the complaint against the alleged violator of the patent. Remedies for patent infringement include injunctions, damages, and attorney's fees. Injunctions are issued to prevent an alleged violator from continuing to use the patented product or process. Compensatory damage is normally based on lost profits, established royalties, and reasonable royalties. The reasonable royalty measure was designed to help judges determine adequate reimbursement for losses incurred through patent infringement in

cases where the patent owner is not able to document specific losses. Traditionally, the judge attempts to determine what the patent owner's profits would have been if a valid license at a "reasonable rate" had been issued for the time the infringer illegally used the product or process. Additionally, a violator may be forced to pay prejudgment interest and increased damages. The Patent Act of 1982 provided a means of settling patent disputes through binding arbitration if both parties agree to do so in writing.

AWARDS AND JUDGMENTS

Judgments in patent infringement cases have frequently resulted in enormous awards for plaintiffs, partly because courts are able to award treble damages in situations where willful infringement occurs. Such a case occurred in 1982 when Johns-Manville was found to have literally copied a fluorescent light fixture from the company brochure of LAM, a small competitor. The judgment against Johns-Manville included triple damages for lost profits, triple damages for reduced profit, and triple damages for projected lost profits, plus prejudgment interest and attorneys' fees for a total award of $1,639,824.21. Other large awards in recent years have included a $56 million award won by Pfizer Pharmaceuticals from International Rectifier which infringed on Pfizer's patent rights to a particular antibiotic. Pfizer also recovered $44 million from American Hospital Supply which infringed on a blood oxygenator patent.

Other awards were even higher. Procter and Gamble was allotted $125 million when Nabisco illegally used a patented cookie recipe. Smith Industries won almost double that amount, which included a $70 million interest payment, from Hughes Tool's infringement of a rock drive bit. Kodak was forced to pay its rival Polaroid $873 million for infringing on a patent for an instant camera design.

Lawyers for defendants in patent infringement cases have the responsibility to raise certain questions to prove to the court that their clients' actions did not infringe on the patent rights of others. A common practice is for defense lawyers to question the validity of the original patent. It is also possible for the alleged infringer to prove that her use of the invention in question was not covered by the owner's patent. Language is particularly important in determining infringement of patent rights. It may be possible for a defendant to show that the language of the original patent did not prevent it from being used in a certain way. Patent infringement cases follow the rule of common law in the United States, drawing on a body of existing decisions or precedents for guidance. While the federal government has the right to use a patented invention without express permission of the patent owner, the government is required to compensate the owner for use of the invention. If the federal government violates a patent, the plaintiff has the option of asking the Court of Claims to award damages. Cases of patent infringement at the federal level may be appealed all the way to the U.S. Supreme Court.

INFRINGEMENT LAWSUITS

Because many of the most impressive technological advances of the last several decades have been involved with computers, a number of prominent patent infringement lawsuits have dealt with these technologies. For example, In 2003, VIA sued Media-Tek for patent infringement, claiming that the company's products used on computers throughout the country infringed on VIA's patent for the process that allowed Media-Tek products to increase the bandwidth of high-speed optical storage devices. A case filed by Multi-Format, a company composed of two inventors located in New Jersey, claimed that Multi-Format has a patent on the entire process of playing DVDs, and the company threatened to sue all DVD retailers, studios, replicators, and manufacturers if they did not obtain licenses for various DVD processes. The technology media and the music industry responded to the threat by suggesting that if the suit were successful, it could raise the price of DVDs beyond the reach of many consumers. In some instances, patent infringement cases are settled without disclosing the terms of the agreement. For example, in June 2003, Silicon Image won an undisclosed amount from Genesis Microchip for violating its patents on the Digital Visual Interface (DVI) and the High-Definition Multimedia Interface (HDMI).

Microsoft may have been sued more than any other company in the computer industry, and both judges and juries have enjoyed attacking the creator of such high-profile products as Windows, Internet Explorer, Microsoft Network, and Microsoft Office. Hundreds of cases have been filed against Mi-

crosoft since the introduction of Windows 95 changed the computer industry in August 1995. In the midst of Microsoft's troubles with the Department of Justice over an antitrust lawsuit, Bill Gates and company were also sued by Sun Microsystems in a trademark infringement suit over Microsoft's use of Sun's Java code that was settled for $20 million in early 2003. In August 2003, a judge in another patent infringement case agreed with InterTrust Technologies that a number of Microsoft products infringed on InterTrust Technologies' digital securities patent. A $521 million settlement was levied against Microsoft for infringing on a process patented by Eolas Technologies that was used in Microsoft Internet Explorer.

The internet has opened new avenues for patents and patent infringement lawsuits. For instance, in May 2003, a Virginia jury found that eBay, an internet auction site, had violated the patent of inventor Thomas Wooten who had developed the process for an online marketplace. Wooten could have insisted that eBay stop using his patented process, which would have put the highly profitable company out of business. The internet also came into play in a battle between America Online (AOL) and Microsoft in the late 1980s when AOL insisted that it had invented the Instant Messenger technology and unsuccessfully tried to prevent Microsoft from using Instant Messenger on the Microsoft Network (MSN).

A number of patent infringement lawsuits have also involved drug companies that have traditionally fought the development of generic drugs, and which have tried to hold onto patents as long as possible, denying consumers the option of choosing between high-priced name brand drugs and cheaper and equally effective generic products Large drug companies have frequently charged generic developers with patent infringement. On August 19, 2003, the Food and Drug Administration (FDA) dealt a blow to the name brand drug companies by announcing that patents would henceforth be issued for no more than 30 months. After that period, developers of generic drugs were free to begin testing products in preparation for their manufacture. The FDA estimated that the move could save consumers as much as $3.5 billion over a 10-year period.

In one case, the Type II diabetes medicine, Glucophage, which sold for 85 cents a tablet in September 2003 could cost as little as 19 cents a tablet in generic form. While the drug companies have a right to protect their intellectual rights through patents of drugs, advocates say consumers also have the right to expect reasonable prices on items that can literally save lives.

SEE ALSO

trademark infringement; industrial espionage; pharmaceutical industry.

BIBLIOGRAPHY. Ward S. Bowman, Jr., *Patent and Antitrust Law: A Legal and Economic Appraisal* (University of Chicago Press, 1973); "Court Upholds Settlement of Silicon Image, Genesis Suit," *Electronic News* (July 21, 2003); Donald M. Dible, *What Everybody Should Know about Patents, Trademarks, and Copyrights* (Entrepreneur Press, 1978); Albert Dorr and Christopher H. Munch, *Protecting Trade Secrets, Patents, Copyrights, and Trademarks* (Wiley Law, 1990); Ellen M. Girt, "Pill Power," *Money* (September 2003); John Gray, "A License to Print Money?" *Canadian Business* (September 12, 2003); Robert L. Harmon, *Patents and The Federal Circuit* (Bureau of National Affairs, 1987); Richard T. Holzmann, *Infringement of United States Patent Rights: A Guide for Executives and Attorneys* (Quorum Books, 1997); Jill Kipnis, "Patent Claim May Hurt DVDs," *Billboard* (June 28, 2003); Roger Parloff, "Microsoft's Patent Problems, *Fortune* (August 11, 2003); Mona Roman, "eBay Lands in Hot Water," *BusinessWeek* (June 9, 2003); Solomon J. Schepps, ed., *The Concise Guide to Patents, Trademarks, and Copyrights* (Bell Publishing, 1980); United States Patent and Trademark Office, "General Information Concerning Patents" www.uspto.gov (2003); VIA Sues Media-Tek for Patent Infringement," *Electronic News* (June 9, 2003).

ELIZABETH PURDY, PH.D.
INDEPENDENT SCHOLAR

pension funds

PENSION FUNDS MAY be defined as forms of institutional investment, which collect and invest funds contributed by sponsors and beneficiaries to provide for the future pension entitlements of beneficiaries. In the United States, a solid majority of Americans own shares in major companies, often through pension funds, and thus have a stake in the market economy. Issues related with pension funds are closely linked with the debate on corporate governance.

Undoubtedly, companies must feel that investors will reward them if they engage in more socially and environmentally responsible behavior. To provide such rewards, various socially responsible investment funds have been created. The conservative behavior of pension funds has persisted, in part, because trustees, however much they might wish to manage the pension funds according to their values, have typically felt that they could not simply vote their conscience.

They also came equipped with a restrictive definition of fiduciary responsibility. The responsibility of the pension fund trustees is to responsibly invest the earnings entrusted to them. The investor liability burden is assumed by pension-fund managers, while pensioners labor in good faith to make consistent contributions allowing long-term growth that will accrue earnings. Fund managers are absolutely accountable to the pensioners, who expectantly depend on the fund to provide for a worthy lifestyle during retirement. Until recently, pension funds have been defined to explicitly exclude making socially and environmentally oriented investments. This definition arose because of a pervasive economic belief that such investments were financially less attractive.

Since the beginning of the 1990s, there has been an ensuing debate on the role and status of pension funds in relation to corporate governance. In part, this debate has been driven by the rising role of institutional investors in the capital of multinational corporations. In the Western world, there has been wide-ranging debate about the role of pension funds in relation to the efficient allocation of resources. For example, there has been a long-running debate about whether the portfolio management practices of pension funds and their investment managers have contributed to (in a positive sense) the long-term efficient allocation of resources in the economy. Some commentators would argue that the preoccupation of institutional investors with short-term outcomes has adversely affected corporate management practice. Likewise, there has been some uneasiness about the capacity of pension funds and their investment managers to make meaningful contributions to the design of agency relationships between managers and shareholders. Every now and again, questions are raised in the financial press about the knowledge, competency, and experience of pension-fund officers in relation to the management of corporations that are, more often than not, complex, multi-jurisdictional institutions.

In American capitalism, the vast majority of shareholders are either small retail investors, or huge pension funds, mutual funds, and insurance firms that manage diversified portfolios through investment managers. And those managers face conflicts of interest, for they have mandates from companies to manage corporate pension funds and provide insurance. The only large shareholders free of such conflicts are public-sector pension funds. They share a general inhibition with other large investors: The benefits of active involvement in steering corporate boards are low, whereas the resources used are high. It has made much more economic sense to be passive, not active.

Performance trends in the nation's 100 largest corporations are, with few exceptions, reporting inaccurate earnings. In the early 2000s, companies were reporting earnings based on growth projections to pension funds when, in reality, the same funds were actually depreciating in value. To make matters worse; the amateur investor has little knowledge of business writing reported in business account statements. The situation in the 1990s was truly exceptional when pension funds reportedly surpassed projected earning expectations. Subsequently, we saw a return to the norm for pension funds where, typically, plans generate an expense instead of a profit.

Since the 1980s, many companies have changed from traditional defined-benefits (DB) plans to defined-contributions (DC) plans such as 401Ks, which limit the company's liability and shift the risk onto the employees and retirees. But this change is only the most visible part of the story. As markets turned down in 2000, most companies with DB continued to bank on optimistic long-term asset return assumptions. DB purportedly reallocated funds to their profit statement even though the earnings will probably not be tangible for multiple years.

For years, pension plans were created to induce loyalty and long service in workers. by the 2000s, long-tenured employees were often deemed liabilities. The idea that pension funds would start failing was never considered. However, given the damage provoked by pension fund scandals, the George W. Bush administration and lawmakers decided to propose new rules for pension plans. The success of pension funds depends on a crucial factor: the investment rate of return.

A downward trending stock market can shrink their value, and in order to bridge the gap between companies' investment needs and the cover of pension liabilities, the Portman-Cardin bill aimed at boosting retirement savings. The bill, known as Protecting Americans' Savings Act, was proposed for consideration to the U.S. Congress in 2003. Subsequent to the Enron and WorldCom corporate accounting scandals, the bill would also impose a 50 percent excise tax on "golden parachute" payment to top managers when a company goes bankrupt.

Although pension funds hold some of the most important blocks of stock of major public companies, the chances of contesting a chief executive officer (CEO) are unlikely, with the exceptions of CalPERS, the California public pension system that names a "watch list" of troubled companies each year, and TIAA-CREF, which tries to push for change by meeting privately with CEOs and boards of directors. Also, many investors now distrust pension accounting because it distorts reported earnings. Criticism centers on the lack of transparency in the management of pension funds, especially in the distribution of profits.

SEE ALSO

Teamster Pension Fund; securities fraud; stock fraud; Enron Corporation; WorldCom.

BIBLIOGRAPHY. Gordon L. Clark, *Pension Fund Capitalism* (Oxford University Press, 2000); David R. Francis, "Pension Funds Pinched, Stirring Calls for Reform," *Christian Science Monitor* (March 9, 2003); Robert Kuttner, "The Great American Pension-Fund Robbery," *BusinessWeek* (September 9, 2003); E. Philip Davis, *Pension Funds, Retirement-Income Security and Capital Markets* (Oxford University Press, 1995).

ALFREDO MANUEL COELHO
UNIVERSITY OF MONTPELLIER, FRANCE

perjury

PERJURY IS INTENTIONALLY lying under oath at an official court proceeding. The false statement could occur in testimony in court, depositions, diverse administrative hearings as well as in written legal documents such as affidavits, deeds, license applications, and tax returns. In societies as diverse as ancient Greece and Rome, the Ashanti in Africa, Native American tribes, early modern England and contemporary Europe and North America, perjury has been considered one of the most despicable of crimes since it involves a brash moral wrongdoing. Usually oaths are sworn in relation to God; breaking such an oath is seen as an offense against God. Moreover, it is regarded as an act of disobedience against the government not unlike tax evasion, contempt, and bribery. It was brought to the public spotlight in the mid-1970s when a number of officials in the Richard M. Nixon administration, such as H. R. Haldeman, John Erlichman, and John Mitchell, became household names for perjuring themselves in relation to covering-up illegal break-ins and surveillance of the Democratic Party. Recent public opinion surveys reveal that it is still considered a particularly odious crime.

Nevertheless, in the modern era convictions for perjury have been extremely rare. A common refrain in the legal community is that perjury is widespread, but is rarely prosecuted. It is particularly difficult to prove since it requires substantial evidence to demonstrate that a statement is false, that it was made intentionally, and that it is relevant to the case. Common defenses by those charged with the crime often center on the argument that they were simply mistaken or confused. Perjury has been frequently associated with serious criminal cases in which witnesses lie on the witness stand. In civil law, perjury has been found largely among corporate and white-collar offenders involved in fraud and illegal financial practices. Due to the complexity of proving perjury, it has been acknowledged that it is quite possible to openly deceive and mislead as long as what you swear is literally true.

HISTORY OF PERJURY

In the Anglo-American tradition, perjury is generally traced back to 16th-century laws established in England. Yet it is valuable to outline what constituted perjury or, more generally, false witness in societies before this period as it illustrates the premium placed on moral behavior under the law, a development within which modern-day formulations have evolved. In the ancient Code of Hammurabi, perjury was punishable by death. In the

Greek city state of Athens, the act of lying in legal proceedings was widely recognized and formed a significant portion of cases brought to the courts. Indeed, one scholar claims that it was much more common than today. While there was no serious criminal sanction against the act, persons alleged to have perjured themselves were subject to serious public disgrace and sometimes fines. Likewise in Roman law, perjury was considered a moral disgrace and in the early period of the empire was sometimes punishable by death. Historians have found evidence that under the reign of the emperor Charlemagne (768-814) perjury was punishable by physical mutilation. There is also considerable evidence in non-Western societies of false witness as a morally abhorrent offense against the deities.

In medieval England, perjury was considered an offense in the various state and church courts. In general, it consisted of all those offenses related to the breaking of an oath in formal legal settings. Although there was no perjury in the modern sense in which a witness intentionally lies on the witness stand, such an infraction was punishable at the time under a different law called maintenance. Perjury in this era was a demonstrably broader offense than today. In the case of lawyers and some government officials, for example, the oath to uphold the law that they swore when they entered office was used to prosecute them for perjury when they were found to have engaged in illegal activities.

An untrue verdict in a common law case was deemed perjury. False financial returns by sheriffs were likewise regarded as perjury and false witness in a church court was subject to punishment. The act of lying in a formal legal setting was thus complex and was interpreted in various manners depending on the nature of the court which was trying the case. In addition, there was still a strong moral element to the term in legal and popular usage associated with dishonor toward God.

In 1563, the Statute of Perjury was passed in England. It was conceived as a way to increase penalties for the existing crime of perjury, but it did little to clarify the ambiguous meanings and interpretations bequeathed from medieval times. According to legal historian Michael Gordon, the notion of perjury as a broad offense committed when persons broke oaths continued into the early 17th century. It also encompassed notions of conspiracy, that is, colluding with others to subvert the law. There was a growing concern among judges, however, that the perjury statute and common law findings on the issue were haphazardly applied and that consequently, it had the potential to deter witnesses from coming forward and testifying truthfully. It was for this reason that judges in the 17th century sharpened the meaning of the statute, creating in the process a common law notion of perjury which exists in its basic form to the present.

During the long reign of Queen Elizabeth (1533–1603), perjury maintained a strong moral component related to religion. The church courts still in existence at this time had responsibility for perjury committed under its auspices. In state courts, however, it was gradually systematized and later added to existing statutes.

The first key principle developed at the time was that perjury had to be willfully intended; it could not result from mistakes or even from misleading and equivocal statements. This had originated in religious teachings that were intended to give witnesses and defendants a way out of the so-called perjury trap, the act of implicating yourself in false statements. A second requirement was that perjury had to originate in proper judicial procedures, that is, in a formal legal proceeding.

You could not be charged with perjury for something you said outside of a court. Less obvious but still crucial, as Michael Gordon argues, was that the false swearing had to be related to the substance of the court proceeding, a concept later known as materiality. Typical cases involved false financial statements made orally or in writing, forcing others to lie in court, and false affidavits. It was considered a misdemeanor in English law and was regarded as relatively rare due to the increasingly complex nature of the rules.

The early American colonies inherited these common law principles and extended them through laws and constitutional provisions. The federal government and courts drew explicitly on the law of perjury developed by the judiciary in England after the 16th century. In early America, the crime of perjury was regarded in the more serious category of criminal law as a felony.

Typical statutes in the early years of the colonies provided for sanctions of fines, imprisonment, and hard labor as penalties for willful lying before the courts, swearing false statements, and persuading others to commit perjury. In the colony of New York, one of the penalties included the branding of a "P" in the forehead of the person convicted, although this harsh form of punishment was apparently exercised rarely.

PERJURY STATUTES

Modern American law has somewhat extended the scope of perjury and provided for precise definitions of its various components and what is necessary to prove the offense. According to Stuart Green, federal perjury statutes comprise five key elements that are required to prove that perjury was committed: "1) an oath authorized by a law of the United States; 2) taken before a competent tribunal, officer, or person; 3) a false statement; 4) willfully made; 5) as to facts material to the hearing."

At the state level, there are a number of differences. In New York, for instance, the crime of perjury was divided into degrees in 1935 and the requirement of materiality was eliminated. Materiality can, however, be used to decide the degree of the crime. Perjury in the first degree is considered a felony while the lesser second-degree perjury is a misdemeanor. Therefore, proving perjury is a difficult task, involving a number of complex legal principles. The question of morality, especially the differences between lying and misleading statements, continues to be a much-debated question, as does the responsibility of lawyers to allow lies and/or misleading statements to go unchallenged in court.

Take the landmark case of *Bronston v. United States* in 1973. Bronston, a movie company president, was involved in a bankruptcy case. At a hearing, he was asked "Do you have any [Swiss bank accounts]? He replied "No." The follow-up question asked, "Have you ever?" He replied, "The company had an account there for about six months in Zurich." In reality, Bronston had had Swiss bank accounts for five years, but not at the time of the trial. He first answer was strictly correct. If he had said "no" to the second question he would have been found guilty. What he in fact did was give a truthful answer to a question that had not been asked. Bronston was clearly misleading the court, but he had not said anything false. The lawyer failed to pursue Bronston on this misleading statement and the conviction was subsequently overturned.

In a contrasting case, *United States v. DeZarn*, a different conclusion was drawn from a similarly misleading statement from a trial defendant. DeZarn was prosecuted for perjury in a case under the Hatch Act, which bans the solicitation of government employees in political campaigns. DeZarn was present at two horse-racing parties in 1990 and 1991. DeZarn conducted fundraising only at the 1990 party. The lawyer meant to ask DeZarn about events at the 1990 party, but erroneously said "1991." DeZarn truthfully answered that no fundraising activities had occurred at the 1991 event. This misleading statement, however, was regarded by the courts as different from the Bronston case since it entailed a responsive answer given to the question. Hailed by some legal observers as "nudging federal criminal law closer to everyday morality," it has also been criticized as unfairly blurring the distinction between lying and misleading. This debate reveals that competing notions of morality and what role they should play in law continue to be controversial. It furthermore demonstrates that errors by legal counsel may play a crucial role in perjury cases.

CORPORATE PERJURY

Cases involving corporations illustrate the difficulties of securing convictions for perjury. In the mid-1990s, tobacco company executives, for example, appeared before a committee of the House of Representatives claiming that they did not believe nicotine was addictive. Of course, beliefs by themselves do not constitute perjury. Nevertheless, documents made public after these appearances made it abundantly clear that tobacco company officials have long concluded that nicotine is indeed addictive and have built their marketing strategies on this very fact. For decades, tobacco companies have also sworn to state and federal agencies that cigarettes have few health effects, knowing full well that they are harmful. Yet no perjury charges have ever been laid against executives in this industry.

The high-profile tobacco industry has not been the only culprit. In 1991, the secretary of labor stated that there had been a consistent pattern of irregularities on dust sampling tests conducted by coal companies. Five hundred mine operators had submitted tests that supposedly demonstrated that their mines had been properly vacuumed. These tests are used to make sure miners are not exposed to toxic levels of coal dust which lead to a number of debilitating diseases. Yet attempts to prosecute the companies failed because they were able to argue in court that the tests may have been potentially mishandled and therefore they were not guilty of false statements. Successful cases of perjury in recent years include that of Hudson Foods which was indicted in December 1998 for lying to the Department of Agriculture in an attempt to stop a recall of 25 million pounds of hamburger meat, some of it infected with e. coli. Even the unlikely cruise ship company, Royal Caribbean Cruise Lines, was discovered to have illegally dumped oil waste in the Gulf of Mexico as well as disposing of physical evidence related to the crime and revising their log book to hide the discharges.

POLICE PERJURY

Perhaps the most prevalent area of perjury in modern society has emanated from law-enforcement officials themselves. This has long been charged by critics of the justice system. Police departments and officers across the country have been charged with numerous cases of what Christopher Slobigin calls "testilying" in recent years. The Mollen Commission, charged with investigating corruption in the New York City Police Department in the early 1990s, found that it was common for police officers to perjure themselves at various stages of the criminal process. Interviews with police officers found that it was usual to falsely claim in police reports and swear under oath that suspects had committed offenses, such as running a red light or that they saw contraband inside the car. To hide an unlawful search, police may claim they saw a bulge in a person's pocket. To enter apartments, they concoct stories that unidentified civilians had seen drugs inside the residence. To arrest people they believe are guilty of drug trafficking, they falsely contend that the defendants had drugs in their possession when, in reality, drugs were found in a place where the officers were not allowed to search.

False statements by police on the application form and in oral testimony to the warrant magistrate has been noted by many observers. According to Slobigin, "In one survey, defense attorneys, prosecutors, and judges estimated that police perjury at Fourth Amendment suppression hearings occurs in 20 to 50 percent of the cases." He concludes that "Few knowledgeable persons are willing to say that police perjury about investigative matters is sporadic or rare, except perhaps the police, and ... even many of them believe it is common enough to merit a label all its own."

In sum, perjury has long had a strong moral component and for this reason it has been regarded as a particularly heinous crime. For this very same reason, it has evolved into a complex and exceedingly difficult crime to prove. Legal observers have long complained that lying and other forms of false swearing are ubiquitous yet are seldom prosecuted. In the white-collar and corporate crime area, they have argued that the only remedy for this sorry state of affairs is devoting more resources to investigating examples of perjury, and seriously prosecuting suspected cases as well as developing sharper concepts of perjury which punish clearly untruthful statements regardless of legal technicalities.

SEE ALSO

Mollen Commission; coal mining; corporate criminal liability; ethics; police corruption.

BIBLIOGRAPHY. Jay Albanese, *White-Collar Crime in America* (Prentice Hall, 1995); Michael Gordon, "The Invention of a Common Law Crime: Perjury and the Elizabethan Courts," *American Journal of Legal History* (v. 24, 1980); Stuart Green, "Lying, Misleading and Falsely Denying: How Moral Concepts Inform the Law of Perjury, Fraud and False Statements," *Hastings Law Journal* (v.53, 2001–02); Sandra Jackson, "Perjury," *Brooklyn Law Review* (v.24, 1957–58); W. Purrington, "The Frequency of Perjury," *Columbia Law Review* (v.8, 1908); Stephen Rostoff, Henry N. Pontell and Robert Tillman, *Profit Without Honor: White-Collar Crime and the Looting of America* (Prentice Hall, 1998); Christopher Slobogin, "Testilying: Police Perjury and What to Do About It," *University of Colorado Law Review* (v.67, Fall 1996); Richard H. Underwood, "False Witness: A Lawyer's History of the Law of Perjury," *Arizona Journal of International and Comparative Law* (v.10, 1993); "Corporate Perjury and Obstruction of Justice," *Multinational Monitor* (v.19, December 1998).

SEAN PURDY, PH.D.
QUEEN'S UNIVERSITY, CANADA

pesticides

IT IS UNLIKELY that most Americans would voluntarily consume poisonous substances, yet millions of people unknowingly consume poisonous residues on fruit and vegetables that they eat every day. Pesticides are useful tools in agricultural work because they kill insects and reverse conditions that interfere with the growth of agricultural products.

However, it is virtually impossible to remove all residues before products are sold and consumed. While it is advisable to wash all fruit and vegetables thoroughly before consuming them, the process will not remove all pesticide residues. In addition to the dangers that pesticides pose to individuals who consume trace amounts on food products, pesticides that are not handled properly can create a host of problems for agricultural and horticultural workers. Even if it were possible to remove all pesticides from such products, exposure to pesticides would likely continue because traces of pesticides are frequently used both indoors and outdoors in almost all homes, apartments, schools, businesses, hotels, restaurants, parks, golf courses, and other places that people frequent. Pesticide residues are also found in water, sidewalks, bedding, furniture, baby toys, and other items that are part of everyday lives. Numerous studies have shown that exposure to pesticides can cause cancer, respiratory disorders, neural damage (as in Parkinson's Disease), immune system damage, endocrine system dysfunction, reproductive problems, and other less serious problems.

Children are particularly vulnerable to pesticides in foods and the environment. In 1999, the Environmental Protection Agency (EPA) announced strict limitations on methyl parathion and azinphosmethyl, two pesticides that were commonly used in growing peaches and apples, because they were suspected of causing neurological damage in infants and children. A study of pregnant women in New York City released in January 2003 by Dr. Gertrud Berkowitz of Mount Sinai School of Medicine revealed that unborn infants were being exposed to pesticides at 60 to 120 times the EPA tolerance levels. Berkowitz's overall conclusion was that urban homes might be even more toxic than agricultural residences.

A report from the Centers for Disease Control and Prevention (CDC) published in April 2003, which examined the presence of 116 separate chemicals (including 34 pesticides) in thousands of participants, revealed that metabolites of chlorpyrifos were twice as likely to be found in children aged 6 to 11 than in adults. While infants and children are at greater risk from pesticide exposure, pesticides also affect the health and lives of the adult population on a global basis. In 2003, a controversial Belgian study found pesticide residue in the blood of 159 women with breast cancer. Studies in North Carolina and Iowa uncovered a correlation between exposure to pesticides and the risk of prostate cancer in males whose work involved pesticide application. Traces of various pesticides, antibiotics, aspirin, and Prozac have been found during tests on wastewater treatment plants. Pollutants from paper mills, power plants, and garbage incinerators that wind their way to the ocean are thought to be responsible for the presence of mercury in fish that continues to be an issue with environmentalists and consumers.

PESTICIDES IN DEVELOPING COUNTRIES

During the period between World War I and World War II, a typhus epidemic led to the deaths of 3 million people in Africa. It is possible that the epidemic would have spread even further had the West not coordinated the effort to stop the disease at its

Orchard workers are the most susceptible to diseases from pesticides sprayed on fruit to make them look appealing.

source. Because typhus is spread by lice, in 1943 the Western countries launched a delousing program in Nigeria. Decontamination was accomplished by mixing DDT with an inert powder and blowing it on to the clothes of Nigerians. It was estimated that within two hours of contact, all body lice had been destroyed, thus, averting a worldwide typhus epidemic. DDT was also used successfully in mitigating the effects of outbreaks of malaria in Kenya in the 1940s and in Uganda in the 1960s. After evidence about the toxic effects of DDT surfaced in the 1970s, the United States and other countries banned its use. Some developing countries, however, continued to use DDT into the 21st century.

While governments in most developed countries have made great strides in regulating the use of pesticides, authorities in developing countries have worked at a much slower pace. Part of the problem is that governments in these countries must balance the danger to residents against the much-desired profits that boost local economies. Foreign businesses have proved mixed blessings for developing countries by using pesticides that are banned in their own countries. One example of this practice can be found in the floriculture industry, which has provided around 190,000 jobs in countries like Columbia, Mexico, and India. While these jobs boost local economies, workers in the floriculture industry have been exposed to pesticides such as organophospates that may negatively affect the reported to produce infertility, miscarriages, and birth defects. Approximately two-thirds of such workers also regularly complain of headaches, dizziness, and blurred vision.

The fruit-growing industry has also produced health problems for workers in developing countries. In the early 1990s, a class action lawsuit was filled by banana workers from Costa Rica, Ecuador, Guatemala, Honduras, Nigeria, and the Philippines, charging Amvac, Dow Chemical, Occidental Chemical, and Shell Oil Company with exposing them to the dangers of DBCP (dibromochloropropane). In 1993, a $25 million settlement was announced. In the winter of 2003, Dow Chemical, Shell Oil Company, and Standard Fruit Company (Dole Food Company) were ordered to pay $490 million to 583 Central American banana workers who had been exposed to the highly toxic Nemagon that had caused infertility.

Some workers also experienced impotence, depression, and stomach cancer when exposed to the substance. Other cases against Dole, Chiquita, and Del Monte continued to wind their way through the courts.

The use of pesticides in developing countries was brought home to many Americans during the Persian Gulf War in 1991. After returning to the United States, a number of veterans complained of health-related problems that included joint pains, sleep disorders, memory loss, and fatigue. It has been documented that at least 35 separate pesticides were used during the war, and a number of these have received special attention from the Office for Special Assistance for Gulf War Illnesses (OS-AGWI) because of known toxicities or frequency of complaints by Gulf War veterans.

Lindane, which was used as a delousing agent, has been known to cause hyperactivity, excitability, tremors, seizures, and comas. Organophosphate compounds, used to exterminate flies, spiders, cockroaches, and other sucking and chewing insects, was credited with causing tremors, severe muscle contractions, dizziness, shortness of breath, vomiting, sleep disorders, depression, and anxiety. Carbamates, used to kill a wide range of insects were believed to cause fatigue, joint pain, sleep disorders, headaches, and skin problems as well as cognitive, mood, and other neurological effects.

FEDERAL REGULATION

The first federal efforts to regulate the manufacture, distribution, and use of pesticides resulted in the Insecticide Act of 1910 that banned the manufacture, sale, and transport of the misbranded, toxic, and useless pesticides that were available. Regulations on pesticides were strengthened with the passage of the Food, Drug, and Cosmetic Act of 1938. One section of the law, known as the Federal Insecticide, Fungicide and Rodenticide Act (FIFRA), gave the government the authority to pull illegal pesticides from the market and to suspend or deny licenses to violators.

A 1954 amendment to the law called for the establishment of tolerance levels for all pesticides used in food and food products. In the wake of the consumer rights movement of the 1960s, increased attention was paid to the use of pesticides in food. This was partly due to the publication of Rachel Carson's *The Silent Spring* in 1962 that served as an environmentalist wake-up call to the American public. The public was also outraged when re-searchers began documenting the impact of using pesticides on farm workers and rural residents. The Environmental Pest Control Act of 1972 gave the government even more authority, and amendments in 1975 and 1978 further strengthened the government's role in protecting consumers from harmful pesticides.

Congress reacted to increase public attention on environmental issues by passing the National Environmental Policy Act (NEPA) of 1969, which established the Council for Environmental Quality and mandated an emphasis on integrated pest management (IPM). Regulation of pesticides suffered a setback in the 1980s when the agricultural sector fell victim to the economic crisis that resulted from Ronald Reagan's trickle-down economics. In 1986, Reagan proposed eliminating funding for the Extension Services and the IPM implementation program, but Congress refused to comply. In 1994, the Department of Agriculture announced renewed federal efforts toward controlling pesticides, stipulating that IPM methods must be employed on at least 75 percent of all crop acreage by 2000.

In 1996, Congress passed the Food Quality Protection Act (FQPA), which gave the EPA the authority to regulate pesticides by requiring that producers and users of pesticides show with reasonable certainty that no harm would result from aggregate use of a product. The new law required the EPA to re-regulate pesticides every 15 years based on most recent data. Congress ordered the EPA to produce a revised list of the most toxic pesticides, with special attention to the impact of toxins on infants and children.

While environmentalists and consumer advocates discourage the widespread use of pesticides because of their harmful affects on human health and the global environment, the agricultural sector defends pesticide use, insisting that pesticides promote better quality food products that are more esthetically appealing.

SEE ALSO

water pollution; Environmental Protection Agency; Food, Drug and Cosmetic Act; United States.

BIBLIOGRAPHY. "Applying Certain Agricultural Pesticides Increases the Risk of Prostate Cancer," *Women's Health Weekly* (July 3, 2003); Gary Cecchine, *A Review of the Scientific Literature as it Pertains to Gulf War Illness* (Rand, 1998); Thomas Degregori, *Agriculture and Modern*

Technology: A Defense (Iowa State University Press, 2001); David Hosansky, "Does the New Crackdown Go Far Enough, Or too Far?" *CQ Researcher* (August 6, 1999); Thomas Kerns, *Environmentally Induced Illnesses: Ethics, Risk Assessment, and Human Rights* (McFarland, 2001); Michael D. Lemonick," In Our Streams: Prozac and Pesticides," *Time* (August 25, 2003); Amy Ling and Martha Olson Jarocki, "Pesticide Justice," *Multinational Monitor* (January/February 2003); Betsy Mason, "Murky Picture on Fish Mercury," *Science* (August 28, 2003); Victoria McGovern, "Prevalent Risk to Pregnant Women," *Environmental Health Perspectives* (January 2003); "Poisoned Petals," *Mother Earth News* (April/May 2003); T.J. Sheets and David Pimentel, eds., *Pesticides: Contemporary Roles in Agriculture* (Health, and Human Press, 1979); "Toxic Americans," *The Ecologist* (April 2003).

ELIZABETH PURDY, PH.D.
INDEPENDENT SCHOLAR

pharmaceutical industry

HEALTHCARE in the United States has become a megabillion-dollar business. It is responsible for over 12 percent of the gross national product. Revenues from the health industry, which currently exceed $360 billion a year, are second only to those of the defense industry. True profits are much higher. In 1991, the United States spent $750 billion on healthcare and the level of spending is increasing each year.

A key component of the health industry, the pharmaceutical business has one of the worst records when it comes to breaking the law. John Braithwaite, in his extensive and illuminating study, shows the profundity and gravity of the crime problem in the pharmaceutical industry. Bribery, corruption, the unsafe manufacturing of drugs, fraud in testing, false advertising, and price-fixing are just a few of the numerous crimes the pharmaceutical industry has engaged in. Braithwaite's research was conducted between 1977 and 1980 and published in 1984, over 20 years ago; unfortunately, not much has changed. The pharmaceutical industry is still involved in malfeasance.

According to the Multinational Monitor which listed the top 100 corporate crimes during the 1990s, 31 of the top 100 involved pharmaceutical companies. Some pharmaceutical makers have a long history of inadequately testing new drugs and products that eventually harm others, particularly women or their children. The organization and operation of the pharmaceutical industry may be a salient factor in understanding the crimes that are committed.

RESEARCH AND PATENTS

The pharmaceutical business incurs tremendous costs in bringing a new drug or medical device from concept to market. These costs generally fall into four areas: Research & Development (R & D), the Food and Drug Administration (FDA) approval process, manufacturing, and advertising. Research and development is by far the most costly of the four and an area that is most open for fraud.

Pharmaceutical companies face great temptations to mislead health authorities, the FDA in particular, about the safety of their products. The companies expend an enormous amount of money, upfront, in the research of new drugs and are in great competition to be the first that obtains approval and a patent for the new discovery. With drug development, potentially hundreds of millions of dollars must be invested for a new compound that may never return a profit and, in a best-case scenario, will only begin returning money 12 to 15 years out. If another company gets its product on the market first, then a massive amount of money and time, already expended, is lost, not to mention the loss of future profits the company would have received if its drug were the one to obtain the market's share.

Currently, patents last for 20 years. The 20-year term is codified in 35 U.S.C. Sec. 154. Twenty years may seem like a lengthy and sufficient amount of time, but the 20-year term begins on the date of the patent application. This is very important for drug manufacturers, because drugs are generally patented before beginning the FDA approval process. Because the approval process can take so long, the "effective life" of the patent (the number of years left on a patent) is often less than half the original life once the product is actually available.

This creates a race to be the first company with the new drug on the market. In 2002, Pharmaceutical Research and Manufacturers of America (PhRMA) member companies invested an estimated $32 billion on research to develop new treatments for diseases. PhRMA member companies spend more on R&D than the National Institutes of Health and the international pharmaceutical industry. The industry invested more than $30 billion in 2001 in discovering and developing new medicines.

CLINICAL TRIALS

Given the enormous amount of money at stake, clinical trials are extremely important in order to move from research and development to obtaining a patent and FDA approval. Clinical trials are another place where fraud may manifest itself given the financial stakes. Research has shown that data from clinical trials have been falsified and adverse effects have been ignored, and in some egregious cases, covered up. According to Braithwaite, between 1977 and 1980 the FDA discovered 62 doctors who had submitted manipulated or downright falsified clinical data. A study conducted by the FDA revealed that one in five doctors investigated, who carry out field research of new drugs, had invented the data they sent to the drug companies, and pocketed the fees.

According to the FDA, if the data proves to be unsatisfactory toward the drug being investigated, it is not unusual for the drug company to continue trials elsewhere until satisfactory results and testimonials are achieved. Unfavorable results are rarely published and those who conducted the tests with adverse findings are pressured into keeping quiet about such data. It is very easy for the drug company to arrange appropriate clinical trials by approaching a sympathetic clinician to produce the desired results. The incentive for clinical investigators to fabricate data is enormous. As much as $1,000 per subject is paid by American companies, which enables some doctors to earn up to $1 million a year from drug research, and investigating clinicians know all too well that if they do not produce the desired results, then the loss of future grants and work is to be expected.

Even if data obtained from clinical trials is not falsified, it may be of little worth, because the trials may not have been performed appropriately. Many trials involve relatively small numbers of people and the true harmful side effects of a new drug may not appear in those small numbers. Harmful side effects may only appear once the drug has been mass marketed and widely used and, by then, it may be too late for the general populace. Furthermore, the subjects taking part in the trial usually do not represent those who will use the drug after its approval. Very young or elderly people, women of child-bearing age and people with liver or kidney disease are usually not included in clinical trials, although such people may be given the drug after it is marketed.

Optimal dosages for adults are calculated based on what is most effective for an average-sized adult. Many adults differ from this average, and many may react atypically to some classes of drugs. Many of these reactions are adverse and can cause great harm. According to the FDA, every year, an estimated 140,000 Americans are killed because of the drugs they are taking. Patients suffering from adverse drug reactions take up one in seven hospital beds in the United States. These estimates are probably much lower than actual estimates given that many adverse drug reactions go unreported or undiagnosed.

DRUG MARKETING

Once a drug makes it through the trials and is approved by the FDA, then it needs to be produced and marketed. The major effort of marketing campaigns is done through the help of physicians, since they will be prescribing the medications to their patients. There is a vast amount of available drugs on the market and the goal of each pharmaceutical company is to have its drug recommended by the prescribing physician. According to Dr. Alan Levin, as stated in his book, *Dissent in Medicine: Nine Doctors Speak Out*, a major reason why health care is in such a shambles is that the medical establishment has allowed itself to be "bought off" by the pharmaceutical industry.

Drug companies expend a great amount of effort to attract the allegiance of practicing physicians, which is done through various aggressive advertising efforts. These advertising efforts can vary from modest gifts to extravagant grants. Drug companies employ many means in bribing medical students, doctors, medical schools, and hospital administrators. Some drug companies have been known to woo young medical students by offering them gifts, including expense-paid trips to conferences and offers of student research grants. Medical schools are given large sums of money for clinical trials and basic pharmaceutical research.

Drug companies regularly host lavish dinner and cocktail parties for groups of physicians. They

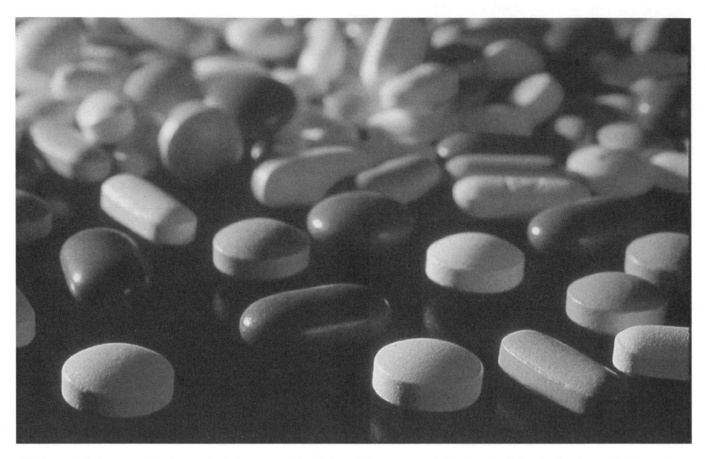

All phases of pharmaceutical manufacturing are subject to fraud, from research funding to clinical testing to marketing and distribution. The act of fraud in these cases often leads to tragic, life-threatening consequences.

provide funding for the establishment of hospital buildings, medical school buildings, and "independent" research institutes. These "gifts" have become a massive marketing tool and campaign to help mold the attitudes, thoughts of students, and policies of practicing physicians.

Fifty percent of drugs on the market today did not exist 10 years ago. With so many new drugs, doctors do not have time to learn about them in medical school or have the time to keep up with all the changes once they are practicing physicians. The busy physicians, therefore, rely mainly on the drug company's sales representatives to inform them about new medications and devices. Drug companies hire sales representatives who regularly and frequently visit physicians' offices to dole out drug samples. They explain the indications for these drugs and try to persuade physicians to utilize their products.

Like any other salesperson, they disparage the products of their competitors while glossing over the shortcomings, or potential strong side effects of

their own product. Most sales representatives do not have formal medical or pharmacological training and are not regulated by any state or federal agencies.

According to the *American Journal of Medicine* in 1982, 46 percent of physicians reported that drug representatives are moderately to very important in influencing their prescribing habits. In a 2003 study, one-third of medical residents reported that they change their practice based on information provided by drug reps. In another study, 61 percent of medical residents stated that industry promotions did not influence their own prescribing, but only 16 percent believed other physicians to be similarly uninfluenced.

In addition to the billions of dollars pharmaceutical companies spend on research and development, and incentives to physicians, drug makers spent an estimated $1.9 billion on direct-to-consumer (DTC) advertising in 1999. Prior to the 1990s, DTC advertisements of prescription drugs were severely restricted. Prior to 1997, advertising had to be accompanied by all of the fine print that would normally go on a label and package insert, but in August 1997, the FDA relaxed restrictions on DTC advertising, leading to a boom in television and radio ads and advertising spending.

According to the National Institute for Health Care Management Research and Educational Foundation, $2.5 billion was spent on advertising to consumers in 2000. Increases in the sales of the 50 drugs most heavily advertised to consumers were responsible for almost half (47.8 percent) of the $20.8 billion increase in spending in 2000. In 2000, Merck spent $161 million on advertising for Vioxx. That is more than Pepsico spent advertising Pepsi ($125 million), and more than Anheuser-Busch spent advertising Budweiser ($146 million). The increase in Vioxx sales in 2000 accounted for 5.7 percent of the one-year increase in drug spending. According to industry estimates, drug companies spent $15.7 billion on promotion in 2000. Also in that year, $7.2 billion worth of free samples were distributed.

UNSAFE PRODUCTS

Unsafe medical devices or drugs can have a devastating effect on many people; historically, women and their unborn babies have been the most victimized. A long list of drugs that have had major complications, including causing death, would cite: Paracetamol (a painkiller) caused 1,500 people to be hospitalized in Great Britain in 1971; Orabilex caused kidney damages with fatal outcomes; MEL/29 caused cataracts; Methaqualone caused severe psychic disturbances leading to at least 366 deaths, mainly through murder or suicide; Isoproterenol (for asthma) caused 3,500 deaths in the 1960s; Stilboestrol (for prostate cancer) caused cancer in young women; Trilergan (anti-allergy) caused viral hepatitis; Phenformin (for diabetes) caused 1,000 deaths annually until withdrawn; Debendox (for nausea) and Accutane (for acne) both caused birth defects. Two of the most egregious cases of corporate malfeasance in relation to unsafe drugs include DES and thalidomide.

Diethylstilbestrol (DES) was initially hailed as a wonder drug that could do everything, including curing the problems of menopause, treating prostate cancer, preventing miscarriages, and making babies healthier. But DES turned out to have tragic consequences, especially for babies who were exposed to DES in the womb. Two major studies that were conducted and published in 1953 showed that DES was definitely not a wonder drug. The studies concluded that the drug did not decrease the number of miscarriages; it had no effect on lowering the rate of prematurity; and it did not increase the health of premature babies. On follow-up studies, the effects were even more disturbing. There was a statistically significant increase in the number of miscarriages, premature births, and neonatal deaths, not the opposite as the drug was marketed. The pharmaceutical manufacturers focused on positive information and downplayed all negative findings. Twelve years after the first studies were conducted, more than 100,000 prescriptions of DES were still given to pregnant women.

Another drug that caused an enormous amount of irreparable harm to pregnant women and their children across the globe was thalidomide. It was used as a tranquilizer or sleeping pill and was being touted as a drug with no side effects. It was also used to treat morning sickness during pregnancy. With its lack of side effects, it was deemed safe enough that it did not require a prescription; therefore, it was widely available over the counter. Numerous women who used thalidomide during pregnancy bore children with extreme congenital abnormalities. Many of the children were born with their extremities attached in odd places. For example, toes attached to the hips or their hands and feet were attached directly to the torso, there was no development of arms and legs. Shortly after the birth defects were observed, thalidomide was banned worldwide, but it was too late for thousands of babies. An estimated 8,000-80,000 children in nearly 50 counties were born deformed because thalidomide had been marketed as being safe to use by pregnant women. Because of this, it became known as the "drug that deformed." The FDA never approved the distribution of thalidomide in the United States until recently in controlled circumstances, and not for pregnant women.

Another area of concern in the testing of new drugs and/or products is the use of pregnant animals to test for human pregnancy effects; the efficacy of these tests are questionable. Because of the thalidomide tragedy, there has been a massive increase in the use of animals that are pregnant in drug testing, but this has failed to prevent further deformities. On the contrary, malformations have increased. It has been found that every year more than a quarter of a million babies (1 in 12) are born with birth defects in the United States. Research has shown that the animals that are used in the testing phase do not really simulate human biology and therefore are not really showing the possible effects the drugs may have on unborn human children and the women who are pregnant.

The production and distribution of unsafe drugs is only one of the many areas controlled by the pharmaceutical companies. Unsafe products have also had devastating effects, as in the case of the Dalkon Shield. The Dalkon Shield was seen as a revolutionary and extremely effective IUD contraceptive device in the 1960s. The device was supposed to be almost 100 percent effective in preventing pregnancy and it was reversible, and did not have the side effects of the birth control pill. Unfortunately, the Dalkon Shield created pelvic infections in women and had a devastating effect on their future reproductive health. In addition, the Dalkon Shield was not effective as a method of birth control and those women who became pregnant, had septic abortions, and many of the women died from septic infections after becoming pregnant. Approximately 5 percent of the women wearing the Shield, 110,000 women, became pregnant and an estimated 60 percent suffered miscarriages.

With a better understanding of how the pharmaceutical industry operates, it is not surprising to see the endless possibilities for fraud and other malfeasance or criminal activity. Falsifying data in trials is only one of the many types of criminal activity the pharmaceutical industry has been accused of, and from which prosecutions have resulted.

Price fixing is another type of fraud committed. In April 2000, three former executives of BASF AG and one former executive of Hoffmann-La Roche Ltd. agreed to plead guilty, serve time in U.S. prisons, and pay criminal fines for their roles in an international conspiracy to suppress and eliminate competition in the vitamin industry. The conspiracy lasted from 1990 until 1999 and affected the vitamins most used as nutritional supplements, or to enrich human food and animal feed.

SEE ALSO

healthcare fraud; Dalkon Shield; Food and Drug Administration; thalidomide; Braithwaite, John.

BIBLIOGRAPHY. John Braithwaite, *Corporate Crime in the Pharmaceutical Industry* (Routledge, 1984); Food and Drug Administration, www.fda.gov (2003); Stephen Fried, *Bitter Pills: Inside the Hazardous World of Legal Drugs* (Bantam Books, 1999); Alan S. Levin, 1985. "Corruption in American Medicine," Dissent in Medicine: Nine Doctors Speak Out (Contemporary Books, 1985); M.A. Steinman, M.G. Shlipak, and S.J. McPhee, "Of Principles and Pens: Attitudes and Practices of Medicine Housestaff toward Pharmaceutical Industry Promotions," *American Journal of Medicine* (v.110/7, 2001); National Institute for Health Care Management, www.nihcm.org (2003); Pharmaceutical Research and Manufacturers of America, www.phrma.org (2003).

DEBRA E. ROSS, PH.D.
GRAND VALLEY STATE UNIVERSITY

Poland

AFTER THE COLLAPSE of the Soviet Union, Poland moved with alacrity to establish a market-oriented economy. The transition was problematic. While elected officials were instituting new legal frameworks for business, including commercial codes, and tort, civil and contract law, white collar and organized criminal gangs in Poland quickly garnered significant profits through a wide array of illicit activities.

Like other former Soviet Union-dominated communist countries throughout Eastern Europe, Polish regulators and law enforcement agencies were ill-equipped to differentiate between legitimate and illegal profit-seeking activities, especially in an era where legal and regulatory standards were slowly evolving. As a result, white-collar and organized crime flourished in Poland throughout the 1990s, and efforts to combat criminal activities were sporadic and ineffectual.

Despite increased efforts to combat criminal activity, Poland remains a major transit point for narcotics trafficking to Western Europe. Criminal gangs also routinely raise illicit proceeds through auto theft, extortion and counterfeiting schemes, and securities fraud. Polish criminal networks are also linked to the smuggling of alcohol, tobacco, fuel, and bulk commodities, especially coal and metallurgical products. According to Polish government estimates, organized crime activity generates criminal proceeds in the range of $1.5 billion to $3 billion annually. This money is laundered through

Polish banks, currency exchange businesses, and casinos. Although Poland is not the leading jurisdiction of choice to launder proceeds for major criminal organizations from Russia, and Ukraine, the weak regulatory environment during most of the 1990s also enabled organized criminal gangs from neighboring states to transfer funds through Polish financial institutions to offshore financial centers.

Poland also suffers from widespread white-collar crime. The large degree of white-collar crime is linked to historical factors, especially an entrenched pattern of bribery, originating during the Soviet era, that remains an integral part of the political and economic process, and an immense civil servant class that makes governmental processes obscure and impede transparency. White-collar crime is also facilitated by elite cronyism and clan-like connections in the Polish business community. Consequently, Poland is routinely targeted by Polish media groups, non-governmental organizations, and international agencies, including the World Bank Group, which issue reports highlighting the link between white-collar criminals and government officials in the judiciary, law enforcement, and security services.

The proceeds of white-collar and organized crime are routinely laundered through Polish financial institutions. Launderers use Polish financial institutions to transfer funds to Western European states that are in close proximity to Poland. The Polish economy, large by regional standards, offers many avenues to launder illicit proceeds through its correspondingly large gray economy, promoted by a complex tax regime. Moreover, as a transit state between the European Union and the former Soviet Union, with a port on the Baltic, Poland has attracted organized crime groups from Western Europe and the Russian Federation. Funds are placed in banks, insurance companies, currency exchange shops, real estate, and short-term bonds. Although some of the proceeds of crime almost certainly leave the country, illicit profits are routinely invested in legal businesses, such as hotels, restaurants, and gambling parlors.

Since the mid-1990s, efforts to combat white-collar collar and organized crime in Poland have improved substantially. To limit the passage of illicit funds from organized criminal and white-collar crime through domestic banking and non-banking financial institutions, Poland initiated a rudimentary anti-money laundering regime with the passage of the 1992 banking regulation, Resolution Number 16, which required Polish banks to report suspicious transactions. Additional measures were adopted through the 1990s. In 2000, the Sejm, the Polish Parliament, instituted a comprehensive anti-money laundering policy with the adoption of the Law on Counteracting the Introduction of Funds From Illegal or Unrevealed Sources Into Financial Turnover.

This law, which came into effect on June 23, 2001, established a financial intelligence unit, and mandated the reporting of all transactions worth more than approximately $8,800. The law also mandated reporting requirements to include a broad range of non-bank financial institutions, especially brokers, investment and trust funds, insurance companies, casinos, money exchange shops, the Polish Post Office, leasing and factoring companies, pension funds, notaries, and real estate agents. Record keeping requirements for such transactions requires the maintenance in a database of information regarding the identity of the account holder owner of the funds for five years.

Additional steps taken by Poland to combat white-collar and organized criminal activities were instituted to meet international norms, and ensure entrance into the European Union. To combat domestic white-collar and organized criminal activity, Poland increased international cooperation with the ratification of a series of significant international conventions, including The Convention on Laundering, Search, Seizure and Confiscation of the Proceeds from Crime in December 2000, and the United Nations Convention Against Transnational Crime in December 2001. The ratification of major international conventions in Poland formalized links to European law enforcement agencies, and ensures international cooperation in the battle against transnational criminal groups, and the passage of illicit funds across European borders.

SEE ALSO

money laundering; corruption; bribery; public corruption; Russia; human trafficking; organized crime.

BIBLIOGRAPHY. Eberhard Bort, *Illegal Migration and Cross-Border Crime* (European University Institute, 2000); Edgar L. Feige, and Katarina Ott, eds., *Underground Economies in Transition: : Unrecorded Activity, Tax Evasion, Corruption And Organized Crime* (Aldershot, 1999). Martin Krygier and Adam Czarnota, eds., *The Rule of Law*

After Communism: Problems and Prospects in East-Central Europe (Aldershot, 1999).

TRIFIN ROULE
JOURNAL OF MONEY LAUNDERING CONTROL

police brutality

USE OF FORCE by the police falls under the Fourth Amendment to the Constitution because it involves the "seizure" of a free citizen. Whether a use of force is "brutal" (or excessive) is case-specific and hinges on whether the act was objectively reasonable under the circumstances (*Graham v. Connor*, 490 U.S. 386, 1989). Excessive force by jail and prison personnel constitutes "cruel and unusual punishment" under the Eighth Amendment.

Excessive use of force by officers of the criminal justice system, if found to be intentional, is punishable by state statutes covering crimes of violence (assault, rape, and homicide) and by the federal statute 18 U.S.C. §242. The latter covers "Deprivation of Rights Under Color of Law," and punishes by up to a year in federal prison any person acting under color of law who intentionally and wrongfully uses excessive force, or by as many as 10 years if there is bodily harm or a dangerous weapon is used, or by as much as life imprisonment or the death penalty if the harm inflicted caused death, was intended to cause death, or involved or was intended to involve kidnapping or aggravated sexual abuse. A person need only be working under legal authority during the use of force to be punishable by Section 242. It covers both full and part-time justice system workers and those who do not work for the justice system but who have lawful arrest or other detention powers (for example, private police and correctional officials, deputized persons).

Nonfederal offending officers and their agencies may be civilly liable in state court, or in federal court under 42 U.S.C. §1983. Because §1983 does not cover federal officers, it was established that they may be held personally civilly liable in federal court for unreasonable force or other rights deprivation under a "Bivens Claim" (*Bivens v. Six Unknown Federal Narcotic Agents*, 91 S.Ct. 1999, 1971). Federal government agencies can only be held liable for rights violations under the Federal Tort Claims Act (28 U.S.C. Chapter 171).

Unreasonable fatal and nonfatal violence perpetrated by police against citizens sometimes has been attributed to stress-inducing job factors, most notably life-threats, social isolation, peer pressures, departmental policies (or lack of them), discretionary decision-making pressures, physiological stress, and anticipatory fear in responding to calls. These conditions contribute to what Jerome Skolnick has termed the "policeman's working personality." This personality is said to be nurtured on the job and includes the elements of authoritarianism, suspicion, racism, insecurity, hostility, and cynicism. Police are expected to establish authority immediately in a tense situation. They sometimes resort to physical force to achieve that authority.

Police are constantly exposed to danger, so they are likely to become suspicious about those who are not part of the police fraternity. Suspicion and authority, coupled with hostility and insecurity, can easily promote the use of unreasonable force. Role socialization may also partly explain brutality by prison authorities; Phillip Zimbardo demonstrated that even ordinary citizens will develop authoritarian personalities while temporarily in the role of human custodians.

THE DIRTY HARRY PROBLEM

Police and prison personnel often become cynical about the social value of many citizens with whom they come in contact, thereby promoting the use of certain "techniques of neutralization," including the "denial of victim" neutralization for brutality (the person had it coming). Further, because the court system is often seen as impotent, an "appeal to higher (justice) loyalties" may be used to help render brutal officer behavior acceptable. Some police and prison personnel believe that bending or breaking the law is acceptable in order to get their job done, and this would include the protection of fellow officers from brutality accusations.

Carl Klockars has termed these tendencies among police the "Dirty Harry Problem" (after the Clint Eastwood movie character). Officers believe that it is acceptable to use "dirty" means to achieve "good ends" (that is, justice), and only "dirty means will work" in attaining those ends. In terms of differential association theory, such attitudes are often transmitted to new officers and assimilated into a shared departmental value system. There may be an excess of definitions favorable to the justification

Police brutality can be understood in terms of differential association and self-control theories.

for criminal brutality that have been learned by officers who employ it. Such schooling may encompass various ways of inflicting brutality.

Group socialization, coupled with job stress, then, has generally been seen to be the major explanations behind police brutality. There also may be nonoccupational factors associated with individuals' personalities that provide an additional explanation.

Self-control theory would conceptualize brutality as an attempt by police to gain "revenge without court delays." Self-control theory would argue that brutality contains many elements of low self-control behavior—it provides excitement, thrills, and risks; there are few long-term benefits associated with it; it takes little skill; it results from a low frustration tolerance; and it demonstrates a lack of attachment to the feelings of others. The theory

would also emphasize that situations in which brutality occurs invariably are perceived to have low visibility, thereby decreasing offenders' perceptions of being punished.

For self-control to be supported as an explanation of brutality over occupational differential association, it would have to be demonstrated that pre-employment levels of self-control are lower among officers who ultimately are more likely to use excessive force. This finding would support self-control theory's notion of stability, and demonstrating that assaulting officers also are involved in other occupational deviance would support the theory's notion of versatility.

SEE ALSO

differential association; self-control theory.; Sutherland, Edwin H.; police corruption; Mollen Commission; Knapp Commission.

BIBLIOGRAPHY. Carl Klockars, "The Dirty Harry Problem," *The Annals of the American Academy of Political and Social Science* (v.425, November 1980); Albert J. Reiss, Jr., "Police Brutality: Answers to Key Questions," *Society* (v.5/8, 1968); Jerome Skolnick, *Justice Without Trial: Law Enforcement in a Democratic Society* (Wiley, 1966).

GARY S. GREEN
CHRISTOPHER NEWPORT UNIVERSITY

police corruption

WHEN POLICE officers intentionally misuse their authority for personal aims, it is termed police corruption. It is a problem that has occurred since modern policing evolved, and it is international in scope. While all criminal experts agree that it is an important social problem, there is less agreement about the extent of corruption.

Some individuals see the majority of police as corrupt, while others believe that only a handful of officers engage in corrupt activities. Three reasons limit our ability to determine the extent of police corruption: conceptual factors, methodological issues, and cultural factors.

In conceptual factors, there is great disparity in the ways that experts define police corruption. Some scholars follow strict definitions of corruption and suggest that any time a police officer violates the rules of her department, corruption has occurred.

The problem is that the rules police are expected to follow are quite extensive. Rulebooks for police departments in major cities are up to one foot thick. There are rules about when to wear a hat, how to get out of a car, how to question suspects, whether to accept a free cup of coffee, among thousands of others. In the end, it is virtually impossible to follow all of the rules all of the time. So, are they committing misconduct when they violate department rules?

At the other end of the continuum are those scholars who define police corruption in rather liberal terms. Members of this camp would allow the police to commit an assortment of transgressions, so long as no one is directly or unfairly harmed by their actions. After all, in most jobs individuals commit what is referred to as occupational deviance. People take longer breaks than they are supposed to; workers take things from work that are supposed to stay at work; sick leave and vacation time are routinely used inappropriately; restaurant workers often take food without paying for it—what is wrong with police officers engaging in similar acts? Thus, some conceptual confusion exists regarding what should be characterized as misconduct and what should be characterized as just a part of the job.

Methodological issues exist that also make it difficult to determine the precise extent of police corruption. It is essentially impossible to study police corruption with traditional research strategies. Researchers have tried to survey police officers regarding their experiences with corruption. These studies have proven to be difficult: Police officers are particularly distrustful of surveys, and when asked about misconduct, honest officers are offended and dishonest officers are not going to be open with researchers. Known as the "Thin Blue Line," it is difficult for researchers to cross over into the world of policing and get access to their activities, lives, and routines when it comes to police corruption.

Similar problems arise when researchers conduct field studies with police officers. Known as the Hawthorne Effect, officers will alter their behavior in the presence of researchers. Researchers, then, are not able to observe true police work. Rather, they are being presented with a staged production that will bias any possibility of obtaining an accurate portrayal of life in the streets.

Cultural problems also limit our ability to accurately understand police corruption. Within the United States, cultural variation exists in individuals' beliefs about appropriate and inappropriate police behavior. Minorities are especially distrusting of the police. Consequently, members of minority groups have been known to routinely call into question all police activities. These cultural issues extend past the boundaries of the United States and exist on an international level. Types of police behavior tolerated in various countries varies significantly. Consider the following:

In Haiti, the wife of a police commissioner of Jacmel hired eight men to kill a 17-year-old boy after the boy littered in her yard.

A survey of households in Bangladesh found the police department was the country's most corrupt public institution. Three-fourths of respondents interacting with police in the prior year indicated that they had paid bribes to the police.

In Bolivia, a criminal gang committed a series of horrific robberies. Eventually authorities learned that the gang included a colonel and major from the local police department.

In Kenya, students and others protest regularly about the extent of corruption on the Kenyan police force.

In Mexico City, a police officer on a motorcycle pretended that a car hit him in an attempt to extort thousands of dollars from the driver. Two other cops pretended to be civilian witnesses to this incident.

These are just a handful of the cases that represent the enormous number of corruption incidents across the world. While it is difficult to determine the extent of police misconduct, researchers have considered the varieties of misconduct, as well as the causes and consequences of the behavior.

VARIETIES OF POLICE MISCONDUCT

One of the first police corruption typologies was developed by J. Roebuck and T. Barker in 1974 in an article appearing in *Social Problems*. The authors identified eight different types of corruption including the following: corruption of authority, kickbacks, opportunistic theft, fixes, protection of illegal activities, direct criminal acts, internal payoffs, and flaking. Corruption of authority is acceptance of free or discounted meals, as one example. Note that it is not always seen as corruption, however. Some departments have policies stating that it is wrong for officers to accept free or discounted meals, while others say such activity is entirely appropriate because it builds good relationships between the police and the public. Many business owners support these policies because it allows them an extra layer of protection—nobody will rob an establishment where police are present. Those who say it is wrong worry about the possibility that police would not provide the same degree of public services to stores that did not provide the free or discounted meals. When police officers force individuals to offer the free or discounted services, many agree that police misconduct has occurred.

Kickbacks occur when police officers get reimbursed for referrals they make. Police officers are in a position to make a host of referrals to citizens. Citizens may want to know who to call to have their car towed. Others may want to know who the best attorney or bail bonds agent is. Depending on department rules, it may be entirely appropriate to offer a referral of some sort. It becomes inappropriate when officers make referrals and receive money or some other favor from the party that benefited from the referral. These practices promote dishonesty and undermine a free market economy.

Opportunistic theft occurs when officers take things to keep for themselves, but they did not necessarily plan the theft. An officer can commit all kinds of opportunistic theft from "borrowing" a newspaper on the subway to stealing money from citizens and drugs from offenders. These aren't planned robberies; officers just take advantage of situations that presented themselves.

A fix occurs when officers accept certain favors or bribes in exchange for decisions that would benefit offenders. Consider a case where a police officer accepts money for not arresting a crack cocaine dealer. Or, consider instances where police officers accept sexual favors for not writing a traffic ticket. These are each examples of fixes. In essence, police accept money, services, sexual favors, or something else in exchange for not enforcing the law.

Protection of illegal activities is a fifth type of corruption described by Roebuck and Barker. This occurs when police offer protection to individuals or groups involved in criminal enterprises. Those often cited as receiving police protection illegally include prostitutes, drug dealers, gangs, and organized offenders. This type of corruption is doubly problematic because those receiving protection may commit crimes beyond supposedly victimless offenses.

Direct criminal activities are acts that are illegal for everyone to commit. If a police officer robs someone, then a direct criminal activity has occurred. If a police officer uses drugs on the job, then a direct criminal activity has occurred. Perhaps the easiest way to think of it is that these actions involve offenses that could get any individual arrested.

Internal payoffs are a seventh type of police corruption. These occur when police officers buy, sell, or barter certain benefits of their job. They may sell their shift to another officer, or trade vacation time. This is basically misuse of administrative policies.

Finally, flaking, also known as padding, occurs when officers plant or add evidence to cases. Some experts think that this is more common in drug cases than any other type of case. Related flaking are instances where police officers lie during trial. The process of lying during testimony is called "testilying" by New York City police officers. It is justified on the grounds that if the offender is guilty, all measures should be taken to ensure they are found guilty.

Los Angeles Police Office Mark Furham, who as accused of planting evidence in the O. J. Simpson case one remarked, "if you find a needle mark [on a drug suspect] that looks like three days old, pick the scab. Squeeze it. Looks like serum's coming, as if it were hours old. That's not falsifying a report. That's putting a criminal in jail. That's being a police officer."

CAUSES OF POLICE MISCONDUCT

Researchers at the Home Office in the United Kingdom cite three possible reasons why police corruption occurs: "bad apples" theory, police organizational explanations, and structural explanations. Bad apples theory suggests that just a few officers are generally corrupt, and those few make the whole department look bad. Recent research has discredited this approach, in part, because corruption, when uncovered, is usually widespread in various departments.

Police organizational explanations look at how the organization of police work may contribute to corruption. There is generally no oversight over police officers in the streets. They are free to do as they wish. They are underpaid, and opportunities to interact with "bad" people are a part of officers' daily routines. The public is not able to watch over the police so they have an enormous amount of discretion, and misuse is, to some, inevitable.

Structural explanations refer to the fact that some values, norms, and practices of certain cultures and subcultures may promote misconduct. In the United States, it is customary to tip those who help us out. Why not tip a police officer for a job well done? We tip hair dressers, taxi cab drivers, delivery people. The norm (standard rule in our culture) is that tipping is an appropriate way to display our satisfaction with others. As well, cultures that have high levels of political corruption generally have higher levels of police corruption.

CONSEQUENCES OF CORRUPTION

A number of consequences occur as a result of police misconduct. One consequence has to do with the decreased amount of trust that individuals have in the police as a result of occasional indiscretions by law enforcement officers. When the public hears about a particular officer engaging in inappropriate activities, the image of the profession is tarnished, and public trust is hindered.

A second and related consequence is fear. When the public loses trust in the police, fear ensues. For example, rumors of corrupt officers in Tijuana, Mexico, abound. Imagine being a tourist in Tijuana and seeing a police officer. Are you going to trust that officer? Are your perceptions of trust going to influence your perceptions of safety?

A third consequence has to do with the fact that police corruption potentially lowers the faith that individuals have in the law. If police don't obey the law, why would ordinary members of society? In effect, those sworn to enforce the law, may actually be criminogenic agents rather than deterrent agents when they commit misdeeds on the job.

It is important to note that the majority of police officers do not engage in illicit activities on the job. The few who do, however, wreak havoc on the profession and society.

SEE ALSO

police brutality; corruption; Knapp Commission; Mollen Commission; bribery; Mexico; organized crime; consequences of white-collar crime; fear of crime.

BIBLIOGRAPHY. Gill Donovan, "Bishops Claim Police Involvement in Killings," *National Catholic Reporter* (v.39/24, 2003); Mertineh Kebede, "Police Corruption: Shame on You the Police," *New African* (v.38/1); J. Roebuck and T. Barker, "A Typology of Police Corruption," *Social Problems* (1974); Tamara Rolef, *Police Corruption* (Greenhaven, 2003); "Policing the Police," *The Economist* (May 4, 2002); "Bangladesh Cops, Courts Most Corrupt," *Washington Report on the Middle Eastern Affairs* (v.22/48, 2003); Alan Zerembo, "The Worst Job in the World," *Newsweek International* (December 4, 2000).

BRIAN K. PAYNE, PH.D.
OLD DOMINION UNIVERSITY

political assassination

WITH A LONG LEGACY throughout history, political assassination has more recently come under the study of crime, and has been delineated between assassinations of a specific individual person or group, or assassinations of persons targeted by chance but with a political agenda. These two main groups may be distinguished by a dozen typologies, which overlap often or describe escalating phases of a conflict.

Assassinations to get rid of a ruling politician and to destabilize the political situation within a country are widely known in democratic and nondemocratic societies. The best known examples are the assassinations of John and Robert Kennedy and of Martin Luther King, Jr., in the United States during the 1960s, or the shooting of Mahatma Gandhi in 1948. Although the moral and sometimes political impact of those assassinations is large, in democracies the political system is seldom changed by such events. Though in dictatorial regimes the elimination of a ruling person may change the regime itself, democracies tend to be able to survive such assassinations as they have proper and accepted rules for succession in place. A recent case of an assassination to change (in the view of the assassin) the course of national politics was the Yitzhak Rabin murder during what was believed to be an Israeli-Palestinian peace process.

Assassinations to start or complete a military coup may be used to overthrow a weak democratic system or to change one dictatorial regime for another. Sometimes it is done by local military forces alone, but other cases have had heavy involvement from Western intelligence agencies.

Assassinations as a tool of war within a civil war are known in many countries all over the world. After Germany became a republic following its defeat in World War I, a large campaign of political murder was engaged by elements of the extreme right, which claimed the lives of several leading politicians. A starting point for the civil war in El Salvador was the shooting of Archbishop Oscar Romero by a murder squad of the extreme right-wing paramilitary. More recent cases include the shooting of Serbian Prime Minister Zoran Djindjic as part of the fading Yugoslav civil war (allegedly linked to mafia involvement), or the killing of Afghan warlord Ahmed Shah Massoud by a suicide assassin of Taliban or al-Qaeda origin, in a nearly coincident timing with the attacks of September 11, 2001.

Assassinations by separatist groups are a common tool to underline their political goals. Some examples include the bombing of Lord Louis Mountbatten by Catholic separatists from Northern Ireland, or the killings of Indira and Rajiv Gandhi by Sikh and Tamil separatists in India.

Assassinations of political opponents or dissidents by totalitarian regimes in the country or abroad became prevalent especially during the fascist period. Although Benito Mussolini made this part of fascist policy, Adolf Hitler epitomized it during the so-called Roehm-Putsch when he personally ordered and supervised the killing of dissidents within the Nazi party in 1934 (Ernst Roehm, a high-ranking and brutal Nazi official, was killed during this internal purge).

Communist regimes, especially during the Stalinist era employed the same tools; the most famous victim was Leon Trotsky, who was brutally murdered in his Mexican exile. Another example is the killing of opposition leader Benigno Aquino upon his return from exile to the Philippines. An assassination of this type could also happen as a formal death penalty by a court, for example many victims of the Nazi terror were sentenced to death for minor "crimes" by the so-called Volksgerichtshof (Court of the People).

Assassinations of people coming to importance not by their political role, but because they witnessed, by whatever circumstances, an event which might be harmful to the assassins if it would be made public: Usually these cases are hardly de-

tected and fall within conspiracy theories. A famous case is the still unsolved murder of the West German prostitute Rosemarie Nittribitt in 1957, who is believed to have had several lovers within the ranks high officials.

Assassinations of political figures or members of the judiciary by the Sicilian Mafia were commonplace in Italy in the 1970s and 1980s. Not only conspiracy theorists, but others linked the murders of the two Kennedy brothers to the Mafia, citing the rigorous anti-Mafia policy of Robert Kennedy as a possible reason. Organized crime assassinations of politicians for their stand against drug trafficking is a dominant part of politics in countries like Colombia.

Assassinations of civilians of a certain origin, religion or political nomination were common in Lebanon and in Northern Ireland in the 1970s and 1980s. Usually those events prepare for or culminate a civil war, which in some cases is a low-intensity armed conflict. Such assassinations take place regularly on a large scale by Palestinian suicide-bombers. An example of an incident where terror was executed in another country is the slaughter of the Israeli Olympic team in Munich in 1972 by Palestinian terrorists.

Assassinations by resistance groups during an occupation against enemy forces and especially against some of their own people viewed as "traitors," can be seen in the American occupation of Iraq in 2003–04 as a U.S.-approved Iraqi police chief was targeted.

Assassinations by mentally ill persons can target anybody. Whereas the murder of John Lennon only had minor political impact, the shooting of President James Garfield was planned by an insane person without any "reasonable" political intent, but was political by virtue of the victim.

Assassinations of civilians chosen at random to provide a climate of terror and fear in the public mood for internal reasons are much more often employed by right-wing extremists than by left-wing counterparts. Terrible examples were the bombings of the Bologna, Italy, railway station in 1980 or the more recent Oklahoma City bombing in 1998. As with terror against individual representatives within democracies, the long-term effect of such attacks can only be attained if the democracy itself was weak even before the killing took place.

Terror attacks against civilians chosen at random by terrorist groups from abroad were brought to a new dimension by al-Qaeda during the events of September 11, 2001. Assassinations on such large scale changed not only threat perceptions, but also questioned many traditional approaches to terror and law. Assassinations and terror attacks before were seen only as a problem for the police and the judiciary. After September 11, the distinction between assassins, terror organizations, and rogue states is fading.

Mass murders or even genocide by totalitarian regimes are, in fact, assassinations on a large scale. The 20th century was marked by such monstrosities from the Armenian genocide during World War I to the Holocaust and the killing fields of Cambodia. Although those mass murder actions need far more factors to happen (people, material, preparation) compared to a single assassination, they can be regarded as the culmination of political assassinations.

Political assassinations may have short term impacts like a change of government or regime, but even in stable democracies, where the effect is limited to the replacement of the victim by another democratically legitimated person, they may poison the political climate for years to come.

SEE ALSO

elite crime; United Fruit; South America; Central America; Cuba.

BIBLIOGRAPHY. Harris M. Lentz, *Assassinations and Executions: An Encyclopedia of Political Violence, 1865-1986* (St. James Press, 1988); Franklin L. Ford, *Political Murder: From Tyrannicide to Terrorism* (Harvard University Press, 1985); Stephen J. Spignesi, *In the Crosshairs* (New Page Books, 2003); Norman Mailer, *Oswald's Tale: An American Mystery* (Random House, 1994); Michael Benson, *Encyclopedia of the JFK Assassination* (Facts on File, 2002); Walter Laqueur, *No End to War* (Continuum, 2003).

OLIVER BENJAMIN HEMMERLE, PH.D.
MANNHEIM UNIVERSITY, GERMANY

polyvinyl chlorides

FOR MANY YEARS a component of plastic, polyvinyl chlorides (PVCs) have been used in products ranging from construction materials to children's toys, and from mini-blinds to intravenous and blood bags.

Polyvinyl chloride was first discovered in 1835 and was one of the first commercially developed plastics. The white powder is made from 57 percent salt and 43 percent oil. It can be blended with a wide variety of stabilizers, lubricators, softeners, and pigments to make a versatile range of products.

There is increasing evidence that there are hazards associated with this material. One problem is that PVC is partly based on chlorine, which is linked to such highly toxic substances as dioxin. Another problem with PVC is that the additives used in it are frequently toxic. Soft PVC requires the addition of plasticizers, the most common of which are phthalates. One phthalate is DEHP, an additive to make PVC softer and more flexible, which has been found to have adverse effects in laboratory animals. The Food and Drug Administration, in September 2002, recommended limiting exposure to DEHP as much as possible.

AGGRAVATED BATTERY

Five Chicago Magnet Wire senior executives were charged with aggravated battery, conspiracy, and reckless conduct in a case in which more than 40 company employees suffered nerve and lung disorders resulting from exposure to hazardous chemicals at the company's Elk Grove Village, Illinois, facility. These chemicals included polyvinyl chlorides. The charges were first dismissed in 1985 by an Illinois state judge. That decision was upheld by a state appellate court, but it finally was reversed by the Illinois Supreme Court in February 1989. The following October, the U.S. Supreme Court refused to hear the five-year-old case, thus letting the conviction stand. The court's decision to not hear the case cleared the way for all state prosecutors to proceed against executives for crimes regarding the health and safety of their employees, an issue which had up to that time been decided differently in different state courts.

In November 2001, an Italian court acquitted former chemical company managers of criminal charges ranging from mass manslaughter to environmental damage. The charges had been brought against the EniChem and Montedison managers three years earlier on behalf of 157 workers who had died of cancer and another 103 who had died of other illnesses between 1965 and 1985. These deaths were alleged to have occurred because of the workers' exposure to vinyl chloride monomer (VCM) at the Porto Marghera, Italy, chemical complex. Environmental charges resulted from the company's allowing the effluent to pollute the famed Venice Lagoon. The court's ruling to dismiss charges was based on the fact that the workers originally became ill in the 1950s and 1960s, but it was 1973 before the potential dangers of VCM were discovered. VCM is used in the production of PVC. Montedison, in a separate agreement with Italy's environmental ministry and the prime minister's office, agreed to help fund clean up of Porto Marghera and the lagoon.

In July 2000, the European Commission issued a Green Paper with its evaluation of PVC environmental issues. The Green Paper stated that PVC is one of today's most widespread plastics with about 5.5 million tons produced in Europe alone in 1998. Lead, cadmium, and organotins are stabilizers in PVC products which are used to prevent deterioration from heat and light. Lead stabilizers are classified as toxic and carcinogenic; cadmium is classed as harmful, toxic, or highly toxic, carcinogenic, and dangerous to the environment.

The commission, however, asserted there was no assessment at that time of the hazard of these chemicals in PVC. It also asserted that information available indicated these chemicals remain bound in PVC while it is in use; potential damage is during the elimination of the PVC materials. When PVCs are burned, almost all the lead and cadmium remains in the residue.

SEE ALSO

Nader, Ralph; Consumer Product Safety Act; unsafe products; workplace deaths.

BIBLIOGRAPHY. "Playing with Polymers," *Design Week* (January 16, 2003); Sean Fenske, "A Move toward Being DEHP-Free (The Way Ahead)," *Medical Design Technology* (September 2002); Ian Young, "Italian Court Clears Managers of Criminal Charges in VCM Case," *Chemical Week* (November 14, 2001); "Environment: Green Paper on Environmental Issues of PVC," *European Report* (July 29, 2000); Michael A. Verespej, "Executives' Criminal Liability Upheld," *Industry Week* (October 16, 1989); "Matel Moves Against PVC Children's Products While Health Canada Still Refuses to Take Action," Canada NewsWire (September 28, 1998); "Real Science Opposed PVC: Greenpeace's Matthew Bramley Says the Campaign Against PVC Is Scientifically Sound, But Michael LeGault Insists It's 'Junk Science,'" *National Post* (May 4, 1999).

LINDA M. CREIBAUM
ARKANSAS STATE UNIVERSITY

Pontell, Henry N. (1950–)

HENRY N. PONTELL is a modern pioneer in white-collar crime research. His writings have covered all aspects of white-collar crime, from medical fraud to the savings and loan crisis to international issues surrounding white-collar crime. As an undergraduate student, Pontell received the New York State Regents Scholar Incentive Award to pursue his studies in sociology and political science at the State University of New York, Stony Brook (SUNY). In graduate school, he received a State University of New York Graduate Research Fellowship and U.S. Department of Justice Research Fellowship. He also worked as a lecturer and as a research associate in the School of Health Sciences at SUNY. Pontell received his Ph.D. in sociology from SUNY Stony Brook in 1979. His dissertation was titled, "Deterrence and System Capacity: Crime and Punishment in California."

In 1979, Pontell was hired as an assistant professor in the social ecology department at the University of California, Irvine (UCI). He has served in several different capacities at the university, including chair of the Department of Criminology, Law and Society at UCI.

While his research has covered an assortment of topics, his white-collar crime research has been especially illuminating. In the early 1980s, he began publishing several studies on white-collar crime topics: One study examined police chiefs' perceptions of white-collar crime, another examined how flight attendants are victimized on the job, and another examined strategies used to detect and investigate Medicaid fraud. This third study was the groundwork for a plethora of other studies on Medicaid fraud. These studies eventually culminated in *Prescription for Profit*, a book he co-authored with Paul Jesilow and Gilbert Geis.

Pontell's white-collar crime research also focused on the cause of the savings and loan crisis. Along with Kitty Calavita, he conducted the most comprehensive investigation of the role of white-collar crime in the savings and loan fiasco. One of their articles was reprinted in the *Hearings of the U.S. Senate's Permanent Subcommittee on Investigations*. They also provided written testimony to the U.S. Senate's Subcommittee on Consumer and Regulatory Affairs, Committee on Banking, Housing, and Urban Affairs. With Robert Tillman, Pontell and Calavita published *Big Money Crime*, a book detailing their savings and loan research. In 2001, Pontell received the Albert J. Reiss Jr. Distinguished Scholarship Award from the Crime, Law, and Deviance section of the American Sociological Association for his efforts.

In the same year, to honor his contributions to increasing understanding about white-collar crime, Pontell was the recipient of the Donald R. Cressey Award from the Association of Certified Fraud Examiners. He has remained active in his discipline and his community, including a four-year stint as the public safety commissioner for the city of Irvine, California.

SEE ALSO

Geis, Gilbert; Jesilow, Paul; Medicare and Medicaid fraud; healthcare fraud; savings and loan fraud.

BIBLIOGRAPHY. Kitty Calavita, Henry Pontell, and Robert Tillman, *Big Money Crime* (University of California Press, 1998); Paul Jesilow, Henry Pontell, and Gilbert Geis, *Prescription without Profit* (University of California Press, 1998); Stephen Rosoff, Henry Pontell, and Robert Tillman, *Profit Without Honor* (Prentice Hall, 2002).

BRIAN K. PAYNE, PH.D.
OLD DOMINION UNIVERSITY

Ponzi scheme

A PONZI SCHEME is an investment fraud in which returns are paid to earlier investors at a great profit entirely out of money paid from a wave of newer investors, who are encouraged to make investments in response to the handsome returns received. Ponzi schemes are similar to pyramid schemes, but differ in that Ponzi schemes are operated by a central company or person, who may or may not be making other false claims about how the money is being invested, and where the returns are coming from. Ponzi schemes do not necessarily involve a hierarchal structure, as in a pyramid scheme; there is merely one person or company that is collecting money from new participants and using this money to pay off promised returns to earlier participants. Because the Ponzi scheme requires an ever-increasing number of investors to keep going, there always comes a point at which the money coming in is insufficient to pay off the previous wave of investors, and they all lose their money.

The scheme is named after Charles Ponzi, who ran such a scheme in 1919–20. The backdrop of his scheme was international postal reply coupons (IPRCs), which could be redeemed for stamps in other countries. Ponzi realized that by purchasing IPRCs in a country whose currency was weak, he could redeem them for stamps in a country whose currency was strong, making a small profit on the differing exchange rates. He found that he could purchase Spanish IPRCs for a penny and redeem them in the United States for 10 cents. Ponzi thought he could take advantage of differences between U.S. and foreign currencies used to buy and sell international mail coupons.

Ponzi told investors that he could provide a 40 percent return in just 90 days compared with 5 percent annually for savings accounts. After his investors' three-month period was up, they were reimbursed with interest not at the guaranteed 40 percent, but at 50 percent.

The investors gladly reinvested the entire amount, and spread the word that Ponzi was the man with whom to do business. While continuing with his scheme, Ponzi discovered that IPRCs were issued only for the convenience of postal customers who used international mail, therefore only a limited number of coupons were issued each year, not nearly enough to finance an investment system like the one he had in mind.

In fact, the Spanish government issued fewer than $1 million worth of these coupons. Ponzi received orders that were so huge that there was no possible way for him to purchase enough IPRCs to cover them. So, he "robbed Peter to pay Paul," reimbursing earlier investors with funds taken from later investors.

As Ponzi paid the matured notes held by early investors, word of enormous profits spread through the community, whipping greedy and credulous investors into a frenzy. He had no trouble finding increasing numbers of investors necessary to keep the operation running smoothly. Happy investors convinced their friends that Ponzi's operation was a safe, easy, and quick way to multiply their savings.

When the swindle was discovered by authorities, Ponzi was exposed through the newspapers. However, people didn't believe the authorities and continued to send money to Ponzi. When the operation was shut down, investors blamed the Massachusetts authorities for victimizing Ponzi and sabotaging their chances of getting their investment back. All told, he took in over $10 million in less than a year.

Though a few early investors were paid off to make the scheme look legitimate, an investigation found that Ponzi had purchased less than $50 worth of the international mail coupons. The simplicity and grand scale of his scheme linked Ponzi's name with a particular form of fraud. A swindle of this nature, once a "bubble," is now referred to as a Ponzi scheme. The engine of Ponzi's postal coupon fraud was a simple accounting misclassification. Money paid to investors, described as income, was actually distribution of capital. Although the economics of such schemes are simple, contemporary swindlers conceal this fact with sophisticated marketing.

The classic Ponzi scheme is still popular today and works in the same way. And unlike pyramid schemes, where one's potential gain is measured by the active and conscious practice of participant recruitment, Ponzi schemes attribute their money-making abilities to some elaborate and inventive investment or business process, with the influx of new depositors the result of word-of-mouth only.

There are several other distinctions between Ponzi schemes and a pyramid selling scheme. A requirement of a Ponzi scheme is the promotion of what starts out to be, or appears to be, a real investment opportunity which investors may passively contribute to. The pyramid scheme involves a person making an investment for the right to receive compensation for finding and introducing other participants into the scheme. There is a clear understanding among the participants that the success of the opportunity is dependent upon attracting these additional participants.

SEE ALSO

scams; Stavisky, Serge; securities fraud; investment trust fraud; Securities and Exchange Commission.

BIBLIOGRAPHY. M. Bertrand, *Fraud! How to Protect Yourself from Schemes, Scams, and Swindles* (American Management Association, 2000); M. Darby, "In Ponzi We Tru$t," *Smithsonian Magazine* (December 1998); M. Fleming, "Crimes of Persuasion: Schemes, Scams, Frauds," www.crimes-of-persuasion.com (2002); M. Allen Henderson, *How Con Games Work* (Citadel Press, 1985); J. Wilker, *Classic Cons and Swindles* (Chelsea House Publishers, 1997); Securities and Exchange Commission, "Ponzi Scheme," www.sec.gov (2000).

PATRICK D. WALSH
LOYOLA UNIVERSITY NEW ORLEANS

pornography

A CLASSIFICATION of crime peripherally related to white-collar and corporate crime, pornography refers to sexually explicit materials produced to induce sexual arousal in a viewer or reader. Pornography, as an illegal revenue source for enterprises ranging from organized crime to internet entrepreneurs, crosses into white-collar crime with tax evasion, money laundering, corruption, and a variety of frauds in accounting and banking that are spread all over the world.

The regulation of pornography evolved from early obscenity laws originally enacted to protect political and religious views. The concept of suppressing sexual expression in the media became a concern in the 19th century following the invention of photography, and the staging of theatrical performances with sexual themes. Anthony Comstock was among the first moral reformers to call for the suppression of sexual expression. Over the years, the manufacture, distribution, and sale of pornographic materials has been either forbidden or regulated in various jurisdictions, however possession of pornography by an adult in the privacy of one's home is generally legal.

To the extent the manufacture or sale of most pornography is illegal, it is viewed as censual crime. Whether viewing pornography has harmful effects or not has been debated for decades with passionate arguments, but with little conclusive evidence on either side. A case can be made for or against it depending on the industry perspective, images depicted, or whether pornography affects the viewer's subsequent behavior.

Two government commissions have addressed the issue of harm from pornography, arriving at different conclusions. Formed in 1970 under President Richard M. Nixon, the Commission on Obscenity and Pornography initiated the scientific approach to the issue. Researchers representing mostly behavioral sciences conducted studies under the auspices of a $2 million grant. Attempts have been made to classify pornography, with the simplest scheme being the three categories used in the 1986 Commission. Class I is adult erotica that may depict images of sexually explicit nudity but not actual intercourse or violence. Class II depicts intercourse, and Class III depicts images of intercourse in conjunction with violence.

The 1970 Commission concluded viewing and the availability of pornography had little measurable effect on the public. Feminists and conservative politicians subsequently challenged its findings. After the early 1970s, the nature and distribution of pornography changed. The 1970 commission examined only popular erotic materials such as *Playboy* and *Penthouse* magazines. By the late 1970s, the number of pornographic publications vastly increased along with the increasing use of videotapes depicting more depraved images.

Rape scenes were and are common, and this is the basis for the feminist argument that pornography encourages violence against women. At the extreme, is the so-called snuff film in which the actress is murdered on camera. Also in the mid-1970s, child pornography became more prevalent. No one doubts child pornography and snuff films are extremely harmful to those involved in production. They remain in the province of organized crime, and though penalties are substantial, profits are high. The appearance of such materials and the content of mainstream pornographic magazines and videos caused many to question whether the 1970 Commission findings still applied.

During the early 1980s, feminists such as Andrea Dworkin and Catharine MacKinnon successfully led crusades against the sale of pornographic images that depict the degradation of women, resulting in city ordinances in Minneapolis, Minnesota. The feminist anti-pornography crusade combined with an unlikely ally of conservative politicians to further question the effect of pornography on the public. To again evaluate the question, the Attorney General's Commission on Pornography was created under President Ronald Reagan and submitted its conclusions in 1986, contradicting those of the 1970 Commission.

Along with debates over the effects of pornography are legal battles. Those who manufacture and sell pornography seek to have the industry protected by the First Amendment of the Constitution. The hardest part is trying to define something that is as subjective as pornography. On this topic, Supreme Court Justice Potter Stewart stated in 1964 (and is often quoted): "I know it when I see it." The Supreme Court has applied the First Amendment quite broadly. The legal battles over pornography are extensive and complex. Three of the most prominent cases in the 20th century have generally afforded First Amendment protection. In *Roth v. United States* (354 U.S. 476, 1957) the Supreme Court ruled that only materials "utterly without redeeming social importance" do not have First Amendment protection. What constitutes redeeming social importance is debatable and can be minimal.

The Supreme Court in *Stanley v. Georgia* (394 U.S. 557) granted First Amendment protection to individuals to read or watch whatever they want in private. In *Miller v. California* (413 U.S. 15, 1973) the Supreme Court stated material is pornographic that is by law "patently offensive" such that the average person viewing it using "contemporary community standards" would feel it appeals only to "prurient" sexual "interests." In addition to these criteria, the work taken as a whole "lacks serious literary, artistic, political, or scientific value." Once again these are open to interpretation.

While organized crime once controlled virtually all production and sale of pornographic materials, Supreme Court decisions and changes in technology have made the pornography market very accessible. Virtually anyone with a video camera can get into the business to some degree. The production of pornographic videos requires relatively low production costs and a strong market exists regardless of any artistic merits of the film. The change from 8mm films to videotape and VCRs in the late 1970s revolutionized the industry.

The pornography industry is composed of many sizable media distribution companies vying for control of product distribution. Regular video stores often, depending on local ordinances, offer adult videos along with mainstream films (albeit in back rooms). Video is the major market, but adult bookstores, peep shows running short films, or live-model dancing are common in large cities. More recently, the internet has afforded virtually unlimited access to pornographic materials without any censuring. The use of the internet to display, market, and sell the most debased and prurient materials, has raised new questions of regulating the internet.

SEE ALSO
organized crime; Justice, Department of; money laundering; reform and regulation.

BIBLIOGRAPHY. Attorney General's Commission on Pornography, *Final Report* (Government Printing Office, 1986); Susan Gubar and Joan Hoff, *For Adult Users Only: The Dilemma of Violent Pornography* (Indiana University Press, 1989); Laurence O'Toole, *Pornocopia: Porn, Sex, Technology and Desire* (Serpent's Tail, 1998); Gary W. Potter, *The Porn Merchants* (Kendall Hunt Publishing, 1986); *Report of the Special Commission on Obscenity and Pornography* (Bantam Books, 1970); Robert J. Stoller, *Porn: Myths for the Twentieth Century* (Yale University Press, 1991); Yaron Svoray, *Gods of Death* (Simon & Schuster, 1997).

MICHAEL SIEGFRIED
COKER COLLEGE

predatory practices

PREDATORY PRACTICES are forms of unfair competition. In consumer markets, they mostly involve exploiting the public's lack of information about products, often financial products such as home loans or credit terms, thereby obtaining unjustifiable fees and unfair contractual conditions. In business markets, predatory practices involve attempts by one company to use its market power or influence to take advantage of a smaller company or companies. Making a large order from a small company and then not making payments so that the supplier is forced into bankruptcy is one example of a predatory practice.

In consumer markets, predatory practices most commonly focus on the attempt to exploit people's lack of information about lending practices, thereby obtaining more money from them. This includes such practices as flipping, which involves causing customers to renegotiate loan details repeatedly, possibly in a short period of time, while charging high fees on each occasion. Another practice is asset-stripping, which is making loans based on equity in a property rather than the loanee's ability to repay the loan. This is designed to lead to default on behalf of the customer and the transfer of the property (or other asset) to the lending company. Packing involves adding supplementary costs such as credit insurance to a loan, which therefore increases its value without the informed consent of the loanee.

Many of these practices are not in themselves illegal; it is possible and quite common for a lender and loanee to renegotiate the terms of a loan, for example. However, predatory practitioners take advantage of those people unable to provide informed consent. Vulnerable groups include the elderly, those for whom the language of the agreement is not the native language and those with a legal status that prevents them from taking full recourse of the protection of the law.

This last category includes migrant workers who may have documents or agreements that, with or without their knowledge, are not wholly legal. Such people may be forced to meet additional payments to job agents or else required to participate in occupations they would not wish to take or live in conditions they would not have considered suitable. An additional segment of this market is the issuing of loans to people in high risk categories, because of poor credit records or borrowing defaults. Loans made to this group attract very high fees.

Owing to the huge expansion of personal debt in recent years associated with the growth in credit card usage, the Federal Trade Commission has estimated that this practice resulted in loans to the value of $56 billion in 2000 alone. The expansion of credit card usage in Korea and Japan has already led to massive personal indebtedness for many people who have then become vulnerable to debt collectors who may require them to undertake tasks or jobs they would not wish to undertake.

The growth of the internet and the penetration of e-mail throughout all sections of developed societies has provided opportunities for unscrupulous lenders to identify potential victims at a relatively low cost. People responding to advertisements likely to lead to such practices are added to others matching profiles believed likely to lead to high levels of vulnerability on so-called sucker lists which may be traded among unscrupulous lenders for high prices.

Airlines have been accused of predatory practices in how they charge tourist versus business customers.

One difficulty that regulators have faced in tackling predatory practices has been in the lack of adequate definitions of what it is and what scope it has. The growth of communications technology and sophisticated financial instruments in the consumer market as well as industrial markets have together enabled predatory practitioners to continue to innovate new schemes and methods a step ahead of regulators.

In business markets, accusations of predatory practices have been leveled at airlines in the United States and Japanese corporations seeking to undermine the international patent system, among others. Such accusations may result from complaints about tough but essentially fair business practices or may be part of fairly regular cross-border trade diplomacy. Some American commentators, for example, have labeled the practices of competitors from Korea or Taiwan as predatory when they are able to provide goods to the American market at lower costs than domestic competitors are able to achieve.

Complaints against the airline industry focus on the use of hub premiums; large airlines have greater market power at strategic travel centers and may charge competitors extra to use them, especially in the case of low-cost carriers seeking to focus on niche markets. Other complaints focus on the possibility of signaling prices to competitors (via computer systems) to maintain comparable rates on all routes, which again disadvantages many smaller competitors.

The payment of excessive salaries and compensation to executives has also been termed a predatory practice, as has excessive profit-making in a variety of industries, although there is generally no consensus on what constitutes an acceptable level of profit.

SEE ALSO

Federal Trade Commission; illegal competition; price-fixing; antitrust; bank fraud.

BIBLIOGRAPHY. Federal Trade Commission, Prepared Statement of the Federal Trade Commission before the House Committee on Banking and Financial Services on Predatory Lending Practices in the Subprime Industry, www.ftc.gov/os (May 24, 2000); Clinton V. Oster, Jr. and John S. Strong, "Predatory Practices in the U.S. Airline Industry," report for the U.S. Department of Transportation, www.ostpxweb.dot.gov (January 15, 2001).

JOHN WALSH, PH.D.
MAHIDOL UNIVERSITY, THAILAND

price discrimination

PRICE DISCRIMINATION IS DEFINED as the act of selling the same product to different consumers at different prices even though the cost of supplying the product is the same. Price discrimination is widespread in the economy. Airlines charge lower prices for travelers who book seats well in advance or who are willing to stay over on a Saturday night in order to differentiate between recreational travelers who often have low budgets for vacations and business travelers who have a high willingness to pay for flights. Movie theaters give discounts to students, senior citizens, and matinee viewers. Frequent flyer programs, supermarket membership cards, store coupons and even college tuition financial aid packages are other common examples of price discrimination.

When a firm can set prices such that each individual customer is paying their maximum willingness to pay, this is known as perfect price discrimination or first-degree price discrimination. Under first-degree price discrimination, the customer is left with no consumer surplus, that is no value in excess of the purchase price of the good. Third-degree price discrimination occurs when the market can be broken up into a several distinct groups each of which faces a different price. Second-degree price discrimination occurs when the firm charges different prices to different consumers depending on the quantity purchased by each consumer. Price discrimination is often confused with predatory pricing. Predatory pricing occurs when a firm charges a price below cost in order to drive rivals from the market with the intention of raising the price again once the competition has been eliminated. Unlike price discrimination, which is usually an acceptable practice, predatory pricing is prohibited by Section 2 of the Sherman Antitrust Act (1890).

THIRD-DEGREE PRICE DISCRIMINATION

In most cases, economists believe that price discrimination, while it increases firm profits at the expense of some consumers, actually increases societal welfare by allowing the firm to maximize profits while serving a variety of customers. The sale of AIDS drugs in the United States and Africa is an excellent case in point. If forced to sell AIDS drugs to all consumers in the world at the same price, drug manufacturers would likely choose a price that exceeded that which a typical African consumer could afford. By engaging in third-degree price discrimination, a pharmaceutical firm will charge high prices in rich countries but then lower the price to victims in poorer countries expanding the number of patients able to afford treatment. Similarly, book publishers immediately provide access to an author's latest work for those willing to pay the premium for a hardcover edition while later expanding the market to additional readers with the subsequent publication of a paperback.

Economists note that successful price discrimination requires several conditions to be in place. First, the firm or provider must have some degree of market power in order to be able to set prices above the equilibrium price determined in the marketplace. Next, the firm must have the ability to identify those willing to pay a high price for the good from those not willing to pay a premium. This can be accomplished in many ways from geographical pricing (as in the AIDS drug example) or age related pricing (student or senior discounts) to directly collecting information on buyers (direct disclosure of economic information on college financial aid applications.) Finally, the seller must

have way to prevent those who purchase the good at a low price from reselling the good to others with a higher willingness to pay. This can be done through contractual prohibitions or the voiding of warrantees following resale. Services tend to be difficult to resell, and high transaction or transportation costs may also reduce resale. While generally legal, price discrimination is prohibited under the Robinson-Patman Act (1936) in cases where there is a substantial likelihood of a significant reduction of competition. This reduction of competition can take two forms. Primary line discrimination occurs when the price discrimination reduces competition in the market of the good itself.

Secondary line discrimination occurs when competition is reduced among the customers of the good so that a favored buyer has a competitive advantage over its rivals in a downstream market. A firm has two primary defenses against a charge of illegal price discrimination. Price discrimination is always legal if it is the direct result of differences in the cost of supplying the good to different customers. Differences in transportation costs are one obvious example, and volume discounts are another if it is truly cheaper to supply the good in larger quantities. Second, price discrimination is legal if the firm is cutting its price to one customer in a legitimate attempt to meet an equally low price of a rival company. In other words, if a competitor offers a low price to one of a company's clients, the company need not lower its price to all of its clients in order to meet to this single challenge.

PRICE DISCRIMINATION CASES

The economic history and the case law of the United States are full of examples of price discrimination. Most famously, John D. Rockefeller's Standard Oil Company solidified its monopoly hold on the American oil business by demanding that the railroads charge Standard Oil a lower price for transporting its products than those of its consumers. The railroads, who could ill-afford to lose the business of such a large shipper, acquiesced to Rockefeller's request for this type of secondary line discrimination.

The higher transportation costs faced by these rival companies left them at a competitive disadvantage compared to Standard Oil, and ultimately either led to their acquisition by Rockefeller or simply drove them out of business entirely. By

1900, the Standard Oil Trust "had obtained complete mastery over the oil industry, controlling 90 percent of the business of producing, shipping, refining, and selling petroleum and its products, and thus was able to restrain and monopolize all interstate commerce in those products" (*Standard Oil Company of New Jersey et al. vs. United States*, 1911) While Standard Oil's actions occurred before such practices were declared illegal, it is important to note that a charge of discriminatory pricing can be leveled either against the seller or against the buyer, as would have been done in this particular case.

Other cases are less well-known but equally instructive. In *Utah Pie v. Continental Baking* (1967), a small, locally owned baker in Salt Lake City, filed suit against its three major competitors in the rapidly expanding frozen pie market, Continental Baking, Pet Milk, and Carnation. While Utah Pie only operated in the Salt Lake City area, the other three firms had nationwide operations. The three national companies charged lower wholesale prices for their pies in the Salt Lake City area than in other areas of the country and often charged prices below cost. The court ruled that this type of primary line price discrimination was anticompetitive with the intent to drive Utah Pie from the market, although dissenting justices argued that the market structure in Salt Lake City following the actions of the three firms was more competitive than before their price wars. Many observers note that basic economic models would show that markets where four major competitors compete should have lower prices than markets where only three competitors exist. Price differentials between Salt Lake City and other markets may, therefore, be due to effective competition rather than anti-competitive behavior. Perhaps the court should have asked why the three national brands charged so much in other cities rather than why they charged so little in Utah.

Matsushita Electric v. Zenith Radio (1986) combines the concepts of predatory pricing and price discrimination. Zenith argued that, from 1960 to 1985, a cartel of Japanese consumer electronics manufacturers conspired to sell their products in the United States at below cost in order to drive American manufacturers from the market. These predatory pricing schemes were made possible by the higher prices the cartel charged to domestic consumers in the Japanese market. While agreeing that Japanese firms did engage in primary line price discrimination by charging higher prices to Japanese

consumers than American consumers, the court found it unreasonable that a cartel of companies would be content to suffer losses for 25 years in order to attain a monopoly position that even after 25 years they were far from achieving. Thus, the court ruled that it was unlikely that predatory pricing had occurred and that the price discrimination was not illegal since it did not lead to a reduction in competition.

In *FTC v. Morton Salt* (1948), the government examined Morton's practice of offering discounts of up to 20 percent on sales to customers purchasing large quantities of salt. The court stated that quantity discounts are only legal to the extent that quantity sales lower costs to the seller. While the discounts were potentially available to any customer, in reality they were available only to a select few customers who could buy in quantity. Therefore, this secondary line price discrimination reduced the ability of small businesses to compete with giant firms.

Similarly, in *United States v. Borden Company* (1962), the Borden company was unable to prove that the costs of providing milk to the stores in the two large Chicago grocery chains, Jewel and A&P, were lower than the cost of providing milk to independent stores, and therefore their secondary line price discrimination was declared illegal. While the average cost of supplying milk was lower in the large chains, the court ruled that "proof by average" was an inadequate defense since it failed to recognize instances where the cost a providing milk to a single particular independent store could be far lower than the cost of providing milk a single chain store. Borden came out on the right side of the law in a later case regarding milk prices.

In the 1970s, Great Atlantic solicited bids from milk producers to provide an in-house milk brand for its A&P stores. Borden submitted the winning bid and offered to provide milk to A&P at a substantial discount over the price it charged to other firms. In *Great Atlantic & Pacific Tea v. FTC* (1979), the court ruled that since Borden was simply bidding for a contract, it could not possibly be guilty of illegal price discrimination. Borden was clearly acting to meet competition. While the Robinson-Patman Act declares it to be illegal for a firm to use its market power to secure a discriminatory price from a supplier, since Borden was not guilty of illegal price discrimination, Great Atlantic could also not be guilty of securing a discriminatory price. In *Stan-*

dard Oil Company v. FTC (1951), Standard Oil sold gasoline to four large "jobbers" in the Detroit area at a price substantially below the price at which it sold its gasoline to regular retailers in the area. The difference in price was more than the cost differential to Standard Oil. Standard argued that it only charged a lower price to these jobbers in order to retain their business in the face of competition from other oil firms. Again, the court granted that a firm may make price changes in order to meet competition for a major customer without simultaneously cutting its prices to all its other customers.

Government action against price discrimination has become increasingly rare as it is being seen more as special interest legislation designed to protect small businesses from more efficient larger firms.

SEE ALSO

price fixing; antitrust; Sherman Antitrust Act; Robinson-Patman Act; Standard Oil; Rockefeller, John D.; robber barons; predatory practices.

BIBLIOGRAPHY. Dennis Carlton and Jeffery Perloff, *Modern Industrial Organization* (Addison-Wesley, 2000); William Breit and Kenneth Elzinga, *The Antitrust Casebook: Milestones in Economic Regulation* (Harcourt, Brace, 1996); Robert Bork, *The Antitrust Paradox* (Simon & Schuster, 1978).

VICTOR MATHESON, PH.D.
WILLIAMS COLLEGE

price fixing

PRICE FIXING REFERS to any usually unlawful practice in which competing corporations join together and agree to set or maintain an artificially high price, for commodities or services, to maximize profits. It may take place at either the wholesale or retail level and, although it need not involve every competitor in a particular market, it usually involves most of the competitors. According to the Antitrust Division of the U.S. Department of Justice, it is not necessary that the competitors agree to charge exactly the same price, or that every competitor in a given industry join the conspiracy. Price fixing can take many forms including, for example, establishing or adhering to price discounts, holding prices firm, eliminating or reducing discounts, adopting a standard formula for computing prices, maintaining certain price differentials between different types, sizes, or quantities of products, adhering to a minimum fee or price schedule, and fixing credit terms.

A number of price-fixing cases, however, do not involve explicit agreements, but rather takes the form of parallel pricing in which there is a tacit understanding that if one or a few companies raise their prices, the others will adjust their own prices accordingly. It is normally difficult for a court to successfully identify agreements in parallel pricing cases just by applying the common judicial definitions of agreement. Some economists estimate that parallel pricing, which is mostly beyond the reach of law, may cost consumers over $100 million annually.

THE PRICE-FIXING DEBATE

There has been an academic debate about whether price-fixing agreements should be outlawed. Some economists in the libertarian tradition argue that price-fixing cartels are inherently unstable and unlikely to be effective in maintaining artificially high prices. Successful price collusion would be of negligible proportions, even without antitrust legislation. They also employ a "natural rights" theory of property and defend a right to fix prices as part of a person's natural right to freely use her property. They argue that any interference in the freedom to contract is a violation of natural rights. The benefit most often claimed for price fixing is a method for firms to reduce uncertainty and thereby to reduce the cost of investment and marketing mistakes.

Most economists and law professors, however, remain almost unanimous in condemning all price fixing as a harmful practice. They provide empirical evidence which suggests that price-fixing agreements can, in fact, be quite long-lived. They note that it is always possible that the members of an industry might succeed in getting together and fixing a price. By raising prices and restricting supply, price fixing makes commodities and services unavailable to some consumers and unnecessarily expensive for others.

A price-fixing agreement, therefore, distorts the functioning of the marketplace by causing resources to be switched from production of the affected product to other less highly valued uses. Elimination of pricing uncertainty, as claimed by

Price fixing suggests a conspiracy or collusion among competing companies to set an artificially high price.

the libertarian economists, can easily be achieved by the use of legally permissible information sharing among members of an industry. In this view, an effective way to deter price fixing is strong legislative and enforcement systems with severe penalties for price fixing.

Much evidence suggests that price fixing has been extremely common across a broad range of industries. Edwin H. Sutherland identified at least six different methods for fixing prices and found evidence of numerous suits alleging this activity. One recent study concludes that the illegal activity of price fixing was costing U.S. consumers an estimated $60 billion annually during the 1980s. Over the years, price-fixing conspiracies have been uncovered for virtually every imaginable product or service, including oil, sugar, beer, infant formula, steel wheels, cardboard cartons, industrial chemicals, long-distance phone companies, and airlines.

One of the most celebrated price-fixing cases involved heavy electrical equipment manufacturers, including General Electric and Westinghouse, who conspired over a period of decades to fix prices for their products. Fairly substantial fines were imposed on the companies, and a number of mid-level executives, who denied the charges, went to jail briefly (for less than a month).

OTHER CONSPIRACIES

Price fixing conspiracies are, in fact, not limited to industrial sales. Price fixing, in one form or another, often occurs in real estate fees, doctors' fees, lawyers' fees, tax accountants' fees, and even university tuition fees and financial-aid packages. Until recently, it was common practice for local bar associations to publish schedules of minimum fees and to punish attorneys who charged less. Because they have the authority to control admission to the practice of law, such associations actually have a much greater power to fix their price schedules than do business associations.

The American Bar Association used to hold that the "habitual charging of fees less than those established in suggested or recommended minimum fee schedules, or the charging of such a fee without proper justification, may be evidence of unethical conduct." A lawyer, therefore, could be disciplined or disbarred for failing to charge clients a high enough price. This brought the application of the antitrust laws to the legal profession.

In the United States, the Sherman Act of 1890 prohibits explicit price fixing that happens via communication and specific agreement between corporations. Violation of the Sherman Act is a felony punishable by a fine of up to $10 million for corporations, and a fine of up to $350,000 or three years' imprisonment (or both) for individuals. Price fixing is subject to criminal prosecution by the Antitrust Division of the U.S. Department of Justice, with the assistance of the Federal Bureau of Investigation (FBI) in some cases. In addition to receiving a criminal sentence, a corporation or individual convicted of a Sherman Act violation may be ordered to make restitution to the victims for all overcharges. Victims of price-fixing conspiracies also may seek civil recovery of up to three times the amount of damages suffered.

As a weapon against price fixing, however, the Sherman Antitrust Act was rarely used to crack down on price-fixing conspiracies. Until recent years, a hands-off approach was found in investigations and prosecutions of price-fixing cases. Throughout the world, broad deregulation based on *laissez-faire* (unrestricted) capitalism had begun to make many governments care little about price-fixing. In 1991, in recognition of the widespread violation of the price-fixing prohibition, Congress moved to reform the law to make the practice more difficult. For example, vertical price fixing, in which some manufacturers attempt to dictate retail price levels and lock out discounters, became vulnerable to lawsuits as a result of this reform. Maximum fines grew from $50,000 in 1955 to a virtually unlimited amount by 1991.

Despite this reform, the Justice Department lost many battles in its war on price fixing cartels. While more than 90 percent of the cases wind up with plea agreements, the department has only a mixed record in cases that are tried. Among the antitrust indictments filed from 1992 to 1997 that went to trial, for example, there were four convictions and 15 acquittals. At the Antitrust Division, meanwhile, a new corporate leniency program, granting significant incentives for early cooperation, was adopted in August 1993. The new policy made amnesty automatic if the company came in before an investigation began, and permitted broad amnesty afterward to the first company to offer assistance.

SLIM CHANCES

Price-fixing cases pursued by the Justice Department represent only a small portion of the actual amount of price fixing in U.S. industry. The potential profits are too attractive for many business executives, and the chances of getting caught are slim. Price fixing cases have proved difficult to establish in court. The likelihood of escaping conviction, if caught, is great because of two factors: 1) the deals are made in secret and masked by apparently legal activity; and 2) the government's antitrust budget is very small. For those few convictions, they were typically resolved with fines rather than prison sentences.

Similar examples of leniency for price fixing can be found in many other countries. Unlike other criminal cases, executives in price fixing cases are often respected by the community. Executives in most price-fixing cases are generously compensated by their companies, and thus can afford to hire the best criminal lawyers. Some jurors have trouble understanding why price fixing should be a crime.

Since price fixing poses a broad threat to U.S. business and consumers, the U.S. government has been developing a more vigorous approach to price-fixing enforcement since the late 1990s. The Justice Department has successfully prosecuted regional, national, and international price-fixing conspiracies affecting construction, agricultural products, manu-facturing, service industries, consumer products, and many other sectors of economy. Many of these prosecutions resulted from information uncovered by members of the general public who reported the information to the Antitrust Division.

During four fiscal years from 1997 to 2000, the Antitrust Division collected $1.7 billion in fines for price fixing. In the same period, more than 75 years of imprisonment have been imposed on price fixing and other antitrust offenders, with more than 30 defendants receiving jail sentences of one year or longer. Following the United States, governments in Europe and Asia are also beginning to combat price fixing more seriously than before. More countries that historically have not been troubled by price fixing are toughening their laws.

SEE ALSO

elite crime; capitalism; free enterprise; Sherman Antitrust Act; price discrimination; predatory practices.

BIBLIOGRAPHY. David O. Friedrichs, *Trusted Criminals: White Collar Crime in Contemporary Society* (Wadsworth Publishing Company, 1996); James W. Coleman, *The Criminal Elite: The Sociology of White-Collar Crime* (St. Martin's Press, 1994); David R. Simon, *Elite Deviance* (Allyn and Bacon, 1999); Laureen Snider, *Bad Business: Corporate Crime in Canada* (Nelson Canada, 1993); Antitrust Division, *Price Fixing, Bid Rigging, and Market Allocation Schemes: What They Are and What to Look For* (U.S. Department of Justice, 2001); Margaret Levenstein, Valerie Suslow and Lynda Oswald, *International Price-Fixing Cartels and Developing Countries: A Discussion of Effects and Policy Remedies* (University of Massachusetts, 2003); Dominick T. Armentano, *Antitrust Policy: The Case for Repeal* (Cato Institute, 1986).

HONGMING CHENG
ST. THOMAS UNIVERSITY
ZHEJIANG WANLI UNIVERSITY

prisoners

IN THE ANNALS of white-collar crime, the ethics of medical experimentation on prisoners has been a contested issue since the early 20th century, when the anti-vivisectionist movement began protesting human subject experimentation, and in particular, experimentation on those populations deemed vulnerable to manipulation or coercion, such as prisoners, children, and the mentally ill. The central concern underlying the movement's protest was whether these populations could offer voluntary consent to experiments, consent having been an ethical principle long accepted by most doctors as a requirement for human experimentation. Although much experimentation on prison populations has been regulated out of existence since then, the ethical question the anti-vivisectionists posed remains a contested issue.

Through the first half of the century, experimentation on prisoners was somewhat belittled by the scientific community in the United States. Despite that, several infamous exceptions have been documented. In 1906, Dr. Richard Strong experimented on a group of Philippine prisoners, exposing them to the cholera virus and, mistakenly, to the bubonic plague, when a bottle of the plague serum was accidentally substituted for the cholera serum. Thirteen prisoners died as a result. Strong, later a professor at Harvard University, continued his experiments with the Philippine prisoners six years later, when he exposed a group of subjects to beriberi. More prisoners died from these experiments. In payment for their participation, prisoners were offered supplies of cigars and cigarettes.

In Mississippi, in 1915, Dr. Joseph Goldberger attempted to discern the cause of pellagra, a disease of unknown origins that caused disfigurement and often death in its victims. The cause of pellagra was in doubt, but Goldberger thought it originated from a lack of adequate protein in the diet. In order to prove this, Goldberger created the necessary dietary conditions among a group of convicts at Rankin Farm prison by feeding the subjects a diet comprised strictly of starch. The subjects soon began to experience the traditional symptoms of pellagra, including dizziness, pain, and skin lesions. The men, some of whom became severely ill, received pardons for their participation in the experiment.

Following the advent of World War II, however, prison populations began to be seen by scientists as legitimate, and even especially valuable, subjects for medical experimentation. Generally, the populations were relatively healthy, unlike patients in hospitals, and willing in many cases to volunteer for dangerous and even lethal experiments in exchange for small amounts of money or for letters written on their behalf to parole boards. Prisoners also had,

for scientists, the advantage of being easily regulated.

Experiments ranging from injections of animal blood to exposure to dengue fever and gonorrhoea were performed on "volunteer" prison populations. In a famous case in Illinois, over 400 inmates of Stateville Penitentiary were infected with malaria. Prisoners were bitten by infected mosquitoes and experienced all of the symptoms of malaria, including vomiting, unconsciousness, and fever. Often more lethal, however, were the countless untested medicines given to the prisoners.

THE NUREMBERG CODE

The public generally supported these efforts which were seen as patriotic, given that American soldiers were dying overseas in vast numbers, sometimes of the diseases that were being studied in the prisons. After the war, when experimentation on prisoners might have been expected to decrease, a huge boom in experimentation on inmates occurred, lasting through the early 1970s. Ironically, the first international code of ethics on the subject of human-subject experimentation, the Nuremberg Code, had just been adopted. The code was a response to the Nazi doctors' trials in Nuremberg, Germany, during which the horrific experimentation on inmates of concentration camps and mental hospitals was revealed. In fact, during the trial, several Nazi doctors defended themselves by citing experiments conducted by American doctors on prison populations, such as the experiments on the Philippine prisoners in the early part of the century.

The Nuremberg Code established 10 ethical standards necessary for humane experimentation on human subjects, including the principle that the human subject "should have legal capacity to give consent … exercise free power of choice, without the element of force … constraint or coercion." This principle seemed to rule out experimentation on prisoners, who could not be said to be free of constraint or coercion.

In the United States, however, the Nuremberg Code was virtually ignored. Prisoners participated in experiments involving everything from malaria and cancer to skin creams and toothpaste. Some of the more dangerous experiments included the injection of live cancer cells into inmates of the Ohio prison system, and radiation exposure to the testicles of inmates in Oregon and Washington. Years later, survivors of the radiation experiments reported prostate cancer, vision loss, pain, rashes, and other problems that were traced to the radiation.

One of the more reprehensible research programs, begun by Dr. Austin Stough, involved the removal of plasma from prisoners to sell to pharmaceutical companies. Stough pioneered a process that allowed donors to contribute more frequently by separating the donated plasma from the red blood cells which were then re-injected into the donor's body. Indifference to the prisoners' health resulted in poorly trained staff, contaminated supplies, and dirty rooms for withdrawing the plasma. Some prisoners were mistakenly re-injected with the wrong type of blood, a potentially fatal mistake. Other prisoners succumbed to viral hepatitis and sickened or died as a result. Stough's operations were eventually shut down as the deaths were publicized, but not before he made millions of dollars from his work.

AWARENESS AND REGULATION

Public opinion on prisoner experimentation was gradually shifting, helped along by the publication in 1973 of Jessica Mitford's indictment of the penal system, *Kind and Usual Punishment*. Mitford's damning chapter on prisoner experimentation, "Cheaper than Chimpanzees" compared the excesses of the U.S. research programs to the Nazi medical experiments revealed at the Nuremberg Trials. Newspapers and government agencies alike began looking seriously at the practice of prisoner experimentation, and, in 1974, a commission was created to study research conducted on human subjects and to identify ethical principles that should govern such experimentation.

In 1976, the director of the Bureau of Prisons, Norman Carlson, banned all medical research on federal prisoners. State prison systems also began shutting down research programs in their prisons. By the 1980s, most of the experimentation on inmates had ceased. New federal regulations were adopted in 1981 to protect prisoners and children as research subjects. The rules provided for review boards to insure that subjects were not exposed to unnecessary risks and to restrict all "unnecessary physical and mental suffering." The new rules also dealt with the issue of informed consent, though not with the strictness of the Nuremberg Code. Instead, the rules required only that the researcher make an effort to "minimize the possibility of coercion or undue influence." Specific to the issue of prisoners, the new regulations required that in cases dealing with prison experimentation, at least one member of the review board should be a prisoner. Researchers were forbidden to offer incentives such as improved food, living conditions, or other enticements that would unduly influence a prisoner to risk participating in an experiment. The rules also mandated that the research must have some beneficial or relevant application to the prison population. Researchers now needed a valid reason for choosing prisoners as subjects, other than their ready availability.

With these restrictions in place, the lure of prison populations as fertile ground for experimentation and profiteering effectively ended. While experimentation on prisoners remains legal in some cases, it is severely limited in its application in the United States.

SEE ALSO
World War II; medical malpractice; ethics; research fraud.

BIBLIOGRAPHY. Allan Brandt and Lara Freidenfelds, "Research Ethics after WWII," *Kennedy Institute of Ethics Journal* (v.6/3, 1996); Annas Grodin, *The Nazi Doctors and the Nuremberg Code* (Oxford University Press, 1992); Allen Hornblum, *Acres of Skin: Human Experiments at Holmesburg Prison* (Routledge, 1998); J. S. Horner, "Retreat From Nuremberg," *Public Health* (v.113, 1999); Jay Katz, "The Nuremberg Code and the Nuremberg Trial," *JAMA* (v.276/20, 1996); Dennis Maloney, *Protection of Human Research Subjects* (Plenum, 1984); Jessica Mitford, *Kind and Usual Punishment: the Prison Business* (Knopf, 1973); Seymour Shubin, "Research Behind Bars," *The Sciences* (v.81/1, 1981).

REGAN BRUMAGEN
GEORGIA COLLEGE & STATE UNIVERSITY

Procter & Gamble

PROCTER & GAMBLE (P&G) has been accused since 1980 of associating with the devil. Problems over their man-in-the-moon and stars trademark surfaced in that year when people began calling the company to ask if it was owned by the followers of

Reverend Sun Myung Moon. The company responded to this assault by writing to news organizations in the Midwest, the origin of most of the telephone calls.

The emphasis of the rumors changed from Moon's church to Satanism, and December 1981 brought the company 1,152 questions/comments on the subject. Tales spread of Procter & Gamble's owner admitting on television that he had traded his soul to the devil in return for the company's success, and the company president announcing on the Phil Donahue Show that 10 percent of their earnings went to a Satanic religion.

The rumors did not die despite a second mailing, this time to the West Coast, statements by Procter & Gamble executives on television shows, and clarifications of the fact that P&G is a corporation and thus profits go to shareholders, not any individual who could send them to a religious group. In the spring of 1982, P&G reportedly was contacted 12,000 times per month regarding its relationship with the devil. Because of indications that some clergy were urging their congregations to boycott P&G products, the corporation sent letters to clergy. These letters contained support for Procter & Gamble from well-known clerics including Reverend Jerry Falwell, leader of the church-based Moral Majority.

By June 1982, more than 15,000 inquiries were made regarding the trademark, and in July, P&G, which produces over 70 household products including Tide, Folgers Coffee, and Oil of Olay, filed lawsuits in an attempt to control these widespread rumors which could potentially cost the company customers, sales, and loss of profit. Most of these defendants sold products, including Amway and Shaklee, which compete with P&G's products. The suits brought publicity and perhaps some understanding by the public because inquiries to P&G dropped by half. By 1990, Satan-related queries were again spiking and the corporation filed its 13th suit charging defendants with spreading false and malicious statements.

In 1995, P&G filed its 15th suit, this time against a Texas Amway distributor who repeated the rumor in a voicemail available to other distributors for a fee. The basis for this suit was that it violated the Lanham Act, a federal law protecting companies from unfair competition in many forms, including misleading representations in commercial advertising. In 1995, P&G named Michigan-based

Amway, not just its distributors, for the first time in a suit filed in the U.S. District Court in Utah.

In August 2000, the Denver, Colorado, federal appeals court dismissed the Utah suit against Amway but revived previously dismissed cases against some of its distributors. In 2001, the federal appeals court in New Orleans, Louisiana, revived the suit against Amway based on the 1970 federal Racketeer Influenced and Corrupt Organizations Act (RICO), and sent it back to Texas for retrial. In January 2003, a federal appeals panel in Utah, then a U.S. District judge in Texas, separately affirmed the lower courts' dismissals of P&G's suits against Amway. At that time, the Utah and Texas suits against Amway distributors were still unsettled. P&G won some suits, including gaining a 1991 $75,000 settlement from a Kansas couple who were Amway distributors.

CORPORATE HISTORY

Procter & Gamble was founded in Cincinnati, Ohio, in 1837 by brothers-in-law William Procter, a candle maker, and James Gamble, a soap maker. The company expanded, and by the mid 1850s it was shipping to other areas of the country by river and railway. Shipping containers were identified with trademarks because many dockworkers were illiterate at that time. Company tradition has it that Procter & Gamble's boxes were first marked with a simple cross on their Star brand candles.

Later the cross was changed to a circled star, and then William Procter elaborated on the trademark making it 13 stars (for the original 13 colonies) and the man in the moon. Because trademarks were the main mode of company identification, when another soap maker began using a very similar emblem in 1875, P&G sued to have him stop. P&G won the suit and registered the symbol in 1882 with the U.S. Patent Office. The familiar bearded man-in-the-moon and stars, slightly changed since 1882, was developed by sculptor and artist Ernest Bruce Haswell.

The International Directory of Company Histories states, "In 1985, the company reluctantly removed the logo from product packages. The logo began to reappear on some packages in the early 1990s, and the company continued to use the trademark on corporate stationery and on its building." In 1991, P&G removed from its trademark the swirls which, when viewed in a mirror, appear to render "666," a number which many people associate with the devil.

SEE ALSO

patent infringement; trademark infringement; unfair trade practices; marketing fraud.

BIBLIOGRAPHY. Sandra Salmans, "P&G's Battles with Rumors," *New York Times* (July 22, 1982); Kevin Kerr, "Corridor Talk," *Adweek* (August 6, 1990); Bill Mintz, "P&G Still Fights Satan Rumors; Local Amway Distributors Sued for Allegedly Spreading Claims," *The Houston Chronicle* (July 18, 1997); Zachary Schiller, "P&G Is Still Having a Devil of a Time," *BusinessWeek* (September 11, 1995); John Accola, "Federal Appeals Court Returns Defamation Suit against Amway," *Denver Rocky Mountain News* (August 25, 2000); "Voicemail Jail: Lanham Act's Broad Reach," *Marketing News* (January 15, 2001); Geanne Rosenberg, "Procter & Gamble Suit over Satan Rumor Resurrected," *New York Times* (March 27, 2001); Thomas M. Tucker and Apral Dougal Gasbarre, *International Directory of Company Histories* (v.26, St. James Press, 1999).

LINDA M. CREIBAUM
ARKANSAS STATE UNIVERSITY

product liability

PRODUCT LIABILITY refers to the legal responsibility of manufacturers, wholesalers, and retailers to compensate buyers and users who have suffered damages or injuries as a result of defective goods. A more detailed definition is provided by Patricia Peppin:

"A breach of the standard of care in the manufacturing, bottling, assembling, distributing, or inspecting of products, which causes foreseeable harm to the ultimate consumer, where there has been no possibility of intermediate examination, will give rise to liability." Products subject to liability include a wide range of consumer goods such as food, drugs, home appliances, automobiles, tobacco, and medical devices.

According to the National Commission on Product Safety, over 20 million Americans have suffered injuries as a result of unsafe consumer products; 110,000 have been permanently disabled and over 30,000 have died. It comes as little surprise, therefore, that product liability cases constitute one of the principal areas of civil law.

As with the general concepts of torts, negligence, and liability, product liability laws have been shaped by shifting political and social attitudes toward the consumer society and the obligations of corporations. In the 19th and early 20th centuries, legal discourse centered on an individualist ethic that tended to absolve corporations of responsibility for their products. There were few cases of successful actions against corporations for defective products. In the mid- to late 20th century, however, notions of corporate liability expanded and judges and lawmakers gradually began to implement broader legal definitions that held businesses liable for a range of offenses related to the goods they produced and sold. Recent years, however, have seen somewhat of a backlash as judges and politicians have gradually decreased the scope of product liability law in response to concerted tort reform lobbies initiated by industry and conservatives.

HISTORY OF LIABILITY

The common law origins of the concept of liability date from 1763 in England and 1791 in the United States. In the British and American legal tradition, the concept of legal liability was hedged by strict boundaries in the 18th and 19th centuries An ethic of individualism was dominant in legal thinking which held that only individuals involved in direct contractual agreements. or who were victims of personally inflicted damage. were eligible to sue on the basis of liability or negligence. Until the early 20th century, Valerie P. Hans writes, "a variety of legal rules and societal and judicial attitudes supported the ethic of individual responsibility."

This was very much in tune with the dominant ideology of free-market capitalism, that is, a belief in unrestrained economic growth, free trade, and a minimal role for the state and courts in business activities. The product liability of manufacturers was thus severely restricted since the sale of a good was regarded solely as a commercial transaction between seller and buyer. Legal historians argue that this restricted definition of liability with regard to products was one of the most uniform and strictly followed laws in both England and America.

For much of the 19th and 20th centuries, courts followed the precedents of the 1842 English case *Winterbottom v. Wright*. Winterbottom, a coach driver, was severely injured when the poorly built vehicle he was driving collapsed. The coach had been bought by the postmaster general from the manufacturer, Wright. Winterbottom worked for a company which was contracted by the postmaster general to provide horses and drivers for its coaches. In other words, he was not employed directly by the company that bought the defective product. Winterbottom's case against Wright was dismissed on the basis that the seller of the product cannot be sued, even for demonstrable negligence, by a party with whom no contractual agreement existed. In legal terms, Winterbottom was not "in privity" with Wright.

Justification for the dismissal of the suit provides a clear illustration of legal thinking on corporate responsibility at the time. Justice Baron Alderson expressed: "If we were to hold that [Winterbottom] could sue in such a case, there is no point at which actions would stop. The only safe rule is to confine the right to recover to those who enter into the contract: if we go one step beyond that, there is no reason why we should not go fifty." Chief Baron Lord Abinger seconded this line of thinking: "We ought not to permit a doubt to rest upon this subject, for our doing so might be the means of letting in upon us an infinity of actions ... Unless we confine the operation of such contracts as this to the parties who entered into them, the most absurd and outrageous consequences, of which I can see no limit, would ensue." In the words of Denis W. Stearns, "with the Winterbottom decision, the doors of the courthouse were locked to any one who did not possess the key of 'privity.'"

20TH CENTURY

In the 20th century, however, broader and more detailed definitions of tort law expanded notions of product liability. This largely resulted from shifting social and political beliefs regarding the responsibility of businesses to their consumers, especially in an era in which a mass, consumer economy was emerging. One of the first significant court cases in this larger social development occurred in 1916 in *MacPherson v. Buick Motor Company* decided in the New York Court of Appeals. A man was injured because a wooden wheel collapsed and he successfully sued the manufacturer. Up to this time, only the dealer was held liable in such cases of product-related injury, not the manufacturer.

Even with this precedent-setting case, the possibility of winning suits against manufacturers remained small although there were a number of important cases in the food industry. Yet notions of liability gradually expanded as the century progressed. In *Escola v. Coca Cola Bottling Company of Fresno* in 1944, Gladys Escola, a worker in a California restaurant, was badly injured when a coke bottle exploded. She won a jury verdict that was later affirmed by the Supreme Court. One of the Supreme Court judges dealt at length with why an expanded concept of liability was necessary in a modern, complex society with a consumer economy based on mass-produced goods.

Throughout the first half of the 20th century, plaintiffs could base their case for product liability damages on two legal doctrines: negligence or breach of warranty. Negligence requires the plaintiff to demonstrate that a manufacturer, seller, or wholesaler of the product was responsible for exercising reasonable care in the manufacturing or retail process and failed to perform that duty, resulting in injuries to the plaintiff. The plaintiff, however, must show that a company had a duty to exercise reasonable care and that it was the failure to exercise this care that led to the injury. Negligence cases, therefore, require substantial evidence to be provided by the plaintiff.

Breach of warranty claims are governed by contract law, specifically Article 2 of the federal Uniform Commercial Code which all states have followed. The law assumes that manufacturers and sellers provide a formal or informal promise about the quality, type, safety, and performance of a product which constitutes a type of contract between maker or seller and buyer. If the product does not live up to the promise of the "warranty" and causes injury, a plaintiff may make a claim for damages on this basis. Both doctrines are complex, vary somewhat by state and continue to be used today in product liability cases.

It was in the food industry that a third and more expanded concept of product liability first arose in the early 1900s. Strict liability is defined as liability for injuries caused by defective and unreasonably safe products. To establish strict liability, the plaintiff must only prove that the product was defective and that the product defect led to the injury. Strict liability originated in a particular kind of warranty claim that developed through a series of cases involving food products. In 1905, crusading journalist

Upton Sinclair published *The Jungle*, an explosive exposé of unsanitary practices in the meatpacking industry which sparked the first federal food product inspection acts in 1906. Sinclair's shocking report also touched off a heated debate on food manufacturer liability in the courts. By the World War I period, a number of cases against food manufacturers argued successfully that the manufacturer and retailer of food has a particular responsibility to consumers, known as a "special implied warranty."

Historically, this notion only applied to the immediate purchaser of food. In the wake of the scandals in the meatpacking industry, courts soon accepted the argument that the implied warranty was associated with the product itself. Consequently, all persons injured, not just the buyer of the product, could launch suits. Furthermore, it would not be necessary to prove that the food maker had been negligent in preparing the food; sufficient proof of negligence was provided by the fact that the product was defective.

LANDMARK CASE

This evolving concept of strict liability was confined to food products and gradually extended on a case to case basis until the 1960s. In 1963, a landmark case in the California Supreme Court altered the legal landscape of products liability. In *Greenman v. Yuba Power Products, Inc.* the presiding judges once again expanded the concept of product liability by arguing, in the words of Justice Robert J. Traynor, "that the liability is not one governed by the law of contract warranties but by the law of strict liability in tort." In the years after this decision, all states adopted some form of the doctrine of strict liability which reflected a generalized sentiment among the wider population that corporations should be more responsible to consumers. Furthermore, both the federal government and states established various agencies to regulate the manufacture and sale of products in this period.

From the 1960s to the 1980s, product liability cases dominated the headlines. Cases for damages based on negligence, breach of warranty and strict liability were brought against the most powerful American corporations. Vietnam veterans suffering from the chemical defoliant, Agent Orange, launched suits in the 1970s and settled out of court in 1985 for $200 million. The Ford Motor Company lost several key cases in relation to deadly design defects in its popular Pinto model in the late 1970s. Asbestos manufacturers, who have already paid hundreds of millions in damages, still face over 100,000 cases. Significant cases were also brought against products that were particularly harmful to women such as contraceptive devices and silicone breast implants. Dow-Corning's Dalkon Shield, an intrauterine device intended to prevent pregnancy not only failed to work properly (110,000 users became pregnant). It was also found to cause miscarriages, stillbirths, children with birth defects, and pelvic inflammatory disease. Eighteen women died as a result of using the product. Nevertheless, the company spent millions in successful defenses; only in 1992 was a woman awarded $43,000 in a case against Dow Corning. Class action suits were then launched by thousands of women, some of whom settled out of court for $200 million.

Despite multimillion dollar awards for product liability, empirical studies have revealed that product liability cases can still be quite difficult to prove by plaintiffs. Large companies have shown that they are willing to spend years in court at great cost to defend themselves which may deter potential claimants.

The limited use of jury trials and the reduction of the power of juries, judicial revisions of jury awards, and caps on "pain and suffering" awards have made product liability litigation a protracted, expensive, and risky course of action. As a result of recent tort reforms, moreover, many states now protect retailers from strict liability; plaintiffs must prove the much more difficult case of negligence to recover damages from the retailer. Corporate reorganization under bankruptcy laws has also allowed companies facing suits to limit liability claims.

In the 21st century, potential sources of tort litigation related to products are diverse and extensive. New technologies are particularly open to legal claims, a process reinforced by substantial pressures from economic interests, social movements, and environmental groups. Products based on scientific advances in genetics and biotechnology, such as genetically engineered foods, have the potential to bring both substantial benefits and harm to economic, social and environmental health, and therefore will likely be highly contested in the courts and legislatures. As in the past, product liability law will certainly be shaped by a complex interplay of social, political, economic, and legal forces.

SEE ALSO

consumer deaths; Ford Pinto; Dalkon Shield; Dow Chemical; unsafe products; corporate criminal liability.

BIBLIOGRAPHY. Jay Albanese, *White-Collar Crime in America* (Prentice-Hall, 1995); Stephen Daniels and Joanne Martin, *Civil Juries and the Politics of Reform* (Northwestern University Press, 1995); Jeffery A. Foran, Bernard D. Goldstein, John A. Moore and Paul Slovic, "Predicting Future Sources of Mass Toxic Tort Litigation," *Risk* (v.7/15, 1996); Lawrence Friedman, *American Law in the Twentieth Century* (Yale University Press, 2002); Valerie P. Hans, *Business on Trial: The Civil Jury and Corporate Responsibility* (Yale University Press, 2000); *Meeson & Welsby Reports* (v.109, 1842); Patricia Peppin, "Feminism, Law and the Pharmaceutical Industry," *Corporate Crime: Debates* (University of Toronto Press, 1995); Stephen Rostoff, Henry N. Pontell, and Robert Tillman, *Profit Without Honor: White-Collar Crime and the Looting of America* (Prentice-Hall, 1998); Sally Simpson, Corporate Crime, Law and Social Control (Cambridge University Press, 2002); Denis W. Stearns, *An Introduction to Product Liability Law* (Marler Clark, 2001).

SEAN PURDY, PH.D.
QUEEN'S UNIVERSITY, CANADA

prosecution

WHITE-COLLAR AND corporate crime cases may be prosecuted one of four ways—through criminal prosecutions, civil prosecutions, *qui tam* lawsuits, or administrative hearings. The prosecution stage refers to the strategies used to determine whether offenders are culpable. Tied into the prosecutions are the sanctions to be administered to those who are found guilty or liable.

CRIMINAL PROSECUTIONS

In the past, criminal prosecutions of white-collar crime cases were rare. However, more currently, a growing number of white-collar and corporate crime cases are being prosecuted by criminal justice officials. While most of these prosecutions are done at the federal level, some are done by local prosecutors. Regardless of where criminal prosecutions occur, a number of issues arise that must be addressed by prosecutors in white-collar crime

cases. *In Crime in the Home Health Care Field* (2003), Brian K. Payne addresses 10 problems that routinely arise in home health care fraud prosecutions: proof problems, witness problems, record chasing, complexity, insufficient statutes, minor losses, offender sympathy, time, victim bias, and funding. These problems can also be seen as occurring in other white-collar crime cases.

Proof problems refer to the fact that criminal prosecutors have an uphill battle proving beyond a reasonable doubt that white-collar offenders are culpable for their actions. First, they must prove that a crime occurred. Second, they must prove that the offender was the one who committed the act. Third, criminal prosecutors must prove that the offender intended to commit the actions. Finally, the prosecutor must dispute any defenses put forth by the defense team.

Witness problems also arise in these cases. On one level, there may simply be no witnesses available. Most individuals do not know it when they have been victimized by a white-collar or a corporate offender. On another level, witnesses may have personal relationships with the defendants, thereby decreasing their desire to cooperate with prosecutors who are seen as the enemy.

Record chasing is another problem that arises. The typical white-collar crime case will require prosecutors to review complex files and evidence. These cases are not the kind highlighted on the evening television shows. They require a great deal of patience, fortitude, and knowledge about different kinds of occupations. In conducting these record chases, a great deal of time and resources must be dedicated to the case.

Most white-collar and corporate crime cases are quite complex. When an individual holds a gun to someone's head and steals her money, it is clear that a crime has been committed. When an individual loses another person's investments, it is not always clear whether a crime has been committed, or simply bad business transactions. Other white-collar crimes are equally complex. When a doctor provides certain services and bills Medicaid for those services, all doctors may not necessarily agree on the utility of those services. It becomes quite complex to determine whether transgressions occurred.

Insufficient statutes are another problem. In many cases, criminal laws may not exist prohibiting certain violations. Computer crimes, for example, were not crimes until recently. Sending viruses, spam, and other problematic e-mails were crimes in just a handful of states in 2003. Prosecutors have gone after contractors who committed fraud with burglary charges (that is, breaking and entering with the intent to commit a crime) because their fraud statutes were flawed.

Another problem that surfaces is one of minor losses. Many white-collar crime cases in and of themselves may actually be "small potatoes." Consider an mechanic who charges customers $10 more than she should for services. Even if the mechanic did this to 100 people, the crimes do not usually amount to a felony because they would be separate misdemeanors, or violations, depending the state's codes. In order for prosecutors to take on the cases, large losses must be involved.

Offender sympathy is another problem. In particular, judges, the jury, and some prosecutors may sympathize with offenders. Some judges are able to relate to white-collar offenders, but cannot relate to crack dealers, burglars, or other street offenders. Juries also understand some of the neutralizations offered by white-collar offenders.

They tend to believe that all doctors write badly, therefore the pharmacist could not read the writing. They tend to agree that the government does not reimburse fairly, therefore it is okay if individuals steal from the government every now and then. They tend to see white-collar offenders as upstanding members of their community who are not harmful or violent offenders.

The problem of time refers to the fact that white-collar and corporate crime cases can take years to resolve. With the resources to hire strong defense teams and the already long paper chase, these cases can drag on for years. As political officials, prosecutors are judged based on their win/loss record. Too many losses or unending cases could result in a prosecutor losing his job, and dismantling a political future. Consequently, some prosecutors may avoid these difficult, time-consuming cases.

Victim bias occurs when the public tends to be sympathetic to white-collar and corporate offenders, but a similar level of sympathy does not exist for victims. Some individuals see white-collar crime victims as somewhat aloof, unintelligent individuals who deserved what they got. Others see them as money hungry, especially if victims are seeking legal redress in civil court. Thus, judges and juries may discount the words of victims in favor of the words

or testimony of offenders, with whom they can relate socially and intellectually.

Funding is a final problem that comes up in white-collar crime cases. These cases can be quite time-consuming and resource intensive. Most of the criminal justice system budget has historically been dedicated to handling drug offenses and street offenses. More recently, budgets have been increased to battle terrorism; this means that less resources are available for white-collar crime prosecutions.

CIVIL PROSECUTIONS

Civil prosecutions are substantively and pragmatically different from criminal prosecutions. Generally, civil prosecutions are known as lawsuits. In white-collar crime cases, lawsuits could be filed either by the government or the victim. The party filing the lawsuit is known as the plaintiff. Plaintiffs may prefer civil prosecutions over criminal prosecutions for a number of reasons. These reasons include concerns about proof, evidentiary factors, and penalty recoupment.

In terms of proof, the level of proof needed in civil cases is lower than what is needed in criminal prosecutions. In civil prosecutions, the level is generally what is known as "beyond a preponderance of evidence" while in criminal cases the proof level is "beyond a reasonable doubt." The preponderance of evidence standard is basically a "more likely than not" standard while the beyond a reasonable doubt standard approaches virtual certainty. It is easier for prosecutors and plaintiffs to prove beyond a preponderance of evidence than beyond a reasonable doubt.

Evidentiary factors also make civil prosecutions especially advantageous. For example, offenders do not have the Fifth Amendment privilege against self-incrimination in civil proceedings. This means that defendants can be forced to testify in civil cases. In addition, because civil prosecutions can occur after criminal prosecutions, prosecutors are afforded access to a great deal of evidence that may have already been presented in a criminal case.

As an example, consider the O.J. Simpson case. While not a white-collar crime case, it is illustrative of the importance of lower proof and increased evidence. Simpson was accused of killing his former wife, Nicole Brown Simpson, and her friend, Ron Goldman. He was acquitted in a criminal trial that caught the attention of America. Shortly thereafter, Goldman's father filed a civil lawsuit against Simpson. With the lower level of proof, and the fact that the attorneys were able to force Simpson to testify on his behalf, Simpson was found liable in the civil case.

Civil lawsuits are also advantageous in the kinds of penalties that can be assessed. In white-collar crime cases in particular, large monetary penalties can be assessed against offenders. These penalties are usually referred to as damages. Some states allow for what are called "treble damages." Treble damages refer to penalties that triple the amount of the profit that the offender obtained from the crime.

Punitive damages are also permitted in civil cases. Punitive damages are monetary awards, sometimes issued by juries and sometimes by judges, that the defendant is ordered to pay the plaintiff. These damages are designed to punish the offender and are justified by the Supreme Court on deterrence grounds. In effect, the Supreme Court, time and time again, has said that large punitive damage awards can be levied against organizations in order to make sure that organization, as well as other organizations, refrain from similar misconduct.

While there may be certain intuitive appeal to justifying punitive damages on deterrence ideals, in reality research suggests that punitive damages do nothing to meet deterrence ideals. In order for a punishment to be a deterrent, three criteria must be met. First, the punishment must be certain. If a company knows that it will be punished for wrongdoing, then theoretically it should be less likely to engage in wrongdoing. Second, the punishment must be just enough so that it is worse than the pleasure (profit) that the company would get from misconduct. Third, the punishment should be swift.

According to Stevens and Payne (1998), four problems exist in justifying punitive damages on deterrence ideals. First, the penalties are not certain; rather they are better characterized by their arbitrariness. This is especially the case with corporate and white-collar crime prosecutions. There is a high degree of uncertainty in detection and punishment. Second, the penalties are often either not severe enough or too severe. Consider environmental laws as examples of penalties that are too lenient.

It is common to hear of companies committing these offenses because it is cheaper to break the law

than it is to develop mechanisms that would protect the environment. As far as penalties that are too stiff, large damages could actually cause some businesses to close. When the business closes, people are out of work and may then do things that are worse than the original offense. Rather than deterring crime, punitive damages may actually lead to more crime. Third, the penalties are rarely swift, especially for those cases in which large penalties are awarded. In those cases, attorneys usually file appeals which slow the case down tremendously. The Exxon *Valdez* incident occurred in the late 1980s, causing great destruction at the time. As of 2003, various aspects of the case were still being appealed.

A fourth problem with punitive damages in corporate misconduct cases is that they present the public with an unrealistic view of the civil justice process. Many likely recall the case in which a woman was awarded millions of dollars because she spilled hot coffee on herself. Individuals hear of cases such as this and may assume that the vast majority of lawsuits are equally questionable. Most don't realize that the award in this case was reduced significantly, and it usually is in other cases as well.

While there are problems with justifying punitive damages on deterrence ideals, civil prosecutions remain an integral and important part of the response to corporate and white-collar misconduct.

QUI TAM SUITS

Another important prosecutorial tool in the response to corporate misconduct is the *qui tam* lawsuit. In a *qui tam* suit, a third party who is not necessarily directly involved in the corporate wrongdoing files the lawsuit. These are also known as whistleblower lawsuits because the individual who files this type of lawsuit is often a whistleblower from within the company. In these cases, the whistleblower is awarded a portion of the punitive damages and the government attorneys serve as the plaintiff's attorneys. *Qui tam* suits have been especially common in healthcare fraud cases.

ADMINISTRATIVE HEARINGS

Administrative proceedings are also used as a tool to adjudicate corporate misconduct. Hundreds of federal and state agencies exist whose sole responsibility is to oversee a particular industry's activities. All industries have rules and regulations they must follow, the violation of which may not necessarily be a crime in the legal sense of the word. Consider the Environmental Protection Agency (EPA). Companies are expected to abide by certain rules to protect the environment. Auditors and inspectors will routinely review the company's files and practices to see if any adjustments are made. If the company is violating regulations (regulatory codes), an administrative proceeding may be initiated to determine how to get the company to stop its practices. Compliance is generally the goal of these proceedings.

Note also that virtually every occupation has a governing board that helps to police members of that occupation. Lawyers are members of the state bar. If they commit certain acts, administrative proceedings could be initiated. Doctors are members of the medical bar. If they commit harmful acts, administrative proceedings could be initiated against them. Of course, administrative proceedings are generally seen as less serious than the other kinds of prosecutions.

SEE ALSO
Green, Mark; Giuliani, Rudolph; Exxon *Valdez*; Environmental Protection Agency.

BIBLIOGRAPHY. Michael Benson and Francis Cullen, *Local Prosecutors at Work* (Northeastern Press, 1998); Gary Green, *Occupational Crime* (Nelson-Hall, 1998); Paul Jesilow, Henry Pontell, and Gilbert Geis, *Prescription for Profit* (University of California Press, 1993); Brian K. Payne, *Crime in the Home Health Care Field* (Charles C. Thomas, 2003); Brian K. Payne, *Incarcerating White-Collar Offenders* (Charles C. Thomas, 2002); Stephen Rosoff, Henry Pontell, and Robert Tillman, *Profit Without Honor* (Prentice Hall, 2002).

BRIAN K. PAYNE, PH.D.
OLD DOMINION UNIVERSITY

prostitution

PROSTITUTION HAS BEEN called the oldest profession, and while there is some truth to this statement, how prostitution or sex work is culturally and legally defined varies from one culture to another and over time. The word, prostitute, originates in Latin and means "up front" or "to expose."

This referred to the early Roman female prostitutes who were not required to cover their faces like other women. However, this was not considered a plus, but rather a sort of public shaming, even though prostitutes were free from male domination or patriarchy.

MALE CULTURE

Usually, Roman prostitutes were slaves who were owned and controlled through the brothels. However, other prostitutes were also performers who operated freely in selling their services. Additionally, males were also prostitutes in ancient Rome. Although free from state regulation in Rome, both male and female prostitutes were under the control of the dominant wealthy and politically powerful male culture.

In ancient Greece, several classes of prostitutes existed including the lowest, the brothel prostitutes; second, the street prostitutes; third, the *aluetrides*, the dancers or performers who are equivalent today to pornography workers, massage parlor workers, and nude dancers. The *aluetrides* were dancers, acrobats, and musicians and were hired to perform at orgies and other social events. They were the next-to-the-highest class of prostitute.

The highest class of prostitute was the *hetaera*, the Greek courtesan prostitute or cultivated companion who associated with the most powerful men of Greece. They were well read, had very proper social graces, and were supposedly very beautiful women who were showered with gifts. However, the *hetaera* also had a number of other skills that she sold, and was engaged in prostitution as a sideline.

From the 4th century through the Reformation, there was some degree of tolerance for prostitution in Western society. Mary Magdalene became a reformed prostitute after her relationship with Jesus, and this redeemed her in the eyes of others. Similarly, many other prostitutes became holy women and saints. In the ancient Near East, India, and southeast Asia, temple prostitution was considered a religious duty for women. Similarly, during medieval England as well as in 19th-century America, becoming a prostitute provided more social and economic freedom and less oppression than doing other kinds of women's work, such as being a servant or textile worker, and even more freedom than being a wife subject to the total control of the husband.

FREEDOM AND STIGMA

Freedom from a husband did not always translate into freedom from social stigma or legal repercussions. For example, in England in 1822, the English Vagrancy Act was passed and was used to control the movements of poor street prostitutes who were actually referred to as "common women." Then in 1864, 1866, and 1869, the Contagious Diseases Act was passed in England stating that it was the prostitutes who were spreading sexually transmitted diseases, thus creating the discretionary power of police to arrest any woman thought to have a sexually transmitted disease. The attitude that she was the root of the problem rather than her customer, was prominent in English law until 1985.

Throughout England and other European countries, as conservative religious and cultural attitudes spread, prostitution became even more likely to be banned or criminalized. Many cities attempted to eliminate prostitution, or to socially control women by labeling economically independent women as prostitutes as they moved about in public space. For example, in 1566, the Pope banned all prostitutes from Rome but withdrew the proclamation when approximately 25,000 people prepared to leave the city. But generally speaking, across time and place, the free common women or poor women have been controlled by being socially constructed as prostitutes even if they weren't, through criminal legislation, while male customers often remained less seriously punished.

Clearly, this method of control was used to limit ordinary women's movement in public space. For example, in Western Europe as well as during the settling of the western United States, brothels or houses of prostitution were often licensed and protected by law enforcement, while women selling sex for money on the streets was defined as criminal and disallowed. In western America, public displays of sexuality were viewed as distasteful and keeping such behavior hidden from public view within the brothel was much preferred. Additionally, the head of the brothel, or madam, often had much political clout in the community and preferred not to have substantial competition from the streetwalker.

However, both in medieval England as well as early western America, women who were sexually active outside of marriage, even if not for pay, were socially constructed as prostitutes. Moreover, sometimes women's movement in public space at particular times was constructed as "vagrancy" or prostitution and thus subject to social control. These social processes provided a method of controlling women's sexuality and prohibiting women's full participation in open society, often characterized as both patriarchal and misogynistic (an ideology promoting hatred of women).

THE MANN ACT

For example, in antebellum St. Louis, Missouri, the idea was promoted that street women corrupted the middle class morals of innocent men by coercing them into illicit sexual acts. Similarly, in 1908, the United States signed an international treaty agreeing to end the slave trade in white women. Nation-states were required to pass and implement domestic legislation in response to agreeing to specific international treaties or conventions. In response, then, the White Slave Traffic Act or the Mann Act was passed in 1910.

Generally, the law stated that it was illegal to transport women across state lines for "immoral purposes." While the intent of the law may have been to control forced transportation of women and coerced prostitution, the law was misused to punish a variety of perceived moral issues, such as sexual activities between unmarried couples who traveled across state lines. Additionally, it was aimed at African-American men who were dating white women, as such behavior was considered a usurpation of the "black man's place" and an infringement upon white male privilege. However, the Mann Act was also used to target real criminals, mostly gangsters, or con men, and occasionally prostitutes who crossed state lines to do business.

The effect of such laws aimed at controlling crime often have unanticipated effects. One such effect of the Mann Act was the victimization of innocent women, and another was the creation of an entire blackmailing industry aimed at the men who crossed the state lines with a non-marital partner for a secret liaison. It wasn't until 1986 that Congress changed the wording of the Mann Act and eliminated the requirement that federal judges define what "immoral purpose" meant.

Prostitution in urban colonial America was a "fringe phenomena" until about 1820, and in large cities most prostitutes served sailors and men involved in the waterfront marketplace. However, prostitution also thrived in the rural west in the

19th-century mining towns where many men traveled to make their fortune in gold or silver.

NEW YORK CITY

Timothy Gilfoyle's historiography of New York City prostitution clearly demonstrates that prostitution has been an accepted and normative part of America's history, and provided pathways to wealth for a variety of New York realtors and their families who gleaned profits based on land ownership of the brothels run by a variety of notable Madams all over the city during the 19th century.

Even politicians owned brothels in the 19th century and many madams became quite rich from sex work business. In the 1820s, approximately 200 brothels existed in New York City while, by the end of the Civil War in 1865, there were over 600 brothels in the City. These were located in various geographic areas from the middle-class East Side to Broadway to the wealthier West Side, near local male-only colleges and universities where students abounded, near hotels where businessmen were staying, and the poorer areas of The Five Points and Water Street, the area known for serving sailors and other travelers.

During the 1830s, prostitution in the New York City Five Points area was publicly acted out in the streets. Also, prostitution was commonly interracial prior to the 1830s in New York City with sex workers and customers doing a great deal of mixing among both the higher-paid brothel prostitutes and the poorer salon and cellar prostitutes. African-Americans enjoyed a great deal of economic and political autonomy in both licit and illicit economies prior to the 1830s. Also during the 19th century, lower-class prostitutes were not fortunate enough to have the luxury of a brothel, but rather performed sex work in the upper or lower floors of liquor stores and dance saloons. Many even took advantage of the new ferry system by selling sex on or near the ferry.

THE SANGER STUDY

The *History of Prostitution*, based upon interviews with 2,000 prostitutes in 1859 is considered the world's first authoritative, scientific study of prostitution. William Sanger's study contains a variety of important findings that have been replicated even in the 21st century with regard to prostitution. His interviews reveal that these women believed that the following factors led to their involvement in prostitution: harsh treatment by parents; parental death; being seduced into false promises of marriage and/or being deserted by their paramour; having no other means of subsistence; being forced into prostitution; or being a drug addict.

While Sanger's work is notable, his work, and substantial work since then, reveals that only among street prostitutes, that is, those who are most likely to end up in jail are such traumatic backgrounds common. Sanger reports that the average female remained a street prostitute for approximately four years during the middle of the 19th century. He found that many women street prostitutes were new immigrants who had often been swindled or criminally victimized by former immigrants who merely repeated the cycle of their own initial victimization on newer immigrants. As has been true for hundreds of years, most women immigrants who became street prostitutes came to the United States in order to improve their condition in life, but many spent their last bit of money to get to America, and thus were forced to choose to engage in sex work to survive after their arrival. Half of the women involved in prostitution in 1859 were married. But many women reported that they had been deserted by their husbands, abused by their husbands, or had husbands who were alcoholics.

Almost half the 2,000 institutionalized prostitutes Sanger interviewed had children, but about half of those children were born before they became prostitutes, while the others were born as the result of involvement in prostitution. Few of these children actually lived with their mothers; most lived with other relatives, including the father, in institutions or in adoptive homes.

Similarly, in more modern times, two-thirds of sex workers arrested in Manhattan in 1984 and 1990 had children, many of whom lived with them. In the 20th and early 21st centuries, street-level sex workers are more likely to be high school dropouts with a history of drug abuse, beginning in adolescence before or in conjunction with participation in prostitution. Female street prostitutes report dependency on drugs with use including heroin, cocaine, and marijuana. Street sex workers are also more likely to be recipients of government subsistence (welfare).

These patterns are replicated among male street prostitutes. Male sex workers are often labeled as hustlers, apparently a less demeaning label. However, like their female counterparts, male street sex workers are often drug addicts or alcoholics, report a history of dysfunctional families including a history of substance abuse. These males are often high school dropouts, have few vocational skills, and were also physically or sexually abused as children. While some research reflects that male hustlers are coerced into prostitution or engage in prostitution to survive, other work indicates that hustlers report that engaging in sex work is a choice based upon making money.

CALL GIRLS

The modern call girl often has some college education and provides from five hours of services to overnight services that range from emotional intimacy and conversation to sexual acts. Her services are usually purchased by wealthy white or Asian males. Conversely, street sex workers are more likely to provide less time to clients who are more representative of the general population in terms of race, and more likely to be middle class.

Call girls today engage in sex work within the private space of their home or the client's home, unlike the sex work of street prostitutes who engage in their work in public spaces like cars or hotel rooms. Interestingly, both groups sometimes report long-term commercial relationships with regular clients anywhere from five to 30 years. Today, most prostitutes are not street sex workers, but it is the street worker who is most likely to be violently victimized and arrested by police.

Additionally, sex workers in the United States are not the most frequent source of the spread of HIV-Aids, as they are in many third world nations. However, just as women prostitutes in the 19th century were victimized in brothel riots in New York City, when brothels were attacked by local men under the influence of alcohol who were envious of the economic success of the brothels, street prostitutes today are often very often victimized by robbery or violence usually perpetrated by their customers.

While Sanger's 19th-century research was predominantly focused on street prostitutes who were adults, other work reveals that both in the 19th century and in modern times, young girls and adolescents are also involved in sex work, some voluntarily for reasons of economic freedom or simply excitement and adventure, while others have been forced into sex work, sometimes by their own families.

International sex trafficking by force, deceit, or coercion is a multimillion-dollar industry mostly serving Western wealthy males with third world women and girls in the role of the sex worker. Sometimes, this global trade also involves organized crime syndicates. Most customers remain male and, generally, in the United States approximately 16 to 18 percent of men report getting at least one service from a prostitute over their life course. Finally, it is street-level sex workers who are more likely to be users of intravenous drugs, and who are also more likely to have a childhood history of sexual abuse or physical abuse. Many teen runaways who leave home as the result of a family history of sexual or physical abuse end up the street, and to survive engage in prostitution.

REGULATION

While much sex work remains criminalized throughout the world, it is legal and highly regulated within 10 counties in Nevada where brothels are licensed by the state. In these counties, it is mostly female sex workers who are mandated to get weekly and monthly health exams certifying that they are free of sexually transmitted diseases.

Taxable profits are at about $40 million a year from 35 licensed Nevada brothels. However, Nevada sex workers are often treated like inmates as their personal movements are quite restricted by law, limiting the benefits that could be gained from more liberal forms of legalization. Moreover, the hierarchy of the brothel business is being taken over by men who treat the women with less respect and dignity than the former madam owners.

Across the globe, prostitution was recently legalized in the Netherlands in 2000 partially in order to provide sex workers with employee benefits including health and pension plans, and to ensure lower rates of sexually transmitted diseases. In some parts of Germany, prostitution is also legal. While there is a growing movement around the world in which sex workers are organizing for a variety of workers rights as well as the decriminalization of their profession, they appear more successful in garnering public and political support for decriminalization in the Netherlands than in the United States. Public attitudes are more favorable to decriminalization in the Netherlands and where prostitution is viewed in less punitive moral terms than here in America. However, prostitution is also the marketplace mechanism for the growing global trade in human trafficking.

Most victims are women and girls but both adult males and male children are also exploited. Often, this involves kidnapping and sometimes involves government cooperation in trafficking women and girls from underdeveloped countries into Western nations. Deception or kidnapping is often used to coerce these women into sex work. The number of trafficked persons is estimated to be in the range of at least 200,000. The illegal industry provides profit to organized crime in the range of more than $10 billion annually. In 2000, the United Nations adopted the Protocol to Prevent, Suppress and Punish Trafficking in persons as a part of a supplement to the recent Convention Against Transnational Organized Crime.

Although more than 120 nations have signed the protocol, 40 nations must also legally ratify it in order to become international law. Also in 2000, the U.S. Congress passed the Victims of Trafficking and Violence Protection Act that increases penalties for traffickers and improves protections for victims. It includes protection from victimization for consensual prostitutes as well, and thus conforms to the United Nations protocol.

SEE ALSO

19th-century regulation; organized crime; Asia; United States; human trafficking.

BIBLIOGRAPHY. Jeffrey S. Adler, Jeffrey, "Streetwalkers, Degraded Outcasts, and Good-For-Nothing Huzzies: Women and the Dangerous Class in Antebellum St. Louis," *Journal of Social History* (2001); Deborah R. Baskin and Ira B. Sommers, "Casualties of Community Disorder Women's Careers in Violent Crime," *Crime and Society* (Westview Press, 1998); Timothy J. Gilfoyle, *City of Eros: New York City Prostitution and the Commercialization of Sex, 1790–1820* (W. W. Norton, 1992); Nanette Graham and Eric D. Wish, "Drug Use Among Female Arrestees: Onset, Patterns, and Relationship to Prostitution," *Journal of Drug Issues* (v.24/1, 1994); Kathryn Hausbeck and Barbara G. Brents, "Inside Nevada's Brothel Industry," *Sex for Sale: Prostitution, Pornography and the Sex Industry* (Routledge, 2000); David J. Langum, *Crossing Over the Line: Legislating Morality and the Mann Act* (University of Chicago Press, 1994); Janet Lever and Deanne Dolnick, "Clients and Call Girls: Seeking Sex and Intimacy," *Sex for Sale: Prostitution, Pornography and the Sex Industry* (Routledge, 2000); Alice Leuchtag, "Human Rights, Sex Trafficking and Prostitution," *Humanist* (v.63/1, 2003); William W. Sanger, *The History of Prostitution: Its Extent, Causes and Effects throughout the World* (1859).

REBECCA S. KATZ
MOREHEAD STATE UNIVERSITY

Public Citizen Health Research Group

IN 1971, CONSUMER advocate Ralph Nader founded Public Citizen, a national nonprofit group designed to protect democracy and to keep consumer health, safety, and financial interests before Congress, the executive branch, and the courts. The Health Research Group (PCHRG) was established as a branch of Public Citizen to promote "research-based, system-wide changes in health care policy" and to provide "oversight concerning drugs, medical devices, doctors and hospitals and occupational health." In practice, PCHRG's efforts to protect the public involve making sure that government, the health profession, drug and device manufacturers, and employers remain aware of threats to human health. In addition, PCHRG vigorously pursues any necessary changes on health-related activities, including calling for investigations and criminal charges whenever harmful or illegal practices are suspected. In order to maintain its objective integrity, PCHRG receives no funding from the government or from corporations.

Throughout its history the Public Citizen Research Health Group has been successful in identifying major threats to the health of Americans. In 1976, the organization effectively petitioned the Food and Drug Administration (FDA) to ban the use of chloroform in various toothpastes and cough medicines after it was identified as a cause of cancer. In 1978, PCHRG discovered that the airline industry was failing to provide adequate seating for non-smokers. The following year, PCHRG led a lobby against the use of a DDT spray that was used to kill Japanese beetles in the passenger sections of airplanes. In 1979, PCHRG finally succeeded in its efforts to force the Environmental Protection

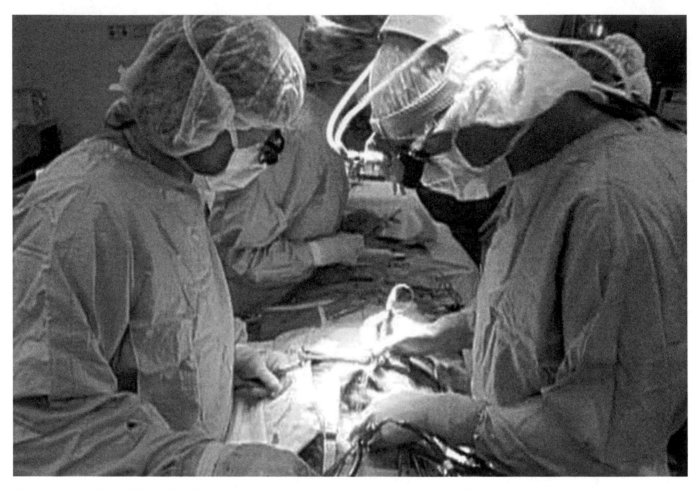

Ralph Nader's Public Citizen Health Research Group keeps tabs on a variety of healthcare dangers, and has had notable success in identifying medical malpractice in its Questionable Doctors *series.*

Agency (EPA) to prohibit the use of DBCP, which was known to cause male sterility.

In the following decade, PCHRG helped to convince the U.S. Congress to pass the Superfund law that funded cleanup of toxic waste sites. In 1981, PCHRG published *Pills That Don't Work*, which became a classic guide to consumers and a thorn in the side of drug manufacturers. This was followed two years later with *Over The Counter Pills That Don't Work*.

A three-year battle by PCHRG resulted in labels on aspirin bottles warning parents and other caretakers of the dangers of Reye's Syndrome in children, and a two-year campaign against tobacco products produced warning labels on chewing tobacco and snuff in 1986. PCHRG's efforts to make the workplace safer for Americans led to Occupational Safety and Health Administrator (OSHA) warnings against the industrial use of cancer-causing ethylene oxide in 1988 and the identification of

250 work sites in which workers had been exposed to hazardous chemicals.

In 1991, the PCHRG published the first issue of *6,836 Questionable Doctors*, a compilation of information on doctors who had been taken to task by the federal and sates governments. It was updated two years later with *10,289 Questionable Doctors*. The list was again updated in 1998 as *16,638 Questionable Doctors*. Charges against the various doctors include overcharging, falsifying records, insurance fraud, sexual misconduct, practicing without a license, professional misconduct, incompetence, negligence, drug and alcohol abuse, misprescribing or over prescribing medications, and criminal convictions.

When criminal or negligent actions on the part of drug manufacturers are suspected, PCHRG can be relentless in its efforts to protect the public. For example, PCHRG called for Health and Human Services (HHS) to insist that Abbot Laboratories be found criminally liable for withholding information about the diet drug Meridia, which has been linked to at least eight deaths and to various to birth defects. PCHRG also prodded HHS to investigate Schering-Plough over the possibility that the company intentionally distributed asthma drug inhalers that lacked the active ingredients necessary to protect the lives and health of asthma sufferers.

PCHRG also insisted that the FDA recall a clot-busting drug called Abbokinase because it may have been tainted. Any time that drug companies or product manufacturers have been found guilty of criminal wrongdoing, PCHRG continues to keep a watchful eye on their activities. For instance, PCHRG continues to monitor Warner Lambert, a company, which has been involved in 64 recalls of products since 1990. Even though the company pleaded guilty to criminally withholding information about its "sloppy manufacturing practices" from the FDA, the recalls have continued. PCHRG has also been instrumental in pushing for a criminal investigation into Smith, Kline, French for neglecting to report adverse reactions to the drug selacryn. PCHRG played an active role in gathering evidence for the criminal prosecution against the Upjohn Company, which manufactured the drug Halcion, after it was revealed that two of the company's long-term studies contained fraudulent or misrepresented data. Eli Lilly has also been continuously monitored since the company suppressed date about the drug Oraflex, including the number of deaths and injuries that resulted from use of the drug.

Other campaigns by PCHRG include a demand for a "Do not use" warning on a new statin drug called Crestor that has been linked to kidney disease and muscle damage, and a sustained effort to convince the federal government to investigate unethical research being conducted by medical students. In October 2003, PCHRG announced that a possible lift on the ban against silicone gel breast implants was reckless, and followed it up with a warning against the antidepressant Serzone that had been linked to several deaths and injuries.

The deregulation of the dietary supplement and herbicide industries resulted in a renewed call by PCHRG for governmental oversight into these substances that are readily available to consumers with little knowledge of potential toxicities. PCHRG maintains a web site (www.citizen.org) that provides up-to-date information on health-related alerts to assist consumers in identifying potential health hazards and issues periodic announcements about health-related issues.

SEE ALSO

medical malpractice; healthcare fraud; pharmaceutical industry; Environmental Protection Agency; Food and Drug Administration.

BIBLIOGRAPHY. Joel Kaufman, *Over The Counter Pills That Don't Work* (Pantheon, 1983); PCHRG, "Corporate Crime and Public Accountability" www.worstpills.org (2003); PCHRG, "Dietary and Herbal Supplements," "Latest News and Alerts," "Public Citizen: 30 Years," www.citizen.org (2003); Sidney M. Wolfe, *Pills That Don't Work* (Farrar, Straus, and Giroux, 1981); Sidney M. Wolfe, et al., *10,289 Questionable Doctors Disciplined by States or the Federal Government* (Public Citizen Health Research Group, 1993).

ELIZABETH PURDY, PH.D.
INDEPENDENT SCHOLAR

public corruption

PUBLIC corruption does not have a single definition in the literature. The meaning of public corruption differs across individuals and academic disciplines. For instance, in criminal law public corruption seems to be confined to the act of bribery. In other disciplines, most scholars have taken bribery as the paradigm for a corrupt act and broadened the definition to include a variety of illegal acts. Public corruption is sometime viewed as rent-seeking activities, and some other time as the violation of a public official's duty of faith towards her community.

Most often, public corruption will take place when a public official is offered a payoff in exchange for a favorable decision. By "public officials" we mean any individual who is either appointed, hired, elected, or working for the service of her constituency. Hence public corruption can take place at the federal, state, local levels.

Public corruption can also be defined as acts of nepotism where promotions are based on personal affiliations and not on merit; it can finally be defined as misappropriations of public funds for personal gain and usage.

It is worth pointing out that some scholars have restricted the definition of public corruption to an act of bribery only, but have broadened the definition of bribery to encompass a variety of corrupt behaviors that falls outside the traditional bribery arena. For example, bribery, in this case, is defined to include payoffs to gain access to public goods, to gain access to the use of public physical or financial assets, to be allowed to engage in illegal trade in goods banned for security or health reasons, in money laundering, or to be able to influence the judicial process.

Essential characteristics of public corruption are generally the following: first, two or more parties that include a public official act in mutual agreement; second their decisions violate the law. Third they illegally benefit from the benefit and finally they try to conceal their behavior. Basically, the process can be decomposed into the following parts: a public official, the actual favor provided by the official, the payoff gained by the official, and the payoff gained by the recipient of the act.

The definitions and characteristics mentioned so far seem to suggest that public corruption requires the presence of at least two parties. It should be pointed out that this does not need to always be the case. Indeed the public official can engage in auto-corruption. Though difficult to define, auto-corruption encompasses a situation in which an official acts both as an offeror and a decision-maker and make use of his position to gain benefits to which he was not entitled.

There are many types of public corruption: Indeed the Federal Bureau of Investigation (FBI) defines five major categories of corruption. They are the legislative, regulatory, contractual, judicial, and law enforcement corruptions. Law enforcement corruption has to do with any attempt to bribe law officers or any corrupt behavior of the latter. Examples of such corruption are bribery of law enforcement officials to prevent enforcement of drug laws; other examples include unconstitutional (police) searches and seizures, the provision of false testimony, and the submission of false crime reports. There is legislative corruption when a legislator is paid a bribe to promote a piece of legislation.

Likewise judicial corruption occurs when a judge is paid a bribe for a favorable ruling in a judicial proceeding. Also, there is regulatory corruption when regulatory inspectors are paid bribes to overlook violations of regulatory codes. And finally

kickbacks associated with public contracts are an example of contractual corruption.

CURBING CORRUPTION

Many efforts have been undertaken to curb and eliminate public corruption. In the United States, the Foreign Corrupt Practices Act (FCPA) was enacted by Congress in 1977 in an effort to criminalize transnational bribe payments of foreign officials by U.S. companies and individuals. By doing so, the United States stood as the only nation in the world to punish its companies or citizens engaged in bribery abroad. Since other countries did not adopt this rule, it was clear that U.S. firms were placed at a disadvantage in international markets. Congress thus asked the president to encourage U.S. trading partners to adopt anti-corruption measures similar to the FCPA. Three important institutions that are mostly composed of trading partners adopted such anti-corruption laws. They are the Organization of Economic Cooperation and Development (OECD), the Council of Europe, and the Organization of American States (OAS).

Founded on April 30, 1948 and based in Washington, D.C., the OAS is comprised of 35 nations. In 1996, as a result of negotiations by the United States, the Inter-American Convention Against Corruption (IACAC) was adopted and sent to country members for signature and ratification. The IACAC was ratified by 21 countries, including the United States. The IACAC provisions clearly specified that an act of public corruption has occurred whenever: 1) there is the solicitation or acceptance by the government official of any article of monetary value or other benefit in exchange for an act pertaining to his functions; 2) there is an act or omission in the performance of his duties for the purpose of illicitly obtaining benefits for himself or a third party. It is thus clear that the IACAC provisions make use of the traditional definition of corruption, but also condemn the misuse of authority for personal gain, even if there is no other party involved.

The OECD was founded on December 14, 1960 and is based in Paris, France. In 2003, the OECD was composed of 30 member nations that are the leading exporters in the world economy. The organization is dedicated to fostering economic growth and development and is therefore a platform for anti-corruption measures. In 1997, the 29 members along with 5 nonmember nations signed the OECD Convention (Convention on Combating Bribery of Foreign Public Officials in International Business Transactions) that criminalizes the bribery of foreign officials. Bribes as defined in Article 1 of the OECD Convention can be either payments or any use of the public official's position similar in nature to influence-peddling. Article 1 mainly focuses on the prosecution of the entity paying the bribes; the prosecution of the corrupt foreign public official is not the focus of Article 1 and is left to the legislations and laws of the foreign country. The OECD Convention had an effect on the 1998 amendments of the FCPA. Indeed these amendments expanded the scope of the FCPA to cover "any person" who engages in bribery on U.S. soil. Before the amendments only American individuals or companies that offered bribes could be prosecuted.

Like the OECD and the OAS, the Council of Europe, which is composed of 45 countries and based in Strasbourg, France, adopted the Criminal Law Convention on Corruption in 1999 and asked all member nations to fight and eliminate all forms of corruption. Corruption was defined to include both bribery and "trading in influence" similar to influence-buying. The Council Convention prosecutes both the "person" giving the bribe and the receiver of the latter. It was signed by 36 member nations and 3 non-members, which include the United States. The Council and OECD Conventions, along with the IACAC, are major examples of efforts to address transnational corruption.

U.S. REGULATION

At the domestic level, developed countries such as the United States have adopted a multi-dimensional approach in their fight against bribery. In the United States, two laws that address public corruption are Section 201 of Title 18 and the Mail Fraud statute. Section 201, enacted in 1962, addresses both the offeror of the bribe and the receiver of "anything of value." The term "anything of value" includes actual financial payments and the promise of future benefit such as employment. In its initial draft, Section 201 was mainly dealing with federal employees bribery prohibition. By 1984, Congress extended the prohibition to state and local officials who receive $10,000 or more in federal money in a 12-month period; public officials who have been nominated or appointed to a public office but have not yet assumed office are also subject to the prohibition. Unlike the international conventions, Section 201 also addresses the issue of gratuity provision. Since one cannot bribe an official for a decision that is already made, bribery is forward looking while gratuities can be either forward or backward looking. Section 201 makes after-the-fact gratuities an illegal act, as the official clearly benefits from the exercise of his functions and the offeror of the gratuity increases the likelihood of his future demands to be met by the public official.

The Mail Fraud statute was first adopted in 1872 to protect the post office from being abused as part of a fraudulent scheme, and later adapted to prevent individuals from using the post office to perpetrate frauds on unsuspecting victims. However, in the early 1970s the Mail Fraud statute was largely used by federal prosecutors to attack political corruption (fraud) at the federal, state, and local levels. A public official is said to have committed an act of fraud when he puts his personal, private interests above the public interest; that is a fraud by an official is a violation of his fiduciary duties. Hence, even in the absence of a two-party transaction, the Mail Fraud statute is an effective means as an anti-corruption law.

Experts agree public corruption is not easy to eliminate in any country, whether it is developed or developing. Developed countries should encourage developing countries to adopt or sign-up to conventions such as the OECD or the Council of Europe Conventions and to develop their own regional conventions. Since public corruption flourishes in the dark, transparency should be developed: developing countries should promote greater openness and independence of the media, expand the audit system to all levels of the government, punish corrupt officials but reward honest ones. The international community should be actively involved in the fight against corruption in developing countries by making the allocations of funds conditional on the implementation of concrete anti-corruption measures, or channeling funds through non-government sources. Finally the fight against public corruption should be done at all levels, including the institutional, political, and legal levels.

SEE ALSO

bribery; Foreign Corrupt Practices Act; mail fraud; corruption; Central America; government contract fraud.

BIBLIOGRAPHY. Kimberly Ann Elliott, *Corruption and the Global Economy* (IIE, 1997); Susan Rose-Ackerman, *Corruption: A Study in Political Economy* (Academic Press, 1978); Miguel Schloss, *Symposium Fighting International Corruption and Bribery in the 21st Century, Luncheon Address* (Cornell International Law Journal, 2000); World Bank, *Governance: The World Bank's Experience* (World Bank, 1994).

ARSENE AKA
CATHOLIC UNIVERSITY OF AMERICA

puffery

A FORM OF deceptive advertising, puffery has immense consequences. The term refers to the practice of making exaggerated claims for a product. Although advertisers routinely make such false claims, and the result is deception, the law considers such practices to be legal. Puffery claims are communicated in the form of unprovable superlatives (that is adjectives such as the best, super, new and improved), often in the form of various advertising slogans:

> Blatz is Milwaukee's finest beer
> Nestle makes the very best chocolate
> Ford gives you better ideas
> You can be sure if it's Westinghouse
> Barnum and Bailey, the greatest show on earth
> Coke is the real thing
> Seagram's, America's number one gin
> Winston tastes good like a cigarette should
> BMW: the ultimate driving machine
> Apple Computers: the power to be your best

None of the slogans are based on objective, factual evidence, and, as such, these claims are either false or unsubstantiated. Even though they are considered legal, their intent is to deceive. The goal, as is always in advertising, is to use whatever tactic will sell a product or service. If that includes distorting the truth, so be it.

Even though knowledge concerning puffery in advertising is far from complete, some important facts have emerged from research on this topic. People perceive more content in ads than the ads actually contain. Additional values are perceived by consumers and attached to products. For example, one study of sweaters concluded that, when sweaters were shown with belts and captions were read by someone with a Scottish accent, consumers were twice as likely to perceive that the sweaters were imported. Implied deceptions (puffery claims) are believed more than outright lies. In one study of 17 puff claims, 70 percent of respondents felt the claims were either wholly or partially true.

Puffery claims are often indistinguishable from factual claims. In another study, a sample of 100 people were placed in a room and presented with both real and puff claims. The researchers found that "many of the puff claims were believed by a large proportion of the respondents. The subjects could not tell that these puffs might not be literally true." Researchers found that the factual claims were believed just as often as the puff claims used in their survey.

Consumers fed a constant diet of puffery ads may confuse fact and fiction. Moreover, they may actually come to distrust advertising, on the one hand, yet unconsciously be manipulated by it on the other. Puffery claims are most often found in lifestyle advertising. These ads usually contain photos of young, attractive men and women depicted in opulent surroundings (for example, beautiful white beaches, penthouse apartments, or luxurious mansions). The photos contain implied promises concerning popularity, sex appeal, power, success, and love—if one uses the product being advertised. The puff claims along with the implied promises in the ads constitute a major form of social structural alienation known as inauthenticity.

Inauthenticity consists of positive overt appearances (that is, the puffery slogans and implied promises) coupled with negative underlying realities that come from a mass consumption lifestyle. This lifestyle includes, for example, consuming dangerous products, generating pollution, depleting resources, chronic indebtedness, envy crimes, and even bankruptcy from spending too much money on mass consumption.

SEE ALSO
advertising fraud; False Claims Act.

BIBLIOGRAPHY. Hal Hemmelstein, *Understanding Television* (Praeger, 1984); Ivan Preston, *The Great American Blow-Up: Puffery in Advertising and Selling* (University of Wisconsin Press, 1975); J. Rotfeld and K.B. Rotzall, "Is Advertising Puffery Believed?" *Journal of Advertising Re-*

search (v.9, 1980); David R. Simon, *Elite Deviance* (Allyn & Bacon, 2002); R.C. Wyckham, "Implied Superiority Claims," *Journal of Advertising Research* (v.27, 1987).

DAVID R. SIMON
UNIVERSITY OF NORTHERN FLORIDA
UNIVERSITY OF CALIFORNIA, BERKELEY

Pure Food, Drug and Cosmetics Act

THE PURE FOOD movement, which surfaced in the decade after the Civil War and the appointment of Dr. Harvey W. Wiley as the sixth head of the Department of Chemistry, was the motivating force behind the early call to prevent the sale of harmful, tainted, or misbranded food and drugs being sold in the United States. In response to these efforts, Congress passed the Food and Drug Act of 1906 over the objections of the whiskey distilleries and the patent food industry which were afraid the new law would put them out of business. With the passage of the law, federal officials had the authority to seize illegal products and to prosecute those who manufactured them. By 1908, Wiley employed 28 food and drug inspectors. A separate law was also passed to regulate the quality of meat in response to Upton Sinclair's exposé of the meat packing industry in *The Jungle*. The Insecticide Act of 1910 placed restrictions on the use of pesticides, banning the manufacture, sale, and transport of harmful and ineffective pesticides. In 1913, Congress mandated uniform weights and measures on food and drug labels.

Drawing on a his extensive research, Wiley faced down legal challenges to the 1906 law, convincing the courts to uphold the right of the federal government to protect American consumers. Wiley also drew up the first *Inspector's Manual*, which provided federal inspectors with scientific methods to test the safety of products. In 1926, the authority to regulate food and drugs was transferred to the newly created Food, Drug, and Insecticide Administration, which became the Food and Drug Administration (FDA) in 1931. The election of Franklin D. Roosevelt in 1932 helped to provide the FDA with the support it needed to protect Americans from harmful and unwholesome foods, and from drugs

that could be fatal or which failed to live up to their claims.

Under Wiley's leadership, the FDA gathered together what became known as the "American Chamber of Horrors" to convince legislators and the public of the need for reform in the food and drug industries that went beyond the 1906 act. His display included: Banbar, a product that falsely promised to cure diabetes; Lash-Lure, a mascara that blinded a number of women; Radithor, a lethal tonic that contained radium; Wilhide Exhaler, which was inaccurately advertised as a cure for tuberculosis and a host of other illnesses; and a variety of foods that had been falsely labeled and/or packaged. Before his death in 1930, Wiley synthesized his research and his goals into a six-page proposal for what became the 1938 Federal Food, Drug and Cosmetic Act. The new law banned the manufacturing and interstate shipment of tainted and falsely labeled food and drugs.

During the five-year battle to pass the Food, Drug, and Cosmetic Act, Arthur Kallet and F. J. Schlink, published *One Hundred Million Guinea Pigs: Dangers in Everyday Foods, Drugs, and Cosmetics*, creating further public outcry about the dangers of a number of products that Americans consumed on a daily basis. This work, coupled with the efforts of Wiley and the FDA were still not enough to push Congress toward consumer reform until a major medical catastrophe occurred. In 1937, a Tennessee company, Massengil, sold a tonic that it claimed was safe enough for pediatric use. In reality, the tonic contained ethylene glycol, an element used in engine antifreeze, and its use resulted in the deaths of at least 100 Americans, many of them children. No safety testing had been performed on the product before it had been unleashed on unsuspecting consumers.

The Federal Food, Drug and Cosmetics Act of 1938 required that drug manufacturers provide scientific proof of drug safety and regulated cosmetics and medical devices for the first time. After the law went into effect, the federal government no longer had to prove fraud to stop manufacturers of drugs from making false claims about their products. The law also banned the addition of any kind of poisonous substances to food, except in the rare case when it was either necessary or unavoidable. For example, residues of pesticides used on fruits and vegetables might be considered unavoidable. For the first time, the FDA was given the authority to obtain injunctions to prevent the manufacture and marketing of illegal products.

In the decades following the passage of the Pure Food, Drug and Cosmetics Act, the widespread use of amphetamines and barbiturates claimed a lion's share of the FDA's attention. A number of amendments to the 1938 law were passed as a result of the agency's continued efforts to protect consumers. In 1954, Congress passed the first laws regulating the use of pesticides on food products. Food additives were regulated in 1958, followed by regulation of color additives two years later. In 1962, in response to the threat of thalidomide, a European tranquilizer that produced horrific birth defects in babies born to women who had taken the drug, the Kefauver-Harris Amendment required the FDA to re-evaluate all drugs that had been introduced in the United States since 1938.

The FDA was also given greater authority over drug trials and improved access to manufacturer's records for purposes of verification. The amendment transferred control of drug advertising from the Federal Trade Commission to the FDA. In 1968, Congress created the Drug Enforcement Administration and brought veterinary medicine under FDA authority. In 1976, the scandal that erupted over the use of the Dalkon Shield, an intrauterine device that caused deaths, birth defects, infertility, and a number of other problems for its users, led to the Medical Device Amendment that gave the FDA the right to regulate medical devices.

In contemporary terms, the 1938 Pure Food, Drug, and Cosmetics Act and its amendments have given the FDA the authority to regulate the contents, manufacture, distribution, and advertising of food, drugs, medical devices, and cosmetics and to mandate scientific testing as ways to ensure safety and effectiveness, along with civil and criminal enforcement authority. FDA authority over food includes the authority to regulate food-borne illnesses, and changes in labeling requirements for food have mandated information about vitamins, minerals, and calories as well as specific weights and measures of products. The FDA has regulatory authority over both biological and therapeutic substances that are classified as drugs, including all prescription and over-the-counter (OTC) drugs. The inclusion of medical devices has provided FDA oversight for devices from contact lenses and hearing aids to pacemakers and breast implants.

Mandates for cosmetic labeling have included content labeling, adverse reactions that have been noted in testing, and the presence of alphahydroxy acids in the product. Penalties for violation of the laws include fines from $50,000 to $1,000,000, depending on the number of charges.

The FDA also has the authority to confiscate illegal products, to obtain injunctions to prevent the manufacture and distribution of illegal products, to force the recall of faulty products, and to debar drug manufacturers who have committed serious violations of drug regulations. While the FDA has the task of ensuring the safety of foods, drugs, medical devices, and cosmetics, consumers share a responsibility for educating themselves about potential hazards.

SEE ALSO

pesticides; Dalkon Shield; A. H. Robins; pharmaceutical industry; Environmental Protection Agency; Food and Drug Administration.

BIBLIOGRAPHY. John G. Fuller, *Two Hundred Million Guinea Pigs: New Dangers in Everyday Foods, Drugs, and Cosmetics* (G.P. Putnam's Sons, 1972); Arthur Kallet and F.J. Schlink, *One Hundred Million Guinea Pigs: Dangers in Everyday Foods, Drugs, and Cosmetics* (Grossett and Dunlap, 1933); Food and Drug Administration, "History of the FDA," www.fda.gov (2003); Food and Drug Administration, "The Story of the Laws Behind the Labels," www.fda.gov (2003).

ELIZABETH PURDY, PH.D.
INDEPENDENT SCHOLAR

R

racial discrimination

PREJUDICE IS the attitudinal element in enforcing racial and ethnic stratification, while discrimination is the active, or behavioral, element. Discrimination involves behavior aimed at denying members of particular ethnic groups equal access to societal rewards. It may be of an individual or institutional nature and *de jure* (in law) or *de facto* (in fact).

Actions taken by individuals or groups of limited size to injure or deny members of minority ethnic groups are perhaps the most easily understood form of discrimination. The employment manager who refuses to hire Asians, the judge who metes out unusually harsh sentences to African Americans, and the homeowners' group that agrees not to sell in the neighborhood to Jews are examples of discriminators at this level.

In these cases, actions are taken by one or few with the intent to harm or restrict in some way members of minority groups. In cases of individual discrimination, the actions taken against minority groups' members are intentional. At first glance, we might assume that the employment manager thinks unfavorably of Asians, the judge dislikes African-Americans, and the homeowners hate Jews. This may, in fact, be the motivating force behind the discrimination in all these cases, but we cannot be certain until we understand more fully the context in which these actions occur. The employment manager, for example, may have no ill feeling toward Asians but may feel compelled to carry out what he perceives to be the unwritten, yet generally understood company policy of not hiring Asians. The judge may feel that sentencing African-Americans more harshly will gain her votes among her predominantly white constituency in the next election. And the members of the homeowners' group may simply be responding to what they fell are neighborhood pressures.

Discrimination, however, may be legal or customary, in which case it is not socially unexpected or disapproved of, but is legitimized. This is called *de jure* (in law) discrimination. In the United States before the 1960s, there were centuries of a well-institutionalized system of racial discrimination in the law. This blocked the access of African-Americans and other racial minorities to economic, political, and social opportunities afforded to whites.

AFRICAN AMERICANS

In *de jure* racial discrimination, racism has been an integral part of American law since the first slaves arrived in Virginia in 1619. A century and a half later, a new nation, composed in large part of slaveholders, made a Declaration of Independence in which they bore witness to the world that "all men are created equal." Twenty years after Columbus reached the New World, African natives, transported by Spanish, Dutch, and Portuguese traders, were arriving in the Caribbean Islands. Almost all came as slaves. By 1600, there were more than half million slaves in the Western Hemisphere.

In Colonial America, the first African Americans landed at Jamestown, Virginia with the earliest settlers. Within 40 years, they had become a group apart, separated from the rest of the population by custom and law. Treated as servants for life, forbidden to intermarry with whites, deprived of their African traditions, and dispersed among Southern plantations, African Americans lost tribal, regional, and family ties. Colonial legislation generally barred marriage between whites and African Americans. These laws were intended to provide "a perpetual and impassible barrier" between whites and African Americans.

Through massive importation, slave numbers increased rapidly. By 1776, some 500,000 African Americans were held in slavery and indentured servitude in the United States. Nearly one of every six persons in the country was a slave. The earliest slave statutes arose in New York, Connecticut, Massachusetts, and Virginia. Black slaves were treated in law as property, and this became part of the Constitution, given that slavery a well-established institution by that time. Slave laws allowed masters total control over their property, including whipping and killing their slaves. White Northern states abolished slavery in the early 1800s, they still maintained legal restriction on free slaves regarding employment, education, and voting. They were not equal in the eyes of the law. Slavery remained a major economic and social institution in the South and the Dred Scott decision by the Supreme Court of the United States in 1857 affirmed their inferior status.

CIVIL WAR

The Civil War was begun largely for Constitutional and economic reasons, due to the secession of the South from the Union. President Abraham Lincoln issued a preliminary warning to states that had seceded and joined the Confederacy that he would free their slaves January 1, 1863 if they did not rejoin the Union. The Proclamation Emancipation was declared on January 1, 1863 freeing slaves in the Confederate states. The campaigning to enact the Thirteenth Amendment abolishing slavery began in 1864 while large numbers of African Americans soldiers were in combat. By the time the Thirteenth Amendment was signed by Lincoln on February 1, 1865, there were 200,000 African Americans in the Union army.

While African-Americans made progress immediately after the Civil War, they were again subjugated by law and violence. Within a decade it became apparent that the Thirteenth Amendment abolishing slavery was obsolete. Southern planter could achieve the same benefits with less burden through the sharecropping system and stark violence. The Fifteenth Amendment, politically obsolete at its birth, was not effectively enforced for almost a century. The Fourteenth Amendment, impassable as specific protection for African-American rights, was enacted finally as a general guarantee of life, liberty, and property of all "persons."

Corporations, following a period of ambivalence, were deemed persons under the Fourteenth Amendment, and for several generations received far more protection from the courts than did African-Americans. Indeed, African-Americans became victims of judicial interpretation of the Fourteenth Amendment and legislation based on it so narrow as to render the promised protection meaningless in virtually all situations. Violence against freed slaves abounded, and the Ku Klux Klan arose in the 1870s as an expression of prevailing attitudes.

The Civil War Amendments and the Civil Rights Acts in the 1860s and 1890s were to remain empty as federal government tools; the courts and state laws allowed a "separate but equal" policy to arise in the United States. Segregation laws were legitimated in 1896 in the case of *Plessey v. Ferguson* by the U.S. Supreme Court allowing the country to maintain an apartheid, segregationist system until the civil rights movement and legal changes beginning in the 1950s and 1960s.

NATIVE AMERICANS

Building on models already tested by the Spanish, the French, and the British, America advanced its takeover of the American landscape through treaties (easily made and as easily abandoned), open warfare waged with, first, superior weapons and, later, with overwhelming numbers, and, ultimately, through genocide. The absence from the Constitution of the general power over Native American affairs is not surprising to students of history, for at the time the Constitution was drafted, the framers regarded Native American tribes as sovereign nations, albeit nations that would soon either move west, assimilate, or become extinct. The judiciary further solidified the analogy of Native American affairs to foreign affairs. Although courts analogized tribe nations to foreign nations in finding Congressional power to deal with them, it is important to note that the courts did not view tribes as possessing all the attributes of a sovereign foreign nation.

In the first Cherokee case, *Cherokee Nation v. Georgia*, the Supreme Court held that Native American nations were not foreign states for the purpose of invoking the court's original jurisdiction. The nation was neither a state of the Union nor a foreign state, but a "domestic dependent nation" incapable of conditioned foreign relations with countries other than the United States. Instead, "their relation to the United States resembles that of a ward to his guardian."

In *Cherokee Nation v. Georgia* (1831) Chief Justice John Marshall suggested Native American tribes were "domestic dependent nations" whose relationship was later to be implemented through the paternalistic colonialism manifest in the reservation system. Furthermore, laws and treaties made by the United States government with the Native American tribes were infamous for their "flexibility." Under the legal Doctrine of Discovery, the U.S. Supreme Court in *United States v. Kagana* (1886), gave Congress the power to govern reservations. Although nominally protected by the individual rights provisions of the Constitution, like other non-citizens, Native Americans and their tribes, in fact, could not vindicate their rights in the courts. The General Allotment Act of 1887 provided that Native Americans receiving allotments under any treaty or statute would become citizens. The act also declared Native Americans living separate and apart and "adopting the habits of civilized life" to be citizens. It was not until 1960 that all Native Americans received citizenship.

CHINESE

The Chinese were the first Asians to immigrate to California. Primarily laborers from Kwantung Province, they emigrated from China to escape the great hardships that followed the Taiping Rebellion of 1850 to 1864. The discovery of gold at Sutter's Mill in 1848 greatly increased the attractiveness of California for the Chinese. Much of the immigration was the product of the "coolie trade," an arrangement by which Chinese laborers were imported under contract that amounted to a form of slavery.

By 1860, they outnumbered the other immigrant groups in California and had earned the animosity of white labor groups by being "too efficient." The California legislature passed laws and regulations designed specifically to create social and economic hardships for the Chinese. The statues ranged from a "foreign miner's tax" to a "police tax" and a "cubic air" ordinance.

Two important court decisions, however, were sources of particular trouble to the Chinese. In 1854, the California Supreme Court ruled that the laws of the state exclude all people of color from giving evidence in court either for or against a white person, and, in 1867, a federal court held that the Chinese aliens were not eligible for naturalization.

The Chinese Exclusion Action of 1882 became the first exclusively racial immigration law. The Geary Act of 1892 extended the suspension for an additional 10 years, and, in 1902, the suspension was converted into permanent exclusion. The Act of 1892 provided that all Chinese laborers lawfully in the United States were required to obtain certificates of residence or face deportation. The Chinese raised large sums of money to sponsor litigation challenging the constitutionality of the act, but the Supreme Court upheld the Geary Act. The court held that he determination of Congress was conclusive on the judiciary, and that the government has the inalienable right to expel all of any class of aliens, "absolutely or upon certain conditions, in war or in peace."

In 1927, the court found that no equal protection violation resulted form the exclusion of a child with some Chinese blood from white schools under state law. Due in part to China being an American ally in World War II, an act of 1943 repealed all previous exclusion acts and established a token quota of 100 Chinese immigrants. This act was also to counter Japanese propaganda against the United States. The Chinese gained the right of naturalization and were taken out of the category of citizens "ineligible for naturalization," a phrase used in discriminatory law against Asians.

The law remained prejudicial, however, in that only Asians did not fall under the national origins system. A Chinese immigrant was put under the Chinese quota even though his national origin was English or Malayan. It was not until 1965 that an amendment to the 1952 Act eliminated discrimination against Asians in the immigration laws.

JAPANESE

The Japanese, who in 1890 began immigration to the United States in large numbers, arrived on the West Court at one of the most inopportune periods in American history. Anti-Chinese feeling had reached its peak, and this hostility was easily transferred to the new Asians arrivals.

In 1906, the San Francisco Board of Education then controlled by the Labor Party, decided to enforce an ordinance passed the previous year that would segregate the city's Asian children. Racism and exclusion did not take the form of only exclusion acts in 1913; California enacted the Alien Land Laws. Many states followed suit. The laws were designed to prevent Japanese immigrants from earning a living in agriculture, thereby driving them out of the state.

But in the 1920s, the Alien Land Laws did not seem sufficiently restrictive to many Americans, and in 1924 an exclusion act was passed. The Quota Act of 1924 excluded from immigration "aliens ineligible to citizenship." Japanese aliens were not to gain the right to citizenship until the Walter-McCarren Act of 1952.

On February 19, 1942, President Franklin D. Roosevelt issued Executive Order 9066, "giving authority to certain military commanders to prescribe military areas from which any or all persons may be excluded, and with respect to which the right to enter, remain in, or leave, shall be subject to the discretion of the military commander." The War Relocation Authority relocated Americans of Japanese ancestry into internment camps. On March 18, 1942, this segregation was upheld by the U.S. Supreme Court in *Korematsu v. United States*.

In addition to loss of freedom, property, education opportunities, businesses, and employment income, the 120,000 people of Japanese ancestry interned (more than two-thirds native-born Americans citizens) were subjected to onerous living conditions. After great pressure decades later, President Ronald Reagan signed the Civil Liberties Act of 1988, setting in motion the statutory means by which Japanese Americans who were interned

would receive federal reparations payments. Government implementation of the measure has been slow, and it is estimated that only about 60,000 survivors or their next of kin will be paid. About half of the internment survivors died before the legislation was passed.

De facto racial discrimination is the situation in the United States since the civil rights movement of the 1950s and 1960s and the elimination of most of the exclusionary and segregation laws. These discriminations may not be lawful as in employment or housing discrimination, yet segregated housing patterns, racial profiling, high rates of incarceration and unemployment of African-Americans and Hispanics reflect *de facto* discrimination. This remains the major challenge in race and ethnic relations.

SEE ALSO

gender discrimination; age discrimination; United States; American Civil War.

BIBLIOGRAPHY. Charles E. Reasons and Jack L. Kurykendall, *Race, Crime and Justice* (Pearson, 2001); Reid Luhman, *Race and Ethnicity in the United States* (Wadsworth, 2002); Derrick Bell, *Race, Racism and American Law* (Aspen Law, 200); Randall Kennedy, *Race, Crime and the Law* (Random House, 1998); Martin N. Marger, *Race and Ethnic Relations* (Wadsworth, 2003); Charles E. Reasons, Darlene J. Carley, Julius Debro, Race, Class, *Gender and Justice In the United States* (Pearson, 2002; Samuel Walker, Cassia Spohn, and Miriam De Lane, *Color of Justice* (Wadsworth, 2004).

CHARLES E. REASONS, PH.D.
CENTRAL WASHINGTON UNIVERSITY

racketeering

RACKETEERING CAN BE generally defined with reference to an individual (a racketeer) who uses extortion, loan sharking, bribery, or obstruction of justice to further her illegal activities. Often, an individual who practices racketeering may also use her formal authority or some type of formal or informal power to illegally persuade others to further her interests. Although definitions of the term racketeering are contained within U.S. Federal statutes, these definitions have been criticized by legal scholars, who have argued that the definitions are too vague and ambiguous. The official definition of racketeering can be found in the Organized Crime Control Act of 1970, or Public Law 91-452. Interestingly, a synonym for racketeer is fraudster, a label that is often used to describe white-collar and corporate offenders.

In the field of criminology, racketeering almost immediately brings to mind images of organized crime, as opposed to white-collar or corporate crime. The same image tends to hold for the related and often interchangeable term, racketeering activity. However, researchers focused on this area of study have readily acknowledged that the line between white-collar crime, corporate crime, and organized crime is often blurred. To successfully operate a criminal organization, also known as a mafia, at least some amount of support from the larger society is needed. Organized crime members may further their criminal interests by involving legitimate businesses and their representatives in their activities.

For example, corrupting legal officials such as police, judges, and legislative officials may occur through bribery or blackmail. Available research on this topic demonstrates that certain industries have historically been more likely to become involved in the activities of organized criminal groups. These industries have included gambling, trash collecting, and freight loading. Many of the racketeering activities associated with these industries have been referred to as white-collar crime, rather than organized crime.

A CHALLENGING ENDEAVOR

The overlap between white-collar crime, corporate crime, and organized crime can also be seen more clearly by examining the legal responses to a variety of criminal and civil violations. Many of these acts occur within the context of legitimate business operations, making their detection and eventual punishment a very challenging endeavor. Studies of corporate crime have documented the numerous difficulties that may be associated with the prosecution of organizations.

For example, determining punishment for an organization can be problematic when offenses include several individuals acting on behalf of the legitimate business. Unlike the case of a single offender, some of the more severe sanctions, such as incarceration, cannot be levied against an entire

organization. Historically, one of the most common available sanctions for organizational defendants has been in the form of a monetary fine.

Over the last two decades, additional punishment options for organizational defendants, as well as criminal individuals, have become available through the Racketeer Influenced Corrupt Organizations (RICO) Act. A provision of the aforementioned Organized Crime Control Act, the RICO statute was originally enacted by Congress to target the criminal enterprises of organized crime families. In fact, it is viewed legally as the primary means of convicting known mobsters or gangsters.

In addition to enabling prosecutors to file charges against criminal groups, RICO has allowed the seizure of assets that are the product of criminal activities and has permitted harsher punishment of offenders. A variety of offenses fall within the boundaries of RICO, and a "pattern of racketeering activity" includes involvement in two acts within a 10-year span. The acts that may be included within this time frame vary considerably. To be charged with racketeering under the RICO Act, a person must be employed or associated with a criminal enterprise. The statute of limitations for prosecuting a RICO violation is five years for criminal prosecution and four years for civil prosecution.

Although RICO covers violent crimes such as murder and kidnapping, several of the offenses encompassed within the statute may be viewed as synonymous with white-collar and corporate crime. These include counterfeiting, financial institution fraud, money laundering, mail fraud, securities fraud, wire fraud, embezzlement from welfare funds, theft by deception, and extortionate credit fraud. RICO has also been used in the successful prosecution of individual and corporate offenders charged with various forms of consumer fraud, such as false advertising.

In a variety of business disputes and commercial litigation consistent with white-collar and corporate crime, such as fraud, civil RICO is more likely to be used against a defendant than criminal RICO. Such claims are often attached to a suit by the plaintiffs as a means of increasing the defendant's exposure to the public. One of the most well-known individuals prosecuted under the RICO Act was junk bond magnate Michael Milken, whose crimes included bond market manipulation, securities fraud, and tax fraud. In 1990, Milken was sentenced to 10 years in prison for these offenses.

SEE ALSO
Racketeering Influenced Corrupt Organizations; prosecution; organized crime; Milken, Michael.

BIBLIOGRAPHY. Dennis J. Kenney and James O. Finckenauer, *Organized Crime in America* (Wadsworth, 1995); Sally S. Simpson, *Corporate Crime, Law, and Social Control* (Cambridge University Press, 2002); Michael Tonry and Albert J. Reiss, Jr., *Beyond the Law: Crime in Complex Organizations* (University of Chicago Press, 1993); Department of Justice, www.usdoj.gov (2004).

KRISTY HOLTFRETER, PH.D.
FLORIDA STATE UNIVERSITY

Racketeer Influenced Corrupt Organizations

IN THE UNITED STATES, the Racketeer Influenced Corrupt Organizations (RICO) statute is considered the most significant piece of legislation targeting organized and white-collar crime ever enacted. While derided in many circles as an unfair infringement on such ingrained constitutional rights as due process, it has been used extensively and successfully to prosecute thousands of individuals and organizations in the United States.

Part of the Organized Crime Control Act of 1970, RICO makes it unlawful to acquire, operate or receive income from an enterprise through a pattern of racketeering activity. Geared toward ongoing, organized criminal activities, the underlying tenet of RICO is to prove and prohibit a pattern of crimes conducted through an "enterprise," which the statute defines as "any individual, partnership, corporation, association, or other legal entity, and any union or group of individuals associated in fact, although not a legal entity."

Under RICO, it is a crime for an individual to belong to an "enterprise" that is involved in a pattern of racketeering, even if the racketeering was committed by other members. Specifically, Section 1962 of RICO prohibits "any person" from: a) using income received from a pattern of racketeering activity or from the collection of an unlawful debt to acquire an interest in an enterprise affecting interstate commerce; b) acquiring or maintaining through a pattern of racketeering activity or through collection of an unlawful debt an interest in an enterprise affecting interstate commerce; c) conducting or participating in the conduct of the affairs of an enterprise affecting interstate commerce through a pattern of racketeering activity or through collection of an unlawful debt; or d) conspiring to participate in any of these activities.

In order for an individual or organization to be convicted of racketeering under RICO, there must be proof of a "pattern" of illegal offenses, which RICO defines as the commission of at least two identified criminal offenses within a 10-year period. RICO defines racketeering in an extremely broad manner and includes many offenses that do not ordinarily violate federal statutes: "any act or threat involving murder, kidnapping, gambling, arson, robbery, bribery, extortion, or dealing in narcotic or other dangerous drugs, which is chargeable under state law and punishable by imprisonment for more than one year."

In addition, RICO lists numerous federal offenses that the statute defines as racketeering: bribery, sports bribery, counterfeiting, embezzlement from union funds, loan sharking, mail fraud, wire fraud, obstruction of justice, contraband cigarettes, prostitution and trafficking in people, bankruptcy fraud, drug violations, and obscenity. As long as the "racketeering activity" is "chargeable" or "indictable" under an applicable criminal statute, the substantive RICO charge is available.

RICO creates offenses and penalties, above and beyond those proscribed for specific criminal offenses, for those involved in an ongoing illegal enterprise that engages in racketeering. The maximum criminal penalties for violating RICO include a $25,000 fine and imprisonment for 20 years.

These penalties are imposed on top of the criminal penalties resulting from two or more substantive offenses that the individual or organization has committed in the 10-year period. In addition to the criminal penalties, there are forfeiture provisions requiring the violators to forfeit any business or property derived from their illegal offenses.

In addition to criminal actions, RICO permits private plaintiffs and the government to seek redress in a civil action. Indeed, perhaps the most controversial aspect of RICO is that the government can seize and confiscate what it deems to be the proceeds of crime through the civil courts. RICO allows the government or a private citizen to file a civil suit requesting the court to forfeit assets, order sanctions, or to provide injunctive relief against an individual or organization involved in a "pattern of racketeering." The civil action provisions of RICO can: force a defendant to forfeit any interest in property, restrict a defendant from engaging in certain future activities or investments, or dissolve or reorganize an enterprise. These penalties were intended to address the economic roots and organizational infrastructure of ongoing criminal conspiracies.

With respect to asset forfeiture, the state can seize property without notice, upon an *ex parte* application of probable cause that the property is associated with criminal activity. In this case, criminal charges need not be provided against a defendant. In contrast to criminal prosecutions, where the burden of proof is beyond a reasonable doubt, only the lesser standard of proof—a balance of probabilities—is required under the civil provisions of RICO. The attraction of this approach is that the onus of proof is shifted to the defendant who must prove that assets were acquired through legitimate means. Civil RICO injunctions can prohibit individuals from owning or becoming involved in certain legitimate or illegitimate businesses or activities. Moreover, if successful, the victim may be able to recoup treble damages (that is, the defendant must pay to the plaintiff three times the amount of damages, as well as legal expenses, that have been determined by a court).

While it took some time for federal prosecutors to fully understand and incorporate RICO into their array of prosecutorial tools, the statute has been increasingly used and has realized much success. By 1990, more than 1,000 major and minor organized crime figures had been convicted and given lengthy prison sentences under RICO. "The hierarchies of the five New York LCN [La Cosa Nostra] Families have been prosecuted, and similar prosecutions have dented the LCN hierarchies in Boston, Cleveland, Denver, Kansas City, Milwaukee, New Jersey, Philadelphia, Pittsburgh and St. Louis," the Pennsylvania Crime Commission reported in 1991. Rudolph Giuliani, the former U.S. attorney for the Southern District of New York, who successfully used RICO in prosecuting organized crime cases, points out:

> The federal prosecutor derives a variety of benefits from the RICO statute's definitions of enterprise and racketeering activity. For example, it

is the only criminal statute that enables the government to present a jury with the whole picture of how an enterprise, such as an organized crime family, operates. Rather than pursuing the leader of a small group or subordinates for a single crime or scheme, the government is able to indict the entire hierarchy of an organized crime family for the diverse criminal activities in which that "enterprise" engages. Instead of merely proving one criminal act in a defendant's life, it permits proof of a defendant's whole life in crime.

Giuliani provides an example of the successful RICO prosecution of one of New York's five LCN crime families, arguing it constituted a criminal enterprise that engaged in an ongoing pattern of racketeering. Fourteen defendants were indicted under RICO as leaders, members, or associates of the Colombo crime family. In establishing that an "enterprise" existed, the indictment identified three bosses and five under-bosses of the family, all of whom were all charged with supervising and protecting the criminal activities of the subordinates of the criminal enterprise. The ongoing nature of the enterprise was demonstrated by the fact that the Colombo family selected an acting boss to direct its criminal activities while the head of the family was in jail. According to Giuliani, relying entirely upon traditional conspiracy laws without RICO would not have enabled the government to include all of these individuals within a single prosecution.

In addition, RICO's requirement of proving a "pattern of racketeering activity" and its broad definition of "racketeering activity" allowed the prosecution to join in a single indictment the widely diverse state and federal crimes the Colombo family had engaged in over the past 15 years. Thus, the indictment included charges that the criminal organization had engaged in extortion, labor racketeering, drug trafficking, gambling, loan sharking, and both state and federal bribery violations.

THE COMMISSION CASE

The use of the RICO statute by the U.S. government resulted in one of the most important prosecutions ever brought against organized crime in the United States. On November 19, 1986, in what became known at the Commission Case, several New York Mafia bosses were convicted of conducting the affairs of "the Commission of La Cosa Nostra" in a pattern of racketeering that violated the RICO statutes.

The theory behind the government's case was that the LCN Commission constituted a criminal enterprise and that each defendant had committed two or more racketeering acts in furtherance of the commission's goals. According to the prosecution, the defendants' predicate racketeering acts fell into three categories: 1) management of a multi-family bid-rigging and extortion scheme in the New York concrete industry; 2) conspiracy to organize loan sharking territories on Staten Island; and 3) the murders of Bonanno family boss Carmine Galante and two of his associates in furtherance of the commission's effort to resolve a Bonanno family leadership dispute.

During the course of the trial that resulted from the RICO indictments, defense counsel admitted the existence of the LCN and the Commission. They denied, however, the Commission's involvement in criminal activity, but to no avail: in 1986 all of the defendants, including Carmine Persico, boss of the Colombo Family, Anthony Salerno, boss of the Genovese Family, and Anthony Corallo, boss of the Lucchese Family were found guilty.

While the original purpose of RICO was to address organized crime, the broad wording of the RICO statute, and its failure to define "racketeering," has meant that both the criminal and civil provisions of RICO have been applied to a number of offenses and defendants, and not just those typically associated with organized crime. Other RICO defendants include terrorists, anti-obscenity protesters, adult video and bookstore owners, financial institutions, politicians, doctors, law enforcement personnel, husbands who have been sued by their ex-wives for defrauding them of marital property, construction workers who sexually harassed a female co-worker, and the drivers of a bus company who inflicted property damage during a strike.

THE REACH OF RICO

Court cases have also expanded the reach of RICO. In *Sedima, S.P.R.L. v. Imrex Co.*, the U.S. Supreme Court concluded that RICO is not limited to organized crime, but may be applied to legitimate commercial enterprise businesses. The Belgian company Sedima filed an action against rival Imrex in the U.S. District Court in 1982, alleging that Imrex inflated its purchase prices and costs by preparing fraudulent purchase orders and credit memos. The action was originally dismissed by a lower court on the grounds that no RICO injury occurred, and the court's decision was upheld on appeal.

A PLETHORA OF SUITS

However, the Supreme Court reversed the appellate decision, considerably broadening RICO's scope, and initiating a plethora of civil and criminal suits involving legitimate companies. Following this decision, RICO was increasingly used by the government to prosecute white-collar and corporate crime offenses, as well as unfair trade practices, committed by legitimate companies not associated with organized crime groups.

For example, in 1988 federal prosecutors brought a RICO indictment against a securities firm called Princeton/Newport Partners. Although prosecutors sought less than $500,000 in illegal profits, they required the firm to post a bond of $24 million, which forced the company to declare bankruptcy. Many of the civil suits launched by RICO have not been undertaken by the government, but by private citizens and private sector companies. Arguably, RICO-based legal actions directed toward white-collar and corporate crime are most frequently undertaken by private citizens and companies as civil suits, no doubt attracted by the prospect of treble damages. In a *New York Times* opinion piece, privacy and consumer rights advocates argued that RICO:

> ... is among the few effective tools against economic crime. Law enforcers have used its enhanced criminal penalties against insider trading and government corruption. ... Civil RICO has been a powerful tool against white-collar crime. For example, federal bank regulators have brought suits against those who purportedly looted savings and loans. ... Civil RICO's multiple damages let moderate-income consumers have their day in court too. Victims of retirement home fraud, home improvement fraud, and investment scams have successfully used the law to recover their losses when no other effective remedy was available to them.

Critics of the civil application of RICO to legitimate commercial enterprises argue that RICO is a statute run amok and no one is beyond its reach. Many times a day, unsuspecting citizens and businesses are shocked to find that they are targets of RICO suits. The law's broad civil suit provisions cast a net so wide that virtually any commercial dispute becomes a candidate for civil RICO jurisdiction. ... Most cases involve the kind of commercial disputes that are part and parcel of the complex web of relationships that define the American economy.

In the last few years, hundreds and perhaps thousands of RICO civil suits have been launched alleging white-collar and corporate crime. Some actions initiated in recent years and summarized in the June 2003 edition of the RICO *Law Reporter* include the following:

Health management organizations launched a RICO civil suit against drug manufacturers, claiming that the defendants released inflated average wholesale prices for their drugs on which Medicare-based payments were unable to allege a proper RICO enterprise.

A plaintiff, who claimed he had been fraudulently deprived of control over a corporation by his nephew launched a civil suit under the mail fraud provisions of RICO.

Plaintiffs claiming that they had been defrauded by their company president's moonlighting for another firm sued the president under RICO. An importer sued a bank under RICO asserting that the bank's adverse credit actions had caused it to default on a supply contract.

All of these suits were unsuccessful, primarily because the plaintiffs could not establish that the defendants were engaged in a pattern of racketeering. Despite the frequent civil actions undertaken through RICO, significant limitations remain on the availability of private civil RICO claims. Civil RICO is not available to compensate the economic consequences of personal injuries sustained as a result of a RICO predicate criminal act. Additionally, the Supreme Court has decided that plaintiffs are required to prove that the alleged RICO violation was the proximate cause of their injury. In 1992, the Seventh Circuit Court ruled that civil RICO was also limited by a requirement that either the enterprise or the racketeering activity be economically motivated. However, the Supreme Court eliminated this requirement, allowing for the possibility that purely political, non-economic criminal activity may now fall within the ambit of RICO.

As a result of this decision, civil RICO actions have been undertaken to address non-economic "criminal" activity. For example, RICO have been used successfully by abortion clinics to sue anti-abortion protest groups for damages. A jury in the case awarded the plaintiff abortion clinics $86,000 in April 1998, based on RICO claims of extortion, conspiracy, and threats of violence. The court also retained jurisdiction for 12 years to enforce a permanent injunction barring the defendants from further blockades of abortion clinics.

RICO has also been used in the context of labor prosecutions. In June 1988, the U.S. district attorney for the Southern District of New York filed a motion under RICO seeking to have the entire executive board of the International Brotherhood of Teamsters (IBT) removed from office and replaced by a federally appointed trustee. The premise underlying this action was that the IBT was so extensively influenced and controlled by organized crime as to constitute a corrupt organization, and its officers were so involved in racketeering that they must be removed from office.

CRITICISMS

RICO has been at the center of vociferous criticisms. Author Howard Abadinsky cites four basic criticisms of RICO that have been raised: First, RICO is overreaching, leading to the prosecution of individuals who, although they may have been involved in criminal behavior, are not by any stretch of the imagination connected to organized crime.

Second, invoking RICO can result in assets being frozen even before a trial begins, an action that can effectively put a company out of business. The threat of freezing assets can induce corporate defendants to plead guilty even when they believe themselves to be innocent.

Third, a RICO action brings with it the stigma of being labeled a racketeer which may be inappropriate given the circumstances at issue.

Fourth, RICO permits lawsuits for triple damages when ordinary business transactions, not organized crime or racketeering, are at issue.

To these four, we can add one more: the application of the civil legal process to criminal offenses, which is an easier way for the government to combat organized crime, yet may contravene the right of the defendant to her right to due process accorded as part of a criminal charge.

SEE ALSO
organized crime; racketeering; corruption, Giuliani, Rudolph; Green, Mark; bribery; prosecution.

BIBLIOGRAPHY. Howard Abadinsky, *Organized Crime* (Wadsworth Publishing, 2003); Rick Boucher, "Trying to Fix a Statute Run Amok," *New York Times* (March 12, 1989); Richard L. Bourgeois, Jr., S.P. Hennessey, Jon Moore, and Michael E. Tschupp, "Racketeer Influenced and Corrupt Organizations," *American Criminal Law Review* (v.37/2, 2000); Rudolph Giuliani, (1986). "Legal Remedies for Attacking Organized Crime," *Major Issues in Organized Crime Control* (U.S. Department of Justice, 1986); T.F. Harrison, "Look Who's Using RICO," *ABA Journal* (February, 1989); G.L. Mangum, "RICO versus Landrum-Griffin as Weapons against Union Corruption: The Teamster Case," *Labor Law Journal* (v.40/2, 1989); Joseph Nocera, "Drexel Hanged Without a Trial, *New York Times* (December 30, 1988); Abdon Pallasch and Judy Peres, "Abortion Foes Suffer a Big Setback," *Chicago Tribune* (April 21, 1998); Pennsylvania Crime Commission, *A Decade of Change: 1990 Report* (Pennsylvania Crime Commission, 1991); F..Shah, "Broadening the Scope of Civil RICO: Sedima S.P.R.L. v. Imrex Co.," *University of San Francisco Law Review* (v.20/2, 1986); Waldman and Gilbert, "RICO Goes to Congress: Keep the Teeth in White Collar Law," *New York Times* (March 12, 1989).

STEPHEN SCHNEIDER, PH.D.
RYERSON UNIVERSITY, CANADA

Reagan, Ronald (1911–2004)

RONALD REAGAN SERVED as the 40th President of the United States from 1981 to 1989. The former film actor turned to politics after serving in various positions such as the president of the Screen Actors Guild (SAG) and as the spokesmen for General Electric. Then in 1967, he was elected governor of California, which would eventually open the doors that led him to the White House.

His politics were conservative, focusing heavily on tax cuts, pro-military government, and anti-communism. "Reaganomics," as his economic policy was usually referred to, was supposedly similar to the traditional principles that helped form the foundation of the American way of life. Unfortunately, Reagan's economic policy suffered from numerous contradictions, the chief among these being that increased defense spending together with cuts in taxes for corporations and rich individuals would somehow result in a balanced federal budget. The result was a quadrupling of the federal debt in just eight years. Aside from his support of big business interests, Reagan is most widely known for yet another declaration of a war on drugs, the fourth such war in the last century.

Reagan's involvement in political scandal was widespread. In fact, over 120 of his appointees resigned due to being indicted, convicted, or being under an unethical cloud. This is the largest number of corruption cases of any administration in American history.

IRAN-CONTRA

In 1986, the Reagan administration was faced with the Iran-Contra scandal that dealt with policy decisions based on anti-communism, covert operations and, a subsequent cover up. The controversy arose when members of Reagan's administration agreed to sell arms to the Iranian government for the release of American hostages held in Lebanon and elsewhere. The administration gave the revenue from the sale to the anti-communist rebels, the Contras in Nicaragua. These events were investigated and there was a national hearing in 1987. The Congressional investigating committee stated that Colonel Oliver North, a White House staffer, had violated the law, but later court trails failed to convict him. This act by the Reagan administration violated the Arms Export Control Act, the Boland Amendment, and the National Security Act of 1947.

Previously, Congress had declared that it was unlawful to sell arms for hostages and to support civil wars on foreign soil without Congressional approval. Under the Boland Amendment, Congress also ordered all military aid to the Contras ceased (after it was discovered that the CIA mined the harbor in Nicaragua's capital). The Reagan White House hired an entire group of ex-military members, along with arms dealers and former CIA officials, that became known as the Enterprise to sell arms to Iran and send some of the profits from that sale to the Contras. Reagan's administration also solicited secret contributions from rich Republicans and foreign governments, in violation of the Boland Amendment.

The Tower Commission that investigated the Iran-Contra scandal did not feel that the President was directly responsible for the scandal. The commission did, however; criticize Reagan for his lack of supervision over his subordinates. They argued that it was his supervision deficiency in this area that created the atmosphere for the scandal to occur. Special prosecutor Lawrence Walsh was quoted as saying that Iran-Contra will be remembered in history "as a non-sordid disregard of constitutional restraints. ... I think the president was wrong, he was defiant, he was deliberate, but he wasn't dirty."

THE S&L SCANDAL

In the mid-1980s, the Reagan administration was faced with another scandal, the savings and loan (S&L) debacle. Reagan believed in a *laissez-faire* government, which would let private enterprise expand with minimal government interference. Reagan wanted state and local governments to assume more responsibility for government programs, decreasing the power of the national government over the American people. This idea was labeled New Federalism; it was not very successful.

The savings and loan industry, prior to the Reagan administration, was heavily restricted in the types of loans that bankers could make. During the 1980s, the restrictions were taken off and extensive, unsound loans were made throughout the S&L industry. When the various banks went bankrupt, investors lost practically all of their money as the government insurance policy only covered $100,000 their deposits. Reagan's belief in a free economy motivated him to remove the restrictions that had been placed on the lending policies of the S&L industry. Sixty percent of all the S&L failures at the time involved fraud. Some even involved the Central Intelligence Agency and organized crime laundering money, the sale of worthless junk bonds, and corrupt S&Ls trading properties on paper in order to fool auditors. There were also many bad loans made to real estate developers and foreign countries.

The administration's timid enforcers repeatedly blocked or slowed attempts by regulators in the field to clamp down on reckless S&Ls. Reagan's actions, which were designed to fuel the economy, unfortunately ultimately undermined the entire S&L industry. Reagan hoped to go back to a classical,

A popular president, Reagan nevertheless "sleepwalked" through various scandals that compromised his presidency.

free-enterprise, capitalist system. Often referred to as supply-side economics, Reagan anticipated decreasing or removing government regulation of industry and to cut both corporate and individual taxes. It was ideally planned that the lower amount of regulation and lower taxes would encourage both businesses and people to invest more and spend more.

THE HUD SCANDAL

The Housing and Urban Development (HUD) scandal dealt with influence peddling in low-income housing program. The Reagan administration viewed federal housing programs as little more than welfare handouts, and would have preferred eliminating HUD from government completely. The Reagan budget slashed HUD staff from 16,000 to 11,000, as well as reduced federal housing subsidies over a period of years from $26 billion to less than $8 billion. HUD had been turned into "grab-bag" for the politicians in the Reagan administration. They allegedly used the money, which was meant for the housing of the poor to further enrich themselves. Reagan administration officials and some of their friends were paid outrageous fees while acting as consultants to HUD. HUD funds were used as political ploys to obtain votes for Republican candidates. While it is a felony to use federal grant money for political purposes, while campaigning for New Jersey Republican Milicent Fenwick, Reagan said he would award HUD grants to New Jersey but only if Fenwick was elected.

THE EPA SCANDAL

The Environmental Protection Agency (EPA) scandal occurred when the Reagan administration claimed executive privilege to withhold agency documents from Congressional committees. A House committee claimed that in 1983 that Theodore B. Olson, an assistant attorney general had given false and misleading testimony in a bitter dispute about Congressional access to EPA enforcement documents. It was a political fight concerning whether the Reagan administration was adequately enforcing hazardous waste cleanup provisions of the Superfund law. Critics contend Reagan opened acre upon acre of government land for commercial purposes and protected corporations that were dumping and poisoning the environment. Reagan watched out for commercial interests of big business to the detriment of the environmental interest. The large amount of money taken and used for personal use by the Reagan administration in both the HUD and the EPA was suspiciously criminal.

One leading interpretation of the Reagan era is Haynes Johnson's *Sleep Walking Through History*. This book argues that Reagan was a true believer in his conservative philosophy, but had a hands-off attitude when it came to supervising his subordinates. Idealism and cynicism, claims Johnson, motivated the admittedly zealous young men in the White House to conspire and force upon the president their newly discovered principles of economic truth. They seemed divided between a sincere belief that they were creating a better way and a simultaneous conscious pursuit of self-interest and greed. This idea of a "sleepwalking" approach to management style may be an effective way to understand how so many scandals occurred during the Reagan era.

The Reagan administration was certainly not unique in its legacy of scandals. Numerous public opinion polls revealed that a majority of Americans liked Reagan's personally, but disagreed with his policies, and were alarmed by the Reagan era scandals.

SEE ALSO

HUD scandals; Boland Amendment; savings and loan fraud; Iran-Contra; North, Oliver.

BIBLIOGRAPHY. Jack Anderson, *War, Peace, and Politics: An Eyewitness Account* (Tom Doherty, 1999); Haynes Johnson, *Sleepwalking Through History: The Reagan Years* (Simon & Schuster, 1991); David R. Simon, *Elite Deviance* (Allyn & Bacon, 2002); Lawrence Walsh, *Iran-Contra: The Final Report* (Times Books, 1994).

DAVID R. SIMON, JAMES FANNING
UNIVERSITY OF NORTH FLORIDA

real estate fraud

REAL ESTATE AND LAND swindles have been the dark side of the important American aspiration of property ownership for all. While some schemes seem to emphasize the opportunity to speculate, to get rich for little investment, others target the average homeowner with the vision of a vacation or retirement paradise. Fraudulent deals have ranged from vacation land in Maine which appears to be solid ground only in the winter, to promises of prosperity in land surrounding the Hoover dam near Las Vegas, Nevada.

All of these schemes seem minor compared to perhaps the original American land fraud: the Yazoo lands of western Georgia, (now comprising the states of Alabama and Mississippi.) In 1789, members of the Georgia legislature authorized the sale of more than 25 million acres to three land companies for $237,580. Six years later they sold some 35 million acres to four more companies for $500,000, basically given away land for 1-1/2 cents an acre. The land companies sold shares in the land back to legislators, who stood to profit when promoters sold to northern investors. One of the victims was Robert Morris, signer of the Declaration of Independence. Even after a new legislature was voted in and rescinded the deal, the land companies continued to sell tracts to unsuspecting speculators in New England and the mid-Atlantic states. The problem passed to the U.S. government when Georgia ceded the land to the United States. Eventually, the Supreme Court found in favor of land holders, ruling that original land grants were valid contracts, and that the later attempt to rescind was in violation of constitutional protection of contracts. In 1814 shareholders were awarded $4.7 million. One author characterized this as a decision that "the land had been originally stolen fair and square."

FRONTIER FRAUD

Western town-site fraud became synonymous with the frontier. Perhaps the earliest was Rolling Stone Colony, Minnesota territory in 1852, promoted by William Haddock. He advertised and promoted the town as a thriving metropolis with lecture hall, library, and hotel and actually sold land to some 400 buyers who attempted to find the site, only to be told that it was on Sioux land.

But on the frontier, the line between town booster and outright con could be a very thin one. Visionary and political maverick Ignatious Donnelly was forever linked to a land deal gone bad in the Minnesota territory in the 1850s. Donnelly himself moved to the community and produced a prospectus depicting a thriving new city with courthouse, churches, and stores. A newspaper, the *Nininger Daily Bugle*, was full of ads for all kinds of business. Like most good fiction, this one relied on the wealth of colorful detail, invoking the image of a prime lot "just west of the dry goods store on First Street."

While Donnelly always maintained that Nininger was the beginning of a futuristic utopian community, after a monetary crash in 1857, he found himself as the only inhabitant and his enemies later depicted the entire affair as a classic swindle. "Every name and every business was entirely fictitious." In fact, Donnelly later became famous for a book of fiction, which made the famous lost continent of Atlantis seem like a reality.

Although Donnelly may have been a true and well-meaning futurist caught in one of the 19th century's frequent monetary crashes, some would argue that American railroads in the 19th century did much the same thing, promoting and selling farm land along their lines far west of known arable land. Meanwhile, town-site fraud and town-lot jumping was more than common; it was ubiquitous in the new boomtowns of the mining west, communities where there was little established law. Land fraud, especially in the west is closely related to mining swindles, especially those involving salted mines. Both types of fraud relied on and elaborate prospectus, the promise of outsized profits, and fast-talking salespeople.

CLASSIC FLORIDA FRAUD

The classic American real estate swindle is the great Florida land boom of the 1920s. At its height, in 1925-26, more than $7 billion changed hands. Whole communities platted on maps, described in detail prospectuses, and pictured in colorful brochures, but never built, lured northerners with promises of low down-payments and low monthly payments. While Charlie Ort developed Key Largo City, Kenneth Roberts planned Wyldewood Park near Ft. Lauderdale, erecting a sign, "Million dollar hotel to be built here," and unloading the surrounding property at highly inflated prices.

The Mizner Brothers, Addison and Wilson, became the symbols of this boom, planning the most extravagant communities and promoting them with the most extravagant promises. Their El Camino Real was to be the broadest highway in the world, leading to their new Mecca, Boca Raton, Florida. While still awaiting construction of the grand canal, investors were induced to purchase expensive lots in the exclusive new community. In what was afterward seen to be a classic bubble, the prices skyrocketed. Addison Mizner himself offered $50,000 to buy back a lot he had previously sold, but owner Lytle Hull would not sell for $100,000. After the bust, the lot was worth only $200.

One con led inevitably to another, and to promote his land, Mizner once buried some gold doubloons in Boca Raton harbor and generated much publicity when they later found "pirate gold." Ort, not to be outdone, buried a crock of gold at Key Largo Sands. This first Florida boom victimized mostly the wealthy and upper middle class, but ironically, the Florida land in Boca Raton did become valuable, though many decades later. When land prices recovered after World War II, it led only to another boom, this one targeting retirees.

Land frauds did not end with town site frauds, or with real estate bubbles like the Florida land boom. In fact, with the advent of the internet, a

Both the financing and construction of homes can be subject to real estate fraud and scams.

whole new generation of real estate swindles are being perpetrated every day.

A NEW CRIME WAVE

In December 2003, the Internal Revenue Service (IRS) reported the booming real estate market helped increase mortgage fraud and other phony real estate related schemes. The perpetrators of these schemes ranged from mortgage brokers looking to make a fast buck to drug dealers laundering illegal revenues. "Every year, these fraudulent schemes victimize individuals and businesses from many walks of life, including struggling low-income families lured into home loans they cannot afford, legitimate lenders saddled with over-inflated mortgages, and honest real estate investors fleeced out of their investment dollars."

Through federal tax fraud investigations and money-laundering charges, the IRS is trying to fight real estate fraud. The number of real estate fraud investigations initiated by IRS Criminal Investigation (CI) doubled from 2001 to 2003. Similarly, the average prison term handed out by federal judges to defendants in these schemes nearly doubled over the same period (from 24 months in 2001 to 46 months in 2003). Some of the more common real estate fraud schemes cited by the IRS include:

Land flipping: A buyer pays a low price for property, then resells it quickly for a much higher price. While this may be legal, when it involves false statements to the lender, it is not.

Two sets of settlement statements: One settlement statement is prepared and provided to the seller accurately reflecting the true selling price of the property. A second fraudulent statement is given to the lender showing a highly inflated purported selling price. The lender provides a loan in excess of the property value, and after the loans are settled, the proceeds are divided among the conspirators.

Fraudulent qualifications: Real estate agents assist buyers who would not otherwise qualify by fabricating employment history or credit records.

In these real estate fraud cases, money laundering is often the mechanism used to hide income from the government. Money laundering is the process of attempting to make money earned illegally appear to be legitimate. The IRS says many criminal tax investigations focus on money laundering schemes because it is often inseparable from tax evasion.

A FEW CASES

Two convictions from the IRS case files help illustrate some of the more recent scams:

The settlement of the vast American plains was replete with town-site fraud and deceptive advertising.

On August 18, 2003, in Greenbelt, Maryland, Alton F. Bivins was sentenced to 57 months in prison, three years of supervised release and ordered to pay restitution of $297,188. As the loan officer for the First Capital Acceptance Corporation and Mortgage Corporation of Maryland, Bivins assisted his sister, Karen Bivins, and Donald Osorio in spending their drug proceeds to purchase real estate. As the loan officer, Alton Bivins submitted false loan applications and documentation, including false tax records and false employment verification, to obtain the mortgage loans. The drug proceeds of Osorio and Karen Bivins were used for down payments and closing costs to complete the transactions. The properties involved were valued at over $1.1 million.

On September 17, 2003, in Des Moines, Iowa, Steven Tod Davis was sentenced to 37 months in prison on bank fraud and money laundering charges. Davis was also ordered to serve five-years supervised release, fined $10,000 and ordered to pay restitution of $1,860,403.50. At his plea, Davis said he formed a company called Eastgate Development to purchase and develop a 40-acre parcel of land in Ames, Iowa. The land was to be developed into commercial lots for resale. During November and December 1997, he raised a total of $1.2 million from 24 investors, each of whom contributed about $50,000 for the purchase of the land. Davis further admitted that in May 1998, he obtained a $1.8 million line of credit from the First National Bank, and in June of 1999 obtained a $1.5 million line of credit from the Hardin County Savings Bank. He explained to both financial institutions that the purpose of the loans was to develop the infrastructure of the property. Davis said he used about $1.8 million of the loan money for purposes other than developing the property, including using the money for his own personal use and injecting funds into other business ventures. He also admitted that he used $300,000 of the money to make a payment on a jet aircraft loan with another financial institution.

SEE ALSO

bank fraud; forgery; scams; savings and loan fraud; contractor fraud.

BIBLIOGRAPHY. Ralph Hancock and Henry Chafetz, *The Compleat Swindler* (Macmillan, 1968); M.C. Bob Leonard, "Florida in the 1920s," www.floridahistory.org (2003); Carl Sifakis, *Hoaxes and Scams: A Compendium of Deceptions, Ruses, and Swindles* (Facts On File, 1993); Internal Revenue Service, "Real Estate Fraud Investigations Increase," www.irs.gov (February 2004).

JANE G. HAIGH
UNIVERSITY OF ARIZONA

redlining

THE TERM *redlining* originated in the insurance industry where insurance executives would draw a red line around a neighborhood to be excluded or treated differently. Defined as the refusal or an inequality of service to a specific geographic region based upon income and/or race, it has been common in the banking and insurance industries. Banks practice redlining when they refuse to accept checks over a certain amount from customers, or when they assign disproportionately higher loan costs, interest rates, loans greater than real value, loans with no regard to borrower's income, loan/property flipping, balloon payments, or negative amortization. Neighborhoods where such practices are commonplace can become devastated by loss of equity and mortgage foreclosure.

The disparity of loan refusals between whites and minorities has been on a steady rise. African-Americans are twice as likely to be turned down for loans when compared to white applicants of similar circumstances. Latinos are one-and-a-half times more likely to be turned down compared to white applicants. And residents, regardless of race, in low-income areas are three times more likely to be turned down as those in upper-income areas when applying for a conventional mortgage. But even when income is held constant, racial redlining is still present.

For example, upper-income African Americans are more likely to be denied a loan or mortgage than middle-income whites. Legislation passed to curb the practice of redlining includes Home Ownership Protection Act (HOEPA), the Community Reinvestment Act (CRA), and the Home Mortgage Disclosure Act (HMDA).

Insurance companies, on the other hand, are not regulated by the laws of Congress but by the states. The states have mostly left laws that govern the practice of insurance sales largely unenforced.

Because of this, it is hard to obtain data needed to calculate and plot the depth and seriousness of insurance redlining.

In the late 1990s and early 2000s, technological advances brought a new type of redlining called electronic redlining. Electronic redlining is defined as the refusal of broadband, high-speed internet access to a poor and/or minority neighborhood. In 2002, a lawsuit was filed against AT&T for discriminatory practices in favoring white neighborhoods.

Redlining is not exclusive to the United States. For example, in South Africa, with its unique history, this is an especially prevalent problem. Since the country is still recovering from a long period of apartheid, there are generations of animosity and hostility along racial lines. The South African Parliament attempted to introduce the Community Reinvestment Bill that would prohibit redlining. But after stiff opposition from the banking community and lobbyists, the bill was withdrawn for further consideration. In 2002, the Banking Council agreed that it is not feasible or acceptable to issue loans to "anarchic" areas. On the other hand, in areas where this is not the case, it is not acceptable to refuse lending based on race or income.

SEE ALSO

insurance fraud; racial discrimination; Consumer Product Safety Commission Act.

BIBLIOGRAPHY. U.S. Congress, "Consumer Product Safety Act," www.herc.org/library (2003); "Reporting Requirements Under the Consumer Product Safety Act," Lectric Law Library, www.lectlaw.com/files (2003); "Consumer Product Safety Act," U.S. Consumer Product Safety Commission, www.cpsc.gov/businfo (2003); David Jones "AT&T Broadband Faces Redlining Suit," United Press International (August 16, 2002).

ARTHUR HOLST, PH.D.
WIDENER UNIVERSITY

reform and regulation

EARLY SCHOLARS of white-collar crime, including Edwin Sutherland, recognized that the dominant legal response to crimes by businesses was regulatory rather than penal. Regulatory enforcement occurs in only a very small percentage of the cases in which it could be applied, and it has far less of the moral outrage and stigma associated with the criminal justice system. The regulatory justice system has a lower profile and is less likely to involve an adversarial confrontation between two parties than the criminal and civil justice systems.

Regulation has been very broadly defined as any attempt by the government to control the behavior of citizens, corporations, or sub-governments, but there is no real consensus on its meaning. Regulation typically involves the imposition of official standards and rules on some form of productive human activity, and it includes an enforcement mechanism and some type of sanctions. It can involve rate-setting, licensing, and financial disclosure requirements, among other stipulations.

A distinction is often made between economic regulation, which addresses market relations (for example, securities, antitrust matters, interstate commerce) and attempts to ensure stability in this realm, and social (or protective) regulation, which addresses harmful consequences to workers, consumers, and citizens of productive activities. Although significant interaction occurs between these two forms of regulation, the social form in particular has expanded greatly since the early 1970s. Because social or protective regulation is much less likely than economic regulation to serve business interests and involves an inherent conflict between the regulator and the regulated, it is met with far more resistance from business interests. Social regulation typically arises following a crisis, tragedy, or panic over some industrial condition or practice. In response to public pressure, the government reluctantly develops regulatory agencies and rules, which the affected industry initially resists and then lobbies to limit in scope. Regulatory laws and enforcement practices are often weak at the outset but may become more potent over time.

MODELS OF REGULATION

There is no single theory or model of regulation. One approach views regulation primarily as a rational means of protecting the public interest. A second, economic approach to regulation emphasizes a cost/benefit analysis oriented toward efficiency. (Although this perspective does not necessarily address the important question of how costs and benefits are defined). A third approach is essentially political; it views regulation primarily in terms of competing interests and the extension of power. Neo-Marxist versions of a political approach to regulation see it as a mechanism for maintaining elites' power and privileges; in this view regulated agencies are dominated by the industries they are supposed to regulate.

AMERICAN REGULATION

The American experience with regulation has been one of ongoing tension between calls for more and calls for less regulation of a wide range of activities. Regulatory and deregulatory cycles have occurred throughout U.S. history. The first major period of federal regulatory expansion in the 20th century occurred during the Progressive Era (1900-14), when populist sentiments against the abuses of big business became sufficiently intense to promote significant government intervention in harmful corporate and occupational activities on behalf of the public interest. In reality, however, much of the regulation developed during this period was supported by and benefited the newly regulated big businesses. For example, the implementation of the Pure Food and Drug Act (1906) that exposed the horrendous conditions in meatpacking plants clearly benefited the larger meat producers by promoting consumer confidence in "government inspected" meat while smaller meatpacking firms that were unable to absorb the added cost of regulation frequently went out of business.

A second major period of regulatory initiatives occurred during the New Deal Era of the 1930s, at least in part inspired by the belief that the 1929 stock market crash and the economic Depression that followed had resulted from unregulated abuses by financiers and major corporations. In an effort to re-establish confidence in failed banks and in the stock market, the Federal Home Loan Bank Board (FHLBB), the Federal Deposit Insurance Corporation (FDIC), the Securities and Exchange Commission (SEC), and the National Labor Relations Board (NLRB) were established during this period. These agencies were granted considerable autonomy, although this hardly made them immune to either political pressures or lobbying by corporate and business interests.

A third, major period of expanding federal regulation began in the relatively affluent Great Society Era of the 1960s and early 1970s. The predominantly social regulation of this time was responsive to a growing awareness of, and organized protest by consumers, environmentalists, and workers against harmful corporate activities. The Consumer Product Safety Commission (CPSC), the Environmental Protection Agency (EPA), the Occupational Safety and Health Administration (OSHA), and the Mining Enforcement and Safety Administration were all established between 1970 and 1973. These agencies operate under more direct control of the Executive branch than is true of the New Deal agencies, and they tend to be more directly responsive to the political agenda of the incumbent administration.

A reasonably high level of consensus on the desirability of government regulation in many new areas eroded in the second half of the 1970s. This period of deterioration of the economy (including rising inflation and declines in industrial productivity and U.S. competitiveness abroad) enabled critics of government regulation to advance much more effectively the argument that federal regulation had become oppressive and economically harmful.

COSTS AND BENEFITS

In 1980, Ronald Reagan ran for president on a platform that was highly critical of a bloated government, and his election was a major factor in the deregulatory era of the 1980s. During this decade regulation was scaled back or severely constrained in many areas (for example, consumer protection and antitrust), especially when politically dominated agencies were able to act on a discretionary basis.

The general tendency in an expanding and increasingly complex society is for regulation to grow. An ongoing debate centers on the moral rightness, desirability, and expedience of such regulation, whether there is currently too much or too little regulation, and whether specific regulatory statutes, agencies, policies, and actions are or are not defensible. Opponents of regulation have claimed that it is an infringement on the individual's freedom and economic rights; that at least some of the regulated activity (for example, insider trading) is essentially victimless; that regulation is economically inefficient; and that alternative processes exist for dealing with harmful activities that are organizationally and more efficient than regulation, and incorporate greater accountability and due process.

More specifically, governmental regulation has been accused of stifling innovation, accelerating inflation, increasing unemployment, and decreasing international competitiveness.

The direct costs of regulation have increased exponentially since the early 1970s, and industries and businesses frequently complain about the excessive paperwork and cost ($100 billion in 1980) involved in compliance. Social or protective regulation was especially criticized as unreasonable, contradictory, counterproductive, and administered by self-interested regulatory bureaucracies.

The accurate measurement of the costs and benefits of regulation is complex. Various parties have incentives to inflate costs or conceal benefits, and there is no single way of interpreting either costs or benefits. It is especially difficult to measure some long-term benefits of regulation, particularly in matters of health, safety, and environmental protection.

Furthermore, there is no complete consensus on regulatory purposes and goals. A leftist or progressive critique has argued that the principal objective of regulatory agencies in a capitalist society is to maintain broad popular legitimacy of the system which is accomplished by adopting regulation that only symbolizes governmental oversight, because regulatory agency effectiveness is severely limited by inadequate budgets and pro-industry regulatory board members who develop specific rules that favor industry interests.

Proponents of regulation contend that it is absolutely necessary in a complex society in which anticompetitive forces with economically undesirable consequences can develop unless the state intervenes, because individuals and communities don't have the means to protect themselves from a wide range of directly harmful or threatening corporate and business activities. Furthermore, corporations have an uncommon measure of power in shaping perceptions of risks, because the capabilities of assessing both risk-related information and realistic options for self-protection are not equally distributed in society. Defenders of regulation argue that factors ranging from bad management to declining markets, not the great expansion of federal regulation in the 1970s, were the principal causes of the economic distress of that period.

In this view, businesses actually benefit from federal regulation because without it they would likely face a much greater number of conflicting state regulations and more civil suits from workers, consumers, and citizens. Even if such regulation cannot be shown to pay in terms of short-term market efficiency, other interests, such as protecting workers and the environment, should take precedence. Many polls reveal general public support for regulatory protection, especially in health, safety, and environmental matters. Altogether, the pro-regulatory argument holds that this activity prevents and deters much activity that could be labeled white-collar crime, and that in its absence, much harm occurs.

REGULATORY AGENCIES

Federal regulatory agencies are created by Congressional action, or specifically by an enabling statute. Some agencies are structured as executive branch departments, whereas others are set up as relatively independent entities, although it is not clear that the latter structure is less susceptible to political influence than the former.

Regulatory agencies are typically directed by a commission, the members of which are appointed by the president and subject to Congressional confirmation. Because they are political appointees, these top agency administrators generally serve only during the term of their presidential sponsor; the managerial personnel below them, however, are more often civil servants who work for the agency over an extended period of time. The managerial personnel of these agencies may be required to have appropriate technical expertise, although the degree of emphasis on expertise and the autonomy of the agency varies.

Regulatory agencies have three basic functions: rule-making, administration, and adjudication. Regulatory rule-making has been supported on the grounds that it allows for more flexible responses to developing circumstances and often requires specialized scientific or technical knowledge that resides in regulatory agencies. It also frees the Congress of the enormous burden of passing thousands of rules, and it diminishes the political consequences of unpopular or contested rules. On the other hand, the legislative oversight process for regulatory rule-making has become quite cumbersome, and it has been recognized that the rule-making process can be distorted by many political or other inappropriate considerations. Industry and business lobbying groups, for example, often succeed in delaying the implementation of new rules they find threatening to their interests.

In recent years federal regulatory agencies have been issuing as many as 7,000 rules and regulations annually, as compared with some 300 public laws enacted annually by Congress. Many of these regulatory rules are relatively minor. In contrast to criminal laws, regulatory rules are likely to be more ambiguous, tend to focus on the risk (not the occurrence) of harm, and are geared toward liability, not criminal intent.

The investigatory process of regulatory agencies typically involves a mixture of reactive and proactive strategies; more visible offenses (especially those involving formal complaints) generally take priority over the more complex, costly proactive investigations in which agencies take the initiative. Violations come to the attention of regulatory agencies from many sources, including consumer complaints, government investigations, Congressional committee investigations, business competitors, the media, and employees.

When it is determined that hearings are appropriate, regulatory agencies can act quite informally in many circumstances without observing due-process guidelines. A fairly large body of law, codified in a basic way by the Administrative Procedures Act (APA) in 1946, governs formal agency proceedings. Agency hearings most typically take the form of quasi-criminal proceedings and are less formal then regular court hearings and trials.

Such hearings are presided over by an administrative judge or hearing examiner, who is independent of agency personnel. Defendants can have attorneys, but they are not entitled to a jury trial. Administrative judges and hearing examiners are empowered to impose various orders or sanctions on defendants, including cease-and-desist orders (equivalent to injunctions); special orders (for example, directives intended to correct past conduct, or product recalls); consent orders (negotiations regarding certain actions); summary orders (for example, prevention of the sale of food); and license suspension or revocation.

Administrative agencies can impose some direct sanctions or civil fines. Cases may also be referred for criminal action or may lead to civil suits. Appeals from hearing decisions must first go through an internal agency appeal process and only then are eligible for appellate court review, although appellate courts have typically been reluctant to overturn agency decisions. When agency decisions are overturned, the basis for such reversals is likely to be a determination that the decision was fundamentally arbitrary, capricious, or discriminatory; was not based on substantial evidence; violated applicable constitutional safeguards; or exceeded the statutory authority of the agency.

Regulatory enforcement and decision-making styles vary greatly in terms of regulatory philosophy, regulatory officials' assessment of compliance and noncompliance, and the actions officials take when they identify violations. Many cases are dropped because it is impractical to pursue them further; cases that are pursued may be dealt with by administrative action, civil action, or referral for criminal prosecution. In the 1970s in particular, federal regulatory agencies seemed more willing to support the application of criminal sanctions.

Regulatory agencies confront a basic choice between emphasizing compliance (persuasion and cooperation) or deterrence (prosecution and punishment). In one conceptual scheme, regulatory agencies extend along a continuum from non-enforcers (who engage in cooperative fostering of self-regulation) to rulebook enforcers (who emphasize command and control). In another scheme, four regulatory agency policing styles have been characterized as service, watchman, legalistic, and free agent.

The first two styles favor persuasion; the service style displays greater proactive initiative and technical competence than the watchman style, which is industry dominated and reactive. The legalistic and free agent styles are prosecutorial, but the legalistic is more mechanistic and formal, whereas and the free agent style is more informal and autonomous.

Regulatory agencies adopt some mixture of cooperative and punitive approaches. Informality and bargaining, and a norm of accommodation, take precedence over the strict implementation of legal rules for most regulatory agencies. Still, the degree to which cooperative versus punitive strategies should be adopted has been heatedly debated. Many different interacting factors shape regulatory enforcement styles.

These factors include the technical, economic, and legal problems encountered in regulatory implementation; features of the "task environment" (for example, detectability); and the political environment of the regulatory agency. Regulatory laws vary considerably in their stringency and specificity, and the objectives they are promoting in the pursuit of curbing white-collar crime..

REGULATION AND INDUSTRY

Politics is often a potent element in the regulatory agency appointment process, at least in the higher levels of agency staffing. Perhaps unsurprisingly, the ideological commitments of agency administrators apparently have important impacts on agency policies and practices.

If, on the one hand, regulatory agencies have been criticized as too responsive to a political agenda, they have also been criticized on the grounds that they are run by appointed bureaucrats with too much power, too little competence, and too little accountability. On the competence issue, it has been claimed that because government salaries cannot generally compete effectively with private sector salaries, regulatory agencies (especially in lower-level jobs) disproportionately attract individuals with mediocre qualifications. Industry representatives claim that this leads to inefficient, even absurd, over-regulation, whereas critics of industry claim that regulatory personnel are too easily misled and tend to under-regulate.

It is commonly conceded that regulatory agencies are greatly under-staffed and under-funded, given their responsibilities. Public pressure for agency action is small relative to that for conventional crime, and business interests have traditionally lobbied for various limitations on agency powers and budgets. OSHA, for example, has several hundred inspectors with responsibilities relating to several million businesses; the SEC has an annual budget in the tens of millions of dollars to police financial transactions in the hundreds of billions of dollars. These agencies increasingly rely on computers to uncover illegal activities, but this use of computer technology raises concern about excessive government intrusion and invasion of privacy.

Even though small businesses may indeed be intimidated by government regulatory agencies, there is good reason to believe that the larger corporations often have an advantage over regulatory agencies. In view of the enormous economic consequences of many regulatory actions, the potential and the reality of corruption are ever-present on all levels. Corruption may be direct or indirect, ranging from outright bribes to prospects of post-government-service jobs with lucrative salaries. The meat industry provides the salaries for inspectors, and this arrangement (however cost-effective for the government) is obviously conducive to corruption. Regulatory personnel may also be compromised by their subservience to powerful political officials, who may in turn put pressure on them on behalf of corporate and individual benefactors. This pattern was exemplified in the Keating Five case involving five prominent U.S. Senators who pressured thrift regulators on behalf of Charles Keating, the head of a major thrift who had donated heavily to their political campaigns.

AGENCY CAPTURE

The concept of agency capture—signified by close and cooperative relationships with regulated industries—has been one part of the critique of regulatory agencies, although there has been considerable disagreement about whether it is appropriately applied to contemporary regulatory agencies. There is no single definition of the agency capture concept, and it has been variously applied to situations when little disruption of industry profits occurs; when the level of regulation is minimal and acceptable to industry; and when enforcement of regulatory law is lenient. More specifically, suspicions of agency capture occur when regulatory agency officials with a pro-industry bias are appointed (or when such officials can anticipate lucrative private-industry perks following their government service), and when various forms of inducement or influence, political or psychological, are evident. Other observers have argued that agency capture cannot simply be equated with corruption and does not necessarily lead to corruption.

Some of the typical criteria for identifying agency capture have been criticized. Industry interests are not necessarily unified or in conflict with public interests, although non-industry interests may not be adequately represented within regulatory agencies. Regulatory agency policies that may appear to signify capture may instead reflect a distaste for confrontation and a view of social welfare shared by the regulators and the regulated alike.

Despite such reservations about the notion of agency capture, regulatory agencies (for example, the EPA and the FDIC) have, in various instances, been co-opted by the industries or businesses they are supposed to be regulating. Since at least the 1970s, a number of policies and strategies have been adopted to minimize the chances of agency capture, including prohibiting entry into regulated industries for a significant period of time after regulatory agency service, limiting agency discretion with more specific statutes, and professionalizing agency personnel. Such measures may have diminished but have not eliminated the problem of agency capture.

Altogether, regulatory agencies often find themselves contending with countervailing pro-regulatory and anti-regulatory forces, and as a matter of survival they may have to steer a middle course between these forces. A complex mix of factors, ranging from political pressures to professional pride to greed, are involved in the regulatory process.

SELF-REGULATION

One manifestation of government regulation of business is the notion of self-regulation, or private policing directed at one's own company or professional peers. Self-regulation generally distinguishes white-collar crime from conventional crime; that is conventional criminals are not typically expected to police or regulate their own illegal conduct. Self-regulation is important because government does not even begin to have either the resources or the expertise to police or regulate fully all the activities of corporations, retail businesses, professionals, and legitimate white- and blue-collar entrepreneurs.

Many corporate crimes are instigated or inspired by the highest levels of authority in the corporation, and obviously these executives are unlikely to encourage any investigation of such activity. On various levels, however, corporate executives may cultivate "concerted" or "strategic" ignorance of certain specific, culpable actions as a way of protecting themselves (and the corporation as a whole) from criminal charges. White-collar crime lawyers advise top executives to avoid involving themselves too directly in internal investigations, when allegations of corporate wrongdoing arise, as a way of minimizing the executives' exposure in any subsequent prosecution. Thus, the chief executives may discourage self-policing or distance themselves from any self-policing inquiries.

On the other hand, corporations often expend resources to police themselves because: 1) they are not uniformly indifferent to an ethical obligation to do so; 2) they have a powerful self-interest in maintaining a good public reputation; and 3) they want whenever possible to pre-empt the imposition of the less palatable alternative of governmental regulation.

SEE ALSO
regulatory enforcement; Securities and Exchange Commission; Environmental Protection Agency; Keating Five; compliance programs.

BIBLIOGRAPHY. Hazel Croall, *Understanding White Collar Crime* (Open University Press, 2001); David O. Friedrichs, *White-Collar Crime: Trusted Criminals in Contemporary Society* (Wadsworth Publishing, 1995); Gilbert Geis, Robert F. Meier, and Lawrence M. Salinger, eds., *White Collar Crime: Classic and Contemporary Views* (The Free Press, 1995); Edwin H. Sutherland, *White-Collar Crime* (Yale University Press, 1983); Sally S. Simpson, *Corporate Crime, Law, and Social Control* (Cambridge University Press, 2002).

MICHAEL MCGREGOR
GEORGE MASON UNIVERSITY

regulatory enforcement

EDWIN SUTHERLAND, the noted sociologist who coined the term *white-collar crime*, observed that not only were the criminal activities of business persons less likely to be subject to criminal penalties, but the corporate and business person was likely to be subject to less severe penalties imposed by a regulatory agency. The use of regulatory agencies and administrative measures to punish white-collar criminals is the most marked distinction between white-collar and other criminals. The involvement of agencies other than the police underlines these distinctions.

The term, *regulation*, generally used to describe the structure of law, enforcement, and sanctions surrounding most offenses, is accompanied by different language from that used in conventional crimes. Fraud and financial offenses are more readily regarded as criminal, subject to criminal law and sanctions and more likely to be subject to police investigations.

Laws are enforced by a variety of enforcement agencies, whose main role is the maintenance of standards and public protection. What is often called social regulation is therefore associated with a distinct set of laws and procedures and regulations. Many scholars have distinguished activities that threaten the interests of capital as fraud and theft and ultimately are likely to be subject to stronger criminalization than those that do not threaten the pursuit of profitability.

Traditionally, criminal justice scholars assumed the less severe nature of white-collar crime reflected the influence of high-status and powerful offenders. More recently, scholars have found it difficult to substantiate direct class bias in the regulatory enforcement of white-collar crimes. Others also dispute that regulation is less stringent, arguing instead that the differences between white-collar and other crimes necessitate different laws and enforcement. In turn, however, these arguments have been strongly criticized for accepting the ideological distinction between white-collar crimes and other crimes. Regulation has been subject to considerable research, theorizing, and academic and political discussion. Studies in the sociology of law have examined the nature and development of regulatory law along with the activities of enforcers and the role of class and powers. Discussions have also focused on the most appropriate means of preventing white-collar crime.

HISTORICAL CONTEXT

Regulatory enforcement can be appreciated more clearly by understanding its historical context, which involves the tension between free market, *laissez-faire* principles under which legal intervention is resisted, and liberal, welfare values under which legal intervention is justified as necessary for public protection.

To advocates of free-market principles, intervention is seen as unnecessary because market forces can themselves ensure high standards of production and protect the public. Workers, it is argued, will refuse to work in unsafe workplaces and consumers will avoid buying substandard or unsafe goods. On the other hand, industrial development has continually presented dangers that have not been prevented by market forces. Protective legislation has been premised on an assumed need to strike a balance between the interests of public protection and industrial or commercial development and profitability.

The aims of regulatory laws and agencies tend to stress the need to secure a fair balance between the interests of business, industry, or commerce and those of consumers, workers, or the general public. Moreover, regulators' main aim is said to be to protect the public by encouraging high standards of trading or commerce, with the detection and prosecution of offenses being one among many strategies. Regulatory agencies are not seen as, nor do they see themselves as industrial police officers but as expert advisers or consultants whose aim is to secure compliance to laws and regulations.

Particular legal problems have also surrounded the criminal liability of companies. It is often very difficult to establish that corporations are legally liable. Considerable difficulties surround establishing intent, or *mens rea*, along with the recklessness or gross negligence, where companies rather than individuals are involved because corporations are legal abstractions and have no "soul" or "mind."

One of the most immediate features of white-collar law enforcement is the large number of different agencies involved. Providing a full list of these would be a prohibitive task. However, these agencies have a number of common characteristics. Principal among these common characteristics is the tendency of most agencies to see prosecution as a last resort, reserved for a relatively small proportion of detected offenses. This is particularly true in the area of social regulation, where only a small number of complaints and incidents eventually lead to prosecution.

COMPLIANCE PROGRAMS

The lack of prosecutions is attributed to the use of what are described as compliance strategies, which are most often associated with social regulation but also, apply to financial regulatory bodies. These derive from the nature of regulatory law, which produces a situation in which an agency's main role is seen to be the maintenance of high standards and compliance with regulations. Many agencies pursue advisory and educational roles in which visits or inspections are used to offer expert advice as well as to detect violations.

Enforcement officers and businesses are involved in a continuing relationship in which persuasion is seen to be a better means of encouraging cooperation and compliance. It is often argued that a strict prosecutorial approach would damage this relationship and alienate businesses. When offenses are detected, a typical approach is to persuade businesses to remedy the situation before resorting to formal measures. These measures range from verbal advice, warnings, and cautions to more formal written notices requiring improvements, and official cautions. Prosecution is considered only if those options fail and offenses persist.

Compliance strategies are also related to the range of powers possessed by agencies, many of which are seen as more effective, and on occasion more Draconian, than prosecution. Some agencies have powers to grant or withdraw licenses necessary for a business to operate, and others can close a business, particularly where it poses a direct danger to public health or where previous warnings have been ignored. These powers are considerable because they directly threaten the profitability or survival of a business, although they are often used sparingly. Other regulatory bodies have powers to disqualify company directors, and professional bodies can also "strike off" or otherwise disqualify members. Some agencies can, additionally, negotiate out of court financial settlements and impose financial penalties. In companies, individual offenders may be dismissed rather than prosecuted because companies may fear that publicity could damage their public reputation. Many offenders are therefore dealt with and sanctioned without resort to criminal proceedings.

Many of these strategies are based on considerations of cost-effectiveness. In addition to being seen as less appropriate, prosecution may be avoided on the grounds that it is costly and often risky. Many offenses are complex in nature, which makes them difficult and costly to investigate, detect, and prosecute. These investigations involve time and resources. Serious frauds are particularly costly to investigate because they often involve many participants and have taken place over long periods of time. They may also require the collection and examination of a long paper chain of thousands of documents or interviews with many witnesses, many of whom may be located abroad. These problems are exacerbated where prosecution is contemplated because evidence must be carefully prepared to satisfy legal requirements that are often complex. Trials have gained the reputation of being risky. Therefore, agencies balance the time and costs of protection in less serious regulatory cases with the lower costs of persuasive strategies, especially where a small fine may result from a prosecution.

The low rates of prosecution inevitably raise questions about which offenses and offenders are most likely to be prosecuted, particularly in relation to class bias. Regulatory enforcement was subject to considerable research in the 1970s and 1980s, in which the attitudes and day-to-day practices of enforcement agents were studied to explore the relationship between the "law in books" and "law in action." These studies revealed how the tension between prosecutions and persuasion are played out in practice and variations between and within agencies. These studies largely confirmed that, in general terms, prosecution was reserved for cases with high public profit. Judgments were made about the character of the criminal.

PROSECUTIONS AND CRITICISMS

Enforcers also have stereotypes about types of businesses where offenses are most likely to occur. This leads to some businesses being visited more often and being seen as deserving prosecution. These studies found no conclusive evidence of class bias, however this issue must be placed in the wider political and economic context of business regulation.

The nature and practice of regulatory enforcement have been subject to extensive public and academic debate. The effectiveness of regulatory enforcement has been questioned and the low rate of prosecutions is said to be an insufficient deterrent, although to advocates of free market principles the same rates of prosecution can be seen as excessive. It is seen to constitute favorable treatment for one class of offenders, which raises questions about the fairness and impartiality of criminal law and justice. At the same time, however, the extent to which it does constitute lenient or unfair treatment can be questioned, and it can also be argued that the regulatory approach is necessitated because offenses are more difficult to detect and prosecute than other crimes along with the rationales for regulatory enforcement. These different views are linked to alternative approaches to the reform of regulation.

Criticisms of ineffectiveness have been leveled at both financial and social regulation, although financial regulation attracts stronger public reaction. Financial regulators are often criticized for the length of time required to take actions in fraud cases. Some high-profile cases have also attracted critical attention to social regulation. The failure to prosecute companies for corporate manslaughter following mass deaths and injuries has led to considerable public and academic criticism, and also draws attention to the policies of enforcement agencies. If the threat of prosecution is to be seen as a deterrent, it is argued, it should be a real one, and the widespread use of out-of-court settlements (meaning many offenders are not publicly prosecuted), compounds these problems.

Although allegations of direct class bias are difficult to substantiate, it can nonetheless be argued that higher-status offenders are structurally advantaged. In general terms, the outcome of compliance strategies is that white-collar offenders, who are more often of middle-class status, are less likely to be prosecuted than conventional offenders and it is also the case that some, often more respectable or large businesses, are less likely to be targeted for surveillance or prosecution.

The use of negotiated settlements can also be seen as advantageous, because, irrespective of their effectiveness, they result in fewer prosecutions and may lead to a situation in which wealthy offenders can "buy" themselves out of public prosecution, which carries a greater stigma. Some offenders may also be able to exert political pressure in relation to investigation and prosecution, as has been the case where the investigation of serious fraud has been subject to political intervention.

In addition, although the law, particularly in relation to social regulation, is seen primarily as a deterrent, the criminal law also carries implications of moral disapproval and its legitimacy rests on assumptions of equal treatment. Therefore, whether or not prosecution is cost effective, it is justifiable on moral grounds. Moreover, arguments about the cost-effectiveness of prosecution are applied less to conventional offenders. It could be argued, for example, that it is not particularly cost-effective to prosecute a burglar in that it may not compensate victims, stop the individual from burgling, or deter other burglars, yet few would dispute that burglars should be prosecuted.

The rationale for compliance strategies therefore rests on assumptions that differentiate white-collar offenses and offenders from other offenders. In addition to pointing to the complexity, organizational location, and invisibility of offenses which hamper law enforcement, advocates of compliance strategies make a number of assumptions about offenders. It has been argued, for example, that white-collar and particularly organizational offenders differ from conventional offenders because their activities are socially productive and should not be curtailed, and that they are not recalcitrant criminals but law-abiding citizens who are amenable to

persuasion. Offenses are seen to be a result of incompetence or lack of expertise rather than criminal or deliberate intent, and as incidental rather than central to the operations of the business. Businesses can be persuaded to comply because, ultimately, offending is not in their long-term interests, despite being motivated by short-term desires to avoid the costs of regulation. Corporations are seen as being capable of being socially responsible and are not therefore necessarily only amoral calculators.

These assumptions have been contested by those adopting a Marxist approach, who relate white-collar crime to capitalism and the profit motive. To such critics, regulation must be located in the political and economic structure of capitalism. In particular, the Marxists challenged the contention that businesses are not amoral calculators. Although individual managers and corporations claim to be socially responsible, they nonetheless have a legal responsibility to act in the interests of shareholders and are continually under pressure from shareholders and competitive considerations to maximize profits at all costs.

These pressures necessarily push managers to develop an amoral, calculative attitude to economic activity, to try to act as rational economic actors. Moreover, Marxists argue, the assumption that businesses are persuadable is related to a view that illegalities are marginal to business operations, which accept business rationalizations and is contradicted by the widespread and normal nature of law violations.

The regulation of white-collar crime therefore involves complex issues. The debates and analyses surrounding regulation and cooperative or compliance models, which have dominated the study of white-collar law enforcement, tend to focus on the contrast between policing crime and regulating business.

SEE ALSO

prosecution; compliance programs; reform and regulations; Securities and Exchange Commission; Environmental Protection Agency.

BIBLIOGRAPHY. B. Fisse, J. Braithwaite, and K. Hawkins, "Compliance Strategy, Prosecution Policy and Aunt Sally: A Comment on Pearce and Tombs," *British Journal of Criminology* (v.30, 1990); M. Levi, "The Regulation of Fraud Revisited," *Invisible Crimes: Their Victims and Their Regulation* (Macmillan, 1999); F. Pearce, and S. Tombs, "Ideology, Hegemony, and Empiricism: Compliance Theories and Regulation," *British Journal of Criminology* (v.30, 1990); F. Pearce, and S. Tombs, "Hazards, Law and Class: Contextualizing the Regulation of Corporate Crime," *Social and Legal Studies* (v.6, 1997); F. Pearce and S. Tombs, *Toxic Capitalism: Corporate Crime and the Chemical Industry* (Ashgate, 1998); G. Slapper and S. Tombs, *Corporate Crime* (Addison-Wesley, 1999).

MICHAEL MCGREGOR
GEORGE MASON UNIVERSITY

religious fraud

FROM JOSEPH SMITH, who founded Mormonism after a revelation that still brings charges of a hoax to L. Ron Hubbard and the lawsuit-prone Scientologists, religion and fraud have been inextricably mixed, either as fact or in the perception of non-believers and skeptics. As religion has become more lucrative and media coverage has expanded, the frauds have as well. The particular type of fraud, the huckstering televangelist, peaked in the 1980s. But other sorts of fraud persist. Fraud against the religious can take the form of affinity fraud. And virtually every religion has those who claim that its origins are fraudulent. Further, there are frauds outside organized religion, in the New Age movement, and elsewhere. Finally, frauds arise from true belief: pious fraud.

The 19th century was a time of religious ferment. The Second Great Awakening emphasized the personal religious experience and potential perfectibility. New religions arose, as did new philosophies and reform movements. Mormonism came into being in New York, and millennial cults and utopian communities were scattered across the country. Reform movements such as temperance and abolitionism had religious underpinnings. At the same time, the United States began to commercialize its entertainments, and religion changed to meet the competition from cheap literature and theater and other amusements.

People who wanted to believe were susceptible to charlatans and frauds, who arose as the purveying of religion became profitable. Late in the century the personal religion mixed with science to create pseudoscientific cults such as spiritualism and

brought into being such sects as the Christian Scientists, Seventh Day Adventists, and Jehovah's Witnesses.

Initially, the new commercial religion was free of fraud, and tent and early radio evangelists prospered greatly. From Dwight Moody to Billy Sunday to Father Divine, the charismatic evangelists kept their business dealings legitimate. By the time of Aimee Semple McPherson in the 1920s through the 1930s, the lines were beginning to blur. The evangelists became able to bring in incredible amounts of money through media pitches and the sales of questionable goods.

Effective use of radio and mass solicitation, and the switch from free public access to paid time after the 1960s, meant that evangelists needed more money and had fewer Federal Communications Commission (FCC) restraints on their television programming. The televangelists became looser, more flamboyant, more aggressive in marketing. The crash of the televangelists in the early 1980s would not diminish fraud.

THE 19TH CENTURY

The Church of Jesus Christ of Latter Day Saints, the Mormons, was created in the 1820s when Joseph Smith, Jr., was visited by supernatural creatures, including the Angel Moroni who revealed to Smith the existence of a set of golden plates. Using "magic" spectacles, Smith translated the tablets into the Book of Mormon. Those who regard the story as fraudulent note that Smith had a reputation for telling stories and pulling pranks. He also was a treasure hunter with a "magic stone." And he did have one conviction of disorderly conduct as well, and an 1826 appearance in court on charges of fraud. Smith was accused of fraud, forgery of the book and the tablets, and eventually bank notes. He attempted faith healing, laying on of hands, but reportedly failed.

Christian Science practiced faith healing. Even today, Christian Science rejects modern medicine, preferring a laying on of hands and the healing power of God to cure sickness. Christian Science was founded by Mary Baker Eddy in 1879 on the work of Phineas Parkhurst Quimby who called it the Science of Man. Critics note that Eddy was a heavy abuser of morphine and was a believer in mesmerism. She also supposedly copied or plagiarized Quimby's writings.

In 1884, Charles T. Russell founded the Zion's Watch Tower Tract Society, the Jehovah's Witnesses. Russell had frequent occasions to defend himself on charges of swindling. And he ran afoul of the U.S. government, which debunked his "miracle wheat," as but another of his money-making schemes. Russell also perjured himself in a 1912 libel suit by exaggerating his academic credentials and his knowledge of biblical languages. Apparently, he also lacked ministerial standing in any church other than the one he created.

Spiritualism was also popular in the 1870s and 1880s. At the end of the century, spiritualists were anticipating the millennium and the onset of a utopian New Age. Spiritualists believed in angels and trance-channeling as a means of communicating with the deceased by way of mediums. The spirit table-rapping medium had its origins in upstate New York in 1848 with Margaretta and Kate Fox, who claimed that spirits communicated by rapping tables. Thirty years later, the Fox sisters confessed that they produced the rapping by cracking their toe knuckles. By then, there were tens of thousands of mediums holding séances where objects materialized or levitated and the "spirits" made noises of communication. In the 1920s, Harry Houdini, the escape artist, spent considerable time looking for a legitimate medium, but he found none. Spiritualism remains the belief of many people into the 21st century.

THE 20TH CENTURY

The courts opened the floodgates in 1925 by ruling in *Hygrade Provision Co. v. Sherman* that only intentional fraud was punishable. Good faith, even if in false belief, was sufficient defense. The 1944 case of *United States v. Ballard* affirmed that sincerity was a matter for juries to decide, but truth of belief was not.

The sea change came in the 1930s with radio evangelism, which could reach numbers unimagined by the tent revivalists. The technology changed, but the grift was the same: play on emotions such as fear, anger, passion and induce mass hysteria and rake in the money. Among the most notable of the era was McPherson, the first evangelist to broadcast a sermon. She wore long white gowns, flowers in her hair, and passion in her voice. She eschewed coin, so she hung a clothesline over the believers' heads so they could pin bills and she could reel them in. She was buried with a telephone in her coffin so she could call if God resurrected her.

The radio evangelists were generally more staid. More typical was Father Charles Coughlin, who made his money fighting the left rather than skinning the gullible. The big scams came after World War II, with the switch from radio to television.

TELEVANGELISTS

By definition, the televangelist is a minister, commonly fundamentalist or evangelical Protestant, whose ministry may include a congregation in a physical building but the largest number of whose followers are in a radio or television audience. The prototype was the Catholic Coughlin, anti-communist and eventually anti-New Deal, in the 1930s. Televangelists may or may not be officially ordained. Televangelists may or may not be honest or orthodox. They may practice pseudosciences such as faith healing, or they may be straight frauds. The unscrupulous may provide false promises in return for donations from the gullible. Or they may embezzle or divert funds to personal use.

The televangelism phenomenon boomed and culminated in the 1980s when 45 million "born again" Christians spent $1 billion a year on religious literature and music, and supported 5,000 evangelical schools. The revival tent gave way to the mass revival in the domed stadium, the regular program over one of the four fundamentalist networks broadcasting around the clock. The United States had 1,400 all-gospel radio stations and 30 gospel television stations. And the political clout of the born-again showed in the 1980 Washington for Jesus demonstration that brought 200,000 to the capital. Their political power was evident in the electoral defeats of Senators Dick Clark of Iowa and Thomas McIntyre of New Hampshire who ran afoul of the born-agains, and in the rewriting of public school books. Religion was a huge phenomenon, a gold mine for those who chose to fleece the flock.

The scams of 1978–79 included James Roy Whitby of Oklahoma who swindled an elderly widow out of $25,000 in 1978, and in 1979 was charged with selling $4 million in worthless bonds. One of his associates in the second case, the Reverend Tillman Sherron Jackson, had been involved in the 1973 the Baptist Foundation of America case, whose $26 million fraud led to a 1973 Congressional inquiry. The case ended in acquittals.

Garner Ted Armstrong raked in $75 million a year from the Worldwide Church of God, run by Garner Ted and his father, Herbert W. Followers sometimes donated 30 percent of their incomes to allow Garner to live royally until 1976 when followers protested the son's sexual habits and the father's self-enrichment. Later, the church leaders faced charges of embezzlement and pilfering. The believers had little to show for the upward of $1 billion they had given over the years.

LeRoy Jenkins of South Carolina brought in $3 million a year from selling prayer cloths, healing t-shirts, and miracle water to viewers on 67 television stations. Even after he went to prison for conspiracy to burn the homes of a state trooper and a creditor and to mug a newspaperman, his staff continued to broadcast his taped revival program.

Praise the Lord (PTL) grossed over $50 million at its peak. The Justice Department wanted to look at its books and the FCC had suspicions that the PTL was engaging in fraud and misleading appeals, as it begged for money to save the overseas missions and the PTL itself. Meanwhile its leader, Jim Bakker, and his wife Tammy, were spending extravagantly. One station mockingly referred to PTL as the Pass the Loot club.

The Reverend Hakeem Abdul Rasheed (alias Clifford Jones) and a female associate went to jail for mail fraud in California in 1980 after running a Ponzi scheme, where new donors' contributions paid the old members, with enough left over for the minister. Ponzi schemes are pyramids that inevitably crumble when the requirement for new donors becomes overwhelming.

False claims that its $15.95 Cross of Lourdes product was dipped in a "miracle pool" and had a Papal blessing cost American Consumer Inc. a fine of $25,000 in 1979 for 1,000 counts of mail fraud. The company also refunded $103,000.

Consumer Companies of America was a 20-state chain founded by the Front Brothers Gospel Quartet. For $535, believers bought merchandise and the right to sign up others, receiving commissions on their orders in the manner of Amway and other companies. After living generously, the brothers were convicted of stock violations, sued for fraud, and hit with a tax lien of $370,000. The pyramid scheme collapsed in 1979, and losses were widespread. Embezzlement was the crime of the

Reverend Jerry Duckett of Williamson Church of God in West Virginia, who stole $40,000 from the church building fund.

Jim Jones's People's Temple required members to donate 40 percent of their income and sign over savings accounts, insurance policies, homes, and Social Security and welfare checks. Jones staged phony cancer cures using stooges and sleight of hand removal of chicken gizzard "tumors." Two disillusioned former members revealed Jones' fakery to *New West* magazine. Jones and 900 followers went to Guyana and died, most committing suicide in a paranoid frenzy. People's Temple assets totaling over $13 million were found afterward.

In the early 1970s, A.A. Allen maintained the tent tradition, adding jars of embalmed bodies he said were demons he had removed from the sick (skeptics said they were frogs). His "love offerings" reached $2.7 million a year. He died of alcoholism, and was the one who supposedly said, "When you can turn people on their head and shake them and no money falls out, then you know God's saying 'Move on, son.'"

The Reverend James Eugene Ewing of Los Angeles, California, solicited donations with promises of Cadillacs and other material wealth. He had believers mailing pledges through "God's Gold Book Plan for Financial Blessings." His gross was $4 million a year until a 1977 bankruptcy.

The Reverend Guido John Carcich of the Pallottine Fathers in Baltimore, Maryland, embezzled $2.2 million. He was convicted in 1978. Only 3 percent of the $20 million the group collected reached the "starving, sick, and naked." Carcich told workers in his warehouse to discard prayer requests without money. His sentence was a year as a prison counselor.

In 1973, Rex Humbard's ongoing attempt to sell $12 million worth of "gospel bonds" ran up against a Securities and Exchange Commission (SEC) cease-and-desist order because the commission concluded that Humbard lacked the assets, even though he had a multimillion dollar real estate holding. Humbard begged for donations, and the believers gave, until the millions were sufficient to satisfy the SEC.

In 1979, Julie Titchbourne won a $2 million verdict against the Church of Scientology after the church fraudulently claimed it could increase her I.Q. And Los Angeles jazz guitarist Gabor Szabo sued the church for embezzling $15,000 from him, kidnapping him, and forcing him to spend $12,000 on a "life repair course."

L. Ron Hubbard, founder of Scientology, suffered a French fraud conviction in 1979, and Scientology had a 1980s investigation of charges that it had obtained millions of dollars through fraudulent bank loans.

The top 12 money-makers as of 1980, the heyday of televangelism, grossed a total of between $400 and $425 million, with Garner Ted Armstrong's The World Tomorrow leading with $75 million. Evangelists do not have to disclose their assets because evangelistic enterprises are churches and exempt. Congressman Mark Hatfield and others tried in 1977 to enact disclosure legislation, but it failed. In 1979, Billy Graham led three dozen other revivalists in creating the Evangelical Council for Financial Accountability, and the Better Business Bureau cited 50 ministries that fell below its ethical standards. The FCC used fraud-by-wire law interpretation in ruling that it was illegal to ask for money for one purpose but spend it for another, and the FCC had the power to pull licenses or not renew them. State attorneys general occasionally attempt to cite consumer protection statutes against the televangelists. And the Internal Revenue Service watches excess salaries and expenses and possessions, but not to any great extent.

THE BUBBLE BURSTS

What finally broke the televangelism bubble was excess and scandal in the mid-1980s, particularly the shenanigans of Jim Bakker. Between 1984 and 1987, Bakker and his associates at the PTL Club offered lift-time partnerships to pay for the building of Heritage USA, a Christian resort and activity center in Fort Mill, South Carolina. Donors, known as Lifetime Partners, received free lodging at the resort on a space-available basis. Unfortunately, the demand exceeded the supply, and regular paying guests had priority for lodging. Accusers said the organization deliberately underbuilt and that they oversold—that constituted a fraud. Convicted and sentenced to 45 years in prison, Bakker served almost 5 years before his 1993 parole. Bakker also had to resign from the PTL in 1987 because of his scandalous affair with Jessica Hahn.

Peter Popoff had a lucrative career in faith healing. Claiming that God healed through his hands, Popoff cured illnesses through a laying on of hands—touching and healing through God's miracles. In the 1980s, James Randi and Johnny Carson exposed Popoff on national television, costing Popoff popularity and audience. Popoff used an in-ear radio to get messages from his wife off-stage as she read cards that the audience filled out beforehand. His ministry went through bankruptcy in 1987.

Over 70 percent Mormon, Utah has a long history of hosting scams. In 1984, one estimate was that 75 percent of the country's investment scams originated in the Salt Lake-Provo area. Fifteen years earlier, Salt Lake City already had the attention of the Wall Street Journal as "a locus for shell operations." And the Journal anointed Salt Lake City the stock fraud capital. Again, in 1984 the label stuck, this time in Newsweek. Even with the publicity, the fraud continued into the 1990s. Presumably the Mormons were victimizing themselves through their absolute loyalty to the church, their willingness to accept any recommendation by another Mormon. Hucksters brought church officials, perhaps unknowingly, into their scams. Utah's governor, Scott Matheson, established a securities task force in 1984 to fight the Mormon connection. His task force included a prominent Mormon, Hugh Pinnock, member of the General Authorities since 1977. By 1985, reportedly the Mormon people were wiser. However, not long after that Pinnock got conned into signing a loan to buy non-existent documents. The Mormons were long vulnerable to document fraud; this one cost $185,000. The wiser people of the fraud capital had begun preying on each other. In the 1980s, fraud cost 10,000 Utah investors over $200 million.

TURN OF THE MILLENNIUM

The televangelists took the people by giving them hope; 20 years later, the racket was simply a matter of taking the people and giving them nothing in the manner established in Utah decades before. In Arizona in 2001, the Baptist Foundation of Arizona offered a good return of 6.7 percent on investments. It attracted Baptists by using sales people who seemed to share their values. Then it went bankrupt and three of its officials pled guilty to fraud. More than 13,000 investors lost $590 million through a case of affinity fraud.

The 1990s and after were a time when increasingly sophisticated investment rackets used reli-

Religious fraud often involves raising millions of dollars in the name of pious efforts, only to see the believers' money end up in the minister's bank account, paying for a lavish lifestyle.

gious loyalty to bring in the believers' money. And it was a national problem, continuing despite the frequent exposure and the common-sense reminders from securities officials that investment and faith were better kept separate. Between 1998 and 2001, affinity fraud cases involving over 90,000 investors spanned 27 states. Another case, the $448 million fraud of Greater Ministries International Church, based in Tampa, Florida. ended with Gerald Payne, an ailing, 65-year-old minister sentenced to 27 years in prison on fraud charges, having bilked 20,000 believers who had to mortgage homes, cash in retirement funds, or run up credit card debt for the promise of large returns on investments in mines and cargo ships.

In 2001, the Philip Kronzer Foundation for Religious Research sued three national groups based in New Jersey, Alabama, and Indiana for fraudulently using phony Papal indulgences and visions of the Virgin Mary to conceal tax evasion, smuggling, and money-laundering. Purportedly the Alabama-based Caritas organization and leader Terry Co-

lafrancesco used mind control and false promises as well as other deceptions to bilk Californians through the internet. The other groups sued were the Children of Medjugorje of South Bend, Indiana, and the Children of War, of New Jersey.

In Bosnia, in 2003, the contributions of believers in the miracle of the Blessed Virgin Mary of Medjugorje were given to the local Franciscans, who, through various companies and a sympathetic bank, were financing a Bosnian Croat nationalist, that is, terrorist group. The Franciscans controlled the shrine, which since 1981 drew millions of pilgrims and brought in the money of millions of other Catholics and Protestants. This case included both cult abuse and religious fraud. And those who chose not to reveal the fraud were willing to use violence against investigators and reporters.

In 2002, a Utah jury found the True and Living Church of Jesus Christ of the Saints of the Last Days guilty of failure to produce Jesus Christ in the flesh. The leaders had to pay nearly $300,000 to two victims for breach of contract, fraud, and emotional distress. The jury rejected claims of racketeering and unjust enrichment. The church had required the victims to provide property in return for other unnamed property, membership in a heavenly elite, and the aforesaid meeting with Jesus. The church split from the Mormons in 1994 over the issue of polygamy. Another phenomenon was the revival of the late 19th century mix of loose science and religion in the New Age movement. A typical case occurred in California when two psychics swindled clients, charging thousands of dollars to rid the sufferers of their bad karma. The federal term for it is mail fraud. The investigation revealed that one man with bad karma went for a tarot card reading after a romantic disappointment in 1996. The "psychics" convinced him to participate in ever more expensive sessions, culminating in an all night gathering of psychics costing $750,000. Before that, in the three years he believed, he had given over $500,000 as well as possessions. Only after watching a television program on psychic fraud, did the man investigate the psychics and turn away from them.

INTERNATIONAL FRAUD

The American way of fraud spread overseas. A cult fraud in Japan in 2000 had members believing that the leaders could cure disease by examining the people's soles. The foot diagnostic cost believers hundreds of thousands of dollars. And, in Taiwan in 1996, Sung Chi-li was accused of selling believers phony photos of him performing supernatural acts. Convicted of fraud, his case was overturned on appeal in 2003 when the high court ruled that the constitution protected religion and there was no proof that he didn't have supernatural powers. This ruling was consistent with U.S. law that truth or falsity was not subject to jury scrutiny but sincerity was. Good faith made fraud unintentional and not actionable.

Belief also allowed the perpetration of frauds such as psychic surgery. Psychic surgery is actually not surgery and it's performed by a non-surgeon. The healer creates a psychic or fake incision by running a finger along the patient's body, penetrating the skin through magic or faith. The healer takes something from the patient's insides, either a tumor or a chicken liver, depending on the perspective. Blood squirts from a hand-hidden balloon. The surgeon closes the psychic incision, and the patient goes to either live or die. Psychic surgery is more common in Brazil and the Philippines, but one popular practitioner, Tony Agpaoa of the Philippines, was indicted in the United States in 1967 for fraud. He fled, forfeiting a $25,000 bond. Psychic healing "works" because patients have faith in the healers. And, at least some of the healers believe their methods work—rather than fakes, they are pious healers, instruments of God or Christ. Among these is Stephen Turoff of England, also noted for the therapeutic touch, a laying on of hands. Psychic dentistry is also popular, most notably Willard Fuller who has healed over 40,000 people since 1960.

Pious frauds let excess religious zeal lead them into deception. Various stigmatics, those who have seemingly inexplicable bloody wounds mimicking those of the crucified Jesus, have been accused of being frauds, including Sister Lucia dos Santos of Fatima (1917), who claimed that she and two others had a visitation from the Virgin Mary. Although she is suspected of having been hallucinating or under the influence of religious books, she has maintained a cult following from the 1940s, and Fatima in Portugal is a site of prayer, penance, and money donations.

A 21st-century alleged pious fraud is Catalina Rivas of Mexico, who has the stigmata wounds and claims to receive messages from Jesus, Mary, and angels in Latin, Greek, Polish, and Spanish. She also channels books through automatic writing, going into a trance and letting the spirits guide her hand as it writes.

As long as people believe and as long as believers have money and as long as religious freedom includes the right to collect money in the name of God, fraud will flourish.

SEE ALSO
Bakker, Jim and Tammy; wire fraud; mail fraud; United States; tax evasion.

BIBLIOGRAPHY. Bob Allen, "Scams Targeting Faithful On Rise, State Security Regulators Warn," *Biblical Recorder* (August 10, 2001); Associated Press, "Jury Awards $290,000 in Religious Fraud Case," (January 30, 2002); Better Business Bureau, "1930: Revival Tent Fraud," www.pittsburgh.bbb.org (2003); Rick Branch, "Scams and the Latter-day Saints," *The Watchman Expositor* (1990); California Department of Corporations, "Volatile Economy Makes 2001 a Prime Year For Affinity Frauds," www.corp.ca.gov (2003); Robert Todd Carroll, "Psychic Surgery," *The Skeptic's Dictionary*, www.skepdic.com (2003); Chuck Fager, "Defrauding the

Faithful," *Christianity Today* (March 5, 2001); Laurence R. Moore, *Selling God; American Religion in the Marketplace of Culture* (Oxford University Press, 1994); Ross Institute for the Study of Destructive Cults, Controversial Groups and Movements, "'Mystic' Acquitted by High Court," *The China Post* (January 29, 2003); David Rosenzweig, "Pychics Bilked and Badgered Clients, Indictment Says," *Los Angeles Times* (March 30, 2002).

JOHN BARNHILL, PH.D.
INDEPENDENT SCHOLAR

research fraud

SCIENCE IS ALWAYS in motion and falsification is an inseparable and even constituent part of science (as Karl Raimund Popper and others pointed out). Research fraud can be divided into at least four major groups: 1) false titles or non-existing publications; 2) plagiarism; 3) forged material, invented experiments and non-existing or exaggerated research results; and 4) pseudo-science.

False titles or nonexistent publications are probably the most basic case of research fraud, whereby the results could be harmful for society, but are usually not for science itself. Forged diplomas of real universities, or awards from fake educational entities are increasingly commonplace. Anybody with access to the internet and a laser printer can create reasonable facsimiles of awards and diplomas.

Some forgers believe careers may be accelerated by such gimmicks. The more dangerous cases involve medical doctors actually operating on real-life patients without any proper training to do so. It should be pointed out that such cases usually only have success outside the scientific community, when the title or degree is not checked against the actual knowledge of the person bearing (or boasting) the title.

Nonexistent publications in a professional background list may open the door to a scientific career, but will sooner or later end abruptly when somebody searches for the publication or a new paper is required from the swindler. Examples range from a student-employee at Harvard University forging letters of recommendation, to a scientist at Stanford University quoting from his own articles, which were never written or published.

Plagiarism is probably the most common case of research fraud. Since the invention of the internet, some students write their school or college papers with the "help" of publications in the public domain. Plagiarism in its crude form, that is the total copy of a paper or article and just changing the name of the author, is easily detected. More sophisticated cases like partial use from several sources, or the paraphrasing of one source are more problematic. The line between plagiarism and cumulative scientific writing is always thin, but the borderline is crossed when sources are not quoted at all or are downplayed in significance. Plagiarism is not just a recent phenomenon, but modern information technology has facilitated new forms of plagiarism; conversely, the same technology allows for easier and quicker detection of plagiarism.

Forged research materials, invented experiments, and nonexistent or exaggerated research results are usually the most important threat to science itself, as other (innocent) scientists may come to wrong conclusions following up false leads based on faked results. The danger is usually most acute when the forger holds a high position within the scientific community. These forgeries are sometimes hard to detect as the replication of fraudulent experiments may involve big laboratory facilities and major funding. Sometimes minor changes in small numbers may signify success or failure of an experiment, so one replication at another laboratory may not be enough to prove fraud beyond a reasonable doubt.

Examples of this kind of research fraud include Ptolemy, who "invented" measurements he never did, and Isaac Newton, who brightened up some of his results to improve its prognostic efficiency. John Dalton's atomic theory was fundamental to nuclear science, yet some of the experiments he described seem to be singularities, if they ever happened at all the way he claimed. In 1912, fossils found in Piltdown made Great Britain the birthplace of humanity, unfortunately all were forgeries.

Three Indian "scientists" forged microscope pictures in 1961, and in a more recent case, a German physicist nearly ruined the longstanding fame of Bell Laboratories by making up research results on a large scale. Biomedicine and cancer research are at the cutting edge of science and are especially vulnerable to fraud.

Pseudo-science is a threat to the uneducated public, not to the scientific community itself. Fraud is inherent to certain forms of self-appointed "scientific" areas like parapsychology, astrology, or UFO research. Whereas some questions within these fields are asked by serious scientists, a large percentage of the publications covering these subjects use a "scientific" language, but invent their basic materials and neglect every aspect of a methodological scientific approach.

TOTALITARIAN SCIENCE

It has to be pointed out that totalitarian regimes tend to hinder science (extending up to frauds to avoid unpleasant new results) or even to create fields of pseudo-science. The best example is Nazi Germany, where Rassenlehre (race science according to the Nazi ideology) led to such strange things as Arische or Deutsche Physik (Aryan or German physics), whereby the racially motivated refutation of Einstein's theory of relativity was declared to be the guiding principle in "science."

In the Soviet Union under Josef Stalin, biology was transformed by communist ideological preconditions. The Catholic Church, for many centuries and for ideological reasons, hindered the development of a modern astronomy (Galileo's trial, for example). In the late 1980s, East German Communist Party chief Erich Honecker presented at one of his last meetings with Soviet leader Mikhail Gorbachev a certain microchip as the latest development of East German industry, which was, in fact, a dummy. In such cases, the fraud is not necessarily a product of one scientist, but comes from within the system itself and is enforced by the authorities with drastic measures (everything from funding shortages to a threat to the life of the opposing scientist).

Reasons for research fraud are to be found in personal misbehavior and vanity, but are probably better explained by the competition within the modern scientific community. This competition is for jobs and, even more importantly, for research funds. Although research fraud can never be excused for any reason, the modern financing system of science nevertheless has to bear part of the blame. As personal careers and sometimes sheer subsistence depends more and more on grants and short-term engagements instead of lifelong university or research jobs, the pressure to present better, results comes with each grant or job application.

The countermeasures against research fraud are as simple in theory as they sometimes are difficult to install in practice: Only an open scientific community presenting research results on an international basis is, at least in the long run, an effective safeguard against research fraud. Only if research results can be checked by other researchers and can be questioned in the case of serious doubt without any institutional or hierarchical hindrance, science then can detect, correct, research fraud. The framework must be set by criminal law and by self-regulations of scientific institutions or communities.

New dangers arise from events not linked to science in the first place. Competition between companies or national industries may enforce secrecy around new scientific results, as a safeguard against industrial espionage. New protective measures had to be taken after the terrorist attacks of September 11, 2001 in high-risk fields of science with potential dual-use-facility (parts of chemistry, biology, physics, etc.).

No one would question the legitimate desire to protect such research results or new technologies, which could be brutally abused if they fall into the hands of terrorists, but this new culture of secrecy for national security reasons may be the source for new dangers in the prevention of research fraud. Yet, as science is always work in progress, so is the prevention of research fraud.

SEE ALSO

forgery; counterfeiting; healthcare fraud; Center for Science in the Public Interest.

BIBLIOGRAPHY. William Broad and Nicholas Wade, *Betrayers of the Truth: Fraud and Deceit in the Halls of Science* (Simon and Schuster, 1982); Anthony Grafton, *Forgers and Critics: Creativity and Duplicity in Western Scholarship* (Princeton University Press, 1990); Thomas S. Kuhn, *The Structure of Scientific Revolutions* (University of Chicago Press, 1962).

OLIVER BENJAMIN HEMMERLE, PH.D.
MANNHEIM UNIVERSITY, GERMANY

respondeat superior

THE PRIMARY DOCTRINE by which organizations have been held legally responsible for their employees' actions is taken from civil tort law, and is known as *respondeat superior* (let the superior respond). The rule originated in England in the late 17th century (although it is traceable to more ancient times), and was meant to deter employers from escaping financial responsibility for the actions of their employees. *Respondeat superior* was first used in England in the mid-19th century to justify a criminal indictment, and it was first used for that purpose in America a short time later.

By the end of the 19th century, there was ample precedent to prosecute corporations under *respondeat superior*. Congress passed the Elkins Act in 1903, which outlawed shipper rebating and contained an explicit statutory clause for corporate criminal liability. Modern theories based on *respondeat superior* impose both civil and criminal liabilities on organizations. They are meant to force superiors to be vigilant of the behavior of people who work under them. *Respondeat superior* requires three elements: 1) the agent of the organization committed the crime; 2) while acting within the scope of his or her authority; 3) with an intent to benefit the corporation.

An organizational criminal liability that is different from *respondeat superior* is strict liability. Strict liability allows for the punishment of individuals and organizations who may not have intended to commit the illegal act. Most criminal statutes require that the perpetrator have an intention to commit the offense. However, strict-liability administrative civil and criminal penalties impose no requirement of intent on organizations or individuals. In essence, strict liability is blame without fault.

There are two basic purposes for imposing strict liability. First, strict liability supposedly encourages people to find out about the law, however obscure it may be, and to follow it. As in cases of respondeat superior, strict liability is supposed to act as a deterrent to a claim of non-responsibility for the offense, and it precludes corporate executives from purposely insulating themselves from knowledge of their employees' activities. The second major justification for strict liability is that it simplifies the prosecution of offenses because intent, which is potentially a very complex issue associated with behavior occurring within larger organizations, does not have to be proved. An organization is expected to know about wrongdoing within its ranks, and "should know" about it. Even accidental offenses, such as environmental or fair trade mishaps, are punishable by strict liability.

To exemplify the stringent legal precedents that have been established for corporate criminal liability, organizations are punishable when employees' collective actions constitute a crime, but each person's individual action does not. This model, known as collective intent or collective knowledge, imputes intent to an organization that never existed among its human actors. Unlike *respondeat superior*, liability for a collective intent offense is not vicarious because the crime arises only out of activities by a plurality of the organization's parts.

Until the 1960s, corporate criminal liability was generally limited to instances where higher level managers were directly involved in or willfully ignorant of the legal infraction. Throughout the 1970s and 1980s, organizational criminal liability was more stringently applied under strict liability and collective knowledge concepts.

However, the advent of the U.S. Sentencing Guidelines in 1991 limited criminal liability when there is non-involvement by higher-level personnel, and the existence of a compliance program to help prevent violations. This allows sophisticated organizations to shift the risks previously associated with *respondeat superior* onto lower-level "rogue" employees by blaming them for illegalities that occur, thereby insulating themselves from vicarious legal liability.

SEE ALSO
Sentencing Guidelines; corporate criminal liability; prosecution; employee crimes.

BIBLIOGRAPHY. Barbara Belbot, "Corporate Criminal Liability," *Understanding Corporate Criminality* (Garland, 1993); L.H. Leigh, "The Criminal Liability of Corporations and Other Groups," *Michigan Law Review* (v.80, 1982); William Laufer, "Corporate Bodies and Guilty Minds," *Emory Law Review* (v.43, 1994); William Laufer, "Corporate Liability, Risk Shifting, and the Paradox of Compliance," *Vanderbilt Law Review* (v.54, 1999).

GARY S. GREEN
CHRISTOPHER NEWPORT UNIVERSITY

Revco

ON JULY 28, 1977, Revco Drug Stores, Inc., was found guilty of a computer-generated double-billing scheme that defrauded the Ohio Department of Public Welfare out of $500,000 in Medicaid funds. At the time, Revco was one of the largest drug retailers in the United States with 825 stores in 21 states.

This case was uncovered by accident in May 1976 when a pharmacist in one of Revco's Ohio stores was puzzled by the large number of prescriptions for narcotics and tranquilizers written by a local podiatrist. A vice president at Revco headquarters called the pharmacy board in support of a thorough inquiry; the pharmacy board contacted the Ohio Department of Public Welfare and by August 1976, the Revco records and the Public Welfare records for this podiatrist were being compared manually.

In October 1976, the investigation was expanded and by March 1977, a pattern of double-billing using transposed prescription numbers regardless of prescribing physician by multiple Revco outlets, was documented. The unraveling of this fraud involved a number of agencies and enormous effort due to the complexities of two different computer systems—Ohio Public Welfare and Revco. The intricacies read like a good mystery story. Revco finally revealed that a vice president and a program manager under his supervision decided to "make good" claims rejected by Ohio Public Welfare. They hired six clerks to alter the rejected claims—not by correcting them—but by double-billing with falsified prescription numbers to get money they felt the state of Ohio "owed" Revco.

Throughout this investigation, "Revco assumed the role of the victim, not the offender," explains author Diane Vaughan in *Controlling Unlawful Organizational Behavior*. It is true that Revco's rate of claims rejections was higher than other providers (24 percent compared to 2 to 6 percent for other companies); Revco's solution was systematic fraud rather than the programmed pre-submission screening system suggested by the welfare department.

Vaughan mentions that the "maintenance of a reliable pre-submission edit system is expensive. Once installed, the provider's system requires constant adjustment as the information needed by the welfare department frequently changes. Allowable claims vary. Recipient eligibility requirements may be altered. New drugs on the market necessitate constant revision of the drug formulary." Interestingly, the welfare department kept Revco as a Med-icaid provider and, "the negotiations were concluded. Revco agreed to enter a plea of no contest to 10 counts of falsification, a misdemeanor of the first degree.

Under the organizational criminal liability statute, the prosecution would recommend imposition of the maximum fine of $5,000 per count. [$50,000]. In addition, Revco would make restitution in the amount of $521,521.12 to the Ohio Department of Public Welfare. As for the two executives, each would plead no contest to two counts of falsification," Vaughan reported. Later, Revco did institute pre-edits as required by the welfare department.

In 1997, a buyout by CVS drugstores was approved by the Federal Trade Commission. Revco systems were simply converted to CVS systems. This merger made CVS second only to Walgreen's in revenue in the drugstore industry. Now a big player, Revco paid $4 million in 2001 to settle allegations of submitting false prescription claims to government health insurance groups.

SEE ALSO

Medicare and Medicaid fraud; healthcare fraud; pharmaceutical industry.

BIBLIOGRAPHY. Helmut K. Anheier, *When Things Go Wrong: Organizational Failures and Breakdowns* (Sage Publications, 1999); Christopher Koch. "Cold Fusion," *CIO Magazine* (November 15, 1999); *Lubbock Avalanche Journal* (February 8, 1997); "Antitrust/Trade Regulation," *Judicial Legislative Watch Report* (October 2001); Bonnie Schreiber, Andrea Prasow, and Rachel S. Martin, "Healthcare Fraud," *American Criminal Law Review* (v.39/2, 2002); Diane Vaughan, *Controlling Unlawful Organizational Behavior: Social Structure and Corporate Misconduct* (University of Chicago Press, 1983).

CAROLE MAKEIG CARROLL
MIDDLE TENNESSEE STATE UNIVERSITY

revolving door

THE EXPRESSION *revolving door* is applied to the flow of employees between the public and private sectors of the economy. Upon leaving their jobs, high level public officials are able to translate their expertise into equally prestigious and often higher paying jobs in the private sector. The watchdog agency Common Cause defines the revolving door as "the practice of government officials cashing in on their public service by leaving public office and going to work for the same special interests who were seeking favors from them while they were in office." Thus, this is an issue that raises important ethical questions because it breeds tight relationships between private sector organizations, bureaucrats, and elected officials that are perceived as threats to democratic government. The revolving door increases the likelihood that public officials will succumb to already pervasive incentives to accept kickbacks meant to sway official decision-making.

Common Cause led a 1989 effort to pass the Ethics in Government Act that applied post-employment laws to members of Congress. The subsequent one-year ban represented an effort to quell suspicion that moneyed interests wield a disproportionate amount of influence over the government decision-making process. Public servants departing from service in 1992 constituted the first group to face the one-year ban on assuming private sector positions requiring them to lobby former colleagues still in public service. According to an investigative article written by Jackie Calmes, of the 25 percent of the 435 House members who stepped down or suffered electoral defeat that year, approximately 40 percent landed positions lobbying or consulting after the one-year ban ended.

The effectiveness of the ban was challenged on the basis of the ease with which former public servants were still able to find a position after a year, and the fact that the ban does not prohibit them from devising strategies for clients during the year-long waiting period. Further, former public officials could and did gather with legislators socially.

At the beginning of the Bill Clinton administration, the president issued an executive order that extended the ban on federal government officials and White House staff from lobbying former colleagues to five years, and forever barred them from lobbying foreign governments. This move was seen as symbolic of the new Democratic administration's commitment to clean government. As the Clinton administration waned, the president undermined the image of having run a clean administration when he revoked this order.

Common Cause keeps the public updated on the content of the most recent legislation in this area. Under the existing law in 2004, high-level officials were prohibited from lobbying their own agency for one year. They were prohibited from lobbying on matters specific to the area that they supervised while in office for a period of two years. They faced a lifetime ban on ever lobbying on matters that they were personally and substantially involved in while in office. Former members of Congress were barred from lobbying other members for a period of one year. High-level members stepping down from the Congressional staff had to wait one year before lobbying the members who they worked for.

There are those who claim that the overall impact of the revolving door is positive, or at least not as harmful as opponents assert. Proponents of the revolving door argue that without it, private industry and interest groups would be at a disadvantage because the sheer volume of legislation that is passed poses a barrier to any individual or group being able to discern which decisions will directly impact them with enough time to actually lobby decision-makers. On the other side of the coin, interest groups provide a valuable service to government actors as well. Interest groups are a source of valuable information for decision-makers who need to consider the long-term impact of potential policy changes from a variety of perspectives within a limited amount of time in order to reach conclusions. Staunch opponents argue that the existence of a revolving door itself is enough of an incentive to ensure that government officials worried about their jobs after each election will rule in favor of powerful interests with a eye toward future employment and benefits.

SEE ALSO

government contract fraud; government procurement fraud; ethics; corruption; military-industrial complex.

BIBLIOGRAPHY. Phillip D. Brady, "Regulatory Chokehold: Our Friend, the Revolving Door," *Wall Street Journal* (May 11, 1993); Jackie Calmes, "Revolving Door between Congress and Lobbyists Spins on Despite Yearlong Cooling-off Period," *Wall Street Journal* (January 24, 1994); Sean Paige, "Revolving Door Spinning Again," Insight on the News (January 29, 2001); Common Cause, www.commoncause.org (2003).

S. MARTIN, PH.D.
CORNELL UNIVERSITY

Rich, Marc (1934–)

INDICTED FUGITIVE financier Marc Rich (a.k.a. Marc David Reich) was born in Belgium in 1934. His family fled the Nazis in 1942 and emigrated to America. Rich served his apprenticeship as a commodities trader under the tutelage of his millionaire father (a burlap-sack producer) and later, Philipp Brothers, a broker in raw metals. His tenure with Philipp Brothers taught Rich the dynamics of trading in natural resources with third world nations.

Rich's involvement with highly suspect business deals brought him to the attention of the U.S. federal government, and in the early 1980s, he was indicted for income tax fraud and breaking a U.S. embargo by selling oil to Iran during the hostage crisis. A criminal indictment was filed against Rich and his partner, Pincus Green, by U.S. Attorney Rudolph Giuliani in 1983. Rich and Green, however, fled the country for Switzerland before the pair could be brought to court to answer the charges. Both Rich and Green remained on the Most Wanted list of the Justice Department for 18 years.

That is, until January 20, 2001. A few hours before leaving office, President Bill Clinton fully pardoned Rich and Green, thereby nullifying the indictment against them. The presidential pardon was controversial because Rich had a long history of questionable transactions with third world nations and because Denise Rich, Rich's ex-wife, had lobbied hard for the pardon. The lobbying effort included donations of $70,000 to Hillary Clinton's Senate campaign, several hundred thousand dollars to the Democratic Party, and $450,000 to Clinton's presidential library. The president denied any connection between the lavish contributions and his decision to pardon Rich and Green. The U.S. Senate Judiciary Committee held hearings to review the legality of the pardon in February 14, 2001, but the results were inconclusive.

Rich had not returned to the United States since 1983. A billionaire commodities trader, Rich claimed citizenship status in Spain, Israel, and Switzerland, rejecting the idea that the United States has any jurisdiction over possible delinquent taxes while he resided there. The issue of citizenship is significant as it reflected both Rich's *modus operandi* in business and his philosophy toward the laws of other nations. He specialized in dealing with "outlawed" or dictatorial countries, regardless of world opinion, embargoes, and legal restraints.

Since 1979, Rich brokered deals in raw products to the following nations: Iran (oil and metals), Libya (oil), South Africa (oil), Cuba and Russia (sugar for oil), and Nigeria (oil). In an interesting turn of events. Rich used one of his American companies to secure 21 contracts with the U.S. mint. From roughly 1989 to 1992, Rich's firm supplied nickel, copper, and zinc to the U.S. mint to cast coins for distribution in the American economy.

Because he was pardoned by Clinton, Rich is not liable for prosecution in the United States for the original 1983 charges. It is possible that he could be held responsible in civil court for tax evasion if he were to return to the United States. Rich claimed that he denounced his American citizenship, but the matter remained unresolved.

As of 2004, Rich resided in Meggen, Switzerland, but the Swiss government has repeatedly refused to extradite him. Tax evasion is not a crime in Switzerland.

SEE ALSO
tax evasion; Giuliani, Rudolph; Switzerland; prosecution; Clinton, William J.

BIBLIOGRAPHY. A. Craig Copetas, *Metal Men* (Perennial Publishing, 2001); "Marc Rich," *Mother Jones* (March 5, 2001); Timothy P. Carney, "The Story of Clinton's Marc Rich Pardon," *World Net Daily* (February 5, 2001); Ian Christopher McCaleb, "Senators Hear details of Clinton's Last-Minute Pardon of Rich" *Inside Politics* (February 14, 2001).

DANIEL S. CAMPAGNA, PH.D.
MOUNT MARY COLLEGE

risk analysis

THE SOCIETY for Risk Analysis defines risk analysis as "risk assessment, risk characterization, risk communication, risk management, and policy relating to risk." The risks being assessed and considered are, in this context, risks to human health from activities and agents as diverse as bioterrorism, neglecting to use sunscreen, working at a location where soil is contaminated, eating improperly stored food, and driving while intoxicated.

Risk is a measure of the probability of harm from a given activity or agent, often calculated as the likelihood of one additional death per one million people. It is important to note that nothing is completely free of risk. The role of risk analysis is to measure and manage acceptable risks, not to eliminate harms completely.

Risk assessment is a statistical modeling technique that uses known exposures and harms to predict unknown exposures and harms. The Food Safety Risk Analysis Clearinghouse defines a four-step process of hazard identification, hazard characterization, exposure assessment, and risk characterization that is typical of risk assessment in general. At each stage, it is possible for false assumptions or misunderstood analysis to result in an incorrect assessment of risks.

Hazard identification involves discovering what potential causes of harm could be present in the substance or situation being assessed. Accurate hazard identification depends both on knowing what substances cause what harms and on knowing which of those substances is likely to be present. In West Chicago, Illinois, for example, homeowners used radioactive thorium tailings from an old American Potash plant as garden fill because they did not know that a hazardous substance was present. Many companies who are now responsible for contaminated site clean-ups aver that, although they knew they were dumping chemicals into the local groundwater, they did not know that the chemicals were harmful. Because hazard identification has become refined over the past 50 years, it is now a standard part of major property transactions to have include a document search, survey of aerial photos, and walk of the grounds, looking for signs of potential contamination. Similarly, the Environmental Protection Agency (EPA) is requiring chemical manufacturers to document the qualities of substances that have been manufactured and used for years but about which little is known.

LONG-TERM HAZARDS

Hazard characterization focuses on evaluating potential adverse health effects from exposure. Two facts are at issue: whether any harms are caused and, if there is a harm, what dose causes it? Some hazards cause harms that only become visible many years later, making short-term health studies useless in characterizing the hazard. For example, asbestos in Georgia-Pacific's Ready-Mix joint compound caused a form of cancer that became apparent in victims more than 20 years after exposure; hormones in a popular anti-miscarriage medication of the 1940s turned out to cause cancer in daughters whose mothers took the drug, with symptoms appearing only as the daughters reached their early 20s. In both of these cases, earlier studies had indicated possible health risks, but the studies were concealed or deemed inapplicable. Similarly, the Dalkon Shield contraceptive was marketed as safe based on a study that was too short to properly measure risks of pregnancy.

Exposure assessment measures how big a dose potential victims are likely to receive. The dangerous dose of a hazardous substance is often smaller for children, the elderly, or women than for adult males, due to lower body rate, lower resistance, or (for children) less developed nervous systems. The EPA thus demands a higher standard of clean-up if a contaminated site is to be used as a park for children than if it is to be used as a factory and parking garage, where most earth is covered with soil and most people exposed are adults.

Finally, risk characterization quantifies the risks to whole populations, given their qualities and exposure. This characterization is always based on assumptions; for example, the EPA's formula for calculating the risks to a child from contaminated soil assumes that a child will routinely consume or inhale a certain amount of dirt. If the contaminated area is paved over, the assumption no longer holds and the risk must be recalculated.

POLITICS OF RISK ANALYSIS

Recalculating acceptable risks can become a political football put in play to prevent a company from having to reduce exposures. Thus, when the James River in Virginia became contaminated with the dangerous pesticide kepone, two governors at two different times petitioned the EPA to raise the acceptable level of kepone in fish for the good of the local fishing industry. (Both attempts were unsuccessful.) Industries routinely argue that the costs of reducing a risk are prohibitively high.

Acceptable levels of exposure can become political partly because risk analysis is always based on extrapolations from incomplete data and partly because the public usually misunderstands risk. While the Harvard Center for Risk Analysis quotes the Centers for Disease Control's findings that the annual risk of dying from alcohol is 9,000 times greater than the annual risk of dying from bioterrorism, it is the lesser risk that dominates public attention. One factor that statistics cannot fully capture is that some risks feel more acceptable than others. The same person who eschews sunscreen in search of a golden tan (7,800 skin cancer deaths in the U.S. per year) may find it unacceptable to be exposed at work to a chemical that bears a considerably lower risk.

SEE ALSO

insurance fraud; Environmental Protection Agency; Justice, Department of; asbestos; kepone.

BIBLIOGRAPHY. Joyce Bichler, *DES Daughter: The Joyce Bichler Story* (Avon, 1981); Patti Bond and Anne Hardie, "Georgia-Pacific's Asbestos Nightmare," *Atlanta Journal and Constitution* (September 15, 2002); "Ecological Risk Analysis: Guidance, Tools, and Applications," www.esd.ornl.gov (2003); Harvard Center for Risk Analysis, www.hcra.harvard.edu (2003); Morton Mintz, *At Any Cost* (Pantheon, 1985); Society for Risk Analysis, www.sra.org (2003); Sandra Sugawara, "10 Years After Kepone Dumping, Problems Persist," *Washington Post* (July 29, 1985); Ron Suskind, "Illinois Town's Battle Over Radioactive Waste," *The New York Times* (March 11, 1985); Environmental Protection Agency, www.epa.gov (2003); Food Safety Risk Analysis Clearinghouse. www.foodriskclearinghouse.umd.edu (2003).

WENDE VYBORNEY FELLER, PH.D.
ST. MARY'S COLLEGE OF CALIFORNIA

Rite Aid

RITE AID CORPORATION was founded by Alex Grass, who, beginning with a discount store in 1962, founded a chain that by 1995 was the number one drugstore chain in store numbers and second in sales. In May 1989, Alex Grass' son, Martin, was named president of Rite Aid. Rite Aid had purchased Lane Drug two months earlier, and the Ohio Pharmacy Board was dissatisfied with Rite Aid's intrusion into Ohio, and penalized Rite Aid for security violations in the Lane Drug deal.

Martin Grass met with Melvin Wilcznski, a member of the Ohio Pharmacy Board and offered him a bribe to resign from the board. Unknown to Grass, the police were videotaping the meeting at Wilcznski's request. The judge dismissed the charges on the grounds that Ohio's bribery law covered bribes of public officials, but not bribes to resign public office. Grass countersued for defamation and won.

According to Frank Portnoy in his book, *Infectious Greed*, in 1996, when Rite Aid sold 189 stores for $90 million profit, the company used the money to "absorb operating expenses." This $90 million was a third of the total 1996 income and stockholders were told in the annual report that "gains from drugstore closing and dispositions were not significant." After that successful scheme, Rite Aid systematically overstated its profits by $2.3 billion in all. The Securities and Exchange Commission (SEC) reported in 2002 that the fraud included "inflated revenues, reductions of previously recorded expenses, inflated deductions for damaged and outdated products, and unwarranted credits to various stores at the end of particular quarters."

The SEC charges included a new element: related-party transactions. Grass commingled Rite Aid accounts with other accounts to which he was a "related party" and used Rite Aid funds for personal debts. By 1999, Grass was inventing phony minutes to nonexistent meetings to support loan applications.

Where were Rite Aid's auditors? KPMG was their accounting firm and when they raised questions about irregular accounting practices, Grass threatened that "skeletons would come out of KPMG's closet" if they did not ignore the problematic issues. Grass also gave them an additional consulting contract to sweeten the deal.

Rite Aid paid Grass millions in options; at their peak, his options were estimated at $100 million in value. Finally, in 2002, charges were brought against Rite Aid and Grass. While prosecutors were preparing their case, Grass and a company lawyer were taped fabricating testimony and discussing tampering with documents and destroying the computer that generated them. In 2003, the judge decided the tapes could be used at the trial. Rite Aid stock rose to $50 a share in 1999 before collapsing. By May 2002, it was selling for less than $2 a share.

When new management was brought into the company in 1999 to replace Grass, managers learned that Rite Aid had overstated profits in the late 1990s by $1.6 billion dollars. "U.S. authorities alleged that Rite Aid's former management had orchestrated a massive accounting fraud that rivaled the scandals that helped topple Enron Corporation," reporter James F. Peltz wrote in the *Los Angeles Times*. Grass and four other Rite Aid officers were indicted on criminal charges in June 2002. In June 2003, Grass pleaded guilty to a conspiracy charge in exchange for "an eight-year prison sentence, a fine of $500,200, and forfeiture of $3 million in connection with a real estate deal. [He also] promised to testify against remaining defendants," the Associated Press reported.

SEE ALSO

accounting fraud; Securities and Exchange Commission; Enron Corporation.

BIBLIOGRAPHY. Tom Dochot, "Guilty Plea Tarnishes Reputation of Rite Aid's Founding Family," *The Patriot News* (June 18, 2003); James F. Peltz, "Rite Aid Team Seeks Prescription for Growth," *Los Angeles Times* (May 11, 2003); Frank Portnoy, *Infectious Greed* (Henry Holt, 2003); Mark Scolforo, "Former Rite Aid chief Martin Grass Agrees to Plea Deal that Calls for Eight Year Sentence," Associated Press (June 17, 2003).

CAROLE MAKEIG CARROLL
MIDDLE TENNESSEE STATE UNIVERSITY

John Jacob Astor, America's first robber baron, made his fortune exploiting the fur trade with Native Americans.

robber barons

ALTHOUGH WHITE-COLLAR crime and unethical business practices are certainly not unique to American companies, there is a prolifically fertile landscape for the roots of such behavior in the country's indefatigable pursuit of capitalism, its unapologetic emphasis on success and the accumulation of material wealth, and the precedence set by America's early capitalist tycoons.

Howard Abadinsky, one of America's foremost scholars on organized crime, goes so far as to characterize the capitalist pioneers of the United States—men like John Jacob Astor, James Fisk, Leland Stanford, John D. Rockefeller, Cornelius Vanderbilt, and J. Pierpont Morgan, among others—as the "antecedents" to organized crime in the country. "While contemporary organized crime has its roots in Prohibition (1920 to 1933), unscrupulous American business entrepreneurs provided role models and created a climate conducive to its growth." These so-called robber barons trans-

formed the wealth of the American frontier into vast financial empires, amassing their fortunes by monopolizing such essential industries as oil, railroads, liquor, cotton, and other textiles. In turn, these monopolies were built upon the liberal use of tactics that are today the hallmark of organized crime: intimidation, violence, corruption, conspiracies, and fraud.

Based partially on characterizations provided by Abadinsky, a description of the some of America's earliest tycoons, and the qualities that have earned them the label of robber baron, includes the following profiles.

John Jacob Astor (1763–1848), a fur magnate, amassed a fortune through the monopoly held by his American Fur Company over the trade in central and western United States during the first 30 years of the 19th century. This monopoly was achieved, in part, by crushing rivals and systematically cheating Native Americans of fur pelts. When his competitors complained to the government, Astor's agents resorted to violence. With his riches, Astor routinely paid off politicians to protect his business interests. At the time of his death, Astor was considered the richest person in the country.

James Fisk (1834–72) was one Wall Street's first great financiers, accumulating much of his fortunes by fraudulent stock market practices. Fisk invested much of the considerable money he made from smuggling Southern cotton to Northern mills during the Civil War into Confederate bonds. He then swindled European investors by selling short when the fall of the Confederate Army was imminent, but before Europe learned the Confederate currency had collapsed.

In 1866, he formed the brokerage firm Fisk and Belden, and the following year he and his colleagues protected their control over the Erie Railroad by issuing fraudulent stock. Along with his associates, Fisk attempted to corner the gold market by inflating the price, which was accomplished by bribing public officials to keep government gold off the market. The venture brought them vast sums but led to a securities market panic that began on September 24, 1869, a day that has long been remembered as Black Tuesday. At the time, the negative repercussions of the gold hoarding shook the economy and the scandal-plagued government of Ulysses S. Grant.

Leland Stanford (1852-93) became involved in Republican politics in California and was elected governor in 1861. While governor, Stanford approved millions of dollars in state grants for the construction of a transcontinental railroad line, during a period he was also president of the Central Pacific Railroad. With three colleagues, he formed the Pacific Association and used their combined assets to bribe Congressmen and others with political influence in the nation's capital. In return, the association was provided 9 million acres and a $24 million loan financed by federal bonds.

In addition, Stanford and his associates intimidated local governments into providing millions of dollars in subsidies by threatening to have the rail line bypass their communities. In 1885, Stanford was elected to the U.S. Senate by the legislature and re-elected in 1890. In 1885 also, he established what would later become Stanford University. Stanford died in 1893 worth more than $18 billion in 2004 dollars.

John D. Rockefeller (1839–1937) made his immense riches from monopolizing America's oil industry. Conspiring with refinery owners, he helped found what became known as the Standard Oil monopoly. In league with the railroads, the consortium had a stranglehold over the delivery of oil, forcing competitors to sell out to Standard Oil, or pay exorbitant shipping costs that would render them non-competitive. These who were stubborn enough to resist were harassed with price wars, and if that did not work, dynamite. By 1890, the Rockefeller trust controlled approximately 90 percent of the petroleum production in the United States, a situation that led to the passage of the Sherman Antitrust Act that same year.

Some have argued that these early American capitalists created a business culture that places the importance of success, capital accumulation, and the realization of the American dream far above ethical behavior. Gus Tyler (1962) was one of the first writers to argue that the roots of organized and economic crime in the United States lie deep within the American culture, drawing nourishment from traditional virtues as well as the popularized vices and excesses of American civilization.

SEE ALSO
Rockefeller, John D.; Sherman Antitrust Act; antitrust; Stanford, Leland; organized crime; United States; capitalism; free trade.

BIBLIOGRAPHY. Matthew Josephson, *The Robber Barrons* (Harvest Books, 1962); Howard Abadinsky, *Organized Crime* (Wadsworth Publishing, 2000); Gus Tyler, *Organized Crime in America* (University of Michigan Press, 1962).

STEPHEN SCHNEIDER, PH.D.
RYERSON UNIVERSITY, CANADA

Roberts, Oral (1918–)

EVANGELIST ORAL ROBERTS is considered by millions of Americans to be a prophet straight from God. Scores of other Americans, however, believe that Roberts is a silver-tongued crook who has bilked millions of dollars from an unsuspecting American public in the name of religion. Regardless of their perceptions of him, few would fail to agree that Roberts has a knack for reading people and for using them to further his goal of becoming an internationally known evangelist. Roberts is the founder of Oral Roberts University chartered in 1963 in Tulsa, Oklahoma, which represents itself as a "Christian university with a liberal arts focus" and which is a major name in college basketball.

Roberts began his ministry in 1947. Over the course of the next several decades, he wrote over 100 books, amassing millions of dollars in profits. In 1979, Jerry Sholes, the son of a Presbyterian minister, who worked with the Roberts' operation for more than three years, wrote an exposé of Roberts and his empire. Sholes wrote that Roberts' representatives had offered him millions of dollars and a lucrative contract to write a book in support of Roberts rather than the exposé. When he refused, Sholes says that he was beaten to the point that he was forced to have plastic reconstructive surgery on his face.

The book offered a devastating look at Roberts who reportedly wore thousand-dollar Brioni suits and drove $25,000 cars, replacing both every six months. Roberts' home in Tulsa was valued at $250,000, and a second home in Palm Springs, California, was valued at over $1 million. Sholes maintained that Roberts had photographers airbrush out his expensive jewelry so that he did not look too prosperous to his followers. While working for Roberts, Sholes attended a number of religious seminars where attendees were pressured to make donations from $250 to $100,000. The average take at the seminars, according to Sholes, was from $1.5 million to $3 million.

On September 7, 1977, Roberts announced to the world that God had sent him a vision in the desert telling him to build the City of Faith, a complex that would eventually include a hospital, a medical school, and a research center. The City of Faith opened its doors in 1981. Records show that Roberts had, in fact, discussed the City of Faith project with members of his staff months before he had the "vision." As much as 20 years earlier, Roberts had said in several interviews that he had already purchased land to build the City of Faith. The project was short-lived.

In March 1986, Roberts announced to his 1.6 million television followers that God had told him that if he did not raise $8 million dollars by March 31, God would strike him down. A number of television stations around the country reacted to

Roberts' announcement by canceling their broadcasts of his shows. Reportedly, more than $160,000 a day poured into the Roberts empire over the next few weeks. Roberts announced that when the devil entered his bedroom to strangle him, his wife Evelyn intervened. He than proclaimed that he had raised the necessary amount and that God would spare his life.

Before an audience of 6,000 followers at Oral Roberts University in July 1987, Roberts boasted that he could raise people from the dead. Ironically, Sholes tells a gripping story of the death of an infant child of one of the faculty members at Oral Roberts University who tried to pray his child into returning from the dead while Roberts refused to put in an appearance. Roberts followed his resurrection announcement by mailing out 1 million packets of "healing water" to his followers. Public reaction to Roberts' announcement was swift and negative, and Roberts' evangelical credibility fell drastically.

Between 1989 and 1990, Roberts laid off at least 10 percent of his staff. Despite his financial problems, Roberts offered $6.5 million for Jim and Tammy Bakker's PTL television network in 1990 but was outbid by fellow evangelist Morris Cerullo, who bid $52 million for the entire PTL unit. After turning over his religious empire to his son Richard, Roberts retired to his home in Palm Springs, California.

SEE ALSO

religious fraud; Bakker, Jim and Tammy; advertising fraud; embezzlement.

BIBLIOGRAPHY. David Edwin Harrell, Jr., *Oral Roberts: An American Life* (Indiana University Press); Richard Ostling, "Raising Eyebrows and The Dead," *Time* (July 13, 1987); Richard Ostling, "Your Money or Your Life: Oral Roberts Delivers an Ultimatum to Bolster His Sagging Empire," *Time* (January 26, 1987); "Questionable Fundraising Practices," *Time* (January 26, 1987); Richard Ostling and T. Curry, "A New Preacher for PTL," *Time* (June 11, 1990); Jerry Sholes, *Give Me That Prime-Time Religion: An Insider's Report on Oral Roberts Evangelistic Association* (Hawthorn Books, 1979); K. Woodward, "Evangelist Making Bizarre Claims," *Newsweek* (January 13, 1987).

ELIZABETH PURDY, PH.D.
INDEPENDENT SCHOLAR

Robinson-Patman Act

THE ROBINSON-Patman Act (RPA) enacted in 1936 is part of the antitrust legislation found in the Clayton Act of 1914. It prohibits discrimination in pricing, promotional allowances, and advertising. Better known as the Anti-Chain-Store Act or Anti-Megastore Act, the RPA is designed to protect small businesses from being driven out of the marketplace by giant franchised companies. It is also intended to protect wholesalers from being excluded from the purchasing chain. Wholesalers do not want such franchises bypassing them to buy products directly from manufacturers.

The logic behind the RPA is simple: Large corporations and businesses receive substantial discounts from their wholesale suppliers. If smaller businesses do not receive the same discounts, they cannot offer the same products at competitive prices. Eventually, these small businesses will be forced out of the market. For example, a giant hardware depot locates itself in a city that has two similar, but smaller, stores. To acquire a controlling share of the market, the megastore continuously undercuts its two competitors by offering much lower prices on popular, high-volume items such as supplies and tools. The smaller businesses cannot match the advertised prices of their competitor because they cannot sustain persistent losses in their operating revenues.

This practice is referred to as predatory pricing. The megastore absorbs short-term losses as a necessary function of driving out its local competitors. The outcomes are twofold. First, area competitors are eliminated, thus securing the megastore's profit margin. Second, once the newcomer has increased its market power, prices are set at a higher level than before. In the long run, revenues are restored.

A retail monopoly-by-default may result as prices are inflated to recoup earlier losses. For the megastore management, predatory pricing resembles "aggressive marketing" in an intensely competitive environment. Price discrimination, however, may result in small business closures and bankruptcy filings.

Claims of price discrimination and predatory pricing are hard to prove. The RPA has ten basic requirements that must be established for an effective claim of discrimination. These include, among others, evidence of intent, interstate commerce, goods of "like grade and quality," and adverse effect(s) on competition. As a result, the RPA is complex, difficult to apply, and open to multiple interpretations. Claims of price discrimination, for example, have been brought against booksellers, grocery store chains, agricultural co-operatives, and franchised retailers.

Litigation is typically brought by individuals and small businesses claiming predatory pricing and discrimination. Several aggressive defenses to the RPA exist, however, and include cost justification, meeting competition, truth in advertising, availability, and functional discounts. The Federal Trade Commission is responsible for upholding provisions of the RPA, but it is seldom enforced by the government.

SEE ALSO

antitrust; Clayton Antitrust Act; Sherman Antitrust Act; predatory practices; price discrimination.

BIBLIOGRAPHY. Executive Legal Summary No. 18 (Business Laws, Inc., 2000); Robinson-Patman Act (15 U.S.C.A. Section 13, 1936); U.S. Department of Justice and The Federal Trade Commission, "Antitrust Enforcement Guidelines For International Operations," (Department of Justice, April 1995).

DANIEL S. CAMPAGNA, PH.D.
MOUNT MARY COLLEGE

Rockefeller, John D. (1839–1937)

JOHN D. Rockefeller, founder of the Standard Oil Trust, was the archetypal robber baron of late 19th-century America. The label signalled public disapproval of the business methods and attitudes of Rockefeller and fellow industrialists and financiers such as Andrew Carnegie, William Vanderbilt, Jay Gould and J. Pierpont Morgan. Political demagogues and muck-raking journalists criticized Rockefeller and Standard Oil for colluding with railroad companies on freight rates, making covert company acquisitions, and predatory price-cutting or threatening to cut prices.

Rockefeller, born in Richford, New York on July 8, 1839, was the son of William Avery Rockefeller and Eliza Davison. His father was a travelling salesman dealing in horses, timber, salt, patent medicines, and herbal remedies, and was an occasional money lender. The family moved several times during Rockefeller's childhood before settling in Cleveland, Ohio. Rockefeller attended Cleveland Central High School (1853–55) before studying business at Folsom's Commercial College.

On leaving Folsom's in 1855, Rockefeller took a job as a clerk and bookkeeper in Isaac Hewitt and Henry Tuttle's wholesale produce commission house. In the spring of 1859, Rockefeller left his first job because he was unhappy with his salary. He went into partnership with Maurice Clark to establish their own commission house after borrowing $1,000 at 10 percent interest from his father. The new business flourished during the Civil War.

In 1863, Clark and Rockefeller entered the oil-refining business after forming a partnership with Samuel Andrews. Andrews had experience in oil refining and handled the technical operations, leaving finance, marketing, and distribution to Clark and Rockefeller. The new company Andrews, Clark & Company was a commercial success, owning and operating the largest oil refinery in Cleveland. In 1865 Rockefeller bought out Clark after a dispute over Rockefeller's expansion plans. Not long after the formation of Rockefeller & Andrews, Clark and Rockefeller dissolved their partnership. Rockefeller & Andrews proceeded to build a second refinery and formed a second company to handle marketing and distribution in New York.

In 1867, the company was renamed Rockefeller, Andrews & Flagler after Henry Flagler and Stephen Harkness invested in the company. Flagler negotiated reduced rail freight rates for the company due to the high volume of the company oil transported by the railroad companies. This accorded with Rockefeller's ambition to increase the company's market share and form an alliance of oil refiners. In 1870, the company was reorganized as the Standard Oil Company, a joint stock company with Rockefeller as president.

Under Rockefeller's guidance, Standard grew through acquisition, and the company participated in the ill-fated National Refiners Association to allocate crude oil between refiners, thus controlling production and pricing. The company successfully defeated attempts to challenge its market dominance and integrated vertically, acquiring assets. Standard's attempts to gain and maintain a monopoly over the U.S. oil industry fell foul of Ohio state law. To circumnavigate the statutory limitations on Ohio companies owning property in other states or stock in non-Ohio companies, Standard Oil adopted a system whereby company officials held stock in other companies as trustees. This was the first and the largest of the "trusts." In 1879, the system was simplified so that only three people acted as trustees. Three years later, the trust was reorganized again.

Under the Standard Oil Trust agreement, a nine-member Board of Trustees held the stock of the Ohio company and its subsidiaries. These trustees gave former stockholders certificates entitling them to a certain proportion of the share dividends. After the Ohio Supreme Court annulled the charter of the Ohio company in 1892, control of the trust was transferred to the Standard Oil (New Jersey) and several other units.

In 1899, the trust was reorganized for the last time when Standard Oil (New Jersey) became the sole holding company. Rockefeller had retired from day-to-day management of the trust two years earlier, although he continued to hold the title of company president until the Supreme Court ordered the company to be broken up in May 1911. Not surprisingly, Rockefeller remained closely identified with the trust and was the focus of its public criticism. Rockefeller chose not to respond to his critics, preferring to refute their image of him through his philanthropic works.

SEE ALSO

antitrust; Standard Oil Company; Sherman Antitrust Act; robber barons.

BIBLIOGRAPHY. Allan Nevins, *Study in Power: John D. Rockefeller, Industrialist and Philanthropist* (Scribner, 1953); Ron Chernow, *Titan: The Life of John D. Rockefeller, Sr.* (Little, Brown, 1998); Daniel Yergin, *The Prize: The Epic Quest for Oil, Money and Power* (Simon & Schuster, 1991).

MARK ROODHOUSE, PH.D.
UNIVERSITY OF YORK, ENGLAND

Rockwell International

ROCKWELL INTERNATIONAL, the largest contractor working with the National Aeronautics and Space Administration (NASA), was indicted in 1991 for over-billing the U.S. government for space shuttle repair and production work. It marked the fourth time in a decade that Rockwell was accused of mischarging the government. The company pleaded guilty in two of the earlier cases and agreed to an injunction against submitting false claims to the government in the third.

The NASA case involved allegations that Rockwell's Collins avionics operation, based in Cedar Rapids, Iowa, inflated records of the amount of time spent on NASA contracts by padding employee time cards and sending the agency false bills. The Cedar Rapids grand jury indictment charged the firm with 15 counts of conspiracy, mail, and wire fraud, and failed to specify when the alleged conspiracy took place, but suggested it started by 1979 and continued at least through August 1987. Two individuals were also indicted, one a current Collins manager and one a former Collins manager, who allegedly told employees to "soak the shuttle," "hose NASA," and "fix the numbers.".

The government suspended the Collins division from obtaining further government contracts because of the unit's indictment, but the Air Force soon lifted its suspension in the belief that Rockwell took a number of actions to prevent a recurrence of the false billings. NASA continued to investigate. Rockwell then agreed in 1992 to pay $1.4 million as part of a compliance agreement with the government to drop charges. It could have been fined as much as $7.5 million.

SEE ALSO

government contract fraud; compliance programs.

BIBLIOGRAPHY. Rhonda L. Rundle, "Rockwell Will Pay $1.4 Million to End NASA Billing Case," *Wall Street Journal* (July 22, 1992); Rick Wartzman, "Rockwell Division Gets Suspension on U.S. Contracts," *Wall Street Journal* (November 11, 1991).

CARYN E. NEUMANN, PH.D.
OHIO STATE UNIVERSITY

Roosevelt, Franklin D. (1882–1945)

IN NOVEMBER 1932, Franklin Roosevelt, popularly known as FDR, won the presidential election in the midst of the worst depression the country has ever known. Ignoring the tradition of a two-term limit on the office begun in 1799 by George Washington (1732–99), Roosevelt also won the next three elections. Roosevelt led the United States through the twin crises of the Great Depression and World War II and is ranked along with Abraham Lincoln (1809–65) as the two best presidents in American history. Lincoln was often called a "constitutional dictator" because of the extensive powers he used to deal with the Civil War. In turn, Roosevelt reshaped the office of the presidency by amassing extensive emergency executive powers that changed presidential powers and defined the modern presidency.

With the stock market and the banking industry reeling from the effects of the Depression early in the Roosevelt administration, the Department of Justice (DOJ) began intensive investigations of white-collar crimes. In 1933, Congress passed the Securities Act of 1933, which became popularly known as the Truth in Securities Act. Since the bill had been designed "to prohibit deceit, misrepresentation," and other kinds of securities fraud, DOJ was frequently involved with prosecuting violations of the act.

In 1942, after the Japanese attack on Pearl Harbor, the Roosevelt administration cited emergency powers against espionage and sabotage in rounding up and interning Japanese Americans in California Federal lawmakers on the West Coast spent a good deal of time rounding up those who refused to comply with the restrictions on their activities. Roosevelt issued Executive Order 9066, "giving authority to certain military commanders to prescribe military areas from which any or all persons may be excluded, and with respect to which the right to enter, remain in, or leave, shall be subject to the discretion of the military commander." This order was upheld by the U.S. Supreme Court in *Korematsu v. United States*, and was not finally resolved until 1988 when the government paid reparations to surviving internees.

Roosevelt was well aware of the problems with war profiteering that had plagued Woodrow Wilson during World War I, and he forcefully announced throughout World War II that he did not want to see a single millionaire made by exploiting war production. Much of the information about war profiteering as well as abuses and waste in government contracts was derived from a Senate Committee chaired by Senator Harry Truman (D-Missouri). Federal lawmakers were vigilant in enforcing bans against war profiteering and policing American interaction with Axis countries. Nevertheless, records released in the late 1990s revealed that a number of American businesses (IBM, for one) had been either overtly or covertly involved with Nazi Germany.

THE NEW DEAL

Roosevelt was a pragmatist and responded to the economic and social emergency of the Depression. He believed that the government had a responsibility to do everything that was possible to turn the country around, and he was willing to do anything within his presidential power to bring this about, regardless of whether that power exceeded his Constitutional authority.

Roosevelt made the banking crisis his first priority. He called Congress into special session and declared a four-day bank holiday and established control over the export of gold. He would later remove the United States from the gold standard. Within five days of FDR's inauguration, the Emergency Banking Act had become law. An upswing in public confidence was immediate, and the stock market reopened after the banking holiday in a "bullish mood."

Roosevelt's next move was to curb federal payments by cutting the salaries of Congress members and all federal personnel and decreasing the benefits paid to veterans. FDR estimated that these cuts would slash half a billion dollars from the federal budget. In response to campaign promises, Roosevelt asked Congress to authorize a modification of the Volstead Act, legalizing the sale of beer and light wine. He had promised in the 1932 campaign to promote passage of the 21st Amendment, which repealed Prohibition, and it was ratified on December 5, 1933.

In what became known as the first Hundred Days, Roosevelt initiated a number of additional major policy reforms: The Federal Emergency Relief Act, Agricultural Adjustment Act, Emergency Farm Act, Tennessee Valley Authority (TVA) Act, Truth in Securities Act, Emergency Conservation Work Act, Home Owners' Loan Act, National Recovery Act, National Recovery Administration, Glass-Steagall Banking Act, Farm Credit Act, and Railroad Coordination Act, all quickly passed in a flurry of legislation.

After the Hundred Days, Roosevelt succeeded in implementing an enormous amount of social welfare legislation that included: social security, public housing, unemployment compensation, and public works projects. Many of FDR's policies were accomplished through executive order. For example, Roosevelt established the Fair Employment Practices Commission to prohibit discrimination in hiring among government agencies and military suppliers. FDR was also active in establishing foreign policy initiatives. He opened diplomatic relations with the Soviet Union, announced the Good Neighbor Policy toward South America, and promoted a Reciprocal Trade Agreement, lowering tariffs and extending free trade.

When Roosevelt was blocked, he reacted by bulldozing his enemies. While members of the Democratic Caucus usually supported New Deal legislation, Southern Democrats and Republicans quire often did not. In retaliation, FDR launched a campaign in the 1938 elections to convince voters to remove recalcitrant members of Congress from office and endorsed other candidates that were Roosevelt supporters. He was only partially successful.

PACKING THE COURT

When the Supreme Court found early New Deal legislation unconstitutional, Roosevelt devised a court-packing scheme that would have added a new, liberal justice for every current justice over the age of 70 who would not retire. Despite the general outrage and the refusal of Congress to fall in line with this clear abuse of executive power, Roosevelt's scheme worked. In what became known as "the switch in time that saved nine," members of the court decided to change their position on New Deal policies, and the number of the court remained at nine.

In the wake of Pearl Harbor, Roosevelt's executive style was more welcome and Congress passed the first War Powers Act, giving FDR an incredible amount of power to oversee the fitting of the nation for war. It was up to the president to establish defense priorities, control rationing and supplies, and identify what could and what could not be produced by American manufacturing plants. If a plant refused to cooperate, the president was given the authority for the government to take it over for the war effort. By executive order, Roosevelt established the Office of Price Administration (OPA) and the Office of Economic Stabilization, giving them extensive power over prices, wages, and profits. OPA was also in charge of rationing war goods and scarce items, such as butter, sugar, shoes, automobile tires, and gasoline. FDR also created the War Labor Board and gave them extensive powers to regulate labor and impose sanctions when necessary. In 1942, the Emergency Price Control Act retroactively endorsed FDR's emergency agencies. During the war, other agencies sprang up like wildfire, creating continued contention between the president and Congress.

In a major leap forward toward ending gender discrimination, the Roosevelt administration was much more open to employing women than previous administrations of either major party had been. Since FDR had not been supportive of women's suffrage as a young senator, much of the credit for his turnaround has been given to his wife Eleanor (1884–1962). At her urging, FDR appointed Frances Perkins (1882–1965) as the Secretary of Labor, the first American woman ever to serve in a Cabinet position. Women made great strides during World War II. Actively recruited by the government, women entered the work force in unprecedented numbers and engaged in jobs that had previously been closed to them. For example, female pilots did most of the ferrying of planes and military equipment to release men for active military work. Thousands of women also served at the frontlines as nurses or as representatives of various organizations, and at home, women worked in factories, government, businesses, and the defense industry.

Roosevelt's near-dictatorial powers, contrary to the spirit and the laws of the U.S. Constitution, extended to the world stage by the closing days of World War II. As negotiations began for planning a post-war world, the leaders of the United States, Great Britain, the Soviet Union met at the Yalta Conference from February 4 to 11, 1945, at a remote location on the Black Sea.

Carving up the postwar world not unlike any cabal of capitalists, the conference established territorial changes and postwar governments for Germany and other Axis countries. Hindsight has shown that Soviet leader Josef Stalin entered the conference determined to acquire territory for the Soviet Union that would provide opportunities for expanding communism throughout Europe. This strategy proved successful in paving the way for Poland, Czechoslovakia, Hungary, Rumania, and Bulgaria to become Soviet satellites. Germany was divided into separate occupation zones, with the United States, Britain, the Soviet Union, and France each in charge of a section. By 1945, 13 years of steering the United States through the twin crises of the Great Depression and World War II had taken a great physical toll on Roosevelt who had developed polio in 1921. In the final days of the war, the president died on April 12, 1945.

SEE ALSO

World War II; Truman, Harry; reform and regulation; United States; gender discrimination; elite crime.

BIBLIOGRAPHY. George C. Edwards, et al., *The Presidency and Public Policy Making* (University of Pittsburgh Press, 1985); Alvin M. Josephey, Jr., *The Congress of The United States* (American Heritage, 1975); Cabell Phillips, *The 1940s: Decade of Triumph and Trouble* (Macmillan, 1975); Norman Polmar and Thomas B. Allen, *World War II: America at War, 1941–45* (Random House, 1991); Arthur M. Schlesinger, *The Coming of the New Deal* (Houghton Mifflin, 1958); Norman C. Thomas, et al., *The Politics of the Presidency* (Congressional Quarterly, 1993); Daniel Ernest White, *The United States Presidency in Perspective* (Nova Publishers, 1996).

ELIZABETH PURDY, PH.D.
INDEPENDENT SCHOLAR

Roosevelt, Theodore (1858–1919)

AS SCION of a prominent and wealthy New York family, Theodore Roosevelt was an unlikely candidate to become a corporate reformer. Roosevelt began his reform career in 1888, serving on the National Civil Service Commission, appointed by Republican Benjamin Harrison and continuing for two more years under Grover Cleveland. Under Republican Mayor William L. Strong, Roosevelt served as president of the New York City Police Commission, where he made a name for himself as a reformer, going after the department's notorious ties to criminal elements and demanding increased professionalism. He was named assistant secretary of the navy during the first William McKinley administration, but resigned to embark on his brief-but-exciting adventures in Cuba during the Spanish American War. Beginning training with his Rough Riders in May, he was home by August. This enhanced his public image and assured his nomination as Republican party candidate for governor of New York, provided he promised to consult the Grand Old Party (GOP) Republican machine, led by Senator Thomas C. Platt.

Roosevelt won a relatively narrow victory over his Democratic opponent. He was never a follower, and he had an independent streak that was apparent even during his tenure as governor, with his early efforts to control corporate greed and with his political appointments. New York Republicans were glad to see him move on to Washington, D.C., as vice presidential candidate for the second McKinley campaign. In a party that did not like surprises, Roosevelt's wide personal appeal trumped his reputation as a wild card. Few could foresee that he would assume the presidency, as he did in September 1901 following McKinley's assassination.

Less than six months after taking office, Roosevelt launched his first salvo against the great corporations when his attorney general announced pending action toward the Northern Securities Company. The result of an attempted takeover of the J. P. Morgan-controlled Northern Pacific by the upstart E. H. Harriman had turned into a fateful stock market corner in May 1901. As a compromise to "protect their assets," the Northern Securities Company combined the assets of the Northern Pacific, the Great Northern Railroad, and the Chicago Burlington and Quincy under the ownership of Morgan, Harriman, and James J. Hill, three of the era's most formidable financiers.

Roosevelt knew that if his action was upheld, it would overturn a 19th-century precedent that limited the ability of government regulation of interstate commerce. When Roosevelt authorized Attorney General Philander Knox to file an antitrust suit, thus signaling his intentions to test the limits of the Sherman Antitrust Act, he placed himself in direct opposition to J.P. Morgan, who, under the McKinley administration, had acted without restraint as the country's *de facto* central banker.

By the summer of 1902, Roosevelt was campaigning in the midterm elections using his bully pulpit to gain advantage in the public relations battle, stating: "The great corporations which we have grown to speak of rather loosely as trusts are the creatures of the State, and the State not only has the

right to control them, but is duty-bound to control them, wherever the need of such control is shown."

As the antitrust action made its way through the courts, Roosevelt planned to increase the pressure on railroad trusts. Roosevelt's first success was an increased appropriation for the new antitrust division of the Justice Department. Congress passed the Elkins Law outlawing rebating shortly thereafter, which was supported by the Railroads themselves against whom shippers had used rebate threats to lower rates. The rest of Roosevelt's program would prove more difficult.

To move things along, Roosevelt sought the assistance of Morgan lieutenant George Perkins. The Senate passed a bill creating the Department of Commerce and Labor in January 1903. Only the House version, passed on January 17, 1903, allowed for a Bureau of Corporations that would specifically investigate corporations and report to the president, giving Roosevelt a certain amount of executive discretion.

OREGON LAND SCANDALS

While Roosevelt's conservation efforts are well known, the Oregon Land scandals, which partially precipitated action to transfer authority over land from the general land office to a new Bureau of Forestry, are often overlooked. Commissioner of Public Lands Binger Hermann, working with public officials including Senator John H. Mitchell, had assisted the fraudulent transfer of public lands to large mining and lumber companies in the Pacific Northwest. Roosevelt appointed a new commissioner, William A. Richards, former governor of Wyoming, and while visiting Oregon in May 1903, ordered Richards to investigate. The dimensions of the scandal grew over next several years.

This mishap set the stage for Roosevelt's creation of a Public Lands Commission, to which he appointed Gifford Pinchot, Richards, and Frederick H. Newall. The commission was directed to report on the condition and operation of existing land laws and to recommend public land policy.

These efforts did not end the Roosevelt administration's reliance on major lumber and cattle corporations in developing public land policy, which favored sustained yield and grazing leases over preservation as advocated by John Muir and others, and excluded small-scale stockmen and lumber operators.

A Post Office Department scandal became public in spring 1903, leading to the resignation of the superintendent in charge of salaries, followed by an assistant attorney general charged with destroying documents. Charles Emory Smith, postmaster general under McKinley, and his assistant Perry S. Heath faced accusations of using political corruption, but lack of evidence prevented prosecution.

Roosevelt won the 1904 election on the basis of his immense popularity. However, the Democrats raised the issue of contributions from the very corporations that Roosevelt had been trying to regulate. This issue would continue to brew during Roosevelt's second term, as the public began to perceive the tremendous political power of the new corporations. Popular publications including *McClures Magazine*, *World's Work*, and *Colliers* focused pubic attention on corruption in cities, unsafe products, diseased food, and unscrupulous business practices.

As a result, the public was ready to back Roosevelt's progressive program of business regulation. A major target continued to be the railroads. While previous legislation had outlawed rebates, there remained a perception that rates unfairly discriminated against certain localities and even regions, particularly the South and Midwest. The Pure Food and Drug Act and regulation of the meat industry followed. Legislation had been proposed since the mid-1890s, but stalled through 1903 due to pressure from the food industry. Muckrakers' efforts to expose patent drugs coupled with the work of the new Consumers League and American Medical Association resulted in a Pure Food and Drug bill that was introduced by Senator Heyburn of Idaho in December, 1905.

Nearly simultaneously, publication of Upton Sinclair's *The Jungle* sparked investigation of Chicago, Illinois, stockyards, which were dangerously unclean and unsafe. A meat inspection law was introduced May 1906 and was signed into law on June 30 along with the Pure Food and Drug Act. Senator Albert J. Beveridge pronounced it "the most pronounced extension of federal power in every direction ever enacted, including even the rate bill itself."

In 1906, Garfield had begun an inquiry into monopolistic practices of Standard Oil, which threatened independent oilmen in Kansas, and concluded that Standard Oil had been receiving secret rebates and other illegal discriminations. This culminated in a move by Department of Justice to dissolve Standard Oil of New Jersey in November 1906. The department also investigated and threatened action against International Harvester, an American Tobacco Company accused of ruthless tactics toward independent wholesalers and retailers. The Department of Justice sued American Tobacco in July 1907, as the White house urged abandonment of the planned suit against International Harvester, another Morgan holding. By now the Roosevelt administration doubted that the Sherman Antitrust Act could truly be enforced.

Roosevelt preferred a middle way of fighting monopoly while respecting the economic and social contributions of big corporations. At Roosevelt's direction, James R. Garfield of the new Bureau of Corporations conducted investigations and then "reached understandings" with the corporate leaders. Sometimes these agreements prevented legitimate prosecution by the Department of Justice.. In the case of the beef industry, Garfield actually promised immunity to companies, eventually thwarting their prosecution by the Justice Department.

SEE ALSO

Justice, Department of; antitrust; Sherman Antitrust Act; Sinclair, Upton; Food and Drug Administration; tobacco industry; monopoly.

BIBLIOGRAPHY. Ron Chernow, *The House of Morgan* (Touchstone, 1990); Lewis L. Gould, *The Presidency of Theodore Roosevelt* (University Press of Kansas, 1991); Jean Strouse, *Morgan: American Financier* (Random House, 1999).

JANE G. HAIGH
UNIVERSITY OF ARIZONA

Ross, Edward (1866–1951)

E. A. ROSS was a very influential sociologist of his time. He was well known as one of the founding fathers of American sociology. Ross attended Coe College in Iowa where he earned a A.B. degree in 1886. Awarded his Ph.D. from Johns Hopkins University in 1891, his career spanned over 35 years and his influence is still felt today. The basic elements of Ross's extensive work can best be examined in his *Foundations of Sociology* (1905), *Social Control* (1901), *Social Psychology* (1908), *Principles of Sociology* (1920, 1930, 1938), and *Sin and Society: An Analysis of Latter-Day Inequity* (1907). Ross explored the subject matter of sociology and the nature of sociology in relation to the other social sciences.

Although he never conducted research on crime or developed specific criminological theories, his research on social control has had a major impact on criminology. In fact, he provided the first separate dialogue on the subject. Ross outlined the theory of social control by identifying the grounds of control, the means of control, and the system of control.

His book, *Sin and Society*, vividly expressed his dismay about corrupt business practices. Ross conceptualized the idea of the criminaloid as a social type who enjoys a public image as a pillar of the community and a paragon of virtue; but beneath this veneer of respectability is actually a very different persona, one that is committed to personal gain through any means. The criminaloids encounter feeble opposition and since their practices are often more lucrative than the typical criminal act, they distance their more scrupulous rivals in business and politics and reap an uncommon worldly prosperity. The key to the criminaloid is not evil impulse, but moral insensibility.

The criminaloid prefers to prey on the anonymous public and is therefore an even greater threat. He even goes beyond this by convincing others to act instead of acting himself, which protects him from liability and being labeled a criminal, and is instead immune to such scrutiny. The criminaloid practices a protective impersonation of the good. The criminoloid counterfeits the good citizen.

The criminaloid plays the support of his local or special group against the larger society. He identifies with some legitimate group and, when necessary, he calls upon this group to protect its own. He will use guile and political connections to rebuke reforms which would have an impact on his practices. Ross believed so long as the public conscious is lazy, the criminaloid has no sense of immorality. The criminaloid flourishes until the growth of morality overtakes the growth of opportunities to prey upon.

Ross regarded these criminaloids as men who lacked morals and he believed that they were directly accountable for unnecessary deaths of consumers and workers. Ross believed that these actions needed to be examined and they were just as, if not more, harmful than the ordinary criminal. The criminaloid personifies the corporate criminal and is an antecedent of Edwin H. Sutherland's white-collar criminal.

SEE ALSO

Sutherland, Edwin H.; differential association theory; self-control theory.

BIBLIOGRAPHY. J.O. Hertzler, "Edward Alsworth Ross: Sociological Pioneer and Interpreter," *American Sociological Review* (v.16/5, 1951); Stephen Rosoff, Henry N. Pontell, and Robert Tillman, *Profit Without Honor: White-collar Crime and the Looting of America* (Prentice-Hall, 2002); E.A. Ross, *Sin and Society: An Analysis of Latter-Day Inequity* (Houghton, Mifflin, 1965); E.A. Ross, *Foundations of Sociology* (Macmillan, 1905); E.A. Ross, *Social Control: A Survey of the Foundations of Social Order* (Macmillan, 1901); E.A. Ross, *Social Psychology: An Outline and Sourcebook* (Macmillan, 1908); E.A. Ross, *The Principles of Sociology* (Century, 1938); E.A. Ross, "The Criminaloid," *The Atlantic Monthly* (v.99/44, 1907).

DEBRA E. ROSS, PH.D.
GRAND VALLEY STATE UNIVERSITY

Rostenkowski, Daniel (1928–)

AN ILLINOIS Democrat, Dan Rostenkowski served 18 terms in the U.S. House of Representatives between 1958 and 1994. He used the Congressional seniority system to eventually assume the chairmanship of the House Ways and Means Committee which controls the government's purse strings. In that role, Rostenkowski became one of the most powerful figures in Washington, D.C. He also used his influential position to plunder the government on behalf of himself, his family, and his friends.

17 COUNTS OF GREED RUN AMOK

Rostenkowski's bid for a 19th term ended in defeat in 1994 at the hands of a political unknown after he had been indicted earlier that year on 17 felony counts of corruption. The indictment painted a devastating picture of greed run amok. The charges included placing "ghost" employees, who did little or no work, on the Congressional payroll, using government employees to remodel his home at taxpayers' expense, charging expensive gifts for friends to his Congressional account and falsely representing them as official items, illegally billing the government for fraudulent car leases, converting campaign money to personal use, and obstructing justice by asking grand jury witnesses to withhold evidence. The most flagrant of the allegations, and the one that spoke volumes of his petty larceny, involved Rostenkowski's routine practice of exchanging stamps from the Congressional Post Office for cash. Added together, the cost of Rostenkowski's embezzlement and misappropriations was nearly $700,000.

On April 9, 1996, Rostenkowski entered into a plea bargain in federal court under which he agreed to plead guilty to two counts of mail fraud in exchange for the government dropping the remaining counts. He was sentenced to 17 months in prison and fined $100,000. He was paroled in 1998 after serving 13 months in a federal penitentiary. When she imposed his sentence, the presiding judge declared Rostenkowski's misconduct a "reprehensible breach of trust."

Rostenkowski later worked as a political consultant and commentator. He received a presidential pardon in 2000 during the waning hours of the Bill Clinton administration.

SEE ALSO
corruption; mail fraud; wire fraud.

BIBLIOGRAPHY. Toni Locy, "Rostenkowski Fraud Plea Brings 17-Month Sentence," *Washington Post* (April 10, 1996); Stephen M. Rosoff, Henry N. Pontell, and Robert Tillman, *Profit Without Honor: White-Collar Crime and the Looting of America* (Prentice Hall, 1998).

STEPHEN M. ROSOFF
UNIVERSITY OF HOUSTON, CLEAR LAKE
HENRY N. PONTELL
UNIVERSITY OF CALIFORNIA, IRVINE

Rusnak, John (1964–)

A FORMER TRADER for Allfirst Bank (a U.S. mid-Atlantic regional bank known in 2004 as M&T Bank), John Rusnak pleaded guilty to bank fraud on October 24, 2002, in connection with the $691.2 million the bank lost through his foreign-currency trading.

Rusnak, hired by Allfirst as a trader in 1993, suffered trading losses buying yen for the bank in 1997. He then began to hide some losses, and the size of reported losses by using fictitious options and changing the currency exchange rates which came into the bank's trading system. False trades disguised the fact that Rusnak was also trading over his limit and taking risks that were too high. The 2002 Ludwig Report on the incident found that Rusnak broke rules that should have offered safeguards, and that he manipulated personnel who should have been supervising and checking on his activities.

Among other points, the report also determined that the bank's internal auditing was deficient and Rusnak's supervisors were not sufficiently experienced or competent to supervise him. Trading was done with Allfirst's funds rather than that of bank customers so it was Allfirst itself that took the losses. Rusnak earned performance bonuses of more than $650,000 beyond his salary due to the appearance of profitable trading.

In January 2003, Rusnak was sentenced as part of a plea agreement to 90 months (7.5 years) in prison and ordered to pay restitution to the bank or its successor. The judge also ordered that during the five years he was on probation following the incarceration, Rusnak enter substance abuse and gambling programs, and pay $1,000 per month restitution. Unless the federal government gave permission, Rusnak was also forbidden to ever work at a bank. Also dismissed by Allfirst were co-workers, supervisors, and managers who did not notice the fraud and losses.

SEE ALSO
bank fraud; securities fraud; Allied Irish Banks; Securities and Exchange Commission.

BIBLIOGRAPHY. Larry Rullison, "Allfirst Trader Rusnak Sentenced to 7.5 Years in Prison," *Washington Business Journal* (January 13, 2003); Sanjay Bhandari, "Treasury: Allied Irish Bank: How to Lose OE500M," *Accountancy* (June 1, 2002); Bill Atkinson and Gail Gibson, "Rusnak Indicted for Bank Fraud in Allfirst Scandal," *Baltimore Sun* (June 6, 2002).

LINDA M. CREIBAUM
ARKANSAS STATE UNIVERSITY

Russia

WHITE-COLLAR, corporate, and organized crime in Russia literally exploded in the years following the disintegration of the Soviet state in the late 1980s and early 1990s. By 2003, the statistics were staggering: In addition to controlling conventional illegal practices such as drug trafficking, prostitution, and money laundering, it is estimated that the Russian Mafia controls as many as half the banks in the country as well as key economic sectors such as petroleum distribution, pharmaceuticals, and consumer products distribution.

Their influence reaches into the highest levels of government and industry. It is widely acknowledged that the Mafia has close links with ranking members of the Russian government. The arrest and forced exile of leading business figures such as Boris Berezovsky, Vladimir Gusinsky and, most notably, the arrest in 2003 of Mikhail Khodorkovsky, Russia's richest man and the dominant figure in Russia's petroleum industry, signals less a crackdown on organized crime than a power play between rival power factions at the top of society. The dominance of organized crime in Russia reflects the deep crisis in the Russian economy.

Some commentators see the rise of organized crime as part of a semi-feudal system inherited from Soviet totalitarianism. Others contend that it is somehow rooted in the Russian character itself, flowing from the "backwardness" and "underdevelopment" of primitive "Eastern" economies. While these interpretations go some way in capturing the shocking extent of corruption, violence, and inequality linked to organized crime, they resolutely miss the mark in understanding the origins and development of the Russian Mafia. It is necessary to firmly place organized crime within the context of late-20th century capitalism as a whole, as well as within the specific trajectory of the Russian economy and society from the Soviet regime to the 21st century. As Boris Kagarlitsky persuasively argues, "In the 1990s, post-communist capitalism was not being 'civilized,' but Western capitalism was turning savage. It was simply that the scale and consequences of the reforms on the periphery were far more striking than in the center."

The crisis is certainly rooted in the nature of the Soviet system. Yet the rise of the Mafia should also be situated in the shock therapy program of privatizations, structural adjustment programs, and gutting of social welfare urged on by Western politicians and corporations. Indeed, Vadim Volkov argues convincingly that organized crime "rests on the division between the legitimate world and the underworld." To understand organized crime in the former Soviet Union, thus requires looking at the connection between and overlapping of both traditional areas of criminal activity and so-called legitimate economic activities.

ORIGINS OF CRIME

Severe economic problems existed in Russia long before the reform programs of Soviet Premier Mikhail Gorbachev brought them to world attention in the mid-1980s. What Mike Haynes calls the "centrally directed, military industrialization" program of the command economy and the competitive pressures of the world market led to a top-heavy and inefficient economy from the 1960s onward: "Too often, from a global point of view, Russia had the wrong type of industry in the wrong place; plants were too large, turning out too diversified a range of products with equipment that was less efficient than that elsewhere in the world economy." Consequently, parallel economic structures mushroomed, creating power centers that gradually became independent of the state. As the bureaucratic machine disintegrated, a barter market proliferated which further weakened the system of centralized production and supply of goods.

In the wake of the crumbling of the state-controlled economy, Russian governments in the 1990s based their economic policies on three key planks: privatization, liberalization, and macro-economic stabilization. Abolishing price controls led to rapid inflation and a monetary crisis. Newly privatized companies were short of cash and forced to expand the existing barter economy to secure financing and supplies. Productivity and productive output fell precipitously: both industrial and agricultural production declined by almost half from 1989 to 1995. Few companies paid their taxes which led to a crisis in state finances, savage cuts to social services and massive layoffs or failure to pay wages in the public sector. The "shadow" economy of smuggling and black markets grew to represent some 40 percent of the gross domestic product.

The effects of economic crisis have been devastating on the Russian population. The United Nations' UNICEF agency laments the "demographic implosion," "appalling numbers of excess deaths" and spiraling suicide rate among young people. Real wages have fallen by 40 percent. A majority of the population lives below the basic poverty line. Life expectancy for Russian males in the late 1990s was lower than in India.

It was the Russian Mafia and its political allies in the state and legitimate business that stepped in to fill the vacuum resulting from economic chaos. It is worthwhile first underscoring the links between the old Soviet ruling class and the new political and economic elite. Many current politicians, business leaders, and Mafia figures cut their teeth in the ministries and economic agencies of the Soviet state. As Mike Haynes states, "There is an irresistible body of evidence to indicate that the people now in charge in Russia are substantially the same as those who ran it in Soviet times." Citing Russian academic Olga Kryshtanovskaya, he observes that former Soviet officials accounted for 74.3 percent of the government and 75 percent of President Boris Yeltsin's presidential team in 1995, including Yeltsin himself. The figure reaches as high as 82.3 percent among the regional state chiefs. Among the new business elite, the figure is 61 percent, but Kryshtanovskaya admits that this is probably an underestimate since many of the current business oligarchs and their deputies were unofficial agents of state bosses in the Soviet regime.

In the old Soviet system, black marketing, bribery, and corruption of officials had become widespread by the 1970s and expanded through the early 1990s. Controlled by a tightly knit corps of leaders nicknamed "sharks," they had, according to Aleksandr Gurov, "diversified criminal organizations with quite extensive regional connections … They included representatives of the administration of various [state] enterprises who often were [Communist] party members and had high positions." Many of the organizations began first with illegal protection rackets and smuggling. When the Soviet state collapsed, these small-scale criminal outfits, along with a range of other semi-legal and legitimate business people, many of them former state officials, were best placed to take advantage of the economic chaos that resulted from neo-liberal economic policies.

The process of privatization of state industries in the 1990s provided the most lucrative access for organized criminal elements, allowing them to consolidate and expand their traditional illegitimate business interests as well as venture into "legitimate" endeavors. The process went as follows: A state company would be abolished and replaced by a joint-stock company with the same personnel and assets as before. The controlling shares would pass into the hands of the state and be sold at deflated prices to a new cadre of leaders largely comprised of existing officials tied to Mafia interests. Windfall profits would be gained from these fire sales.

This process occurred in the huge raw material and natural resource industries as well as banks; in some cases, deals have then been made with Western companies as in the case of the mega-merger of British Petroleum and the Tyumen Oil Company of Siberia. The latter company has been suspected of numerous legal violations since it was formed in 1997 out of the privatization of a Soviet-era state company. The billions of dollars in profits made by these turnovers and by the export of goods produced in these industries have, moreover, been spirited away into Western bank accounts, garnering huge fortunes for a small minority of business tycoons. As much as 65 percent of Western aid in the 1990s was also stolen by such elites and ended up in private bank accounts in Switzerland and elsewhere.

ELITE CRIME

This new business elite, considered legal and democratic, but with close ties to organized crime organizations, has, according to James Hughes, "succeeded in dramatically eclipsing other social groups" in local, regional and national politics. Leading criminals have even been elected as deputies in the Russian Duma (legislature) where they use their influence to dole out tax breaks and other benefits to friends and allies.

A similar process of corruption by organized crime in concert with local politicians has occurred among those private companies that sprung up in the 1990s to pick up the slack of the declining state companies. Organized crime and/or local political leaders would force companies into bankruptcy by cutting off credit or disrupting production and sales. They would then coerce managers and buy the company at rock-bottom prices, relying on the promise of contracts with cozy regional governments to gain large profits. Other types of economic crime include transfer pricing, the act of insider or parent holding companies purchasing goods at below market prices and then reselling them at higher prices. Yet another consists of buying raw materials and natural resources at domestic prices and then illegally reselling them in the higher-priced international market. In these ways, by early 1997, 41,000 companies, 400 banks and 80 percent of all joint ventures were controlled by organized crime.

CASE IN POINT

The banking industry is an interesting case in point. Large banks and the state are interdependent. The state, as emitter of bonds and as the regulating agency of the monetary system, is an important customer of the banks. The state, in turn, relies on banks to finance the deficit and stabilize financial markets. In this environment, extensive networks of corruption have developed. The banks gain preferential treatment from the state through sales of bonds at low prices and return the favor by financing political campaigns.

Banks have also been given control of managing state funds and the privatization process. With the control of the auctions of state industry, the banks ended up buying many privatized companies for negligible prices and have in this manner developed into powerful financial-industrial groups. Banks not yet powerful enough to gain favors from the state focus on the profits to be gained from investment fraud, forgery, money laundering, and transfer of capital to the West.

Capital flight, estimated at $100 billion since the early 1990s, meant fewer taxes for state coffers (only 15 percent of companies paid their taxes in full and on time in 1998) and a drain on hard currency which is used to pay off the spiraling state debts to Western banks. The state itself was thus weakened through this process of privatization and liberalization. In addition to the effective loss of power in economic planning, tax and monetary policy, even the security forces themselves (military and police) lost the capacity to investigate and prosecute organized crime. Private security forces hired to protect enterprise and composed of ex-members of the Soviet military and secret police blossomed under the auspices of organized crime. Intimidation of competitors and the few state security agencies that remain have led to violence, including beatings, arson, and assassinations.

The state defense industry that sells military hardware, including nuclear technology, to foreign governments has been pilfered of billions since the early 1990s. In 2002 alone, $5 billion in profits were made through the sales of arms yet only a tiny fraction ended up in government accounts since well-placed government officials, tied to organized crime, intervened to skim off the majority of profits. Huge brokerage and freight fees are paid to foreign intermediaries or dummy companies and production costs are exaggerated so that most of the profits end up in the hands of a few insiders.

The money is then laundered in foreign countries, such as Cyprus, and divided up among the players. While the state is the nominal producer of these defense products, it ends up with almost nothing. The assassinations of two leading directors of state defense industries in June 2003 signaled that the ferocious competition among criminal organizations to muscle in on arms sales has moved to a violent stage.

In addition to infiltration and dominance of legitimate business, organized crime has considerably expanded its traditional criminal activities, using connections and profits from one to finance and support the other. Activities run the gamut from drug trafficking and prostitution to money laundering and credit-card fraud. Many of these activities have expanded to include extensive operations in other Eastern European countries, North America, Europe, Israel, and South America. The extent of the power of organized crime outside Russia's borders is shown by the well-documented takeover of legitimate business in Russian emigré communities in the West.

HUMAN TRAFFICKING

Perhaps one of the most worrying developments is the growth in trafficking of women for the purpose of sexual exploitation. Under the control of organized crime in Russia, it has expanded in recent years into a multi-billion dollar market. Estimates suggest that as many as 500,000 women, largely from Russia, the Ukraine, Belarus and Latvia have been literally sold into prostitution to countries around the world. Mafia organizations falsely advertise in newspapers offering lucrative job opportunities abroad for women and then kidnap them and force them into prostitution. Other methods include recruitment to mail-order bride schemes, or entertainment tours where women have legal visas and are supposedly part of touring entertainment companies. Researchers stress that this form of modern-day slavery exists because of demand from the receiving countries which include many European, North American, and Asian nations.

There are few signs that organized crime will be broken or even reduced in the coming decade. The extent of the economic crisis in the former Soviet Union is so deep that criminal elements have infiltrated the highest echelons of economic and political power. Western nations, too, have largely turned a blind eye to such activities as they rely on the diplomatic support of the Russian government, and are firm supporters of the shock-therapy programs that have aided the consolidation of organized crime. Most observers admit that the only chance for reform will come from the mass of the population itself through the creation of a reliable legal and tax system, effective law enforcement, and socioeconomic policies which reduce the massive disparity between rich and poor. Yet the type of social and political movements required to turn the tide of corruption, violence and crime have only recently begun to organize.

SEE ALSO

public corruption; corruption; organized crime; prostitution; human trafficking.

BIBLIOGRAPHY. Pavel Felgengauer, "Organized Crime Declares War on the Kremlin's Secret Service Agents," *Novaya Gazeta* (June 16, 2003); Ben Fowkes, *The Post-Communist Era: Change and Continuity in Eastern Europe* (Macmillan, 1999); Kevin Flynn, "Rich Get Richer While the Poor Die Young," *The Guardian* (October 17, 2003); Tanya Frisby, "The Rise of Organized Crime in Russia: Its Roots and Social Significance," *Europe-Asia Studies* (v.50/1, 1998); Mike Haynes, *Russia: Class and Power, 1917-2000* (Bookmarks, 2000); Donna M. Hughes, "The Natasha Trade: The Transnational Shadow Market of Trafficking in Women," *Journal of International Affairs* (Spring 2000); Boris Kagarlitsky, *Russia under Yeltsin and Putin: Neo-Liberal Autocracy* (Pluto Press, 2002); Henry McDonald, "Mafia's Eircom Card Scam Cracked," *The Observer* (September 14, 2003); T.V. Parasuram, "Mobsters Control Half of Russia's Banks: FBI," *Financial Express* (October 24, 1998); "Nick Paton Walsh, "Moscow Crooks Turn to Arson in Property Boom," *The Observer* (March 9, 2003); Nick Paton Walsh, "Black Market Missiles Raise Terror Fears," *The Guardian* (August 13, 2003); Nick Paton Walsh, "Turning Point: Putin Shows his Authoritarian Hand," *The Guardian* (October 27, 2003); Heiko Pleines, "Corruption and Crime in the Russian Banking Sector," *Bericht des Biost* (June 1998); Louise Shelley, "Transnational Organized Crime: The New Authoritarianism," *The Illicit Global Economy and State Power* (Rowan & Littlefield, 1999); Vadim Volkov, *Violent Entrepreneurs: The Use of Force in the Making of Russian Capitalism* (Cornell University Press, 2002); Global Organized Crime Project, *Russian Organized Crime and Corruption* (Center for Strategic and International Studies, 2000).

SEAN PURDY, PH.D.
QUEEN'S UNIVERSITY, CANADA

S

Salomon Smith Barney

DESPITE ITS REPUTATION as an investment company that has produced solid results for its clients, Salomon Smith Barney (SSB) became mired in the corruption and greed that shook the securities industry in the 1990s. Smith Barney, which was founded in the late 19th century when the firms of Edward B. Smith and Charles Barney combined, was bought by Travelers Group in 1992. Travelers united Smith Barney with Salomon, Inc. Scandal hit the company in 1991 when Salomon's Paul Mozer set up a scam in which he used unsuspecting clients to buy more two-year Treasury notes than the legal limit allowed by the federal government. Of the $12.26 billion sold at a Treasury auction on May 22, 1991, Salomon bought 90 percent. As a result, the company was forced to pay a $290 million fine for defrauding the U.S. Treasury.

While Salomon Smith Barney was still recovering from the Treasury fiasco, government regulators levied a $300 million fine when it was discovered that SSB's telecom research analyst, Jack Grubman, had falsified company reports to make certain companies appear healthier than they actually were, causing a number of investors to lose substantial amounts of money. Federal and state regulators had little trouble tracing the actions in which Grubman promoted a number of companies that later went bankrupt, because he left a substantial e-mail trail. Investigators also uncovered information that led them to believe that the company's rivals had been paid to issue misleading reports to make designated companies look inviting to investors. Although he never admitted any wrongdoing, Grubman was ultimately banned from the securities industry for life and was forced to pay a $15 million fine.

Sandy Weill, chairman of Salomon Smith Barney, who was once known as the most powerful person on Wall Street, also fell victim to the scandal. Investigators learned that Weill had made a $1 million donation to an exclusive nursery school to ease the way for the application of Grubman's child. Weill has since been allowed to speak to SSB analysts only in the presence of lawyers.

He was also taken to task for not properly supervising Grubman and other individuals who provided misleading financial analysis, and he was required to issue a public apology to SSB clients. Evidence revealed that other SSB executives had also turned a blind eye to tainted research. For example, Michael Carpenter, who headed up SSB's global equity research team, was warned in a December 2000 memo that "legitimate concerns" had been raised "about the objectivity of [SSB] analysts."

While SSB was only one of 10 investment companies caught up in securities scandals in the 1990s, the company received the stiffest fine and was severely taken to task by federal and state regulators

As if financial scandals were not enough, the Los Angeles, California, office of SSB also became caught up in a sexual discrimination case in 1997. Around 2,000 female employees accused the company of creating a sexually hostile working environment. In December 2002, the women were awarded $3.2 million in compensatory and punitive damages after it was revealed in court that male employees had engaged in intimidation, ridicule, and insults in addition to playing pornographic videos, and engaging in other sexual activities.

One-fourth of the money from the securities fines was allotted to states, and the rest was distributed among various investors who were able to document that their losses derived from tainted research given them by Salomon Smith Barney. Investigators have also been interested in SSB's ties to the Enron Corporation scandal. Perhaps to distance itself from its scandalous past, Salomon Smith Barney became officially known in 2003 as Citigroup Global Markets.

SEE ALSO
securities fraud; Securities and Exchange Commission; Enron Corporation.

BIBLIOGRAPHY. Matthew Benjamin, "Wall Street Pays for Its Sins," *U.S. News and World Report* (May 12, 2003); David Colbert, *Eyewitness to Wall Street: 400 Years of Dreamers, Schemers, Busts, and Booms* (Broadway Books, 2001); Paula Dwyer, "Will It Matter?" *BusinessWeek* (May 12, 2003); "Top Wall Street Firm to Pay $3.2 Million in Discrimination Case," *Feminist Daily News* (December 27, 2002); "Under Fire," *BusinessWeek* (January 13, 2003); Nicolas Varchaver and Katherine Bonamici, "The Perils of Email," *Fortune* (February 17, 2003).

ELIZABETH PURDY, PH.D.
INDEPENDENT SCHOLAR

Saudi Arabia

THE KINGDOM of Saudi Arabia (KSA) was created in 1932 from a region that had historically been the home of the spiritual and temporal rulers of Arabia and many of the holiest places in Islam. The traditional form of rule in KSA has been autocracy, with the appointed leader taking counsel from a variable group of elders and advisers, many of whom are drawn from the leader's family. Decisions and policies have been left deliberately opaque. This method extends not just to the government service but also to the private sector, in which many decisions are made on the basis of mutual connections or of family trust and, hence, not subject to wider scrutiny. This has led to many opportunities for corruption and white-collar crime.

ABOVE SUSPICION

In common with other parts of the Middle East, many members of the ruling family consider themselves and the positions they occupy in society to be above suspicion. Each of the approximately 5,000 princes, for example, receives a royal pension and expects various privileges.

The unwillingness of the elite to be held accountable for business decisions means that bankruptcies and other failures are rarely disclosed, and so creditors and foreign workers are frequently left without compensation in such cases. This is exacerbated by the refusal of the KSA government to permit dealings with any business that also has dealings with Israel. This policy contravenes international trade law, which requires impartiality of treatment and, consequently, the KSA has not been bound to international conventions. Opposition to organized labor in the country has further meant that international labor standards cannot be enforced or even effectively monitored by the International Labor Organization (ILO). There are many reports of the abuse of domestic migrant workers and other service sector workers.

The KSA has operated under a strong policy of religious leadership in the Muslim world and this has manifested itself in the funding of various religious organizations. This funding is related to the Muslim practice of charitable giving, yet it supports the extreme form of Islamic thought, Wahhabism, which has led to tensions with Western countries. The West is considered by Wahhabite thinkers to maintain decadent and corrupt societies. Indeed, many people believe that it is their duty to combat such decadence and that they should be supported by their country and its institutions.

With the current monarch, King Fahd, and his family identified strongly with the West, particularly because of the decision to permit the stationing of U.S. troops in the KSA as part of the 1991 Gulf War against Iraq, extremist Islamic movements have gained strength and support. This has been manifested in terrorist attacks against Western interests by religious groups, some of which may have been supported through charitable giving. The alarming decline of the Saudi economy and the difficulties faced by educated Saudis in finding jobs they believe suitable has intensified tensions. Calls for reform of the corruption practiced by the elite have become more noticeable, and the state is reluctant to act too openly against religious dissent for fear of sparking a major uprising.

The KSA was the home of Osama bin Laden and many of the hijackers who committed the 2001 terrorist attacks on the United States. Bin Laden was a very wealthy industrialist who seems to have been able to sponsor acts of terrorism internationally from his own resources. The complexity of modern finance operations, conducted through the internet, has demonstrated the difficulties involved in tackling such terrorist money laundering.

The lack of transparency with respect to charitable giving and the anti-Western sentiment aroused by many of the religious recipients of Saudi state support have brought the kingdom under much greater scrutiny. International pressure on the Saudis to reform corporate and other practices in the early 2000s were compromised by the presence of so many of U.S. President George W. Bush's closest advisers who benefited from association with the Saudi oil industry.

Many investment deals in the oil industry require associated offset agreements by which the investing company makes additional contracts with local companies, many of which are controlled by members of the ruling elite. Some deals in industries such as armaments and aerospace are shrouded in additional layers of secrecy due to the need for security. However, it is allegedly apparent that local agents have been employed by the British government in the KSA, and elsewhere in the region, with a mandate to use bribery to obtain arms sales. One arms deal, the al Yamamah arms accord has resulted in a number of companies opening facilities in the KSA through offset arrangements, including Rolls Royce, Glaxo Wellcome and Tate & Lyle.

This Western interest has contributed to the large community of migrant Western workers in the kingdom, largely based in compounds, who were the victims of violence in 2003. Western com-

pounds have been linked with large-scale illegal alcohol drinking operations and a number of people have been arrested and imprisoned as a result of such allegations.

A number of large arms sales have also come under scrutiny as a result of suspicion that illegal commissions have been paid. The leadership and control which the kingdom exerts over the region means that the American-led reconstruction of Iraq and Afghanistan includes significant inputs from Saudi organizations, corporations, and individuals.

SEE ALSO
elite crime; multinational corporations; bribery; corruption; Arab nations.

BIBLIOGRAPHY. Said Aburish, "The Coming Arab Crash," *The Guardian* (October 18, 2001); Ed Blanche, "The Labyrinthine Money Trail of Osama Bin Laden," *Middle East* (January 2002); Rob Evans, Ian Traynor, Luke Harding, and Rory Carroll, "Web of State Corruption Dates Back 40 Years," *The Guardian* (June 13, 2003); Maggie Mulvihill, Jack Meyers, and Jonathan Wells, "Bush Advisers Cashed in on Saudi Gravy Train," *Boston Herald* (December 11, 2001); Dexter Jerome Smith, "Non-Oil Industry in the GCC," *Middle East* (May, 1998); Brian Whitaker, "Saudis Open a Can of Words," *The Guardian* (February 14, 2001).

JOHN WALSH, PH.D.
MAHIDOL UNIVERSITY, THAILAND

savings and loan fraud

SAVINGS and loan fraud refers to false representations or failure to disclose significant information with the intent of denying the savings and loan association of assets that legally belong to the savings and loan association. Perpetrators of savings and loan fraud are employees, owners, or persons closely affiliated with a savings and loan, who are in a position of trust and violate that trust for the purpose of enriching themselves at the expense of the owners and depositors of the savings and loan.

A savings and loan is a type of financial institution that takes deposits and, as originally conceived in the 1930s, uses the deposits for making mortgage loans to consumers. Examples of savings and loan fraud include trading stock on inside information, usurping opportunities or profits, engaging in self-dealing, or otherwise using the institution for personal gain.

Specific examples of insider abuse include loans to insiders in excess of that allowed by regulation; high risk speculative ventures; payment of exorbitant dividends at times when the institution is at or near insolvency; payment from institution funds for personal vacations, automobiles, clothing, and art; payment of unwarranted commissions and fees to companies owned by a shareholder; payment of "consulting fees" to insiders or their companies; use of insiders' companies for association business; and putting friends and relatives on the payroll of the savings and loan associations.

The varieties and possible permutations of criminal activity perpetrated by thrift operators are seemingly endless. By and large, however, fraud in the savings and loan industry fell into three general categories, classified as unlawful risk taking, looting, and covering up.

UNLAWFUL RISK TAKING

Deregulation made it legal for thrifts to invest in nontraditional, higher-risk activities, but regulations and laws were often broken in the process, either by extending these investment activities beyond permissible levels or by compounding the level of risk by, for example, inadequate marketability studies or poor supervision of loan disbursements

The deregulation of savings and loans' investment powers unleashed an escalating competitive process in which brokered deposits were a key ingredient. Overnight, ailing savings and loans could obtain huge amounts of cash to stave off their impending insolvency. As brokerage firms shopped across the country for the best return on their money, thrifts had to offer ever-higher interest rates to attract them. In this environment, the weakest thrifts grew the fastest.

By 1984, Edwin Gray, chairman of the Federal Home Loan Bank Board (FHLBB), became alarmed over the rate of growth of brokered deposits that he had attempted unsuccessfully to re-regulate. Broker deposits often entail huge sums, at high rates for the short term—not infrequently passing through an institution in 24 hours, then moving on to the next highest bidder. Institutions whose survival depends on such jumbo deposits are clearly vulnerable to the

effects of unexpected withdrawals. Large cash infusions facilitate risky speculative ventures, but conversely and more importantly, long-shot investments with the potential for high payoffs are undertaken by institutions desperate to offset the costs of high-interest deposits.

Among the most popular of high-risk strategies used in conjunction with brokered deposits are acquisition, development and construction loans (ADC). The power of federally chartered savings and loans to invest in commercial real-estate projects was expanded with the deregulation of 1982, so that thrifts could invest up to 40 percent of their total assets in such ventures. Increasingly, high-risk loans were made to developers to acquire and develop projects for commercial use, more than tripling such loans between 1980 and 1986. As long as a high-risk ADC loan remained within the 40 percent limit stipulated by federal regulations, they did not, by themselves, constitute misconduct. The problem was that, given the competitive pressure exerted on thrifts by the new deregulation and the proliferation of high-interest brokered deposits, some thrifts exceeded the federal ceiling on ADC loans and/or committed misconduct in handling them.

NO-RISK INVESTING

Because these high-risk loans have potential (although are unlikely) to be very profitable in the long run, and because they provide a desperately needed cash flow in the short run (in the form of percentage points paid up front), they are an extremely attractive source of investment to which faltering savings and loans increasingly turned in the early and mid-1980s. But it was the "no-risk" federally insured nature of these high risk investments that ensured their proliferation and abuse. For, should developers default on these loans, they suffered no personal liability; and deposits were protected by the Federal Savings and Loan Insurance Corporation (FSLIC) insurance. The short-term and long-term potential of these ADC loans, in combination with their low risk for the investor, triggered a scramble among savings and loans to enter the world of speculative development (particularly in Texas and other states where no ceiling existed for ADC lending).

Deregulation started an ever-escalating competition for deposits, and pressed some thrift operators

Detection of savings and loan fraud comes from uncovering the layers of deception like multiple amounting books.

into high-risk, often unlawful, loan arrangements. As deregulation lifted the ceiling on interest rates and intensified competition, it provided a primary incentive for fraud, and by opening up investment powers, it provided the opportunity; by simultaneously deviating from the free market model upon which these moves were ostensibly based, and increasing the level of protective FSLIC insurance, would-be "deregulators" added the irresistible force of temptation.

LOOTING

Collective embezzlement, also called looting, refers to the siphoning-off of funds from a savings and loan institution for personal gain, at the expense of the institution itself and with the implicit or explicit sanction of its management. This robbing one's own bank is estimated to be the single most costly category of crime in the thrift industry, having precipitated a significant number of thrift insolvencies to date. In some cases, thrift embezzlement takes the form of buying sprees, in which thrift operators, and others with inside access to thrift funds, purchase luxury goods and services and charge them to the institution. For example, when Erwin Hansen took over Centennial Savings and

Loan in California at the end of 1980, he threw a Centennial-funded, $148,000 Christmas party for 500 friends and invited guests that included a 10-course sit-down dinner, roving minstrels, court jesters, and pantomimes. Hansen and his companion Beverly Haines, a senior officer at Centennial, traveled extensively around the world in the thrift's private airplanes, purchased antique furniture at the thrift's expense, and "renovated" an old house in the California countryside at a cost of over $1 million, equipping it with a gourmet chef at an annual cost of $48,000. A fleet of luxury cars was put at the disposal of Centennial personnel, and the thrift's offices were adorned with art from around the world. Hansen died before he could be formally charged, but Haines was eventually convicted of having embezzled $2.8 million. Centennial's inevitable insolvency cost the FSLIC an estimated $160 million.

Other, more subtle forms of collective embezzlement include a variety of schemes to obtain excessive compensation for the institution's directors and officers. Compensations include salaries as well as bonuses, dividend payments, and perquisites for

Personal expenses beyond the norm for savings and loan executives now come under intense scrutiny.

executives. The most widespread techniques of looting discovered involve an array of special deals. For example, in "nominee loan" schemes, a "straw borrower" outside of the thrift obtains a loan for a third person, who is usually affiliated with the thrift from which the loan is received. Such nominee loans are a popular device for disguising violations of the regulation which limits unsecured commercial loans to affiliated persons to $100,000.

A related system for violating the loans-to-affiliated-persons regulation is reciprocal loan arrangements. Reciprocal loans are loans in which insiders from one bank authorizes loans to the insiders of another bank in return for similar loans. This scam has resulted in losses to taxpayers of $26 million when the loans defaulted and the institutions failed.

So called land flips use real estate deals as the mechanism for looting. Land flips are defined as transfers of land between related parties to fraudulently inflate the value of the land. The land is used as collateral for loans based on the inflated or fraudulent valuation. Loan amounts typically greatly exceed the actual value of the land. Loan broker J. William Oldenburg bought a piece of property in Richmond, California, in 1979 for $874,000. Two years later, after a number of flips, he had the land appraised at $83.5 million. After buying State Savings and Loans in Salt Lake City for $10.5 million, he sold the property to the newly acquired thrift for $416 million in outstanding deposits.

Linked financing, or daisy chains as it is known in the industry, is perhaps the most subtle and complex of the special deals used for embezzling. Linked financing is the practice of depositing money into a financial institution with the understanding that the financial institution will make a loan conditioned upon receipt of the deposits. It often involves large brokered deposits, made by a business. The brokers can then default on their loans, essentially obtaining free cash (these are called drag loans, because the borrower simply drags away the loan, with no intention of repayment); middlemen obtain a generous finder's fee; and thrift operators record hefty deposits and inflated assets, which spell extra bonuses and dividends for thrift executives.

Looting is not confined to inside operators of thrifts. More often than not, the scheme requires intricate partnerships with those outside the industry, usually in real estate or loan brokerage. In some cases the outsiders initiate the fraud by identifying weak thrifts as easy targets that are ripe for plucking. In one infamous deal, loan broker Charles J. Bazarian, Jr., engaged in fraudulent real estate transactions that contributed to the insolvency of two large California thrifts, Consolidated Savings Bank of Irvine and American Diversified Savings Bank of Costa Mesa. According to charges brought against Bazarian, in one instance he borrowed more than $9.5 million from Consolidated, putting close to $5 million of it in a partnership in which the owner of the thrift, Robert Ferrante, had a direct interest. The same year, Bazarian arranged a reciprocal transaction with American Diversified in which the thrift bought $15 million of worthless investor notes from Bazarian's brokerage firm, in exchange for Bazarian's purchase of $3.85 million in promissory notes and two pieces of real estate from the thrift. When federal regulator's finally closed the two thrifts, together they registered close to $200 million in losses.

Daisy chains, dead cows for dead horses, land flips, cash for trash, cash for dirt, kissing the paper, white knights—this playful jargon reflects the make-believe, candy-store mentality of this breed of white-collar criminal and belies the devastating consequences of their actions.

COVER UP

The most widespread criminal activity of thrift operators is the manipulation of accounting books and records, as well as engaging in transactions to cover up, or hide, from the regulator the fact that the thrift lacked sufficient capital required by statute and regulation. The thrift knows the regulator will close the thrift and the illegal activities will be brought to light.

In the cases of Manning Savings and Loan, American Heritage Savings and Loan of Bloomingdale and First Suburban Bank of Maywood, when the nominee loans became non-performing, the assets were taken back into the institution, again sold at inflated prices to straw purchasers, financed by the institution, in order to inflate the net worth of the bank or savings and loan. The clear purpose was to keep the federal regulatory agencies at bay by maintaining a net worth above the trigger point for forced reorganization or liquidation.

Probably most common, however, is simply adjusting the accounting books to shield the thrift from regulatory action. At one savings and loan, three irreconcilable sets of records were kept, two on different computer systems and one manually. The FHLBB aided ailing thrifts engaged in fraud to cover-up their illegal and unethical activity by establishing a number of bookkeeping strategies during the deregulatory period that provided the industry with the tools to juggle their books.

In 1981, the FHLBB developed and encouraged the use of new accounting procedures known as regulatory accounting procedures (RAP). The new procedures entailed a complex formula allowing for the understating of assets and the overstating of capital. The sole purpose of the new RAP techniques was to inflate an institution's capital-to-assets ratio, thereby bolstering its image of financial health, and warding off reorganization, which the FSLIC increasingly could not afford. The procedures created a gray area where the thrifts could commit fraud without detection, but it also sent the message that the board permitted deceptive accounting. The FHLBB failure to issue appropriate guidance on how to treat ADC transactions for accounting purposes resulted in the FHLBB sending the implicit message that it implicitly condoned accounting practices that increased a thrift's net worth, that is, encouraged accounting treatments of ADC transactions that inflated the net worth of thrifts.

Thrift fraud went relatively undetected by regulators, and was generally not dealt with through formal actions. This was partly due to the regulator's belief in deregulation and that the market would regulate thrifts, and that government intervention was not necessary.

Compounding the problem was that the resources of the FHLBB for examining thrifts remained constant for 20 years, despite the increased number of thrifts. In 1966, when the total assets of thrift institutions were $133.8 billion, FHLBB had a field examination staff of 755 persons; by 1985, when total assets had soared to $1 trillion, the examination staff stood at 747. Despite repeated requests by the FHLBB for budget increases, the Office of Management and Budget (OMB) refused to increase the FHLBB's budget. In 1985, OMB finally agreed to increase the FHLBB's budget, but this was too little too late.

It is clear that politics played an important role in the fraud committed by savings and loans: It has been charged that M. Danny Wall, head of the FHLBB at the time, met personally with Charles

Keating, owner of Lincoln Savings and Loan, and intervened on behalf of Keating to ward off FHLBB regulators in the San Francisco district who were investigating the thrift. Wall managed to move the investigation from the San Francisco office to Washington, D.C. and to delay closure of the insolvent thrift for two years, a delay that is estimated to have cost the FSLIC insurance fund $2 billion.

Thrifts used their tremendous influence to enlist members of Congress to their cause of covering-up fraudulent activity. For example, just before the Lincoln case was moved to Washington, D.C. five U.S. Senators who had received campaign and other contributions from Charles Keating, called San Francisco regulators to Washington, D.C. to "discuss" their prolonged examination of Lincoln.

Political influence and corruptions were not the only factors that allowed the use of thrifts as an instrument of illegal fraud. There were more general structural forces complicating the uncovering of the fraud by federal regulators. The basic structural flaw permeating the FHLBB system was the conflicting responsibility of promoting the industry, while regulating the industry, and simultaneously insuring deposits of those thrifts.

The FSLIC, charged with insuring thrift deposits and paying depositors of any thrift that became insolvent or unable to pay its depositors, had no legal authority to monitor or supervise the institutions and had to receive approval from the Bank Board before it could take any final action. Making matters worse, the FHLBB was responsible for chartering new thrifts and promoting the general welfare of the savings and loan system, yet at the same time was the main thrift regulator.

Another structural problem that resulted in the FHLBB and its examiners being reluctant to close a failing thrift was that the FSLIC lacked the money to pay off all depositors of thrifts, that it would close. By 1986, the FSLIC itself was insolvent (its liabilities exceeded its assets by an estimated $3 billion to $7 billion), drained of its resources by the epidemic of thrift failures.

Throughout the 1980s, the FHLBB had extended forbearance to ailing thrifts, forestalling their closure or reorganization, either because it believed the thrift to be capable of recovery in the new deregulated environment, or because the regulators desired to postpone using insurance fund reserves. When the fund itself became insolvent in 1986, forbearance became a matter of necessity. As the

FSLIC stopped closing insolvent thrifts, not only did the final costs escalate, but fraud, which in many cases had contributed to the insolvency in the first place, went undeterred. With nothing to lose, careless risk-taking and looting permeated the institutions until they were finally, mercifully put out of their misery.

Savings and loan fraud is clearly white-collar crime on a grand scale, although it does not fit neatly into one of the categories of white-collar crime defined by sociologists and criminologists of state crime, corporate crime, and financial crime. However, it does underscore that the problem of defining white-collar crime continues today.

SEE ALSO
scams; Keating Five; Keating, Charles; bank fraud; accounting fraud.

BIBLIOGRAPHY. Bruce A. Green, "Financial Institutions and Regulations, the S&L Crisis: Death and Transfiguration: After the Fall: The Criminal Law Enforcement Response to the S&L Crisis," *Fordham Law Review* (v.59, 1991); Martin Meyer, *The Greatest-Ever Bank Robbery* (Charles Scribner's Sons, 1990); Frederic S. Mishkin and Stanley G. Eakins, *Financial Markets and Institutions* (Addison-Wesley, 2000); Michael Waldman, *Who Robbed America?* (Random House, 1990).

MICHAEL MCGREGOR
GEORGE MASON UNIVERSITY

scams

SCHEMES, FRAUDS, scams, and cons are devices by which one party defrauds another of a desired object, usually cash. In some scams, victims are willing participants, hoping to gain an unfair advantage over someone else (Nigerian fraud, winning lottery ticket, etc.) while in other scams victims are unwilling participants (home repair, bank examiner, bumper cars, etc.)

Unwilling participants are often selected because of their age, ethnic heritage, or apparent naivete. Often willing participants are hesitant to file criminal charges, as are other scam victims who are too embarrassed to admit they were duped. Scams range in nature from the feasibly possible (merchandise at slightly under cost, lost pet) to those that are physically impossible (money-making machine.)

The people perpetrating the scams are hoping to identify certain characteristics in their victims: desire for excitement, greed, compassion, or lack of confidence. Perpetrators of scams and cons become quite adept at quickly identifying their next victim or "mark." Similarly, they will often quickly cancel an attempted scam if they note hesitancy by the potential victim. Many scams often follow a scripted format, with each step designed to draw the victim further into the scam. The steps are put into operation as follows: locating a mark, a victim is identified both by personal characteristics and the amount of money they control; playing the con, gaining the confidence of the mark through various subterfuges; roping the mark, drawing the mark further into the scam often through the use of partners, sometimes acting as uninterested bystanders and other times as participants; telling the tale, giving the victim "the inside scoop" on how they can profit from the venture; putting on the touch, the scam is executed and the victim is relieved of funds; losing the mark, the victim is separated from the scam operation, often not realizing that she has been the victimized.

Some common, specific types of perpetrated scams are described below.

Advance fee scam: This is a generic scam, sometimes identified as the Nigerian 419 scam, in which a person is requested to pay an advance fee for paperwork processing, taxes, or bribes in order to receive a much larger amount of cash later. In many cases, the money is allegedly coming from less than legitimate business transactions and that is the reason the cash payments are required. The scam is usually repeated, requesting additional payments, as new glitches to the transfer of the larger amount have occurred. The amount of the money promised to the victim is often said to be in the millions, so that payments of only a few thousand dollars seems to be a wise "investment."

Advertising materials scam: Businesses are approached concerning an exceptional deal on advertising materials (placemats, pens, calendars, etc.) but after payment is made no materials are received.

ATM repair: In this scam, an official-looking repair technician arrives at a location (convenience store, gas station, shopping mall, casino) that has an automatic teller machine (ATM) terminal and proceeds to work on it with a computer keyboard.

After some time working on the machine, the fraudster approaches an employee on duty and asks to use the telephone to call the maintenance supervisor. The caller explains that the ATM is in need of shop repair and to send over a service truck. A service truck appears shortly and the technicians remove the ATM and clean up the area. In some cases, the "supervisor" will call to the location to speak to the "technician."

Bank examiner scam: A "bank examiner" contacts the victim notifying him that a teller at their bank branch is suspected of theft from customers, and the examiner is in need of a regular customer to assist in the investigation. The victim is asked to go to the bank and remove a specific amount of money from a specific teller and then meet the examiner.

The examiner will inspect the money and give a receipt as well as the serial numbers of the bills "held" for evidence. In a deviation on the scam, a "bank examiner" will ask persons leaving a bank to allow him to inspect the cash they just received. The bills will be identified as counterfeit and a receipt will be given, along with a promise of contact by a supervisor.

Illegal alien lottery scam: A victim is approached by a person, speaking broken English, who explains that he has a winning lottery ticket but cannot redeem it, as he is an illegal alien. In exchange for a lesser cash amount he will surrender the ticket to the victim. To often convince the victim of the value of the ticket, a copy of the local newspaper with the winning number is shown to the victim; however, the ticket being offered was purchased the day after the drawing.

A variation on the scam is that the holder of the winning ticket of the lottery from his home country (Spain is often mentioned) is either wanted in his homeland or is hiding in the United States due to political persecution and therefore cannot cash the ticket.

Big carrot scam: A scam that usually occurs in a busy shopping mall in which a person affiliated with one of the anchor stores informs you that his store is grossly overstocked with certain items and that they need to sell them out at below cost, but the shopping center has rules concerning under cost sales. The salesperson agrees to take your money, go inside and transact the sale and bring the merchandise back. He enters the store but never returns, escaping out the back of the store.

Begging scams: A generic scam in which a persons assumes any of a multitude of personae (homeless, veteran, unemployed, physical or mental illness) or conditions (vehicle broken down, medical bills, etc.) to plead for money.

Bogus invoices: Companies, especially those with multiple locations, receive invoices for the alleged receipt of goods (office supplies, safety materials, etc.). No goods were ever received but some companies pay the invoices out of lack of internal accounting controls and fear of litigation.

Bumper cars: In this scam, a victim (usually an older driver or someone leaving a bar) is involved in a staged accident and a third party approaches and states that the victim was clearly at fault. The other driver claims some minor injury and vehicle damage. Out of fear of a police report and an insurance claim, the victim pays the other driver the amount requested for damages. In variations of this scam, the victim is contacted again and informed that the actual damages were higher and additional funds are required; and other times, if the victim is low on cash they are encouraged to give a credit card as collateral until they can get the cash.

Catalog 10-and-10 scam: In this scam, a representative of a nationally known company approaches homeowners advising them of a national sale going in their area to improve the company's market share. In an attempt to increase sales, the representative is authorized to give discounts up to 50 percent off the usual price, and the customer only has to pay 10 percent down and 10 percent shipping costs to the representative and the order will be placed. Of course, no such shipment ever occurs.

Chain letter scams: A deviation of a pyramid scheme in which a recipient is encouraged to send money to the names on the list and add her name to the list. The letter promises a large return on the "investment" in a short time; however the original names on the mailing are the names of the scam operators.

Change machine scam: A scam in which an authentic-looking change machine is placed near vending machines. The machine will accept bills but returns no change. As most losses are low, the majority of victims either walk away or may leave a note advising that the machine is not working properly. The person running the scam removes the note after the victim leaves. In a technological improvement on this scam, authentic-looking ATM machines are placed in high foot-traffic areas. Victims place their credit cards in the machine as well as type in their personal identification numbers (PINs) but are advised that the ATM is out of money. The operator of the fraudulent ATM later removes the machines and has the victims' credit card information as well as their PIN.

Coin con: A person is approached by a young man, who often appears to be confused, and is shown a roll of coins with a note advising to call the listed number for a reward. Upon calling the number, the person is advised that there is a $500 or more reward. Most victims mention the person who handed the roll to them. The caller is asked to give the "confused" young man $100 and is given an address to bring the coins where they will be reimbursed for the $100 and paid the remaining reward. Of course, no such address exists.

Fast change scam: In this scam, a customer at a retail location makes a purchase and pays with one denomination bill and, as the cashier begins to make change, offers another denomination bill instead. This occurs several times during the transaction and when the change-making process is finally completed the cashier's register is short.

Fortune teller handkerchief scam: A fortune teller, who has slowly been gaining the customer's confidence, advises the customer that the only way to rid themselves of bad luck or karma is to dispose of a large sum of money; which they will reap tenfold in other ways. The fortune teller produces a handkerchief, sewn at two ends, into which the money is placed. After sewing the handkerchief entirely closed and speaking some words over it, the customer is advised to go to a nearby disposal point (bridge, cemetery, body of water) and get rid of the handkerchief. Unbeknownst to the customer the fortune teller switched the handkerchief with the money for another containing paper.

Gold brick scam: A person is approached by someone who asks them to hold a gold ingot for them for an indeterminate period of time, as the owner will be incapacitated for some time. In a gesture of good faith a small amount of money is asked for as "good faith" money. When the victim closely inspects the gold bar, it is discovered to be an iron ingot plated with a gold-colored material.

Home inspector scams: A generic scam type, often perpetrated upon older homeowners, in which a person posing as a municipal inspector (from the water, gas, or electric company, for example) approaches a homeowner and advises her that the residence is in violation of an ordinance. The scam can proceed to several directions at this point, with the inspector referring a contractor that he knows is in the neighborhood, or collects the money himself agreeing to send a municipal crew the following day to make the repairs.

Home repair scams: In this generic scam usually executed upon older homeowners, itinerant laborers offer to perform various home repairs for exceptionally low prices. The scam has many variations: they simply use the ploy to enter the house and steal valuables; they fail to finish the job the first day and request payment promising to return tomorrow; one of the workers injures himself and demands money for medical treatment; or once the work is completed the price is inflated (owner heard wrong, additional repairs had to be performed, extra materials were required, etc.) In cases where repairs are actually performed, the work and the materials are often substandard.

Jamaican handkerchief/envelope scam: A variation of the pigeon drop scam in which two persons impersonate newly arrived Jamaican immigrants. The scam works as follows: Con man 1 approaches the victim and asks (in broken English) for directions and pulls out a large roll of bills and gives the mark $50; con man 2 approaches the pair and states that it is unsafe for a newly arrived immigrant to carry that much money and offers to hold it; con man 1 states that he doesn't trust con man 2 but for some reason trusts the victim; he pulls out the roll of money placing it in a handkerchief and gives it to the victim; he then mentions he would feel more secure if the victim placed his cash in the handkerchief also—so the victim would protect the handkerchief like it was his own; after the victim places the handkerchief in his pocket one of the con men explains that it should be positioned differently and they remove the handkerchief; after a sleight of hand the victim is given the handkerchief again (now with no money, just paper).

Money-making machine scam: This is a scam that, in spite of its improbability, has been successfully executed upon business persons. In the operation, an inventor has created a machine that not only perfectly reproduces money, it scrambles the serial numbers to circumvent the problems counterfeiters encounter, that is, multiple bills with the same serial number. The only "drawback" to the process is the time (1–2 hours) it takes to process a bill. To convince the victim that the process does work, the fraudster allows the victim to insert two paper trays, one with plain paper and one with actual currency into the machine. Then, both leave. Unknown to the victim, the machine actually works from a second concealed tray, in which another real bill has been placed.

When both the inventor and victim return to the machine, the victim is allowed to check the machine and finds both the bill originally placed there as well as the newly "made" bill. The victim is encouraged to go to his bank and check the authenticity of the second bill. Once the customer is convinced that the machine works as promised, the sale is made. In many cases, the inventor has placed a few other legitimate bills in the hidden compartment delaying the discovery of the con.

Lamborghini test drive: A scam often offered around the winter holiday season in which individuals are offered the opportunity to drive a Lamborghini for 30 minutes in exchange for a small payment (for insurance purposes only) to do some "street advertising" for the car. If an hour block of time is purchased, for $400 the purchaser will also get an hour in a Dodge Viper as part of the package. Payment is made and the buyer is told to be at a prescribed location, with his valid driver's license, the following day. In some cases, advertisements are run in local newspaper, later found to be paid with forged checks.

Lonely hearts scam: A scam in which, after a mail relationship has been established, money is requested in ever-increasing amounts to facilitate efforts for the romantic pair to finally meet. This is a scam often run by prison inmates who create elaborate stories to obtain additional funding, while normally concealing the fact that the letter writer is incarcerated. In one noted scam form Angola Prison in Louisiana, over $500,000 was made using this format.

The victim would first send airfare, then receive a telephone from the airport police advising that his friend was arrested due to a fight and bail money was needed. The victim would receive a subsequent call noting that the friend was injured in an altercation in jail and medical expenses were needed. If the victim became aware of the scam or refused to pay additional monies, the scam sometimes progressed to extortion.

Lost pet scam: A scam that is performed upon pet owners who have posted lost pet ads. In one common adaptation of this scam, a caller informs the owner that she has found the lost pet—in their moving van now several states away. The caller explains that the pet must have jumped into the moving van as it was being loaded near the owner's residence. In order to "swing" back to the owner and return the pet, the fraudster needs some fuel money wired immediately.

The caller recommends Western Union, and to make sure the caller isn't scammed out of her money, the pet-owner should send the money with a test question, for example, the pet's name. By sending money in this manner, the caller is able to collect the money without showing identification and can retrieve it at any Western Union outlet, often in the city where the funds were sent.

Fax fraud: Businesses receive a request for pricing on services or sales, and the information must be returned via fax. The letter indicates a serious interest in conducting business and an immediate response is required. The out-going fax number turns out to be from a foreign country resulting in an exorbitant long-distance phone line charge.

Melon drop scam: A scam often perpetrated on tourists in which a person intentionally "bumps" into the victim and drops an item, often a champagne bottle filled with water. The scammer then proceeds to accost the person who "made" them drop the champagne until the victim is so intimidated that he pays for the damaged merchandise. Another participant may intercede as a witness agreeing that the victim caused the accident. This scam is often perpetrated on Japanese tourists using melons for the merchandise. Japanese nationals are accustomed to paying as much as $35 to $50 for melons in their country.

Murphy game: A scam that originally had involved prostitutes, but now has extended to other areas. In the original scam, a person posing as a pimp would bring the victim to a hotel lobby and say that, to avoid problems with the police, he would handle the money transaction. After the agreed upon price is paid, the victim is sent to a hotel room soon to find that no prostitute was waiting for him. In a variation of this scam, a prostitution date was arranged but a "police officer" would burst into the room before any sexual activity took place. The police officer would agree to accept a cash bribe in exchange for not making an arrest.

A current version of the scam now involves a "middleman" story in which high priced electronics, clothing, or equipment can be purchased from a friend on the loading dock. The victim, sometimes renting a truck in expectation of a large purchase, and the middleman drive to the warehouse where the victim is informed that for secrecy reasons, the victim cannot meet the inside man, and must give the middleman the cash to bring inside to the inside man. The middleman proceeds to enter the loading dock area as if looking for his contact but once out of sight leaves through another door.

Nigerian 419 scam: A scam in which a person is contacted, usually by e-mail or fax, and is informed that for his cooperation in removing a large sum of money (proceeds of illegal oil sale, hidden assets of deposed leader, overage on government contract) from, Nigeria he will be given a percentage of the gross amount. All that is needed from the victim is a bank account into which the funds can be transferred; and possibly some other banking information all sent back to the Nigerian contact. The scam sometimes evolves to the Nigerian advance fee scam, when due to complications, some upfront money is now required. Once the victim's bank account routing number is gained, the account is depleted of funds rather than funds being placed in it.

Obituary scam: This is a swindle in which information is obtained from a local newspaper obituary column and a package is then brought to the home of the deceased, or relative of the deceased noted in the column. The package was insured and came with a small amount due, which has to be paid before the package is released. Another variation of the scam involves services that were partially paid for by the deceased, but for which there is an outstanding balance.

Pager/cell phone scams: A digital or voice message is left on an individual's cellphone or pager indicating an urgent matter. When the return call is made to the number given, the caller is placed on hold; and later when the bill arrives a charge is noted for either a service charging a per-minute fee or an international call.

Pedigree dog scam: A person enters a business, often a bar, and pays the bartender to watch his dog for a few minutes as he is going to a "very" profitable business appointment. After the "businessman" leaves, another patron arrives shortly thereafter and begins admiring the dog, stating that he has been looking for that exact dog for some time and would pay handsomely, dropping the figure of $600, leaving his business card and telephone number. That patron departs and shortly thereafter the "businessman" returns looking sullen saying that his deal fell through and he is totally broke. If the mark has been properly selected (subject to greed) the bartender will offer to help the businessman by purchasing the dog (for much less than the other patron had offered.) The other patron is not to be found, however.

Pigeon drop scam: A commonly run street scam in which a participant of the scam "notices" a bag/bundle/wallet on the ground just as the mark approaches. Upon opening the package, a large amount (several hundred to several thousand dollars) of money is noted. While discussing what to do, another participant of the scam arrives posing as a bystander. He happens to know a lawyer who they can contact. After making a call to the lawyer, it is learned that they must hold the money for 30 days (state law) and if no claims are made, they can keep it. The decision is made to let the victim hold the money, but so they can all trust each other each should put up an equal sum of money. The two participants of the scam just happen to have their share on them. They agree to go with the mark to get his share, and once it is obtained all the money is placed in a cloth sack and handed to the mark with details given to meet again in 30 days. However, as the result of sleight of hand, the mark is now in possession of a folded cloth containing cut up newspaper.

PBX phone scams: A business receives a telephone call advising the PBX (telephone system) operator who answers that a problem exists on the line and the PBX operator needs to punch in 90# so the line can be tested and repaired. Later, several unauthorized long-distance charges will be noted as the PBX operator unintentionally granted long-distance access to the caller.

Slamming: Without approval of anyone in authority, a company's telephone service has been switched resulting in excessive charges. As an offer of proof of authorization to make the change, the offending company may offer an audio tape of an employee saying "yes," but not to the authorization, but rather some inane question posed of the employee in an innocuous conversation, and tape-recorded.

Charity scams: A request to make a donation to an apparent worthy cause, for example, police department, fire department, disaster survivors, disabled children groups, etc. However, the group making the solicitation has no official connection to the causes the fraudster claims to represent.

Ponzi/pyramid schemes: Two different scams which are somewhat similar in nature in that both profess that wealth will be produced by the entrance of either more people or more levels into the operation. Victims are promised great returns and are often paid with the monies supplied by new victims. As the scam proceeds, the victims are encouraged to leave their monies in the operation to achieve even greater returns. As the scam cannot mathematically succeed due to the ever-increasing number of new members needed, the scam eventually fails and the participants lose their "investments."

Recovery operation fraud: An individual, who is the victim of an earlier scam is contacted, by a recovery specialist who is involved in efforts to either recover the victim's prior losses through a fee-based operation or through the continued "cooperation" with the original scam to assist in apprehending the original fraudster. Either operation causes the victim to scammed a second time.

Spanish prisoner scam: This is a scam that date back to the 1500s in which an unjust imprisonment has occurred in a foreign country, and unless funding is received for both legal defense and bribes, the prisoner will probably die in prison. The letter, which has been smuggled out of prison, has the name and post office box of a friend of the prisoner where money can be sent. The letter further states that the generous souls who donate money will be repaid "multiple times over," as after the prisoner obtains his release he will have access to a large cache of money in the United States, and will generously reward his benefactors. Thousands of copies are mass mailed and the response rate is amazingly high.

Three card monte/shell game: A street scam in which the position of a card or token is wagered upon. Through sleight of hand maneuvers, the victim is allowed to win several times with the bet slowly being raised. After the bet has been risen sufficiently, to a point where the victim may leave if it goes much higher, the same sleight of hand now causes the victim to start losing. Due to his earlier winning streak the victim attempts to recoup his "winnings" only to continue to lose.

You have won a prize scam: In this generic scam type, a victim is informed that she has won a prize of substantial value and must only pay a small amount for shipping to receive the prize. In some cases, the scam is perpetrated a second time explaining that the item was shipped to the wrong location and a small additional fee is needed.

SEE ALSO

Ponzi schemes; telemarketing fraud; bait-and-switch; contractor fraud; sweepstakes offers; savings and loan fraud; bank fraud; Better Business Bureaus.

BIBLIOGRAPHY. M. Chesbro, *Don't Be A Victim! How to Protect Yourself from Hoaxes, Scams, and Frauds* (Loompanics Unlimited, 2002); M. Allen Henderson, *How Con Games Work* (Citadel Press, 1985); T. Lesce, *Modern Frauds and Con Games* (Loompanics Unlimited, 2002); L.R. Mizelli, Jr., *Masters of Deception* (John Wiley & Sons, 1997); J. Wilker, *Classic Cons and Swindles* (Chelsea House Publishers, 1997); U.S. Securities Exchange Commission, "Pyramid Scheme," www.sec.gov (2003).

PATRICK D. WALSH
LOYOLA UNIVERSITY NEW ORLEANS

Scandinavia

SCANDINAVIA IS A region of northern Europe consisting of Sweden, Norway, Finland and Denmark, with Iceland also included occasionally for reasons of cultural proximity. In recent decades, these countries generally have established a reputation for a high-class welfare state, funded by comparatively high levels of taxation and with neutralist international tendencies that have not hampered efforts to contribute to international peace and reconciliation efforts but does translate into a certain skepticism about international political organizations such as the European Union. Welfare state provision has meant a comparatively low level of underground economic activities and low misuse of migrant workers.

The Scandinavian countries consistently rate amongst the nations with the lowest levels of corruption and other forms of white-collar crime. They have frequently taken a leadership role in the promotion of social responsibility in business ethics and have looked to shape international organizations such as the European Union according to their principles. The ideas that they favor include the use of regulation to require firms to take their social responsibilities seriously and the use of shareholder and stakeholder interests representatives at board level for similar reasons.

However, research has indicated that there is, nevertheless, a quite high level of fraud throughout the region in some sectors. To try to identify the extent of fraud and to introduce joint policies to help to reduce that level, industries such as the insurance industry have established cross-border initiatives. On some occasions, corporate wrongdoing has been attached to Scandinavian firms as a result of mergers and acquisitions.

For example, the Swedish pharmaceutical company AstraAB merged in 1999 with the British firm Zeneca Pharmaceuticals to form AstraZeneca, which was subsequently prosecuted and fined for conspiring with medical practitioners in the United States to defraud the Medicare system by making false claims for drugs it marketed. In other cases, a more familiar predilection for greed and a febrile internet-backed atmosphere, that provided the opportunity to indulge it, produced a familiar result.

The innovative use of technology has also been a feature of fraud in the region, with one notable case involving the planting of fake automatic teller machines (ATMs) in central Copenhagen, Denmark, used to extract money from unwary individuals.

Scandinavian firms have also been among those accused of wrongdoing in connection with mining practices in resource-rich, but economically underdeveloped areas, although such allegations are also made against mining companies in most world regions.

SEE ALSO

Medicare and Medicaid fraud; healthcare fraud; insurance fraud.

BIBLIOGRAPHY. "AstraZeneca Pleads Guilty to Health-Care Fraud Scheme," Knight Ridder Tribune Business News (June 21, 2003); "Dankort Fraud Highlights Flaws in System," The Copenhagen Post (June 13, 1999); "Nordic Countries Look into Fraud Jointly," International Insurance Monitor (v.53/1, 2000); Morten P. Broberg, "Corporate Social Responsibility in the European Communities: a Scandinavian Perspective," Journal of Business Ethics (v.15/6, 1996); Jayaraman Ntiyanand, "Norsk Hydro: Global Compact Violator," Special Corp-Watch Series on Campaign for a Corporate-Free UN, www.corpwatch.org (October 18, 2001); Thomas Watson, "The Man Who Ambushed Open Text," Canadian Business (June 10, 2002).

JOHN WALSH, PH.D.
MAHIDOL UNIVERSITY, THAILAND

Securities and Exchange Commission

THE SECURITIES and Exchange Commission, commonly referred to as the SEC, is the primary regulator of the U.S. financial securities markets, and has the overall responsibility for overseeing the federal regulation of the securities industry.

The SEC enforces, among other acts, the Securities Act of 1933, the Securities Exchange Act of 1934, the Public Utility Holding Company Act of 1935, the Trust Indenture Act of 1939, the Investment Company Act of 1940, and the Investment Advisers Act of 1940. The SEC works closely with many other institutions, including Congress, other federal departments and agencies, the self-regulatory organizations (the stock exchanges), state securities regulators, and various private sector organizations.

The SEC was created in 1934 as a governmental response to the massive stock manipulations and frauds that helped lead to the famous 1929 stock market crash. During the 1920s, the American dream of rags-to-riches was very successful in bringing millions of individual investors into the stock market. When the stock market crashed in October 1929, the market lost almost 89 percent of its value. Thousands of shareholders lost extraordinary sums of money and soon banks and businesses started to collapse.

The stock market crash and the subsequent Great Depression led to a massive loss of confidence among the millions of Americans who had invested on Wall Street. After the crash, Congress conducted hearings to determine the public's faith, or lack of faith, in the capital markets. Based on the findings, Congress passed the Securities Act of 1933 (the 1933 Act) and the Securities Exchange Act of 1934 (the 1934 Act).

The SEC was established as a result of the 1934 Act, which empowered the SEC with broad authority over all aspects of the securities markets. The commission's main purpose was to restore investor confidence by ending misleading trading practices and stock manipulations. President Franklin D. Roosevelt appointed Joseph P. Kennedy, future President John F. Kennedy's father, as its first chairman. The power of the commission extends to registration, regulation, and oversight of brokerage firms, transfer agents, clearing agencies, and self-regulatory agencies. Most importantly, the SEC is responsible for investigating and initiating action when federal securities laws are violated and securities frauds are committed.

There are five commissioners who are appointed by the president with the advice and consent of the Senate. To ensure the commission's impartiality, no more than three of the commissioners can belong to the same political party. The commissioners cannot engage in any other business, vocation, or employment. The commissioners cannot participate in any stock market operations or transactions which are regulated by the SEC. Each term for a commissioner is five years and is staggered relative to the other commissioners. The president appoints one of the commissioners as chairman, the SEC's top executive. The SEC is an independent policing agency with quasi-legislative and quasi-judicial powers.

The commissioners meet to discuss and resolve a variety of issues the staff members bring to their attention. They are responsible for interpreting federal securities laws, amending existing rules, proposing new rules, and enforcing laws and rules. The SEC is supposed to be independent from any influence by representatives of the Executive or Legislative branches of the government. The president has no power to remove any member of the SEC unless he is "inefficient in neglect of duty or malfeasant in office."

STRUCTURE AND ENFORCEMENT

There are four divisions under the commissioners: the divisions of corporate finance, enforcement, investment management, and market regulation. The commission also has 18 offices, including the offices of administrative law judges, the chief accountant, compliance inspections and examinations, economic analysis, investor education and assistance, and 11 regional and district offices throughout the country. Altogether approximately 3,100 staff members are spread throughout the SEC headquar-

ters in Washington, D.C. and regional and district offices. Crucial to the SEC's effectiveness is its enforcement authority. The division of enforcement, the largest division in the SEC, is responsible for investigating possible violations of securities laws, recommending commission action when appropriate, either in a federal court or before an administrative law judge, negotiating settlements on behalf of the commission, and reviewing cases for possible referral to the U.S. Department of Justice for criminal prosecution. The enforcement division also cooperates with other divisions and offices in the SEC, as well as other domestic and foreign authorities and organizations, for its enforcement work.

There are primarily three sources from which the SEC enforcement division detects or becomes aware of possible violations of the securities laws. A large part of the SEC cases are the result of referrals by the self-regulatory organizations (SROs) which include the securities exchanges such as the New York Stock Exchange (NYSE) and the American Stock Exchange (AMEX), and the National Association of Securities Dealers (NASD) which regulates the over-the-counter securities market. Many of the cases have come from tips provided by informants or complainants. Insiders, such as company executives, who suspect possible violations, may call to inform the SEC of the unusual trades. To encourage more people to report illegalities, the SEC provided a bounty for informants whose tips lead to the conviction of an offender. Finally, the enforcement division, in cooperation with other relevant divisions and offices in the SEC, proactively searches for illegal behavior by scanning the press reports for clues, or conducts its own surveillance activities.

Whatever the source that reports the potential illegalities, the enforcement division must make the decision whether or not to investigate. The division's staff will check to see if the person under investigation has had problems in her trading history. They may also obtain facts through informal inquiries, interviewing witnesses, examining trading records, and other methods. If the facts show that no violation has been found, the informal inquiry is concluded. If the staff members find it necessary to proceed, they will present a staff report to the commissioners for their approval for a formal order of investigation. Once the commission issues a formal order of investigation, the enforcement officials have the power to subpoena individuals or entities to obtain sworn testimony and relevant documents. In most cases, since it is difficult to find eyewitnesses to testify against a potential violation of securities laws, cases are primarily based on circumstantial evidence. For example, in insider trading cases, telephone records of insiders may be subpoenaed to see if there were conversations between certain individuals.

Illegalities originating in foreign countries make detection and enforcement even more difficult because some countries have bank secrecy laws or blocking laws which prevent the SEC from obtaining a trading account or the account holder's information. The SEC has made great effort to deal with such problems by signing agreements with foreign exchanges, and memoranda of understanding and treaties for mutual assistance in criminal cases. However, not every country has an agreement with the SEC regarding mutual assistance for investigating transnational cases. Even with the agreements, the SEC must present a very clear case before a foreign country is willing to provide assistance.

GOING TO COURT

Following an investigation, the SEC staff will close the case if they decide that sanctions are not necessary, or otherwise make a recommendation to the commissioners that enforcement action be taken. The staff presents to the commission the facts of the case and its reasons for pursuing sanctions. SEC commissioners determine not only whether to take actions against the perpetrators, but also the options of action to be taken. The commissioners' deliberation in prosecutorial discretion is conducted confidentially. The kinds of issues considered by the commission in deciding how to proceed include: the available evidence, the technical nature of the case, the seriousness of the wrongdoing, the type of sanction or relief to obtain, the deterrent effect a prosecutorial decision might have on potential law breakers, and the impact of prosecutorial decisions on the development of policy.

After their deliberation, the commissioners may authorize the staff to file a civil case in federal court, bring an administrative action before an administrative law judge, or refer the case to the Justice Department for criminal prosecution. For civil cases, the commissioners review the material before them and decide whether charges should be laid or amended. The administrative proceeding is a public or private hearing, ordered by the commission, and presided by an administrative law judge, who is independent of the commission. Administrative law judges consider the evidence presented by the enforcement staff and the subject of the proceeding. Following the hearing, they recommend a disposition based on their findings of fact to the SEC commissioners, who determine the final disposition. Among other actions, administrative law judges issue subpoenas, rule on motions, and rule on the admissibility of evidence.

The commissioners may affirm the decision of the administrative law judge, reverse the decision, or remand it for additional hearings. The defendant may request an oral argument before the commission or appeal all or any portion of the SEC decision to the federal courts. The administrative sanctions include cease-and-desist orders, suspension or revocation of broker-dealer and investment advisor registrations, temporary suspensions of business and employment, censures, bars from association with the securities industry, alterations in the management structure of the organization, restrictions on business practices, payment of civil monetary penalties, and return of illegal profits.

Civil actions are initiated by SEC staff in the federal district courts. The staff files a complaint with a federal district court that describes the misconduct, indicates the laws and regulations violated, and proposes the sanctions or remedies. Typically, the commission requests the court to issue an injunction decree, which enjoins offenders from future violations of the securities laws or SEC rules.

The commission may also request the court to impose ancillary remedies, such as asset freezing, civil monetary penalties and the return of illegal profits, known as disgorgement, and suspension of an individual from employment. Failure to abide by an injunctive decree can result in criminal contempt proceedings. Each year the SEC brings 400 to 500 civil actions against securities lawbreakers. Typical offenses pursued by the SEC include insider trading, accounting fraud, and misleading statements about securities and the companies that issue them.

The person charged may alternatively choose to settle the case before the charges are filed in court. In fact, a settlement is a typical result of enforcement actions by the SEC. In most settlement arrangements, the defendant agrees to a civil penalty without admitting or denying the SEC's allegations.

Such a settlement is a benefit to both the defendant and the SEC in terms of cost and time saved. The terms of a settlement must be approved by the commissioners in administrative cases, and by both the commissioners and the U.S. District Court in civil cases.

Normally, a settlement with the SEC does not preclude criminal prosecution. In some cases, however, a defendant will propose a civil settlement which provides that the SEC shall not pursue the case criminally. The SEC's litigation experience is relatively rare, with only about 12 percent of the cases litigated and approximately 80 percent settled by consent.

PROSECUTION

In most cases, SEC staff decides whether criminal prosecution is appropriate, and the commission formally refers the case to the Justice Department, which has the discretion to accept or decline the case for criminal prosecution in the federal district courts. Some researchers who examined the SEC's prosecutorial discretion found that only about 10 percent of the SEC cases are referred for criminal prosecutions.

The reasons may include the difficulty in proving the case, limited enforcement powers, limited resources, and the commission's lenient ideology against securities law violations. Driven by high service fees, in contrast, attorneys for securities offenses usually get involved in such cases as early as the investigation begins. They prepare their cases with painstaking attention to detail, often employ the services of other professionals, and spend great effort to prevent charges from being filed.

Because there are various checks to ensure that the cases pursued are clearly strong ones, defense attorneys have various opportunities at each stage to encourage the SEC to drop the cases. Therefore, the SEC prefers instead to resolve cases by various other means, especially by administrative proceedings. In many decades of its operation, the SEC has been criticized by some as unnecessary, but by others as insufficiently effective. In the years before the late 1970s, it was seen as retreating from its traditional role as protector of investors and progressed little in its enforcement. In the 1980s, however, the SEC achieved power and respect for its vigorous pursuit of insider trading. In the 1990s, it further strengthened its enforcement efforts against various forms of financial crime. Political heat stoked by corporate scandals has made the SEC reluctant to settle or close out cases without imposing fines or some other punishment.

By the 2000s, the growing volume of enforcement actions by the SEC was putting the policing agency in a real bind, because it did not have enough staff to keep up with the volume of cases it had already opened. Congress was on its way to help the SEC with the caseload problem by substantially increasing the agency's budget. With its long tradition of aggressive actions, it is possible that the SEC will achieve more efficient and effective enforcement of the U.S. federal securities laws.

SEE ALSO

insider trading; securities fraud; accounting fraud; bank fraud; prosecution; reform and regulation; United States; Roosevelt, Franklin D.; capitalism.

BIBLIOGRAPHY. David O. Friedrichs, *Trusted Criminals: White-Collar Crime in Contemporary Society* (Wadsworth, 1996); Elizabeth Szockyj, *The Law and Insider Trading: In Search of A Level Playing Field* (William S. Hein, 1993); Shen-Shin Lu, *Insider Trading and the Twenty-Four Hour Securities Market: A Case Study of Legal Regulation in the Emerging Global Economy* (Christopher Publishing House, 1994); Gerry Moore, "Growing Case Backlog Slows SEC Enforcement," (Kiplinger Washington Editors 2002); Securities and Exchange Commission, www.sec.gov (2003).

HONGMING CHENG
ST. THOMAS UNIVERSITY
ZHEJIANG WANLI UNIVERSITY

securities fraud

SECURITIES FRAUD refers to the criminal conduct of persons involved in the purchase and/or sales of stock shares in both publicly and privately held companies, as well as other financial instruments, including bonds and commodities. The word security refers to a monetary interest in a company, such as: an investment contract, voting trust certificate, options to purchases stock in a company, interest in oil, gas, water, or mineral rights; as well as stocks and bonds. Federal securities laws, primarily the Securities Act of 1933 and

Collusion to raise a stock's price can include false claims of breakthroughs.

Corporate tax evasion using offshore entities is a form of securities fraud.

Corporate debacles, such as Enron, cause share prices to plummet.

the Securities Exchange Act of 1934, regulate the conduct of both brokers and stock exchanges. Shares of publicly held companies are normally purchased and sold on one of several exchanges, including: the New York Stock Exchange (NYSE), NASDAQ which is operated by the National Association of Securities Dealers, Inc. (NASD) and handles many high technology stocks as well as "over the counter" (OTC) shares; and other smaller exchanges. Security fraud can involve the actions of individual stockbrokers, company officers, internal or external auditors, or joint efforts of multiple brokers at the same or different firms. Security fraud cases can result in both civil and criminal sanctions. In the early 2000s, due to downward stock market trends, an increase in security fraud allegations was noted; however, security fraud does not apply to all losses incurred in the stock market, only those with criminal actions attributable to persons involved in fraud.

The crime of securities fraud was much publicized with the cases of Adelphia Communications, Enron, ImClone, Tyco, and WorldCom. Another noted case involved a 15-year-old from New Jersey who generated $285,000 in profits from a pump and dump scheme. Profits and greed are the drivers behind securities fraud as articulated by stock trader Ivan Boesky in his quote to the 1986 commencement address at the University of California, Berkeley: "Greed is all right, by the way ... I think greed is

healthy. You can be greedy and still feel good about yourself." Specific security fraud crimes cases are delineated as follows.

PUMP AND DUMP

A securities fraud type often utilized in "boiler-room" operations (stock sales operations specifically established to perform pump and dump scams), and on internet bulletin boards. In a typical pump and dump scheme, the operation purchases large blocks of stocks in small, thinly traded companies, and then promotes the company's stock with misrepresentations and false statements. Comments such as the following are often utilized: "this is a sure thing; the company is about to announce a merger"; "we will monitor your account and control your losses"; and "our owner just made a large under the table purchase himself."

Once the widespread high-pressure selling begins to increase the price, the stock becomes a self-fulfilling prophecy and more buyers purchase blocks of stocks. The fraudulent information campaign continues until the operators decide to sell their large blocks of stocks. Once the boiler-room/bulletin board operation stops, the price of the investment falls as it is no longer pushed for investment. At that point the investors lose their money as the price returns to the point it was before the fraud was initiated. Pump and dump schemes have been conducted by single individuals, groups of collusive brokers, and by organized crime groups.

In some cases, owners of the involved companies have orchestrated the pump and dump. The Securities Exchange Commission (SEC) obtained several criminal convictions and recovered approximately $11 million in a case against the owners of Systems of Excellence, Inc. The owners sent out false press releases over the internet and bribed stock analysts to tout the stock; after they secretly distributed over 40 million shares to friends and family. In another SEC case, Sloane Fitzgerald, Inc. sent out six million unsolicited e-mails and created a phony online newsletter to promote two thinly traded companies. Sloane Fitzgerald had been contracted by the two pumped companies and paid in cash for their services.

INSIDER TRADING

In this securities fraud, the purchase or sale of shares is made subsequent to acquisition of information not known to the general public. Insider trading is the use of pertinent, nonpublic information to impact the sales of securities. The guilty parties can be insiders (owners, officers, directors, employees) of the company involved; the persons who make the purchases for themselves or as "shills" for the insiders; or independent parties (printers, couriers, outside legal contractors) who have obtained inside information.

Within SEC regulations, the parties to fraud are labeled as to their involvement: persons who pass-on insider information but do not trade shares themselves are called tippers; persons who acquire insider information themselves, or through the others who have breached their fiduciary responsibilities, are called tippees. Another classification, misappropriators, refers to persons outside the involved corporation, who steal non-public information in violation of fiduciary rules.

A highly publicized insider-trading case involved ImClone Chief Executive Officer Samuel Waksal, media giant Martha Stewart, and her stock broker. According to SEC filings and press reports, Waksal allegedly learned of a pending report form the U.S. Food and Drug Administration (FDA) concerning a medication the company had hoped to sell in the United States. Once the information was made public, the stock price plummeted and in-

vestors lost millions. However, several investors were able to sell their shares before the news release and the subsequent price decline. The investors included members of Waksal's family, as well as Waksal friend, Stewart. It was additionally alleged that, in an attempt to portray Stewart's sale of approximately $225,000 of ImClone shares the day before the press release as unrelated to the negative FDA report, her stock broker and his assistant were charged with falsifying brokerage house records to show that a previously agreed, pending sale order was in the file.

RESEARCH AND INVESTMENT COLLUSION

In this potential fraud situation the investment banking (sales) department of a brokerage house utilizes inappropriate influence over the research analysis department. Potentially negative analysis concerning preferred customers is either suppressed or altered to conceal certain negative aspects of the analysis. The inappropriate influence leads to investors being misled about the strengths of the involved companies.

In some cases, analysts are compensated either by the management of the brokerage house or by the company in question for positive research recommendations. An example of this fraud type concerned the continued sales efforts of some brokerage houses to recommend Enron stock while their internal analysis departments determined the stock to be a risky investment. In April 2003, the SEC announced $1.4 billion in fines and penalties against 10 of the nation's top investment firms for alleged improper activities between research and investment divisions.

STOCK CHURNING

This type of fraud refers to a securities scam in which a broker performs multiple trades in a client's account not for the advantage of the client, but only to generate additional sales commissions. Churning can occur in both accounts where a broker has discretionary authority from the account holder to make trades on her behalf, and on accounts where the broker does not have discretionary trading authority. In accounts where the broker has discretionary authority, excessive, unnecessary, and detrimental trades are transacted simply to generate sales commissions. In accounts where discretionary authority is not granted, trades are transacted in selective accounts (those with high profits and minor review by the account holder) so that the trades and subsequent commissions will probably not be noticed. Investors are not only impacted by commissions, but often short-term capital gains taxes if the stocks are held less than the prescribed time.

UNAUTHORIZED TRADES

This is a securities scam similar to churning but the focus isn't necessarily commission-driven. In some cases, stocks are sold between accounts to cover misappropriation by a stockbroker, that is, if an account holder requests a statement for an account that the broker has stolen from, the broker needs to replace those stocks back into the account. If the account holder notices the in-and-out transaction the broker can claim an accounting error that was caught internally. The account the stocks were obtained from doesn't need to be covered until a statement is requested for that account.

Unauthorized trades may also be conducted by brokers to cover margin calls (stocks that were purchased on credit against the portfolio need to paid for as the stock price dropped) in their personal accounts; or to simply steal money from accounts.

PENNY STOCKS

Also referred to as micro-cap and chop stocks trading, these names all refer to the trading of low-priced stocks often involving start-up companies (even though they are labeled penny stocks, the title refers to stocks priced at less than $5). These stocks are traded on the over-the-counter bulletin board (OTCBB), which on a typical day lists approximately 70,000 stocks.

Micro-cap/penny stock fraud became popular in the 1950s with the sales of uranium mining shares in Utah. In the 1980s, the focus shifted to oil and gas stocks, again in companies with little or no track record. These types of stocks are often sold by unregistered brokers sometimes out of "boiler-room" operations, with limited knowledge of the company's operations and tightly controlled trading. There has been a noted increase in organized crime in the sales of micro-cap stocks. One noted case involved Uniprime Capital Acceptance Inc., which in 1996 began as an auto-financing and insurance company with a daily average of 10,000 shares

at 50 cents. In 1999, an attempt was made to increase the value of the company by touting an HIV (AIDS virus) medical breakthrough in one of its affiliated companies. With the assistance of online chat rooms and bulletin boards, Uniprime increased its daily volume to 5 million shares and traded at a high of almost $8. Once later information revealed that no breakthrough or affiliated company existed, the stock rapidly collapsed.

AFFINITY FRAUD

This securities fraud is focused on identifiable groups whose members are chosen as victims because of their membership. The group (church, social group, professional organization) is approached and offered an opportunity that other groups will not be offered. When focusing on church groups, the sales pitch may focus on the good the proceeds can do to help others, or similar religious backgrounds will be professed.

One noted case was *SEC v. Oracle Trust Fund*, in which approximately $7 million was raised from just over 120 church members. The promoters gained the confidence of the members by claiming to have been born-again Christians, and a prophecy sent them to these particular church members.

ACCOUNTING FRAUD

This securities scam is often perpetrated by the management of a company, rather than individual brokers; sometimes with the assistance or negligence of internal or external auditors. Specifically, these acts violate several SEC doctrines and laws, including:

Bespeaks caution doctrine: forecasts, opinion, or projections must disclose specific risks.

Duty to disclose: persons who have made misleading statements must issue corrective statements as soon as they are aware of the misstatement.

Breach of fiduciary duty: reasonable decisions must be made concerning corporate and stockholder investments.

The management structure of an organization has an understood duty to both the company (board members and employees), as well as to the stockholders; and as such all statements made by officers of a company must be made in good faith and all accounting information supplied to analysts and stockholders must be accurately presented. In 2002, the SEC investigated several cases of alleged financial manipulation.

Members of the management teams of Enron, Tyco, WorldCom, and Adelphia, among others, were investigated for various frauds and securities violations. Enron Corporation Chairman and Chief Executive Officer Kenneth Lay encouraged Enron employees to buy Enron stock as the company prospects were very positive. In August 2000, Enron reached an all-time high of $90.75, and while Lay was encouraging employees and investors to purchase more stock, he was selling his stock (approximately $100 million according to the SEC).

As Enron stock began to fall, Lay still strenuously encouraged employees to purchase additional stock. Employees eventually were blocked from selling the Enron stock held in their 401K plans. In November 2001, Enron shares closed at 26 cents. Also involved in the Enron accounting scandal were chief financial officer Andrew Fastow and external audit firm Arthur Andersen LLP. Fastow allegedly generated over $25 million in profits for himself through off-the-balance-sheets partnerships named after his wife and children. Audit firm Arthur Andersen LLP paid a $7 million fine for obstruction of justice charges for destroying internal memos at the request of Enron after the investigation began and subpoenas were issued.

UNQUALIFIED REPORTS

The SEC also cited Arthur Andersen for its auditing work with Waste Management Inc., noting that that Andersen repeatedly issued unqualified audits reports of the company. The SEC alleged that the audit firm agreed to conceal past accountings frauds committed by Waste Management if Waste Management agreed to make accounting changes in the future.

Tyco chairman Dennis Kozlowski was charged with criminal enterprise and grand larceny concerning securities fraud and thefts committed through his position with Tyco. His actions allegedly involved the procurement of unauthorized "sweetheart" loans from various accounts at Tyco, and concealing the transactions from board members by ordering the internal auditors to report their findings directly to him.

Several members of WorldCom upper management were charged with securities fraud after multiple accusations of accounting irregularities surfaced, including carrying over approximately $5 million in expenses from one operating year to the next. There were allegations of collusion between WorldCom management and external stock analysts who continued to recommend World Com stock as more and more accounting irregularities surfaced.

Additionally, it was alleged that one such analyst advised WorldCom management beforehand of questions he would ask during financial conference calls. Chief Executive Officer Dennis Ebbers allegedly obtained $408 million in loans from the company, contrary to accepted practices. WorldCom stock closed in 2002 at 35 cents after reaching $90 in 1999. Review of the auditing procedures at the company revealed that the internal audit department was looking for inefficiency in operations and not reviewing accounting procedures.

Several members of the Rivas family, the founders and operators of Adelphia Communications were indicted for securities fraud at their company. According to SEC records $3.1 billion was hidden through off-balance-sheet loans, and the debts were allegedly concealed from other board members.

SEE ALSO

Arthur Andersen; stock fraud; stock churning; accounting fraud; Tyco International; WorldCom; Enron Corporation; Securities and Exchange Commission.

BIBLIOGRAPHY. Howard Schilit, *Financial Shenanigans* (McGraw-Hill, 2002); U.S. Securities and Exchange Commission, www.sec.gov/investor (2003); Federal Bureau of Investigations Economic Crime Unit, www.fbi.gov/hq/cid (2003); S. Weisman, *Need and Greed: The Story of the Largest Ponzi Scheme in American History* (Syracuse University Press, 1999); F. Partnoy, *Infectious Greed* (Henry Holt, 2003); K. Eichenwald, *Serpent on the Rock* (HarperBusiness, 1995); M. Binstein, *Trust Me: Keating and the Missing Billions* (Random House, 1993)

PATRICK D. WALSH
LOYOLA UNIVERSITY NEW ORLEANS

self-control theory

THE PRESUMPTION THAT virtually everyone in society is capable of illegal or criminal and other deviant behavior because people are clever enough to see their advantages, is the basis of self-control theory. People have no trouble inventing wrongful behaviors and then discovering the easiest ways to commit them, with no special motivation or learning required for their completion. Why, then, is not everyone a criminal? Michael Gottfredson and Travis Hirschi's self-control theory, found in their *A General Theory of Crime*, stresses the importance of studying the factors that cause most individuals generally to obey the law, factors that center on a fear of the consequences for bad behavior.

Virtually all crimes promise to net the perpetrator some expression of immediate self-gratification, be it money without work, sex without courtship, revenge without court delays, or simply excitement itself. It follows that persons likeliest to commit crime are those who are most unable to self-control pursuit of these outcomes. An individual's general level of self-control varies from very high (or little tendency for short-term gratification) to very low (great tendency for short-term gratification), and all of us fall somewhere within those extremes.

CRIME SIMILARITY

Self-control theory's approach represents three major departures from other criminological postulations. Most fundamentally, because virtually all criminal acts promise the same thing—relatively immediate gratification—self-control theorists believe that distinctions such as white-collar and corporate crime or even violent and property crime have little utility, and, in fact obscure the similarity among criminal acts and among criminals. To illustrate this similarity, all of the following are looking for money (or its equivalent) based on the least amount of honest work: robbers, corporate polluters, shoplifters, bank embezzlers, doctors who perform unnecessary surgery, lawyers who over-bill, burglars, and price-fixers. Self-control theory therefore supposes that all of these offenders should be viewed as essentially the same.

A second important divergence of self-control theory is that it considers the division between criminal and noncriminal behavior to be a false distinction for theoretical purpose, because both crime and noncriminal deviant acts reveal manifestations of the same trait. Tobacco and alcohol use, lying, low academic performance and cheating, adultery, high debt, checkered work histories, unsafe sex, car

accidents from risky driving, gambling, and a host of other noncriminal behaviors will occur at rates based on how low one's self-control is, as will larceny, assault, embezzlement, rape, fraud, and murder. By transcending legalistic designations of which behaviors and individuals are criminal, self-control theory avoids many of the entanglements associated with figuring out such designations, and is able instead to concentrate on overall behavior patterns. Many of these noncriminal acts of self-gratification can contribute to financial and other stresses for an individual, increasing further the motivations and frustrations that lead a person to commit property crime, violent crime, and to use drugs. Indeed, extremely low self-control ravages a person's life far beyond the pains associated with official punishments, and official punishments are often the least of such persons' daily worries. However, self-control theory does not believe that involvement in one form of deviance leads to involvement in other forms. Rather, high involvement in both criminal and noncriminal deviant behaviors are caused by the same thing—lower self-control.

Third, the vast majority of popular criminological perspectives presume that something bad must happen to make someone a criminal. A person must be taught how to commit crime, or inherit bad genes, or be pressured by a bad economic situation. In a significant departure from this supposition, self-control theory believes that all people are born with innate tendencies to gratify themselves, and will act out those impulses unless something is done to help them control themselves. Parenting is seen as the major source for teaching self-control, through emphasizing respect for the feelings and rights of others and reinforcing the belief that society's rules are legitimate. Good parental teachings, regardless of who inculcates them, encourage people to delay immediate gratifications, most notably through child discipline and forming attachments to the parents.

ASPECTS AND SYMPTOMS

Symptoms associated with low self-control are: risk-taking, or a quest for exciting and dangerous behavior; simplicity, or an avoidance of difficult tasks; low frustration tolerance, which is manifested in both having a temper and easy boredom; physicality, or a preference for physical rather than mental activity; impulsiveness, which involves more concern with here-and-now pleasures than future outcomes; and self-centeredness, or looking out for oneself first and tending to blame oneself last. People who strongly exhibit these symptoms are, according to Gottfredson and Hirschi, "relatively unable or unwilling to delay gratification; they are relatively indifferent to punishment and to the interests of others." However, even those with the lowest control do not commit crimes under all circumstances. And those with the highest control are not infallible, but will commit crime at an extremely low rate.

Self-control theory does not attempt to explain those relatively few criminal acts which do not involve immediate gratification. Mercy killing by physicians is a crime, but it is not based on the self-gratification of the offender, so it would be outside the purview of the theory. The same would be true for any illegal behaviors that are committed because of a higher principle rather than gaining some personal advantage. Thus, self-control theory is an atypical general theory of crime in that it explains some noncriminal behavior while at the same time does not attempt to explain some criminal behavior.

Self-control has an invariant and curvilinear life-course relationship with a person's age. Self-control is at it lowest in every person's life—regardless of where that person's general level of self-control may be—from early adolescence through about age 30, and then slowly rises into later years. Self-control is stable—from early adolescence onward, people do not change their levels of self-control relative to others their age. People with lower levels of self-control will exploit a variety of opportunities, people, and animals to satisfy their self-gratification.

Opportunity is assumed to be ubiquitous—people are limited only by the opportunities with which they are confronted and that they invent. Deterrence is a strong component in self-control theory in that most normal people are able to take inventory of what they have to lose for committing the crime. They will also have some idea, correct or not, about what their probability of apprehension will be. We would expect crime to occur when the tendency for short-term gratification is coupled with both physical opportunity and a perception on the part of the potential offender that he is immune from at least immediate formal and nonformal sanctions. The absence of any one of these three conditions nullifies the theory's prediction that crime is

very likely to occur. Making criminal opportunity physically more difficult (such as by installing locks or increasing the scrutiny in account audits), known as "target hardening," is likely to fend off low self-control offenders because overcoming such barriers may be seen as involving too much effort since such persons are easily frustrated and avoid difficult tasks.

MORE TO LOSE

As noted, the theory dismisses the notion that white-collar and corporate crime are meaningful groupings. However, Gottfredson and Hirschi do predict that the rate of occupational and other offenses by persons toward the high end of the occupational structure will be lower than that by persons toward the low end of the occupational structure, because selection processes inherent to the high end tend to recruit people with relatively higher self-control. As one goes higher in the occupational structure, one is also more likely to find persons who have reached long-term goals because of their greater self-control.

These in-hand achievements (such as an education, a career, a nice home, a respectable reputation within and outside of one's family) are held dearly, and such persons therefore are less likely to commit crime because they have more to lose by doing so. They perceive much greater negative consequences for their criminal behavior than people situated much lower on the occupational ladder, and therefore would be more likely to be deterred. Lower self-control individuals, on the other hand, have very little to lose, and therefore are less responsive to sanction threats of all kinds.

To support self-control theory, research must account for age and demonstrate that people exhibit versatility and stability in their immediate gratification behaviors (both criminal and noncriminal) that vary inversely with measures of their self-control. The theory would predict that doctors who purposely perform unnecessary surgery also would be more likely to be involved in other medical crimes. Police who commit brutality should prove more likely to take bribes and have patrol car accidents. And corporate executives who cheat on their wives should be more likely also to cheat on their taxes.

The theory rejects the general notion of differential association that non-corrupt business people and women become corrupted later in life by the corporate culture. Although self-control theory readily acknowledges that organizational structures and processes can either encourage or discourage the commission of offenses, it would nevertheless assert that levels of self-control can predict criminal rates in organizations better than criminogenic organizational environments can predict them. This would be true both for crime benefiting an organization and for crime against it. Such studies have yet to be done.

In addition to transcending the entanglements of theories that depend on the legalisms of criminal and noncriminal behavior, self-control theory's main contribution lies in having found the middle ground between two of criminology's most timeless findings—deterrence and early socialization.

SEE ALSO
differential association; conflict theory; critical theory; employee crimes.

BIBLIOGRAPHY. Michael Gottfredson and Travis Hirschi, *A General Theory of Crime* (Stanford University Press, 1990); Travis Hirschi and Michael Gottfredson, "Causes of White-Collar Crime," *Criminology* (v.27, 1987); Gary Reed and Peter Yeager, "Organizational Offending and Neoclassical Criminology: Challenging the Reach of A General Theory of Crime," *Criminology* (v.43, 1996); Carey Herbert, Gary Green, and Victor Larragoite, "Clarifying the Reach of A General Theory of Crime for Organizational Offending: A Comment on Reed and Yeager," *Criminology* (v.36, 1998); Gilbert Geis, "On the Absence of Self-control as the Basis for A General Theory of Crime: A Critique," *Theoretical Criminology* (v.4, 2000); Travis Hirschi and Michael Gottfredson, "In Defense of Self-Control," *Theoretical Criminology* (v.4, 2000).

GARY S. GREEN
CHRISTOPHER NEWPORT UNIVERSITY

Sentencing Guidelines

THROUGHOUT THE 1970s, a great deal of attention was focused on disparities in sentencing—people who committed the same crime rarely received the same sentence. This disparity also produced many cases in which persons received very little punishment for serious crimes. The response to fed-

eral sentencing disparity was the Sentencing Reform Act of 1984 (Title II of the Comprehensive Crime Control Act of 1984), which established the U.S. Sentencing Commission. Congress's objective was to enhance the ability of the federal criminal justice system to combat crime through an effective and fair sentencing system. Congress wanted honesty in sentencing so that potential offenders know the punishments that they were likely to receive. Congress also wanted uniformity in sentencing to promote fairness. The U.S. Sentencing Commission was established to review the existing practices of the federal law enforcement system and to create the Guidelines that were relatively concrete and equitable—the U.S. Sentencing Guidelines ("Guidelines"). The Guidelines have not only resulted in more equitable punishments for like offenders, they have also punished more severely many white collar criminals and corporations who otherwise would have escaped such sanctioning.

There are two sets of Guidelines, one for individuals (effective October 1, 1987) and one for organizations (effective November 1, 1991). Both individuals and organizations are separately punishable for crimes committed by persons working on behalf of an organization, and when the organization is owned by the offender(s), considerations are made to reduce the organizational punishment in light of the punishment given to the individual(s).

PUNISHMENT OF INDIVIDUALS

Two factors determine an individual's sentence length: the offense level (ranging from a low of 1 to a high of 43) and the person's criminal history score. The offense level is generally based upon the harmfulness of the offense (bodily injury, monetary loss, property damage, and any other resulting harm) and the blame attributable to the offender for the crime in question. Dominant offense roles are more punishable than peripheral ones and negligent behavior is less punishable than willful behavior, for instance. The criminal history score is generally based upon the extent and recentness of one's officially documented criminal past.

If the individual has a long-standing previous criminal record, the incarceration length and amount of fine are increased substantially. Such enhancements were justified by the Commission on the grounds that repeat offenders are more blameworthy when they commit subsequent offenses and that increased punishments are needed to deter them from future illegalities and to isolate them from society for longer periods.

The Guidelines for individuals work as follows. Most felonies and Class A misdemeanors in the several volumes of the United States Code have been assigned an offense level, although many regulatory violations are not included. However, price fixing, money laundering, mishandling of toxic substances, mail and wire fraud, bribery, and a host of other crimes that are committed for the benefit of an organization are punishable under the Guidelines for individuals. Depending upon explicitly defined aggravating and mitigating factors, the level can be increased or decreased, respectively.

AGGRAVATING FACTORS

The greatest monetary value associated with the crime (amount stolen or bribed, criminal profit to the offender, loss to the victim), the vulnerability of the victim, and the offender's role in the offense are some of the factors that will increase or decrease the base offense level. The extent to which the offense endangered public welfare (national security, public health or safety) would enhance the level of the offense. Whether the offender abused a position of trust or special skill in the commission of the offense is also an aggravating factor.

Cooperation by the defendant will lessen the sentence slightly, but a guilty plea is not supposed to be treated as a demonstration of cooperation. Both *no lo contendre* pleas ("I neither admit nor deny the charges") and Alford pleas ("I do not admit the offense but acknowledge that there is enough evidence to convict me") are considered to be guilty pleas by the Guidelines. The final offense level is then located on a row in the Sentencing Table (in Guidelines, Chapter 5). The final incarceration range is determined by the offender's criminal history score in that row.

Offense levels, but not criminal history scores, equate also with monetary penalties for a given offense or set of offenses—a fine up to $250,000 (or more if allowed by statute; found in Guidelines Chapter 5), victim restitution, prosecution costs, and in some cases, forfeiture of assets related to criminal behavior. Restitution is the pre-eminent concern. The U.S. District Court judge then sentences to any incarceration and monetary penalties within the ranges allowed. The U.S. District Court

"shall" impose a fine within the specified range, but can reduce or eliminate the fine if the offender is unable to pay it and is unlikely to be able to pay it sometime in the future. The adverse effects of a fine on a defendant's dependents are also a consideration. The Guidelines expressly prohibit a reduction in sentence based on any "lack of guidance" the defendant experienced as a youth. Probation for individuals is allowed only when the offense level is very low.

Two offenses may be vastly different in terms of harm and culpability, even though they violate the same statute. To help ensure that the penalty is proportional to the offense, the Guidelines attempt to punish on the basis of "real offense sentencing"— the actual conduct in which the offender engaged. Further, in sentencing for multiple crimes, the cumulative harm associated with the "same course of conduct" or a "common scheme or plan" is used in the determination of offense levels. A "common scheme or plan" involves common victims, common accomplices, a common purpose, or a similar modus operandi. Multiple offending which may not qualify as a common scheme or plan may nevertheless be considered to be part of a "same course of conduct" when a spree or series of ongoing offenses can be viewed as similar and occurring at relatively short time intervals.

PUNISHMENT OF ORGANIZATIONS

Chapter 8 of the Guidelines covers organizations, and it is also based upon real offense sentencing. "Organizations" include any legal entity other than an individual: corporations, partnerships, associations, joint-stock companies, unions, trusts, pension funds, unincorporated organizations, governments and political subdivisions thereof, and non-profit organizations. As in the case of Guidelines for individuals, organizational penalties consider offense harm, organizational culpability, and previous organizational criminality in determining the monetary penalty that is to be paid by the organization. Historically, more than 90 percent of organizations sentenced under the Guidelines have been "closely held" organizations with a small number of owners. Less than 5 percent of organizations sentenced under the Guidelines are larger, publicly traded corporations. Research shows the majority of sentenced organizations, close to four-fifths, have fewer than 50 employees. About 1 in 10 is a recidivist.

The Guidelines punish organizations based on vicarious liability, or *respondeat superior*. Vicarious liability covers the illegal acts of any director, officer, employee, or independent contractor authorized to act on behalf of the organization. Offense levels for organizations are based essentially on the same criteria as individual offense levels, including aggravating and mitigating factors. Probation is also possible for organizations, especially when necessary to collect a fine or to restructure the organization to prevent future offenses.

The Chapter 8 fines for organizations have been enormous in a few select cases, having reached into several hundreds of millions of dollars. However, the vast majority of fines are associated with small organizations where the dollar values are consistently much less. Some larger organizations have avoided criminal prosecution under the Guidelines because they have the resources to leverage prosecutors into accepting civil and administrative sanctions. Or, they have circumvented vicarious liability by redirecting blame to their employees based on the leeway of the Guidelines.

ORGANIZATIONAL FINING PROCEDURES

Generally, the Guidelines provide that some combination of the following be paid by convicted organizational offenders: 1) victim restitution and any other costs that would be associated with righting the harm of the offense (restitution is paramount); 2) a fine; 3) payment (or "disgorgement") of any criminal profits beyond the value of restitution that has been or will be paid, including any social losses (such as harm to a marketplace in an antitrust crime); and 4) costs of prosecution. The disgorgement of profits realized from the offense must be added to the fine, so the monetary penalty will always exceed the financial benefits of organizational criminal behavior. In addition, organizations can be sentenced to community service (which can involve expenditures) and they may be forced to make expensive structural changes designed to preclude future offending.

If an organization cannot pay its proper fine either because it has no assets or because paying the fine will jeopardize full payment of victim restitution, the court can waive the fine entirely (under Guidelines §8C3.3). Research has shown that two-thirds of convicted organizations that cannot pay receive no fine whatsoever; if they do receive a fine,

it is substantially less than the prescribed minimum. Organizations are allowed up to five years to pay their fines.

FINE RANGES

Determining the fine range for organizations is much more complicated than determining it for individuals. First, a base fine must be decided, and it is the greatest of the following: the fine associated with a specific offense level (found in Chapter 8), pecuniary gain (pre-tax profit from the offense), or financial harm to victim(s). Base fines are high because they need to demonstrate the seriousness of the offense and that the fine is punitive, and they need to act as just punishment and as a deterrent to the organization (and to others). In no case can a fine be more than is allowed by statute. Currently, base fines cover an array from $5,000 (for an offense level of 6 or less) to $72.5 million (for an offense level of 38 or more). Actual fine ranges are determined by a "culpability score" and each score has a specific minimum and maximum multiplier that is applied to the base fine in order to determine the fine range in which the sentence will fall. The score begins at five and can be reduced to as low as zero or increased to as high as ten.

The culpability score will be increased if the organization's management either "participated in," "condoned," or was "willfully ignorant" of the offense. The amount of the increase for this provision is based on the size of the organization, ranging from 1 point (10-49 employees) to 5 points (5,000 or more employees). The larger the organization, the higher the government's expectation that management create formal structures to eliminate the organization's participation in illegality.

Criminal history is also an aggravator, adding one point if a similar offense had occurred within the past 10 years, and two points if it had occurred within the past five. If the crime involves a violation of a previous court order or condition of probation, one or two points are added, depending on the situation. If the organization in any way obstructed justice related to the investigation or prosecution of the offense, including failure to prevent obstruction, 3 points are added.

Reductions in the culpability score are based on the following: 1) the organization had an effective compliance program to detect, prevent, and report violations at the time of the offense (subtract 3 points); and 2) the organization brought the offense to the attention of appropriate government officials before outside discovery was imminent, it accepted responsibility for the offense, and it fully cooperated with authorities in the investigation of the offense (subtract 5 points). Cooperation and acceptance entitles the organization to a 2-point reduction, and acceptance of responsibility alone entitles it to a 1-point reduction.

The culpability score, in essence, punishes according to the inverse of the probability that an offense will be officially detected. Higher probabilities of detection—based on compliance programs, reporting the offense to the authorities, and cooperating in investigations—equate with lower culpability. Lower probabilities of detection—when management participates in, condones, or is willfully ignorant of the offending, or there is obstruction of justice—equate with higher culpability.

Minimum multipliers for the base fine vary from .05 (culpability score ? 0) to 2.0 (culpability score ? 10). Maximum multipliers vary from 0.2 (culpability score ? 0) to 4.0 (culpability score ? 10). The presumptive culpability score of five equates to multipliers of 1.0 and 2.0. As an example, if an organization's base fine is $10,000 and the culpability score remains at the presumptive five, the fine range would be $10,000 to $20,000 (based on its minimum and maximum multipliers). If its culpability score is 0 or less, the fine range is $500 to $1,000, and it is $20,000 to $40,000 if the culpability score is 10 or more. Thus, based on the culpability score, a fine can vary by as much as a factor of eighty (.05 to 4.0). Organizations will be fined within the prescribed range according to various criteria, including victim vulnerability or psychological harm, the role of the organization in the offense, and whether there is recidivism associated with the current offense(s). Any monies paid previously in civil or criminal proceedings because of the offense should be deducted from the fine.

The determination of the culpability score becomes especially important with the highest base fines. Before the Guidelines were put forth, there was a strong and quite reasonable concern about the lessening in culpability scores related to the 3-point reduction for the existence of a compliance program to detect, prevent, and report violations. It was believed that devious corporations would construct merely cosmetic façades for such programs, and then redirect risks of vicarious liability onto

their employees, thereby reaping both the benefits of crime and the benefits of reductions in culpability. The U.S. Sentencing Commission was very sensitive to this possibility, and put forth explicit criteria about what constitutes an effective compliance program that would qualify under the Guidelines. Even with these well defined criteria for compliance, the commission's earliest fears about the misuse of this culpability mitigation have not proved to be unfounded.

COMPLIANCE PROGRAMS

The U.S. Sentencing Commission equates the requirements for compliance programming with being a "good corporate citizen." The criteria for qualifying compliance programs have come to be known as the "Seven Steps," and the government hallmark is whether the organization used "due diligence" to prevent, detect, and report legal violations. the Guidelines assert that the failure to prevent or detect an offense will not, by itself, render a compliance program ineffective. However, the Guidelines also imply that the only real way to measure whether a program was designed, implemented, and enforced with due diligence is in the scarcity of violations.

The "Seven Steps" involve: 1) the establishment of compliance standards and procedures; 2) the designation of high-level personnel as having responsibility to oversee the program; 3) the avoidance of delegating authority to persons known to have a propensity to engage in illegalities; 4) taking steps to communicate effectively the standards and procedures; 5) the establishment of monitoring and auditing systems to detect violations and of a reporting system by which employees can report criminal conduct of others within the organization without fear of reprisal; 6) consistent enforcement of standards through disciplinary mechanisms, including the discipline of individuals responsible for overseeing compliance structures when there is a failure to detect an offense; and 7) the organization taking all reasonable steps to respond appropriately to an offense that has occurred and to prevent further similar offenses, including any necessary modifications to its program.

The Guidelines further emphasize that the larger an organization, the more stringent the expectations for effective compliance programming. Organizations must also anticipate violations that are known or probable based on their organizational history and their sector or industry, and design their programs accordingly. Further, an organization's failure to follow industry practice or a legal regulation is contrary to a finding that its program was effective.

Despite the importance the Guidelines places on effective compliance, research for the U.S. Sentencing Commission has found that most employees working in very large corporations believe that the Guidelines have had a limited, insignificant, or negative effect on compliance efforts. Commission research has also concluded that the two most important environmental factors in an organization contributing to noncompliance are remuneration incentives for unethical behavior and employees' perceived threats of reprisal for reporting violations.

ORGANIZATIONAL PROBATION

Before its codification in the Guidelines, organizational probation was used for the first time in a federal criminal case in 1971 in *United States v. Atlantic Richfield Co.* (465 F.2d 58). U.S. District Court Judge James B. Parsons, Jr. broke jurisprudential ground by placing ARCO on probation so that he could monitor the company's progress in complying with his order to develop an oil spill response program. Parsons's innovation was widely copied by his colleagues, and by the middle 1980s, probation was ordered in approximately a fifth of all federal corporate convictions. However, many of these probation orders were successfully appealed because, although probation for individuals had been well entrenched in the federal law for 60 years, there were no legal provisions to justify this type of sentence for organizations, until the Guidelines §8D1.1.

Under the Guidelines, a convicted organization can be placed on probation for between one and five years to ensure that it will pay its fine and that it will rehabilitate its compliance structure to help prevent future violations. Such rehabilitation includes submitting to the court a viable compliance program, including a schedule for implementation. To monitor whether the organization is following the program, the organization must submit to regular audits and interrogations of key individuals by outsiders, the costs of which will be paid by the organization. The organization will also be required to notify its employees and shareholders of its crimi-

nal behavior and of its new compliance structure. Any failure to follow these or other conditions of probation will result in the revocation of probation and resentencing to more punitive sanctions. Early research indicates that about two-thirds of organizations convicted under the Guidelines are placed on probation, about one in five of which were also ordered to create a compliance program. Organizations of all sizes have been placed on probation under the Guidelines.

One of the most interesting features of organizational probation under the Guidelines is the possibility for court-imposed adverse publicity. The court can, as a condition of probation, order the convicted organization to publicize the nature of the offense committed, the fact of conviction, the nature of the punishment imposed, and the steps that will be taken to prevent the occurrence of similar offenses. There is a befitting poetic justice in the fact that the organization will have to pay for its own adverse publicity. Forced adverse publicity penalties are analogous to a "corporate pillory," for they place organizational offenders at public ridicule. The primary purposes of this sanction is shaming the organization and as a deterrent, but it is seldom imposed.

In conclusion, in order for the Guidelines to act as its intended deterrent, decision makers in large corporations must perceive a high probability of being implicated in and convicted for organizational criminal behavior. To help encourage this perception, federal prosecutors must be willing to spend their resources pursuing rich corporations in protracted criminal court battles, and they should not acquiesce to negotiations for a civil settlement in *prima facie* criminal cases.

Experts agree that prosecutors should also be critical in their acceptance of corporate assertions that lower level employees are responsible for offending when there is an "effective compliance program" in place to detect, prevent, and report violations. For persons making decisions in small and powerless organizations (the vast majority sentenced under the Guidelines) the deterrent value of fine threats will work only to the point that the potential offender is able to pay. Threats beyond that capability offer no additional deterrent.

SEE ALSO

reform and regulation; prosecution; corporate liability; consent decrees and orders; compliance programs.

BIBLIOGRAPHY. Amitai Etzioni, "The U.S. Sentencing Commission on Corporate Crime: A Critique," *Annals of the American Academy of Political and Social Science* (v.525, 1993); Peter French, "Publicity and the Control of Corporate Conduct," *Corrigible Corporations and Unruly Law* (Trinity University Press, 1985); William Laufer, "Corporate Liability, Risk Shifting, and the Paradox of Compliance," *Vanderbilt Law Review* (v.54, 1999); William Lofquist, "Organizational Probation and the U.S. Sentencing Commission" *Annals of the American Academy of Political and Social Science* (v.525, 1993); Gary Green and Madhu Bodapati, "The Deterrence Trap in the Federal Fining of Organizations" *Criminal Justice Policy Review* (v.10, 1999); Mark Pastin, "A Study of Organizational Factors and their Effect on Compliance," *Proceedings, Corporate Crime in America: Strengthening the Good Citizen Corporation* (U.S. Sentencing Commission, September 7, 1995); Gary Green, "Organizational Probation Under the Federal Sentencing Guidelines," *Federal Probation* (v.62, 1998); Jeffrey Kaplan, Joseph Murphy, and Winthrop Swenson, eds., *Compliance Programs and the Corporate Sentencing Guidelines* (West Group, 2002).

GARY S. GREEN
CHRISTOPHER NEWPORT UNIVERSITY

sexual discrimination

SEE gender discrimination.

sexual harassment

SEXUAL HARASSMENT is unwanted sexual behavior that interferes with occupational or educational functioning and is a form of white-collar crime. However, there is no statutory law criminalizing sexual harassment, but court cases against harassers in civil court have been won based upon Title VII of the 1964 Civil Rights Act prohibiting sex discrimination.

The term *sexual harassment* was coined in 1970 when Carmita Wood, an administrative assistant at Cornell University sued the university for unemployment compensation after she left the university due to an illness, precipitated as the result of ongoing sexual advances from a university professor. In 1972, Congress passed the Equal Opportunity Employment Act extending the coverage of Title VII to state and local governments and empowering the Equal Employment Opportunity Commission to enforce, via lawsuits, the 1964 prohibition on sex and race discrimination in employment.

In 1980, the chair of the Equal Employment Opportunity Commission issued a set of guidelines detailing prohibited behavior that applied to all federal agencies and to private businesses with 15 or more employees. The guidelines included the prohibition of three general types of behaviors: 1) physical or verbal behaviors that are sexual in nature, including comments, photographs, jokes, or cartoons; 2) unwanted sexual behaviors; and 3) sexual behaviors that interfere with the ability to complete work or studies or that make the subject feel uncomfortable or threatened.

Generally sexual harassment is characterized by two types, *quid pro quo* harassment, and the creation of a hostile work or educational environment. Quid pro quo harassment occurs when an employee's initial or continued employment or advancement is conditioned on the performance of sexual favors. A hostile environment is the result of unwelcome or offensive conduct of a sexual nature that makes working conditions uncomfortable for a reasonable person.

Specifically, a hostile work environment charge of sexual harassment may consist of verbal or physical conduct of a sexual nature that unreasonably interferes with the employee's work, or creates an intimidating, hostile, or offensive work environment. Sexual harassment has been shown to lead to high rates of job turnover, lower productivity, and negative health consequences.

Sexual harassment in federal agencies alone costs the government approximately $327 million from 1992to 1994. In 1994, 44 percent of women and 19 percent of men employed in civilian federal government agencies reported experiencing unwanted sexual attention over the last two years. While in a 1994–95 survey of military personnel, 71 percent of women and 36 percent of men were sexually harassed in the last 12 months. Crude and offensive behavior is most common among military personnel, but women are five times as likely as men to report experiencing unwanted sexual attention or coercion.

Twelve percent of military women report experiencing sexual coercion, and 41 percent reported unwanted sexual attention. Similarly, surveys in the private sector reveal that 45 to 68 percent of women experienced sexual harassment over a two-year period.

CASE STUDIES

In order to bring a successful lawsuit, the harassment needs to pervasive, frequent, repetitive, and a part of an overall environmental pattern of behavior. In 1976, the U.S. District Court for New Jersey recognized a cause for sexual harassment in *Tompkins v. Public Services Electric and Gas Company*. Also in 1976, the first *quid pro quo* sexual harassment case was decided in *Williams v. Saxbe*. In this case, Diane Williams was fired from the Department of Justice after refusing sexual advances from a supervisor. Federal judges established sexual harassment as a cause for sex-based discrimination civil suits making employers liable (413 F. Supp. 654 D.D.C. 1976).

In 1981, the first successful lawsuit arguing hostile environment was *Bundy v. Jackson* in which Sandra Bundy was harassed by a barrage of sexual insults and propositions leading to anxiety and debilitation. In 1985, in *Hicks v. Gates Rubber Company* and *McKinney v. Dole*, the court stated that sex-based harassment (not incorporating sexual language or activity) can violate Title VII if it is "sufficiently patterned or pervasive" and targeted toward an employee because of his sex.

In 1986, *Meritor Savings Bank v. Vinson* (U.S. 57), the U.S. Supreme Court held that willful submission to sexual conduct does not suppress a claim of sexual harassment and that such harassment is a form of sex discrimination. The court also stated that *quid pro quo* and hostile environment violated Title VII of the Civil Rights Act. These legal precedents prohibit employment discrimination based on race, color, national origin, religion, or sex in any educational program or activity that receives federal funds and by all private employers.

Sexual harassment is also cause of action based upon Title IX of the Education Amendments of 1972 and under the Equal Protection Clause of the Fourteenth Amendment. In 1992, in *Franklin v. Gwinett County Public Schools*, the Supreme Court found that Title IX of the Educational Amendments of 1972 had been violated due to the sexual harassment of several students by teachers and inaction by the school administration. One student, Christine Franklin, was forcibly kissed by a teacher and subjected to sexually oriented conversation.

Subsequently, the school principal was told about the harassment. But the principal discouraged Franklin from making a complaint even though several other students had made similar complaints. The court stated that this behavior by a teacher and the inaction by the principal was a form of gender discrimination.

However, in another court case in 1993, the Supreme Court found that an initial warning to a teacher for inappropriate sexual remarks to students and a later dismissal after rape charges were filed were sufficient corrective measures and did not classify as a violation of student rights under Title IX (*Gebser v. Lago Vista Independent School District*). Finally, in 1999 in *Davis v. Monroe County Board of Education*, a student was subjected to sexual remarks and sexual touching by a male classmate and reported it. However, school officials failed to act on reports and thus were found liable since they received federal assistance, and were deliberately indifferent to depriving the victim of educational opportunities and benefits provided by the school.

HARASSMENT AT WORK

Several lower federal court decisions are also important in understanding sexual harassment at work. Employers are not liable if they establish and implement preventative policies on sexual harassment, take prompt action to remedy the harassment situation, or when the victim knew or should have known that the employer did not tolerate sexual harassment. Another court case (*Lipsett v. University of Puerto Rico* 864 F.2d 881) also ruled that conduct that men consider unobjectionable may offend many women. Similarly, in 1987, (*Barbetta v. Chemlawn Services Corporation*) the court found that the "proliferation of pornography may be found to create an atmosphere where women are viewed as men's sexual playthings rather than their equal coworkers if it is sufficiently continuous and pervasive."

Also in *Berkman v. City of New York* (775 F.2d. 913) the court decided that harassing conduct of a non-sexual nature could also constitute sexual harassment if the environment is hostile to women in other ways. Other causes of action include workplace behavior that includes gossip about workplace affairs, use of unwelcome foul language, or sexual innuendo. In 1998 (*Burlington Industries Inc. v. Ellerth* and *Faragher v. City of Boca Raton*), the courts decided that employers are subject to vicarious liability for a victimized company employee in hostile environment cases.

A federal circuit court determined that lower level *(Parkins v. Civil Constructors of Illinois Inc.)* employees are subject to negligent charges rather than vicarious liability. Finally, in 1998, a federal regulation established guidelines for workplace conduct that are actionable for a civil tort under Title VII and these include "unwelcome sexual advances, requests for sexual favors, and other verbal or physical conduct of a sexual nature." However, substantive law or statutes as well as case law (court cases) require that, while the employer must demonstrate that she made reasonable efforts to prevent and correct such harassment, the employee or victim or plaintiff must also show that he made an effort to avoid or prevent harm from the harassment. Employers who subsequently discharge demote, or reassign the victim also make the employer liable for the harassment.

In a 1999 case, the New Jersey Supreme Court *(Blakely v. Continental Airlines)* ruled that sexual harassment and other types of sex discrimination that occur on the internet outside the workplace, but connected to the workplace, still make the company liable under sex discrimination statutes. In this case, a commercial airline pilot, Tammy Blakely, was sexually harassed at work through the placement of pornography in her cockpit as well as a variety of verbal comments. This was followed by further retaliatory behavior by her male coworkers on the company's internet bulletin board site.

With regard to the internet, the court ruled that employers must remedy any retaliatory harassment even in cyberspace. Finally, in 2002, the Ninth Circuit Court of Appeals ruled in favor of an openly gay male who was sexually harassed by his male coworkers by whistling, blowing kisses, telling crude jokes, and forcing him to look at pictures of men having sex. Six out of 10 judges ruled that the behavior was actionable under Title VII, first under physical sexual assault provisions, and secondly under gender stereotyping theory that recognizes that same sex harassment is actionable.

HARASSMENT REPORTING

Research indicates that there exists a gross under-reporting of sexual discrimination and harassment, but the experience of sexual harassment remains quite common among women, with most offenders being men. Women's responses to harassment and discrimination are varied. About half of all women will likely experience sexual harassment at work from male coworkers, supervisors, clients, or customers while about 30 to 66 percent of female students can expect to be harassed by teachers, administrators, staff, or peers. Anywhere from 44 to 85 percent of U.S. women and 78 percent of Canadian women are sexually harassed, whereas only 12 to 19 percent of U.S. men experience sexual harassment.

Similarly, there is some evidence that women who occupy non-traditional roles at work may more likely to be sexually harassed than women in more traditional workplace positions. Studies also reveal that less than 12 percent of women actually file complaints, and only about 24 percent ever even disclose the event. Additionally, less than 1 percent of sexual harassment claims are heard in court and only about one third of these outcomes favor the victim.

Costs of sexual harassment among federal employees have been estimated as high as $300 million, and among Fortune 500 companies it has cost more than $6 million in productivity. Feminists argue that sexual harassment by men reflects the patriarchal nature of the workplace characterized by an environment where men have more economic and institutional power, and thus engage in behavior that attempts to further subordinate and disempower women. However, it should be noted that men in female dominated positions are also more likely to experience sexual harassment than other men. The Federal Equal Employment Opportunity Commission's annual report indicates that the filing of formal complaints by victims remains very limited. Specifically, in 1999, only 23,907 complaints were filed under Title VII alleging sex-based discrimination; similarly 15,222 sexual harassment complaints were filed in 1999 (12 percent of the charges were filed by men).

However, only 7 percent of the sexual harassment cases resulted in findings of reasonable causes; 2 percent were successfully conciliated; 7 percent were withdrawn with benefits; and 23 percent resulted in a merit resolution. In regard to the sex discrimination filings, only 6 percent of the cases resulted in findings of reasonable cause; 2 percent were successfully conciliated; 4 percent were withdrawn with benefits; and 17 percent resulted in a merit resolution.

PREDICTORS AND EFFECTS

The best predictors of harassment are the gender composition of the work place, that is, a male-dominated workplace with men holding supervisory positions and women occupying less powerful roles. However, there is some evidence that when gender roles are reversed sexual harassment is also likely to occur. But today, generally, victims are more likely to be female, unmarried, to have some college and to be supervised by men.

Women with lower level positions in the workplace and less college education are more likely to be sexually harassed. Men who are harassed are more likely to be harassed by coworkers, whereas women are more likely to be harassed by supervisors. Empirical evidence reveals that women who work in male-dominated workplaces or in traditional male jobs are more likely to be harassed than women in other types of jobs, as are white and minority women who work in particularly low level positions. However, recent research reveals that about 1 percent of females are also harassed by other women while 35 percent of men are harassed by women. Recently in Papa v. Domino's Pizza, the first EEOC trial in which a male employee won $237,000, the case was won after proving that his female supervisor sexually harassed him.

Research indicates that many women victims of harassment often simply change jobs. Women who do file complaints often report experiencing counterclaims and in fighting against such claims are often re-victimized. This retaliation, combined with the fact that women tend to avoid risk-taking, makes it understandable that women are reluctant to file formal complaints of sex discrimination or sexual harassment. In fact, reporting or filing a sexual harassment or sexual discrimination complaint may be the least likely response of most women. Some evidence indicates that women who report are more likely to have experienced extremely offensive sexual harassment and that these women are less likely to perceive disadvantages to reporting, and are more likely to be white and to have access to more workplace power.

Moreover, the effects of harassment on the victim include harming both physical and mental well-being, as well as increasing feelings of helplessness and lowered self-esteem. Students who are harassed often have lower grades and may avoid certain classes in order to avoid the perpetrator.

In 1996, the Equal Opportunity Employment Commission sued Mitsubishi Motor Corporation's American Division on behalf of more than 400 women who reported that the company had allowed the creation and maintenance of a hostile work environment. These incidents included pervasive physical groping of female workers by male coworkers and sexual graffiti scrawled on bathroom walls.

Dial Soap Company also settled a class action sexual harassment lawsuit. In this situation, 100 women reported that sexual harassment had been a part of their daily experience in an Aurora, Illinois, factory for over 10 years. Dial agreed to pay $10 million and to comply with 30 months of independent monitoring. The EEOC reported that its investigation revealed that women at Dial experienced all types of sexual harassment and described the Aurora plant as free-for-all with regard to the degree and quantity of harassment. Similarly, 14 women at a Ford plant in Chicago, Illinois, also settled a $7.5 million sexual harassment case that was later increased to $9 million in a district court review. The women reported being verbally harassed with catcalls, swearing, and suggestive language while working on the assembly line.

Sexual harassment is a form of white-collar crime that is being treated more seriously by the civil court system. However, sexual harassment remains a pervasive problem in the workplace.

SEE ALSO
gender discrimination; racial discrimination.

BIBLIOGRAPHY. Heather Antecol and Deborah Cobb-Clark, "Men, Women, and Sexual Harassment in the U.S. Military," *Gender Issues* (Winter 2001); Greg Burns, "Dial Settles Sexual Harassment Case," *Chicago Tribune* (April 30, 2003); "Mitsubishi Plant Better Place for Women, Monitors Report," *Chicago Tribune* (May 23, 2001); "Judge Agrees to $9 million Settlement in Sexual Harassment Suit Against Ford," *Chicago Tribune* (November 18, 2000); Equal Opportunity Employment Commission, "Sex-Based Charges and Sexual Harassment Charges," www.eeoc.gov/stats (2000); Michelle Higgins, "*Blakely v. Continental Airlines Inc.*: Sexual Harassment in the New Millennium," *Women's Rights Law Reporter* (v.23/2, 2002); Catherine MacKinnon, "The

Logic of Experience: Reflections on the Development of Sexual Harassment Law," *The Georgetown Law Review* (v.90, 2002); Phoebe Morgan, "Sexual Harassment Violence Against Women at Work," *Sourcebook on Violence Against Women* (Sage Publications, 2001); Kimberly Pruett, *Sexual Harassment in the Workplace: A Legal Research Guide* (William S. Hein, 2001); Charles J. Russo, "Recent Developments in the United States. Supreme Court Update on Sexual Harassment in Schools," *Education and the Law* (v.13/1, 2001).

REBECCA S. KATZ
MOREHEAD STATE UNIVERSITY

Sherman Antitrust Act

THE SHERMAN Antitrust Act of 1890 provided the first, and what remains the most important legal basis for efforts to break up exploitative monopolies and commercial behaviors, such as price-fixing agreements, that produce concentrations of economic power. The act was sponsored by Senator John Sherman (1823–1900) of Ohio, who had declared: "If we will not endure a king as a political power, we should not endure a king over the production, transportation, and sale of any of the necessities of life." The Sherman Act, as Lawrence Friedman has noted, was surprisingly brief: less than two pages in length. The law is, Friedman observes, "terse," "vague," and "ambiguous." Notably absent are definitions of such key terms as "monopoly" and "restraint of trade."

The heart of the Sherman Act is Section 1 which reads: "Every contract, combination in restraint of trade or commerce among the several states, or with foreign nations, is hereby declared to be illegal. Every person who shall make any such contract or engage in any such combination or conspiracy, shall be deemed guilty of a misdemeanor, and, on conviction thereof, shall be punished by a fine not exceeding $5,000, or by imprisonment not exceeding one year, or by both said punishments, in the discretion of the court."

In 1914, Congress added the Clayton Act and the Federal Trade Commission Act to strengthen the Sherman Act. The Clayton Act specifically prohibited four practices: 1) price discrimination, that is, selling products more cheaply to a favored customer; 2) exclusive-dealing contracts, tying a purchaser to deal exclusively with a single supplier and often on a long-term basis; 3) mergers that unduly restricted competition; and 4) interlocking directorates in which the same person sits on the boards of companies supposed to be in competition. Some agricultural combinations were exempted from the Clayton Act so that farmers' cooperatives could retain their legal status.

The new laws were a response to the Supreme Court's 1911 decision in *Standard Oil of New Jersey v. United States* (221 U.S. 1) which, though it favored the government's position, opened up a number of loopholes in antitrust regulation. These new statutes extending the reach of the Sherman Act relied on administrative rather than criminal law to deal with unfair competition. The Federal Trade Commission, made up of five members, was established to help the Department of Justice to prevent unfair and deceptive practices.

Further amendments and additions followed, including the Robinson-Patman Act of 1936 which shored up the ban on price discrimination ban, and the Celler-Kefauver Act of 1950, which toughened anti-merger rules and prohibited the purchase of the plant, equipment, or assets of a competitor. In 1975, Congress changed violations of the Sherman Act from misdemeanors to felonies and raised the ceiling on fines significantly.

During the first decades of the Sherman Act, enforcement was virtually non-existent. This situation reinforced the view of those who believed that the law had been passed to calm public resentment while, at the same time, not interfering greatly with business-as-usual, since the politicians in Congress relied heavily upon the support of the corporate world for campaign contributions. The Department of Justice filed only nine cases during the first five years of the Sherman Act, and only 22 in the first 15 years. These early cases often resulted in verdicts favoring the accused.

In 1892, for example, a district judge dismissed an indictment against five lumber dealers alleged to have conspired to charge an additional 50 cents on 1,000 feet of pine in the five states where they marketed their product. The court held that such price-fixing was permissible unless it could be proven that the agreement had influenced all lumber dealers in the area to follow its example (*United States v. Nelson*, 52 Fed. 646. 1852).

Critics insisted that it was obvious that the lumber dealers had acted as they did because they knew that their tactics would increase their profits. The following year, in 1893, a prosecution of the National Cash Register Company (NCR) also fizzled. James Henry Patterson, owner of NCR, had vanquished his competitors, occasionally buying them out, but more often employing predatory pricing tactics and nastily aggressive salesmanship to undercut them. Patterson had his salesforce seek to convince employers that they needed his cash registers in order to avoid tempting, and being ripped-off by employees. So effective were Patterson's methods that, in a later decade, one-fourth of all the chief executives of Fortune 500 companies had received their indoctrination into business at NCR.

Though he had driven out of business or gobbled up a significant portion of NCR's competition, a federal court found that the Sherman Act did not prohibit what Patterson had done. "It must appear somewhere in the indictment that there was a conspiracy in restraint of trade by. . .monopolizing the market, and it is not sufficient to allege a purpose to drive certain competitors out of the field by violence, annoyance, intimidation, or otherwise (*United States v. Patterson*, 55 Fed. 605, 641, 1893).

The Supreme Court was no less ready to strike down merger prosecutions. The facts in *United States v. E.C. Knight Co.* (156 U.S. 1, 1895) show that the American Sugar Refining Company was busily absorbing its remaining few competitors, four businesses in Pennsylvania that controlled 33 percent of the refinery business with the Revere company in Boston having 2 percent of the market. American Sugar had bought out the Pennsylvania group, which gave it 98 percent control of sugar refining in the United States. The Supreme Court decreed, however, that American Sugar was a monopoly of manufacture and not of interstate or international commerce and that only the latter was forbidden by the Sherman Act. "Commerce succeeds to manufacture and is not part of it," the court declared. The opinion in passing mentioned a doctrine that was to come to dominate thinking about monopolies nearly a century later. According to political economists, declared Chief Justice Melville Fuller, "aggregates of capital may reduce prices."

In an elegant dissent, Justice John Harlan offered a view not wrapped in legalistic hair-splitting but based on a commonsense understanding of what was required to control monopolies: "It will be cause for regret that the patriots who framed the Constitution did not foresee the necessity of investing the national government with power to deal with gigantic monopolies holding in their grasp, and injuriously controlling in their own interest, the entire trade among the States in food products that are essential to every household in the land."

Not a single violator of the Sherman Antitrust Act went to jail until 1921, more than 30 years after the enactment of the law. During the first 50 years of the act, only 24 cases led to jail sentences out of 252 prosecutions. Eleven of these cases involved businessmen; the others were trade union leaders. Significantly, 10 of the 11 sentences of businessmen involved acts of violence, threats, or other forms of intimidation.

Matters changed dramatically as Franklin D. Roosevelt's presidency ushered in a period of vigorous antitrust enforcement. Many of the cases arose during World War II and were directed against companies headquartered in Germany, Italy, and the United States that supported America's wartime enemies.

The first prison sentence for price-fixing was imposed in the 1950s in a hand-tools industry case, though the case did not differ markedly from many that preceded it. Throughout the 1950s, however, antitrust enforcement tended to be inconsistent. But the heat on business clearly stepped up as time went by because of the combined influences, among other developments, of the Ralph Nader movement, the Watergate scandal, the rise of the counterculture, and the press reporting on those excluded from the mainstream for a fairer deal. From 1981 to 1985 there was, for the first time, a greater number of criminal than civil antitrust case filed in federal courts. Particularly notable in that period was the 1984 breakup of the American Telephone & Telegraph (AT&T) in a decision that forced AT&T to reshape itself as a long-distance company and create seven "Baby Bells."

This tough stance abated when economists, primarily from the University of Chicago, successfully pressed the argument that monopolies were not necessarily harmful. They based their position on the declaration in a 1920 Supreme Court ruling that illegal monopolies were to be judged in terms of whether they were "unreasonable." The economists maintained that the test ought to be framed in terms of the actual consequences of the control that a monopolistic entity exerted over the marketplace. The burden then fell on prosecutors to demonstrate higher prices existed than those that would have prevailed under freer competitive circumstances, a task that often resulted in mind-numbing testimony by well-paid corporate expert witnesses whose fancy mathematical analyses were well beyond the reach of judges and jurors.

Some monopolies, the pro-business economists insisted, are beneficial because, among other things, they reduce operating costs. The courts listened, and the criminal prosecution of antitrust cases became a much more difficult enterprise than it had been when monopolization alone was regarded as illegal.

Recent antitrust charges against Microsoft represent one of the better-known invocations of the Sherman Act. The government claimed that Microsoft's overwhelming market share in the personal computer operating system market had given it an unfair advantage over competitors such as RealNetworks and American Online. Microsoft, it was said, had tried to monopolize the internet browser market by unlawfully tying its Internet Explorer software to its Windows operating system in order to exclude rival products by Netscape.

"Because of its monopoly Microsoft can skimp on quality," former Senator Howard Metzenbaum declared. " It ships products with avoidable defects, sells upgrades that often are of marginal value ... and it has repeatedly imitated the innovative leaders in the industry and then driven them out of the market."

A decision by district court judge Thomas Penfield Jackson called Microsoft "untrustworthy" and an "unrepentant lawbreaker." Jackson ruled that Microsoft had to be broken into two companies as a penalty for inhibiting consumer choices and breaking antitrust law. But an appeals court reversed the breakup order, and the case was assigned to another judge. This resulted in a settlement in which Microsoft agreed to disclose more technical information about its Windows operating system so that competitors can write programs that work with Microsoft equipment.

SEE ALSO

antitrust; Clayton Act; Federal Trade Commission; Microsoft; Robinson-Patman Act; Celler-Kefauver Act.

BIBLIOGRAPHY. C. Thomas, *Federal Trade Commission: An Experiment in the Control of Business* (Columbia University Press, 1932); Donald J. Dewey, *The Antitrust Experiment in America* (Columbia University Press, 1990); Jack C. High and Wayne E. Gable, eds., *A Century of the Sherman Act: American Economic Opinion, 1890-1990* (George Mason University Press, 1992); Katherine M. Jamieson, *The Organization of Corporate Crime: Dynamics of Antitrust Violation* (Sage Publications, 1994); David D. Martin, *Mergers and the Clayton Act* (University of California Press, 1959); George A. Sigler, "The Origins of the Sherman Act," *Journal of Legal Studies* (v.14, 1935); Hans B. Thorelli, *The Federal Antitrust Policy: Organization of an American Tradition* (Johns Hopkins University Press, 1955).

GILBERT GEIS, PH.D.
UNIVERSITY OF CALIFORNIA, IRVINE

Short, James F., Jr. (1924–)

JAMES SHORT GREW up in a small Illinois town where his father was the principal of the rural community school that he attended for 12 years. During his formative years, Short's educational experiences instilled a deep sense of personal responsibility and respect for the virtues of learning. His strong work ethic developed at the age of six when he began toiling at odd jobs on nearby farms. Though thankful for the opportunities, Short quickly realized that he would seek an alternative area of expertise for his life's work.

After graduating from high school, he enrolled at Shrutleff College, a small Baptist institution, in Alton, Illinois. Short enlisted in the U.S. Marine Corps Reserve while attending college and in 1943 was sent to a training program at Denison University in Granville, Ohio, and then to Parris Island for boot camp in 1943. Short eventually became part of the occupying forces in Japan after the bombing of Hiroshima and Nagasaki. His return to the United States marked an illustrious and fruitful career in sociology and criminology.

Short's contributions on the sociology of risk and organizational theory have had a substantial impact on the study of white-collar crime. In the early 1980s, Short and Donna Randall's exploration of women working in a toxic environment inspired his interest and research in risk analysis studies and his presidential address to the American Sociological Association ("The Social Fabric at Risk: Toward the Social Transformation of Risk Analysis"). In 1991, he joined a research team established to study the effects of a proposed nuclear waste facility in Nevada's Yucca Mountain. His research on risk analysis (a field that generally explores technical problems; for example, location of toxic waste disposal sites), refocused efforts to include the impact of technology on social constructs and public policy. Short notes that his "enlightenment model" perspective includes knowledge of fundamental personal, interpersonal, group, and organizational structures and processes of human behavior and cultures in order to fully understand deviance in a highly advanced technological world.

SUICIDE AND HOMICIDE

Short received his Ph.D. in 1951 from the University of Chicago under the tutelage of renowned sociologists William F. Ogburn and Ernest Burgess. When Short began his graduate studies in 1947, the Chicago School was well on its way to becoming the most famous sociology department in the world—unsurpassed in scholarship and research. During his studies, Short grappled with the unresolved dilemma of social science versus social action. He credits Ogburn for persuading him that the scientific study of social ills offers more effective input toward solutions than individual efforts at reform. Burgess further instilled in him the virtues of tenacity, courage, and intellectual flexibility in the exploration of problems and the use of methodology. His dissertation work, *Suicide and Homicide*, was published in 1964.

Short's scholarship endeavors also have included delinquency, gangs, suicide, homicide, and theory. As of 2003, he was a professor emeritus in sociology at Washington State University and has served as president of the American Society of Criminology. He was the recipient of the Edwin Sutherland Award in 1979. In retirement, Short continues to pursue his career and publications.

SEE ALSO
risk analysis; Toxic Substance Control Act; employee safety.

BIBLIOGRAPHY. James F. Short, Jr., "A Natural History of One Sociological Career," *Sociological Self-Images: A Collective Portrayal* (Sage Publications, 1969); James F. Short, Jr., "Characterizing and Managing Environmental and Technological Risks: Some Requirements for a New Paradigm," *Social Problems and Public Policy* (1999); James F. Short, Jr., "Unwinding: Reflections on a Career," *Lessons of Criminology* (Anderson, 2002).

MARY DODGE, PH.D.
UNIVERSITY OF COLORADO, DENVER

Shover, Neal (1940–)

A LEADING FIGURE in research and publication concerning white-collar and corporate crime, Neal Shover was raised in Columbus, Ohio, and went to public schools in an inner city, working class, racially diverse neighborhood. He received his B.S. degree in social welfare from Ohio State University in 1963. From 1964 to 1966, he was a prison sociologist at Illinois State Penitentiary at Joliet. He completed his M.A. degree in sociology at the University of Illinois, Urbana-Champaign in 1969, subsequently completing his Ph.D. there in 1971. In the early 2000s, Shover was a professor of sociology at the University of Tennessee, Knoxville, where he started his career in 1971.

Shover began publishing in 1978 with the book chapter, "Defining Organizational Crime" in a text on corporate and governmental deviance. This was a significant work in terms of establishing the parameters of the field. A major amount of his early writings concerned regulatory laws and surface-coal mining, including the role of inspectors.

While there has been much written on police roles and behavior, little was known about inspectors in the regulatory arena. This was particularly significant since workplace deaths and injuries take a larger toll than criminal deaths and injuries and many are the consequence of negligence. Thus, he was one of the early advocates of criminalizing such behavior. He has also contributed to developing the theoretical explanations of corporate crime through his published work.

Shover's book, *Crimes of Privilege: Readings in White-Collar Crime*, helped to further the work in this area. In 2004, Shover published *Doing Deals and Making Mistakes: The Challenge of White Collar Crime*. He has also published in the area of telemarketing crimes, and tax avoidance and evasion. Besides the white-collar and corporate crime area, Shover is also widely published in the areas of career thieves and corrections (prisons). He published one of the early texts in corrections, *A Sociology of American Corrections,* in 1979 and later published a book on career thieves, *Pursuit and Careers of Persistent Thieves,* in 1996. He has been a visiting fellow or scholar at numerous institutions ranging from the U.S. Department of Justice and the National Institute of Justice to the Australian National University in Canberra.

SEE ALSO

prisoners; workplace deaths; negligence; Justice, Department of.

BIBLIOGRAPHY. Neal Shover and Paul Wright, eds., *Crimes of Privilege: Readings in White-Collar Crime* (Oxford University Press, 2001); Neal Shover, *Great Pretenders: Pursuits and Careers of Persistent Thieves* (Westview,1996); Neal Shover, Donald A. Clelland, and John P. Lynxwiler, *Enforcement or Negotiation? Constructing a Regulatory Bureaucracy* (State University of New York Press, 1986); Neal Shover, Glenn S. Coffey, and Dick Hobs, "Crime on the Line: Telemarketing and the Changing Nature of Professional Crime," *British Journal of Criminology* (v.43, 2003); Neal Shover and Andy Hochstetler, *Doing Deals and Making Mistakes: The Challenge of White-Collar Crime* (Cambridge University Press, 2004).

CHARLES E. REASONS, LL.B., PH.D.
CENTRAL WASHINGTON UNIVERSITY

Silkwood, Karen (1946–1974)

KAREN SILKWOOD was killed in a car accident on November 13, 1974, while on her way to meet with officials to expose the physical negligence occurring at the Kerr-McGee's plutonium fuels production plant in Crescent, Oklahoma, where she worked as a chemical technician. The attempt to destroy her reputation and the subsequent cover-ups are worthy of the best mystery thrillers. Indeed, a Hollywood movie was made of her life story. Several crimes were committed in the Silkwood case: she was purposely exposed to radiation, harassed, then allegedly murdered.

Silkwood was born in Longview, Texas, the daughter of William and Merle Silkwood. She was a straight-A student throughout school and particularly enjoyed chemistry. She studied medical tech-

nology at Lamar College in Beaumont, Texas. In 1972, Silkwood was employed as a metallography laboratory technician at the Kerr-McGee Nuclear Corporation's plant at the Cimarron River site near Crescent, Oklahoma.

Kerr-McGee's business tentacles reached up to the highest government levels. Silkwood had participated in the union strike against the company and thereafter served on the union's bargaining committee. Her task was to monitor the plant's health and safety practices which she found to be problematic with leaks, spills, falsification of records, inadequate training, health regulation violations, poor quality control, and even some missing amounts of plutonium. The Atomic Energy Commission (AEC) inquiry led to her testimony about the dangerous safety practices at the plant. Kerr-McGee deemed Silkwood a troublemaker.

RADIATION EXPOSURE

During the week of November 5, 1972, Silkwood was repeatedly exposed to radiation on various parts of her body. Traces of plutonium were found by Kerr-McGee officials in Silkwood's apartments; she attributed this to spilling her urine sample and trying to clean it up. She was sent to the Los Alamos, New Mexico, laboratory on November 11 for testing and found to be within range of the acceptable levels of radiation. Unknown to her, Silkwood had been followed, watched, and had her telephone bugged for a number of months.

On November 13, Silkwood planned to meet a union official and a *New York Times* reporter and to provide them with evidence concerning negligent safety regulations. She carried a brown manila envelope that contained her documentation. On her way to the meeting, Silkwood was allegedly run off the road, crashed her car on a concrete abutment and sustained fatal injuries. According to state troopers, the cause of death was due to falling asleep at the wheel. Her autopsy revealed that Silkwood had been exposed to dangerously high levels of radiation. The documentation she was carrying was never found. Although a considerable amount of evidence exists that she was purposely killed, a conspiracy to cover up the faulty company practices and Silkwood's death have never been confirmed.

The resulting Silkwood estate civil suit, charging for personal injury and punitive damages against Kerr-McGee, was awarded $10.5 million in 1979.

However, this amount was reduced to $5,000 for personal injury upon appeal. The case was not settled until 1986 when an out-of-court settlement awarded the estate $1.3 million. The Kerr-McGee industrial plant at Cimarron River was closed in 1975.

SEE ALSO
Kerr-McGee; employee safety; whistleblowers; employee safety; unions.

BIBLIOGRAPHY. Richard Rashke, *The Killing of Karen Silkwood: The Story Behind the Kerr-McGee Plutonium Case* (Penguin Books, 1982); Howard Kohn, *Who Killed Karen Silkwood?* (Summit Books, 1981).

ANNETTE RICHARDSON, PH.D.
UNIVERSITY OF ALBERTA, CANADA

Simpson, Sally (1954–)

AFTER RECEIVING A Ph.D. in sociology from the University of Massachusetts, Amherst, Sally Simpson secured a post-doctoral research fellow position at Harvard University's business school and then joined the faculty at the University of Maryland. Her research in corporate crime has spanned a wide range of topics including: the intersection of criminological theories and explanations of corporate criminality, measurement of corporate crime, antitrust offending, and corporate crime control.

In addition to numerous studies directly testing the assumptions of traditional criminological theories' (such as deterrence, strain, and low self-control) applicability to corporate offending, Simpson, along with Raymond Paternoster, posited a rational choice model of corporate crime (1993). Their subjective, expected utility model privileges individuals over organizations as actors and decision-makers, but recognizes that the individual's calculation of cost and benefits will incorporate both personal and organizational factors.

In order to overcome the paucity of corporate crime data sources, Simpson has engaged in several data collection efforts. On two separate occasions, she administered vignette surveys to M.B.A. and executive education students as well as to a group of managers from a Fortune 500 company. Addition-

ally, she has amassed one of the few longitudinal data sets that details antitrust offending.

More recently, Simpson assessed the effectiveness of corporate crime control with attention focused on the increasing use of criminalization and punitive legal penalties for corporate violators. Her research examines a corporate crime deterrence model juxtaposed against compliance strategies, and she concludes that deterrence strategies are ineffective in controlling corporate misbehaviors, but that compliance strategies built on a foundation of self-regulation and cooperation may hold some promise for effective control.

In addition to her work in corporate crime, Simpson also works in the areas of criminological theory and gender and crime.

SEE ALSO
compliance programs; prosecution; antitrust.

BIBLIOGRAPHY. Raymond Paternoster and Sally Simpson, "A Rational Choice Theory of Corporate Crime," *Routine Activities and Rational Choice: Advances in Criminological Theory* (Transaction Publishers, 1993); Sally Simpson, "The Decomposition of Antitrust: Testing a Multi-level Longitudinal Model of Profit-Squeeze," *American Sociological Review* (v.51, 1986); Sally Simpson, *Corporate Crime, Law, and Social Control* (Cambridge University Press, 2002).

NICOLE LEEPER PIQUERO
UNIVERSITY OF FLORIDA

Sinclair, Upton (1878–1968)

AMERICAN NOVELIST, essayist, muckraker, and socialist economic reformer, Upton Sinclair was born in Baltimore, Maryland, to Upton Beall and Priscilla (Harden) Sinclair. His father's alcoholism severely affected the family's stability and living conditions; his mother hated alcohol and caffeine. Sinclair began publishing dime novels when he was 15 (five years after the family moved to New York City), and while attending New York City College, he wrote pulp fiction to finance his education.

He enrolled at Columbia University in 1897, producing under pseudonyms in his spare time, the Clif Faraday and Mark Mallory, stories for boys' publications. Sinclair began reading the *Appeal to*

Reason, a socialist-populist newspaper, and then joined the American Socialist Party when he was 24 years old.

Sinclair's most famous work and only best-seller, the historical fiction novel *The Jungle* (1906), is much more remembered for its political effects than for its literary contribution. In 1905, *The Jungle* was serialized in *Appeal to Reason*. Doubleday agreed to publish its entirety in 1906. It was dedicated to the workingmen of America, and educated the public about the horrors of the meatpacking industry in Chicago ("Packingtown"), including the ways in which meats delivered to consumers were contaminated. Widespread outrage and boycotting aimed at the meat industry shortly followed, and the government quickly passed in 1906 the Pure Food and Drug Act and the Meat Inspection Act. The legislation occurred during the Progressive Era, representing America's first national consumer protection laws, and it was a clear indication that the federal government was no longer following a hands-off attitude toward business.

The Pure Food and Drug Act may be seen as an example of "structural Marxism"—when laws are enacted in order to promote the viability of a capitalistic system. Unless confidence was restored in the marketplace, all of the economic role participants in the meat industry—farmers, butchers, railroads, grocery stores, packing houses—would be adversely affected. Even though the initial cost of implementing the law may not have been in participants' best interests, the law was nevertheless necessary to prevent economic disaster.

The Jungle depicts the experience of protagonist Jurgus Rudkus, a Lithuanian immigrant who came to America with dreams of wealth, success, and happiness. Rudkus found only price-gouging, corruption, wage-slavery, and unsafe working conditions, causing him ultimately to become a socialist. Sinclair tried to demonstrate in *The Jungle* that capitalism is an attack on the American Dream that states that hard work leads to financial success. He also tried to convince the reader that socialism is the remedy for the evils of capitalism. The slaughterhouses and pens at Packingtown were to symbolize the plight of the working class—both the animals and the workers were at the mercy of the owners of Packingtown.

The Jungle is a metaphor for capitalism, portraying it as a system based on competition and self-gratification, in which only the strongest survive. As a historical novel, *The Jungle* is said to have had the most significant political impact since Harriet Beecher Stowe's *Uncle Tom's Cabin*. President Theodore Roosevelt, moved by *The Jungle*, ordered federal investigations of the meatpacking industry which led to the passage of the pure food laws. It was soon translated into 17 languages and became a worldwide bestseller.

Although only a dozen of the more than 300 pages in Sinclair's novel were devoted to the horrors of the meatpacking industry, the book had a profound effect on public opinion. A familiar rhyme was parodied in the press after the publication of *The Jungle*: "Mary had a little lamb, and when she saw it sicken, she shipped it off to Packingtown, and now it's labeled chicken!" Sinclair later said, "I aimed at the public's heart and by accident I hit it in the stomach."

Income from *The Jungle* enabled Sinclair in 1906 to establish and support a commune for left-wing writers called the Helicon Home Colony in Englewood, New Jersey. It burned to the ground within four months, and Sinclair claimed the fire to be arson committed by political opponents. After a short residence in Croton-on-Hudson, New York, Sinclair moved to Pasadena, California, in 1915 where he lived for almost 40 years. Having set an exposé style based on *The Jungle*, Sinclair wrote *The Metropolis* in 1908 (about New York high society), *King Cole* in 1917 (about the 1914 Colorado miners' strike), *Oil!* in 1927 (about the Warren Harding administration's Teapot Dome scandal), and *Boston* in 1928 (about the controversial 1920-21 Sacco-Vanzetti robbery-murder case in that city; Sacco and Vanzetti were executed in 1927). Right after World War 1 ended, *Jimmie Higgins* (1919) was published as a representation of the internal conflicts experienced by American leftists who felt a duty to support the most prosperous citizens of England and France during war. In the 1920s, Sinclair was a major contributor to the founding of the American Civil Liberties Union.

Sinclair ran for the California governor's office in 1924 as a socialist and again in 1934 as a Democrat. In the 1934 race, Sinclair put forth his EPIC Plan (End Poverty in California), a proposed solution to the Depression that pushed the state of California to rent idle lands and factories to the impoverished for self-survival. He easily won the primary, but lost the election (with 43 percent of the vote) when conservative Democrats supported the anti-New Deal Republican candidate, Frank Merriman. Sinclair's candidacy was smeared badly by Merriman through contrived newsreels showing hoards of homeless Americans invading California and by associating EPIC with socialism, including alleging Sinclair favored the "nationalization" of children.

His writing continued to be fertile during 1940 to 1953 when his *Lanny Budd* series of 11 contemporary anti-fascist historical novels was published. Budd was the illegitimate son of a munitions tycoon, later an American secret agent, who always found himself around important people at critical points in history. *Dragon's Teeth* (1942), about the rise of Nazi Germany, won the Pulitzer Prize for fiction in 1943 (Sinclair's only major literary award). The last novel in the series, *The Return of Lanny Budd* (1953), centers on Cold War politics between America and the former Soviet Union.

Sinclair moved to Buckeye, Arizona, in 1953. He published *My Lifetime in Letters* in 1960 and *The Autobiography of Upton Sinclair* in 1962. Sinclair died in his sleep on November 25, 1968 in Bound Brook, New Jersey.

SEE ALSO

Meat Inspection Act; Pure Food and Drug Act; Roosevelt, Theodore.

BIBLIOGRAPHY. Dell Floyd, *Upton Sinclair: A Study in Social Protest* (AMS Press, 1970); Upton Sinclair, *The Autobiography of Upton Sinclair* (Harcourt, Brace, 1962); Upton Sinclair, *The Jungle* (Vanguard Press, 1906).

GARY S. GREEN
CHRISTOPHER NEWPORT UNIVERSITY

Singapore

SINGAPORE IS A SMALL island city state that was, until its separation in 1965, part of Malaysia. As a former British colony, much of its legal system and business practices are based on British models. In the case of Singapore, it has been the government that has been the leading driver of economic development and government-linked companies (GLCs), together with multinational enterprises, have been the most influential actors in business. The economic downturn of the mid-1980s persuaded the Singaporean government of the importance of entrepreneurship in addition to the existing driving forces, and thus, it has encouraged Singaporeans to conduct their own overseas foreign investment. In doing so, some entrepreneurs have used their own personal networks and, while there is no suggestion of impropriety, it has reduced the level of transparency in Singaporean business dealings.

The majority of Singapore's more than three million people are ethnic Chinese, with smaller numbers of Malays, Indians, and others. Singapore has become known as one of the most economically and technologically advanced societies in Asia; it has been run by the People's Action Party (PAP) since its founding and that party has become almost institutionalized as the government, albeit in free and fair elections. The PAP is well-known for its paternalistic style and its sponsorship of Asian values. Partly as a result of this and partly because of an earlier perceived need to defend Singapore against the twin dangers of mainland Chinese triad gangs and communism, Singapore has a strict criminal justice system with sentences readily enacted.

To maintain business confidence, Singaporean leaders are keen to make it known that the city has a very low crime rate and is secure for multinational companies. However, it is ironic that any opposition to the PAP from trade unionists, or even non-political figures, has regularly been met with official revelations that the dissidents are in some ways part of international conspiracies and guilty of a wide array of crimes. Foreign media disseminating stories that the ruling party considers detrimental to the party or to individuals within it have been struck with severe financial penalties, resulting from libel actions in which Singaporean courts interpret the law in ways which are generous towards plaintiffs.

The current vogue for promoting business interests above social ones, which has long been attractive to Singaporean leaders, requires a reduction in regulations and bureaucracy which has made it easier for businesses and business people to commit crimes. The introduction of e-commerce and other information technology systems has also provided avenues for new crimes such as cybercrimes, which include online fraud, credit card theft, and theft of identities, as well as hacking websites, and cracking software and systems. A survey by KPMG in 2002 found that fraud in business was considered to be a growing threat and was an ever-present aspect of business, with nearly half of the business executive

Singapore's business district has links to organized crime and smuggling operations, but overall remains a relatively secure and civil society in which to conduct business in southeast Asia.

respondents acknowledging that they had witnessed fraud of some sort in their own organizations. Singapore has strongly emphasized the development of information technology skills as part of its development model. Ironically, the skills engendered offer opportunities for crime for which international policing protocols have yet fully to be established.

The desire by Singaporean authorities to promote the island as a secure home for international business has meant that most sectors are adequately regulated and policed. However, regulation itself cannot prevent instances of poor management practices leading to fraud, as the activities of Nick Leeson at Barings Bank demonstrated. Leeson's futures trading losses were catastrophic for his employers but there was also culpability in the firm's own internal management practices in allowing Leeson to hide his activities for so long. Singapore has a sex industry linked to organized crime and some intellectual property piracy of computer software and CD entertainment disks. However, a more important issue is that of smuggling and trans-shipment of smuggled goods, which in some cases have been linked with piracy in the South China Sea. Nevertheless, Singapore remains a comparatively secure base for business in southeast Asia.

SEE ALSO

Barings Bank; Leeson, Nick; Asia; public corruption.

BIBLIOGRAPHY. Heidi Dahles, "Transborder Business: The 'Capital' Input in Singapore Enterprises Venturing into ASEAN and Beyond," *Sojourn* (v.17/2, 2002); KPMG, *KPMG Fraud Survey Report 2002* (KPMG, 2002): Anatoly Kuprianov, "Derivatives Debacles," *Economic Quarterly: Federal Reserve Bank of Richmond* (v.81/1, 1995); Gordon P. Means, "Soft Authoritarianism in Malaysia and Singapore," *Democracy in East Asia* (Johns Hopkins University Press, 1998).

JOHN WALSH, PH.D.
MAHIDOL UNIVERSITY, THAILAND

small-business fraud

ACCORDING TO the Association of Certified Fraud Examiners (ACFE), a leading anti-fraud organization, small businesses are particularly vulnerable to fraud, and are even more likely to become the victims of fraud than larger businesses. The classification of a business as small usually refers to those businesses with a total of less than 100 employees. In a 2002 study conducted by the ACFE, losses to small businesses that were estimated on a per-employee basis were approximately 100 times greater than those losses in large businesses (classified as having 10,000 or more employees).

The average fraud loss in small businesses was approximately $127,000 in 2002. Other estimates state that losses due to fraud may cost small businesses around 6 percent of their annual revenue. The ACFE and other anti-fraud professional organizations provide extensive information on the topic of small-business fraud, including examples of different forms of fraud, and also potential steps that businesses can take to prevent fraud victimization.

Like any company, small businesses may be victimized by fraud both within and from outside the organization. Fraud from within is committed by employees against the business, while fraud from outside often is committed by vendors or potential vendors offering to provide services to the business. Regardless of the type of fraud that occurs, experts in the field agree that the key to prevention starts with awareness. If small businesses begin by recognizing that fraud is a possibility, they can then take the appropriate steps to detect and prevent fraud. Businesses should accept the fact that fraud is very common, and can happen to anyone at any time. An appropriate ethical standard should be developed to deal with both employees and outside associates even if the business feels very close to them. Many recent examples have shown that fraud may be more likely when there is too much trust by businesses.

INSIDE THE COMPANY

According to the ACFE, fraud from within takes three common schemes: asset misappropriation, corruption, and fraudulent statements. Asset misappropriation is broader than simple employee theft, and can be sub-divided into two forms: the misappropriation of cash, and the misappropriation of non-cash (such as company supplies). The misappropriation of cash occurs more often than the misappropriation of non-cash, and the ACFE estimates that this is because cash is easily expendable—there is always a readily available market for spending money, but other assets may not be so easily discarded or translated into cold, hard cash. The cash funds of any business can be vulnerable in three distinct areas: skimming, larceny, and fraudulent disbursements.

Skimming takes place when an employee steals money from the business before it is ever accepted and recorded by the business. For example, a salesperson could take cash for a transaction without entering the transaction into a business cash register. Another potential perpetrator of skimming could be an employee in the business accounting department, who similarly does not record a transaction on the books and instead pockets the cash. Alternatively, larceny refers to the theft of cash or currency that occurs after a business has already received or recorded the transaction. In a small business setting, larceny is most often perpetrated by cashiers, or other employees who are given easy access to currency. However, the ACFE states that larceny schemes are uncommon and do not typically result in large losses, because currency typically is closely monitored.

In comparison, fraudulent disbursements represent the greatest cash losses to small businesses. This type of scheme refers to actual fraudulent disbursements from the business accounts. Unlike skimming and larceny, the nature of this form of fraud usually means it is limited to employees in the accounting or bookkeeping department of the business. A likely example is a fake invoice submitted to the company for reimbursement, which is then unsuspectingly paid by the business. Common fraudulent disbursement schemes identified through the ACFE's research have involved false billing for services to the business that are never rendered. The perpetrator of this kind of scheme can conceal such illegal reimbursements by directing checks to be paid out to friends, relatives, or even fictitious companies.

Non-cash asset misappropriation is not as common, but when it occurs, it may involve the theft of a commodity that is personally appealing to the perpetrator. Typical examples include such assets as electronic devices and computers, clothing and jewelry, or a variety of other valuables.

Corruption, the second type of occupational fraud perpetrated from within, is not as likely as asset misappropriation, but can be even more costly to the small business. Corruption differs from asset misappropriation in that it involves some form of a conspiracy between an employee and one or more parties outside the business. The ACFE discusses examples of corruption that include attractive offers from vendors such as free trips, enticements or discounts that result in the occurrence of a bribe. The small business is victimized when it ends up paying higher prices for the vendor's services, or alternatively, receives inferior services.

Finally, fraudulent statements, the third kind of fraud that is perpetrated from within, occurs when employees mis-state the organization's financial information. This type of fraud is costly, but occurs mainly in larger organizations and is therefore not a significant risk to the small business.

OUTSIDE THE COMPANY

Fraud against small businesses that is committed from outside the company is typically perpetrated by vendors or potential vendors seeking a relationship with the business. Small businesses have increasingly been targeted by a variety of scam artists, many of whom fraudulently induce the business to pay for services never rendered or products never delivered. Much like the different ways in which employees can perpetrate fraud, outside offenders may use a number of deceptive techniques to victimize a small business. For example, they may send fake invoices requesting payment for items never or-

If a cashier in a small retail business "skims" from the cash register, it may constitute the commission of larceny. Such employee crimes are one kind of fraud facing small businesses.

A typical small business owner contends with fraud within the company and from outside relationships.

dered, offer prizes as an inducement to purchase overpriced supplies and office equipment, or even send fake yellow page directory advertisement renewal forms which are actually contracts for the business to advertise in other directories.

With recent increases and advances in technology, small businesses may also be particularly vulnerable to outside fraud schemes involving computers and other common electronic transactions. These types of fraud can be perpetrated by vendors and customers of the small business. For example, various forms of check fraud can occur in many kinds of businesses, but the small business may find it more difficult to recover from a resulting loss. Check fraud may include counterfeit checks or forged checks, which are used to purchase merchandise or other products from the small business. This form of fraud from outside has increased considerably due to technological advances like laser printers and sophisticated computer software programs, both of which now make a phony check

less likely to be detected. Similarly, credit card fraud is also often perpetrated against the small business. Stolen credit cards may be used to purchase merchandise from the business. Additionally, credit cards that are altered to represent non-valid or non-existent accounts may be used in a small business. The recent increase in cases of identity theft makes the possibilities of both check fraud and credit card fraud even more likely. In these situations, the perpetrator illegally obtains identifying information, such as a driver's license or social security number, from an unsuspecting individual. The offender then fraudulently obtains credit in the victim's name. Resulting sources of credit, such as major credit cards, may then be used for transactions with the business.

FRAUD RISK

How does a company identify whether it is at risk for fraud? Executives should be made aware of three major risk factors that contribute to small-business fraud. These include inadequate employee pre-screening, limited controls, and too much trust. The first factor applies to cases of fraud from within, while the second factors apply equally to both internal and external frauds that may be perpetrated against a small business.

Inadequate employee pre-screening, the first risk factor, often occurs because small businesses rarely have the funds needed to complete thorough screenings of potential employees. Although small businesses may limit pre-screening to save costs, this may ultimately result in great losses due to fraud. Unlike larger companies, small businesses do not consistently check background information such as prior work references or criminal records of potential employees. Additionally, other pre-employment practices that are common in larger businesses, such as drug-testing or psychological testing, are rarely performed by small businesses due to the costs of these procedures. This fact may be obvious to the fraudster, who will take advantage of the limitation and seek employment at a small business. While it estimated that only less than 10 percent of employees actually have a criminal record that includes prior acts of fraud, it is this small proportion that can end up doing the most damage in a small business. Investment in thorough pre-screening practices is therefore vital to the small business seeking to prevent fraud victimization. The second risk factor for fraud, limited controls, refers to the

The abuse of trust in a small business environment, where owners and employees become well acquainted, can lead to employers overlooking key fraud signs from a particularly likeable worker.

common division of labor in a small business setting. While larger organizations often have an entire, multi-staffed department that is responsible for accounting and bookkeeping functions, the nature of the small business dictates that this role is often performed by a single employee. Even if the small business does not regularly conduct audits, a more limited consultation with a Certified Public Accountant (CPA) can show the employer potential fraudulent schemes. The CPA may also perform verification functions by certifying the information reported by the company's internal accountant. The ACFE suggests that small businesses consider conducting regular, external audits. If this oversight is made known to small business employees, particularly the one-person accounting department, the mere knowledge that an audit will occur can serve as a powerful fraud deterrent. Studies have also shown that an unexpected audit can be a valuable tool in detecting fraud, because deceitful employees

will not attempt to cover up their fraudulent activities if they do not expect an investigation.

THE TRUST FACTOR

The third risk factor for fraud in small businesses, too much trust, can potentially be remedied without a great deal of financial expense to the business. Referred to as the human element of the workplace, trust is an important factor in any business setting. While large businesses may be less intimate because various employees rarely interact with one another, the small business setting holds a greater degree of intimacy. In fact, it is this element that may make working at a small business particularly desirable to potential employees. In a small business setting, employees are more likely to be well acquainted with each other, and interact on a regular basis inside and outside the workplace. The majority of the time, trusting and believing in one's employees is a valuable asset, but can sometimes lead to large fraud losses. Just as a complete lack of trust may be detrimental, so, too, is absolute faith in one's employees. As the ACFE's extensive study revealed, trust can be both an essential element in sound business transactions as well as a critical element in fraud.

To prevent other forms of fraud from within, research has shown that small businesses can benefit from implementing a code of ethics: the ethical tone, or climate, in businesses is set by the employer. It is particularly important that employees are treated fairly, because feelings of inequity or anger toward the business can lead directly to fraud. Employers or owners can prevent potential, perceived inequity by regularly interacting with their employees, and even engaging in interactive discussions about fraud. A clearly defined policy on fraud from within is also a critical step.

In addition to the trust factor between employees and employers, trust relationships with outside vendors are also subject to fraud victimization for the small business. Several strategies may be used to avoid being a victim of fraud by outside entities. For instance, one simple step that small businesses can take is the verification of all invoices. All incoming invoices sent to the small business should go through a verification procedure before a payment is made. Employees responsible for the reimbursement function can be assisted in this process by providing them with a list of the contact names, addresses, and phone numbers for all vendors that the company contracts with.

With regard to various frauds that may be perpetrated by customers, the small business also has several relatively simple options to protect itself. For example, check fraud and credit fraud can be easily prevented with education. If small businesses do not intimately know their customers by name, training for employees who accept checks and credit cards can make detection more likely. Counterfeit checks tend to be of very poor printing quality. Personal checks will always have one perforated edge, so employees should make sure this is the case for all non-government checks, which have four smooth sides. Signatures on checks should also be closely examined by cashiers or other employees who accept payments.

Numerous investigations of check forgery have shown that forged signatures may often reach past the regular signature line on the check, due to the fact that the forger has limited experience in signing the victim's name. Another common tip to a forged check is a newly opened account, which investigations have found are more vulnerable to fraud. It may be possible for cashiers to determine the age of an account if this information is printed on the check. Lower numbers on checks may also indicate a newer account, and thus, a potentially forged check.

There are also several signs to look for in detecting credit card fraud. Just like check fraud, the key line of defense for the small business is the education of its employees. The small business cashier should be wary of alterations in a credit card's signature panel, which may suggest that the signature has been removed and replaced with a fake one. If the signature does not appear to be altered, another line of defense for the small business is to verify the signature by asking the customer for a form of photo identification.

In addition to obvious signature abnormalities, alterations on the face of a credit card can be a noticeable sign of fraud. This may be in the form of obviously changed numbers or expiration dates on the card. A limited amount of numbers may appear to be altered, or a phony card could even be flattened and then re-stamped with an entire set of new numbers. In some cases, stolen or invalid credit cards may be badly discolored, or even show signs of glue or paint on their surfaces. Electronic verification systems for both checks and credit cards may be initially costly to implement, but could be invaluable to the retail business.

Regardless of whether fraud is perpetrated from within or outside the small business, it is apparent that many of the obvious red flags and warning signs are often ignored. Education is one of the most effective methods small businesses can use in preventing fraud. Relatively minor investments in education, training, and awareness in the short term can result in the elimination of potentially devastating, long-term fraud losses to the small business.

SEE ALSO

employee crimes; embezzlement; contractor fraud; bribery; forgery; bad checks; credit card fraud; identity fraud.

BIBLIOGRAPHY. Association of Certified Fraud Examiners, www.cfenet.org (2003); *How to Prevent Small-Business Fraud: A Manual for Business Professionals* (Association of Certified Fraud Examiners, 2002); W.

Steve Albrecht, *Fraud Examination* (Thompson-Southwestern, 2003); *Report to the Nation on Occupational Fraud and Abuse* (Association of Certified Fraud Examiners, 2002); Joseph T. Wells, *Occupational Fraud and Abuse* (Obsidian Publishing, 1997); "Preventing Small-Business Fraud," www.inc.com (2003).

KRISTY HOLTFRETER, PH.D.
FLORIDA STATE UNIVERSITY

South America

IN THE LATE 20th century and into the early 21st century, organized and white-collar crime became a major issue South America. Much of this criminal activity has revolved around the illegal drug trade and associated money laundering. There have also been concerns that international terrorists will be able to take advantage of the continent's financial systems to launder money. In response to these problems, in 2002 the Inter-American Development Bank approved $1.2 billion to fight money laundering in eight South American countries. Carried out through the Organization of American States, the countries apply the funds to create or strengthen financial intelligence units that will track suspicious transactions of suspected money launders.

BOLIVIA

Most organized crime in Bolivia is related to the cocoa growing industry. Since the 1960s, Bolivian governments have pledged to eradicate cocoa crops. Despite such promises, cocoa cultivation has expanded and transnational criminal organizations have played a growing role in the country. Often family-based, these organizations have established links to the police, the armed forces, politicians, and international criminal networks. International attention to organized crime related to the drug trade has concentrated on Colombia, allowing Bolivian groups to expand and take a more active role than is often assumed.

Organized crime associated with cocoa and cocaine production in Bolivia dates back to 1940. There was an increase in international criminal activity in the country during the 1950s due to improved communications capabilities, particularly air traffic in and out of Bolivia, which in turn allowed Cuban drug traffickers to import cocoa paste from Bolivia. This criminal activity grew even more during the military governments from 1964 to 1982, as international demand for cocaine grew and Bolivians made connections with Colombian drug cartels.

The Santa Ana cartel, sometimes known simply as *La Corporación* (The Corporation), dominated organized crime in Bolivia starting in the 1970s. Led by wealthy cattle rancher Roberto Suarez Gómez, the Santa Ana cartel got its start by supplying cocoa paste to Colombian drug traffickers. By the late 1970s, the cartel was monopolizing the production and commercialization of cocaine in Bolivia. Soon, the organization became independent of the Colombians, shipping cocaine to the United States through Mexico and bringing back millions of dollars to launder. *La Corporación* was also increasingly involved in politics and the armed forces, and was apparently behind the 1980 military coup that brought General Luis García Meza to power. The Santa Ana cartel also has been linked to former Nazi Klaus Barbie, who arrived in Bolivia in the 1950s and was involved in many illicit activities.

VENEZUELA

During the 1980s, oil revenue in petroleum-rich Venezuela declined sharply. The economy became increasingly affected by the drug trade and money-laundering because Colombian cartels, the Sicilian Mafia, and Venezuelan politicians and bankers all sought to profit. Large amounts of the cocaine shipped to the United States and Europe passed through Venezuela, and those involved earned perhaps $2 billion in narcotics profits.

Much of the illicit activity came to light during the administration of Carlos Andrés Pérez (1989-1993). Pérez appointed Thor Halvorssen as his anti-drug czar. Halvorssen also became the special overseas investigator for the Venezuelan Senate's Anti-money Laundering Commission. He began investigating Banco Latino, Venezuela's second largest bank. Halvorssen soon discovered that the president and his mistress had put away $19 million in secret accounts, which led to the impeachment of Pérez in May 1993. Later that year, clear evidence of money-laundering schemes in Venezuelan banks came to light, especially those involving Banco Latino. Banco Latino and numerous other Venezuelan banks had shifted many of their assets to offshore facilities to avoid the country's currency controls. In turn, Colombian drug traffickers used the Venezuelan banking system and its offshore subsidiaries to launder their earnings. Banco Latino and other banks collapsed, Pérez was indicted in the money-laundering operations, and more than 300 bankers and businessmen were arrested, while others fled the country.

In addition to these money-laundering operations by Venezuelan bankers, organized criminals connected to the Italian Mafia have operated in Venezuela. The most well known was the family of Pasquale Cuntrera. These Italian citizens operated in Venezuela as businessmen and have been routinely accused of Mafia connections in Italy. Cuntrera was removed from Venezuela by Italian officials and sentenced to 21 years in prison. However, he disappeared from an appeals hearing in 1998, only to be arrested later that year while trying to board a plane to Venezuela. A major Italian-Venezuelan narcotics operation also led to the arrest of 50 others. These criminals connected to the Italian Mafia transport cocaine and heroin through the Caribbean to Europe. Much of their money is then laundered in the Caribbean and elsewhere.

PERU

Organized crime centered around the drug trade has been active in Peru since its transition to democracy in 1980. The administration of Fernando Belaunde Terry (1980–85) was marked by charges of corruption and connections to the drug traffickers. The situation became worse during the administration of Alan Garcia (1985–90). The nationalistic Garcia deposited large sums of Peru's foreign exchange reserves in the Bank of Credit and Commerce International (BCCI) as part of a plan to renounce the country's foreign debt. Garcia used such offshore facilities to protect the funds from the International Monetary Fund (IMF) and commercial creditors.

In 1991, an indictment against BCCI claimed that the bank had paid $3 million in bribes to top officials at Peru's Central Bank. In exchange, Peruvian authorities agreed to deposit government funds into BCCI accounts in New York. The New York District Attorney's office raised this issue, which led to investigation in Peru. Rumors abounded that Garcia knew about the bribes. To make matters worse, accusations by Peruvian legis-

lators claimed that the former president stole as much as $50 million while channeling the funds through BCCI. Rumors even circulated that Garcia had been introduced to BCCI by Panamanian strongman Manuel Noriega. Indeed, Garcia apparently deposited funds in BCCI accounts in Panama before transferring them to other accounts in his wife's name.

Garcia claimed that political opponents who were trying to discredit his possible presidential campaign in 1995 made the accusations. Nevertheless, Garcia fled to Paris, France, rather than face charges and his APRA political party was largely discredited. In a turn of events, Garcia returned to Peru and ran for president in 2001. While he did not win, he made an impressive showing despite his checkered past.

COLOMBIA

Organized and white-collar crime in Colombia centers around the production and sale of illegal drugs, particularly cocaine. Due to the large amount of money involved in the illegal narcotics trade, money laundering has also become a key issue in Colombia. Furthermore, there is pervasive manipulation of the country's political system by those in the drug trade. Colombian traffickers consistently bribe high-level officials of the central government to create a more crime-friendly environment in which authorities protect and support illegal activity. The power and wealth of organized crime in Colombia can be seen in activities that include being able to negotiate judicial leniency, creating paramilitary groups to fight leftist insurgents, and the contribution of drug money to political campaigns.

The presence of drug cartels in Colombia has led to numerous money-laundering operations in the country. Among the more famous was La Mina, which operated from 1985 to 1988. Associated with the Medellín cartel, La Mina was the largest cocaine money-laundering operation up to that time, washing more than $1 billion. The system revolved around gold trading, because the sale of the precious metal could justify large cash transactions. Early in the operation, gold-plated lead was shipped from Uruguay to the United States and "sold" to drug traffickers. The gold seller then transferred the funds to cartel accounts. In a later phase, Colombian traffickers in the United States purchased gold in Los Angeles with drug profits and sent the gold to New York City, where it was then resold to banks. The Colombians then wired the money to banks in Panama. This sophisticated operation was eventually broken up by U.S. law enforcement.

Another prominent Colombian money-laundering scheme was organized by José Santacruz Londoño, one of the leaders of the Cali cartel. Between 1988 and 1990, this operation laundered hundreds of millions of dollars from drug sales in New York. The organization deposited the profits in U.S. banks or shipped them to Panama. Then the money was funneled into a front company known as the Siracusa Trading Company. This company then transferred the funds to European accounts. Finally, from these European accounts, the money was sent back to Colombia, where it was converted to pesos by money exchangers for use by the cartel.

An additional money-laundering trend that arose in the 1990s was the washing of funds through trade. Colombian "peso-brokers" bought drug dollars at a discount in the United States and stored them in stash houses until they could gradually deposit the money into bank accounts.

The brokers then sold the dollars to Colombian business people who needed them for imports. The importers were given a discount off the official exchange rate and also were able to avoid taxes. They then bought goods ranging from clothing and liquor to computers and appliances from U.S.-based companies. Thus, the laundered money ends up in the hands of U.S. corporations.

SEE ALSO
Brazil; organized crime; drug trafficking; money laundering; corruption.

BIBLIOGRAPHY. Robert E. Grosse, *Drugs and Money: Laundering Latin America's Cocaine Dollars* (Praeger, 2001); David Jordan, *Drug Politics: Dirty Money and Democracies* (University of Oklahoma Press, 1999); Rensselaer W. Lee III and Francisco Thoumi, "The Political-Criminal Nexus in Colombia," *Trends in Organized Crime* (Winter 1999); Francisco Thoumi, "Illegal Drugs in Colombia: From Illegal Economic Boom to Social Crisis," *The Annals of the American Academy of Political and Social Science* (v.582, July 2002); Francisco Thoumi, "The Impact of the Illegal Drug Industry on Colombia," *Transnational Crime in the Americas* (Routledge, 1999).

RONALD YOUNG
GEORGIA SOUTHERN UNIVERSITY

Spain

A DECADE AGO, corruption was a serious problem in Spain, but acts of high-level corruption are far less evident today. Other forms of white-collar crime, however, are a serious problem in Spain. Media and domestic government reports routinely cite the proliferation of embezzlement, insider trading, consumer fraud, counterfeiting and tax evasion. Unfortunately, Spanish agencies that investigate white-collar crimes must compete for resources earmarked to prevent all forms of criminal behavior. Consequently, most government funds are budgeted to combat violent crimes, especially crimes linked to the influx of organized criminal networks into Spain over the past two decades.

The cultural and linguistic ties to Latin and South America and close proximity to Eastern Europe and Africa make Spain a haven for organized criminal gangs from disparate parts of the globe. Since the 1980s, organized criminal groups routinely traffic cocaine from Latin and South America to Spain.

Another grave problem arose in the mid-1990s, as organized criminal gangs from Eastern Europe purchased real estate and other assets in Spain with the proceeds of corruption, stolen state property, and money laundering from their home countries. Currently, Spain maintains a substantial presence of criminal gangs from Colombia, Italy, France, Great Britain, Morocco Portugal, and Turkey. Criminals from the former Soviet Union have also taken up residence in Spain, and some have been arrested for such activities as extortion, document fraud, and money laundering. Organized criminals and corrupt businessmen from the former Soviet Union and surrounding countries live in Spain and have also invested the proceeds of illicit activity in Spain, especially in real estate.

Organized criminal groups routinely transfer illegal proceeds through Spanish financial institutions. Spanish authorities conclude that nearly 23 percent of organized criminal activity pertains to money-laundering schemes. The value of laundered money held by organized crime in Spain amounts to about $7.2 billion. The illicit funds are transferred through the sophisticated Spanish financial sector, which provides a wide array of institutions to launder illicit profits. Money changing at exchange bureaus, which exchange more than $20 billion annually, is among the most important means of laundering money in Spain. Moreover, internet gambling in Spain is a growing concern for domestic and international regulators and law enforcement agencies. Spain permits both physical and virtual gambling establishments, both lacking stringent oversight mechanisms, to operate from Spanish territory.

Spanish authorities respond to threats from organized criminal groups in a timely fashion. As a result, Spain's formal anti-money laundering system is as good as that of any country in the world, with broad sectoral coverage and inclusion of all serious crimes. The 1993 Spanish anti-money laundering law covers the acquisition, use, conversion, or transfer of property derived from drug trafficking, terrorism, and organized crime.

Penalties to institutions or businesses for serious violations may include a private warning, a public warning, plus a fine of up to 1 percent of the equity capital of the entity, and other penalties. Penalties for individuals involved in serious offenses include a private warning, a public warning, or suspension of a license to practice business for one year. In addition, there is a mandatory fine for persons involved in serious offenses, of between 500,000 to 10 million pesatas per person, ranging from approximately $3,000 to $57,000.

The funneling of illicit profits from transnational organized criminal groups is a major concern for Spanish authorities. To assist in quelling the passage of illicit proceeds from abroad through Spanish financial institutions, Spain ratified a number of regional and international agreements. Spain is a member of the Financial Action Task Force (FATF), and an observer in the Caribbean Financial Action Task Force (CFATF).

Spain is also a signatory to the 2000 United Nations Convention Against Transnational Organized Crime. Spain signed mutual legal assistance treaties or bilateral counternarcotics agreements with most countries in Latin America, as well as with Morocco, and Turkey. Spain also has a mutual cooperation agreement with Russia for the exchange of information on money-laundering matters.

The domestic legislation and international conventions illustrate the high level of commitment to combat crime in Spain. Significant numbers of domestic and transnational criminal groups continue to challenge Spanish authorities, but the pro-active efforts to enforce Spanish and international laws will slow the illegal efforts of a host of white-collar

criminals and organized criminal gangs established throughout Spain.

SEE ALSO
corruption; public corruption; reform and regulation.

BIBLIOGRAPHY. Francesca Longo, ed., *The European Union and the Challenge of Transnational Organized Crime: Towards a Common Police and Judicial Approach* (Milano, 2002); Ernesto U. Savona, *European Money Trails* (Routledge, 1999) Petrus C. Van Duyne, et al., *Cross-Border Crime in a Changing Europe* (Nova Science, 2001).

TRIFIN ROULE
JOURNAL OF MONEY LAUNDERING CONTROL

Spitzer, Eliot (1959–)

ELECTED NEW York attorney general in 1999, Eliot Spitzer gained national attention for his aggressive legal actions against Wall Street giant, Merrill Lynch. In 2001, Spitzer began investigating Merrill Lynch for promoting stocks of companies to which it had financial ties.

CRAP AND JUNK

Spitzer's investigation turned up e-mails from Merrill Lynch stock analysts indicating that the company routinely published favorable stock ratings for certain companies that they privately thought were of dubious value. One of Merrill's most famous analysts, Henry Blodget, was found to have called stocks "crap" and "junk" that had been given a strong recommendation to investors.

All told, Spitzer's office subpoenaed about 30,000 e-mails from which investigators pulled a number of similarly incriminating messages. To force Merrill Lynch to the bargaining table, Spitzer released the e-mails, outraging investors who had relied on Merrill Lynch investment reports, and causing the company's stock to drop by 12 percent over the next week.

Merrill's chief executive officer, David Kamensky, apologized to shareholders for the situation and several weeks later settled with Spitzer's office for $100 million. More significantly perhaps for investors, Spitzer forced Merrill Lynch to agree to stop the practice of paying analysts for the number of companies they attracted to Merrill's investment banking arm.

Spitzer's interest in advocacy first took shape in college, when he lobbied the Princeton University administration to raise salaries for custodial and other service employees on campus. Upon earning his law degree from Harvard University in 1984, Spitzer bounced between public and private practice for several years, working as a clerk for a U.S. District Court judge, as an assistant district attorney in Manhattan, and, ironically, as a defense attorney for white-collar criminals at a prestigious private firm in New York.

In 1994, Spitzer, finding private practice uninteresting, ran for the New York state attorney general's office, using money borrowed from his wealthy father. Despite spending an estimated $10 million, Spitzer lost in the primary. Four years later, however, after spending a considerable amount of time campaigning, Spitzer narrowly won the next election for the office by fewer than 25,000 votes.

One of Spitzer's first triumphs in office was bringing to conclusion a lengthy 30-year case between General Electric (GE) and the state over pollutants in the Hudson River. GE had allegedly used the river to dump PCBs (a chemical pollutant), creating a potential health risk for humans and wildlife. Spitzer's prosecution of GE led to the Environmental Protection Agency's ruling that GE was required to clean up the PCB pollution from the river.

Spitzer also brought environmental cases against sewage treatment plants and against several midwestern and southern power plants whose pollution drift, Spitzer alleged, created smog and acid rain in New York. He used the Clean Air Act to force those companies to improve their emission standards. Several of the companies settled and agreed to reduce emissions. Many New Yorkers see Spitzer as a champion of the common person over the corporate giant, a particularly compelling image in the wake of the corporate scandals of Enron Corporation, Global Crossing, and others.

SEE ALSO

Merrill Lynch; General Electric; Giuliani, Rudolph.

BIBLIOGRAPHY. "Eliot Spitzer," *Current Biography* (v.64/3, 2003); Michael Freedman, "Witch Hunt," *Forbes* (v.170/12, 2002); Adi Ignatius, "Wall Street's Top Cop," *Time* (v.160/27, 2003); Noam Scheiber, "Consumer Party," *New Republic* (v.227/23, 2002); James Traub, "The Attorney General Goes to War," *New York Times Magazine* (v.151/52151, 2002).

REGAN BRUMAGEN
GEORGIA COLLEGE & STATE UNIVERSITY

sports scandals

MOST sports, from tennis to cricket, have seen their fair share of white-collar crime, most notably bribery and illegal gambling. Perhaps the most famous sports scandal in American history, the 1919 Baseball World Series between the Cincinnati Reds and the Chicago White Sox, was corrupted by members of the White Sox being bribed to lose the World Series. A year later, eight members of the White Sox, including superstar Shoeless Joe Jackson, were banned from the game for life. However, while there is no doubt that players were bribed, there is great debate as to whether Jackson, who has the third-highest lifetime batting average in history (.356), under-performed to lose the series.

SOX SCANDAL

Three of the prominent gamblers involved in the scandal were William Burns, Billy Maharg, and Joseph Sullivan. Burns and Maharg approached pitcher Ed Cicotte and first baseman Arnold Gandil, who agreed to the fix. In order to ensure that the series was indeed lost, more players needed to be a part of the bribe, which thus meant that more money was needed to pay off the added players. More gamblers were brought in to finance the scam, and because of the increase of people involved, word of the incident spread. It became obvious that something peculiar had occurred as heavy bets were being placed on the Reds winning, and the betting odds kept changing.

With the World Series then set in a best-of-nine format, Cincinnati won the first game, 9-1, with Cicotte pitching and giving up five runs in the fourth inning. The Reds also won game 2, but the White Sox were victorious in game 3. Cicotte was again the losing pitcher in game 4, and the Reds also won game 5. Chicago responded by then winning games

6 and 7, before Cincinnati won game 8, and thus the World Series. During the series, problems arose as the players who had been bribed were not receiving the money that they were promised. The victories in games 6 and 7 were a response by the Chicago players to try to win the series because they felt like they were being cheated by the gamblers who had not yet honored their agreement. However, prior to game 8, Chicago's starting pitcher, Lefty Williams, was threatened before the game by a thug hired by gambler Arnold Rothstein: if he did not lose, then something tragic would happen to his wife. A frightened Williams ensured a Reds' victory. It was a massive upset as Chicago was the much superior team.

In September 1920, a grand jury in Chicago's Cook County began an investigation into possible game fixing by the Chicago Cubs, and included the 1919 World Series. Cicotte and Jackson admitted their parts in the scandal, while Gandil remained silent. Baseball Commissioner Kenesaw Mountain Landis banned all eight players for life on August 2, 1921, following a not-guilty decision from the court. The other five players who were banned for life were Buck Weaver, Swede Risberg, Fred Mc-Mullin, Oscar Felsch, and Lefty Williams.

The biggest controversy over the fixed series was the involvement of Shoeless Joe Jackson. It is believed that Jackson was aware of the fix but initially refused to take any bribes. Gandil offered him $10,000 to take part, but Jackson still refused. Jackson ended up taking $5,000, largely because the fix was already in place. However, his play in the series was never in question. He batted .375 for the series, with a homerun, six runs batted in, and no fielding errors. Even more so, Jackson informed the White Sox owner, Charles Comiskey, that the bribe was on and asked for advice. Comiskey turned his back on Jackson.

The scandal deeply hurt America, and was compounded by the loss of one of its brightest stars. Jackson died on December 5, 1951 from a heart attack. His story has been retold many times, including in the movie *Eight Men Out*, which helped to spark a resurgence in a public push to see Jackson reinstated into the game, thus allowing him a place in Baseball's Hall of Fame.

DANNY ALMONTE

The belief that America's youth sporting leagues and associations were free from corruption ended in the aftermath of the 2001 Little League World Series. Danny Almonte and the rest of the Rolando Paulino All-Stars burst onto the scene of the 2001 Little League World Series led by Almonte's dominating pitching. The team from the Bronx, New York City, finished third in the tournament and Almonte was crowned the game's brightest star. The young phenomenon threw a perfect game against Apolea, Florida, on August 18, with a fastball that reached 70 miles per hour. The team from the Bronx only lost when Almonte was not pitching. However, after the tournament finished, *Sports Illustrated* magazine revealed that Almonte's birth certificate had been forged, making the Dominican-born pitcher actually 14 years old. Little League rules strictly prohibit any child over the age of 12 from participating, thus the Rolando Paulino All-Stars were stripped of their Little League accomplishments, including their third place finish in the tournament.

This revelation shocked many people, since the media had glorified the team. Almonte's father, Felipe de Jesus Almonte, and the Bronx league's founder, Rolando Paulino, came under serious scrutiny. Paulino received a lifetime ban from Little League baseball. The elder Almonte was believed to have falsified his son's birth certificate and also received a lifetime ban. The team fell from grace as America was awakened to the fact that its most beloved sporting institutions were not safe from the tentacles of scandal that was thought to be far from the sacred grounds of Little League baseball.

THE BRONX BULL

One of boxing's toughest and fiercest middleweight fighters of all-time was Bronx native Giacobe "Jake" LaMotta. From 1949 to 1951, the Bronx Bull held the middleweight crown. Born on July 10, 1921, LaMotta was revered for his ability to absorb punches and for having a rock-hard chin that allowed him to constantly press his opponents. He was the first boxer to defeat the legendary Sugar Ray Robinson, winning in 1943. On June 16, 1949, he defeated Marcel Cerdan in Detroit, Michigan, to win the middleweight belt. His championship reigned until February 14, 1951, when Robinson defeated him in Chicago, Illinois, in a fight nicknamed the St. Valentine's Day Massacre.

LaMotta's career is as much remembered for his ability to withstand a punch as it was for his notorious November 14 fight against Billy Fox in 1947. Fighting in New York City, LaMotta lost a fourth round technical knockout to Fox in which he took a dive to ensure that the weaker fighter would win. The incident was revealed in 1953, when LaMotta was called to testify in front of the Federal Bureau of Investigation, which was holding a series of investigations into local mafia affiliations. LaMotta freely admitted the fact that he took the dive, insisting that it was the only way in which he could gain a title shot at the middleweight crown.

Boxing has long been associated with gambling and bribes, and this was particularly prevalent in the 1940s and 1950s. A strong organized-crime influence gripped the sport, and in order for title shots to be granted, the mafia would have to approve them. LaMotta more than deserved a title shot based on his world ranking, but found himself unable to get the opportunity. He agreed to lose to Fox as a favor to the underworld chiefs in order to guarantee himself a title opportunity, which he received in 1949. LaMotta retired from boxing in 1954, then as a light heavyweight, with a career record of 83-19-4, with 30 knockouts. The trials and tribulations of his life were made into the 1981 movie classic, *Raging Bull*.

OLYMPIC SCANDALS

While baseball scandals tend to have the most saddening affect on the American public, perhaps nothing can be as disgraceful as being caught cheating on the world's stage at the Olympics. In 1988, Canadian sprinter Ben Johnson felt first-hand the disgrace of being caught cheating in his sprint, the 100-meter dash.

With a star-studded line-up that included Olympic great and reigning gold medalist Carl Lewis, as well as future champion Linford Christie, Johnson blew his competition away by setting a world record time of 9.79. This beat his own world record, set a year earlier, of 9.83. However, doubts had been growing as to whether the muscular Johnson had been using steroids. Only two hours after his Olympic glory, Johnson was shocked to hear that he had failed a steroid drug test. His gold medal was stripped and awarded to Lewis, and his two world record times were erased from the record books. In 1993, he again tested positive for steroids and received a lifetime ban from track and field. He has since become a spokesperson for the problems

and dangers of drugs in sports, and claims that especially in track and field, performances enhancing illegal substances are common. In 1999, Christie received a two-year ban for testing positive for nandrolone. Even the great Lewis was not safe from drug controversy, as he has remained the subject of much debate as to whether or not he had tested positive for three banned substances prior to the 1988 games in South Korea.

The 1988 Summer Olympics was the scene of even more controversy than the 100-meter dash. In the boxing ring, American light middleweight Roy Jones, Jr. was the victim of corrupt boxing judges. Fighting for the gold medal against South Korean Park Si-Hun, Jones out-punched his overmatched opponent 86 to 32. His performance was so dominating that he was awarded the Val Barker Cup, an award given to the Olympics' best boxer. Yet, in a startling turn of events, at the conclusion of his match, the judges awarded the fight and thus the gold medal to the South Korean. Jones was left devastated, as were the live audience and viewers from home. Referee Aldo Leoni was equally as shocked by the result. Bitter justice was later served when it was revealed that South Korean businessmen had bribed the judges. While Jones was cheated out of his taste of Olympic glory, he left the Olympics and became one of the greatest pound-for-pound fighters of all-time, winning belts at the middleweight, super middleweight, light heavyweight, and heavyweight divisions.

INTERNATIONAL SCANDALS

One of South Africa's most celebrated cricket players was born September 25, 1969. Wessel Johannes "Hansie" Cronje became South Africa's captain at age 25 and held this role until he was removed for alleged match-fixing in April 2000. In October 2000, he received a lifetime ban from cricket for admitting that he took money bribes from bookmakers over an unspecified period of years. He also admitted to asking his teammates to under-perform for money. Two of these players, Herschelle Gibbs and Henry Williams, received six-month cricket suspensions.

Cronje's problems became apparent when he was recorded talking with an Italian bookmaker. A self-proclaimed devout Christian, Cronje at first denied the allegations, but later admitted foul play. He claimed that his greed had consumed him, and while he acknowledged taking bribe money, he denied match-fixing. On June 1, 2002, Cronje died in a plane crash at age 32. At the time, it was still not certain if he would face prosecution. Regardless of his acts, Cronje remained popular among his former teammates, who dedicated the 2003 Cricket World Cup, in South Africa, to their late captain. His popularity among South Africans remained divided, however, as for many, regardless of his skill and ability, Cronje violated the time-honored traditions of the sport.

WORLD CUP

Two of the biggest soccer scandals that damaged the integrity of international football (or soccer) both involve the Argentinean national team. With one of the greatest international records, including three World Cup championships, the Argentines have been surrounded with their share of controversy. In 1978, a year that Argentina would go on to win the World Cup, the team faced an upward climb in order to reach the final group. At the time, the format for the World Cup had 16 teams in groups of four. Each team within a group played each other, and the two top teams in the group advanced to the second round. The second round consisted of two groups of four, and once again, each team would play each other within their group. The top two teams of each group would meet in the World Cup final. In case two teams finished with the same record in a group, goal difference was a deciding factor to break the tie.

Argentina advanced to the second round of the 1978 World Cup, and found itself in a group along with Peru, Brazil, and Poland. Argentina beat Poland by two goals, and then drew with Brazil. The Brazilians, meanwhile, beat Peru 3-0 and Poland 3-1, giving them a goal differential of 6 goals to 1. Argentina against Peru was the last game of the group, and the Argentines knew beforehand that in order to reach the finals, they would have to beat Peru by at least 4 goals. When the final whistle blew, Argentina had won 6-0 which allowed them to advance to the final. However, immediately following the game, it was widely speculated that Peru had been bribed. Their goalkeeper, who played one of the worst matches of any goalkeeper, denied having thrown the game. The problem with his denial is that he made it prior to anyone accusing him of being bribed. Argentina went on to defeat Holland

in the finals, in what in all likelihood should have been Brazil against Holland. For Peru, however, it was rumored that the Argentine military placed $50 million in a trust account for Peruvian players, their families, and soccer officials.

Sixteen years after the Peru incident, Argentina's biggest star was disgracefully sent home from the 1994 World Cup. Diego Maradona was without question one of the greatest soccer stars to ever grace the pitch. Born October 30, 1960, in Buenos Aires, Argentina, Maradona led his country to glory by winning the 1986 World Cup, in which he distinguished himself as the premier player of his era. He also found much success in both the Italian League and Spanish League, winning league titles for Barcelona (Spain) in 1982 and for Napoli (Italy) in 1987 and 1989. Known as much for his dazzling dribbling skills as well as his sometimes volatile temper and grandiose arrogance, Maradona's brilliant career soured as he was twice suspended for failing drug tests.

His first suspension was issued in 1991 and kept the superstar away from the game for 15 months. A surprising comeback in the 1994 World Cup witnessed a revitalized Maradona fall victim to a second failed drug test after he tested positive for the enhancing stimulant ephedrine. He was again banned for 15 months, effectively ending his soccer career. Amid all of his turmoil, including a battle with cocaine, Maradona remained one of the most popular figures to soccer fans worldwide.

SEE ALSO
organized crime; bribery; corruption.

BIBLIOGRAPHY. Eliot Asinof and Stephen J. Gould, *Eight Men Out* (Holtzman, 1981); Jimmy Burns, *Hand of God: The Life of Diego Maradona, Soccer's Fallen Star* (The Lyons Press, 2001); Charlie Francis, *Speed Trap: Inside the Biggest Scandal in Olympic History* (St. Martin's Press, 1991); Donald Gropman, *Say It Ain't So, Joe!: The True Story of Shoeless Joe Jackson* (Carol Publishing, 1999); Andrew Jennings, *The New Lords of the Ring: Olympic Corruption and How to Buy Gold Medals* (Simon & Schuster, 1996); Jake LaMotta, *Raging Bull* (DaCapo Press, 1997); Simon Wilde, *Caught* (Aurum Press, 2001); Associated Press, "Almonte, Bronx Team Records Wiped Away," (September 1, 2001).

DAVID W. MCBRIDE
UNIVERSITY OF NOTTINGHAM, ENGLAND

Standard Oil

IN 1859, WITH $1,000 in savings and a $1,000 loan from his father, Cleveland, Ohio, resident John D. Rockefeller formed a partnership with Maurice B. Clark and became a commission merchant, a go-between who received a percentage of commission on each sale. During the Civil War, Rockefeller prospered from the generous prices the U.S. government paid him, and he used the profits from that business as well as credit to finance his entry into the oil business. In 1863, Rockefeller and his partners founded Rockefeller, Andrew & Flagler. When the partnership split, Rockefeller and Andrews bought out the other partners (by then, three) for $72,500.

By 1868 this oil-refining business was the world's largest, and in 1870 Rockefeller created Standard Oil Company of Ohio, capitalized at $1 million, which began integrating horizontally by buying out the competition, consolidating all oil refining into Standard Oil. Eight years later, the company owned approximately 90 percent of the United States' oil-refining capacity.

Standard bought virtually all the refineries in Cleveland as well as two in New York City. It established its own barrel-making shop to handle the 29,000 barrels of crude it produced each day. It built storage tanks capable of holding several hundred thousand barrels, warehouses for its refined product, and facilities for the manufacture of finished products such as glue and paint. In 1882, Standard consolidated all the businesses into the Standard Oil Trust, capitalized at $70 million, with 42 owners. The next step was to control the entire business through vertical integration, from the well to the kerosene lantern that used much of Standard's oil.

When the Ohio courts dissolved the company after a decade, the companies of the trust formed Standard Oil Company of New Jersey, taking advantage of state law that allowed holding companies, parent companies that held stock in other companies. Although divested of some of its holdings, Standard retained a petroleum market share of 75 percent.

Standard Oil engaged in dubious business practices. Its cutthroat methods and favored treatment in deals with the railroads allowed it to undercut competitors, eventually expanding its control of refining into a stranglehold on the pre-Spindletop oil business. Standard monopolized resources to the extent of buying all components needed for barrels to prevent the competition from making the barrels that they needed to market their products. Rockefeller also undercut the prices of smaller companies, taking a short term loss until the smaller companies either sold out to Standard or went out of business. The company also coerced rebates from railroads by threatening to take its immense business elsewhere. When all else failed, Rockefeller hired goons to break up uncooperative operators' businesses. Standard also opposed organized labor.

UNREASONABLE MONOPOLY

These practices created enemies, an unfavorable reputation, and an incentive for antitrust authorities to act. Legal action in the 1880s proved futile. In 1890, largely in response to Standard Oil, Congress enacted the Sherman Antitrust Act, which outlawed all combinations in restraint of trade. In 1892, the attorney general of Ohio brought an antitrust suit against the company based on Sherman. In 1911, the U.S. Supreme Court ruled that Standard was an unreasonable monopoly in violation of the Sherman Antitrust Act, forcing Standard to break into a cluster of companies. The owners of Standard remained owners of the fragments.

The Supreme Court had dissolved a trust for the first time, sending notice that there would be at least occasional enforcement of the Sherman Act, but it also modified the act by ruling that only "unreasonable" restraints—whether combinations and contracts—were antitrust violations. Before then, the law had provided that "all" restraints of trade were illegal. The concept enunciated by Justice Edward White was known as the rule of reason.

SEE ALSO

antitrust; Sherman Antitrust Act; Rockefeller, John D.; robber barons; predatory practices.

BIBLIOGRAPHY. *Standard Oil Co. v. U.S.*, 221 U. S. 1 1911 www.ripon.edu (2003); *Standard Oil Co. of NJ v. United States*, 221 U.S. 1 1911 Docket Number: 398. Abstract; www.oyez.org (2003); Francois Micheloud, "John D. Rockefeller & the Standard Oil Company; Strategies of John D. Rockefeller and the Standard Oil Company 1863–1911," www.micheloud.com (2003); Lawrence W. Reed, "Witch-Hunting For Robber Barons: The Standard Oil Story," www.libertyhaven.com (2003); Rockefeller Archive Center, "John D. Rockefeller, 1839–1937," www.rockefeller.edu (September 1997); "John D. Rockefeller 1839–1937," www.u-s-history.com (2003).

JOHN H. BARNHILL, PH.D.
INDEPENDENT SCHOLAR

Stanford, Leland, Sr. (1824–1893)

LELAND STANFORD, Sr., was born on the family farm at Watervliet, New York. He studied law, and was admitted to practice in 1848. He moved to Port Washington, Wisconsin, the same year, where he entered into legal practice and where he met and married his wife, Jane, the daughter of a wealthy businessman.

In 1852 he moved to Cold Springs, California, where he became involved in his brothers' mercantile business. In 1855, Stanford moved to Sacramento, California, to pursue other business interests—and he developed an interest in politics. Stanford served as California governor from 1861 to 1863, and later as a Republican U.S. Senator from 1885 until his death in 1893.

While living in California, Stanford became acquainted with fellow businessmen Collis P. Huntington, Mark Hopkins, and Charles Crocker, all of whom would come to be called robber barons, along with men like Jay Gould and Cornelius Vanderbilt. Together they created a venture called Pacific Associates, which looked for mutually beneficial business opportunities. Through Pacific Associates, Stanford and his business partners built the Central Pacific Railroad and later, the Southern Pacific Railroad. Stanford was named president of the Central Pacific Railroad in 1863.

The goal of the Southern Pacific Railroad was to complete the transcontinental link with the Union Pacific Railroad, which was achieved in 1869 at Promontory, Utah. The four Pacific Associates partners invested $200,000 in the venture, but depended on government grants and bond guarantees for most of their funding. Within a short time after the completion of the Central Pacific Railroad, the partners became extremely wealthy, purchasing vast acres of land, lumber, vineyards, and mining properties and interests.

This was possible because they had a monopoly on railroad transportation of goods and passengers from the West Coast to the midwest. Before the railroad, the only means of long-distance travel was via horses or ships—neither of which moved very quickly. The railroad allowed for relatively rapid transportation, but at great cost. Passengers paid 10 cents per mile traveled, and freight was hauled at exorbitant prices.

As a result of the monopoly, farmers and ranchers who wanted to sell their goods in the eastern part of the country had to pay whatever freight prices were set by the railroad. This monopoly also benefited the partners when building the Southern Pacific Railroad to southern California.

During this process, they demanded that local cities and counties pay the cost of construction if they wanted the rail line to run through their areas. Failure to pay the ransom resulted in the railroad being built around those cities and counties. Community leaders knew that reliable transportation was vital to economic growth, so they paid the bill. Stanford's political acumen was also useful in influencing regulation of the railroads. In 1881, the California legislature created a three-member railroad commission to regulate shipping tariffs in the state. Stanford and Huntington were permitted to name two of the members, thus guaranteeing support for their monopoly.

SEE ALSO

robber barons; monopoly; reform and regulation; antitrust.

BIBLIOGRAPHY. Matthew Josephson, *The Robber Barons* (Harcourt, 1962); "Stanford University History," www.stanford.edu; "Leland Stanford, 1924–1893," *Biographical Directory of the United States Congress*, www.bioguide.congress.gov (2003); "Leland Stanford Jr., The Children of California Shall Be Our Children," www.usdreams.com (2003).

LAWRENCE M. SALINGER
GENERAL EDITOR

Stavisky, Serge (1886–1934)

SERGE Stavisky (also known as Serge Alexander) was a French confidence man of diverse talents. His criminal activities spanned decades and culminated in a notorious political scandal known as the Stavisky Affair. This event triggered the downfall of

Camille Chautemps' government in 1934 and had long-term repercussions for the political stability of France.

Stavisky's family left the Ukraine for France in 1899. His aptitude for deceit emerged when he was in his early teens. Stavisky refined and tested his skills to prey on the confidence and trust of others by creating illusory business ventures and soliciting capital investment from friends and clients. It was a recurrent theme throughout his life—profit through misrepresentation.

Stavisky's criminal enterprises took him and his partners into the worlds of entertainment, journalism, mass marketing, politics, finance, and invariably—criminal justice. In 1925, Stavisky and Henri Hayotte formed a company, Le P'tit Pot, that promoted and sold a meat-based bouillon. The pair sold this fictitious product to merchants and retailers, realizing a sizable profit in doing so. Although he fled, Stavisky was eventually captured and served a three-month sentence in prison.

On release, Stavisky conducted many fraudulent activities. These included forging stock certificates and checks, impersonating a stockbroker, counterfeiting, selling a device known as the Martyrscope for detecting pregnancy, bilking cafes and theaters of receipts, bouncing checks, issuing bonds without capital, pawning counterfeit jewelry, and promoting variations of the Ponzi scheme. The regulatory and bureaucratic disorder of post-World War I France created a climate vulnerable to exploitative individuals like Stavisky. The absence, moreover, of effective oversight in the banking and finance industries aggravated the problem of enforcing commercial codes of conduct.

Stavisky's most significant fraud, however, began in 1928. Stavisky created Establissements Alex, a municipal pawnshop, in Orleans. He circulated counterfeit jewels through the pawnshop, financing credit for the items by issuing bonds. Such businesses were only allowed to issue bonds equal to their assets. Stavisky sold million of francs in bonds using bogus jewelry as collateral. When the bonds came due for redemption Stavisky set up an identical firm in Bayonne in 1931, sold bonds, and used the revenues to partially pay back the debts owed in Orleans. He used his substantial profits to buy influence among journalists, the business communities, politicians, and the legal systems. People trusted Stavisky, and advocated on his behalf. Creditors eventually closed in on Stavisky. He could not cover his old debts with new bonds. A compulsive gambler and lavish spender, Stavisky fled criminal and civil charges. On January 8, 1934 in Chamonix, Switzerland, minutes before the police were about to break down his door, Stavisky shot himself (some sources suspect the police had a hand in his death).

The subsequent trials (1935–36) of Stavisky's accomplices uncovered corrupt relationships within government and business. Lax enforcement of the law and official indifference to Stavisky's many duplicitous enterprises drew public outrage and challenged the legitimacy of the Third Republic of France. The Stavisky Affair exposed and discredited the radical Socialist Party and undermined public support for parliamentary government.

SEE ALSO

Ponzi schemes; scams; bond fraud; France.

BIBLIOGRAPHY. John Kenneth Galbraith, *A Short History of Financial Euphoria* (Penguin, 1993); Paul F. Jankowski, *Stavisky: A Confidence Man in the Republic of Virtue* (Cornell University Press, 2002); Benjamin Martin, *The Shame of Marianne: Criminal Justice Under the Third Republic* (Baton Rouge, 1990).

DANIEL S. CAMPAGNA, PH.D.
MOUNT MARY COLLEGE

Steffens, Lincoln (1866–1936)

JOSEPH LINCOLN Steffens was an American author and editor, and one of the first and leading muckrakers. In 1906, President Theodore Roosevelt referred to a group of journalists as muckrakers, liking them to a *Pilgrim's Progress* character in the novel who was only interested in raking muck or dung. These muckrakers exposed corruption, abuse of power, and the suffering of the nation's very poor, and in doing so "provided American journalism with what many regard as one of its finest hours," according to an article by Stephen Goode.

Steffens began reporting in 1892 for New York City's *Evening Post*, then moved to an editorial position at the *Commercial Advertiser*, but continued to write freelance stories for magazines such as *McClure's*. Steffens was hired in 1901 to be editor of *McClure's*, but only held that position a few months before the magazine's owner sent him to St. Louis, Missouri, to investigate tales of corruption in city government. "When I set out to describe the corrupt systems of certain typical cities," Steffens wrote in 1903, "I meant to show simply how the people were deceived and betrayed. But in the very first study—St. Louis—the startling truth lay bare that corruption was not merely political; it was financial, commercial, social; the ramifications of boodle were so complex, various and far-reaching, that one mind could hardly grasp them, and not even Joseph W. Folk, the tireless prosecutor, could follow them all."

THE MUCKRAKING ERA

The writer's findings of wrongdoing in St. Louis were published in *McClure's* in October 1902, the beginning of the muckraking era. A series of articles on Chicago, Minneapolis, Pittsburgh, Philadelphia, and New York City followed. These articles were collected in Steffens' book *The Shame of the Cities* (1904). Subsequent investigations into state and federal government led to more exposè articles and *The Struggle for Self-Government* (1906), and *Upbuilders* (1909).

Unlike some muckrakers who preferred to write about previously unknown wrongs, Steffens emphasized the fact that most government corruption was known and allowed by its constituency. The writer also offered suggestions for reform, rather than just reporting evils. Disappointed that he had not made a difference, Steffens was ready to stop muckraking journalism about the time the style died out around 1911.

Steffens began to lecture on muckraking and politics, and after the death of his wife he traveled widely, including three trips to the Soviet Union between 1917 and 1923. The writer lectured enthusiastically about post-revolutionary Russian life and the Russian system of government. This fostered popular and critical disapproval of his work, but he was selected to be part of a 1919 American-British secret fact-finding mission talking to the Bolsheviks and Soviet leader Vladimir Lenin. It was following this visit to Russia that Steffens uttered, "I have been over into the future, and it works," which later became the oft-quoted, "I have seen the future, and it works."

In 1924, Steffens married his second wife Ella Winter, with whom he had a son. Because most men his age were grandfathers when he was just becoming a father and he believed he would probably not live to see his son become an adult, Steffens began his *Autobiography*, an immediate bestseller. He died 12 years later.

SEE ALSO
Roosevelt, Theodore; corruption; Sinclair, Upton.

BIBLIOGRAPHY. Lincoln Steffens, *The Autobiography of Lincoln Steffens* (Literary Guild, 1931); Stephen Goode, "Muckrakers Made Mounds of Trouble," *Insight on the News* (July 7, 1997); *Twentieth-Century Literary Criticism* (Gale,, 1986); Justin Kaplan, *Lincoln Steffens: A Biography* (Simon & Schuster, 1974).

LINDA M. CREIBAUM
ARKANSAS STATE UNIVERSITY

Stewart, Martha (1941–)

MARTHA KOSTYRA was born and reared in a working-class family in New Jersey. Her mother, a schoolteacher, and her father, a pharmaceutical salesman, held high standards and expectations for their children: ambition, achievement, and perfection were instilled at an early age. Martha, who married and eventually divorced Andrew Stewart, began her successful career as a model and then stockbroker. After leaving Wall Street, Stewart moved to Westport, Connecticut, and began restoration of an 1805 farmhouse that later served as the backdrop for her television appearances and programs.

Within 10 years, her catering business and specialty retail shop became a $1 million enterprise. Her first book, *Entertaining*, was published in 1982 and her merchandising collaboration with Kmart made Martha Stewart a household name that represented the American Dream and the embodiment of a prosperous homemaker-entrepreneur. She was chief executive officer of Martha Stewart Living Omnimedia, and in 1999, when the company became public, she was worth over $1 billion.

Her stalwart image was scorched, however, when accusations of insider-trading emerged. The investigation focused on Stewart's sale of ImClone stock. In 2001, two days after Christmas while on a Mexican vacation, Stewart called her Merrill Lynch stockbroker, Peter Bacanovic, and requested that he sell her 3,928 shares—a move that made her less than $230,000. Samuel Waksal, chief executive of the biotechnology company and friend of Stewart, had just dumped millions of dollars of shares based on information that the Food and Drug Administration (FDA) would deny approval of the company's highly anticipated cancer drug.

After his arrest, Waksal pleaded guilty to insider trading and was sentenced to seven years in prison and $4 million in fines and restitution. After a year-long investigation, Stewart was indicted, not for the alleged crime, but for the cover-up. The U.S. attorney admitted being unable to prove that she knew of the pending FDA announcement and thus had engaged in insider trading. The 40-page, nine-count indictment accused her and Bacanovic of obstruction of justice, conspiracy, making false statements to the government, and securities fraud. In her defense, Stewart maintained that she had pre-arranged a stop-loss order to sell the ImClone stock if the price dropped below $60 a share.

Stewart was found guilty of lying to cover up the stock deal but not guilty of securities fraud. In July 2004, she was sentenced to five months in prison and five months' home confinement. Though Stewart planned to appeal, it seemed the "doyenne of domesticity" was going to jail.

SEE ALSO
insider trading; securities fraud.

BIBLIOGRAPHY. C. M. Byron, *Martha Inc.: The Incredible Story of Martha Stewart Omnimedia* (Wiley, 2002); Jerry Oppenheimer, *Just Desserts: Martha Stewart Unauthorized Biography* (Avon, 1998); Jeffrey Toobin, "Lunch at Martha's: Problems with the Perfect Life," *The New Yorker* (February 3, 2003); www.-marthatalks.com (2004).

MARY DODGE, PH.D.
UNIVERSITY OF COLORADO

stock churning

STOCK CHURNING IS THE excessive trading of securities in a brokerage account. Also called burning and churning and over-trading, churning is done in order to increase the broker's commissions, which are directly related to the volume of trading rather than customer profits. Part, or sometimes all, of the client's potential profit may be absorbed by the broker's commission on some trades even though there would otherwise seem to be a profit. Sometimes, the commission will result in the client actually taking a loss on what would have been a profitable trade. In these cases, the broker makes a profit but the client would have been better off with an unchanged portfolio. Although some changes are necessary or good business for the client, excessive trading or churning is good business only for the financial adviser and her firm.

According to PR Newswire, churning is involved if these conditions are met: "The trading in the customer's account was excessive in the light of the customer's investment objectives; the broker exercised control over the trading in the account; the broker intended to defraud or demonstrated willful and reckless disregard for the customer's interest."

Over-trading is not solely within the realm of stockbrokers. Because the charge, or load, to a client on a mutual fund is typically higher than it is on stock sales, fund advisers can make larger commissions by moving an investor's holdings less often than with stocks. There are several forms this deceit can take.

Mutual fund managers sometimes churn the portfolio of stock holdings within their funds, sometimes on a daily basis. If the fund manager simply exchanges one of a client's funds with a similar one, he reaps the commission but the portfolio's performance does not change significantly. Because the performance is unchanged, the owner might not notice the change, but her value or interest has been lessened or depleted by the manager's commission on the trade.

Another kind of mutual fund churning occurs when a fund manager switches from one kind of fund to another, such as a mutual fund to a unit investment trust then to another mutual fund. Sponsors or families of investment vehicles will usually allow investors to shift money between funds within their group with no commission charge, so if a change is desired or necessary, staying within the same sponsor or family can be beneficial to the fund holder without costing him a commission on the change. Unscrupulous brokers will exchange sponsors simply to get a commission.

A side effect of churning is that it can be problematic for companies whose shares are traded often. Long-term stock holders may provide a company with more stability and options for long-term planning and profits than having a majority of short-term investors.

Although high trading volume is typical of churning or overtrading, all relatively high turnover is not necessarily a concerted effort by a broker or manager to increase commissions. An investment house basing buy and sell decisions on short-term technical and liquidity indicators will have higher turnover than a house with the "buy and hold" approach. Some decisions are also based on an exceptional offer to buy or to sell or other valid investment reasons.

Most brokers and fund managers are honest, but there is much pressure for production performance. Along with greed (broker income is based on commissions and bonuses), motives for churning include performance pressures from within the securities industry and sometimes the firm itself. Unsuccessful individuals will not continue in this line of work very long.

Some of the precautions stock or fund holders can take in preventing or avoiding being taken advantage of by churning include being cautious of pressure to invest or make changes quickly; carefully examining account statements and questioning anything that seems suspicious or unclear (although commissions are not always separated out in fund statements); being suspicious of guarantees in performance or earnings.

Mutual funds are typically considered to be long-term vehicles, so frequent changes of a client's holdings from one fund to another, or one kind to another, might prove to be a red flag to investors. One of the most important steps is to know your broker. The National Association of Securities Dealers (NASD) will provide the full disciplinary record of any broker.

In the United States, churning may have both civil and criminal repercussions, and is under the jurisdiction of states' blue sky laws and the Securities and Exchange Commission (SEC). Brokers convicted of churning can lose their licenses, be required to pay restitution, and/or be incarcerated.

SEE ALSO

stock fraud; securities fraud; National Association of Securities Dealers; Securities and Exchange Commission.

BIBLIOGRAPHY. David L. Scott, *Wall Street Words: An Essential A to Z Guide for Today's Investor* (Houghton Mifflin, 1997); John A. Byrne, "When Capital Gets Antsy," *BusinessWeek* (issue 3646, 1999); Carole Gould, "Churning Is Not Just for Stocks," *The New York Times* (June 7, 1992); Kelvin Tan, "Personal Finance: Is Your Fund Churning Too Much?" *The Edge Singapore* (September 16, 2002).

LINDA M. CREIBAUM
ARKANSAS STATE UNIVERSITY

stock fraud

THE TOPIC OF STOCK fraud were prominently featured in the news media through the 1980s, 1990s, and the beginning of the 21st century. Names like Enron became part of the lexicon, while the terms *penny stocks* and *boiler room* made their way into the public conscience and into Hollywood productions. Because of these events, the public's confidence in the stock markets was predictably affected. Politicians and other public officials have scrambled to devise ways to avoid such large-scale frauds in the future.

Though the term *stock fraud* can encompass numerous illicit activities, there are essentially two key types of stock fraud—insider trading and market manipulation (each with many variants that can fill volumes unto themselves). Unfortunately, there are no valid statistics available to compare the difference in prevalence and significance of these types of stock fraud.

EARLY FRAUDS

Historically, documented stock frauds in the United States date back to the 1800s. These frauds included the gold and silver mines of the American west, in particular the Colorado gold rush in the 1880s. Prospectors had little capital and turned to selling shares to finance their ventures. Those unable to lure more substantial investments sold shares for as little as a penny. Of course, many "prospectors" were nothing of the sort, and frauds were commonplace.

On the heels of the 19th century miners came the oil and gas promoters. By 1918, towns like Fort Worth, Texas, were home to motley armies of "lease sharks, grafters and grabbers, operators, speculators, and gamblers," according to authors Roger

M. Olien and Diana Davids Olien. In Los Angeles, California, the Department of Justice estimated that stock swindlers hawking oil securities, many for little more than $1, were making about $100,000 a week in 1923. The activities leading up to, and including, the stock market crash of 1929 resulted in the Securities Act of 1933, which requires companies going public to register their securities offerings and to supply financial and other material information enabling investors to make informed decisions. The Securities Exchange Act of 1934 followed, creating the Securities and Exchange Commission (SEC) as the primary agency responsible for administering federal securities laws. These measures were intended to restore confidence in securities trading, and have remained the hallmark of regulation and enforcement.

The topic of stock fraud lay dormant, with minor exceptions, until the infamous insider trading cases of the 1980s. These scandals were serious enough to result in the U.S. Senate Committee on Banking, Housing, and Urban Affairs inquiry, "Improper Activities in the Securities Industry." Following the insider trading cases of the 1980s and before the high-profile Enron, Tyco et al. cases the early 2000s, the most commonly discussed frauds were concentrated in the "micro-cap" market, more commonly referred to as the penny-stock industry.

PENNY STOCKS

The U.S. penny-stock market was designed as a "conduit through which money from small investors travels to legitimate young companies in need of venture financing," according to Robert L. Frick and Mary Lynne Vellinga. There is no commonly held definition for penny stocks. In general, penny stocks are considered those securities not listed on a recognized exchange, hence they are traded over-the-counter (OTC), and information about them is only available on the "pink sheets." Some argue, however, penny stocks are those that trade for less than $5.00 per share, and thus can be found on NASDAQ exchange. While there are several types of securities violations (for example, failure to disclose, unauthorized trading, refusal to execute orders, etc.), market manipulation dominates penny-stock fraud.

Until the mid-1980s, criminal penny-stock firms made their money through initial public offerings (IPOs) of phony and/or overvalued securities

(that is, the primary market). The North American Securities Administrators Association (NASAA) noted that criminals then shifted their emphasis "from the primary market of IPOs to the secondary or 'after' market." This was done through the much greater use of what are called blank check blind pools. Stock swindlers tweaked the concept and began conning investors to give them money for investments in unspecified companies. They were asking for what came to be known as a blank check. The blind pool typically stands for a sham corporation which has been created to "merge with other closely-held public companies in order to bypass federal and state securities regulation, gain immediate access to the secondary market and serve as a vehicle for market manipulation," NASAA explains.

Diane Francis describes blind pools as "venture capital outfits" that raise money without needing to tell the investors there was a specific plan in mind for use of their money. One of the most audacious blind pool shams in history was Canada's infamous Bre-X mining scandal, which ran from 1993 to 1997, and involved a Busang, Indonesia, site that failed to produce the expected gold. The stock tumbled from C$28.50 to $.00005 per share, and cost Bre-X's chief geologist his life when he "fell" out of a helicopter over the rain forest in Samarinda, Indonesia.

SCALPING

The secondary market became the arena for making really big money. Generally speaking, it works like this: a public offering is made for the stock of a sham company, which is merging with another usually unspecified firm already registered with the SEC. Investors are not informed, of course, that the swindler's firm owns the bulk of the shares. (This practice is known as scalping and is a violation of the Investment Advisors Act of 1940.)

The price is then driven up, made all the easier when the crooked firm is the sole market maker. At some predetermined peak, the swindlers sell their shares in this new firm, the product of the merger, in what is called the secondary market. For the insiders to hit the peak and get out, the investing public cannot be allowed to sell their shares. The criminal firm simply refuses to execute sell orders on behalf of its clients. The firm's sales representatives, who do the scripted telephoning to hook the unwary, are ordered to either hang up when a client

Stock fraud was mainly the province of "boiler room" operations until the advent, in the 1980s and 1990s, of top Wall Street firms involved in corporate malfeasance and accounting fraud.

calls who wants to sell, or not to answer the phone during "selling" times.

Blank checks and blind pools rely on the most important technical innovation the criminal stock firm has—the telephone, which by the 1980s evolved to include toll-free numbers, call waiting, call screening, the availability of specialized phone lists, and interacted with fax machines and computers. Their methods reveal the kinship between the penny-stock racket and the classic swindler's boiler room operation: high-pressure promotion by telephone of a bogus commodity, often by people who don't have the foggiest idea what it is they are promoting. Perhaps Lorenzo Formato, a high school dropout, represents the best example. Formato started out on the telephone with Mayflower Securities, the progenitor of some of the most important penny-stock criminals in U.S. history.

Though completely ignorant of the brokerage business, he had more clients than anyone else at Mayflower within six months. He didn't know what stocks were, but he did know that selling them could make him a lot of money. He sold and sold "never knowing," he told the U.S. House of Representatives, "whether or not the stock was any good,

whether or not the company had any profits, whether or not the company even existed." Boiler rooms may operate out of homes, warehouses and any number of places, but they are most often operated in offices. Salespeople sit at desks cold-calling potential investors, typically reading off of a script.

THE RATIONAL INVESTOR

In the world of securities, there are several third parties, including private associations of securities dealers at the state and national level, state government regulators, and the SEC, whose work is based on creating sufficient rules to compel broker-dealers to give true disclosure, thereby creating trust between sellers and buyers of securities. Underlying this is the concept of the rational investor. That is, there simply cannot be a rational investor without honest and full disclosure, though no one guarantees the rational investor will be successful and no one knows whether the informed investor is more likely to succeed than the intuitive investor.

What the SEC does is to try and reduce the risks or level the playing field of what is always, essentially a gamble. One of the basic tenets of regulatory agencies is that consumer education is the key to reducing crimes by society's elite. This is particularly the case with securities fraud in the United States, because the SEC and National Association of Securities Dealers (NASD) structure their policies around the "informed," "educated," or "rational" investor paradigm. With the advent of the internet, and the related resources for prospective investors, there has never been a better time for investors gathering information on stocks, firms, shareholders, employees, and other relevant data. And yet, concurrent with the rise in these resources for investors came the explosion in penny-stock fraud, dispelling the notion of the informed investor. If disclosure and investor education have each been stressed without success, what are the other possible remedies?

SEC REGULATION

Susan Shapiro (1984), in her classic study of the SEC, notes that SEC commissioners have three formal legal options in pursuing cases against perpetrators of a particular offense: civil proceedings, administrative proceedings, and referrals to the U.S. Department of Justice. She found that 93 percent of suspects investigated by the SEC have committed securities violations that carry criminal penalties. As Shapiro and many others have noted, the SEC is far more likely to seek civil and administrative proceedings than to seek criminal prosecution. The NASD, similarly, may refer cases involving criminal activity for further investigation and possible indictment, but they are also far more likely to seek civil remedies.

In Shapiro's study, she found that only 46 percent of the total number of cases referred to the Department of Justice for criminal prosecutions resulted in convictions. These findings go a long way to explaining the persistent pattern of utilizing civil and administrative proceedings by regulatory and law enforcement agencies. These proceedings are usually settled when the defendant consents to some penalty, fine, suspension, etc., "without admitting or denying the facts, findings or conclusions contained" in the "offer of settlement," commonly referred to as a consent decree.

Ironically, it was the "Johnny Appleseed of massive penny-stock fraud," Robert E. Brennan, who thought SEC consent decrees meant little in practice. He said that in a consent decree, the SEC proves "nothing, I admit nothing, and they can go tell their bosses in Washington, D.C., they've done a good job." He added, "It's a disgrace."

Studies have frequently identified several reasons that authorities give in defending their preference for non-criminal proceedings. The most common reasons cited are the following: the lower legal threshold in civil cases that enables easier prosecution; the higher likelihood in civil cases that defendants will cooperate to avoid the criminal justice system, and the ensuing labeling, which is advantageous for regulators because it expedites the process and frequently serves as a means of intelligence-gathering to thwart future offenses.

Moreover, there is the prospect for substantial fines in civil proceedings. Thus, while there is general agreement that civil and administrative proceedings are ineffective as a deterrent, there are practical reasons government officials elect these processes. Consider the following exchange between U.S. Senator Max Cleland and Securities and Exchange Commission Chairman Arthur Levitt, Jr.:

Senator Cleland: I understand the importance of injunctions and consent decrees and receivers and trustees and other types of administrative and civil sanctions that can be applied against violators. The media is full of stories about the major frauds perpetrated on our citizens. It is my opinion that the only sanction, quite frankly… that most of the serious violators will understand as a successful deterrence is jail time and the completion of a successful criminal prosecution. Do you have any idea why more of the major fraud cases do not end up in the criminal courts?

SEC Chairman Levitt: Well, I think it is a question of calendars that are so full and commitments that are so great, and these are cases that are difficult cases to bring and to prove. It is only in the most egregious cases that we get to criminal actions. We find that there are very few districts of our Federal courts that are experienced at bringing securities cases. Some of them, such as New York and California, do have that experience and recognize it as a major area for their involvement. Others simply would rather go after bank robbers than they would go through the difficult process of trying to prove what a securities fraud is.

Research has documented the omnipresence of fraud in the stock-market industry since its inception, and media outlets have covered both individual cases and industry-wide activities. No less an authority than Attorney General Robert F. Kennedy wrote in 1964:

> A highly profitable activity for racketeers with legitimate business interests has been stock fraud. Often, rackets figures with considerable at their disposal invest, not only in legitimate securities, but also in questionable stock. Typically, they artificially raise the price of such stock with calculated purchases and then sell large amounts through "boiler room" telephone solicitation. In one case, a leading Eastern rackets figure is now under indictment for evading taxes on more than a million dollars' profit received from sale of such stock.

With the skyrocketing of the securities markets in the 1990s, and with the advent of information technologies, the opportunities for, and actual occurrences of securities fraud came to the public's awareness. The precipitous increase in legitimate stocks drew many uninformed investors into the fold. Thus, stock scammers no longer had to convince prospective "marks" they should invest, since the marks were themselves seeking investment opportunities. In 1999, NASAA President Peter Hildreth stated, "Today we have an ideal climate for fraud. Millions of new investors, many of whom expect unrealistically high returns, are looking for places to put their money. At the same time, we're living through an internet-driven technology revolution that is a boom to investors and con artists alike." Just as regulators were beginning to reign in penny-stock kingpins such as Randolph Pace, Meyer Blinder, and Robert Brennan, they soon became consumed with investigations of worldwide significance. Enron, Worldcom and others soon gained notoriety for their securities discretions, among other noteworthy issues.

As a response to corporate scandals born in the 1990s and early 2000s, the U.S. Congress drafted reform legislation titled the Sarbanes-Oxley Act of 2002. The act created a series of oversight measures, and expanded and increased the sanctions for illicit

For fraudsters and investors alike, the information technology revolution has opened up new opportunities for research and education, or for stock fraud and scams, depending on the objective.

white-collar actions, including stock frauds. President George W. Bush signed the legislation into law on July 30, 2002, and the U.S. Sentencing Commission approved lengthening sentences for stock fraudsters on January 8, 2003. Federal law enforcement agencies, most notably the Federal Bureau of Investigation (FBI), were consumed with terrorism investigations in addition to their normal mandates and responsibilities (organized crime and narcotics trafficking cases). Nevertheless, due in part to the activities enumerated above, the president of the NASAA stated that accounting and stock frauds "have become the hot, sexy cases ... I think a lot of people have changed their focus in terms of how seriously they're taking these cases." According to officials, cases that would normally have been handled exclusively by the SEC now routinely involve federal prosecutors and the FBI.

HEIGHTS OF CORPORATE CRIME

On April 28, 2003, headlines in the United States announced the record settlement between the nation's largest investment firms and the SEC. Ten Wall Street firms settled civil claims for a total of $1.4 billion to end several probes involving various frauds and conflicts of interest. The government used internal e-mails to illustrate how the investment firms touted stocks they knew to be of questionable quality, so their firms could gain investment-banking business.

For instance, one prolific stock analyst at Salomon Smith Barney, Jack B. Grubman, privately called one of the stocks he was publicly recommending a "pig." Another broker at the firm called Grubman a "poster child for conspicuous conflicts of interest." The apparent assault on corporate crime, particularly concerning stock fraud, continued in the summer of 2003. On July 25, the SEC announced a major strategic initiative concerning their primary remedy, consent decrees. Even in cases where the accused "neither admit nor deny wrongdoing," the agency will view defendants as having admitted the facts in the settlement.

Thus, a brokerage that agrees to a court injunction against committing fraud, even if it does not admit to fraud, may not contest the facts in future actions brought by the SEC in connection with the injunction. The "non-denial" denials have thus seen their last days. The new policy will likely make it easier for the SEC to follow injunctions with disciplinary actions. Some questions remain, however; first among them is whether the policy will reduce the number of settlements with the SEC. If so, this would create a problem seemingly ameliorated by the former policy of settlements, namely rising (and likely unmanageable) workloads for SEC investigators that ultimately serve to lessen the deterrent effect on violators.

SEE ALSO

Securities and Exchange Commission; accounting fraud; securities fraud; Enron Corporation; WorldCom; Sarbanes-Oxley Act; Bre-X.

BIBLIOGRAPHY. Alex Berenson, "A U.S. Push on Accounting Fraud," *The New York Times* (April 9, 2003); Diane Francis, *Bre-X: The Inside Story* (Key Porter Books, 1997); Robert L. Frick and Mary Lynne Vellinga, *Keys to Risks and Reward of Penny Stocks* (Barron's, 1990); Sean Patrick Griffin and Alan A. Block, "PennyWise: Accounting for Fraud in the Penny Stock Industry," in Henry N. Pontell and David Shichor, eds., *Contemporary Issues in Crime and Criminal Justice: Essays in Honor of Gilbert Geis* (Prentice-Hall, 2000); Martin Mayer, *Stealing the Market: How the Giant Brokerage Firms, with the Help from the SEC, Stole the Stock Market from Investors* (Basic Books, 1992); National Association of Securities Dealers, Inc., *Securities Regulation in the United States* (1996); North American Securities Administrators Association, *The NASAA Report on Fraud and Abuse in the Penny Stock Industry*, Subcommittee on Telecommunications and Finance, Committee on Energy and Commerce, U.S. House of Representatives (September 1989); Roger M. Olien and Diana Davids Olien, *Easy Money: Oil Promoters and Investors in the Jazz Age* (University of North Carolina Press, 1990); Securities and Exchange Commission, *Penny-Stock Task Force* (1988); Stephen M. Rosoff, Henry N. Pontell, and Robert Tillman, *Profit Without Honor: White-Collar Crime and the Looting of America* (Prentice Hall, 1998); Kip Schlegel, *Securities Lawbreaking: The Enforcement Response*, report submitted to the U.S. Department of Justice (1994); Susan P. Shapiro, *Wayward Capitalists: Target of the Securities and Exchange Commission* (Yale University Press, 1984); Jules Tygiel, *The Great Los Angeles Swindle: Oil, Stocks, and Scandal During the Roaring Twenties* (Oxford University Press, 1994); U.S. House of Representatives, *Hearings: Penny Stock Market Fraud* (1989); U.S. Senate, Committee on Banking, Housing, and Urban Affairs, *Improper Activities in the Securities Industry* (1987); U.S. Senate, Permanent Subcommittee on Investigations (PSI) of the Committee on Governmental Affairs, *Fraud in the Micro-Capital Markets Including Penny Stock Fraud* (U.S. Government Printing Office, 1997); Ben White and Kathleen Day, "SEC Approves Wall Street Settlement," *Washington Post* (April 29, 2003).

SEAN PATRICK GRIFFIN, PH.D.
PENN STATE UNIVERSITY, ABINGTON

Sumitomo Corporation

THE SUMITOMO CORPORATION is a large Japanese company with interests in a wide range of fields. Like many other Japanese companies, Sumitomo has suffered from the effects of excessive diversification in the post-boom period and has subsequently been afflicted with various non-performing loans. In 2003, Sumitomo Mitsui, Japan's second biggest lender reported a loss of Y465 billion (approximately $3.9 billion) and was forced to seek additional funding. Some of its subsidiaries have been linked with poor environmental practices, for example, with respect to stockpiled pesticides which can pose a threat of toxicity.

However, a more startling revelation of corporate malpractice was revealed in 1996 when Yasuo Hamanaka, a trader at Sumitomo, was revealed to have cost the company some $3 billion through losses in the copper market. Hamanaka had, with the apparent collusion of his former supervisor Saburo (Steve) Shimizu, been attempting to make money by cornering a portion of the copper commodity market. They had resorted to this illegal practice in 1985, supposedly to recoup through trading in futures on the London Metal Exchange (LME) money previously lost on physical trading deals.

Cornering the market involves purchasing a large amount of a commodity and then withholding it from sale for a period, thereby reducing the supply and hence inflating the demand and cost for it. By doing so, Hamanaka could make profits by selling the copper he had earlier obtained at a lower price. This practice can only succeed when it is kept secret and when sufficient quantities of the product are obtained to provide a meaningful level of control over market supply. Hamanaka was eventually unable to obtain these criteria for Sumitomo and was obliged to sell some of his product at a loss.

However, rather than accept the loss, Hamanaka attempted to manipulate the market further until his activities came to light and the market plunged into turmoil.

Hamanaka was subsequently jailed for eight years for his part in the deal, but Sumitomo, which brought a criminal complaint against Hamanaka in part to try to distance itself from allegations of its own wrongdoing, was not the only company to be implicated. In 1999, the brokerage house Merrill Lynch was accused of assisting Hamanaka's activities and fined £6.5 million (approximately $10.4 million) by the LME and £9 million (approximately $14.4 million) by the United States Commodity Trading Futures Commission.

Deutsche Bank, the leading German bank, through the actions of a subsidiary, was fined some £1.5 million (approximately $2.4 million) by authorities for failing to exercise sufficient care in purchasing large quantities of copper for a client. As in the case of Nick Leeson at Barings Bank and other scandals, the Hamanaka affair revealed that the complexity of many modern financial transactions and inadequate supervision can lead individuals to believe their activities are undetectable.

SEE ALSO
Yasuo Hamanaka; Leeson, Nick; Barings Bank; Japan.

BIBLIOGRAPHY. Dan Atkinson, "£1.5m Copper Fine for Deutsche," *The Guardian* (January 7, 2000); "Ex-Sumitomo Copper Trader Arrested," Cable News Network (October 22, 1996); Paul Krugman, "How Copper Became a Cropper," *The Accidental Theorist* (Penguin Books, 1999); Cat Lazaroff, "USA: World Health Threatened by Toxic Pesticide Stocks," Environment News Service (CorpWatch.org, May 9, 2001); Jonathan Watts, "Mizuho Loss Hits Hopes of Japanese Banking Turnaround," *The Guardian* (May 27, 2003).

JOHN WALSH, PH.D.
MAHIDOL UNIVERSITY, THAILAND

Sutherland, Edwin H. (1893–1950)

CRIMINOLOGIST, TEACHER, and the person officially credited with the discovery of the white-collar criminal, on December 27, 1939, Edwin H. Sutherland coined the phrase in Philadelphia, Pennsylvania, in a speech he delivered as president of the American Sociological Society. The most often cited of Sutherland's various definitions of white-collar crime, from his 1949 monograph of the same name, conceptualizes it "approximately as a crime committed by a person of respectability and high social status in the course of his occupation."

Born in Gibbon, Nebraska, Sutherland was the fourth of five children of fundamentalist Baptist minister George Sutherland and Lizzie (Pickett) Sutherland. The family moved to Grand Island, Nebraska, in 1893, where Sutherland attended Grand Island College, played football, and graduated with an A.B. in 1904. In 1906, he began study at the preeminent department of sociology at the University of Chicago, the first such department in America (founded in 1890). He finished his Ph.D. in sociology and political economy in 1913. Sutherland taught at Sioux Falls College (1904-06), Grand Island College (1909-11), William Jewell College (1913-19), University of Illinois (1919-26), University of Minnesota (1926-29), and Indiana University (1935-50). He also worked as a researcher for the New York Bureau of Social Hygiene (1929-30) and the University of Chicago (1930-35). Sutherland is remembered as a self-critical scholar and a stimulating teacher.

DIFFERENTIAL ASSOCIATION

Sutherland is best known for his theory of differential association, which focuses on learning from significant others the reasons for violating or not violating the law. Many of his ideas in differential association originated with the intense study of a professional thief, nicknamed Broadway Jones (*The Professional Thief*, 1937). His 1924 textbook, *Criminology*, had only rudimentary antecedents of differential association, but his third edition of the text in 1939 (*Principles of Criminology*) contained seven explicit propositions of the theory. These were expanded to nine in the 1947 edition, the last before his death. Differential association is the most enduring criminological theory of the 20th century, and Sutherland utilized the idea of white-collar crime as evidence for the validity of differential association.

Sutherland was the first to identify white-collar crime systematically, but he was not the first to write about it. He had the benefit of the muckrakers (such as Upton Sinclair and Ida Tarbell) and of

Matthew Josephson's 1934 publication of *The Robber Barons*. Sutherland was also exposed to the works of Charles R. Henderson, Edward Alsworth Ross, and Thorstein Veblen. Veblen's *Theory of the Leisure Class* (1912), for instance, likened captains of industry to typical juvenile delinquents. Sutherland was further anticipated by Albert Morris's "criminals of the upperworld" (1935), which included bankers, stockbrokers, manufacturers, politicians, contractors, and law enforcement officials as examples of the type.

Sutherland's 1939 speech, which was the culmination of his collected materials on white-collar crime over the previous 13 years, had three objectives. Sutherland wanted to emphasize that "white-collar criminality is real criminality" because it is in violation of law. Sutherland also reminded criminologists that poverty-based theories of crime causation—virtually all of the theories popular at that time—were intellectually inadequate because poverty did not differentiate between who committed crime and who did not. The third, and perhaps most important, purpose of Sutherland's speech was to assert that his theory of differential association constituted an approach that explained a general process characteristic of all criminality, including the social business influences that caused persons of high status to violate the law through occupation. It is interesting that Sutherland used white-collar crime primarily as the vehicle to promote differential association, rather than to spotlight white-collar crime.

In the decade that followed Sutherland's address, however, the question of whether his concept of white-collar crime actually dealt with real crime would become the subject of heated intellectual debate. Sutherland published "Is 'White-Collar Crime' Crime?" in 1945 in the *American Sociological Review*, which made more concrete his assertions about the criminal nature of the phenomenon. His main detractor was Paul Tappan, a legalistic sociologist who insisted that the term criminal can only be applied to persons convicted of an offense. Sutherland responded by stating that the penalties in both administrative codes and in penal codes are the same because they were designed by legislatures to invoke suffering for lawbreakers.

In his monograph, *White-Collar Crime*, published in 1949 shortly before his death, Sutherland presented 20 years of his research on the subject, having compiled hundreds of legal violations committed by 70 of the larger American corporations of his day. Sutherland tabulated all officially recorded violations against those organizations from their beginning through the time of his writing (organizational ages ranged from 18 to 150 years). Sutherland was aware of the shortcomings in his method: 1) there may have been violations about which he was unaware; 2) opportunities to commit crime vary with organizational size and age; 3) single adverse decisions sometimes involved large numbers of separate violations; and 4) the kinds of violations committed by organizations are closely related to their location in the economic system.

Sutherland used *White-Collar Crime* as proof for differential association and to announce that "white-collar crime is organized crime." It is organized primarily because white-collar (corporate) criminals manipulate the elections of officials and the focus of enforcement agencies. This represents an underlying anti-capitalistic theme in the monograph. In the original version of *White-Collar Crime* (1949), the names of the organizations were deleted, allegedly because, as Sutherland noted in the preface, "[a] theory of criminal behavior ... can be better attained without directing attention in an invidious manner to the behavior of particular corporations." Sutherland and his publisher were sensitive to libel suits. It was not until 34 years after its original publication that Sutherland's work reappeared in an expanded, "uncut" version that finally included the identities of the 70 corporations he had studied.

DEFINITIONAL PROBLEMS

Sutherland's inexact definition of white-collar crime has been seen as extremely problematic. It is difficult to study something that can not be well defined. Scholars have also pointed out that Sutherland's biggest theoretical problem was his tendency in *White-Collar Crime* to view organizations as the criminal actors, rather to treat the organizations' employees as the criminals. Differential association is explainable in terms of individuals' behaviors, not that of corporations.

Despite the flaws in *White-Collar Crime*, Sutherland succeeded convincingly in his main task—to reform the theory of criminal behavior through demonstrating that crime is abundant in the upper levels of society. He died of a stroke and an ensuing fall while walking to work at Indiana University on

October 11, 1950. At the time of his death, Sutherland had produced more than 50 academic publications in addition to seven books, and his writings on white-collar crime have been considered among the most influential works in the discipline. The Sutherland Award, bestowed annually by the American Society of Criminology, is the most prestigious recognition for an American criminologist.

SEE ALSO
differential association; self-control theory; Sutherland-Tappan Debate; techniques of neutralization.

BIBLIOGRAPHY. Mark Gaylord and John Galliher, *The Criminology of Edwin Sutherland* (Transaction Books, 1988); Schuessler, Karl, ed., *Edwin H. Sutherland: On Analyzing Crime* (University of Chicago Press, 1973); Edwin H. Sutherland, "White-Collar Criminality," *American Sociological Review* (v.5, 1940); Edwin H. Sutherland, "Is 'White-Collar Crime' Crime?" *American Sociological Review* (v.10, 1945); Edwin H. Sutherland, *White-Collar Crime* (Dryden Press, 1949); *White-Collar Crime: The Uncut Version* (Yale University Press, 1983).

GARY S. GREEN
CHRISTOPHER NEWPORT UNIVERSITY

Sutherland-Tappan Debate

MOST ASTUTE STUDENTS of criminology, particularly those interested in the topic of white-collar crime, are quite familiar with Edwin Sutherland's famous definition of the term: "a crime committed by a person of respectability and high social status in the course of his occupation." In focusing on white-collar crime as an area of research, Sutherland's main interest was in critiquing existing criminological theories. At this time, the main theories, such as social disorganization theory, sought to explain crime as a result of various structural factors, including poverty and inequality.

As Sutherland correctly argued, existing theories could easily explain violent, or common crimes committed by unemployed, street criminals. However, factors such as poverty could not accurately explain the criminal activities of educated, higher status individuals working in legitimate organizations. Sutherland's well-known definition of white-collar crime can be considered offender-based, since it includes characteristics of the individual of-fender. However, Sutherland later suggested an alternative, offense-based definition, which broadly defined all white-collar offenses as violations of trust. Although Sutherland's early definitions of white-collar crime focused on individuals, he created further conceptual confusion when his landmark study of white-collar crime actually dealt with sanctions against entire organizations.

Regardless of whether he was interested in individuals or corporations, what is clear is that Sutherland was satisfied to consider white-collar crime behaviors that were punishable by law. Even if such offenses did not result in actual punishment, Sutherland felt they were still white-collar crime. He also did not believe it was not necessary to differentiate between criminal and civil statutes. All that mattered, according to Sutherland, was that some violation of a statute or code was taking place within the organizational setting.

Sociologist Paul W. Tappan, who also had legal training, took offense at Sutherland's position that acts were "crimes" and individuals were "criminals" if they had not been formally charged and adjudicated within the justice system. In particular, Tappan argued that Sutherland was attacking the integrity of the business world by labeling corporations as "white-collar criminals." Contrary to Sutherland, Tappan suggested in his 1947 article that "adjudicated offenders represent the closest possible approximation to those who have in fact violated the law, carefully selected by sieving of the due process of law." Tappan felt that Sutherland's position exemplified an anti-business bias.

In response, Sutherland forcefully and eloquently defended his opinion by arguing that what mattered was what an individual actually did in terms of violating the law, not the way in which the criminal justice system dealt with him. In fact, Sutherland was concerned with the fact that existing statutes did not proscribe penalties for white-collar offenses. Sutherland was also deeply troubled with what he termed "differential implementation of law," the process by which higher status offenders were treated more leniently than their poor, lower-class counterparts. Sutherland felt it was important that all criminologists, not just those interested in white-collar crime, should continue to research why the legal system tends to be biased in favor of the wealthy. Most criminologists at the time, and certainly those today, would side with

Sutherland's position. The main flaw of Tappan's viewpoint is that he was suggesting that criminologists should not study what is referred to as the "dark figure" of crime—those offenses which may not be reported to or detected by the police. Tappan's strict legal interpretation of what types of behavior constitute crime was viewed as too narrow, given that much of what criminologists do view as crime occurs much earlier than the conviction stage of the criminal justice system. Unlike in Sutherland's time, today's modern criminologists now have access to data and other sources of information that provide even more evidence against Tappan's restricted opinion.

The "dark figure" of crime is still very much a topic of study, and attempts to measure this elusive form often take the mode of the self-report survey. Additionally, this data source, and also self-report surveys of crime victims, are now viewed as superior to conviction data for several reasons. Studies have demonstrated that biases in sentencing are common, particularly for certain groups of people and also in specific geographic regions of the United States. At an earlier stage in the criminal justice system, the arrest-procedure research has revealed the occurrence of similar biases. For example, studies of police practices have shown that certain groups, such as minority males in low-income neighborhoods, may be targeted more forcefully by the police. Taken together, the existing literature suggests that the study of only one point in the criminal justice system, whether it is arrest, conviction, or an alternative, can lead to unreliable conclusions about social processes.

Although our research and data collection methods have improved considerably since the time of Sutherland and Tappan, criminologists' concern with differential implementation of law remains a critical issue. The answer to the question of why certain offenders receive favorable treatment remains elusive at best.

SEE ALSO

Sutherland, Edwin H.; prosecution; differential association; self-control theory.

BIBLIOGRAPHY. Henry N. Pontell and David Shichor, *Contemporary Issues in Crime and Criminal Justice: Essays in Honor of Gilbert Geis* (Prentice-Hall, 2001); Edwin Sutherland, *White-Collar Crime* (Dryden Press, 1949); Kip Schlegel and David Weisburd, *White-Collar Crime Recon-*

sidered (Northeastern University Press, 1992); Edwin Sutherland, "Is 'White-Collar Crime' Crime?" *American Sociological Review* (v.10, 1945); Paul W. Tappan, "Who is the Criminal?" *American Sociological Review* (v.12, 1947).

KRISTY HOLTFRETER, PH.D.
FLORIDA STATE UNIVERSITY

sweepstakes fraud

EACH DAY SWEEPSTAKES entries arrive in the homes of millions of people around the world through the telephone, in the mailbox, or in e-mail. Companies promoting sweepstakes offer everything from diamond rings to millions of dollars; and according to the Department of Justice, one out of every six Americans is cheated by sweepstakes scam artists each year. A survey conducted by the National Consumers League (NCL) found that 92 percent of adults had received at least one postcard in the mail telling them they were sweepstakes winners. Approximately one-third of the recipients answered the postcards, but less than 20 percent of the 54 million respondents in the NCL survey won a prize without paying a fee or buying a product.

TARGETING SENIORS

Many sweepstakes are legitimate, but an increasing number are simply scams designed to entice gullible people into sending money, buying unwanted and often inferior merchandise, or giving away personal information that allows scam operators to steal identities.

The Federal Bureau of Investigation (FBI) reports that in almost 80 percent of the sweepstakes fraud cases investigated, victims are elderly. Publishing Clearing House (PCH), the best known of the large sweepstakes companies, estimates that at least 30 percent of its entrants are over 65 years old.

The elderly may be more vulnerable to sweepstake scams because they may be lonely, suffering from cognitive impairment, or simply more trusting. Marketing to the elderly may be as subtle as adding a familiar touch to the sweepstakes offer by addressing the recipient by name, or it may be as blatant as advertising in cemeteries. In August 2003, Alder Woods Group, Inc., installed 8-foot by 10-foot signs at the entrances of its 200 cemeteries, inviting visitors to enter a sweepstakes in which they might win from $2,000 to $25,000.

An elderly person may send money to fraudulent sweepstakes companies for months or years before authorities are notified. An elderly woman in Colorado, for example, wrote more than 2,000 checks totaling $107,000 over a 14-month period before it was reported. A Colorado man in his 70s became so obsessed with entering sweepstakes that he rented a post office box to receive the entries and locked himself in his room each day where he wrote checks from $5 to $50 totaling hundreds of thousands of dollars before his family discovered his secret and reported it.

After being asked to send a map to her home, one 78-year old Florida woman had friends waiting to watch her receive her prize from representatives of Publishers Clearing House. The company, who had no association with PCH, never came. Another elderly woman spent one-half of her social security check each month buying products from companies because she thought that purchasing improved her chances of winning. In an effort to educate the elderly about sweepstake scams, in 1999 Congress passed the Protecting Seniors from Fraud Act (Public Law 106-534), requiring the assistant secretary of Health and Human Services for Aging to work with state attorneys general to educate seniors about sweepstakes fraud.

One of the most common sweepstakes scams involves notifying an individual that she has won millions of dollars that will be transmitted only after the recipient sends a cashier's check, money order, or Western Union transfer to prepay taxes, cover shipping and handling, or make an nonrefundable deposit. Gloria Vettor, a Canadian bookkeeper in her 50s, was so anxious to win the $850,000 that she was told she had won in a sweepstakes that she embezzled the $82,140 "cover fee" from her employer. After responding to the first offer, Vettor was put on a "sucker list" and was contacted by scores of other fraudulent sweepstake companies to which she also sent money. After embezzling $8,768,000 from her employer over ten months, Vettor was arrested and sent to jail. Out of the $2.7 million that Vettor was told she had won, she never received a penny.

States have also passed laws against sweepstakes fraud and have successfully sued a number of sweepstakes companies. West Virginia, which has reported more victims of sweepstakes than any other state, sued 106 companies for sweepstakes fraud in 1994. During that same year, 14 states filed suit against PCH, forcing the company to reform the way it conducts sweepstakes. PCH paid $490,000 to be distributed among thousands of sweepstakes entrants who were misled by wording in their sweepstakes information. Massachusetts won a $250,000 settlement from Direct American Marketers after the company led a number of entrants into thinking each had won $7,500. Over 15,000 respondents paid approximately $15.92 per call to 900 numbers to confirm nonexistent winnings.

Asking sweepstake respondents to call 900 numbers is a common tactic of sweepstake scam artists. Companies ask "winners" to call a 900 telephone number to verify personal information. When the entrant calls the 900 number, the sweepstakes company receives a percentage of the call, netting millions of dollars a day. Investigative journalists have reported that, in some cases, 900 operators are instructed to keep respondents on the phone as long as possible in order to raise costs.

The number of sweepstakes scams has become so extensive that it has taken on international proportions. In July 2001, the Better Business Bureaus in both the United States and Canada warned of a sweepstakes scam asking residents of the two countries to send large amounts of money to an address in Canada. In October 2003, Spain discovered a sweepstakes scam involving American and Canadian victims who were told they had won El Gordo, a legitimate Spanish Christmas sweepstakes. To collect their winnings, some victims traveled to Spain and were bilked out of thousands of dollars.

On December 13, 1999, President Bill Clinton signed the Deceptive Mail Prevention and Enforcement Act (Public Law 106-168), making it illegal to falsely announce that a person has won a sweepstakes or to make it appear that sweepstakes promotions are official government documents. The law also provided civil penalties for sweepstakes promoters who do not include the following information in sweepstake rules and on entry forms: A statement saying that no purchase is necessary to enter and that purchasing products from the company does not improve chances of winning; terms and conditions of the sweepstakes; odds on winning; the quantity, estimated retail value, and nature of each prize; and a schedule of payments for prize winners. Under the law, companies are required to

remove the name of anyone from their lists requesting them to do so, and all sweepstakes information must contain the name and complete address of the promoter as well as a toll-free number to facilitate requested removals. The United States Postal Service was given the authority to prosecute offenses and to levy fines as high as $2.0 million for sweepstakes fraud.

The Federal Trade Commission has established the 900 Number Rule, mandating the inclusion of an introductory message that notifies the entrant of the odds of winning the sweepstakes or how sweepstakes odds are calculated. Advertisements for 900 numbers are required to include: the total cost of calls whenever a flat fee is charged, a per-minute charge where applicable, the range of fees where different rates are applicable, and costs for any transferred 900 number calls. The print size of this information must be at least half the size of the 900 number in the advertisement.

SEE ALSO

mail fraud; telemarketing fraud; internet fraud; scams; Better Business Bureaus.

BIBLIOGRAPHY. Genevieve Anton, "Colorado Attorney General to Crack Down on Sweepstakes Scams," *Colorado Springs Gazette* (November 1, 1999; James Blair, "Post Office's G-Men: Cutting Crime Through The Mail," *Christian Science Monitor* (September 10, 1998); Chuck Grassley, "Crack Down on Sweepstakes Scams," Federal Document Clearing House Press Release (August 20, 1999); Maryrose J. McMahon, "Sweepstakes Scandals," *Consumer's Research Magazine* (September 1995); John Nicol and Jock Ferguson, "Phone Scams," *Maclean's* (October 19, 1998); Dan Rather, "Consumers Warned of Sweepstakes Scams," CBS Evening News (January 3, 2003); "Relatives Object to Sweepstakes Ads in Cemeteries," *Marketing News* (August 18, 2003); "Spain Breaks Up Sweepstakes Fraud Ring," *Community CustomWire* (October 14, 2003).

ELIZABETH PURDY, PH.D.
INDEPENDENT SCHOLAR

Switzerland

A NUMBER OF BOOKS and movies have depicted Swiss banks as the ideal place to hide money from inquisitive Internal Revenue Service agents, criminal prosecutors, or rightful owners of stolen funds. In common with other tax havens, Switzerland levies minimal taxes and encourages large investments by foreign interests. Switzerland has the additional advantage of strict laws on banking security. Swiss law establishes criminal penalties for those who irresponsibly, either through direct action or negligence, violate banking secrecy.

While it is possible to place money in bank accounts in Switzerland that are known to most bank employees only through numbers or passwords, bank officials have always known the names of account holders. In order to provide some protection for themselves, Swiss banks are restricted to opening numbered accounts only for those foreigners who are already customers of Swiss banks or who have passed a rigorous screening process of interviews and reference checks. Because of its banking laws, Switzerland has become one of the leading financial powers in the world.

On January 1, 1983, International Mutual Assistance in Criminal Matters (IMAC) took effect in Switzerland. The law extended the rights of foreign investigators and gave foreign prosecutors the same powers as Swiss prosecutors within Switzerland. IMAC also made it easier for foreign countries to pursue income-tax evaders. Switzerland has historically been the recipient of funds garnered through a number of means used to avoid paying taxes: under-invoicing, which allows firms to hide profits from sales by underreporting them; compensation, which depends on the practice of using third parties in over-invoicing schemes; transferring negotiable assets directly to Swiss banks; and fraudulent accounting, which allows firms to claim losses while depositing hidden profits in Swiss banks. Switzerland has cooperated with other nations in preventing Swiss banks from being used in illegal activities.

Beginning in 1998, Swiss law has considered it a criminal offense for Swiss bankers to refuse to name the sources of wealth behind numbered accounts and has forced bankers to identify any "end beneficiaries" connected to accounts opened by other parties. In addition to Swiss bankers, Switzerland also forces attorneys, stockbrokers, and employees of other financial institutions to comply with the requirement to report suspicions of money laundering. Changes in Swiss banking laws in 1998 arose partly from a banking scandal concerning the Nigerian dictator Sani Abacha in which

banks all over the world had been involved in the deposit of approximately $3 billion of Nigerian funds. Both the Abacha family and Nigeria claimed the funds. Nineteen Swiss banks had accepted more than $660 million from Abacha. Even though the banks had suspected money laundering, they did accept the money. The Swiss Federal Banking Commission particularly criticized Crédit Suisse, Crédit Agricole Indosuez, Union Bancaire Privée, and MM Warburg for failing to run sufficient checks on the Abacha accounts. In 2001, the commission ruled that Swiss banks could not justify their actions by claiming that the money had come from reputable intermediaries, or by insisting that the Abacha family had provided "glowing references."

NAZI TIES

Switzerland's history of banking secrecy arose legitimately from Nazi leader Adolf Hitler's attempt to commandeer the assets of Jews who escaped Germany or who were annihilated during the Holocaust during World War II. Unfortunately, Swiss banking secrecy and the chaos of the Holocaust allowed Swiss banks to hold the money for over 50 years. On August 13, 1998, Switzerland announced a payment of $1.25 billion to be distributed among approximately 100,000 Jews who either survived the Holocaust or who were descendants of those who died. Many people believe that Swiss banks are still holding large amounts of money that should rightfully be theirs. While the original intent of Swiss banking secrecy was laudable, Swiss banks have often become the repository for goods received through fraudulent endeavors such as arms smuggling, narcotics trafficking, computer fraud and theft, consumer fraud, circumvention of export controls, corporate takeovers, and bank frauds.

U.S. tax laws require American citizens who have deposits of over $10,000 in foreign banks to report those deposits to the Internal Revenue Service. Specific agreements with the United States requires Swiss banks to render "unlimited" assistance to representatives of the American government who are pursuing violators of crimes that are also punishable under Swiss law. The issue with using Swiss banks as tax havens is that, in Switzerland, income-tax invasion is a misdemeanor. Changes in Swiss law in 1982 did, however, prohibit all banks from maintaining accounts for individuals and companies that the banks suspect of knowingly using their Swiss accounts to assist in tax evasion. Critics of the attempt to stop Americans from using tax havens argue that the United States should not tax citizens who live outside the United States. This rationale is used to defend the practice of depending on tax havens to shield wealthy Americans from exorbitantly high taxes. In truth, some people will always think that tax rates are too high and will spend a good deal of time finding ways to circumvent paying the government.

SEE ALSO
bank fraud; tax evasion; offshore entities.

BIBLIOGRAPHY. Richard H. Blum, *Offshore Haven Banks, Trusts, and Companies* (Praeger, 1984); Richard B. Miller, *Tax Haven Investing: A Guide to Offshore Banking and Investment Opportunities* (Probus Publishing, 1998); Richard C. Morais, "The Myth of Swiss Bank Secrecy," *Forbes* (November 12, 2001); Jerome Schneider, *Using An Offshore Bank for Profit, Privacy, and Tax Protection* (WFI Publishing, 1982); British Broadcasting Company, "Swiss Banks Rapped over Abacha Loot," www.news.bbc.co.uk (2003).

ELIZABETH PURDY, PH.D.
INDEPENDENT SCHOLAR

T

Tailhook Scandal

THE TAILHOOK Association is a private organization whose membership includes active duty, reserve, and retired U.S. Marine Corps and Navy flyers, defense contractors, and others. The Tailhook symposium, a reunion of flyers, began in 1956. It moved from San Diego, California, to Las Vegas, Nevada, in 1963, becoming more than a reunion by adding seminars and professional development activities. From the initial symposium, the U.S. Navy and defense contractors provided significant support to the annual meeting, and the board of directors and president were customarily active and retired naval flyers. As of 1992, the membership consisted of 10 corporations and over 15,000 individuals.

The activities of the association came under close examination in 1993 when Navy Lieutenant Paula Coughlin publicly disclosed on ABC News what had transpired at the Tailhook convention she attended. Coughlin was a helicopter pilot and admiral's aid. Even if she knew that there was wild partying at the Tailhook conventions, she thought she was "one of the guys." That is, until she stepped off the hotel elevator into the gauntlet of officers who grabbed at her body and clothing and made raucous comments. As it happened she was one of many, male and female, who suffered the same indignities.

It didn't help that Admiral John W. Snyder acknowledged her objection by saying, "That's what you get when you go on the third deck full of drunk aviators."

Coughlin filed charges, got tired of the delays in official channels, and went public. After seven months, the Naval Investigative Service and the inspector general reported that they had investigated 140 cases of misconduct. Tailhook was a debauch, with 80 to 90 victims. H. Lawrence Garrett III, secretary of the navy, ordered the navy and marines to begin disciplinary action against 70, including 50 charged with forcing women to run the gauntlet and six accused of obstructing the investigation. The secretary and Chief of Naval Operations Frank Kelso were at Tailhook but failed to intercede. Both denied being aware of the harassment, but when witnesses placed them near the gauntlet, Garrett resigned immediately and Kelso retired early when the Senate, by a 54 to 43 vote, allowed him to retire with his four admiral stars intact.

Kelso and Garrett had previously tried to improve women's status, to open opportunity, to discourage sexual harassment. And in 1992, Kelso had sought Senatorial permission for women to fly in combat. Tailhook undid all of that.

Immediate damage was extensive. Coughlin's boss, Snyder, was relieved of duty for ignoring her complaints. Three admirals were censured, a career-ending black mark, for not stopping the behavior. Thirty more admirals got letters of caution put into their permanent records. And more than three dozen captains and commanders and marine colonels received fines or letters of censure or reprimand. In total, 117 officers were implicated in one improper behavior or another; only 10 junior grade officers received letters of admonition or fines. There were innocent bystanders, too. One commander was unfairly denied promotion in 1995 because he was in Las Vegas at the time; he was not however at Tailhook, and a court of inquiry exonerated him.

MANHANDLING

Coughlin described her manhandling and harassment by drunken male officers, and the ramifications widened quickly. The story spread, forcing some senior officers into retirement and effectively ending the careers of others. It also generated a controversial investigation. During her testimony, Coughlin came under attack because of discrepancies in her testimony and a lack of corroborating witnesses. Interviewees could not remember or chose not to testify. The investigation ended inconclusively.

Coughlin and six other victims sued the Hilton hotel and the association. The Tailhook Association settled out of court, and Coughlin won $1.7 million in compensatory damages and $5 million in punitive damages, later cut by the judge who removed the Tailhook settlement and reduced the punitive damages to $3.9 million, three times the compensatory. The next chief of naval operations, Michael Boorda, attempted to assist Coughlin by moving her into his office, Naval Personnel. Coughlin resigned in 1995, and the Hilton hotel appealed.

Optimists believed that Coughlin's exposure of Tailhook made the navy unable to pretend that sexual harassment and sexual crimes were not a problem. This case was the beginning of the stepping forward of military women and the exposure of sex discrimination and other abuses that had been occurring since the end of the draft in 1973, and the active recruitment of women.

The increase of women from only 1 percent of the force, and the demands of women for equal opportunity made virtually all jobs unisex (excluding only direct combat, and that was tenuous). The military was stressed by the changes, and the logical culmination was Tailhook. The other services also became more aggressive in tracking such claims.

Meanwhile, at the Air Force Academy, a pattern of comparable behavior persisted, and the services periodically had flare-ups of sexually inappropriate behavior. Tailhook remained controversial a decade later, with defenders of the services and the "old boy culture" finding fault with Coughlin, accusing her of behavior detrimental to the navy and marines, and of distortion of the events for her own advantage. The tensions released by the inclusion of women in virtually every aspect of the military in significant numbers remained unalleviated despite 10 years of promised increased vigilance and education and reform.

SEE ALSO
sexual harassment; gender discrimination.

BIBLIOGRAPHY. Cable Network News, "Navy Investigating Alleged Misconduct at Latest Tailhook Convention," www.cnn.com (August 25, 2000); Elizabeth Frost-Knappman and Kathryn Cullen-DuPont, eds., *Women's Rights on Trial* (Gale, 1997); Maryland Institute for Technology in the Humanities, Women's Studies Database, www.mith2.umd.edu (2003); "A Tale of Two Paulas," www.militarycorruption.com (2003); Office of the OSD Inspector General, *The Tailhook Report: The Official Inquiry Into The Events Of Tailhook 91* (St. Martin's Press, 1993); Public Broadcasting Service, "Tailhook," www.pbs.org (2003).

JOHN H. BARNHILL, PH.D.
INDEPENDENT SCHOLAR

tampons and toxic shock

DOCTOR JAMES K. TODD of the University of Colorado first identified Toxic Shock Syndrome (TSS) in 1978. TSS is a type of blood poisoning caused by the release of toxins from the growth of bacteria. TSS develops from a common bacterium, staphylococcus aureus, which can live on the skin and in the nose, armpit, groin, or vagina.

Though the disease is rare, it can be fatal. Symptoms of TSS include high sudden fever, muscle aches, vomiting, diarrhea, rashes, rapid pulse, fatigue, sore throat, dizziness, fainting, and a drop in blood pressure. Although TSS can arise from wounds or infections and is seen in some men, it normally manifests in women 30 years old and younger. The most common cause of TSS is tied to the use of super absorbent tampons which trap the bacteria and act as a breeding ground when left in place for extended periods.

Super absorbent tampons were being marketed by numerous companies in the mid-1970s, including Procter & Gamble, Playtex, Tampax, Kimberly Clark, and Johnson & Johnson. Initial concerns about the tampons were based on anecdotal evidence and appeared in the absence of scientific research. Court documents suggest, however, that manufacturers were aware of the link between the tampons and TSS but continued to market the dangerous product.

Matters worsened for the manufacturers when the Centers for Disease Control (CDC) entered the fray in 1980. The CDC's investigation focused primarily on the Rely brand tampon. Ultimately, the CDC identified 55 fatal cases and 1,066 nonfatal cases of TSS, though companies continued to sell the product without warnings of the possible risks. A CDC study showed that 70 percent of the victims of TSS reportedly used Rely tampons. Eventually 38 deaths were attributed to the tampon.

Procter & Gamble's ultra-absorbent tampon, Rely, was introduced in 1974. The company released the new, improved product with claims of having conducted extensive research on its safety. Rely was the only tampon that used a highly absorbent synthetic material, polyester foam. The corporation introduced the Rely tampon in a fiercely competitive market but had hopes of out-selling Tampax, the leading product. Procter & Gamble later claimed that the sales of Rely amounted to less than 1 percent of the company's total consolidated annual revenues of $10.8 billion.

When the Rely tampon first was released in a test market, the company logged more than 100 complaints per month. In 1980, Procter & Gamble sent 60 million sample packages directly to households across the nation.

Rely was voluntarily recalled by the company on September 22, 1980 based on the CDC's studies, finished in June 1980, that linked incidents of TSS with the use of tampons. The cost of the recall to the company was estimated at $75 million and was done only under protest. The company continued to claim that the Rely tampon was not defective and that TSS would continue to occur even after the tampon was removed from the market. The company's agreement with the Food and Drug Administration (FDA) also included a massive advertising campaign that began in October with ads on 600 television stations, 350 radio stations, and 1,200 newspapers designed to reach all American households. The agreement included a detailed plan to provide consumer refunds, and prohibited the sale of the tampons overseas or in the United States without prior FDA approval. Nonetheless, Procter & Gamble faced some 400 civil lawsuits.

ON TRIAL

In the first public trial against Procter & Gamble, a federal jury found the company guilty of negligence for failing to conduct adequate testing and for marketing a dangerous product. Deletha Dawn Lampshire, an 18-year-old student at University of Denver, sought $25 million in damages after using Rely in May 1980. Procter & Gamble argued that the plaintiff had the flu (many TSS symptoms are similar to the flu) and denied any definitive link between Rely and TSS. The company also claimed to have acted in a responsible manner by removing the product from the market after solid, scientific evidence of the danger emerged.

The jury found the company negligent but awarded no compensatory or punitive damages to the plaintiff. Both sides in the Lampshire case filed an appeal following the judgment and eventually settled out of court for an undisclosed amount to avoid a second trial. The second major lawsuit against Procter & Gamble was filed by Michael Kehm who sought $30 million in damages after his wife died. Patricia Kehm was a 25-year-old housewife and mother in Cedar Rapids, Iowa, who first used Rely tampons on September 2, 1980. She died four days later. In response to the lawsuit, the company used its multi-million dollar litigation fund to hire a slew of attorneys and scientific experts to defend the Rely tampon. Kehm was awarded a mere $300,000.

Liability for super absorbent tampons haunted other companies as well. A jury in South Carolina found Playtex guilty of recklessness for failing to warn women of the risks. Twenty-four-year-old Linda J. Wooten sued the company after she developed TSS. The jury found that the company had failed to warn women, although Playtex had launched its own advertising campaign that advised consumers of the TSS risks and inserted flyers in its tampon boxes. The plaintiff was awarded $3,870 in compensatory damages and $15,500 in punitive damages; though the award was relatively small it was the first that involved punitive compensation against Playtex.

In February 1985, Betty O'Gilvie's family was awarded $10 million in punitive damages. The jurors were said to have expressed their "outrage" over the company's actions by imposing a high award after finding that Playtex caused or contributed to O'Gilvie's death from TSS. The 10th Circuit U.S. Court of Appeals determined that Playtex's warning simply mentioning an association between TSS and tampon use was inadequate. The court also found that Playtex deliberately disregarded studies and medical reports linking super absorbent tampons and increased risk of TSS while other manufacturers were redesigning or withdrawing the tampons.

Playtex, in fact, deliberately sought to profit from the situation, according to the court, and therefore, was "grossly negligent or recklessly indifferent to the rights of others." An internal memorandum showed that Playtex knew the tampon was more absorbent than what was necessary: "Our tampons are similar to automobiles which can achieve a speed of 300 miles an hour, but with which 90 percent of the drivers will never exceed 55 miles per hour and the remainder will occasionally drive at speeds up to 90 miles per hour." The memo also noted that by "being obsessed with 'absorbency' we lost sight of the fact that 'leakage' complaints did not decrease as the tampon absorbency potentials were increased. Like the definition of a fanatic, one who redoubles his efforts because he has lost sight of his goals, we then converted our heavier weight tampons to PA fiber, providing even more 'absorbency' and in fact threw in a 3.8 g PA 'Super Plus' for good measure."

Lynette West filed suit against Johnson & Johnson after she contracted TSS using the ob brand tampon. Her case alleged that the tampons were defectively designed, that the instructions were inadequate, and that the company was negligent in testing the product. A jury awarded West $500,000 in compensatory damages and $ 10 million in punitive damages. The trial court granted a motion for a new trial on the basis of excessive damages unless West accepted a reduction to $100,000 in compensatory damages and $1 million in punitive damages. During the trial, evidence was presented that, in 1975, Johnson & Johnson began receiving complaints of adverse reactions to ob tampons from consumers and physicians. According to one witness, consumers complained of "irritation, infection, vaginitis, discharge, pain, burning, and rash." Some women complained that the fibers remained in the vagina when the tampon was removed. Others grumbled that the tampons were difficult to remove and in some cases, had to be removed by a doctor. A physician wrote that use of ob tampons had caused severe vaginitis in his daughter, and requested that the company examine its product to "shed some light on the problem."

Consumer complaints attributed bladder infections, vaginal infections, pelvic inflammatory disease to the use of ob tampons. One physician complained that ob tampons swelled too much in the vaginas of young women with intact hymens. Between 1975 and February 1980, the company received approximately 150 complaints, yet Johnson & Johnson made no effort to conduct studies on potential risks. In direct contrast to medical advice, instructions on the ob tampons stated: "Changing tampons too frequently can be uncomfortable," and that users should "try not to change your tampon until it's nearly saturated."

The number of TSS cases has reduced dramatically since the 1980s when super absorbent tampons were removed from the market, though about half the cases reported are still related to tampon use in young women. According to the CDC, in 1997 only five confirmed TSS cases were connected to menstrual-related incidents compared to 814 in 1980. The FDA now requires that all tampon boxes carry a warning that describes the link between TSS and tampon use. The FDA also regulates tampons as medical devices and regulates the absorbency ratings.

SEE ALSO

consumer deaths; Procter & Gamble; juries and wards; unsafe products.

BIBLIOGRAPHY. Tom Riley, *The Price of Life: One Woman's Death from Toxic Shock* (Adler & Adler, 1986); Stephen M. Rosoff, Henry N. Pontell, and Robert Tillman, *Profit Without Honor: White-Collar Crime and the Looting of America* (Prentice Hall, 1998); Joan E. Steinman "A Legal Sampler: Women, Medical Care, and Mass Tort Litigation," *Chicago Kent Law Review* (1992); Alecia

Swasy, *Soap Opera: The Inside Story of Procter & Gamble* (Times Books, 1993).

MARY DODGE, PH.D.
UNIVERSITY OF COLORADO, DENVER

tariff crimes

TARIFF CRIMES REFER broadly to a range of illegal practices associated with the non-payment of one or more of the various taxes that are levied on goods traded across national borders. Specifically, tariffs are taxes usually applied to imports based on a percentage of the value of the product in question. Along with a complex range of other subsidies, duties, and customs (referred to hereafter as trade crimes), they constitute the chief means for national governments to control and benefit from trade.

Crimes against trading laws and regulations may include outright smuggling of goods to evade tariffs and customs, fraudulent reporting of the amount and value of products, and breaches of quota restrictions. Since tariffs are set by national governments in conjunction with other economic regulations, the nature and degree of customs crimes has varied in different jurisdictions and periods according to economic and political changes. It is necessary to emphasize, therefore, that infractions of trading laws cannot be separated from the differing histories of national states themselves.

U.S. DUTIES AND TARIFFS

In industrializing countries such as the United States so-called protectionist policies, in which high tariffs were purposely applied to foster industry and garner revenue, were extensive. Soon after the American Revolution, individual states such as Pennsylvania and Massachusetts levied duties to protect their infant textile industries. These duties were codified in the first federal Tariff Act of 1789 which also established the U.S. Customs Service. In addition, this pioneering piece of legislation provided for tariffs for hemp, nails, glass, and iron manufactures. In this period, revenue from tariffs was the principal source of government finances for the struggling American government. Even as American industry began to dominate in many sectors on an international scale from the 1880s to the 1920s, the U.S. government maintained an extensive tariff system although there were ongoing efforts to establish free trade agreements with Canada. Tariffs were regarded as an important step in the process of economic modernization and national identity. In this context, attempts by smugglers and merchants to skirt tariffs were common and widespread.

During the 1920s and 1930s when alcohol was prohibited, the U.S. concluded a number of bilateral treaties to allow the Customs service to board private vessels. This may have had some deterrent effect on cross-border crimes on a number of products. Yet alcohol smuggling itself skyrocketed during Prohibition, especially between Canada and the United States.

The high tariffs enacted by the United States in the context of the Great Depression of the 1930s, such as the Smoot-Hawley Tariff Act, helped export the economic crisis to the rest of the world as well as to provide economic incentives for smuggling and tariff avoidance. With incomes rapidly declining, however, the market for both legal and illegal goods during the Depression contracted.

GATT AND NAFTA

After the World War II, the General Agreement on Tariffs and Trade (GATT) was established as an international body to monitor merchandise trade and foster reductions in trade restrictions. While there was some progress toward liberalization of trade, especially between developed capitalist countries, many nations continued to use tariffs as a means to develop their own industry and earn much-needed finances for government coffers. More recently, the North American Free Trade Agreement between Canada, Mexico and the United States (NAFTA, 1991) and the European Economic Union (EU, 1961) have restricted opportunities for trade crimes as tariffs have been lowered across the board.

Two high-value commodities, cigarettes and alcohol, have nonetheless continued to worry customs authorities in Canada and the United States. Canada is the largest trading partner of the United States and vice-versa; they share a large border and a long history of intimate trading relations. Excise taxes on cigarettes introduced by Canada as part of a public health campaign against smoking in 1998 led to a massive differential between the price of cigarettes in both countries.

As a result, a huge incentive was created for Canadians to illegally purchase cigarettes manufactured in the United States, or Canadian-made cigarettes that were exported abroad and resold in Canada. The potential profits of such illegal transactions were enormous. One single trip across the border to sell 50 cartons of cigarettes could result in profits of almost $15,000. By 1993, 100 million cartons of contraband cigarettes had been consumed in Canada, constituting nearly one in three cigarettes smoked by Canadians.

A similar pattern developed with alcohol. The Canadian government estimated that differences in the price of alcohol between the two countries had led to a 2,250 percent increase in smuggling over the three-year period from 1991 to 1993. Up to 15 percent of all alcohol drunk from 1991 to 1996 was illegally imported from the United States without the payment of customs duties. Only with the reduction of the excise tax, the application of an export tax, and a substantial increase in funding for Canadian customs under an Anti-Smuggling Initiative were the problems of the illegal sale of alcohol and cigarettes resolved.

Modern trade crimes in the United States occur in a myriad of ways. Many products imported into the country are subject to a very complicated system of tariffs and duties which make it practically difficult to regulate. In the huge U.S. market for imported steel, for instance, businesses have used falsified documents and other illegal practices to undercut the competitiveness of U.S.-made steel. Importers, for example, altered shipping documents to make it appear that products are different from what they really are. In this way, high import duties on particular steel products were avoided. Customs inspection of steel products, moreover, were hampered by the fact that many different products look substantially the same and can only be distinguished by time-consuming and expensive methods.

CUSTOMS FRAUD

In recent years, the food import industry has also been subject to increasing scrutiny for customs evasion. In one of the largest customs fraud cases ever, the directors of a California company were sentenced to jail and forced to pay $93 million in back taxes after it was discovered that tens of millions of dollars in imported foods were falsely reported to evade duties and taxes.

Other recent examples of trade crime include: 1) illegal trans-shipments in which imports made in one country are sold through another country to the United States to avoid import quotas; 2) the pirating of U.S. products by foreign importers; 3) undervaluation of goods to pay less duty; 4) the illegal discounting of products (dumping); 5) transfer pricing, where companies undervalue imported parts which will be assembled in the United States; and 6) violation of rules of origin regulations which favor countries such as Canada and Mexico under NAFTA. Most of these types of violations have become openly political as domestic manufacturers pressure the government to crack down on what they see as "unfair" competition.

With the accelerating globalization of economies in recent decades, customs fraud has become acutely international and much more complex. A widening gap between rich, developed countries and poor, developing nations has resulted in a shifting political economy of trade crime. The unequal distribution of wealth between countries has led to a situation in which developing nations have become centers of international trade crime solely because illegal practices are regarded as the only viable economic activity available. Governments in countries with weak economies often overlook, or are involved in smuggling, or do not have the resources to combat trade violations. Countries such as Paraguay, China, Russia and other East European countries have been singled out in this regard. On the other hand, many developing nations charge, with some justification, that despite the rhetoric of free trade, many rich nations have put up unfair trade barriers that force many businesses to skirt the rules.

The future of trade crime and measures to combat it will continue to be shaped by large political and economic forces such as globalization, inequality between nations, shifting international trade policies, the growing power of trading blocs such as NAFTA and the EU and new methods of law enforcement.

SEE ALSO

corruption; bribery; Foreign Corrupt Practices Act; tax evasion; corporate dumping.

BIBLIOGRAPHY. William P. Alford, "When is China Paraguay? An Examination of the Application of Antidumping and Countervailing Duty Laws of the United

States to China and other 'Nonmarket Economy Nations'," *Southern California Law Review* (v.79, 1987-1988); W.A. Cole, "Trends in 18th-Century Smuggling," *The Economic History Review* (v.10/3, 1958); K. Gillespie and J.B. McBride, "Smuggling in Emerging Markets: Global Implications," *Columbia Journal of World Business* (v.31, 1996); Cynthia Hody, *The Politics of Trade: American Political Development and Foreign Economic Policy* (University Press of New England, 1996); Robert Isaak, *Managing World Economic Change: International Political Economy* (Prentice Hall, 1995); Ruth Jamieson, Nigel South and Ian Taylor, "Economic Liberalization and Cross-Border Crime: The North American Free Trade Area and Canada's Border with the U.S.A. Parts 1-2," *International Journal of the Sociology of the Law* (v.26, 1998); Robert Guy Matthews, "Steel Smugglers Pull Wool Over the Eyes of Customs Agents to Enter U.S. Market," *Wall Street Journal* (November 1, 2001); Alan Milward, "Tariffs as Constitutions," *The International Politics of Surplus Capacity* (Allyn & Unwin, 1981); Bryan D. Palmer, *Cultures of Darkness: Night Travels in the Histories of Transgression* (Monthly Review Press, 2000); "Two Plead Guilty in Massive Tax, Customs Fraud Case," Department of Justice, www.usdoj.gov (2003).

Sean Purdy, Ph.D.
Queen's University, Canada

tax evasion

TAX EVASION IS defined as "the willful attempt to defeat or circumvent the tax law in order to illegally reduce one's tax liability." The crime of tax evasion, defined within 26 U.S.C. §7201 and amended in 1984 under 18 U.S.C. §3623, carries the severest criminal penalties and requires the greatest burden of proof on behalf of the U.S. government in comparison to any other tax crime.

The exact statutory language of 26 U.S.C. §7201, entitled "Attempt To Defeat or Evade Tax" reads, "Any person who willfully attempts in any manner to evade or defeat any tax imposed by this title or payment thereof shall, in addition to other penalties provided by law, be guilty of a felony and, upon conviction thereof, shall be fined not more than $100,000 ($500,000 in the case of a corporation) or imprisoned not more than 5 years, or both, together with the costs of prosecution." The Criminal Fines Enforcement Act of 1984, codified at 18

U.S.C. §3623, substantially increased the maximal permissible fines for both misdemeanors and felonies as set forth in §7201. For felony offenses committed after December 31, 1984, the maximum permissible fine is $250,000 for an individual and $500,000 for a corporation. Moreover, if any person derives financial gain from the offense or if the offense results in a financial loss to a person other than the defendant, "the defendant may be fined not more than the greater of twice the gross gain or twice the gross loss."

According to the U.S. Supreme Court in *Sansone v. United States* (1965) §7201 contains two distinct criminal offenses, "the willful attempt to evade or defeat the assessment of a tax; and the willful attempt to evade or defeat the payment of a tax." Evasion or defeat of an assessment involves an attempt by the taxpayer to prevent the government from determining her true tax liability while evasion or defeat of payment involves an attempt by a taxpayer to evade payment of that liability.

ATTEMPTED EVASION

According to the Internal Revenue Service §7201 contains one distinct criminal offense "attempted evasion of any tax," which can be committed by evading the assessment of a tax or by evading the payment of that tax. Nevertheless, §7201 has been described as the "capstone of a system of sanctions that were intended to induce prompt and forthright fulfillment of every duty under the income tax law and to provide a penalty suitable to every degree of delinquency."

Most commonly, a taxpayer may attempt to evade or defeat the payment of a tax liability by filing a fraudulent tax return that omits or understates taxable income and/or claims deductions to which the taxpayer is not entitled. This falls under the category evasion of assessment. Evasion of payment occurs when a taxpayer attempts to evade payment of her tax liability altogether. Evasion of payment occurs only after the existence of a tax liability has been established. Establishment of a tax liability generally occurs in one of three ways: the taxpayer reports the amount of the taxes owed; the Internal Revenue Service (IRS) assesses the amount of taxes owed; or by operation of law on the date the return is due the taxpayer fails to file a tax return and the government can prove a tax deficiency. Merely failing to pay assessed taxes, however, does not constitute evasion of payment. The taxpayer must have taken some affirmative action. Generally, affirmative acts associated with evasion of payment involve concealment of the taxpayer's ability to pay taxes, dealing in currency, or the removal of assets beyond the reach of the IRS such as placing assets in the names others.

ELEMENTS OF PROSECUTION

To obtain a conviction for tax evasion under §7201 the government is required to prove three elements: the existence of a tax deficiency; an affirmative act constituting evasion or attempted evasion of the tax; and willfulness. As in any criminal prosecution, the government must prove each element beyond a reasonable doubt. Failure to prove any one of the three elements will most likely result in an acquittal.

The first element that must be proven by the government is the existence of a tax deficiency. Therefore, the government must prove beyond a reasonable doubt that the defendant had greater taxable income than reported. Some courts have required the tax deficiency to be substantial. Tax evasion cases, however, are not tax collection cases so the government need not prove the exact amount owed only that a tax deficiency exists. Furthermore, since taxes are paid annually, each tax year is considered a separate offense.

There are two methods of proof used for establishing the existence of a tax deficiency: the direct or specific item method and the indirect method. The direct or specific item method is considered the simplest and most accurate means of proving a tax deficiency. Under this method, the government's case is based on specific, identifiable transactions such as a defendant's books and records providing direct evidence revealing the fact that the defendant has failed to report all taxable transactions, or testimony from a third party revealing money paid to the defendant for goods or services. Proof of unreported taxable income by means of the direct or specific item method, however, is extremely difficult and often impossible for the government to obtain.

Alternatively, the government may prove the existence of a tax deficiency by using indirect methods such as the net worth method, the cash expenditures method, and the bank deposits method. The most common indirect method used by the government to prove the existence of a tax deficiency is the net worth method. The method examines the defendant's net worth or net value of all the defendant's assets on the last day of the tax year immediately preceding the first prosecution year. The defendant's nondeductible expenditures and living expenses are added to these increases. If the resulting figure is substantially greater than the taxable income reported by the defendant for that year, the government claims the excess represents unreported taxable income. To be successful using the net worth method, the government must establish the defendant's net worth at the beginning of the year with "reasonable certainty."

Once an increase in the defendant's net worth has been proven with reasonable certainty, the government must introduce evidence supporting the conjecture that the unreported income is taxable. The government can do so by establishing a "likely source" for the unexplained income or by negating all possible nontaxable sources of income. Moreover, if the defendant offers an explanation for the source of the unreported income, the government has a duty to investigate all reasonable explanations offered by the defendant as proscribed by the reasonable leads doctrine.

The reasonable leads doctrine, established by the Supreme Court in *Holland v. United States* (1954), places on the government the duty of "effective negation of reasonable explanations by the taxpayer inconsistent with guilt" and a duty limited to the investigation of "leads reasonably susceptible of being checked, which, if true would establish the defendant's innocence."

To prove a tax deficiency by means of the cash expenditures method, the government must prove that a defendant's expenditures have exceeded the defendant's reported taxable income. This method is typically used in cases where the defendant does not purchase durable assets but rather consumable items such as vacations, lavish dinner parties, and entertainment. In most cases the defendants are gamblers or involved in the distribution of narcotics. As in the net worth method, the government must introduce evidence supporting the conjecture that the unreported income is taxable.

To prove a tax deficiency by means of the bank deposit method, the government totals the amount of all cash expenditures and all deposits made to the defendant's bank account. The government then simply compares this figure to the defendant's reported taxable income. If the total of cash expenditures and deposits is substantially greater than the defendant's reported taxable income, the excess represents the defendant's unreported taxable income. As in the other indirect methods of proof, the government must introduce evidence supporting the conjecture that the unreported income is taxable.

The second element the government must prove for a conviction under § 7201 is "an affirmative act constituting evasion or attempted evasion of a tax." In other words, the government must prove that the defendant purposely and willfully attempted to evade or defeat a tax payment. The Supreme Court, in *Spies v. United States* (1943), set forth illustrations of conduct, termed "badges of fraud," from which willful attempt could be inferred.

The examples provided by the court were: "keeping a double set of books, making false entries or alterations, or false invoices or documents, destruction of books and records, concealment of assets or covering up sources of income, handling of one's affairs to avoid making the records usual in transactions of the kind, and any conduct, the likely of which would be to mislead or conceal."

The final element the government must prove for a conviction under §7201 is willfulness. The element of willfulness can be the most difficult element to prove since an admission or confession is very seldom available. Therefore, the government generally relies on the defendant's conduct, past record of compliance, knowledge, and education. Examples of willfulness include: failure to provide an accountant with complete and accurate information; making false statements to agents of the IRS; keeping a double set of books; and extensive use of currency or cashiers checks.

The Supreme Court struggled for 43 years to define willfulness. It first attempted to define willfulness in *United States v. Murdock* (1933). According to the court, willfulness "denoted an act which is intentional, or knowing, or voluntary, as distinguished from accidental." Ten years later in *Spies v. United States* (1943), it interpreted willfulness to mean, "An act committed with bad purpose; without justifiable excuse, stubbornly, obstinately… or with bad faith or evil intent." Finally, the Supreme Court ended the confusion in *United States v. Pomponio* (1976), stating that the earlier courts "assumed that the reference to an evil motive meant something more than the specific intent to violate the law." The court then set forth a standard defini-

The U.S. Supreme Court spent four decades trying to define willfulness in tax evasion charges.

tion of the term simply defining willfulness as a "voluntary, intentional violation of a known legal duty."

DEFENSES

After the government has proved beyond a reasonable doubt the three elements necessary to obtain a conviction for tax evasion under §7201, a defendant may assert a number of defenses refuting any one of the three elements proven by the government. The defenses typically used to refute the government's case include: proving the lack of a tax deficiency; proving the lack of willfulness; third party liability or reliance; selective prosecution; and cash on hand or cash hoard defense.

A conviction may be avoided under § 7201 if a defendant can successfully refute the government's claim that a tax deficiency exists by proving that the additional income received was in fact nontaxable in nature. Nontaxable sources include gifts, loans, and inheritances. Moreover, in cases involving the indirect method of proof, a defendant may refute the tax deficiency by identifying errors in the government's analysis or claim that the government failed to fully investigate any explanation offered by the defendant.

A conviction may also be avoided under §7201 if a defendant can prove that the tax deficiency was evaded in a non-willful manner. According to the Supreme Court in *Cheeks v. United States* (1991), a good faith belief that one is not violating the tax law negates the element of willfulness. Furthermore, willfulness can be refuted when there is uncertainty in the tax law. In 1921, the Supreme Court held that a criminal law that fails to establish an ascertainable standard of guilt is unconstitutional on two grounds. First, the statute violates the Due Process Clause of the 5th Amendment. Second, it violates the guarantee of being informed of the nature and causes of the criminal charges brought against the defendant as proscribed by the 6th Amendment.

A conviction may also be avoided under §7201 if a defendant shifts the responsibility of a tax deficiency to a third party such as an attorney or accountant. Reliance on the advice of a third party does establish a complete defense and does negate the element of willfulness, which is a "substantial part of the charge." To be successful using the defense of third party reliance, a defendant must show that he consulted with a competent attorney, made a full and accurate report of all material facts of which he had knowledge, and then acted strictly in accordance with the advice provided to him by the attorney or accountant.

A defendant may claim the defense of selective prosecution to avoid a conviction under §7201. When a defendant claims selective prosecution, she claims that the government's decision to prosecute is based on reasons forbidden by the U.S. Constitution, and in particular the Due Process Clause of the 5th Amendment. The Due Process Clause forbids prosecutions based on "race, religion, or other arbitrary classification."

To be successful, the defendant must clearly present sufficient evidence showing that federal prosecutorial policy has both a discriminatory effect and discriminatory purpose. The mere belief or suspicion on behalf of the defendant is insufficient.

Lastly, the defendant may avoid a conviction under §7201 by claiming the cash on hand defense, commonly referred to as the cash hoard defense. Cash on hand refers to the money that a defendant carries in his pockets as well as money or cash available to the defendant, which is not deposited in a bank or other financial institution. Typically, a cash hoard defense is based on a claim that the defendant received gifts from family members, friends, or an inheritance, received in an earlier year and spent during the prosecution period. The Supreme Court has defined the cash hoard defense as a "taxpayer's claim that the net worth increase shown by the government's statement is in reality not an increase at all because of the existence of substantial cash on hand at the starting point... asserting that the cache is made up of many years' savings, which for various reasons were hidden and not expended until the prosecution period." The government has great difficulty in refuting the cash hoard defense. One way the government does refute the cash hoard defense is by proving to the court that the family member or friend implicated lacks the resources to give the defendant the amount claimed.

HIGH-PROFILE TAX EVASION

Federal taxes are the principal source of revenue for the U.S. government. The federal tax system is based upon the idea of "voluntary compliance." Each person is "expected to account annually for his or her income and deductions and to pay the proper amount of tax." Therefore, in order to foster voluntary compliance, the government must impose taxes that are construed by the American taxpayers as fair and must penalize those who fail to comply. The IRS, a branch of the Department of the Treasury, is responsible for investigating and penalizing those who fail to comply with the system of voluntary compliance.

The Criminal Investigation Unit (CIU) of the IRS is responsible for investigating any potentially criminal violation of the Internal Revenue Code, such as the widespread allegations of tax fraud, including tax evasion, in such a manner that "fosters confidence in the tax system and compliance with the law." Since its inception in 1919, the CIU's conviction rate for federal tax prosecutions has never fallen below 90 percent, a record unmatched in federal law enforcement. The CIU is famous for the financial investigative skills of its special agents; it gained national prominence in 1930 for the conviction of Al Capone, public enemy number one, for income tax evasion. According to the IRS, one of the most effective deterrents in enhancing voluntary compliance in the tax law is by publicly making examples of well-known individuals who fail to comply with the tax law, as was case with Capone.

Between 1988 and 2002, the IRS successfully prosecuted three well-known individuals in the United States for their failure to comply with the tax laws as stipulated within 26 U.S.C. §7201. In April 1988, a federal grand jury indicted Leona Helmsley, a hotel chain executive along with her husband Harold, on 47 counts of attempted tax evasion, conspiracy, filing false tax returns, and mail fraud. The indictment alleged that Helmsley's used various Helmsley-controlled companies to pay for $2.6 million in extravagant restoration improvements to Dunnellen Hall, the couple's 28-room estate in Greenwich, Connecticut.

Her defense suffered immeasurably when a witness testified that Helmsley had boasted, "We don't pay taxes. Only the little people pay taxes."

In a second highly publicized trial, country singer Willie Nelson was found guilty of tax evasion in 1993 and fined $32 million after a criminal investigation revealed that Nelson owed $11 million in back taxes from 1972 to 1983. Moreover, the IRS alleged that Nelson had attempted to hide earnings in a fraudulent tax shelter. The IRS seized Nelson's assets including his 44-acre ranch in order to recoup the $16.7 million Nelson owed in interest and penalties as result of the tax evasion charges. Nelson, who lacked the sufficient resources to satisfy his debt with the Internal Revenue Service, was able to settle the case out of court by agreeing to pay an additional $9 million over a five-year period.

In January 1997, "Hollywood madam" Heidi Fleiss was sentenced to 37 months in prison, fined $400, and ordered to complete 300 hours of community service after being found guilty of tax evasion, pandering, and money laundering. Fleiss, who ran one of the most successful escort services in the United States, reportedly earned millions of dollars and failed to report her income, obtained by improper means, to the IRS. According to District Court Judge Consuelo Marshall described the Fleiss case as "atypical and even the minimum sentence would have been far too harsh," relying on an expert witness who testified that the federal sentencing guidelines for money laundering were drafted with organized criminal enterprises and drug cartels in mind, not madams.

The IRS initiated 3,906 criminal investigations under §7201 for the fiscal year ending 2002. Of the criminal investigations initiated 2,133 were referred for prosecution, 1,926 were convicted, and 1,809 were incarcerated. Voluntary compliance with the tax laws of the United States has declined and according to the IRS, investigating and prosecuting tax crimes is "key in promoting voluntary compliance with the tax laws."

SEE ALSO

offshore banking; offshore entities; United States; Capone, Alphonse; accounting fraud.

BIBLIOGRAPHY. Patricia Morgan, *Procedure and Tax Fraud in a Nutshell* (West Publishing, 1990); Ellen Podgor, *White-Collar Crime in a Nutshell* (West Publishing, 1993); Bryan Garner, ed., *Blacks Law Dictionary* (2003); Department of Justice, "Criminal Tax Manual 1994," (December 15, 1997); Internal Revenue Service, Data Book 2002, Publication 55B, (2003); Larry Seigel, *Criminology* (West Publishing, 1995); Keith Benes, et al., "Tax Violations," *American Criminal Law Review* (v.35, 1998); Ronald Jensen, "Reflections on *United States v. Helmsley*: Should Impossibility be a Defense to Attempted Income Tax Evasion," *Virginia Tax Review* (v.12, 1993); Linda Eads, "From Capone to Boesky: Tax Evasion, "Insider Trading, and Problems of Proof," *California Law Review* (v.79, 1991); Internal Revenue Service, "General Tax Fraud," www.irs.gov (2003); National Archives Records and Administration, www.archives.gov (2003); Leslie Geary, "Tax Troubles of the Rich and Famous," CNN Money (February 20, 2003); ABC News, "Famous Tax Slackers: Famous Celebrities Who Fought the Losing Battle with the Tax Man," abcnews.go.com (2003);

RONALD C. DESNOYERS, JR.
ROGER WILLIAMS UNIVERSITY

Teamsters Pension Fund

THE TEAMSTERS Pension Fund, formally the Central States, Southeast and Southwest Areas Pension Fund, was created in the mid-1950s and came to be known by many as organized crime's bank.

The corrupt use of the fund has been well documented beginning in the 1960s in numerous investigations, commissions, reports, prosecutions and media forums.

The fund gained notoriety because International Brotherhood of Teamsters (IBT) Pension Fund managers would loan money from the fund to organized criminals, usually through straw men, for casinos, hotels, and resorts. The recipients of the fund proceeds included such noteworthy establishments as Las Vegas, Nevada, casinos Circus Circus, Caesar's Palace, the Dunes, and the Sands. So-called finders fees were charged, kickbacks were common, and loans were years delinquent but carried as assets. All the while, organized criminals battled for cuts of the finders fees and other illicit facets of the massive conspiracy.

JIMMY HOFFA

The Central States, Southeast and Southwest Areas Pension Fund was formally set up on March 16, 1955, designed to hold millions (and later billions) of dollars in trust for pensions, life insurance, and disability of Teamsters union members. By 1961, it had assets of approximately $200 million. Infamous IBT leader Jimmy Hoffa used the fund to assist friends in various deals and, more importantly, to court organized criminals who were pleased (and indebted) to have this resource available for their investments. As one observer, Ronald Goldfarb, wryly noted, "the pension fund had become the mob's savings and loan."

Hoffa was convicted of diverting $20 million from the pension fund in a 1964 Chicago case, and sentenced to five years in jail. Teamster corruption did not end with the imprisonment of Hoffa, and underlings took on more prominent roles in the scheme. Furthermore, the fund's value continued to grow. In the mid 1970s, the fund's assets totaled approximately $2.2 billion, and pension payments were almost $325 million per year.

Throughout the 1960s and early 1970s, the Department of Labor, the Internal Revenue Service (IRS) and the U.S. Senate's Permanent Subcommittee on Investigations (PSI) investigated the fund. By 1975, the Department of Labor was the lead investigative body, and thus created its Special Investigations Staff for the sole purpose of exposing the pension fund scandal. Technically, the Labor Department was to coordinate with the IRS and then refer founded cases to the Department of Justice for prosecution. For a variety of reasons, including ambivalence (and possibly corruption) within the Labor Department and the IRS, the investigations stalled as documented in the fall of 1980 by the PSI.

During the 1980 presidential election campaign between Democrat Jimmy Carter and Republican Ronald Reagan, each candidate courted the IBT for its weighty support. The pension fund became a focal point in the IBT's decision on whom to endorse. Following several private meetings with such notorious IBT officials as Frank Fitzsimmons, Roy Williams, and Jackie Presser, the Reagan camp was delighted to know they had won the IBT's support. As described by F.C. Duke Zeller, a Teamsters public relations staff member, the key to their support was Reagan's promise to stall or end the Labor Department's pension fund investigation.

Zeller recalls Presser's impassioned plea to his IBT cohorts to support Reagan: "You Italians, listen up! Especially you Italians! More than anyone else in this room, you should be supporting Reagan! Reagan has agreed to lay off us! The Justice Department will not be on our backs for once!" Following Reagan's victory, the president visited the Teamsters' headquarters and "invited the Teamsters high command to help him select his secretary of labor and other top administration officials," Zeller notes.

Many Reagan critics thought it remarkable that someone being sued by the Labor Department for over $120 million in illegal loans to Las Vegas casinos and gangsters was helping to organize the very department suing him. The Teamsters recommended Raymond J. Donovan for secretary of labor and he became the Reagan nominee and secretary. In the next year, Donovan was asked by the PSI to investigate IBT President Williams regarding "his conduct as a fiduciary of union trust funds." Donovan declined to look into the pension fund scandal, claiming the Labor Department had no authority in the matter.

The legend of the Teamsters Pension Fund, based in large part on real life events, has been promulgated by print media, fiction, and non-fiction authors, and by Hollywood. The 1995 movie *Casino* prominently featured the fund's role in the development of Las Vegas.

SEE ALSO

organized crime; corruption; Reagan, Ronald; fiduciary fraud.

BIBLIOGRAPHY. Steven Brill, *The Teamsters* (Pocket Books, 1979); Victor S. Navasky, *Kennedy Justice* (Atheneum, 1971); Allen Friedman and Ted Schwartz, *Power and Greed: Inside the Teamsters Empire of Corruption* (Franklin Watts, 1989); Ronald Goldfarb, *Perfect Villains, Imperfect Heroes: Robert F. Kennedy's War Against Organized Crime* (Random House, 1995); Dan E. Moldea, *Dark Victory: Ronald Reagan, MCA, and the Mob* (Viking, 1986); James Neff, *Mobbed-Up: Jackie Presser's High-Wire Life in the Teamsters, the Mafia, and the FBI* (Atlantic Monthly Press, 1989); U.S. Senate, Committee on Governmental Affairs, Permanent Subcommittee on Investigations, Oversight Inquiry of the Department of Labor's Investigation of the Central States Pension Fund (Government Printing Office, 1981); F.C. Duke Zeller, *Devil's Pact: Inside the World of the Teamsters* Union (Birch Lane Press, 1996).

SEAN PATRICK GRIFFIN, PH.D.
PENN STATE UNIVERSITY, ABINGTON

Teapot Dome Scandal

WARREN G. HARDING (1865–1923), who is considered by most political scientists and historians to have been one of the worst presidents in the history of the United States, was blamed for the Teapot Dome Scandal, which erupted during the rampant corruption and gaiety of the so-called Roaring Twenties. Although the president was not personally involved in the criminal activities that wrecked his administration, Harding's fierce loyalty to his political cronies and his reluctance to believe in their dishonesty led to his being discredited along with them.

On becoming president, Harding brought what became known as the "Ohio Gang" with him to Washington, D.C. He may have never realized the extent of the corruption practiced by these opportunists who saw the capital as a city ripe for exploitation. While Harding's friends saddled him with a number of scandals, the most serious was Teapot Dome, which came to define the Harding presidency. The scandal involved Harding's cabinet, presidential appointees, the oil industry, and even a few innocent bystanders.

The groundwork for the scandal had been laid during the preceding decades with an increased emphasis on conservation during the presidency of

Theodore Roosevelt and with increased demands for oil during the presidency of William Howard Taft. In 1912, the U.S. Navy began converting its ships from coal to diesel fuel; and in anticipation of the need for increased fuel, Taft decided that government-owned oil reserves or "domes" at Elk Hills and Buena Vista in California should be held in reserve for future naval needs. President Woodrow Wilson further expanded naval oil reserves in 1914 with the addition of a location in Wyoming that came to be known as Teapot Dome because it roughly resembled the shape of a teapot.

ALBERT FALL

As a well-known lawyer and wheeler-dealer, Albert Fall was a name to be reckoned with in New Mexico; he became one of its first senators when the territory achieved statehood in 1912. In 1921, Fall left the Senate to serve as Harding's secretary of interior. Before accepting the position, Fall had suffered a series of financial setbacks. A number of risky investments had left him with a mortgage he couldn't pay and a ranch in need of serious repairs.

Whether he was innately dishonest, or whether he simply grasped the opportunity to solve his financial problems, Fall decided to use his position for personal profit. His first move was to convince Harding that private oil companies were inadvertently draining the government's oil resources. Harding was already under some obligation to the big oil companies because they had been instrumental in his election. According to Fall, the government's response to the drainage should be to allow the oil companies to lease the reserves instead of obtaining oil at the government's expense.

After only three months in office and with the full support of Edwin M. Denby, the secretary of the navy, Harding issued an executive order placing the oil reserves at Teapot Dome in Wyoming and Elk Hills in California under the Department of Interior, with Fall in charge. Congress agreed to the president's request to lease the naval reserves, and Fall made sure that neither the president nor Congress was aware of the details of the deals.

LEASING THE OIL RESERVES

In April 1922, without seeking competitive bids, Fall secretly ceded exclusive rights to the Teapot Dome oil reserves to Harry F. Sinclair of the Mammoth Oil Company. Sinclair was one of the richest oilmen in the country with worldwide holdings. In exchange for a 20-year lease, Sinclair promised to pay the U.S. government from 12.5 to 50 percent of the proceeds from Teapot Dome's oil reserves, depending on how productive the wells proved to be. Payment was to be made with certificates that the government could exchange for fuel oil, gasoline, and other oil-related products at posts on the Atlantic and Gulf Coasts and in Cuba. The government also had the option of using the certificates to have Mammoth build fuel storage facilities for the navy. After taking charge of the Teapot Dome reserve, Mammoth built a pipeline from the Wyoming reserve to Chicago, Illinois.

A week after finalizing the deal with Sinclair, Fall sought various bids for various construction projects, including the installation of a loading mechanism to be used in dredging a channel at Pearl Harbor, Hawaii. Edward L. Doheny, the millionaire owner of Pan-American Petroleum and Transport Company and a personal friend of Fall's, submitted a successful bid to construct oil storage tanks to be paid for with oil certificates that would ultimately give Pan-Am preference at the Elk Hill reserves. Fell further negotiated with Doheny to build additional tanks for the navy and to fill them with oil. The deal also required Pan-Am to build a refinery in San Pedro, California, and to construct a pipeline between Elk Hills and the San Pedro refinery. As a result of the new relationship between Pan-Am and the government, control of most of the naval reserves at Elk Hill was granted to Doheny. Standard Oil retained control of one section of Elk Hills, and Honolulu Oil was in control at the Buena Vista reserve.

Known only to the principals involved in the transactions, Fall received over $3 million in Liberty Bonds and other gifts from Sinclair. For his secret deal with Doheny, Fall received $100,000 in a black bag. Fall later claimed that the payment from Doheny was an interest-free loan. Fall immediately paid his bills, remodeled his ranch, and bought an adjoining piece of property. When questioned about his sudden wealth, Fall insisted that Sinclair had bout a one-third interest in the Three Rivers Ranch. Falls's machinations came to light through a Wyoming oilman who had not been allowed to bid on the naval reserves. Shortly thereafter, a reporter at the *St. Louis Dispatch* newspaper broke the story. Senator Robert M. La Follette of Wisconsin con-

vinced the Senate to appoint a committee to investigate the charges under the leadership of Senator Thomas J. Walsh of Montana. Despite repeated lies, evasions, and a general lack of cooperation from the principals involved in the Teapot Dome scandal, and in the face of repeated attempts by the Harding administration to block the investigation, the Senate dedicated 18 months to uncovering the corruption involved in the scandal. During this period, Walsh's office was ransacked, his telephones were tapped, his mail was opened, his three-year-old daughter was threatened, and his past was investigated. However, Walsh refused to be intimidated by either the Harding administration or the oil magnates.

THE AFTERMATH

On August 2, 1923, Warren G. Harding unexpectedly died. Many people believed that he had committed suicide by taking poison, although the official explanation was that he had died from food poisoning. At any rate, Harding never lived to see his secretary of interior and close friend sent to jail. On June 30, 1924, Fall was indicted on charges of conspiracy and bribery. It took another five years before Fall was found guilty of bribery, sentenced to one year in the New Mexico State Penitentiary, and forced to pay a $100,000 fine. In response to his behavior during the investigation, Congress charged Sinclair with contempt of Congress. During his trial, Sinclair reportedly offered a member of the jury a car "as long as this block" to vote in his favor. Sinclair was then sentenced to three months in jail for contempt and another three months for jury tampering and was fined $1,000. Ironically, both Sinclair and Doheny were cleared of conspiracy and bribery charges.

At the insistence of Congress, Calvin Coolidge, who had succeeded to the presidency on Harding's death, appointed special prosecutors Republican Owen J. Roberts and Democrat Allen Pomerene to investigate all parties implicated in the Teapot Dome scandal.

HARRY DAUGHERTY

Members of Congress had done their best to oust Attorney General Harry Daugherty during their investigations into the Teapot Dome scandal. Many members of Congress had reservations about

Daugherty's character, and they had resented his efforts to protect Fall from the Teapot Dome investigation.

One of the Ohio Gang, Daugherty had been instrumental in convincing Harding to run for president and had been rewarded with the plum job of attorney general. Daugherty had already developed a reputation as a slick promoter, and he was severely criticized for naming con man Jess Smith as his assistant. When Congress and the press reacted to Daugherty's appointment with outrage, the president defended his choice, maintaining that "Henry Daugherty is the best friend I have on earth." After Harding's death, Smith committed suicide, and Daugherty resigned in disgrace in the midst of congressional efforts to impeach him. He was cleared of all charges three years later.

With the investigation of the Teapot Dome scandal completed, Congress nullified the lease on both the Teapot Dome and Elk Hills reserves, declaring them "illegal and fraudulent." In 1927, the Supreme Court upheld the nullification. The U.S. government also received $6 million from Sinclair and Doheny.

SEE ALSO

bribery; corruption; public corruption; conspiracy.

BIBLIOGRAPHY. Frederick Lewis Allen, *Only Yesterday: An Informal History of the Nineteen-Twenties* (Harper and Row, 1957); Margaret L. Davis, *Dark Side of Fortune* (University of California Press, 1998); Charles L. Mee, Jr., *The Ohio Gang* (M. Evans, 1981); Hope Ridings Miller, *Scandals in The Highest Office* (Random House, 1973); Robert K. Murray, *The Harding Era And His Administration* (University of Minnesota Press, 1969); Francis Russell, *The Shadow of Blooming Grove: Warren G. Harding in His Times* (McGraw-Hill, 1968); David H. Stratton, *Tempest over Teapot: The Story of Albert B. Fall* (University of Oklahoma Press, 1998).

ELIZABETH PURDY, PH.D.
INDEPENDENT SCHOLAR

techniques of neutralization

GRESHAM SYKES and David Matza (1958) articulated five techniques of neutralization that were derived from observing recently arrested juvenile delinquents. Neutralizations represent common justifications or excuses for wrongful behavior prior to committing it, in order to alleviate moral guilt. They are: 1) denial of injury (no harm was really done); 2) denial of victim (no crime occurred because the entity against whom the act was committed deserved it); 3) denial of responsibility (it was not the actor's fault); 4) condemnation of condemners (penalizers are hypocrites); and 5) appeals to higher loyalties (the act was done because of an allegiance to a more important principle, like loyalty to a group).

Donald Cressey's classic 1953 work on embezzlers, *Other People's Money*, anticipated by several years the ideas of Sykes and Matza when he found that his subjects had to counteract the criminal nature of the theft before they could steal. Carl Klockars added another neutralization in 1974, the metaphor of the ledger (there are many more good behaviors than bad ones on an individual's behavior balance sheet). Unlike the neutralizations of Sykes and Matza, Klockars's metaphor of the ledger admits that a behavior is wrong. But, it nevertheless shares the fundamental aspect of the other neutralizations—it is an attempt to reduce personal moral guilt. The concept of neutralization makes a plausible contribution to the understanding of many kinds of business crime because most business criminals are generally law-abiding and do not want to think of themselves as immoral.

The term *neutralization* should not be confused with the term *rationalization*, although the two are often used interchangeably. If the excuses described by Sykes and Matza and Klockars are invoked before the offense to repress feelings of guilt, they are neutralizations. If the excuses are used after the offense to repress feelings of guilt, then they are rationalizations. Of the two concepts, only neutralizations can help to explain an offense because they occur prior to the illegal act.

Researchers almost always record these justifications after the crime is committed. This makes it impossible to determine whether a subject used an excuse to neutralize her crime before it was committed, or whether the excuse was created after the crime as a rationalization to avoid self-embarrassment. White-collar criminals have been documented numerous times using denial of injury, especially in defrauding or embezzling from a government or another wealthy entity. In many cases of embezzlement, the thief tries to believe that there is no harm because the money is merely being "borrowed." Corporate criminals also use denial of injury when victimizing the public at large. In such cases, the harm inflicted is mild and diffuse when spread over so many individuals (for example, stockholders), so the perception by the criminal is that there is little discernable injury to any single person.

Denial of victim will be used to defend a crime when there is a sense of injustice, such as workers who believe that they are underpaid. Denials of responsibility have been documented in statements such as: "The tax laws are too complex for me to understand," and "It's not the organization's fault that our employees committed crimes." Condemnation of condemners is used when it is believed that a contemplated victim is in no position to render judgment, such as the water polluter who validates the offense by asserting that government officials are corrupt.

An appeal to higher loyalties often manifests in persons who have strong organizational allegiance—"I did it for the company." Women who embezzle have also repeatedly invoked this neutralization when they try to substantiate their theft because it provides a better lifestyle for their family or mate. Criminals use the metaphor of the ledger when they view their offense as a rare episode in an otherwise law-abiding history. In essence, the metaphor justifies an illegality based on the many criminal opportunities upon which the offender did not act in the past—the offender perceives a fundamentally good self.

An excuse is a neutralization if it is used once or twice before committing a crime. However, as it becomes utilized on a more regular basis, it turns into a personal belief favorable to the violation of law, and it will eventually become a permanent part of one's value system. It is easier for people to believe that a criminal behavior is not wrong when they have seen little or no punishment for it.

Neutralizers may be deterred by the threat of punishment associated with their contemplated illegal behavior. Deterred neutralizers appear as though they are moral individuals, but in reality they would be very likely to commit offenses if they did not fear the consequences.

SEE ALSO

Cressey, Donald; differential association theory; self-control theory.

BIBLIOGRAPHY. Michael Benson, "Denying the Guilty Mind: Accounting for Involvement in White Collar Crime," *Criminology* (v.23, 1985); Donald Cressey, *Other People's Money* (Free Press, 1953); Carl Klockars, *The Professional Fence* (Free Press, 1974); Gerald Mars, "Dock Pilferage: A Case Study in Occupational Theft," *Deviance and Social Control* (Tavistock, 1974); Erwin Smigel and H. Lawrence Ross, eds., *Crimes Against Bureaucracy* (Van Nostrand Reinhold, 1970); Gresham and David Matza, "Techniques of Neutralization," *American Sociological Review* (v.22, 1958).

GARY S. GREEN
CHRISTOPHER NEWPORT UNIVERSITY

Teledyne Industries

FOUNDED IN 1960 by Henry Singleton and George Kozmetsky, Teledyne, Inc. was a communications company created to capitalize on the shift from analog to digital technologies. Teledyne has since branched out into several subsidiaries including companies in the fields of electronics, communications, engineering, aerospace, and energy.

Several of these subsidiaries have continued to branch off into separate units of their own. One of the units, Teledyne Industries, is a military contracting company based out of Newbury Park, California, and has been involved in several cases of defrauding the U.S. government, specifically, the Department of Defense. Most of the cases involve inflated pricing and inadequate testing of military equipment.

Between 1980 and 1986, Teledyne Hydra-Power, a unit of Teledyne Industries, defrauded the U.S. Navy of $4.5 million on a helicopter contract by inflating the price of parts and the number of hours worked. Teledyne paid the U.S. government $11.9 million to cover overcharges, interest, and penalties. Again, in 1992 Teledyne Industries agreed to pay $17.5 million to settle a criminal case in which it was accused of 35 counts of submitting false statements between 1987 and 1990. Teledyne sold over 12 million relay switches to the Pentagon without adequately testing them. The relays normally cost $6 each, but the government paid $26 per relay so that each one could be tested and certified.

In the course of the 10-year contract, the government would have been defrauded of $240 million. In a similar case, Teledyne paid the U.S. government $275,000 in 1993 to settle claims that their Firth Sterling division failed to properly test cluster bomb grenades. Ten months later, Teledyne paid the government $1.5 million and pleaded guilty to three felony counts of submitting false statements about sales to Taiwan in the 1980s. Then, again in 1994, Teledyne Industries paid the U.S. government another $10 million for failing to perform quality-control tests on parts used in the U.S. Army's Stinger missile. The Environmental Protection Agency also fined Teledyne $85,000 in 1994 for violating the federal Clean Water Act by releasing excess metals and cyanide in waste water discharged to city sewer plants.

SETTLING FOR MILLIONS

Perhaps the most noteworthy case against Teledyne Industries is the whistleblower case first filed in 1991 by a former employee. Gerald Dean Woodward, who worked for Teledyne from 1969 to 1990, filed a lawsuit under the federal False Claims Act claiming that Teledyne defrauded the government of millions of dollars between 1986 and 1990. Some of the allegations in the suit included selling military aircraft parts as commercial parts to private individuals and companies, falsifying paperwork to hide these sales, charging the government for parts that they already paid for, and charging the government for time actually spent working on other business. The U.S. government picked up the case in 1996 and Teledyne settled for $4.75 million. Woodward received $831,250 from that settlement.

Teledyne is still a major military contractor for the U.S. government. In March 2001, Teledyne was awarded $17 million for two separate three-year contracts with the U.S. Navy for electron tubes in support of the EA-6B aircraft.

SEE ALSO
government contract fraud; government procurement fraud; water pollution; False Claims Act.

BIBLIOGRAPHY. Paul Flemming, "Teledyne Settles for $4.75 Million," Springfield Business Journal (v.17/25, 1996); Myron Levin, "EPA Fines 5 Firms $750,000 in Toxics Case Environment," Los Angeles Times (September 14, 1994); Andy Pasztor, "Teledyne to Plead Guilty Second Time in 10 Months to Charges of Lying to U.S.," Wall Street Journal (August 24, 1993); "Teledyne Unit Pays Government," Wall Street Journal (December 20, 1993); "Teledyne Unit Settles U.S. False-Price Claim Paying $11.9 Million," Wall Street Journal (November 6, 1989); Ralph Vartabedian, "Teledyne Case Poses a Dilemma for Feds," Los Angeles Times (October 7, 1992).

ANDREA SCHOEPFER
NICOLE LEEPER PIQUERO
UNIVERSITY OF FLORIDA

telemarketing fraud

ACCORDING TO the U.S. Department of Justice, telemarketing fraud "refers to any scheme to defraud in which the persons carrying out the scheme use the telephone as their primary means of communicating with prospective victims and trying to persuade them to send money to the scheme." The first widespread fraudulent telemarketing scheme involved the activities of Fifty States Distributors in the mid-1970s in Las Vegas, Nevada. Initially started as a legitimate company, Fifty States sold office supplies to businesses. Barry Schrader, the owner of Fifty States, learned that his office supplies were easier to sell when jewelry or some other item was falsely promised along with the supplies. Eventually, he employed up to 300 people in the scheme to rip off businesses. Fifty States was raided by the federal government in 1979 and closed.

Telemarketing fraud increased significantly in the 1980s. By the end of the decade, the National American Securities Administration Association estimated that Americans "invest[ed] more than $1 million every hour in fraudulent financial schemes promoted by phone." It is difficult to determine the precise extent of telemarketing fraud, in part because less than 10 percent of victims report their victimization to the authorities. Despite these problems determining the magnitude of this problem, federal officials believe that hundreds of fraudulent telemarketing schemes exist on any given day in the United States. Other estimates from the National Consumers League (NCL) in 2002 suggest that each fraudulent act nets the offender an average of $845, and the federal government suggests that up to $40 billion is lost each year to telemarketing fraud.

To fully understand telemarketing fraud, it is important to consider the types of telemarketing fraud, the patterns surrounding these incidents, and strategies that have been utilized to control these incidents.

TYPES OF TELEMARKETING FRAUD

The U.S. Department of Justice (DOJ) cites nine different kinds of telemarketing schemes. These schemes vary in their patterns, but are similar in that each aims to take money from victims as quickly as possible. They include the following: charity frauds, investment schemes, credit-related schemes, lottery schemes, magazine-promotion schemes, cross-border schemes, prize-promotion schemes, recovery-room schemes, and internet-related schemes.

Charity fraud occurs when offenders contact individuals and use some bogus charity as a justification to ask for donations. Some charity frauds are referred to as "badge frauds" because offenders will claim that the money will be going to police officers or fire fighters. Also, they may use a number of different strategies to take on the appearance of legitimacy.

For example, some charity fraud schemes may donate a small percent of their profits to a charity, usually less than 10 percent of its profit, to make it seem that they have actually fulfilled their obligations. Others may name themselves with identifiable labels that are easily misconstrued with legitimate charities. One charity scheme, for instance, used the name of the National Lung Association in an attempt to get donors to think they were donating to the American Lung Association.

Investment schemes occur when individuals promise get-rich schemes in exchange for sizeable investments on the part of victims. In the 1980s, common fraudulent investment schemes centered around selling fake coins and strategic metals. In the 1990s, the schemes expanded to include luring investors to dump money into an assortment of businesses including wireless cable and ostrich farms.

Credit-related schemes occur when offenders use the victims' credit, or lack of credit, as a part of the offense. Three types of credit-related schemes exist. First, credit-card frauds perpetrated as telemarketing schemes entail offenders promising credit cards to those with bad credit in exchange for an exorbitant fee. The credit is usually denied. Second, credit-repair schemes entail promises of credit reparation. It is very difficult, however, to alter credit reports, making these promises completely

unattainable and bogus. Third, loan schemes occur when the offenders offer the victims a loan for a fee. After they pay this fee, victims are eventually referred to a "turn down" room and told that their bad credit prohibited the company from offering the loan.

Lottery schemes are another type of telemarketing fraud. Two varieties of lottery schemes exist. In one variety, offenders call victims promising to invest their money in foreign lotteries for a small fee. Victims have been known to pay thousands of dollars trying to win these lotteries. In another variety, victims are told that they have won a lottery, but they have to pay an administrative fee in order to recover the award. In one case, a 93-year-old man "paid a $5,000 'processing fee' after being told he'd won a $1 million lottery prize," the *Virginian-Pilot* newspaper reported in 1999. The Associated Press ran the story with an accompanying picture showing the man standing outside of Tampa International Airport with a sign around his neck that read, "I'm John. Meeting Sgt. Moore from Canada."

Magazine promotion schemes are also orchestrated through telemarketing schemes. The most common strategy used in these schemes entails offenders telling victims that they have won a prize that will be supplied if they purchase magazines. The magazines are usually overpriced, and ones that the victim would not select. The problem that arises is that a large number of magazines try to sell their products through telemarketing strategies. The DOJ points out that fraudulent magazine sales can be distinguished from legitimate ones in that they generally do not provide: 1) advance price disclosure, 2) advance magazine title disclosure, or 3) the magazines.

Cross-border schemes originating in other countries are becoming increasingly common. Estimates suggest that one-third of telemarketing complaints are based on calls that originated in Canada. These cross-border scams are more difficult to investigate because of differences in approaches to defining and responding to telemarketing fraud as well as problems getting offenders extradited from their country of origin.

Prize-promotion schemes occur when individuals are told they have won a prize as part of the fraudulent scheme. Three varieties of this scam exist. In the oldest variety, victims are told that they have won something, but they have to pay the taxes on it, upfront. Another variation, the "one in five scheme," entails offenders telling victims that they have won "one of five prizes," but they have to pay an administrative fee. The prize they actually receive is a "gimme prize" that is essentially worthless. The third variety is the "mystery pitch" or "integrity pitch." Victims are told that they have won something, but the offender is not able to disclose the prize lest they be charged with extortion or bribery, which are entirely baseless claims.

The prize they get is worth far less than what they invested into the contest. According to an article in the *FBI Law Enforcement Bulletin* (1998), "most illegal prize rooms operate on a 10 to 1 principle." This means that the prizes received by customers are valued at one-tenth of the price they paid. In one scam, consumers were promised a "car telephone." What they got was a telephone shaped like a car.

Recovery-room schemes target those who have been previously victimized in telemarketing scams. Victims are called by an individual claiming to be a law enforcement official. The caller tells the victim that her money has been recovered from the fraudulent telemarketing ring, but the caller must pay the taxes on the money, or some other fee, in order for the reimbursement to occur. These scams are usually reserved for those victims who have already been bilked out of thousands of dollars. The fact is, however, that law enforcement agencies would never require victims to pay fees for their services.

The DOJ also cites internet-related schemes as a type of telemarketing fraud. Offenders often use telephone lines in these cases, though the communication strategy is usually not oral. The NCL cites the following estimates for the top ten internet frauds occurring in 2002: online auctions (90 percent); general merchandise (5 percent); Nigerian money offers (4 percent); computer equipment or software (.5 percent); internet access services (.4 percent); work-at-home plans (less than .1 percent); information/adult services (less than .1 percent); travel/vacations (less than .1 percent); advance fee loans (less than .1 percent); and prizes/sweepstakes (less than .1 percent).

In 34 percent of the cases, victims paid by credit card, while they sent money orders in about 30 percent of the cases. Checks, bank cards, and debit cards were used in about 27 percent of the cases. With the growth of the internet, these fraud offenses are expected to grow significantly in the coming years.

PATTERNS OF FRAUD

These schemes are often run like any legitimate business, employing dozens if not hundreds of individuals. They are often located in "boiler rooms," low-rent motels, or rundown office buildings. Some of telemarketing schemes even have a customer service department which is designed to deal with complaints from the victims. Others may have reload rooms, which include workers whose aim is to convince past victims to fall for the scheme once again.

Participants in the schemes include lead brokers and individuals called "touts" or "singers." Lead brokers are companies that buy and sell phone numbers of individuals who have been defrauded. The phone numbers they collect are placed on a list euphemistically referred to as a "sucker list." "Touts" and "singers" are individuals who are employed to provide testimonials for the scheme, but they are actually part of the scheme.

Fraudulent telemarketers will do three things to improve their likelihood of successfully completing the offense. First, they will make it appear as if the goods or services they are providing are worth more than they actually are. Steven Rosoff and other scholars cite an example in which consumers were told they would get a clothes dryer that did not use electricity. They got a clothes line and some clothes pins. Second, fraudulent telemarketers will always ask for quick payment. Third, these businesses will try to do something to make their business look legitimate. Some may assume names that sound official, while others will tell the consumer that the phone conversation is being taped for security reasons.

Note that the schemes vary in how often they are perpetrated. NCL points out that the top 10 telemarketing frauds in 2002 were ranked in the following order: credit card offers (27 percent); work-at-home schemes (18 percent); prizes/sweepstakes (16 percent); advance fee loans (8 percent); magazine sales (5 percent); buyers clubs (4 percent); telephone slamming (2 percent); lotteries (2 percent); travel/vacations (2 percent); and Nigerian money offers (1 percent). NCL adds that victims use their bank debit cards in 37 percent of the cases, their checks in about 16 percent of the cases, their credit cards in 13 percent of the cases, and money orders in 10 percent of the cases. In an additional 13 percent of the cases, victims wired the money to offenders.

CONTROLLING FRAUD

The three main strategies used to control telemarketing fraud are enforcement, education, and prevention. In terms of enforcement, state and federal authorities have taken an active role in rooting out fraudulent telemarketers. Operation Disconnect was the first nationwide undercover operation designed solely to detect and investigate telemarketing fraud. Undercover Federal Bureau of Investigation (FBI) agents claimed to possess machines that would allow telemarketers to call thousands of people an hour. The agents contacted telemarketers and offered the calling machine. In order for the machine to be designed appropriately for the telemarketer, the undercover agents told the telemarketer that they would have to describe the ways they did business in detail. This essentially resulted in confessions of telemarketing fraud. In the end, over 300 people were arrested and 79 boiler-room operations were closed.

Authorities have also tried to educate the public about telemarketing fraud in order to protect citizens from victimization. The National Consumers League's National Fraud Information Center and the U.S. Postal Service warn consumers to be on the lookout.

Prevention strategies are also used to try to control telemarketing fraud. Consider the National Do Not Call Registry. On October 1, 2003, the federal government implemented the registry, designed to limit the number of telemarketing calls individuals received. Citizens who placed their names on the registry were not supposed to receive calls from telemarketers, with the exception of charities, political advertisements, and researchers. In limiting telemarketing calls, a consequence of the legislation should be increased control over fraud.

The costs of these crimes have been discussed in economic terms. It is significant, however, to note that the losses go far beyond the dollar losses experienced by victims. Anne Riordan, AARP's director of its anti-telemarketing fraud section, commented, "Telemarketing fraud isn't about money, it's about the human suffering it causes—It's life suffering." To be sure, victims will experience a great deal of pain beyond their economic losses.

SEE ALSO

wire fraud; mail fraud; advance fee scams; credit card fraud; charity fraud.

BIBLIOGRAPHY. John N. Ferguson, "Phone Scams," *Maclean's* (October 19, 1998); Jonathon Harris, 'The Latest Twist in Phone Fraud," *Maclean's* (October 7, 1996); Joyce Jones, "Consumer Fraud: The Telemarketing Hoax," *Black Enterprise* (September 1998); Ann Lallande, "The Troublemakers," *Marketing and Media Decisions* (May, 1989); National Consumer's League, *Telemarketing Fraud* (USGPO, 2003); National Institute of Justice, *Fraudulent Telemarketers in Their Own Words* (USGPO, 1998); Brian K. Payne, *Crime and Elder Abuse* (Charles C. Thomas, 2000); H. Schneider, "Telemarketing Scams Reach Across Borders," *Washington Post* (August 24, 1977); B.T. Seeman, "Swindlers Target Lonely, Unwary Seniors," *Miami Herald* (July 8, 1993); K. Slotter, "Hidden Faces: Combating Telemarketing Fraud," *FBI Law Enforcement Bulletin* (v.73/3, 1998); U.S. Department of Justice, *What Kinds of Telemarketing Schemes Are Out There?* (USGPO, 2003); U.S. Postal Inspection Service, *Characteristics of Telemarketing Fraud Schemes* (USGPO, 2003).

BRIAN K. PAYNE, PH.D.
OLD DOMINION UNIVERSITY

Thailand

THE KINGDOM of Thailand has a long history of strong centralized rule and complicity with authoritarian figures which has increased the likelihood of corruption. Many people consider corruption to be not just pervasive but endemic throughout the entire Thai system.

In the summer of 2003, the prime minister of Thailand, Thaksin Shinawatra, following campaigns against drug trafficking and intellectual-property piracy, launched a campaign designed to eradicate "Dark Influence" throughout the country. Regional officials were instructed to draw up lists of suspected figures who would then be investigated and, if found guilty, dealt with harshly. Attention has been focused on unlicensed bus companies and motor cycle taxis, both of which are important sectors in Bangkok in particular, and both of which have reported paying bribes to the police.

The corruption that is endemic in Thai society has its roots in the feudal patronage system known as *sakdina*, in which a designated regional official was granted wide-ranging powers and discretion to administer an area, and who could reward individuals for their service. The legacy of this method continues to be particularly strong in the rural, agricultural areas in which the majority of Thailand's population of 70 million people live.

Thailand has a highly developed prostitution sector and this has been linked to human trafficking both into and out of the country. High profile declarations of leading massage parlor owners indicate that bribe-taking by police is widespread, while under-reporting of income has attracted the interest of revenue authorities.

Gambling is partly legalized and the underground sector is extremely large, with estimates of its annual value running at 450 billion baht ($11 billion); this includes not just illegal lotteries but also unlicensed casinos located in border regions or river islands. These regions have also witnessed large-scale illegal logging and the manufacture and distribution of illegal drugs, often by ethnic minority people seeking funding for their struggle for independence, as in the case of the Wa in Myanmar (Burma).

The Golden Triangle includes part of northern Thailand and remains a significant producer of opium for distribution internationally. Thailand's drug problems stem from being forced to agree with the United States in 1856 to allow the importation of opium in the name of free trade.

The inability of central authorities to control actions in the regions of the country, combined with the wide-ranging powers given to regional figures, has provided numerous opportunities for graft, vote-buying and collusion between private and public figures. Both army and police officials have been implicated in these kinds of activities. Local politics are routinely run by local "godfather" figures (*chao pho*) who wield considerable influence and who have seemed able to conduct extravagant, violent lifestyles with impunity. The Thai media have yet fully to emerge from an attitude of deference and respect that hampers serious investigation and, in some cases, news executives have been associated with accepting gifts from officials to ignore potentially damaging stories.

The private sector has been quick to take advantage of shortcomings in the Thai regulatory structure and there are numerous examples of money being siphoned off from works, protection rackets, and illegal sales operations. Firearms and explosives are easily obtainable and the violent resolution of turf disputes has been common. There have also been murders of auditors and other regulators. A great many people rely upon the informal sector of the economy and their work is therefore unregulated, and they are frequently unprotected. Reports of the mistreatment of domestic laborers emerged in the early 2000s, while the extortion of money from those wishing to work overseas has been notable for some years.

SEE ALSO
drug trafficking; human trafficking; corruption.

BIBLIOGRAPHY. John Laird, *Money Politics* (Graham Brash, 2000); Duncan McCargo, *Politics and the Press in Thailand: Media Machinations* (Garuda Press, 2002); Ron Renard, "The Making of a Problem: Narcotics in Mainland Southeast Asia," *Development or Domestication: Indigenous Peoples of Southeast Asia* (Silkworm Books, 1997); Sombat Chantornvong, "Local Godfathers in Thai Politics," *Money and Power in Provincial Thailand* (Institute of Southeast Asian Studies and Silkworm Books, 2000); Supradit Kanwanich, "Life's a Gamble," *The Bangkok Post* (September 15, 2002).

JOHN WALSH, PH.D.
MAHIDOL UNIVERSITY, THAILAND

thalidomide

CHEMIE GRUNENTHAL, a West German pharmaceutical company, created thalidomide in 1953. It was used as a tranquilizer or sleeping pill and was being touted as a drug with no side effects. It was also used to treat morning sickness during pregnancy With its lack of side effects, it was deemed safe enough that it did not require a prescription; therefore, it was widely available over the counter. Eventually, the German manufacturer began to license the distribution of thalidomide in other countries.

The American pharmaceutical firm, William S. Merrell Company, wanted to distribute thalidomide in the lucrative U.S. market. On September 12, 1960, the Food and Drug Administration (FDA) received a New Drug Application (NDA) from Merrell requesting approval for thalidomide. The NDA filed by Merrell contained glowing claims that the drug was safe. Animal and human tests had been conducted and there were no known problems.

And since thalidomide was already widely used all over the world, Merrell and the FDA thought the approval process would be routine. The approval was assigned to Dr. Frances Kelsey, the FDA's newest medical officer.

Kelsey reviewed the NDA along with an FDA pharmacologist and chemist. They noticed many inconsistencies with the data and omissions. Kelsey sent Merrell a letter stating that she was concerned about the testing of the drug and the many inconsistencies that were found, and more testing was needed before the FDA would grant Merrell distribution rights. Merrell was anxious to have the drug on the market and put pressure on Kelsey for approval, she declined. Meanwhile, some disturbing reports were surfacing over the drugs' side effects. Kelsey was also concerned about the drug's use by pregnant women. In the early 1960's more research was conducted on the effects of drugs on fetuses. Kelsey raised these questions to Merrell and ordered more testing. Merrell responded by putting intense pressure on Kelsey to approve the drug, but she did not yield.

Prior to the application to the FDA, in 1957, Chemie Grunenthal had early indications of the drug's dangers, as well as limited effectiveness but did not disclose these results. In fact, Grunenthal continued to promote the drug in spite of the growing number of reports of its dangerousness. Numerous women who used thalidomide during pregnancy were bearing children with extreme congenital abnormalities.

Many of the children were born with their extremities attached in odd places. Shortly after the birth defects were observed, thalidomide was banned worldwide, but it was too late for thousands of babies. An estimated 8,000-80,000 children in nearly 50 counties were born deformed because thalidomide had been marketed as being safe to use by pregnant women. Because of this, it became known as the "drug that deformed."

It was not until the considerable scope of harm being done was widely publicized that Grunenthal was forced to withdraw thalidomide from the market in 1962. Because of the various medical journal articles and news reports of the devastating effects of thalidomide and Kelsey's stubbornness for more testing by Merrell, American women and their unborn children averted tragedy. The women outside of the United States, unfortunately were not that lucky. Upon further investigation, much of Grunenthal's behavior, prior to withdrawal of the drug from the marketplace, came under scrutiny.

Grunenthal did not have a strong reputation for thorough research. They did conduct laboratory tests of thalidomide, but the clinical trials were done by doctors on their payroll. Some of the patients experienced side effects like giddiness, nausea, constipation, and loss of feeling in their fingertips and toes. These were recorded and sent on to the company; therefore, Grunenthal had knowledge that thalidomide was not "perfectly safe" with "no side effects."

As time went on, negative reports of the drugs actual side effects began to surface. As negative reports surfaced, Grunenthal had positive reports published swiftly and attempted to discourage more negative scrutiny by exerting pressure on the medical journals not to publish such harmful reports; the drug was making them an enormous amount of money. Nevertheless, negative reports came flooding in, and with very disturbing results. Doctors, who had been told that the drug was completely safe, started contacting Grunenthal about the negative findings.

Because of the overwhelming effects of thalidomide on pregnant women and their children, the public prosecutor's office in West Germany began an investigation into Grunenthal's behavior and knowledge. Nine of Grunenthal managers were criminally tried for committing bodily harm and for involuntary manslaughter. After two-and-half years, the company agreed to an out of court settlement. The criminal hearings were suspended and Chemie Grunenthal agreed to pay 114 million marks into a victim's compensation fund, and 50 million German marks to the national government (about $31 million).

Grunenthal was not the only pharmaceutical company sued. In Britain, thalidomide was distributed by Distillers Company Biochemicals, Ltd. (DCBL). They also advertised the drug as being completely safe, especially for pregnant women. In 1961, Dr. W. McBride of Australia discovered a direct link between pregnancy and the birth of severely deformed children.

He made his results known to DCBL, but they were ignored in Australia, nor were they passed onto their headquarters in London. It was only until McBride published his findings in *The Lancet*, a leading British medical journal, that DCBL seemed to be interested in the findings.

Even though DCBL was not the manufacturer, the many families that were affected by the drug sued the company. The lawsuits against DCBL were motivated by the need for compensation. Many of the families needed the money to help care for the children who were born with defects directly related to the use of thalidomide during pregnancy. The legal battle took 15 years to resolve. The families eventually received approximately $33,000 each.

Early use of thalidomide across the globe had disastrous consequences. However, thalidomide has been recently resurrected. It has been discovered that thalidomide (renamed and marketed as Thalomide) is effective in treating symptoms of diseases such as leprosy and possibly AIDS. Thalomid was approved in 1998 by the U.S. Food and Drug Administration (FDA) to treat leprosy. In order to avoid tragic birth defects as in the past, the FDA has established several severe restrictions.

SEE ALSO

pharmaceutical industry; Food and Drug Administration; unsafe drugs.

BIBLIOGRAPHY. John Braithwaite, *Corporate Crime in the Pharmaceutical Industry* (Routledge, 1984); Maurice Punch, *Dirty Business: Exploring Corporate Misconduct, Analysis and Cases* (Sage Publications, 1996);Elaine Potter, *Suffer the Children: The Story of Thalidomide* (Viking Press, 1979); Trent D. Stephens and Rock Brynner, *Dark Remedy: The Impact of Thalidomide and Its Revival as a Vital Medicine* (Perseus Publishing, 2001); Lisa A. Seidman and Noreen Warren, "Frances Kelsey and Thalidomide in the U.S.," *The American Biology Teacher* (v.64/7, 2002); George J. Annas and Sherman Elias, "Thalidomide and the Titanic: Reconstructing the Technology Tragedies of the Twentieth Century," *American Journal of Public Health* (v.89/1, 1999).

DEBRA E. ROSS, PH.D.
GRAND VALLEY STATE UNIVERSITY

Three Mile Island

THE WORST NUCLEAR accident in the history of the United States occurred at Pennsylvania's Three Mile Island (TMI) nuclear power plant in the predawn hours of March 28, 1979. The plant located approximately 10 miles south of Harrisburg, Pennsylvania, on the Susquehanna River, came dangerously close to a nuclear meltdown that could have had devastating results.

For nearly a year, the TMI plant had been successfully producing electricity. Problems began, however, when TMI's Unit 2 Reactor was hastily opened for operation at the end of December 1987. By January 1979, Unit 2 Reactor had to be shut down for two weeks while operators identified leaks in the piping and pump system. Problems began in the pump system of the Unit 2 Reactor, specifically in the secondary loop feedwater pumps, which are responsible for turning heat and pressure from the primary nuclear sector of the plant into safely emitted steam. Due to unidentified mechanical or electronic failure, the pumps automatically shut down. Without water pushing through the secondary loop, the heat being generated in the radioactive core had no way of escaping. Thus, the water and pressure in the primary loop began to rise. A pressure relief valve opened to release the steam into a holding tank and alleviate the building pressure inside the core. The valve should have closed once the pressure decreased inside the reactor but the valve got stuck ajar. The pressure in the reactor continued decreasing as water and steam drained off the core through the opening. Further compounding the problem, the emergency water pumps, which should have immediately turned on, did not. The cutoff valves connecting the backup pumps to the rest of the system were closed days before during routine tests and never reopened. It took eight minutes for operators to notice that the valves were shut.

In the control room, an indicator light erroneously showed that the pressure relief valve had closed. Since water and steam continued to leak through the open valve, a loss-of-coolant accident was developing. Voids, or areas where there is no water present, began to form. Water was automatically and unsuccessfully redistributed to fill the voids but in the process, the pressurizer filled with water. This caused the level indicator in the control room to register that the system was safely full of water.

Operators had no idea that the pressure and water in the core were continuing to decrease, so they turned off the emergency injection water system despite the fact that the open valve was releasing water and steam. Because of inadequate cooling and the loss of water, the exposed rods warmed to

The Three Mile Island nuclear power plant in Pennsylvania in April 1979, a few weeks after the partial meltdown. Studies are in conflict about how severely local residents were affected by the release of radiation.

roughly 4,300 degrees, dangerously close to the 5,200-degrees meltdown point. It took almost 16 hours for plant operators to fix the valves and pumps and stabilize the temperature and pressure inside the nuclear reactor. However, one more problem had to be dealt with. A hydrogen bubble had formed above the reactor core. There was concern that the bubble would block the flow of water to the core and cause an explosion if the hydrogen were to mix with the oxygen in the water.

Five days after the chain of events began, engineers from the Nuclear Regulatory Commission (NRC) announced they had shrunk the hydrogen bubble and that the threat of a hydrogen blast had been miscalculated. It took another month before Unit 2 Reactor could be shut down completely. Three years later, the full extent of the damage was revealed when a robotic camera provided pictures of the core. Fifty percent of the core had been entirely destroyed and approximately 20 tons of molten uranium had settled on the bottom of the pressure valve.

THE BLAME

A report commissioned by President Jimmy Carter following the incident suggests that the standards surrounding nuclear power, particularly at TMI,

had become grievously relaxed, and the associated dangers were not being taken seriously. Investigators found that the equipment, attitudes, and operating training practices of the plant's owner, Metropolitan Edison, made an accident virtually inevitable. Additionally, the report faulted human error for failing to properly connect the water pumps, neglecting to open the hand-operated valves that would have allowed the emergency water system to save the plant, and for the fatal decision to decrease water pressure to the core when the unprepared control room operators became inundated with a barrage of sirens and data print-outs.

Finally, the report placed some blame with the NRC, the watchdog agency for nuclear power plants, for failing to require replacement of the critical pressure valve that had malfunctioned 11 times before at other power plants.

In addition to the questionable professional environment surrounding the plant prior to the accident, the handling of the public throughout the course of the crisis raised some controversy. Plant officials and operators were reluctant to notify residents that a problem had occurred within the plant. A study conducted after the incident revealed that 24 percent of the sampled residents living within a 15-mile radius of TMI were not aware that anything was amiss until two days after the initial accident had occurred. The citizens who were aware of the accident came to believe that they were intentionally misled by NRC and Metropolitan Edison.

EVACUATION

For two days after the initial incident, residents were officially told that the situation was under control, but on Friday, March 30, they were informed, some for the first time, that the incident was not contained. Many residents were learning not only that there was an accident at TMI, but also that a hydrogen bubble had formed in the reactor's core and was threatening an explosion.

A burst of radiation had to be released into the air, thwarting an explosion by relieving the pressure building up inside the reactor. The governor advised that pregnant women and children should evacuate the area. As NRC debated on whether or not the reactor would detonate, nearly 150,000 residents chose to leave the area.

Even after area residents felt safe enough to return to their homes, many continued to live with the fear that the amount of radiation released from the plant was greater and more damaging than officials had disclosed. The degree to which the partial meltdown physically affected residents of the Three Mile Island area is still unclear. Both the long- and short-term health effects of the accident have repeatedly been researched, but often with contradictory results. A survey conducted by the University of North Carolina in 1997 examined the long-term health consequences of the TMI incident. The study found that in areas downwind of TMI, the rates of lung cancer had doubled and the incidents of leukemia were three times the national average. Meanwhile, additional research on the long-term effects was conducted by Columbia University and the National Cancer Institute which concluded that no long-term public health hazards resulted from the accident.

To further complicate the understanding of the health hazards of TMI, a re-analysis of the Columbia University data identified a relationship of heightened cancer rates across increasing levels of radiation exposure. The most recent long-term study has tracked a group of TMI area residents for 20 years and found no consistent evidence that the radioactivity released during the accident had a significant impact on the overall mortality of residents in the immediate area. The research did, however, note a slightly elevated level in overall mortality and cancer mortality in the TMI area since 1979.

Beyond the lingering health concerns, TMI produced a wave of financial losses. Insurers for the plant's parent electric company, General Public Utilities Corp., settled lawsuits with residents tallying $25 million. There were nearly 2,000 additional claims pending against the company until 2002 when the U.S. Third Circuit Court of Appeals dismissed all further appeals based on a lack of concrete evidence that the accident had direct health consequences. The electric company took an additional financial loss when the one functioning unit of TMI was sold for $100 million, just one-seventh of its estimated market value.

The incident also had a significant impact on the nuclear power industry as a whole. Not one nuclear power plant was constructed in the United States since the accident at TMI to date in early 2004, and 60 other plants have been shut down or abandoned. Higher regulatory standards have been put in place, such as requiring better emergency response planning, more operator training, and general improvements in all other areas of nuclear power plant operations. Since TMI, nuclear power is no longer considered the cheap energy source of the future. It is now a more expensive option than both coal and hydroelectric power, and continues to be viewed with a wary eye.

SEE ALSO
air pollution; Clean Air Act; Carter, James E..

BIBLIOGRAPHY. Stanley D. Brunn, James H. Johnson, and Donald J. Zeigler, *Final Report on a Social Survey of Three Mile Island Area Residents* (Department of Geography, Michigan State University, 1979); David DeKok, "Lawyers Give Up on Health Cases Related to Three Mile Island Nuclear Accident," *The Patriot-News* (2002); "Meltdown at Three Mile Island," www.pbs.org (WGBH Educational Foundation, 1999); Wilborn Hampton, *Meltdown: A Race Against Nuclear Disaster at Three Mile Island: A Reporter's Story* (Candlewick Press, 2001); Thewei Hu, *Health-related Economic Cost of the Three Mile Island Accident* (Center for Research on Human Resources, Institute for Policy Research and Evaluation, Pennsylvania State University, 1980). Marianne Lavelle, "When the World Stopped," *U.S. News & World Report* (1999); David L. Sills, C.P. Wolf, and Vivian B. Shelanski, *Accident at Three Mile Island: The Human Dimension* (Westview Press, 1982); Evelyn Talbott, et al., "Long-Term

Follow-Up of the Residents of the Three Mile Island Accident Area: 1979-1998," *Environmental Health Perspectives* (National Institute of Environmental Health Sciences, 2003).

LYNN LANGTON
NICOLE LEEPER PIQUERO
UNIVERSITY OF FLORIDA

Times Beach

ON THE MERAMEC River in Missouri, Times Beach was primarily a small resort community with a population just over 1,000 citizens. Sadly, it became emblematic of the discovery of the hazard waste problem characterizing the 1980s and, as such, was rendered a "ghost town" in the early part of the decade due to contamination by dioxin, a cancer-producing chemical.

The tortured journey for this community began when Northeastern Pharmaceutical and Chemical Company, Inc. (NEPACCO), while manufacturing hexachlorophene (an antibacterial agent), leased a production facility from Hoffman Taff. Hoffman Taff (which was later acquired by Syntex Corporation) was the manufacturer of the notorious defoliant Agent Orange created to aid ground-based troops in their combat operations in the Vietnam War. The byproducts of these production processes produced both dioxin and TCP (trichlorophenol) carcinogens. NEPACCO and Independent Petrochemical Corporation (IPC) then arranged for disposal of these wastes with Russell Martin Bliss, a St. Louis-based waste oil hauler and operator of Bliss Waste Oil Company.

Bliss mixed these chemical wastes with waste oil at his Frontenac, Missouri, facility and hauled five truckloads between February and October 1971, with each load containing between 3,000-3,500 gallons of dioxin- and TCP-laced oil. The cash-strapped community of Times Beach contracted with Bliss (for six cents per gallon of waste oil sprayed) to spray numerous roads for dust control over several miles in and around Times Beach. Bliss also sprayed the same contents on parking lots, truck terminals, several horse stables, and a horse ring owned by Bliss.

Over 40 horses died as a result of exposure to the dioxin as well as other livestock, dogs, and birds. Several adults and children were also sickened as a result of their exposure, ranging from diarrhea, headaches, nausea, and skin lesions to hospitalizations for kidney and bladder bleeding. At least one death from soft tissue sarcoma (a rare form of cancer) was tied to dioxin exposure. In total, Bliss sprayed the dioxin-laced waste oil at 28 sites throughout eastern Missouri.

The full extent of contamination became apparent in the early 1980s as the nearby Meramec River flooded the city, further spreading the dioxin over a larger area and forcing residents to evacuate their homes. The Centers for Disease Control and Prevention recommended in December 1982 those who were evacuated be permanently relocated in what was dubbed the Christmas Message: "If you are in town it is advisable for your to leave and if you are out of town do not go back." The Environmental Protection Agency (EPA) transferred approximately $30 million to the Federal Emergency Management Agency (FEMA) for permanent relocation of residents and businesses in 1983 (and all were relocated permanently by 1986). Those facing relocation complained bitterly about not receiving fair market value for their homes and the manner in which they were portrayed in the media as "greedy" in seeking compensation for their losses.

These events lead the EPA to place these sites on its initial National Priorities List under the provisions of the Comprehensive Environmental Response, Compensation, and Liability Act (1980). This act was designed to remedy the ravages of hazardous waste contamination common to locales such as Times Beach and Love Canal (New York) and led to an eventual cleanup funded by parties responsible for the generation and transportation of the wastes as well as the state of Missouri and the USEPA. The costs for the cleanup were in excess of $100 million. After contentious litigation involving parties responsible for the generation and disposal of the dioxin wastes (Bliss, NEPACCO, Syntex, IPC and others) as well as citizens contesting the EPA's disposal methods and possibility of additional contamination, these wastes were incinerated in Times Beach. Although dioxin contamination was spread over numerous locations in light of Bliss spraying over such an extensive range, Times Beach was selected for the incineration site because of its small size, the largest concentration of contaminated waste, prior evacuation, and it was not yet cleaned and restored. Times Beach recently became Route

66 State Park and has been hailed as an "environmental success story" and offers visitors a history of the contamination as well as hiking, fishing, and camping. Other eastern Missouri communities contaminated by the dioxin-based materials have become upscale housing developments. However, as a legacy of its polluted past, the failure of realtors to fully disclose the extent of dioxin contamination in eastern Missouri to seven potential home buyers culminated in a jury award in excess of $500,000.

SEE ALSO
Love Canal; Environmental Protection Agency.

BIBLIOGRAPHY. Bureau of National Affairs, *EPA v. Bliss, Environmental Law Reporter* (v.18, 1988); D.M. Richardson, "Cleaning Up the Past: The Waste May Be Gone, But The Stigma Lingers," *Riverfront Times* (November 13, 2002); EPA, Record of Decision for Times Beach, Missouri, www.epa.gov (2003); EPA, Times Beach Site Description, www.epa.gov (2003); EPA, NPL Times Beach, www.epa.gov/superfund (2003).

S. GUNKEL, PH.D.
DOANE COLLEGE

tobacco industry

TOBACCO HAS BEEN around since before the United States was even a small group of colonies, but the negative health effects of tobacco remained unknown until the early 20th century. Then, articles about the detrimental health effects of smoking appeared in medical and scientific journals. A statistical correlation between smoking and cancer had been demonstrated; but no causal relationship was demonstrated until 1952 and the public remained unaware of the growing body of evidence.

Reader's Digest published "Cancer by the Carton," in 1952, the first popular article dealing with the detrimental effects of smoking. The article's appearance resulted in similar reports being published in other publications In 1953, cigarette sales decreased for the first time in more than 20 years. The tobacco industry responded in 1954 by forming the Tobacco Industry Research Council (TIRC). With advice from TIRC, the tobacco industry began marketing filtered and low-tar cigarettes that promised a "healthier" smoke. The public responded, and sales increased again. Then in the early 1960s, the Surgeon General's Advisory Committee on Smoking and Health was formed. Initiated in response to a growing body of scientific evidence suggesting a causal relationship between smoking and cancer, and political pressure, the committee published a 387-page report in 1964 entitled "Smoking and Health." It insisted that cigarette smoking was causally linked to lung cancer in males, and claimed that the data for women, though less complete, pointed to the same conclusion. The report noted that smokers were nine to 10 times more likely to get lung cancer than non-smokers and listed specific carcinogens in cigarette smoke, including arsenic, cadmium, and DDT.

DEFENSIVE, THOUGH PROFITABLE

The tobacco industry has been on the defensive (though profitably) since then. The tobacco industry was also successfully sued by the U.S. Department of Justice for engaging in a 30-year criminal conspiracy to hide information concerning the link between smoking and cancer from the public. In 1965, Congress passed the Federal Cigarette Labeling and Advertising Act requiring the surgeon general's warnings on all cigarette packages. In 1971, all broadcast advertising was banned. In 1990, smoking was banned on all interstate buses and all domestic airline flights lasting six hours or less. In 1994, Mississippi filed the first of 22 state lawsuits seeking to recoup millions of dollars from tobacco companies for smokers' Medicaid bills. And in 1995, President Bill Clinton announced plans to regulate tobacco, especially sales and advertising aimed at minors.

For decades, lawsuits from consumers went nowhere. Tobacco companies, with multiple resources for legal maneuvering, easily defeated early suits, including the first one filed in 1954. Their most serious challenge before the 1990s came in 1983, when Rose Cipollone, a smoker suffering from terminal lung cancer, filed suit against Liggett, charging the company failed to warn her about the dangers of smoking. Cipollone, who did die from smoking effects, initially was awarded a $400,000 judgment, which was later overturned. Cipollone's family was unable to afford the cost of litigation, and abandoned the suit.

Into the 21st century, "big tobacco" faces a new legal environment. Over the past three decades, the law has changed considerably. State laws and legal

The epitome of "cool," Joe Camel was a character created by advertising agencies to entice market segments to smoke Camel cigarettes. The packaging on these cigarette packs is showcased like collectible trading cards for kids.

precedents hold manufacturers more liable for the effects of their products. And the old legal defense of "contributing negligence"—which prevented lawsuits by people with some measure of responsibility for their own condition—is no longer viable in most jurisdictions. Instead, a defendant can be held partially liable and forced to pay a corresponding percentage of damages. Finally, the notion of "strict" liability has developed; this means defendants can be found liable whether or not they are found negligent. If a product such as tobacco causes harm, the company that produced it can be held responsible, even if it wasn't aware of the potential danger.

As smoking has declined among the white non-Hispanic population, tobacco companies have targeted both African-Americans and Hispanics with intensive merchandising, which includes billboards, advertising in media targeted to those communities, and sponsorship of civic groups and athletic, cultural, and entertainment events. The sponsorship of these events and groups may mean that community leaders in minority areas are less like to speak out against the dangers of smoking.

According to the American Lung Association, smoking-related diseases take an estimated 440,000 American lives each year, including those affected indirectly, such as babies born prematurely due to prenatal maternal smoking, and some of the victims of second-hand exposure to tobacco's carcinogens. Smoking costs the United States approximately $150 billion each year in healthcare costs and lost productivity. These costs exceed all tobacco corporation profits and tax revenues from tobacco.

The result is that, until very recently, the costs of smoking have been socialized while tobacco profits are privatized in the hands of wealthy tobacco stockholders. The government has also granted tobacco firms some interesting forms of corporate welfare, including exporting tobacco under the Food for Peace Program, exacting trade concessions from sovereign governments that amount to forcing American cigarettes on foreign markets in the name of free trade, while the blame for tobacco related diseases and the inability to quit smoking on many people's part is viewed as a matter of individual responsibility, or the lack thereof.

Finally, for all their talk about responsibility, the tobacco industry has actually been criminally irresponsible for decades. They have illegally smuggled an increased nicotine-level tobacco plant out of the United States, and tried to grow it in a foreign country. Tobacco firms have sanctioned the selling of cigarettes on the global black market, and have hired organized crime syndicates to peddle black market tobacco products. Tobacco executives committed contempt of Congress by lying under oath about the addictive nature of cigarettes.

The tobacco industry loses close to 5,000 customers every day in the United States alone—including 3,500 who manage to quit and about 1,200 who die. The most promising replacement smokers are young people: 90 percent of smokers begin before the age of 21, and 60 percent before age 14. To find new customers, every day U.S. tobacco companies spend $11 million to advertise and promote cigarettes—more than the U.S. Federal Office on Smoking and Health spends to prevent smoking in an entire year.

INTERNATIONAL SMOKING

Outside the United States, central messages about tobacco are wealth, health, consumption—in short, "USA." In Africa, U.S. tobacco companies capitalize on this by associating smoking with affluence. It's common to hear African children say they start smoking because of the glamorous lifestyle associated with it in the advertisements they see, hear, and read. In emerging markets from eastern Europe to southeast Asia, transnational tobacco giants Philip Morris, RJR Nabisco, and BAT Industries aggressively hawk cigarettes with slogans associated with the American Dream; "L & M: The Way America Tastes," "Winston: The Spirit of the USA" and "Lucky Strikes: An American Original." These themes, and the images that accompany them, expand the appeal beyond what has in many countries been an adult male market, and has now been extended to young people and women.

Globally, per capita cigarette consumption in the developing world has increased by over 70 percent in the past quarter century. In Hong Kong, children as young as seven smoke cigarettes, and the rate of Latin American teen smoking in some cities is 50 percent. In Kenya, it was estimated in 1989 that 40 percent of primary school children smoke. And smoking rates among Korean teen-aged males climbed from 18 percent to 30 percent in a single year following the entrance of an American tobacco firm into that market.

SEE ALSO
advertising fraud; marketing fraud; consumer deaths.

BIBLIOGRAPHY. American Heart Association, www.americanheart.org (2003); American Lung Association, www.lungusa.org (2003); Morton C. Mintz, "Marketing Tobacco to Children," *The Progressive* (v.5, May, 1991); David R. Simon, *Elite Deviance* (Allyn & Bacon, 2002); Larry C. White, *Merchants of Death: The American Tobacco Industry* (Morrow, 1985).

DAVID R. SIMON
UNIVERSITY OF NORTH FLORIDA
UNIVERSITY OF CALIFORNIA, BERKELEY

American tobacco companies are turning to foreign markets after more and more U.S. citizens kick the habit.

Toxic Substances Control Act

PASSED BY THE U.S. Congress and signed into law by President Gerald Ford on October 11, 1976, the Toxic Substances Control Act (TSCA) directed the administrator of the Environmental Protection Agency (EPA) to establish testing procedures for toxic chemicals, publicize the results of chemicals which prove to be dangerous, and to set guidelines for controlling toxic chemicals.

Legislation with a similar aim was originally proposed in 1971 by the President's Council on Environmental Quality. In one of the council's reports, a desire for substantial legislation to examine, to identify, and to regulate potentially harmful toxic chemicals was expressed. In subsequent years, the House and the Senate each passed their own versions of legislation, during both the 92nd and 93rd sessions, to address the concerns raised by the council. Disagreements resulted on the issues of chemical testing and the legislation's relationship to current regulatory laws, leading to inaction on the topic. Enactment of the TSCA finally came after there was a rise in public concern about the contamination of the Hudson River and other waterways by chlorinated biphenyl molecules (PCBs), emissions of chlorofluorocarbons (CFC), and the contamination of food products by polybrominated biphenyls (PBBs). A final version was drafted by U.S. Senator John V. Tunney of California and accepted by the majority of the House and Senate.

At first, there was a major lack of knowledge about which chemicals were toxic and about the potential effects of chemical toxicity. Therefore, the first step of the TSCA was to research and examine various chemicals in order to discover the effects of their use. Even today, the potential health and environmental effects of some chemicals which are being used daily are not completely understood.

To gain knowledge, the TSCA directed the collection of test data from different U.S. industries concerning all the chemicals that they used. Guidelines for which chemicals should be tested were set forth in the TSCA and the EPA was authorized to modify and enforce them. Companies are required to compile test data on chemicals whose manufacture, distribution, and use "may present an unreasonable risk." Testing is also required for chemicals which are produced in large amounts and if there is a possibility that some quantity of the chemical may be released into the environment or be exposed to people. Consequently, a company must compile the data and submit it to the EPA. Then, the EPA is obligated by the TSCA to require further tests if existing data does not sufficiently prove that a certain chemical is safe and if further testing is necessary to even draw conclusions.

Since there were over 55,000 chemicals being manufactured and used at the time of the TSCA's enactment, the U.S. Congress set up a special interagency committee to work with the EPA in deciding which chemicals should be examined first and in coordinating the efforts of various government agencies. Every six months, the Interagency Testing Committee (ITC), as it is known, compiles a list of up to 50 chemicals and submits it to the EPA. In response, the EPA must deal with the list by returning an explanation to the ITC or calling for testing for each chemical on the list. ITC's factors for chemical selection include quantity manufactured, quantity released into the environment, number of exposures, similarity of the chemical to other known toxic chemicals, current information, and the availability of testing resources for the chemicals.

Notification of the manufacture of a new chemical within the United States by any company, except for the U.S. military which is not bound by the TSCA, is required by the TSCA at least 90 days before production begins. Also, the EPA must be informed if a company is using an existing chemical in a new way, different from the uses permitted by the EPA at that time. With this information, the EPA is able to conduct research on the new chemicals or on the new use of the existing chemicals in order to determine if the chemicals are safe. Annually, the EPA looks into more than 1,000 new chemicals submitted by companies. Interestingly, the TSCA bans the EPA from setting uniform testing procedures for new chemicals, being afraid that requirements which were too stringent would prevent companies from innovating for fear of expensive testing and possible bans on their new products.

The TSCA grants the EPA the authority to regulate toxic chemicals. The EPA may ban or limit production, specify acceptable uses, limit the acceptable concentration, require warning labels, and force companies to notify distributors and consumers of potential dangers. Also, the EPA is able to specify that companies must keep thorough records of production, plan safe disposal methods, and force the replacement or refund of products which contain dangerous chemicals.

With the company's records and the EPA's own research, the EPA maintains a massive database of all chemicals, which is required by the TSCA. Any chemical not listed in the EPA's database is considered new and must undergo the notification and research process. With the inventory and all of the EPA's toxic chemical procedures, confidentiality is considered to be very important and EPA officials are forbidden to disclose information. Doing so in serious instances may result in criminal penalties.

Since its passage, the TSCA has been modified by amendments which deal with specific toxic chemicals like radon, asbestos, and lead. Enforcement of regulations concerning these toxic chemicals, as well as all toxic chemical procedures embodied in the TSCA, is the responsibility of the EPA. Companies may have their plants inspected to verify compliance. Chemicals that have been produced illegally may be ceased in manufacture, and destroyed by EPA officials. Civil penalties for violations may result in fines as high as $25,000 per violation each day. For violations that an individual willingly and knowingly commits, criminal penalties are possible. With strict enforcement, the EPA works to fulfill its obligations under the TSCA in order to promote the safety and health of U.S. citizens.

SEE ALSO

Environmental Protection Agency; water pollution; asbestos; General Electric; Love Canal; Times Beach.

BIBLIOGRAPHY. CRS Report RL30022: *Summaries of Environmental Laws Administered by the EPA: Toxic Substances Control Act*, www.ncseonline.org (2003); Environmental Protection Agency, www.epa.gov (2003); Public Law 94-469: Toxic Substance Control Act Summary, www.loc.gov; Thomas P. Sullivan, ed., *Environmental Law Handbook* (Government Institutes, 1997); Toxic Substances Control Act, www.tamu.edu (2003).

ARTHUR HOLST, PH.D.
WIDENER UNIVERSITY

trademark infringement

A TRADEMARK IDENTIFIES a company and its product(s) or service(s) to consumers. Trademarks that are successfully identified with a particular company may be instantly recognizable. For instance, children all over the world, even those who cannot read, know that the golden arch trademark represents McDonald's fast food restaurant.

Trademark infringement deals with commercial use of a trademark "without the consent of the owner with intent to cause confusion or to cause a mistake or to deceive." Trademark infringement may consist of reproducing, counterfeiting, copying, or deceptively imitating a registered trademark.

The infringement may occur through the use of the violating trademark in advertising, packaging, letters, websites, promotional materials, etc. Successful trademarks often imbue consumers with feelings of familiarity and confidence; therefore, when another individual or company infringes on a trademark, consumers may be misled into buying the infringer's product or service. If the product is inferior, it may negatively impact on the trademark holder's business.

HISTORY OF TRADEMARKS

Courts in the United States have protected the rights of patent and copyright holders since the colonial period, but trademarks were unprotected until after the Civil War. In 1870, the U.S. Congress passed the first federal trademark law, but the Supreme Court overturned it eight years later on the grounds that the law was too broad and that it was improperly based on existing patent and copyright laws. A group of interested parties formed the International Trademark Association and lobbied Congress for a new law. Congress responded with the Trade-Mark Act of 1881, which allowed trademark holders to sue for infringement but failed to clarify crucial issues of how trademarks should be defined and who had the right to claim trademark infringement.

In 1945, Representative Fritz Lanham introduced a number of bills in the House of Representatives aimed at providing adequate protection for trademark holders and clarifying the issues left hanging in the earlier legislation. The results of Lanham's efforts were synthesized in the Lanham Act, which was signed into law in July 1946. The Lanham Act, which provided the groundwork for all future trademark legislation, defined a trademark as "any word, name, symbol, device, or any combination thereof adopted by a manufacturer or merchants to identify goods and distinguish them from those manufactured or sold by others." The legislation also created a separate agency under the U.S. Patent Office to deal with the registration of trademarks and established guidelines for proving infringement of federal copyrights.

In 1988, Congress updated the Lanham Act with the Trademark Law Revision Act and changed the period of trademark protection from 20 years to 10 years, with infinite renewals. After five years, the trademark holder is required to file an affidavit showing that the trademark will continue to be used. The name of the regulating agency was officially changed to the Patent and Trademark Office. In 1992, Congress again strengthened trademark protection with the Trademark Dilution Act, which became effective in 2000 and which stipulated that dilution of a trademark occurs when "similar trademarks are used for other products than the one registered to the trademark owner." On March 3, 2003, in *Moseley v. Secret Catalogues* (01-1015), the Supreme Court held that it was necessary for the plaintiff to show actual proof that the trademark had been diluted rather than the likelihood that it would do so.

TRADEMARK HOLDERS

In the United States, trademark holders may be protected from infringement by common law, state law, and federal law. To own a common law right to a trademark, a company or individual must adopt a trademark, affix it to a product or service, and use it in commerce within a restricted territory. On the other hand, trademarks that are registered in a state give the holder exclusive rights throughout the state. Federal trademarks involve trademarks that are used in interstate commerce. Individuals and companies can also file an intent-to-use trademark application with the Patent and Trademark Office.

Most trademarks are words, but they can also be logos, slogans, shapes, artistic designs, packaging, characters, graphic symbols, processes, sounds, or three-dimensional items. A company may also trademark a combination of these. A trademark containing word(s) may be an individual's name like Jean Naté, or the name of a company like Microsoft, or a "fanciful" name made up for the product like Kodak or Advil.

Fanciful names are better protected from infringement claims because they are more distinct than "arbitrary" trademarks that use an existing word like Apple Computers or Camel cigarettes. Words used in trademarks may also be suggestive like Coppertone tanning lotion. Graphic symbols like the Prudential rock or Arm and Hammer's bodiless arm wielding a hammer are so easily recognizable that no company name is really needed to identify those products.

Trademark infringement cases are often personal and highly emotional because both parties feel that their very identities are at stake, and at least one of the parties in the suit may have spent years establishing a reputation based on the trademark. Throughout the history of trademark law, courts have been asked to decide whether infringement has occurred, whether the likelihood of confusion exists, whether the infringement was intentional, whether an infringement resulted in damage to the legal owner of the trademark, and what remedies are available when infringement is upheld. To do these things, court have generally used The Restatement of Torts, which provides guidelines for trademark infringement based on the following tests:

Similarity of appearance may exist in cases such as the internationally known horseman trademark used by Polo Ralph Lauren and the double horseman trademark used by the United States Polo Association that has been challenged by Ralph Lauren.

Phonetic similarity was found in a suit in which Seycos watches were considered to have violated the trademark of Seiko watches because the names sounded so much alike.

Similarity of meaning is possible in cases like the one in which a fence company was denied the right to use the trademark Tornado because it was considered too similar in meaning to the existing Cyclone trademark for wire fences.

Channels of trade are used to determine if consumers might be confused by the same or similar name of a product sold in different markets. For example, both the Bigfoot trademark for snowmobile truck belts and Bigfoot for automobile tires were considered legal trademarks. On the other hand, Nutra Salt was seen as violating the trademark rights of Nutra Sweet because both products were sold to similar markets.

Directly competitive trademarks such as cellophane may take precedence over competitors who wish to use the term with other kinds of wrapping materials.

Degree of care, which is based on the level to which a consumer is committed to a product, would require that a court place more emphasis on the trademark of an automobile that cost several thousand dollars than on a bicycle that cost a few hundred dollars.

Strength of a famous mark gives broader protection to a nationally known trademark than to other trademarks.

Many trademark cases are settled without going to trial, and others are settled when both sides agree on a remedy. In cases that go to trial, the plaintiff may ask for an injunction to stop the sale or use of an infringing item, and the defendant may ask for a declaratory statement to make it clear that no infringement has occurred. Successful plaintiffs may also receive compensatory and/or punitive damages and may force the cancellation of a trademark registration that is considered violative.

SEE ALSO

copyright infringement; forgery; capitalism; United States.

BIBLIOGRAPHY. Donald M. Dible, *What Everybody Should Know about Patents, Trademarks, and Copyrights* (Entrepreneur Press, 1978); Robert C. Dorr and Christopher H. Munch, *Protecting Trade Secrets, Patents, Copyrights, and Trademarks* (Wiley Law, 1990); John. D. Oathout, *Trademarks: A Guide to the Selection, Administration, and Protection of Trademarks in Modern Business Practice* (Charles Scribner's Sons, 1981); Hope Viner Samborn," Who Got There First?" *ABA Journal* (October 2001); United States Patent and Trademark Office, www.uspto.gov (2003); Kimberly Weisul, "Ralph Lauren Isn't Horsing Around," *BusinessWeek* (October 29, 2003).

ELIZABETH PURDY, PH.D.
INDEPENDENT SCHOLAR

Truman, Harry (1884–1972)

BASED ON HIS early life as a Missouri farmer, cattleman, and failed investor, Harry Truman seemed an unlikely candidate for the highest political office in the United States. On April 12, 1945, Franklin D. Roosevelt (FDR, 1882–1945) died at the Little White House in Warm Springs, Georgia, after winning an unprecedented fourth term in November 1944. In that election, Truman had been on the ticket with Roosevelt for the first time. After only a few weeks as vice president and with insufficient time to settle into politics on such a large scale, Truman became the 33rd president of the United States.

One of Truman's major tasks as president was to continue Roosevelt's war on white-collar crime, particularly the ban on war profiteering and the fight against waste and corruption in government contracts. Once the war was over, Truman's Department of Justice turned its attention to policing crimes that evolved from the Cold War. This task was made more complicated by the antics of the House Committee on Un-American Activities, which insisted that there were communists strategically placed at all levels of American government. Federal prosecutors were forced to walk a tightrope between prosecuting genuine white-collar crimes and pursuing the alleged crimes reported by participants in what became known as the Red Scare.

As the new president, Truman accepted the responsibility of leading the country through the final days of World War II and establishing the United States as the major player in a new interdependent world and serving as the guiding force of the newly established United Nations and the North Atlantic Treaty Organization (NATO). Truman's most momentous decision came early in his presidency when he made the decision to drop the atomic bomb on Hiroshima, Japan, on August 6, 1945, and on Nagasaki, Japan, three days later in order to bring World War II to a formal close.

Roosevelt was admittedly a hard act to follow, but Truman had already made a name for himself during his 10 years in the Senate through hard work and ingenuity, often bucking the political machines that ruled political parties in the 1940s. After being notified by a number of sources about the waste and corrupt practices of government contractors and subcontractors, Senator Truman managed to convince his colleagues to establish the Senate Committee to Investigate the National Defense Program, which became known as the Truman Committee that investigated the military and defense industries and ultimately saved the government over $15 billion.

This committee became the vehicle by which Truman received FDR's attention and admiration and launched Truman as a vice presidential candidate. As president, Truman followed many of Roosevelt's plans for postwar America and adhered to almost all of FDR's plans for the United Nations. Truman did, however, develop his own leadership style and implemented new policy initiatives. In addition to his stint in Congress, Truman had served in World War I and as a judge in Missouri. This experience gave him a unique perspective on how the three branches of government worked together.

Although Truman became president through the death of FDR, in the 1948 election he was forced to run on his own record as the leader of the post-war Democratic party. When the Republican

Congress refused to implement his policies, Truman called them into special session. Truman then made their inaction a major element of his campaign. During the election, Truman promised to establish the Fair Deal policy, continuing the liberalism that had turned the country around during the Great Depression. Truman's Fair Deal consisted of over 30 propositions for government initiated reforms that centered around four major groups.

Civil Rights programs and legislation were designed to eliminate the political, social, and economic differences between races, including anti-lynching laws, fair employment and housing practices, an end to restrictions on voting, and the creation of a Civil Rights Commission to oversee implementation of civil rights programs.

Social welfare programs and legislation were intended to continue New Deal policies by passing more equitable tax laws, establishing national health insurance and unemployment compensation, and expanding coverage of social security benefits.

Housing programs were initiated in which the national government subsidized low and moderate housing to deal with the housing shortage that had emerged during World War II. Labor initiatives were directed toward raising the minimum wage from 40 to 75 cents an hour and expressing a strong opposition to the Taft-Hartley Act.

UNCONSTITUTIONAL ACTIONS

In June 1947, Congress passed the Labor Management Relations Act, more commonly known as the Taft-Hartley Act for its congressional sponsors, over Truman's veto. The law banned closed shops, regulated strikes, and made unions liable for damage suits incurred during strikes. In 1952, during the Korean War, Truman threatened to nationalize the railroads during a labor dispute and did seize control of the steel mills to forestall a strike in this crucial industry, acting through an executive order and ignoring the procedure for presidential intervention established in the Taft-Hartley Act. The Supreme Court found Truman's actions unconstitutional.

During Truman's second term, he also oversaw the Berlin Airlift that saved West Germany from communism, engineered U.S. entry into the Korean War, witnessed the fall of China to communism, and established American defenses to battle the Cold War which had developed as tensions with the

Soviet Union increased. Fear of communism in the United States, egged on by Senator Joseph McCarthy and his Red Scare, led to the creation of the President's Commission on Employee Loyalty and the Loyalty Oath that all government employees were required to sign, swearing that they had never been involved with the communist party in any way.

SEE ALSO
World War II; Roosevelt, Franklin D.; United States.

BIBLIOGRAPHY: Robert H. Farrell, *Harry S Truman and the Modern Presidency* (Little, Brown, and Company, 1983); Cabell Phillips, *The 1940s: Decade of Triumph and Trouble* (Macmillan, 1975); Cabell Phillips, *The Truman Presidency: The History of A Triumphant Succession* (Macmillan, 1966); Norman C. Thomas, *The Politics of the Presidency* (Congressional Quarterly, 1993).

ELIZABETH PURDY, PH.D.
INDEPENDENT SCHOLAR

truth in labeling

AMERICANS DEPEND on the national government to protect them from all kinds of potentially damaging substances and devices, and one way that the U.S. Congress has dealt with this issue has been to pass a series of acts mandating truth in labeling in everything from food to drugs to cosmetics to nutritional supplements to medical devices to music to movies to books to toys to blood to electrical appliances to automobiles to industrial hazards.

The history of labeling in the United States began early in the 20th century, when, in 1907 Congress passed the Federal Food and Drug Act and gave the Bureau of Chemistry, later known as the Food and Drug Administration (FDA), the responsibility for ensuring that food products were clean and free of toxins and that medicines were safe.

Later, the government also took on the responsibility of guaranteeing that medicines and products accomplished what the manufacturers promised they would do. In the 1920s, through a series of bills, Congress called for truth in labeling in clothing with the Truth in Fabric Act. This was followed in 1938 with the Federal Seed Act, which mandated truth in the labeling of seeds and seed products, and in 1948, by the Fur Labeling Act, calling for accurate labeling of furs and fur products to avoid misrepresentation. In the 1960s, Congress extended the truth in labeling requirements to include truth in lending, requiring that consumers be notified of specific charges, practices, and penalties when borrowing money to purchase high-priced goods.

In the wake of new attention to consumer rights, a number of government regulatory agencies announced additions to labeling requirements. Many conservatives, such as conservative economist Milton Friedman, argued that the government should not insist on labeling products because the market would take care of the problems; consumers would refuse to purchase and use unsafe products.

However, government agencies, liberals, and most consumers disagreed with Friedman, and the list of products affected by labeling requirements grew. Label requirements for packaging products was strengthened in 1964 with the Truth in Packaging Act in which Congress stipulated that package labels contain information on the weight, volume, or count of the package contents. Congress also mandated that manufacturers include a valid description of the contents of a package and include the name and address of the manufacturer on all packages.

WARNING LABELS

In 1978, the FDA, the U.S. Department of Agriculture, and the Bureau of Consumer Protection of the Federal Trade Commission (FTC) held five joint hearings around the country to ask consumers what information they saw as necessary for food labeling and how they felt it should be presented. The hearings produced over 900 oral commentaries and 9,000 letters. An additional two-day hearing generated another 2,000 comments. Subsequent meetings were also held in 1980 and 1981. Overwhelmingly, consumers wanted information that helped them make decisions about products and called for warnings against harmful products.

Reacting to consumer concerns, the U.S. government has given a number of government agencies the authority to oversee the practice of labeling to help consumers make wise decisions about products they commonly use. The FDA oversees labeling on foods, drugs, cosmetics, veterinary products, medical devices, biologics, and radiation-emitting products. The National Toxicology Program works with the FDA to identify potential toxins. The FTC is charged with oversight of truth in labeling and advertising. The Bureau of Alcohol, Tobacco, and Firearms guarantees truth in labeling of alcohol products. The Consumer Products Safety Division (CPSD) has oversight of most other products, including those commonly used in households such as baby toys or electrical appliances. The Food Safety Inspection Service (FSIS) under the direction of the Department of Agriculture has oversight responsibility for agricultural products.

There are four kinds of labels commonly used to convey information to consumers: content labels, which often contain messages about harmful ingredients such as tar or nicotine, but may also simply inform the consumer about the ingredients in the product such as the nutritional value of food or the fiber content of clothing; informational labels, which tell the consumer how to use a product and identify the possible dangers of misuse, such as using an electrical product around water; warning labels, which caution individuals about possible side effects of using the product as with some medications, or, in some cases, advise the use of protective clothing or conditions of use, such as using certain products only in well-ventilated areas; quality labels, which convey comparative information, such as "prime choice" or "irregular" on meat and clothing respectively.

The medium that is used to convey the message of the label has much to do with how well the consumer receives the message. For example, a consumer may be more likely to read large print than the fine print on the outside of a package, or a consumer may be more inclined to read information placed directly on the label of a medicine bottle than to read the details included on a prescription insert.

While a number of big businesses have continued to fight truth in labeling since its inception because of enormous costs involved in labeling and the loss of profits from unsafe or unwise products, numerous studies have documented the effectiveness of product labeling.

SEE ALSO
False Claims Act; Food and Drug Administration; Federal Trade Commission.

BIBLIOGRAPHY. Food and Drug Administration, www.fda.gov (2003); Michael B. Mazis, "An Overview of

Product Labeling and Health Risks," *Product Labeling and Health Risks* (Cold Spring Harbor Laboratory, 1980); Ira Sager, "The Price of Safety," *BusinessWeek* (September 15, 2003).

ELIZABETH PURDY, PH.D.
INDEPENDENT SCHOLAR

Truth in Lending Act

ON MAY 29, 1968, the U.S. Congress passed the Truth in Lending Act (TILA), Public Law 96-32. TILA was designed to promote economy stability by protecting the credit rights of consumers. Provisions of the act apply to individuals and businesses that on a regular basis offer and extend credit involving finance charges to individuals, families, or households. Credit extended for business and commercial activity and to security and commodities accounts are not covered by TILA. Loans in excess of $25,000 and public utility tariffs are excluded.

The bill came in response to lobbying by consumer groups and the realization that consumers were spending millions of dollars every year in unsuccessful efforts to deal with unfair credit practices. It was understood that in their quest for ever-increasing profits, creditors often ignored the concept of consumer rights. The Federal Reserve and the Federal Trade Commission (FTC) were given the power to enforce provisions of TILA. At the urging of consumer advocate Ralph Nader, Congress created the Consumer Protection Agency in 1971. This agency has the authority to oversee all activities concerned with protecting the rights of consumers. In addition to federal regulations, each state retains the right to establish laws and restrictions concerning interest rates and credit conditions.

Terms of the Truth in Lending Act require timely public disclosure of credit terms in language that consumers can understand. Before the TILA was passed, it was common practice for terms of credit to be placed in fine print and/or in highly legal terms that obscured the real terms of extending credit. The result was often high interest rates and unexpected finance charges for the consumer. Section 106 A of TILA mandates that the amount of finance charges shall be determined as the sum of all charges paid by the consumer. These charges include interest rates, time price differentials, point discount amounts, and other charges included in the loan. Service and carrying charges, finder's fees, credit report charges, and insurance payments are also covered by TILA disclosure requirements.

The Truth in Lending Act spells out specifically what must be included in information given to the consumer at the initial transaction and with each billing. Initially, the creditor must explain all finance charges, dates of accrual, billing cycles, conditions of charges, and use of additional charges. TILA also requires that the consumer be given a statement of consumer rights and information about resolving disputes. In periodic statements, the creditor must inform the consumer of the outstanding balance at the beginning of the billing cycle, amounts, and dates of any additional transactions, the total amount credited through payment or billing errors, itemized explanation of all finance charges, and the balance at the end of the billing cycle.

Credit extended through the use of credit cards is also restricted by TILA. In that instance, the creditor must detail the liability to the consumer for any unauthorized use of the credit card. Fraudulent use of credit cards in excess of $5,000 is punishable by fines up to $10,000 and imprisonment for up to five years or both.

The architects of the Truth in Lending Act recognized that consumers sometimes change their minds. In the case of a home improvement loan not covered by a first loan or mortgage, the consumer may withdraw from the loan within three working days. Truth in advertising credit was also covered under TILA. Creditors are bound to disclose the amount of the required down payment, the amount and due dates of payments, and the true annual percentage of finance charges.

Other provisions of TILA provide the consumer with the right to bring civil charges against creditors who do not comply with truth-in-lending law. Consumers have the right to collect damages up to twice the amount involved in the transaction. When credit abuse identified under TILA is extensive enough to warrant a class-action lawsuit, the creditor may be found liable up to $500,000 or one percent of net worth, whichever figure is lesser. The creditor may also be required to pay all court and legal costs. In some cases, the creditor is able to show that the illegal conduct was unintentional and that corrective measures have been initiated. In cases of criminal liability, the creditor can be fined up to $5,000, imprisoned for up to one year, or both.

The Fair Credit Billing Act of October 29, 1974 amended the Truth in Lending Act to give consumers greater protection by providing a legal platform for complaints and requiring creditors to disclose all billing complaints. In the 1970s, other Congressional efforts to protect the credit rights of consumers included the Fair Credit Reporting Act of 1979, the Equal Credit Opportunity Act of 1975, the Consumer Leasing Act of 1976, and the Fair Debt Collection Practices Act of 1977. Additionally, Congress has frequently extended truth-in-lending consumer protections through updated legislation.

SEE ALSO

bank fraud; credit card fraud; advertising fraud.

BIBLIOGRAPHY. Ira U. Cobleigh, "What Everyone Should Know About Credit Before Buying Or Borrowing Again," *U.S. News and World Report* (1975); Dorothy Cohen, *Consumer Behavior* (Random House, 1981); James Medoff and Andrew Harless, *The Indebted Society* (Little, Brown, 1996); Adam Starchild, *It's Your Money: A Consumer Guide to Credit* (Books for Business, 1978). "Truth in Lending Act," www.smartagreements.com (2003); "Truth in Lending Act 1968," www.lima.ohio-state.edu (2003); "You Can Fight Back!" www.fairdebtcollection.com (2003).

ELIZABETH PURDY, PH.D.
INDEPENDENT SCHOLAR

Tyco International

IN 1960, Tyco was established by Arthur J. Rosenburg, who started it as an investment and holding company in Waltham, Massachusetts (not be confused with the Tyco Toy, Inc., the well-known toy company). The company had two main holdings: the Materials Research Laboratory and Tyco Semiconductor. The company's primary function was performing experimental research for the government sector.

In 1962, Rosenburg incorporated the business, changing its name to Tyco Laboratories and merging Tyco Semiconductor and the Materials Research Laboratory. After the merger, Tyco still relied heavily on U.S. government research contracts. The main concentration of the company soon changed, from governmental research to the commercial sector, for which high-technology materials as well as science and energy conversion products were produced. As the company grew, it became public in 1964, and its expansion continued.

Tyco again altered is focus, and in 1965, it started to purchase other companies to meet its development and distribution network needs. It was during this phase that Tyco's purpose morphed into the manufacturing of industrial products. By 1968, a total of 16 companies had been acquired by Tyco Laboratories.

During the period of 1973-82, the company continued to experience tremendous growth through the acquisition of even more affiliated businesses. In 1974, Tyco's stock was listed on the New York Stock Exchange, and by 1982, its sales exceeded $500 million and its net worth surpassed $140 million. In 1976, the company hired L. Dennis Kozlowski. Major acquisitions of the company during this period included Simplex Technologies (1974); Grinnell Fire Protection Systems (1976); Armin Plastics (1984); and Ludlow Corporation (1981).

Between the years of 1986 and 2000, many significant changes occurred, including a name change from Tyco Laboratories to Tyco International Ltd. in 1993, which was a reflection of its increasingly global presence. These changes set the stage for the company's four business segments: electrical and electronic components, healthcare and specialty products, fire and security services, and flow control. Kozlowski became the company's chief executive officer (CEO) in 1992.

Tyco continued to experience success, attributed in part to the business practices of Kozlowski. In 1999, the Securities and Exchange Commission (SEC) initiated an inquiry into Tyco's practices, resulting in a restatement of Tyco's earnings in 2000. The SEC abandoned its probe in July 2000, and the company boasted revenues in excess of $6 billion for fiscal year 2001. In January 2002, the bright picture changed when its many questionable accounting practices were revealed, adding the name Tyco to a series of corporate crime scandals. It was during this time that Tyco posted a negative cash flow, and subsequently set a plan to break into four companies. This plan was deserted in April, during the course of an investigation by the Manhattan, New York City, district attorney's office.

The investigation revealed Kozlowski's involvement in many questionable activities, such as a $19 million, no-interest loan from Tyco in 1998, which the company forgave as part of a special bonus program. Tyco also covered Kozlowski's income taxes on the forgiven loan, which amounted to $13 million. Kozlowski's extravagant lifestyle, financed by Tyco, included multiple estates in Nantucket, Massachusetts, Rye, New Hampshire, and Boca Raton, Florida, as well as lavish parties, a 130-foot racing yacht, and charitable donations with company funds in Kozlowski's name. Estimates indicated that Kozlowski financed these activities by looting over $75 million from Tyco; none of this was made public to the company's shareholders.

Kozlowski resigned on June 2, 2002, and the following day, charges of evading more than $1 million in New York state sales taxes on art were filed against him. In September 2002, the SEC filed a civil enforcement action against Kozlowski and two other top executives, charging that they failed to disclose the multimillion dollar, interest-free loans from Tyco. Kozlowski's trial resulted in the most serious charges being dismissed, with a mistrial declared on the larceny charge. Expecting a retrial, and in an unusual situation, he has asked that his trial on state charges of sales tax evasion be combined with his federal larceny trial.

SEE ALSO

accounting fraud; embezzlement; fiduciary fraud; forensic auditing; Enron Corporation.

BIBLIOGRAPHY. M. Maremont and L. Cohen, "Tyco Spent Millions for Benefit of Kozlowski, its Former CEO," *Wall Street Journal* (August 7, 2002); "A History of Who We Are," www.tyco.com; "Litigation Release No. 17722," United States Securities and Exchange Commission, www.sec.gov (September 12, 2002),

KRISTY HOLTFRETER, PH.D.
FLORIDA STATE UNIVERSITY

tying arrangements

A TYING arrangement is an agreement by a party to sell one product or service only if the potential buyer: a) also purchases a different product or service, or b) agrees she will not purchase that product or service from another seller. The item the buyer wants to buy is the tying item, and the one she is required to buy in order to get it is the tied item.

A Louisiana hospital required that all surgical patients use the services of one of four anesthesiologists. A competing anesthesiologist charged that this violated the Sherman Antitrust Act, which "prohibits contracts, combinations, and conspiracies in restraint of trade, and monopolization, [and] includes criminal penalties when enforced by the government. Violation can result in substantial fines and, for individual transgressors, prison terms." The U.S. Supreme Court's 1984 decision that this case did not represent an illegal tying arrangement was based on the hospital's lack of dominant position; it only housed 30 percent of the area's hospitalized patients. If a patient did not want to use any of the four anesthesiologists, he could easily go to another hospital.

For many years prior to this *Jefferson Parish Hospital v. Hyde* decision, federal courts had considered tying arrangements to be illegal *per se*, that is, automatically illegal. However, in that landmark decision, five justices retained the traditional *per se* rule but only if an analysis of the market affected by the tying arrangement indicated a "substantial potential for impact on competition." The other four justices were in favor of abandoning *per se* altogether. Associate Justice John Paul Stevens said in the majority opinion that "there is nothing inherently anticompetitive about packaged sales." He went on to say that to have a tying arrangement, there must be two products with distinct markets, and the seller must have sufficient market power for the first product to compel the customer to buy the second product.

The key is the market power. A company that only holds a small share of market for a product or service will not endanger other companies, products, or consumer resources by tying its product or service with another. On the other hand, a company that has a large portion of the market would be much more likely to run afoul of illegal tying charges because consumers would have much less recourse, or other products to choose instead. Because of the actual market conditions and required effect on commerce, each case must be studied on an individual basis. A classic example of a tying arrangement involves Sandoz Pharmaceuticals. The company manufactured Clozaril, which is used in treatment of schizophrenia, and required that the medicine be bought only as a package with an expensive blood-monitoring system and lab-testing services operated by Caremark, Inc.

It was ruled that this was an illegal tying because, although Clozaril patients should have their blood monitored for side effects, those side effects were rare. More importantly, the tests could be performed more quickly and equally effectively by personnel by any hospital or laboratory service provider.

Tying arrangements, which can seriously damage competition, have been associated with many products and services. Charges of illegal tying have been filed in such diverse areas as photocopiers, computer software and systems, games, and banking services.

SEE ALSO

antitrust; Sherman Antitrust Act.

BIBLIOGRAPHY. U.S. Attorney General's Office, www.wa.gov/ago/trust/primer (2003); Linda Greenhouse, "Antitrust Bar to 'Tying' of Sales Eased by Court," *The New York Times* (March 28, 1984); "Preate, Others Sue Maker of Drug for Treatment of Schizophrenia," PR Newswire (December 18, 1990).

LINDA M. CREIBAUM
ARKANSAS STATE UNIVERSITY

U

unfair trade practices

UNFAIR trade practices involve a set of activities that involve one economic actor taking actions that are not consistent with the conditions of free market trade, thus obtaining or hoping to obtain an advantage over competitors. Unfair trade practices are related to but separate from both predatory practices, which involves the exploitation of weaker parties with partial access to information and marketing fraud, which involves making false promises about goods and services. However, there are considerable areas of overlap between the different sets of activities.

Unfair trade practices may be divided into the micro level, which concerns the activities of individual firms, and the macro level, which concerns activities at the industry or state level. In both cases, awareness of unfair trade practices and pressure applied to prevent them has intensified considerably in recent years as concerned people have been able to distribute information and organize protests much more efficiently through the use of the internet and mobile telecommunications technology. This, combined with the significantly reduced costs of international travel, have greatly raised awareness of global inequities and public sentiment has turned against the corporate sector in many cases because of high-profile financial scandals and the payment of huge salaries and bonuses to executives, seemingly irrespective of corporate performance.

MICRO LEVEL

There is a wide range of activities that may be classified as unfair trade practices at the micro level. They include espionage and theft of intellectual property, deliberately breaking business contracts or signing them without intending to adhere to them, or in some other ways undermining the competitive positions of other organizations. The point at which trade practices change from being intensely competitive to being unfair is, of course, difficult to define as it is likely to vary in most cases, and to appear differently to each participant.

For example, the growth in power of large retailers, like supermarket chains, has enabled them to apply considerable pressure on their suppliers to provide fruit and vegetables of regulation size and shape and at ever lower prices. These practices are regarded by the farmers as unfair but by the retailers as a legitimate use of market power to obtain a competitive advantage. Additional activities in which firms might indulge include the attempted creation of monopolistic conditions, discriminatory pricing, and dumping. Monopolistic competition or the attempts to create it may be countered by the use of antitrust legislation in whatever manifestation it appears in a particular country. Discriminatory pricing refers to charging different prices to sets of consumers based on criteria that do not conform to free trade principles. Dumping is a type of discriminatory pricing, in that prices in some export markets are set very low, possibly under the costs of production, so as to undermine the position of domestic competition. Accusations of this practice may be referred to the World Trade Organization (WTO). The tactic may also be employed within a domestic market when one or more products in a product line may be offered at a very low cost in the effort to obtain market share.

MACRO LEVEL

At the macro level, unfair trade practices involve such activities as barriers to entry into the home market, the imposition of taxes and tariffs on a discriminatory basis, and the creation of industry-wide cartels and consortia designed to maintain prices at high levels or else to extract an excessive amount of profit from customers. Perhaps inevitably, many of the practices of this kind are subject to being contested on political grounds, in that governments may plead special circumstances in protecting their own industries, or else that barriers to entry are simply health and safety standards. Examples of this include the insistence by the Korean government that all products imported into the country be packaged wholly in the Korean language and the European Union's (EU) refusal to accept some imports of Thai shrimps on the grounds of possible chemical contamination.

The use of government trade diplomacy in promoting home interests in export markets is also a potential source of contest unfair trade practices. Pressures to conduct these activities are intensifying in some respects because of the increasing need for competitiveness in markets in which large pools of cheap labor are becoming more active and important and states look to compete with each other more directly. Generally, international trade practices are regulated by the WTO, which seeks to act on a multilateral basis in resolving conflicts.

SEE ALSO

illegal competition; tariff crimes; globalization.

BIBLIOGRAPHY. "Lords Back Ban on 'Predatory' Newspaper Pricing," BBC News (February 10, 1998); Ji Zhaojin, A History of Modern Shanghai Banking: The Rise and Decline of China's Finance Capitalism (M.E. Sharpe, 2003); George Monbiot, "Loss Leaders," The Guardian (October 12, 2000); George Monbiot, "The Philosophy of Cant," The Guardian (September 16, 2003);

JOHN WALSH, PH.D.
MAHIDOL UNIVERSITY, THAILAND

Unilever

UNILEVER IS A Dutch-Anglo global company specializing in consumer goods, essentially food and personal care products. Unilever proclaims that every day 150 million people are choosing their brands "to feed their families and clean their homes." Its products are sold in over 150 countries and the company has annual sales of approximately $46 billion. Unilever controls subsidiaries in at least 90 countries and has 295,000 employees (2000).

In spite of Unilever's vast size and presence worldwide, the company's actual visibility is cloaked into appearing relatively small since Unilever does not retail under its own name. The global company creates loyalties to various brand names in various markets. One of the keys of its winning strategy is a substantial dependence on advertising.

Unilever distributes its products all over the world, especially in Europe, the United States, South America, and Asia. Among them are prestigious brands, such as Magnum and Solero and Ben & Jerry's (ice cream). Other recognizable goods are labeled Dove and Lever 2000 (soaps), Gorton's (frozen meals), Slim Fast meal replacement drinks, Lipton (teas), and Vaseline, among the 400 brands the company controls. Shares of Unilever are available for trade in the Netherlands, France, Germany, Great Britain, the United States, and Switzerland.

Unilever has strong ties with the third world thanks to the operation of plantations and agricultural experiments it has carried out in cooperation with national governments. It uncompromisingly controls the virtual food chain. For example, tea is the result of Unilever's agricultural and economic systems in the web of supply and demand worldwide. As a true transnational giant, Unilever has been criticized over time at different levels. For example, in the promotion of its products, Unilever tries to bring as many products as possible to the market without necessarily examining the consequences. The Advertising Standards Authority (ASA) ruled that Unilever misled British consumers in the way the company presented the health benefits of its cholesterol-lowering margarine, Flora pro-activ.

Unilever was accused by Greenpeace of double standards and shameful negligence for allowing its Indian subsidiary, Hindustan Lever, to dump several tons of highly toxic mercury waste in the densely populated tourist resort of Kodaikanal and the surrounding protected nature reserve of Pambar Shola, in Tamilnadu, southern India.

According to Corpwatch, a corporate watchdog group, "In March 2001, residents of Kodaikanal caught Unilever red-handed when they uncovered a dumpsite with toxic mercury-laced waste from a thermometer factory run by Hindustan Lever. The 7.4 ton stockpile of crushed mercury-containing glass was found in torn sacks, spilling onto the ground in a busy scrap yard located near a school."

Corpwatch further states: "Unilever's actions in Kodaikanal violated several United Nations Global Compact principles. Some of their actions, such as the closure of the factory, may appear to be in line with responsible behavior. However, these actions were taken only after the community exposed Unilever's wrongdoings."

Unilever's chief executive officer admitted unethical business practices, confirming the use of "sweeteners" or "facilitation payments," used by local management administration in approximately 90 countries, to seal business deals.

SEE ALSO

bribery; corporate criminal liability.

BIBLIOGRAPHY. David Kenneth Fieldhouse, *Unilever Overseas: The Anatomy of a Multinational, 1895–1965* (Croom Helm, 1978); Geoffrey Jones, "Controls, Performance, and Knowledge Transfers in Large Multinationals: Unilever in the United States, 1945-1980," *Business History Review* (v.76/3, 2002); Floris A. Maljers, "Inside Unilever: The Revolving Transnational Company," *Harvard Business Review* (v.70/5, 1992); Charles Wilson, *The History of Unilever* (Cassel & Company Publishing, 1970).

ALFREDO MANUEL COELHO
UNIVERSITY OF MONTPELLIER, FRANCE

Union Carbide

THE U.S.-BASED chemical company, Union Carbide Corporation, a wholly-owned subsidiary of Dow Chemical Company since 2001, is linked in the minds of many to the 1984 Bhopal disaster. Just after midnight on December 3, 1984 methyl isocyanate gas leaked from a tank at a chemical plant in Bhopal, India, that was owned and operated by Union Carbide India Limited, a joint venture between Union Carbide and a group of Indian companies.

According to the state government of Madhya Pradesh, approximately 3,500 people died, 40 people experienced permanent total disability, and 2,680 people experienced permanent partial disability. The Bhopal People's Health and Documentation Clinic maintains that 8,000 people died in the immediate aftermath of the incident; other estimates range higher as well. Although the number of people killed and injured is disputed, most commentators agree that the Bhopal disaster is the world's worst industrial disaster to date.

The Bhopal disaster has come to dominate popular memory of Union Carbide, obscuring the history of the company prior to the date of the disaster. Although the Union Carbide and Carbon Corporation did not exist until November 1917, its origins date to the formation of the Union Carbide Company to manufacture calcium carbide for acetylene and carriage lamps in 1898. A period of tremendous growth followed, but was soured by events at Hawk's Nest, West Virginia during the late 1920s and early 1930s.

Approximately 700 people died from acute silica poisoning contracted during the construction of a tunnel for a hydroelectric power project near Hawk's Nest, Virginia in 1930. Union Carbide conceived the project in 1927, contracting the construction work to Rinehart and Dennis and forming the New Kanahwa Power Company to operate the hydroelectric plants. Union Carbide engineers directed the work carried out by Rinehart and Dennis, which employed the construction workers. Many of the workers contracted silicosis after inhaling rock dust containing silica while clearing the tunnel of blasted rock.

In 1932 lawyers began legal proceedings on behalf of several of the workers with local residents testifying that the workers left the site covered in dust. The courts ruled in favor of compensating the workers. However, the court cases were settled out of court after the victims' attorneys received secret payments to take no further action.

During the 1940s, Union Carbide played an important role in the U.S. war effort, producing butadiene, styrene and polyethylene; mining and refining uranium; and contributing to atomic weapons research by operating the Oak Ridge, Tennessee, facilities for the U.S. government. In 1970 the world's largest mercury spill occurred at the Oak Ridge plant. Union Carbide used large quantities of mercury in the weapons work. In 1982 health officials warned that fish from an Oak Ridge creek should not be eaten because of high levels of mercury left from a spill in 1966. The following year a declassified report revealed that Oak Ridge plants released an estimated 2.4 million pounds of mercury from the 1950s to the mid-1960s.

By 1984 Union Carbide's fortunes were improving as the global economy recovered from the effects of the 1970s oil shocks. The company was well respected within the chemical industry and operated 1,200 sites around the world.

THE BHOPAL DISASTER

Union Carbide had a long history in India before the Bhopal disaster, opening its first plant, a battery-assembly unit near Calcutta, in 1924. In 1975 the government of India granted Union Carbide a license to manufacture pesticides, which played an essential role in attempts to increase Indian agricultural productivity. Union Carbide and a group of Indian companies formed Union Carbide India Limited (UCIL). This joint venture company was to construct and operate the pesticide plant in Bhopal, Madhya Pradesh. The plant used methyl isocyanate (MIC) to manufacture sevin carbaryl and several other carbamate pesticides. Sometime during the third shift on the night of December 2, 1984 a large quantity of water entered Tank 610. The water reacted with the MIC leading to a rapid increase in temperature and pressure inside the tank. A pressure release valve on the tank blew open, and 41 tons of MIC gas were released into the atmosphere, killing thousands and injuring thousands more in residential areas downwind of the plant.

In the immediate aftermath of events at Bhopal, the media attributed the incident to improper washing of a pipe in the MIC manufacturing unit. It emerged that a worker cleaning pipes in the MIC

manufacturing unit on the day of the incident failed to isolate the section of pipe he was cleaning by inserting a metal slip blind. This account portrayed the plant as poorly run, an impression reinforced by increasing revelations about malfunctioning pressure gauges and thermometers, and the parlous state of the plant's safety system.

The cooling system was not working and the vent gas scrubber was turned off for maintenance, as was the flare tower. It also emerged that a team of Union Carbide engineers inspected the Bhopal plant and indicated that it was unsafe in May 1982. In their Business Confidential safety audit the team identified "61 hazards, 30 of them major and 11 in the dangerous phosgene/MIC units." When it became known that Union Carbide was planning to sell its Indian chemicals and plastics businesses before the incident, there appeared to be a commercial reason for the company's apparent lack of concern about rectifying health and safety issues at the plant.

SABOTAGE OR NEGLIGENCE

The government of India and Union Carbide investigated the incident independently. The official investigation plumped for the water-washing theory and placed the blame for the incident firmly on the shoulders of UCIL, while Union Carbide attributed the incident to employee sabotage and later to a Sikh terrorist group known as Black June. Although the Union Carbide team accepted that the entry of water into Tank 610 caused the leak, the team attributed this to deliberate sabotage, not improper washing of a pipeline in the MIC unit.

The government of India did not share this interpretation of events and sought compensation from Union Carbide. In 1985 the government passed the Bhopal Gas Leak (Processing of Claims) Act making the government the sole representative of the victims and their relatives in dealings with the company. India proceeded to file a civil suit against Union Carbide in a U.S. federal court, seeking $3 billion in compensation. The U.S. court sent the case back to the Indian courts in May 1986. Meanwhile, Bhopal District Court ordered Union Carbide to pay $190 million in interim relief to Bhopal victims.

The Jabalpur High Court upheld the court order after hearing a Union Carbide appeal. In February 1989, the Supreme Court of India ordered Union Carbide and UCIL to pay the government of

India $470 million and $45 million in compensation for Bhopal, settling all litigation relating to Bhopal. The court also quashed all criminal proceedings relating to the incident. In January 1990, the government of India announced it would support victims' attempts to have the Bhopal settlement set aside. Almost two years later, the Indian Supreme Court revoked the criminal immunity granted to the company and its officers. Attempts to bring Warren Anderson and other former executives to trial continue as do efforts to set aside the 1989 settlement.

It is arguable whether Union Carbide ever truly recovered from Bhopal, and the weakened company merged with a subsidiary of Dow Chemical Company in 2001, becoming a wholly owned subsidiary. Dow maintains that the company did not inherit an outstanding liability for the Bhopal disaster despite being the focus of lobbying by Bhopal survivors. However, Dow inherited several other liabilities from Union Carbide, including responsibility for asbestosis and environmental damage.

The U.S. authorities were slow to learn the lessons of Bhopal until a small amount of MIC gas leaked from a Union Carbide plant in Institute, West Virginia, in August 1985. This awakened the American public to the possibility of an incident similar to Bhopal occurring in the U.S. The Environmental Protection Agency (EPA) responded to these concerns by establishing the voluntary Chemical Emergency Preparedness program to encourage state and local authorities to identify hazards and plan for emergencies in their area. In 1986 Congress incorporated many of the elements of this program in the Emergency Planning and Community Right-to-Know Act of 1986, also known as Title III of the Superfund Amendments and Reauthorization Act .

The chemical industry also took steps to prevent another major release of toxic gas and repair the industry's public image. The U.S. Chemical Manufacturers Association (CMA) initiated a Responsible Care initiative in 1988. The initiative was an attempt to improve the safety and environmental performance of the U.S. chemical industry and thus improve the public image of the U.S. chemical industry after Bhopal.

SEE ALSO

India; corporate criminal liability; negligence.

BIBLIOGRAPHY. Martin Cherniack, *The Hawk's Nest Incident: America's Worst Industrial Disaster* (Yale University Press, 1989); Larry Everest, *Behind the Poison Cloud: Union Carbide's Bhopal Massacre* (Banner Press, 1985); Dan Kurtzman, *A Killing Wind: Inside Union Carbide and the Bhopal Catastrophe* (McGraw-Hill, 1987); Robert D. Stief, *A History of Union Carbide Corporation: from the 1890s to the 1990s* (Carbide Retirees Corps, 1998); Union Carbide Corporation, *Our History* (Union Carbide Corporation, 1976); Bruce W. Piasecki, "Change from Above: Union Carbide and Reactive Strategies," *Corporate Environmental Strategy: The Avalanche of Change since Bhopal* (Wiley, 1995).

MARK ROODHOUSE, PH.D.
UNIVERSITY OF YORK, ENGLAND

unions

UNIONS ARE constituted for the aim of collectively negotiating with employers over wages, hours and other terms and conditions of employment. Throughout their history, labor unions have been both perpetrators and challengers of corporate crimes. In his division of corporate crime into white-collar and occupational crimes, Clinard Marshall describes occupational crime as that "committed largely by individuals or small groups of individuals in connection with their occupations. It includes violations of the law by businessman, politicians, labor union leaders, lawyers, doctors, pharmacists, and employees who embezzle money from their employers or steal merchandise and tools."

On the other hand, he also states that corporate crime is indicative of the power relations in our societies and that laws on such crime indicate the influence of big corporations on legislation. It is in this context that unions, together with other interest groups, can challenge illegal corporate activities such as the disregard of workers' safety. The intervention of unions is particularly necessary given the failure of big business to act sufficiently to assure the health and safety of its workers.

Without the pressure of unions for labor legislation, workers could still be paid according to what corporations deem appropriate and working conditions could be more dangerous. In the context of global capitalism, many scholars and economists agree unions are a much needed corrective to the general profit motive.

Despite ties to organized crime and politics, unions have protected the safety and wages of American workers.

As an assistant attorney general put it: "In these times, when important and far-reaching questions are being raised about the ethics of the business community, strong and eloquent voices urging responsible business behavior are vitally needed."

ORIGINS AND SCOPE

The concept of labor unions developed in Europe at the time of the Industrial Revolution, when agricultural activities declined and employment began to move to urban and industrialized areas. An increasing number of people left farming and started to work for employers, often in hideous conditions and for very low wages. The labor movement arose as a result of the disparity between the power of

employers and the powerlessness of individual employees. Predictably, employers did not welcome the appearance of unions on the labor scene. Labor unions were illegal for many years in most countries. There were severe penalties for attempting to organize labor unions, including execution and deportation. However, such an attitude proved, in the long run, to favor rather than hinder the development of labor unions. To quote just one of the most famous examples of this trend, in 1834, six British men from Tolpuddle in Dorset were arrested and deported to Australia for the founding of the Friendly Society of Agricultural Laborers. Yet, they soon became popular heroes and were released two years later with the help of Home Secretary Lord John Russell. Their fame has survived to this day and many memorials and events still celebrate the six Tolpuddle Martyrs as they have become known in labor history.

Labor unions soon developed into important political entities which eventually managed to get approved a body of labor law legalizing organizational efforts and codifying the relationship between employers and those employees who are members of labor unions. Yet, both the function of labor unions and the extent and effectiveness of labor legislation vary greatly from country to country. In Europe, unions have played a greater role in management decisions through participation in corporate boards, while in the United States this practice started later and is still limited. To many, the appointment of union officials to boards of directors is an effective countermeasure to corporate crime. Yet, not everyone believes that union board members will necessarily exhibit greater responsibility than business members. What mainly affects the roles of the unions is the structure of employment laws. In many European countries, wages and work contracts are largely negotiated through governmental action. The American approach, on the other hand, derives from theories of *laissez-faire* capitalism and while, setting some minimum standards, it leaves most workers' salary and benefits to collective bargaining and market forces.

POLITICS AND UNIONS

Unions have also very different relationships with political parties in different countries and such relationships are constantly changing. In many European countries unions were, in the past, integrally associated with a particular political party. During the Cold War era, for example, in countries which had a strong communist party such as Italy and France, trade unions soon split according to their ideological allegiances. In Italy, critics of the leftist union CGIL considered it as the "conveyor belt" of the politics of the Italian Communist Party. In France, in 1948, a group of the leftist union CGT founded the union Force Ouvrière, denouncing the dominance of the French Communist Party within the CGT. With the disappearance of the two contrasting blocks of the Cold War and the definition of a more moderate agenda for the Left, the relationships between unions and parties has turned out to be more fluid. Even in a country like the United Kingdom, where the labor movement has always been an integral part of the Labor Party, this relationship frayed as Prime Minister Tony Blair's New Labor embarked on privatization plans considered irreconcilably at odds with labor's interests.

In the United States, by contrast, while the labor movement has traditionally been aligned with the Democratic Party, labor unions have not been monolithic in their alliances. The International Brotherhood of Teamsters, the big union that was headed for two decades by Jimmy Hoffa, supported Republican Party candidates on a number of occasions. The Professional Air Traffic Controllers Organization endorsed Ronald Reagan in 1980, only to see the president banning all of its striking members from employment the following year.

Images of corruption and crime have also been widely associated with unions in the American collective mind. While efforts were made throughout the 19th century to establish unions, religion, race, ethnicity and gender acted as divisive forces. The early American craft unions founded in the 1820s and 1830s had characteristics more similar to medieval guilds than to modern trade unions: membership, which was refused to women and African Americans, was conceived as a way to avoid the competition of inferior workmen due to the regulation of apprenticeship and the establishment of minimum wages.

Craft unions soon started to gather in umbrella organizations such as the National Trades Union, but the high unemployment and the wage cuts that characterized the late 1830s and early 1840s led to the collapse of the movement. This pull of organization and disorganization was constant throughout the century, making the presence of trade unions in

Union membership steadily declined in the late 20th and early 21st centuries as corporate strengths have grown.

American life extremely weak: only 2 per cent of the total labor force and less than 10 per cent of all industrial workers, were members of unions. Nineteenth century middle-class Americans saw workers' organizations with suspicion.

AMERICAN UNIONIZATION

In 1881, the Federation of Trades and Labor Unions was founded, and five years later the organization changed its name to the American Federation of Labor (AFL). The AFL's first president was Samuel Gompers, who held fairly conservative political views and believed that trade unionists should accept the capitalist economic system. The membership of AFL consisted of about 140,000 workers, most of them skilled and native-born. Gompers purposefully avoided the rhetoric of workers' solidarity and pushed instead for concrete targets such as higher wages, shorter hours and the right to bargain collectively. Gompers's deputy gave an effective view of the AFL stating that they had no ultimate ends, but were fighting only for immediate objects, "objects that can be realized in a few years." In contrast to earlier workers' organizations such as the Knights of Labor, the AFL accepted industrialism and worked to improve working conditions. Though AFL memberships grew steadily under Gompers' leadership, the union suffered several setback in the 1890s due to the outbreak of labor violence, especially in the railroad industry.

In 1905, representatives of 43 groups, who opposed the policies of American Federation of Labor, formed the radical labor organization, the Industrial Workers of the World (IWW). The IWW, whose motto was "An injury to one is an injury to all," shared the Knights of Labor's aim of seeking to unite all workers, including the unskilled who were barred from craft unions. Yet, its members, known as "Wobblies," were more radical than most Knights of Labor: they clearly supported socialism and employed tactics of sabotage. The Wobblies used the rhetoric of class conflict, "The final aim is revolution," to convey their belief that workers should run national industries.

Mary Harris, better known as "Mother Jones," fought against the exploitation of workers in mines and helped miners to organize. Many members and leaders of the Industrial Workers of the World were harassed by the police and suffered legal prosecutions. Mother Jones was arrested following the strike in Paint Creek, West Virginia. During the strike, men employed by the mine-owners opened fire against the strikers and their families.

When a company guard was murdered, Jones, then age 78, was found guilty of being involved in the crime, and sentenced to 20 years in prison (later overturned). In addition, since the IWW opposed America's entry into the First World War, many of its leaders were arrested under the Espionage Act. This tactic of intimidation was highly effective and, by 1925, membership had declined dramatically.

THE ROOSEVELT YEARS

During the presidency of Franklin D. Roosevelt, elected in 1932 with the support of most trade unionists, the labor movement scored important victories. Frances Perkins and Robert Wagner, whose sympathy for the trade union movement was well-known, were appointed respectively as secretary of labor and chairman of the National Recovery Administration. In 1933, Wagner introduced a bill to Congress to help protect trade unionists from their employers. With the support of Perkins, Wagner's proposals became the National Labor Relations Act. It created the National Labor Relations Board which administered the regulation of labor relations in industries engaged in or affecting interstate commerce. The act also sanctioned the rights of workers to join trade unions and to bargain collectively with their employers through representatives of their own choosing. Workers were now protected from their employers and, as a result, union membership grew rapidly. While union membership stood at 3.6 million in 1929, in 1938 it exceeded 7 million.

The New Deal era also witnessed the creation of a new confederation of labor. In 1935, John L. Lewis joined with the heads of seven other unions to form the Congress for Industrial Organization (CIO). Lewis became president of this new organization and, over the next few years, attempted to organize workers in the new mass-production industries, including, for the first time, women and African Americans. This strategy was successful and, only two years later, the CIO had more members than the AFL. The two organizations merged in 1955.

In June 1938, Perkins persuaded Congress to pass the Fair Labor Standards Act, whose main objective was to eliminate "labor conditions detrimental to the maintenance of the minimum standards of living necessary for health, efficiency, and well-being of workers." The act established maximum working hours as 44 per week for the first year, 42 for the second, and 40 thereafter. Minimum wages of 25 cents an hour were established for the first year, 30 cents for the second, and 40 cents over a period of the next six years. The Fair Labor Standards Act also prohibited child labor in all industries engaged in producing goods in inter-state commerce and limited the labor of boys and girls between 16 and 18 years of age in dangerous occupations.

Another important act passed, thanks to the initiative of Perkins and the vice president, Harry S Truman, was the Fair Employment Act. This 1942 act compelled all federal agencies to include in their contracts with private employers a provision obligating such employers not to "discriminate against persons of any race, color, creed, or nationality in matters of employment." The act set up the Committee on Fair Employment Practice (FEPC), a body that was empowered to investigate all complaints of discrimination.

TAFT-HARTLEY

However, at the end of the New Deal, the changed political climate prompted the Republican Party and right-wing elements in the Democratic Party to object to the pro-trade union legislation of the Roosevelt administration. On June 23, 1947, Congress passed the Taft-Hartley Act, over the veto of President Truman, who denounced it as a "slave-labor bill." The act, still in effect, severely limited the power of trade unions.

It forbade jurisdictional strikes and secondary boycotts. It prohibited the closed shop, a workplace where membership of a particular union was a prerequisite for being hired. Other aspects of the legislation included the right of employers to be exempted from bargaining with unions unless they wished to. The act forbade unions from contributing to political campaigns and required union leaders to affirm they were not supporters of the communist party. This aspect of the act was upheld by the Supreme Court in 1950. The Taft-Hartley Act also established the National Labor Relations Board, a body that had the power to determine the issuance or prosecution of a complaint. Under the terms of the act, the U.S. attorney general had the power to obtain an 80-day injunction when a threatened or actual strike was believed to imperil the national health or safety, a proviso that courts have interpreted extremely loosely. During the post-World War II years, the climate of the Cold War also proved damaging for unions and the labor movement. The movement was absorbed by the dominating anti-communism hysteria which pushed unions to disown their class-conscious militancy. In 1949, the CIO expelled 11 unions, amounting to some 900,000 workers suspected of being communist-controlled.

ORGANIZED CRIME

In the postwar period, many U.S. unions lost much of their prestige when links to organized crime were

discovered. An image of trade unions as source of corruption began to take hold in the public mind. Such a characterization was also dramatized in successful Cold War popular culture products such as Elia Kazan's film *On the Waterfront* (1954), where rank and file are exploited and impoverished by the mob-infested union, the International Longshoremen's Association. Some unions progressively acquired the reputation of being groups of thugs who would use even unlawful methods to bring some employers into line.

This was the case, for example, of the Teamsters, the union of truck drivers which was headed from the 1950s through the late 1960s by the famous and controversial labor leader Jimmy Hoffa. Hoffa scored an important success in 1964 when he managed to bring virtually all American truck drivers under a single national master freight agreement. Hoffa's grand design, however, was to bring all transport employees into the union: this ambition obviously worried American government and business alike which understood how devastating a general strike of all the transportation sector could be for the national economy. Hoffa's policy brought benefits to truck drivers, yet several local Teamsters leaders agreed to make deals that contributed more to the wealth of union officers rather than to workers' rights and benefits.

Hoffa also had dangerous ties with the mafia, which, in certain sectors, such as garment delivery, took control of the union and worked to put industries under its control or, at least vulnerable to its blackmail. Some of these mafia racketeers had played an important part in getting Hoffa elected president of the Teamsters. In spite of their many convictions for mob-related crimes, several Teamster chapter presidents often continued serving as union leaders, including Antonio Provenzano, in New Jersey. There is evidence that the Teamsters pension fund was used to fund mob-controlled casinos and hotels.

In the last decades of the 20th century, union membership steadily declined in all sectors except the public one. In the conclusion to her study on the representation of workers in American fiction, Laura Hapke effectively summarizes the predicament of American unions and its leaders who have exchanged "unified labor militancy for a job-security pragmatism" and who "have engaged in their own unfair labor practices by their obliviousness to work-floor and retirement inequities."

Union members were disappointed but not surprised by their leaders' behavior of permanent mismanagement and greed. Yet, Hapke also denounces "the prevailing cultural amnesia," which affected American public awareness about job protests. Unanimous voices state that the working class and the labor movement are progressively fading out from American consciousness, but such reports may be exaggerated: unions at the beginning of the new millennium are still alive and fighting.

SEE ALSO
Teamsters pension fund; capitalism; globalization; labor crimes; Roosevelt, Franklin D.

BIBLIOGRAPHY. Irving Bernstein, *The Lean Years: A History of the American Worker, 1920–33* (Penguin Books, 1960); Irving Bernstein, *Turbulent Years: A History of the American Worker, 1933–41* (Houghton-Mifflin, 1971); Mary H. Blewett, *Women, and Work* (University of Illinois Press, 1988); Lizabeth Cohen, *Making a New Deal: Industrial Workers in Chicago, 1919–39* (Cambridge University Press, 1990); Katherine M. Dudley, *The End of the Line: Lost Jobs, New Lives in Postindustrial America* (University of Chicago Press, 1994); Leon Fink, *Workingmen's Democracy: The Knights of Labor and Americans Politics* (University of Illinois Press, 1983); Nancy Gabin, *Feminism in the Labor Movement* (Cornell University Press, 1990); Herbert Gutman, *Work, Culture, and Society in Industrializing America: Essays in American Working Class and Social History* (Alfred Knopf, 1976); Laura Hapke, *Labor's Text: The Worker in American Fiction* (Rutgers University Press, 2001); Marshall Clinard, *Corporate Crime* (Free Press, 1983); David Montgomery, *Worker's Control in America: Studies in the History of Work, Technology, and Labor Struggles* (Cambridge University Press, 1979); David Roediger, *The Wages of Whiteness: Race and the Making of the American Working Class* (Verso Books, 19910; Willie Thompson and Daniel Nelson, *The St. James Encyclopedia of Labor History Worldwide* (St. James Press, 2003); Sean Wilentz, *Chants Democratic: New York City and the Rise of the American Working Class* (Oxford University Press, 1984).

Unisys

IN SEPTEMBER 1991, Unisys, then the fourth-largest defense contractor in the United States, agreed to pay a record $190 million fine to settle criminal charges stemming from Operation Ill Wind. Among those implicated in the government investigation of Defense Department corruption were six company executives, several consultants, military officials, and Armand D'Amato, brother of Senator Alfonse D'Amato (R-NY).

Formed in the 1986 merger of Burroughs and Sperry, Unisys became a computer industry giant, second only to IBM in size. Late that year, the company sold its Sperry Aerospace division to Honeywell but overstated assets in the $1.025 billion deal, leading to a 1993 settlement in which Unisys paid Honeywell $43.2 million.

Operation Ill Wind was an Federal Bureau of Investigation and Naval Investigative Service project aimed at rooting out fraud in the defense industry. In June 1988, a federal grand jury issued 275 subpoenas; federal agents searched 42 homes and offices in 12 states. Unisys' 1991 guilty plea was the 51st conviction of companies or individuals fingered in the investigation.

Charges against Unisys included bribing Melvyn R. Paisley, an assistant secretary of the navy, and Victor D. Cohen, air force deputy for tactical warfare systems, to gain contracts for the navy's Aegis anti-air warfare system and other military projects. Two years before the Unisys settlement, Garland L. Tomlin Jr., a branch head of the navy's Space and Naval Warfare Systems Command, pled guilty to accepting the largest bribe uncovered in the probe, $400,000 from Unisys and $75,000 from Honeywell. Tomlin was sentenced to 18 months in prison.

As well as direct bribery, Unisys was charged with using consultants to make illegal campaign contributions to members of the House Armed Services and Appropriations committee. Unisys also funneled money to D'Amato, hoping that he would lobby his brother. Senator Alfonse D'Amato was reprimanded by the Senate in 1991 for allowing his brother unrestricted access to his office and letterhead; Armand D'Amato was convicted in 1993 of seven counts of mail fraud. The brains behind Unisys' wrongdoing, Vice-President Charles Gardner, pleaded guilty in 1989 to bribing Paisley; on his release, he testified for the government against the younger D'Amato.

The 1991 settlement cleared the way for Unisys to spin off its troubled defense division as Paramax. This company, briefly owned by Loral and then bought by Lockheed Martin in 1996, had its own woes during multiple rounds of layoffs in the early 1990s. Although still faced with lawsuits from retirees whose health insurance benefits were cut, Unisys is finally showing signs of stability. Among its current products is fraud-prevention software.

SEE ALSO

bribery; defense contract fraud; whistleblowers; False Claims Act.

BIBLIOGRAPHY. "Business Briefs: Honeywell to Get $70 Million to Settle Litigation over Purchase of Sperry Unit," *Wall Street Journal* (April 19, 1993); Robert W. Greene, "Senator's Brother Indicted," *Newsday* (March 12, 1992); Robert F. Howe, "Pentagon Fraud Defendant Given 18 Months in Jail," *Washington Post* (October 28, 1989); Robert F. Howe, "Unisys to Pay Record Fine in Defense Fraud," *Washington Post* (September 7, 1991); Ruth Marcus, "Details of Defense Probe Remain Shrouded," *Washington Post* (June 26, 1988); Steven Pearlstein, "Unisys to Sell McLean Defense Unit in Stock Offering," *Washington Post* (October 1, 1991); Jonathan Rabinovitz, "Trial of Armand D'Amato May Focus on His Brother," *New York Times* (April 19, 1993); Patrick Sweeney, "Suit Says Unisys Defrauded Government By Overcharging," *Saint Paul Pioneer Press* (April 9, 1998); Wendy Tanaka, "Retirees Say Unisys Broke Benefit Pledge," *Philadelphia Inquirer* (April 24, 2003); Michael Weber, "Purchase Order the Key," *Newsday* (May 8, 1993).

WENDE VYBORNEY FELLER, PH.D.
ST. MARY'S COLLEGE OF CALIFORNIA

United American Bank

THE UNITED American Bank (UAB), based in Knoxville, Tennessee, was part of the Butcher brothers' financial empire which collapsed as a result of numerous legal and banking problems. Jake and C. H. Butcher were originally considered to be some of Knoxville's finest residents. Exercising influence from their financial empire which included 27 banks in Tennessee and Kentucky with over $3 billion in assets, the Butcher brothers were responsible for funding Knoxville's two tallest buildings and for attracting the World's Fair in 1982.

The brothers worked together well, with Jake taking care of expansions in larger markets and C.

H. dealing with the more rural areas. Jake could win investment from wealthy industrialists while C. H. was persuasive with small community farmers. However, the situation did not remain perfect for long. During the days leading up to the opening of the World's Fair, politicians and citizens began to question Jake's methods of raising money to attract the fair. On the day after the closure of the fair, November 1, 1982, auditors from the Federal Deposit Insurance Corporation (FDIC) set themselves up at UAB headquarters and began conducting a thorough investigation.

SURPRISING NEWS

To UAB employees, the length of the FDIC auditors' investigation begin to raise concerns. Typical FDIC examinations usually lasted a month or two, but UAB's investigation did not end until February 14, 1983 and on that day, UAB employees were told some surprising news. They were now employees of the FDIC and UAB was served notice of closure by the FDIC for numerous violations.

Depositors had heard of the bank's difficulties and UAB had been paying out large sums of money for weeks leading up to the impending closure. Over the following days, the FDIC shipped in more than $10 million in currency. UAB's closure sparked a chain of collapse throughout the Butcher brother's empire.

Soon after, another one of the brothers' banks, Southern Industrial Banking Corporation went bankrupt, followed by another 21 affiliated banks in the brothers' financial empire. Consequently, the Butcher brothers and many members of their family were also bankrupt and now under federal and state investigations. Charges were eventually brought against the Butcher brothers, three family members, some friends, and an accountant employed by the family.

Both brothers agreed to plea bargains with the government authorities. Jake, who was guilty of stealing $17 million in illegal loans and of cheating on his tax returns, ended up with a 20-year prison term and a massive bill for damages. C. H., who was an alleged cocaine abuser, womanizer, and heavy gambler and was guilty of fraud and money-laundering, ended up with 25 years in prison and large fines. C. H.'s wife, Shirley Butcher, also faced three years in prison for assistance with C. H.'s money-laundering schemes.

C. H. served six years of his 25-year sentence before being paroled. Until his death on April 30, 2002, he assisted his second wife with her real estate business. His wife, Shirley, served eight months of her sentence before parole. Jake Butcher was also paroled after serving six years and eight months of his sentence.

SEE ALSO
Butcher brothers; bank fraud; accounting fraud.

BIBLIOGRAPHY. Steve Baker, "Federal Grand Jury Issues More Indictments Against C. H. Butcher," *Journal Record* (April 22, 1986); Elizabeth A. Davis, "Former Banker C. H. Butcher Jr. Dead at 62," *The Oak Ridger* (May 1, 2002.); Don K. Ferguson, "20 Years Ago, FDIC Closed UAB Banks," *KnoxNews* (January 19, 2003); Irvine Sprague, "Crime Doesn't Pay, Except Where Certain Bankers Are Concerned," *American Banker* (August 12, 1988).

ARTHUR HOLST, PH.D.
WIDENER UNIVERSITY

United Fruit

BEFORE 1970, Chiquita Brands International was known as the United Fruit Company, one of the most storied and controversial business in the history of the Americas. The United Fruit Company was established at the beginning of the 20th century, founded through the merger of four banana importing companies.

United Fruit played a key role in the Central Intelligence Agency (CIA)-sponsored removal from power of Guatemala's democratically elected government in 1954. It also assisted in the attempt to overthrow Cuba's communist Fidel Castro regime in 1961. The company became important in trading, especially tropical bananas and pineapples, from the third world plantations to the United States and Europe.

The company, its predecessors and successors included, is an archetypal case of multinational influence extending deeply into the internal politics and policies of so-called "banana republics" and may well provide an example of neo-colonialism. The United Fruit Company owned vast tracts of land in Central America, and sometimes the company had real power of those nations, with national governments doing the company's bidding.

The company owes its existence to Captain Lorenzo Dow Baker who transported a group of miners to Venezuela from Boston, Massachusetts, in 1870 on his schooner. He put into Port Morant, Jamaica, on his homeward voyage to find a cargo to pay his expenses on the northbound trip. He purchased 160 bunches of unripe bananas there for $40 which he sold in Jersey City, New Jersey, for $320. The following year he returned to Jamaica and started steadily shipping bananas to Boston.

In 1884, Baker with J. H. Freeman and A. Preston formed the Boston Fruit Company and acquired their own steamship. Boston Fruit Co. merged with leading banana operators in 1899 to form the world's biggest banana importer, the United Fruit Company of New Jersey with plantations in Colombia, Costa Rica, Cuba, Jamaica, Nicaragua, Panama, and Santo Domingo. Along with rail lines, the company had telegraph lines and plantations all over Central America. United Fruit owned a fleet of white steamships called the Great White Fleet. The company continued to expand into Caribbean and Central American territories and to absorb competing companies.

In 1901, the Guatemalan dictator Manuel Estrada Cabrera ensured United Fruit's exclusive rights to transport postal mail between Guatemala and the United States. Cabrera allowed the company to establish a subsidiary, the Guatemalan Railroad Company, and build a railroad and telegraph lines between Puerto Barrios and the capital, Guatemala City. Furthermore, he gave permission to United Fruit Company to acquire land very reasonably and gave the company a land grant 500 yards wide and one mile long on either side of the municipal pier.

Also, the United Fruit Company was exempted from taxes for 99 years. By 1910, United Fruit Company had won a controlling stake in the British owned Elders & Fyffes Co. and ships were regularly transferred between the two fleets. United Fruit merged with Cuyamel Fruit Company in 1929. In 1970, United Fruit was absorbed into United Brands and subsequently divested itself of its American flagged ships.

The company has a long history of vigilantly political activism. For example, in 1910 a ship of armed hired thugs was sent from New Orleans, Louisiana, to Honduras to install a new president by force when the incumbent failed to grant the fruit company tax breaks. The newly installed Honduran president granted the company a waiver from paying any taxes for 25 years. By 1918, United Fruit Company and two other companies controlled 75 percent of the nation's banana-growing land, much of it taken through threats or violence.

THE GUATEMALAN COUP

In Guatemala, in 1944, a group of liberal military leaders seized power and inaugurated a program of land reform under successive presidents, Juan Jose Arevalo and Jacobo Arbenz. They began redistributing United Fruit Company land to citizens. According to some intelligence sources, the Guatemalan government of Guzman was overthrown by covert action by the U.S. government in 1954 at the request of United Fruit because of Guzman's plans to redistribute uncultivated land owned by the United Fruit Company among native peasants. The United Fruit Company and others charged that Guatemala had turned communist and convinced President Dwight Eisenhower to overthrow Guzman's government. As many as 100,000 people may have died in the ensuing war.

In order to administer its distant and dispersed activities, United Fruit became a major developer of radio technology, which it later pooled with other companies to form the Radio Corporation of America. The company had a mixed record of encouraging and discouraging development in the countries in which they had operations. For example, in Guatemala, the company built schools for the people who lived and worked on the company land, while at the same time, for many years, disallowed the Guatemalan government from constructing highways, because this would lessen the profitable transportation monopoly of the railroads, which were owned by United Fruit.

Richard Allen LaBarge (1968) reached a different conclusion from the studies that had prevailed up to that moment. According to his study, United Fruit Company had a positive impact on local economies: As the gross national product per capita increased, the countries got a more developed infrastructure (trains, telegraphs, roads, camps, and plantations).

Thus, the banana-produce industry enabled the developing nations to gain international trade status. LaBarge also argues that the negative criticism toward the United Fruit Company negates the prevailing business environment in the Central Americas of the era.

The contemporary use of banana labels in the United States dates from the early 1960s when the United Fruit Company began placing its familiar blue Chiquita labels on fruit. In 1970, United Fruit Company merged with AMK Corp. to form United Brands Co., which took the Chiquita Brands International name in 1990. Chiquita's name has been additionally tainted by alleged preferential treatment by the Bill Clinton administration. With its heavy involvement in any Latin American country that was friendly to its policies, United Fruit gave birth to the term "banana republic." Even in 1996, United Fruit/Chiquita evicted 100 Honduran families and grazed their homes after declaring their land "infertile."

The successor of United Fruit has interests in Colombia, Costa Rica, Cuba, Guatemala, Honduras, and Panama. So overwhelming has the impact been on the fabric of history and Central American society that it has inspired poet Pablo Neruda to express this relationship through verse in a poem entitled "United Fruit Company."

SEE ALSO

Central America; South America; capitalism; free trade.

BIBLIOGRAPHY. Richard Allen LaBarge, "Impact of the United Fruit Company on Economic Development of Guatemala, 1946–54," *Studies in the Middle American Economics* (Middle American Research Institute, 1968); Steve Striffler, *In the Shadows of State and Capital*, (Duke University Press, 2002); Stephen Schlesinger and Stephen Kinzer, *Bitter Fruit: the Untold Story of the American Coup in Guatemala* (Anchor Press, 1990); Aviva Chomsky, *West Indian Workers and the United Fruit Company in Costa Rica, 1870–1940* (Louisiana State University Press, 1996); Chiquita, www.chiquita.com (2003).

ALFREDO MANUEL COELHO, PH.D.
UNIVERSITY OF MONTPELLIER, FRANCE

United Kingdom

IN 2002, the Association of British Insurers estimated that fraud alone cost the United Kingdom (UK) economy £14 billion. Estimating the cost of white-collar and corporate crime is a favorite pastime for researchers and policymakers as well as insurers. Invariably, these educated guesses "prove" that the cost of white-collar and corporate crime is vast, implying that the economic performance of the UK would be dramatically improved if government directed more resources to the plethora of agencies responsible for enforcing economic and social regulations. These attempts to estimate the extent of white-collar and corporate crime reflect increasing public awareness of the problem brought about by a series of high-profile scandals since the late 1970s.

INVISIBLE CRIMES

Policymakers, law-enforcement officers and social scientists paid little attention to the phenomenon of white-collar crime and corporate crime until the 1970s. These crimes were invisible crimes insofar as many people were unaware that such crimes were being committed, there was little statistical data and what there was related to a handful of offenses. There was very little research into occupational and organizational crime, and responsibility for controlling such crimes was divided among a large number of agencies; controlling white-collar and corporate crime was not on the political agenda and the public was relatively unconcerned. Given the North American origins of the terms *white-collar, white-collar crime,* and *corporate crime,* it is not surprising that academic study of white-collar and corporate crime in the UK was slow to develop.

These crimes remained invisible until a series of high-profile cases pushed control of occupational and organizational crime up the political agenda. The scandals of the Lonhro, Guinness takeover of Distillers (1986); Blue Arrow share dealings (1987); Harrods takeover; the Bank of Credit and Commerce International collapse (BCCI, 1991); the posthumous discovery that Robert Maxwell misappropriated funds in the Mirror Newspaper Group pension scheme (1991); Polly Peck (1993); the hostile takeover bid for the Co-op; and the Barings Bank collapse (1995) forged the impression that financial crime was rife in the kingdom.

The sinking of the ferry *Herald of Free Enterprise* at Zeebrugge, Holland (1987), the fire on the *Piper Alpha* oil platform in the North Sea (1988), the Lyme Regis Bay tragedy (1994), and several major train crashes, notably at Potters Bar in 2002,

also drew public attention to industrial health and safety regulations. The contamination of the Camelford water supply with 20 tons of aluminum sulphide in 1988 had the same effect on British public consciousness of environmental protection.

Food crime also became of increasing concern after a series of food scares about salmonella in eggs, *e. coli* outbreaks in Lancashire and Lanarkshire, BSE (Bovine Spongiform Encephalopathy) in cattle and its human variant CJD (Creutzfeldt-Jakob Disease), and GM (genetically modified) food. The 2001 BSE foot-and-mouth outbreak exacerbated worries about food crime after it emerged that infected meat imported illegally into the UK might have caused the outbreak, and that illegal movements of livestock facilitated the spread of disease.

The extensive media coverage of these cases shaped public perception of the incidence of white-collar and corporate crime in the UK. The focus on the most dramatic of cases obscures petty white-collar and corporate crime that occurs more frequently. Despite the best efforts of consumer affairs programs such as the BBC Television's *Watchdog,* securities-trading offenses receive far less attention in the media, although British subjects are far more likely to be the victims of an unscrupulous trader than a major financier. Equally, tax evasion receives very little media coverage.

British criminologists have also played a significant role in the increasing visibility of white-collar and corporate crime. Studies of the policing and prosecution of such crimes have had a significant influence on policymakers and administrators, as well as making a significant contribution to the theory of white-collar and corporate crime. As a result of increased awareness, there are now a plethora of agencies responsible for the prevention, detection, prosecution, and conviction of corporate criminals.

BRITISH REGULATORS

The Crown Prosecution Service (CPS), the Financial Services Authority (FSA), the Serious Fraud Office (SFO), the Metropolitan Police Fraud Squad, and the Department of Trade and Industry (DTI) share responsibility for policing and prosecuting financial crime. The National Criminal Intelligence Service (NCIS) gets involved in some of the most serious cases of financial crime. The CPS, HM Customs and Excise and HM Inland Revenue deal with the various aspects of tax evasion.

Although many companies lump health, safety and environmental issues together, the responsibility for enforcing regulations governing health and safety in the workplace and the regulations protecting the environment are shared by many agencies. Health and safety crimes fall under the purview of the Health and Safety Executive established in 1974, while the bulk of environmental crimes fall within the remit of the Environment Agency and Local Authority Environmental Health Departments.

Food law is also enforced by a variety of specialist agencies. The Food Standards Agency and its executive agency the Meat Hygiene Service, and the Pesticides Safety Directorate, Veterinary Medicines Directorate and the Dairy Hygiene Inspectorate of the Department of Environment, Food and Rural Affairs tackle food crime at a national level. Their auxiliaries at the local level are the Local Authority Environmental Health Departments, Local Authority Trading Standards Department and Public Analysts.

A whole host of agencies protect consumers from avaricious traders dealing in goods apart from foodstuffs under the watchful eye of consumer groups like the Consumers Association. The DTI, the Office of Fair Trading (OFT) and the Monopolies and Mergers Commission (MMC) deal with antitrust issues. A series of agencies perform a similar function for the privatized utilities, while the OFT and Local Authority Trading Standards Departments deal with trading offenses.

Given limited resources, the size of the task and the consequent need for co-operation from businesses, the specialist enforcement agencies follow a policy of regulatory compliance. Although there are differences of emphasis, these agencies prefer to issue warnings or to impose administrative penalties, rather than prosecute offenders, a process viewed as time-consuming, expensive and unpredictable. Prosecution is reserved for serious offenses and persistent offenders.

Nevertheless, groups representing business interests have lobbied successive governments to reduce the regulatory burden. Both the Conservative governments of Margaret Thatcher and John Major, and the Labor government of Tony Blair have attempted to simplify the administration and enforcement of economic and social regulations. Deregulation was important to the Thatcher and Major governments as reducing state intervention in the economy was central to the Conservative

agenda. Consequently, the Conservative government encouraged "business-friendly enforcement" in the Deregulation and Contracting Out Act, 1994. In 1997, the incoming Labor government emphasized "better regulation" as opposed to "deregulation." However, this change in rhetoric did not reflect a shift in policy. *The Principles of Good Regulation*, published by the Better Regulation Task Force in 1998, and the Enforcement Concordat with Local Authorities and Government departments agreed to shortly thereafter, emphasized the use of persuasive rather than punitive strategies. Government attempts to deregulate business and emphasize persuasive strategies efforts have met with limited success.

REGULATION REFORM

In 1997, the Labor government reformed financial services regulation merging banking supervision and investment services regulation into the Securities and Investments Board (SIB). The Bank of England, severely criticized in the official report on the BCCI collapse, was stripped of its responsibilities for bank regulation. Within a few months of taking over these duties, the SIB changed its name to the Financial Services Authority (FSA).

A similar process of simplification and strengthening of regulation can be seen in the areas of environmental protection and food law with the creation of the Environment Agency in 1995 and the Food Standards Agency in 2001. The establishment of the Environment Agency simplified the enforcement of environmental regulations, merging HM Inspectors of Pollution with the National Rivers Authority and a handful of smaller agencies. The creation of the Food Standards Agency was, however, more of a public relations exercise than a tidying-up exercise after successive food scares and the foot-and-mouth outbreak in the 1990s. The creation of the Pesticides Safety Directorate and the Meat Hygiene Service of the Ministry of Agriculture, Fisheries and Food (MAFF) in 1993 and 1995 respectively, did not reassure the public who felt that MAFF put the producer interest before the consumer interest. Consequently, the Labor government created the Food Standards Agency.

The origins of the modern food law, environmental law and the law governing trading standards, health and safety at work and financial regulation, as well as the agencies responsible for enforcing these laws, can be traced back to the 19th century. Nevertheless, discussion of white-collar and corporate crime in contemporary Britain took place in an historical vacuum until recently. Although white-collar crime and corporate crime have been touched upon in historical studies of the development of economic and social regulation, electoral and political corruption, and the informal economy, white-collar crime and corporate crime did not become the subject of historical study in their own right until the 1990s.

SEE ALSO
reform and regulation; capitalism; free trade; Bank of Credit and Commerce International; Barings Bank; Maxwell, Robert.

BIBLIOGRAPHY. Ingeborg Paulus, *The Search for Pure Food* (Martin Robertson, 1974); Michael Levi, *Regulating Fraud* (Tavistock, 1987); George Robb, *White-Collar Crime in Modern England: Financial Fraud and Business Morality 1845–1929* (Cambridge: Cambridge University Press, 1992); Tony Freyer, *Regulating Big Business: Antitrust in Great Britain and America 1880–1990* (Cambridge University Press, 1992); David J. Moss, "Business and Banking: Ethics and White-Collar Crime in Norwich, 1825–1831," *Albion* (1997); Barry S. Godfrey and John P. Locker, "The Nineteenth Century Decline of Custom and Its Impact on Theories of Workplace Theft" and "White-Collar Crime," *Northern History* (2001); Gary Slapper and Steve Tombs, *Corporate Crime* (Longman, 1999); UK agencies: www.fsa.gov.uk; www.food.gov.uk; www.oft.gov.uk; www.hse.gov.uk (2004).

MARK ROODHOUSE, PH.D.
UNIVERSITY OF YORK, ENGLAND

United States

WHITE-COLLAR CRIME most often involves a network of people in legitimate occupations assisting one another for profit and covering-up wrongdoing. Individually, this often includes lawyers, accountants, stockbrokers, boards of directors, chief executive officers, government regulators, and thrift or banking insiders.

Since 1949 when Edwin H. Sutherland first defined white-collar crime, it has not been a uniquely American phenomenon. Yet, as the United States has been and remains the pre-eminent capitalist economic power, the nation is also the world leader in corporate criminality, as well as in this relatively new study of criminology.

THE AMERICAN WAY

Criminal acts by corporations in the United States, rather than resulting in arrest are typically managed by regulatory agencies. They can be referred to the federal Department of Justice if the regulatory agency is unable to get the corporation to comply with the regulation. These regulations are designed to control or manage an offending corporation's behavior. Controlling, managing, and punishing corporate crime has been a difficult challenge in American history. During first major federal attempt, the 1898 Sherman Antitrust Act, passed to prevent monopolies from fixing prices on goods sold to consumers, the Department of Justice only filed 9 cases, and only 16 in the first twelve years. No violators were imprisoned until 1921. During the first 50 years of the law, of 252 prosecutions only 24 perpetrators went to prison. Eleven of these were businessmen and the remainder were union leaders who were being controlled by the laws sponsored by the elite controlled politicians.

Before cases are brought to criminal court, federal and sometimes state regulatory agencies may manage the company through an administrative hearing and a consent decree asking the company to stop its behavior. Subsequently, the company may offer to clean up its mess or perform restitution to victims. Part of the problem in trying to make corporations accountable for the harms that they commit is that a Supreme Court decision in 1886, in *Santa Clara v. California*, declared that a private corporation is a natural person. Thus, they have the same rights as a natural person under the law to freedom of speech, to sue, and to borrow money but unfortunately, finding culpable parties in white-collar crime cases is often quite difficult.

Harm done to workers by corporations in their work environment has been a common white-collar offense in American industry. These offenses ranged from knowingly exposing coal miners to harmful coal dust and lying about it, to improperly locked employee-exit doors. One example of corporate negligence occurred in 1991 at the Imperial Food Products chicken-processing plant fire in

Hamlet, North Carolina, where 25 employees were killed. The employees died because company management had locked the exit doors, allegedly due to suspected employee theft. However, additional problems included the fact the building was over 100 years old and had an inadequate sprinkler system, too few windows, and the plant had not been inspected by the state regulatory agency, the Occupational Safety and Health Administration in its 11 years of operation. In the end, the state hired new inspectors and legislated 12 new workplace safety laws. The state Labor Department fined the company $800,000 and the owner, plant manager, and his son were indicted on 25 counts of manslaughter. Eventually the owner, Emmett Roe, pleaded guilty to all 25 counts and was sentenced to almost 20 years; but was eligible for parole in less than 3 years.

State-sponsored crime committed by the U.S. government has been problematic for many years. Early, extreme examples include the enslavement of hundreds of thousands of African-American slaves for over 100 and the genocide committed against the Native American tribes. More recent incidents include the Challenger Space Shuttle explosion in 1986, killing all 8astronauts. Later investigations revealed that engineers and managers knew that at a certain temperature, an O-ring would not function properly but estimated that postponing the launch to repair or replace the faulty ring was not cost-effective and may have endangered NASA's schedule. Therefore, managers and engineers knowingly risked the lives of all the astronauts.

CONSUMER AND FINANCIAL FRAUD

Consumer fraud or the death of consumers caused by corporate America knowingly producing and selling unsafe products are also a commonly committed white-collar crime. One such case includes Ford Motor Company's 1970 development of the Ford Pinto, an automobile the company knew would explode when rear-ended because of the location of the gas tank, but calculated the cost of lawsuits for wrongful deaths as cheaper than changing the design of the automobile. Similarly in 2001, both Ford Motor Company and Firestone Tires were implicated in a number of automobile accidents involving the Ford Explorer SUV. Eventually, the responsibility was found to lie with the tires constructed by Firestone. Other instances of crimes against consumers include the silicon breast im-

plant developed by Dow Corning and approved by the Food and Drug Administration initially as safe.

Some of the most pervasive instances of white-collar crime included the 1980s financial crimes in the savings and loan (S&L) industry, as well as the insider trading and accounting theft in a number of cases of stock fraud. Insider trading involves the illegal use of important nonpublic information about the sale of stocks or securities, or trading in them, by providing tips to others about forthcoming transactions. In many instances, the stock market has become a market not of products but of information and speculation. Michael Milken committed one of the largest white-collar crimes in history when he created a junk bond market for his company Drexel Burnham Lambert. Milken also provided confidential inside information about deals and then helped clients conceal ownership of huge blocks of stock in anticipation of the deal he already knew was forthcoming. Insider trading is prohibited by a federal regulatory agency, the Securities and Exchange Commission (SEC).

Other prohibitions on stock trading in America include an SEC rule that prohibits individuals from engaging in any act of business that operates as a fraud or deceives any person in connection with the purchase or sale of a securities product. These regulatory laws are aimed at preventing insiders from gaining an unfair advantage in a capitalist market, that is supposed to be neutral where all parties have an equal standing. While this notion of equal standing is true ideologically, in practice it is far from the truth. The landmark Supreme Court decision laying out this rule was the SEC v. Texas Gulf Sulphur Company, in which executives in the Texas company purchased large quantities of their own stock before making public their discovery of minerals. Once this information was made public, the stock shot up and the executives made huge profits.

SAVINGS AND LOANS

Also in the 1980s, frauds committed by savings and loan institutions and the bailout of these institutions by the federal government amounted to what one author referred to as corporate welfare. The regulatory agency responsible for financial institutions like banks and savings and loans companies is the Federal Deposit Insurance Association (FDIC). The federal system of insured savings and loan institutions was enacted in the 1930s in response to the economic Depression, and to oversee federally chartered savings and loan institutions. The FDIC insures the deposits of federally chartered banks for premiums paid by each bank to the federal government. Basically, the criminal and fraudulent actions of the S&Ls was made possible by federal deregulation of the industry. From 1989 through 1990, over 7,000 cases were referred by the regulatory agency to the Department of Justice. The Federal Bureau of Investigation and sometimes the Secret Service or specialized task forces investigated these suspected crimes. By 1991, 764 defendants were charged, 95 of them were board chairmen, chief executives, or presidents, and 131 were other management personnel. Ninety-three percent of those tried (550) were convicted and 42 were acquitted.

RULES AND REGULATIONS

In response to the debacles of the mid-1980s, Congress enacted two pieces of legislation in 1984 defining insider trading and securities fraud as a public wrong. The 1984 Insider Trading Sanctions Act of mandates that individuals "found guilty of insider trading violations may face financial penalties of up to three times the profits made (or losses avoided) as a result of the unlawful trading." Prior to the enactment of this law offenders could only loose their profits. Second, Congress passed the Insider Trading and Securities Fraud Enforcement Act of 1988. This established a bounty program to enhance the detection of insider trading, increased the penalties, broadened the right to private civil action, and imposed a criminal penalty of up to five years, mandated preventative rules for brokerage dealers, investment advisors and firms in order to prevent insider trading.

Under this act, civil remedies can include in injunctions or prohibitions of engaging in any more stock trading and can also require changes in the structure and personnel of an offending organization. Moreover, the SEC also can order financial penalties and other administrative remedies. This includes court orders to cease and desist from stock market activities.

For example in 1985, the SEC forced Ivan Boesky to give up $50 million of his profits gained from his insider training activities, this money is held in a trust and provided to those individuals harmed by the financial crime. Under these SEC laws and the Supreme Court case of *Dirks v. SEC*

(1986), corporate employees are financially responsible to their shareholders and thus cannot trade that stock without disclosing that they have the nonpublic information. Also, any person who has gained such inside nonpublic information based on a connection to that company and trades on that information is responsible. In this case, culpability can extend beyond individuals directly involved in profiting from trading.

For example, in *U.S. v. Winans* (1985), a newspaper reporter was convicted of securities fraud for publishing insider information provider by an insider who profited from the release of the information in the article. In 1991, even a psychiatrist had charges filed against him for revealing a patient's disclosure of stock information to others. Nancy Reichman analyzed a variety of SEC litigation cases involving insider trading from January 1, 1989, through October 15, 1991, and found that SEC actions included civil complaints, administrative hearings, and criminal sanctions.

For the SEC, catching white-collar criminals is difficult, but punishing them is even more problematic. For example, in 1991, the Federal Sentencing Guidelines became law providing federal judges with a specific set of guidelines to follow in white-collar crime sentencing. While these guidelines mandated the harshest financial penalties ever up to that time, up to $500 million, this law also provided corporations with an opportunity to police themselves by mandating ethics training and an internal compliance policy structure. But ultimately, these mandates for internal policing encourage companies to scapegoat a particular employee without addressing the corporate culture that encourages increasing profit without taking into account harms against others.

More punitive laws governing corporate crimes were legislated in 2002 as the result of several of the largest corporate bankruptcies in America's history. The story behind the bankruptcies included theft and fraud. Specifically, Enron Corporation, a multinational energy and oil company created a number of executive partnerships to hide the company's financial losses. The SEC began an investigation into Enron and it's accounting firm, Arthur Anderson. Subsequently, the accounting firm began destroying paperwork detailing previous audits of Enron's accounting books. It has been alleged that Enron's board of directors were receiving cash payments from illicit partnerships used to hide Enron's debt, and to make tax-deductible contributions to a variety of philanthropic organizations. During this same time period, Enron executives prevented lower-level employees from cashing in their shares while executives sold their shares at a higher value just prior to filing of the company's bankruptcy. Kenneth Lay, the company's president was selling his own shares while he told non-executive Enron employees to continue to buy Enron shares. Enron executives also bullied analysts who were questioning the value of Enron's stock. Anderson refused to downgrade Enron's credit rating even as bankruptcy loomed. This accounting firm also assisted Waste Management Inc. in developing misleading financial reports. Anderson also performed similar functions for Sunbeam Corporation in 2001 and paid $110 million to shareholders to settle a fraud lawsuit. Similar bankruptcies and illegal accounting methods were found in dozens of companies.

These crimes resulted public outcry and created pressure on the House, Senate, and the president resulting in the most stringent corporate crime laws to be generated in many years. The passage of the Sarbanes-Oxley Act addressed accounting oversight in order to prevent cheating on the books. The new law also improved criminal fraud accountability with criminal penalty enhancements. The penalty enhancement portion of the bill is referred to as the White Collar Crime Penalty Enhancement Act. It contains five major sections covering attempt and conspiracy to commit criminal fraud; criminal penalties for mail and wire fraud, criminal penalties for violations of the employee retirement income security Act of 1974; Amendment to Sentencing Guidelines Relating to Certain White collar Offenses; and Corporate Responsibility for Financial Reports. Additionally, these new laws also provide the Sentencing Commission with the power to increase the punitiveness of any sentence based upon how much money has been lost to employees or ordinary shareholders.

White-collar crime has characterized the history of the United States since the country's founding. Only in the last 50 years have white-collar offenses been treated and studied as a serious criminology that can financially harm workers and consumers as well as result in serious injury and death.

SEE ALSO

antitrust; Sherman Antitrust Act; Clayton Act; Sentencing Guidelines, U.S.; reform and regulation; corporate liability; air pollution; water pollution; unions; Justice, Department of; Securities and Exchange Commission; Food and Drug Administration; Sutherland, Edwin H.

BIBLIOGRAPHY. Patrick Akard, "Book Review of *Corporate Welfare Policy and the Welfare State*," *American Journal of Sociology* (v.103/5, 1998); Barbara Ettore, "Crime and Punishment a Hard Look at White Collar Crime," *Management Review* (v.83/5, 1994); David O. Friedrichs, "Enron et al: Paradigmatic White-Collar Crime Cases for the New Century," Paper Presented at the American Society of Criminology Meetings (November, 2002); Nancy Reichman, "Insider Trading," *Beyond the Law, Crime in Complex Organizations* (University of Chicago Press, 1993); Edwin H. Sutherland, "White-Collar Crime," *Corporate and Governmental Deviance Problems of Organizational Behavior in Contemporary Society* (Oxford University Press, 2002); Jennifer S. Recine, "Examination of the White Collar Crime Penalty Enhancements in the Sarbanes-Oxley Act," *American Criminal Law Review* (v.29, 2002); David Weisburd, et al., *White-Collar Crime and Criminal Careers* (Cambridge University Press, 2001); John F. Wozniak, "Assessing Contemporary White Collar Crime Textbooks: A Review of Common Themes and Prospects for Teaching," *Journal of Criminal Justice Education* (v.12/2, 2001).

Rebecca S. Katz
Morehead State University

unnecessary surgery

FROM THE STANDPOINT of the criminal law, willfully committing unnecessary surgery (or other unnecessary medical treatments) is fraud because it obtains money from the patient under the false pretense that the medical procedure is necessary. It is also a crime against the person because, depending upon the extent of the intrusion, the unnecessary surgery or treatment would involve battery, mayhem, or criminal homicide.

The victim's consent cannot be used as a defense by the offender because consent was obtained under false pretenses. In cases of unnecessary surgeries and treatments by veterinarians, the behavior would comprise fraud and cruelty to animals. Insurance companies who are asked to pay for willfully committed unnecessary surgeries and treatments would also be fraud victims. Concerns about unnec-

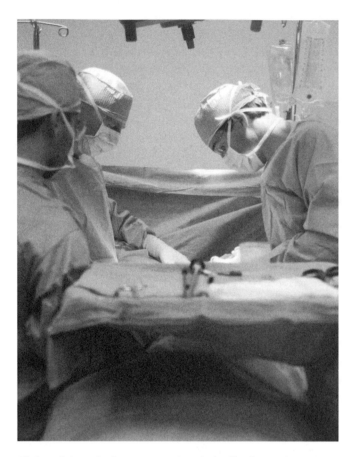

Determining whether a procedure is ineffective or inappropriate is the crux of defining unnecessary surgery.

essary medical procedures in America go back as far as 1775, but standards regulating American physicians' decisions to perform surgeries and treatments were not forthcoming for at least a century and a quarter later.

It was not until the first decade of the 20th century that Ernest Amory Codman proposed to assess the competency of hospitals and physicians through his "end-result plan," which tracked hospital patients after medical procedures. Codman was appointed as chairperson of the Clinical Congress of Surgeons' (the forerunner to the American College of Surgeons) Committee on Hospital Standardization, a role in which he crusaded for a national standardization in hospital medical care. In 1920, John G. Bowman, the first director of the American College of Surgeons, advocated "minimum standardization" to identify unnecessary surgery and lax diagnoses.

Defining exactly what is "unnecessary" surgery or treatment is problematic. Whether a medical procedure is ineffective or inappropriate for a given medical circumstance is the crux of what is meant by unnecessary. Yet, any operation or treatment that fails to produce its desired result can later be judged as ineffective and inappropriate, though there initially was a presumed potential to help the patient.

Perhaps the best way to define a criminal unnecessary medical procedure is when a doctor knowingly lies by telling a patient that her condition requires a particular surgery or treatment. This approach includes nearly all connotations of intentional fraud in the delivery of medical procedures by legally practicing physicians. It would include the delivery of procedures known by the physician to be ineffective. It would also encompass delivering procedures without advising the patient about other methods known to the physician that would have the same outcome and be less expensive or less intrusive.

Unintentional unnecessary medical procedures should not be confused with the intentional ones; the former are civil wrongs (torts) and result from incompetence while the latter are crimes that result from intents to defraud. Of the many billions of dollars paid each year for unnecessary physician procedures, a portion is spent because of incompetence and the rest is the product of doctors' willful attempts to defraud and to maim. Incompetent decisions to perform unnecessary surgery may be so plainly bad that they meet a prosecutor's legal threshold for charges of criminal negligence.

The primary type of research documenting unnecessary surgery involves a geographic comparison of surgical rates. Huge differences in surgical rates for certain geographic areas have been found especially for tonsillectomies, hemorrhoidectomies, hysterectomies, heart surgeries, and hernia operations. Researchers have also documented higher surgery rates among physicians who charge a fee for each service compared to HMO physicians who do not. "Second opinion" studies have shown that as many as a fifth of prescribed surgeries are not validated by peers. And expert specialists have often been found to disagree with their colleagues' diagnoses.

These four methods of studying unnecessary surgery have presented information of varying strength to support the idea that many operations need not happen, but none of them allow us to infer the extent of doctors' criminal intent to perform unneeded operations. However, when gross discrepancies—such as a tenfold higher rate of a surgery type in one area compared to another—are present, it is difficult to explain away the difference without acknowledging that at least some would have been known to have been unnecessary before they were performed.

There have been several reasons put forth that try to explain wrong decisions to deliver unnecessary medical treatment, including training (doctors practice the way they were taught in medical school); insufficient knowledge to make competent diagnoses (doctors often do not pay attention to all of the relevant symptoms or keep abreast of medical developments); individual physician characteristics (age, experience, personality, and medical specialty); and the practice of "defensive medicine" (doctors over-prescribe medical procedures as a defense against possible future medical malpractice lawsuits). None of these ideas purporting to explain unnecessary treatments and surgeries involve intentional fraud by the doctor.

It would be difficult to argue for the differential association theory that says physicians learn from their peers and mentors specific attitudes favorable to the delivery of unnecessary surgeries and treatments, given the strong normative system in medicine that emphasizes the best interests of the patient. Self-control theory would probably be most relevant as an explanation, because criminal unnecessary surgery is not only an example of "easy money," but also reflects an extreme insensitivity to the feelings and rights of others.

To demonstrate self-control theory as a correct explanation, research would have to indicate that physicians who willfully lie to patients about the necessity of their surgery or treatment are also more likely than their colleagues to be involved in other medical crimes (such as prescription violations, insurance fraud, patient sexual assault). Those who fraudulently deliver unnecessary treatments and surgeries should also be more likely than those who do not to be involved in non-medical criminal behaviors such as tax evasion, and various risky and deviant noncriminal behaviors, such as gambling, alcohol abuse, and sexual abuse.

The self-regulating nature of the medical community accords great deference to the validity of individual physician opinion. This circumstance will continue to insulate those who willfully defraud and maim patients, because there will be little perceived probability of being exposed as a criminal by one's fellow doctors. Reaching any reliable figure of criminal unnecessary surgery is extremely problematic because the included acts must involve either criminal intent or criminal negligence, both of which may only be determinable after legal conviction.

SEE ALSO

healthcare fraud; insurance fraud; Medicare and Medicaid; differential association; self-control theory.

BIBLIOGRAPHY. Paul Jesilow, Henry N. Pontell, and Gilbert Geis, *Prescription for Profit: How Doctors Defraud Medicaid* (University of California Press, 1993); Lucian L. Leape, "Unnecessary Surgery," *Health Services Research* (v.24, 1989); John Liederbach, Francis Cullen, Jody Sundt, and Gilbert Geis, "The Criminalization of Physician Violence: Social Control in Transformation," *Justice Quarterly* (v.18, 2001).

GARY S. GREEN
CHRISTOPHER NEWPORT UNIVERSITY

Unsafe at Any Speed

IN 1965, Ralph Nader, a 31-year-old attorney, published *Unsafe at Any Speed: The Designed-in Dangers of the American Automobile* (Grossman), excoriating the Detroit, Michigan, automotive industry for its privileging of style and design over consumer safety. Nader's book eventually became a bestseller and, many believe, helped pass what became the country's first automobile safety legislation.

Nader had been interested in issues of consumer safety since he was a law school student at Harvard University and the editor of the *Harvard Law Record*. While editor, he published an article entitled, "American Cars: Designed for Death," the first of several articles Nader wrote on this subject. He subsequently published articles in *The Nation* and in *Personal Injury Annual*, calling attention to Detroit's deliberate choice of making style a priority over safety.

The rising death toll from traffic accidents was also driving Congressional and governmental leaders to look at the issue of automobile safety. For years, driver error had been the sole focus in investigations of traffic accidents. Nader and others suggested, however, that the cars themselves might be to blame in many cases. Nader's interest in this cause attracted the attention of Daniel Patrick Moynihan, then assistant secretary of labor, who hired Nader as staff consultant for highway safety. Nader's assignment was to research and write a report on this issue for a Congressional audience.

Unsafe at Any Speed was the result of this assignment. In his book, Nader attacked the entire Detroit auto industry, but General Motors (GM) and its Chevrolet Corvair came under particular fire. The Corvair had been a controversial issue in the courts since 1961 when a woman lost an arm after her Corvair flipped over and subsequently sued GM for selling cars with unsafe steering designs. The case was settled out of court before a decision was reached, but other cases followed. In fact, by 1967 around 150 lawsuits had been filed against GM and its Corvair. Many of these were also settled out of court, but GM won several judgments in cases that actually went to trial. Nader also noted problems with other automobiles such as the Buick Roadmaster and the Ford Mustang. He described features such as steering wheels whose design could easily impale a driver in a crash, poor exhaust systems, and the unnecessary pollution produced by badly engineered cars.

Ironically, the driving public that Nader hoped to outrage with his detailed assault on Detroit virtually ignored the publication of the book until GM took a hand. Apparently worried about Nader's influence in Washington, D.C., and afraid the public might take notice of his book, GM hired private investigators to look into Nader's financial and private life in hopes of smearing his reputation, which to date had been spotless. Nader discovered the investigation and publicly denounced GM's tactics, alleging that the "investigators" had even hired several young women to lure him into a sexual liaison. Nader quickly sued GM for harassment. GM settled the court case for $425,000.

The first safety legislation was passed in 1966 with the National Traffic and Motor Vehicle Safety Act and the Highway Safety Act. A range of safety standards for automobiles followed, including padded steering wheels, shoulder belts, safety glass, rear "back-up" lights, emergency flashers, and other design features. The 1966 laws also established an agency to regulate the automobile industry and protect consumers. This agency eventually became the National Highway Traffic Safety Administration.

Nader went on to become the most recognizable and influential champion of the consumer advocacy movement. In 1968, he founded the Center for the Study of Responsive Law with money from the GM settlement. The Center's staff quickly became known as Nader's Raiders as they focused their investigations on issues relating to consumer safety and health. Nader also founded other consumer rights groups, including the Public Interest Research Group, the Center for Auto Safety, the Clean Water Action Project, and many others.

Although the influence of these consumer advocacy groups has waned somewhat since the 1980s, no one denies the impact Nader and his book *Unsafe at Any Speed* had in establishing standards for consumer safety. The title of his book has been used repeatedly to describe products from baby carriages to cell phones whose design somehow imperils the safety of its user.

SEE ALSO
Corvair; General Motors; Nader, Ralph; National Highway Traffic Safety Administration.

BIBLIOGRAPHY. "Meet Ralph Nader: Everyman's Lobbyist and his Consumer Crusade," *Newsweek* (v.71, 1968); "Nader Damned Chevy's Corvair and Sparked a Safety Revolution," *Automotive News* (v.70, 1996); Joseph Page, "Unsafe at Any Speed," *California Law Review* (v.54, 1966); "Ralph Nader," *Current Biography Yearbook* (1986); Ralph Nader, "Profits vs. Engineering: the Corvair Story," *Nation* (v.201, 1965); Martha May, *American Reform and Reformers* (Greenwood, 1996).

REGAN BRUMAGEN
GEORGIA COLLEGE & STATE UNIVERSITY

V

Vatican Bank

THE VATICAN Bank scandal is one of those affairs which will not fade away and still haunts the media, because the secrecy of the authorities (in this case, especially of the independent Vatican state) provides the breeding ground for conspiracy theories of all kinds. As time goes by, fact, semifact, fiction, and pure nonsense become inextricable. In the beginning of the Vatican Bank scandal some major factors linked together: unprofessional management by Catholic clergy not trained for the high-risk banking business, a profit orientation of a Catholic institution not bound by the high moral standards proclaimed by the Catholic church, criminal elements within and outside the bank, and last, but not least, the chaotic Italian political system since World War II.

To get to the indisputable core of the scandal, one has to focus on Roberto Calvi, president of the Banco Ambrosiano, and on Archbishop Paul Marcinkus, head of the Istituto per le Opere di Religione (sometimes referred as Istituto per le Opere Religiose; the Vatican bank). The third person was a certain Italian financier and banker, Michele Sindona, who had strong Italian Mafia links.

These three persons interacted financially on a large scale, the details of those operations still remain a mystery. Disaster happened when high-risk

currency deals by Calvi failed in the early 1980s and the Italian National Bank had to intervene. On June 18, 1982, Calvi was found hanging from the Blackfriars Bridge in London, England; Archbishop Marcinkus went into exile within the borders of Vatican City (or state), which was extraterritorial for the Italian police and judiciary. The financial collapse and the loss of money for the Vatican (and others) was gigantic and involved not only institutions in the Vatican state and Italy, but worldwide (especially in distant tax safe-havens in exotic places). Although judicial investigations in several countries and parliamentary inquiries in Italy tried to get a clear picture, the special status of the Vatican as a sovereign entity hindered a proper and thorough clearing-up of the mess.

The conspiracy theories came in, which cannot be dismissed out of hand: The most influential book on this subject was published by the journalist David A. Yallop in 1984. Yallop linked the Vatican Bank scandal directly to the sudden death of Pope John Paul I after only 33 days in office in 1978.

He claimed that John Paul I was murdered, because this new Pope was on the way to get rid of Marcinkus as head of the financial operations of the Vatican, and because he would have discovered the improper deals with elements of the Mafia via Calvi and Sindona, which were at least tolerated by Marcinkus. The background for Yallop's highly speculative story is the political situation in Italy since the late 1940s: Faced with a large Italian Communist Party, the United States, during the Cold War period, fostered all sorts of anti-communist groups, including former personalities of the fascist Benito Mussolini rule (such as Prince Junio Borghese).

The Italian democracy was riddled for decades not only by Mafia crimes, but also by attempted coups from the military and intelligence community, and by terrorism of the extreme left and the extreme right. The main player of the rightwing anti-democracy plot(s) in the 1970s was Licio Gelli and his secret organization Propaganda 2, which was outlawed when it was discovered by chance by the authorities. A main part of the argument of Yallop is the link between Italian politics, Gelli, Sindona, Calvi and the Vatican, which led by his speculation to the murder of a Pope.

Other authors near the Vatican situation, like John Cornwell in his 1988 book *A Thief in the Night*, disputed Yallop's Pope thesis. But even at the publication of Yallop's book in 1984, the Vatican Bank scandal was overshadowed, in real life and in conspiracy theory circles, by the attempt to kill Pope John Paul II on May 13, 1981. Although the marksman, Ali Mehmet Agca, was arrested on the spot and later convicted, his motivations and possible handlers remain a mystery. The murder case became part of the last period of the Cold War propaganda battles, when the late Claire Sterling published *The Time of Assassins* in 1983. This pamphlet accusing Eastern intelligence organizations from Bulgaria and the Soviet Union of the attempted murder of the Pope of Polish origin is by now generally dismissed as at least unofficial Western disinformation.

Nevertheless this unrelated case and many "minor" incidents (like unsolved kidnapping cases within the Vatican community or a murder/suicide involving three persons within the Swiss Guards corps of the Vatican in 1998) add to the perpetuation of the Vatican Bank scandal mystery. In July 2003, the Italian authorities officially blamed the Mafia for the death of Calvi. The only certainty in these cases is the demonstrated will of the Vatican not to lift the veil of secrecy.

SEE ALSO

Banco Ambrosiano; Italy; organized crime; extortion; bribery.

BIBLIOGRAPHY. Nino Lo Bello, *The Vatican Papers* (New English Library, 1982); Claire Sterling, *The Time of Assassins* (Holt, Rinehart and Winston, 1983); David A. Yallop, *In God's Name* (Poetic Products, 1984); Victor J. Willi, "Im Namen des Teufels?" (Christiana, 1987); John Cornwell, *A Thief in the Night* (Viking Penguin, 1988).

OLIVER BENJAMIN HEMMERLE, PH.D.
MANNHEIM UNIVERSITY, GERMANY

Vaughan, Diane (1951–)

DIANE VAUGHAN IS BEST known for her extensive work on the organizational deviance and the development of a general theory of the normalization of deviance. Much of her research explores mistakes and misdeeds that have resulted in disaster—the dark side of organizations. Her seminal work on the space shuttle disaster, *The Challenger Launch Decision: Risky Technology, Culture, and Deviance at NASA*, was published in 1996. Vaughan, along with millions of Americans, watched as the space shuttle exploded on national television. The tragedy prompted her search for an explanation of why the National Aeronautic and Space Administration (NASA) had failed to prevent the tragedy.

Vaughan's nine-year research endeavor found that common speculations that NASA had ignored potential risks were superficial at best. Based on over 200,000 pages of interviews and internal NASA documents housed at the National Archive, Vaughan discovered officials and managers at the space organization had not violated agency policy and procedures in their decision to launch the Challenger. In fact, the strict adherence to rules and protocol took precedence over indications that forecasted any potential for disaster. "The decision to launch Challenger was, incredibly and sadly, a mistake embedded in the banality of organizational life," according to Vaughan.

"No fundamental decision was made at NASA to do evil; rather, a series of seemingly harmless decisions were made that incrementally moved the space agency toward a catastrophic outcome." The book has received numerous accolades, including the Rachel Carson Prize, Alpha Sigma Nu National Book Award, Robert K. Merton Book Award, along with nominations for a Pulitzer Prize and National Book Award. Vaughan received her Ph.D. in 1979 from the department of sociology at Ohio State University. She first established her career as a post-doctoral fellow in the sociology of social control at Yale University and then as a research associate at Wellesley College Center for Research on Women from 1982 until 1984. She began teaching at Boston College in 1984 and was 20 years later a professor in the department of sociology. Vaughan received the Donald R. Cressey Memorial Award in 1995 and was a visiting fellow at the American Bar Foundation in Chicago and the Centre for Socio-Legal Studies, Wolfson College at the University of Oxford, England.

Vaughan's areas of specialty in research include organizational theory, cultural sociology, qualitative methods, and science, knowledge, and technology. Her contributions to the field of white-collar crime are numerous, including victimology studies; organization, motivation and control of fraud; and social deviance. Vaughan's book, *Controlling Unlawful Organizational Behavior*, was published in 1983. *Uncoupling* is a highly acclaimed book on intimate relationships that examines breakups from sociological and psychological perspectives.

SEE ALSO
Morton Thiokol; *Challenger* Disaster; negligence.

BIBLIOGRAPHY. Diane Vaughan, *The Challenger Launch Decision: Risky Technology, Culture, and Deviance at NASA* (Chicago University Press, 1996); Diane Vaughan, *Uncoupling: Turning Points in Intimate Relationships* (Oxford University Press, 1986); Diane Vaughan, *Controlling Unlawful Organizational Behavior: Social Structure and Corporate Misconduct* (University of Chicago Press, 1983).

MARY DODGE, PH.D.
UNIVERSITY OF COLORADO, DENVER

Vietnam War

IN THE VIETNAM WAR of the 1960s and early 1970s, both the Americans and the North Vietnamese were the protagonists of brutal war crimes, though the more advanced American arsenal took by far the greatest toll. The main aerial strategy adopted by the Americans to win the war, which Congress never officially declared, was an infringement of the Fourth Geneva Convention of 1949. From the very start of the conflict, the American aerial campaigns took the form of the so-called carpet or area bombing, a practice which contravenes all the norms about civilian protection in the 1949 convention. Particularly infamous examples were the Christmas bombing of 1972 against Hanoi and Haiphong, cities in North Vietnam.

These area bombers were incapable of precision and they had never been employed in attacks against cities before. In addition to indiscriminate bombings, the American government was responsible for the practice of declaring whole villages and populated areas as "free fire zones," thus destroying them altogether and killing their residents. In the eyes of military officers, this practice was justified by the conviction that many South Vietnamese villages provided a safe shelter for Vietcong.

In fact, investigations carried out after the destruction had already taken place revealed that many of these zones had been peaceful and should not have been targeted. In the confusion of the Vietnam War, it was virtually impossible for the American troops to establish with certainty whether a village was siding with the North or the South Vietnamese. The most gruesome example of these military assaults was the My Lai Massacre in 1968, when the military unit led by Lieutenant William Calley entered the hamlet of My Lai and for hours savagely destroyed it and killed its inhabitants. Although Calley was court-martialed in 1971, President Richard Nixon ordered him released from jail.

The American military-industrial complex (first warned of by President Dwight Eisenhower) was fundamental to the atrocities of the Vietnam War. Dow Chemical, for example, became a notorious symbol of the brutality and ruthlessness of the American military assaults. The company perfected napalm, the jellied gasoline first developed by American chemists during World War II, at its laboratory in Midland, Michigan, and became the sole supplier of this destructive chemical during the war. Napalm inflicts particularly horrible injuries, burning its victims and melting their skin so that the substance remains in their bodies leading to a slow death.

Huge quantities were dropped over Vietnam on suspected enemy targets such as villages or hamlets rumored to be sympathetic to the North's cause.

The savagery of this weapon was captured in the famous photograph of a young, naked Vietnamese girl screaming in pain as she fled a U.S. air strike which dropped napalm on her village. (The girl has since become a physician.) Dow's role in the manufacture of napalm brought it worldwide notoriety, and made it a target of the antiwar movement.

Dow's other contribution to the Vietnam War arsenal, Agent Orange, is famous as much for its effects on American soldiers as for the toll of death and suffering among the Vietnamese. Agent Orange was a defoliant sprayed from 1965 to 1975 over millions of acres of Vietnamese jungle to deny cover to the North's infiltration. These were called "area denial missions" (ADM) and resulted in the complete destruction of the vegetation of entire areas of the country. Agent Orange is made of dioxin, one of the most toxic substances ever devised by American industry. This lethal weapon was sadly effective on people, too. Tens of the thousands of American soldiers and airmen who were exposed to Agent Orange were subsequently diagnosed with diseases resulting from chemical poisoning such as cancers, brain and nerve damage, and damage to reproductive organs. From 1975 onward, it became apparent that an unusual number of Vietnam veterans were affected with non-Hogdkins lymphoma and skin sarcoma. Vietnamese citizens were obviously exposed to the chemical in vast numbers and experienced similar consequences in terms of disease, death and birth defects, but there has never been an official and comprehensive study of the Vietnamese victims of Agent Orange.

Vietnamese doctors, however, have reported significant increases in birth defects among the communities located in the affected areas. In the same way, there has never been an official survey of the environmental impact of Agent Orange, but huge regions of Vietnam are described as looking like a moonscape and are deemed unsuitable for agricultural use. The testimony of George Claxton, a Vietnam veteran, exposed the wide use of Agent Orange in the U.S. military campaign and the scarce information among soldiers on its deadly effects: "I took showers in the stuff. We had wooden stalls with a tub overhead filled with rainwater that was tinged slightly orange. We would pull the string hanging in the shower and bathe in it. We knew it was Agent Orange because we saw the planes spraying it on the jungle every day. We didn't think anything of it really and at first we thought, the army is spraying for mosquitoes."

Public opinion worldwide began to denounce the American behavior in southeast Asia. As a result of these protests, the Pentagon tried to limit the atrocities, issuing, for example, stricter rules to declare a free fire zone. Yet, legal scholars and historians agree that these rules were completely ineffective. This failure to contain the propensity of the troops to commit war crimes resulted in the international conviction that American soldiers were undisciplined, and even Vietnamese who were not sympathetic to the communist cause started to feel that Americans did not value Vietnamese lives.

Finally, a cease-fire agreement was signed in January 1973 in which the Americans consented to withdraw all their troops within 60 days and to the formation of a coalition government in South Vietnam which would also include the communists. The violations to the agreement by both North and South led to continued conflict between the two countries which ended in 1975 with the collapse of the South Vietnamese government and the unification of the whole country under a communist regime.

SEE ALSO

war crimes; military-industrial complex.

BIBLIOGRAPHY. William Colby with James McCargar, *Lost Victory* (Contemporary Books, 1989); Elizabeth Becker, *America's Vietnam War: A Narrative History* (Clarion, 1992); Marc Jason Gilbert, ed., *Why the North Won the Vietnam War* (Palgrave, 2002); Roy Gutman and David Rieff, eds., *Crimes of War: What the Public Should Know* (W. W. Norton, 1999); Neil L. Jamieson, *Understanding Vietnam* (University of California Press, 1993).

LUCA PRONO, PH.D.
UNIVERSITY OF NOTTINGHAM, ENGLAND

W-Z

wage crimes

WAGE CRIMES ARE violations of laws, treaties, or international conventions (hereafter simply, laws) that govern wage rates, work hours, and other aspects of employment for specific categories of workers. The concept is sometimes used more generally to cover any abusive practices related to wages or working hours. Wage laws are based on the idea that there is an inequality of bargaining power between workers and employers, with employers holding a stronger position than workers.

As a result, wages might be "too low," while other working conditions, such as working hours, might also be worse than they should be. Such inequality of bargaining power is most pronounced when workers are less skilled and less informed about their options in the labor market. Because highly skilled workers are usually paid far more than the legally mandated wage rates, wage laws usually come into play only for the benefit of those workers least able to defend their own interests.

The standards by which wages are judged to be too low or working conditions too bad vary depending on the context, and are not always well-defined. Often, such judgments can be moralistic. Sometimes, they are based on economic, legal, or social theories. From the viewpoint of mainstream (neoclassical) economic theory, each worker's wage is determined by the marginal product of labor for a worker in that category. This is equal to the extra revenue that a company would receive from one additional unit of labor by a worker of that type. As a result, many mainstream economists often dismiss wage laws as either superfluous or harmful. How-

A wage earner's pay slip, usually attached to the check, should explain all income and deductions for a pay period.

ever, the mainstream theory of wage determination has definite flaws. It is based on a model of competitive labor markets that never exists in the real world, and assumes that employers can determine worker productivity with a precision that is impossible except in very simple situations which are not the norm.

From the viewpoint of some worker advocates, including some economists, wages are determined not by the marginal product of labor but by the relative bargaining power of businesses and workers. Because the individual worker's livelihood depends on securing employment, while a business can almost always be profitable without a particular worker, the worker is in an inherently weaker bargaining position than the employer. As a result, wages are set below the marginal productivity of labor, whatever it is, while any surplus is reaped by the employer as additional profit. This view also has its problems, but it has the merit of being closer to reality than the neoclassical theory.

LEGAL FRAMEWORK

In the United States before the 1930s, wage laws were rarely enacted and were almost always struck down by the courts. During the Great Depression of the 1930s, however, massive unemployment led the federal government and courts to take a more supportive view of wage laws. In 1931, the U.S. Congress passed the Davis-Bacon Act, which required that government contracts include a clause specifying the minimum wages to be paid to workers in various categories. Wages were to be "no less than the locally prevailing wages and fringe benefits paid on projects of a similar character." Though it applied only to workers employed under government contracts, Davis-Bacon was the first U.S. federal wage law.

In 1938, the U.S. Congress passed the Fair Labor Standards Act (FLSA), which was amended in 1949 and in later years. This law established a national minimum wage for most private employers, as well as rules governing working hours, overtime pay, and the employment of minors. Certain categories of employees, such as managers, are not covered by the law. In theory, only companies with at least two employees and whose business affects interstate commerce fall under the FLSA. However, the government construes almost all private business activities to affect interstate commerce, so very

few firms are exempt from the minimum wage and other FLSA requirements. The FLSA is enforced by the Wage and Hour Division of the U.S. Department of Labor. Violations of the law can be punished by civil actions, injunctions, or criminal prosecution, though the latter is seldom pursued.

In 1963, the U.S. Congress passed the Equal Pay Act, which forbids wage discrimination based on sex. Employers must pay the same wages to both sexes for work that requires similar skill, effort, and responsibility under the same working conditions. The Equal Pay Act launched a new view of what wage levels should be, apart from the marginal-product and bargaining theories: the so-called comparable worth theory, which asserted that jobs requiring the same skills and working conditions were of comparable worth. This was the job-market counterpart of the labor theory of value in goods markets. Just as the labor theory of value held that the value of goods was determined not by market forces but by the amount of labor required to produce them, comparable-worth theory held that the value of work was determined not by market forces but by the skill required to perform it.

In 1964, Congress passed the Civil Rights Act, Title VII of which went beyond the Equal Pay Act to forbid wage discrimination based on race, religion, sex, or national origin. This, too, had far-reaching implications. Internationally, wage and hour laws vary widely. In developing countries, they are almost non-existent. In European countries, they are more demanding than U.S. laws. France, for example, enacted in 2001 a law mandating a 35-hour work week. Predictions of economic disaster based on mainstream economic theory have not come true, and French workers' productivity has actually increased. Thus, the effects of wage and hour laws are still a matter of dispute.

NOTABLE CASES

Notable wage-crime cases would fill several volumes. A few of the most influential cases are:

Lochner v. New York (198 U.S. 45, 1905). Lochner, owner of a bakery, was convicted of violating a New York state law that prohibited requiring bakers to work more than 10 hours per day or more than 60 hours per week. The U.S. Supreme Court found in favor of Lochner and struck down the New York law, stating that it violated the Due Process Clause and the 14th Amendment.

Corning Glass Works v. Brennan (417 U.S. 188, 1974). Corning Glass Works paid its night-shift inspectors, all of whom were male, a higher wage than its day-shift inspectors, all of whom were female. The U.S. Department of Labor sued Corning under the Equal Pay Act. The Supreme Court ruled against Corning, and held that the time of day when work was done did make jobs different under the comparable-worth doctrine.

Dalheim v. KDFW-TV (918 F.2d 1220, 5th Circuit, 1990). A group of editors, reporters, producers, and directors of the station's local-news show sued the station, arguing that they were wrongfully denied overtime pay required by the FLSA; the station argued that they were not covered by the FLSA because they were professionals. The court held that based on the nature of the work the employees did, they were indeed covered.

SEE ALSO

labor crimes; gender discrimination; racial discrimination; globalization.

BIBLIOGRAPHY. Jeffrey D. Sachs and Howard J. Schatz, "International Trade and Wage Inequality in the United States: Some New Results," (Brookings Institution Press, 1998); *The Economist* (June 13, 2002); Richard G. Lipsey and Alex Chrystal, *Principles of Economics* (Oxford University Press, 1999); Gregory Mankiw, *Principles of Economics* (Harcourt College, 2001); Thomas I. Palley, *Plenty of Nothing* (Princeton University Press, 1998); Mark A. Rothstein and Lance Liebman, *Employment Law* (West Publishers, 2003); John Sloman, *Economics* (Pearson, 2000); U.S. Department of Labor, "What Are the Davis-Bacon and Related Acts?" www.dol.gov (2003).

SCOTT PALMER, PH.D.
RGMS ECONOMICS

war crimes

THE MAJORITY OF the literature on white-collar and corporate crime generally focuses on financial and commercial crimes. Yet, the historical conditions in the last decades of the 20th century and the beginning of the 21st, such as the bloody, ethnic wars in the Balkans, Africa, and the Middle East as well as state-organized terrorism, have prompted a growing interest in the area of state and governmental crimes.

Although numberless treaties, protocols and conventions regulate the laws of war, images of concentration camps, ethnic cleansing, torture and execution of prisoners and civilians, rape, bombing of cities and of their monumental patrimony are still a very vivid part of our collective memory. All these actions can be defined as war crimes, as violations of the laws of war, or International Humanitarian Law (IHL). While our familiarity with war crimes has been dramatically enhanced and disseminated by media coverage of more recent wars, legal limitations on the behaviors of soldiers and armies were first contemplated by the Greeks and by the Hindu code of Manu (200 B.C.E.).

The early theories of war were elaborated by philosophers as a reaction to the religious wars that devastated Europe in the 16th and 17th centuries. Equally, while tribunals and reconciliation committees for war and military crimes have been widely invoked after the Second World War, the first trial for war crimes dates back to the 15th century when Peter von Hagenbach was sentenced to death for wartime atrocities.

As a result of the atrocities suffered by prisoners and expeditionary forces during 19th century conflicts such as the Crimean War and other struggles for national independence; calls for drafts that would codify the rules of military engagement began to multiply. During the American Civil War, President Abraham Lincoln appointed to this task the New York professor, Francis Lieber, whose Lieber Code had a deep impact on all subsequent conventions and protocols. These were mainly held and signed in two European cities: The Hague, Holland (in 1899, 1907 and 1954) and Geneva, Switzerland (in 1925, 1929, 1949, and 1977). These conferences, while remaining silent on the legitimacy of war itself, addressed problems raised by the conflicts that had taken place just before their assemblies.

Atrocities included the use of poisonous gases and biological weapons, the fate of the wounded and sick on land and at sea and of prisoners of war, the destiny of civilian noncombatants, and the protection of cultural monuments. In addition to the rules codified during these events, the Nuremberg tribunals of Nazi leaders (1945–49) theorized the concept of crime against humanity, which was reinforced by the 1948 United Nations Convention on the Prevention and Punishment of the Crime of Genocide.

The 1945 Charter of the international military tribunal at Nuremberg classified war crimes as "violations of the laws or customs of war," and included under this rubric murder, ill-treatment, or deportation of civilians in occupied territory; murder or ill-treatment of prisoners of war; killing of hostages; looting of public or private property; willful destruction of municipalities and gratuitous devastation.

All the conventions and the protocols of the 20th century testify to the commitment of several generations of diplomats and legal advisers. Yet, while the principles behind this impressive monument to international humanitarian law are difficult to question, its effectiveness has been routinely challenged. What all the agreements and codes have left unanswered, at least until the establishment of the tribunals for the wars in the former Yugoslavia and in Rwanda, is key to their existence: how to enforce their norms and, subsequently, how to prosecute effectively the individuals or the states found guilty of war crimes. Although prosecutions have been carried out following the fall of cruel military dictatorships such as the ones in Greece, Chile, Argentina and several governments have been found guilty of breaching human rights norms, the bulk of international humanitarian law has remained in a state of severe paralysis throughout last century.

Another problematic aspect of the legislation concerning war crimes is that civil wars are almost completely ignored it since many states consider the conduct of internal wars as part of their jurisdiction. In many cases, it is difficult to determine the point at which a violent confrontation within a single state goes beyond the sphere of domestic jurisdiction and becomes a case for international law. States are usually unwilling to admit that the situation has progressed out of their control, while dissidents usually appeal to the international community claiming theirs is a cause for international concern.

This is the case, for example, of the conflict in Chechnya: while Russians define it as simply an anti-terrorist police action, international observers have argued that it is an internal armed conflict as defined in international law. In 1977, the second Additional Protocol to the Geneva Convention provided basic rules for the conduct of internal conflicts but did not contain any provisions on the criminal liability for their breaches. Therefore, the tribunals which were set up among general skepticism for the crimes in the former Yugoslavia and Rwanda had to refer directly only to Article 3 of the Geneva Convention (the only article in the Convention that does refer to civil war) and the added protocols, so that the list of grave breaches to be considered war crimes turned out to be considerably shorter than that applicable to interstate conflicts.

The case of civil wars points to the weakest part of International Humanitarian Law. For all its conventions and protocols, the legislation regarding war crimes is difficult to enforce and its mere existence does not guarantee that criminals will be arrested and prosecuted. The implementation of the laws regarding war crimes are left to the good will of the single states, although, given the shocking reports of the wars of the 1990s, the United Nations as well as other international organization are increasingly advocating this role for themselves. The Geneva Convention states that governments have the duty to search for all persons suspected of committing war crimes. Once caught, they should either be extradited or tried. All states have the legal right to prosecute war criminals thanks to the principle of universal jurisdiction. Yet, this all-embracing universalism clashes with the scarcity of prosecutions. In spite of the obligations to prosecute, governments have often granted impunity or simple administrative punishment to war criminals. The few court cases have become historical events such as the American trial related to the My Lai incident in March 1968, in which American soldiers had shot several hundred unresisting Vietnamese non-combatants in Quang Ngai Province.

In this climate, the tribunals for the crimes in Rwanda and Yugoslavia came as surprises. Yet, the five permanent members of the Security Council delayed the appointment of a permanent prosecutor for more than a year and forced several administrative and financial restrictions, endangering the activity of the tribunals. The UN has always showed an ambiguous relationship to the regulations of the Geneva Convention and states have often used their participation in UN actions to escape legal obligations regarding war crimes. This may happen because the forces entrusted with peacekeeping duties answer uniquely to the Security Council and the UN is not a party to the conventions. In this way, the UN can display its troops without remembering to issue statements reminding states of the relevant applicable rules of the Geneva Convention and of the duty to punish violations. Examples of this failure to remind states of their obligations under the Geneva Convention include the operations in Kuwait, Bosnia, and Cambodia.

One of the sanctions following the liberation of Kuwait in 1991 even violated the rule of the Geneva Convention that grants free passage of humanitarian aid intended for civilians. Critics of the UN position toward war crimes argue that without the control of an international legal regime, the ones effectively in charge of accomplishing the UN's often ill-defined directives (ranging from passive peacekeeping to active peace-enforcing) are the military on the battlefields. Obviously, with a Security Council far away and incapable of carrying out their monitoring tasks, commanders always keep the priorities of their own governments clear in mind and interpret their mandate accordingly. War crimes often get quickly dismissed. Particularly infamous cases include the 1992 UN personnel's visit to Sonja's Kon-Tiki, a pension outside Sarajevo, Yugoslavia, which the Bosnian government had denounced as a cover-up for a Serbian concentration camp, and the shooting of a Somali intruder in cold blood in 1993 by Canadian troops. During the same year, hundreds of Somalis were also detained and denied the assistance of the Red Cross.

The implementation of the laws of armed conflict and the prosecution of perpetrators of war crimes relies entirely on the will of the political leaders of the main world powers. Yet, their record on the matter is far from being flawless and their interests often control international organizations and entities that should account for war crimes. For example, following the Yugoslavian example, North Atlantic Treaty Organization (NATO) forces were charged of war crimes for its 1999 bombing campaign. Carla Del Ponte, chief prosecutor at the former Yugoslavia tribunal rejected the option of opening an inquiry into NATO's role, saying that there had been no targeting of civilians or other illegal activity by NATO during the 78-day assault. One should perhaps bear in mind that the tribunal's former presiding judge referred to Madeline Albright, then US. secretary of state, as the court's "mother."

An independent and unofficial European tribunal, held in Berlin, Germany, in 2001, came to a very different conclusion. It cited NATO officials and provided as examples of war crimes the strategy of targeting civilians to pressure them to rise against their own government, the destruction of the Belgrade Radio Television Serbia Studios, which killed 16 journalists, as well as the use of cluster bombs and depleted uranium, whose harmful effects are still visible.

Though these unofficial tribunals have no real legal power, their verdicts should alert public opinion of the lack of any existing body for unprejudiced institutional recourse and the risk that war criminals will not be prosecuted thanks to the vetoes of world powers. In this bleak overview, a hopeful note is provided by the enforcement in 2002 of the Statute of the International Criminal Court at the Hague.

SEE ALSO

Vietnam War; American Civil War; American Revolution; prisoners.

BIBLIOGRAPHY. Hazel Croall, *Understanding White-Collar Crime* (Open University Press, 2001); Yoram Dinstein and Mala Tabory, *War Crimes in International Law* (M. Nijhof Publishers, 1996); Roy Gutman and David Rieff, eds., *Crimes of War: What the Public Should Know* (W. W. Norton, 1999); Erwin Knoll and Judith Nies McFadden, *War Crimes and the American Conscience* (Holt, Rinehart and Winston, 1970); Howard S. Levie, *Terrorism in War: The Law of War Crimes* (Oceana Publications, 1993); Aryeh Neier, *Brutality, Genocide, Terror, and the Struggle for Justice* (Times Books, 1998); Naomi Roht Arriaza, ed., *Impunity and Human Rights in International Law and Practice* (Oxford University Press, 1995); Stephen R. Ratner and Jason S. Abrams, *Accountability for Human Rights Atrocities in International Law* (Oxford University Press, 1997); Adam Roberts and Richard Guelff, eds., *Documents on the Laws of War* (Oxford University Press, 1989); N. Tutorow, *War Crimes, War Criminals, and War Crimes Trials* (Greenwood Press, 1986).

LUCA PRONO, PH.D.
UNIVERSITY OF NOTTINGHAM, ENGLAND

Waste Management, Inc.

WASTE MANAGEMENT, Inc. (WMI) is one of the largest refuse companies in the United States and a chronic corporate criminal offender. Waste Management controls approximately 22 percent of North American waste business. This includes the transport of millions of tons of waste on roads and waterways to waste disposal landfills in Virginia and Pennsylvania, the top two importers of trash, primarily from New York, Washington, D.C., and Delaware. WMI was sued but recently settled out of court with the state of Virginia for violating the state's environmental waste transport laws that prohibited water transport of waste. WMI can legally use barges to transport interstate waste to Virginia. Virginia was one of the first states that tried to protect its waterways from exposure to waste, however a federal court struck down the state law.

MINORITY NEIGHBORHOODS

WMI operates a landfill in Sun Valley, California, where residents sought in the early 2000s to stop the company's landfill expansion. Expansion plans would increase the amount of waste in the landfill from 1 million to 3.3 million cubic yards. Critics say WMI, like other waste companies, often exploits geographic areas like this one that involve lower costs and where resident resistance is less powerful. Typically, this often involves placement of facilities in poor or predominately minority neighborhoods.

From 1970 to 2004, Waste Management was criminally convicted 10 times and was fined over $5 million. Additionally, it was convicted of 23 price-fixing crimes in 23 states, and has violated 22 environmental regulations and 87 other administrative regulations. WMI also was found guilty of defrauding its investors. In a civil settlement, Waste Management was forced to pay $220 million in damages for lying about its earnings to inflate its stock prices.

In 2002, the Securities and Exchange Commission (SEC) filed a lawsuit against former executives of the company for inflating earnings by almost $2 million, an accounting fraud scheme designed to deceive shareholders. The accounting firm, Arthur Anderson, assisted in perpetrating the fraud and as with Enron Corporation, also destroyed the paper trail of evidence in the fraud. The lawsuit alleged that WMI defrauded shareholders of more than $6 million.

Meanwhile, Waste Management announced in February 2003 that it was cutting full-time jobs and contracts across North America and expanding its operations globally. Like the early predecessors in the cartage or garbage industry that were owned and operated by a number of organized crime families, WMI also was convicted of price-fixing charges in Wisconsin and California and pleaded no contest to similar charges in Florida and Georgia. It has also settled out of a court a class action lawsuit for price fixing in a number of local markets, paying over f$50 million. WMI was also sued by the town of South Elgin, Illinois, for trying to open a waste transfer station on top of a closed landfill that it had previously promised to not expand in 1988.

In the wake of the company's international expansion, one WMI subsidiary, Waste Management Siam Limited, is headquartered in Thailand. This plant is the first Thai facility to be owned by private investors rather than the state, and currently has the capacity to process 2 million cubic meters of waste.

Forty percent of the plant's waste revenues come from the United States, 40 percent from Japan, 15 percent from other countries, and only 5 percent from Thailand. Much of the current waste dumped in Thailand is dumped illegally. Clearly, states appear to make more money (or no money) by storing other people's garbage rather than their own, or illegally receiving it without any safety measures to protect the environment or the people.

SEE ALSO
water pollution; air pollution; hazardous waste; Environmental Protection Agency.

BIBLIOGRAPHY. Harry Glasbeek, *Wealth by Stealth Corporate Crime, Corporate Law, and the Perversion of Democracy* (Between the Lines, 2002); "Waste Management Accused of Massive Accounting Fraud," *Toronto Star* (March 27, 2002); Kurt Eichenwald, "Anderson Misread Depths of the Government's Anger," *New York Times* (March 18, 2002); "Waste Management to Cut Workforce," *New York Times* (v.152/52399, 2003); "Sun Valley, California Residents to Fight Proposed Expansion of Landfill," *Los Angeles Daily News* (February 13, 2003); "Wisconsin-Based Recycler Joins Waste Management in Alliance," *Duluth News-Tribune* (January 14, 2003); Peter Reuter, "The Cartage Industry in New York," *Beyond the Law, Crime in Complex Organizations* (University of Chicago Press, 1993); "South Elgin Sues over Waste," *Chicago Tribune* (August 14, 2002).

Rebecca S. Katz
Morehead State University

water pollution

POLLUTING THE WATER in the United States is an environmental crime. The Environmental Protection Agency (EPA) monitors and regulates approximately 80 chemicals in finished drinking water as stipulated by the Safe Drinking Water Act. When analyzed samples contain the specified chemicals above a preset maximum contamination level, then the water is considered unsafe.

Corporations are chronic offenders in this category of white-collar crime. Some of the biggest corporate offenders of such environmental crimes include, General Electric (GE), Westinghouse, Ford, DuPont, the U.S. government, and Union Carbide. Estimates are that corporations illegally dump about 8 million tons of toxic wastes into rivers and coastal waters annually.

As just one example from the industrial polluters list, during the 1950s, General Electric's two manufacturing plants in New York, one at Fort Edward and the other at Hudson Falls made electrical capacitators for electricity plants. A capacitator saves electric companies' money by producing more electricity with less power or amps. However, these capacitators only work because of the use of polychlorinated biphenyls or PCBs. Monsanto developed PCBs in 1929, and in 1970 Monsanto warned GE to keep PCBs from entering the environment. PCBs are listed as a persistent organic pollutant that does not break down over time. A variety of research also shows that PCBs are carcinogenic, cause birth defects, miscarriages, and cloracne (a severe skin disease that covers the body with pustules and darkens the skin), impairs vision, leads to impotence, fever, and diarrhea.

Both GE plants began dumping the castings used to make the capacitators, covered with PCBs, into the Hudson River. The Hudson at the time provided drinking water, commercial fishing, and recreational fishing to the local population. It is estimated that over 500,000 pounds of PCBs were dumped into the river. GE also had a policy to sell or give away PCB contaminated dirt, including selling it as fertilizer. One such place is the Dewey Loeffel Landfill in Nassau, New York, where GE dumped more than 46,000 tons of PCBs, other heavy metals, and toxic wastes in the 1950s and 1960s. This is more than twice the amount dumped at the Love Canal, New York, catastrophe in 1984 in what is referred to as the worst industrial accident on record. The Dewey site continues to be classified as a significant health risk by the state of New York.

Pollution of the Hudson continued until 1975 when the Clean Water Act began to be enforced. Subsequently, the federal government ordered the company to begin to reduce the amount of PCBs released into the Hudson. In 1976, the U.S. Congress outlawed PCB manufacture, sale, and distribution (except in "totally enclosed systems"). Finally, GE agreed to pay $3 million to clean up the Hudson and to discontinue use of PCB by the year 1977. Since that time, GE has managed to get 77 of its plant sites on the EPA Superfund list, areas that must be cleaned up as the result of severe pollution. Superfund sites are contaminated areas requiring cleanup by the company that did the polluting whether or not the pollution was legal at the time. The Comprehensive Environmental Response, Compensation and Liability Act created such sites in 1980.

POLAR BEARS TO DOLPHINS

At least 500,000 pounds of PCBs are estimated to still set at the bottom of the Hudson. In the early 2000s, the EPA had a five-year plan to complete a dredging program aimed at removing 2.65 million cubic yards or 100,000 pounds of PCBs from the Hudson River. The cost was estimated at $460 million dollars. Fish still remain contaminated and unsafe to eat, and on land, animals such river otters, turtles and mink also have high levels of PCBs in their bodies. As far as 40 miles away from GE's two plants, PCBs were also being found in water falling from the Troy Dam. Moreover, PCBs have been found higher up the food chain in polar bears and dolphins and in human tissue and blood samples.

GE has spent millions fighting the government and unsuccessfully refuting these research findings while donating millions of dollars to local communities to garner support for a no-dredge or no-clean up order. Nonetheless, the EPA made a decision in 2002 requiring GE through the Superfund program to clean up the Hudson River. There are at least 40 sites along the river that are contaminated with PCBs, 13 of which have been designated as a "threat to public health or the environment" by the New York Department of Environmental Conservation.

GE also has similar sites like the Hudson River plants in Pittsfield, Massachusetts, and Rome,

Georgia, communities with similar pollution problems and clean up mandates.

HAZARDOUS WASTES

What may begin as air pollution at work, may also result in groundwater pollution. A company called Rentokil Wood Preserving Division in Henrico County, Virginia, treated wood with chemicals from 1957 until 1990 when the plant was closed. Employees were regularly unprotected from a variety of airborne chemicals that were used to treat the wood, including copper arsenate (CCA), creosote, chromated zinc arsenate, pentachlorophenol (PCP), xylene, and fire retardants in solutions of ammonium phosphates and sulfates from 1982-1990. Until 1980, these chemicals dripped from the treated wood into the ground. Employees also reported that similar wastes were discharged into a sump from 1957 through 1963. CCA was also dumped into a ditch near the company during the mid 1970s.

Additionally, hazardous waste was generally put in drums and buried on the property for many years as well as dumped openly into the soil. Several employees (the company only employed 20 people) developed cancer after working for many years at the plant. Carcinogenic chemicals were discovered in excess of the mandated levels in the soil, and groundwater near the plant. These included PCPs, polynulcear aromatic hydrocarbons, dioxins, zinc, and furans. While the authors of one study report that an appropriate negotiation process for the clean up of this site followed, the EPA really capitulated to pressure from the industry. The company was allowed to use the cheapest method of clean up involving capping the materials in the ground and then allowing for the re-development of the land (including a playground). From discovery in 1982 to clean up, this Superfund project took 17 years to complete at a cost of $15.5 million.

Similarly, Union Carbide is also responsible for water pollution. In Ocean County, New Jersey, between 1979 and 1991, a number of underground water wells became contaminated from a Union Carbide Superfund site. The site had been used for the disposal of industrial waste beginning in 1971 and was later condemned after leaking was discovered in 1975. In 1987, the same volatile organic pollutants that are known to be carcinogenic and were in the Superfund site were also found in the water.

The groundwater underneath the Superfund site was collected by two of the wells that provided water to the community.

INTERNATIONAL WATERS

Internationally, the World Health Organization estimates that a lack of safe water kills over two million people each year. While some of this is simply due to poor sanitation, much of it is also the result of polluting Western industries taking advantage of third world nations with lax environmental laws. For example, a study recently completed in Taiwan found that exposure to contaminated groundwater was associated with cancer risks for 382 residents of several communities. These communities were located from near the site of a former electronic appliance factory responsible for on-site soil and underground water contamination over a 10-year period. The Taiwan EPA declared the area a hazardous waste site in 1994. A variety of distinct types of chemicals were found at the Taiwan site and are referred to generally as chlorinated hydrocarbons associated with increased risk for liver cancer. Sixty-one percent of the problems associated with liver cancer were the result of inhaling the chemicals during showering (local residents boiled their water thus eliminating carcinogenic risks from contamination).

In 2002, the United Nations (UN) Committee on Economic, Social and Cultural Rights declared access to safe, sufficient, physically accessible and affordable water to be a human right. The UN goal is to decrease by half the number of people who still do not have access to clean water around the globe by 2015.

SEE ALSO

Environmental Protection Agency; air pollution; General Electric; Love Canal; Clean Water Act.

BIBLIOGRAPHY. Russell Mokhiber, *Corporate Crime and Violence. Big Business Power and the Abuse of the Public Trust* (Sierra Club Books, 1988); Charlie Cray, "Toxics on the Hudson," *Multinational Monitor* (v.22/7–8); Jack Griffith, et al., "Cancer Mortality in U.S. Counties with Hazardous Waste Sites and groundwater Pollution," *Archives of Environmental Health* (v.44/2, 1989); Peter Iadicola and Anson Shupe, "Violence and Inequality and Human Freedom," *Economic Violence* (Rowman and Littlefield, 2003); Jyuhn-Hsiar Lee, et al., "Health Risk Assessment on Residents Exposed to Chlorinated Hydrocarbons Contaminated in Groundwater of a Hazardous Waste Site," *Journal of Toxicology and Environmental Health* (v.65, 2002); Susan D. Richardson, et al., "Identification of Drinking Water Contaminants in the Course of a Childhood Cancer Investigation in Toms River, New Jersey," *Journal of Exposure Analysis and Environmental Epidemiology* (v.9, 1999); Jennifer Smith Esway and Margot Garcia, Margot, "From Superfund Site to Developable Property: The Case of Rentokil," *Journal of Environmental Planning and Management* (v.45/2, 2002); Jonathan Watts, "Forum Debates Private Sector Role in Global Water Supply," *Lancet* (v.361, 2003).

REBECCA S. KATZ
MOREHEAD STATE UNIVERSITY

Watergate

THE WATERGATE scandal generally refers to all offenses committed during the Richard Nixon administration. The unraveling of the Watergate incident originally pursued by investigative reporters Carl Bernstein and Bob Woodward of the *Washington Post* led to the revelation of extensive illegal acts by members of the White House staff and others closely associated with, or employed by the Nixon administration. As a totality of all crimes by the Nixon administration, Watergate is better understood broken down into three phases.

The first includes illegal acts sanctioned by the White House prior to the break-in at Democratic National Campaign (DNC) headquarters in the Watergate apartment complex in Washington, D.C. Second is the Watergate burglary itself which was a failed attempt to tap the telephone lines of the DNC chairman on June 17, 1972. Third is the conspiracy to cover up the Watergate burglary and prevent any connection between it and the White House from being discovered.

The question was how much did Nixon know about the plan before its commission? The notion Nixon may have had prior knowledge of the burglary seems plausible by the fact that the Watergate burglary was not the only one associated with his administration. The burglary of Daniel Ellsberg's psychiatrist's office preceded Watergate, and involved some of the same people who played subsequent roles in Watergate. (Moreover, in 2003, one of the indicted participants in the Watergate scandal, Jeb Stuart Magruder, told a Public Broadcasting Service reporter that Nixon, indeed, had authorized the plan for the Watergate break-in.)

As a Defense Department consultant who personally supported the War, Ellsberg was commissioned by the Rand Corporation to write a history of U.S. involvement in the conflict, *The Pentagon Papers*. The publication of the *Papers* infuriated Nixon because they could appear to imply he was not handling the war as promised. To identify the source of the *Papers* leak and to prevent others in the White House from leaking information, Nixon created a special investigative unit known as the Plumbers under the supervision of John Ehrlichman with Egil Krogh in charge. The Plumbers unit included G. Gordon Liddy and E. Howard Hunt. They identified Ellsberg to be responsible for leaking the *Papers* to the press. Liddy and Hunt were put in charge of burglarizing Ellsberg's psychiatrist's office o obtain incriminating information.

Many other factors played a part leading up to the Watergate break-in that make an explanation of it much more complex than a simple order from the president. The overall mentality of the Nixon administration was a factor. Nixon's goal in anything he undertook was to win at all costs. This went so far as placing anyone who opposed him, or who was unfriendly, on the White House "enemies list." In such an environment subordinates felt secure in doing just about anything to attain presidential goals, even if the actions were unethical or illegal.

The win-at-all-costs outlook, and certain amount of paranoia about leaks, certainly would shape the thinking and acts of Nixon's campaign officials. Unlike previous presidential incumbents up for re-election, Nixon did not leave his campaign to his party, but instead created the Committee to Re-elect the President (CREEP). CREEP was devoted entirely to ensuring Nixon's re-election. John Mitchell, attorney general of the United States, was appointed to head CREEP with Magruder serving as deputy director. Mitchell reported to John Dean III, White House counsel, who in turn reported to H. R. "Bob" Haldeman the White House chief of staff. Rather than focusing on publicity and raising campaign contributions, CREEP set about to gather political intelligence.

The idea to break into Democratic headquarters was possibly suggested to John Mitchell by G. Gorden Liddy CREEP's "intelligence chief." The object was to wiretap the telephone line of Larry O'Brien, the DNC chairman, to gather intelligence on the Democrats' campaign strategy. As the persons in charge of the operation Liddy and Hunt directed the burglary from a hotel room across the street from the Watergate apartment complex. On night of June 17, five burglars, Bernard L. Barker, Virgilio Gonzalez, Eugenio R. Martinez, Frank A. Sturgis, and James W. McCord (CREEP's security consultant) entered the DNC offices. A security guard noticed a taped-open door and lights, and called police. The day after the burglary, Ehrlichman, Haldeman, and the president were informed of the ill-fated attempt. Nixon was extremely aggravated at his subordinates' failure, but referred to the incident as "the caper." The burglary and additional crimes the investigation exposed led to Nixon's resignation as president of the United States on August 9, 1974.

CENTER OF THE PLOT

Two points of law made Nixon culpable. First, laws on criminal conspiracy state if someone becomes aware of a plan to commit crime and takes action to further it, he is culpable because the actions place him among the plotters, and can thus be criminally charged. He also ordered the Federal Bureau of Investigation to stop inquiries into the Watergate burglary thus obstructing justice. Second, one must have something to gain or an interest in the object of the conspiracy. A burglary aimed at ensuring Nixon's re-election placed his personal interests at the center of the plot.

The case of the *United States v. Mitchell et. al.* began January 8, 1973, before Judge John J. Sirica. The Watergate incident, as a whole, resulted in the indictment of more than 40 of Nixon's subordinates and supporters. Each served minimal time, with Liddy serving the longest actual sentence of four years. President Gerald Ford pardoned Nixon, arguing that losing the presidency was punishment enough and a prison term would serve no purpose.

SEE ALSO

elite crime; Nixon, Richard M; corruption.

BIBLIOGRAPHY. Carl Bernstein and Bob Woodward, *All the President's Men* (Simon & Schuster, 1974); Fred J. Cook, *The Crimes of Watergate* (Franklin Watts, 1981); John Dean, *Blind Ambition: The White House Years* (Simon & Schuster, 1976); F. Emery, *Watergate* (Times Books, 1994); Barbara S. Feinberg, *Watergate: Scandal in the White House* (Franklin Watts, 1990); Leon Jaworski, *The Right and the Power: The Prosecution of Watergate* (Gulf Publishing Company, 1976); Stanley I. Kutler, *Abuse of Power: The New Nixon Tapes* (The Free Press, 1997); "Newshour: What the President Knew," www.pbs.org (2003).

MICHAEL SIEGFRIED
COKER COLLEGE

Weisburd, David (1947–)

IN 2003, David Weisburd was a professor and senior research fellow in the department of criminology and criminal justice at the University of Maryland, a position held since 2000. Weisburd also held a joint appointment at the Institute of Criminology at the Hebrew University in Jerusalem, Israel, where he was on the faculty of law. Weisburd obtained his Ph.D. in sociology at Yale University, where he also earned a Master of Philosophy degree in sociology, and a M.A. in sociology. Weisburd earned his B.A. degree in sociology from Brandeis University.

Before his 2003 academic position, Weisburd held a number of posts and visiting positions in the field of criminology and criminal justice, including as a research associate on the well-known Yale Studies in White-Collar Crime at Yale Law School during the periods of 1979–81 and again in 1983–84.

Weisburd has conducted research in several distinct criminal justice topics, including policing, research, and statistical methods, and white-collar crime. He has received numerous grants and fellowships to support his individual and collaborative research projects. One such project was an extensive, National Institute of Justice-funded study to assess sanctioning effects in the area of white-collar criminal careers, under which he served as a co-principal investigator with Ellen Chayet. The research examined whether white-collar offenders shared the characteristics commonly associated with the career criminal and criminal career paradigms, such as onset, prevalence, specialization in offending, frequency of offending, and duration of offending.

This unique study was the first of its kind in white-collar crime, and contributed to a number of significant journal articles and books. Some of his major contributions in this area of research include *White-Collar Crime and Criminal Careers* (co-authored with Elin Waring and Ellen Chayet in 2001); *White-Collar Crime Reconsidered* (co-edited with Kip Schlegel in 1992); and *Crimes of the Middle Classes: White-Collar Offenders in the Federal Courts* (co-authored with Stanton Wheeler, Elin Waring, and Nancy Bode in 1991).

SEE ALSO

Wheeler, Stanton; differential association theory; self-control theory; Sutherland, Edwin H.

BIBLIOGRAPHY. Kip Schlegel and David Weisburd, *White-Collar Crime Reconsidered* (Northeastern University Press, 1992); David Weisburd, Elin Waring, and Ellen Chayet, *White-Collar Crime and Criminal Careers* (Cambridge University Press, 2001); David Weisburd, Stanton Wheeler, Elin Waring and Nancy Bode, *Crimes of the Middle Classes: White-Collar Offenders in the Federal Courts* (Yale University Press, 1991).

KRISTY HOLTFRETER, PH.D.
MICHIGAN STATE UNIVERSITY

Wheeler, Stanton (1930–)

IN 2003, Stanton Wheeler was a Ford Foundation professor emeritus of law and the social sciences and professorial lecturer in law at Yale University Law School. Although he is well known for his research contributions in areas such as administration of justice, white-collar crime, and sociology of law, Wheeler's research has also included the areas of sports and law as well as music and law.

Wheeler began his education at Pomona College, where he graduated with a B.A. in 1952. Subsequently, he enrolled in graduate school at the University of Washington in Seattle, where he earned a M.A. in sociology in 1956, followed by a Ph.D. in 1958. Before joining the faculty at Yale, Wheeler's professional and academic positions including assistant professor in the department of social relations at Harvard University (1961–63). While employed at Harvard, Wheeler was also a Fulbright research scholar at the Institutes of Sociology and Criminology, University of Oslo, Norway, where he served from 1960 to 1961. Wheeler

has also held many official positions related to his research, such as a member of many journals' editorial boards.

Wheeler is the author of numerous books and articles based on his funded research. His major writings on white-collar crime emerged during the course of his direction of the largest-ever research study on white-collar crime, the Yale Studies. For students of white-collar crime, the Yale Studies have provided some of the most influential findings in the field. From 1983 to 1991, Wheeler directed the project, and served as the general editor of *Yale Studies in White-Collar Crime*, a series of books that reported the major findings from the research project. A series of articles based on preliminary findings from the project were also published, and the data from the studies have been re-analyzed by several other researchers.

The topics of the Yale series books are related, but each investigates a unique area of interest to white-collar crime researchers, such as offender characteristics, theory, and sentencing and punishment. In 1988, Wheeler (along with Kenneth Mann and Austin Sarat) published *Sitting in Judgment: The Sentencing of White-Collar Criminals*. This book summarizes and discusses comprehensive interviews of federal district court judges. Another significant contribution in the series is *Crimes of the Middle Classes: White-Collar Offenders in the Federal Courts*, which Wheeler co-authored with David Weisburd, Elin Waring, and Nancy Bode in 1991. Perhaps most notable of its findings, this book revealed that the larger portion of white-collar crime is not committed by upper-class individuals, as commonly assumed, but instead by those offenders who can be described as "ordinary people."

Examination of the sentencing data showed that common offenders still received harsher sanctions than white-collar offenders, a finding that supported previous ideas. Common offenders were also more likely to lose their jobs after sentencing. The major policy lesson learned from this book is that white-collar crime can be reduced through procedures that reduce temptation and also make it difficult to accumulate debt.

SEE ALSO

Sutherland, Edwin H.; differential association theory.

BIBLIOGRAPHY. David Weisburd, Stanton Wheeler, Elin Waring, and Nancy Bode, *Crimes of the Middle*

Classes: White-Collar Offenders in the Federal Courts (Yale University Press, 1991); Stanton Wheeler, Kenneth Mann, and Austin Sarat, *Sitting in Judgment: The Sentencing of White-Collar Criminals* (Yale University Press, 1988). Stanton Wheeler and Leon Lipson, *Law and the Social Sciences* (Russell Sage Foundation, 1986); www.law.yale.edu (2003).

KRISTY HOLTFRETER, PH.D.
FLORIDA STATE UNIVERSITY

whistleblowers

THE ORIGINS OF whistleblowing have been compared to English common law notions of raising the "hue and cry" to create a public uproar when a crime was discovered. Other scholars have traced the term to a referee who blows the whistle to halt action or to a police officer who blows a whistle and yells "stop thief." Gerald Vinten notes that the first known use of the term was in reference to the 1963 Otto Otopeka case.

Otopeka provided classified documents concerning security risks to the U.S. Senate Subcommittee on Internal Security that resulted in the firing of the Secretary of State Dean Rusk. Whistleblowing is defined under the Whistleblower Protection Act as the "disclosure of information that an employee reasonably believes is evidence of illegality, gross waste, gross mismanagement, abuse of power, or substantial and specific danger to public health or safety."

The efforts of whistleblowers have resulted in the exposure of dangerous workplace environments and deviant organizational practices that have served as the impetus for major organizational changes and government prosecutions of malfeasance. Infamous whistleblowers include, for example, Frank Serpico who reported widespread corruption in the New York City police department in the late 1960s. Ernest Fitzgerald was fired by the Pentagon in the 1970s after he revealed a billion-dollar waste overrun on military aircraft contracts.

In 2002, *Time* magazine named three whistleblowers as Persons of the Year. Sherron Watkins was a vice president at Enron who first warned the chairman of improper accounting methods. Coleen Rowley was a Federal Bureau of Investigation (FBI) staff attorney who reported negligence within the agency on the investigation of a man who later was charged as a co-conspirator in the September 11, 2003, terrorist attacks. Cynthia Cooper helped uncover WorldCom's attempt to cover up $3.8 billion in losses when she informed the company's board members of the "creative" accounting. Though these whistleblowers have been designated heroes for uncovering fraud and malfeasance, traditionally, companies and colleagues have viewed employees who report wrongdoing as disloyal rats who are prone to tattle-telling.

Motives of whistleblowers often are difficult to disentangle from the circumstances and complexities surrounding each unique case. While the motivations and ethics of whistleblowing often are difficult to generalize, similarities are noted in the literature. Researchers have discovered that whistleblowers are likely to have a high level of moral development, high self-esteem, and an internal locus of control. Whistleblowers consider themselves loyal employees who are committed to their organizations. Often, they have attempted to rectify the situation through internal reporting, but as a result of the negative labels and retaliation resort to external sources. When deciding to report, observers of illegal or immoral actions also consider the personal costs of reporting.

In certain circumstances, whistleblowers pay a high price for dissenting. They may suffer retaliation through demotions or firing. Their family life may be disrupted; they can become targets of scorn and be alienated from friends and colleagues. Research suggests that retaliation is more likely to occur when the reported wrongdoing harms the organization, hurts the public, or when the illegal activity continues despite complaints. Organizations typically discourage and resist recognition of whistleblowers; consequently, their decision to report wrongdoing through external channels often result in public scandals that further damage the reputation of the organization.

Efforts to legitimize the reporting of workplace malfeasance through legislation appear to have little effect on eradicating views that whistleblowing is a pejorative act. The False Claims Act (FCA) protects employees from retaliation and allows private citizens who suspect fraud to file suit on behalf of the government. The FCA was enacted during the Civil War to control fraud in government contracts. Whistleblower protection can be found in 35 federal laws and in individual state legislation—the

FCA represents the most effective source for recovery and protection from retaliation.

A *qui tam* suit involves private individuals who sue on behalf of the government to recover damages for criminal or fraudulent actions. *Qui tam* is Latin for "he who brings an action for the king as well as for himself." The whistleblower complaint is filed under seal in the U.S. District Court. The Justice Department then has 60 days to investigate the allegations and decide whether or not to join in the lawsuit. The Government Accountability Project, which has defended thousands of whistleblowers against retaliation, however, warns of the odds of profiting from a whistleblower claim are similar to those of winning a lottery. As of late 2001, the Department of Justice (DOJ) reported that 3,194 *qui tam* cases have been filed since 1986. Ninety-five percent of the cases in which DOJ intervened resulted in some type of monetary recovery. Through September 2000 the total recovered reached $5.204 billion.

SEE ALSO
corporate liability; Witness and Victim Protection Act; differential association theory.

BIBLIOGRAPHY. Myron Peretz Glazer and Penina Migdal Glazer, *The Whistleblowers: Exposing Corruption in Government and Industry* (Basic Books, 1989); Stephen M. Kohn, *Concepts and Procedures in Whistleblower Law* (Quorum, 2000); Janet Near and Marcia Miceli, *Blowing the Whistle* (Lexington Books, 1992); Gerald Vinten, *Whistleblowing: Subversion or Corporate Citizenship* (St. Martin's Press, 1994); Alan F. Westin, *Whistleblowing: Loyalty and Dissent in the Corporation* (McGraw-Hill 1981); www.whistleblowers.org (2003).

MARY DODGE, PH.D.
UNIVERSITY OF COLORADO, DENVER

Whitewater

THE TERM *Whitewater* has two meanings. In its literal sense, it refers to the Whitewater Development Corporation, an unsuccessful real estate partnership between former president and first lady Bill and Hillary Clinton and James and Linda McDougal to develop a resort on the White River in Arkansas. In its broader sense, Whitewater was a partisan attempt to use a "scandal" to bring down a president.

The real estate deal can only be understood in the deregulation environment of the 1980s in what became known as the "me decade." The "scandal" makes sense only in the highly charged environment of political campaigns and subsequent partisan attacks on a political opponent. Within the context of Whitewater, neither Bill nor Hillary Clinton was ever found guilty of anything worse than misjudgment. The investigations never proved that Arkansas Governor Clinton (at the time of the Whitewater transactions) used his position to help the McDougals. Nor did it prove that either of the Clintons engaged in a cover-up. Clinton opponents maintain that the Clintons lied, and even some Clinton supporters believe that both Clintons should have been more forthcoming on details of Whitewater.

James and Susan McDougal, who allegedly illegally diverted over $17 million from Madison Guaranty funds, were convicted on charges of conspiracy and mail fraud. James McDougal died in prison in 1998. Susan McDougal was also charged with contempt because she would not provide requested information on the Clintons. Arkansas Governor Guy Tucker was also convicted of conspiracy and fraud.

In an unsecured loan, the Union National Bank of Arkansas provided the Clintons $20,000 to invest in the deal to turn 230 acres of undeveloped land into a resort. The Citizen's Bank and Trust of Arkansas financed an additional $182,000 for the Whitewater Development Corporation to buy the land, which the president of the bank owned. Even though the McDougals put up most the money involved, the Clintons were considered equal partners.

In the early 1990s, investigations began into various failed savings and loan institutions (S&Ls), which had cost the taxpayers millions of dollars. Charged with investigating the S&L scandals, the Resolution Trust Corporation examined Madison Guaranty Savings and Loan in Arkansas, which had collapsed in 1989 and which was owned by James and Susan McDougal. Even after filing for bankruptcy, Madison Guaranty continued to make payments to the Whitewater account. Initially, the Clintons were seen as witnesses against the McDougals; but as details about the partnership were made public, the media and Clinton critics called for hearings into the Clinton's finances. Matters were complicated by the fact that Hillary Clinton had served as the lawyer for Madison Guaranty Savings and Loan, and more complications arose when Vince Foster, White House counsel and guardian of the Clinton's personal financial papers, committed suicide in July 1993 under mysterious circumstances.

After both the Senate and House Banking Committees held hearings on Whitewater, Kenneth Starr, a staunch Republican, was appointed as independent counsel to investigate the Clinton connection to Whitewater. Starr extended his investigation to include information about Bill Clinton's sexual activities. Ultimately, the House of Representatives impeached the president on charges that arose from Starr's investigation.

SEE ALSO
investment trust scandals; Clinton, William J.

BIBLIOGRAPHY. Joseph R. Blaney and William L. Benoit, *The Clinton Scandals and the Politics of Image Restoration* (Praeger, 2001); Elizabeth Drew, *Showdown: The Struggle Between the Gingrich Congress and the Clinton White House* (Simon & Schuster, 1996); Gene Lyons and the Editors of *Harper's* Magazine, *Fools for Scandal: How the Media Invented Whitewater* (Franklin Square Press, 1996); James B. Stewart, *Blood Sport: The President and His Adversaries* (Simon & Schuster, 1996); Martin Walker, *The President We Deserve* (Crown Publishers, 1996).

ELIZABETH PURDY, PH.D.
INDEPENDENT SCHOLAR

wire fraud

THE FEDERAL WIRE fraud statute, originally enacted in 1952, is codified under 18 U.S.C. §1343, and has two essential elements: 1) using, or trying to use, signal transmission that occurs in interstate or foreign commerce; 2) transmission that is in furtherance of defrauding someone.

The law has been utilized against virtually every new electronic method of fraud as well as less sophisticated schemes. Federal jurisdiction over wire fraud originates in the Constitution under Article 1, Section 8, and is based on Congress's right to make laws affecting interstate and foreign commerce. It is titled *Fraud By Wire, Radio, or Television*:

> Whoever, having devised or intending to devise any scheme or artifice to defraud, or for obtaining money or property by means of false or fraudulent pretenses, representations, or promises, transmits or causes to be transmitted by means of wire, radio, or television communication in interstate or foreign commerce, any writings, signs, signals, pictures, or sounds for the purpose of executing such scheme or artifice, shall be fined under this title or imprisoned not more than five years, or both. If the violation affects a financial institution, such person shall be fined not more than $1,000,000 or imprisoned not more than 30 years, or both.

Many of the legal theories associated with the application of the mail fraud statute (18 U.S.C. 1341) are also applicable to wire fraud. One major difference between wire and mail fraud is that the federal government can criminalize any use or intended use of the mails both interstate and intrastate, according to its right to regulate the post office, which it owns and operates. In contrast, the federal government does not own the wires over which fraud is conducted and therefore is not allowed to criminalize intrastate wire use. It is restricted by the Commerce Clause to criminalize only wire transmissions that affect interstate and foreign commerce.

Four years after its passage, Congress changed the statute to explicitly reflect the federal jurisdictional criterion and to eliminate any challenges to the law based on constitutionality. The change involved substituting "transmitted by means of wire, radio, or television communication in interstate or foreign commerce" for the original statutory wording of "transmitted by means of interstate wire, radio, or television communication." The other major revision of the statute occurred in 1989 when the clause related to effects on a financial institution was added, and for which the maximum punishment was increased by 10 years in 1990.

The underlying legal crime of wire fraud is not that associated with the fraud, but rather the crime in using wires or signals in interstate or foreign commerce, or trying to use them, as an instrument of crime. This allows extremely distinctive enforcement interpretations. First, the statute does not consider the harm inflicted by the fraud. Rather, it cares only about how many times signals were used, or were tried, in interstate or foreign commerce to in any way further the fraud.

Second, the statute allows merely a "scheme" to be prosecuted, regardless of whether the fraud actually took place. The interpretation is in this sense similar to a conspiracy to commit a crime, but a conspiracy necessitates at least two participants; there need be only one participant in the scheme to be prosecuted under wire fraud. Further, whereas conspiracy can be charged only once, wire fraud law punishes each act of signal transmission as a separate count.

ENOUGH TO CONVICT

The intent to violate §1343 only need involve a broadly interpreted "foreseeable" use of wires or radio/television signals, and the offender need not even have foreseen their use in interstate or foreign commerce. In one case, for instance, there was a fraud-related Western Union communication between two small cities in Texas, but the message happened to be routed, as were all such communications, through West Virginia. Even though the defendant did not "foresee" the use of wires in interstate or foreign commerce, he should have foreseen at least the use of wires, which is enough to convict. This broad interpretation of "foreseeing" is especially idiosyncratic to both mail and wire fraud statutes, because most offenses require that the perpetrator have knowledge of the commission of the act and also intends its commission.

Wire fraud must go beyond obtaining something under false pretenses and include harm to victims. An illustrative case involved employees of an office-supply company who lied to potential customers when they sold stationery over the telephone, by stating that they were physicians who needed to dispose of unwanted supplies, or that the goods to be sold belonged to a friend who had died. Because the goods were delivered, as promised for the agreed price, no harm, and therefore no fraud, was found, despite the creative false pretenses under which the sales were made. Wire fraud, then, must involve the use of false pretenses.

For many years, §1343 was interpreted as covering bribe-taking by officials and private citizens who used wires or signals in interstate commerce to effect the bribery scheme. The legal basis was that the bribe-takers were depriving others of their intangible right for honest services. This prosecutorial basis for wire fraud was overturned by the Supreme Court in 1987, because the fraud did not necessarily involve an intent to deprive a person of property or property rights. In 1988, Congress responded by passing 18 U.S.C. §1346, which explicitly defined wire and mail fraud in terms of depriving a person of her intangible right to honest services. In 1994, Congress passed 18 USC §2326, which added as many as five years to the punishment of federal wire and mail frauds associated with a telemarketing scheme, including the unauthorized use of identity, credit card, or bank information gained from telemarketing. If the telemarketing either victimized more than 10 persons over 55 years of age, or generally targeted those seniors, then the penalty for these federal frauds could be increased by as many as 10 years.

Another statute related to wire fraud, 18 USC §1029, was passed in 1984 and concerns the use of any card, device, or code that is used in fraudulent credit card or bank account schemes, many of which involve wire or signals in interstate commerce. Using electronic scanners to intercept signals for fraudulent purposes or using equipment to receive unauthorized telecommunication services are also punishable under §1029.

SEE ALSO

mail fraud; telemarketing fraud; Federal Trade Commission; credit card fraud.

BIBLIOGRAPHY. Richard Beckler and Maury Epner, "Principal White-Collar Crimes," *Business Crimes: A Guide for Corporate and Defense Counsel* (Practicing Law Institute, 1982); Pamela H. Bucy, *White Collar-Crime: Cases and Materials* (West, 1992).

GARY S. GREEN
CHRISTOPHER NEWPORT UNIVERSITY

Witness and Victim Protection Act

IN 1982, Congress initiated the Victim and Witness Protection Act (VWPA) as a means of providing restitution for victims of financial crimes. With the passing of this act, federal courts are allowed to provide for victims of crimes by sanctioning the defendant with fines directly intended for the victim. This differs from prior legislation in that traditionally fines were paid to the court and then used to offset court costs, fees, and other legal costs. Under the modifications provided by the VWPA, victims of crimes are entitled to receive compensation for their pain, suffering, or loss.

While victim restitution is one of the more important aspects of the act, it is not for restitution that the act is best known. Rather, it is the witness protection clauses that have received the most notable attention. Sections 1512 and 1513 allow for the protection of witnesses, potential witnesses, notable investigators, and any other individual who testifies against a defendant and then fears for their safety or life.

The protection extended to witnesses is twofold. Witnesses are provided protection from coercion during the trial and are occasionally provided protection after the trial. Traditionally, the witness was protected during the trial from any form of knowing intimidation, threat, misleading conduct or coercion that was accomplished through threat of physical force. However, tampering with a witness, as prohibited by section 1512, has been extended to acts other than physical force and includes acts that could be interpreted as an attempt to bribe a witness to change her testimony or refuse to present evidence at trial.

Interestingly, the government is not required to provide evidence that a defendant was successful in coercing a witness into failing to testify. The prosecution must only prove that acts took place that could be considered threatening or coercive. Should the coercion of the witness be successful, and the prosecution can demonstrate that the defendant was aware of the coercion, then the defendant is considered to have vacated his right to face his accuser and may not challenge the admission of statements made by a witness prior to the coercion. This is an important consideration because of the traditional ban on the admission of hearsay statements, which are statements made outside the court that cannot be confirmed through the questioning of the individual who made the statement.

In an effort to prevent a witness from being coerced, or physically harmed, witnesses who are preparing for trial are provided with around-the-clock security. The witness is normally housed at an unknown location during the trial, and once the trial is completed the witness is given several choices; whether the choices are offered is contingent upon several factors such as the importance of the witness and the nature of the prosecution.

If the court determines that the defendant is not a threat to the safety of the witness, or if the witness declines to accept continued federal protection, then the witness is released into her own custody. If, however, the court determines that the defendant, or perhaps individuals who work with or for the defendant, pose a threat to the safety of a witness, and the individual in question desires protection, then the individual is placed into the protective custody of the Witness Protection Program with a new identity. The use of the Witness Protection Program is rather expensive and is therefore normally reserved for cases that involve serious violent criminal acts and defendants who are believed to be capable of causing harm to a witness either during or after their incarceration.

SEE ALSO

prosecution; sentencing guidelines; Justice, Department of; United States.

BIBLIOGRAPHY. E. Lent and M. Williams, "Obstruction of Justice," *American Criminal Law Review* (v.39, 2002); G. Lynch, G. (1987). "RICO: The Crime of Being a Criminal," (v.87, 1987); P. Earley and G. Shur, *Witsec: Inside The Federal Witness Protection Program* (Bantam Books, 2003).

ROBERT MOORE, PH.D.
DELTA STATE UNIVERSITY

workplace deaths

IN 2001, 5,900 people in the United States were killed at work. The ways people died included motor vehicle deaths, accidents with machines, falls, being struck by objects, electrocutions, and homicides. The number of workplace homicides (the killing of one human being by another) was the lowest since the federal Occupational Health and Safety Administration (OSHA) began collecting data on workplace homicides.

To fully understand workplace homicides, it is necessary to consider the characteristics of the offenses, victims, and offenders; the causes of workplace homicide; reasons for decreases in workplace homicides; and strategies to deal with offenses.

A number common patterns have been found in workplace violence cases. For instance, offenders and victims tend to be males. According to the Department of Justice (2001), between 1993 and 1999, 80 percent of victims were males. Victims also tend to be between the ages of 25 and 44, as do offenders in these cases. Also, guns are used in 86 percent of the cases and robbery is the most common motive in workplace homicides, according to the Office of Victims of Crime (2001). Taxi cab drivers have the highest risk of workplace homicide. In fact, in the mid-1990s, they were 60 times more likely to be killed at work than the rest of the population.

In *Workplace Homicide: A Continuum from Threat to Death*, criminologist Mittie Southerland and her co-authors identify the following possible causes of workplace homicides. These causes include: 1) low self-control theory, 2) routine activities theory, 3) strain theory, and 4) domestic violence theory.

Low self-control theory suggests that individuals with low self-controls are more likely to commit crime than are those with high self-controls. Routine activities theory assumes that victims are engaged in normal activities and a level of vulnerability and risk may increase the likelihood of victimization. According to this theory, three elements must be present for a crime to occur: 1) a motivated offender, 2) a suitable target, and 3) the absence of a capable guardian. Strain theory is traced to sociologist Robert Merton who argued that individuals work to attain goals by any means set by society.

Domestic violence theory considers the way that intimates commit workplace homicides against their partners. Violence is believed to be a loss of control and the aggressor feels disobeyed or rejected. Tying in routine activities theory, the offender knows the victim's whereabouts at all times when she is at work. Indeed, when domestic violence is the source of the workplace homicide, it is usually a man killing a woman.

In addition to these causes, other authors have identified certain themes that address some reason why these offenses occur. Kelly McMurry (1996) stresses that 75 percent of workplace homicides are robbery-related, while just 9 percent of homicides outside of the workplace are robbery-related. The

study further points out that victims who are at risk are those who work alone, work very late, have a great deal of contact with the public, and exchange money. T.S. Duncan, in the article "Death in the Office," (1995) identifies some other themes that help to explain workplace offenses. The article suggests that these offenses more often involve: 1) a man with a gun, 2) a man with a mid-life crisis, 3) disgruntled employees, 4) civil servants, and 5) offenders who are suicidal.

The number of workplace homicides decreased in the late 1990s. In full, workplace homicides decreased 44 percent in the 1990s, a significant measure. Two explanations for these changes exist: organizational changes and structural factors. Organizational changes have to do with things that companies did in response to the high workplace homicide rate of the mid-1990s. Companies developed zero-tolerance policies in dealing with workplace violence.

HAPPY WORKERS

Structural factors look at societal characteristics in an attempt to explain changing crime rates. From this perspective, the trend of workplace violence decreasing in the 1990s and stabilizing into the new decade is not surprising. All types of violence followed the same pattern. Some criminologists attribute violence rates to the percentage of 18- to 21-year-olds in the population. More young people means more violence. This, however, would not necessarily explain the changes in workplace violence. One explanation for the changes in the workplace could stem from the changes in the economy; better economy, happier workers; struggling economy, less happy workers.

Three separate strategies have been used to prevent workplace violence: careful hiring practices, environmental changes, and training. With regard to careful hiring practices, companies have strengthened their background checks, drug tests, and other procedures designed to determine who has a propensity toward violence. These measures are believed to protect workers from violence perpetrated by fellow workers.

Environmental changes refer to changes that are made to the physical structure where the business is located in order to protect workers. Training has been another strategy used to prevent workplace homicides. Some experts recommend that training should focus on decision-making drills and skills training. A growing number of retail outlets have their workers participate in training sessions in which they role-play a robbery. A consultant who conducts workplace violence training session suggests that workers and management should learn how to do the following: understand the causes of workplace violence; understand the consequences of the violence; understand the characteristics of high-risk individuals; understand how to deal with confrontation; understand the costs management experiences; identify the warning signs of workplace violence..

The fact that workplace homicides has decreased significantly in the 1990s is promising. The task at hand is to continue to find ways to make the workplace as safe as possible for workers.

SEE ALSO
workplace violence; Occupational Safety and Health Act.

BIBLIOGRAPHY. Terry Becker-Fritz, "Violence in the Workplace," www.beckerfritz.com (2003); T.S. Duncan, "Death in the Office," (v.64/4, 1995); Dan Emerson, "Safe Driver on Board," *Safety and Health* (v.157/6, 1998); Marilynn Larkin, (2002), "Better Methods Needed to Prevent Workplace Homicides," *Lancet* (v.359/9308, 2002); Kelly McMurry, "In Harm's Way," *Trial* (v.32/9, 1996); "Violence in the Workplace," National Institute for Occupational Safety and Health (Government Printing Office, 1997), "Homicide in the Workplace," OSHA (GPO, 1998); "Risk Factors and Protective Measures for Taxi and Livery Drivers," OSHA (GPO, 2000); Mittie Southerland, Pamela Collins, and Kathryn Scarborough, *Workplace Violence: A Continuum from Threat to Homicide* (Anderson Publishing, 1997); Flora Tartakovsky, "You're Safer at the Office," *Time* (November 15, 1999); "Violence in the Workplace, 1993–99," U.S. Department of Justice (GPO, 2001).

BRIAN K. PAYNE
OLD DOMINION UNIVERSITY

workplace violence

WORKPLACE VIOLENCE has become a common occurrence in workplaces across the world. The types of violence range from simple assaults to violent homicides committed against workers. Esti-

mates from the National Institute for Occupational Safety and Health (NIOSH) suggest that nonfatal assaults cost 876,000 lost workdays and $16 million in lost wages each year.

Workplace-violence incidence can be categorized based on victim-offender relationships or by the actual type of harm inflicted on victims. Researchers at the University of Iowa (2000) have described workplace violence in terms of the victim-offender relationships. Based upon their categorization, they cite four general types of workplace violence.

Type I workplace violence refers to those crimes that are committed as part of a broader criminal act. The offender would have absolutely no personal relationship with the victim. As an illustration, consider instances where offenders harm workers in the process of robberies or other thefts. According to the Iowa researchers, 85 percent of workplace homicides are the result of these sorts of interactions.

Type II workplace violence incidents involve situations in which the offender has a business relationship with the workplace, usually in the form of a customer, consumer, or client. The offender becomes violent during the transaction, and there is generally no other crime committed during these interactions.

Type III incidents refer to those situations in which the offender is a worker in the business. Workers could be violent against fellow workers, their bosses, or their customers. Less than one in 15 of workplace fatalities are committed by employees of a business.

Type IV incidents refer to those that are committed by offenders who have no work relationship with the victims. Consider as an example an offender who commits a violent offense in the workplace against his girlfriend or wife. In *Workplace Violence: A Continuum from Threat to Death*, criminologists Mittie Southerland and her colleagues argue that offenders commit domestic violence in the workplace for two reasons. First, they want to expand or gain control over their victims, and harming them in the workplace allows them to accomplish this. Second, in terms of vulnerability, abusive mates know where their victims are when they are at work. Thus, they know when their partners are at risk.

Violence can also be characterized by the kinds of harm committed by aggressors. These types of harm include homicides, non-fatal assaults, and sexual assaults. With regard to homicide, NIOSH estimates 20 people are murdered in the workplace every week. These figures mean that homicides are the third-highest cause of death in the workplace in the United States. Some industries are more at risk than others. Police officers, private security guards, and taxi drivers are especially vulnerable.

Non-fatal assaults entail instances in which one individual physically harms another. Attempts to harm individuals are included in this category. It is difficult to estimate the precise extent of assaults occurring in the workplace for a number of reasons. Victims may choose not to report the incident because they may see violence simply as part of the job. Others may be afraid of the abusers and fear losing their jobs. Still others may be afraid of retaliation. There are patterns surrounding reporting decisions. The U.S. Department of Justice (2001) reported that about one-fourth of workplace sexual assaults are reported to the police, about 70 percent of robberies are reported to the police, about two-thirds of aggravated assaults are reported, and about 40 percent of simple assaults occurring in the workplace are reported to the police. In the end, of 2 million workplace crimes committed between 1993 and 1999, 936,000 were not reported to the police.

Despite these obstacles to obtaining an accurate estimate of the extent of abuse, researchers are still able to offer some estimates. According to the U.S. Department of Justice, the following patterns exist in workplace violence incidents: workplace violence offenders are more likely to be white than African-American; 13 out of 1,000 white workers in the workplace were violent between 1993 and 1999, while 10 out of 1,000 African-American workers were violent in the workplace during the same time frame; workplace violence incidents tend to be committed against members of the same race; the victimization rate among private sector and federal government employees is virtually identical; elementary school teachers face a lower risk of violence than do junior and senior high school teachers; males, while making up less than half of the U.S. population.

Researchers have also considered the kinds of strategies used to commit the violence in the workplace. A review of workplace homicides between 1980 and 1992 by NIOSH reveals that over three-fourths of the cases involved guns, 12 percent involved knives or other cutting instruments, 2 percent involved strangulations, and the remaining 10 percent involved an assortment of other strategies.

CAUSES OF VIOLENCE

Sutherland and colleagues (1997) cite five theories that potentially explain violence occurs in the workplace. First, using the self-control theory, they point out that some workers may have low self-controls. Individuals learn self-control during their childhood from their parents. Those who learn a low self-control as child will, theoretically have a low self-control as an adult. When opportunities present themselves in the workplace, low self-control individuals may respond with violence.

Second, citing the routine activities theory, the authors note that victims can be seen as vulnerable targets who are doing their normal activities during structured times. In cases where offenders have a personal relationship with the victim, offenders are able to be violent because they know the victim's whereabouts. Also tied into the equation is the importance of capable guardians. Victims' risks of workplace violence theoretically decrease when more security is present.

A number of risk factors increase the likelihood that violence will occur in a particular job environment. According to NIOSH, these risk factors include: interacting with the public, exchanging money, delivering goods or services, working late at night or during early morning hours, working alone, guarding valuable goods or property, and dealing with violent people or volatile situations.

Most government agencies have developed guidelines that are designed to prevent workplace violence, as well as policies that dictate their response to such incidents. The Occupational Safety and Health Administration (OSHA) has made a number of recommendations to increase the safety of workers. For instance, OSHA recommends that the companies policy on violence must be communicated clearly to clients, consumers, and employees. This policy should be based on zero-tolerance ideals. They also recommend that workers be trained how to respond to possible violent situations. OSHA also recommends that a reporting policy be developed. Workers should be familiar with the reporting strategies, and ties should be developed with local police and state prosecutors so response mechanisms are in place should violence occur. Also, companies should provide both crisis intervention and long-term assistance to its employees who are victims of workplace violence. In addition, companies should keep track of the reports of violence so that records are available if they are needed. OSHA also recommends that should violence occur, a comprehensive post-incident evaluation should be conducted.

SEE ALSO
workplace deaths; Occupational Safety and Health Act.

BIBLIOGRAPHY. Bruce Blythe, *Blindsided: A Manager's Guide to Catastrophic Incidents in the Workplace* (Portfolio, 2002); "Violence in the Workplace," National Institute for Occupational Safety and Health (GPO, 1997): Brian K. Payne, *Crime in the Home Healthcare Field* (Charles C. Thomas, 2003); Mittie Southerland, Pamela Collins, and Kathryn Scarborough, *Workplace Violence: A Continuum from Threat to Homicide* (Anderson Publishing, 1997); U.S. Department of Justice, *Violence in the Workplace, 1993–99* (GPO, 2001); "Workplace Violence: A Report to the Nation," (University of Iowa Press, 2001).

BRIAN K. PAYNE
OLD DOMINION UNIVERSITY

World War I

AS WORLD War I raged in Europe, President Woodrow Wilson's re-election campaign theme in 1916 was "He kept us out of war." In fact, the United States had already entered the war because American industry had converted in large part to a wartime economy in order to provide Europe with the necessities of war. Initially, the Wilson administration used the incentive of huge profits to encourage American industries to provide the war materials needed in Europe.

While many Americans saw the war effort as a way to help save the world for democracy without giving up its cherished position of neutrality, profiteers and other opportunists viewed World War I as a time of huge profits and unchecked greed. Scholars have estimated that military spending during World War I rose as high as $11 billion, providing unprecedented opportunities for profiteers. It was often difficult to draw the line between legitimate profits and illegal profiteering; and once the United States entered World War I in 1918, it became even more incomprehensible that American businessmen and industrialists were getting rich while young men died to protect the capitalist system that fostered profiteering and opportunism.

By 1915, the American public was calling for the establishment of some controls on profiteering. On November 24, 1915, William C. McAdoo, the secretary of the treasury, responded by proposing an income tax bill designed to curb inflated profits. The bill called for a two-cent tax on the production of dynamite, gunpowder, and nitroglycerine. Wilson nixed the tax. In 1917, allegations began surfacing that some American businesses had gone beyond simple profit-making to engaging in criminal profiteering in securing illegal contracts and ignoring government restrictions of war trading.

WILSON AND PROFITEERING

On May 27, 1918, Wilson addressed a joint session on Congress to warn that "There is such profiteering now, and the information with regard to it is available and indisputable." According to Wilson, profiteers were out of control, and the president received advice on what to do from all sides. Theodore Roosevelt, both a former president and a former assistant secretary of the navy, argued that outfitting the navy was more important than worrying about profiteering. On the other hand, future president and current Food Administrator Herbert Hoover advised Wilson that wartime profits were both unreasonable and unjust.

Within two months of Wilson's address to Congress, the Federal Trade Commission (FTC) issued a report simply entitled "Profiteering," documenting extensive cases of "inordinate greed," "barefaced fraud," deceptive accounting practices, and artificial price inflation that were allowing American industrialists and financiers to become wealthy by exploiting the tragedy of war. The report identified the steel, oil, and gas industries as being particularly responsible for the profiteering problem.

The public was outraged, and even the American Legion called for controls on war profits, suggesting that the government draft war materials rather than purchase them at inflated prices. In the 1924 presidential election, both the Democratic and Republican parties added anti-profiteering planks to their party platforms.

To serve as an incentive to American industry, the government had negotiated contracts on cost-plus-profit basis. The government agreed to reimburse the contractor for all the costs of a project, plus a hefty profit. This plan was beneficial to the government because it saved time to bypass the process of competitive bidding and removed the need for the government to worry about the costs of labor, preparation, and changing prices. On the other hand, it allowed companies to profit at the expense of taxpayers who had seen their wages rise only slightly throughout the war. Because so many young men were at the battlefront and so many young women were involved in a number of war-relation occupations, the pool of workers was somewhat diminished. Cases were documented where government contracts were awarded to companies that hired untrained workers who knew little about what they were doing and who sometimes produced low-quality products.

A legal kind of profiteering also occurred after the war when industries were allowed to purchase facilities built on the cost-plus-profit basis for a fraction of what the government had paid for constructing the buildings. For instance, during World War I, the United States government had built a $14 million facility on land belonging to the New York Shipping Company. After the war, the government allowed the company to purchase the $14 million facility for $500,000.

FINANCIAL PROFITEERING

The munitions industry received a good deal of criticism for profiteering during and after World War I, and some companies were accused of bribing foreign officials to buy their products and of selling munitions to the enemy. The growth of munitions companies during World War I was phenomenal. For instance, Du Pont, the country's largest supplier of munitions and the foremost member of what was known as the "Powder Trust," increased it employees from 5,000 before World War I to over 100,000 by 1919, raking in profits of $266 million.

John Pierpont Morgan, the son of the noted financier of the same name, epitomized the financier who saw a profit to be made from financing foreign belligerents. His father had left him a $70 million fortune in 1913, which Morgan more than doubled by the end of World War I. Morgan became a purchasing agent for the British government and negotiated with American suppliers to supplement Britain's dwindling resources. In addition to his banking interests, J.P. Morgan was also the head of United States Steel Corporation. The steel industry took in profits that exceeded those of any other industry during World War I, making an average profit of $20 million a year.

The outcry against profiteering continued for two decades after World War I ended; and in 1934, the U.S. Senate established a special committee to investigate the munitions industry. The committee was chaired by Gerald P. Nye (R-ND) who had chaired the investigation into the Teapot Dome scandal a decade before. The three-year investigation uncovered extensive proof that profiteering had been rampant throughout World War I. In addition to the Senate Committee's investigation into World War I profiteering, the House of Representatives set up the Graham Committee that also found extensive profiteering during the war. The Graham Committee discovered that taxpayers had lost more than $78.5 million through excess profits during World War I.

Because the profits from World War I were so enormous and because so many fortunes were made during the war, a number of scholars believe World War I was more about finances than democracy.

SEE ALSO

war crimes; kickbacks; price-fixing; government contract fraud; government procurement fraud.

BIBLIOGRAPHY. Stuart D. Brandes, *Warhogs* (University Press of Kentucky, 1997); H. C. Engelbrecht and F.C. Hanighen, *Merchants of Death: A Study of the International Armament Industry* (Dodds Mead, 1934); Richard F. Kaufman, *War Profiteers* (Bobbs-Merrill, 1970); Richard Lewisohn, *The Profits of War Through The Ages* (Dutton, 1937).

ELIZABETH PURDY, PH.D.
INDEPENDENT SCHOLAR

World War II

FROM THE TIME that Adolf Hitler began the campaign that led to the outbreak of World War II in Europe in 1939, most Americans realized that U.S. involvement was a distinct possibility. On Sunday morning, December 7, 1941, the Japanese attacked Pearl Harbor in Hawaii with a devastating loss of American lives and property. The following day, President Franklin Roosevelt asked Congress to declare war. From that time until the war ended in August 1945, the Unites States was in a state of emergency. The president believed that the burdens of war should be shared equally among the population.

While he was sincerely dedicated to eradicating profiteering during World War II, Roosevelt also used anti-profiteering policies to pacify isolationists who used profiteering as one reason for remaining neutral. When FDR sent legislation to Congress asking for increased military spending, it was usually accompanied by legislation for the "prevention of profiteering and equalization of the burdens of a possible war." In October 1942, Roosevelt issued an anti-profiteering executive order limiting personal salaries to $25,000 after taxes except for movie stars and sports figures, but Congress repealed it the following year. Roosevelt considered and then discarded a 100 percent tax on excess profits. In order to prevent possible cheating in reporting excess profits taxes, around 6,400 federal auditors were employed to monitor tax fraud.

Roosevelt was determined to find ways to curtail profiteering without handicapping the American military. He knew that it was also necessary to differentiate between legal and illegal war profits, while rewarding superior performance in military production. The president charged the Office of War Mobilization with eliminating all illegal war profiteering in the United States. In 1941, the Office of Price Administration (OPA) was created and was given responsibility for preventing speculation, hoarding, profiteering, and price manipulation. Roosevelt believed that controlling wages, rents, and prices would curb inflation and serve to mitigate war profiteering. The chief task of the OPA, therefore, was to stabilize rents and prices and to oversee the quality of war-related materials. The national government used price controls as a major tool in anti-profiteering from 1941 until the end of World War II and pursued violators vigorously.

After price controls were put into effect in the United States, black markets sprang up almost overnight to provide Americans with goods that were rationed or restricted at prices that ignored legal price limits. Black market goods included meat, tires, gasoline, silk stockings, sugar, refrigerators, automobiles, washing machines, and radios. Because black market goods were illegal, no ration stamps were required to purchase them. The Roosevelt administration established severe penalties for black market activities that included injunctions, fines, and prison sentences.

WAR PRODUCTION

Between 1940 and 1944, over $175 billion were awarded in government contracts. In order to meet the needs of a world at war, the U.S. government had to depend on thousands of American businesses to manage production. In 1940, around 175,000 companies controlled 70 percent of the manufacturing output of the United States, with some 100 companies managing the other 30 percent. By 1943, these positions had shifted, with the top 100 companies controlling 70 percent of all production. Within the top 100 companies, one-third of all government contracts went to only ten major corporations. These Top Ten were in unique positions in their relationship to the national government during World War II. Financial benefits were an essential part of the benefits package awarded to the Top Ten in payment for providing essential war goods.

From 1939 to 1945, the federal government covered two-thirds of the $26 billion spent for constructing new facilities or modernizing existing plants and for purchasing the equipment needed to run those facilities. Privileged companies were allowed to write off major construction and improvements in five years rather than having to wait the traditional 20 to 30 years. In addition to operating their own facilities at government expense during the war, favored companies also operated a number of government-owned facilities with options to buy at reduced costs after the war. On the average, most companies reported World War II earnings from 20 to 40 times that of pre-war earnings. In one case, a company reported a war profit of over 800 percent.

TRUMAN COMMITTEE

After the election of 1940, Senator Harry Truman, a Democrat from Missouri, was contacted by several constituents who were concerned about the waste, possible fraud, and profiteering that was taking place on military bases. Truman convinced his Senate colleagues to create the Senate Special Committee to Investigate the National Defense Program, which became known as the Truman Committee. The committee found that many American companies were involved in international cartels that were feathering their nests by dealing either directly or indirectly with the Axis countries. The Truman Committee ultimately saved the government $15 billion and brought Truman to the forefront of national politics.

DEALING WITH THE ENEMY

In 1998, the United States Congress passed the Nazi War Disclosure Act, which declassified over three million pages of military and intelligence material. West Germany and the Soviet Union also declassified their World War II files. Together, the records revealed hundreds of incidences where American financial institutions had been secretly involved with financing Hitler's Third Reich either directly or indirectly. For example, the declassified records show that in the fall of 1942, under the Trading with the Enemy Act, Leo T. Crowley, FDR's Alien Property Custodian, seized the assets of the Union Banking Corporation in New York City, along with the assets of several other financial institutions. The files revealed that the Union Banking Corporation was owned by Prescott Bush (the father of future President George H.W. Bush), Prescott Bush's father-in-law George Herbert Walker, Averill Harriman, and several Nazi executives.

In the early 2000s, declassified Central Intelligence Agency documents explained how insurance companies had cooperated with various banks and shipping companies to use neutral countries to engage in illegal relationships with the Axis. Incidences of companies that chose profit over patriotism involved insurance companies that provided the Japanese with material that helped them plan the attack on Pearl Harbor.

SEE ALSO

military-industrial complex; government procurement fraud; bribery; kickbacks; corruption.

BIBLIOGRAPHY. Bernard Baruch, *American Industry in the War: A Report of the War Industries Board* (Prentice Hall, 1941); John Morton Blum, *V Was for Victory: Politics and American Culture During World War II* (Harcourt Brace Jovanovich, 1976); Stuart D. Brandes, *Warhogs* (University Press of Kentucky, 1997); Colin D. Campbell, ed., *Wage-Price Controls in World War II* (American Enterprise Institute, 1972); Leo M. Cherne, "America's Black Market," *Wage-Price Controls in World War II* (American Enterprise Institute, 1972); Mark Fritz, "Cloaked Business, Part VII: Files Reveal How Allied Firms Dealt with Axis Through Cover of Other Companies," www.boston.com (2003); Richard F. Kaufman, *The War Profiteers* (Bobbs-Merrill, 1970); Norman D. Livergood, "War Crimes and War Profiteering," www.hermespress.com (2003); C. Wright Mills, *The Power Elite* (Oxford University Press, 1971); Donald H. Riddle, The Truman Committee (Rutgers University Press, 1964); "War Profiteering," *The Nation* (May 12, 2003).

ELIZABETH PURDY, PH.D.
INDEPENDENT SCHOLAR

WorldCom

DURING THE financial boom of the 1990s, Bernard J. Ebbers, a former basketball coach, bought up a number of telecommunications companies under the WorldCom umbrella. From 1999 to 2000, World Com engaged in the largest accounting fraud in history. The company systematically billed billions of dollars of routine business costs as capital expenditures to make it appear that the company was making enormous profits while it was actually losing millions of dollars a year. Investors who bought stocks according to the inflated prices discovered that their stocks were virtually worthless. Overall, WorldCom's accounting fraud amounted to approximately $11 billion.

Discovery of WorldCom's fraud led to investigations by the Department of Justice, the Securities and Exchange Commission (SEC), several states, Canada, and Mexico. Investigators also investigated a $400 million loan that WorldCom's board of directors made to Ebbers. Although Ebbers was not initially charged, it soon became evident that he had been aware of the fraudulent accounting practices all along.

Ebbers and former CEO Scott Sullivan were charged on 15 counts by both federal prosecutors and prosecutors in Oklahoma and New York. The charges included lying to investors about WorldCom's worth. If convicted of the charges, Ebbers and Sullivan could each face at least ten years in jail and fines of up to $10 million on each charge. Former WorldCom employees David Myers, Bedford Yates, Betty Vinson, and Troy Nomand all pleaded guilty to charges of fraud and agreed to cooperate with prosecutors. Prosecutors in Oklahoma charged WorldCom/MCI with 15 violations of the Oklahoma Securities Law on charges that the company's bankruptcy cheated investors out of millions of dollars. The state lost at least $64 million in state-pension funds that were invested in WorldCom stocks. WorldCom filed for bankruptcy in July 2002, creating chaos among its investors and playing havoc with the American economy. In October 2003, a federal judge approved a redesigned settlement of $750 million. The settlement included a civil penalty of $2.25 billion to be paid by an initial payment of $500 million in cash and $250 million in common stock to shareholders and bondholders to be distributed after WorldCom emerged from the Chapter 11 bankruptcy proceedings. Trade creditors were set to receive 52.7 cents on a dollar rather than the 36 cents on a dollar originally negotiated.

Microwave Communications Incorporation (MCI) took over WorldCom on October 1, 1997, although WorldCom continued to operate under its own name. In an effort to avoid being associated with the negative publicity that followed the WorldCom scandal, WorldCom officially became known as MCI.

Congress passed the Sarbanes-Oxley Act in July 2003 in response to various accounting scandals over a period of years. The law required all businesses to include internal controls, ethics codes, and information about audit committees in annual reports. While Congress intended to prevent unethical conduct, many businesses claimed that it was difficult to comply with all the regulations of Sarbanes-Oxley. As proof of its own intention to comply with the new law, MCI promised that it would heed the recommendations of a former chairman of the SEC who was assigned to monitor the company. The company emerged from bankruptcy in 2004.

SEE ALSO

accounting fraud, stock fraud; consequences of white-collar crime; reform and regulation.

BIBLIOGRAPHY. G. Bischoff, "WorldCom Performs A Great Escape," *Telephony* (May 26, 2003); "Matt Hamblen, "WorldCom Defends Federal IT Contracts," *Computer World* (June 9, 2003); S. Mehta, "Mike Capellas Has His Plate Full Cleaning up MCI," *Fortune* (October 27, 2003); "Passages," *Maclean's* (September 8, 2003); S. Resenbush, "MCI's Under a New Cloud, But it Can Weather the Storm," *BusinessWeek* (August 1, 2003); C. Stern, "FCC Opens Probe into WorldCom Access-Fee Violations," *Washington Post* (July 31, 2003); C. Stern, "WorldCom Plan Goes to Creditors," *Washington Post* (September 13, 2003); C. Stern, "WorldCom Tells of Snarled Records," *Washington Post* (September 16, 2003); "WorldCom Investigations Paint Portrait of Incompetence," *Philadelphia Inquirer* (October 19, 2003); "WorldCom's Revenge," *The Economist* (August 30, 2003).

ELIZABETH PURDY, PH.D.
INDEPENDENT SCHOLAR

Appendix A
Resource Guide

Selected sources for more information; please see article bibliographies for complete references.

Books

A Short History of Financial Euphoria by John Kenneth Galbraith (Penguin Books, 1993)

American Reform and Reformers by Martha May (Greenwood, 1996)

Anatomy of a Fraud: Inside the Finances of the PTL Ministries by Gary Tidwell (Wiley, 1993)

Antitrust Experiment in America by Donald Dewey (Columbia University Press, 1990)

Antitrust Revolution by John E. Kwoka, Jr. and Lawrence J. White (Oxford University Press, 1999)

Art Crime by John Conklin (Praeger, 1994)

At Any Cost: Corporate Greed, Women, and the Dalkon Shield by Morton Mintz (Pantheon Books, 1985)

Bribes by John T. Noonan, Jr. (Macmillan, 1984)

Class Action: The Story of Louise Jenson and the Landmark Case That Changed Sexual Harassment Law by Clara Bingham and Laura Leedy Gansler (Doubleday, 2002)

Combating Corporate Crime: Local Prosecutors at Work by Michael L. Benson and Francis T. Cullen (Northeastern University, 1998)

Constitution and Campaign Finance Reform:

An Anthology edited by Frederick G. Slabach (Carolina Academic Press, 1998).

Contemporary Issues in Crime and Criminal Justice: Essays in Honor of Gilbert Geis edited by Henry Pontell and David Schicor (Prentice Hall, 2001)

Controlling Unlawful Organizational Behavior: Social Structure and Corporate Misconduct by Diane Vaughn (University of Chicago Press, 1983)

Corporate Board: Confronting the Paradoxes by Ada Demb and F.-Friedrich Neubauer (Oxford University Press, 1992)

Corporate Corruption: The Abuse of Power by Marshall B. Clinard (Praeger, 1990)

Corporate Crime and Violence: Big Business Power and the Abuse of the Public Trust by Russell Mokhiber (Sierra Club Books, 1988)

Corporate Crime by Marshall B. Clinard and Peter Cleary Yeager, with collaboration of Ruth Blackburn Clinard (Free Press, 1980)

Corporate Crime Corporate Violence A Primer by Nancy K. Frank and Michael J. Lynch (Harrow and Heston Publishers, 1992)

Corporate Crime Under Attack: The Ford Pinto Case and Beyond by Francis T. Cullen, William J. Maakestad, and Gray Cavender (Anderson, 1987)

Corporate Crime, Law, and Social Control by Sally S. Simpson (Cambridge University Press, 2002)

Corporate Violence: Injury and Death for Profit by Stuart Hills (Bowman and Littlefield, 1988)

Crimes of Privilege: Readings in White-Collar Crime by Neal Shover and John Paul Wright (Oxford University Press, 2001)

Crimes of the Middle Classes: White-Collar Offenders in the Federal Courts by David Weisburd, Stanton Wheeler, Elin Waring, and Nancy Bode (Yale University Press, 1991)

Criminal Behavior Systems: A Typology by Marshall B. Clinard and Richard Quinney (Holt, Rinehart, and Winston, 1967)

Criminal Elite: The Sociology of White-Collar Crime by James W. Coleman (St. Martin's Press, 1998)

Criminal Organization: Its Elementary Forms by Donal R. Cressey (Harper and Row, 1972)

Criminological Theory: Context and Consequences by J. Robert Lilly, Francis T. Cullen, and Richard A. Ball (Sage Publications, 2002)

Criminology of Edwin Sutherland by Mark Gaylord and John Galliher (Transaction Books, 1988)

Dangerous Ground: The World of Hazardous Waste Crime by Donald J. Rebovich (Transaction Press, 1992)

Department of Justice, The by Luther A. Huston (Praeger, 1967)

Dying for Growth: Global Inequality and the Health of the Poor by Jim Yong Kim, Joyce Millen, Alec V. Irwin, and John Gershman (Common Courage Press, 2000)

Elite Deviance by David R. Simon (Allyn and Bacon, 1999)

Environmental Crime: Enforcement, Policy and Social Responsibility by Mary Clifford (Aspen Publications, 1998)

Environmental Crime: The Criminal Justice System's Role in Protecting the Environment by Yingyi Situ and David Emmons (Sage Publications, 2000)

Federal Trade Commission: An Experiment in the Control of Business by C. Thomas (Columbia University Press, 1932)

Fraud Examination by W. Steve Albrecht (Thompson-Southwestern, 2003)

Government Racket 2000: All New Washington Waste from A to Z by Martin L. Gross (Avon, 2001)

Illegal Corporate Behavior by Marshall B. Clinard and Peter Cleary Yeager (Government Printing Office, 1979)

Impact of Public Policy on Corporate Offenders, The by Brent Fisse and John Braithwaite (State University of New York Press, 1983)

In the Wake of the Exxon Valdez by Art Davidson (Sierra Club Books, 1990)

Inequality, Crime, and Public Policy by John Braithwaite (Routledge, 1979)

Informed Consent by John A. Byrne (McGraw-Hill, 1996)

Knapp Commission Report on Police Corruption, The (George Brazilier, 1973)

Law and Insider Trading: In Search of A Level Playing Field by Elizabeth Szockyj (William S. Hein & Co., 1993)

Masters of Deception: The Worldwide White-Collar Crime Crisis and Ways to Protect Yourself by Louis Mizell (Wiley, 1997)

Medical Malpractice: Theory, Evidence, and Public Policy by Patricia M. Danzon (Cambridge University Press, 1985)

Merchants of Death: The American Tobacco Industry by Lawrence White (Beech Tree, 1988)

Occupational Fraud and Abuse by Joseph T. Wells (Obsidian Publishing, 1997)

On White-Collar Crime by Gilbert Geis (D.C. Heath, 1982)

Organization of Corporate Crime: Dynamics of Antitrust Violation by Katherine M. Jamieson (Sage Publications, 1994)

Organized Crime by Gary W. Potter and Michael D. Lyman (Prentice Hall, 2002)

Organized Crime: A Compilation of U.N. Documents 1975–1998 by M. Cherif Bassiouni and Eduardo Vetere (Transnational Publishers, 1998)

Organizing the Breathless: Cotton Dust, Southern Politics, & the Brown Lung Association by Robert E. Botsch (University Press of Kentucky, 1993)

Other People's Money by Donald R. Cressey (Free Press, 1953)

Outrageous Misconduct: The Asbestos Industry on Trial by Paul Bradeur (Pantheon Books, 1985)

Prescription for Profit: How Doctors Defraud Medicaid by Paul Jesilow, Henry Pontell, and Gilbert Geis (University of California Press, 1993)

Profit Without Honor: White Collar Crime & the Looting of America by Stephen M. Rosoff, Robert Tillman, and Henry Pontell (Prentice Hall, 2001)

Regulating Fraud: White-Collar Crime and the Criminal Process by M. Levi (Tavistock, 1987)

Restorative Justice and Responsive Regulation by John Braithwaite (Oxford University Press, 2002)

Road to Love Canal: Managing Industrial Waste before EPA by Craig E. Colten and Peter Skinner (University of Texas Press, 1996)

Silent Spring by Rachel Carson (Houghton Mifflin, 1962)

Sin and Society: An Analysis of Latter-Day Inequity by E.A. Ross (Houghton Mifflin, 1965)

Sitting in Judgment: The Sentencing of White-Collar Criminals by Stanton Wheeler, Kenneth Mann, and Austin Sarat (Yale University Press, 1988)

Stealing Dreams: A Fertility Clinic Scandal by Gilbert Geis (Northeastern University Press, 2004)

Swindled! Classic Business Frauds of the Seventies by Donald Moffitt (Dow Jones Books, 1976)

The Jungle by Upton Sinclair (Bantam Classics, reprint 1981)

Theft of the Nation: The Structure and Operations of Organized Crime in America by Donald R. Cressey (Harper and Row, 1969)

To Punish or Persuade: Enforcement of Coal Mine Safety by John Braithwaite (State University of New York Press, 1985)

Tony Soprano's America: The Criminal Side of the American Dream by David R. Simon (Westview, 2002)

Trusted Criminals: White Collar Crime in Contemporary Society by David O. Friedrichs (Wadsworth Publishing Company, 2004)

Understanding Corporate Criminality edited by Michael Blankenship (Garland, 1993)

Unsafe at Any Speed: The Designed-In Dangers of the American Automobile by Ralph Nader (Grossman, 1972)

Utilization-Focused Evaluation: The New Century Text by Michael Quinn Patton (Sage Publications, 1997)

Wall Street Words: An Essential A to Z Guide for Today's Investor by David L. Scott (Houghton Mifflin, 1997)

Warhogs: A History of War Profits in America by Stuart D. Brandes (University Press of Kentucky, 1997)

Wealth by Stealth: Corporate Crime, Corporate Law and the Perversion of Democracy by Harry Glasbeck (Between the Lines, 2002)

Whistleblowers: Exposing Corruption in Government and Industry by Myron Peretz Glazer and Penina Migdal Glazer (Basic Books, 1989)

Whistleblowing: Loyalty and Dissent in the Corporation by A. F. Westin (McGraw-Hill, 1981)

White Collar Crime Reconsidered edited by K. Schlegel and D. Weisburd (Northeastern University Press, 1992)

White Collar Crime: Cases and Materials by Pamela H. Bucy (West Publishing, 1992)

White-Collar Crime and Criminal Careers by David Weisburd, Elin Waring, and Ellen Chayet (Cambridge University Press, 2001)

White-Collar Crime by Edwin H. Sutherland (Holt, Rinehart, and Winston, 1949)

White-Collar Crime in a Nutshell by Ellen S. Podgor and Jerold H. Israel (West Publishing, 1997)

White-Collar Crime in America by Jay Albanese (Prentice Hall, 1994)

White-Collar Crime: Classic and Contemporary Views edited by Gilbert Geis, Robert F. Meier, and Lawrence M. Salinger (Free Press, 1995)

White-Collar Crime: The Uncut Version by Edwin H. Sutherland (Yale University Press, 1983)

White-Collar Deviance by David R. Simon and Frank E. Hagan (Allyn & Bacon, 1998)

Women Who Embezzle or Defraud: A Study of Convicted Felons by Dorothy Zeitz (Praeger, 1981)

Journals

Advances in Criminological Theory (Rutgers University Press)

American Criminal Law Review (Georgetown University Press)

American Journal of Criminal Law (University of Texas Press)

American Journal of Sociology (University of Chicago Press)

American Sociological Review (American Sociological Association)

Corporate Counsel's Guide to White-Collar Crime (Business Laws, Inc.)

Criminal Justice (Sage Publications)

Criminology (American Society of Criminology)

Environmental Law Reporter (Environmental Law Institute)

FBI Law Enforcement Bulletin (Federal Bureau of Investigation)

FDA Consumer (Food and Drug Administration)

Harvard Journal of Law and Public Policy (Harvard University)

Journal of Business Ethics (Kluwer Academic Publishers)

Journal of Contemporary Criminal Justice (Sage Publications)

Journal of Criminal Law and Criminology
    (Nothwestern University School of Law)
Journal of Financial Economics
    (University of Rochester Press)
Justice Quarterly
    (Academy of Criminal Justice Sciences)
Law and Society Review
    (Law and Society Association)
Management Review
    (Massachusetts Institute of Technology Press)
Social Problems
    (Society for the Study of Social Problems)
The British Journal of Criminology
    (Oxford University Press)
Theoretical Criminology
    (Sage Publications)
Western Criminology Review
    (Western Society of Criminology)
International Journal of Social Economics
    (Emerald Academic)
International Journal of the Economics of Business
    (Routledge, Taylor & Francis)

Magazine and Newspapers

Advertising Age (Crain Communications)
Adweek (VNU Business Publications)
American Demographics (Primedia Publishing)
Black Enterprise (Earl G. Graves, Ltd.)
Bloomberg Markets (Bloomberg LP)
Business 2.0 (Business 2.0 Media, Inc.)
BusinessWeek (McGraw-Hill Companies, Inc.)
Corporate Crime Reporter
    (American Communications)
Crain's Chicago Business (Crain Communications)
Crain's New York Business (Crain Communications)
Euromoney (Euromoney Institutional Investor PLC)
Far Eastern Economic Review
    (Dow Jones & Compaay, Inc., Hong Kong)
Fast Company (Gruner + Jahr USA Publishing)
Financial Times (The Financial Times, Ltd.)
Forbes (Forbes, Inc.)
Fortune (Time, Inc.)
Harvard Business Review (Harvard University Press)
Inc. (Gruner + Jahr USA Publishing)
Industry Week (Penton Media, Inc.)
International Herald Tribune
    (The New York Times Company)
Investor's Business Daily (Investors' Business Daily)
Kiplinger's (The Kiplinger Washington Editors)

New York Times
    (The New York Times Company)
Money (Time Inc., Time Warner)
Smart Money (Dow Jones & Company)
The Economist (The Economist Group, Inc.)
Wall Street Journal
    (Dow Jones & Company, Inc.)
Washington Post
    (The Washington Post Company)
White-Collar Crime Fighter
    (White Collar Crime 101 LLC)
White-Collar Crime Reporter (Andrews Publications)
Worth (Worth Media)

Internet Websites

Almost all journals, magazines, newspapers, and associations have dedicated websites that can be easily located using standard internet search engines. One rule of caution in using internet research tools in white-collar and corporate crime: rely on "branded" media, that is, websites associated with known media and institutions. Some recommended websites include:

www.bbb.org (Better Business Bureau)
www.commerce.gov
    (U.S. Department of Commerce)
www.cpsc.gov
    (Consumer Product Safety Commission)
www.epa.gov
    (U.S. Environmental Protection Agency)
www.fda.gov
    (U.S. Food and Drug Administration)
www.hoovers.com
    (Hoover's Handbook of American Business)
www.loc.gov (U.S. Library of Congress)
www.nber.org
    (National Bureau of Economic Research)
www.nw3c.org
    (National White-Collar Crime Center)
www.sec.gov
    (U.S. Securities and Exchange Commission)
www.un.org/english (United Nations)
www.doj.gov (U.S. Department of Justice)
www.treas.gov (U.S. Treasury Department)
www.whitehouse.gov/omb/budget/fy2004/
    (Budget of the United States)
www.whitecollarcrimefyi.com
    (Lawyershop, Inc.)

Appendix B
Glossary

Italics refer to cross-referenced Glossary entries.

Abuse: In some cultures, a minor *Fraud* or infraction.

Accomplice: In fraud, a partner to the fraud scheme. See also *Perpetrator* and *Shill*.

Advance Fee Scheme: The *Fraudster* collects fees in advance without ever intending to fulfill the agreement to provide services or products.

Affidavit: A sworn statement.

Affiliate Bidding: A condition in purchasing when multiple bids are tendered for a contract from a single company under various names to give the appearance of competition.

Agent: A person with an agency relationship (employee or independent contractor).

At will: An employment situation where the employee is not protected from arbitrary firing — the employee works only at the pleasure of management and may be terminated at any time for no reason. Contrast *For cause*.

Backdate: To post a date on a document earlier than the actual creation date for purposes of deception.

Back Door: In computer fraud, unauthorized entry point or weakness discovered by a *Hacker*. Similar to *Trapdoor*, except that back doors are usually pre-existing weaknesses.

Bait-and-Switch: In consumer fraud, advertising a low cost item and then steering customers to a higher-priced item when they come to buy, claiming the low priced item was sold out.

Bank Examiner Scheme: The *Fraudster* poses as a bank examiner who is trying to catch a dishonest teller. The bank examiner needs the victim to withdraw a substantial sum from her account to test the teller. The examiner then asks the victim to hand over the cash for a receipt while he uses the cash as evidence. The fraudulent examiner then disappears with the cash, and the receipt turns out to be worthless.

Bankruptcy Fraud: The *Perpetrator* files a notice of bankruptcy. He then approaches each of his creditors (who have received a cop of the notice of bankruptcy) and tells each one in turn that they are the special one that he wants to see get paid at least something. The creditor often settles for 10 percent of the amount owed. Once a settlement with one creditor is reached, the perpetrator approaches the next creditor, and so on until all creditors have been settled at a small fraction of the outstanding amounts owed. The perpetrator then withdraws his petition for bankruptcy, have extinguished most of his debt for a small fraction of the original amount.

Bid Rigging: In purchasing, any scheme that gives the appearance of competitive bids but is actually not competitive because the participants establish the winner before submitting bids for the contract. See *Affiliate Bidding* and *Bid Rotation*.

Bid Rotation: In purchasing, when bidders for contracts *Collude* to distribute work among themselves by establishing which among them will win particular bids.

Boiler Room Operation: A fraud scheme that attempts to sell worthless securities (or similar assets) over the telephone through high pressure sales tactics. If the money is sent in or the credit card number given out, there is nothing of value received.

Bribery: To offer money in exchange for favorite treatment or to compel or influence some action. Official (government employee or elected official) bribery involves a promise for acting or withholding some official act. Official bribery (*Corruption*) is unlawful in most cultures. *Commercial Bribery* is known as "facilitating payments" in some cultures and is not a crime in most cultures, although it often is against the organization's policies and procedures.

Bucket Shop: A securities fraud scheme that pretends to buy and sell securities for customers, but actually never invests the money it receives. The scheme depends upon stock price manipulation or a continuously rising market to encourage more buyers than sellers. Also associated sometimes with the *Pump-and-Dump* scheme.

Case Method: In fraud *Investigation*, a six-step process of gathering evidence in order to identify a *Suspect*.

Chain of Custody: In evidentiary matters, the record of possession from original discovery until produced at trial. If the chain of custody is broken or unclear, the *Evidence* may be challenged as not the original or not in its original condition.

Chain Letter Schemes: Letters with names listed and claims that the recipient of the letter, by putting their name on the list, removing the top name and sending them some nominal amount, then mailing the new list to some number of friends and acquaintances, will receive a lot of riches in the mail. There is usually also a "curse" or bad luck associated with individuals who "break the chain."

Check Kiting: See *Kiting*.

Code of Ethics: A document adopted by an organization that describes the expectations of the organization of employee and management behavior to all employees, suppliers, customers, the government, and the community.

Coerce: To influence action against someone's will, usually by threat.

Collateral Frauds: Fraudulent representing collateral for loans that 1) does not exist, 2) is not owned by the loan applicant, or 3) is grossly over-valued, or all of these.

Collude: In the context of *Fraud*, to act together for a fraudulent purpose.

Commercial Bribery: Giving and accepting payments to favor or not favor a commercial transaction or relationship. See also *Bribery* and *Corruption*.

Computer Virus: See *Virus*.

Con: Short form of *Confidence Game*.

Conceal(ment): The second step in committing a *Fraud*. To hide from view.

Confidence Game: A fraud scheme where the *Perpetrator* gains the confidence of the *Mark* to defraud the Mark in some way. Perfect confidence games are so effective that Marks do not report them to the authorities for fear of looking foolish or because the game involved something unlawful (such as illegal gambling).

Conflict of Interest: An employee owes a duty to the employer to act in the interest of the employer (and no other) when carrying out the duties of an employer. A conflict exists when the employee has some personal kinship, friendship or financial interest in the transaction that may divide the employee's interests and put his duty to his employer in jeopardy.

Conspiracy: Two or more persons come together for the purpose of committing a *Fraud*.

Conversion: The third step in a *Fraud*. To exchange for personal gain.

"Cooking the Books": Altering the official accounts to deceive. See also *Journal Entry Fraud*.

Corruption: *Bribery* of a government official. See also *Commercial Bribery*.

Cost of Goods Sold changes: Unusual changes in cost of goods sold as a percentage of sales may be an indicator of the theft of revenue or theft of finished goods inventory. See *Fictitious Refunds Fraud*.

Covert: Hidden or secret, as in *Covert Operations*.

Covert Operation: A plan or activity to obtain evidence through *Operatives* or *Agents* whose true role is undisclosed to the target. Examples of covert operations include *Undercover* work and *Pretense*. See also *Ruse*.

Cyber-crime: Referring to frauds perpetrated on the Internet or through the use of computers.

Cycle Counts: In inventory control, counting various portions of the inventory frequently until it is all counted (vs. counting once a quarter or year).

Defalcation: A word for *Fraud*, theft, or other dishonest act relating to a position of trust in an organization.

Defamation: The act of knowingly uttering *Slander* or printing *Libel* that is untrue but harms another person's character and reputation.

Denial of Access attack: A computer *Virus* or computer program run to generate many thousands of requests to the central computer, thereby tying up the processor and denying legitimate requests of access.

Deposition: A pre-trial legal proceeding in which a person is questioned under oath by an attorney, usually witnessed and recorded by audio, video, and/or written verbatim notes. The purpose of the deposition is to discover *Evidence* that may be used later at trial or to induce the person to make statements of fact that can be used at trial.

Directory Advertising Schemes: Fraudulent invoices claiming that the company is listed in a business directory and requesting payment. There may or may not be such a directory, and the directory may or may not ever be distributed or distributed as widely as claimed. For certain, no one ever ordered or authorized the directory advertisement. See also *Shipping Short*.

Documentary Evidence: Written or photographic representations of fact.

Dual Custody: A method of protecting cash by requiring all cash assets handled by two people (two signatures, two keys, two people counting, etc.).

Dummy: Fictitious.

"Dumpster Diving": Rummaging through someone's trash to obtain information.

Electronic Surveillance: Listening and/or recording activities using electronic means (audio and video) without being detected. In some jurisdictions, electronic surveillance is unlawful without permission from all parties.

Embezzlement: Theft of money from an employer by an employee using false entries in accounting records to cover up the crime. See also *Journal Entry Fraud*.

Employee Account Fraud: When employees are also customers, employees may make unauthorized adjustments to their accounts (including write-off).

Entrapment: Unlawfully lured into a crime by a police officer. A common defense in a criminal activity where the criminal claims they were innocent and would not have been involved in the crime otherwise.

Expense Report Fraud: Charging unauthorized or fictitious amounts on an expense report. See *Padding Expense Accounts*.

Exposure: The potential for loss.

Extortion: The offer to keep from harm in exchange for money or other consideration. The demand for *Restitution* in exchange for not prosecuting a crime is a form of extortion.

Factors of Fraud: Opportunity (an opening or control weakness to be able to commit the fraud), Pressure (a problem that cannot be shared or resolved), and Attitude (a propensity to steal or the ability to rationalize fraudulent behavior). All frauds have these three factors as a cause.

False Claims: Claims for reimbursement by an employee or contractor for nonexistent or inflated expenses. False claims can be for business expenses or personal expenses (such as medical). See *Padding Expense Accounts*.

False Credentials: Misrepresenting education or experience or professional certification to fraudulently obtain and hold employment.

False Imprisonment: During an *Interrogation*, blocking the subject's avenue of escape, essentially holding the person against their will. Unless the person has been arrested, they may not be detained against their will at any time.

False Pretense: See *Pretense, Ruse* or *Subterfuge*.

Fictitious Refunds Scheme: Preparing false documents of refunds to cover thefts of cash. A retail cashiering fraud. See *Cost of Goods Sold changes*.

Fictitious Sales: A scheme to record sales to fictitious customers or fictitious sales to existing customers at the end of one period and reversing the transactions at the beginning of the next period. The purpose of the scheme is to inflate sales to create false profit statements or earn unwarranted bonuses. Excessive credit memos or sales cancellations at the beginning of an accounting period can be an indicator of this fraud.

Fiduciary Duty: The acts necessary (usually of an authorized employee or agent) to carry out a responsibility to care for assets prudently. See *Embezzlement*.

Firewall: A software program that protects direct access to a local area network by establishing a public network in front of the trusted network. The purpose of the program is to secure data and systems from *Hackers*.

For Cause: An employment arrangement where employees may only be terminated for a proven cause. For contrast, see *At will*.

Forensic: Suitable for use in a court proceeding.

Forensic Auditing: Examination of a business process for evidence of *Fraud*.

Forgery: Creation of false documents or altering existing documents, especially financial instruments or other authorizations.

Fraud: A theft, concealment and conversion to personal gain of another's money, physical assets, information, or time.

Fraud Scenarios: A method of developing mental models of possible *Frauds*.

Fraudster: One who commits the *Fraud*.

Ghost Employees: Fictitious employees on the payroll, for whom the supervisor or manager receives the extra paychecks.

Hacker: (Old) One who enjoys unraveling the mysteries of the computer. (Modern) A person who attacks another's computer and seeks to gain unauthorized access by hacking (breaking down) the computer's logical security.

Hearsay: A weak form of evidence that is an opinion of the witness or that is not personally and directly known to her.

Hidden Bank Accounts: A possible indication of *Embezzlement*, *Bribery* or *Kickback* frauds.

Hot Line: A telephone number to report suspected Fraud. Often hot lines are handled as anonymous tips.

Impeach: In *Testimony*, to catch the person in a lie or contradiction of fact.

Improprieties: A polite word for *Frauds* and wrongdoings.

Inflated Inventory: An indication of *Embezzlement* or possible theft of inventory. See *Inventory Shrinkage*.

Influence Peddling: The offer by a government official to use their office to influence actions for a private party in return for something of value.

Informant: A person, such as a co-worker or friend of the accused, used in the investigation of a fraud who may know something about the crime but is otherwise not involved.

Insider Trading: Using business information not released to the public to reap profits trading in the financial markets.

Interrogation: An interview of a suspect conducted for the main purpose of obtaining an admission of guilt, to identify and neutralize defenses the target may raise, and to obtain information used to impeach the *Suspect*.

Interview: A structured (planned) question and answer session with a person designed to elicit information.

Inventory Shrinkage: Theft of physical inventory.

Investigation: A structured gathering of *Documentary Evidence* and *Testimony* to solve a reported *Fraud*.

Irregularity: A polite word for *Fraud*.

Journal Entry Fraud: Using accounting journal entries to fraudulently adjust financial statements. See also *Embezzlement*.

Kickback: A payment by a vendor to an employee at the request of the employee in order for the vendor to receive favorable treatment.

Kiting: Using several bank accounts in different banks, making deposits and writing checks against the accounts before the deposit checks clear the banking system, creating a "float" of money out of nothing more than the lag time while checks clear and post to their respective accounts.

Lapping: Stealing a customer payment and then using a subsequent customer payment to cover the previous customer's account. This overlapping payments creates a "float" of money that can be used as long as all payments are eventually posted. What usually occurs is that the lapping process builds up like a giant pyramid until it falls apart when not enough payments are available to cover the amounts owed.

Libel: Knowingly publishing false statements about another person that creates harm.

Lie Detector: See *Polygraph*.

Lifestyle changes: A possible indicator of theft is the sudden change in lifestyle such as exhibiting more than usual wealth.

Lowballing: Placing an unusually low bid to win the business. Often with the intent to inflate the price later with extras or change orders. Also can indicate a defective *Request for Proposal*.

Malicious Prosecution: Targeting someone for prosecution without reasonable grounds for suspicion.

Mark: The intended victim of a *Swindle* or *Confidence Game*.

Misappropriation: A polite word for theft.

Multi-Level Marketing: A form of *Pyramid Scheme*, not necessarily fraudulent, where sales are made to retail customers and commissions earned through many levels of the chain within the pyramid. The chain is built and expanded by each layer constantly recruiting more people to sell the product.

Negative Invoicing: Using an invoice for a negative

amount to cover a theft of a customer payment. The negative invoice is less noticeable than a credit memorandum and usually under less stringent control. A negative invoice is a symptom of possible theft.

Nigerian Letter: A fraud scheme that now includes fax and email versions of a letter from a supposed official in Nigeria. The official has a large sum of money (often stated as $20 to $30 million) to transfer out of the country. Due to exchange controls, the official asks for the victim's help with the transfer. All that is required to earn a hefty reward/commission is to furnish the Nigerian official with your bank account number, and they will handle the rest. What actually happens is that the *Perpetrator* depletes the victim's account.

Obstruction of Justice: Impeding a lawful Investigation by such acts as providing false documents, false testimony, destruction of evidence, and intimidating witnesses.

Ombudsman: A person who acts as an advocate for employee grievances against the organization. Also, a neutral party to whom employees can turn to report *Fraud*.

Operative: A person acting on one's behalf or under care, custody or control in a specific manner. A source or *Informant* working *Undercover* in *Covert Operations* is an operative. There is no agency relationship with an operative as with an *Agent*.

Overbilling schemes: Padding invoices with extraneous or fictitious items. Intentional duplicate billing, such as billing two parties for the same work is also an overbilling scheme.

Overt: Open, not hidden. See *Covert* for contrast.

Out-of-Route: Outside sales or service workers who deviate from their normal route or time schedule, such as conducting personal errands or taking excessively long coffee or lunch breaks.

Outstanding Items: In checking operations, checks that have been written but not cleared through the bank. An equivalent banking term for interbank transactions.

Padding Expense Accounts: Adding extra expense items or inflating the value of legitimate expense items to obtain unwarranted reimbursements.

Padding Overtime: Adding extra hours to falsely inflate the payroll and earn unwarranted pay.

Palming: To conceal in the hand.

Perjury: Lying under oath, including sworn court *Depositions*, *Affidavits*, statements, and documents.

Perpetrator: The person who commits the *Fraud*.

Personal Identification Number: A code used to access personal data or accounts.

Pilfering: *Theft*, usually referring to theft of physical goods. In retail business, customer theft is known as *Shoplifting* and employee theft is called pilfering. Occasionally used also with theft of cash, especially petty cash or for small thefts.

PIN: See Personal Identification Number.

Pigeon Drop: A fraud scheme that involves a wallet/purse/envelope with a large sum of money in it but no identification. The *Perpetrator* and *Accomplice*, together with the victim "finds" the wallet, and the victim is persuaded to withdraw a sum of money as "good faith" to share in the cache. The victim is distracted and the Perpetrators steal the money and disappear with it.

Pingponging: In medical insurance or *Workers Compensation Fraud*, referring patients to other doctors in the same clinic in order to claim reimbursement for "consultations" rather than for actual treatment. See also *False Claims*.

Polygraph: A machine for recording a number of life signs (breathing rate, pulse, etc.) to aid in determining if a *Suspect* is lying. Also known as a *Lie Detector*.

Ponzi Scheme: A fraud in which a high rate of return is promised on investments. The first few investors receive the high rate of return from part of the investments of later victims. At no time is any actual investment made.

Pretense: Also *False Pretense*. To represent something to be what it is not. See *Ruse* and *Subterfuge*.

Pump-and-Dump: Manipulating stock prices by artificially creating demand through rumor, high pressure sales tactics, or multiple large orders. The price is pumped upwards and then when other investors join the trend, the original investors dump the stock in a rapid sell-off. See also *Bucket Shop*.

Pyramid Scheme: A commercial version of the *Chain Letter* scheme where the *Fraudster* sells bogus distributorships, franchises or business opportunity plans to people who are in turn induced to do the same. See also *Multi-Level Marketing*.

Razoring: Removing the last check, invoice, purchase order or other sequentially numbered item from a pad of items by carefully cutting with a razor around the staple holding the pad together. In this manner, fictitious transactions can be documented on official forms.

Reconciliation: A process of comparing details with control totals, such as checks paid during the month and deposits made that month with the change in bank balance at end of the month.

Red Flags: Symptoms and indicators (of *Fraud*).

Remote Access Unit: See *Maintenance Port*.

Request for Proposal: A request to potential vendors for tender offers or bids to perform a service or provide a product (or both) to solve a particular business problem. See also *Request for Quote*.

Request for Quote: A request to potential vendors for price quotes and delivery terms, usually for much simpler procurement requirements than a *Request for Proposals*.

Restitution: Restoring money or property to the victim of a *Fraud*.

Resume Inflation: See *False Credentials*.

Rube: A slang term for a *Mark* or victim, especially someone who appears naïve.

Ruse: A scheme that tries to make something appear as something else. Hiding the true meaning or acting out a lie. A *Subterfuge* or *Pretense*.

Sabotage: Destroying or delaying some part of the business process.

Salami: In banking, a fraud that involves taking all of the round-down fractional cents from periodic interest payments and crediting them to a single account. Thus each transaction has only a thin slice removed.

Salting cash: Testing accounts receivable employee honesty by placing some cash in the customer receivables process to see if it is reported as cash or stolen.

Secure Socket Layer: A protocol used in electronic commerce to afford more security to transactions on the Internet.

Self-Approval: The act of authorizing a transaction for one's own benefits or gains, or an act of approval for an activity in which the approval authority participated.

Sewer Service: Many consumer frauds rely on litigation to win judgments to collect the proceeds of the fraud. These organizations limit the ability of the victim to defend against this litigation by not informing them of the suit (literally dropping the *Subpoena* "down the sewer") and filing false *Affidavits* in court that the litigation papers had been properly served.

Shadowing: Following the suspect or target of *Surveillance* from place to place to observe activities without being detected.

Shell Game: A game where a pebble or dried pea is hidden under one of three shells or cans. The *Perpe-*trator moves the shells around quickly, often *Palming* the pebble, and then asks the *Mark* to choose the shell where the pea is located. A common street *Confidence Game*. See also *Sleight-of-hand*.

Shill: A person in a *Confidence Game* who acts as a participant to draw in the *Mark*. An *Accomplice* — one who is paid to play as part of a *Swindle*. Derived from casino gambling, where the shill is a paid employee used to attract other gamblers.

Shoplifting: Customer theft from retail inventory. See also *Pilfering*.

Short-and-Over: An account used in cashiering operations to track the imbalance of cash to sales recorded. A perfectly balanced cash operation day-after-day, with no shorts or overs, is a symptom of possible theft. It is unusual to never make mistakes handling money.

Shorting: In medical frauds, delivering less prescription medicine than actually charged to the insurance company or government.

Short Shipping: Shipping less than the quantity shown on the invoice (or shipping nothing at all; see *Directory Advertising Scheme*).

Shoulder Surfing: Observing someone using a *PIN* (*Personal Identification Number*) by covertly looking over her shoulder, sometimes with the aid of binoculars or a video camera with zoom lens.

Shrinkage: See Inventory Shrinkage.

Slander: Knowingly uttering false statements about another person that causes harm.

Sleight-of-hand: A magician's trick. The ability to conceal a physical action by distracting the participant. See also *Palming*.

Spying: See *Surveillance*.

Stationary Surveillance: Observation of activities of a suspect from one vantage point. Also known as a *Stakeout*.

Statutory Employee: An employee by action and tax law, but not actually on the payroll. There are potential violations of U.S. tax and employment benefits laws if independent contractors and consultants are found to be statutory employees instead.

Suborn: The act of *Bribery*.

Subterfuge: Masking the true nature or reason for an action.

Surveillance: Gathering evidence through observation from outside of the operation (contrasted with Undercover). Surveillance can be *Moving Surveillance*, *Stationary Surveillance* or *Electronic Surveillance*. Also known as *Spying*.

Suspect (n.): The target of the fraud Investigation. See also *Perpetrator* and *Fraudster*.

Suspect (v.): To place under suspicion of wrongdoing.

Swindle: A scheme to obtain money by *Ruse* or *False Pretense*. See also *Confidence Game*.

Tailing: See *Shadowing*.

Testimony: Oral evidence (representations of fact) taken by *Interview* or *Interrogation*. Testimonial evidence is necessarily weaker than *Documentary Evidence*.

Theft: The first step in a *Fraud*. Unlawfully taking.

Thief's Calculator: A collection of innocent-looking bits and pieces near the cash register for the purpose of tracking the amount of cash stolen by *Skimming*.

Tone at the Top: The messages and actions of senior management in relation to *Fraud* detection and deterrence.

Trapdoor: In computer fraud, a means of unauthorized access to the computer operating system or files, usually placed by a *Hacker*.

Trojan Horse: A type of computer program that remains inert (and possibly hidden) until activated by an external event such as a date. Used as *Viruses* to disrupt or destroy computer operations, or used to open a *Trapdoor* for unauthorized access.

Unauthorized Use: Policies should be in place to determine what business resources may be used for personal business and at what times. Other use constitutes *Theft*.

Undercover: Secret or *Covert Operations* where a person works under an assumed identity, adopts a disguise, or takes on an assumed role in order to gather evidence for prosecution.

Under-ring: To record less than the actual sales price. Usually refers to a cashier ringing a sale on a cash register. Under-rings may be a method used in *Skimming* cash by the cashier, or they may be used to give unauthorized discounts to an Accomplice.

Unethical: Behavior that does not meet community standards for "right behavior," but that does not violate any laws either.

Unlawful: Behavior that violates established laws.

Virus: In computer operations, a program that is deliberately released to a system with the ability to replicate itself and spread by attaching unauthorized data to files. Viruses can be benign, just taking up disk storage space, or they may be vicious and actually destroy data or deny access.

Voids: In cashiering, ringing a Void to cancel a previous sale. Excessive voids may be a sign of theft.

Whistleblowing: The act of an employee revealing suspected fraud (usually involving senior management) to an outside third party.

Witnesses: People who may have information of a *Fraud* based on observation.

Worker's Compensation Fraud: False claims for on-the-job injuries. Usually takes the *Collusion* of employee and unscrupulous doctors to submit false diagnoses. Back injuries (soft tissue strains) and stress are the most common ailments used in this scheme.

DAVID MCNAMEE, PRESIDENT
MC² MANAGEMENT CONSULTING
WWW.MC2CONSULTING.COM

Appendix C
Law Summaries

Contents

Clayton Antitrust Act 1914
Title 15. Commerce and Trade
Chapter 1. Monopolies and Combinations in Restraint of Trade

§ 12. Words defined; short title

(a) "Antitrust laws," as used herein, includes the Act entitled "An Act to protect trade and commerce against unlawful restraints and monopolies," approved July second, eighteen hundred and ninety [15 USCS §§ 1 et seq.]; sections seventy-three to seventy-six, inclusive, of an Act entitled "An Act to reduce taxation, to provide revenue for the Government, and for other purposes," of August twenty-seventh, eighteen hundred and ninety-four [15 USCS §§ 8-11]; an Act entitled "An Act to amend sections seventy-three and seventy-six of the Act of August twenty-seventh, eighteen hundred and ninety-four, entitled 'An Act to reduce taxation, to provide revenue for the Government, and for other purposes,'" approved February twelfth, nineteen hundred and thirteen [amending 15 USCS §§ 8, 11]; and also this Act.

"Commerce," as used herein, means trade or commerce among the several States and with foreign nations, or between the District of Columbia or any Territory of the United States and any State, Territory, or foreign nation, or between any insular possessions or other places under the jurisdiction of the United States, or between any such possession or place and any State or Territory of the United States or the District of Columbia or any foreign nation, or within the District of Columbia or any Territory or any insular possession or other place under the jurisdiction of the United States: Provided, That nothing in this Act contained shall apply to the Philippine Islands.

The word "person" or "persons" wherever used in this Act shall be deemed to include corporations and associations existing under or authorized by the laws of either the United States, the laws of any of the Territories, the laws of any State, or the laws of any foreign country.

(b) This Act may be cited as the "Clayton Act."

§ 13. Discrimination in price, services, or facilities

(a) Price; selection of customers. It shall be unlawful for any person engaged in commerce, in the course of such commerce, either directly or indirectly, to discriminate in price between different purchasers of commodities of like grade and quality, where either or any of the purchases involved in such discrimination are in commerce, where such commodities are sold for use, consumption, or resale within the United States or any Territory thereof or the District of Columbia or any insular possession or other place under the jurisdiction of the United States, and where the effect of such discrimination may be substantially to lessen competition or tend to create a monopoly in any line of commerce, or to injure, destroy, or prevent competition with any person who either grants or knowingly receives the benefit of such discrimination, or with customers of either of them: Provided, That nothing herein contained shall prevent differentials which make only due allowance for differences in the cost of manufacture, sale, or delivery resulting from the differing methods or quantities in which such commodities are to such purchasers sold or delivered: Provided, however, That the Federal Trade Commission may, after due investigation and hearing to all interested parties, fix and establish quantity limits, and revise the same as it finds necessary, as to particular commodities or classes of commodities, where it finds that available purchasers in greater quantities are so few as to render differentials on account thereof unjustly discriminatory or promotive of monopoly in any line of commerce; and the foregoing shall then not be construed to permit differentials based on differences in quantities greater than those so fixed and established: And provided further, That nothing herein contained shall prevent persons engaged in selling goods, wares, or merchandise in commerce from selecting their own customers in bona fide transactions and not in restraint of trade: And provided further, That nothing herein contained shall prevent price changes from time to time where in response to changing conditions affecting the market for or the marketability of the goods concerned, such as but not limited to actual or imminent deterioration of perishable goods, obsolescence of seasonal goods, distress sales under court process, or sales in good faith in discontinuance of business in the goods concerned.

(b) Burden of rebutting prima-facie case of discrimination. Upon proof being made, at any hearing on a complaint under this section, that there has been discrimination in price or services or facilities furnished, the burden of rebutting the prima-facie case thus made by showing justification shall be upon the person charged with a violation of this section, and unless justification shall be affirmatively shown, the Commission is authorized to issue an order terminating the discrimination: Provided, however, that nothing herein contained shall prevent a seller rebutting the prima-facie case thus made by showing that his lower price or the furnishing of services or facilities to any purchaser or purchasers was made in good faith to meet an equally low price of a competitor, or the services or facilities furnished by a competitor.

(c) Payment or acceptance of commission, brokerage or other compensation. It shall be unlawful for any person engaged in commerce, in the course of such commerce, to pay or grant, or to receive or accept, anything of value as a commission, brokerage, or other compensation, or any allowance or discount in lieu thereof, except for services rendered in connection with the sale or purchase of goods, wares, or merchandise, either to the other party to such transaction or to an agent, representative, or other intermediary therein where such intermediary is acting in fact for or in behalf, or is subject to the direct or indirect control, of any party to such transaction other than the person by whom such compensation is so granted or paid.

(d) Payment for services or facilities for processing or sale. It shall be unlawful for any person engaged in commerce to pay or contract for the payment of anything of value to or for the benefit of a customer of such person in the course of such commerce as compensation or in consideration for any services or facilities furnished by or through such customer in connection with the processing, handling, sale, or offering for sale of any products or commodities manufactured, sold, or offered for sale by such person, unless such payment or consideration is available on proportionally equal terms to all other customers competing in the distribution of such products or commodities.

(e) Furnishing services or facilities for processing, handling, etc. It shall be unlawful for any person to discriminate in favor of one purchaser against another purchaser or purchasers of a commodity bought for resale, with or without processing, by contracting to furnish or furnishing, or by contributing to the furnishing of, any services or facilities connected with the processing, handling, sale, or offering for sale of such commodity so purchased upon terms not accorded to all purchasers on proportionally equal terms.

(f) Knowingly inducing or receiving discriminatory price. It shall be unlawful for any person engaged in commerce, in the course of such commerce, knowingly to induce or receive a discrimination in price which is prohibited by this section.

§ 14. Sale, etc., on agreement not to use goods of competitor

It shall be unlawful for any person engaged in commerce, in the course of such commerce, to lease or make a sale or contract for sale of goods, wares, merchandise, machinery, supplies or other commodities, whether patented or unpatented, for use, consumption or resale within the United States or any Territory thereof or the District of Columbia or any insular possession or other place under the jurisdiction of the United States, or fix a price charged therefor, or discount from, or rebate upon, such price, on the condition, agreement or understanding that the lessee or purchaser thereof shall not use or deal in the goods, wares, merchandise, machinery, supplies or other commodities of a competitor or competitors of the lessor or seller, where the effect of such lease, sale, or contract for sale or such condition, agreement or understanding may be to substantially lessen competition or tend to create a monopoly in any line of commerce.

§ 15. Suits by persons injured

(a) Amount of recovery; prejudgment interest. Except as provided in subsection (b), any person who shall be injured in his business or property by reason of anything forbidden in the antitrust laws may sue therefor in any district court of the United States in the district in which the defendant resides or is found or has an agent, without respect to the amount in controversy, and shall recover threefold the damages by him sustained, and the cost of suit, including a reasonable attorney's fee. The court may award under this section, pursuant to a motion by such person promptly made, simple interest on actual damages for the period beginning on the date of service of such person's pleading setting forth a claim under the antitrust laws and ending on the date of judgment, or for any shorter period therein, if the court finds that the award of such interest for such period is just in the circumstances. In determining whether an award of interest under this section for any period is just in the circumstances, the court shall consider only—

(1) whether such person or the opposing party, or either party's representative, made motions or asserted claims or defenses so lacking in it as to show that such party or representative acted intentionally for

delay, or otherwise acted in bad faith;

(2) whether, in the course of the action involved, such person or the opposing party, or either party's representative, violated any applicable rule, statute, or court order providing for sanctions for dilatory behavior or otherwise providing for expeditious proceedings; and

(3) whether such person or the opposing party, or either party's representative, engaged in conduct primarily for the purpose of delaying the litigation or increasing the cost thereof.

(b) Amount of damages payable to foreign states and instrumentalities of foreign states.

(1) Except as provided in paragraph (2), any person who is a foreign state may not recover under subsection (a) an amount in excess of the actual damages sustained by it and the cost of suit, including a reasonable attorney's fee.

(2) Paragraph (1) shall not apply to a foreign state if—

(A) such foreign state would be denied, under section 1605(a)(2) of title 28 of the United States Code [28 USCS § 1605(a)(2)], immunity in a case in which the action is based upon a commercial activity, or an act, that is the subject matter of its claim under this section;

(B) such foreign state waives all defenses based upon or arising out of its status as a foreign state, to any claims brought against it in the same action;

(C) such foreign state engages primarily in commercial activities; and

(D) such foreign state does not function, with respect to the commercial activity, or the act, that is the subject matter of its claim under this section as a procurement entity for itself or for another foreign state.

(c) Definitions. For purposes of this section—

(1) the term "commercial activity" shall have the meaning given it in section 1603(d) of title 28, United States Code [28 USCS § 1603(d)], and

(2) the term "foreign state" shall have the meaning given it in section 1603(a) of title 28, United States Code [28 USCS § 1603(a)].

§ 15a. Suits by United States; amount of recovery; prejudgment interest

Whenever the United States is hereafter injured in its business or property by reason of anything forbidden in the antitrust laws it may sue therefor in the United States district court for the district in which the defendant resides or is found or has an agent, without respect to the amount in controversy, and shall recover threefold the damages by it sustained and the cost of suit. The court may award under this section, pursuant to a motion by the United States promptly made, simple interest on threefold the damages for the period beginning on the date of service of the pleading of the United States setting forth a claim under the antitrust laws and ending on the date of judgment, or for any shorter period therein, if the court finds that the award of such interest for such period is just in the circumstances. In determining whether an award of interest under this section for any period is just in the circumstances, the court shall consider only—

(1) whether the United States or the opposing party, or either party's representative, made motions or asserted claims or defenses so lacking in merit as to show that such party or representative acted intentionally for delay or otherwise acted in bad faith;

(2) whether, in the course of the action involved, the United States or the opposing party, or either party's representative, violated any applicable rule, statute, or court order providing for sanctions for dilatory behavior or otherwise providing for expeditious proceedings;

(3) whether the United States or the opposing party, or either party's representative, engaged in conduct primarily for the purpose of delaying the litigation or increasing the cost thereof; and

(4) whether the award of such interest is necessary to compensate the United States adequately for the injury sustained by the United States.

15b. Limitation of actions

Any action to enforce any cause of action under section 4, 4A, or 4C [15 USCS §§ 15, 15a, 15c] shall be forever barred unless commenced within four years after the cause of action accrued. No cause of action barred under existing law on the effective date of this Act shall be revived by this Act.

§ 16. Judgments

(a) Prima facie evidence; collateral estoppel. A final judgment or decree heretofore or hereafter rendered in any civil or criminal proceeding brought by or on behalf of the United States under the antitrust laws to the effect that a defendant has violated said laws shall be prima facie evidence against such defendant in any action or proceeding brought by any other party against such defendant under said laws as to all matters respecting which said judgment or decree would be an estoppel as between the parties thereto: Provided, That this section shall not apply to consent judgments or decrees entered before any testimony has been taken. Nothing contained in this section shall be construed to impose any limitation on the application of collateral estoppel, except that, in any action or proceeding brought under the antitrust laws, collateral estoppel effect shall not be given to any finding made by the Federal Trade Commission under the antitrust laws or under section 5 of the Federal Trade Commission Act [15 USCS § 45] which could give rise to a claim for relief under the antitrust laws.

(b) Consent judgments and competitive impact statements; publication in Federal Register; availability of copies to the public. Any proposal for a consent judgment submitted by the United States for entry in any civil proceeding brought by or on behalf of the United States under the antitrust laws shall be filed with the district court before which such proceeding is pending and published by the United States in the Federal Register at least 60 days prior to the effective date of such judgment. Any written comments relating to such proposal and any responses by the United States thereto, shall also be filed with such district court and published by the United States in the Federal Register within such sixty-day period. Copies of such proposal and any other materials and documents which the United States considered determinative in formulating such proposal, shall also be made available to the public at the district court and in such other districts as the court may subsequently direct. Simultaneously with the filing of such proposal, unless otherwise instructed by the court, the United States shall file with the district court, publish in the Federal Register, and thereafter furnish to any person upon request, a competitive impact statement which shall recite—

(1) the nature and purpose of the proceeding;

(2) a description of the practices or events giving rise to the alleged violation of the antitrust laws;

(3) an explanation of the proposal for a consent judgment, including an explanation of any unusual circumstances giving rise to such proposal or any provision contained therein, relief to be obtained thereby, and the anticipated effects on competition of such relief;

(4) the remedies available to potential private plaintiffs damaged by the alleged violation in the event that such proposal for the consent judgment is entered in such proceeding;

(5) a description of the procedures available for modification of such proposal; and

(6) a description and evaluation of alternatives to such proposal actually considered by the United States.

(c) Publication of summaries in newspapers. The United States shall also cause to be published, commencing at least 60 days prior to the effective date of the judgment described in subsection (b) of this section, for 7 days over a period of 2 weeks in newspapers of general circulation of the district in which the case has been filed, in the District of Columbia, and in such other districts as the court may direct—

(i) a summary of the terms of the proposal for the consent judgment,

(ii) a summary of the competitive impact statement filed under subsection (b),

(iii) and a list of the materials and documents under subsection (b) which the United States shall make available for purposes of meaningful public comment, and the place where such materials and documents are available for public inspection.

(d) Consideration of public comments by Attorney General and publication of response. During the 60-day period as specified in subsection (b) of this section, and such additional time as the United States may request and the court may grant, the United States shall receive and consider any written comments relating to the proposal for the consent judgment submitted under subsection (b). The Attorney General or his designee shall establish procedures to carry out the provisions of this subsection, but such 60-day time period shall not be shortened except by order of the district court upon a showing that (1) extraordinary circumstances require such shortening and (2) such shortening is not adverse to the public interest. At the close of the period during which such comments may be received, the United States shall file with the district court and cause to be published in the Federal Register a response to such comments.

(e) Public interest determination. Before entering any consent judgment proposed by the United States under this section, the court shall determine that the entry of such judgment is in the public interest. For the purpose of such determination, the court may consider—

(1) the competitive impact of such judgment, including termination of alleged violations, provisions for enforcement and modification, duration or relief sought, anticipated effects of alternative remedies actually considered, and any other considerations bearing upon the adequacy of such judgment;

(2) the impact of entry of such judgment upon the public generally and individuals alleging specific injury from the violations set forth in the complaint including consideration of the public benefit, if any, to be derived from a determination of the issues at trial.

(f) Procedure for public interest determination. In making its determination under subsection (e), the court may—

(1) take testimony of Government officials or experts or such other expert witnesses, upon motion of any party or participant or upon its own motion, as the court may deem appropriate;

(2) appoint a special master and such outside consultants or expert witnesses as the court may deem appropriate; and request and obtain the views, evaluations, or advice of any individual, group or agency of government with respect to any aspects of the proposed judgment or the effect of such judgment, in such manner as the court deems appropriate;

(3) authorize full or limited participation in proceedings before the court by interested persons or agencies, including appearance amicus curiae, intervention as a party pursuant to the Federal Rules of Civil Procedure, examination of witnesses or documentary materials, or participation in any other manner and extent which serves the public interest as the court may deem appropriate;

(4) review any comments including any objections filed with the United States under subsection (d) concerning the proposed judgment and the responses of the United States to such comments and objections; and

(5) take such other action in the public interest as the court may deem appropriate.

(g) Filing of written or oral communications with the district court. Not later than 10 days following the date of the filing of any proposal for a consent judgment under subsection (b), each defendant shall file with the district court a description of any and all written or oral communications by or on behalf of such defendant, including any and all written or oral communications on behalf of such defendant, or other person, with any officer or employee of the United States concerning or relevant to such proposal, except that any such communications made by counsel of record alone with the Attorney General or the employees of the Department of Justice alone shall be excluded from the requirements of this subsection. Prior to the entry of any consent judgment pursuant to the antitrust laws, each defendant shall certify to the district court that the requirements of this subsection have been complied with and that such filing is a true and complete description of such communications known to the defendant or which the defendant reasonably should have known.

(h) Inadmissibility as evidence of proceedings before the district court and the competitive impact statement. Proceedings before the district court under subsections (e) and (f) of this section, and the competitive impact statement filed under subsection (b) of this section, shall not be admissible against any defendant in any action or proceeding brought by any other party against such defendant under the antitrust laws or by the United States under section 4A of this Act [15 USCS § 15a] nor constitute a basis for the introduction of the consent judgment as prima facie evidence against such defendant in any such action or proceeding.

(i) Suspension of limitations. Whenever any civil or criminal proceeding is instituted by the United States to prevent, restrain, or punish violations of any of the antitrust laws, but not including an action under section 4A [15 USCS § 15a], the running of the statute of limitations in respect of every private or State right of action arising under said laws and based in whole or in part on any matter complained of in said proceeding shall be suspended during the pendency thereof and for one year thereafter: Provided, however, That whenever the running of the statute of limitations in respect of a cause of action arising under section 4 or 4C [15 USCS §§ 15, 15c] is suspended hereunder, any action to enforce such cause of action shall be forever barred unless commenced either within the period of suspension or within four years after the cause of action accrued.

§ 17. Antitrust laws not applicable to labor organizations

The labor of a human being is not a commodity or article of commerce. Nothing contained in the antitrust laws shall be construed to forbid the existence and operation of labor, agricultural, or horticultural organizations, instituted for the purposes of mutual help, and not having capital stock or conducted for profit, or to forbid or restrain individual members of such organizations from lawfully carrying out the legitimate objects thereof; nor shall such organizations, or the members thereof, be held or construed to be illegal combinations or conspiracies in restraint of trade, under the antitrust laws.

§ 18. Acquisition by one corporation of stock of another
See Celler-Kefauver Act 1950

§ 19. Interlocking directorates and officers
(a) (1) No person shall, at the same time, serve as a director or officer in any two corporations (other than banks, banking associations, and trust companies) that are—

(A) engaged in whole or in part in commerce; and

(B) by virtue of their business and location of operation, competitors, so that the elimination of competition by agreement between them would constitute a violation of any of the antitrust laws;

if each of the corporations has capital, surplus, and undivided profits aggregating more than $ 10,000,000 as adjusted pursuant to paragraph (5) of this subsection.

(2) Notwithstanding the provisions of paragraph (1), simultaneous service as a director or officer in any two corporations shall not be prohibited by this section if—

(A) the competitive sales of either corporation are less than $ 1,000,000, as adjusted pursuant to paragraph (5) of this subsection;

(B) the competitive sales of either corporation are less than 2 per centum of that corporation's total sales; or

(C) the competitive sales of each corporation are less than 4 per centum of that corporation's total sales.

For purposes of this paragraph, "competitive sales" means the gross revenues for all products and services sold by one corporation in competition with the other, determined on the basis of annual gross revenues for such products and services in that corporation's last completed fiscal year. For the purposes of this paragraph, "total sales" means the gross revenues for all products and services sold by one corporation over that corporation's last completed fiscal year.

(3) The eligibility of a director or officer under the provisions of paragraph (1) shall be determined by the capital, surplus and undivided profits, exclusive of dividends declared but not paid to stockholders, of each corporation at the end of that corporation's last completed fiscal year.

(4) For purposes of this section, the term "officer" means an officer elected or chosen by the Board of Directors.

(5) For each fiscal year commencing after September 30, 1990, the $ 10,000,000 and $ 1,000,000 thresholds in this subsection shall be increased (or decreased) as of October 1 each year by an amount equal to the percentage increase (or decrease) in the gross national product, as determined by the Department of Commerce or its successor, for the year then ended over the level so established for the year ending September 30, 1989. As soon as practicable, but not later than January 31 of each year, the Federal Trade Commission shall publish the adjusted amounts required by this paragraph.

(b) When any person elected or chosen as a director or officer of any corporation subject to the provisions hereof is eligible at the time of his election or selection to act for such corporation in such capacity, his eligibility to act in such capacity shall not be affected by any of the provisions hereof by reason of any change in the capital, surplus and undivided profits, or affairs of such corporation from whatever cause, until the expiration of one year from the date on which the event causing ineligibility occurred.

§ 21. Enforcement provisions
(a) Commission, Board, or Secretary authorized to enforce compliance. Authority to enforce compliance with sections 2, 3, 7, and 8 of this Act [15 USCS §§ 13, 14, 18, 19] by the persons respectively subject thereto is hereby vested in the Surface Transportation Board where applicable to common carriers subject to jurisdiction under subtitle IV of title 49, United States Code [49 USCS §§ 10101 et seq.]; in the Federal Communications Commission where applicable to common carriers engaged in wire or radio communication or radio transmission of energy; in the Secretary of Transportation where applicable to air carriers and foreign air carriers subject to the Federal Aviation Act of 1958 [49 USCS §§ 40101 et seq.]; in the Federal Reserve Board [Board of Governors of the Federal Reserve System] where applicable to banks, banking associ-

ations, and trust companies; and in the Federal Trade Commission where applicable to all other character of commerce to be exercised as follows:

(b) Issuance of complaints for violations; hearing; intervention; filing of testimony; report; cease and desist orders; reopening and alteration of reports or orders. Whenever the Commission, Board, or Secretary vested with jurisdiction thereof shall have reason to believe that any person is violating or has violated any of the provisions of sections 2, 3, 7, and 8 of this Act [15 USCS §§ 13, 14, 18, 19], it shall issue and serve upon such person and the Attorney General a complaint stating its charges in that respect, and containing a notice of a hearing upon a day and at a place therein fixed at least thirty days after the service of said complaint. The person so complained of shall have the right to appear at the place and time so fixed and show cause why an order should not be entered by the Commission, Board, or Secretary requiring such person to cease and desist from the violation of the law so charged in said complaint. The Attorney General shall have the right to intervene and appear in said proceeding and any person may make application, and upon good cause shown may be allowed by the Commission, Board, or Secretary, to intervene and appear in said proceeding by counsel or in person. The testimony in any such proceeding shall be reduced to writing and filed in the office of the Commission, Board, or Secretary. If upon such hearing the Commission, Board, or Secretary, as the case may be, shall be of the opinion that any of the provisions of said sections have been or are being violated, it shall make a report in writing, in which it shall state its findings as to the facts, and shall issue and cause to be served on such person an order requiring such person to cease and desist from such violations, and divest itself of the stock, or other share capital, or assets, held or rid itself of the directors chosen contrary to the provisions of sections 7 and 8 of this Act [15 USCS §§ 18, 19], if any there be, in the manner and within the time fixed by said order. Until the expiration of the time allowed for filing a petition for review, if no such petition has been duly filed within such time, or, if a petition for review has been filed within such time then until the record in the proceeding has been filed in a court of appeals of the United States, as hereinafter provided, the Commission, Board, or Secretary may at any time, upon such notice and in such manner as it shall deem proper, modify or set aside, in whole or in part, any report or any order made or issued by it under this section. After the expiration of the time allowed for filing a petition for review, if no such petition has been duly filed within such time, the Commission, Board, or Secretary may at any time, after notice and opportunity for hearing, reopen and alter, modify, or set aside, in whole or in part, any report or order made or issued by it under this section, whenever in the opinion of the Commission, Board, or Secretary conditions of fact or of law have so changed as to require such action or if the public interest shall so require: provided, however, That the said person may, within sixty days after service upon him or it of said report or order entered after such a reopening, obtain a review thereof in the appropriate court of appeals of the United States, in the manner provided in subsection (c) of this section.

(c) Review of orders; jurisdiction; filing of petition and record of proceeding; conclusiveness of findings; additional evidence; modification of findings; finality of judgment and decree. Any person required by such order of the commission, board, or Secretary to cease and desist from any such violation may obtain a review of such order in the court of appeals of the United States for any circuit within which such violation occurred or within which such person resides or carries on business, by filing in the court, within sixty days after the date of the service of such order, a written petition praying that the order of the commission, board, or Secretary be set aside. A copy of such petition shall be forthwith transmitted by the clerk of the court to the commission, board, or Secretary and thereupon the commission, board, or Secretary shall file in the court the record in the proceeding, as provided in section 2112 of title 28, United States Code. Upon such filing of the petition the court shall have jurisdiction of the proceeding and of the question determined therein concurrently with the commission, board, or Secretary until the filing of the record, and shall have power to make and enter a decree affirming, modifying, or setting aside the order of the commission, board, or Secretary and enforcing the same to the extent that such order is affirmed, and to issue such writs as are ancillary to its jurisdiction or are necessary in its judgment to prevent injury to the public or to competitors pendente lite. The findings of the commission, board, or Secretary as to the facts, if supported by substantial evidence, shall be conclusive. To the extent that the order of the commission, board, or Secretary is affirmed, the court shall issue its own order commanding obedience to the terms of such order of the commission, board, or Secretary. If either party shall apply to the court for leave to adduce additional evidence, and shall show to the satisfaction of the court that such additional evidence is material and that there were reasonable grounds for the failure to adduce such evidence in the proceeding before the commission, board, or Secretary, the court may order such additional evidence to be taken before the commission, board, or Secretary, and to be adduced upon the hearing in such manner and upon such terms and conditions as to the court may seem proper. The commission, board, or Secretary may modify its findings as to the facts, or make new findings, by reason of the additional evidence so taken, and shall file such modified or new findings, which, if supported by subsantial evidence, shall be conclusive, and its recommendation, if any, for the modification or setting aside of its original order, with the return of such additional evidence. The judgment and decree of the court shall be final, except that the same shall be subject to review by the Supreme Court upon certiorari, as provided in section 1254 of title 28 of the United States Code.

(d) Exclusive jurisdiction of Court of Appeals. Upon the filing of the record with it the jurisdiction of the court of appeals to affirm, enforce, modify, or set aside orders of the commission, board, or Secretary shall be exclusive.

(e) Liability under antitrust laws. No order of the commission, board, or Secretary or judgment of the court to enforce the same shall in anywise relieve or absolve any person from any liability under the antitrust laws.

(f) Service of complaints, orders and other processes. Complaints, orders, and other processes of the commission, board, or Secretary under this section may be served by anyone duly authorized by the commission, board, or Secretary, either (1) by delivering a copy thereof to the person to be served, or to a member of the partnership to be served, or to the president, secretary, or other executive officer or a director of the corporation to be served; or (2) by leaving a copy thereof at the residence or the principal office or place of business of such person; or (3) by mailing by registered or certified mail a copy thereof addressed to such person at his or its residence or principal office or place of business. The verified return by the person so serving said complaint, order, or other process setting forth the manner of said service shall be proof of the same, and the return post office receipt for said complaint, order, or other process mailed by registered or certified mail as aforesaid shall be proof of the service of the same.

(g) Finality of orders generally. Any order issued under subsection (b) shall become final—

(1) upon the expiration of the time allowed for filing a petition for review, if no such petition has been duly filed within such time; but the commission, board, or Secretary may thereafter modify or set aside its order to the extent provided in the last sentence of subsection (b); or

(2) upon the expiration of the time allowed for filing a petition for certiorari, if the order of the commission, board, or Secretary has been affirmed, or the petition for review has been dismissed by the court of appeals, and no petition for certiorari has been duly filed; or

(3) upon the denial of a petition for certiorari, if the order of the commission, board, or Secretary has been affirmed or the petition for review has been dismissed by the court of appeals; or

(4) upon the expiration of thirty days from the date of issuance of the mandate of the Supreme Court, if such Court directs that the order of the commission, board, or Secretary be affirmed or the petition for review be dismissed.

(h) Finality of orders modified by Supreme Court. If the Supreme Court directs that the order of the commission, board, or Secretary be modified or set aside, the order of the commission, board, or Secretary rendered in accordance with the mandate of the Supreme Court shall become final upon the expiration of thirty days from the time it was rendered, unless within such thirty days either party has instituted proceedings to have such order corrected to accord with the mandate, in which event the order of the commission, board, or Secretary shall become final when so corrected.

(i) Finality of orders modified by Court of Appeals. If the order of the commission, board, or Secretary is modified or set aside by the court of appeals, and if (1) the time allowed for filing a petition for certiorari has expired and no such petition has been duly filed, or (2) the petition for certiorari has been denied, or (3) the decision of the court has been

affirmed by the Supreme Court, then the order of the commission, board, or Secretary rendered in accordance with the mandate of the court of appeals shall become final on the expiration of thirty days from the time such order of the commission, board, or Secretary was rendered, unless within such thirty days either party has instituted proceedings to have such order corrected so that it will accord with the mandate, in which event the order of the commission, board, or Secretary shall become final when so corrected.

(j) Finality of orders issued on rehearing ordered by Court of Appeals or Supreme Court. If the Supreme Court orders a rehearing; or if the case is remanded by the court of appeals to the commission, board, or Secretary for a rehearing, and if (1) the time allowed for filing a petition for certiorari has expired, and no such petition has been duly filed, or (2) the petition for certiorari has been denied, or (3) the decision of the court has been affirmed by the Supreme Court, then the order of the commission, board, or Secretary rendered upon such rehearing shall become final in the same manner as though no prior order of the commission, board, or Secretary had been rendered.

(k) "Mandate" defined. As used in this section the term "mandate," in case a mandate has been recalled prior to the expiration of thirty days from the date of issuance thereof, means the final mandate.

(l) Penalties. Any person who violates any order issued by the commission, board, or Secretary under subsection (b) after such order has become final, and while such order is in effect, shall forfeit and pay to the United States a civil penalty of not more than $ 5,000 for each violation, which shall accrue to the United States and may be recovered in a civil action brought by the United States. Each separate violation of any such order shall be a separate offense, except that in the case of a violation through continuing failure or neglect to obey a final order of the commission, board, or Secretary each day of continuance of such failure or neglect shall be deemed a separate offense.

§ 22. District in which to sue corporation

Any suit, action, or proceeding under the antitrust laws against a corporation may be brought not only in the judicial district whereof it is an inhabitant, but also in any district wherein it may be found or transacts business; and all process in such cases may be served in the district of which it is an inhabitant, or wherever it may be found.

§ 23. Suits by United States; subpoenas for witnesses

In any suit, action, or proceeding brought by or on behalf of the United States subpoenas for witnesses who are required to attend a court of the United States in any judicial district in any case, civil or criminal, arising under the antitrust laws may run into any other district: Provided, That in civil cases no writ of subpoena shall issue for witnesses living out of the district in which the court is held at a greater distance than one hundred miles from the place of holding the same without the permission of the trial court being first had upon proper application and cause shown.

§ 24. Liability of directors and agents of corporation

Whenever a corporation shall violate any of the penal provisions of the antitrust laws, such violation shall be deemed to be also that of the individual directors, officers, or agents of such corporation who shall have authorized, ordered, or done any of the acts constituting in whole or in part such violation, and such violation shall be deemed a misdemeanor, and upon conviction therefor of any such director, officer, or agent he shall be punished by a fine of not exceeding $ 5,000 or by imprisonment for not exceeding one year, or by both, in the discretion of the court.

§ 25. Restraining violations; procedure

The several district courts of the United States are invested with jurisdiction to prevent and restrain violations of this Act, and it shall be the duty of the several district attorneys of the United States [United States attorneys], in their respective districts, under the direction of the Attorney General, to institute proceedings in equity to prevent and restrain such violations. Such proceedings may be by way of petition setting forth the case and praying that such violation shall be enjoined or otherwise prohibited. When the parties complained of shall have been duly notified of such petition, the court shall proceed, as soon as may be, to the hearing and determination of the case; and pending such petition, and before final decree, the court may at any time make such temporary restraining order or prohibition as shall be deemed just in the premises. Whenever it shall appear to the court before which any such proceeding may be pending that the ends of justice require that other parties should be brought before the court, the court may cause them to be summoned whether they reside in the district in which the court is held or not, and subpoenas to that end may be served in any district by the marshal thereof.

§ 26. Injunctive relief for private parties; exception; costs

Any person, firm, corporation, or association shall be entitled to sue for and have injunctive relief, in any court of the United States having jurisdiction over the parties, against threatened loss or damage by a violation of the antitrust laws, including sections two, three, seven and eight of this Act [15 USCS §§ 13, 14, 18, and 19], when and under the same conditions and principles as injunctive relief against threatened conduct that will cause loss or damage is granted by courts of equity, under the rules governing such proceedings, and upon the execution of proper bond against damages for an injunction improvidently granted and a showing that the danger of irreparable loss or damage is immediate, a preliminary injunction may issue: Provided, That nothing herein contained shall be construed to entitle any person, firm, corporation, or association, except the United States, to bring suit for injunctive relief against any common carrier subject to the jurisdiction of the Surface Transportation Board under subtitle IV of title 49, United States Code [49 USCS §§ 10101 et seq.]. In any action under this section in which the plaintiff substantially prevails, the court shall award the cost of suit, including a reasonable attorney's fee, to such plaintiff.

§ 27. Effect of partial invalidity

If any clause, sentence, paragraph, or part of this Act shall, for any reason, be adjudged by any court of competent jurisdiction to be invalid, such judgment shall not affect, impair, or invalidate the remainder thereof, but shall be confined in its operation to the clause, sentence, paragraph, or part thereof directly involved in the controversy in which such judgment shall have been rendered.

Celler-Kefauver Act 1950 (amending § 7 of the Clayton Antitrust Act)
Title 15. Commerce and Trade
Chapter 1. Monopolies and Combinations in Restraint of Trade

§ 18. Acquisition by one corporation of stock of another

No person engaged in commerce or in any activity affecting commerce shall acquire, directly or indirectly, the whole or any part of the stock or other share capital and no person subject to the jurisdiction of the Federal Trade Commission shall acquire the whole or any part of the assets of another person engaged also in commerce or in any activity affecting commerce, where in any line of commerce or in any activity affecting commerce in any section of the country, the effect of such acquisition may be substantially to lessen competition, or to tend to create a monopoly.

No person shall acquire, directly or indirectly, the whole or any part of the stock or other share capital and no person subject to the jurisdiction of the Federal Trade Commission shall acquire the whole or any part of the assets of one or more persons engaged in commerce or in any activity affecting commerce, where in any line of commerce or in any activity affecting commerce in any section of the country, the effect of such acquisition, of such stocks or assets, or of the use of such stock by the voting or granting of proxies or otherwise, may be substantially to lessen competition, or to tend to create a monopoly.

This section shall not apply to persons purchasing such stock solely for investment and not using the same by voting or otherwise to bring about, or in attempting to bring about, the substantial lessening of competition. Nor shall anything contained in this section prevent a corporation engaged in commerce or in any activity affecting commerce from causing the formation of subsidiary corporations for the actual carrying on of their immediate lawful business, or the natural and legitimate branches or extensions thereof, or from owning and holding all or a part of the stock of such subsidiary corporations, when the effect of such formation is not to substantially lessen competition.

Nor shall anything herein contained be construed to prohibit any common carrier subject to the laws to regulate commerce from aiding in the construction of branches or short lines so located as to become feeders to the main line of the company so aiding in such construction or from acquiring or owning all or any part of the stock of such branch lines, nor to prevent any such common carrier from acquiring and owning all or any part of the stock of a branch or short line constructed by an independent company where there is no substantial competition between the company owning the branch line so constructed and the company owning the main line acquiring the property or an interest therein, nor to prevent such common carrier from extending any of its lines through the medium of the acquisition of stock or otherwise of any other common carrier where there is no substantial competition between the company extending its lines and the company whose stock, property, or an interest therein is so acquired.

Nothing contained in this section shall be held to affect or impair any right heretofore legally acquired: Provided, That nothing in this section shall be held or construed to authorize or make lawful anything heretofore prohibited or made illegal by the antitrust laws, nor to exempt any person from the penal provisions thereof or the civil remedies therein provided.

Nothing contained in this section shall apply to transactions duly consummated pursuant to authority given by the Secretary of Transportation, Federal Power Commission, Surface Transportation Board, the Securities and Exchange Commission in the exercise of its jurisdiction under section 10 of the Public Utility Holding Company Act of 1935 [15 USCS § 79j], the United States Maritime Commission, or the Secretary of Agriculture under any statutory provision vesting such power in such Commission, Board, or Secretary.

Sherman Antitrust Act
United States Code Service
Title 15. Commerce and Trade
Chapter 1. Monopolies And Combinations In Restraint Of Trade

§ 1. Trusts, etc., in restraint of trade illegal; penalty

Every contract, combination in the form of trust or otherwise, or conspiracy, in restraint of trade or commerce among the several States, or with foreign nations, is hereby declared to be illegal. Every person who shall make any contract or engage in any combination or conspiracy hereby declared to be illegal shall be deemed guilty of a felony, and, on conviction thereof, shall be punished by fine not exceeding $ 10,000,000 if a corporation, or, if any other person, $ 350,000, or by imprisonment not exceeding three years, or by both said punishments, in the discretion of the court.

§ 2. Monopolization; penalty

Every person who shall monopolize, or attempt to monopolize, or combine or conspire with any other person or persons, to monopolize any part of the trade or commerce among the several States, or with foreign nations, shall be deemed guilty of a felony, and, on conviction thereof, shall be punished by fine not exceeding $ 10,000,000 if a corporation, or, if any other person, $ 350,000, or by imprisonment not exceeding three years, or by both said punishments, in the discretion of the court.

§ 3. Trusts in Territories or District of Columbia illegal; combination a felony

(a) Every contract, combination in form of trust or otherwise, or conspiracy, in restraint of trade or commerce in any Territory of the United States or of the District of Columbia, or in restraint of trade or commerce between any such Territory and another, or between any such Territory or Territories and any State or States or the District of Columbia, or with foreign nations, or between the District of Columbia and any State or States or foreign nations, is declared illegal. Every person who shall make any such contract or engage in any such combination or conspiracy, shall be deemed guilty of a felony, and, on conviction thereof, shall be punished by fine not exceeding $ 10,000,000 if a corporation, or, if any other person, $ 350,000, or by imprisonment not exceeding three years, or by both said punishments, in the discretion of the court.

(b) Every person who shall monopolize, or attempt to monopolize, or combine or conspire with any other person or persons, to monopolize any part of the trade or commerce in any Territory of the United States or of the District of Columbia, or between any such Territory and another, or between any such Territory or Territories and any State or States or the District of Columbia, or with foreign nations, or between the District of Columbia, and any State or States or foreign nations, shall be deemed guilty of a felony, and, on conviction thereof, shall be punished by fine not exceeding $ 10,000,000 if a corporation, or, if any other person, $ 350,000, or by imprisonment not exceeding three years, or by both said punishments, in the discretion of the court.

§ 4 Jurisdiction of courts; duty of United States attorneys; Procedure

The several circuit [district] courts of the United States are hereby invested with jurisdiction to prevent and restrain violations of this act [15 USCS §§ 1 et seq.]; and it shall be the duty of the several district attorneys of the United States [United States attorneys], in their respective districts, under the direction of the Attorney General, to institute proceedings in equity to prevent and restrain such violations. Such proceedings may be by way of petition setting forth the case and praying that such violation shall be enjoined or otherwise prohibited. When the parties complained of shall have been duly notified of such petition the court shall proceed, as soon as may be, to the hearing and determination of the case; and pending such petition and before final decree, the court may at any time make such temporary restraining order or prohibition as shall be deemed just in the premises.

§ 5. Bringing in additional parties

Whenever it shall appear to the court before which any proceeding under section four of this Act [15 USCS § 4] may be pending, that the ends of justice require that other parties should be brought before the court, the court may cause them to be summoned, whether they reside in the district in which the court is held or not; and subpoenas to that end may be served in any district by the marshal thereof.

§ 6. Forfeiture of property in transit

Any property owned under any contract or by any combination, or pursuant to any conspiracy (and being the subject thereof) mentioned in section one of this Act [15 USCS § 1], and being in the course of transportation from one State to another, or to a foreign country, shall be forfeited to the United States, and may be seized and condemned by like proceedings as those provided by law for the forfeiture, seizure, and condemnation of property imported into the United States contrary to law.

§ 6a. Conduct involving trade or commerce with foreign nations

This Act [15 USCS §§ 1 et seq.] shall not apply to conduct involving trade or commerce (other than import trade or import commerce) with foreign nations unless—

(1) such conduct has a direct, substantial, and reasonably foreseeable effect—

(A) on trade or commerce which is not trade or commerce with foreign nations, or on import trade or import commerce with foreign nations; or

(B) on export trade or export commerce with foreign nations, of a person engaged in such trade or commerce in the United States; and

(2) such effect gives rise to a claim under the provisions of this Act [15 USCS §§ 1 et seq.], other than this section.

If this Act [15 USCS §§ 1 et seq.] applies to such conduct only because of the operation of paragraph (1)(B), then this Act [15 USCS §§ 1 et seq.] shall apply to such conduct only for injury to export business in the United States.

§ 7. "Person" defined

The word "person," or "persons," wherever used in this Act [15 USCS §§ 1 et seq.] shall be deemed to include corporations and associations existing under or authorized by the laws of either the United States, the laws of any of the Territories, the laws of any State, or the laws of any foreign country.

Sarbanes-Oxley Act 2002
United States Code Service
Title 15. Commerce and Trade
Chapter 98. Public Company Accounting Reform and Corporate Responsibility

§ 7201. Definitions

In this Act, the following definitions shall apply:

(1) Appropriate State regulatory authority. The term "appropriate State regulatory authority" means the State agency or other authority responsible for the licensure or other regulation of the practice of accounting in the State or States having jurisdiction over a registered public accounting firm or associated person thereof, with respect to the matter in question.

(2) Audit. The term "audit" means an examination of the financial statements of any issuer by an independent public accounting firm in accordance with the rules of the Board or the Commission (or, for the period preceding the adoption of applicable rules of the Board under section 103 [15 USCS § 7213], in accordance with then-applicable generally accepted auditing and related standards for such purposes), for the purpose of expressing an opinion on such statements.

(3) Audit committee. The term "audit committee" means—

(A) a committee (or equivalent body) established by and amongst the board of directors of an issuer for the purpose of overseeing the accounting and financial reporting processes of the issuer and audits of the financial statements of the issuer; and

(B) if no such committee exists with respect to an issuer, the entire board of directors of the issuer.

(4) Audit report. The term "audit report" means a document or other record—

(A) prepared following an audit performed for purposes of compliance by an issuer with the requirements of the securities laws; and

(B) in which a public accounting firm either—

(i) sets forth the opinion of that firm regarding a financial statement, report, or other document; or

(ii) asserts that no such opinion can be expressed.

(5) Board. The term "Board" means the Public Company Accounting Oversight Board established under section 101 [15 USCS § 7211].

(6) Commission. The term "Commission" means the Securities and Exchange Commission.

(7) Issuer. The term "issuer" means an issuer (as defined in section 3 of the Securities Exchange Act of 1934 (15 U.S.C. 78c)), the securities of which are registered under section 12 of that Act (15 U.S.C. 78l), or that is required to file reports under section 15(d) (15 U.S.C. 78o(d)), or that files or has filed a registration statement that has not yet become effective under the Securities Act of 1933 (15 U.S.C. 77a et seq.), and that it has not withdrawn.

(8) Non-audit services. The term "non-audit services" means any professional services provided to an issuer by a registered public accounting firm, other than those provided to an issuer in connection with an audit or a review of the financial statements of an issuer.

(9) Person associated with a public accounting firm.

(A) In general. The terms "person associated with a public accounting firm" (or with a "registered public accounting firm") and "associated person of a public accounting firm" (or of a "registered public accounting firm") mean any individual proprietor, partner, shareholder, principal, accountant, or other professional employee of a public accounting firm, or any other independent contractor or entity that, in connection with the preparation or issuance of any audit report—

(i) shares in the profits of, or receives compensation in any other form from, that firm; or

(ii) participates as agent or otherwise on behalf of such accounting firm in any activity of that firm.

(B) Exemption authority. The Board may, by rule, exempt persons engaged only in ministerial tasks from the definition in subparagraph (A), to the extent that the Board determines that any such exemption is consistent with the purposes of this Act, the public interest, or the protection of investors.

(10) Professional standards. The term "professional standards" means—

(A) accounting principles that are—

(i) established by the standard setting body described in section 19(b) of the Securities Act of 1933 [15 USCS § 77s(b)], as amended by this Act, or prescribed by the Commission under section 19(a) of that Act (15 U.S.C. 17a(s) [77s(a)] [15 USCS § 77s(a)]) or section 13(b) of the Securities Exchange Act of 1934 (15 U.S.C. 78a(m) [78m(b)] [15 USCS § 78m(b)]); and

(ii) relevant to audit reports for particular issuers, or dealt with in the quality control system of a particular registered public accounting firm; and

(B) auditing standards, standards for attestation engagements, quality control policies and procedures, ethical and competency standards, and independence standards (including rules implementing title II) that the Board or the Commission determines—

(i) relate to the preparation or issuance of audit reports for issuers; and

(ii) are established or adopted by the Board under section 103(a) [15 USCS § 7213(a)], or are promulgated as rules of the Commission.

(11) Public accounting firm. The term "public accounting firm" means—

(A) a proprietorship, partnership, incorporated association, corporation, limited liability company, limited liability partnership, or other legal entity that is engaged in the practice of public accounting or preparing or issuing audit reports; and

(B) to the extent so designated by the rules of the Board, any associated person of any entity described in subparagraph (A).

(12) Registered public accounting firm. The term "registered public

accounting firm" means a public accounting firm registered with the Board in accordance with this Act.

(13) Rules of the Board. The term "rules of the Board" means the bylaws and rules of the Board (as submitted to, and approved, modified, or amended by the Commission, in accordance with section 107 [15 USCS § 7217]), and those stated policies, practices, and interpretations of the Board that the Commission, by rule, may deem to be rules of the Board, as necessary or appropriate in the public interest or for the protection of investors.

(14) Security. The term "security" has the same meaning as in section 3(a) of the Securities Exchange Act of 1934 (15 U.S.C. 78c(a)).

(15) Securities laws. The term "securities laws" means the provisions of law referred to in section 3(a)(47) of the Securities Exchange Act of 1934 (15 U.S.C. 78c(a)(47)), as amended by this Act, and includes the rules, regulations, and orders issued by the Commission thereunder

(16) State. The term "State" means any State of the United States, the District of Columbia, Puerto Rico, the Virgin Islands, or any other territory or possession of the United States.

§ 7202. Commission rules and enforcement

(a) Regulatory action. The Commission shall promulgate such rules and regulations, as may be necessary or appropriate in the public interest or for the protection of investors, and in furtherance of this Act.

(b) Enforcement.

(1) In general. A violation by any person of this Act, any rule or regulation of the Commission issued under this Act, or any rule of the Board shall be treated for all purposes in the same manner as a violation of the Securities Exchange Act of 1934 (15 U.S.C. 78a et seq.) or the rules and regulations issued thereunder, consistent with the provisions of this Act, and any such person shall be subject to the same penalties, and to the same extent, as for a violation of that Act or such rules or regulations.

(2)—(4) [Omitted]

(c) Effect on Commission authority. Nothing in this Act or the rules of the Board shall be construed to impair or limit—

(1) the authority of the Commission to regulate the accounting profession, accounting firms, or persons associated with such firms for purposes of enforcement of the securities laws;

(2) the authority of the Commission to set standards for accounting or auditing practices or auditor independence, derived from other provisions of the securities laws or the rules or regulations thereunder, for purposes of the preparation and issuance of any audit report, or otherwise under applicable law; or

(3) the ability of the Commission to take, on the initiative of the Commission, legal, administrative, or disciplinary action against any registered public accounting firm or any associated person thereof.

Public Accounting Oversight Board

§ 7211. Establishment; administrative provisions

(a) Establishment of Board. There is established the Public Company Accounting Oversight Board, to oversee the audit of public companies that are subject to the securities laws, and related matters, in order to protect the interests of investors and further the public interest in the preparation of informative, accurate, and independent audit reports for companies the securities of which are sold to, and held by and for, public investors. The Board shall be a body corporate, operate as a nonprofit corporation, and have succession until dissolved by an Act of Congress.

(b) Status. The Board shall not be an agency or establishment of the United States Government, and, except as otherwise provided in this Act, shall be subject to, and have all the powers conferred upon a nonprofit corporation by, the District of Columbia Nonprofit Corporation Act [unclassified]. No member or person employed by, or agent for, the Board shall be deemed to be an officer or employee of or agent for the Federal Government by reason of such service.

(c) Duties of the Board. The Board shall, subject to action by the Commission under section 107 [15 USCS § 7217], and once a determination is made by the Commission under subsection (d) of this section—

(1) register public accounting firms that prepare audit reports for issuers, in accordance with section 102 [15 USCS § 7212];

(2) establish or adopt, or both, by rule, auditing, quality control, ethics, independence, and other standards relating to the preparation of audit reports for issuers, in accordance with section 103 [15 USCS § 7213];

(3) conduct inspections of registered public accounting firms, in ac-

cordance with section 104 [15 USCS § 7214] and the rules of the Board;

(4) conduct investigations and disciplinary proceedings concerning, and impose appropriate sanctions where justified upon, registered public accounting firms and associated persons of such firms, in accordance with section 105 [15 USCS § 7215];

(5) perform such other duties or functions as the Board (or the Commission, by rule or order) determines are necessary or appropriate to promote high professional standards among, and improve the quality of audit services offered by, registered public accounting firms and associated persons thereof, or otherwise to carry out this Act, in order to protect investors, or to further the public interest;

(6) enforce compliance with this Act, the rules of the Board, professional standards, and the securities laws relating to the preparation and issuance of audit reports and the obligations and liabilities of accountants with respect thereto, by registered public accounting firms and associated persons thereof; and

(7) set the budget and manage the operations of the Board and the staff of the Board.

(d) Commission determination. The members of the Board shall take such action (including hiring of staff, proposal of rules, and adoption of initial and transitional auditing and other professional standards) as may be necessary or appropriate to enable the Commission to determine, not later than 270 days after the date of enactment of this Act [enacted July 30, 2002], that the Board is so organized and has the capacity to carry out the requirements of this title [15 USCS §§ 7211 et seq.], and to enforce compliance with this title [15 USCS §§ 7211 et seq.] by registered public accounting firms and associated persons thereof. The Commission shall be responsible, prior to the appointment of the Board, for the planning for the establishment and administrative transition to the Board's operation.

(e) Board membership.

(1) Composition. The Board shall have 5 members, appointed from among prominent individuals of integrity and reputation who have a demonstrated commitment to the interests of investors and the public, and an understanding of the responsibilities for and nature of the financial disclosures required of issuers under the securities laws and the obligations of accountants with respect to the preparation and issuance of audit reports with respect to such disclosures.

(2) Limitation. Two members, and only 2 members, of the Board shall be or have been certified public accountants pursuant to the laws of 1 or more States, provided that, if 1 of those 2 members is the chairperson, he or she may not have been a practicing certified public accountant for at least 5 years prior to his or her appointment to the Board.

(3) Full-time independent service. Each member of the Board shall serve on a full-time basis, and may not, concurrent with service on the Board, be employed by any other person or engage in any other professional or business activity. No member of the Board may share in any of the profits of, or receive payments from, a public accounting firm (or any other person, as determined by rule of the Commission), other than fixed continuing payments, subject to such conditions as the Commission may impose, under standard arrangements for the retirement of members of public accounting firms.

(4) Appointment of Board members.

(A) Initial board. Not later than 90 days after the date of enactment of this Act [enacted July 30, 2002], the Commission, after consultation with the Chairman of the Board of Governors of the Federal Reserve System and the Secretary of the Treasury, shall appoint the chairperson and other initial members of the Board, and shall designate a term of service for each.

(B) Vacancies. A vacancy on the Board shall not affect the powers of the Board, but shall be filled in the same manner as provided for appointments under this section.

(5) Term of service.

(A) In general. The term of service of each Board member shall be 5 years, and until a successor is appointed, except that—

(i) the terms of office of the initial Board members (other than the chairperson) shall expire in annual increments, 1 on each of the first 4 anniversaries of the initial date of appointment; and

(ii) any Board member appointed to fill a vacancy occurring before the expiration of the term for which the predecessor was appointed shall be appointed only for the remainder of that term.

(B) Term limitation. No person may serve as a member of the Board, or as chairperson of the Board, for more than 2 terms, whether or not such terms of service are consecutive.

(6) Removal from office. A member of the Board may be removed by the Commission from office, in accordance with section 107(d)(3) [15 USCS § 7217(d)(3)], for good cause shown before the expiration of the term of that member.

(f) Powers of the Board. In addition to any authority granted to the Board otherwise in this Act, the Board shall have the power, subject to section 107 [15 USCS § 7217]—

(1) to sue and be sued, complain and defend, in its corporate name and through its own counsel, with the approval of the Commission, in any Federal, State, or other court;

(2) to conduct its operations and maintain offices, and to exercise all other rights and powers authorized by this Act, in any State, without regard to any qualification, licensing, or other provision of law in effect in such State (or a political subdivision thereof);

(3) to lease, purchase, accept gifts or donations of or otherwise acquire, improve, use, sell, exchange, or convey, all of or an interest in any property, wherever situated;

(4) to appoint such employees, accountants, attorneys, and other agents as may be necessary or appropriate, and to determine their qualifications, define their duties, and fix their salaries or other compensation (at a level that is comparable to private sector self-regulatory, accounting, technical, supervisory, or other staff or management positions);

(5) to allocate, assess, and collect accounting support fees established pursuant to section 109 [15 USCS § 7219], for the Board, and other fees and charges imposed under this title [15 USCS §§ 7211 et seq.]; and

(6) to enter into contracts, execute instruments, incur liabilities, and do any and all other acts and things necessary, appropriate, or incidental to the conduct of its operations and the exercise of its obligations, rights, and powers imposed or granted by this title [15 USCS §§ 7211 et seq.].

(g) Rules of the Board. The rules of the Board shall, subject to the approval of the Commission—

(1) provide for the operation and administration of the Board, the exercise of its authority, and the performance of its responsibilities under this Act;

(2) permit, as the Board determines necessary or appropriate, delegation by the Board of any of its functions to an individual member or employee of the Board, or to a division of the Board, including functions with respect to hearing, determining, ordering, certifying, reporting, or otherwise acting as to any matter, except that—

(A) the Board shall retain a discretionary right to review any action pursuant to any such delegated function, upon its own motion;

(B) a person shall be entitled to a review by the Board with respect to any matter so delegated, and the decision of the Board upon such review shall be deemed to be the action of the Board for all purposes (including appeal or review thereof); and

(C) if the right to exercise a review described in subparagraph (A) is declined, or if no such review is sought within the time stated in the rules of the Board, then the action taken by the holder of such delegation shall for all purposes, including appeal or review thereof, be deemed to be the action of the Board;

(3) establish ethics rules and standards of conduct for Board members and staff, including a bar on practice before the Board (and the Commission, with respect to Board-related matters) of 1 year for former members of the Board, and appropriate periods (not to exceed 1 year) for former staff of the Board; and

(4) provide as otherwise required by this Act.

(h) Annual report to the Commission. The Board shall submit an annual report (including its audited financial statements) to the Commission, and the Commission shall transmit a copy of that report to the Committee on Banking, Housing, and Urban Affairs of the Senate, and the Committee on Financial Services of the House of Representatives, not later than 30 days after the date of receipt of that report by the Commission.

§ 7212. Registration with the Board

(a) Mandatory registration. Beginning 180 days after the date of the determination of the Commission under section 101(d) [15 USCS § 7211(d)], it shall be unlawful for any person that is not a registered public accounting firm to prepare or issue, or to participate in the preparation or issuance of, any audit report with respect to any issuer.

(b) Applications for registration.

(1) Form of application. A public accounting firm shall use such form as the Board may prescribe, by rule, to apply for registration under this section.

(2) Contents of applications. Each public accounting firm shall submit, as part of its application for registration, in such detail as the Board shall specify—

(A) the names of all issuers for which the firm prepared or issued audit reports during the immediately preceding calendar year, and for which the firm expects to prepare or issue audit reports during the current calendar year;

(B) the annual fees received by the firm from each such issuer for audit services, other accounting services, and non-audit services, respectively;

(C) such other current financial information for the most recently completed fiscal year of the firm as the Board may reasonably request;

(D) a statement of the quality control policies of the firm for its accounting and auditing practices;

(E) a list of all accountants associated with the firm who participate in or contribute to the preparation of audit reports, stating the license or certification number of each such person, as well as the State license numbers of the firm itself;

(F) information relating to criminal, civil, or administrative actions or disciplinary proceedings pending against the firm or any associated person of the firm in connection with any audit report;

(G) copies of any periodic or annual disclosure filed by an issuer with the Commission during the immediately preceding calendar year which discloses accounting disagreements between such issuer and the firm in connection with an audit report furnished or prepared by the firm for such issuer; and

(H) such other information as the rules of the Board or the Commission shall specify as necessary or appropriate in the public interest or for the protection of investors.

(3) Consents. Each application for registration under this subsection shall include—

(A) a consent executed by the public accounting firm to cooperation in and compliance with any request for testimony or the production of documents made by the Board in the furtherance of its authority and responsibilities under this title [15 USCS §§ 7211 et seq.] (and an agreement to secure and enforce similar consents from each of the associated persons of the public accounting firm as a condition of their continued employment by or other association with such firm); and

(B) a statement that such firm understands and agrees that cooperation and compliance, as described in the consent required by subparagraph (A), and the securing and enforcement of such consents from its associated persons, in accordance with the rules of the Board, shall be a condition to the continuing effectiveness of the registration of the firm with the Board.

(c) Action on applications.

(1) Timing. The Board shall approve a completed application for registration not later than 45 days after the date of receipt of the application, in accordance with the rules of the Board, unless the Board, prior to such date, issues a written notice of disapproval to, or requests more information from, the prospective registrant.

(2) Treatment. A written notice of disapproval of a completed application under paragraph (1) for registration shall be treated as a disciplinary sanction for purposes of sections 105(d) and 107(c)[15 USCS §§ 7215(d), 7217(c)].

(d) Periodic reports. Each registered public accounting firm shall submit an annual report to the Board, and may be required to report more frequently, as necessary to update the information contained in its application for registration under this section, and to provide to the Board such additional information as the Board or the Commission may specify, in accordance with subsection (b)(2).

(e) Public availability. Registration applications and annual reports required by this subsection, or such portions of such applications or reports as may be designated under rules of the Board, shall be made available for public inspection, subject to rules of the Board or the Commission, and to applicable laws relating to the confidentiality of proprietary, personal, or other information contained in such applications or reports, provided that, in all events, the Board shall protect from public disclosure information reasonably identified by the subject accounting firm as proprietary information.

(f) Registration and annual fees. The Board shall assess and collect a registration fee and an annual fee from each registered public accounting firm, in amounts that are sufficient to recover the costs of processing and reviewing applications and annual reports.

§ 7213. Auditing, quality control, and independence standards and rules

(a) Auditing, quality control, and ethics standards.

(1) In general. The Board shall, by rule, establish, including, to the extent it determines appropriate, through adoption of standards proposed by 1 or more professional groups of accountants designated pursuant to paragraph (3)(A) or advisory groups convened pursuant to paragraph (4), and amend or otherwise modify or alter, such auditing and related attestation standards, such quality control standards, and such ethics standards to be used by registered public accounting firms in the preparation and issuance of audit reports, as required by this Act or the rules of the Commission, or as may be necessary or appropriate in the public interest or for the protection of investors.

(2) Rule requirements. In carrying out paragraph (1), the Board—

(A) shall include in the auditing standards that it adopts, requirements that each registered public accounting firm shall—

(i) prepare, and maintain for a period of not less than 7 years, audit work papers, and other information related to any audit report, in sufficient detail to support the conclusions reached in such report;

(ii) provide a concurring or second partner review and approval of such audit report (and other related information), and concurring approval in its issuance, by a qualified person (as prescribed by the Board) associated with the public accounting firm, other than the person in charge of the audit, or by an independent reviewer (as prescribed by the Board); and

(iii) describe in each audit report the scope of the auditor's testing of the internal control structure and procedures of the issuer, required by section 404(b) [15 USCS § 7262(b)], and present (in such report or in a separate report)—

(I) the findings of the auditor from such testing;

(II) an evaluation of whether such internal control structure and procedures—

(aa) include maintenance of records that in reasonable detail accurately and fairly reflect the transactions and dispositions of the assets of the issuer;

(bb) provide reasonable assurance that transactions are recorded as necessary to permit preparation of financial statements in accordance with generally accepted accounting principles, and that receipts and expenditures of the issuer are being made only in accordance with authorizations of management and directors of the issuer; and

(III) a description, at a minimum, of material weaknesses in such internal controls, and of any material noncompliance found on the basis of such testing.

(B) shall include, in the quality control standards that it adopts with respect to the issuance of audit reports, requirements for every registered public accounting firm relating to—

(i) monitoring of professional ethics and independence from issuers on behalf of which the firm issues audit reports;

(ii) consultation within such firm on accounting and auditing questions;

(iii) supervision of audit work;

(iv) hiring, professional development, advancement of personnel;

(v) the acceptance and continuation of engagements;

(vi) internal inspection; and

(vii) such other requirements as the Board may prescribe, subject to subsection (a)(1).

(3) Authority to adopt other standards.

(A) In general. In carrying out this subsection, the Board—

(i) may adopt as its rules, subject to the terms of section 107 [15 USCS § 7217], any portion of any statement of auditing standards or other professional standards that the Board determines satisfy the requirements of paragraph (1), and that were proposed by 1 or more professional groups of accountants that shall be designated or recognized by the Board, by rule, for such purpose, pursuant to this paragraph or 1 or more advisory groups convened pursuant to paragraph (4); and

(ii) notwithstanding clause (i), shall retain full authority to modify, supplement, revise, or subsequently amend, modify, or repeal, in whole or in part, any portion of any statement described in clause (i).

(B) Initial and transitional standards. The Board shall adopt standards described in subparagraph (A)(i) as initial or transitional standards, to the extent the Board determines necessary, prior to a determination of the Commission under section 101(d) [15 USCS § 7211(d)], and such standards shall be separately approved by the Commission at the time of that determination, without regard to the procedures required by section 107 [15 USCS § 7217] that otherwise would apply to the approval of rules of the Board.

(4) Advisory groups. The Board shall convene, or authorize its staff to convene, such expert advisory groups as may be appropriate, which may include practicing accountants and other experts, as well as representatives of other interested groups, subject to such rules as the Board may prescribe to prevent conflicts of interest, to make recommendations concerning the content (including proposed drafts) of auditing, quality control, ethics, independence, or other standards required to be established under this section.

(b) Independence standards and rules. The Board shall establish such rules as may be necessary or appropriate in the public interest or for the protection of investors, to implement, or as authorized under, title II of this Act.

(c) Cooperation with designated professional groups of accountants and advisory groups.

(1) In general. The Board shall cooperate on an ongoing basis with professional groups of accountants designated under subsection (a)(3)(A) and advisory groups convened under subsection (a)(4) in the examination of the need for changes in any standards subject to its authority under subsection (a), recommend issues for inclusion on the agendas of such designated professional groups of accountants or advisory groups, and take such other steps as it deems appropriate to increase the effectiveness of the standard setting process.

(2) Board responses. The Board shall respond in a timely fashion to requests from designated professional groups of accountants and advisory groups referred to in paragraph (1) for any changes in standards over which the Board has authority.

(d) Evaluation of standard setting process. The Board shall include in the annual report required by section 101(h) [15 USCS § 7211(h)] the results of its standard setting responsibilities during the period to which the report relates, including a discussion of the work of the Board with any designated professional groups of accountants and advisory groups described in paragraphs (3)(A) and (4) of subsection (a), and its pending issues agenda for future standard setting projects.

§ 7214. Inspections of registered public accounting firms

(a) In general. The Board shall conduct a continuing program of inspections to assess the degree of compliance of each registered public accounting firm and associated persons of that firm with this Act, the rules of the Board, the rules of the Commission, or professional standards, in connection with its performance of audits, issuance of audit reports, and related matters involving issuers.

(b) Inspection frequency.

(1) In general. Subject to paragraph (2), inspections required by this section shall be conducted—

(A) annually with respect to each registered public accounting firm that regularly provides audit reports for more than 100 issuers; and

(B) not less frequently than once every 3 years with respect to each registered public accounting firm that regularly provides audit reports for 100 or fewer issuers.

(2) Adjustments to schedules. The Board may, by rule, adjust the inspection schedules set under paragraph (1) if the Board finds that different inspection schedules are consistent with the purposes of this Act, the public interest, and the protection of investors. The Board may conduct special inspections at the request of the Commission or upon its own motion.

(c) Procedures. The Board shall, in each inspection under this section, and in accordance with its rules for such inspections—

(1) identify any act or practice or omission to act by the registered public accounting firm, or by any associated person thereof, revealed by such inspection that may be in violation of this Act, the rules of the Board, the rules of the Commission, the firm's own quality control policies, or professional standards;

(2) report any such act, practice, or omission, if appropriate, to the Commission and each appropriate State regulatory authority; and

(3) begin a formal investigation or take disciplinary action, if appropriate, with respect to any such violation, in accordance with this Act and the rules of the Board.

(d) Conduct of inspections. In conducting an inspection of a registered public accounting firm under this section, the Board shall—

(1) inspect and review selected audit and review engagements of the firm (which may include audit engagements that are the subject of ongoing litigation or other controversy between the firm and 1 or more third parties), performed at various offices and by various associated persons of the firm, as selected by the Board;

(2) evaluate the sufficiency of the quality control system of the firm, and the manner of the documentation and communication of that system by the firm; and

(3) perform such other testing of the audit, supervisory, and quality control procedures of the firm as are necessary or appropriate in light of the purpose of the inspection and the responsibilities of the Board.

(e) Record retention. The rules of the Board may require the retention by registered public accounting firms for inspection purposes of records whose retention is not otherwise required by section 103 [15 USCS § 7213] or the rules issued thereunder.

(f) Procedures for review. The rules of the Board shall provide a procedure for the review of and response to a draft inspection report by the registered public accounting firm under inspection. The Board shall take such action with respect to such response as it considers appropriate (including revising the draft report or continuing or supplementing its inspection activities before issuing a final report), but the text of any such response, appropriately redacted to protect information reasonably identified by the accounting firm as confidential, shall be attached to and made part of the inspection report.

(g) Report. A written report of the findings of the Board for each inspection under this section, subject to subsection (h), shall be—

(1) transmitted, in appropriate detail, to the Commission and each appropriate State regulatory authority, accompanied by any letter or comments by the Board or the inspector, and any letter of response from the registered public accounting firm; and

(2) made available in appropriate detail to the public (subject to section 105(b)(5)(A) [15 USCS § 7215(b)(5)(A)], and to the protection of such confidential and proprietary information as the Board may determine to be appropriate, or as may be required by law), except that no portions of the inspection report that deal with criticisms of or potential defects in the quality control systems of the firm under inspection shall be made public if those criticisms or defects are addressed by the firm, to the satisfaction of the Board, not later than 12 months after the date of the inspection report.

(h) Interim Commission review.

(1) Reviewable matters. A registered public accounting firm may seek review by the Commission, pursuant to such rules as the Commission shall promulgate, if the firm—

(A) has provided the Board with a response, pursuant to rules issued by the Board under subsection (f), to the substance of particular items in a draft inspection report, and disagrees with the assessments contained in any final report prepared by the Board following such response;   or

(B) disagrees with the determination of the Board that criticisms or defects identified in an inspection report have not been addressed to the satisfaction of the Board within 12 months of the date of the inspection report, for purposes of subsection (g)(2).

(2) Treatment of review. Any decision of the Commission with respect to a review under paragraph (1) shall not be reviewable under section 25 of the Securities Exchange Act of 1934 (15 U.S.C. 78y), or deemed to be "final agency action" for purposes of section 704 of title 5, United States Code.

(3) Timing. Review under paragraph (1) may be sought during the 30-day period following the date of the event giving rise to the review under subparagraph (A) or (B) of paragraph (1).

§ 7215. Investigations and disciplinary proceedings

(a) In general. The Board shall establish, by rule, subject to the requirements of this section, fair procedures for the investigation and disciplining of registered public accounting firms and associated persons of such firms.

(b) Investigations.

(1) Authority. In accordance with the rules of the Board, the Board may conduct an investigation of any act or practice, or omission to act, by a registered public accounting firm, any associated person of such firm, or both, that may violate any provision of this Act, the rules of the Board, the provisions of the securities laws relating to the preparation and issuance of audit reports and the obligations and liabilities of accountants with respect thereto, including the rules of the Commis-

sion issued under this Act, or professional standards, regardless of how the act, practice, or omission is brought to the attention of the Board.

(2) Testimony and document production. In addition to such other actions as the Board determines to be necessary or appropriate, the rules of the Board may—

(A) require the testimony of the firm or of any person associated with a registered public accounting firm, with respect to any matter that the Board considers relevant or material to an investigation;

(B) require the production of audit work papers and any other document or information in the possession of a registered public accounting firm or any associated person thereof, wherever domiciled, that the Board considers relevant or material to the investigation, and may inspect the books and records of such firm or associated person to verify the accuracy of any documents or information supplied;

(C) request the testimony of, and production of any document in the possession of, any other person, including any client of a registered public accounting firm that the Board considers relevant or material to an investigation under this section, with appropriate notice, subject to the needs of the investigation, as permitted under the rules of the Board; and

(D) provide for procedures to seek issuance by the Commission, in a manner established by the Commission, of a subpoena to require the testimony of, and production of any document in the possession of, any person, including any client of a registered public accounting firm, that the Board considers relevant or material to an investigation under this section.

(3) Noncooperation with investigations.

(A) In general. If a registered public accounting firm or any associated person thereof refuses to testify, produce documents, or otherwise cooperate with the Board in connection with an investigation under this section, the Board may—

(i) suspend or bar such person from being associated with a registered public accounting firm, or require the registered public accounting firm to end such association;

(ii) suspend or revoke the registration of the public accounting firm; and

(iii) invoke such other lesser sanctions as the Board considers appropriate, and as specified by rule of the Board.

(B) Procedure. Any action taken by the Board under this paragraph shall be subject to the terms of section 107(c) [15 USCS § 7217(c)].

(4) Coordination and referral of investigations.

(A) Coordination. The Board shall notify the Commission of any pending Board investigation involving a potential violation of the securities laws, and thereafter coordinate its work with the work of the Commission's Division of Enforcement, as necessary to protect an ongoing Commission investigation.

(B) Referral. The Board may refer an investigation under this section—

(i) to the Commission;

(ii) to any other Federal functional regulator (as defined in section 509 of the Gramm-Leach-Bliley Act (15 U.S.C. 6809)), in the case of an investigation that concerns an audit report for an institution that is subject to the jurisdiction of such regulator; and

(iii) at the direction of the Commission, to—

(I) the Attorney General of the United States;

(II) the attorney general of 1 or more States; and

(III) the appropriate State regulatory authority.

(5) Use of documents.

(A) Confidentiality. Except as provided in subparagraph (B), all documents and information prepared or received by or specifically for the Board, and deliberations of the Board and its employees and agents, in connection with an inspection under section 104 [15 USCS § 7214] or with an investigation under this section, shall be confidential and privileged as an evidentiary matter (and shall not be subject to civil discovery or other legal process) in any proceeding in any Federal or State court or administrative agency, and shall be exempt from disclosure, in the hands of an agency or establishment of the Federal Government, under the Freedom of Information Act (5 U.S.C. 552a), or otherwise, unless and until presented in connection with a public proceeding or released in accordance with subsection (c).

(B) Availability to government agencies. Without the loss of its status as confidential and privileged in the hands of the Board, all information referred to in subparagraph (A) may—

(i) be made available to the Commission; and

(ii) in the discretion of the Board, when determined by the Board to be necessary to accomplish the purposes of this Act or to protect investors, be made available to—

(I) the Attorney General of the United States;

(II) the appropriate Federal functional regulator (as defined in section 509 of the Gramm-Leach-Bliley Act (15 U.S.C. 6809)), other than the Commission, with respect to an audit report for an institution subject to the jurisdiction of such regulator;

(III) State attorneys general in connection with any criminal investigation; and

(IV) any appropriate State regulatory authority, each of which shall maintain such information as confidential and privileged.

(6) Immunity. Any employee of the Board engaged in carrying out an investigation under this Act shall be immune from any civil liability arising out of such investigation in the same manner and to the same extent as an employee of the Federal Government in similar circumstances.

(c) Disciplinary procedures.

(1) Notification; recordkeeping. The rules of the Board shall provide that in any proceeding by the Board to determine whether a registered public accounting firm, or an associated person thereof, should be disciplined, the Board shall—

(A) bring specific charges with respect to the firm or associated person;

(B) notify such firm or associated person of, and provide to the firm or associated person an opportunity to defend against, such charges; and

(C) keep a record of the proceedings.

(2) Public hearings. Hearings under this section shall not be public, unless otherwise ordered by the Board for good cause shown, with the consent of the parties to such hearing.

(3) Supporting statement. A determination by the Board to impose a sanction under this subsection shall be supported by a statement setting forth—

(A) each act or practice in which the registered public accounting firm, or associated person, has engaged (or omitted to engage), or that forms a basis for all or a part of such sanction;

(B) the specific provision of this Act, the securities laws, the rules of the Board, or professional standards which the Board determines has been violated; and

(C) the sanction imposed, including a justification for that sanction.

(4) Sanctions. If the Board finds, based on all of the facts and circumstances, that a registered public accounting firm or associated person thereof has engaged in any act or practice, or omitted to act, in violation of this Act, the rules of the Board, the provisions of the securities laws relating to the preparation and issuance of audit reports and the obligations and liabilities of accountants with respect thereto, including the rules of the Commission issued under this Act, or professional standards, the Board may impose such disciplinary or remedial sanctions as it determines appropriate, subject to applicable limitations under paragraph (5), including—

(A) temporary suspension or permanent revocation of registration under this title [15 USCS §§ 7211 et seq.];

(B) temporary or permanent suspension or bar of a person from further association with any registered public accounting firm;

(C) temporary or permanent limitation on the activities, functions, or operations of such firm or person (other than in connection with required additional professional education or training);

(D) a civil money penalty for each such violation, in an amount equal to—

(i) not more than $ 100,000 for a natural person or $ 2,000,000 for any other person; and

(ii) in any case to which paragraph (5) applies, not more than $ 750,000 for a natural person or $ 15,000,000 for any other person;

(E) censure;

(F) required additional professional education or training; or

(G) any other appropriate sanction provided for in the rules of the Board.

(5) Intentional or other knowing conduct. The sanctions and penalties described in subparagraphs (A) through (C) and (D)(ii) of paragraph (4) shall only apply to—

(A) intentional or knowing conduct, including reckless conduct, that results in violation of the applicable statutory, regulatory, or professional standard; or

(B) repeated instances of negligent conduct, each resulting in a violation of the applicable statutory, regulatory, or professional standard.

(6) Failure to supervise.

(A) In general. The Board may impose sanctions under this section on a registered accounting firm or upon the supervisory personnel of such firm, if the Board finds that—

(i) the firm has failed reasonably to supervise an associated person, either as required by the rules of the Board relating to auditing or quality control standards, or otherwise, with a view to preventing violations of this Act, the rules of the Board, the provisions of the securities laws relating to the preparation and issuance of audit reports and the obligations and liabilities of accountants with respect thereto, including the rules of the Commission under this Act, or professional standards; and

(ii) such associated person commits a violation of this Act, or any of such rules, laws, or standards.

(B) Rule of construction. No associated person of a registered public accounting firm shall be deemed to have failed reasonably to supervise any other person for purposes of subparagraph (A), if—

(i) there have been established in and for that firm procedures, and a system for applying such procedures, that comply with applicable rules of the Board and that would reasonably be expected to prevent and detect any such violation by such associated person; and

(ii) such person has reasonably discharged the duties and obligations incumbent upon that person by reason of such procedures and system, and had no reasonable cause to believe that such procedures and system were not being complied with.

(7) Effect of suspension.

(A) Association with a public accounting firm. It shall be unlawful for any person that is suspended or barred from being associated with a registered public accounting firm under this subsection willfully to become or remain associated with any registered public accounting firm, or for any registered public accounting firm that knew, or, in the exercise of reasonable care should have known, of the suspension or bar, to permit such an association, without the consent of the Board or the Commission.

(B) Association with an issuer. It shall be unlawful for any person that is suspended or barred from being associated with an issuer under this subsection willfully to become or remain associated with any issuer in an accountancy or a financial management capacity, and for any issuer that knew, or in the exercise of reasonable care should have known, of such suspension or bar, to permit such an association, without the consent of the Board or the Commission.

(d) Reporting of sanctions.

(1) Recipients. If the Board imposes a disciplinary sanction, in accordance with this section, the Board shall report the sanction to—

(A) the Commission;

(B) any appropriate State regulatory authority or any foreign accountancy licensing board with which such firm or person is licensed or certified; and

(C) the public (once any stay on the imposition of such sanction has been lifted).

(2) Contents. The information reported under paragraph (1) shall include—

(A) the name of the sanctioned person;

(B) a description of the sanction and the basis for its imposition; and

(C) such other information as the Board deems appropriate.

(e) Stay of sanctions.

(1) In general. Application to the Commission for review, or the institution by the Commission of review, of any disciplinary action of the Board shall operate as a stay of any such disciplinary action, unless and until the Commission orders (summarily or after notice and opportunity for hearing on the question of a stay, which hearing may consist solely of the submission of affidavits or presentation of oral arguments) that no such stay shall continue to operate.

(2) Expedited procedures. The Commission shall establish for appropriate cases an expedited procedure for consideration and determination of the question of the duration of a stay pending review of any disciplinary action of the Board under this subsection.

§ 7216. Foreign public accounting firms

(a) Applicability to certain foreign firms.

(1) In general. Any foreign public accounting firm that prepares or furnishes an audit report with respect to any issuer, shall be subject to this Act and the rules of the Board and the Commission issued under this Act, in the same manner and to the same extent as a public accounting firm that is organized and operates under the laws of the United States or any State, except that registration pursuant to section 102 [15 USCS § 7212] shall not by itself provide a basis for subjecting such a foreign public accounting firm to the jurisdiction of the Federal or State courts, other than with respect to controversies between such firms and the Board.

(2) Board authority. The Board may, by rule, determine that a foreign public accounting firm (or a class of such firms) that does not issue audit reports nonetheless plays such a substantial role in the preparation and furnishing of such reports for particular issuers, that it is necessary or appropriate, in light of the purposes of this Act and in the public interest or for the protection of investors, that such firm (or class of firms) should be treated as a public accounting firm (or firms) for purposes of registration under, and oversight by the Board in accordance with, this title [15 USCS §§ 7211 et seq.].

(b) Production of audit workpapers.

(1) Consent by foreign firms. If a foreign public accounting firm issues an opinion or otherwise performs material services upon which a registered public accounting firm relies in issuing all or part of any audit report or any opinion contained in an audit report, that foreign public accounting firm shall be deemed to have consented—

(A) to produce its audit workpapers for the Board or the Commission in connection with any investigation by either body with respect to that audit report; and

(B) to be subject to the jurisdiction of the courts of the United States for purposes of enforcement of any request for production of such workpapers.

(2) Consent by domestic firms. A registered public accounting firm that relies upon the opinion of a foreign public accounting firm, as described in paragraph (1), shall be deemed—

(A) to have consented to supplying the audit workpapers of that foreign public accounting firm in response to a request for production by the Board or the Commission; and

(B) to have secured the agreement of that foreign public accounting firm to such production, as a condition of its reliance on the opinion of that foreign public accounting firm.

(c) Exemption authority. The Commission, and the Board, subject to the approval of the Commission, may, by rule, regulation, or order, and as the Commission (or Board) determines necessary or appropriate in the public interest or for the protection of investors, either unconditionally or upon specified terms and conditions exempt any foreign public accounting firm, or any class of such firms, from any provision of this Act or the rules of the Board or the Commission issued under this Act.

(d) Definition. In this section, the term "foreign public accounting firm" means a public accounting firm that is organized and operates under the laws of a foreign government or political subdivision thereof.

§ 7217. Commission oversight of the Board

(a) General oversight responsibility. The Commission shall have oversight and enforcement authority over the Board, as provided in this Act. The provisions of section 17(a)(1) of the Securities Exchange Act of 1934 (15 U.S.C. 78q(a)(1)), and of section 17(b)(1) of the Securities Exchange Act of 1934 (15 U.S.C. 78q(b)(1)) shall apply to the Board as fully as if the Board were a "registered securities association" for purposes of those sections 17(a)(1) and 17(b)(1) [15 USCS § 78q(a)(1), (b)(1)].

(b) Rules of the Board.

(1) Definition. In this section, the term "proposed rule" means any proposed rule of the Board, and any modification of any such rule.

(2) Prior approval required. No rule of the Board shall become effective without prior approval of the Commission in accordance with this section, other than as provided in section 103(a)(3)(B) [15 USCS § 7213(a)(3)(B)] with respect to initial or transitional standards.

(3) Approval criteria. The Commission shall approve a proposed rule, if it finds that the rule is consistent with the requirements of this Act and the securities laws, or is necessary or appropriate in the public interest or for the protection of investors.

(4) Proposed rule procedures. The provisions of paragraphs (1) through (3) of section 19(b) of the Securities Exchange Act of 1934 (15 U.S.C. 78s(b)) shall govern the proposed rules of the Board, as fully as

if the Board were a "registered securities association" for purposes of that section 19(b) [15 USCS § 78s(b)], except that, for purposes of this paragraph—

(A) the phrase "consistent with the requirements of this title and the rules and regulations thereunder applicable to such organization" in section 19(b)(2) of that Act [15 USCS § 78s(b)(2)] shall be deemed to read "consistent with the requirements of title I of the Sarbanes-Oxley Act of 2002 [15 USCS §§ 7211 et seq.], and the rules and regulations issued thereunder applicable to such organization, or as necessary or appropriate in the public interest or for the protection of investors"; and

(B) the phrase "otherwise in furtherance of the purposes of this title" in section 19(b)(3)(C) of that Act [15 USCS § 78s(b)(3)(C)] shall be deemed to read "otherwise in furtherance of the purposes of title I of the Sarbanes-Oxley Act of 2002 [15 USCS §§ 7211 et seq.]".

(5) Commission authority to amend rules of the Board. The provisions of section 19(c) of the Securities Exchange Act of 1934 (15 U.S.C. 78s(c)) shall govern the abrogation, deletion, or addition to portions of the rules of the Board by the Commission as fully as if the Board were a "registered securities association" for purposes of that section 19(c) [15 USCS § 78s(c)], except that the phrase "to conform its rules to the requirements of this title and the rules and regulations thereunder applicable to such organization, or otherwise in furtherance of the purposes of this title" in section 19(c) of that Act [15 USCS § 78s(c)] shall, for purposes of this paragraph, be deemed to read "to assure the fair administration of the Public Company Accounting Oversight Board, conform the rules promulgated by that Board to the requirements of title I of the Sarbanes-Oxley Act of 2002 [15 USCS §§ 7211 et seq.], or otherwise further the purposes of that Act, the securities laws, and the rules and regulations thereunder applicable to that Board".

(c) Commission review of disciplinary action taken by the Board.

(1) Notice of sanction. The Board shall promptly file notice with the Commission of any final sanction on any registered public accounting firm or on any associated person thereof, in such form and containing such information as the Commission, by rule, may prescribe.

(2) Review of sanctions. The provisions of sections 19(d)(2) and 19(e)(1) of the Securities Exchange Act of 1934 (15 U.S.C. 78s(d)(2) and (e)(1)) shall govern the review by the Commission of final disciplinary sanctions imposed by the Board (including sanctions imposed under section 105(b)(3) of this Act [15 USCS § 7215(b)(3)] for noncooperation in an investigation of the Board), as fully as if the Board were a self-regulatory organization and the Commission were the appropriate regulatory agency for such organization for purposes of those sections 19(d)(2) and 19(e)(1) [15 USCS § 78s(d)(2), (e)(1)], except that, for purposes of this paragraph—

(A) section 105(e) of this Act [15 USCS § 7215(e)] (rather than that section 19(d)(2) [15 USCS § 78s(d)(2)]) shall govern the extent to which application for, or institution by the Commission on its own motion of, review of any disciplinary action of the Board operates as a stay of such action;

(B) references in that section 19(e)(1) [15 USCS § 78s(e)(1)] to "members" of such an organization shall be deemed to be references to registered public accounting firms;

(C) the phrase "consistent with the purposes of this title" in that section 19(e)(1) [15 USCS § 78s(e)(1)] shall be deemed to read "consistent with the purposes of this title and title I of the Sarbanes-Oxley Act of 2002 [15 USCS §§ 78a et seq., 7211 et seq.]";

(D) references to rules of the Municipal Securities Rulemaking Board in that section 19(e)(1) [15 USCS § 78s(e)(1)] shall not apply; and

(E) the reference in section 19(e)(2) of the Securities Exchange Act of 1934 [15 USCS § 78s(e)(2)] shall refer instead to section 107(c)(3) of this Act [15 USCS § 7217(c)(3)].

(3) Commission modification authority. The Commission may enhance, modify, cancel, reduce, or require the remission of a sanction imposed by the Board upon a registered public accounting firm or associated person thereof, if the Commission, having due regard for the public interest and the protection of investors, finds, after a proceeding in accordance with this subsection, that the sanction—

(A) is not necessary or appropriate in furtherance of this Act or the securities laws; or

(B) is excessive, oppressive, inadequate, or otherwise not appropriate to the finding or the basis on which the sanction was imposed.

(d) Censure of the Board; other sanctions.

(1) Rescission of Board authority. The Commission, by rule, consistent with the public interest, the protection of investors, and the other

purposes of this Act and the securities laws, may relieve the Board of any responsibility to enforce compliance with any provision of this Act, the securities laws, the rules of the Board, or professional standards.

(2) Censure of the Board; limitations. The Commission may, by order, as it determines necessary or appropriate in the public interest, for the protection of investors, or otherwise in furtherance of the purposes of this Act or the securities laws, censure or impose limitations upon the activities, functions, and operations of the Board, if the Commission finds, on the record, after notice and opportunity for a hearing, that the Board—

(A) has violated or is unable to comply with any provision of this Act, the rules of the Board, or the securities laws; or

(B) without reasonable justification or excuse, has failed to enforce compliance with any such provision or rule, or any professional standard by a registered public accounting firm or an associated person thereof.

(3) Censure of Board members; removal from office. The Commission may, as necessary or appropriate in the public interest, for the protection of investors, or otherwise in furtherance of the purposes of this Act or the securities laws, remove from office or censure any member of the Board, if the Commission finds, on the record, after notice and opportunity for a hearing, that such member—

(A) has willfully violated any provision of this Act, the rules of the Board, or the securities laws;

(B) has willfully abused the authority of that member; or

(C) without reasonable justification or excuse, has failed to enforce compliance with any such provision or rule, or any professional standard by any registered public accounting firm or any associated person thereof.

§ 7218. Accounting standards

(a) [Omitted]

(b) Commission authority. The Commission shall promulgate such rules and regulations to carry out section 19(b) of the Securities Act of 1933 [15 USCS § 77s(b)], as added by this section, as it deems necessary or appropriate in the public interest or for the protection of investors.

(c) No effect on Commission powers. Nothing in this Act, including this section and the amendment made by this section, shall be construed to impair or limit the authority of the Commission to establish accounting principles or standards for purposes of enforcement of the securities laws.

(d) Study and report on adopting principles-based accounting.

(1) Study.

(A) In general. The Commission shall conduct a study on the adoption by the United States financial reporting system of a principles-based accounting system.

(B) Study topics. The study required by subparagraph (A) shall include an examination of—

(i) the extent to which principles-based accounting and financial reporting exists in the United States;

(ii) the length of time required for change from a rules-based to a principles-based financial reporting system;

(iii) the feasibility of and proposed methods by which a principles-based system may be implemented; and

(iv) a thorough economic analysis of the implementation of a principles-based system.

(2) Report. Not later than 1 year after the date of enactment of this Act [enacted July 30, 2002], the Commission shall submit a report on the results of the study required by paragraph (1) to the Committee on Banking, Housing, and Urban Affairs of the Senate and the Committee on Financial Services of the House of Representatives.

§ 7219. Funding

(a) In general. The Board, and the standard setting body designated pursuant to section 19(b) of the Securities Act of 1933 [15 USCS § 77s(b)], as amended by section 108 [15 USCS § 7218], shall be funded as provided in this section.

(b) Annual budgets. The Board and the standard setting body referred to in subsection (a) shall each establish a budget for each fiscal year, which shall be reviewed and approved according to their respective internal procedures not less than 1 month prior to the commencement of the fiscal year to which the budget pertains (or at the beginning of the Board's first fiscal year, which may be a short fiscal year). The budget of the Board shall be subject to approval by the Commission. The budget for the first fiscal year of the Board shall be prepared and approved

promptly following the appointment of the initial five Board members, to permit action by the Board of the organizational tasks contemplated by section 101(d) [15 USCS § 7211(d)].

(c) Sources and uses of funds.

(1) Recoverable budget expenses. The budget of the Board (reduced by any registration or annual fees received under section 102(e) [15 USCS § 7212(e)] for the year preceding the year for which the budget is being computed), and all of the budget of the standard setting body referred to in subsection (a), for each fiscal year of each of those 2 entities, shall be payable from annual accounting support fees, in accordance with subsections (d) and (e). Accounting support fees and other receipts of the Board and of such standard-setting body shall not be considered public monies of the United States.

(2) Funds generated from the collection of monetary penalties. Subject to the availability in advance in an appropriations Act, and notwithstanding subsection (i), all funds collected by the Board as a result of the assessment of monetary penalties shall be used to fund a merit scholarship program for undergraduate and graduate students enrolled in accredited accounting degree programs, which program is to be administered by the Board or by an entity or agent identified by the Board.

(d) Annual accounting support fee for the Board.

(1) Establishment of fee. The Board shall establish, with the approval of the Commission, a reasonable annual accounting support fee (or a formula for the computation thereof), as may be necessary or appropriate to establish and maintain the Board. Such fee may also cover costs incurred in the Board's first fiscal year (which may be a short fiscal year), or may be levied separately with respect to such short fiscal year.

(2) Assessments. The rules of the Board under paragraph (1) shall provide for the equitable allocation, assessment, and collection by the Board (or an agent appointed by the Board) of the fee established under paragraph (1), among issuers, in accordance with subsection (g), allowing for differentiation among classes of issuers, as appropriate.

(e) Annual accounting support fee for standard setting body. The annual accounting support fee for the standard setting body referred to in subsection (a)—

(1) shall be allocated in accordance with subsection (g), and assessed and collected against each issuer, on behalf of the standard setting body, by 1 or more appropriate designated collection agents, as may be necessary or appropriate to pay for the budget and provide for the expenses of that standard setting body, and to provide for an independent, stable source of funding for such body, subject to review by the Commission; and

(2) may differentiate among different classes of issuers.

(f) Limitation on fee. The amount of fees collected under this section for a fiscal year on behalf of the Board or the standards setting body, as the case may be, shall not exceed the recoverable budget expenses of the Board or body, respectively (which may include operating, capital, and accrued items), referred to in subsection (c)(1).

(g) Allocation of accounting support fees among issuers. Any amount due from issuers (or a particular class of issuers) under this section to fund the budget of the Board or the standard setting body referred to in subsection (a) shall be allocated among and payable by each issuer (or each issuer in a particular class, as applicable) in an amount equal to the total of such amount, multiplied by a fraction—

(1) the numerator of which is the average monthly equity market capitalization of the issuer for the 12-month period immediately preceding the beginning of the fiscal year to which such budget relates; and

(2) the denominator of which is the average monthly equity market capitalization of all such issuers for such 12-month period.

(h) [Omitted]

(i) Rule of construction. Nothing in this section shall be construed to render either the Board, the standard setting body referred to in subsection (a), or both, subject to procedures in Congress to authorize or appropriate public funds, or to prevent such organization from utilizing additional sources of revenue for its activities, such as earnings from publication sales, provided that each additional source of revenue shall not jeopardize, in the judgment of the Commission, the actual and perceived independence of such organization.

(j) Start-up expenses of the Board. From the unexpended balances of the appropriations to the Commission for fiscal year 2003, the Secretary of the Treasury is authorized to advance to the Board not to exceed the amount necessary to cover the expenses of the Board during its first fiscal year (which may be a short fiscal year).

Auditor Independence

§ 7231. Exemption authority

The Board may, on a case by case basis, exempt any person, issuer, public accounting firm, or transaction from the prohibition on the provision of services under section 10A(g) of the Securities Exchange Act of 1934 [15 USCS § 78j-1(g)] (as added by this section), to the extent that such exemption is necessary or appropriate in the public interest and is consistent with the protection of investors, and subject to review by the Commission in the same manner as for rules of the Board under section 107 [15 USCS § 7217].

§ 7232. Study of mandatory rotation of registered public accounting firms

(a) Study and review required. The Comptroller General of the United States shall conduct a study and review of the potential effects of requiring the mandatory rotation of registered public accounting firms.

(b) Report required. Not later than 1 year after the date of enactment of this Act [enacted July 30, 2002], the Comptroller General shall submit a report to the Committee on Banking, Housing, and Urban Affairs of the Senate and the Committee on Financial Services of the House of Representatives on the results of the study and review required by this section.

(c) Definition. For purposes of this section, the term "mandatory rotation" refers to the imposition of a limit on the period of years in which a particular registered public accounting firm may be the auditor of record for a particular issuer.

§ 7233. Commission authority

(a) Commission regulations. Not later than 180 days after the date of enactment of this Act [enacted July 30, 2002], the Commission shall issue final regulations to carry out each of subsections (g) through (l) of section 10A of the Securities Exchange Act of 1934 [15 USCS § 78j-1], as added by this title.

(b) Auditor independence. It shall be unlawful for any registered public accounting firm (or an associated person thereof, as applicable) to prepare or issue any audit report with respect to any issuer, if the firm or associated person engages in any activity with respect to that issuer prohibited by any of subsections (g) through (l) of section 10A of the Securities Exchange Act of 1934 [15 USCS § 78j-1], as added by this title, or any rule or regulation of the Commission or of the Board issued thereunder.

§ 7234. Considerations by appropriate State regulatory authorities

In supervising nonregistered public accounting firms and their associated persons, appropriate State regulatory authorities should make an independent determination of the proper standards applicable, particularly taking into consideration the size and nature of the business of the accounting firms they supervise and the size and nature of the business of the clients of those firms. The standards applied by the Board under this Act should not be presumed to be applicable for purposes of this section for small and medium sized nonregistered public accounting firms.

Corporate Responsibility

§ 7241. Corporate responsibility for financial reports

(a) Regulations required. The Commission shall, by rule, require, for each company filing periodic reports under section 13(a) or 15(d) of the Securities Exchange Act of 1934 (15 U.S.C. 78m, 78o(d)), that the principal executive officer or officers and the principal financial officer or officers, or persons performing similar functions, certify in each annual or quarterly report filed or submitted under either such section of such Act that—

(1) the signing officer has reviewed the report;

(2) based on the officer's knowledge, the report does not contain any untrue statement of a material fact or omit to state a material fact necessary in order to make the statements made, in light of the circumstances under which such statements were made, not misleading;

(3) based on such officer's knowledge, the financial statements, and other financial information included in the report, fairly present in all material respects the financial condition and results of operations of the issuer as of, and for, the periods presented in the report;

(4) the signing officers—

(A) are responsible for establishing and maintaining internal controls;

(B) have designed such internal controls to ensure that material information relating to the issuer and its consolidated subsidiaries is made known to such officers by others within those entities, particu-

larly during the period in which the periodic reports are being prepared;

(C) have evaluated the effectiveness of the issuer's internal controls as of a date within 90 days prior to the report; and

(D) have presented in the report their conclusions about the effectiveness of their internal controls based on their evaluation as of that date;

(5) the signing officers have disclosed to the issuer's auditors and the audit committee of the board of directors (or persons fulfilling the equivalent function)—

(A) all significant deficiencies in the design or operation of internal controls which could adversely affect the issuer's ability to record, process, summarize, and report financial data and have identified for the issuer's auditors any material weaknesses in internal controls; and

(B) any fraud, whether or not material, that involves management or other employees who have a significant role in the issuer's internal controls; and

(6) the signing officers have indicated in the report whether or not there were significant changes in internal controls or in other factors that could significantly affect internal controls subsequent to the date of their evaluation, including any corrective actions with regard to significant deficiencies and material weaknesses.

(b) Foreign reincorporations have no effect. Nothing in this section 302 [this section] shall be interpreted or applied in any way to allow any issuer to lessen the legal force of the statement required under this section 302 [this section], by an issuer having reincorporated or having engaged in any other transaction that resulted in the transfer of the corporate domicile or offices of the issuer from inside the United States to outside of the United States.

(c) Deadline. The rules required by subsection (a) shall be effective not later than 30 days after the date of enactment of this Act [enacted July 30, 2002].

§ 7242. Improper influence on conduct of audits

(a) Rules to prohibit. It shall be unlawful, in contravention of such rules or regulations as the Commission shall prescribe as necessary and appropriate in the public interest or for the protection of investors, for any officer or director of an issuer, or any other person acting under the direction thereof, to take any action to fraudulently influence, coerce, manipulate, or mislead any independent public or certified accountant engaged in the performance of an audit of the financial statements of that issuer for the purpose of rendering such financial statements materially misleading.

(b) Enforcement. In any civil proceeding, the Commission shall have exclusive authority to enforce this section and any rule or regulation issued under this section.

(c) No preemption of other law. The provisions of subsection (a) shall be in addition to, and shall not supersede or preempt, any other provision of law or any rule or regulation issued thereunder.

(d) Deadline for rulemaking. The Commission shall—

(1) propose the rules or regulations required by this section, not later than 90 days after the date of enactment of this Act [enacted July 30, 2002]; and

(2) issue final rules or regulations required by this section, not later than 270 days after that date of enactment [enacted July 30, 2002].

§ 7243. Forfeiture of certain bonuses and profits

(a) Additional compensation prior to noncompliance with commission financial reporting requirements. If an issuer is required to prepare an accounting restatement due to the material noncompliance of the issuer, as a result of misconduct, with any financial reporting requirement under the securities laws, the chief executive officer and chief financial officer of the issuer shall reimburse the issuer for—

(1) any bonus or other incentive-based or equity-based compensation received by that person from the issuer during the 12-month period following the first public issuance or filing with the Commission (whichever first occurs) of the financial document embodying such financial reporting requirement; and

(2) any profits realized from the sale of securities of the issuer during that 12-month period.

(b) Commission exemption authority. The Commission may exempt any person from the application of subsection (a), as it deems necessary and appropriate.

§ 7244. Insider trades during pension fund blackout periods

(a) Prohibition of insider trading during pension fund blackout periods.

(1) In general. Except to the extent otherwise provided by rule of the Commission pursuant to paragraph (3), it shall be unlawful for any director or executive officer of an issuer of any equity security (other than an exempted security), directly or indirectly, to purchase, sell, or otherwise acquire or transfer any equity security of the issuer (other than an exempted security) during any blackout period with respect to such equity security if such director or officer acquires such equity security in connection with his or her service or employment as a director or executive officer.

(2) Remedy.

(A) In general. Any profit realized by a director or executive officer referred to in paragraph (1) from any purchase, sale, or other acquisition or transfer in violation of this subsection shall inure to and be recoverable by the issuer, irrespective of any intention on the part of such director or executive officer in entering into the transaction.

(B) Actions to recover profits. An action to recover profits in accordance with this subsection may be instituted at law or in equity in any court of competent jurisdiction by the issuer, or by the owner of any security of the issuer in the name and in behalf of the issuer if the issuer fails or refuses to bring such action within 60 days after the date of request, or fails diligently to prosecute the action thereafter, except that no such suit shall be brought more than 2 years after the date on which such profit was realized.

(3) Rulemaking authorized. The Commission shall, in consultation with the Secretary of Labor, issue rules to clarify the application of this subsection and to prevent evasion thereof. Such rules shall provide for the application of the requirements of paragraph (1) with respect to entities treated as a single employer with respect to an issuer under section 414(b), (c), (m), or (o) of the Internal Revenue Code of 1986 [26 USCS § 414(b), (c), (m), or (o)] to the extent necessary to clarify the application of such requirements and to prevent evasion thereof. Such rules may also provide for appropriate exceptions from the requirements of this subsection, including exceptions for purchases pursuant to an automatic dividend reinvestment program or purchases or sales made pursuant to an advance election.

(4) Blackout period. For purposes of this subsection, the term "blackout period", with respect to the equity securities of any issuer—

(A) means any period of more than 3 consecutive business days during which the ability of not fewer than 50 percent of the participants or beneficiaries under all individual account plans maintained by the issuer to purchase, sell, or otherwise acquire or transfer an interest in any equity of such issuer held in such an individual account plan is temporarily suspended by the issuer or by a fiduciary of the plan; and

(B) does not include, under regulations which shall be prescribed by the Commission—

(i) a regularly scheduled period in which the participants and beneficiaries may not purchase, sell, or otherwise acquire or transfer an interest in any equity of such issuer, if such period is—

(I) incorporated into the individual account plan; and

(II) timely disclosed to employees before becoming participants under the individual account plan or as a subsequent amendment to the plan; or

(ii) any suspension described in subparagraph (A) that is imposed solely in connection with persons becoming participants or beneficiaries, or ceasing to be participants or beneficiaries, in an individual account plan by reason of a corporate merger, acquisition, divestiture, or similar transaction involving the plan or plan sponsor.

(5) Individual account plan. For purposes of this subsection, the term "individual account plan" has the meaning provided in section 3(34) of the Employee Retirement Income Security Act of 1974 (29 U.S.C. 1002(34), except that such term shall not include a one-participant retirement plan (within the meaning of section 101(i)(8)(B) of such Act (29 U.S.C. 1021(i)(8)(B))).

(6) Notice to directors, executive officers, and the Commission. In any case in which a director or executive officer is subject to the requirements of this subsection in connection with a blackout period (as defined in paragraph (4)) with respect to any equity securities, the issuer of such equity securities shall timely notify such director or officer and the Securities and Exchange Commission of such blackout period.

(b) Notice requirements to participants and beneficiaries under ERISA.

(1) [Omitted]

(2) Issuance of initial guidance and model notice. The Secretary of Labor shall issue initial guidance and a model notice pursuant to sec-

tion 101(i)(6) of the Employee Retirement Income Security Act of 1974 [29 USCS § 1021(i)(6)] (as added by this subsection) not later than January 1, 2003. Not later than 75 days after the date of the enactment of this Act [enacted July 30, 2002, the Secretary shall promulgate interim final rules necessary to carry out the amendments made by this subsection.

(3) [Omitted]

[(4)](3) Plan amendments. If any amendment made by this subsection requires an amendment to any plan, such plan amendment shall not be required to be made before the first plan year beginning on or after the effective date of this section, if—

(A) during the period after such amendment made by this subsection takes effect and before such first plan year, the plan is operated in good faith compliance with the requirements of such amendment made by this subsection, and

(B) such plan amendment applies retroactively to the period after such amendment made by this subsection takes effect and before such first plan year.

(c) Effective date. The provisions of this section (including the amendments made thereby) shall take effect 180 days after the date of the enactment of this Act [enacted July 30, 2002]. Good faith compliance with the requirements of such provisions in advance of the issuance of applicable regulations thereunder shall be treated as compliance with such provisions.

§ 7245. Rules of professional responsibility for attorneys

Not later than 180 days after the date of enactment of this Act [enacted July 30, 2002], the Commission shall issue rules, in the public interest and for the protection of investors, setting forth minimum standards of professional conduct for attorneys appearing and practicing before the Commission in any way in the representation of issuers, including a rule—

(1) requiring an attorney to report evidence of a material violation of securities law or breach of fiduciary duty or similar violation by the company or any agent thereof, to the chief legal counsel or the chief executive officer of the company (or the equivalent thereof); and

(2) if the counsel or officer does not appropriately respond to the evidence (adopting, as necessary, appropriate remedial measures or sanctions with respect to the violation), requiring the attorney to report the evidence to the audit committee of the board of directors of the issuer or to another committee of the board of directors comprised solely of directors not employed directly or indirectly by the issuer, or to the board of directors.

§ 7246. Fair funds for investors

(a) Civil penalties added to disgorgement funds for the relief of victims. If in any judicial or administrative action brought by the Commission under the securities laws (as such term is defined in section 3(a)(47) of the Securities Exchange Act of 1934 (15 U.S.C. 78c(a)(47)) the Commission obtains an order requiring disgorgement against any person for a violation of such laws or the rules or regulations thereunder, or such person agrees in settlement of any such action to such disgorgement, and the Commission also obtains pursuant to such laws a civil penalty against such person, the amount of such civil penalty shall, on the motion or at the direction of the Commission, be added to and become part of the disgorgement fund for the benefit of the victims of such violation.

(b) Acceptance of additional donations. The Commission is authorized to accept, hold, administer, and utilize gifts, bequests and devises of property, both real and personal, to the United States for a disgorgement fund described in subsection (a). Such gifts, bequests, and devises of money and proceeds from sales of other property received as gifts, bequests, or devises shall be deposited in the disgorgement fund and shall be available for allocation in accordance with subsection (a).

(c) Study required.

(1) Subject of study. The Commission shall review and analyze—

(A) enforcement actions by the Commission over the five years preceding the date of the enactment of this Act [enacted July 30, 2002] that have included proceedings to obtain civil penalties or disgorgements to identify areas where such proceedings may be utilized to efficiently, effectively, and fairly provide restitution for injured investors; and

(B) other methods to more efficiently, effectively, and fairly provide restitution to injured investors, including methods to improve the collection rates for civil penalties and disgorgements.

(2) Report required. The Commission shall report its findings to the

Committee on Financial Services of the House of Representatives and the Committee on Banking, Housing, and Urban Affairs of the Senate within 180 days after of the date of the enactment of this Act [enacted July 30, 2002], and shall use such findings to revise its rules and regulations as necessary. The report shall include a discussion of regulatory or legislative actions that are recommended or that may be necessary to address concerns identified in the study.

(d) [Omitted]

(e) Definition. As used in this section, the term "disgorgement fund" means a fund established in any administrative or judicial proceeding described in subsection (a).

Enhanced Financial Disclosures

§ 7261. Disclosures in periodic reports

(a) [Omitted]

(b) Commission rules on pro forma figures. Not later than 180 days after the date of enactment of the Sarbanes-Oxley Act fo [of] 2002 [enacted July 30, 2002], the Commission shall issue final rules providing that pro forma financial information included in any periodic or other report filed with the Commission pursuant to the securities laws, or in any public disclosure or press or other release, shall be presented in a manner that—

(1) does not contain an untrue statement of a material fact or omit to state a material fact necessary in order to make the pro forma financial information, in light of the circumstances under which it is presented, not misleading; and

(2) reconciles it with the financial condition and results of operations of the issuer under generally accepted accounting principles.

(c) Study and report on special purpose entities.

(1) Study required. The Commission shall, not later than 1 year after the effective date of adoption of off-balance sheet disclosure rules required by section 13(j) of the Securities Exchange Act of 1934 [15 USCS § 78m(j)], as added by this section, complete a study of filings by issuers and their disclosures to determine—

(A) the extent of off-balance sheet transactions, including assets, liabilities, leases, losses, and the use of special purpose entities; and

(B) whether generally accepted accounting rules result in financial statements of issuers reflecting the economics of such off-balance sheet transactions to investors in a transparent fashion.

(2) Report and recommendations. Not later than 6 months after the date of completion of the study required by paragraph (1), the Commission shall submit a report to the President, the Committee on Banking, Housing, and Urban Affairs of the Senate, and the Committee on Financial Services of the House of Representatives, setting forth—

(A) the amount or an estimate of the amount of off-balance sheet transactions, including assets, liabilities, leases, and losses of, and the use of special purpose entities by, issuers filing periodic reports pursuant to section 13 or 15 of the Securities Exchange Act of 1934 [15 USCS § 78m or 78o];

(B) the extent to which special purpose entities are used to facilitate off-balance sheet transactions;

(C) whether generally accepted accounting principles or the rules of the Commission result in financial statements of issuers reflecting the economics of such transactions to investors in a transparent fashion;

(D) whether generally accepted accounting principles specifically result in the consolidation of special purpose entities sponsored by an issuer in cases in which the issuer has the majority of the risks and rewards of the special purpose entity; and

(E) any recommendations of the Commission for improving the transparency and quality of reporting off-balance sheet transactions in the financial statements and disclosures required to be filed by an issuer with the Commission.

§ 7262. Management assessment of internal controls

(a) Rules required. The Commission shall prescribe rules requiring each annual report required by section 13(a) or 15(d) of the Securities Exchange Act of 1934 (15 U.S.C. 78m or 78o(d)) to contain an internal control report, which shall—

(1) state the responsibility of management for establishing and maintaining an adequate internal control structure and procedures for financial reporting; and

(2) contain an assessment, as of the end of the most recent fiscal year of the issuer, of the effectiveness of the internal control structure and procedures of the issuer for financial reporting.

(b) Internal control evaluation and reporting. With respect to the inter-

nal control assessment required by subsection (a), each registered public accounting firm that prepares or issues the audit report for the issuer shall attest to, and report on, the assessment made by the management of the issuer. An attestation made under this subsection shall be made in accordance with standards for attestation engagements issued or adopted by the Board. Any such attestation shall not be the subject of a separate engagement.

§ 7263. Exemption

Nothing in section 401 [15 USCS § 7261], 402, or 404 [15 USCS § 7262], the amendments made by those sections, or the rules of the Commission under those sections shall apply to any investment company registered under section 8 of the Investment Company Act of 1940 (15 U.S.C. 80a-8).

§ 7264. Code of ethics for senior financial officers

(a) Code of ethics disclosure. The Commission shall issue rules to require each issuer, together with periodic reports required pursuant to section 13(a) or 15(d) of the Securities Exchange Act of 1934 [15 USCS § 78m(a) or 78o(d)], to disclose whether or not, and if not, the reason therefor, such issuer has adopted a code of ethics for senior financial officers, applicable to its principal financial officer and comptroller or principal accounting officer, or persons performing similar functions.

(b) Changes in codes of ethics. The Commission shall revise its regulations concerning matters requiring prompt disclosure on Form 8-K (or any successor thereto) to require the immediate disclosure, by means of the filing of such form, dissemination by the Internet or by other electronic means, by any issuer of any change in or waiver of the code of ethics for senior financial officers.

(c) Definition. In this section, the term "code of ethics" means such standards as are reasonably necessary to promote—

(1) honest and ethical conduct, including the ethical handling of actual or apparent conflicts of interest between personal and professional relationships;

(2) full, fair, accurate, timely, and understandable disclosure in the periodic reports required to be filed by the issuer; and

(3) compliance with applicable governmental rules and regulations.

(d) Deadline for rulemaking. The Commission shall—

(1) propose rules to implement this section, not later than 90 days after the date of enactment of this Act [enacted July 30, 2002]; and

(2) issue final rules to implement this section, not later than 180 days after that date of enactment.

§ 7265. Disclosure of audit committee financial expert

(a) Rules defining "financial expert". The Commission shall issue rules, as necessary or appropriate in the public interest and consistent with the protection of investors, to require each issuer, together with periodic reports required pursuant to sections 13(a) and 15(d) of the Securities Exchange Act of 1934 [15 USCS §§ 78m(a), 78o(d)], to disclose whether or not, and if not, the reasons therefor, the audit committee of that issuer is comprised of at least 1 member who is a financial expert, as such term is defined by the Commission.

(b) Considerations. In defining the term "financial expert" for purposes of subsection (a), the Commission shall consider whether a person has, through education and experience as a public accountant or auditor or a principal financial officer, comptroller, or principal accounting officer of an issuer, or from a position involving the performance of similar functions—

(1) an understanding of generally accepted accounting principles and financial statements;

(2) experience in—

(A) the preparation or auditing of financial statements of generally comparable issuers; and

(B) the application of such principles in connection with the accounting for estimates, accruals, and reserves;

(3) experience with internal accounting controls; and

(4) an understanding of audit committee functions.

(c) Deadline for rulemaking. The Commission shall—

(1) propose rules to implement this section, not later than 90 days after the date of enactment of this Act [enacted July 30, 2002]; and

(2) issue final rules to implement this section, not later than 180 days after that date of enactment.

§ 7266. Enhanced review of periodic disclosures by issuers

(a) Regular and systematic review. The Commission shall review disclosures made by issuers reporting under section 13(a) of the Securities Exchange Act of 1934 [15 USCS § 78m(a)] (including reports filed on Form 10-K), and which have a class of securities listed on a national securities exchange or traded on an automated quotation facility of a national securities association, on a regular and systematic basis for the protection of investors. Such review shall include a review of an issuer's financial statement.

Federal Trade Commission Act 1914
Title 15. Commerce and Trade
Chapter 2. Federal Trade Commission; Promotion of Export Trade and Prevention of Unifair Methods of Competition

§ 41. Federal Trade Commission established; membership; vacancies; A commission is created and established, to be known as the Federal Trade Commission (hereinafter referred to as the commission), which shall be composed of five commissioners, who shall be appointed by the President, by and with the advice and consent of the Senate. Not more than three of the commissioners shall be members of the same political party. The first commissioners appointed shall continue in office for terms of three, four, five, six, and seven years, respectively, from the date of taking effect of this Act, the term of each to be designated by the President, but their successors shall be appointed for terms of seven years, except that any person chosen to fill a vacancy shall be appointed only for the unexpired term of the commissioner whom he shall succeed: Provided, however, That upon the expiration of his term of office a Commissioner shall continue to serve until his successor shall have been appointed and shall have qualified. The commission [President] shall choose a chairman from its own [the commission's] membership. No commissioner shall engage in any other business, vocation, or employment. Any commissioner may be removed by the President for inefficiency, neglect of duty, or malfeasance in office. A vacancy in the commission shall not impair the right of the remaining commissioners to exercise all the powers of the commission.

§ 44. Definitions
The words defined in this section shall have the following meaning when found in this Act, to wit:
"Commerce" means commerce among the several States or with foreign nations, or in any Territory of the United States or in the District of Columbia, or between any such Territory and another, or between any such Territory and any State or foreign nation, or between the District of Columbia and any State or Territory or foreign nation.
"Corporation" shall be deemed to include any company, trust, so-called Massachusetts trust, or association, incorporated or unincorporated, which is organized to carry on business for its own profit or that of its members, and has shares of capital or capital stock or certificates of interest, and any company, trust, so-called Massachusetts trust, or association, incorporated or unincorporated, without shares of capital or capital stock or certificates of interest, except partnerships, which is organized to carry on business for its own profit or that of its members.
"Documentary evidence" includes all documents, papers, correspondence, books of account, and financial and corporate records.
"Acts to regulate commerce" means the Act entitled "An Act to regulate commerce," approved February 14, 1887, and all Acts amendatory thereof and supplementary thereto [49 USCS §§ 10101 et seq.] and the Communications Act of 1934 and all Acts amendatory thereof and supplementary thereto.
"Antitrust Acts" means the Act entitled "An Act to protect trade and commerce against unlawful restraints and monopolies," approved July 2, 1890; also sections 73 to 76 inclusive, of an Act entitled "An Act to reduce taxation, to provide revenue for the Government, and for other purposes," approved August 27, 1894 [15 USCS §§ 8-11]; also the Act entitled "An Act to amend sections 73 and 76, of the Act of August 27, 1894, entitled 'An Act to reduce taxation, to provide revenue for the Government, and for other purposes,'" approved February 12, 1913 [amending 15 USCS §§ 8, 11]; and also the Act entitled "An Act to supplement existing laws against unlawful restraints and monopolies, and for other purposes," approved October 15, 1914.
"Banks" means the types of banks and other financial institutions referred to in section 18(f)(2) [15 USCS § 57a(f)(2)].
§ 45. Unfair methods of competition unlawful; prevention by Commission
(a) Declaration of unlawfulness; power to prohibit unfair practices; inapplicability to foreign trade.
  (1) Unfair methods of competition in or affecting commerce, and unfair or deceptive acts or practices in or affecting commerce, are

hereby declared unlawful.
  (2) The Commission is hereby empowered and directed to prevent persons, partnerships, or corporations, except banks, savings and loan institutions described in section 18(f)(3) [15 USCS § 57a(f)(3)], Federal credit unions described in section 18(f)(4) [15 USCS § 57a(f)(4)], common carriers subject to the Acts to regulate commerce, air carriers and foreign air carriers subject to the Federal Aviation Act of 1958 [49 USCS §§ 40101 et seq.], and persons, partnerships, or corporations insofar as they are subject to the Packers and Stockyards Act, 1921, as amended [7 USCS §§ 181 et seq.], except as provided in section 406(b) of said Act [7 USCS § 227(b)], from using unfair methods of competition in or affecting commerce and unfair or deceptive acts or practices in or affecting commerce.
  (3) This subsection shall not apply to unfair methods of competition involving commerce with foreign nations (other than import commerce) unless—
    (A) such methods of competition have a direct, substantial, and reasonably foreseeable effect—
      (i) on commerce which is not commerce with foreign nations, or on import commerce with foreign nations; or
      (ii) on export commerce with foreign nations, of a person engaged in such commerce in the United States; and
    (B) such effect gives rise to a claim under the provisions of this subsection, other than this paragraph.
  If this subsection applies to such methods of competition only because of the operation of subparagraph (A)(ii), this subsection shall apply to such conduct only for injury to export business in the United States.
(b) Proceeding by Commission; modifying and setting aside orders. Whenever the Commission shall have reason to believe that any such person, partnership, or corporation has been or is using any unfair method of competition or unfair or deceptive act or practice in or affecting commerce, and if it shall appear to the Commission that a proceeding by it in respect thereof would be to the interest of the public, it shall issue and serve upon such person, partnership, or corporation a complaint stating its charges in that respect and containing a notice of a hearing upon a day and at a place therein fixed at least thirty days after the service of said complaint. The person, partnership, or corporation so complained of shall have the right to appear at the place and time so fixed and show cause why an order should not be entered by the Commission requiring such person, partnership, or corporation to cease and desist from the violation of the law so charged in said complaint. Any person, partnership, or corporation may make application, and upon good cause shown may be allowed by the Commission to intervene and appear in said proceeding by counsel or in person. The testimony in any such proceeding shall be reduced to writing and filed in the office of the Commission. If upon such hearing the Commission shall be of the opinion that the method of competition or the act or practice in question is prohibited by this Act, it shall make a report in writing in which it shall state its findings as to the facts and shall issue and cause to be served on such person, partnership, or corporation an order requiring such person, partnership, or corporation to cease and desist from using such method of competition or such act or practice. Until the expiration of the time allowed for filing a petition for review, if no such petition has been duly filed within such time, or, if a petition for review has been filed within such time then until the record in the proceeding has been filed in a court of appeals of the United States, as hereinafter provided, the Commission may at any time, upon such notice and in such manner as it shall deem proper, modify or set aside, in whole or in part, any report or any order made or issued by it under this section. After the expiration of the time allowed for filing a petition for review, if no such petition has been duly filed within such time, the Commission may at any time, after notice and opportunity for hearing, reopen and alter, modify, or set aside, in whole or in part, any report or order made or issued by it under this section, whenever in the opinion of the Commission conditions of fact or of law have so changed as to require such action or if the public interest shall so require, except that (1) the said person, partnership, or corporation may, within sixty days after the service upon him or it of said report or order entered after such a reopening, obtain a review thereof in the appropriate court of appeals of the United States, in the manner provided in subsection (c) of this section; and (2) in the case of an order, the Commission shall reopen any such order to consider whether such order (including any affirmative relief provision contained in such order)

should be altered, modified, or set aside, in whole or in part, if the person, partnership, or corporation involved files a request with the Commission which makes a satisfactory showing that changed conditions of law or fact require such order to be altered, modified, or set aside, in whole or in part. The Commission shall determine whether to alter, modify, or set aside any order of the Commission in response to a request made by a person, partnership, or corporation under paragraph [clause] (2) not later than 120 days after the date of the filing of such request.

(c) Review of order; rehearing. Any person, partnership, or corporation required by an order of the Commission to cease and desist from using any method of competition or act or practice may obtain a review of such order in the [circuit] court of appeals of the United States, within any circuit where the method of competition or the act or practice in question was used or where such person, partnership, or corporation resides or carries on business, by filing in the court, within sixty days from the date of the service of such order, a written petition praying that the order of the Commission be set aside. A copy of such petition shall be forthwith transmitted by the clerk of the court to the Commission, and thereupon the Commission shall file in the court the record in the proceeding, as provided in section 2112 of title 28, United States Code. Upon such filing of the petition the court shall have jurisdiction of the proceeding and of the question determined therein concurrently with the Commission until the filing of the record and shall have power to make and enter a decree affirming, modifying, or setting aside the order of the Commission, and enforcing the same to the extent that such order is affirmed and to issue such writs as are ancillary to its jurisdiction or are necessary in its judgment to prevent injury to the public or to competitors pendente lite. The findings of the Commission as to the facts, if supported by evidence, shall be conclusive. To the extent that the order of the Commission is affirmed, the court shall thereupon issue its own order commanding obedience to the terms of such order of the Commission. If either party shall apply to the court for leave to adduce additional evidence, and shall show to the satisfaction of the court that such additional evidence is material and that there were reasonable grounds for the failure to adduce such evidence in the proceeding before the Commission, the court may order such additional evidence to be taken before the Commission and to be adduced upon the hearing in such manner and upon such terms and conditions as to the court may seem proper. The Commission may modify its findings as to the facts, or make new findings, by reason of the additional evidence so taken, and it shall file such modified or new findings, which, if supported by evidence, shall be conclusive, and its recommendation, if any, for the modification or setting aside of its original order, with the return of such additional evidence. The judgment and decree of the court shall be final, except that the same shall be subject to review by the Supreme Court upon certiorari, as provided in section 240 of the Judicial Code [28 USCS § 1254].

(d) Jurisdiction of court. Upon the filing of the record with it the jurisdiction of the [circuit] court of appeals of the United States to affirm, enforce, modify, or set aside orders of the Commission shall be exclusive.

(e) Extension from liability. No order of the Commission or judgment of court to enforce the same shall in anywise relieve or absolve any person, partnership, or corporation from any liability under the Antitrust Acts.

(f) Service of complaints, orders and other processes; return. Complaints, orders, and other processes of the Commission under this section may be served by anyone duly authorized by the Commission, either (a) by delivering a copy thereof to the person to be served, or to a member of the partnership to be served, or the president, secretary, or other executive officer or a director of the corporation to be served; or (b) by leaving a copy thereof at the residence or the principal office or place of business of such person, partnership, or corporation; or (c) by mailing a copy thereof by registered mail or by certified mail addressed to such person, partnership, or corporation at his or its residence or principal office or place of business. The verified return by the person so serving said complaint, order, or other process setting forth the manner of said service shall be proof of the same, and the return post office receipt for said complaint, order, or other process mailed by registered mail or by certified mail as aforesaid shall be proof of the service of the same.

(g) Finality of order. An order of the Commission to cease and desist shall become final—

(1) Upon the expiration of the time allowed for filing a petition for review, if no such petition has been duly filed within such time; but the Commission may thereafter modify or set aside its order to the extent provided in the last sentence of subsection (b).

(2) Except as to any order provision subject to paragraph (4), upon the sixtieth day after such order is served, if a petition for review has been duly filed; except that any such order may be stayed, in whole or in part and subject to such conditions as may be appropriate, by—

(A) the Commission;

(B) an appropriate court of appeals of the United States, if (i) a petition for review of such order is pending in such court, and (ii) an application for such a stay was previously submitted to the Commission and the Commission, within the 30-day period beginning on the date the application was received by the Commission, either denied the application or did not grant or deny the application; or

(C) the Supreme Court, if an applicable petition for certiorari is pending.

(3) For purposes of subsection (m)(1)(B) and of section 19(a)(2) [15 USCS § 57b(a)(2)], if a petition for review of the order of the Commission has been filed—

(A) upon the expiration of the time allowed for filing a petition for certiorari, if the order of the Commission has been affirmed or the petition for review has been dismissed by the court of appeals and no petition for certiorari has been duly filed;

(B) upon the denial of a petition for certiorari, if the order of the Commission has been affirmed or the petition for review has been dismissed by the court of appeals; or

(C) upon the expiration of 30 days from the date of issuance of a mandate of the Supreme Court directing that the order of the Commission be affirmed or the petition for review be dismissed.

(4) In the case of an order provision requiring a person, partnership, or corporation to divest itself of stock, other share capital, or assets, if a petition for review of such order of the Commission has been filed—

(A) upon the expiration of the time allowed for filing a petition for certiorari, if the order of the Commission has been affirmed or the petition for review has been dismissed by the court of appeals and no petition for certiorari has been duly filed;

(B) upon the denial of a petition for certiorari, if the order of the Commission has been affirmed or the petition for review has been dismissed by the court of appeals; or

(C) upon the expiration of 30 days from the date of issuance of a mandate of the Supreme Court directing that the order of the Commission be affirmed or the petition for review be dismissed.

(h) Modification or setting aside of order by Supreme Court. If the Supreme Court directs that the order of the Commission be modified or set aside, the order of the Commission rendered in accordance with the mandate of the Supreme Court shall become final upon the expiration of thirty days from the time it was rendered, unless within such thirty days either party has instituted proceedings to have such order corrected to accord with the mandate, in which event the order of the Commission shall become final when so corrected.

(i) Modification or setting aside of order by Court of Appeals. If the order of the Commission is modified or set aside by the [circuit] court of appeals, and if (1) the time allowed for filing a petition for certiorari has expired and no such petition has been duly filed, or (2) the petition for certiorari has been denied, or (3) the decision of the court has been affirmed by the Supreme Court, then the order of the Commission rendered in accordance with the mandate of the court of appeals shall become final on the expiration of thirty days from the time such order of the Commission was rendered, unless within such thirty days either party has instituted proceedings to have such order corrected so that it will accord with the mandate, in which event the order of the Commission shall become final when so corrected.

(j) Rehearing upon order or remand. If the Supreme Court orders a rehearing; or if the case is remanded by the [circuit] court of appeals to the Commission for a rehearing, and if (1) the time allowed for filing a petition for certiorari has expired, and no such petition has been duly filed, or (2) the petition for certiorari has been denied, or (3) the decision of the court has been affirmed by the Supreme Court, then the order of the Commission rendered upon such rehearing shall become final in the same manner as though no prior order of the Commission had been rendered.

(k) "Mandate" defined. As used in this section the term "mandate," in case a mandate has been recalled prior to the expiration of thirty days from the date of issuance thereof, means the final mandate.

(l) Penalty for violation of order; injunctions and other appropriate equitable relief. Any person, partnership, or corporation who violates an order of the Commission after it has become final, and while such order is in effect, shall forfeit and pay to the United States a civil penalty of not more than $ 10,000 for each violation, which shall accrue to the United States and may be recovered in a civil action brought by the Attorney General of the United States. Each separate violation of such an order shall be a separate offense, except that in the case of a violation through continuing failure to obey or neglect to obey a final order of the Commission, each day of continuance of such failure or neglect shall be deemed a separate offense. In such actions, the United States district courts are empowered to grant mandatory injunctions and such other and further equitable relief as they deem appropriate in the enforcement of such final orders of the Commission.

(m) Civil actions for recovery of penalties for knowing violations of rules and cease and desist orders respecting unfair or deceptive acts or practices; jurisdiction; maximum amount of penalties; continuing violations; de novo determinations; compromise or settlement procedure.

(1) (A) The Commission may commence a civil action to recover a civil penalty in a district court of the United States against any person, partnership, or corporation which violates any rule under this Act respecting unfair or deceptive acts or practices (other than an interpretive rule or a rule violation of which the Commission has provided is not an unfair or deceptive act or practice in violation of subsection (a)(1)) with actual knowledge or knowledge fairly implied on the basis of objective circumstances that such act is unfair or deceptive and is prohibited by such rule. In such action, such person, partnership, or corporation shall be liable for a civil penalty of not more than $ 10,000 for each violation.

(B) If the Commission determines in a proceeding under subsection (b) that any act or practice is unfair or deceptive, and issues a final cease and desist order, other than a consent order, with respect to such act or practice, then the Commission may commence a civil action to obtain a civil penalty in a district court of the United States against any person, partnership, or corporation which engages in such act or practice—

(1) after such cease and desist order becomes final (whether or not such person, partnership, or corporation was subject to such cease and desist order), and

(2) with actual knowledge that such act or practice is unfair or deceptive and is unlawful under subsection (a)(1) of this section.

In such action, such person, partnership, or corporation shall be liable for a civil penalty of not more than $ 10,000 for each violation.

(C) In the case of a violation through continuing failure to comply with a rule or with section 5(a)(1) [subsec. (a)(1) of this section], each day of continuance of such failure shall be treated as a separate violation, for purposes of subparagraphs (A) and (B). In determining the amount of such a civil penalty, the court shall take into account the degree of culpability, any history of prior such conduct, ability to pay, effect on ability to continue to do business, and such other matters as justice may require.

(2) If the cease and desist order establishing that the act or practice is unfair or deceptive was not issued against the defendant in a civil penalty action under paragraph (1)(B) the issues of fact in such action against such defendant shall be tried de novo. Upon request of any party to such an action against such defendant, the court shall also review the determination of law made by the Commission in the proceeding under subsection (b) that the act or practice which was the subject of such proceeding constituted an unfair or deceptive act or practice in violation of subsection (a).

(3) The Commission may compromise or settle any action for a civil penalty if such compromise or settlement is accompanied by a public statement of its reasons and is approved by the court.

(n) Definition of unfair acts or practices. The Commission shall have no authority under this section or section 18 [15 USCS § 57a] to declare unlawful an act or practice on the grounds that such act or practice is unfair unless the act or practice causes or is likely to cause substantial injury to consumers which is not reasonably avoidable by consumers themselves and not outweighed by countervailing benefits to consumers or to competition. In determining whether an act or practice is unfair, the Commission may consider established public policies as evidence to be considered with all other evidence. Such public policy considerations may not serve as a primary basis for such determination.

§ 45a. Labels on products

To the extent any person introduces, delivers for introduction, sells, advertises, or offers for sale in commerce a product with a "Made in the U.S.A." or "Made in America" label, or the equivalent thereof, in order to represent that such product was in whole or substantial part of domestic origin, such label shall be consistent with decisions and orders of the Federal Trade Commission issued pursuant to section 5 of the Federal Trade Commission Act [15 USCS § 45]. This section only applies to such labels. Nothing in this section shall preclude the application of other provisions of law relating to labeling. The Commission may periodically consider an appropriate percentage of imported components which may be included in the product and still be reasonably consistent with such decisions and orders. Nothing in this section shall preclude use of such labels for products that contain imported components under the label when the label also discloses such information in a clear and conspicuous manner. The Commission shall administer this section pursuant to section 5 of the Federal Trade Commission Act [15 USCS § 45] and may from time to time issue rules pursuant to section 553 of title 5, United States Code, for such purpose. If a rule is issued, such violation shall be treated by the Commission as a violation of a rule under section 18 of the Federal Trade Commission Act (15 U.S.C. 57a) regarding unfair or deceptive acts or practices. This section shall be effective upon publication in the Federal Register of a Notice of the provisions of this section. The Commission shall publish such notice within six months after the enactment of this section [Sept. 13, 1994].

§ 46. Additional powers of Commission

The commission shall also have power—

(a) Investigation of persons, partnerships, or corporations. To gather and compile information concerning, and to investigate from time to time the organization, business, conduct, practices, and management of any person, partnership, or corporation engaged in or whose business affects commerce, excepting banks, savings and loan institutions described in section 18(f)(3) [15 USCS § 57a(f)(3)], Federal credit unions described in section 18(f)(4) [15 USCS § 57a(f)(4)], and common carriers subject to the Act to regulate commerce, and its relation to other persons, partnerships, and corporations.

(b) Reports of persons, partnerships, and corporations. To require, by general or special orders, persons, partnerships, and corporations engaged in or whose business affects commerce, excepting banks, savings and loan institutions described in section 18(f)(3) [15 USCS § 57a(f)(3)], Federal credit unions described in section 18(f)(4) [15 USCS § 57a(f)(4)], and common carriers subject to the Act to regulate commerce, or any class of them, or any of them, respectively, to file with the commission in such form as the commission may prescribe annual or special, or both annual and special, reports, or answers in writing to specific questions, furnishing to the commission such information as it may require as to the organization, business, conduct, practices, management, and relation to other corporations, partnerships, and individuals of the respective persons, partnerships, and corporations filing such reports or answers in writing. Such reports and answers shall be made under oath, or otherwise, as the commission may prescribe, and shall be filed with the commission within such reasonable period as the commission may prescribe, unless additional time be granted in any case by the commission.

(c) Investigation of compliance with antitrust decrees. Whenever a final decree has been entered against any defendant corporation in any suit brought by the United States to prevent and restrain any violation of the antitrust Acts, to make investigation, upon its own initiative, of the manner in which the decree has been or is being carried out, and upon the application of the Attorney General it shall be its duty to make such investigation. It shall transmit to the Attorney General a report embodying its findings and recommendations as a result of any such investigation, and the report shall be made public in the discretion of the commission.

(d) Investigations of violations of antitrust statutes. Upon the direction of the President or either House of Congress to investigate and report the facts relating to any alleged violations of the antitrust Acts by any corporation.

(e) Readjustment of business of corporations violating antitrust statutes. Upon the application of the Attorney General to investigate and make recommendations for the readjustment of the business of any corporation alleged to be violating the antitrust Acts in order that the corporation may thereafter maintain its organization, management, and conduct of business in accordance with law.

(f) Publication of information; reports. To make public from time to time such portions of the information obtained by it hereunder as are in the public interest; and to make annual and special reports to the Congress and to submit therewith recommendations for additional legislation; and to provide for the publication of its reports and decisions in such form and manner as may be best adapted for public information and use: Provided, That the Commission shall not have any authority to make public any trade secret or any commercial or financial information which is obtained from any person and which is privileged or confidential, except that the Commission may disclose such information to officers and employees of appropriate Federal law enforcement agencies or to any officer or employee of any State law enforcement agency upon the prior certification of an officer of any such Federal or State law enforcement agency that such information will be maintained in confidence and will be used only for official law enforcement purposes.
(g) Classification of corporations; regulations. From time to time to classify corporations and (except as provided in section 18(a)(2) of this Act [15 USCS § 57a(a)(2)]) to make rules and regulations for the purpose of carrying out the provisions of this Act.
(h) Investigations of foreign trade conditions; reports. To investigate, from time to time, trade conditions in and with foreign countries where associations, combinations, or practices of manufacturers, merchants, or traders, or other conditions, may affect the foreign trade of the United States, and to report to Congress thereon, with such recommendations as it deems advisable.
(i) With respect to the International Antitrust Enforcement Assistance Act of 1994, to conduct investigations of possible violations of foreign antitrust laws (as defined in section 12 of such Act [15 USCS § 6211]). Provided, That the exception of "banks, savings and loan institutions described in section 18(f)(3) [15 USCS § 57a(f)(3)], Federal credit unions described in section 18(f)(4) [15 USCS § 57a(f)(4)], and common carriers subject to the Act to regulate commerce" from the Commission's powers defined in clauses (a) and (b) of this section, shall not be construed to limit the Commission's authority to gather and compile information, to investigate, or to require reports or answers from, any person, partnership, or corporation to the extent that such action is necessary to the investigation of any person, partnership, or corporation, group of persons, partnerships, or corporations, or industry which is not engaged or is engaged only incidentally in banking, in business as a savings and loan institution, in business as a Federal credit union, or in business as a common carrier subject to the Act to regulate commerce.
The Commission shall establish a plan designed to substantially reduce burdens imposed upon small businesses as a result of requirements established by the Commission under clause (b) relating to the filing of quarterly financial reports. Such plan shall (1) be established after consultation with small businesses and persons who use the information contained in such quarterly financial reports; (2) provide for a reduction of the number of small businesses required to file such quarterly financial reports; and (3) make revisions in the forms used for such quarterly financial reports for the purpose of reducing the complexity of such forms. The Commission, not later than December 31, 1980, shall submit such plan to the Committee on Commerce, Science, and Transportation of the Senate and to the Committee on Energy and Commerce of the House of Representatives. Such plan shall take effect not later than October 31, 1981.
No officer or employee of the Commission or any Commissioner may publish or disclose information to the public, or to any Federal agency, whereby any line-of-business data furnished by a particular establishment or individual can be identified. No one other than designated sworn officers and employees of the Commission may examine the line-of-business reports from individual firms, and information provided in the line-of-business program administered by the Commission shall be used only for statistical purposes. Information for carrying out specific law enforcement responsibilities of the Commission shall be obtained under practices and procedures in effect on the date of the enactment of the Federal Trade Commission Improvements Act of 1980 [enacted May 28, 1980], or as changed by law.
Nothing in this section (other than the provisions of clause (c) and clause (d)) shall apply to the business of insurance, except that the Commission shall have authority to conduct studies and prepare reports relating to the business of insurance. The Commission may exercise such authority only upon receiving a request which is agreed to by a majority of the members of the Committee on Commerce, Science,

and Transportation of the Senate or the Committee on Energy and Commerce of the House of Representatives. The authority to conduct any such study shall expire at the end of the Congress during which the request for such study was made.
§ 47. Reference of suits under antitrust statutes to Commission
In any suit in equity brought by or under the direction of the Attorney General as provided in the antitrust Acts, the court may, upon the conclusion of the testimony therein, if it shall be then of opinion that the complainant is entitled to relief, refer said suit to the commission, as a master in chancery, to ascertain and report an appropriate form of decree therein. The commission shall proceed upon such notice to the parties and under such rules of procedure as the court may prescribe, and upon the coming in of such report such exceptions may be filed and such proceedings had in relation thereto as upon the report of a master in other equity causes, but the court may adopt or reject such report, in whole or in part, and enter such decree as the nature of the case may in its judgment require.
§ 49. Documentary evidence; depositions; witnesses
For the purposes of this Act the commission, or its duly authorized agent or agents, shall at all reasonable times have access to, for the purpose of examination, and the right to copy any documentary evidence of any person, partnership, or corporation being investigated or proceeded against; and the commission shall have power to require by subpoena the attendance and testimony of witnesses and the production of all such documentary evidence relating to any matter under investigation. Any member of the commission may sign subpoenas, and members and examiners of the commission may administer oaths and affirmations, examine witnesses, and receive evidence.
Such attendance of witnesses and the production of such documentary evidence, may be required from any place in the United States, at any designated place of hearing. And in case of disobedience to a subpoena the commission may invoke the aid of any court of the United States in requiring the attendance and testimony of witnesses and the production of documentary evidence.
Any of the district courts of the United States within the jurisdiction of which such inquiry is carried on may, in case of contumacy or refusal to obey a subpoena issued to any person, partnership, or corporation, issue an order requiring such person, partnership, or corporation to appear before the commission, or to produce documentary evidence if so ordered, or to give evidence touching the matter in question; and any failure to obey such order of the court may be punished by such court as a contempt thereof.
Upon the application of the Attorney General of the United States, at the request of the commission, the district courts of the United States shall have jurisdiction to issue writs of mandamus commanding any person, partnership, or corporation to comply with this Act or any order of the commission made in pursuance thereof.
The commission may order testimony to be taken by deposition in any proceeding or investigation pending under this Act at any stage of such proceeding or investigation. Such depositions may be taken before any person designated by the commission and having power to administer oaths. Such testimony shall be reduced to writing by the person taking the deposition, or under his direction, and shall then be subscribed by the deponent. Any person may be compelled to appear and depose and to produce documentary evidence in the same manner as witnesses may be compelled to appear and testify and produce documentary evidence before the commission as hereinbefore provided.
Witnesses summoned before the commission shall be paid the same fees and mileage that are paid witnesses in the courts of the United States, and witnesses whose depositions are taken and the persons taking the same shall severally be entitled to the same fees as are paid for like services in the courts of the United States.
§ 50. Offenses and penalties
Any person who shall neglect or refuse to attend and testify, or to answer any lawful inquiry or to produce any documentary evidence, if in his power to do so, in obedience to an order of a district court of the United States directing compliance with the subpoena or lawful requirement of the commission, shall be guilty of an offense and upon conviction thereof by a court of competent jurisdiction shall be punished by a fine of not less than $ 1,000 nor more than $ 5,000, or by imprisonment for not more than one year, or by both such fine and imprisonment.
Any person who shall willfully make or cause to be made, any false entry or statement of fact in any report required to be made under this

Act, or who shall willfully make, or cause to be made, any false entry in any account, record, or memorandum kept by any person, partnership, or corporation subject to this Act, or who shall willfully neglect or fail to make, or cause to be made, full, true, and correct entries in such accounts, records, or memoranda of all facts and transactions appertaining to the business of such person, partnership, or corporation, or who shall willfully remove out of the jurisdiction of the United States, or willfully mutilate, alter, or by any other means falsify any documentary evidence of such person, partnership, or corporation, or who shall willfully refuse to submit to the commission or to any of its authorized agents, for the purpose of inspection and taking copies, any documentary evidence of such person, partnership, or corporation in his possession or within his control, shall be deemed guilty of an offense against the United States, and shall be subject, upon conviction in any court of the United States of competent jurisdiction, to a fine of not less than $ 1,000 nor more than $ 5,000, or to imprisonment for a term of not more than three years, or to both such fine and imprisonment. If any persons, partnership or corporation required by this Act to file any annual or special report shall fail so to do within the time fixed by the commission for filing the same, and such failure shall continue for thirty days after notice of such default, the corporation shall forfeit to the United States the sum of $ 100 for each and every day of the continuance of such failure, which forfeiture shall be payable into the Treasury of the United States, and shall be recoverable in a civil suit in the name of the United States brought in the case of a corporation or partnership in the district where the corporation or partnership has its principal office or in any district in which it shall do business, and in the case of any person in the district where such person resides or has his principal place of business. It shall be the duty of the various district attorneys [United States attorneys], under the direction of the Attorney General of the United States, to prosecute for the recovery of forfeitures. The costs and expenses of such prosecution shall be paid out of the appropriation for the expenses of the courts of the United States.

Any officer or employee of the commission who shall make public any information obtained by the commission without its authority, unless directed by a court, shall be deemed guilty of a misdemeanor, and, upon conviction thereof, shall be punished by a fine not exceeding $ 5,000, or by imprisonment not exceeding one year, or by fine and imprisonment, in the discretion of the court.

§ 52. Dissemination of false advertisements

(a) Unlawfulness. It shall be unlawful for any person, partnership, or corporation to disseminate, or cause to be disseminated, any false advertisement—

(1) By United States mails, or in or having an effect upon commerce, by any means, for the purpose of inducing, or which is likely to induce, directly or indirectly the purchase of foods, drugs, devices, services, or cosmetics; or

(2) By any means, for the purpose of inducing, or which is likely to induce, directly or indirectly, the purchase in or having an effect upon commerce of food, drugs, devices, services, or cosmetics.

(b) Unfair or deceptive act or practice. The dissemination or the causing to be disseminated of any false advertisement within the provisions of subsection (a) of this section shall be an unfair or deceptive act or practice in or affecting commerce within the meaning of section 5 [15 USCS § 45].

§ 53. False advertisements; injunctions and restraining orders

(a) Power of Commission; jurisdiction of courts. Whenever the Commission has reason to believe—

(1) that any person, partnership, or corporation is engaged in, or is about to engage in, the dissemination or the causing of the dissemination of any advertisement in violation of section 12 [15 USCS § 52], and

(2) that the enjoining thereof pending the issuance of a complaint by the Commission under section 5 [15 USCS § 45], and until such complaint is dismissed by the Commission or set aside by the court on review, or the order of the Commission to cease and desist made thereon has become final within the meaning of section 5 [15 USCS § 45], would be to the interest of the public, the Commission by any of its attorneys designated by it for such purpose may bring suit in a district court of the United States or in the United States court of any Territory, to enjoin the dissemination or the causing of the dissemination of such advertisement. Upon proper showing a temporary injunction or restraining order shall be granted without bond. Any suit may

be brought where such person, partnership, or corporation resides or transacts business, or wherever venue is proper under section 1391 of title 28, United States Code. In addition, the court may, if the court determines that the interests of justice require that any other person, partnership, or corporation should be a party in such suit, cause such other person, partnership, or corporation to be added as a party without regard to whether venue is otherwise proper in the district in which the suit is brought. In any suit under this section, process may be served on any person, partnership, or corporation wherever it may be found.

(b) Temporary restraining orders; preliminary injunctions. Whenever the Commission has reason to believe

(1) that any person, partnership, or corporation is violating, or is about to violate, any provision of law enforced by the Federal Trade Commission, and

(2) that the enjoining thereof pending the issuance of a complaint by the Commission and until such complaint is dismissed by the Commission or set aside by the court on review, or until the order of the Commission made thereon has become final, would be in the interest of the public the Commission by any of its attorneys designated by it for such purpose may bring suit in a district court of the United States to enjoin any such act or practice. Upon a proper showing that, weighing the equities and considering the Commission's likelihood of ultimate success, such action would be in the public interest, and after notice to the defendant, a temporary restraining order or a preliminary injunction may be granted without bond: Provided, however, That if a complaint is not filed within such period (not exceeding 20 days) as may be specified by the court after issuance of the temporary restraining order or preliminary injunction, the order or injunction shall be dissolved by the court and be of no further force and effect: Provided further, That in proper cases the Commission may seek, and after proper proof, the court may issue, a permanent injunction. Any suit may be brought where such person, partnership, or corporation resides or transacts business, or wherever venue is proper under section 1391 of title 28, United States Code. In addition, the court may, if the court determines that the interests of justice require that any other person, partnership, or corporation should be a party in such suit, cause such other person, partnership, or corporation to be added as a party without regard to whether venue is otherwise proper in the district in which the suit is brought. In any suit under this section, process may be served on any person, partnership, or corporation wherever it may be found.

(c) Service of process of the Commission; proof of service. Any process of the Commission under this section may be served by any person duly authorized by the Commission—

(1) by delivering a copy of such process to the person to be served, to a member of the partnership to be served, or to the president, secretary, or other executive officer or a director of the corporation to be served;

(2) by leaving a copy of such process at the residence or the principal office or place of business of such person, partnership, or corporation; or

(3) by mailing a copy of such process by registered mail or certified mail addressed to such person, partnership, or corporation at his, or her, or its residence, principal office, or principal place or business. The verified return by the person serving such process setting forth the manner of such service shall be proof of the same.

(d) Exception of periodical publications. Whenever it appears to the satisfaction of the court in the case of a newspaper, magazine, periodical, or other publication, published at regular intervals—

(1) that restraining the dissemination of a false advertisement in any particular issue of such publication would delay the delivery of such issue after the regular time therefor, and

(2) that such delay would be due to the method by which the manufacture and distribution of such publication is customarily conducted by the publisher in accordance with sound business practice, and not to any method or device adopted for the evasion of this section or to prevent or delay the issuance of an injunction or restraining order with respect to such false advertisement or any other advertisement, the court shall exclude such issue from the operation of the restraining order or injunction.

§ 54. False advertisements; penalties

(a) Imposition of penalties. Any person, partnership, or corporation who violates any provision of section 12(a) [15 USCS § 52(a)] shall, if the use of the commodity advertised may be injurious to health because of results from such use under the conditions prescribed in the advertisement thereof, or under such conditions as are customary or usual, or if such violation is with intent to defraud or mislead, be guilty of a misdemeanor, and upon conviction shall be punished by a fine of not more than $ 5,000 or by imprisonment for not more than six months, or by both such fine and imprisonment; except that if the conviction is for a violation committed after a first conviction of such person, partnership, or corporation, for any violation of such section, punishment shall be by a fine of not more than $ 10,000 or by imprisonment for not more than one year, or by both such fine and imprisonment: Provided, That for the purposes of this section meats and meat food products duly inspected, marked, and labeled in accordance with rules and regulations issued under the Meat Inspection Act approved March 4, 1907, as amended, shall be conclusively presumed not injurious to health at the time the same leave official "establishments."

(b) Exception of advertising medium or agency. No publisher, radio-broadcast licensee, or agency or medium for the dissemination of advertising, except the manufacturer, packer, distributor, or seller of the commodity to which the false advertisement relates, shall be liable under this section by reason of the dissemination by him of any false advertisement, unless he has refused, on the request of the Commission, to furnish the Commission the name and post-office address of the manufacturer, packer, distributor, seller, or advertising agency, residing in the United States, who caused him to disseminate such advertisement. No advertising agency shall be liable under this section by reason of the causing by it of the dissemination of any false advertisement, unless it has refused, on the request of the Commission, to furnish the Commission the name and post-office address of the manufacturer, packer, distributor, or seller, residing in the United States, who caused it to cause the dissemination of such advertisement.

§ 55.   Additional definitions

For the purposes of sections 12, 13 and 14 [15 USCS §§ 52, 53, 54]—

(a) False advertisement.

(1) The term "false advertisement" means an advertisement, other than labeling, which is misleading in a material respect; and in determining whether any advertisement is misleading, there shall be taken into account (among other things) not only representations made or suggested by statement, word, design, device, sound, or any combination thereof, but also the extent to which the advertisement fails to reveal facts material in the light of such representations or material with respect to consequences which may result from the use of the commodity to which the advertisement relates under the conditions prescribed in said advertisement, or under such conditions as are customary or usual. No advertisement of a drug shall be deemed to be false if it is disseminated only to members of the medical profession, contains no false representation of a material fact, and includes, or is accompanied in each instance by truthful disclosure of, the formula showing quantitatively each ingredient of such drug.

(2) In the case of oleomargarine or margarine an advertisement shall be deemed misleading in a material respect if in such advertisement representations are made or suggested by statement, word, grade designation, design, device, symbol, sound, or any combination thereof, that such oleomargarine or margarine is a dairy product, except that nothing contained herein shall prevent a truthful, accurate, and full statement in any such advertisement of all the ingredients contained in such oleomargarine or margarine.

(b) Food. The term "food" means (1) articles used for food or drink for man or other animals, (2) chewing gum, and (3) articles used for components of any such article.

(c) Drug. The term "drug" means (1) articles recognized in the official United States Pharmacopoeia, official Homoeopathic Pharmacopoeia of the United States, or official National Formulary, or any supplement to any of them; and (2) articles intended for use in the diagnosis, cure, mitigation, treatment, or prevention of disease in man or other animals; and (3) articles (other than food) intended to affect the structure or any function of the body of man or other animals; and (4) articles intended for use as a component of any article specified in clause (1), (2), or (3); but does not include devices or their components, parts, or accessories.

(d) Device. The term "device" (except when used in subsection (a) of this section) means an instrument, apparatus, implement, machine, contrivance, implant, in vitro reagent, or other similar or related article, including any component, part, or accessory, which is—

(1) recognized in the official National Formulary, or the United States Pharmacopeia, or any supplement to them,

(2) intended for use in the diagnosis of disease or other conditions, or in the cure, mitigation, treatment, or prevention of disease, in man or other animals, or

(3) intended to affect the structure or any function of the body of man or other animals, and which does not achieve any of its principal intended purposes through chemical action within or on the body of man or other animals and which is not dependent upon being metabolized for the achievement of any of its principal intended purposes.

(e) Cosmetic. The term "cosmetic" means (1) articles to be rubbed, poured, sprinkled, or sprayed on, introduced into, or otherwise applied to the human body or any part thereof intended for cleansing, beautifying, promoting attractiveness, or altering the appearance, and (2) articles intended for use as a component of any such article; except that such term shall not include soap.

(f) Oleomargarine or margarine. For the purpose of this section and section 407 of the Federal Food, Drug, and Cosmetic Act, as amended [21 USCS § 347], the term "oleomargarine" or "margarine" includes—

(1) all substances, mixtures, and compounds known as oleomargarine or margarine;

(2) all substances, mixtures, and compounds which have a consistence similar to that of butter and which contain any edible oils or fats other than milk fat if made in imitation or semblance of butter.

§ 57.   Separability clause

If any provision of this Act or the application thereof to any person, partnership, corporation, or circumstance, is held invalid, the remainder of the Act and the application of such provision to any other person, partnership, corporation, or circumstance, shall not be affected thereby.

§ 57b. Civil actions for violations of rules and cease and desist orders respecting unfair or deceptive acts or practices

(a) Suits by Commission against persons, partnerships, or corporations; jurisdiction; relief for dishonest or fraudulent acts.

(1) If any person, partnership, or corporation violates any rule under this Act respecting unfair or deceptive acts or practices (other than an interpretive rule, or a rule violation of which the Commission has provided is not an unfair or deceptive act or practice in violation of section 5(a) [15 USCS § 45(a)]), then the Commission may commence a civil action against such person, partnership, or corporation for relief under subsection (b) in a United States district court or in any court of competent jurisdiction of a State.

(2) If any person, partnership, or corporation engages in any unfair or deceptive act or practice (within the meaning of section 5(a)(1) [15 USCS § 45(a)(1)]) with respect to which the Commission has issued a final cease and desist order which is applicable to such person, partnership, or corporation, then the Commission may commence a civil action against such person, partnership, or corporation in a United States district court or in any court of competent jurisdiction of a State. If the Commission satisfies the court that the act or practice to which the cease and desist order relates is one which a reasonable man would have known under the circumstances was dishonest or fraudulent, the court may grant relief under subsection (b).

(b) Nature of relief available. The court in an action under subsection (a) shall have jurisdiction to grant such relief as the court finds necessary to redress injury to consumers or other persons, partnership, and corporations resulting from the rule violation or the unfair or deceptive act or practice, as the case may be. Such relief may include, but shall not be limited to, rescission or reformation of contracts, the refund of money or return of property, the payment of damages, and public notification respecting the rule violation or the unfair or deceptive act or practice, as the case may be; except that nothing in this subsection is intended to authorize the imposition of any exemplary or punitive damages.

(c) Conclusiveness of findings of Commission in cease and desist proceedings; notice of judicial proceedings to injured persons, etc.

(1) If (A) a cease and desist order issued under section 5(b) [15 USCS § 45(b)] has become final under section 5(g) [15 USCS § 45(g)] with respect to any person's, partnership's, or corporation's rule violation or unfair or deceptive act or practice, and (B) an action under this section is brought with respect to such person's, partnership's, or corporation's rule violation or act or practice, then the findings of the Commission as to the material facts in the proceeding under section 5(b) [15 USCS § 45(b)] with respect to such person's, partnership's, or corporation's rule

violation or act or practice, shall be conclusive unless (i) the terms of such cease and desist order expressly provide that the Commission's findings shall not be conclusive, or (ii) the order became final by reason of section 5(g)(1) [15 USCS § 45(g)(1)], in which case such finding shall be conclusive if supported by evidence.

(2) The court shall cause notice of an action under this section to be given in a manner which is reasonably calculated, under all of the circumstances, to apprise the persons, partnerships, and corporations allegedly injured by the defendant's rule violation or act or practice of the pendency of such action. Such notice may, in the discretion of the court, be given by publication.

(d) Time for bringing of actions. No action may be brought brought by the Commission under this section more than 3 years after the rule violation to which an action under subsection (a)(1) relates, or the unfair or deceptive act or practice to which an action under subsection (a)(2) relates; except that if a cease and desist order with respect to any person's, partnership's, or corporation's rule violation or unfair or deceptive act or practice has become final and such order was issued in a proceeding under section 5(b) [15 USCS § 45(b)] which was commenced not later than 3 years after the rule violation or act or practice occurred, a civil action may be commenced under this section against such person, partnership, or corporation at any time before the expiration of one year after such order becomes final.

(e) Availability of additional Federal or State remedies; other authority of Commission unaffected. Remedies provided in this section are in addition to, and not in lieu of, any other remedy or right of action provided by State or Federal law. Nothing in this section shall be construed to affect any authority of the Commission under any other provision of law.

§ 57b-2. Confidentiality

(a) Definitions. For purposes of this section:

(1) The term "material" means documentary material, tangible things, written reports or answers to questions, and transcripts of oral testimony.

(2) The term "Federal agency" has the meaning given it in section 552(e) of title 5, United States Code.

(b) Procedures respecting documents, tangible things, or transcripts of oral testimony received pursuant to compulsory process in investigation.

(1) With respect to any document, tangible thing, or transcript of oral testimony received by the Commission pursuant to compulsory process in an investigation, a purpose of which is to determine whether any person may have violated any provision of the laws administered by the Commission, the procedures established in paragraph (2) through paragraph (7) shall apply.

(2) (A) The Commission shall designate a duly authorized agent to serve as custodian of documentary material, tangible things, or written reports or answers to questions, and transcripts of oral testimony, and such additional duly authorized agents as the Commission shall determine from time to time to be necessary to serve as deputies to the custodian.

(B) Any person upon whom any demand for the production of documentary material has been duly served shall make such material available for inspection and copying or reproduction to the custodian designated in such demand at the principal place of business of such person (or at such other place as such custodian and such person thereafter may agree and prescribe in writing or as the court may direct pursuant to section 20(h) [15 USCS § 57b-1(h)]) on the return date specified in such demand (or on such later date as such custodian may prescribe in writing). Such person may upon written agreement between such person and the custodian substitute copies for originals of all or any part of such material.

(3) (A) The custodian to whom any documentary material, tangible things, written reports or answers to questions, and transcripts of oral testimony are delivered shall take physical possession of such material, reports or answers, and transcripts, and shall be responsible for the use made of such material, reports or answers, and transcripts, and for the return of material, pursuant to the requirements of this section.

(B) The custodian may prepare such copies of the documentary material, written reports or answers to questions, and transcripts of oral testimony, and may make tangible things available, as may be required for official use by any duly authorized officer or employee of the Commission under regulations which shall be promulgated by the Commission. Notwithstanding subparagraph (C), such material, things, and

transcripts may be used by any such officer or employee in connection with the taking of oral testimony under this section.

(C) Except as otherwise provided in this section, while in the possession of the custodian, no documentary material, tangible things, reports or answers to questions, and transcripts of oral testimony shall be available for examination by any individual other than a duly authorized officer or employee of the Commission without the consent of the person who produced the material, things, or transcripts. Nothing in this section is intended to prevent disclosure to either House of the Congress or to any committee or subcommittee of the Congress, except that the Commission immediately shall notify the owner or provider of any such information of a request for information designated as confidential by the owner or provider.

(D) While in the possession of the custodian and under such reasonable terms and conditions as the Commission shall prescribe—

(i) documentary material, tangible things, or written reports shall be available for examination by the person who produced the material, or by any duly authorized representative of such person; and

(ii) answers to questions in writing and transcripts of oral testimony shall be available for examination by the person who produced the testimony or by his attorney.

(4) Whenever the Commission has instituted a proceeding against a person, partnership, or corporation, the custodian may deliver to any officer or employee of the Commission documentary material, tangible things, written reports or answers to questions, and transcripts of oral testimony for official use in connection with such proceeding. Upon the completion of the proceeding, the officer or employee shall return to the custodian any such material so delivered which has not been received into the record of the proceeding.

(5) If any documentary material, tangible things, written reports or answers to questions, and transcripts of oral testimony have been produced in the course of any investigation by any person pursuant to compulsory process and—

(A) any proceeding arising out of the investigation has been completed; or

(B) no proceeding in which the material may be used has been commenced within a reasonable time after completion of the examination and analysis of all such material and other information assembled in the course of the investigation;

then the custodian shall, upon written request of the person who produced the material, return to the person any such material which has not been received into the record of any such proceeding (other than copies of such material made by the custodian pursuant to paragraph (3)(B)).

(6) The custodian of any documentary material, written reports or answers to questions, and transcripts of oral testimony may deliver to any officers or employees of appropriate Federal law enforcement agencies, in response to a written request, copies of such material for use in connection with an investigation or proceeding under the jurisdiction of any such agency. The custodian of any tangible things may make such things available for inspection to such persons on the same basis. Such materials shall not be made available to any such agency until the custodian receives certification of any officer of such agency that such information will be maintained in confidence and will be used only for official law enforcement purposes. Such documentary material, results of inspections of tangible things, written reports or answers to questions, and transcripts of oral testimony may be used by any officer or employee of such agency only in such manner and subject to such conditions as apply to the Commission under this section. The custodian may make such materials available to any State law enforcement agency upon the prior certification of any officer of such agency that such information will be maintained in confidence and will be used only for official law enforcement purposes.

(7) In the event of the death, disability, or separation from service in the Commission of the custodian of any documentary material, tangible things, written reports or answers to questions, and transcripts of oral testimony produced under any demand issued under this Act, or the official relief of the custodian from responsibility for the custody and control of such material, the Commission promptly shall—

(A) designate under paragraph (2)(A) another duly authorized agent to serve as custodian of such material; and

(B) transmit in writing to the person who produced the material or testimony notice as to the identity and address of the successor so designated.

Any successor designated under paragraph (2)(A) as a result of the requirements of this paragraph shall have (with regard to the material involved) all duties and responsibilities imposed by this section upon his predecessor in office with regard to such material, except that he shall not be held responsible for any default or dereliction which occurred before his designation.

(c) Information considered confidential.

(1) All information reported to or otherwise obtained by the Commission which is not subject to the requirements of subsection (b) shall be considered confidential when so marked by the person supplying the information and shall not be disclosed, except in accordance with the procedures established in paragraph (2) and paragraph (3).

(2) If the Commission determines that a document marked confidential by the person supplying it may be disclosed because it is not a trade secret or commercial or financial information which is obtained from any person and which is privileged or confidential, within the meaning of section 6(f) [15 USCS § 46(f)], then the Commission shall notify such person in writing that the Commission intends to disclose the document at a date not less than 10 days after the date of receipt of notification.

(3) Any person receiving such notification may, if he believes disclosure of the document would cause disclosure of a trade secret, or commercial or financial information which is obtained from any person and which is privileged or confidential, within the meaning of section 6(f) 15 USCS § 46(f)], before the date set for release of the document, bring an action in the district court of the United States for the district within which the documents are located or in the United States District Court for the District of Columbia to restrain disclosure of the document. Any person receiving such notification may file with the appropriate district court or court of appeals of the United States, as appropriate, an application for a stay of disclosure. The documents shall not be disclosed until the court has ruled on the application for a stay.

(d) Particular disclosures allowed.

(1) The provisions of subsection (c) shall not be construed to prohibit—

(A) the disclosure of information to either House of the Congress or to any committee or subcommittee of the Congress, except that the Commission immediately shall notify the owner or provider of any such information of a request for information designated as confidential by the owner or provider;

(B) the disclosure of the results of any investigation or study carried out or prepared by the Commission, except that no information shall be identified nor shall information be disclosed in such a manner as to disclose a trade secret of any person supplying the trade secret, or to disclose any commercial or financial information which is obtained from any person and which is privileged or confidential;

(C) the disclosure of relevant and material information in Commission adjudicative proceedings or in judicial proceedings to which the Commission is a party; or

(D) the disclosure to a Federal agency of disaggregated information obtained in accordance with section 3512 of title 44, United States Code, except that the recipient agency shall use such disaggregated information for economic, statistical, or policymaking purposes only, and shall not disclose such information in an individually identifiable form.

(2) Any disclosure of relevant and material information in Commission adjudicative proceedings or in judicial proceedings to which the Commission is a party shall be governed by the rules of the Commission for adjudicative proceedings or by court rules or orders, except that the rules of the Commission shall not be amended in a manner inconsistent with the purposes of this section.

(e) Effect on other statutory provisions limiting disclosure. Nothing in this section shall supersede any statutory provision which expressly prohibits or limits particular disclosures by the Commission, or which authorizes disclosures to any other Federal agency.

(f) Exemption from disclosure. Any material which is received by the Commission in any investigation, a purpose of which is to determine whether any person may have violated any provision of the laws administered by the Commission, and which is provided pursuant to any compulsory process under this Act or which is provided voluntarily in place of such compulsory process shall be exempt from disclosure under section 552 of title 5, United States Code.

Federal Food, Drug, And Cosmetic Act
Title 21. Food and Drugs
Chapter 9. Federal Food, Drug, And Cosmetic Act Definitions

§ 331. Prohibited acts
The following acts and the causing thereof are hereby prohibited:
(a) The introduction or delivery for introduction into interstate commerce of any food, drug, device, or cosmetic that is adulterated or misbranded.

(b) The adulteration or misbranding of any food, drug, device, or cosmetic in interstate commerce.

(c) The receipt in interstate commerce of any food, drug, device, or cosmetic that is adulterated or misbranded, and the delivery or proffered delivery thereof for pay or otherwise.

(d) The introduction or delivery for introduction into interstate commerce of any article in violation of section 404 or 505 [21 USCS § 344 or 355].

(e) The refusal to permit access to or copying of any record as required by section 412, 414, 504, 703, or 704(a) [21 USCS § 350a, 350c, 354, 373, or 374(a)]; or the failure to establish or maintain any record, or make any report, required under section 412, 414(b), 504, 505(i) or (k), 512(a)(4)(C), 512(j), (l), or (m), 515(f), or 519 [21 USCS § 350a, 350c(b), 354, 355(i) or (k), 360b(a)(4)(C), 360b(j), (l), or (m) 360e(f), or 360i] or the refusal to permit access to or verification or copying of any such required record.

(f) The refusal to permit entry or inspection as authorized by section 704 [21 USCS § 374].

(g) The manufacture, within any Territory of any food, drug, device, or cosmetic that is adulterated or misbranded.

(h) The giving of a guaranty or undertaking referred to in section 303(c)(2) [21 USCS § 333(c)(2)], which guaranty or undertaking is false, except by a person who relied upon a guaranty or undertaking to the same effect signed by, containing the name and address of, the person residing in the United States from whom he received in good faith the food, drug, device, or cosmetic; or the giving of a guaranty or undertaking referred to in section 303(c)(3) [21 USCS § 333(c)(3)], which guaranty or undertaking is false.

(i) (1) Forging, counterfeiting, simulating, or falsely representing, or without proper authority using any mark, stamp, tag, label, or other identification device authorized or required by regulations promulgated under the provisions of section 404 or 721 [21 USCS § 344 or 379e].

(2) Making, selling, disposing of, or keeping in possession, control, or custody, or concealing any punch, die, plate, stone, or other thing designed to print, imprint, or reproduce the trademark, trade name, or other identifying mark, imprint, or device of another or any likeness of any of the foregoing upon any drug or container or labeling thereof so as to render such drug a counterfeit drug.

(3) The doing of any act which causes a drug to be a counterfeit drug, or the sale or dispensing, or the holding for sale or dispensing, of a counterfeit drug.

(j) The using by any person to his own advantage or revealing, other than to the Secretary or officers or employees of the Department, or to the courts when relevant in any judicial proceeding under this Act [21 USCS §§ 301 et seq.], any information acquired under authority of section 404, 409, 412, 414, 505, 510, 512, 513, 514, 515, 516, 518, 519, 520, 704, 708 or 721 [21 USCS § 344, 348, 350a, 350c, 355, 360, 360b, 360c, 360d, 360e, 360f, 360h, 360i, 360j, 374, 379, or 379e], concerning any method or process which as a trade secret is entitled to protection; or the violating of section 408(i)(2) [21 USCS § 346a(i)(2)] or any regulation issued under that section.[.] This paragraph does not authorize the withholding of information from either House of Congress or from, to the extent of matter within its jurisdiction, any committee or subcommittee of such committee or any joint committee of Congress or any subcommittee of such joint committee.

(k) The alteration, mutilation, destruction, obliteration, or removal of the whole or any part of the labeling of, or the doing of any other act with respect to, a food, drug, device, or cosmetic, if such act is done while such article is held for sale (whether or not the first sale) after shipment in interstate commerce and results in such article being adulterated or misbranded.

(l) [Deleted]

(m) The sale or offering for sale of colored oleomargarine or colored margarine, or the possession or serving of colored oleomargarine or colored margarine in violation of sections 407(b), or 407(c) [21 USCS § 347(b) or (c)].

(n) The using, in labeling, advertising or other sales promotion of any reference to any report or analysis furnished in compliance with section 704 [21 USCS § 374].

(o) In the case of a prescription drug distributed or offered for sale in interstate commerce, the failure of the manufacturer, packer, or distributor thereof to maintain for transmittal, or to transmit, to any practitioner licensed by applicable State law to administer such drug who makes written request for information as to such drug, true and correct copies of all printed matter which is required to be included in any package in which that drug is distributed or sold, or such other printed matter as is approved by the Secretary. Nothing in this paragraph shall be construed to exempt any person from any labeling requirement imposed by or under other provisions of this Act [21 USCS §§ 301 et seq.].

(p) The failure to register in accordance with section 510 [21 USCS § 360], the failure to provide any information required by section 510(j) or 510k, [21 USCS § 360(j) or (k)], or the failure to provide a notice required by section 510(j)(2) [21 USCS 360(j)(2)].

(q) (1) The failure or refusal to (A) comply with any requirement prescribed under section 518 or 520(g) [21 USCS § 360h or 360j(g)], (B) furnish any notification or other material or information required by or under section 519 or 520(g) [21 USCS § 360i or 360j(g)], or (C) comply with a requirement under section 522 [21 USCS § 360l].

(2) With respect to any device, the submission of any report that is required by or under this Act [21 USCS §§ 301 et seq.] that is false or misleading in any material respect.

(r) The movement of a device in violation of an order under section 304(g) [21 USCS § 334(g)] or the removal or alteration of any mark or label required by the order to identify the device as detained.

(s) The failure to provide the notice required by section 412(c) or 412(e) [21 USCS § 350a(c) or (e)], the failure to make the reports required by section 412(f)(1)(B) [21 USCS § 350a(f)(1)(B), the failure to retain the records required by section 412(b)(4) [21 USCS § 350a(b)(4)], or the failure to meet the requirements prescribed under section 412(f)(3) [21 USCS § 350a(f)(3)].

(t) The importation of a drug in violation of section 801(d)(1) [21 USCS § 381(d)(1)], the sale, purchase, or trade of a drug or drug sample or the offer to sell, purchase, or trade a drug or drug sample in violation of section 503(c) [21 USCS § 353(c)], the sale, purchase, or trade of a coupon, the offer to sell, purchase, or trade such a coupon, or the counterfeiting of such a coupon in violation of section 503(c)(2) [21 USCS § 353(c)(2)], the distribution of a drug sample in violation of section 503(d) [21 USCS § 353(d)], or the failure to otherwise comply with the requirements of section 503(d) [21 USCS § 353(d)], or the distribution of drugs in violation of section 503(e) [21 USCS § 353(e)] or the failure to otherwise comply with the requirements of section 503(e) [21 USCS § 353(e)].

(u) The failure to comply with any requirements of the provisions of, or any regulations or orders of the Secretary, under section 512(a)(4)(A), 512(a)(4)(D), or 512(a)(5) [21 USCS § 360b(a)(4)(A), (4)(D), or (5)].

(v) The introduction or delivery for introduction into interstate commerce of a dietary supplement that is unsafe under section 413 [21 USCS § 350b].

(w) The making of a knowingly false statement in any statement, certificate of analysis, record, or report required or requested under section 801(d)(3) [21 USCS § 381(d)(3)]; the failure to submit a certificate of analysis as required under such section; the failure to maintain records or to submit records or reports as required by such section; the release into interstate commerce of any article or portion thereof imported into the United States under such section or any finished product made from such article or portion, except for export in accordance with section 801(e) or 802 [21 USCS § 381(e) or 382], or with section 351(h) of the Public Health Service Act [42 USCS § 262(h)]; or the failure to so export or to destroy such an article or portions thereof, or such a finished product.

(x) The falsification of a declaration of conformity submitted under section 514(c) [21 USCS § 360d(c)] or the failure or refusal to provide data or information requested by the Secretary under paragraph (3) of such section.

(y) In the case of a drug, device, or food—

(1) the submission of a report or recommendation by a person ac-

credited under section 523 [21 USCS § 360m] that is false or misleading in any material respect;

(2) the disclosure by a person accredited under section 523 [21 USCS § 360m] of confidential commercial information or any trade secret without the express written consent of the person who submitted such information or secret to such person; or

(3) the receipt by a person accredited under section 523 [21 USCS § 360m] of a bribe in any form or the doing of any corrupt act by such person associated with a responsibility delegated to such person under this Act [21 USCS §§ 301 et seq.].

(z) The dissemination of information in violation of section 551 [21 USCS § 360aaa].

(aa) The importation of a covered product in violation of section 804 [21 USCS § 384], the falsification of any record required to be maintained or provided to the Secretary under such section, or any other violation of regulations under such section.

(bb) The transfer of an article of food in violation of an order under section 304(h) [21 USCS § 334(h)], or the removal or alteration of any mark or label required by the order to identify the article as detained.

(cc) The importing or offering for import into the United States of an article of food by, with the assistance of, or at the direction of, a person debarred under section 306(b)(3) [21 USCS § 335a(b)(3)].

(dd) The failure to register in accordance with section 415 [21 USCS § 350d].

(ee) The importing or offering for import into the United States of an article of food in violation of the requirements under section 801(m) [21 USCS § 381(m)].

(ff) The importing or offering for import into the United States of a drug or device with respect to which there is a failure to comply with a request of the Secretary to submit to the Secretary a statement under section 801(o) [21 USCS § 381(o)].

(gg) The knowing failure of a person accredited under paragraph (2) of section 704(g) [21 USCS § 374(g)] to comply with paragraph (7)(E) of such section; the knowing inclusion by such a person of false information in an inspection report under paragraph (7)(A) of such section; or the knowing failure of such a person to include material facts in such a report.

§ 332. Injunction proceedings

(a) Jurisdiction of courts. The district courts of the United States and the United States courts of the Territories shall have jurisdiction, for cause shown to restrain violations of section 301 [21 USCS § 331], except paragraphs (h), (i), and (j).

(b) Violation of injunction. In case of violation of an injunction or restraining order issued under this section, which also constitutes a violation of this Act, trial shall be by the court, or, upon demand of the accused, by a jury.

§ 333. Penalties

(a) Violation of 21 USCS § 331.

(1) Any person who violates a provision of section 301 [21 USCS § 331] shall be imprisoned for not more than one year or fined not more than $ 1,000, or both.

(2) Notwithstanding the provisions of paragraph (1) of this section, if any person commits such a violation after a conviction of him under this section has become final, or commits such a violation with the intent to defraud or mislead, such person shall be imprisoned for not more than three years or fined not more than $ 10,000 or both.

(b) Imprisonment and fines.

(1) Notwithstanding subsection (a), any person who violates section 301(t) [21 USCS § 331(t)] by—

(A) knowingly importing a drug in violation of section 801(d)(1) [21 USCS § 381(d)(1)],

(B) knowingly selling, purchasing, or trading a drug or drug sample or knowingly offering to sell, purchase, or trade a drug or drug sample, in violation of section 503(c)(1) [21 USCS § 353(c)(1)],

(C) knowingly selling, purchasing, or trading a coupon, knowingly offering to sell, purchase, or trade such a coupon, or knowingly counterfeiting such a coupon, in violation of section 503(c)(2) [21 USCS § 353(c)(2)], or

(D) knowingly distributing drugs in violation of section 503(e)(2)(A) [21 USCS § 353(e)(2)(A)], shall be imprisoned for not more than 10 years or fined not more than $ 250,000, or both.

(2) Any manufacturer or distributor who distributes drug samples by means other than the mail or common carrier whose representative, during the course of the representative's employment or association

with that manufacturer or distributor, violated section 301(t) [21 USCS § 331(t)] because of a violation of section 503(c)(1) [21 USCS § 353(c)(1)] or violated any State law prohibiting the sale, purchase, or trade of a drug sample subject to section 503(b) [21 USCS § 353(b)] or the offer to sell, purchase, or trade such a drug sample shall, upon conviction of the representative for such violation, be subject to the following civil penalties:

(A) A civil penalty of not more than $ 50,000 for each of the first two such violations resulting in a conviction of any representative of the manufacturer or distributor in any 10-year period.

(B) A civil penalty of not more than $ 1,000,000 for each violation resulting in a conviction of any representative after the second conviction in any 10-year period. For the purposes of this paragraph, multiple convictions of one or more persons arising out of the same event or transaction, or a related series of events or transactions, shall be considered as one violation.

(3) Any manufacturer or distributor who violates section 301(t) [21 USCS § 331(t)] because of a failure to make a report required by section 503(d)(3)(E) [21 USCS § 353(d)(3)(E)] shall be subject to a civil penalty of not more than $ 100,000.

(4) (A) If a manufacturer or distributor or any representative of such manufacturer or distributor provides information leading to the institution of a criminal proceeding against, and conviction of, any representative of that manufacturer or distributor for a violation of section 301(t) [21 USCS § 331(t)] because of a sale, purchase, or trade or offer to purchase, sell, or trade a drug sample in violation of section 503(c)(1) [21 USCS § 353(c)(1)] or for a violation of State law prohibiting the sale, purchase, or trade or offer to sell, purchase, or trade a drug sample, the conviction of such representative shall not be considered as a violation for purposes of paragraph (2).

(B) If, in an action brought under paragraph (2) against a manufacturer or distributor relating to the conviction of a representative of such manufacturer or distributor for the sale, purchase, or trade of a drug or the offer to sell, purchase, or trade a drug, it is shown, by clear and convincing evidence—

(i) that the manufacturer or distributor conducted, before the institution of a criminal proceeding against such representative for the violation which resulted in such conviction, an investigation of events or transactions which would have led to the reporting of information leading to the institution of a criminal proceeding against, and conviction of, such representative for such purchase, sale, or trade or offer to purchase, sell, or trade, or

(ii) that, except in the case of the conviction of a representative employed in a supervisory function, despite diligent implementation by the manufacturer or distributor of an independent audit and security system designed to detect such a violation, the manufacturer or distributor could not reasonably have been expected to have detected such violation,

the conviction of such representative shall not be considered as a conviction for purposes of paragraph (2).

(5) If a person provides information leading to the institution of a criminal proceeding against, and conviction of, a person for a violation of section 301(t) [21 USCS § 331(t)] because of the sale, purchase, or trade of a drug sample or the offer to sell, purchase, or trade a drug sample in violation of section 503(c)(1) [21 USCS § 353(c)(1)], such person shall be entitled to one-half of the criminal fine imposed and collected for such violation but not more than $ 125,000.

(6) Notwithstanding subsection (a), any person who is a manufacturer or importer of a covered product pursuant to section 804(a) [21 USCS § 384(a)] and knowingly fails to comply with a requirement of section 804(e) [21 USCS § 384(e)] that is applicable to such manufacturer or importer, respectively, shall be imprisoned for not more than 10 years or fined not more than $ 250,000, or both.

(c) Exceptions in certain cases of good faith, etc. No person shall be subject to the penalties of subsection (a)(1) of this section, (1) for having received in interstate commerce any article and delivered it or proffered delivery of it, if such delivery or proffer was made in good faith, unless he refuses to furnish on request of an officer or employee duly designated by the Secretary the name and address of the person from whom he purchased or received such article and copies of all documents, if any there be, pertaining to the delivery of the article to him; or (2) for having violated section 301(a) or (d) [21 USCS § 331(a), (d)], if he establishes a guaranty or undertaking signed by, and containing the name and address of, the person residing in the United States from

whom he received in good faith the article, to the effect, in case of an alleged violation of section 301(a) [21 USCS § 331(a)], that such article is not adulterated or misbranded, within the meaning of this Act, designating this Act, or to the effect, in case of an alleged violation of section 301(d) [21 USCS § 331(d)], that such article is not an article which may not, under the provisions of section 404 or 505 [21 USCS § 344 or 355], be introduced into interstate commerce; or (3) for having violated section 301(a) [21 USCS § 331(a)], where the violation exists because the article is adulterated by reason of containing a color additive not from a batch certified in accordance with regulations promulgated by the Secretary, under this Act, if such person establishes a guaranty or undertaking signed by, and containing the name and address of, the manufacturer of the color additive, to the effect that such color additive was from a batch certified in accordance with the applicable regulations promulgated by the Secretary under this Act; or (4) for having violated section 301(b), (c) or (k) [21 USCS § 331(b), (c) or (k)] by failure to comply with section 502(f) [21 USCS § 352(f)] in respect to an article received in interstate commerce to which neither section 503(a) [21 USCS § 353(a)] nor section 503(b)(1) [21 USCS § 353(b)(1)] is applicable, if the delivery or proffered delivery was made in good faith and the labeling at the time thereof contained the same directions for use and warning statements as were contained in the labeling at the time of such receipt of such article; or (5) for having violated section 301(i)(2) [21 USCS § 331(i)(2)] if such person acted in good faith and had no reason to believe that use of the punch, die, plate, stone, or other thing involved would result in a drug being a counterfeit drug, or for having violated section 301(i)(3) [21 USCS § 331(i)(3)] if the person doing the act or causing it to be done acted in good faith and had no reason to believe that the drug was a counterfeit drug.

(d) Exceptions involving misbranded food. No person shall be subject to the penalties of subsection (a)(1) of this section for a violation of section 301 [21 USCS § 331] involving misbranded food if the violation exists solely because the food is misbranded under section 403(a)(2) [21 USCS § 343(a)(2)] because of its advertising.

(e) Distribution of or possession with intent to distribute human growth hormone; exception.

(1) Except as provided in paragraph (2), whoever knowingly distributes, or possesses with intent to distribute, human growth hormone for any use in humans other than the treatment of a disease or other recognized medical condition, where such use has been authorized by the Secretary of Health and Human Services under section 505 [21 USCS § 355] and pursuant to the order of a physician, is guilty of an offense punishable by not more than 5 years in prison, such fines as are authorized by title 18, United States Code, or both.

(2) Whoever commits any offense set forth in paragraph (1) and such offense involves an individual under 18 years of age is punishable by not more than 10 years imprisonment, such fines as are authorized by title 18, United States Code, or both.

(3) Any conviction for a violation of paragraphs (1) and (2) of this subsection shall be considered a felony violation of the Controlled Substances Act for the purposes of forfeiture under section 413 of such Act [21 USCS § 853].

(4) As used in this subsection the term "human growth hormone" means somatrem, somatropin, or an analogue of either of them.

(5) The Drug Enforcement Administration is authorized to investigate offenses punishable by this subsection.

(f) Civil penalties.

(1) (A) Except as provided in subparagraph (B), any person who violates a requirement of this Act which relates to devices shall be liable to the United States for a civil penalty in an amount not to exceed $ 15,000 for each such violation, and not to exceed $ 1,000,000 for all such violations adjudicated in a single proceeding. For purposes of the preceding sentence, a person accredited under paragraph (2) of section 704(g) [21 USCS § 374(g)] who is substantially not in compliance with the standards of accreditation under such section, or who poses a threat to public health or fails to act in a manner that is consistent with the purposes of such section, shall be considered to have violated a requirement of this Act that relates to devices.

(B) Subparagraph (A) shall not apply—

(i) to any person who violates the requirements of section 519(a) or 520(f) [21 USCS § 360i(a) or § 360j(f)] unless such violation constitutes (I) a significant or knowing departure from such requirements, or (II) a risk to public health,

(ii) to any person who commits minor violations of section

519(e) or 519(f) [21 USCS § 360i(e) or (f)] (only with respect to correction reports) if such person demonstrates substantial compliance with such section, or

(iii) to violations of section 501(a)(2)(A) [21 USCS § 360(a)(2)(A)] which involve one or more devices which are not defective.

(2) (A) Any person who introduces into interstate commerce or delivers for introduction into interstate commerce an article of food that is adulterated within the meaning of section 402(a)(2)(B) [21 USCS § 342(a)(2)(B)] shall be subject to a civil money penalty of not more than $ 50,000 in the case of an individual and $ 250,000 in the case of any other person for such introduction or delivery, not to exceed $ 500,000 for all such violations adjudicated in a single proceeding.

(B) This paragraph shall not apply to any person who grew the article of food that is adulterated. If the Secretary assesses a civil penalty against any person under this paragraph, the Secretary may not use the criminal authorities under this section to sanction such person for the introduction or delivery for introduction into interstate commerce of the article of food that is adulterated. If the Secretary assesses a civil penalty against any person under this paragraph, the Secretary may not use the seizure authorities of section 304 [21 USCS § 334] or the injunction authorities of section 302 [21 USCS § 332] with respect to the article of food that is adulterated.

(C) In a hearing to assess a civil penalty under this paragraph, the presiding officer shall have the same authority with regard to compelling testimony or production of documents as a presiding officer has under section 408(g)(2)(B) [21 USCS § 346a(g)(2)(B)]. The third sentence of paragraph (3)(A) shall not apply to any investigation under this paragraph.

(3) (A) A civil penalty under paragraph (1) or (2) shall be assessed by the Secretary by an order made on the record after opportunity for a hearing provided in accordance with this subparagraph and section 554 of title 5, United States Code. Before issuing such an order, the Secretary shall give written notice to the person to be assessed a civil penalty under such order of the Secretary's proposal to issue such order and provide such person an opportunity for a hearing on the order. In the course of any investigation, the Secretary may issue subpoenas requiring the attendance and testimony of witnesses and the production of evidence that relates to the matter under investigation.

(B) In determining the amount of a civil penalty, the Secretary shall take into account the nature, circumstances, extent, and gravity of the violation or violations and, with respect to the violator, ability to pay, effect on ability to continue to do business, any history of prior such violations, the degree of culpability, and such other matters as justice may require.

(C) The Secretary may compromise, modify, or remit, with or without conditions, any civil penalty which may be assessed under paragraph (1) or (2). The amount of such penalty, when finally determined, or the amount agreed upon in compromise, may be deducted from any sums owing by the United States to the person charged.

(4) Any person who requested, in accordance with paragraph (3)(A), a hearing respecting the assessment of a civil penalty and who is aggrieved by an order assessing a civil penalty may file a petition for judicial review of such order with the United States Court of Appeals for the District of Columbia Circuit or for any other circuit in which such person resides or transacts business. Such a petition may only be filed within the 60-day period beginning on the date the order making such assessment was issued.

(5) If any person fails to pay an assessment of a civil penalty—

(A) after the order making the assessment becomes final, and if such person does not file a petition for judicial review of the order in accordance with paragraph (4), or

(B) after a court in an action brought under paragraph (4) has entered a final judgment in favor of the Secretary, the Attorney General shall recover the amount assessed (plus interest at currently prevailing rates from the date of the expiration of the 60-day period referred to in paragraph (4) or the date of such final judgment, as the case may be) in an action brought in any appropriate district court of the United States. In such an action, the validity, amount, and appropriateness of such penalty shall not be subject to review.

§ 334. Seizure

(a) Grounds and jurisdiction.

(1) Any article of food, drug, or cosmetic that is adulterated or misbranded when introduced into or while in interstate commerce or while held for sale (whether or not the first sale) after shipment in interstate commerce, or which may not, under the provisions of section 404 or 505 [21 USCS § 344 or 355], be introduced into interstate commerce, shall be liable to be proceeded against while in interstate commerce, or at any time thereafter, on libel of information and condemned in any district court of the United States or United States court of a Territory within the jurisdiction of which the article is found. No libel for condemnation shall be instituted under this Act [21 USCS §§ 301 et seq.], for any alleged misbranding if there is pending in any court a libel for condemnation proceeding under this Act [21 USCS §§ 301 et seq.] based upon the same alleged misbranding, and not more than one such proceeding shall be instituted if no such proceeding is so pending, except that such limitations shall not apply (A) when such misbranding has been the basis of a prior judgment in favor of the United States, in a criminal, injunction, or libel for condemnation proceeding under this Act [21 USCS §§ 301 et seq.], or (B) when the Secretary has probable cause to believe from facts found, without hearing, by him or any officer or employee of the Department that the misbranded article is dangerous to health, or that the labeling of the misbranded article is fraudulent, or would be in a material respect misleading to the injury or damage of the purchaser or consumer. In any case where the number of libel for condemnation proceedings is limited as above provided the proceeding pending or instituted shall, on application of the claimant, seasonably made, be removed for trial to any district agreed upon by stipulation between the parties, or, in case of failure to so stipulate within a reasonable time, the claimant may apply to the court of the district in which the seizure has been made, and such court (after giving the United States attorney for such district reasonable notice and opportunity to be heard) shall by order, unless good cause to the contrary is shown, specify a district of reasonable proximity to the claimant's principal place of business, to which the case shall be removed for trial.

(2) The following shall be liable to be proceeded against at any time on libel of information and condemned in any district court of the United States or United States court of a Territory within the jurisdiction of which they are found: (A) Any drug that is a counterfeit drug, (B) Any container of a counterfeit drug, (C) Any punch, die, plate, stone, labeling, container, or other thing used or designed for use in making a counterfeit drug or drugs, and (D) Any adulterated or misbranded device.

(3) (A) Except as provided in subparagraph (B), no libel for condemnation may be instituted under paragraph (1) or (2) against any food which—

(i) is misbranded under section 403(a)(2) [21 USCS § 343(a)(2)] because of its advertising, and

(ii) is being held for sale to the ultimate consumer in an establishment other than an establishment owned or operated by a manufacturer, packer, or distributor of the food.

(B) A libel for condemnation may be instituted under paragraph (1) or (2) against a food described in subparagraph (A) if—

(i) (I) the food's advertising which resulted in the food being misbranded under section 403(a)(2) [21 USCS § 343(a)(2)] was disseminated in the establishment in which the food is being held for sale to the ultimate consumer,

(II) such advertising was disseminated by, or under the direction of, the owner or operator of such establishment, or

(III) all or part of the cost of such advertising was paid by such owner or operator; and

(ii) the owner or operator of such establishment used such advertising in the establishment to promote the sale of the food.

(b) Procedure; multiplicity of pending proceedings. The article, equipment, or other thing proceeded against shall be liable to seizure by process pursuant to the libel, and the procedure in cases under this section shall conform, as nearly as may be, to the procedure in admiralty; except that on demand of either party any issue of fact joined in any such case shall be tried by jury. When libel for condemnation proceedings under this section, involving the same claimant and the same issues of adulteration or misbranding, are pending in two or more jurisdictions, such pending proceedings, upon application of the claimant seasonably made to the court of one such jurisdiction, shall be consolidated for trial by order of such court, and tried in (1) any district selected by the claimant where one of such proceedings is pending; or (2) a district agreed upon by stipulation between the parties. If no order for consolidation is so made within a reasonable time, the claimant may apply to the court of one such jurisdiction, and such court (after giving the United States attorney for such district reasonable notice and opportunity to be heard) shall by order, unless good cause to the contrary is shown, specify a district of reasonable proximity to the claimant's principal place of business, in which all such pending proceedings shall be consolidated for trial and tried. Such order of consolidation shall not apply so as to require the removal of any case the date for trial of which has been fixed. The court granting such order shall give prompt notification thereof to the other courts having jurisdiction of the cases covered thereby.

(c) Availability of samples of seized goods prior to trial. The court at any time after seizure up to a reasonable time before trial shall by order allow any party to a condemnation proceeding, his attorney or agent, to obtain a representative sample of the article seized and a true copy of the analysis, if any, on which the proceeding is based and the identifying marks or numbers, if any, of the packages from which the samples analyzed were obtained.

(d) Disposition of goods after decree of condemnation; claims for remission or mitigation of forfeitures.

(1) Any food, drug, device, or cosmetic condemned under this section shall, after entry of the decree, be disposed of by destruction or sale as the court may, in accordance with the provisions of this section, direct and the proceeds thereof, if sold, less the legal costs and charges, shall be paid into the Treasury of the United States; but such article shall not be sold under such decree contrary to the provisions of this Act [21 USCS §§ 301 et seq.] or the laws of the jurisdiction in which sold. After entry of the decree and upon the payment of the costs of such proceedings and the execution of a good and sufficient bond conditioned that such article shall not be sold or disposed of contrary to the provisions of this Act [21 USCS §§ 301 et seq.] or the laws of any State or Territory in which sold, the court may by order direct that such article be delivered to the owner thereof to be destroyed or brought into compliance with the provisions of this Act [21 USCS §§ 301 et seq.] under the supervision of an officer or employee duly designated by the Secretary, and the expenses of such supervision shall be paid by the person obtaining release of the article under bond. If the article was imported into the United States and the person seeking its release establishes (A) that the adulteration, misbranding, or violation did not occur after the article was imported, and (B) that he had no cause for believing that it was adulterated, misbranded, or in violation before it was released from customs custody, the court may permit the article to be delivered to the owner for exportation in lieu of destruction upon a showing by the owner that all of the conditions of section 801(e) [21 USCS § 381(e)] can and will be met. The provisions of this sentence shall not apply where condemnation is based upon violation of section 402(a)(1), (2), or (6) [21 USCS § 342(a)(1), (2), or (6)], section 501(a)(3) [21 USCS § 351(a)(3)], section 502(j) [21 USCS § 352(j)], or section 601(a) or (d) [21 USCS § 361(a) or (d)]. Where such exportation is made to the original foreign supplier, then subparagraphs (A) and (B) of section 801(e)(1) [21 USCS § 381(e)(1)(A), (B)] and the preceding sentence shall not be applicable; and in all cases of exportation the bond shall be conditioned that the article shall not be sold or disposed of until the applicable conditions of section 801(e) [21 USCS § 381(e)] have been met. Any person seeking to export an imported article pursuant to any of the provisions of this subsection shall establish that the article was intended for export at the time the article entered commerce. Any article condemned by reason of its being an article which may not, under section 404 or 505 [21 USCS § 344 or 355] be introduced into interest to commerce, shall be disposed of by destruction.

(2) The provisions of paragraph (1) of this subsection shall, to the extent deemed appropriate by the court, apply to any equipment or other thing which is not otherwise within the scope of such paragraph and which is referred to in paragraph (2) of subsection (a).

(3) Whenever in any proceeding under this section, involving paragraph (2) of subsection (a), the condemnation of any equipment or thing (other than a drug) is decreed, the court shall allow the claim of any claimant, to the extent of such claimant's interest, for remission or mitigation of such forfeiture if such claimant proves to the satisfaction of the court (i) that he has not committed or caused to be committed any prohibited act referred to in such paragraph (2) and has no interest in any drug referred to therein, (ii) that he has an interest in such equipment or other thing as owner or lienor or otherwise, acquired by him in good faith, and (iii) that he at no time had any knowledge or reason to believe that such equipment or other thing was being or would be used in, or to facilitate, the violation of laws of the United States relating to counterfeit drugs.

(e) Costs. When a decree of condemnation is entered against the article, court costs and fees, and storage and other proper expenses, shall be awarded against the person, if any, intervening as claimant of the article.

(f) Removal of case for trial. In the case of removal for trial of any case as provided by subsection (a) or (b)—

(1) The clerk of the court from which removal is made shall promptly transmit to the court in which the case is to be tried all records in the case necessary in order that such court may exercise jurisdiction.

(2) The court to which such case was removed shall have the powers and be subject to the duties, for purposes of such case, which the court from which removal was made would have had, or to which such court would have been subject, if such case had not been removed.

(g) Administrative restraint; detention orders.

(1) If during an inspection conducted under section 704 [21 USCS § 374] of a facility or a vehicle, a device which the officer or employee making the inspection has reason to believe is adulterated or misbranded is found in such facility or vehicle, such officer or employee may order the device detained (in accordance with regulations prescribed by the Secretary) for a reasonable period which may not exceed twenty days unless the Secretary determines that a period of detention greater than twenty days is required to institute an action under subsection (a) or section 302 [21 USCS § 332], in which case he may authorize a detention period of not to exceed thirty days. Regulations of the Secretary prescribed under this paragraph shall require that before a device may be ordered detained under this paragraph the Secretary or an officer or employee designated by the Secretary approve such order. A detention order under this paragraph may require the labeling or marking of a device during the period of its detention for the purpose of identifying the device as detained. Any person who would be entitled to claim a device if it were seized under subsection (a) may appeal to the Secretary a detention of such device under this paragraph. Within five days of the date an appeal of a detention is filed with the Secretary, the Secretary shall after affording opportunity for an informal hearing by order confirm the detention or revoke it.

(2) (A) Except as authorized by subparagraph (B), a device subject to a detention order issued under paragraph (1) shall not be moved by any person from the place at which it is ordered detained until—

(i) released by the Secretary, or

(ii) the expiration of the detention period applicable to such order, whichever occurs first.

(B) A device subject to a detention order under paragraph (1) may be moved—

(i) in accordance with regulations prescribed by the Secretary, and

(ii) if not in final form for shipment, at the discretion of the manufacturer of the device for the purpose of completing the work required to put it in such form.

(h) Administrative detention of foods.

(1) Detention authority

(A) In general. An officer or qualified employee of the Food and Drug Administration may order the detention, in accordance with this subsection, of any article of food that is found during an inspection, examination, or investigation under this Act [21 USCS §§ 301 et seq.] conducted by such officer or qualified employee, if the officer or qualified employee has credible evidence or information indicating that such article presents a threat of serious adverse health consequences or death to humans or animals.

(B) Secretary's approval. An article of food may be ordered detained under subparagraph (A) only if the Secretary or an official designated by the Secretary approves the order. An official may not be so designated unless the official is the director of the district under this Act [21 USCS §§ 301 et seq.] in which the article involved is located, or is an official senior to such director

(2) Period of detention. An article of food may be detained under paragraph (1) for a reasonable period, not to exceed 20 days, unless a greater period, not to exceed 30 days, is necessary, to enable the Secretary to institute an action under subsection (a) or section 302 [21 USCS § 332]. The Secretary shall by regulation provide for procedures for instituting such action on an expedited basis with respect to perishable foods.

(3) Security of detained article. An order under paragraph (1) with respect to an article of food may require that such article be labeled or

marked as detained, and shall require that the article be removed to a secure facility, as appropriate. An article subject to such an order shall not be transferred by any person from the place at which the article is ordered detained, or from the place to which the article is so removed, as the case may be, until released by the Secretary or until the expiration of the detention period applicable under such order, whichever occurs first. This subsection may not be construed as authorizing the delivery of the article pursuant to the execution of a bond while the article is subject to the order, and section 801(b) [21 USCS § 381(b)] does not authorize the delivery of the article pursuant to the execution of a bond while the article is subject to the order.

(4) Appeal of detention order.

(A) In general. With respect to an article of food ordered detained under paragraph (1), any person who would be entitled to be a claimant for such article if the article were seized under subsection (a) may appeal the order to the Secretary. Within five days after such an appeal is filed, the Secretary, after providing opportunity for an informal hearing, shall confirm or terminate the order involved, and such confirmation by the Secretary shall be considered a final agency action for purposes of section 702 of title 5, United States Code. If during such five-day period the Secretary fails to provide such an opportunity, or to confirm or terminate such order, the order is deemed to be terminated.

(B) Effect of instituting court action. The process under subparagraph (A) for the appeal of an order under paragraph (1) terminates if the Secretary institutes an action under subsection (a) or section 302 [21 USCS § 332] regarding the article of food involved.

§ 335b. Civil penalties

(a) In general. Any person that the Secretary finds—

(1) knowingly made or caused to be made, to any officer, employee, or agent of the Department of Health and Human Services, a false statement or misrepresentation of a material fact in connection with an abbreviated drug application,

(2) bribed or attempted to bribe or paid or attempted to pay an illegal gratuity to any officer, employee, or agent of the Department of Health and Human Services in connection with an abbreviated drug application,

(3) destroyed, altered, removed, or secreted, or procured the destruction, alteration, removal, or secretion of, any material document or other material evidence which was the property of or in the possession of the Department of Health and Human Services for the purpose of interfering with that Department's discharge of its responsibilities in connection with an abbreviated drug application,

(4) knowingly failed to disclose, to an officer or employee of the Department of Health and Human Services, a material fact which such person had an obligation to disclose relating to any drug subject to an abbreviated drug application,

(5) knowingly obstructed an investigation of the Department of Health and Human Services into any drug subject to an abbreviated drug application,

(6) is a person that has an approved or pending drug product application and has knowingly—

(A) employed or retained as a consultant or contractor, or

(B) otherwise used in any capacity the services of, a person who was debarred under section 306 [21 USCS § 335a], or

(7) is an individual debarred under section 306 [21 USCS § 335a]and, during the period of debarment, provided services in any capacity to a person that had an approved or pending drug product application, shall be liable to the United States for a civil penalty for each such violation in an amount not to exceed $ 250,000 in the case of an individual and $ 1,000,000 in the case of any other person.

(b) Procedure.

(1) In general.

(A) Action by the Secretary. A civil penalty under subsection (a) shall be assessed by the Secretary on a person by an order made on the record after an opportunity for an agency hearing on disputed issues of material fact and the amount of the penalty. In the course of any investigation or hearing under this subparagraph, the Secretary may administer oaths and affirmations, examine witnesses, receive evidence, and issue subpoenas requiring the attendance and testimony of witnesses and the production of evidence that relates to the matter under investigation.

(B) Action by the Attorney General. In lieu of a proceeding under subparagraph (A), the Attorney General may, upon request of the Secretary, institute a civil action to recover a civil money penalty in the amount and for any of the acts set forth in subsection (a). Such an action may be instituted separately from or in connection with any other claim, civil or criminal, initiated by the Attorney General under this Act.

(2) Amount. In determining the amount of a civil penalty under paragraph (1), the Secretary or the court shall take into account the nature, circumstances, extent, and gravity of the act subject to penalty, the person's ability to pay, the effect on the person's ability to continue to do business, any history of prior, similar acts, and such other matters as justice may require.

(3) Limitation on actions. No action may be initiated under this section—

(A) with respect to any act described in subsection (a) that occurred before the date of the enactment of this section [enacted May 13, 1992], or

(B) more than 6 years after the date when facts material to the act are known or reasonably should have been known by the Secretary but in no event more than 10 years after the date the act took place.

(c) Judicial review. Any person that is the subject of an adverse decision under subsection (b)(1)(A) may obtain a review of such decision by the United States Court of Appeals for the District of Columbia or for the circuit in which the person resides, by filing in such court (within 60 days following the date the person is notified of the Secretary's decision) a petition requesting that the decision be modified or set aside.

(d) Recovery of penalties. The Attorney General may recover any civil penalty (plus interest at the currently prevailing rates from the date the penalty became final) assessed under subsection (b)(1)(A) in an action brought in the name of the United States. The amount of such penalty may be deducted, when the penalty has become final, from any sums then or later owing by the United States to the person against whom the penalty has been assessed. In an action brought under this subsection, the validity, amount, and appropriateness of the penalty shall not be subject to judicial review.

(e) Informants. The Secretary may award to any individual (other than an officer or employee of the Federal Government or a person who materially participated in any conduct described in subsection (a)) who provides information leading to the imposition of a civil penalty under this section an amount not to exceed—

(1) $ 250,000, or

(2) one-half of the penalty so imposed and collected, whichever is less. The decision of the Secretary on such award shall not be reviewable.

§ 342. Adulterated food

A food shall be deemed to be adulterated—

(a) Poisonous, insanitary, or deleterious ingredients.

(1) If it bears or contains any poisonous or deleterious substance which may render it injurious to health; but in case the substance is not an added substance such food shall not be considered adulterated under this clause if the quantity of such substance in such food does not ordinarily render it injurious to health.[; or] (2)(A) if it bears or contains any added poisonous or added deleterious substance (other than a substance that is a pesticide chemical residue in or on a raw agricultural commodity or processed food, a food additive, a color additive, or a new animal drug) that is unsafe within the meaning of section 406 [21 USCS § 346]; or (B) if it bears or contains a pesticide chemical residue that is unsafe within the meaning of section 408(a) [21 USCS § 346a(a)]; or (C) if it is or if it bears or contains (i) any food additive that is unsafe within the meaning of section 409 [21 USCS § 348]; or (ii) a new animal drug (or conversion product thereof) that is unsafe within the meaning of section 512 [21 USCS § 360b]; or (3) if it consists in whole or in part of any filthy, putrid, or decomposed substances, or if it is otherwise unfit for food; or (4) if it has been prepared, packed, or held under insanitary conditions whereby it may have become contaminated with filth, or whereby it may have been rendered injurious to health; or (5) if it is, in whole or in part, the product of a diseased animal or of an animal which has died otherwise than by slaughter; or (6) if its container is composed, in whole or in part, of any poisonous or deleterious substance which may render the contents injurious to health; or (7) if it has been intentionally subjected to radiation, unless the use of the radiation was in conformity with a regulation or exemption in effect pursuant to section 409 [21 USCS § 348].

(b) Absence, substitution, or addition of constituents. (1) If any valuable constituent has been in whole or in part omitted or abstracted therefrom; or (2) if any substance has been substituted wholly or in part therefor; or (3) if damage or inferiority has been concealed in any manner; or (4) if any substance has been added thereto or mixed or packed therewith so as to increase its bulk or weight, or reduce its quality or strength, or make it appear better or of greater value than it is.

(c) Color additives. If it is, or it bears or contains, a color additive which is unsafe within the meaning of section 721(a) [21 USCS § 379e(a)].

(d) Confectionery containing alcohol or nonnutritive substance. If it is confectionery, and—

(1) has partially or completely imbedded therein any nonnutritive object, except that this subparagraph shall not apply in the case of any nonnutritive object if, in the judgment of the Secretary as provided by regulations, such object is of practical functional value to the confectionery product and would not render the product injurious or hazardous to health;

(2) bears or contains any alcohol other than alcohol not in excess of one-half of 1 per centum by volume derived solely from the use of flavoring extracts, except that this clause shall not apply to confectionery which is introduced or delivered for introduction into, or received or held for sale in, interstate commerce if the sale of such confectionery is permitted under the laws of the State in which such confectionery is intended to be offered for sale; or

(3) bears or contains any nonnutritive substance, except that this subparagraph shall not apply to a safe nonnutritive substance which is in or on confectionery by reason of its use for some practical functional purpose in the manufacture, packaging, or storage of such confectionery if the use of the substance does not promote deception of the consumer or otherwise result in adulteration or misbranding in violation of any provision of this Act [21 USCS §§ 301 et seq.], except that the Secretary may, for the purpose of avoiding or resolving uncertainty as to the application of this subparagraph, issue regulations allowing or prohibiting the use of particular nonnutritive substances.

(e) Oleomargarine containing filthy, putrid, etc., matter. If it is oleomargarine or margarine or butter and any of the raw material used therein consisted in whole or in part of any filthy, putrid, or decomposed substance, or such oleomargarine or margarine or butter is otherwise unfit for food.

(f) Safety of dietary supplements and burden of proof on FDA.

(1) If it is a dietary supplement or contains a dietary ingredient that—

(A) presents a significant or unreasonable risk of illness or injury under—

(i) conditions of use recommended or suggested in labeling, or

(ii) if no conditions of use are suggested or recommended in the labeling, under ordinary conditions of use;

(B) is a new dietary ingredient for which there is inadequate information to provide reasonable assurance that such ingredient does not present a significant or unreasonable risk of illness or injury;

(C) the Secretary declares to pose an imminent hazard to public health or safety, except that the authority to make such declaration shall not be delegated and the Secretary shall promptly after such a declaration initiate a proceeding in accordance with sections 554 and 556 of title 5, United States Code, to affirm or withdraw the declaration; or

(D) is or contains a dietary ingredient that renders it adulterated under paragraph (a)(1) under the conditions of use recommended or suggested in the labeling of such dietary supplement.

In any proceeding under this subparagraph, the United States shall bear the burden of proof on each element to show that a dietary supplement is adulterated. The court shall decide any issue under this paragraph on a de novo basis.

(2) Before the Secretary may report to a United States attorney a violation of paragraph (1)(A) for a civil proceeding, the person against whom such proceeding would be initiated shall be given appropriate notice and the opportunity to present views, orally and in writing, at least 10 days before such notice, with regard to such proceeding.

(g) Good manufacturing practices.

(1) If it is a dietary supplement and it has been prepared, packed, or held under conditions that do not meet current good manufacturing practice regulations, including regulations requiring, when necessary, expiration date labeling, issued by the Secretary under subparagraph (2).

(2) The Secretary may by regulation prescribe good manufacturing practices for dietary supplements. Such regulations shall be modeled after current good manufacturing practice regulations for food and may

not impose standards for which there is no current and generally available analytical methodology. No standard of current good manufacturing practice may be imposed unless such standard is included in a regulation promulgated after notice and opportunity for comment in accordance with chapter 5 of title 5, United States Code [5 USCS §§ 500 et seq.].

(h) If it is an article of food imported or offered for import into the United States and the article of food has previously been refused admission under section 801(a) [21 USCS § 381(a)], unless the person reoffering the article affirmatively establishes, at the expense of the owner or consignee of the article, that the article complies with the applicable requirements of this Act [21 USCS §§ 301 et seq.], as determined by the Secretary.

§ 343.   Misbranded food

A food shall be deemed to be misbranded—

(a) False or misleading label. If (1) its labeling is false or misleading in any particular, or (2) in the case of a food to which section 411 [21 USCS § 350] applies, its advertising is false or misleading in a material respect or its labeling is in violation of section 411(b)(2) [21 USCS § 350(b)(2)].

(b) Offer for sale under another name. If it is offered for sale under the name of another food.

(c) Imitation of another food. If it is an imitation of another food, unless its label bears, in type of uniform size and prominence, the word "imitation" and, immediately thereafter, the name of the food imitated.

(d) Misleading container. If its container is so made, formed, or filled as to be misleading.

(e) Package form. If in package form unless it bears a label containing (1) the name and place of business of the manufacturer, packer, or distributor; and (2) an accurate statement of the quantity of the contents in terms of weight, measure, or numerical count, except that under clause (2) of this paragraph reasonable variations shall be permitted, and exemptions as to small packages shall be established, by regulations prescribed by the Secretary.

(f) Prominence of information on label. If any word, statement, or other information required by or under authority of this Act [21 USCS §§ 301 et seq.] to appear on the label or labeling is not prominently placed thereon with such conspicuousness (as compared with other words, statements, designs, or devices, in the labeling) and in such terms as to render it likely to be read and understood by the ordinary individual under customary conditions of purchase and use.

(g) Representation as to definition and standard of identity. If it purports to be or is represented as a food for which a definition and standard of identity has been prescribed by regulations as provided by section 401 [21 USCS § 341], unless (1) it conforms to such definition and standard, and (2) its label bears the name of the food specified in the definition and standard, and, insofar as may be required by such regulations, the common names of optional ingredients (other than spices, flavoring, and coloring) present in such food.

(h) Representation as to standards of quality and fill of container. If it purports to be or is represented as—

(1) a food for which a standard of quality has been prescribed by regulations as provided by section 401 [21 USCS § 341], and its quality falls below such standard, unless its label bears, in such manner and form as such regulations specify, a statement that it falls below such standard;

(2) a food for which a standard or standards of fill of container have been prescribed by regulations as provided by section 401 [21 USCS § 341], and it falls below the standard of fill of container applicable thereto, unless its label bears, in such manner and form as such regulations specify, a statement that it falls below such standard; or

(3) a food that is pasteurized unless—

(A) such food has been subjected to a safe process or treatment that is prescribed as pasteurization for such food in a regulation promulgated under this Act [21 USCS §§ 301 et seq.]; or

(B) (i) such food has been subjected to a safe process or treatment that—

(I) is reasonably certain to achieve destruction or elimination in the food of the most resistant microorganisms of public health significance that are likely to occur in the food;

(II) is at least as protective of the public health as a process or treatment described in subparagraph (A);

(III) is effective for a period that is at least as long as the shelf life of the food when stored under normal and moderate abuse conditions; and

(IV) is the subject of a notification to the Secretary, including effectiveness data regarding the process or treatment; and

(ii) at least 120 days have passed after the date of receipt of such notification by the Secretary without the Secretary making a determination that the process or treatment involved has not been shown to meet the requirements of subclauses (I) through (III) of clause (i). For purposes of paragraph (3), a determination by the Secretary that a process or treatment has not been shown to meet the requirements of subclauses (I) through (III) of subparagraph (B)(i) shall constitute final agency action under such subclauses.

(i) Label where no representation as to definition and standard of quality. Unless its label bears (1) the common or usual name of the food, if any there be, and (2) in case it is fabricated from two or more ingredients, the common or usual name of each such ingredient and if the food purports to be a beverage containing vegetable or fruit juice, a statement with appropriate prominence on the information panel of the total percentage of such fruit or vegetable juice contained in the food; except that spices, flavorings, and colors not required to be certified under section 721(c) [21 USCS § 379e(c)] unless sold as spices, flavorings, or such colors, may be designated as spices, flavorings, and colorings without naming each. To the extent that compliance with the requirements of clause (2) of this paragraph is impracticable, or results in deception or unfair competition, exemptions shall be established by regulations promulgated by the Secretary.

(j) Representation for special dietary use. If it purports to be or is represented for special dietary uses, unless its label bears such information concerning its vitamin, mineral, and other dietary properties as the Secretary determines to be, and by regulations prescribes as, necessary in order fully to inform purchasers as to its value for such uses.

(k) Artificial flavoring, artificial coloring, or chemical preservatives. If it bears or contains any artificial flavoring, artificial coloring, or chemical preservative, unless it bears labeling stating that fact, except that to the extent that compliance with the requirements of this paragraph is impracticable, exemptions shall be established by regulations promulgated by the Secretary. The provisions of this paragraph and paragraphs (g) and (i) with respect to artificial coloring shall not apply in the case of butter, cheese, or ice cream. The provisions of this paragraph with respect to chemical preservatives shall not apply to a pesticide chemical when used in or on a raw agricultural commodity which is the produce of the soil.

(l) Pesticide chemicals on raw agricultural commodities. If it is a raw agricultural commodity which is the produce of the soil, bearing or containing a pesticide chemical applied after harvest, unless the shipping container of such commodity bears labeling which declares the presence of such chemical in or on such commodity and the common or usual name and the function of such chemical, except that no such declaration shall be required while such commodity, having been removed from the shipping container, is being held or displayed for sale at retail out of such container in accordance with the custom of the trade.

(m) Color additives. If it is a color additive, unless its packaging and labeling are in conformity with such packaging and labeling requirements, applicable to such color additive, as may be contained in regulations issued under section 721 [21 USCS § 379e].

(n) Packaging or labeling of drugs in violation of regulations. If its packaging or labeling is in violation of an applicable regulation issued pursuant to section 3 or 4 of the Poison Prevention Packaging Act of 1970 [15 USCS § 1472 or 1473].

(o) [Repealed]

(p) [Deleted]

(q) Nutrition labeling; information required.

(1) Except as provided in subparagraphs (3), (4), and (5), if it is a food intended for human consumption and is offered for sale, unless its label or labeling bears nutrition information that provides—

(A) (i) the serving size which is an amount customarily consumed and which is expressed in a common household measure that is appropriate to the food, or

(ii) if the use of the food is not typically expressed in a serving size, the common household unit of measure that expresses the serving size of the food,

(B) the number of servings or other units of measure per container,

(C) the total number of calories—

(i) derived from any source, and

(ii) derived from the total fat, in each serving size or other unit of measure of the food,

(D) the amount of the following nutrients: Total fat, saturated fat, cholesterol, sodium, total carbohydrates, complex carbohydrates, sugars, dietary fiber, and total protein contained in each serving size or other unit of measure,

(E) any vitamin, mineral, or other nutrient required to be placed on the label and labeling of food under this Act [21 USCS §§ 301 et seq.] before October 1, 1990, if the Secretary determines that such information will assist consumers in maintaining healthy dietary practices.

The Secretary may by regulation require any information required to be placed on the label or labeling by this subparagraph or subparagraph (2)(A) to be highlighted on the label or labeling by larger type, bold type, or contrasting color if the Secretary determines that such highlighting will assist consumers in maintaining healthy dietary practices.

(2) (A) If the Secretary determines that a nutrient other than a nutrient required by subparagraph (1)(C), (1)(D), or (1)(E) should be included in the label or labeling of food subject to subparagraph (1) for purposes of providing information regarding the nutritional value of such food that will assist consumers in maintaining healthy dietary practices, the Secretary may by regulation require that information relating to such additional nutrient be included in the label or labeling of such food.

(B) If the Secretary determines that the information relating to a nutrient required by subparagraph (1)(C), (1)(D), or (1)(E) or clause (A) of this subparagraph to be included in the label or labeling of food is not necessary to assist consumers in maintaining healthy dietary practices, the Secretary may by regulation remove information relating to such nutrient from such requirement.

(3) For food that is received in bulk containers at a retail establishment, the Secretary may, by regulation, provide that the nutrition information required by subparagraphs (1) and (2) be displayed at the location in the retail establishment at which the food is offered for sale.

(4) (A) The Secretary shall provide for furnishing the nutrition information required by subparagraphs (1) and (2) with respect to raw agricultural commodities and raw fish by issuing voluntary nutrition guidelines, as provided by clause (B) or by issuing regulations that are mandatory as provided by clause (D).

(B) (i) Upon the expiration of 12 months after the date of the enactment of the Nutrition Labeling and Education Act of 1990 [enacted Nov. 8, 1990], the Secretary, after providing an opportunity for comment, shall issue guidelines for food retailers offering raw agricultural commodities or raw fish to provide nutrition information specified in subparagraphs (1) and (2). Such guidelines shall take into account the actions taken by food retailers during such 12-month period to provide to consumers nutrition information on raw agricultural commodities and raw fish. Such guidelines shall only apply—

(I) in the case of raw agricultural commodities, to the 20 varieties of vegetables most frequently consumed during a year and the 20 varieties of fruit most frequently consumed during a year, and

(II) to the 20 varieties of raw fish most frequently consumed during a year.

The vegetables, fruits, and raw fish to which such guidelines apply shall be determined by the Secretary by regulation and the Secretary may apply such guidelines regionally.

(ii) Upon the expiration of 12 months after the date of the enactment of the Nutrition Labeling and Education Act of 1990 [enacted Nov. 8, 1990], the Secretary shall issue a final regulation defining the circumstances that constitute substantial compliance by food retailers with the guidelines issued under subclause (i). The regulation shall provide that there is not substantial compliance if a significant number of retailers have failed to comply with the guidelines. The size of the retailers and the portion of the market served by retailers in compliance with the guidelines shall be considered in determining whether the substantial-compliance standard has been met.

(C) (i) Upon the expiration of 30 months after the date of the enactment of the Nutrition Labeling and Education Act of 1990 [enacted Nov. 8, 1990], the Secretary shall issue a report on actions taken by food retailers to provide consumers with nutrition information for raw agricultural commodities and raw fish under the guidelines issued under clause (A). Such report shall include a determination of whether there is substantial compliance with the guidelines.

(ii) If the Secretary finds that there is substantial compliance with the guidelines, the Secretary shall issue a report and make a determination of the type required in subclause (i) every two years.

(D) (i) If the Secretary determines that there is not substantial compliance with the guidelines issued under clause (A), the Secretary shall at the time such determination is made issue proposed regulations requiring that any person who offers raw agricultural commodities or raw fish to consumers to provide, in a manner prescribed by regulations, the nutrition information required by subparagraphs (1) and (2). The Secretary shall issue final regulations imposing such requirements 6 months after issuing the proposed regulations. The final regulations shall become effective 6 months after the date of their promulgation.

(ii) Regulations issued under subclause (i) may require that the nutrition information required by subparagraphs (1) and (2) be provided for more than 20 varieties of vegetables, 20 varieties of fruit, and 20 varieties of fish most frequently consumed during a year if the Secretary finds that a larger number of such products are frequently consumed. Such regulations shall permit such information to be provided in a single location in each area in which raw agricultural commodities and raw fish are offered for sale. Such regulations may provide that information shall be expressed as an average or range per serving of the same type of raw agricultural commodity or raw fish. The Secretary shall develop and make available to the persons who offer such food to consumers the information required by subparagraphs (1) and (2).

(iii) Regulations issued under subclause (i) shall permit the required information to be provided in each area of an establishment in which raw agricultural commodities and raw Fish are offered for sale. The regulations shall permit food retailers to display the required information by supplying copies of the information provided by the Secretary, by making the information available in brochure, notebook or leaflet form, or by posting a sign disclosing the information. Such regulations shall also permit presentation of the required information to be supplemented by a video, live demonstration, or other media which the Secretary approves.

(E) For purposes of this subparagraph, the term "fish" includes freshwater or marine fin fish, crustaceans, and mollusks, including shellfish, amphibians, and other forms of aquatic animal life.

(F) No person who offers raw agricultural commodities or raw fish to consumers may be prosecuted for minor violations of this subparagraph if there has been substantial compliance with the requirements of this paragraph.

(5) (A) Subparagraphs (1), (2), (3), and (4) shall not apply to food—

(i) which is served in restaurants or other establishments in which food is served for immediate human consumption or which is sold for sale or use in such establishments,

(ii) which is processed and prepared primarily in a retail establishment, which is ready for human consumption, which is of the type described in subclause (i), and which is offered for sale to consumers but not for immediate human consumption in such establishment and which is not offered for sale outside such establishment,

(iii) which is an infant formula subject to section 412 [21 USCS § 350a],

(iv) which is a medical food as defined in section 5(b) of the Orphan Drug Act (21 U.S.C. 360ee(b)), or

(v) which is described in section 405(2) [21 USCS § 345(2)].

(B) Subparagraphs (1) and (2) shall not apply to the label of a food if the Secretary determines by regulations that compliance with such subparagraphs is impracticable because the package of such food is too small to comply with the requirements of such subparagraphs and if the label of such food does not contain any nutrition information.

(C) If a food contains insignificant amounts, as determined by the Secretary, of all the nutrients required by subparagraphs (1) and (2) to be listed in the label or labeling of food, the requirements of such subparagraphs shall not apply to such food if the label, labeling, or advertising of such food does not make any claim with respect to the nutritional value of such food. If a food contains insignificant amounts, as determined by the Secretary, of more than one-half the nutrients required by subparagraphs (1) and (2) to be in the label or labeling of the food, the Secretary shall require the amounts of such nutrients to be stated in a simplified form prescribed by the Secretary

(D) If a person offers food for sale and has annual gross sales made or business done in sales to consumers which is not more than $ 500,000 or has annual gross sales made or business done in sales of food to consumers which is not more than $ 50,000, the requirements of subparagraphs (1), (2), (3), and (4) shall not apply with respect to food sold by such person to consumers unless the label or labeling of food offered by such person provides nutrition information or makes a nutrition claim.

(E) (i) During the 12-month period for which an exemption from subparagraphs (1) and (2) is claimed pursuant to this subclause, the requirements of such subparagraphs shall not apply to any food product if—

(I) the labeling for such product does not provide nutrition information or make a claim subject to paragraph (r),

(II) the person who claims for such product an exemption from such subparagraphs employed fewer than an average of 100 full-time equivalent employees,

(III) such person provided the notice described in subclause (iii), and

(IV) in the case of a food product which was sold in the 12-month period preceding the period for which an exemption was claimed, fewer than 100,000 units of such product were sold in the United States during such preceding period, or in the case of a food product which was not sold in the 12-month period preceding the period for which such exemption is claimed, fewer than 100,000 units of such product are reasonably anticipated to be sold in the United States during the period for which such exemption is claimed.

(ii) During the 12-month period after the applicable date referred to in this sentence, the requirements of subparagraphs (1) and (2) shall not apply to any food product which was first introduced into interstate commerce before May 8, 1994, if the labeling for such product does not provide nutrition information or make a claim subject to paragraph (r), if such person provided the notice described in subclause (iii), and if—

(I) during the 12-month period preceding May 8, 1994, the person who claims for such product an exemption from such subparagraphs employed fewer than an average of 300 full-time equivalent employees and fewer than 600,000 units of such product were sold in the United States,

(II) during the 12-month period preceding May 8, 1995, the person who claims for such product an exemption from such subparagraphs employed fewer than an average of 300 full-time equivalent employees and fewer than 400,000 units of such product were sold in the United States, or

(III) during the 12-month period preceding May 8, 1996, the person who claims for such product an exemption from such subparagraphs employed fewer than an average of 200 full-time equivalent employees and fewer than 200,000 units of such product were sold in the United States.

(iii) The notice referred to in subclauses (i) and (ii) shall be given to the Secretary prior to the beginning of the period during which the exemption under subclause (i) or (ii) is to be in effect, shall state that the person claiming such exemption for a food product has complied with the applicable requirements of subclause (i) or (ii), and shall—

(I) state the average number of full-time equivalent employees such person employed during the 12 months preceding the date such person claims such exemption,

(II) state the approximate number of units the person claiming the exemption sold in the United States,

(III) if the exemption is claimed for a food product which was sold in the 12-month period preceding the period for which the exemption was claimed, state the approximate number of units of such product which were sold in the United States during such preceding period, and, if the exemption is claimed for a food product which was not sold in such preceding period, state the number of units of such product which such person reasonably anticipates will be sold in the United States during the period for which the exemption was claimed, and

(IV) contain such information as the Secretary may require to verify the information required by the preceding provisions of this subclause if the Secretary has questioned the validity of such information. If a person is not an importer, has fewer than 10 full-time equivalent employees, and sells fewer than 10,000 units of any food product in any year, such person is not required to file a notice for such product under this subclause for such year.

(iv) In the case of a person who claimed an exemption under subclause (i) or (ii), if, during the period of such exemption, the number of full-time equivalent employees of such person exceeds the number in such subclause or if the number of food products sold in the United States exceeds the number in such subclause, such exemption shall extend to the expiration of 18 months after the date the number of full-time equivalent employees or food products sold exceeded the applicable number

(v) For any food product first introduced into interstate commerce after May 8, 2002, the Secretary may by regulation lower the employee or units of food products requirement of subclause (i) if the Secretary determines that the cost of compliance with such lower requirement will not place an undue burden on persons subject to such lower requirement.

(vi) For purposes of subclauses (i), (ii), (iii), (iv), and (v)—

(I) the term "unit" means the packaging or, if there is no packaging, the form in which a food product is offered for sale to consumers,

(II) the term "food product" means food in any sized package which is manufactured by a single manufacturer or which bears the same brand name, which bears the same statement of identity, and which has similar preparation methods, and

(III) the term "person" in the case of a corporation includes all domestic and foreign affiliates of the corporation.

(F) A dietary supplement product (including a food to which section 411 [21 USCS § 350] applies) shall comply with the requirements of subparagraphs (1) and (2) in a manner which is appropriate for the product and which is specified in regulations of the Secretary which shall provide that—

(i) nutrition information shall first list those dietary ingredients that are present in the product in a significant amount and for which a recommendation for daily consumption has been established by the Secretary, except that a dietary ingredient shall not be required to be listed if it is not present in a significant amount, and shall list any other dietary ingredient present and identified as having no such recommendation;

(ii) the listing of dietary ingredients shall include the quantity of each such ingredient (or of a proprietary blend of such ingredients) per serving;

(iii) the listing of dietary ingredients may include the source of a dietary ingredient; and

(iv) the nutrition information shall immediately precede the ingredient information required under subclause (i), except that no ingredient identified pursuant to subclause (i) shall be required to be identified a second time.

(G) Subparagraphs (1), (2), (3), and (4) shall not apply to food which is sold by a food distributor if the food distributor principally sells food to restaurants or other establishments in which food is served for immediate human consumption and does not manufacture, process, or repackage the food it sells.

(r) Labeling required.

(1) Except as provided in clauses (A) through (C) of subparagraph (5), if it is a food intended for human consumption which is offered for sale and for which a claim is made in the label or labeling of the food which expressly or by implication—

(A) characterizes the level of any nutrient which is of the type required by paragraph (q)(1) or (q)(2) to be in the label or labeling of the food unless the claim is made in accordance with subparagraph (2), or

(B) characterizes the relationship of any nutrient which is of the type required by paragraph (q)(1) or (q)(2) to be in the label or labeling of the food to a disease or a health-related condition unless the claim is made in accordance with subparagraph (3) or (5)(D).

A statement of the type required by paragraph (q) that appears as part of the nutrition information required or permitted by such paragraph is not a claim which is subject to this paragraph and a claim subject to clause (A) is not subject to clause (B).

(2) (A) Except as provided in subparagraphs (4)(A)(ii) and (4)(A)(iii) and clauses (A) through (C) of subparagraph (5), a claim described in subparagraph (1)(A)—

(i) may be made only if the characterization of the level made in the claim uses terms which are defined in regulations of the Secretary,

(ii) may not state the absence of a nutrient unless—

(I) the nutrient is usually present in the food or in a food which substitutes for the food as defined by the Secretary by regulation, or

(II) the Secretary by regulation permits such a statement on the basis of a finding that such a statement would assist consumers in maintaining healthy dietary practices and the statement discloses that the nutrient is not usually present in the food,

(iii) may not be made with respect to the level of cholesterol in the food if the food contains, as determined by the Secretary by regulation, fat or saturated fat in an amount which increases to persons in the general population the risk of disease or a health related condition which is diet related unless—

(I) the Secretary finds by regulation that the level of cholesterol is substantially less than the level usually present in the food or in a food which substitutes for the food and which has a significant market share, or the Secretary by regulation permits a statement regarding the absence of cholesterol on the basis of a finding that cholesterol is not usually present in the food and that such a statement would assist consumers in maintaining healthy dietary practices and the regulation requires that the statement disclose that cholesterol is not usually present in the food, and

(II) the label or labeling of the food discloses the level of such fat or saturated fat in immediate proximity to such claim and with appropriate prominence which shall be no less than one-half the size of the claim with respect to the level of cholesterol,

(iv) may not be made with respect to the level of saturated fat in the food if the food contains cholesterol unless the label or labeling of the food discloses the level of cholesterol in the food in immediate proximity to such claim and with appropriate prominence which shall be no less than one-half the size of the claim with respect to the level of saturated fat,

(v) may not state that a food is high in dietary fiber unless the food is low in total fat as defined by the Secretary or the label or labeling discloses the level of total fat in the food in immediate proximity to such statement and with appropriate prominence which shall be no less than one-half the size of the claim with respect to the level of dietary fiber, and

(vi) may not be made if the Secretary by regulation prohibits the claim because the claim is misleading in light of the level of another nutrient in the food.

(B) If a claim described in subparagraph (1)(A) is made with respect to a nutrient in a food and the Secretary makes a determination that the food contains a nutrient at a level that increases to persons in the general population the risk of a disease or health-related condition that is diet related, the label or labeling of such food shall contain, prominently and in immediate proximity to such claim, the following statement: "See nutrition information for ——— content." The blank shall identify the nutrient associated with the increased disease or health-related condition risk. In making the determination described in this clause, the Secretary shall take into account the significance of the food in the total daily diet.

(C) Subparagraph (2)(A) does not apply to a claim described in subparagraph (1)(A) and contained in the label or labeling of a food if such claim is contained in the brand name of such food and such brand name was in use on such food before October 25, 1989, unless the brand name contains a term defined by the Secretary under subparagraph (2)(A)(i). Such a claim is subject to paragraph (a).

(D) Subparagraph (2) does not apply to a claim described in subparagraph (1)(A) which uses the term "diet" and is contained in the label or labeling of a soft drink if (i) such claim is contained in the brand name of such soft drink, (ii) such brand name was in use on such soft drink before October 25, 1989, and (iii) the use of the term "diet" was in conformity with section 105.66 of title 21 of the Code of Federal Regulations. Such a claim is subject to paragraph (a).

(E) Subclauses (i) through (v) of subparagraph (2)(A) do not apply to a statement in the label or labeling of food which describes the percentage of vitamins and minerals in the food in relation to the amount of such vitamins and minerals recommended for daily consumption by the Secretary.

(F) Subclause (i) clause (A) does not apply to a statement in the labeling of a dietary supplement that characterizes the percentage level of a dietary ingredient for which the Secretary has not established a reference daily intake, daily recommended value, or other recommendation for daily consumption.

(G) A claim of the type described in subparagraph (1)(A) for a nutrient, for which the Secretary has not promulgated a regulation under clause (A)(i), shall be authorized and may be made with respect to a food if—

(i) a scientific body of the United States Government with official responsibility for public health protection or research directly relating to human nutrition (such as the National Institutes of Health or the Centers for Disease Control and Prevention) or the National Academy of Sciences or any of its subdivisions has published an authoritative statement, which is currently in effect, which identifies the nutrient level to which the claim refers;

(ii) a person has submitted to the Secretary, at least 120 days (during which the Secretary may notify any person who is making a claim as authorized by clause (C) that such person has not submitted all the information required by such clause) before the first introduction into interstate commerce of the food with a label containing the claim, (I) a notice of the claim, which shall include the exact words used in the claim and shall include a concise description of the basis upon which such person relied for determining that the requirements of subclause (i) have been satisfied, (II) a copy of the statement referred to in subclause (i) upon which such person relied in making the claim, and (III) a balanced representation of the scientific literature relating to the nutrient level to which the claim refers;

(iii) the claim and the food for which the claim is made are in compliance with clauses (A) and (B), and are otherwise in compliance with paragraph (a) and section 201(n) [21 USCS § 321(n)]; and

(iv) the claim is stated in a manner so that the claim is an accurate representation of the authoritative statement referred to in subclause (i) and so that the claim enables the public to comprehend the information provided in the claim and to understand the relative significance of such information in the context of a total daily diet.

For purposes of this clause, a statement shall be regarded as an authoritative statement of a scientific body described in subclause (i) only if the statement is published by the scientific body and shall not include a statement of an employee of the scientific body made in the individual capacity of the employee.

(H) A claim submitted under the requirements of clause (G) may be made until—

(i) such time as the Secretary issues a regulation—

(I) prohibiting or modifying the claim and the regulation has become effective, or

(II) finding that the requirements of clause (G) have not been met, including finding that the petitioner had not submitted all the information required by such clause; or

(ii) a district court of the United States in an enforcement proceeding under chapter III [21 USCS §§ 331 et seq.] has determined that the requirements of clause (G) have not been met.

(3) (A) Except as provided in subparagraph (5), a claim described in subparagraph (1)(B) may only be made—

(i) if the claim meets the requirements of the regulations of the Secretary promulgated under clause (B), and

(ii) if the food for which the claim is made does not contain, as determined by the Secretary by regulation, any nutrient in an amount which increases to persons in the general population the risk of a disease or health-related condition which is diet related, taking into account the significance of the food in the total daily diet, except that the Secretary may by regulation permit such a claim based on a finding that such a claim would assist consumers in maintaining healthy dietary practices and based on a requirement that the label contain a disclosure of the type required by subparagraph (2)(B).

(B) (i) The Secretary shall promulgate regulations authorizing claims of the type described in subparagraph (1)(B) only if the Secretary determines, based on the totality of publicly available scientific evidence (including evidence from well-designed studies conducted in a manner which is consistent with generally recognized scientific procedures and principles), that there is significant scientific agreement, among experts qualified by scientific training and experience to evaluate such claims, that the claim is supported by such evidence.

(ii) A regulation described in subclause (i) shall describe—

(I) the relationship between a nutrient of the type required in the label or labeling of food by paragraph (q)(1) or (q)(2) and a disease or health-related condition, and

(II) the significance of each such nutrient in affecting such disease or health-related condition.

(iii) A regulation described in subclause (i) shall require such claim to be stated in a manner so that the claim is an accurate representation of the matters set out in subclause (ii) and so that the claim en-

ables the public to comprehend the information provided in the claim and to understand the relative significance of such information in the context of a total daily diet.

(C) Notwithstanding the provisions of clauses (A)(i) and (B), a claim of the type described in subparagraph (1)(B) which is not authorized by the Secretary in a regulation promulgated in accordance with clause (B) shall be authorized and may be made with respect to a food if—

(i) a scientific body of the United States Government with official responsibility for public health protection or research directly relating to human nutrition (such as the National Institutes of Health or the Centers for Disease Control and Prevention) or the National Academy of Sciences or any of its subdivisions has published an authoritative statement, which is currently in effect, about the relationship between a nutrient and a disease or health-related condition to which the claim refers;

(ii) a person has submitted to the Secretary, at least 120 days (during which the Secretary may notify any person who is making a claim as authorized by clause (C) that such person has not submitted all the information required by such clause) before the first introduction into interstate commerce of the food with a label containing the claim, (I) a notice of the claim, which shall include the exact words used in the claim and shall include a concise description of the basis upon which such person relied for determining that the requirements of subclause (i) have been satisfied, (II) a copy of the statement referred to in subclause (i) upon which such person relied in making the claim, and (III) a balanced representation of the scientific literature relating to the relationship between a nutrient and a disease or health-related condition to which the claim refers;

(iii) the claim and the food for which the claim is made are in compliance with clause (A)(ii) and are otherwise in compliance with paragraph (a) and section 201(n) [21 USCS § 321(n)]; and

(iv) the claim is stated in a manner so that the claim is an accurate representation of the authoritative statement referred to in subclause (i) and so that the claim enables the public to comprehend the information provided in the claim and to understand the relative significance of such information in the context of a total daily diet.

For purposes of this clause, a statement shall be regarded as an authoritative statement of a scientific body described in subclause (i) only if the statement is published by the scientific body and shall not include a statement of an employee of the scientific body made in the individual capacity of the employee.

(D) A claim submitted under the requirements of clause (C) may be made until—

(i) such time as the Secretary issues a regulation under the standard in clause (B)(i)—

(I) prohibiting or modifying the claim and the regulation has become effective, or

(II) finding that the requirements of clause (C) have not been met, including finding that the petitioner has not submitted all the information required by such clause; or

(ii) a district court of the United States in an enforcement proceeding under chapter III [21 USCS §§ 331 et seq.] has determined that the requirements of clause (C) have not been met.

(4) (A) (i) Any person may petition the Secretary to issue a regulation under subparagraph (2)(A)(i) or (3)(B) relating to a claim described in subparagraph (1)(A) or (1)(B). Not later than 100 days after the petition is received by the Secretary, the Secretary shall issue a final decision denying the petition or file the petition for further action by the Secretary. If the Secretary does not act within such 100 days, the petition shall be deemed to be denied unless an extension is mutually agreed upon by the Secretary and the petitioner. If the Secretary denies the petition or the petition is deemed to be denied, the petition shall not be made available to the public. If the Secretary files the petition, the Secretary shall deny the petition or issue a proposed regulation to take the action requested in the petition not later than 90 days after the date of such decision. If the Secretary does not act within such 90 days, the petition shall be deemed to be denied unless an extension is mutually agreed upon by the Secretary and the petitioner. If the Secretary issues a proposed regulation, the rulemaking shall be completed within 540 days of the date the petition is received by the Secretary. If the Secretary does not issue a regulation within such 540 days, the Secretary shall provide the Committee on Commerce of the House of Representatives and the Committee on Labor and Human Resources of the Sen-

ate the reasons action on the regulation did not occur within such 540 days.

(ii) Any person may petition the Secretary for permission to use in a claim described in subparagraph (1)(A) terms that are consistent with the terms defined by the Secretary under subparagraph (2)(A)(i). Within 90 days of the submission of such a petition, the Secretary shall issue a final decision denying the petition or granting such permission.

(iii) Any person may petition the Secretary for permission to use an implied claim described in subparagraph (1)(A) in a brand name. After publishing notice of an opportunity to comment on the petition in the Federal Register and making the petition available to the public, the Secretary shall grant the petition if the Secretary finds that such claim is not misleading and is consistent with terms defined by the Secretary under subparagraph (2)(A)(i). The Secretary shall grant or deny the petition within 100 days of the date it is submitted to the Secretary and the petition shall be considered granted if the Secretary does not act on it within such 100 days.

(B) A petition under clause (A)(i) respecting a claim described in subparagraph (1)(A) or (1)(B) shall include an explanation of the reasons why the claim meets the requirements of this paragraph and a summary of the scientific data which supports such reasons.

(C) If a petition for a regulation under subparagraph (3)(B) relies on a report from an authoritative scientific body of the United States, the Secretary shall consider such report and shall justify any decision rejecting the conclusions of such report.

(5) (A) This paragraph does not apply to infant formulas subject to section 412(h) [21 USCS § 350a(h)] and medical foods as defined in section 5(b) of the Orphan Drug Act [21 USCS § 360ee(b)].

(B) Subclauses (iii) through (v) of subparagraph (2)(A) and subparagraph (2)(B) do not apply to food which is served in restaurants or other establishments in which food is served for immediate human consumption or which is sold for sale or use in such establishments.

(C) A subparagraph (1)(A) claim made with respect to a food which claim is required by a standard of identity issued under section 401 [21 USCS § 341] shall not be subject to subparagraph (2)(A)(i) or (2)(B).

(D) A subparagraph (1)(B) claim made with respect to a dietary supplement of vitamins, minerals, herbs, or other similar nutritional substances shall not be subject to subparagraph (3) but shall be subject to a procedure and standard, respecting the validity of such claim, established by regulation of the Secretary

(6) For purposes of paragraph (r)(1)(B), a statement for a dietary supplement may be made if—

(A) the statement claims a benefit related to a classical nutrient deficiency disease and discloses the prevalence of such disease in the United States, describes the role of a nutrient or dietary ingredient intended to affect the structure or function in humans, characterizes the documented mechanism by which a nutrient or dietary ingredient acts to maintain such structure or function, or describes general well-being from consumption of a nutrient or dietary ingredient,

(B) the manufacturer of the dietary supplement has substantiation that such statement is truthful and not misleading, and

(C) the statement contains, prominently displayed and in boldface type, the following: "This statement has not been evaluated by the Food and Drug Administration. This product is not intended to diagnose, treat, cure, or prevent any disease."

A statement under this subparagraph may not claim to diagnose, mitigate, treat, cure, or prevent a specific disease or class of diseases. If the manufacturer of a dietary supplement proposes to make a statement described in the first sentence of this subparagraph in the labeling of the dietary supplement, the manufacturer shall notify the Secretary no later than 30 days after the first marketing of the dietary supplement with such statement that such a statement is being made.

(7) The Secretary may make proposed regulations issued under this paragraph effective upon publication pending consideration of public comment and publication of a final regulation if the Secretary determines that such action is necessary—

(A) to enable the Secretary to review and act promptly on petitions the Secretary determines provide for information necessary to—

(i) enable consumers to develop and maintain healthy dietary practices;

(ii) enable consumers to be informed promptly and effectively of important new knowledge regarding nutritional and health benefits of food; or

(iii) ensure that scientifically sound nutritional and health information is provided to consumers as soon as possible; or

(B) to enable the Secretary to act promptly to ban or modify a claim under this paragraph.

Such proposed regulations shall be deemed final agency action for purposes of judicial review.
(s) Dietary supplements
If—

(1) it is a dietary supplement; and

(2) (A) the label or labeling of the supplement fails to list—

(i) the name of each ingredient of the supplement that is described in section 201(ff) [21 USCS § 321(ff)]; and

(ii) (I) the quantity of each such ingredient; or

(II) with respect to a proprietary blend of such ingredients, the total quantity of all ingredients in the blend;

(B) the label or labeling of the dietary supplement fails to identify the product by using the term "dietary supplement", which term may be modified with the name of such an ingredient;

(C) the supplement contains an ingredient described in section 201(ff)(1)(C) [21 USCS § 321(ff)(1)(C)], and the label or labeling of the supplement fails to identify any part of the plant from which the ingredient is derived;

(D) the supplement—

(i) is covered by the specifications of an official compendium;

(ii) is represented as conforming to the specifications of an official compendium; and

(iii) fails to so conform; or

(E) the supplement—

(i) is not covered by the specifications of an official compendium; and

(ii) (I) fails to have the identity and strength that the supplement is represented to have; or

(II) fails to meet the quality (including tablet or capsule disintegration), purity, or compositional specifications, based on validated assay or other appropriate methods, that the supplement is represented to meet. A dietary supplement shall not be deemed misbranded solely because its label or labeling contains directions or conditions of use or warnings.
(t) If it purports to be or is represented as catfish, unless it is fish classified within the family Ictaluridae.
(u) If it purports to be or is represented as ginseng, unless it is an herb or herbal ingredient derived from a plant classified within the genus Panax.
(v) If—

(1) it fails to bear a label required by the Secretary under section 801(n)(1) [21 USCS § 381(n)(1)] (relating to food refused admission into the United States);

(2) the Secretary finds that the food presents a threat of serious adverse health consequences or death to humans or animals; and

(3) upon or after notifying the owner or consignee involved that the label is required under section 801 [21 USCS § 381], the Secretary informs the owner or consignee that the food presents such a threat.
§ 351.   Adulterated drugs and devices
A drug or device shall be deemed to be adulterated—
(a) Poisonous, insanitary, etc., ingredients; adequate controls in manufacture. (1) If it consists in whole or in part of any filthy, putrid, or decomposed substance; or (2)(A) if it has been prepared, packed, or held under insanitary conditions whereby it may have been contaminated with filth, or whereby it may have been rendered injurious to health; or (B) if it is a drug and the methods used in, or the facilities or controls used for, its manufacture, processing, packing, or holding do not conform to or are not operated or administered in conformity with current good manufacturing practice to assure that such drug meets the requirements of this Act as to safety and has the identity and strength, and meets the quality and purity characteristics, which it purports or is represented to possess; or (C) if it is a compounded positron emission tomography drug and the methods used in, or the facilities and controls used for, its compounding, processing, packing, or holding do not conform to or are not operated or administered in conformity with the positron emission tomography compounding standards and the official monographs of the United States Pharmacopoeia to assure that such drug meets the requirements of this Act as to safety and has the identity and strength, and meets the quality and purity characteristics, that it purports or is represented to possess; or (3) if its container is com-

posed, in whole or in part, of any poisonous or deleterious substance which may render the contents injurious to health; or (4) if (A) it bears or contains, for purposes of coloring only, a color additive which is unsafe within the meaning of section 721(a) [21 USCS § 379e(a)], or (B) it is a color additive the intended use of which in or on drugs or devices is for purposes of coloring only and is unsafe within the meaning of section 721(a) [21 USCS § 379e(a)]; or (5) if it is a new animal drug which is unsafe within the meaning of section 512 [21 USCS § 360b]; or (6) if it is an animal feed bearing or contaminating a new animal drug, and such animal feed is unsafe within the meaning of section 512 [21 USCS § 360f].

(b) Strength, quality, or purity differing from official compendium. If it purports to be or is represented as a drug the name of which is recognized in an official compendium, and its strength differs from, or its quality or purity falls below, the standard set forth in such compendium. Such determination as to strength, quality, or purity shall be made in accordance with the tests or methods of assay set forth in such compendium, except that whenever tests or methods of assay have not been prescribed in such compendium, or such tests or methods of assay as are prescribed are, in the judgment of the Secretary, insufficient for the making of such determination, the Secretary shall bring such fact to the attention of the appropriate body charged with the revision of such compendium, and if such body fails within a reasonable time to prescribe tests or methods of assay which, in the judgment of the Secretary, are sufficient for purposes of this paragraph, then the Secretary shall promulgate regulations prescribing appropriate tests or methods of assay in accordance with which such determination as to strength, quality, or purity shall be made. No drug defined in an official compendium shall be deemed to be adulterated under this paragraph because it differs from the standard of strength, quality, or purity therefor set forth in such compendium, if its difference in strength, quality, or purity from such standard is plainly stated on its label. Whenever a drug is recognized in both the United States Pharmacopoeia and the Homoeopathic Pharmacopoeia of the United States it shall be subject to the requirements of the United States Pharmacopoeia unless it is labeled and offered for sale as a homoeopathic drug, in which case it shall be subject to the provisions of the Homoeopathic Pharmacopoeia of the United States and not to those of the United States Pharmacopoeia.

(c) Misrepresentation of strength, etc., where drug is unrecognized in compendium. If it is not subject to the provisions of paragraph (b) of this section and its strength differs from, or its purity or quality falls below, that which it purports or is represented to possess.

(d) Mixture with or substitution of another substance. If it is a drug and any substance has been (1) mixed or packed therewith so as to reduce its quality or strength or (2) substituted wholly or in part therefor.

(e) Devices not in conformity with performance standards.

(1) If it is, or purports to be or is represented as, a device which is subject to a performance standard established under section 514 [21 USCS § 360d], unless such device is in all respects in conformity with such standard.

(2) If it is declared to be, purports to be, or is represented as, a device that is in conformity with any standard recognized under section 514(c) [21 USCS § 360d(c)] unless such device is in all respects in conformity with such standard.

(f) Certain class III devices—

(1) If it is a class III device—

(A) (i) which is required by a regulation promulgated under subsection (b) of section 515 [21 USCS § 360e] to have an approval under such section of an application for premarket approval and which is not exempt from section 515 [21 USCS § 360e] under section 520(g) [21 USCS § 360j(g)], and

(ii) (I) for which an application for premarket approval or a notice of completion of a product development protocol was not filed with the Secretary within the ninety-day period beginning on the date of the promulgation of such regulation, or

(II) for which such an application was filed and approval of the application has been denied, suspended, or withdrawn, or such a notice was filed and has been declared not completed or the approval of the device under the protocol has been withdrawn;

(B) (i) which was classified under section 513(f) [21 USCS § 360c(f)] into class III, which under section 515(a) [21 USCS § 360e(a)] is required to have in effect an approved application for premarket approval, and which is not exempt from section 515 [21 USCS § 360e]

under section 520(g) [21 USCS § 360j(g)], and

(ii) which has an application which has been suspended or is otherwise not in effect; or

(C) which was classified under section 520(l) [21 USCS § 360j(l)] into class III, which under such section is required to have in effect an approved application under section 515 [21 USCS § 360e], and which has an application which has been suspended or is otherwise not in effect.

(2) (A) In the case of a device classified under section 513(f) [21 USCS § 360c(f)] into class III and intended solely for investigational use, paragraph (1)(B) shall not apply with respect to such device during the period ending on the ninetieth day after the date of the promulgation of the regulations prescribing the procedures and conditions required by section 520(g)(2) [21 USCS § 360j(g)(2)].

(B) In the case of a device subject to a regulation promulgated under subsection (b) of section 515 [21 USCS § 360e(b)], paragraph (1) shall not apply with respect to such device during the period ending—

(i) on the last day of the thirtieth calendar month beginning after the month in which the classification of the device in class III became effective under section 513 [21 USCS § 360c], or

(ii) on the ninetieth day after the date of the promulgation of such regulation, whichever occurs later.

(g) Banned devices. If it is a banned device.

(h) Manufacture, packing, storage, or installation of device not in conformity with applicable requirements or conditions. If it is a device and the methods used in, or the facilities or controls used for, its manufacture, packing, storage, or installation are not in conformity with applicable requirements under section 520(f)(1) [21 USCS § 360j(f)(1)] or an applicable condition prescribed by an order under section 520(f)(2) [21 USCS § 360j(f)(2)].

(i) Failure to comply with requirements under which device was exempted for investigational use. If it is a device for which an exemption has been granted under section 520(g) [21 USCS § 360j(g)] for investigational use and the person who was granted such exemption or any investigator who uses such device under such exemption fails to comply with a requirement prescribed by or under such section.

§ 352. Misbranded drugs and devices

A drug or device shall be deemed to be misbranded—

(a) False or misleading label. If its labeling is false or misleading in any particular. Health care economic information provided to a formulary committee, or other similar entity, in the course of the committee or the entity carrying out its responsibilities for the selection of drugs for managed care or other similar organizations, shall not be considered to be false or misleading under this paragraph if the health care economic information directly relates to an indication approved under section 505 [21 USCS § 355] or under section 351(a) of the Public Health Service Act [42 USCS § 262(a)] for such drug and is based on competent and reliable scientific evidence. The requirements set forth in section 505(a) [21 USCS § 355(a)] or in section 351(a) of the Public Health Service Act [42 USCS § 262(a)] shall not apply to health care economic information provided to such a committee or entity in accordance with this paragraph. Information that is relevant to the substantiation of the health care economic information presented pursuant to this paragraph shall be made available to the Secretary upon request. In this paragraph, the term "health care economic information" means any analysis that identifies, measures, or compares the economic consequences, including the costs of the represented health outcomes, of the use of a drug to the use of another drug, to another health care intervention, or to no intervention.

(b) Package form; Contents of label. If in package form unless it bears a label containing (1) the name and place of business of the manufacturer, packer, or distributor; and (2) an accurate statement of the quantity of the contents in terms of weight, measure, or numerical count: Provided, That under clause (2) of this paragraph reasonable variations shall be permitted, and exemptions as to small packages shall be established, by regulations prescribed by the Secretary.

(c) Prominence of information on label. If any word, statement, or other information required by or under authority of this Act to appear on the label or labeling is not prominently placed thereon with such conspicuousness (as compared with other words, statements, designs, or devices, in the labeling) and in such terms as to render it likely to be read and understood by the ordinary individual under customary conditions of purchase and use.

(d) [Repealed]

(e) Designation of drugs or devices by established names.

(1) (A) If it is a drug, unless its label bears, to the exclusion of any other nonproprietary name (except the applicable systematic chemical name or the chemical formula)—

(i) the established name (as defined in subparagraph (3)) of the drug, if there is such a name;

(ii) the established name and quantity or, if determined to be appropriate by the Secretary, the proportion of each active ingredient, including the quantity, kind, and proportion of any alcohol, and also including whether active or not the established name and quantity or if determined to be appropriate by the Secretary, the proportion of any bromides, ether, chloroform, acetanilide, acetophenetidin, amidopyrine, antipyrine, atropine, hyoscine, hyoscyamine, arsenic, digitalis, digitalis glucosides, mercury, ouabain, strophanthin, strychnine, thyroid, or any derivative or preparation of any such substances, contained therein, except that the requirement for stating the quantity of the active ingredients, other than the quantity of those specifically named in this subclause, shall not apply to nonprescription drugs not intended for human use; and

(iii) the established name of each inactive ingredient listed in alphabetical order on the outside container of the retail package and, if determined to be appropriate by the Secretary, on the immediate container, as prescribed in regulation promulgated by the Secretary, except that nothing in this subclause shall be deemed to require that any trade secret be divulged, and except that the requirements of this subclause with respect to alphabetical order shall apply only to nonprescription drugs that are not also cosmetics and that this subclause shall not apply to nonprescription drugs not intended for human use.

(B) For any prescription drug the established name of such drug or ingredient, as the case may be, on such label (and on any labeling on which a name for such drug or ingredient is used) shall be printed prominently and in type at least half as large as that used thereon for any proprietary name or designation for such drug or ingredient, except that to the extent that compliance with the requirements of subclause (ii) or (iii) of clause (A) or this clause is impracticable, exemptions shall be established by regulations promulgated by the Secretary.

(2) If it is a device and it has an established name, unless its label bears, to the exclusion of any other nonproprietary name, its established name (as defined in subparagraph (4)) prominently printed in type at least half as large as that used thereon for any proprietary name or designation for such device, except that to the extent compliance with the requirements of this subparagraph is impracticable, exemptions shall be established by regulations promulgated by the Secretary.

(3) As used in subparagraph (1), the term "established name," with respect to a drug or ingredient thereof, means (A) the applicable official name designated pursuant to section 508 [21 USCS § 358], or (B), if there is no such name and such drug, or such ingredient, is an article recognized in an official compendium, then the official title thereof in such compendium, or (C) if neither clause (A) nor clause (B) of this subparagraph applies, then the common or usual name, if any, of such drug or of such ingredient, except that where clause (B) of this subparagraph applies to an article recognized in the United States Pharmacopeia and in the Homoeopathic Pharmacopoeia under different official titles, the official title used in the United States Pharmacopeia shall apply unless it is labeled and offered for sale as a homoeopathic drug, in which case the official title used in the Homoeopathic Pharmacopoeia shall apply.

(4) As used in subparagraph (2), the term "established name" with respect to a device means (A) the applicable official name of the device designated pursuant to section 508 [21 USCS § 358], (B) if there is no such name and such device is an article recognized in an official compendium, then the official title thereof in such compendium, or (C) if neither clause (A) nor clause (B) of this subparagraph applies, then any common or usual name of such device.

(f) Directions for use and warnings on label. Unless its labeling bears (1) adequate directions for use; and (2) such adequate warnings against use in those pathological conditions or by children where its use may be dangerous to health, or against unsafe dosage or methods or duration of administration or application, in such manner and form, as are necessary for the protection of users, except that where any requirement of clause (1) of this paragraph, as applied to any drug or device, is not necessary for the protection of the public health, the Secretary shall promulgate regulations exempting such drug or device from such

requirement. Required labeling for prescription devices intended for use in health care facilities may be made available solely by electronic means provided that the labeling complies with all applicable requirements of law and, that the manufacturer affords health care facilities the opportunity to request the labeling in paper form, and after such request, promptly provides the health care facility the requested information without additional cost.

(g) Representations as recognized drug; packing and labeling; inconsistent requirements for designation of drug. If it purports to be a drug the name of which is recognized in an official compendium, unless it is packaged and labeled as prescribed therein. The method of packing may be modified with the consent of the Secretary. Whenever a drug is recognized in both the United States Pharmacopoeia and the Homoeopathic Pharmacopoeia of the United States it shall be subject to the requirements of the United States Pharmacopoeia with respect to packaging and labeling unless it is labeled and offered for sale as a homoeopathic drug, in which case it shall be subject to the provisions of the Homoeopathic Pharmacopoeia of the United States, and not to those of the United States Pharmacopoeia, except that in the event of inconsistency between the requirements of this paragraph and those of paragraph (e) as to the name by which the drug or its ingredients shall be designated, the requirements of paragraph (e) shall prevail.

(h) Deteriorative drugs; packing and labeling. If it has been found by the Secretary to be a drug liable to deterioration, unless it is packaged in such form and manner, and its label bears a statement of such precautions, as the Secretary shall by regulations require as necessary for the protection of the public health. No such regulation shall be established for any drug recognized in an official compendium until the Secretary shall have informed the appropriate body charged with the revision of such compendium of the need for such packaging or labeling requirements and such body shall have failed within a reasonable time to prescribe such requirements.

(i) Drug; misleading container; imitation; offer for sale under another name. If it is a drug and its container is so made, formed, or filled as to be misleading, or (2) if it is an imitation of another drug; or (3) if it is offered for sale under the name of another drug.

(j) Health-endangering when used as prescribed. If it is dangerous to health when used in the dosage, or manner or with the frequency or duration prescribed, recommended, or suggested in the labeling thereof.

(k), (l) [Repealed]

(m) Color additives; packing and labeling. If it is a color additive the intended use of which is for the purpose of coloring only, unless its packaging and labeling are in conformity with such packaging and labeling requirements applicable to such color additive, as may be contained in regulations issued under section 721 [21 USCS § 379e].

(n) Prescription drug advertisements: established name; quantitative formula; side effects, contraindications, and effectiveness; prior approval; false advertising; labeling; construction of the Convention on Psychotropic Substances. In the case of any prescription drug distributed or offered for sale in any State, unless the manufacturer, packer, or distributor thereof includes in all advertisements and other descriptive printed matter issued or caused to be issued by the manufacturer, packer, or distributor with respect to that drug a true statement of (1) the established name as defined in section 502(e) [subsec. (e) of this section], printed prominently and in type at least half as large as that used for any trade or brand name thereof, (2) the formula showing quantitatively each ingredient of such drug to the extent required for labels under section 502(e) [subsec. (e) of this section], and (3) such other information in brief summary relating to side effects, contraindications, and effectiveness as shall be required in regulations which shall be issued by the Secretary in accordance with the procedure specified in section 701(e) of this Act [21 USCS § 371(e)], except that (A) except in extraordinary circumstances, no regulation issued under this paragraph shall require prior approval by the Secretary of the content of any advertisement, and (B) no advertisement of a prescription drug, published after the effective date of regulations issued under this paragraph applicable to advertisements of prescription drugs, shall, with respect to the matters specified in this paragraph or covered by such regulations, be subject to the provisions of sections 12 through 17 of the Federal Trade Commission Act, as amended [15 USCS §§ 52-57]. This paragraph (n) shall not be applicable to any printed matter which the Secretary determines to be labeling as defined in section 201(m) of this Act [21 USCS § 321(m)]. Nothing in the Convention on Psychotropic Substances, signed at Vienna, Austria, on February 21, 1971, shall be construed to prevent drug price communications to consumers.

(o) Drugs or devices from nonregistered establishments. If it was manufactured, prepared, propagated, compounded, or processed in an establishment in any State not duly registered under section 510 [21 USCS § 360], if it was not included in a list required by section 510(j) [21 USCS § 360(j)], if a notice or other information respecting it was not provided as required by such section or section 510(k) [21 USCS § 360(k)], or if it does not bear such symbols from the uniform system for identification of devices prescribed under section 510(e) [21 USCS § 360(e)] as the Secretary by regulation requires.

(p) Packaging or labeling of drugs in violation of regulations. If it is a drug and its packaging or labeling is in violation of an applicable regulation issued pursuant to section 3 or 4 of the Poison Prevention Packaging Act of 1970 [15 USCS § 1472 or 1473].

(q) Restricted devices using false or misleading advertising or used in violation of regulations. In the case of any restricted device distributed or offered for sale in any State, if (1) its advertising is false or misleading in any particular, or (2) it is sold, distributed, or used in violation of regulations prescribed under section 520(e) [21 USCS § 360j(e)].

(r) Restricted devices not carrying requisite accompanying statements in advertisements and other descriptive printed matter. In the case of any restricted device distributed or offered for sale in any State, unless the manufacturer, packer, or distributor thereof includes in all advertisements and other descriptive printed matter issued or caused to be issued by the manufacturer, packer, or distributor with respect to that device (1) a true statement of the device's established name as defined in section 502(e) [21 USCS § 352(e)], printed prominently and in type at least half as large as that used for any trade or brand name thereof, and (2) a brief statement of the intended uses of the device and relevant warnings, precautions, side effects, and contra-indications and, in the case of specific devices made subject to a finding by the Secretary after notice and opportunity for comment that such action is necessary to protect the public health, a full description of the components of such device or the formula showing quantitatively each ingredient of such device to the extent required in regulations which shall be issued by the Secretary after an opportunity for a hearing. Except in extraordinary circumstances, no regulation issued under this paragraph shall require prior approval by the Secretary of the content of any advertisement and no advertisement of a restricted device, published after the effective date of this paragraph shall, with respect to the matters specified in this paragraph or covered by regulations issued hereunder, be subject to the provisions of sections 12 through 15 of the Federal Trade Commission Act (15 U.S.C. 52-55). This paragraph shall not be applicable to any printed matter which the Secretary determines to be labeling as defined in section 201(m) [21 USCS § 321(m)].

(s) Devices subject to performance standards not bearing requisite labeling. If it is a device subject to a performance standard established under section 514 [21 USCS § 360d], unless it bears such labeling as may be prescribed in such performance standard.

(t) Devices for which there has been a failure or refusal to give required notification or to furnish required material or information. If it is a device and there was a failure or refusal (1) to comply with any requirement prescribed under section 518 [21 USCS § 360h] respecting the device, (2) to furnish any material or information required by or under section 519 [21 USCS § 360i] respecting the device, or (3) to comply with a requirement under section 522 [21 USCS § 360l].

§ 361. Adulterated cosmetics

A cosmetic shall be deemed to be adulterated—

(a) If it bears or contains any poisonous or deleterious substance which may render it injurious to users under the conditions of use prescribed in the labeling thereof, or under such conditions of use as are customary or usual, except that this provision shall not apply to coaltar hair dye, the label of which bears the following legend conspicuously displayed thereon: "Caution—This product contains ingredients which may cause skin irritation on certain individuals and a preliminary test according to accompanying directions should first be made. This product must not be used for dyeing the eyelashes or eyebrows; to do so may cause blindness.", and the labeling of which bears adequate directions for such preliminary testing. For the purposes of this paragraph and paragraph (e) the term "hair dye" shall not include eyelash dyes or eyebrow dyes.

(b) If it consists in whole or in part of any filthy, putrid, or decomposed substance.

(c) If it has been prepared, packed, or held under insanitary conditions whereby it may have become contaminated with filth, or whereby it may have been rendered injurious to health.

(d) If its container is composed in whole or in part, of any poisonous or deleterious substance which may render the contents injurious to health.

(e) If it is not a hair dye and it is, or it bears or contains, a color additive which is unsafe within the meaning of section 721(a) [21 USCS § 379e(a)].

§ 362. Misbranded cosmetics

A cosmetic shall be deemed to be misbranded—

(a) If its labeling is false or misleading in any particular.

(b) If in package form unless it bears a label containing (1) the name and place of business of the manufacturer, packer, or distributor; and (2) an accurate statement of the quantity of the contents in terms of weight, measure, or numerical count: Provided, That under clause (2) of this paragraph reasonable variations shall be permitted, and exemptions as to small packages shall be established, by regulations prescribed by the Secretary.

(c) If any word, statement, or other information required by or under authority of this Act to appear on the label or labeling is not prominently placed thereon with such conspicuousness (as compared with other words, statements, designs, or devices, in the labeling) and in such terms as to render it likely to be read and understood by the ordinary individual under customary conditions of purchase and use.

(d) If its container is so made, formed, or filled as to be misleading.

(e) If it is a color additive, unless its packaging and labeling are in conformity with such packaging and labeling requirements, applicable to such color additive, as may be contained in regulations issued under section 721 [21 USCS § 379e]. This paragraph shall not apply to packages of color additives which, with respect to their use for cosmetics, are marketed and intended for use only in or on hair dyes (as defined in the last sentence of section 601(a) [21 USCS § 361(a)].

(f)]If its packaging or labeling is in violation of an applicable regulation issued pursuant to section 3 or 4 of the Poison Prevention Packaging Act of 1970 [15 USCS § 1472 or 1473].

§ 371. Regulations and hearings

(a) Authority to promulgate regulations. The authority to promulgate regulations for the efficient enforcement of this Act, except as otherwise provided in this section, is hereby vested in the Secretary.

(b) Regulations for imports and exports. The Secretary of the Treasury and the Secretary of Health and Human Services shall jointly prescribe regulations for the efficient enforcement of the provisions of section 801 [21 USCS § 381], except as otherwise provided therein. Such regulations shall be promulgated in such manner and take effect at such time, after due notice, as the Secretary of Health and Human Services shall determine.

(c) Conduct of hearings. Hearings authorized or required by this Act shall be conducted by the Secretary or such officer or employee as he may designate for the purpose.

(d) Effectiveness of definitions and standards of identity. The definitions and standards of identity promulgated in accordance with the provisions of this Act shall be effective for the purposes of the enforcement of this Act, notwithstanding such definitions and standards as may be contained in other laws of the United States and regulations promulgated thereunder.

(e) Procedure for establishment.

(1) Any action for the issuance, amendment, or repeal of any regulation under section 403(j), 404(a), 406, 501(b), or 502 (d) or (h) of this Act [21 USCS § 343(j), 344(a), 346, 351(b) or 352(d) or (h)], and any action for the amendment or repeal of any definition and standard of identity under section 401 of this Act [21 USCS § 341] for any dairy product (including products regulated under parts 131, 133 and 135 of title 21, Code of Federal Regulations) shall be begun by a proposal made (A) by the Secretary on his own initiative, or (B) by petition of any interested person, showing reasonable grounds therefor, filed with the Secretary. The Secretary shall publish such proposal and shall afford all interested persons an opportunity to present their views thereon, orally or in writing. As soon as practicable thereafter, the Secretary shall by order act upon such proposal and shall make such order public. Except as provided in paragraph (2), the order shall become effective at such time as may be specified therein, but not prior to the day following the last day on which objections may be filed under such paragraph.

(2) On or before the thirtieth day after the date on which an order

entered under paragraph (1) is made public, any person who will be adversely affected by such order if placed in effect may file objections thereto with the Secretary, specifying with particularity the provisions of the order deemed objectionable, stating the grounds therefor, and requesting a public hearing upon such objections. Until final action upon such objections is taken by the Secretary under paragraph (3), the filing of such objections shall operate to stay the effectiveness of those provisions of the order to which the objections are made. As soon as practicable after the time for filing objections has expired the Secretary shall publish a notice in the Federal Register specifying those parts of the order which have been stayed by the filing of objections and, if no objections have been filed, stating that fact.

(3) As soon as practicable after such request for a public hearing, the Secretary, after due notice, shall hold such a public hearing for the purpose of receiving evidence relevant and material to the issues raised by such objections. At the hearing, any interested person may be heard in person or by representative. As soon as practicable after completion of the hearing, the Secretary shall by order act upon such objections and make such order public. Such order shall be based only on substantial evidence of record at such hearing and shall set forth, as part of the order, detailed findings of fact on which the order is based. The Secretary shall specify in the order the date on which it shall take effect, except that it shall not be made to take effect prior to the ninetieth day after its publication unless the Secretary finds that emergency conditions exist necessitating an earlier effective date, in which event the Secretary shall specify in the order his findings as to such conditions.

(f) Review of order.

(1) In a case of actual controversy as to the validity of any order under subsection (e), any person who will be adversely affected by such order if placed in effect may at any time prior to the ninetieth day after such order is issued file a petition with the Circuit Court of Appeals of the United States [United States Court of Appeals] for the circuit wherein such person resides or has his principal place of business, for a judicial review of such order. A copy of the petition shall be forthwith transmitted by the clerk of the court to the Secretary or other officer designated by him for that purpose. The Secretary thereupon shall file in the court the record of the proceedings on which the Secretary based his order, as provided in section 2112 of title 28, United States Code.

(2) If the petitioner applies to the court for leave to adduce additional evidence, and shows to the satisfaction of the court that such additional evidence is material and that there were reasonable grounds for the failure to adduce such evidence in the proceedings before the Secretary, the court may order such additional evidence (and evidence in rebuttal thereof) to be taken before the Secretary, and to be adduced upon the hearing, in such manner and upon such terms and conditions as to the court may seem proper. The Secretary may modify his findings as to the facts, or make new findings, by reason of the additional evidence so taken, and he shall file such modified or new findings, and his recommendations, if any, for the modification or setting aside of his original order, with the return of such additional evidence.

(3) Upon the filing of the petition referred to in paragraph (1) of this subsection, the court shall have jurisdiction to affirm the order, or to set it aside in whole or in part, temporarily or permanently. If the order of the Secretary refuses to issue, amend, or repeal a regulation and such order is not in accordance with the law the court shall by its judgment order the Secretary to take action, with respect to such regulation, in accordance with law. The findings of the Secretary as to the facts, if supported by substantial evidence, shall be conclusive.

(4) The judgment of the court affirming or setting aside, in whole or in part, any such order of the Secretary shall be final, subject to review by the Supreme Court of the United States upon certiorari or certification as provided in section 1254 of title 28, United States Code, as amended.

(5) Any action instituted under this subsection shall survive notwithstanding any change in the person occupying the office of Secretary or any vacancy in such office.

(6) The remedies provided for in this subsection shall be in addition to and not in substitution for any other remedies provided by law.

(g) Copies of records of hearings. A certified copy of the transcript of the record and proceedings under subsection (e) shall be furnished by the Secretary to any interested party at his request, and payment of the costs thereof, and shall be admissible in any criminal, libel for condemnation, exclusion of imports, or other proceeding arising under or in respect to this Act, irrespective of whether proceedings with respect to the order have previously been instituted or become final under subsection (f).

(h) Guidance documents.

(1) (A) The Secretary shall develop guidance documents with public participation and ensure that information identifying the existence of such documents and the documents themselves are made available to the public both in written form and, as feasible, through electronic means. Such documents shall not create or confer any rights for or on any person, although they present the views of the Secretary on matters under the jurisdiction of the Food and Drug Administration.

(B) Although guidance documents shall not be binding on the Secretary, the Secretary shall ensure that employees of the Food and Drug Administration do not deviate from such guidances without appropriate justification and supervisory concurrence. The Secretary shall provide training to employees in how to develop and use guidance documents and shall monitor the development and issuance of such documents.

(C) For guidance documents that set forth initial interpretations of a statute or regulation, changes in interpretation or policy that are of more than a minor nature, complex scientific issues, or highly controversial issues, the Secretary shall ensure public participation prior to implementation of guidance documents, unless the Secretary determines that such prior public participation is not feasible or appropriate. In such cases, the Secretary shall provide for public comment upon implementation and take such comment into account.

(D) For guidance documents that set forth existing practices or minor changes in policy, the Secretary shall provide for public comment upon implementation.

(2) In developing guidance documents, the Secretary shall ensure uniform nomenclature for such documents and uniform internal procedures for approval of such documents. The Secretary shall ensure that guidance documents and revisions of such documents are properly dated and indicate the nonbinding nature of the documents. The Secretary shall periodically review all guidance documents and, where appropriate, revise such documents.

(3) The Secretary, acting through the Commissioner, shall maintain electronically and update and publish periodically in the Federal Register a list of guidance documents. All such documents shall be made available to the public.

(4) The Secretary shall ensure that an effective appeals mechanism is in place to address complaints that the Food and Drug Administration is not developing and using guidance documents in accordance with this subsection.

(5) Not later than July 1, 2000, the Secretary after evaluating the effectiveness of the Good Guidance Practices document, published in the Federal Register at 62 Fed. Reg. 8961, shall promulgate a regulation consistent with this subsection specifying the policies and procedures of the Food and Drug Administration for the development, issuance, and use of guidance documents.

False Claims Act
Title 31. Money and Finance
Subtitle III. Financial Management
Chapter 37. Claims
Subchapter III. Claims Against the United States Government

§ 3729. False claims

(a) Liability for certain acts. Any person who—

(1) knowingly presents, or causes to be presented, to an officer or employee of the United States Government or a member of the Armed Forces of the United States a false or fraudulent claim for payment or approval;

(2) knowingly makes, uses, or causes to be made or used, a false record or statement to get a false or fraudulent claim paid or approved by the Government;

(3) conspires to defraud the Government by getting a false or fraudulent claim allowed or paid;

(4) has possession, custody, or control of property or money used, or to be used, by the Government and, intending to defraud the Government or willfully to conceal the property, delivers, or causes to be delivered, less property than the amount for which the person receives a certificate or receipt;

(5) authorized to make or deliver a document certifying receipt of

property used, or to be used, by the Government and, intending to defraud the Government, makes or delivers the receipt without completely knowing that the information on the receipt is true;

(6) knowingly buys, or receives as a pledge of an obligation or debt, public property from an officer or employee of the Government, or a member of the Armed Forces, who lawfully may not sell or pledge the property; or

(7) knowingly makes, uses, or causes to be made or used, a false record or statement to conceal, avoid, or decrease an obligation to pay or transmit money or property to the Government, is liable to the United States Government for a civil penalty of not less than $ 5,000 and not more than $ 10,000, plus 3 times the amount of damages which the Government sustains because of the act of that person, except that if the court finds that—

(A) the person committing the violation of this subsection furnished officials of the United States responsible for investigating false claims violations with all information known to such person about the violation within 30 days after the date on which the defendant first obtained the information;

(B) such person fully cooperated with any Government investigation of such violation; and

(C) at the time such person furnished the United States with the information about the violation, no criminal prosecution, civil action, or administrative action had commenced under this title with respect to such violation, and the person did not have actual knowledge of the existence of an investigation into such violation; the court may assess not less than 2 times the amount of damages which the Government sustains because of the act of the person. A person violating this subsection shall also be liable to the United States Government for the costs of a civil action brought to recover any such penalty or damages.

(b) Knowing and knowingly defined. For purposes of this section, the terms "knowing" and "knowingly" mean that a person, with respect to information—

(1) has actual knowledge of the information;

(2) acts in deliberate ignorance of the truth or falsity of the information; or

(3) acts in reckless disregard of the truth or falsity of the information, and no proof of specific intent to defraud is required.

(c) Claim defined. For purposes of this section, "claim" includes any request or demand, whether under a contract or otherwise, for money or property which is made to a contractor, grantee, or other recipient if the United States Government provides any portion of the money or property which is requested or demanded, or if the Government will reimburse such contractor, grantee, or other recipient for any portion of the money or property which is requested or demanded.

(d) Exemption from disclosure. Any information furnished pursuant to subparagraphs (A) through (C) of subsection (a) shall be exempt from disclosure under section 552 of title 5.

(e) Exclusion. This section does not apply to claims, records, or statements made under the Internal Revenue Code of 1986.

§ 3730. Civil actions for false claims

(a) Responsibilities of the Attorney General. The Attorney General diligently shall investigate a violation under section 3729. If the Attorney General finds that a person has violated or is violating section 3729, the Attorney General may bring a civil action under this section against the person.

(b) Actions by private persons.

(1) A person may bring a civil action for a violation of section 3729 for the person and for the United States Government. The action shall be brought in the name of the Government. The action may be dismissed only if the court and the Attorney General give written consent to the dismissal and their reasons for consenting.

(2) A copy of the complaint and written disclosure of substantially all material evidence and information the person possesses shall be served on the Government pursuant to Rule 4(d)(4) of the Federal Rules of Civil Procedure. The complaint shall be filed in camera, shall remain under seal for at least 60 days, and shall not be served on the defendant until the court so orders. The Government may elect to intervene and proceed with the action within 60 days after it receives both the complaint and the material evidence and information.

(3) The Government may, for good cause shown, move the court for extensions of the time during which the complaint remains under seal under paragraph (2). Any such motions may be supported by affidavits or other submissions in camera. The defendant shall not be required to respond to any complaint filed under this section until 20 days after the complaint is unsealed and served upon the defendant pursuant to Rule 4 of the Federal Rules of Civil Procedure.

(4) Before the expiration of the 60-day period or any extensions obtained under paragraph (3), the Government shall—

(A) proceed with the action, in which case the action shall be conducted by the Government; or

(B) notify the court that it declines to take over the action, in which case the person bringing the action shall have the right to conduct the action.

(5) When a person brings an action under this subsection, no person other than the Government may intervene or bring a related action based on the facts underlying the pending action.

(c) Rights of the parties to qui tam actions.

(1) If the Government proceeds with the action, it shall have the primary responsibility for prosecuting the action, and shall not be bound by an act of the person bringing the action. Such person shall have the right to continue as a party to the action, subject to the limitations set forth in paragraph (2).

(2) (A) The Government may dismiss the action notwithstanding the objections of the person initiating the action if the person has been notified by the Government of the filing of the motion and the court has provided the person with an opportunity for a hearing on the motion.

(B) The Government may settle the action with the defendant notwithstanding the objections of the person initiating the action if the court determines, after a hearing, that the proposed settlement is fair, adequate, and reasonable under all the circumstances. Upon a showing of good cause, such hearing may be held in camera.

(C) Upon a showing by the Government that unrestricted participation during the course of the litigation by the person initiating the action would interfere with or unduly delay the Government's prosecution of the case, or would be repetitious, irrelevant, or for purposes of harassment, the court may, in its discretion, impose limitations on the person's participation, such as—

(i) limiting the number of witnesses the person may call;

(ii) limiting the length of the testimony of such witnesses;

(iii) limiting the person's cross-examination of witnesses; or

(iv) otherwise limiting the participation by the person in the litigation.

(D) Upon a showing by the defendant that unrestricted participation during the course of the litigation by the person initiating the action would be for purposes of harassment or would cause the defendant undue burden or unnecessary expense, the court may limit the participation by the person in the litigation.

(3) If the Government elects not to proceed with the action, the person who initiated the action shall have the right to conduct the action. If the Government so requests, it shall be served with copies of all pleadings filed in the action and shall be supplied with copies of all deposition transcripts (at the Government's expense). When a person proceeds with the action, the court, without limiting the status and rights of the person initiating the action, may nevertheless permit the Government to intervene at a later date upon a showing of good cause.

(4) Whether or not the Government proceeds with the action, upon a showing by the Government that certain actions of discovery by the person initiating the action would interfere with the Government's investigation or prosecution of a criminal or civil matter arising out of the same facts, the court may stay such discovery for a period of not more than 60 days. Such a showing shall be conducted in camera. The court may extend the 60-day period upon a further showing in camera that the Government has pursued the criminal or civil investigation or proceedings with reasonable diligence and any proposed discovery in the civil action will interfere with the ongoing criminal or civil investigation or proceedings.

(5) Notwithstanding subsection (b), the Government may elect to pursue its claim through any alternate remedy available to the Government, including any administrative proceeding to determine a civil money penalty. If any such alternate remedy is pursued in another proceeding, the person initiating the action shall have the same rights in such proceeding as such person would have had if the action had continued under this section. Any finding of fact or conclusion of law made in such other proceeding that has become final shall be conclusive on all parties to an action under this section. For purposes of the preceding sentence, a finding or conclusion is final if it has been finally

determined on appeal to the appropriate court of the United States, if all time for filing such an appeal with respect to the finding or conclusion has expired, or if the finding or conclusion is not subject to judicial review.

(d) Award to qui tam plaintiff.

(1) If the Government proceeds with an action brought by a person under subsection (b), such person shall, subject to the second sentence of this paragraph, receive at least 15 percent but not more than 25 percent of the proceeds of the action or settlement of the claim, depending upon the extent to which the person substantially contributed to the prosecution of the action. Where the action is one which the court finds to be based primarily on disclosures of specific information (other than information provided by the person bringing the action) relating to allegations or transactions in a criminal, civil, or administrative hearing, in a congressional, administrative, or Government [General] Accounting Office report, hearing, audit, or investigation, or from the news media, the court may award such sums as it considers appropriate, but in no case more than 10 percent of the proceeds, taking into account the significance of the information and the role of the person bringing the action in advancing the case to litigation. Any payment to a person under the first or second sentence of this paragraph shall be made from the proceeds. Any such person shall also receive an amount for reasonable expenses which the court finds to have been necessarily incurred, plus reasonable attorneys' fees and costs. All such expenses, fees, and costs shall be awarded against the defendant.

(2) If the Government does not proceed with an action under this section, the person bringing the action or settling the claim shall receive an amount which the court decides is reasonable for collecting the civil penalty and damages. The amount shall be not less than 25 percent and not more than 30 percent of the proceeds of the action or settlement and shall be paid out of such proceeds. Such person shall also receive an amount for reasonable expenses which the court finds to have been necessarily incurred, plus reasonable attorneys' fees and costs. All such expenses, fees, and costs shall be awarded against the defendant.

(3) Whether or not the Government proceeds with the action, if the court finds that the action was brought by a person who planned and initiated the violation of section 3729 upon which the action was brought, then the court may, to the extent the court considers appropriate, reduce the share of the proceeds of the action which the person would otherwise receive under paragraph (1) or (2) of this subsection, taking into account the role of that person in advancing the case to litigation and any relevant circumstances pertaining to the violation. If the person bringing the action is convicted of criminal conduct arising from his or her role in the violation of section 3729, that person shall be dismissed from the civil action and shall not receive any share of the proceeds of the action. Such dismissal shall not prejudice the right of the United States to continue the action, represented by the Department of Justice.

(4) If the Government does not proceed with the action and the person bringing the action conducts the action, the court may award to the defendant its reasonable attorneys' fees and expenses if the defendant prevails in the action and the court finds that the claim of the person bringing the action was clearly frivolous, clearly vexatious, or brought primarily for purposes of harassment.

(e) Certain actions barred.

(1) No court shall have jurisdiction over an action brought by a former or present member of the armed forces under subsection (b) of this section against a member of the armed forces arising out of such person's service in the armed forces.

(2) (A) No court shall have jurisdiction over an action brought under subsection (b) against a Member of Congress, a member of the judiciary, or a senior executive branch official if the action is based on evidence or information known to the Government when the action was brought.

(B) For purposes of this paragraph, "senior executive branch official" means any officer or employee listed in paragraphs (1) through (8) of section 101(f) of the Ethics in Government Act of 1978 (5 U.S.C. App.).

(3) In no event may a person bring an action under subsection (b) which is based upon allegations or transactions which are the subject of a civil suit or an administrative civil money penalty proceeding in which the Government is already a party.

(4) (A) No court shall have jurisdiction over an action under this section based upon the public disclosure of allegations or transactions in a criminal, civil, or administrative hearing, in a congressional, administrative, or Government [General] Accounting Office report, hearing, audit, or investigation, or from the news media, unless the action is brought by the Attorney General or the person bringing the action is an original source of the information.

(B) For purposes of this paragraph, "original source" means an individual who has direct and independent knowledge of the information on which the allegations are based and has voluntarily provided the information to the Government before filing an action under this section which is based on the information.

(f) Government not liable for certain expenses. The Government is not liable for expenses which a person incurs in bringing an action under this section.

(g) Fees and expenses to prevailing defendant. In civil actions brought under this section by the United States, the provisions of section 2412(d) of title 28 shall apply.

(h) Any employee who is discharged, demoted, suspended, threatened, harassed, or in any other manner discriminated against in the terms and conditions of employment by his or her employer because of lawful acts done by the employee on behalf of the employee or others in furtherance of an action under this section, including investigation for, initiation of, testimony for, or assistance in an action filed or to be filed under this section, shall be entitled to all relief necessary to make the employee whole. Such relief shall include reinstatement with the same seniority status such employee would have had but for the discrimination, 2 times the amount of back pay, interest on the back pay, and compensation for any special damages sustained as a result of the discrimination, including litigation costs and reasonable attorneys' fees. An employee may bring an action in the appropriate district court of the United States for the relief provided in this subsection.

§ 3731. False claims procedure

(a) A subpena [subpoena] requiring the attendance of a witness at a trial or hearing conducted under section 3730 of this title may be served at any place in the United States.

(b) A civil action under section 3730 may not be brought—

(1) more than 6 years after the date on which the violation of section 3729 is committed, or

(2) more than 3 years after the date when facts material to the right of action are known or reasonably should have been known by the official of the United States charged with responsibility to act in the circumstances, but in no event more than 10 years after the date on which the violation is committed, whichever occurs last.

(c) In any action brought under section 3730, the United States shall be required to prove all essential elements of the cause of action, including damages, by a preponderance of the evidence.

(d) Notwithstanding any other provision of law, the Federal Rules of Criminal Procedure, or the Federal Rules of Evidence, a final judgment rendered in favor of the United States in any criminal proceeding charging fraud or false statements, whether upon a verdict after trial or upon a plea of guilty or nolo contendere, shall estop the defendant from denying the essential elements of the offense in any action which involves the same transaction as in the criminal proceeding and which is brought under subsection (a) or (b) of section 3730.

§ 3732. False claims jurisdiction

(a) Actions under section 3730. Any action under section 3730 may be brought in any judicial district in which the defendant or, in the case of multiple defendants, any one defendant can be found, resides, transacts business, or in which any act proscribed by section 3729 occurred. A summons as required by the Federal Rules of Civil Procedure shall be issued by the appropriate district court and served at any place within or outside the United States.

(b) Claims under state law. The district courts shall have jurisdiction over any action brought under the laws of any State for the recovery of funds paid by a State or local government if the action arises from the same transaction or occurrence as an action brought under section 3730.

§ 3733. Civil investigative demands

(a) In general.

(1) Issuance and service. Whenever the Attorney General has reason to believe that any person may be in possession, custody, or control of any documentary material or information relevant to a false claims law investigation, the Attorney General may, before commencing a civil proceeding under section 3730 or other false claims law, issue in writing and cause to be served upon such person, a civil investigative demand

requiring such person—

(A) to produce such documentary material for inspection and copying,

(B) to answer in writing written interrogatories with respect to such documentary material or information,

(C) to give oral testimony concerning such documentary material or information, or

(D) to furnish any combination of such material, answers, or testimony. The Attorney General may not delegate the authority to issue civil investigative demands under this subsection. Whenever a civil investigative demand is an express demand for any product of discovery, the Attorney General, the Deputy Attorney General, or an Assistant Attorney General shall cause to be served, in any manner authorized by this section, a copy of such demand upon the person from whom the discovery was obtained and shall notify the person to whom such demand is issued of the date on which such copy was served.

(2) Contents and deadlines.

(A) Each civil investigative demand issued under paragraph (1) shall state the nature of the conduct constituting the alleged violation of a false claims law which is under investigation, and the applicable provision of law alleged to be violated.

(B) If such demand is for the production of documentary material, the demand shall—

(i) describe each class of documentary material to be produced with such definiteness and certainty as to permit such material to be fairly identified;

(ii) prescribe a return date for each such class which will provide a reasonable period of time within which the material so demanded may be assembled and made available for inspection and copying; and

(iii) identify the false claims law investigator to whom such material shall be made available.

(C) If such demand is for answers to written interrogatories, the demand shall—

(i) set forth with specificity the written interrogatories to be answered;

(ii) prescribe dates at which time answers to written interrogatories shall be submitted; and

(iii) identify the false claims law investigator to whom such answers shall be submitted.

(D) If such demand is for the giving of oral testimony, the demand shall—

(i) prescribe a date, time, and place at which oral testimony shall be commenced;

(ii) identify a false claims law investigator who shall conduct the examination and the custodian to whom the transcript of such examination shall be submitted;

(iii) specify that such attendance and testimony are necessary to the conduct of the investigation;

(iv) notify the person receiving the demand of the right to be accompanied by an attorney and any other representative; and

(v) describe the general purpose for which the demand is being issued and the general nature of the testimony, including the primary areas of inquiry, which will be taken pursuant to the demand.

(E) Any civil investigative demand issued under this section which is an express demand for any product of discovery shall not be returned or returnable until 20 days after a copy of such demand has been served upon the person from whom the discovery was obtained.

(F) The date prescribed for the commencement of oral testimony pursuant to a civil investigative demand issued under this section shall be a date which is not less than seven days after the date on which demand is received, unless the Attorney General or an Assistant Attorney General designated by the Attorney General determines that exceptional circumstances are present which warrant the commencement of such testimony within a lesser period of time.

(G) The Attorney General shall not authorize the issuance under this section of more than one civil investigative demand for oral testimony by the same person unless the person requests otherwise or unless the Attorney General, after investigation, notifies that person in writing that an additional demand for oral testimony is necessary. The Attorney General may not, notwithstanding section 510 of title 28, authorize the performance, by any other officer, employee, or agency, of any function vested in the Attorney General under this subparagraph.

(b) Protected material or information.

(1) In general. A civil investigative demand issued under subsection (a) may not require the production of any documentary material, the submission of any answers to written interrogatories, or the giving of any oral testimony if such material, answers, or testimony would be protected from disclosure under—

(A) the standards applicable to subpoenas or subpoenas duces tecum issued by a court of the United States to aid in a grand jury investigation; or

(B) the standards applicable to discovery requests under the Federal Rules of Civil Procedure, to the extent that the application of such standards to any such demand is appropriate and consistent with the provisions and purposes of this section.

(2) Effect on other orders, rules, and laws. Any such demand which is an express demand for any product of discovery supersedes any inconsistent order, rule, or provision of law (other than this section) preventing or restraining disclosure of such product of discovery to any person. Disclosure of any product of discovery pursuant to any such express demand does not constitute a waiver of any right or privilege which the person making such disclosure may be entitled to invoke to resist discovery of trial preparation materials.

(c) Service; jurisdiction.

(1) By whom served. Any civil investigative demand issued under subsection (a) may be served by a false claims law investigator, or by a United States marshal or a deputy marshal, at any place within the territorial jurisdiction of any court of the United States.

(2) Service in foreign countries. Any such demand or any petition filed under subsection (j) may be served upon any person who is not found within the territorial jurisdiction of any court of the United States in such manner as the Federal Rules of Civil Procedure prescribe for service in a foreign country. To the extent that the courts of the United States can assert jurisdiction over any such person consistent with due process, the United States District Court for the District of Columbia shall have the same jurisdiction to take any action respecting compliance with this section by any such person that such court would have if such person were personally within the jurisdiction of such court.

(d) Service upon legal entities and natural persons.

(1) Legal entities. Service of any civil investigative demand issued under subsection (a) or of any petition filed under subsection (j) may be made upon a partnership, corporation, association, or other legal entity by—

(A) delivering an executed copy of such demand or petition to any partner, executive officer, managing agent, or general agent of the partnership, corporation, association, or entity, or to any agent authorized by appointment or by law to receive service of process on behalf of such partnership, corporation, association, or entity;

(B) delivering an executed copy of such demand or petition to the principal office or place of business of the partnership, corporation, association, or entity; or

(C) depositing an executed copy of such demand or petition in the United States mails by registered or certified mail, with a return receipt requested, addressed to such partnership, corporation, association, or entity at its principal office or place of business.

(2) Natural persons. Service of any such demand or petition may be made upon any natural person by—

(A) delivering an executed copy of such demand or petition to the person; or

(B) depositing an executed copy of such demand or petition in the United States mails by registered or certified mail, with a return receipt requested, addressed to the person at the person's residence or principal office or place of business.

(e) Proof of service. A verified return by the individual serving any civil investigative demand issued under subsection (a) or any petition filed under subsection (j) setting forth the manner of such service shall be proof of such service. In the case of service by registered or certified mail, such return shall be accompanied by the return post office receipt of delivery of such demand.

(f) Documentary material.

(1) Sworn certificates. The production of documentary material in response to a civil investigative demand served under this section shall be made under a sworn certificate, in such form as the demand designates, by—

(A) in the case of a natural person, the person to whom the demand is directed, or

(B) in the case of a person other than a natural person, a person having knowledge of the facts and circumstances relating to such production and authorized to act on behalf of such person.

The certificate shall state that all of the documentary material required by the demand and in the possession, custody, or control of the person to whom the demand is directed has been produced and made available to the false claims law investigator identified in the demand.

(2) Production of materials. Any person upon whom any civil investigative demand for the production of documentary material has been served under this section shall make such material available for inspection and copying to the false claims law investigator identified in such demand at the principal place of business of such person, or at such other place as the false claims law investigator and the person thereafter may agree and prescribe in writing, or as the court may direct under subsection (j)(1). Such material shall be made so available on the return date specified in such demand, or on such later date as the false claims law investigator may prescribe in writing. Such person may, upon written agreement between the person and the false claims law investigator, substitute copies for originals of all or any part of such material.

(g) Interrogatories. Each interrogatory in a civil investigative demand served under this section shall be answered separately and fully in writing under oath and shall be submitted under a sworn certificate, in such form as the demand designates, by—

(1) in the case of a natural person, the person to whom the demand is directed, or

(2) in the case of a person other than a natural person, the person or persons responsible for answering each interrogatory.

If any interrogatory is objected to, the reasons for the objection shall be stated in the certificate instead of an answer. The certificate shall state that all information required by the demand and in the possession, custody, control, or knowledge of the person to whom the demand is directed has been submitted. To the extent that any information is not furnished, the information shall be identified and reasons set forth with particularity regarding the reasons why the information was not furnished.

(h) Oral examinations.

(1) Procedures. The examination of any person pursuant to a civil investigative demand for oral testimony served under this section shall be taken before an officer authorized to administer oaths and affirmations by the laws of the United States or of the place where the examination is held. The officer before whom the testimony is to be taken shall put the witness on oath or affirmation and shall, personally or by someone acting under the direction of the officer and in the officer's presence, record the testimony of the witness. The testimony shall be taken stenographically and shall be transcribed. When the testimony is fully transcribed, the officer before whom the testimony is taken shall promptly transmit a copy of the transcript of the testimony to the custodian. This subsection shall not preclude the taking of testimony by any means authorized by, and in a manner consistent with, the Federal Rules of Civil Procedure.

(2) Persons present. The false claims law investigator conducting the examination shall exclude from the place where the examination is held all persons except the person giving the testimony, the attorney for and any other representative of the person giving the testimony, the attorney for the Government, any person who may be agreed upon by the attorney for the Government and the person giving the testimony, the officer before whom the testimony is to be taken, and any stenographer taking such testimony.

(3) Where testimony taken. The oral testimony of any person taken pursuant to a civil investigative demand served under this section shall be taken in the judicial district of the United States within which such person resides, is found, or transacts business, or in such other place as may be agreed upon by the false claims law investigator conducting the examination and such person.

(4) Transcript of testimony. When the testimony is fully transcribed, the false claims law investigator or the officer before whom the testimony is taken shall afford the witness, who may be accompanied by counsel, a reasonable opportunity to examine and read the transcript, unless such examination and reading are waived by the witness. Any changes in form or substance which the witness desires to make shall be entered and identified upon the transcript by the officer or the false claims law investigator, with a statement of the reasons given by the witness for making such changes. The transcript shall then be signed by the witness, unless the witness in writing waives the signing, is ill, cannot be found, or refuses to sign. If the transcript is not signed by the witness within 30 days after being afforded a reasonable opportunity to examine it, the officer or the false claims law investigator shall sign it and state on the record the fact of the waiver, illness, absence of the witness, or the refusal to sign, together with the reasons, if any, given therefor.

(5) Certification and delivery to custodian. The officer before whom the testimony is taken shall certify on the transcript that the witness was sworn by the officer and that the transcript is a true record of the testimony given by the witness, and the officer or false claims law investigator shall promptly deliver the transcript, or send the transcript by registered or certified mail, to the custodian.

(6) Furnishing or inspection of transcript by witness. Upon payment of reasonable charges therefor, the false claims law investigator shall furnish a copy of the transcript to the witness only, except that the Attorney General, the Deputy Attorney General, or an Assistant Attorney General may, for good cause, limit such witness to inspection of the official transcript of the witness' testimony.

(7) Conduct of oral testimony.

(A) Any person compelled to appear for oral testimony under a civil investigative demand issued under subsection (a) may be accompanied, represented, and advised by counsel. Counsel may advise such person, in confidence, with respect to any question asked of such person. Such person or counsel may object on the record to any question, in whole or in part, and shall briefly state for the record the reason for the objection. An objection may be made, received, and entered upon the record when it is claimed that such person is entitled to refuse to answer the question on the grounds of any constitutional or other legal right or privilege, including the privilege against self-incrimination. Such person may not otherwise object to or refuse to answer any question, and may not directly or through counsel otherwise interrupt the oral examination. If such person refuses to answer any question, a petition may be filed in the district court of the United States under subsection (j)(1) for an order compelling such person to answer such question.

(B) If such person refuses to answer any question on the grounds of the privilege against self-incrimination, the testimony of such person may be compelled in accordance with the provisions of part V of title 18 [18 USCS §§ 6001 et seq.].

(8) Witness fees and allowances. Any person appearing for oral testimony under a civil investigative demand issued under subsection (a) shall be entitled to the same fees and allowances which are paid to witnesses in the district courts of the United States.

(i) Custodians of documents, answers, and transcripts.

(1) Designation. The Attorney General shall designate a false claims law investigator to serve as custodian of documentary material, answers to interrogatories, and transcripts of oral testimony received under this section, and shall designate such additional false claims law investigators as the Attorney General determines from time to time to be necessary to serve as deputies to the custodian.

(2) Responsibility for materials; disclosure.

(A) A false claims law investigator who receives any documentary material, answers to interrogatories, or transcripts of oral testimony under this section shall transmit them to the custodian. The custodian shall take physical possession of such material, answers, or transcripts and shall be responsible for the use made of them and for the return of documentary material under paragraph (4).

(B) The custodian may cause the preparation of such copies of such documentary material, answers to interrogatories, or transcripts of oral testimony as may be required for official use by any false claims law investigator, or other officer or employee of the Department of Justice, who is authorized for such use under regulations which the Attorney General shall issue. Such material, answers, and transcripts may be used by any such authorized false claims law investigator or other officer or employee in connection with the taking of oral testimony under this section.

(C) Except as otherwise provided in this subsection, no documentary material, answers to interrogatories, or transcripts of oral testimony, or copies thereof, while in the possession of the custodian, shall be available for examination by any individual other than a false claims law investigator or other officer or employee of the Department of Justice authorized under subparagraph (B).

Index

Note: Page numbers in **boldface** refer to volume numbers and major topics. Article titles are in **boldface.**

PHOTO CREDITS